Microsoft®

Windows 7
IN DEPTH

Robert Cowart and Brian Knittel

que®

800 East 96th Street
Indianapolis, Indiana 46240

MICROSOFT® WINDOWS 7 IN DEPTH

ISBN 10: 070 0-7097-4199-8

ISBN-10: 0-7897-4199-7

Library of Congress Cataloging-in-Publication Data

Cowart, Robert.

Microsoft Windows 7 in depth / Robert Cowart and Brian Knittel. — 1st ed.

p. cm.

Includes index.

ISBN 978-0-7897-4199-8

1. Microsoft Windows (Computer file) 2. Operating systems (Computers) I. Knittel, Brian. II. Title.

QA76.76.O63C68336 2009

005.4'46 — dc22

2009030029

Printed in the United States of America

Third Printing: March 2010

Trademarks

All terms mentioned in this book that are known to be trademarks or service marks have been appropriately capitalized. Que Publishing cannot attest to the accuracy of this information. Use of a term in this book should not be regarded as affecting the validity of any trademark or service mark.

Microsoft is a registered trademark of Microsoft Corporation.

Warning and Disclaimer

Every effort has been made to make this book as complete and as accurate as possible, but no warranty or fitness is implied. The information provided is on an "as is" basis. The authors and the publisher shall have neither liability nor responsibility to any person or entity with respect to any loss or damages aris-ing from the information contained in this book.

Bulk Sales

Que Publishing offers excellent discounts on this book when ordered in quantity for bulk purchases or special sales. For more information, please contact

U.S. Corporate and Government Sales

1-800-382-3419

corpsales@pearsontechgroup.com

For sales outside the United States, please contact

International Sales

international@pearson.com

Associate Publisher
Greg Wiegand

Acquisitions Editor
Rick Kughen

Development Editor
Rick Kughen

Managing Editor
Patrick Kanouse

Senior Project Editor
Tonya Simpson

Copy Editor
Bill McManus

Indexer
Brad Herriman

Proofreader
Sheri Cain

Technical Editor
Mark Reddin

Publishing Coordinator
Cindy Teeters

Book Designer
Anne Jones

Compositor
Bronkella Publishing, LLC

CONTENTS AT A GLANCE

Introduction 1

I Getting Started with Windows 7

1 Introducing Windows 7 11
2 Installing and Upgrading Windows 7 43
3 The First Hour 77

II Using Windows 7

4 Using the Windows 7 Interface 115
5 Managing Files and Searching 149
6 Printing 187
7 Gadgets and Other Supplied Accessories 207

III Multimedia and Imaging

8 Windows Media Player 231
9 Windows Media Center 251
10 Windows Imaging Tools 277
11 Scanning and Faxing 293
12 Sound Recorder, DVD Maker, and Other Multimedia Tools 313

IV Windows 7 and the Internet

13 Getting Connected 329
14 Using Internet Explorer 8 355
15 Email and Newsgroups with Windows Live Mail 393
16 Troubleshooting Your Internet Connection 417

V Networking

17 Creating a Windows Network 443
18 Mix and Match with Old Windows and Macs 487
19 Connecting Your Network to the Internet 515
20 Using a Windows Network 541
21 Troubleshooting Your Network 575

VI Maintaining Windows 7

22 Windows Management and Maintenance 593
23 Tweaking and Customizing Windows 679
24 Managing Hard Disks 709
25 Troubleshooting and Repairing Problems 737
26 Keeping Windows and Other Software Up to Date 757
27 Installing and Replacing Hardware 779
28 Editing the Registry 805
29 Command-Line and Automation Tools 821

VII Security

30 Protecting Windows from Viruses and Spyware 845
31 Protecting Your Data from Loss and Theft 863
32 Protecting Your Network from Hackers and Snoops 913
33 Protecting Yourself from Fraud and Spam 945

VIII Windows on the Move

34 Wireless Networking 959
35 Hitting the Road 971
36 Meetings, Conferencing, and Collaboration 999
37 Remote Desktop 1013
38 Tablet PC Features 1029

A Using Virtualization on Windows 7 1051

Index 1057

CONTENTS

Introduction 1

Welcome **1**

Why This Book? **2**

How Our Book Is Organized **4**

Conventions Used in This Book **5**
    Text Conventions **5**
    Special Elements **6**

I Getting Started with Windows 7

1 Introducing Windows 7 11

An Overview of Windows 7 **11**

What's New in Windows 7? **13**
    Installation and Setup **16**
    Interface Improvements **17**
    System Security Enhancements **25**
    Improved Web Browsing with IE 8 **27**
    Data Security Enhancements **29**
    Performance Improvements **30**
    New Accessories **31**
    Power Management **32**
    Networking **33**
    System Management and Stability **35**
    New, Improved Applications and
    Services **37**
    Entertainment **37**

Differences Among Windows 7 Versions **38**

Windows 7 on the Corporate Network **41**

**2 Installing and Upgrading
Windows 7 43**

General Considerations for Windows 7 **43**

Windows 7 Hardware Requirements **44**

Option 1: Using What You've Got:
    Ensuring Compatibility via the
    Windows 7 Upgrade Advisor **45**
Option 2: Choosing a Windows 7 Ready PC
    49
Option 3: Upgrading Your
    Computer **50**

Performing a New Installation of
Windows 7 **50**
    Typical Clean Setup Procedure **51**

Upgrading Older Versions of Windows to
Windows 7 **63**

Upgrading One Version of Windows 7 to
Another **65**

Multibooting Windows 7 **66**

Activating Windows 7 **70**

Taking the Virtual Machine Approach **72**

Editing Windows 7 Boot Menu Entries **74**

3 The First Hour 77

The First Things to Do After Starting
Windows 7 **77**

A Quick Tour of Windows 7's Important
Features **78**
    The Welcome Screen **78**
    The New Start Menu **79**
    The New Windows Explorer **80**
    The Redesigned Control Panel **82**
    Devices and Printers **83**
    User Account Control **84**

Setting Up User Accounts **88**
    Create New Accounts **89**
    Change Account Settings **90**
    Before You Forget Your Password **91**

Adjust Your Own User Account **92**

Just One User? **93**

Setting Up Internet Access **93**

Downloading Critical Updates **94**

Personalizing Windows **94**

Personalize Screen Settings **94**

Tune Up the Taskbar **96**

Jump Lists **98**

Adjust the Explorers **98**

Transferring Information from Your Old Computer **101**

Windows Easy Transfer **101**

Logging Off or Shutting Down **104**

More Than You Wanted to Know **106**

Where's My Stuff?: The User Profile Structure **106**

Compatibility and Virtualization **108**

After You Forget Your Password **109**

Using a Password Reset Disk **111**

Accessing the Real Administrator Account **111**

Configuring a Default User Profile **112**

II Using Windows 7

4 Using the Windows 7 User Interface **115**

Who Should Read This Chapter? **115**

Logging In to Windows 7 **116**

Logging On from the Welcome Screen **117**

Using Windows 7—The User Experience **117**

Parts of the Windows 7 Screen **118**

Dialog Boxes **122**

Putting Items on the Desktop **123**

Properties and the Right-Click **124**

Using Windows Explorer **126**

Gestures **131**

The Taskbar, the Start Menu, and Other Tools **131**

Uninstall or Change Programs **134**

Add New Programs **135**

Running Your Applications **136**

How to Launch Your Apps **136**

Using Libraries **140**

Using Speech Recognition **141**

Help and Support **143**

Exiting Windows Gracefully **144**

Dealing with a Crashed Application or Operating System **147**

5 Managing Files and Searching **149**

What's New in Windows Explorer **149**

The Legacy of WebView **152**

How WebView Gives Windows 7 a Browser Look and Feel **154**

Buttons, Breadcrumbs, Toolbars, and More **155**

Breadcrumbs in the Computer Window **156**

Breadcrumbs in Windows Explorer **158**

User Profiles **158**

Navigating the File System **158**

Right-Clicking **161**

Selecting Several Items **162**

Viewing Meta-Information **163**

Turning Panes On and Off **165**

Customizing File and Folder Views **167**

Setting Folder Options **168**

Managing Libraries **170**

Creating a Library **170**

Add Elements to a Library **172**

Remove Elements From a Library **173**

Searching **173**

Types of Searching **174**

Changing Search and Indexing
Settings **174**
Searching As You Type **177**
Grouping and Stacking **181**

Zipping and Packing Files **183**

File and Folder Security **185**

6 Printing 187

Windows Printing Primer **187**

Installing and Configuring a Printer **189**
Adding a New Printer **190**

Installing a Local Printer **191**
If the Printer Isn't Found **192**
What to Do If Your Printer Isn't Listed **194**

Changing a Printer's Properties **196**
Printing Preferences **196**
Printer Properties **198**
Print Server Properties **199**

Removing a Printer **200**

Printing from Your Applications **200**
Printing Offline **202**
Printing from DOS Applications **202**

Working with the Printer Queue **203**
Deleting a File from the Queue **204**
Canceling All Pending Print Jobs on a
Given Printer **204**
Pausing, Resuming, and Restarting the
Printing Process **204**

Advanced Printer Management **205**

XPS Print Output **205**

Faxing **206**

**7 Gadgets and Other Supplied
Accessories 207**

Using Gadgets **207**
Adding New Gadgets **209**

Downloading New Gadgets **211**
Peeking at Gadgets **212**
Adjusting a Gadget's Settings **212**
Moving Gadgets Around **213**
Adding a Gadget More Than Once **214**
Changing Opacity of Gadgets **214**
Removing Gadgets **215**

Using the Snipping Tool **216**

Exploring the Other Accessories **220**
Narrator **220**
Magnifier **220**
XPS Viewer **221**
Calculator **222**
Character Map **224**
Paint **224**
Notepad **225**
Sticky Notes **226**
WordPad **227**

III Multimedia and Imaging

8 Windows Media Player 231

Learning the Basics **231**
Media Types Compatible with WMP **232**
Getting Around in Windows Media
Player 12 **233**
Playing Audio and Video in WMP 12 **239**

Getting Music and Video on Your
Computer **240**
Ripping Songs from CDs onto Your
Computer **240**
Adding Items from Your Computer to
Your Library **243**

Taking Your Music and Video on the Go **243**
Burning Customized CDs **244**
Syncing Files to Your Portable Media
Player **246**
Sharing Media Throughout Your
Home **248**

9 Windows Media Center 251

Windows Media Center—What's the
Hubbub? **251**

What's New in Windows 7 Media
Center? **253**

The WMC Hardware **254**
    The New WMC PC Form Factors **256**
    Is Windows Media Center Based on
    Home or Business Versions? **257**
    Can I Upgrade My Non-WMC PC to a
    WMC PC? **257**
    Basic WMC PC Hookup **258**
    Media Center Extender **261**

The WMC Functions **262**
    Movies **264**
    TV **264**
    Pictures + Videos **266**
    Music **269**

Some Tricks of the Trade **270**
    Playing DVDs and Other Video Files **270**
    Viewing TV Shows on Your HDTV or
    Projector **270**
    Broadcasting TV Shows to Your TV or
    Projector **271**
    Burning DVDs from Recorded TV **273**
    Setting Parental Control Ratings **274**

10 Windows Imaging Tools 277

Image Manipulation in Windows 7 **277**

What's Built in to Windows 7 for
Photographs? **277**

Windows Pictures Library **278**
    Importing Files into the Windows
    Pictures Library from a Media Source **279**
    Organizing Photos and Movies in
    Windows Pictures Library **279**

Working with Scanners and Cameras **279**
    Using Windows Pictures Library with a
    Scanner **279**
    Using Windows Pictures Library with a
    Digital Camera **281**
    Manipulating Pictures in Windows
    Media Player **284**
    Printing Your Masterpiece **286**
    Sharing Your Photos with Others
    Electronically **289**

Burning Your Pictures to CD or DVD **290**
    Writing Photos to CD Using Windows
    Explorer **290**
    Making CDs and DVDs from Windows
    Media Player **291**
    Which Output Option to Use **291**
    What Is This Blu-Ray Thing? **292**

11 Scanning and Faxing 293

Introducing Windows Fax and Scan **293**
    Preparations for Using Windows Fax
    and Scan **294**

Configuring the Fax Service **295**
    Configuring Fax-Receiving Options **295**
    Setting Up Sender Information **296**
    Creating a Customized Cover Page **296**
    Configuring Fax Settings **298**

Sending Faxes from Windows Fax and
Scan **299**
    Adding Scanned Pages **302**
    Previewing the Fax **303**
    Setting Up Dialing Rules **303**
    Sending the Fax **304**
    Monitoring Outgoing Faxes **304**

Receiving Faxes **305**
    Printing Received Faxes
    Automatically **305**

Scanning Documents with Windows Fax
and Scan **305**
    Editing Scan Profile Defaults **306**

Creating a New Scan Profile **308**
Scanning Images **308**
Emailing Scans **310**
Faxing Scans **310**
Manipulating Scanned Images **310**

Scanning and Faxing Slides and
Transparencies **310**

**12 Sound Recorder, DVD Maker, and
Other Multimedia Tools 313**

Become a Recording Star **313**

Windows Sound Recorder **313**

Volume Control **316**

Using the Snipping Tool **319**
Viewing Your "Snipped" Images **320**

Recording to DVD **321**

IV Windows 7 and the Internet

13 Getting Connected 329

Going Worldwide **329**

Connection Technologies **330**
Analog Modem **330**
ISDN **330**
DSL **331**
Cable Modem **331**
Satellite Service **332**
Wireless and Cellular Service **332**
Choosing a Technology **333**

Choosing Equipment **334**

Ordering the Service **335**

Installing a Modem for Dial-Up Service **335**
Changing the Modem Type **338**

Configuring a Dial-Up Internet
Connection **338**
Creating a New Dial-Up Connection **338**

Adjusting Dial-Up Connection
Properties **340**

Making and Ending a Dial-Up
Connection **343**
Hanging Up a Dial-Up Connection **345**

Installing a Network Adapter for
Broadband Service **345**
Installing Filters for DSL Service **346**

Configuring a High-Speed Connection **347**
Configuring a PPPoE Broadband
Connection **347**
Setting Up Dynamic IP Addressing
(DHCP) **349**
Setting Up a Fixed IP Address **350**

Changing the Default Connection **351**

Managing Multiple Internet Connections **352**

14 Using Internet Explorer 8 355

What's New in Internet Explorer 8? **355**

Internet Explorer 8 Quick Tour **357**
Browsing in Tabbed Pages **361**
Browsing with Enhanced Privacy and
Security **365**
Adding Sites to Your Favorites **365**

Using Multimedia Browsing and
Downloading **367**
Images **368**
Audio and Video **368**
Downloading Programs **373**
Protecting Against Bad Downloaded
Programs **374**
Protecting Against "Drive-By"
Downloads of IE Add-Ons **376**

Customizing the Browser and Setting
Internet Options **379**
Setting Default Mail, News, and HTML
Editor Programs **381**
Setting Security and Privacy
Preferences **384**

Blocking Pop-Ups and Pop-Unders 386
Controlling Objectionable Content 388

Effectively Searching the Web 391

15 Email and Newsgroups with Windows Live Mail 393

Choosing an Email Client 393

Windows Live Mail Quick Tour 394
Getting Windows Live Essentials 394
Launching Windows Live Mail 395
Setting Up an Email Account 395
Reading and Processing Incoming
Messages 398
Deleting Messages 401

Creating and Sending New Mail 401
Sending and Receiving Attachments 403
Guarding Yourself Against Email
Viruses 404
Setting Up a Signature 405

Using the Windows Live Mail Contacts 406
Adding, Editing, and Removing
Entries 406
Dealing with Spam 407

Newsgroups and the Internet 408
Locating News Servers 409

Setting Up a Newsgroup Account in
Windows Live Mail 410
Downloading the Newsgroup List 411

Finding and Reading Newsgroups 412
Subscribing to Newsgroups 412
Reading and Posting Messages to a
Newsgroup 414
Managing Messages 415

16 Troubleshooting Your Internet Connection 417

It's Great When It Works, but... 417

Before You Run into Trouble 418

Troubleshooting Step by Step 420

Identifying Software Configuration
Problems 425
Troubleshooting a Dial-Up
Connection 425
Troubleshooting a Cable or DSL Modem
Connection 426
Troubleshooting a LAN Connection 427

Identifying Network Hardware
Problems 429
Identifying Modem Hardware
Problems 430
Identifying Modem Connectivity
Problems 432

Troubleshooting Internet Problems with
Windows TCP/IP Utilities 433
ipconfig 433
ping 434
tracert 435
pathping 437
route 437

Third-Party Utilities 439
Speed Check 439
whois Database 439
Reverse tracert 439
WS_Ping Pro Pack 440

V Networking

17 Creating a Windows Network 443

Creating or Joining a Network 443

Planning Your Network 444
Are You Being Served? 445
When to Hire a Professional 446

Choosing a Network and Cabling
System 447
10/100BASE-T Ethernet 448
1000Mbps Ethernet
(Gigabit Ethernet) 449

Phoneline and Powerline Networking **449**
802.11g and 802.11n Wireless
Networking **451**
Mixed Networking **453**

Additional Networking Functions **453**
Printing and Faxing **453**
Providing Internet Connectivity **454**
Providing Remote Access **454**

Installing Network Adapters **454**
Checking Existing Adapters **455**
Installing Multiple Network Adapters **456**

Installing Network Wiring **457**
Cabling for Ethernet Networks **457**
General Cabling Tips **458**
Wiring with Patch Cables **459**
Installing In-Wall Wiring **460**
Connecting Just Two Computers **461**
Connecting Multiple Switches **462**

Installing a Wireless Network **463**
Wireless Network Setup Choices **464**
Longer Is Better **466**
Setting Up a New Wireless Network **468**
Joining an Existing Wireless Network **472**

Configuring a Peer-to-Peer Network **472**
Configuring the TCP/IP Protocol **473**
Choosing Your Network Location **475**
Setting Your Computer Identification **476**
Configuring Windows Firewall **477**
Setting Up a Homegroup **478**
Alternatives to Using a Homegroup **480**
Wrapping Up **481**

Joining a Windows Domain Network **481**

Checking Out the Neighborhood **483**

Bridging Two Network Types **484**

18 **Mix and Match with Old Windows
and Macs 487**

Networking with Other Operating
Systems **487**

Internetworking with Windows Vista, XP,
and 2000 **489**
Setting TCP/IP as the Default Network
Protocol **490**
Installing the LLDP Responder for
Windows XP **491**
Password Protection and Simple File
Sharing **491**
Using Windows Vista and XP with a
Homegroup **494**

Internetworking with Windows 95, 98, and
Me **496**

Internetworking with UNIX and Linux **497**
Samba **497**
Samba Client Tools **497**
Samba Server Tools **498**
Services for NFS **500**
Subsystem for UNIX-Based
Applications **501**

Internetworking with Macintosh **503**
Compatibility Issues **504**
Working with Mac OS X **506**

Installing Optional Network
Components **510**

The Hosts File **512**

19 **Connecting Your Network to the
Internet 515**

It's a Great Time to Connect Your LAN to
the Internet **515**

Ways to Make the Connection **516**
Managing IP Addresses **518**
NAT and Internet Connection
Sharing **518**
A Warning for Business Users **521**
Special Notes for Wireless
Networking **521**
Special Notes for Cable Service **522**

Configuring Your LAN **523**
  Scheme A—Windows Internet
  Connection Sharing with a Dial-Up
  Connection **523**
  Scheme B—Windows Internet
  Connection Sharing with a Broadband
  Connection **527**
  Scheme C—Connection Sharing Router
  with a Broadband Connection **529**
  Using Universal Plug and Play **531**
  Scheme D—Cable Internet with
  Multiple Computers **531**
  Scheme E—Routed Service Using a
  Router **532**

Making Services Available **533**
  Enabling Access with Internet
  Connection Sharing **533**
  Enabling Access with a Sharing
  Router **537**

20 Using a Windows Network 541

Windows 7 Was Made to Network **541**

Using Shared Folders in Windows 7 **542**
  Browsing Through a Homegroup **542**
  Browsing a Network's Computers **544**
  Viewing a Shared Folder Directly Using
  Its UNC Path **545**

Searching the Network **546**
  Searching for Files or Folders **546**
  Searching for Computers **548**
  Searching for Printers **548**
  Searching Active Directory **549**

Security and File Sharing **550**
  File Permissions and Networking **550**
  Network Permissions **552**

Using Printers on the Network **552**
  Using a Shared Printer **553**
  Using Printers over the Internet with
  IPP **554**
  Using UNIX and LPR Printers **555**
  Using Other Network-Connected
  Printers **556**

Network Power User Topics **556**
  Backing Up Your Computer over the
  Network **557**
  Adding a Network Folder to a
  Library **557**
  Sharing and Using an Entire Drive **557**
  Understanding the UNC Naming
  Convention **558**
  Mapping Drive Letters **559**
  Mapping a Drive to a Subfolder **561**

Sharing Resources **561**
  Sharing with a Homegroup **562**
  Sharing the Public Profile Folder **565**
  Sharing Your Own Folders **566**
  Sharing Folders Independently **566**

Sharing Printers **568**
  Setting Printer Permissions **569**
  Changing the Location of the Spool
  Directory **570**
  Printer Pooling **571**

Managing Your Network **571**
  Monitoring Use of Your Shared
  Folders **572**
  Managing Network Resources Using the
  Command Line **573**

21 Troubleshooting Your Network 575

When Good Networks Go Bad **575**

Getting Started **576**

Diagnostic Tools **577**
  The Network and Sharing Center **577**
  Network Map **579**
  Network Diagnostics **581**
  Windows Firewall **582**
  Event Viewer **582**
  Device Manager **584**

Testing Network Cables **585**

Checking Network Configuration **585**
  `ipconfig` **585**

Computer **587**

Network Connections **588**

Testing Network Connectivity **588**
ping **588**

Diagnosing File and Printer Sharing
Problems **589**

VI Maintaining Windows 7

22 Windows Management and Maintenance 593

The Windows 7 Control Panel **594**
Breaking Down Category View **595**
What Should You Use? **600**
Action Center **604**
AutoPlay **607**
Color Management **609**
Date and Time **609**
Default Programs **611**
Device Manager **612**
Devices and Printers **619**
Ease of Access Center **623**
Fonts **627**
Notification Area Icons **631**
Performance Information and Tools **632**
Power Options **642**
Programs and Features **643**
Region and Language **646**
System **647**

Computer Management **652**
Task Scheduler **654**
Event Viewer **655**
Shared Folders **658**
Services **659**

Administrative Tools **660**
Component Services **661**
iSCSI Initiator **663**
Print Management **664**
System Configuration **664**

System Tools Folder in Start Menu **666**
Character Map **667**
Private Character Editor **670**
System Information **670**

Additional Tools **671**
Task Manager **672**

Third-Party Tools **677**

23 Tweaking and Customizing Windows 679

GUI: To Tweak or Not to Tweak **679**

Start Menu Pizzazz! **680**
Tweaking the Start Menu **680**
Tweaking the Taskbar **682**

Display Properties **683**
Themes **684**
Desktop Background **685**
Window Color and Appearance **688**
Sounds **690**
Screen Savers **693**
Setting Desktop Icons **695**
Account Picture **696**
Display Settings **696**

Miscellaneous GUI Tips **703**
Fonts Preview Trick **704**
Which Windows Are You Using? **704**
Limiting Flip 3D **705**
More Visual Effects **705**
Administrator Tools Not Showing
Up **706**
Cascading Elements from the Start
Menu **707**

Configuring the Recycle Bin **707**

24 Managing Hard Disks 709

The Nature of Hard Disks **709**

Windows 7 File and Storage Systems **710**
Basic Disks **710**
Dynamic Storage **710**

Organizational Strategies **712**

Disk Management **713**
    Assigning Drive Letters and Joining
    Volumes **714**
    Dynamic Disk Management **717**
    Extending a Disk **717**
    Shrinking a Disk **718**
    Creating a Spanned Volume **718**
    Creating a Striped Volume **719**
    Creating and Attaching VHDs **721**

Convert from FAT to NTFS **722**

Windows 7 Disk Maintenance Tools **723**
    Disk Cleanup **724**
    Detecting and Repairing Disk Errors **728**
    Disk Defragmenter **730**

Compression: How It Works, How to Use
It **731**

Third-Party Management Tools **732**

Hard Disk Troubleshooting **733**
    Take the Mental Approach First **733**
    Problems and Solutions **735**

**25 Troubleshooting and Repairing
    Problems 737**

Troubleshooting 101 **737**

Easy Repair Options at Boot Time **738**
    Using System Recovery **738**

Startup Repair **739**

System Restore **740**
    Configuring System Restore **740**
    Creating Restore Points **741**
    Restoring Your System to an Earlier
    Time **743**

System Image Recovery **743**

Windows Memory Diagnostic **745**

Command Prompt **746**

Using Regedit to Repair a System That
Won't Start **747**

Boot Options **748**

As a Last Resort **751**

Using Problem Reports and Solutions **752**

Black Magic of Troubleshooting **753**

Recovering Data from the System Recovery
Options Menu **755**

**26 Keeping Windows 7 and Other
    Software Up to Date 757**

Introducing Updates **757**

Windows Update **758**
    Windows Automatic Updates **758**
    Windows Update Applet and
    Functions **760**
    Other Windows Update Settings **761**
    Viewing and Changing Installed
    Updates **763**

Updating Drivers **764**
    Using Device Manager to Update
    Drivers **765**

Service Packs **767**
    Basic Service Pack Information **768**
    Installation of Service Packs **768**

Installing and Removing Software **769**
    Installation via CD or DVD **770**
    Installation via Downloaded
    Program **771**
    Viewing and Changing Programs **771**
    Uninstalling Software **772**
    Compatibility Issues in 64-Bit Version **774**
    Other Program Compatibility Issues **774**
    Side-by-Side Installs and Virtual
    Registries **776**

27 Installing and Replacing Hardware 779

Upgrading Your Hardware **779**
 ReadyBoost **780**
 BIOS Settings **781**
 Upgrading Your Hard Disk **782**
 Adding RAM **783**

Adding Hardware **784**
 Providing Drivers for Hardware Not in the List **787**

Removing Hardware **789**

Installing and Using Multiple Monitors **790**

Installing a UPS **795**
 Choosing a UPS **797**
 Installing and Configuring a UPS **798**
 Testing Your UPS Configuration **799**

How Do Upgrades Affect a Windows 7 License? **799**

Upgrading Hardware in the Same Box and Complying with EULA **800**

Upgrading and Optimizing Your Computer **801**
 Keep an Eye on Hardware Compatibility **801**
 Sleuthing Out Conflicts **802**
 Optimizing Your Computer for Windows 7 **802**

28 Editing the Registry 805

What Is the Registry? **805**

How the Registry Is Organized **805**

New Registry Features **806**
 Registry Virtualization **806**
 Registry Redirection and Reflection **808**

Backing Up and Restoring the Registry **808**
 Backing Up the Registry **809**
 Restoring the Registry **810**

Using Regedit **812**
 Viewing the Registry **812**
 Searching in the Registry **814**
 Editing Keys and Values **814**
 Editing Registry Entries for Another User **816**
 Editing Registry Entries for Another Windows Installation **817**
 Editing Registry Security **010**

Other Registry Tools **819**
 X-Setup Pro **819**
 Registry Toolkit **819**
 Registrar Registry Manager **820**
 Tweak-7 **820**

Registry Privileges and Policies **820**

29 Command-Line and Automation Tools 821

Command-Line Tools **821**

The Windows 7 Command Prompt Environment **822**
 Running Commands with Elevated Privileges **823**
 Learning About Command-Line Programs **824**
 Cutting and Pasting in the Command Prompt Window **825**

Setting Environment Variables **825**
 Setting the PATH Environment Variable **827**

The MS-DOS Environment **828**
 Editing Advanced Settings for a DOS Application **829**
 Customizing autoexec.nt and config.nt **830**
 Issues with DOSKEY and ANSI.SYS **831**

Batch Files **832**
 Batch File Tips **833**

Windows Script Host **834**

Creating Scripts 834

Some Sample Scripts 836

Windows PowerShell 837

Task Scheduler 839

VII Security

30 Protecting Windows from Viruses and Spyware 845

Malicious Software: Ignorance Is Not Bliss 845

Viruses Past and Present 846

Worms: "Look, Ma! No Hands!" 846

Spyware 847

Rootkits and Beyond 847

Antimalware Strategy: Defense in Depth 848

Windows Action Center 848

Choosing and Installing an Antivirus Client 850

Windows Defender for Spyware Protection 852

Personal Firewalls: A Layer of Protection from Worms 856

Automatic Updates: Remove the Side Doors 857

Data Execution Prevention 857

User Account Control Options 859

Service Hardening 860

Internet Explorer 8 Malware Protection 861

31 Protecting Your Data from Loss and Theft 863

The All New Backup and Restore 863

Improvements in the Backup and Restore Features in Windows 7 864

File and Folder Backups Versus System Images 865

Creating a File and Folder Backup 866

Working with Removable Media During Backups 871

How Backups Created with Windows Backup Are Stored 871

Restoring Data from a File and Folder Backup 872

Restoring the Current User's Data 872

Performing an Advanced Restore 875

Creating a System Image (Complete PC Backup) 878

WBADMIN Command-Line System Backup and Restore 879

Using Disk Management with System Images 882

Restoring a System Image 883

Encrypted File System (EFS) 884

Encrypting Offline Files 886

Using CIPHER 887

Rules for Using Encrypted Files 889

Suggested Folders to Encrypt 891

Protecting and Recovering Encrypted Files 891

Disk Organization for Data Safety 894

BitLocker Disk Encryption 895

BitLocker System Requirements 895

BitLocker To Go 896

Enabling the TPM 897

Encrypting the Drive with BitLocker 898

BitLocker Drive Encryption Recovery 899

How BitLocker Protects Your Information 900

Differences Between BitLocker and EFS Encryption 900

Recovering Previous Versions of a File 901

NTFS File Permissions 903

Inheritance of Permissions 905

Advanced Security Settings 906

Viewing Effective Permissions **907**
Access Auditing **907**
Taking Ownership of Files **908**
Assigning Permissions to Groups **908**
Securing Your Printers **910**

Security Policy Configuration Options **910**

Third-Party Disc-Backup Tools **911**

32 Protecting Your Network from Hackers and Snoops 913

It's a Cold, Cruel World **913**
Who Would Be Interested in My Computer? **914**
Types of Attack **915**
Your Lines of Defense **917**

Preparation: Network Security Basics **917**

Active Defense **919**
Firewalls and NAT (Connection-Sharing) Devices **919**
Windows Firewall **920**
Packet Filtering **921**
Using NAT or Internet Connection Sharing **923**
Add-On Firewall Products for Windows **923**
Secure Your Router **923**
Configure Passwords and File Sharing **924**
Set Up Restrictive Access Controls **926**

Testing, Logging, and Monitoring **927**
Test Your Defenses **927**
Monitor Suspicious Activity **929**

Disaster Planning: Preparation for Recovery After an Attack **929**
Make a Baseline Backup Before You Go Online **930**
Make Frequent Backups When You're Online **930**
Write and Test Server Restore Procedures **930**

Write and Maintain Documentation **931**
Prepare an Incident Plan **931**

Specific Configuration Steps for Windows 7 **932**
Windows 7's Security Features **932**
If You Have a Standalone Windows 7 Computer **933**
If You Have a LAN **934**
Keep Up-to-Date **934**
Tightening Local Security Policy **934**

Configuring Windows Firewall **937**
Enabling and Disabling Windows Firewall **938**
Allow a Program or Feature Through Windows Firewall **939**
Change Notification Settings, Turn Windows Firewall On or Off **940**
Restore Defaults **941**
Advanced Settings **941**

More About Security **943**

33 Protecting Yourself from Fraud and Spam 945

Phishing (Fishing) for Information **945**
Live Phish: A Real-World Example **945**
More Help from Internet Explorer **949**
Two-Way Authentication **950**
Two-Factor Authentication **951**
Identity-Management Software **951**

Fighting Spam **952**

Take Action Against Email Abuse **955**

VIII Windows on the Move

34 Wireless Networking 959

Wireless Networking in Windows 7 **959**
Types of Wireless Networks **960**
Take Care When You Share **960**

Joining a Wireless Network **961**
  In the Corporate Environment **961**
  At Home or the Small Office **961**
  In Someone Else's Office **963**
  At a Public Hot Spot **964**

Ad Hoc Networks and Meetings **965**

Managing Wireless Network
Connections **966**
  Changing Wireless Settings **966**
  Switching Between Wireless
  Networks **966**
  Prioritizing Wireless Network
  Connections **967**
  Copying Wireless Profiles to Other
  Computers **968**
  Adding a Network Manually **968**
  Deleting Network Profiles **969**

35 Hitting the Road 971

Windows Unplugged: Mobile and Remote
Computing **971**

Managing Mobile Computers **972**
  Windows Mobility Center **972**
  Getting the Most Out of Your Battery **974**

VPN and Dial-Up Networking **977**
  Virtual Private Networking **977**
  Setting Up a VPN or Dial-Up
  Networking Connection **978**
  Setting a VPN or Dial-Up Connection's
  Properties **980**
  Managing Dial-Up Connections from
  Multiple Locations **982**
  Establishing a VPN or Dial-Up
  Connection **983**
  Using Remote Network Resources **985**
  Email and Network Connections **986**
  Monitoring and Ending a VPN or Dial-
  Up Connection **986**
  Advanced Routing for Remote
  Networks **986**

Incoming VPN and Dial-Up Access **987**
  Setting Up VPN and Dial-Up Access **988**
  Enabling Incoming VPN Connections
  with NAT **989**
  Disabling Incoming Connections **990**

Offline Files **991**
  Identifying Files and Folders for Offline
  Use **992**
  Using Files While Offline **993**
  Sync Center **995**
  Managing and Encrypting Offline
  Files **997**
  Making Your Shared Folders Available
  for Offline Use by Others **997**

Multiple LAN Connections **998**

**36 Meetings, Conferencing, and
Collaboration 999**

Windows 7 Plays Well with Others **999**

Making Presentations with a Mobile
Computer **1000**
  Adjusting Presentation Settings **1000**
  Controlling External Display **1001**
  Connecting to Network Projectors **1003**

Remote Assistance **1003**
  Enabling Remote Assistance **1004**
  Requesting Remote Assistance **1004**
  Responding to an Assistance
  Request **1007**
  Working with Remote Assistance **1008**
  Using Third-Party Tools **1009**

Online Meeting Tools **1010**

37 Remote Desktop 1013

Using Your Computer Remotely **1013**

Setting Up Access to Your Own
Computer **1015**
  Enabling Remote Desktop Access to
  Your Computer **1015**

Establishing 24×7 Access **1016**
Setting Up Dynamic DNS **1017**
Configuring Port Forwarding **1018**

Connecting to Other Computers with
Remote Desktop **1021**
Connection Options **1022**
Using the Remote Connection **1024**
Keyboard Shortcuts **1025**

Third-Party Remote Control Tools **1027**

38 Tablet PC Features 1029

Importance of Handwriting **1029**

History of Tablet PCs **1029**

Who Needs a Tablet? **1032**

What Does a Windows 7 Tablet PC Have
That Regular PCs Don't? **1033**

What's New in Tablet Windows 7? **1033**

Choosing a Tablet PC **1035**

Using Your Tablet PC—Differences and
Similarities of Functions **1035**

Input Methods Using the Input Panel **1036**
Writing Methods Using the Input
Panel **1037**

Using the Stylus Pen **1038**
Input Panel Options **1039**

Gestures and Pen Flicks **1040**
Scratch-Out Gestures **1040**
Pen Flicks **1040**

Handwriting Recognition **1041**
Specific Handwriting Recognition
Errors **1042**
Teach the Recognizer Your Style **1042**

AutoComplete **1043**

Windows Journal **1043**

Tweaking Your Tablet PC Settings **1045**
Tablet PC Settings Dialog Box **1045**
Pen and Touch Dialog Box **1047**

**A Using Virtualization on Windows 7
1051**

Windows XP Mode in Windows 7 **1052**
Installing Microsoft Virtual PC **1052**
Installing Windows XP Mode **1053**
Installing Applications into the
XP VM **1055**

Index 1057

About the Contributing Authors

Eric Butow has authored or co-authored 14 books, most recently *User Interface Design for Mere Mortals*, *How to Succeed in Business Using LinkedIn*, *File Virtualization for Dummies*, and the upcoming *Blogging to Drive Business* to be published by Que Publishing. He is also the CEO of Butow Communications Group (BCG), a Web design and online marketing firm based in Roseville, California. When Eric isn't working he enjoys time with friends and visiting family in California's Gold Country.

Greg Dickinson lives in Birmingham, Alabama, and has 10 years experience with computer networking. He works for one of the top 30 banks in the country, packaging and distributing software packages and updates to the bank's 6,000 desktops. When not wrestling with the intricacies of enterprise networks, Greg likes to spend his time recording training videos and singing in a barbershop chorus.

Justin Korelc lives in San Marcos, Texas, and began his computing experience on the DOS command line more than 15 years ago. Justin now writes about his computing experiences as a full-time freelance writer of numerous articles, whitepapers, and co-author of books including home entertainment, security, and networking topics.

Tyler Regas lives in Mission Viejo, California, with his wife and daughter. He is a 20-year technology professional, consultant, enterprise operations manager, the occasional pundit and author, and a rabid blogger, and has an inordinate love of small, electronic devices.

Mark Edward Soper is a technical writer, trainer, and consultant. He is the president of Select Systems & Associates, Inc. Mark blogs at ww.maximumpc.com. He also writes for *Maximum PC* magazine and is the author of many books, most recently *The Shot Doctor: The Amateur's Guide to Taking Great Digital Photos* and *Easy Windows 7*.

Ed Tittel lives in Round Rock, Texas, and has been working with and around computers for 30 years. A veteran of such companies as Burroughs, Schlumberger, Novell, and Tivoli Systems, Ed now works as a full-time freelance writer. He has contributed to more than 100 computer books and writes regularly for Tom's Hardware, InformIT.com, and other websites. When he's not writing, Ed likes to shoot pool, cook, play with his boy, Gregory, and hang on to his lovely wife, Dina.

DEDICATION

In memory of my mother, Geraldine, for teaching me that the devil is in the details.
—Bob

To my mother and father, for their encouragement. —Brian

ACKNOWLEDGMENTS

This book, as much as the product it covers, is the product of a team effort. We couldn't have produced this without the great team at Que, the assistance of contributing writers, the patience and support of our friends, and so...

We feel privileged to be part of the consistently professional Que family. Producing these highly technical, state-of-the art books requires a dedicated and knowledgeable staff, and once again the staff at Que did an amazing job. Executive Editor Rick Kughen has provided unflagging, cheerful support and guidance through our four *SE Using* volumes and now this *In Depth* title. Rick and our copy editor, Bill McManus, pored over every word on every page and offered invaluable direction and tuning. This is a much better book than it could have been without them.

We'd like to acknowledge the efforts of our technical editor, Mark Reddin. We also would like to thank the editorial, indexing, layout, art, proofing, and other production staff at Que—Tonya Simpson, Brad Herriman, Sheri Cain, and Tricia Bronkella. You did a marvelous job.

We'd like to thank Ed Tittel, Justin Korelc, Greg Dickinson, Mark Soper, Tyler Regas, and Eric Butow for their contributions: Your efforts made this a better book and let it get to press on time (more or less!). You were a great writing team to work with. No book could make it to market without the real-world personal relationships developed between booksellers on the one hand, and the sales and marketing personnel back at the publishers. We've had the opportunity to meet sales and marketing folks in the computer publishing world and know what a difficult job selling and keeping up with the thousands of computer titles can be. Thanks to all of you for your pivotal role in helping us pay our mortgages!

Finally, we should acknowledge those who made it possible for us to get through the many months of writing. Bob first offers many thanks to John Prendergast, Dr. Steven Feig, Dr. Julie Griffith, and Dr. Christine Green for keeping him ticking. Second, thanks to agent Carole McClendon of Waterside Productions for representing me in contractual matters. And finally, as always, thanks to friends and family who, even though used to seeing me disappear for months on end, let me back in the fold when it's over, especially Diane Zaremba, Kathy Geisler, Heidi Page, Kirsten Spalding, and Michael Callahan.

Brian adds thanks to Dave, Frank, Todd, Bubba, and Lucy.

WE WANT TO HEAR FROM YOU!

As the reader of this book, *you* are our most important critic and commentator. We value your opinion and want to know what we're doing right, what we could do better, what areas you'd like to see us publish in, and any other words of wisdom you're willing to pass our way.

As an associate publisher for Que Publishing, I welcome your comments. You can email or write me directly to let me know what you did or didn't like about this book—as well as what we can do to make our books better.

Please note that I cannot help you with technical problems related to the topic of this book. We do have a User Services group, however, where I will forward specific technical questions related to the book.

When you write, please be sure to include this book's title and author as well as your name, email address, and phone number. I will carefully review your comments and share them with the author and editors who worked on the book.

Email: feedback@quepublishing.com

Mail: Greg Wiegand
          Associate Publisher
          Que Publishing
          800 East 96th Street
          Indianapolis, IN 46240 USA

READER SERVICES

Visit our website and register this book at informit.com/register for convenient access to any updates, downloads, or errata that might be available for this book.

Introduction

Welcome

Thank you for purchasing or considering the purchase of *Windows 7 In Depth*. It's amazing the changes that 20-odd years can bring to a computer product such as Windows. When we wrote our first Windows book back in the mid-1980s, our publisher didn't even think the book would sell well enough to print more than 5,000 copies. Microsoft stock wasn't even a blip on most investors' radar screens. Boy, were they in the dark! Who could have imagined that a little more than a decade later, anyone who hoped to get hired for even a temp job in a small office would need to know how to use Microsoft Windows, Office, and a PC. Fifteen or so Windows books later, we're still finding new and exciting stuff to share with our readers.

Who could have imagined in 1985 that a mass-market operating system two decades later would have to include support for so many technologies, most of which didn't even exist at the time: DVD, DVD±RW, CD-R and CD-RW, Internet and intranet, MP3, MPEG, WMA, DV, USB, FireWire, APM, ACPI, RAID, UPS, PPOE, Gigabit Ethernet, 802.11g, WPA2, IPv6, Teredo, speech recognition, touch and pen interfaces, fault tolerance, disk encryption and compression…? The list goes on. And that 8GB of disk space Windows 7 occupies? It would have cost about half a million dollars in 1985. Today, it costs less than a dollar.

In 1981, when we were building our first computers, the operating system (CP/M) had to be modified in assembly language and recompiled, and hardware parts had to be soldered together to make almost any new addition (such as a video display terminal) work. Virtually nothing was standardized, with the end result being that computers remained out of reach for average folks.

Together, Microsoft, Intel, and IBM changed all that. Today you can purchase a computer, a printer, a scanner, an external disk drive, a keyboard, a modem, a monitor, and a video card over the Internet, plug them in, install Windows, and they'll work together. The creation and adoption (and sometimes forcing) of hardware and software standards that have made the PC a household appliance the world over can largely be credited to Microsoft, like it or not. The unifying glue of this PC revolution has been Windows.

Yes, we all love to hate Windows, but it's here to stay. Linux and Mac OS X are formidable alternatives, but for most of us, at least for some time, Windows and Windows applications are "where it's at." And Windows 7 ushers in truly significant changes to the landscape. That's why we were excited to write this book.

Why This Book?

We all know this book will make an effective doorstop in a few years. You probably have a few already. (We've even written a few!) If you think it contains more information than you need, just remember how helpful a good reference can be when you need it at the 11th hour. And we all know that computer technology changes so fast that it's sometimes easier just to blink and ignore a phase than to study up on it. Windows 7 is definitely a significant upgrade in Windows' security and sophistication—one you're going to need to understand.

If you're moving up to Windows 7 from Windows XP, you should know that Windows 7 is a very different animal. Yes, the graphics and display elements are flashier, but it's the deeper changes that matter most. With its radically improved security systems, revamped Control Panel, friendlier network setup tools, new problem-tracking systems, improved power management and usability tools for mobile computers, and completely revamped networking and graphics software infrastructures, Windows 7 leaves XP in the dust.

And if you're moving up from Vista, you'll be *very* pleasantly surprised at the improvements. Vista got a bad rap, perhaps for some good reasons: It was slow, required too much RAM, had driver issues, and annoyed users with its User Account Control prompts. Windows 7 fixes all of that, thank goodness! Think of Windows 7 as Vista after three years at a spa/reform school. It's leaner, stronger, more refined, and ever so polite. In all ways, Windows 7 is superior to any operating system Microsoft has ever produced.

Is Windows 7 so easy to use that books are unnecessary? Unfortunately, no. True, as with other releases of Windows, online help is available. As has been the case ever since Windows 95, however, no printed documentation is available (to save Microsoft the cost), and the Help files are written by Microsoft employees and contractors. You won't find criticisms, complaints, workarounds, or suggestions that you use alternative software vendors, let alone explanations of *why* you have to do things a certain way. For that, you need this book! We will even show you tools and techniques that Microsoft's insiders didn't think were important enough to document at all.

You might know that Windows 7 comes in a bewildering array of versions: primarily Home Premium, Professional, Enterprise, and Ultimate (not to mention Starter, intended for relatively primitive "netbook" computers and emerging markets; Home Basic, sold only in emerging markets; and several extra versions sold in the European Union to comply with antitrust court-mandated restrictions). But Windows 7 is Windows 7, and all that really distinguishes the versions is the availability of various features. *Most* of the differences matter only in the corporate world, where Windows 7 will be managed by network administrators, so most corporate users won't need to worry about them. For the remaining features, we tell you when certain features do or don't apply to your particular version of Windows 7. (And we show you how to upgrade from one version to a better version, if you want the features your copy doesn't have!)

In this book's many pages, we focus not just on the gee-whiz side of the technology, but why you should care, what you can get from it, and what you can forget about. The lead author on this book has previously written 17 books about Windows, all in plain English (several bestsellers), designed for everyone from rank beginners to full-on system administrators deploying NT Server domains. The coauthor has designed software and networks for more than 20 years and has been writing about Windows for 10 years. We work with and write about various versions of Windows year in and year out. We have a clear understanding of what confuses users and system administrators about installing, configuring, or using Windows, as well as (we hope) how to best convey the solutions to our readers.

While writing this book, we tried to stay vigilant in following four cardinal rules:

- Keep it practical.

- Keep it accurate.

- Keep it concise.

- Keep it interesting, and even crack a joke or two.

We believe that you will find this to be the best and most comprehensive book available on Windows 7 for intermediate through advanced users. And whether you use Windows 7 yourself or support others who do, we firmly believe this book will address your questions and needs.

Our book addresses both home and business computer users. We assume you probably are not an engineer, and we do our best to speak in plain English and not snow you with unexplained jargon. As we wrote, we imagined that you, our reader, are a friend or co-worker who's familiar enough with your computer to know what it's capable of, but might not know the details of how to make it all happen. So we show you, in a helpful, friendly, professional tone. In the process, we also hope to show you things that you might not have known, which will help make your life easier—your computing life, anyway. We spent months and months poking into Windows 7's darker corners so you wouldn't have to. And, if you're looking for power-user tips and some nitty-gritty details, we make sure you get those, too. We try to make clear what information is essential for you to understand and what is optional for just those of you who are especially interested.

We're also willing to tell you what we don't cover. No book can do it all. As the title implies, this book is about Windows 7. We don't cover setting up the Server versions of this operating system, called Windows 2000 Server, Windows Server 2003, and Windows Server 2008. However, we do tell you how to connect to and interact with these servers, and even other operating systems, including Mac OS X, Linux, and older variants of Windows, over a local area network.

Because of space limitations, there is only one chapter devoted to coverage of Windows 7's numerous command-line utilities, its batch file language, Windows Script Host, and Windows PowerShell. For that (in spades!), you might want to check Brian's book *Windows 7 and Vista Guide to Scripting, Automation, and Command Line Tools*, which is due to be published in the fall of 2009.

Even when you've become a Windows 7 pro, we think you'll find this book to be a valuable source of reference information in the future. Both the table of contents and the very complete index will provide easy means for locating information when you need it quickly.

How Our Book Is Organized

Although this book advances logically from beginning to end, it's written so that you can jump in at any location, quickly get the information you need, and get out. You don't have to read it from start to finish, nor do you need to work through complex tutorials.

This book is broken down into seven major parts. Here's the skinny on each one:

Part I, "Getting Started with Windows 7," introduces Windows 7's new and improved features and shows you how to install Windows 7 on a new computer or upgrade an older version of Windows to Windows 7. It also shows you how to apply service packs to keep your version of Windows 7 up-to-date. Finally, we take you on a one-hour guided tour that shows you the best of Windows 7's features and walks you through making essential settings and adjustments that will help you get the most out of your computer.

In Part II, "Using Windows 7," we cover the core parts of Windows 7, the parts you'll use no matter what else you do with your computer: managing documents and files, using the Windows desktop, starting and stopping applications, searching through your computer's contents, printing, and using the desktop gadgets and other supplied accessories. Don't skip this section, even—or rather, *especially*—if you've used previous versions of Windows. Windows 7 does many things differently, and you'll want to see how to take advantage of it!

Windows 7 has great tools for viewing, playing, creating, editing, and managing music, movies, and pictures. In Part III, "Multimedia and Imaging," we show you how to use the new Windows Media Player, burn CDs, extract and edit images from cameras and scanners, send faxes, and create DVDs. Finally, we show you how to use Windows Media Center, which lets you view all that stuff and, on a properly equipped computer, record and play back your favorite TV shows. We even show you how to burn DVDs from your recorded shows and discuss compression options for storage considerations and format options for playback on other devices.

In Part IV, "Windows 7 and the Internet," we first help you set up an Internet connection and then move on to explain Windows 7's Internet tools. We provide in-depth coverage of the new and improved (and safer!) Internet Explorer. The final chapter shows you how to diagnose Internet connection problems.

Networks used to be found only in high-falutin' offices and corporate settings. Now, any home or office with two or more computers should have a network. A LAN is inexpensive, and with one you can share an Internet connection, copy and back up files, and use any printer from any computer. In Part V, "Networking," we walk you through setting up a network in your home or office, and show you how to take advantage of it in day-to-day use. We also show you how easy it is to share a DSL or cable Internet connection with all your computers at once, show you how to network with other operating systems, and, finally, help you fix it when it all stops working.

Part VI, "Maintaining Windows 7," covers system configuration and maintenance. We tell you how to work with the Control Panel and System Administration tools, provide tips and tricks for customizing the graphical user interface to maximize efficiency, explain how to manage your hard disk and other hardware, and describe a variety of ways to upgrade your hardware and software (including third-party programs) for maximum performance. We show you how to troubleshoot hardware and software problems, edit the Windows Registry, and, for real power users, how to use and tweak the command-line interface.

When Windows was introduced over two decades ago, computer viruses, online fraud, and hacking were only starting to emerge as threats. Today (thanks in great part to *gaping* security holes in previous versions of Windows), computer threats are a worldwide problem, online and offline. In Part VII, "Security," we provide a 360-degree view of Windows 7's substantial improvements in security. Here you'll find out both what Windows 7 will do to help you, and what you must do for yourself. We cover protection against viruses and spyware, loss and theft, hackers and snoops, and fraud and spam—in that order.

Part VIII, "Windows On the Move," shows you how to get the most out of Windows 7 when either you or your computer, or both, are on the go. We show you how to use wireless networking safely, how to get the most out of your laptop, and how to connect to remote networks. We also show you how to use Remote Desktop to reach and use your own computer from anywhere in the world. We finish up with a chapter about the cutting edge in laptops and desktops—pen and touch computing using the Tablet-PC features of Windows 7.

Appendix A, "Using Virtualization on Windows 7," explains how to use a newly released, free version of the Microsoft Virtual PC program to run older XP programs under Windows 7. For some users, this can be an excellent alternative to creating a dual-boot system with XP and Windows 7.

Conventions Used in This Book

Special conventions are used throughout this book to help you get the most from the book and from Windows 7.

Text Conventions

Various typefaces in this book identify terms and other special objects. These special typefaces include the following:

Type	Meaning
Italic	New terms or phrases when initially defined
`Monospace`	Information that appears in code or onscreen
`**Bold monospace**`	Information you type

Words separated by commas—All Windows book publishers struggle with how to represent command sequences when menus and dialog boxes are involved. In this book, we separate commands using a comma. Yeah, we know it's confusing, but this is traditionally how Que's books do it, and traditions die hard. So, for example, the instruction "Choose Edit, Cut" means that you should open the Edit menu and choose Cut. Another, more complex example is "Click Start, Control Panel, System and Security, Change Battery Settings."

Key combinations are represented with a plus sign. For example, if the text calls for you to press Ctrl+Alt+Delete, you would press the Ctrl, Alt, and Delete keys at the same time.

Special Elements

Throughout this book, you'll find Notes, Tips, Cautions, Sidebars, Cross-References, and Troubleshooting Notes. Often, you'll find just the tidbit you need to get through a rough day at the office or the one whiz-bang trick that will make you the office hero. You'll also find little nuggets of wisdom, humor, and lingo that you can use to amaze your friends and family, not to mention making you cocktail-party literate.

 tip

We specially designed these tips to showcase the best of the best. Just because you get your work done doesn't mean you're doing it in the fastest, easiest way possible. We show you how to maximize your Windows experience. Don't miss these tips!

 note

Notes point out items that you should be aware of, but you can skip them if you're in a hurry. Generally, we've added notes as a way to give you some extra information on a topic without weighing you down.

 caution

Pay attention to cautions! They could save you precious hours in lost work.

 ## Something Isn't Working

Throughout the book, we describe some common trouble symptoms and tell you how to diagnose and fix problems with Windows, hardware, and software. These troubleshooting notes are sure to make your life with Windows 7 a bit easier.

We Had More to Say

We use sidebars to dig a little deeper into more esoteric features of Windows, settings, or peculiarities. Some sidebars are used to explain something in more detail when doing so in the main body text would've been intrusive or distracting. Sometimes, we just needed to get something off our chests and rant a bit. Don't skip the sidebars, because you'll find nuggets of pure gold in them (if we do say so ourselves).

Cross-References

Cross-references are designed to point you to other locations in this book (or other books in the Que family) that will provide supplemental or supporting information. Cross-references appear as follows:

➡ *To learn how to copy user accounts and files from your old computer to Windows 7,* ***see*** *"Windows Easy Transfer,"* ***p. 101.***

GETTING STARTED WITH WINDOWS 7

IN THIS PART

1   Introducing Windows 7   11

2   Installing and Upgrading Windows 7   43

3   The First Hour   77

INTRODUCING WINDOWS 7

An Overview of Windows 7

Windows 7 is the successor to Windows Vista. As such, it takes its place as the latest corporate desktop and workstation upgrade, and also sets its sights on the home office and even home entertainment/gaming console, as Microsoft did with its ill-fated Windows Vista. This time, though, Microsoft has gotten it right. In fact, we're sure you'll really grow to like Windows 7 as you use it.

The goal Microsoft set for Windows Vista was quite ambitious. That probably explains why it took Microsoft so long to get it to market. During development, more and more features worked their way into Microsoft Vista and the project became increasingly unwieldy. The code kept ballooning, and the process couldn't be stopped. This pushed out the delivery date of Vista, first to 2005, then to early 2006, and finally to late 2006.

Worse, when Vista did appear, its reception was lukewarm at best, and customers complained long and loud about their preference for Windows XP, even as it remained an older, less-attractive interface with more security problems. Even six months past its January 2007 public release, it was clear that Vista wasn't attracting widespread adoption. To satisfy a continued desire for Windows XP, Microsoft ended up trying to fix Vista while simultaneously working on XP Service Pack 3 (released in mid-2008).

In an attempt to convince customers that Vista was better than its industry reputation, Microsoft remarketed it as "Mojave," a campaign that highlighted the many superb features of this system. It didn't work, so plans for a follow-on to Vista were accelerated. That successor is what has been released as Windows 7.

Think of Windows 7 as "Vista, fixed" and you'll have a pretty good idea of how it compares to both Windows XP and Windows Vista.

Many of the most important improvements in Windows 7 are under the proverbial hood, including dramatic performance improvements and a far greater level of reliability over a similarly configured Vista system. Enough history, though! Let's talk about what Windows 7 is and is not.

Following in the footsteps of Windows XP Professional and Windows XP Home Edition, Windows 7 comes in six flavors (perhaps more, if versions without Internet Explorer are created for the European market as with Vista):

- Windows 7 Starter (available only pre-installed on netbook class PCs)

- Windows 7 Home Basic

- Windows 7 Home Premium

- Windows 7 Professional

- Windows 7 Enterprise

- Windows 7 Ultimate

As with Windows Vista, Windows 7 flavors benefit from being very much the same under the hood. Recall that between 1993 and the release of XP, there were very separate home-oriented (Windows 3.*x*/9*x*/Me) and corporate-oriented (Windows NT/2000) Windows versions with drastically different internals. A common core for all Windows 7 versions makes program and device driver development much easier because device drivers and software programs need to be created only once, not twice.

Vista's design mandate was a tough one: to create a more-secure, flashy-looking, reliable, easy-to-use operating system with functionality ranging from an excellent gaming and home entertainment platform all the way to a full-blown highly secure, mission-critical business networking machine. Vista needed to be more attractive, more capable, and much more robust than XP; incorporate all the latest technologies; and be far less susceptible to attack from viruses, phishing, spam, and the like. Malware has kept legions of IT professionals in business, but it has grown nightmarish for all Windows-based IT departments.

Vista succeeded for the most part, but at the price of performance and compatibility. That's where Windows 7 comes in. Thus, for example, many of the apps previously included in Vista are now in a separate Windows Live Essentials bundle available online, including Windows Calendar, Windows Photo Gallery, Windows Movie Maker, and Windows Mail.

Unlike the completely reworked user interface (UI) that we saw when making the jump from XP to Vista, Windows 7's UI is quite similar to Vista. Windows 7 adds enough nuances to deliver a better computing experience, but enough basic similarities that if you've used Vista, you'll be ready to go instantly. If you're coming from Windows XP, however, you might be surprised that many of the menus XP users have grown accustomed to are gone, replaced by a much more web-like view of the computer, with phrase-like links that imply their functions—for example, "See what happens when I press the Power button."

Vista also included the option of switching to a "Classic" Start menu, but Windows 7 axes that. If you move to Windows 7, you'll need to get used to the new Start menu, even if it feels a bit odd at first.

Windows XP was designed for application and hardware compatibility with products made for older versions of Windows, even MS-DOS games and graphics applications. Windows 7, like Vista, carries this same compatibility over in its 32-bit versions, but Windows 7 64-bit versions have abandoned that legacy. The time has come to put those old dogs to rest. There are ways around this, using Virtual PC, for example, so you don't have to jettison your favorite Windows 9x or DOS programs in Windows 7 64-bit versions. We'll talk about Virtual PC in Chapter 2, "Installing and Upgrading Windows 7."

If you've worked in the Windows XP world, you'll also be glad to know that Microsoft listened to its customer base and added a Windows XP compatibility mode that you can install into some Windows 7 versions (Professional, Enterprise, and Ultimate) to run your favorite Windows XP programs. At some point in the future, Microsoft's vendors will upgrade these apps and Windows XP will take the Big Sleep, but until then, this will doubtless be a lifesaver for many.

What's New in Windows 7?

One question people ask us as we write books about each new version of Windows is whether the new version is improved enough to justify the hassle of upgrading. We don't always answer "yes." For example, Windows Me was no major improvement over Windows 98. For that matter, Windows 98 wasn't much to write home about, either (in our opinion, it was much less stable than Win 95). By contrast, XP was a major upgrade from any preceding Windows version. Likewise, Windows 7 is a major upgrade if you haven't jumped onto Vista, mostly because it's been so long since XP made its debut. If you haven't migrated from Win 9x yet, consider this: Microsoft no longer produces security fixes or provides any other support for Windows 95, 98, and Me. Time to jump!

The jump from Windows Vista to Windows 7 is more of an incremental leap (like the jump from Windows 95 to 98), but it brings significant improvements and many changes. Although Windows 7 is a much-improved version of the Windows XP family, preserving many of Windows XP's corporate networking and security features, it also carries many multimedia capabilities from Vista, including support for digital projectors, slideshows, movie making, and DVD burning. Furthermore, in its Ultimate and Home versions, Windows 7 supports Media Center. But of course, Vista also upped the Windows security ante considerably, and introduced the slick, animated Aero interface, which are also part of Windows 7 as well.

 note

In this section, we discuss what's new in Windows 7. We don't bother telling you about boatloads of features and internals that Windows 7 inherits from Vista (and Vista from XP, XP from Win 2000, NT, and so on). Please see our previous books for those dirty little details. (See *Special Edition Using Windows Vista, Second Edition*, for specifics about Vista, *Special Edition Using Windows XP Professional* and *Platinum Edition Using Windows XP* for specifics about XP, *Using Windows 2000* for details about Windows 2000, and so on.) An Amazon search for "Cowart and Knittel" will fetch you a list of our almost 20 years of output as coauthors.

How big a change is Windows 7? Estimates are that by the time it was released, it contained about 50 million lines of code. That's about 12% more code than Windows XP, but about 10% less code than its immediate predecessor, Windows Vista.

Because Windows 7 offers so many improvements and new features compared to Windows Vista, XP, 9x, Me, and 2000, in this section, we highlight some of its new and improved features and what each feature does. Table 1.1 highlights some key improvements found in Windows 7 and points you to the chapter(s) in which each one is covered. Most of them are introduced only briefly in this chapter.

 note

For the first time ever, Windows 7 features a code base smaller than the code base in the preceding version. Microsoft was able to achieve this astonishing reversal thanks to ruthless pruning of old and obsolete code, but also thanks to a new generation of programming tools designed in part to produce more compact code that is also highly secure and reliable.

Table 1.1 Coverage of New and Improved Windows 7 Features

New Windows 7 Features	Covered in Chapters...
Installation and Setup	
Improved Windows Easy Transfer Wizard, User State Migration Tool	1, 3
Faster, easier install and setup	2
Faster, easier Anytime Upgrade	2
User Interface Improvements	
New taskbar	4
Large, animated task thumbnails	4
Jump lists	3
Libraries	4
Aero Snap and Aero Shake	4, 5
Desktop enhancements	4, 5
Improved Start menu search	5
Less cluttered Explorer windows	4
Revised role for gadgets	7
System Security Enhancements	
Improved User Account Control	3
BitLocker to Go	31
AppLocker	1, 30
Multiple active firewall profiles	1, 32
DirectAccess	1

Table 1.1 Continued

New Windows 7 Features	Covered in Chapters...
Improved Web Browsing with IE 8	
Web Slices	14
Accelerators	14
InPrivate Browsing	14
Tab Groups	14
Crash recovery	14
Data Security Enhancements	
Back up to network drive	31
Create System Repair disc	1, 25
Improved Volume Shadow Copy	25, 31
Include/exclude specific backup folders	31
BitLocker to Go	31
VPN Reconnect	1, 35
Performance improvements	
Improved overall performance	1
Improved Windows ReadyBoost	1
Improved Reliability Monitor	1
Improved SSD support	1
New Accessories	
Math Input Panel	1
Sticky Notes	1
Connect to a Projector	1
Power Management	
Reduced power consumption	1, 22, 35
Improved power plans	1, 22, 35
Networking	
Improved Network and Sharing Center	17, 19, 20, 21
Enhanced wireless networking	17, 37
Simplified sharing via homegroups	1, 17, 20
System Management and Stability	
Manage AutoPlay feature for CD/DVD	22
Improved notification area displays	1, 4
Automated third-party troubleshooting	1
Improved system restore and repair	31
One-stop management with Action Center	1, 22

Table 1.1   Continued

New Windows 7 Features	Covered in Chapters...
New, Improved Applications and Services	
Multitouch support	38
PowerShell 2.0	22, 29
Windows Live access	35
Windows XP Mode	1, 2, Appendix A
WordPad enhanced	7
Entertainment	
Media Center versions	9
Launch TV from Start menu	1, 9
Floating Media Center Gadget	1
Copy remote content	1, 9
Play to streaming media	1
Windows Media Player 12	8

Now on to a brief description of these new and/or improved features to brief you on what the Windows 7 hoopla is all about.

Installation and Setup

When it comes to installing and configuring Windows 7, changes are evolutionary rather than revolutionary. Even so, a typical Windows 7 install usually completes in around 30 minutes — almost twice as fast as a typical Vista install. Migrating from older Windows versions and upgrading Windows 7 versions are also improved.

Improved Windows Easy Transfer and Migration Tools

In Windows Vista, you could use either the Windows Easy Transfer Wizard, or the User State Migration Tool (aka USMT) to move user preferences and settings from older versions of Windows into Vista. You could also generate considerable frustration during the process, and still wind up with inconsistent or incomplete results. In Windows 7, both of these tools work more or less as they should, and help transfer user environments from older Windows versions into Windows 7, including Vista and older Windows versions. But neither tool moves applications over, while some applications that require logins, such as Outlook, still require user accounts to be re-created and passwords re-assigned.

Faster, Easier Install and Setup

Windows 7 normally takes less than half an hour to install, which is faster than any versions we've worked with since the 1990s. It also involves fewer reboots, less user interaction, and generally less muss and fuss. You'll get the chance to follow several installation step-by-step in Chapter 2, but we think you'll be pleasantly surprised as you do your own Windows 7 installations.

Faster, Easier Anytime Upgrade

Here again, Windows 7 delivers what Windows Vista promised and failed to do. The concept in Vista with Anytime Upgrade was: get an upgrade key, perform the upgrade, done! In practice with Vista, this proved a bit more difficult and often involved using install media, Internet, or phone interaction with Microsoft for a new install key, and an hour or more to run through the upgrade install. In practice with Windows 7, the whole process can complete in under ten minutes, and obtaining a key can go even faster.

Interface Improvements

Hands down, Windows 7 is the best-looking version of Windows ever, even better than Vista. Even before you have time to check out all the improved functionality listed in Table 1.1, you'll notice the flashy glassy look of Windows 7, called Aero, which carries over from Vista. Microsoft took Vista one better in Windows 7, with a cleaned-up and better-looking GUI.

New Taskbar

The Windows 7 taskbar features larger, more-attractive icons than in Vista or previous versions (see Figure 1.1). It's often much easier to tell what's what by looking at the taskbar, where the Start menu icon remains at the far left, followed by icons for programs pinned to the taskbar and programs that are currently running. In Figure 1.1, the Snipping Tool (scissors) is running to the right of the Windows Media Player icon (fourth from left). To its right is a generic program icon for Spyware Blaster.

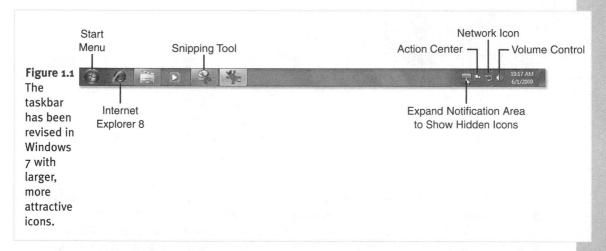

Figure 1.1
The taskbar has been revised in Windows 7 with larger, more attractive icons.

At the far right of the taskbar you see the revised system tray, which is known as the notification area. The flag icon proffers access to the new Windows 7 Action Center (more on this later in the chapter), with the network icon and volume control icon to its right. All other notification area icons are readily accessible through the upward-pointing arrow to the left of the Action Center icon.

You'll have to work with the new taskbar to learn to appreciate it, but you'll find it quite convenient as you get to know it better. One particular favorite, carried over from Vista, is the Search box in the Start menu; we'll discuss this further later in this chapter.

Large Animated Task Thumbnails

When you move the mouse cursor over an icon on the left side of the taskbar, it displays a large icon for the highlighted item (see Figure 1.2). These icons are actually large enough to give you a sense of what's going on inside the program. In Figure 1.2, we highlighted Windows Explorer opened to the My Pictures folder, and you can read the folder name and see how many files are inside the folder in its current Details view (if a Thumbnail view were turned on, you could see thumbnails of those thumbnails, in fact).

...and a large icon appears, enabling you to see the contents of the folder or file.

Figure 1.2
Windows 7 improves upon the taskbar icons by making them bigger and easier to read.

Hover your mouse over an icon in the taskbar...

This feature comes in handy to let you know what your minimized programs are doing, and to help remind you about what's what if you have numerous windows active on your desktop.

Jump Lists

If you right-click an icon in the taskbar, you get a pop-up window that Microsoft calls a Jump List. It provides access to frequently used commands associated with that particular icon, or to frequently visited locations associated with its applications. Figure 1.3 displays the Jump List for Windows Explorer, which shows a list of frequently visited folders and drives above the dividing line, and a set of commands below. This a handy way to use programs pinned to the taskbar and programs open on your desktop.

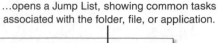

...opens a Jump List, showing common tasks associated with the folder, file, or application.

Figure 1.3
Jump Lists provide easy access to commonly performed tasks related to the item in the taskbar.

Right-clicking an icon in the taskbar...

Libraries

A library is a new grouping construct in Windows 7. It lets you grab files, documents, or whatever you want from anywhere on your system and put it in a container, presumably with other items of the same general kind, or perhaps for a single project or task. In Figure 1.4, you see the four default libraries that Windows 7 provides automatically: Documents, Music, Pictures, and Videos.

What makes these libraries different from the old Documents, Pictures, Music, and Videos entries for each user account (or My Documents, My Pictures, and so forth) is that you can add content from anywhere on your system to them, yet access and search their contents through a single, consistent Explorer window. Although music files might be located in multiple folders on multiple drives on a Windows 7 system, for example, you can see and access all of them through the Music library.

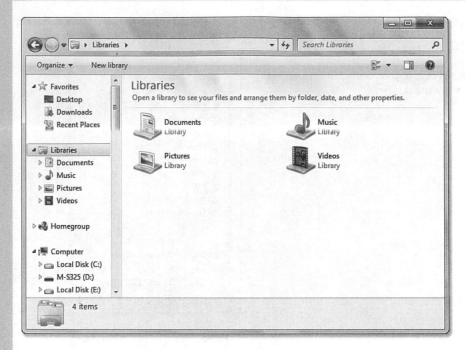

Figure 1.4
Libraries group com-
mon file types for
easy access.

Homegroups

A homegroup is a local network sharing tool that Windows 7 sets up automatically. The first
Windows 7 machine to join a network establishes a password, after which any other Windows 7
machine that joins the network can supply that password to share content. By default, all predefined Windows 7 libraries may be shared, though Documents is disabled and Music, Videos, and
Pictures are enabled by default, and the Printers homegroup is enabled as well. Figure 1.5 shows
part of the Music library on another Windows 7 machine in a local homegroup, which has an external USB drive with an entire music collection attached to it.

Homegroups simplify network sharing on small-scale networks. In older versions of Windows, users
had to supply a login and password for a target machine, or map a network drive to access shared
content or devices. In Windows 7, users need only join the homegroup and access to everything
shared within that group comes along with that membership. You'll find more information on this
topic in Chapters 17 and 20.

Figure 1.5
Homegroups provide an easy way to set up multiple networks and share specific files with specific users.

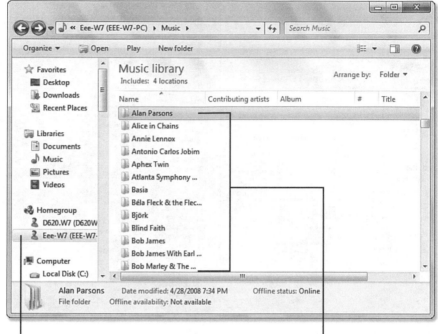

Clicking on this homegroup…   …enables the homegroup member to access these files.

Aero Snap Behavior

"Aero Snap" refers to windows placement and sizing behaviors new to Windows 7. By dragging a window to the left or right side of your display, you can force it to fit itself to the right or left half of your screen. By dragging a window to the top of your display, you can maximize it to fill the whole screen. These functions can be helpful on large displays, when you want to split the viewing area between two open windows, as shown in Figure 1.6. Notice that Internet Explorer occupies the left half, and Windows Explorer the right half. Depending on your monitor's resolution, you might have more real estate than what is shown here.

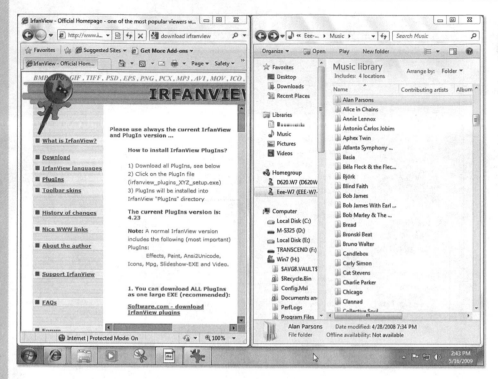

Figure 1.6
Aero Snap enables you to easily size more than one window to fit onscreen.

Desktop Enhancements

Windows 7 includes some desktop eye candy that's both attractive and interesting. Several sets of Aero Themes are provided as part of Windows 7, which rotate your desktop background among a collection of gorgeous photographs that size all the way up to HD monitor resolution (1920×1200) without stretching or tiling. You'll find numerous themes, including

- **Architecture**—A set of photographs of outstanding modern architecture

- **Characters**—Computer graphics depicting fanciful scenes and cartoon-inspired figures

- **Landscapes**—Knockout nature photographs of postcard-worthy vistas and scenes

- **Nature**—Lush photos of various forms of plant life

- **Scenes**—More fanciful computer graphics, with a distinctly Peter Max feel

- **United States**—More postcard-worthy photos of American landscapes

To access this window, right-click on your Windows 7 desktop, and select Personalize from the resulting pop-up menu. When you select an Aero Theme, you'll find that window color, sounds, and the screen saver all also change with the rotating set of backgrounds. These various themes are depicted inside the Personalization window shown in Figure 1.7.

Figure 1.7
Windows 7 includes a variety of attractive themes you can use to alter how your desktop and windows appear.

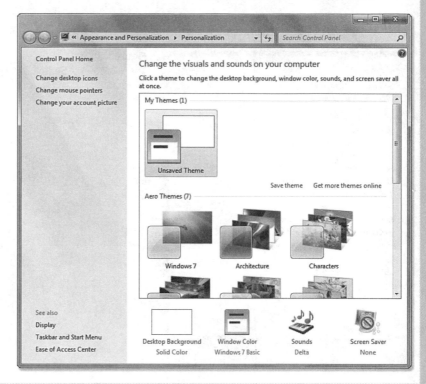

Improved Start Menu Search

Although the Start menu in Vista added the Search box to its bag of tricks, those tricks have been refined considerably in Windows 7. It's easier than ever to find programs, utilities, or other system features by searching for them. With Vista you had to know some part of your search target's filename or window name to get a solid hit while searching. In Windows 7, any good descriptive phrase will often work even if you can't remember some utility's complete or correct name. For example, look at Figure 1.8 to see all the backup-related entries and items that pop up simply by typing **back** into the Search box. You can use Windows 7's improved search capabilities to very good effect, right from the Start menu.

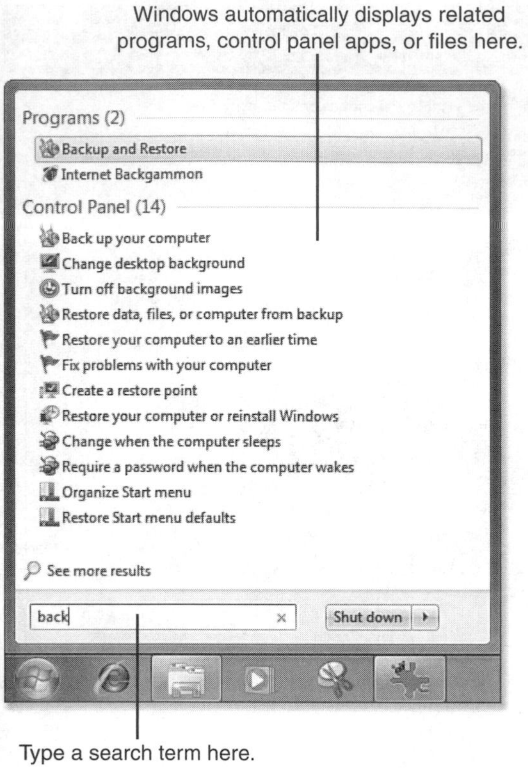

Windows automatically displays related
programs, control panel apps, or files here.

Programs (2)

- Backup and Restore
- Internet Backgammon

Control Panel (14)

- Back up your computer
- Change desktop background
- Turn off background images
- Restore data, files, or computer from backup
- Restore your computer to an earlier time
- Fix problems with your computer
- Create a restore point
- Restore your computer or reinstall Windows
- Change when the computer sleeps
- Require a password when the computer wakes
- Organize Start menu
- Restore Start menu defaults

See more results

back   ✕   Shut down ▶

Type a search term here.

Figure 1.8
The Windows 7 Search function has received a needed overhaul.

Less Cluttered Explorer Windows

Hopefully, you've noticed Windows 7's spare and uncluttered interface windows in Explorer in many of the preceding screenshots. The same look and feel applies to anything that uses the Explorer UI to manage its onscreen appearance. Thus, this applies to everything from Control Panel, to Games, to Network, Library, Homegroup, and other information display windows. As you work with Windows 7, you should come to appreciate its spare but attractive design.

Revised Role for Gadgets

Windows Vista introduced Windows Sidebar, an area at the right edge of the primary display on the desktop reserved for small programs called *gadgets*. By default, Vista included in Windows Sidebar a clock, a calendar, a rotating photo display, and an RSS feed area for headlines, but countless other gadgets were also available for Vista.

Oodles of gadgets are likewise available for Windows 7, too (and most Vista gadgets run on Windows 7), but there's no Sidebar anymore. By default, gadgets still migrate to the right edge of your primary display, but if you don't like them there you can drag and drop them anywhere on your desktop. There's also no default set of gadgets for Windows 7, so you get to pick whichever ones you like and place them where you like them (though a base set of gadgets similar to the Vista default set is supplied with Windows 7). Figure 1.9 shows some personal favorites on the right edge of the screen. You can interact with gadgets on a Windows 7 system by typing **gadget** into the Start menu search box, and then selecting View List or Add Gadgets from the search results.

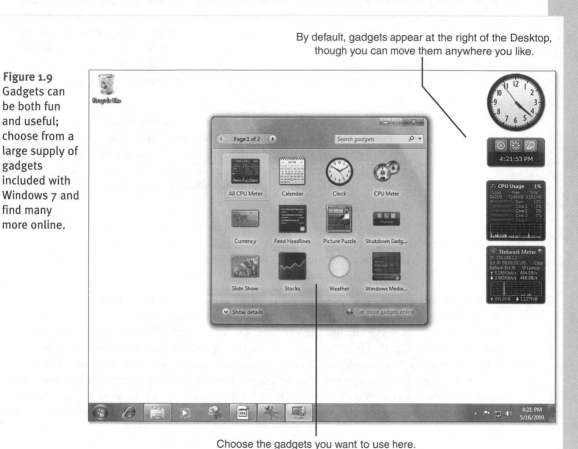

By default, gadgets appear at the right of the Desktop, though you can move them anywhere you like.

Figure 1.9
Gadgets can be both fun and useful; choose from a large supply of gadgets included with Windows 7 and find many more online.

Choose the gadgets you want to use here.

System Security Enhancements

Certainly, the most often-heard beef about Windows (even XP) is that it's too fragile and vulnerable to malware and hackers. Some say it's simply not robust enough. Microsoft hears it, too, from ordinary users and experts alike. Imagine their support calls. So with each new iteration of Windows, Microsoft tries to harden it against onslaught. (Of course, if it were not for the popularity of Windows, hacking it wouldn't be an issue, so the naysayers have a somewhat specious argument, in our opinion.) For each new and creative plan of attack, a counterattack or defense emerges. Thus, Windows 7 has a new batch of security enhancements:

- **Improved User Account Control (UAC)**—In XP, users too often give themselves administrative privileges, which sometimes lets malicious programs run amok. Windows 7 gives *everyone* low levels of privilege until they need more. This will result in dialog boxes asking you to confirm certain things can run before they're let loose. It's not as intrusive as it was with Vista, but it still helps prevent secretive programs from running without your knowledge. Even better, you can adjust the level of confirmations that Windows 7 requests, so that only programs seeking elevated privileges cause alerts, but you're allowed to install programs, change settings, and so forth (as long as your account possesses the necessary rights, of course). This is a big improvement over Vista, for sure!

- **BitLocker to Go**—Vista introduced BitLocker, an encrypted and secure form of on-disk storage that only those with the right password can access. In Windows 7, BitLocker to Go extends this capability to USB drives, including USB flash drives (UFDs), so that you can secure some or all of the contents on drives or devices that you take with you on the road. This is a great way to protect against unwanted disclosure resulting from theft or loss of a notebook or a portable storage devices of some kind.

- **AppLocker**—Windows 7 lets system administrators apply a kind of "whitelist" control to applications on user desktops. In other words, they can create lists of valid applications and use Group Policy objects to apply them to what users can see and launch on their desktops. If an application isn't on the list, users can't run it: What better way to keep them out of trouble?

- **Multiple active firewall profiles**—In the Windows 7 environment, Windows Firewall settings depend on the firewall profile in use. Previous versions of Windows allowed only one firewall profile to be active at any one time. In Windows 7, each network adapter on a PC can apply whichever firewall profile is most appropriate for the type of network to which it connects (which will differ considerably from home, to office, to public/unsecured networks). Thus, if you're working in an airport coffee shop and using a virtual private network (VPN) connection to access a server at your office, the firewall rules for the office VPN will apply to all traffic to and from that location, and the firewall rules for a public network will apply to all other traffic to and from your PC.

- **DirectAccess**—This applies only to Windows 7 computers that belong to an Active Directory domain on a Windows Server 2008 R2 server. Within that framework, however, users can connect to office/domain network resources whenever they access the Internet. Connection speed aside, such Internet users have the same experience accessing office/domain network elements that they would if they were locally attached to that network. This technology also lets system administrators manage Windows 7 computers remotely, no matter where they may be at any given moment.

- **VPN Reconnect**—This facility lets Windows 7 users automatically reestablish VPN connections as soon as they regain Internet access. This lets users turn off or disconnect their machines from the Internet at will, yet re-creates their secure office network connections as soon as they regain Internet access, using secure protocols that require no user interaction to set up and maintain.

Improved Web Browsing with IE 8

Internet browsing remains the most widely used application on the PC desktop. As such, it behooves Microsoft to make its browser ever better. Ironically, Internet Explorer has been the bane of Microsoft's (and users') existence, constantly being one-upped by Netscape, Opera, Mozilla Firefox, and others. IE is a constant target for hackers, so Windows Update regularly doles out updates to harden IE; still, it's a game of catch-up, for the most part. As mentioned earlier in this chapter, Windows 7 lowers the privilege level of IE now to help protect your PC. On the user end of things, IE 8 ups the bar on performance by keeping up with the Joneses again. Here's what IE delivers (you must upgrade other versions, but Windows 7 has it built right in):

- **Web Slices**—These items let you keep up with regularly updated sites from the Favorites bar. When a Web Slice is available on a page, a green Web Slices icon appears in the upper-right corner of the browser. Click it to add it to the Favorites, and it's never more than a click away at any time.

- **Accelerators**—IE 8 offers a built-in collection of web add-ons and enhancements that Microsoft calls Accelerators. To use any Accelerator, right-click a word or phrase on any web page, and then click the Accelerator button that pops up, or use the All Accelerators entry in the pop-up menu. There, you'll find tools for blogging, web searching, email, maps, translating, and more, as shown in Figure 1.10.

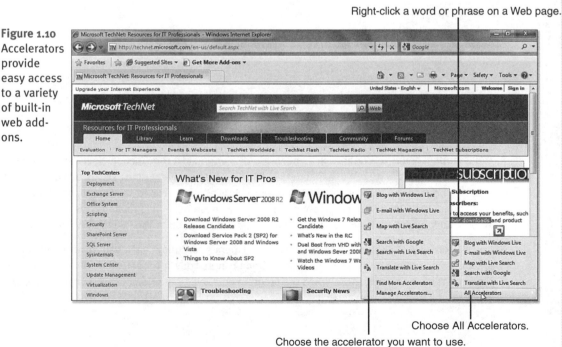

Figure 1.10 Accelerators provide easy access to a variety of built-in web add-ons.

Right-click a word or phrase on a Web page.

Choose All Accelerators.

Choose the accelerator you want to use.

- **InPrivate Browsing**—This new mode of operation lets you surf the Web without leaving any trail behind in Internet Explorer: no history, no cookies, no URLs, no nothing. To use InPrivate Browsing, you must use the New Tab control (Click File, New Tab), and then select Use InPrivate Browsing. Or, click the Safety entry in the IE Command bar (top right above main window), then select InPrivate Browsing. Either way, a new IE window opens that reads "InPrivate is turned on," as shown in Figure 1.11.

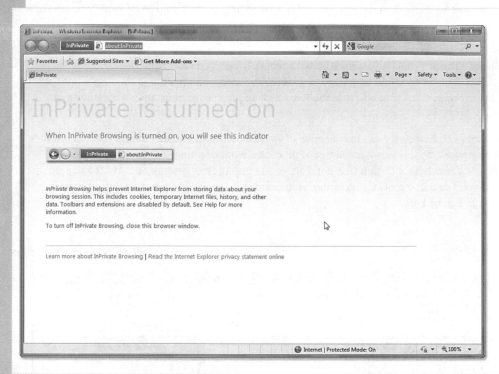

Figure 1.11
InPrivate Browsing allows you to surf without leaving a trail of your online activities.

- **Tab Groups**—When you right-click a link inside IE 8 and select the Open in New Tab menu item, the browser opens another tab as requested. This repeats as many times as you use this facility from any page in the current set of tabs. IE also colors all such related tabs green, so that any time you look at a page in that group, you can tell all those pages are related. This makes it easy to tell which pages are interlinked as you jump around from tab to tab inside IE. Very handy.

- **Crash Recovery**—Call this a "catch-up" feature: Opera and Firefox have had this capability for some time now. But now, when you close IE 8 you can instruct it to remember all tabs and open pages on the next restart. Also, when the program crashes, IE 8 automatically restores all open pages on the next restart as well.

Data Security Enhancements

Maintaining data integrity on the PC is a constant job for IT people. Independent businesspeople without the aid of an IT professional worry about this just as much as the IT folks, if not more so, partly because they don't know what to do when things go south. In addition to the stability improvements listed earlier, there are two areas of significant improvement in data security (outlined here and in Part VII of this book).

- **Back up to network drive**—On previous Windows versions, the only drives to which you could back up were those attached directly to your PC, either internally or via eSATA or USB. On Windows 7, any network-accessible drive becomes a valid backup target. For those (like us) with a MediaSmart Server already on their home networks, this is fantastic!

- **Manage AutoPlay behavior for CDs/DVDs**—Recently, worms and viruses triggered by AutoPlay for CDs and DVDs have surfaced on the Internet, primarily in the form of BitTorrent-based ISO downloads. Burn a DVD from such a download, and you'll contract a virus as soon as you run the setup or other default executable from that image file. Most antivirus programs, and thus most Windows systems, are defenseless against this kind of attack. Windows 7 lets you block AutoPlay behaviors on optical disks, and sidestep this kind of vulnerability. Bravo, Microsoft!

- **Create System Repair Disc**—To create a bootable DVD that you can use to repair your system, click Create a System Repair Disc in the left column of the Backup and Restore Center and insert a blank DVD (see Figure 1.12). This option is much easier than finding the installation media for Windows Vista—especially if you bought a machine with Windows 7 preinstalled and didn't get an install disc! To access the Backup and Recovery center, type **backup** into the Start menu search box, and select that utility from the search results.

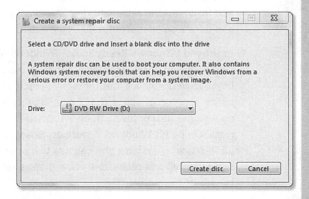

Figure 1.12
Creating a system repair disc now could save you major headaches down the road!

- **Improved Volume Shadow Copy**—Windows Volume Shadow Copy Service (VSS) is responsible for creating restore points and for making copies of files as they change on your system. On Windows Vista, VSS could sometimes impose onerous burdens on a drive: 15% or more might get allocated to the System Volume Information folder (we had a situation once where 120GB on a 750GB drive went into that folder). For Windows 7, shadow copy space is limited to 5% of total drive space for drives over 64GB in size, and 3GB for drives 64GB and under in size. This helps keep shadow copy storage under control by default.

- **Include/exclude specific backup folders**—When backing up in Windows 7, you now have the option of including or excluding specific folders from the volumes you elect to back up. This provides much greater control over backup content and activity, and allows you to set up and schedule multiple backup tasks to capture different data for each task.

Table 1.1 also mentions BitLocker to Go and VPN Reconnect as data security enhancements. Because they're also system security enhancements, we don't repeat the information on those topics we provided in our earlier section ("System Security Enhancements").

Performance Improvements

Computers always seem to slow down over time, and no matter how fast the hardware gets, things always seem to run at the same speed. What we might have called a supercomputer a few years ago now runs word processing and email apps about as fast as it did when CPUs ran at a fraction of their current speeds. This is because code has grown larger and more complex to take advantage of added processing power, so that users haven't experienced serious perceptual performance gains. But by comparison with Vista, several speed-ups in Windows 7 are worth mentioning.

- **Improved overall performance**—As previously mentioned, Windows 7 requires less memory and less computing horsepower than Windows Vista. Case in point: Windows 7 works nicely on net-book PCs with 1- or 2GB of RAM, 1.6GHz Intel Atom processors, and minimal disk space (less than 32GB is pushing things, but 32GB works just fine); Vista drags or hangs on that resource budget. Windows 7 also runs nicely in Microsoft Virtual PC 2007, where virtual machines get only single-processor access, even on dual- or quad-core computers; Windows Vista runs slowly and fitfully in the same situation. All in all, you'll find that Windows 7 boots faster, runs faster, and uses less memory and disk space than Vista. How's that for improved overall performance?

- **Improved Windows ReadyBoost**—Windows Vista introduced ReadyBoost, which lets users allocate space on a UFD or SD card for extra system cache space. We all know that adding RAM can improve performance, but for many people, this is difficult to do and might violate a maintenance contract or annoy the IT people at a company. On Vista, ReadyBoost was limited to 4GB on a single UFD or SD card; on Windows 7, ReadyBoost cache size limits apply only to 32-bit systems. On 64-bit Windows 7 systems, ReadyBoost can be about as big as you want to make it; on all Windows 7 systems you can use two or more UFDs or memory cards to create a single mono-lithic ReadyBoost cache. See www.grantgibson.co.ukmisc/readyboost for test results for many brands of flash drive.

- **Improved Reliability Monitor**—Windows Vista introduced the Reliability Monitor, which reports on system problems, errors, and stability. In Windows 7, this useful facility is expanded and improved. For one thing, it updates the reliability index (a number between 1 and 10 that reflects the system's reliability over time) whenever errors or problems occur (the Vista version didn't update until midnight on the day of occurrence). For another, the Reliability Monitor now integrates the search for solutions to problems right into its interface (in Vista, you had to use the Problems and Solutions applet in Control Panel to do this). Overall, the Windows 7 Reliability

Monitor takes a good concept and makes it better. As Figure 1.13 shows, all reliability info now falls under a single interface. To access this tool, type `reli` into the Start menu search box, then select View Reliability History from the results.

Figure 1.13
The Reliability Monitor tracks your computer's problem history and helps you locate solutions.

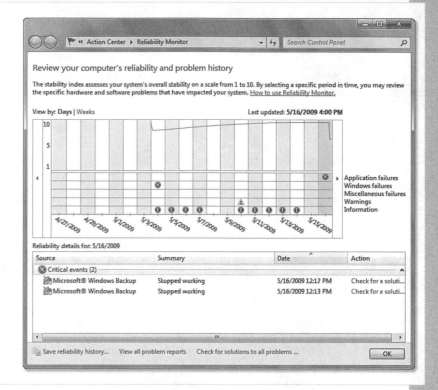

- **Improved SSD support**—A solid-state disk (SSD) is a type of storage device that uses flash memory chips to store data instead of common hard drives. Windows 7 can recognize and work with SSDs much more effectively and directly than previous versions of Windows could, mostly by disabling disk access behaviors that are suitable or necessary for rotating media but unsuitable or unnecessary on solid-state devices (such as turning off defragmentation, which isn't needed on SSDs, adding better support for lazy write/erase operations, disabling SuperFetch, ReadyBoost, and boot or application launch prefetching because access times on SSDs are so fast). If you use Windows 7 on a PC with an SSD, you'll notice faster performance and an increased lifetime for the drive.

New Accessories

Historically, Microsoft has packed ever-increasing globs of accessories into Windows. In the olden days of Windows 1.0 you were lucky to get a clock and one game. Windows 7 departs from tradition and adds only a few items to its software offerings and, almost unbelievably, removes some supplied applications (many applications are now offloaded into the Windows Live service online). To access these and other Windows Accessories, click Start, All Programs, Accessories. Here's what's new for accessories in Windows 7:

- **Math Input Panel**—Lets you use the mouse to enter mathematical formulas of all kinds. This tool takes a little practice to learn but offers a handier way to create formulas than using MathML or formula entry in Word or Excel.

- **Sticky Notes**—Use this to drop a note onto your screen view anywhere you like. The note stays visible until you decide to close it, and works well as an editable addition to your gadgets. Figure 1.14 shows a simple to-do list, but you can use Sticky Notes for whatever you want.

Figure 1.14
Use Sticky Notes to jot notes—useful for grocery lists, reminders, phone notes, anything you can think of!

- **Connect to a Projector**—Lets you direct video to a DVI- or VGA-attached video projector. You can duplicate what you see on your screen (typical for a presentation) or extend your desktop from the current display(s) to include a projector. This is handy for those who must work in conference rooms giving presentations.

Power Management

As energy conservation and consumption loom ever larger in assessing true costs of computer ownership, and users seek to cut those costs, Windows power management tools have gained considerable importance. Windows 7 makes some nice additions and enhancements to power management features already present in Windows Vista (and to some extent in Windows XP as well).

Reduced Power Consumption

By paying closer attention to Windows activity levels, Windows 7 can implement sleep or hibernation features in modern PCs, and even shut down system components that aren't in use. Most users can turn these capabilities to best advantage on battery-powered PCs, where conserving energy translates directly into longer battery life. But even for computers plugged into a wall socket, reduced power consumption translates into lower overall costs for electricity.

Improved Power Plans

The Power Options item in Control Panel remains the primary means of access to power plans and their behavior in Windows 7, just as it was in Vista and XP. Users who spend some time investigating this utility will find only two basic plans (Balanced and Power User) rather than the three from earlier versions (Balanced, Power Saver, and High Performance in Vista, and six or more Power Schemes in XP) but many more options and more nuanced controls in the Advanced Settings window. Click Start, Control Panel, System and Security, Power Options, Change Plan Settings, Change Advanced Power Settings. There's a new Desktop Background Settings (to enable/disable rotating desktop backgrounds) entry, many more Sleep options, and even a System Cooling Policy option in Processor Power Management. Some early testing indicates that Windows 7 can extend battery life by as much as 10% as compared to Vista on identical hardware.

Networking

Windows 7 networking includes a variety of new features. Chief among these is a reworked version of the Network and Sharing Center, but you'll also find some nice improvements to wireless networking, and simplified resource sharing on home networks thanks to homegroups.

Improved Network and Sharing Center

The Network and Sharing Center is a single location that lets you easily perform common network tasks, much as the Mobility Center does for portable computers:

- Set up a new connection or network

- Connect to a network

- Choose homegroup and sharing options

- Troubleshoot problems

The Network and Sharing Center also provides some great functionality upgrades, including

- **Change Adapter Settings**—Click this entry in the left pane of the Network and Sharing Center and get right to work on adapter configuration settings.

- **Change Advanced Sharing Settings**—Also located in the left pane of the Network and Sharing Center, this is another way into homegroup setup and sharing instructions.

- **See Full Map**—Lets you see the entire network you're connected to in a visual display, with icons that include routers and switches (see Figure 1.15). This helps the network make more sense, especially if you are troubleshooting. To see this map, right-click the network icon in the notification area, select Network and Sharing Center in the pop-up menu, and click See Full Map in that window's upper-right corner.

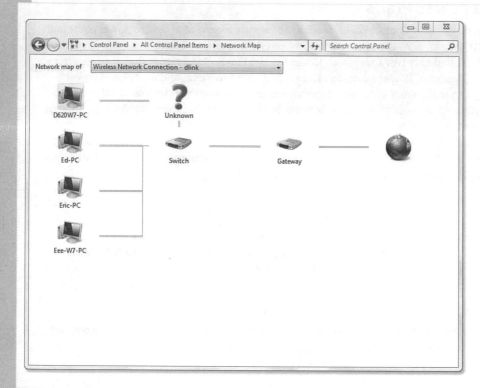

Figure 1.15
The Network Map displays your network visually, which makes troubleshooting easier.

Enhanced Wireless Networking

Just click the network icon in the notification area and you get instant access to all nearby wireless networks (see Figure 1.16), and one-click access to all important networking functions from there. This is much simpler than in earlier versions of Windows, where you had to click through the system tray icon, into any of several utilities (disconnect or connect commands in Vista, View Available Wireless Networks or Open Network Connections in XP) to micro-manage wireless networking tasks.

Figure 1.16
Instantly see and connect to available networks via the network icon in the notification area.

Other available networks appear here.
The currently connected network appears here.

Click the Network icon

Simplified Sharing via Homegroups

We've already introduced homegroups in the "Interface Improvements" section earlier in this chapter, but it's worthwhile to observe in a networking context that sharing resources is both incredibly simple and entirely automatic for Windows 7 computers. Once you join a local homegroup, you automatically gain access to all resources shared with that group—by default, this includes the contents of the pre-defined Videos, Music, and Pictures libraries, plus any shared printers (but not people's Documents libraries). All of this material is easily and naturally available to all homegroup members through their own libraries. It simply doesn't get any easier than that!

System Management and Stability

Stability is probably the most important issue when considering whether to upgrade to a new OS or buy a computer with it installed. Early adopters have a choice about this, but as an OS becomes ubiquitous and new PCs come with it already installed, we must make peace with the thing. After the likes of Windows Me (we liked to call it Windows 666), the real question we always want answered is, "Does it crash less?" Windows 7 has some pretty impressive anticrash technology. Think of them as antilock brakes and airbags for your computer:

- **Manage AutoPlay feature for CD/DVD**—With the recent introduction of malware that exploits Windows AutoPlay to install itself on unprotected systems, Microsoft made some important changes to AutoPlay behavior. You can now instruct the OS to prompt you for permission before automatically running programs from an optical disc, which you may wish to deny for untrusted media on systems that don't yet have anti-malware software installed. A nasty variant introduced a Trojan horse into the Windows 7 setup.exe file on some BitTorrent sites while the operating system was still in pre-release, in fact. If you must run an ISO or other bootable DVD on an unprotected system, be sure to scan the media or the ISO image on another protected system first and only run those that are provably clean on vulnerable PCs.

- **Improved notification area displays**—Windows 7 presents quicker, easier access to key status and troubleshooting information in its notification area. Most notably, this includes the Action Center, which unifies security, troubleshooting, and maintenance alerts in a single window.

- **Automated third-party troubleshooting**—Microsoft opened up its Help and Support APIs to third-party vendors for Windows 7. This might not sound like a big deal, but it means that vendors can build their own troubleshooting utilities, then plug them directly into the Help and Support environment. In the best cases, which we hope includes most responsible vendors, you'll be able to troubleshoot third-party devices much more easily with this latest Windows OS.

- **Improved system restore and repair**—As we worked with Windows 7 we found ample reason to admire its stability and resilience. No single incident impressed us more than this one: After we applied a beta graphics driver, we found ourselves looking at a black screen (which basically means the graphics driver failed miserably). By pressing Ctrl+Alt+Esc we were able to launch the Task Manager, from whence we typed `restrui.exe` to launch the System Restore utility. From there, we rolled back to the most recent restore point and kept right on working. No previous version of Windows, to our knowledge, has ever been able to support this kind of repair and restore operation. Factor in the built-in Create a System Repair Disc option in the Backup and Restore Center (Vista requires you to find and use the installation media to run repairs on an otherwise unbootable machine) and you've got an unbeatable combination. When it comes to repair, we *like* Windows 7!

- **One-stop management with Action Center**—The Windows 7 Action Center brings security and maintenance handling together under a single umbrella. By providing a single place to view, access, and address all system issues, whether security- or stability-related, Windows 7 improves your ability to recognize, identify, and solve problems on your system.

New, Improved Applications and Services

Windows 7 makes numerous additions to its applications and services arsenal, including the following:

- **Multitouch support**—Vista added Tablet PC support for Business, Enterprise, Home Premium, and Ultimate Editions. Windows 7 builds on this platform with support for Multitouch, a way to use visual gestures on touchscreens to instruct Windows 7 what to do, and how to behave. To better understand this capability, watch the Microsoft video demo at http://video.msn.com/video.aspx?vid=8700c7ff-546f-4e1d-85f7-65659dd1f14f.

- **PowerShell 2.0**—PowerShell is a scripting language that you can use to automate just about anything that Windows can do, especially at the command line. With Vista, you can download and install PowerShell 1.1 from the Windows Download Center; PowerShell 2.0—which is both more powerful and more flexible than 1.x versions—is bundled as part of Windows 7. Check out the PowerShell Pro demo at www.powershellpro.com/powershell-tutorial-introduction for all the details.

- **Windows Live access**—Whereas earlier versions of Windows, including both XP and Vista, included e-mail, messaging, photo handling, and address book functionality as part of the OS, Windows 7 pushes all this functionality onto the Internet. Although registration is required, you can use Windows Live for all kinds of activities for free. Check it out at http://home.live.com.

- **Windows XP Mode**—For compatibility with legacy applications that work in Windows XP, users of Windows 7 Professional, Enterprise, and Ultimate can all download the free Windows XP Mode package. It not only provides a tailored version of Microsoft Virtual PC with a pre-fab Windows XP virtual hard disk (VHD), it also provides a free license for the XP OS you run inside that machine. Designed to make it easy to run older applications that don't work on Vista or Windows 7, this utility makes it easy to keep older code operational in a virtual machine. See Appendix A, "Using Virtualization on Windows 7," for details.

- **WordPad**—This venerable alternative to Microsoft Word comes free with modern Windows versions and gets a complete makeover in Windows 7. Whereas the older versions let you read and work with DOC files, this latest version also understands XML-based formats (DOCX) and provides a ribbon interface that looks and behaves very much like (a stripped-down version of) Word 2007.

Entertainment

A few odds and ends in the entertainment department are worth noting. Though this is not the full list, these are the notables:

- **Media Center versions**—The Ultimate and Home Premium editions include Media Center, including support for Media Center Extender and Media Center Games. Media Center, just as in Vista (or in XP Media Center Edition), marries to a specific kind of computer that meets Media Center specifications. As always, Media Center PCs are designed for home entertainment, are typically more quiet than normal PCs, and come with remote controls and other goodies. They can connect easily to projectors and TV sets so you can record and watch TV, see slick slideshows of your digital images, watch movies, listen to your MP3 songs, and so on, all using a hand-held remote control. Windows 7 Media Center supports improved HDTV recording (if you have an HDTV source, that is) and built-in Blu-ray playback support. It has a better menuing system that is easier to navigate, and handles multiple displays (usually HDTV set and PC monitor) much better than Vista or XP Media Center versions.

- **Launch TV from Start menu**—You can put Media Center at the head of the Start menu, or on the taskbar, and use its Jump List features to see (and play back) recently recorded shows as well as regularly used features and commands.

- **Floating Media Center gadget**—Drop this gadget on your desktop, and you don't even need to hit the Start menu or taskbar to access Media Center commands and controls.

- **Copy remote content**—When browsing several media libraries (Music, Videos, Pictures, and so on) you can view or save content for later use by instructing Windows 7 to make a copy. As long as no digital rights restrictions adhere to the item you choose, it gets copied to your local hard disk, where you can play it back at your leisure.

- **Play to streaming media**—In a long-overdue move, Windows 7 adds support for DLNA (Digital Living Network Alliance) devices to Media Center. This gives the OS the information it needs to enroll any DLNA devices on your network in its database, whereupon it can push media to that device on your command (given multiple DLNA devices on a network, things get even more interesting in that Windows 7 Media Center can pull the stream from one DLNA device and play it back itself, or push it to another DLNA devices instead). This makes streaming media on home networks with Media Center much easier and, in fact, fun. Good job, Microsoft!

- **Windows Media Player 12**—Windows Media Player 12 comes standard with Windows 7. It has numerous new features, including support for Libraries. It also supports numerous media-streaming options, including local network and Internet-based access to your media collection. Version 12 doesn't represent quite the facelift we saw in version 11, but there are some nice changes here for mediaphiles.

Differences Among Windows 7 Versions

Windows 7 comes in six basic versions in the U.S. market:

- Windows 7 Starter
- Windows 7 Home Basic
- Windows 7 Home Premium

- Windows 7 Professional

- Windows 7 Enterprise

- Windows 7 Ultimate

Although all versions contain the same integrated applications and many of the same multimedia features, Professional and Enterprise editions include greater security and emphasize the needs of the business sector (Enterprise is available only through special corporate licensing agreements, not via retail). The Starter version is available only pre-installed on low-end PCs (primarily netbook PCs). Home versions emphasize the multimedia experience. For the buyer who has to have it all, the Ultimate version leaves nothing out.

Furthermore, 64-bit versions are available for all platforms. As of this writing, most users will be running the x86 code base because their computers have 4GB or less RAM installed. But as more computers begin to ship with 4GB or more RAM installed, that will change. Then 64-bit CPUs, such as AMD's Athlon 64 and Opteron, or Intel's Core Duo and i7 families, can take advantage of their speed and other enhancements.

The 64-bit versions use an emulation layer called WOW64 to run Win32-based applications, although, for best performance, Microsoft recommends using 32-bit software on 32-bit Windows systems. The emulation feature enables organizations to use their Itanium-based systems with existing Windows applications until they create 64-bit versions created internally or purchase them from software vendors.

Table 1.2 compares the features in the various versions of Windows 7.

Table 1.3 outlines the upgrade options mapped to the different Windows 7 editions.

note

Certain limitations apply to 64-bit Windows versions. For example, there is no Win16 or MS-DOS support, so you cannot run 16-bit Windows (3.*x* and 9*x*) or DOS applications. You might occasionally encounter issues with availability of 64-bit device drivers for the 64-bit platform. Many experts believe that home/small office users should install the 32-bit version of Windows 7 even if they have x64 processors, and should use the 64-bit versions only if they must run specific 64-bit apps with huge memory requirements (such as Adobe PhotoShop or Flash Professional). We think the dawn of the 64-bit age has finally started, and with Windows 7 you can go either way (32- or 64-bit, that is).

note

The *N* versions of the Home Basic and Professional editions (available in Europe) are similar to U.S. versions, but omit multimedia features such as Windows Media Player and IE. The Windows 7 Starter edition is available in 139 countries with emerging technology markets and leaves out some features found in Windows 7 Home Basic. This book does not cover these editions.

Table 1.2   Various Versions of Windows 7 Compared

Some information in this table was adapted from information found on Paul Thurrott's incredibly informative Windows Supersite (www.winsupersite.com).

Feature	Starter	Home Basic	Home Premium	Professional	Enterprise/ Ultimate
Windows Basic UI	Yes	No	Yes	Yes	Yes
Windows Standard UI	No	Yes	Yes	Yes	Yes
Windows Aero UI	No	No	Yes	Yes	Yes
Aero Peek	No	No	Yes	Yes	Yes
Aero Shake	No	No	Yes	Yes	Yes
Aero Background	No	No	Yes	Yes	Yes
Windows Flip 3D	No	No	Yes	Yes	Yes
Live Taskbar Previews	No	Yes	Yes	Yes	Yes
Fast User Switching	No	Yes	Yes	Yes	Yes
Number of CPUS	1	1	2	2	2
Maximum RAM (32-bit)	4GB	4GB	4GB	4GB	4GB
Maximum RAM (64-bit)	8GB	8GB	16GB	192GB	192GB
Backup to network	No	No	No	Yes	Yes
BitLocker (& To Go)	No	No	No	No	Yes
Premium Games	No	No	Yes	Yes	Yes
Snipping Tool	No	No	Yes	Yes	Yes
Anytime Upgrade	Yes	Yes	Yes	Yes	N/A
Windows Media Player Remote Experience	No	No	Yes	Yes	Yes
MPEG-2 decoding	No	No	Yes	Yes	Yes
Dolby Digital compatible	No	No	Yes	Yes	Yes
DVD playback	No	No	Yes	Yes	Yes
Windows Media Center	No	No	Yes	Yes	Yes
Windows DVD Maker	No	No	Yes	Yes	Yes
HomeGroup sharing	Join only	Join only	Yes	Yes	Yes
Remote desktop host	No	No	No	Yes	Yes
IIS Web server	No	No	Yes	Yes	Yes
Internet Connection Sharing	No	Yes	Yes	Yes	Yes
Offline files	No	No	No	Yes	Yes
Windows Mobility Center	No	Yes (limited)	Yes (limited)	Yes	Yes
Windows Sideshow	No	No	Yes	Yes	Yes
Tablet PC capability	No	No	Yes	Yes	Yes

Table 1.2 Continued

Feature	Starter	Home Basic	Home Premium	Professional	Enterprise/ Ultimate
Multitouch	No	No	Yes	Yes	Yes
Join AD domain	No	No	No	Yes	Yes
XP Mode licensed	No	No	No	Yes	Yes
Boot from VHD	No	No	No	No	Yes
Branch Cache	No	No	No	No	Yes
DirectAccess	No	No	No	No	Yes

Available in all Windows 7 versions are Aero Snap, Windows Flip, Jump Lists, more granular UAC, Action Center, Windows Defender, Windows Firewall, Parental Controls, Windows ReadyDrive, Windows ReadyBoost, SuperFetch, 64-bit support, unlimited processor core support, Windows Backup, System Image, disk defragmentation, create and attach VHD, IE 8, Windows Gadgets and Gallery, basic games, Windows Photo Viewer, basic photo slideshows, Windows Media Player 12, AAC and H.264 decoding, Device Stage, Sync Center, 20 SMB connections, Network and Sharing Center, improved power management, connect to projector, remote desktop, and RSS support.

Table 1.3 Windows 7 Upgrade Paths

Windows 7 Editions	Starter	Home Basic	Home Premium	Professional	Ultimate/ Enterprise
From Windows XP (all versions)	1	1	1	1	1
From Windows Vista Home Basic	1	2	2	1	1
From Windows Vista Home Premium	1	1	2	1	1
From Windows Vista Business	1	1	1	2	1
From Windows Vista Ultimate	1	1	1	1	2
From Windows Vista Enterprise	1	1	1	1	2
From Windows 2000	1	1	1	1	1

Some information in this table adapted from information found on Paul Thurrott's Windows Supersite (www.winsupersite.com).

1 = Requires clean install.

2 = In-place installation option available.

Windows 7 on the Corporate Network

Because Windows 7 Professional is designed as a replacement for Windows XP Professional and Vista, it is designed to work well on corporate networks. Thus, it contains all the network and security features of Windows XP Professional and Vista, including these:

- Support for IP Security (IPSec), to protect data being transmitted across VPNs

- Kerberos v5 support for authentication

- Group Policy settings for administering networks and users

- Roaming user profiles to let users see their own files and preference settings on any computer

- Offline viewing of network data when not connected to the network

- Synchronization of local and network files

- Easy dial-up and VPN networking setup, plus Remote Desktop Connection, DirectAccess, and more

- Support for Active Directory (Microsoft's directory service feature that helps manage users and resources on large networks)

- Disk quotas, to prevent a few storage-hog users from running the server out of space

- Internet Information Services, including FTP, World Wide Web service, and scriptable management interfaces

- Fax services for sending and receiving faxes

- Simple Network Management Protocol (SNMP) support

- Print services for UNIX

However, if you want to enjoy the maximum possible feature set, choose Windows 7 Ultimate Edition. It is equally at home in corporate networks and as a part of a home entertainment system.

INSTALLING AND UPGRADING WINDOWS 7

General Considerations for Windows 7

You learned about Windows 7's new features, and some details of its design and architecture, in Chapter 1, "Introducing Windows 7." The question at this point is, "Will you install it?" If you plan to, go ahead and read this chapter and the next one. In this chapter, I coach you on preparing for installation and checking hardware and software requirements; then I discuss compatibility issues that might affect your product-purchasing decisions. Chapter 3, "The First Hour," covers post-installation issues, such as personalizing Windows 7. In this chapter, I also walk through the setup procedure.

Of course, if Windows 7 is already running on your PC, you might want to skip to Chapter 3. However, please at least scan this chapter because it covers information that might affect software and hardware installation decisions when using Windows 7 in the future. Understanding what you can do with and shouldn't expect from an operating system is always good when you use a tool as complex as a computer. Pay particular attention to the section about RAM and hard disk upgrades, and how to research hardware compatibility and find the Windows 7–approved applications in the Windows 7 Compatibility Center.

As you learn later in this chapter, the Windows 7 Setup program automatically checks your hardware and software, and reports on potential conflicts. Using it is one way to find out whether or not your system is ready for this new OS. It can be annoying; but that's better than learning something is wrong at midnight when doing an installation, especially when you could have purchased RAM or some other item the previous day while you were at the computer store. Likewise, you don't want to be technically able to run Windows 7, only to experience disappointing performance. To help prevent problems or surprises, this chapter's first part covers hardware compatibility issues.

Windows 7 Hardware Requirements

Let's start with the basics. The principal (and minimal) hardware requirements for running Windows 7 are as follows:

With Windows 7, Microsoft defines two different levels of minimum hardware requirements. In a sense, though, this is something that most power users routinely do for themselves. Microsoft defines these levels as Windows 7 Minimum and Windows 7 Recommended. A Windows 7 Minimum computer is one that meets the minimum requirements listed here. Although Windows 7 runs on a computer with these specifications, the experience is less positive compared to running Windows 7 on a computer that meets Recommended levels. The Windows 7 Minimum hardware requirements are as follows:

- At least 800MHz 32-bit (x86) or 64-bit (x64) processor

- 512MB of RAM

- A video card capable of at least 800×600 resolution and DirectX 9 with at least 32MB of graphics RAM

- A DVD drive

- Audio output capability

- A hard drive that is at least 40GB in total size, with at least 16GB of free space

These are Microsoft's suggested minimums, not what provides satisfactory or exceptional performance. Even so, some users report installing Windows 7 on less powerful machines. Microsoft tries to frame minimum requirements that deliver performance that average users can live with. As its Minimum specifications now indicate, you'll want at least 32MB of video RAM to allow your system to choose 24- and 32-bit color depths at 1024×768 resolution, and sound circuitry that works with Windows Media Player.

By comparison, here are the Windows 7 Recommended specifications:

- A 1GHz (or faster) 32-bit (x86) or 64-bit (x64) processor

- A minimum of 1GB of RAM

- A video card that supports DirectX 9 graphics with a WDDM driver and has at least 128MB of graphics memory

- Video card support for Pixel Shader 2.0 and 32 bits per pixel

- A hard drive that is at least 80GB in total size, with at least 40GB of free space

- A DVD drive

- Audio output capability

- Internet connectivity for product activation

Based on what's available these days, you don't have to pay too much for a machine that runs Windows 7 quite nicely. Despite rapid de-escalation in prices and remarkable increases in computing speed, putting together a machine to run Windows 7 successfully for your needs might not be as easy as you think. Whenever I build a new system, I'm always surprised by twists I hadn't considered, new hardware standards I didn't know about, and so on. In general, I believe that buying a complete, preconfigured system is smarter than building one from parts that you buy from separate manufacturers, unless you are a serious hardware geek. You probably know the story.

 tip

Given plummeting prices for CPUs and RAM, you could upgrade your CPU and motherboard, or just get a whole new system for Windows 7. The price wars between Intel and AMD might be brutal on those corporations, but consumers are big winners. You can find 2GHz–3GHz desktop computers with 320GB or larger hard disks and 3GB of RAM for under $400 as I write this.

Option 1: Using What You've Got: Ensuring Compatibility via the Windows 7 Upgrade Advisor

If you have a fairly new computer that meets the requirements listed earlier and you want to check compatibility before moving ahead with Windows 7 installation, this is the option to choose. Microsoft has put together the Windows 7 Upgrade Advisor for just this purpose. By downloading, installing, and running the Upgrade Advisor, you can create an easy-to-read report that lists all system and device compatibility issues with your current computer. Additionally, and perhaps most usefully, the Upgrade Advisor recommends ways to resolve any issues it uncovers. Finally, the Upgrade Advisor helps you choose the correct version of Windows 7 to meet your needs.

To get started with the Windows 7 Upgrade Advisor, visit the Upgrade Advisor page at www.microsoft.com/windows/Windows-7/upgrade-advisor.aspx and download the program. After you've downloaded the Upgrade Advisor, follow these steps to get it installed and start using it:

 note

Depending on the software configuration of the computer on which you are running the Upgrade Advisor, you may be prompted to install MSXML 6.0 and/or the .NET Framework before you will be able to run the program. This program works for both 32- and 64-bit operating systems.

1. Locate the Windows 7UpgradeAdvisor.msi file and double-click it to start the installation process.

2. When prompted, click the Run button to start the installer.

3. In the opening dialog box of the Windows 7 Upgrade Advisor Wizard, click Next to continue.

4. In the License Agreement dialog box, select I Accept The License Terms and then click Next to continue.

5. In the Select Installation Folder dialog box, shown in Figure 2.1, select a location where the Upgrade Advisor should be installed. Also, you can check the box next to Create A Shortcut On My Desktop. After making these selections, click Install to continue.

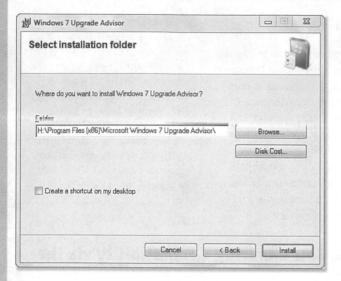

Figure 2.1
You can specify where the Upgrade Advisor is installed and put a shortcut on your desktop.

6. In the Installation Complete dialog box, click Close. You must then launch the Upgrade Advisor from the Start menu, as shown in Figure 2.2.

Figure 2.2
The Microsoft Windows 7 Upgrade Advisor scans your computer for upgrade and compatibility issues.

7. Click the Start Scan link to begin the scan process.

8. The Upgrade Advisor will spend some time scanning your computer. During this time, you can click on the link to the Windows 7 home page, as shown in Figure 2.3, to learn more about different Windows 7 versions.

Figure 2.3
You must wait a few minutes to allow the Upgrade Advisor to scan your computer.

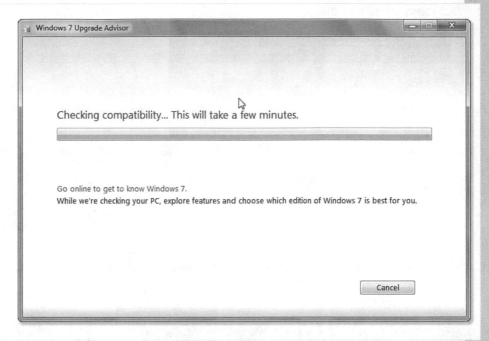

9. When the scan is complete, you can view the results of the scan and how your system fares in the System Requirements, Devices, and Programs categories, as shown in Figure 2.4.

10. Click on any live links that appear in the window to see whether Upgrade Advisor has identified problems for Windows 7, as in Figure 2.5. Note the instructions to update this system's ACPI facility.

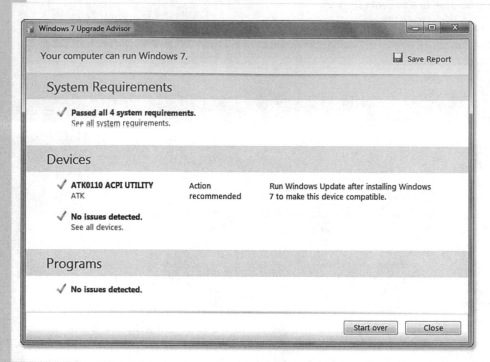

Figure 2.4
The Microsoft Windows 7 Upgrade Advisor shows you how your system stacks up in various categories.

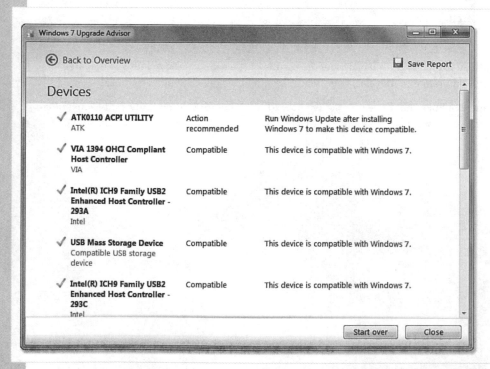

Figure 2.5
You will be alerted to problems that must be addressed.

11. Use the Save Report button at the upper-right, shown in Figure 2.5, to retain a consolidated list of all actions you must perform. The Save Report dialog appears as shown in Figure 2.6.

Figure 2.6
Save the report to retain access to a consolidated list of actions that need to be performed.

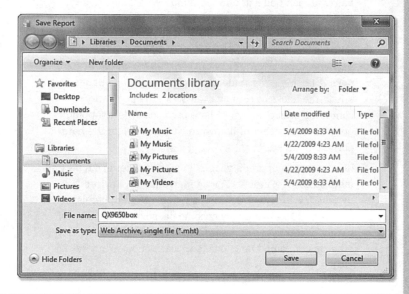

12. After you've saved the report, click the Close button at the bottom of the page.

Based on the results of the Upgrade Advisor scan, you should have a good idea of what, if any, issues you'll encounter when you install Windows 7 on your system.

 tip

To find general information about Windows 7, including compatibility, check out www.microsoft.com/Windows7.

Option 2: Choosing a Windows 7 Ready PC

It isn't a bad idea to bite the bullet and shell out for a new Windows machine every two or three years. When you do upgrade to a new computer, you'll notice lots of improvements across the board, including quicker response; improved power management so your idle system uses less power (and cuts your utility bills); reduced energy consumption owing to lower chip counts; more hardware settings; a faster optical drive; faster, higher-resolution video displays; and so on.

If you decide to purchase new PCs for your personal or corporate arsenal, let me suggest an easier way to choose them than to research each piece separately. Visit the Windows Marketplace website at www.windowsmarketplace.com to browse the desktop and portable computers that meet Windows 7 requirements. There's no shortage of systems there, so get ready to do some digging.

 tip

If you have a PC guaranteed to run Windows Vista (even if it's running Windows XP), chances are good that it will also run Windows 7.

Option 3: Upgrading Your Computer

Don't want to purchase a whole new computer, but your hardware isn't all listed in the Windows 7 Compatibility Center (formerly known as the HCL)? Or do you have some old, stodgy disk drive, SCSI controller, video adapter, motherboard, or some other piece of gear that you want to upgrade anyway? You're not alone. The PC upgrade business is booming, as evidenced by the pages and pages of ads in the backs of computer rags and the popularity of computer "swap meets," where precious little swapping goes on except that of hardware components for the hard-earned green stuff.

If you want to upgrade your existing computer to support an installation of Windows 7, it can have no ISA devices installed. Windows 7 does not support ISA peripherals, so it seems that ISA has finally become passé. Also, be wary of potential compatibility issues: research motherboards and other major components online to learn about Windows 7 issues.

Performing a New Installation of Windows 7

The three basic types of clean installation procedures are as follows:

- Install on a brand new disk or computer system

- Erase the disk, format it, and install

- Install into a new directory for dual-booting (see the multiboot discussion later in this chapter)

If you intend to use either of the first two methods, be sure your computer can boot from a DVD (most newer computers support booting from a DVD drive). Doing so might require changing the drive boot order in the BIOS or CMOS, but try it first as-is. With no floppy disk inserted and a clean hard disk, try the DVD drive next. The Windows 7 DVD is bootable and should run the Setup program automatically.

Installation takes 15–30 minutes, depending on the speed of your machine. Refer to the following sections if you have questions about any steps in this process.

 tip

The HCL mentioned to the left stands for Hardware Compatibility List, and is a historical term that Microsoft has used in the past to refer to a database of hardware that's been checked for compatibility with specific OSes. For Vista and Windows 7, there are Compatibility Centers to serve this function. Visit the Windows 7 Compatibility Center. The Windows Catalog also mentioned there is now called the Windows Logo'd Products List; visit it at www.microsoft.com/windows/compatibility/windows-7/.

 tip

If you plan to upgrade, see Scott Mueller's book *Upgrading and Repairing PCs* (Que, 2007; ISBN 0789736970) for the best (and most complete) information available on how to do the job right the first time. Check for regular updates to this perennial classic at www.upgradingandrepairingpcs.com.

 tip

Any time you do a clean install of Windows 7 with a prior Windows installation from which you must grab files, settings, or other stuff, consider using the Windows Easy Transfer Wizard to archive accounts and files (it works with XP, Vista, and Windows 7). If you save this archive file to an external hard disk, do your clean install, and then use the Windows Easy Transfer Wizard, accounts and files will appear in their usual or required directories. It can't save and restore applications, or passwords associated with individual accounts, but it eases the pain and effort involved in migrating from an old Windows installation to a new one.

Typical Clean Setup Procedure

If you're installing into an empty partition and you can boot an operating system that is supported for the purpose of Setup (Windows Vista or XP), just boot up, insert the DVD, and choose Install Now from the resulting dialog box, shown in Figure 2.8. Then you can follow the installation step-by-step procedure.

 note

Windows 7 automatically applies the NTFS format to any disk partition upon which it is installed during a clean installation.

Figure 2.7
Installing Windows 7 from an existing Windows installation is easy to start.

 Install now

What to know before installing Windows

Copyright © 2009 Microsoft Corporation. All rights reserved.

If Windows doesn't detect the DVD automatically upon insertion, you must run the Setup program, `setup.exe`, from the Start, Run dialog box (after opening the Run dialog box, type `D:/setup.exe`; on Vista use the Start menu Search box instead). The `setup.exe` application is located in the Sources directory on the DVD. After the Setup routine starts, you can follow the installation procedure step by step.

 note

When using the Run box, substitute the actual drive letter for your DVD drive. We used D: in our examples here; yours might differ.

If your computer has a blank hard disk or your current OS isn't supported, this process changes. You must launch the installation process from the Windows 7 DVD (this works only if you can boot from the DVD drive). Setup automatically runs if you boot from the DVD.

Yet another setup method involves the network. To initiate a network installation, you must create a network share of the distribution DVD or a copy of the DVD on a hard drive. The destination system must have network access, and the user account must have at least read access to the installation files. Initiate Setup by executing `setup.exe` from the network share. For example, from the Start, Run command, or the Vista Start menu Search box, type this path: `\\<servername>\<sharename>\sources\Setup`. Setup recognizes an over-the-network installation and automatically copies all files from the network share to the local system before the first reboot.

Clean Install from DVD, Step by Step

A typical clean installation (on a blank hard disk) step-by-step procedure is as follows:

1. Insert the Windows 7 DVD into your computer's DVD-ROM drive, and restart the computer. Windows 7 Setup should start automatically, as shown in Figure 2.8. If Setup does not start automatically, ensure that your computer is configured to boot from the DVD drive.

 tip

All versions of Windows 7, 32 or 64 bit, are included on the same DVD. The product key that you enter during setup determines which actual version of Windows 7 you end up with after the installation completes. Keep your Windows 7 DVD and product key in a safe location after you've performed your installation. It's useful for repairs of all kinds!

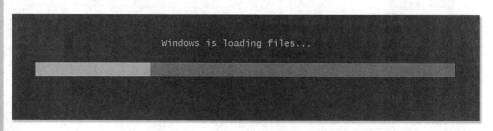

Windows is loading files...

Figure 2.8
This screen is one of only two text-based setup screens you'll see in Windows 7.

2. You are asked to select regional options for the Windows 7 installation, as shown in Figure 2.9. Make your selections and click Next to continue.

Figure 2.9
You make regional selections early in the Windows 7 installation process.

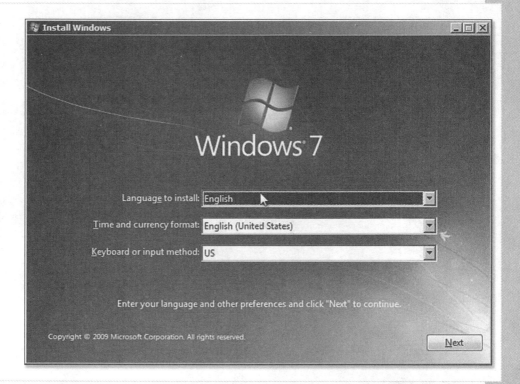

3. In the next dialog box, you are prompted to start the installation. Click Install Now to begin the installation. This produces a screen that tells you that Setup is starting.

4. In the Software License Terms dialog box, ensure that you read and understand the End User Licensing Agreement (EULA). When you're ready, select the I Accept the License Terms option and click Next to continue.

5. In the Which Type of Installation Do You Want? dialog box, shown in Figure 2.10, you can select only the Custom (Advanced) option because you're performing a new installation on a blank hard disk. Click Custom (Advanced) to continue.

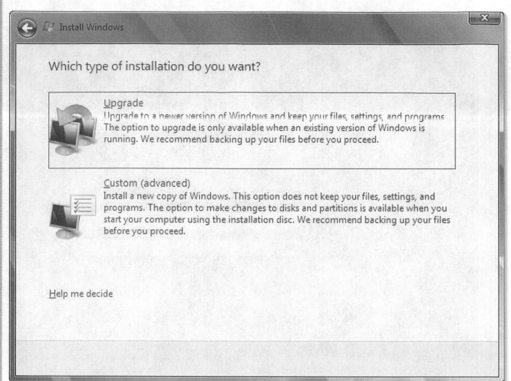

Figure 2.10
For new installations, only the Custom (Advanced) option is available.

6. In the Where Do You Want to Install Windows? dialog box, shown in Figure 2.11, select the partition onto which you'll install Windows 7. When you're ready to proceed, click Next. If you need to provide a RAID or SCSI driver, now is the time to do it.

7. The Installing Windows dialog box appears and gives you an updated status of the upgrade process.

8. After some time, your computer restarts and the newly installed Windows 7 loads. Windows 7 resumes the installation process. Before the restart, a warning appears.

9. After the restart, you'll see a notification telling you that Windows 7 is preparing the new installation. Windows 7 moves back into a graphical display after a few minutes and tells you it's updating Registry settings and starting services, after which it lets you know it's completing the installation.

10. After completing the installation, Windows 7 asks you to provide a username and a computer name, as shown in Figure 2.12. After providing this information, click Next to continue.

Figure 2.11
You must select an empty partition for the installation of Windows 7.

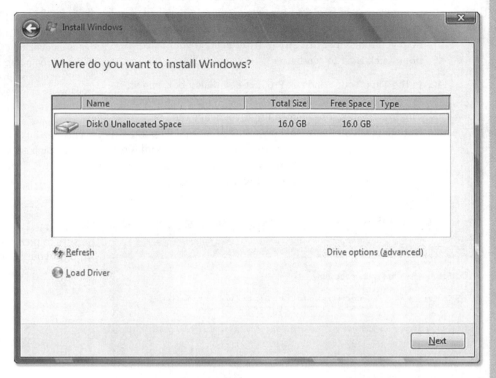

Figure 2.12
Be sure to choose a unique name for your computer.

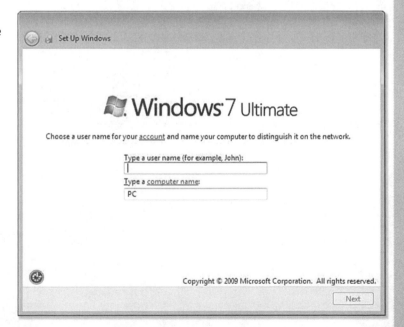

11. In the next dialog box, shown in Figure 2.13, you are asked to supply a password for your user account (which you must reenter as a double-check) and a password hint to help you remember that string. After making your selections, click Next to continue.

12. In the Type Your Windows Product Key dialog box, shown in Figure 2.14, enter the product key that came with your Windows 7 DVD. I recommend that you leave the Automatically Activate Windows When I'm Online option checked to take care of Windows Product Activation within the three days after the Windows 7 installation. After entering this information, click Next to continue.

note

Always choose a computer name that is unique. It must differ from any other computer, workgroup, or domain names on the network. You'll probably want to enter your name or a name of your own choice, although Setup supplies a recommendation. You might want to coordinate naming your computer with your LAN administrator, if you have one.

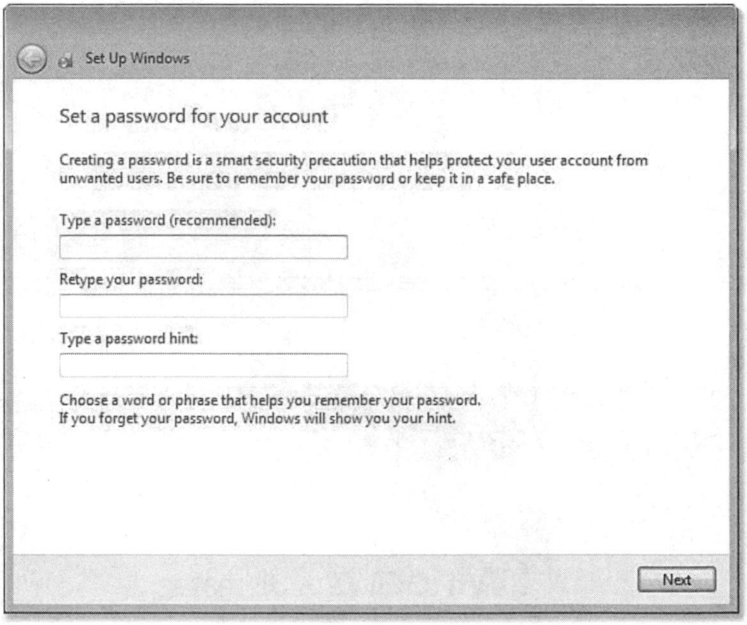

Figure 2.13
Be sure to pick a strong password for your user account.

Set Up Windows

Set a password for your account

Creating a password is a smart security precaution that helps protect your user account from unwanted users. Be sure to remember your password or keep it in a safe place.

Type a password (recommended):

Retype your password:

Type a password hint:

Choose a word or phrase that helps you remember your password.
If you forget your password, Windows will show you your hint.

Next

Figure 2.14
Enter your product key and ensure that Windows 7 can automatically activate itself.

More About Product Keys

You can also leave the Product Key box blank. If you do this, you'll be asked which version of Windows 7 you want to install, and you can select any version from Starter to Ultimate. You'll have to provide a valid product key, however, within 30 days for whatever version you install or else Windows 7 will nag you regularly and often about registration. (If you install a "slip-streamed" copy of Windows 7 Service Pack 1, or use the Windows Update service to upgrade to SP-1, you'll be reminded to register rather than receiving constant nags.)

You can use the no-key method to play around with different versions of Windows 7, but be careful if you select a version for which you don't have a key; you must perform a clean install every time you reinstall Windows 7, and you must eventually install a version for which you have a license, or erase it. You'll lose your applications and data every time you reinstall.

13. In the Help Protect Your Computer and Improve Windows Automatically dialog box, shown in Figure 2.15, you configure the base security for Windows 7. In most cases, you should select Use Recommended Settings. To make your selection, click it.

14. In the Review Your Time and Date Settings dialog box, shown in Figure 2.16, select your time zone, daylight savings option, and current date options. Click Finish to complete the upgrade process.

 caution

You should definitely not play with alternate versions if you are upgrading from an older version of Windows. After the first such install, there's no way to go back and repeat the upgrade with your licensed version of Windows 7!

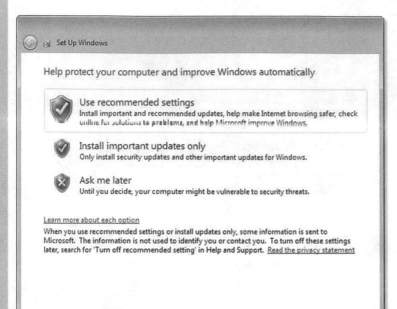

Figure 2.15
Windows 7 encourages you to be secure upon installation.

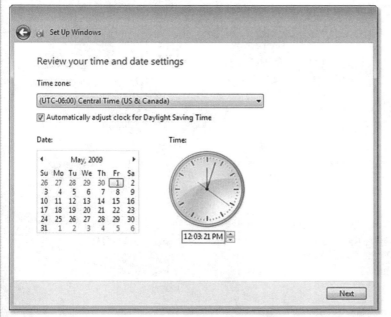

Figure 2.16
Be sure to set your location's current date and time information.

15. In the Select Your Computer's Current Location dialog box, shown in Figure 2.17, tell Windows where you'll be using your computer. As with Windows Vista, Windows 7 configures your network adapters for DHCP and does not ask you what to do.

Figure 2.17
The different location choices correspond to different levels of security on your Windows 7 computer.

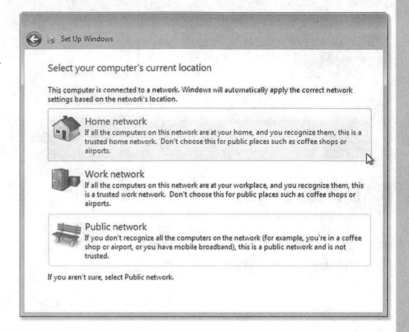

16. Windows prompts you one last time—after you click Start, you're finished with the installation.

17. After a few more minutes, you are finally presented with your brand new Windows 7 login screen, as shown in Figure 2.18. Congratulations, you've completed the installation of Windows 7!

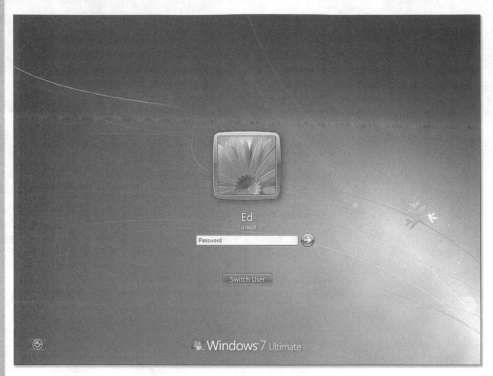

Clean Install from Inside Windows, Step by Step

If you initiate the Setup routine from within Windows XP or Windows Vista, the step-by-step procedure is as follows:

1. Insert the Windows 7 DVD into your computer's DVD-ROM drive. It should AutoPlay and present the Install Windows dialog box. If not, locate and double-click the setup.exe program in the Sources folder on the DVD.

2. To download, install, and use the Windows 7 Upgrade Advisor, as detailed previously, click the Check Compatibility Online link. Otherwise, to begin the in-place upgrade to Windows 7, click the Install Now link.

3. In the Get Important Updates for Installation dialog box, shown in Figure 2.19, you are asked whether you want to download updates to the Windows 7 install files. Typically, for computers that have an active Internet connection, you're better off getting the updates. Make your selection by clicking it.

 tip

If you plan to perform a clean installation on your computer that is currently running some earlier Windows version, be sure to get your data and other files off the computer beforehand. You can perform this process manually, or you can opt to use Windows Easy Transfer to automatically copy all your files and settings to an external hard drive or network location. After the clean installation of Windows 7 has completed, you can run Windows Easy Transfer again to reload your files and settings on the new installation of Windows 7. Chapter 3 discusses using Windows Easy Transfer.

Figure 2.19
You should typically allow the Windows 7 Setup routine to download updates.

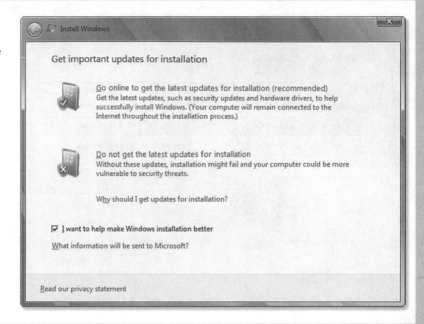

4. In the Please Read the License Terms dialog box, ensure that you read and understand the End User Licensing Agreement (EULA). When you're ready, select the I Accept the License Terms option and click Next to continue.

5. In the Type Your Product Key for Activation dialog box, you are asked to enter your Windows 7 product key. Enter the key and ensure that the Automatically Activate Windows When I'm Online option is checked, to enable Windows Product Activation. After entering the product key, click Next to continue.

6. In the Which Type of Installation Do You Want? dialog box, shown previously in Figure 2.10, select Custom (Advanced) because you're performing a clean installation here on top of an existing Windows XP installation.

7. In the Where Do You Want to Install Windows? dialog box, shown in Figure 2.20, select the partition onto which you'll install Windows 7. When you're ready to proceed, click Next.

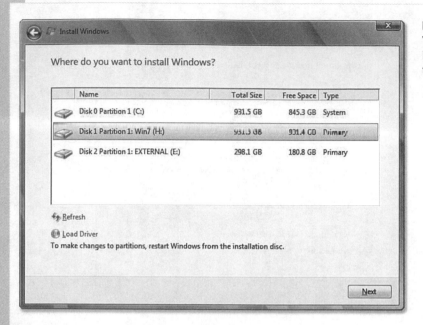

Figure 2.20
You need to select an existing partition for the installation of Windows 7.

8. The Setup application warns you that the selected partition contains files from another Windows installation, as shown in Figure 2.21. After you read this information, click OK to continue.

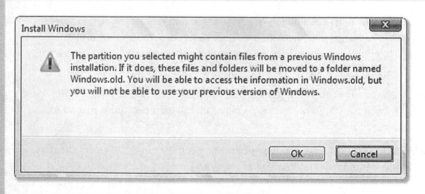

Figure 2.21
Windows 7 Setup moves all your old Windows files to a new directory—you must delete that directory later to reclaim that disk space.

9. The Installing Windows dialog box appears and updates the status for the upgrade process.

10. From here, the rest of the process is just like that for a clean installation (on a blank hard disk), starting with step 9. After some time, your computer restarts and the newly installed Windows 7 loads.

Upgrading Older Versions of Windows to Windows 7

Although doing a new installation of Windows 7 is almost always the best plan, you might prefer to perform an in-place upgrade on your computer. Before you attempt any in-place upgrade to Windows 7, perform the following tasks:

- Ensure that a valid, working backup exists of all important data and other files stored on your computer.

- Ensure that your hardware meets the requirements discussed previously in the "Windows 7 Hardware Requirements" section of this chapter.

- Run the Windows 7 Upgrade Advisor to verify that your hardware and software environment is ready for an upgrade. Take special note of any software issues, such as drivers needing updates for Windows 7. Be sure to print a copy of the Upgrade Advisor's final report so you'll have it handy after the Windows 7 upgrade installation has completed.

Windows 7 supports only a few in-place upgrade paths, and only for Vista (32-bit to 32-bit only, and 64-bit to 64-bit only):

- Windows Vista Home Premium to Windows 7 Home Premium

- Windows Vista Business to Windows 7 Professional

- Windows Vista Ultimate (or Enterprise) to Windows 7 Ultimate (or Enterprise)

Other versions of Windows don't support in-place upgrades, so you'll have to do clean installs for all the following items:

- **Windows XP (all versions)**—An upgrade license from XP to Windows 7 will be available from Microsoft, but requires users to perform a clean install (information is not yet available on source and target mappings for Windows XP and Windows 7, nor about pricing).

- **Windows 2000**—Requires a clean install for any installation of Windows 7.

- **Windows 95/98/Me**—Requires a clean install for any installation of Windows 7.

> **tip**
>
> You can get more information about upgrading to Windows 7 by visiting www.microsoft.com/ Windows7/getready/ upgradeinfo.mspx.

The process to perform an in-place upgrade from an already installed instance of Windows Vista is as follows:

1. Insert the Windows 7 DVD into your computer's DVD-ROM drive. It should AutoPlay and present the Install Windows dialog box. If not, locate the `setup.exe` program in the Sources folder on the DVD and double-click it.

2. To download, install, and use the Windows 7 Upgrade Advisor, as detailed previously, click the Check Compatibility Online link. Otherwise, to begin an in-place upgrade to Windows 7, click the Install Now link.

3. In the Get Important Updates for Installation dialog box, shown previously in Figure 2.19, decide whether to download updates to the Windows 7 install files. Typically, for computers with an active Internet connection, you're better off getting the updates. Make your selection by clicking it.

4. In the Please Read the License Terms dialog box, ensure that you read and understand the End User Licensing Agreement (EULA). When you're ready, select the I Accept the License Terms option, and click Next to continue.

5. In the Type Your Product Key for Activation dialog box, you are asked to enter your Windows 7 product key. Enter the key and ensure that the Automatically Activate Windows When I'm Online option is checked, to enable Windows Product Activation. After entering the product key, click Next to continue.

6. In the Which Type of Installation Do You Want? dialog box, previously shown in Figure 2.10, select Upgrade because here you're performing an in-place upgrade of Windows Vista.

7. In the Compatibility Report dialog box, shown in Figure 2.22, note what items Windows 7 Setup flags as needing attention after the installation is complete. When you're ready to proceed, click Next.

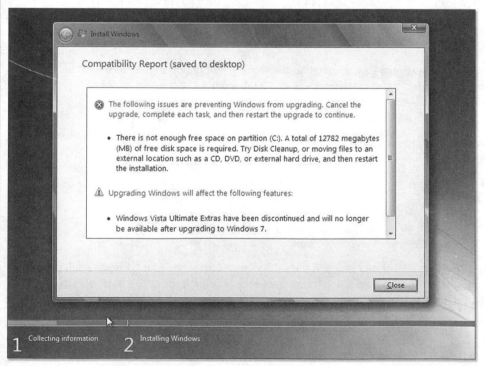

Figure 2.22
You might need to upgrade some hardware drivers after the Windows 7 upgrade has completed.

8. The Upgrading Windows dialog box appears and gives you an updated status of the upgrade process.

9. You are next asked to select the regional options for the Windows 7 installation. Make your selections and click Next to continue.

10. After some time, your computer restarts and the newly installed Windows 7 loads. Windows 7 resumes the installation process. Windows typically restarts once more before it finally completes the installation process.

11. In the Help Protect Your Computer and Improve Windows Automatically dialog box, shown previously in Figure 2.16, you are asked how to configure the base security for Windows 7. In most cases, you should select Use Recommended Settings. Make your selection by clicking it.

12. In the Review Your Time and Date Setting dialog box, select your time zone, daylight savings option, and current date. Click Finish to complete the upgrade.

13. After a few more minutes, you are finally presented with your brand new Windows 7 login screen. You've completed the upgrade to Windows 7.

When your upgrade is complete, be sure to spend some time reading through Chapter 3, which takes you on a tour of key settings and features you need to check out before getting started with your new Windows 7 installation.

> **tip**
>
> It's worth noting that a clean install from Windows XP Professional SP3 to Windows 7 Ultimate uses approximately 10GB of disk space; an upgrade install from Vista SP2 uses about 12GB. Plan accordingly for your upgrades. All of these consume a fair bit of disk space, so please plan ahead!

Upgrading One Version of Windows 7 to Another

If you want to upgrade from one version of Windows 7 to another (for example, from the Home Basic version that came on a new computer to the Home Premium or Ultimate editions), you don't need to start over from scratch—you can simply purchase an upgrade kit and update the version of Windows 7 with all your files, applications, and settings intact (see Figure 2.23).

When Windows Vista was first released, Microsoft offered a feature called Windows Anytime Upgrade that let you purchase a new product key over the Internet. With the new product key and your original Windows DVD in hand, you could be up and running with a new version in an hour or so.

In Windows 7, Microsoft has improved this upgrade service. All you need is a valid upgrade key, and the whole process takes 10 minutes or less. You can go online and obtain a key by paying for it, or if you already have one, you need only enter that key to begin the upgrade process.

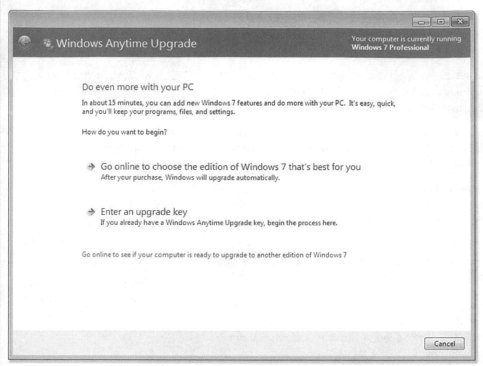

Figure 2.23
Windows Anytime Update is located in the System and Security option of the Control Panel.

Multibooting Windows 7

In today's world of advanced OSs and low hard-disk prices, it certainly is not unusual for some users to experiment with different OSs. The world of consumer computing is ripe with many options. Along with just plain curiosity and experimentation, here are other good reasons to switch among or between OSs:

- Many users use two or more OSs because of application-compatibility issues. Hardware support issues occur, too: Windows 2000 and Windows XP might have drivers for older hardware that Windows 7 doesn't support.

- Some users want to run specific applications or games in an optimal environment for their use.

- A developer might swap among Windows XP Professional, Windows Vista, and maybe even several different versions of Windows 7, to test application compatibility.

- Website developers need to use different OS versions to see how pages look and behave with corresponding web browser versions.

Other than buying multiple computers, there are two ways to accommodate such needs. You can multiboot (that is, select the desired OS at bootup) or you can run one OS in a "virtual" computer inside another OS (that is, in a special application program that lets the alternate OS think it's running on a PC of its own). A "virtual" approach can be quite useful; we cover it later in this chapter in a section titled "The Virtual Machine Approach."

Windows 7 uses a boot scheme introduced with Windows Vista based on so-called "Boot Configuration Data," usually abbreviated as BCD. BCD is more complex than and incompatible with the boot scheme used in previous versions of Windows. While Windows 2000 and XP let you set up a boot menu from which you could select any version of Windows, as well as other OSs, Windows 7's boot menu only lets you select Windows Vista or 7 versions, or "something else," and all "something else" selections must be managed separately.

The Skinny on Boot Scheme Changes

Here's a rough sketch of what's changed: In the boot scheme used by the Intel x86 versions of Windows 2000 and XP, the boot partition's boot sector program loaded `ntldr`, which read the menu file `boot.ini`, and then loaded Windows. Aside from the boot sector, all of the stuff was in "super hidden" files (files marked with the `system` and `hidden` attributes), stored in the root directory. The Windows Vista and Windows 7 boot sectors load a file called `bootmgr` from the root directory, which loads a set of programs and DLLs in the `\boot` folder, which then reads the BCD file (actually a Registry hive), and then loads Windows. The BCD hive is also loaded into and visible in the Windows Registry after bootup. In a Windows 7 multiboot configuration, the root directory file `bootsect.bak` is a copy of the pre–Windows 7 boot sector (XP's version of the boot sector). Choosing "Legacy" from the Windows 7 boot menu loads and runs the original boot sector program, which carries on as before.

The reason for making this change was to create a common boot system that would work on both BIOS-based computers and computers using the newer EFI configuration system (built around Intel's Extensible Firmware Interface). The impact of this new scheme is that the Windows 7 boot menu can offer only Windows 7, Windows Vista, and Windows Server 2008 versions, where anything using the older boot loader gets lumped under the "Legacy" entry. The `boot.ini` file is used *only* to list and load non-BCD operating systems.

As a result of the boot manager changes, if you want to set up a computer that can boot several different versions of Windows and/or other OSs, you need to follow these guidelines:

- You must install each OS into a separate disk volume (drive letter). To get these separate volumes, you can create multiple partitions on one disk drive, or use multiple disk drives, or a combination of these two organizing principles.

- If you install multiple versions of Windows 7 on the same computer, the same rule applies: You must install each version in a separate disk volume.

  (If you do install multiple versions of Windows 7, see the "Editing Windows 7 Boot Menu Entries" section at the end of this chapter to learn how to tell them apart in the boot menu.)

- Install versions of Windows starting with the oldest and working toward the newest. For example, to set up a computer that can boot into Windows Me, Windows XP, and Windows 7, install Me first, then XP, then Windows 7.

  You *must* install Windows 7 last!

- To install OSs other than Windows, such as Linux, you might need a boot manager that can recognize all the different OSs in use. Linux offers a choice of several different boot managers. Their use is beyond the scope of this book, but you should be able to find instructions on the Web for multibooting Linux and Windows 7.

To create a multiboot installation on a computer that already has Windows Vista installed, follow this procedure. These steps are quite similar to the "clean install" procedure described earlier.

1. Insert the Windows 7 DVD into your computer's DVD-ROM drive. It should AutoPlay and present the Install Windows dialog box. If not, locate the `setup.exe` program in the Sources folder on the DVD, and double-click it.

   (Alternatively, you can restart your computer and boot from the DVD.)

2. To download, install, and use the Windows 7 Upgrade Advisor, as detailed previously, click the Check Compatibility Online link. Otherwise, to begin the in-place upgrade to Windows 7, click the Install Now link.

3. In the Get Important Updates for Installation dialog box, shown previously in Figure 2.20, you are asked whether you want to download updates to the Windows 7 install files. Typically, for computers that have an active Internet connection, you are better off getting the updates. Make your selection by clicking it.

4. In the Please Read the License Terms dialog box, ensure that you read and understand the End User Licensing Agreement (EULA). When you're ready, select the I Accept the License Terms option, and click Next to continue.

5. In the Type Your Product Key for Activation dialog box, you are asked to enter your Windows 7 product key. Enter the key and ensure that the Automatically Activate Windows When I'm Online option is checked, to enable Windows Product Activation. After entering the product key, click Next to continue.

6. In the Which Type of Installation Do You Want? dialog box, shown previously in Figure 2.11, select Custom (Advanced) because here you're performing a clean, multiboot installation of Windows 7, not an upgrade.

7. In the Where Do You Want to Install Windows? dialog box, shown in Figure 2.24, select the partition into which you'll install Windows 7. This must be a partition that does not already have a version of Windows installed on it. When you're ready to proceed, click Next.

8. Follow the rest of the procedure described previously under "Typical Clean Setup Procedure," from step 6 on through the end.

9. If you plan on installing another version of Windows 7 on this same computer, skip ahead to the "Editing Windows 7 Boot Menu Entries" section at the end of this chapter to rename the current version's title in the boot menu.

10. You can check out the new Windows 7 boot menu, shown in Figure 2.25, on the next restart of your computer.

When your installation is complete, spend some time reading through Chapter 3.

Figure 2.24
You must select an empty partition for multiboot installation of Windows 7.

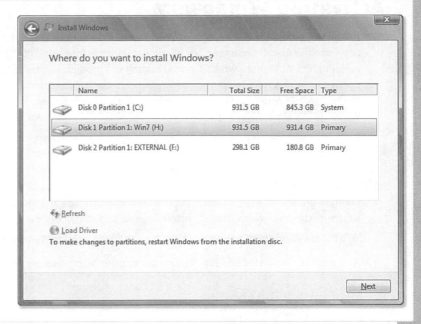

Figure 2.25
The Windows 7 boot menu has changed a lot from Windows XP but not much from Vista.

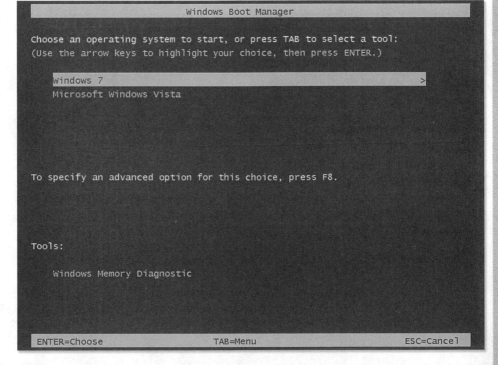

Activating Windows 7

Product Activation is one feature in Windows 7 that ensures that a software product key has not been used to install more than the allowed number of instances of that specific software. In general, Product Activation works by transmitting the product key used during the Windows 7 installation along with a nonidentifying hardware hash that is generated from the computer's configuration to Microsoft. Product Activation typically occurs via the Internet, and occurs automatically in Windows 7 after 3 days, but you can opt to perform activation earlier if desired, as we discuss next.

Please understand that Product Activation is not intended to prevent you from reinstalling Windows 7 on the same computer more than once—it's intended to prevent you from installing Windows 7 on more computers than the license covers (usually, one installation for any given key). As such, you should typically have no issues with reactivating your instance of Windows 7 on the same computer multiple times—at least, as long as the hardware configuration stays more or less the same (it's the source of the hash value that Microsoft uses as part of its checks).

To activate Windows 7 yourself, before it does so automatically, follow these steps:

1. Open the Computer window, shown in Figure 2.26, by clicking Start, Computer.

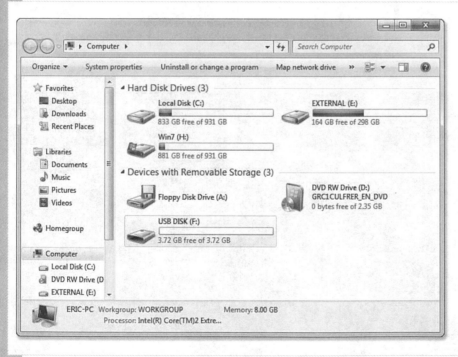

Figure 2.26
The My Computer look has been updated for Windows 7.

2. In Computer, click the System Properties link. The system properties are displayed, as shown in Figure 2.27.

Figure 2.27
You can easily view basic properties of your Windows 7 computer.

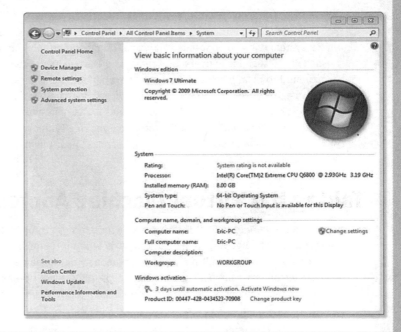

3. At the bottom of the Properties dialog box, click the link to Activate Windows Now. The Activate
   Windows Now dialog box opens, as shown in Figure 2.28.

4. Click the Activate Windows Online Now link to get activation going.

Figure 2.28
Windows Activation has been streamlined in
Windows 7.

You must activate Windows 7 within 30 days of installation, or it will begin to nag you to perform this task.

For Windows 7, computers that fail its activation or validation tests will bug their users much like an XP system does when it fails validation. Upon logging in, a pop-up dialog box that can't be dismissed for 15 seconds appears, and reappears every hour by changing the desktop wallpaper or background to plain black and flashing activation and balloon help dialog boxes near the system tray. You can ignore the pop-ups and change the background back to your favorite photo, but it all repeats again in another hour. The good news is that you won't lose any real functionality, as with Reduced Functionality Mode (RFM) and non-genuine Windows mode (NGM) in Windows Vista prior to the release of Service Pack (SP1). Microsoft heard users' complaints and showed some mercy.

Taking the Virtual Machine Approach

If you need access to multiple OSs primarily for testing purposes rather than for long periods of work, there's another way to use multiple OSs without the hassle inherent to multiboot setups. In fact, you can even use multiple OSs simultaneously on the same computer. It's done with a setup called a *virtual machine*. This is an old concept—IBM used it on its mainframes as far back as the 1970s—and it's making a big comeback, thanks to today's fast processors and huge hard disks.

A virtual machine program emulates (simulates) in software all the hardware functions of a PC. It lets an entire operating system (called a *guest* operating system) run as an ordinary application program on a *host* operating system such as Windows 7. Because all the hardware functions are emulated, the guest OS doesn't "know" it's not in complete control of a real physical computer. When the guest OS requests access to a hard disk, display card, network adapter, or serial port, the virtual machine program calls upon the host OS to actually carry out the necessary operations.

Even though software might occasionally need to execute hundreds of instructions to emulate a single hardware operation, the overall speed penalty is only 5%–10%. And if a guest OS crashes, it won't take down your system. You can simply click a Reset menu choice and "reboot" the virtual machine. Figure 2.29 shows a typical Virtual PC window.

Another advantage of the virtual machine programs currently on the market is that they don't allow a guest OS unfettered access to your real disk drives. Instead, you create a *virtual disk*, a single large file on your host OS that contains what a virtual machine sees as a hard drive. With today's large hard drives, it's no big deal to create a 15GB–30GB file to serve as a virtual hard drive for an older version of Windows or even Linux.

If you make a backup copy of the file after installing a guest OS on a virtual disk drive, you can return the guest OS to its original, pristine state just by copying the backup over the virtual disk file. You can even boot up a guest OS, start a bunch of applications, and save the virtual machine in this exact state. When you want to use it again, just fire up the whole system from that point. If you're a tester or experimenter, a virtual computer can save hours of time installing, reinstalling, and rebooting.

Figure 2.29
Virtual PC
running
Windows XP
Professional
SP3 inside a
virtual
machine on
Windows 7.

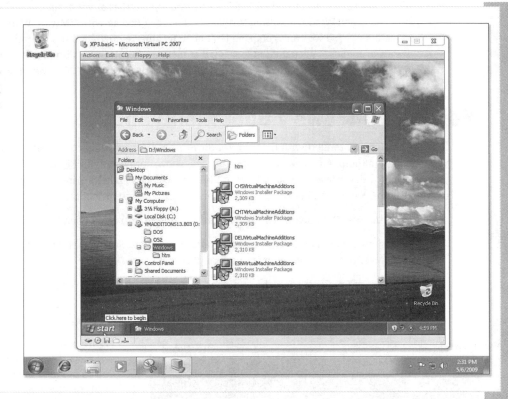

Of course, you still need separate licenses for all the extra OSs
you install, but a virtual machine can let you run as many OSs
and as many configurations of these OSs as you like, separately
or simultaneously. And all this comes without the hassle of editing the Windows 7 boot menu or worrying about partitions.

If full-blown virtualization sounds interesting, check into these
products:

- VMware, now an EMC company, located at
  www.vmware.com. VMware Workstation was the first commercial system to emulate a PC on a PC. It's the most
  "industrial-strength" PC emulator available. You can get a
  30-day free trial of VMware Workstation from the VMware
  site. Or, you can use the free VMware Player version to run
  virtual computers set up by others.

- Microsoft Virtual PC. Microsoft bought this program from
  Connectix Corporation. Versions are available for Windows
  and for the Mac; check out www.microsoft.com/virtualpc.

 tip

With each copy of Windows 7
Professional, Ultimate, and
Enterprise comes the ability to use a
Microsoft download called XP Mode,
aka XPM. Basically, this includes
Virtual PC plus a virtual machine
image (VHD) and settings (VMC)
files with Windows XP SP3 preinstalled. Microsoft also grants a
"free" license to use this guest OS,
thereby saving users the expense of
acquiring one of their own. One
word of warning, though: The XPM
version of Virtual PC requires host
processors to support hardware virtualization, which means that older
PCs can't run it.

The Windows version of Virtual PC 2007 is a free download that anyone can use. In general, the experience for non-Windows OSs on Virtual PC is not as good as with VMware Workstation. However, it's free, so we can't complain too much. Be sure to download the Virtual PC extensions and give a Windows 7 Virtual PC at least 1GB of memory (a setting in Virtual PC) for it to run with any appreciable speed. This requires that at least 1.5GB of physical RAM in your host PC.

Editing Windows 7 Boot Menu Entries

If you're not exactly thrilled with the way Windows 7 has prepared your boot menu options for you, you can change them. As if the rather plain entries, shown previously in Figure 2.26, aren't enough, you can easily get confused if you have multiple instances of Windows 7 installed on your computer in a multiboot scenario. To change boot menu entries in Windows 7, simply follow these steps:

1. Boot into the first Windows 7 instance whose boot menu entry you wish to change.

2. Open a command prompt by typing **cmd** into the Start menu Search box. Your current account needs Administrative permissions to perform this task.

3. At the command prompt, enter the command **bcdedit** to produce an output similar to that shown in Figure 2.30.

Figure 2.30
The bcdedit command enables you to manage the Windows 7 boot menu.

4. Note that in the `Windows Boot Loader` section, you can see the name for the Windows 7 boot menu entry.

5. To change the boot menu entry displayed for this installation of Windows 7, enter the following command, as shown at the bottom of Figure 2.31: **bcdedit /set description** "*New boot menu text*".

Figure 2.31
You can easily change one Windows 7 boot menu entry at a time using bcdedit.

6. To continue renaming other Windows 7 installations on the computer, simply reboot into each installation and repeat steps 2–4.

Be aware that you cannot edit any other boot menu entries for any other OSs using the bcdedit command. The boot menu entries for older versions of Windows that you have installed on the computer, as well as those for other OSs (such as versions of Linux), are still managed through the Windows XP or Windows 2000 boot.ini file. When you select the Earlier Versions of Windows option on the Windows 7 boot menu, you get another boot menu displayed using the information in the boot.ini file to help you select and launch any of those other OSs installed on your computer.

One more thing: `bcdedit` isn't exactly user-friendly; not surprisingly, people have built better tools for editing Windows 7's boot configuration data. We've used and like VistaBootPro, available at www.vistabootpro.org. NeoSmart Technologies EasyBCD is also a winner, available at www.neosmart.net (scroll down and look for the "Recent Software Releases" heading on their home page).

3

THE FIRST HOUR

The First Things to Do After Starting Windows 7

If you just installed Windows 7, or have just purchased a new computer that came with Windows 7 already installed, you're probably itching to use it. This chapter is designed to help get you off to a good start. We're going to take you and your computer on a guided tour of Window 7's new and unusual features, and walk you through making some important and useful settings. Here's our itinerary:

- A quick tour of Windows 7's important features

- Setting up user accounts

- Personalizing system settings to make using Windows 7 more comfortable and effective

- Where's my stuff?—or, an introduction to Windows 7's new file location scheme

- Transferring information from your old computer

- Setting up Internet access and automatic updates

- Logging off and shutting down

Our hope is that an hour or so invested in front of your computer following us through these topics will make you a happier Windows user in the long run.

A Quick Tour of Windows 7's Important Features

Windows 7 is in many ways similar to its predecessors Windows Vista, XP, and 2000. The differences that do exist range from fun to peculiar to irritating (at least, irritating at first). This section discusses some of the most important features and the most significant differences between Windows 7 and its predecessors. It would be best if you read this while seated in front of your computer and follow along. That way, when you run into these features and topics later in this book and in your work with Windows, you'll already have "been there, done that" at least once. We'll start with the Welcome screen, which appears after you finish installing Windows 7, or when you turn on your computer for the first time (if Windows 7 came preinstalled on your new PC).

 note

If you're using Windows 7 in a corporate setting and your computer was set up for you, some of the steps in this chapter won't be necessary, and they may not even be available to you. Don't worry—you can skip over any parts of this chapter that have already been taken care of, don't work, or don't interest you.

The Welcome Screen

When Windows starts, you see the Welcome screen, shown in Figure 3.1. On your computer, of course, you'll see different usernames.

Figure 3.1
The Welcome screen is the starting point for logging on. Choose a user and enter the appropriate password or use the icon at the lower right to log off, restart, shut down, or place your computer in hibernation mode.

The Welcome screen lists all the people (*users*, in computer parlance) who have been authorized to use the computer. Click your name, and if asked, enter the account's password. After you enter the password, press Enter, or click the right arrow button to complete the logon process.

The first time you log on, it may take a minute or two for Windows to prepare your *user profile*, the set of folders and files that holds your personal documents, email, pictures, preference settings, and so on. Logging on should take only a few seconds from the second time on. After the logon process is complete, Windows displays the desktop.

The New Start Menu

As with every version of Windows since Windows 95, the route to Windows applications and functions is through the Start menu. To open it, click Start and…wait a minute. Start?

The Start button doesn't say Start on it. It's a round icon bearing the Windows logo, initially at the lower-left corner of the screen, as shown in Figure 3.2. (If move your mouse pointer over it, after a moment the word Start actually will appear, to reassure you I guess.)

 note

If you just purchased a new computer, the first screen you see might be from the tail end of the installation process described in the previous chapter. Your computer's manufacturer set it up this way so that you could choose settings such as your local time zone and keyboard type. If you do see something other than the Welcome screen, scan back through Chapter 2, "Installing and Upgrading Windows 7." If you recognize the screen you see in one of that chapter's illustrations, carry on from here.

If Windows jumps right up to the desktop, your computer's manufacturer set up Windows not to require an initial logon. In that case, skip to the following section in this chapter, in which we show you how to set up a user login.

Figure 3.2
The Start button doesn't read Start anymore.

The Button Formerly Known as Start

So: Click

the Start button. The Start menu appears as a large panel with a list of frequently used programs at the left and a list of locations and tools at the right. The items in the right list that were called My Computer, My Documents, and so on in Windows XP are still present, but the names are now just Computer, Documents, and so on. (We'll show you later in this tour how to select which items appear in this list.)

tip

If you click on your username at the top of the Start menu list, Windows Explorer will display your user profile folder. Your profile folder contains your personal files and settings.

Windows 7 adds a new feature to the list of programs at the left side of the Start menu: *Jump Lists*. Notice the arrows next to some of the program names at the left side of Figure 3.3. If you click an arrow, the Start menu will display a list of files recently opened by or saved by this application. If you click one of those document names, Windows will start the program and open the selected document. You can right-click any of these names to remove them from the recent document list, or permanently "pin" them to the list.

Jump List Pointers

Figure 3.3
Click a Jump List pointer to open a document recently used with an application.

Now, click All Programs, Accessories, and notice that the menus don't expand out in a series of pop-up panels as they did in older versions of Windows. The idea now is to reduce visual clutter. Instead, only one menu at a time is shown in its entirety. The "back" link that appears at the bottom of the list takes you back to the previous menu list. Try it, and watch how the menu display returns to the original Start menu.

The Windows Search tool is also integrated into the Start menu. Under the words All Programs, notice the box that says Search Programs and Files. You can type a part of a filename or a phrase from a document into this box, and Windows attempts to locate the file or document. Results are displayed in the upper part of the Start menu panel.

A similar Search box appears in Windows Explorer, as you'll see in the next section.

The New Windows Explorer

To continue our tour, let's take a quick look at Windows Explorer, which got a major facelift in the jump from Windows XP to Windows Vista. It's the same in Windows 7. Click Start, Computer, and Windows will display the Windows Explorer file manager, shown in Figure 3.4.

Figure 3.4
Windows Explorer sports a new look.

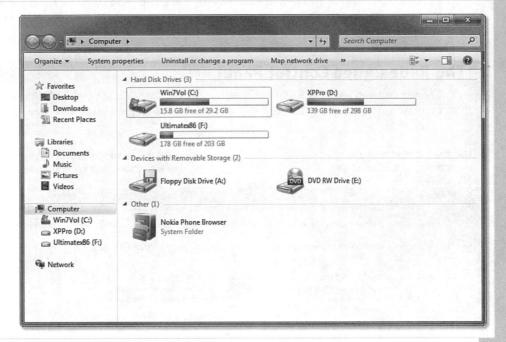

In the left pane, under Computer, click the C: drive, or whichever drive you used when you installed Windows. Double-click Users, then double-click the folder name that corresponds to your user account. (This is usually the same name that you selected on the Welcome screen when you logged on to Windows.) Finally, double-click My Documents.

Notice that as you dig into these folders on your hard disk, the path is displayed at the top of the window, like this: Computer → *diskname* (C:) → Users → *yourname* → My Documents. The names in this list are called *breadcrumbs* (after the breadcrumbs dropped by the children in the fairy tale *Hansel and Gretel*). These breadcrumbs serve to show the way back through the path you took as you dug into the folders. The important thing to remember is that you can always click any of the names in the list to immediately jump back to that particular folder. Besides the standard concept of browsing through files by folder, Windows 7 lets you browse through files by type, through the new Libraries feature. A library is a combined view of several folders that all hold the same type of file. For example, by default, the Documents library lists the combined contents of your personal My Documents folder and the shared Public Documents folder. You can add additional locations to libraries, and you

 tip

When you have several applications running at once, Windows 7 makes it a lot easier to find a particular open window.

You're probably familiar with the Alt+Tab key combination that steps through open windows, which dates back to Windows 3.1. Alt+Tab still works in Windows 7, but it's learned a new trick: While you're holding down Alt+Tab, you can hover your mouse over any of the small snapshot views of the windows, and you'll be treated to a full view of the window's contents.

If you press the Windows key+Tab, Windows rolls through open windows like a Rolodex.

Finally, you can hover your mouse over the icon for any active application in the taskbar, and Windows will display snapshot views of the application's window(s). Click on one to make it the active window. Notice that these snapshot views also have close buttons, so you can quickly close windows you don't need.

can construct new libraries of your own devising. We'll talk more about Libraries and Windows Explorer in Chapter 5, "Managing Files and Searching." Close Windows Explorer now and we'll go on.

The Redesigned Control Panel

The wordy "web page" look and feel used all over Windows 7 reaches its penultimate in the Control Panel. Click Start, Control Panel, and you see the window shown in Figure 3.5.

Use the back button if you end up following a dead-end path.

Use this to switch between this category view and an icon view.

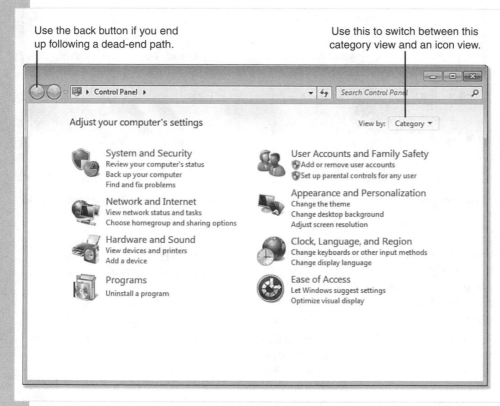

Figure 3.5
The new Control Panel's Category View looks and acts a lot like a web page. You can switch back and forth between this view and the old-style icon view using the View By drop-down box.

Whereas the old Control Panel model used icons to identify little configuration and control programs, the new Control Panel uses phrases—dozens and dozens of phrases—that describe various tasks. The major titles in large type, such as System and Security, Network and Internet and so on, are links to other pages with many subheadings and numerous tasks. The two or three tasks that appear under each title on the main Control Panel page, such as Back Up Your Computer under System and Security, are there as convenient shortcuts, and they appear on the subpages as well.

Now, click the green title System and Security. Notice that this System and Security page has its own long list of headings, such as Action Center, Windows Firewall, System, Windows Update, and so on, with tasks under each heading. On these pages, both the green headings *and* the task descriptions lead to various dialog boxes that let you configure and adjust Windows. Notice also that the Back and Forward buttons in the upper-left corner of the window work just as on a web page, and let you retrace your steps.

Personally, we think that the new Control Panel uses too many words. If you have a hard time finding a control panel applet that you know should be there, try either of these two techniques:

- In the search box, type a word related to the applet you want. For example, the easiest way to get to the Phone and Modem setup dialog is to type the word `modem` into the search box (no need to press Enter), then click Phone and Modem in the list of search results.

- Click the View By drop-down list in the upper-right part of the window, and select Small Icons or Large Icons. The resulting list of icons looks like the Control Panel from Windows XP.

note

The Back button is found all over the place in Windows 7. It can come in handy, so make a mental note to remember to look for it as you use various control panels, Windows Explorer views, setup wizards, and so on.

tip

If you have trouble finding a setting, check this book's index, which should lead you to instructions for finding the correct links in the Control Panel or elsewhere. You can also use the Search box at the top of the Control Panel window.

That View By drop-down item lets you instantly switch back and forth between the Category view and an icon view. (By the way, in this book, almost all instructions will refer to the Category view.)

Before proceeding, be sure View By is set to Category. Next, we're going to look at user accounts and security in Windows 7.

Devices and Printers

A new feature in Windows 7 is the Devices and Printers window, which Microsoft also calls the Device Stage. Click Start, Devices and Printers to display it. A typical display is shown in Figure 3.6.

You can manage a device by right-clicking its icon. The pop-up menu will contain selections appropriate for each type of device. You can poke around the icons on your computer's Devices and Printer window to see what's available. Later in the book there are specific instructions for managing devices using this window.

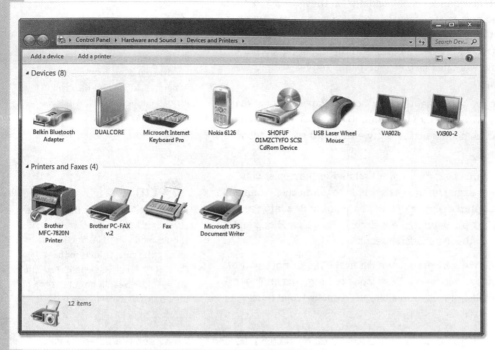

Figure 3.6
The Devices and Printers window is new to Windows 7. It provides a single place to manage printers, monitors, imaging devices, Bluetooth devices, and so on.

User Account Control

We need to stop, at this point, to give you some background on the next feature that we'll show you.

One area where Microsoft justifiably received a great deal of criticism over the past 15 years or so was its handling of security. Windows 95, 98, and Me had no security scheme at all—any user could modify any file or program.

Windows NT, 2000, and XP did have the necessary structure to secure the operating system. The way Windows security works, any program that a user runs gains the privileges associated with the user's logon account; this determines what folders the user can save files in, what settings the user can change, and so on. Computer Administrator accounts, in particular, have the capability to change any system setting, change any file, or install any software.

Unfortunately, in Windows XP, *all* user accounts were by default created as Computer Administrator accounts, and it took a lot of effort and training to work with Windows any other way. So, for most home and small office users, Windows security was essentially bypassed. The consequences of this were, in turn

- Any program run by hundreds of millions of Windows 95, 98, Me, and XP users had complete access to the computer.

- When anyone was duped into running bad software downloaded from the Internet or received a bogus program by email, that software also had the complete run of the computer.

- Some tens of millions of Windows computers are, as a result, infected with spam-sending software, unbeknown to their owners.

- Criminals remotely control those computers and use them to send about 80% of more than 100 billion or so spam emails that are sent every day.

So, the next time you clear out your email inbox, consider that most of the spam in there got there because for 15 years Microsoft made no effort to make Windows Internet-secure "out of the box," meaning, as delivered to the consumer. And few people knew how to take the complex steps needed to tighten things up.

Windows Vista and now Windows 7 change that in a big way. Out of the box, Windows 7 and Vista enforce security through several means, including these:

- The disk on which Windows is installed uses the NTFS disk formatting system so that access to files and folders can be tightly controlled.

- As initially installed, the security system is actually used and ensures that users do not have the ability to randomly create, delete, or modify files in the Windows program folders. This protects Windows not only from accidents but also from rogue software.

- Programs and system control panels that can make changes that have security implications use a special feature called User Account Control to ensure that changes can't be made without your knowing it.

This latter part is what we want to talk about and show you now.

As mentioned earlier, Windows programs run with the permissions associated with a user account. Permissions include things such as the ability to create or modify files in each folder, change settings on features such as networking and hard disk management, install software and hardware device drivers, and so on. Computer Administrator accounts can do any of these things.

What changed starting with Windows Vista is that programs run even by users with Administrator accounts *don't* automatically get all those privileges. The potential is there, but by default, programs run with a reduced set of privileges that lets them modify files in the user's own folders but *not* in the Windows folder or the Program Files folder. Likewise, by default, programs run even by a Computer Administrator cannot change networking settings, install applications, install device drivers, or change system software services.

Instead, you have to take a special step to run a program with *elevated privileges*—that is, with the full complement of Computer Administrator privileges. And, on Vista, whenever you try to do this, Windows requires that you confirm that you actually do want to run that specific program with elevated privileges. Windows displays a dialog box, and you have to click a yes or no response before the program is allowed to run (or not). On Windows 7, as we'll explain shortly, this mechanism is still there, but Windows requires this sort of confirmation in fewer circumstances.

What is important is that when this "go or no go" dialog box is displayed, it's displayed by Windows in a secure way, from a deep, protected part of Windows, and there is no way for rogue software to bypass it, block it, or fake your approval. Thus, there is no way for rogue software to install itself *without your consent*. This is called *User Account Control (UAC)*, and it's the most important distinction between Windows 7 and Vista and any of their predecessors.

Another important feature of the UAC prompt is this: If you are logged on using a Computer Administrator account, Windows just asks you to consent to running the program. However, if you logged on using a Standard User account, Windows *can still run the administrative program*—the UAC prompt asks you to select the username and enter the password of a Computer Administrator account.

All this makes Windows more secure *and* usable. It makes it safer to let people have and use Computer Administrator accounts. And, it is now reasonable to set up Standard User accounts for everyday use, for anyone, and especially for people whom you'd rather not be asked to judge which programs should run—for example, children or non-computer-literate employees. Should they actually need to change some setting that brings up a UAC prompt, you can simply reach over their shoulders, type in a privileged account name and password, let them make the one change, and poof!—they're back to being a limited-privilege user.

Of course, this type of intervention is required only for programs that involve security-related settings. And this brings us to the reason that the new Control Panel and other Windows management tools are so complex and fractured.

Microsoft had to go through all the Windows settings and adjustments and decide which ones could pose security risks and which were benign. For example, installing a device driver is a risky task, and selecting a desktop background picture is benign. Risky and benign settings had to be put into separate programs or Control Panel elements. The benign ones are packaged as nonprivileged programs so that they can be run by any user. The risky ones have been put into separate programs that are marked as requiring elevated privileges. So, Control Panel items that used to have dozens of settings on one dialog box had to be split into many smaller pieces.

This seemed to us to be a small price to pay for such a huge increase in security. But, Vista got a bad rap because these pop-ups popped up fairly often, especially in the first few weeks of using a new computer, when lots of software and hardware changes take place. It annoyed people who were used to the "Wild West" days of Windows 98. We think the bad rap was completely unjustified, but it stuck.

So, for Windows 7, Microsoft has softened UAC somewhat. By default, Windows now automatically grants elevated privileges to many less-risky Control Panel programs and dialog boxes, and pops up the confirmation box in only two situations: if it's not sure that the requested program is absolutely safe, or if you are not using a Computer Administrator account, in which case an administrator's password is needed. And, you can control how rigid UAC is, from turning it off entirely to requesting the Windows Vista–style of prompting before every change.

A program can be run with elevated privileges in three ways:

- Some programs are "marked" by their developers as *requiring* elevated privileges. These programs display the UAC prompt whenever you try to run them.

 caution

The default setting makes Windows 7 much less annoying than Vista, without compromising security too much. We *strongly* urge you *not* to reduce the UAC warning level below the default setting. Doing so makes your computer much more vulnerable to being taken over by criminals. If you have specific programs that don't work well with UAC enabled, you can work around this *just for those specific programs*.

- You can right-click *any* program's icon and select Run As Administrator. Generally, you need to do this only if you attempt some task and are told that you don't have permission. This can happen, for instance, if you try to delete some other user's document from the printer's queue.

- If you have an old program that you find doesn't work correctly with UAC, right-click its icon and select Properties. On the Shortcut tab, click the Advanced button, and check Run As Administrator. This will make the program run with elevated privileges every time you run it.

So...that was a long explanation for something that will help you tremendously but in practice won't take up much of your time. Let's go on with the tour.

note

If you're interested in reading about the nitty-gritty details about how User Account Control works in Windows 7, go to technet. microsoft.com and search for "Inside Windows 7 User Account Control." Look for the article of this name written by Mark Russinovich, who's one of the Windows gurus behind sysinternals.com, and who's now employed by Microsoft.

If you aren't looking at the Control Panel, now, click Start, Control Panel. Click on System and Security, and notice that some of the tasks are shown with a small shield icon. This is the indication that a task requires elevated privileges. By default, on Windows 7, most of these items will *not* bring up a UAC prompt; Windows will elevate most management tools automatically.

When you do get a UAC prompt, it will display one of the dialog boxes shown in Figure 3.7.

If you are currently logged on to a Computer Administrator account, you see dialog box A shown in Figure 3.7. The dialog shows the name and the origin of the program, if it can be determined. You can click Show Details to see more information about the program file, if any is available.

A   B

Figure 3.7
User Account Control asks for confirmation or asks you to provide an Administrator password.

If you are logged on to a Standard User account, Windows displays dialog box B shown in Figure 3.7. Here, you can also click Show Details to see more information about the program that caused the UAC pop-up. To proceed, you (or someone else) must select one of the Administrator account names and enter its password.

In either case, this is your chance to verify that you intended to run the program that caused the pop-up, and that you trust it to be safe to run.

In the next part of our tour, we will help you set up user accounts for the people who will be using your computer.

Setting Up User Accounts

As mentioned previously, distinct user accounts identify each person who uses the computer and regulate what settings and files the users can change. Windows 2000 and XP provided three types of user accounts:

- **Computer Administrator**—Could change any setting, view any file

- **Power User**—Could change many settings, view own files only

- **Limited User**—Could change virtually no settings, view own files only

The problem with this scheme was that Limited Users were constantly frustrated by being unable to make changes as trivial as choosing a screen saver. The Power User category should have been the right one to use for day-to-day use, but it wasn't available on Windows XP Home Edition. Even on XP Professional, it wasn't easy to create Power User accounts. The result was that most users were created as Computer Administrators, and we discussed in the previous section what a disaster *that* has turned out to be.

On Windows 7, this situation has improved dramatically. First, the Limited User category is now named Standard User, to reflect its "mainstream" role. Most settings that don't have security implications—such as changing the screen resolution—can now be changed by Standard Users. Plugging in a new USB device used to require Administrator privileges, but now, if a Microsoft-verified driver is preinstalled, a Standard User can add the device without any trouble. And for any tasks that *do* require Administrator privileges, the UAC system makes it easy to perform the task without having to completely log off and log back on.

As a result, it's perfectly reasonable to use a Standard User account for your day-to-day work. And should you choose to use an Administrator account, *even that* is relatively safe now. So,

 caution

Don't get in the habit of just clicking Yes every time one of these dialog boxes appears. Read it and consider it every time.

If you have any doubts about the program listed in the dialog box, especially if a UAC pop-up appears when you didn't expect it, click No.

 tip

If you want to transfer user accounts and files from an older computer to your Windows 7 computer using the Windows Easy Transfer program that is described later in this chapter, do that first, then come back to this section to set passwords on each of the transferred accounts.

 tip

If you purchased a computer with Windows 7 preinstalled, the manufacturer might have set Windows up to skip the Welcome screen logon process entirely. There actually is a user account set up for you, and when you start Windows it automatically logs on to that one account.

If you expect to have others people use your computer, go ahead and create more user accounts now, and we'll show you how to make the Welcome screen work later in the chapter, under "Just One User?"

while the Power User category is still present, it's neither needed nor useful.

At this point on our tour, let's add user accounts for the people who will be using your computer.

Create New Accounts

If you aren't looking at the Manage Accounts screen now, click Start, Control Panel, and then click Add or Remove User Accounts under the heading User Accounts and Family Safety. You should see the Manage Accounts window shown in Figure 3.8—of course, it shows your names instead of mine.

tip

When you first installed Windows, Windows setup created a Computer Administrator account. We recommend that you create perhaps one additional Computer Administrator account, and that you create a Standard User account for yourself for day-to-day use. This gives you maximum protection against viruses and other malware.

From the Manage Accounts screen, you can select an account to modify, or you can click Create a New Account. You'll find that it's best if each person who uses the computer has his or her own account so that each person's email can be kept separate, settings and preferences can be personalized, and so on.

Figure 3.8
Manage Accounts lets you create or modify user accounts.

To create a new user account, perform the following steps:

1. Click Create a New Account.

2. Type a name for the account. Use just letters, numbers, and optionally spaces or hyphens. We typically use each person's first initial and last name, but you can use any scheme you want.

3. If you want to create a Computer Administrator account, select Administrator; otherwise, leave the selection at Standard User. I recommend that you use Standard accounts for most users, and even for your own day-to-day use.

4. Click Create Account.

The new user appears in the Manage Accounts screen.

Now, you can make adjustments to each account.

note

Before logging on to any other accounts for the first time, see the "Configuring a Default User Profile" section at the end of this chapter.

Change Account Settings

To change an account's settings, view the Manage Accounts screen, as shown in Figure 3.8, and click an account name. The screen lists several tasks, including the following:

- **Change the Account Name**—Click to edit the account's username. (Note: If the user has already logged on, this actually changes the name of his or her profile folder in the \Users folder. If this doesn't make sense to you right now, don't worry about it.)

- **Create a Password** or **Change the Password**—Click to create or change the account's password. We *strongly* recommend that you set a password on every user account, or at the very least on *every* Administrator account.

- **Change the Picture**—Click to select a different picture to appear on the Start menu and the Welcome screen. You can select one of the pictures supplied by Microsoft or click Browse for More Pictures to locate one of your own images.

- **Set Up Parental Controls**—Click to control when this user can use the computer, and what games and applications the user can use. (Unlike Windows Vista, website filtering and activity tracking are not standard features with Windows 7—you have to install third-party software for that.)

- **Change the Account Type**—Click to change the account type from Administrator to Standard User or vice versa.

- **Delete the Account**—Click to delete the account. You can elect to keep or delete the account's files (documents, pictures, and so on).

You can also select and enable the Guest account. The Guest account is a Standard User account that requires no password, and it should be enabled only if you want to provide a computer to guests in your home or office.

tip

Before logging on to other accounts for the first time, see "Configuring a Default User Profile" at the end of this chapter.

At this point on our tour of Windows 7, we recommend that you take a moment now to add a user account for each person who will be using your computer. Definitely set a password on each Administrator account. We recommend that you set a password on each Standard User account as well.

After you add your user accounts, continue to the next section.

Before You Forget Your Password

If you forget your account's password, you could be in serious trouble. On a corporate domain network, you can ask your network administrator to save you. But, on a home computer or in a small office, forgetting your password is serious. It can put your encrypted files at risk, and you could lose any passwords that you've stored for automatic use on websites. (Do you even remember them all?)

And if you can't remember the password to any Computer Administrator account, you'll really be stuck. You'll most likely have to reinstall Windows, and all of your applications, and you'll be *very* unhappy.

There is something you can do to prevent this disaster from happening to you. You can create a password reset disk *right now*, and put it away in a safe place. A password reset disk is linked to your account and lets you log in using data physically stored on the disk. It's like a physical key to your computer. Even if you later change your account's password between making the disk and forgetting the password, the reset disk will still work to unlock your account.

So...make a password reset disk now! Here's how. You need a blank, formatted floppy disk, recordable CD, removable USB thumb drive, or other such removable medium. Follow these steps:

1. Click Start, Control Panel, User Accounts and Family Safety; then click the (usually green) User Accounts title at the top of the right-hand pane.

2. In the Tasks list at the left side of the window, choose Create a Password Reset Disk.

3. When the wizard appears, click Next.

4. Select a removable disk drive from the list and click Next.

5. Enter your current password and click Next.

6. Follow the wizard's instructions. When the wizard finishes writing data, click Next and then click Finish.

The disk will now contain a file called userkey.psw, which is the key to your account. (You can copy this file to another medium, if you want.) Remove the disk, label it so that you'll remember what it is, and store it in a safe place.

 tip

If you are in a home or small office environment, have more than one computer, and plan on setting up a local area network, we suggest that you create accounts for every one of your users on each of your computers, using the *same name and same password* for each person on each computer. This makes it possible for anyone to use any computer, and it makes it easier for you to manage security on your network.

 caution

A password reset disk, or rather the file userkey.psw that's on it, is as good as your password for gaining access to your computer, so store the reset disk in a safe, secure place. By "secure," I mean something like a locked drawer, filing cabinet, or safe-deposit box.

You don't have to re-create the disk if you change your password in the future. The disk will still work regardless of your password at the time. However, a password disk works only to get into the account that created it, so each user should create one.

If you forget your password and can't log on, see "After You Forget Your Password" toward the end of this chapter.

 note

Be absolutely sure to create a password reset disk for at least one Computer Administrator account on your computer.

Adjust Your Own User Account

Windows has a few settings that are set on a per-user basis, and some of them can be set in only one particular way, using the following steps. You don't necessarily need to do this now. If you want to, you can skip ahead to the next section.

To see the list of user account settings you can change, click Start, Control Panel, User Accounts and Family Safety; then click the User Accounts title at the top of the right-hand pane.

The most common tasks are listed in the window's larger pane. These include options to change your password and the picture associated with your account, which we discussed earlier.

 note

Each user should create his own password reset disk. In theory, a computer Administrator could always reset any other user's password, but that user would then lose his or her encrypted files and stored passwords. Better to have a password reset disk for *every* user account.

Look through the Tasks list on the left side of the screen. These selections appear only when you open the User Accounts control panel this particular way, and they have the following uses:

- **Create a Password Reset Disk**—Creates a disk that you can use to log on if you forget your password, as discussed in the previous section.

- **Manage Your Network Passwords**—Lets you add, delete, or change passwords that have been remembered by Windows for use on remote servers or websites. One useful feature here is that you can back up these passwords to a disk and copy them to your account on another computer.

- **Manage Your File Encryption Certificates**—Use this wizard to create, back up, or restore the certificates (keys) used to encrypt your files, on Windows 7 Professional, Enterprise, or Ultimate editions only.

  ➡ *For more information on file encryption,* **see** *"Encrypted File System (EFS)," p. 884.*

- **Configure Advanced User Profile Properties**—If your computer is on a domain network, you can select whether your user profile should be copied back and forth to the file server (a roaming profile) or just kept on the computer in front of you (a local profile).

- **Change My Environment Variables**—You can customize environment variables for your account here. Environment variables tell Windows applications where to look for executable files, where to store temporary files, and so on.

  ➡ *For more information,* **see** *"Setting Environment Variables," p. 825.*

Just One User?

If you are the only person who is going to use your computer, there is a setting that you can use so that Windows starts up and goes directly to your desktop without asking you to log on. You may find that your computer does this anyway; some computer manufacturers turn on this setting before they ship the computer to you. Technically, a password is still used; it's just entered for you automatically.

We recommend that you don't use this automatic logon option. Without a password, your computer or your Internet connection could be abused by someone without your even knowing it.

Still, in some situations it's reasonable to change this setting—for example, if your computer manufacturer set your computer up this way, you can disable it. Or you may want to use the feature in a computer that's used in a public place, or in an industrial control setting. To change the startup setting, follow these steps:

1. Click Start, and in the Search box, enter `control userpasswords2` and press Enter.

2. To require a logon, check Users Must Enter a Username and Password to Access This Computer, and click OK.

   Alternately, to make Windows go to the desktop automatically, uncheck Users Must Enter a Username and Password to Access This Computer, and click OK. Then, type the username and password of the account that you want to log on automatically and click OK.

The change takes effect the next time Windows starts up.

Setting Up Internet Access

Although you'll probably want to change a number of settings, you should start by making sure that your computer has a working Internet connection, for two reasons. First, critical Windows security or device driver updates might have been released since your computer's copy of Windows was made. You definitely want to get those updates installed as quickly as possible. Second, at least one setting, which we're going to discuss later in this chapter, requires a functioning Internet connection.

If you have existing dial-up or broadband Internet service or, better still, have an existing network that you can just plug your computer into, this should be easy. We actually devote entire chapters in this book to the topic, but you might be able to get on the air in just a few seconds, so let's give it a shot. Here's what to try:

1. If your home or office has a wired Ethernet network (for example, a router) that provides shared Internet access, just plug in your computer. That's all you should need to do. Open Internet Explorer (IE) and see whether it works.

2. If you have a wireless network adapter in your computer and a wireless network available that provides Internet access, turn on your wireless adapter. Windows should pop up a notice that wireless networks are available. If it doesn't, click Start, Control Panel, Network and Internet, and then, under Network and Sharing Center, click Add a Wireless Device to the Network.

A list of available networks should appear. If your wireless network's name appears in the list, click the name and then click the Connect button. The Connection Wizard then walks you through establishing the connection.

3. If you have broadband cable or DSL service and you plan to connect your computer directly to the cable or DSL modem, connect your computer's network adapter to the modem now.

4. If you have cable Internet service, this might be enough to get your connection going...open Intornot Exploror and coo.

If you have dial-up or DSL service, click Start, Control Panel, Network and Internet, Network and Sharing Center, and then click Set Up a New Connection or Network. Select Connect to the Internet and click Next. Then follow the wizard to set up a PPPoE (DSL) or dial-up connection.

If this seat-of-the-pants procedure doesn't work for you, jump ahead to Chapter 13, "Getting Connected," to get your connection working.

When your Internet connection is set up, you're ready to continue with the rest of this chapter.

Downloading Critical Updates

After your Internet connection is up and running, click Start, All Programs, Windows Update. In the left pane, click Check for Updates.

If no updates are available, and the screen says that Windows is up to date, you can close this window and skip ahead to the next section.

If there are any Critical or Important updates to download, click Install Updates and wait for the process to complete before continuing the tour. If Windows has to restart, log on, and immediately return to Windows Update and see whether any *additional* updates are available. It's essential that you get all security fixes installed before proceeding.

Personalizing Windows

For the next part of your first hour with Windows, we want to help you make changes to some settings that make Windows a bit easier to use, and a little easier to understand. So, let's tear through them.

As initially installed, Windows might set your screen's resolution to a lower resolution than your monitor supports. You might also want to change the screen background from the picture you chose during installation or set up a screen saver. Let's start personalizing Windows by adjusting these settings.

Personalize Screen Settings

Now we're ready to make a couple of quick selections to the settings that control Windows' appearance. To do this, right-click the desktop anywhere but on an icon and select Personalize. The window shown in Figure 3.9 appears.

Figure 3.9
Windows 7's
Personalization screen
lets you change display
and sound settings.

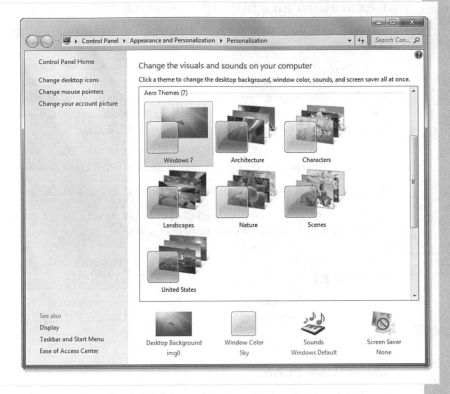

You can select a Theme, which is a collection of desktop and sound settings, and/or you can customize individual settings by clicking the icons at the bottom of the window. The two important settings to consider now are

- **Desktop Background**—Click to select a different desktop picture. If you check more than one picture, Windows will change the background every so often—the timing is set at the bottom of the window. You can also change the Picture Location to Solid Colors to select a plain, uniform background, or to Pictures Library to select one of your own pictures; or click Browse to locate a favorite picture of your own.

- **Screen Saver**—Click to select a screen saver and set the timeout. If you want your computer to lock itself if you go away long enough for the screen saver to activate, check On Resume, Display Logon Screen.

 note

You can put those unused computer processor cycles to better use than making the Windows logo swim around your screen. Several worthy screen-saver alternatives actually might help find a cure for cancer or eavesdrop on ET phoning home. Our favorites can be found at http://boinc.berkeley.edu.

Resolution and Multiple Monitors

On Windows 7, the display's physical settings are changed through a different window. Right-click the desktop and select Screen Resolution.

Click the Resolution value, and drag the slider up or down to set the resolution of your monitor. If Windows looks a little blurry, especially on an LCD monitor, it could be that Windows guessed too low a resolution. Drag the resolution button up to set it to the exact native resolution of your LCD monitor; then click Apply to check the setting. If it works, click OK to keep it. (If the type is too small to read, don't worry; we'll get to the fix for that shortly.)

If you have two or more monitors attached to your computer, Windows should have offered you the option of extending your desktop onto all of them. If not, follow these steps:

1. Next to Multiple Displays, select Extend These Displays, and then click Apply.

2. Click the Identify button, and drag the numbered icons in the Screen Resolution pane so that they are in the same arrangement as your monitors. Click Apply again.

Font Size

If you have trouble reading the type on the screen, at the bottom of the window select Make Text and Other Items Large or Smaller, and select either Medium or Larger. Click Apply to check the setting.

ClearType Tuner

Finally, if you have an LCD monitor, use the nifty ClearType Tuner tool to ensure that the text displayed on your monitor is sharp and easy to read. Here's what to do:

1. Click Start, Control Panel, Appearance and Customization, Adjust ClearType Text (under Fonts).

2. Be sure that Turn On ClearType is checked, and then click Next. Follow the wizard's instructions to select the text layout that looks best to you.

3. When the wizard has finished, click the small icon at the top of the Control Panel's left margin to restore the web layout, then close it.

Now, we'll make some other adjustments to the desktop.

Tune Up the Taskbar

The taskbar at the bottom of the desktop has the Start button at the far left and the notification area at the far right. The middle section shows an icon for each running application. This much hasn't changed since Windows 95. You might also recall the Quick Launch bar from previous versions of Windows, which had little icons you could use to start up commonly used programs with a single click.

 note

The old Show Desktop icon that parks all applications in the taskbar is now the unlabeled rectangle at the far right.

In Windows 7, the Quick Launch bar and the taskbar have been combined and enhanced, and now there is just one set of icons: they represent applications that *are* running, and those that represent programs you *could* run, as shown in Figure 3.10.

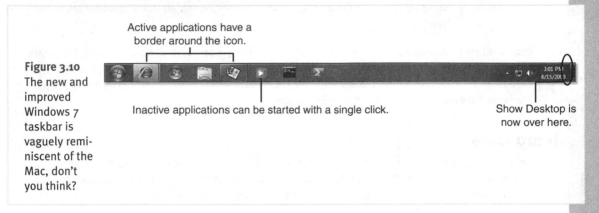

Active applications have a
border around the icon.

Figure 3.10
The new and improved
Windows 7
taskbar is
vaguely reminiscent of the
Mac, don't
you think?

Inactive applications can be started with a single click.

Show Desktop is
now over here.

This new arrangement might seem strange at first, but it's actually pretty handy, and we think you'll like it a lot. (And if it seems vaguely familiar, it might be because the Apple Mac has worked this way for more than eight years!)

Follow these steps to see it in action:

- Click the blue **e** icon for Internet Explorer. (If it's not present on your computer, use another of the icons.)

    When you click the icon for an application that isn't running, Windows starts it.

- Click the blue **e** icon two more times.

    When you click the icon for an application that's already running, Windows hides or brings up the application's window, in alternation.

- Right-click the blue **e** icon, and select Internet Explorer.

    This opens up another, separate instance of the application.

- Click the blue **e** icon.

    When you click the icon for an application that has more than one instance open, Windows displays thumbnail views of the various windows, so you can select which one you want to use.

In practice, you won't have to think about it. When you want to use a program, you just click its icon, and you get it, whether it was already running or not.

You can also easily organize the icons on the taskbar:

- You can drag the icons around to reorder them any way you want.

- To put an application in the taskbar permanently, if it's already running, right-click the icon and select Pin This Program to Taskbar.

If the program isn't currently running, you can locate it in the Start menu, right-click and select Pin to Taskbar, or, just drag the icon down to the taskbar.

- To remove an icon, right-click and select Unpin This Program from Taskbar. (Use this technique to get rid of icons that some application installers insist on putting on the taskbar whether you want them or not.)

You might want to take a moment now to add icons for the programs you use frequently. Personally, I always add icons for the Command Prompt, Windows Explorer, and Microsoft Word, but you might have other favorites. To add Windows Explorer, click Start, All Programs, then Accessories. Drag Windows Explorer down to the taskbar and release it.

Jump Lists

Another neat new feature of the taskbar is the Jump List. Remember the old Recent Documents list from previous versions of Windows? In Windows 7, this feature is now part of the taskbar, and recently used documents are linked to the icons for the applications that opened them.

Right-click the taskbar's Internet Explorer icon, for example, and you'll see a list of recently visited websites. Right-click Microsoft Word or WordPad or Notepad, and you'll see the last several documents you saved using those programs. It's all very intuitive and natural. (Although, it only works with applications that know about this feature. Older applications may not create a Jump List.)

Jump lists also appear in the Start menu, except there, you click the small arrow that appears next to an icon instead of right-clicking the icon itself.

tip

If you want to keep a website or document in the Jump List permanently, right-click it and select Pin to This List.

Adjust the Explorers

You're probably familiar with Internet Explorer, Microsoft's web browser. The other Explorer you need to know about is Windows Explorer, the program behind the desktop itself, and the Start Menu, Computer, Documents, Music, and other file management windows. You're using Windows Explorer when you use any of those tools. You can also use it by itself to manage files. By default, though, it hides some information about files, and we want to give you the option of seeing that hidden information.

Disable Hide Extensions for Known File Types

By default, Windows Explorer hides the file extension at the end of most filenames: This is the .doc at the end of a Word document, the .xls at the end of an Excel spreadsheet, or the .exe at the end of an application program. Hiding the extension makes it more difficult for you to accidentally delete it when renaming the file, but we think it also makes it more difficult to tell what a given file is. It can also make it easier to fall for ruses, as when someone sends an email virus in a file named payroll.xls.exe. If Explorer hides the .exe part, you may fall for the trick and think the file is just an Excel spreadsheet.

To make Explorer show filenames in all their glory, follow these steps:

1. Click Start, Computer.

2. Click the Organize button at the top, left side of the window, and select Folder and Search Options.

3. Select the View tab. In the Advanced Settings list, find Hide Extensions for Known File Types and uncheck it.

4. This one is optional: If you're curious about Windows' internal files and folders, and plan on investigating them, also select Show Hidden Files and Folders. You can change this setting after you finish looking around.

5. Click OK.

Customize the Start Menu

There are some Windows maintenance tools that, for some reason, Microsoft doesn't put into the Start menu by default. We suggest that you enable them now so that you don't have to dig through the Control Panel to get to them. Here's how:

1. Right-click the Start button and select Properties.

2. Click the Customize button.

3. Scroll down through the list to find System Administrative Tools near the bottom. Select Display on the All Programs menu.

4. If you're interested, check out the rest of this list for other Start menu options. If you find that you *never* use the Music link, for example, you can remove it from the Start menu here.

   Or if you find that you miss the old Run command that lets you start programs by typing their name, you can enable it here. (Although, you can start a program by typing its name into the Search box on the Start menu, so Run isn't as necessary anymore. Still, the Search window can run only programs that are in the search path, so for hardcore command-line users, the Run option is still useful.)

5. Click OK twice, closing both of the open dialog boxes in turn.

Set Internet Explorer's Home Page

By default, whenever you open Internet Explorer, it immediately displays a Microsoft website, or a website specified by your computer manufacturer. Personally, I prefer to have Internet Explorer open to a blank page because I rarely start my browsing in the same place twice. You may also prefer to select a different "home" page, one that *you* want to visit rather than one selected by some company's marketing department. To take control of your Internet Explorer home page, take the following steps:

1. Click Start, All Programs, Internet Explorer. (Or click the little **e** icon on the taskbar.)

2. To start IE with a blank page every time, in the upper-right corner of the window, click Tools, Internet Options. Then, click the Use Blank button.

   Or to select a page that you prefer to see each time IE starts, view that page now. Then, in the upper-right corner of the window, click Tools, Internet Options. Click the Use Current button.

3. Click OK to close the Internet Options dialog box.

If you prefer to use a different web browser entirely, Safari, Chrome, Firefox, and Opera are popular alternatives to IE. For more information, see Chapter 14, "Using Internet Explorer 8."

Set Internet Explorer's Search Provider

Internet Explorer has a search tool built into the upper-right corner of the window. When you type something into this box and press Enter, IE sends the text to an Internet search engine and displays the result. This saves you having to open the search engine page first, type the search text, and then wait for the results.

However, by default IE sends you to Microsoft's own search engine, called Windows Live. Or your computer manufacturer may have specified a different default search engine. Again, we suggest that you take control and tell IE what search engine *you* want to use. You can use Windows Live, of course, but you can also select a different default site.

To change the default search site, follow these steps:

1. Internet Explorer should still be open from the previous section, but if it's not, click Start, All Programs, Internet Explorer.

2. At the upper-right corner of the window, locate the little magnifying glass icon and click the small down-pointing arrow just to its right.

3. Select Find More Providers.

4. Click the name of one of the providers in the Web Search or Topic Search lists. When the Add Provider dialog appears, check Make This My Default Search Provider. Then, click Add Provider.

5. Test the new search tool: Type your name into the Search box and press Enter.

That's the end of our list of "must-do" Windows settings. You can, of course, change hundreds of other things, which is why we went on to write Chapters 4 through 38.

 note

Normally, you have to go through most of these same setup steps for each user account on your computer. At the end of this chapter, under "Configuring a Default User Profile," we show you how you can do all of your setup, tweaking, and adjusting just once, and have your finely tuned setup be the default setup for all of your computer's user accounts.

If that sounds interesting, skip ahead to the end of the chapter now, *before* you or anyone else logs on to any other account on your computer.

Transferring Information from Your Old Computer

If you have set up a new Windows 7 computer rather than upgrading an old one, you probably have files that you want to bring over to your new computer. Windows 7 has a tool called Windows Easy Transfer that will help you do that. The next several sections show you how to use it. (Corporate network managers can use a program called the User State Migration Tool, but it's beyond the scope of this book.)

Windows Easy Transfer

The Windows Easy Transfer program lets you copy documents and preference settings from an older computer running Windows 7, Vista, or XP to a new computer running Windows 7. You can use several different means to transfer the data:

- If you can plug both computers into the same local area network (LAN), the transfer can occur directly over the network.

- If you don't have a network but both of your computers have Ethernet network adapters, you can connect them using an Ethernet crossover cable. **See** "Connecting Just Two Computers," **p. 461**. Then, you can use the network transfer method.

- You can connect the two computers using a special Easy Transfer USB cable, which you can buy for about $30 US.

- You can elect to copy data using a Flash drive, a removable, external USB, FireWire, or SATA hard disk, or a network folder.

- The system doesn't make it easy to use a recordable CD or DVD drive. If you have a small enough amount of data to copy, you could, however, use the "external drive" method, save the user data file on your hard disk, and then burn this to a DVD or CD.

The wizard is self-explanatory, so we won't give you step-by-step instructions here, but we do have some pointers that might make the process smoother and easier to follow.

The process goes like this:

- First, copy the Windows Easy Transfer program to your old computer. Then, run the program on your old computer.

- If you're using a direct network connection or an Easy Transfer Cable, start up the Easy Transfer program on your new computer as well, select the user accounts and files you want to copy, and the program goes to town.

 note

Be aware that Windows Easy Transfer doesn't transfer your application programs. Some third-party programs, such as LapLink PCMover, do purport to transfer applications, but I can't vouch for them.

By default, if you elect to copy Shared Items, Windows Easy Transfer *will* copy data stored outside the usual My *Whatever* folders on *all* of your hard drives; that is, everything except the \Windows, \Program Files, and \Program Data folders.

 caution

Passwords are *not* set up for user accounts copied by the transfer program, even though the Users control panel makes it seem that they are. Be sure to read the section "Password Issues" that follows shortly.

 tip

The Windows Easy Transfer program and our instructions here refer to an "old computer" and a "new computer." But, you can use it to save your user accounts and files and then restore them on the *same computer*. You might do this if you want to install a fresh copy of Windows 7 on a new or erased hard disk. Use Windows Easy Transfer to save your user files on an external disk, set up Windows on a clean hard disk, then run the program again to restore your files. Again, this doesn't save your application software, but it does preserve user accounts and files.

- If you're using a flash drive, an external disk, or a shared folder, select the user accounts and files you want to transfer. The program will create one big file containing all the user data. Then take this file to the new computer and run the Easy Transfer program there. Tell it where the big file is. The program will re-create the selected user accounts and documents from the data stored in the file.

Now, we'll give you some tips for each of these stages.

Copying the Easy Transfer Program

If your old computer is running the *same version* of Windows 7 as your new computer, you already have the program on both machines. Start at your *old* computer. Click Start, type the word **easy** into the Search box, click Windows Easy Transfer, and follow the instructions from there.

Otherwise, you have to get the transfer program into your old computer.

If you have your Windows 7 setup DVD handy, you can save some time using this trick: Start at your *old* computer, log on as a Computer Administrator user, and insert the Windows 7 setup DVD. If an AutoPlay dialog box pops up, select Open Folder or Browse Files; otherwise, open [My] Computer. Browse to `\support\migwiz` on the DVD drive, and double-click the `migsetup` or `migsetup.exe` icon. Follow the instructions from there. When you later run the transfer program on your *new* computer, tell it that the program is already installed on the old computer.

If you don't have the setup DVD or if you don't want to use it, you'll need a USB Flash drive, a removable external USB, FireWire, or SATA hard drive that works with both your new and old computer, or network access to a shared folder. Start at your *new* computer. Click Start, type **easy** into the Search box, then click Windows Easy Transfer. Follow the instructions, and select I Need to Install It Now to copy the program onto your removable drive. Then, take that drive over to your old computer. Be sure to log on using a Computer Administrator account. Find and double-click the Windows Easy Transfer shortcut on the removable drive.

Selecting a Transfer Method

As previously mentioned, you can use a direct network connection, an Easy Transfer USB cable, or some sort of disk medium that can carry a file from your old computer to your new computer.

The direct network connection and the Easy Transfer Cable methods are the easiest, because they let the old computer talk directly to the new computer, you don't have to worry about having enough room on the external disk for all of the files you'll transfer, and it saves you a few steps.

But the external disk method is just fine too, and it's the only method you can use if the old and new computers are physically the same computer—that is, if you want to store your user accounts and documents while you perform a fresh installation of Windows 7.

You can also use the external disk method if you want to use a recordable DVD or CD to transfer your data. (Remember, though, that a DVD can only hold 4GB to 5GB of data, and a CD can only hold about 700MB. Is that enough room for all of your files?) To use these media, have the transfer program save your information to the old computer's hard disk. Then, burn a DVD or CD with the file that the transfer program creates. By default, this file is named `Windows Easy Transfer - Items from old computer.MIG`.

Selecting Accounts and Content

The Windows Easy Transfer program lets you select which user accounts to copy and, if you want to get picky, decide which files to copy from each account, as shown in Figure 3.11. By default, the program will transfer all accounts and all files and folders under each account (that is, My Documents, My Pictures, and so on). In addition, the Shared Items entry copies the files under \Users\Public on Vista and Windows 7 or under \Documents and Settings\All Users on Windows XP, as well as *all other folders on all of your hard drives* except \Windows, \Program Files, and \Program Data. The total amount of data to be copied is displayed under the list of accounts.

Figure 3.11
Select which user accounts to copy. Shared Items copies all shared user files plus all other folders on all of your hard drives.

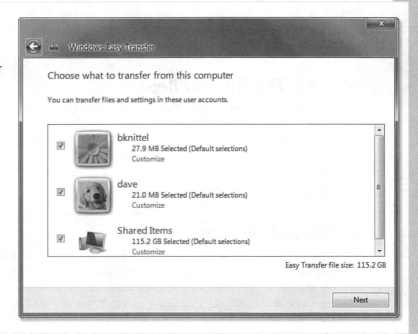

If you use a direct network or Easy Transfer Cable connection, you'll make these selections from the *new* computer. Note that there is an Advanced Options link under the list of user accounts. If you click this, you can select alternate names for the user accounts that are copied. It makes sense to do this if you already have accounts with the same names on the new computer.

And if your old computer has multiple hard drives, click Advanced Options, then click the Map Drives tab to select which drives on the new computer to use for data from your old computer.

 tip

Under each user account, you can click Customize to select categories of documents and file types to copy, or not copy. Click Customize then Advanced to select folders and files on an individual basis.

If you use the external disk method to transfer accounts, you'll select which accounts to copy when you run the Easy Transfer program on the *old* computer. You won't have the option to set Advanced

Options there; you're just deciding what to store in the big data file. When you later run the transfer program on your new computer, you'll see the account list again. This time, you can select Advanced Options, and you can rename the accounts or change drive letters if necessary.

Running Easy Transfer On the New Computer

If you're using an external disk to transfer your data, when the transfer program instructs you to, unplug the external disk from the old computer and plug it into the new one. To run the Windows Easy Transfer program on your new computer, click Start, type the word **easy** into the Search box, then click Windows Easy Transfer. Follow the instructions it presents. The program will help you locate the transfer file that was stored on the external disk.

 tip

You can also start the transfer program by locating and double-clicking the .MIG file that the old computer created on your external disk or in a shared folder yourself; this will automatically start up the transfer program.

Viewing The Transfer Report

When the process is complete, the Easy Transfer program will display a window that lets you browse through the list of user accounts, documents, and program settings it copied. Another tab lets you see the list of application programs it detected on your old computer. You can use this list to remind you what to install on your new computer.

To view this transfer report again later on, click Start, type the word **easy** into the Search box, and click Windows Easy Transfer Reports.

Setting Passwords

When the old computer's user accounts have been copied to your new computer, the Users control panel makes it appear that these accounts have passwords set. However, they *do not*. No password will be required when you select these accounts from the Welcome screen. Windows will prompt the users to create one the first time they log on. Therefore, it's a good idea to use the Users control panel to set a password for each transferred account right after you finish with the Windows Easy Transfer program—otherwise the user accounts are unprotected.

Also, once you've copied accounts to your new computer, you might want to log on and create password reset disks for them, as described previously under "Before You Forget Your Password."

You might then want to jump back to "Change Account Settings" earlier in this chapter to tune up the settings for each added user account.

Logging Off or Shutting Down

We end our tour and setup marathon by showing you how to log off and turn off your computer.

Windows 7 still requires you to stop by clicking the Start button, but at least it doesn't say "Start" anymore. And, the Windows 7 shutdown options are a little clearer than Vista's. So, click Start and look at the bottom of the Start menu, as shown in Figure 3.12.

Figure 3.12
Shutdown and other logoff options on the Start
menu.

The Shut Down option is the first one you see. Click this, and the computer will shut down completely. If you click the small arrow to the right of Shut Down, you can make other selections, which should be familiar if you've used Windows XP or Vista:

- **Switch User**—Displays the Welcome screen so another user can log on and work. You remain logged on, and your applications keep running, invisibly.

- **Log Off**—Logs your account off entirely, and returns to the Welcome screen.

- **Lock**—Hides the desktop. You have to type your password to resume working. It's about the same as Switch User, and the Windows+L hotkey does the same thing.

- **Restart**—Logs you off, shuts down Windows, and reboots.

- **Sleep**—Puts the computer in a lower-power mode, where it's mostly off, except that Windows remains in memory, and can be restarted in a few seconds.

Sleep is a great way to save energy if you're leaving your computer for more than 10 minutes and plan to come back. But, if the computer loses power, Windows will not have a chance to shut down properly, and you could lose data if you hadn't saved your documents. By default, if you leave the computer "asleep" for three hours, Windows will automatically turn the computer back on, save its memory to disk, and then really power itself off. This is called *hibernation*. When you turn the computer back on, it'll take longer to restart, but it's still usually faster than a regular Windows startup.

This ends our tour. To close the book, so to speak, click the arrow next to the Start menu's Shut Down button, select Sleep, and watch Windows power off. When it's asleep, press your computer's power button briefly and see how fast it powers back up.

More Than You Wanted to Know

In the remainder of this chapter, we cover some more advanced topics that some of you may want to know about, and some of you won't. Feel free to skim the rest of the chapter and read just what interests you. You're probably itching to start poking around with Windows 7 now anyway, and you can always come back to these items later on if the need arises.

Now, let's go on to learn where Windows 7 stores your documents, music, and so on, and how this differs from previous versions of Windows.

 note

On desktop computers, Hibernate isn't shown as an option on this Shut Down menu because the automatic hibernate-after-sleep mechanism, called *Hybrid Sleep*, is enabled by default. If you disable Hybrid Sleep in the Advanced Power Settings control panel, Hibernate will appear as an option on this Shut Down menu. On laptops, Hibernate should appear on the Shut Down menu because Hybrid Sleep is disabled by default.

 caution

Always use Shut Down or put your computer into hibernation before you unplug it.

Where's My Stuff?: The User Profile Structure

Windows 7 and Vista store your documents, music, and pictures in a different folder layout than did Windows XP and earlier versions of Windows.

In Windows 7, each user's personal files are stored in a folder with the same name as the user account inside folder \Users. (In some cases, Windows adds other letters or numbers to the username to create a unique folder name.)

This folder is called a *user profile*, and it contains not only your personal documents but also some hidden files that contain your personal Windows Registry data (which contains information used by Windows and application programs), temporary files used by Internet Explorer, and so on. Another folder inside \Users is named Public, and this folder can be used by any of the computer's users. It's a place to put files that you want to share with anyone else.

In Windows 7 and Vista, you *can't* store your own files inside \Program Files, \Windows, or the root (top) folder of the drive on which Windows is installed, although you can create folders there and put files in the new folders.

The directory structure looks like this:

```
C:\
   Windows
   Program Data
   Program Files
```

```
Users
   myname
   yourname
   ⋮
   Default
   Public
```

Here's a brief tour:

- The `Windows` and `Program Files` folders have the same purpose as older versions of Windows—to hold Windows and application programs, respectively.

- The `Program Data` folder is hidden, so you won't see it unless you elected to show hidden files earlier in the chapter in the section "Disable Hide Extensions for Known File Types." In it, the `Start Menu` subfolder contains Start Menu items that are displayed to all users. This was folder `\Documents and Settings\All Users\Start Menu` on Windows XP.

- The `Users` folder contains user profiles, the `Public` folder (which contains the rest of what was `\Documents and Settings\All Users` in Windows XP), and the `Default` user profile, which is discussed in "Configuring a Default User Profile" at the end of this chapter.

- A user profile folder for a given account is created only when the user logs on for the first time. The hidden `Default` folder is copied to create the new profile.

The user profile folder for the account named "myname" is `c:\Users\myname`, the folder for the account named "yourname" is `c:\Users\yourname`, and so on.

Inside each user's profile folder is a series of subfolders, which are listed in Table 3.1.

Table 3.1 User Profile Folders

Folder Name	Purpose
AppData (hidden folder)	Per-user application data. Subfolders Local, LocalLow, and Roaming are used to separate data that will never leave this computer from data that should be copied back to a central server if the account is on a corporate network with roaming profiles.
Contacts	Address book data.
Desktop	Files and shortcuts that appear on the desktop.
Documents	Personal documents. This folder was named My Documents in Windows XP, and on Window 7 its name is displayed in Windows Explorer as My Documents or *Username's* Documents; but in reality, the folder is named just Documents.
Downloads	Files downloaded from the Internet.
Favorites	Favorites links for Internet Explorer.
Links	Shortcuts to important Windows folders.
Music	Personal folder for music files.
Pictures	Personal folder for images.
Saved Games	Data saved by games.
Searches	Saved search queries.
Videos	Personal folder for multimedia files.

These folders are organized differently than in Windows XP, but correctly written application programs won't need to know about the differences; Windows has mechanisms to provide to programs the paths to these various folders based on their function rather than their location. Still, for those applications whose programmers "wired in" the old XP structure, Windows 7 has a mechanism to let them run without problems, as we'll show you in the next section.

Profile Compatibility Junction Points

Windows 7 setup creates *junction points* and *symbolic links* in the Windows drive that provide a measure of compatibility with applications that were hard-wired to expect the Windows XP user profile structure. Junction points and symbolic links are special "virtual" folders that point to other, real folders. When a program attempts to examine files in the virtual folder, Windows shows it the files in the real folder. If older applications attempt to read from folder \Documents and Settings, for example, Windows shows them the contents of \Users.

You should ignore these special link folders; don't delete them, and to the extent possible, forget that they exist. They are hidden system files by default, so you only see them, in fact, when you instruct Windows Explorer or use the dir command-line command to display both hidden and system files.

Compatibility and Virtualization

In previous versions of Windows, applications could store files inside the \Program Files and \Windows folders, and they often took advantage of this to store common data that was shared among all users. The same was true for the Registry, a database of user and setup information—programs frequently stored information in the HKEY_LOCAL_MACHINE Registry section.

To make Windows more secure, user programs are no longer allowed to store files or Registry data in these areas unless their setup programs explicitly change Registry security settings to permit it. (And this has to happen while the program is being installed under elevated privileges.)

Most of the applications that ship with Windows are subject to these restrictions. Try it yourself—open Notepad, type a few words, and try to save a file in \Program Files. You can't. Any application that Windows deems as "modern" or "should know better" is entirely blocked from saving information in these protected areas. (Technically, the presence of a *manifest file* in the program's folder or inside the program file itself is what tells Windows that the program is "modern.")

Older programs, however, expect to write in these privileged directories and Registry areas, and to maintain compatibility Windows 7 gives them an assist called *file and Registry virtualization*. What happens is that if an older program attempts to create a file in one of the protected folders or Registry areas and access is blocked, and the program is not running with elevated permissions and the file doesn't have a manifest file, Windows stores the file or Registry data in an alternate, safer location. Whenever an older program tries to read a file or Registry data from a protected location, Windows first checks the alternate location to see whether it had been shunted there earlier and, if so, returns the data from that location.

Thus, the application doesn't actually store information in the secure locations but thinks it has.

Why are we explaining this to you? There are two reasons:

- One consequence of virtualization is that programs that try to share data between users can't. Each user will see only his or her private copy of the files that should have been stored in a common place. For example, in the "high score" list in a game, each user may see only his or her own name and scores. This may also cause problems with programs that track licensing or registration.

If you view a folder in `\Windows` or `\Program Files` in Windows Explorer, a button named Compatibility Files appears in the window's taskbar If you click this button, Explorer displays the corresponding subfolder in your `VirtualStore` folder. This is an easy way to examine your virtualized files.

- If you go searching for files in Windows Explorer or the command-line prompt, you won't see the files that got virtualized where you expected them to be because `explorer.exe` and `cmd.exe` have manifests—they don't get the virtualization treatment, so they see only the files stored in their intended locations.

The first problem can't be helped; the older programs just have to be redesigned and replaced. Knowing that virtualization occurs, you can work around the second problem by knowing where to look.

Files intended for `\Windows` or `\Program Files` (or any of their subfolders) will be placed into `\Users\`*`username`*`\AppData\Local\VirtualStore\Windows` or `...\Program Files`, respectively.

Registry data intended for `HKEY_LOCAL_MACHINE` will be shunted to `HKEY_CURRENT_USER\Software\Classes\VirtualStore\Machine`. There is no quick-view button in the Registry editor, so to find this data, you have to browse to it.

Some Registry keys are not virtualized in any case. For example, most keys under `HKEY_LOCAL_MACHINE\Software\Microsoft\Windows` will not be virtualized; attempts to write data in this key or most of its subkeys will simply fail. This prevents rogue applications from creating startup program Run entries.

After You Forget Your Password

Forgetting the password to your computer account is an unpleasant experience. It's definitely no fun to have your own computer thumb its proverbial nose at you and tell you it's not going to let you in to get your own files. If this happens to you, take a deep breath. You might recover from this. Here are the steps to try, in order of preference:

1. If you created a password reset disk, as described earlier in the chapter in the section "Before You Forget Your Password," you're in good shape. Follow the instructions in the next section, "Using a Password Reset Disk."

2. If you are a member of a domain network, contact the network administrator to have him or her reset your password. The administrator *might* be able to recover any encrypted files you created.

3. Log on as a Computer Administrator user and use the User Accounts control panel to change your primary account's password.

4. If you don't remember the password to any Administrator account, or you can't find someone else who does, you're in big trouble. Programs are available that can break into Windows and reset one of the Computer Administrator account's passwords. It's a gamble—there's a chance these programs might blow out your Windows installation. Still, if you're in this situation, you probably will want to risk it. Here are some programs you might look into:

   - Windows Key (www.lostpassword.com) creates a Linux boot disk, which pokes through your NTFS disk volume, finds the Windows security Registry file, and replaces the administrator's password so that you can reboot and log on.

   - Active@ Password Changer (www.password-changer.com) works on a similar principle, booting up in Free-DOS from a CD or floppy disk. The program finds the security Registry file on your Windows installation and deletes the password from selected accounts.

   - There are several free password-reset programs that you can download from the Internet. The ones we tested did not work with Windows 7 or Vista, and we found that some of them didn't even work on earlier versions of Windows as they claimed to. We'd try to get one of the for-sale products if possible and would attempt a free program only if we were *really* desperate.

5. If you need to retrieve only files, you can remove the hard drive and install it in another Windows 7, Vista, XP, or Windows 2000 computer as a *secondary* drive. Boot it up, log on as an Administrator, and browse into the added drive. You probably need to take ownership of the drive's files to read them. (If the hard drive is encrypted with BitLocker, this technique won't work either).

6. If you get this far and are still stuck, things are pretty grim. You'll need to reinstall Windows using the Clean Install option, which will erase all your user settings. Then, as an Administrator, you can browse into the \Users folder to retrieve files from the old user account folders. Again, you'll need to take ownership of the files before you can give yourself permission to view or copy them.

If you are not a member of a domain network, you can avoid all this by creating a password reset disk ahead of time.

 caution

If you have to resort to option number three (logging on as an administrator and changing your primary account's password), you will lose any stored website passwords linked to your account and, worse, any files that you encrypted using Windows file encryption (a feature found on Windows 7 Professional, Enterprise, and Ultimate only). There will be absolutely *no way* to recover the encrypted files.

 caution

The existence of such programs that allow you to reset passwords should raise your eyebrows. The fact is that with physical possession of your computer, people can get into it. However, these break-in tools won't work if your hard drive is encrypted with BitLocker, a feature available in the Enterprise and Ultimate editions.

Using a Password Reset Disk

If you have lost your password but have a password reset disk that you made earlier, you can use it to log on. Just attempt to sign on using the Welcome screen. When the logon fails, click Reset Password. Then, follow the Password Reset Wizard's instructions to change your password and store the password reset disk away for another rainy day. You don't need to remake the disk after using it.

Accessing the Real Administrator Account

In Windows NT, 2000, and XP, there was an account named Administrator that was, by definition, a Computer Administrator account. You may have noticed that it's nowhere to be seen in Windows 7.

Actually, it's still there, but hidden. There's a good reason for this. It's disabled by default and hidden on the Welcome screen and even in Safe Mode. And it requires no password to log on. This was done to provide a way to recover if you somehow manage to delete the last (other) Computer Administrator account from your computer. In this case, Windows will automatically enable the Administrator account so that you can log on (without having to remember a password) and re-create one or more Computer Administrator accounts, or turn a Standard User into an Administrator. (You would then immediately log off and use the restored regular account.)

This is a good fail-safe scheme, and we recommend that you leave it set up this way. Still, if for some reason you want to set a password on the Administrator account or use it directly, here's how:

1. Click Start, right-click Computer, and select Manage.

2. Select Local Users and Groups, and open the Users list.

3. Right-click Administrator and select Properties. Uncheck Account Is Disabled and click OK.

4. Log off or Switch Users; then log on as Administrator (which now appears on the Welcome screen).

5. Press Ctrl+Alt+Del, and click Change a Password.

6. We strongly urge you to click Create a Password Reset Disk and make a password reset disk for the Administrator account, as described earlier in this chapter. Be sure to store it in a secure place.

7. Back at Change a Password, leave the old password field blank and enter a new password as requested. Press Enter when you finish.

> **caution**
>
> When you are logged on using the real Administrator account, User Account Control is bypassed, and all privileged programs run with elevated privileges.

Now, the Administrator account is accessible and secured.

If you're worried that the default passwordless Administrator account is a security risk, remember that by default it can't be accessed unless all other Administrator accounts have been deleted, and only an Administrator user could manage to do that. So, a nonadministrator can't do anything personally to get to Administrator. If you enable the Administrator account, then, yes, you really *must* set a password on the account.

Configuring a Default User Profile

As you saw in this chapter, it can take quite a bit of time to tune up a user account and set it up "just so." There are taskbar icons to add, things to change in Windows Explorer and Internet Explorer, and potentially dozens of other applications to configure. It's bad enough doing this once, but if you have many accounts on your computer and you want them all to be set up more or less the same way (at least initially), you're looking at a *lot* of setup time.

Fortunately, you can do this just once and have Windows use your settings as the base settings for other accounts. You can set up one account as you want it and copy that account's profile to the Default user profile so that all future accounts start with a copy of your finely tuned setup. The trick is that you have to do this before other users have logged on to the computer for the first time. It's also best to do this after setting up, but before really using, your own account.

To use this technique to set up nicely pre-tweaked accounts on your computer, follow these steps:

1. Log on to a Computer Administrator account and set it up just as you want all the accounts to look. (Of course, other users can change things after they log on; you're just setting up their account's initial look and feel.)

   In addition to setting preferences, you can add icons to the desktop and taskbar and add documents to the Documents folder and favorites to the Favorites list in Internet Explorer. You can also delete marketing junk installed by Microsoft or your computer manufacturer.

2. Create a new Computer Administrator user account named **xyz**. Don't bother setting a password for it.

3. Log out or switch users, and then log in using the new xyz account. Don't bother making any changes.

4. Click Start, Computer. Click Organize, Folder, and Search Options. Select the View tab and select Show Hidden Files and Folders. Click OK; then close Computer.

5. Click Start, Control Panel, System and Security, System; then in the left Tasks list, select Advanced System Settings.

6. In the middle User Profiles section, click Settings.

7. Select the entry for the account that you originally logged on to and set up. Click Copy To. Then click Browse.

8. In the Browse for Folder dialog box, open the drive that Windows is installed on, dig into Users, and select Default. Click OK to close the Browse for Folder dialog box; then click OK to close the Copy To dialog box.

9. When prompted, click Yes to overwrite the original default profile.

10. When the copying finishes, close all the windows and log out.

11. Log back in to the original account.

12. Click Start, Control Panel, User Accounts and Family Safety, Add or Remove User Accounts.

13. Select account xyz and click Delete the Account. Click Delete Files; then click Delete Account.

Now, when any other user logs on for the first time, his or her user profile will be created with the settings, files, and icons exactly as you set them.

USING WINDOWS 7

IN THIS PART

4   Using the Windows 7 User Interface   115

5   Managing Files and Searching   149

6   Printing   187

7   Gadgets and Other Supplied Accessories   207

4

USING THE WINDOWS 7 USER INTERFACE

Who Should Read This Chapter?

Many readers might wonder why an advanced book such as this includes coverage of something as basic as the Windows user interface (UI). The decision was primarily driven by the knowledge that many users of Windows 7 will be upgrading from Windows 2000, XP, and even Vista. For those users, savvy as they might be with Windows concepts, the Windows 7 UI is different enough that they'll need a roadmap to get started. When you are familiar with it, you'll wonder how you ever got around in those old clunky environments. In addition to the newer look of Windows 7, many new functions are woven into the fabric of the new UI—we don't want you to miss out on them. We've also included some UI tips and tricks that you might not know about. So even if you consider yourself a Windows veteran, at least take the time to skim through this chapter before you move on.

Don't just take our word for it. Experiment with the new UI as you read this chapter. We've found that nothing can substitute for direct hands-on operation to get an understanding and a feel for the new user environment. Most of the information in this chapter is not of a level or type that can damage your system, but whenever caution is needed, we spell it out clearly.

We aren't able to cover everything about the new environment in this chapter, but we do a good job of covering the important aspects and those of interest to most readers. If you run across a button or command that you don't recognize, don't be afraid to explore the Windows Help service for details and instructions. The Windows 7 Help system builds upon the help and support available in Windows Vista, and expands upon the articles previously available.

> ➥ *For those looking for ways to tweak and customize the new GUI,* **see** *Chapter 23, "Tweaking and Customizing Windows."*

If at any time you want to put this book down and walk away from your system, jump to the "Exiting Windows Gracefully" section near the end of this chapter to find out how to log off with aplomb.

 note

Upgrading might not be just for the fun of it. Microsoft stopped offering support for MS-DOS, Windows 1.0-3.x, Windows for Workgroups, and Windows 95 on December 31, 2001. Support for Windows 98 (OSR2 and SE), Me, and Windows NT 4 Workstation was dropped on June 30, 2003. Support for Windows 2000 Professional ended on June 30, 2005. And support for Windows XP Service Pack 1 ended on October 10, 2006. When Microsoft says it will be dropping support, that means the Microsoft technical support system will not respond to calls or email with questions regarding these OSs. In addition, and more importantly, Microsoft will no longer locate and fix security problems in these older OSs. In addition to Windows 7, Microsoft still supports Windows XP Service Packs 2 and 3, as well as Windows Vista Service Packs 1 and 2—at least for the time being.

Logging In to Windows 7

In Chapter 3, "The First Hour," we briefly showed you how to log on, and gave you a quick tour of the OS. We'll cover the logon process and the Welcome screen in more detail in this section.

When Windows 7 starts up, you need to log on before you can start to work. There are three ways that this logon process can occur, depending on how your computer was set up:

- In most cases, you will see the Welcome screen, which displays a list of user account names and pictures. Locate and click your account name. If asked for a password, type in your password, then press Enter.

- If your computer is a member of a domain network (as is usually the case in a corporate setting), the screen may instruct you to press Ctrl+Alt+Del to log on. Hold down the Ctrl and Alt keys, and then press the Del key. Then, when prompted, enter your logon information, as provided by your network administrator. This will include a username, password, and location, which is the network's domain name. To use a local account instead of a domain account—that is, a user account that is defined only in your computer—enter the name of your computer as the location.

- If your computer's bootup process takes you right to the Windows desktop, it's been set up to log on to an account automatically. You can leave it like this, if you want, and still use the Log Off or Switch Users feature to log on with other user accounts. Alternatively, you can disable the automatic logon feature and have Windows display the Welcome screen at startup.

> ➥ *For more information about automatic logons,* **see** *"Just One User?," p. 93.*

By the way, it's likely that shortly after installing Windows, or upon booting the first time and logging in, you'll see a "balloon" notification at the bottom of your screen, warning you that your computer might be at risk because you do not have antivirus protection. Clicking the balloon brings up the Windows Action Center (which replaces the Windows Security Center that you have come to know and love in previous versions of Windows). The Action Center can also be accessed by opening the Control Panel and choosing the System and Security section.

Logging On from the Welcome Screen

On most systems, you'll see the Welcome screen every time Windows starts up. You may also see it when another user has logged off, when someone has disconnected from Windows using Switch User, when the system has been locked, or after the screen saver has kicked in.

If you see the Welcome screen, just click on your user account to log on. The Welcome screen presents a list of available user accounts that can be used to access this system. If a password is associated with a selected account, you are prompted to provide it.

If you have forgotten your password, click the question mark. (Note: The question mark appears only if you have previously defined a password hint in the Users section of the Control Panel.) If there was a hint defined for your account, Windows will display the hint so that you might remember the password.

If you forget your password, and you previously created a password reset disk, you can use the reset disk to gain access to your account. If you don't have a password reset disk, you'll have to have another user log on using a Computer Administrator account and reset your account's password for you. This process could make you lose access to some information in your account, including website passwords that Windows remembered for you, and if you were using the Encrypted Files feature on Windows 7 Professional, Enterprise, or Ultimate edition, you could lose your encrypted files too. So, we strongly urge you to create a password reset disk for your account.

➡ *To learn how to create and use a password reset disk,* **see** *"Before You Forget Your Password,"* *p. 91.*

After you've logged in, it's time to explore the user interface—or, as Microsoft likes to call it, the *user experience*.

Using Windows 7—The User Experience

Windows 7 has a familiar yet different user interface. Most of the visual aspects of the desktop environment have been updated, but you'll find most of the tools and applications you remember from Windows XP and Windows Vista right where you expect. As with Windows Vista, the user interface in Windows 7 is Aero. While substantially the same as Windows Vista, there have been a number of tweaks and improvements to the Aero UI, which make the Windows 7 experience subtly different from the Windows Vista experience. A few new features in the UI are so attractive that they will be very gratifying if you have just switched from Vista to Windows 7. If you want the older stylings of previous Windows versions (mainly Windows 2000–era visual stylings), revert to the "Classic" style. However, we highly recommend giving the new look and feel a try for a week or so before ditching it.

Microsoft's visual palette now has three different user styles to choose from:

- **Windows Classic**—Contains the same user interface as Windows 2000 and earlier versions, if you still prefer that interface. It is important to note, however, that even though the visual theme might be set to Windows Classic, you will still have the Windows 7 Start menu, with no easy way to revert to the "old school" Start menu.

- **Windows 7 Basic**—Gives you the Aero look and feel, but without all the semitransparent glass effects that can cause old graphics hardware to become a bit overwhelmed.

- **Aero**—Provides a semitransparent "glass" look for the taskbars, menu bars, and window frames, as well as advanced features. Those features include Flip, which shows thumbnails of open programs when you move the mouse pointer over an application button in the button bar, Aero Peek, which allows you to see the contents of windows before selecting them, animated windows when opening and closing windows, and Flip 3D for "flipping" between 3D representations of your windows. Aero is processor intensive and, therefore, needs a high-grade video graphics card installed on your computer to work.

But even with all the enhancements, everything still seems to have a similar function or placement to that of Windows 2000, XP, and Vista, and it's not too different from Windows 9x or Me. Thus, you'll easily leverage your existing experience and expertise in navigating and operating Windows 7. After a few days, you'll soon forget how you got by without all these useful improvements.

However, Windows is more than just an OS and GUI. Like other versions of Windows, Windows 7 includes a broad collection of useful programs, from a simple arithmetic calculator to a fancy system and network-management tools. This list also includes a word processing program called WordPad, a drawing program called Paint, Internet Explorer for cruising the Web, CD-burning software that lets you create your own CDs, DVD-burning and playback tools, utilities for keeping your hard disk in good working order, and a data-backup program—just to name a few. See Chapter 7, "Gadgets and Other Supplied Accessories," to learn more about some of the accessories included with Windows 7.

 note

For a nearly exhaustive list of keyboard shortcuts for navigating and controlling aspects of Windows 7, check out the "Keyboard Shortcuts" document, available through the Help and Support Center. Just click Start, Help and Support; type **keyboard shortcuts** in the title in the Search field; and then click the blue magnifying glass icon. The document should appear under Best 30 Results, so click that link in the Search Results to get to it.

Parts of the Windows 7 Screen

At this point, you should be booted up and signed in. After you've logged in, Windows 7 deposits you in its basic environment (called the *desktop*). You'll probably notice two things almost immediately: first, the taskbar at the bottom of the screen, and second, an empty (or nearly so) desktop (see Figure 4.1). The taskbar is the central control mechanism for the Windows 7 user experience. It hosts the Start menu, the taskband area, active program buttons, the notification area (sometimes called the system tray by users that have been using Windows for a while), and the clock. The only item that is present on your desktop is the Recycle Bin, although if you purchased a computer system with Windows 7 preinstalled, you might see other icons as well. Unlike previous versions of Windows, with a default installation of Windows 7, the Recycle Bin is located in the top-left corner of the desktop and not in the lower right, as with Windows XP and Vista. The location of the Recycle Bin might change, however, depending on how you sort icons on the Desktop.

Figure 4.1
The default desktop with the Start menu open.

All you really must know to use Windows 7's interface are these essential building blocks and how to manipulate a window and its commands. If you've been using any recent version of Windows, you already know the latter. You just need to be brought up to speed on the advanced Windows 7 interface specifics.

The Desktop

The desktop is your home base while doing your work in Windows. It is always on the screen as the backdrop (whether you see it or not) and you can deposit files and folders right on it for storage. It's analogous to a real desktop in this way. It also serves as a handy temporary holding area for files you might be copying from, say, a floppy disk to a hard disk folder. The *Recycle Bin* holds deleted work objects, such as files and folders, until you empty it (with caveats). Just as in previous versions of Windows (or the

 note

You might also see some items on the right edge of your desktop, such as a clock or calendar, or a news or stock ticker. These are clever desktop add-ons called Windows Desktop gadgets and are covered in Chapter 7, "Gadgets and Other Supplied Accessories."

Mac, for that matter, if you're coming from that background), you'll do all your work in Windows 7 using graphical representations of your files and applications, called *icons*.

All the desktop icons you are familiar with from Windows XP and 2000 have been moved to the Start menu. (And if you upgraded from Windows XP or Vista, the Windows 7 Start menu will look *very* familiar.) You can gain access to Computer, Documents, and Network with a simple click on the Start button. You can easily control which items appear on the taskbar, or on the desktop (see Chapter 23).

The Recycle Bin

The Recycle Bin acts a bit like the waste paper basket at the side of your desk. After you throw something into it, it's basically trash to be thrown out; however, you can still retrieve items from it if you get there before the cleaning staff takes it and throws it away for good. Within Windows 7, the Recycle Bin holds those files you've deleted using Windows Explorer or Computer. It does not capture files deleted by third-party tools, files deleted from floppy disks or network drives, files removed with an uninstall program or from DOS boxes, or DOS files running in a DOS box.

The Recycle Bin has limited storage capacity. However, Windows 7 provides each user with a default amount of Recycle Bin space, specified in megabytes. When the maximum size of the Recycle Bin is reached, the oldest files are permanently removed from the hard drive to make room for newly deleted files. The size of the Recycle Bin can be customized as a percentage across all drives or as a unique size on each individual volume. The Recycle Bin is customized through its Properties dialog box (see Figure 4.2). The configuration options are discussed in Chapter 23, but if you want to get to them now, right-click the Recycle Bin icon and select Properties from the pop-up menu.

After a file is removed from the Recycle Bin, it cannot be recovered using native tools. You must restore the files from a backup, use a third-party recovery tool (which often needs to be in place before the file is deleted), or live without the lost files. If you don't want your excess trash sitting around, you can also configure the system to bypass the Recycle Bin entirely so that it permanently deletes files immediately instead of granting you a recovery period.

To restore a file still retained in the Recycle Bin, double-click the desktop icon to open the Recycle Bin, locate and select the file to restore, and then click the Restore This Item button in the toolbar (see Figure 4.3). The file/folder(s) then are returned to the original location.

 caution

Don't try moving program files unless you know that they have not registered themselves with the OS and that they can harmlessly be moved between folders. If you must move applications, use a tool specifically designed for this.

If you delete files in folders shared by other computers on a network, or delete files by typing commands into the Command Prompt window, the files are *not* moved to the Recycle Bin. They're deleted instantly and permanently.

Options can be set for
each drive or partition
on your computer.

Set the maximum size
of the Recycle Bin here.

Figure 4.2
The Recycle Bin Properties
dialog box.

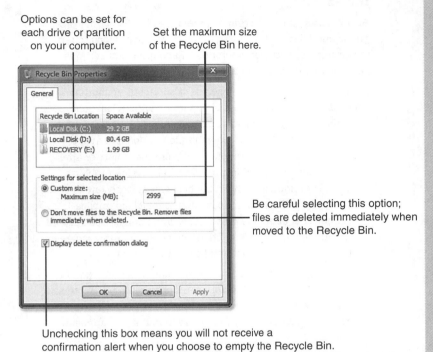

Be careful selecting this option;
files are deleted immediately when
moved to the Recycle Bin.

Unchecking this box means you will not receive a
confirmation alert when you choose to empty the Recycle Bin.

Figure 4.3
Restoring a
file from the
Recycle Bin.

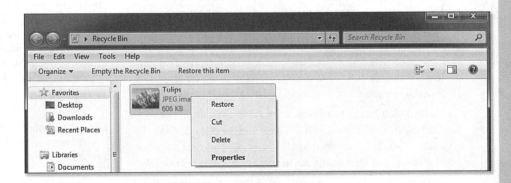

You can also manually empty the Recycle Bin. This is often a useful activity before defragmenting your hard drive or if you just want to permanently delete files and folders. The Empty Recycle Bin command, found in the right-click pop-up menu for the Recycle Bin icon, the File menu if the menu bars are enabled (be sure no items are selected—otherwise, the File menu's context changes to file/folder restore operations), and the Recycle Bin Tasks list of the Recycle Bin interface, is used to clear out all files that are being retained.

Icons

As you know, the small graphical representations of your programs and files are called *icons*. Windows 7 uses icons to represent folders, documents, programs, and groups of settings (such as dial-up connections).

Icons are either objects themselves or shortcuts. A shortcut is a means to gain access to an object from multiple locations throughout the environment. Shortcuts are the preferred way to access the same object from multiple locations, to avoid having to make duplicate copies of the original object or application. Duplicating the object often causes version problems, such as never knowing which one has your most recent changes, and difficulties in upgrading or replacing applications. Shortcuts eliminate these issues and take up less space. You could have thousands of shortcuts pointing to the same application or document and still save drive space.

Additionally, a shortcut can define alternative launching parameters, such as default directories, command-line parameters, compatibility mode, and so on. To alter the settings of a shortcut, right-click it and select Properties from the pop-up menu.

Dialog Boxes

The Open and Save dialog boxes (also known as file or browse dialog boxes) for most applications still offer the same shortcuts and controls as those of previous versions of Windows. This typically includes a shortcut menu to Recent Places (the new name for Internet Explorer history), Desktop, Documents, Computer, and Network. Not all applications that function on Windows 7 offer a fully enhanced file dialog box.

Many dialog boxes have tabs. These often appear at the top of a dialog box, as the tabs for General and Security do (see Figure 4.4). Tabs are used to offer multiple pages or displays of controls within a single smaller window. Many of the configuration settings dialog boxes have tabs, so watch for them. To select another tab, just click on it. In some cases, tabs are easy to miss; the new color scheme and display enhancements don't always direct your eyes to tabs.

 note

In recent versions of Windows, Microsoft began using the term *folder* instead of *directory*. It wants to focus your thoughts toward the idea of your files being stored on the hard drive in a manner similar to that of a filing cabinet for manila folder. Although this analogy helps, we don't always stick to Microsoft-speak. So if you see *folder* or *directory* in this book, know that we consider them to be the same.

 note

Compatibility mode is a nifty feature that enables Windows 7 to support a wider range of software products than Windows 95 and Windows NT combined. A compatibility mode is simply a designation for a software platform-emulation environment. In other words, when an application is launched with compatibility mode enabled, a virtual machine representing that application's native environment (Windows 9*x*, Windows NT, Windows 2000, Windows XP, or Windows Vista) is created in such a way that the application is fooled into thinking that it is the only application present on the computer system running its preferred OS.

If you have installed a 64-bit version of Windows 7, you cannot run MS-DOS or Windows 16-bit (Windows 3.*x*) applications. However, if you have installed a 32-bit version of Windows 7, MS-DOS or Windows 16-bit applications are automatically launched into their own virtual machine called WOW (Windows on Windows). Microsoft also makes available a free download called Windows XP Compatibility Mode, which allows even the most die-hard Windows XP application to run on Windows 7. For more information, see Appendix A.

Figure 4.4
A Properties dialog box containing tabs that you can click to see additional settings.

Putting Items on the Desktop

The desktop is a convenient location for either permanent or temporary storage of items. Many folks use the desktop as a home for often-used documents and program shortcuts. I'm quite fond of using the desktop as an intermediary holding tank when moving items between drives or computers, or to and from removable media. It's particularly good for pulling found items out of a search window or other folder while awaiting final relocation elsewhere.

Here are some quick helpful notes about using the desktop:

- You can send a shortcut of an object to the desktop very easily by right-clicking it and choosing Send To, Desktop (thus creating the shortcut).

- The desktop is nothing magical. Actually, it's just another folder with a few additional properties. Prime among them is the option to have live, active, Internet-based information on the desktop using Windows gadgets, such as stock tickers, weather reports, and the like.

- Each user on the machine can have his or her own desktop setup, with icons, background colors, screen saver, and such.

- Whatever you put on the desktop is always available by minimizing or closing open windows, or more easily by clicking the Show Desktop button on the far right of the taskbar. It is for just this reason that almost every application enables you to save files directly to the desktop, and many programs default to saving files on the desktop. Keep in mind that some items cannot be moved onto the desktop—only their shortcuts can. (For example, if you try to drag a Control Panel applet to the desktop, you'll see a message stating that you cannot copy or move the item to this location.)

If you want to be able to access a Control Panel applet from the desktop, you have only one choice: create a shortcut to the applet and place it on the desktop. However, in other cases, when you're copying and moving items, particularly when using the right-click method, you'll be presented with the options of copying, moving, or creating a shortcut to the item. What's the best choice?

Here are a few reminders about shortcuts:

- They work just as well as the objects they point to (for example, the program or document file), yet they take up much less space on the hard disk. For this reason, they're generally a good idea.

- You can have as many shortcuts scattered about for a given object as you want. Therefore, for a program or folder you use a lot, put its shortcuts wherever you need them—put one on the desktop, one on the Taskband, one on the Start menu, and another in a folder of your favorite programs on the desktop.

- Make up shortcuts for other objects you use a lot, such as folders, disk drives, network drives and printers, and web links. From Internet Explorer, for example, drag the little blue *E* icon that precedes a URL in the Address bar to the desktop, to save it as a shortcut. Clicking it brings up the web page.

- The link between shortcuts and the objects they point to can be broken. This happens typically when the true object is erased or moved. Clicking the shortcut can result in an error message. In Windows 7, this problem is addressed in an ingenious way. Shortcuts automatically adjust when linked objects are moved. The OS keeps track of all shortcuts and attempts to prevent breakage. Shortcut "healing" is built into Windows 7 for situations in which the automated recovery mechanism fails.

- If you're not sure about the nature of a given shortcut, try looking at its properties. Right-click the shortcut and choose Properties. Clicking Find Target locates the object that the shortcut links to and displays it in a folder window.

> **caution**
>
> Remember that shortcuts are not the item they point to. They're aliases only. Therefore, copying a document's shortcut to a floppy or a network drive or adding it as an attachment to an email doesn't copy the document itself. If you want to send a document to some colleagues, don't make the mistake of sending them the shortcut unless it's something they'll have access to over the LAN or Web. If it's a shortcut to, say, a word processing document or folder, they'll have nothing to open.

> **tip**
>
> To quickly bring up the Properties dialog box for most objects in the Windows GUI, you can highlight the object and press Alt+Enter.

Properties and the Right-Click

Ever since Windows 95, a common theme that unites items within Windows is the aspect called *properties*. Properties are pervasive throughout Windows 9*x*, NT 4, 2000, XP, Vista, and now Windows 7. The Properties dialog boxes provide a means of making changes to the behavior, appearance, security level, ownership, and other aspects of objects throughout the OS. Object properties apply to everything from individual files to folders, printers, peripherals, screen appearance, the computer itself, or a network or workgroup. All these items have a Properties dialog box that enables you to easily change various settings. For example, you might want to alter whether a printer is the default printer or whether a folder on your hard disk is shared for use by co-workers on the LAN.

A typical set of properties is shown in Figure 4.5, which displays the Properties dialog box for the D: drive (hard disk) on a computer. Notice that there are several tab pages in this dialog box. Some Properties dialog boxes have only a single page, whereas others have many.

Figure 4.5
A typical Properties dialog box for a hard disk.

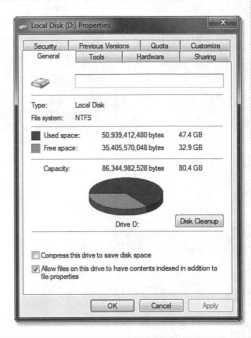

Properties dialog boxes are very useful and often serve as shortcuts for modifying settings that otherwise would take you into the Control Panel or through some other circuitous route. With some document files (for example, Word files), you can examine many settings that apply to the file, such as the creation date, author, editing history, and so forth.

Here are some typical uses of right-click context menus:

- Sharing a folder on the network

- Changing the name of your hard disk and checking its free space

- Changing a program's icon

- Creating a new folder

- Setting the desktop's colors, background, screen saver, and so on

- Adjusting the date and time of the clock quickly

- Closing an application

- Displaying a font's technical details

- Renaming an object

As an example of the right-click, simply get to an empty place on the desktop and right-click on it. Right by the cursor, you'll see a menu that looks like the one shown in Figure 4.6. Notice that you can slide your cursor up and down the menu to make choices. Choose Personalize down at the bottom of the list. You'll see the Personalization settings for your desktop (as well as general video display, screen saver, and other related items). By the way, many menus (Start, menu bar, pop-up, and so on) have commands with a small arrow to one side. If you highlight one of these commands, a submenu flies out—hence, the term *flyout menu*.

Figure 4.6
An example of a right-click menu, this one from an empty location on the desktop. Notice that it contains flyout menus.

If you want to use Windows most efficiently, make a habit of right-clicking on objects to see what pops up. You might be surprised to see how much time you save with the resulting shortcuts.

Using Windows Explorer

For a bird's-eye view of your computer, many users prefer Folder view over the usual folder system, which can clutter your screen with numerous overlapping windows when you have lots of them open. Using the folders in the left pane makes copying, moving, and examining all the contents of your computer easier. If you're doing housekeeping, copying and moving items from one folder to another or across the network, or hopping back and forth between viewing web pages and your local hard disk, mastering this view will serve you well.

 note

Starting with this chapter, we're going to assume that you understand the choice between single-click mode and double-click mode. Some of the figures in the book might have icons, files, or other object names underlined, whereas others might not, based on what mode the computer was set in when the screenshots were grabbed. Don't let it throw you. When we say "double-click something," we mean run it or open it by whatever technique is applicable based on your click setting. Also, when we say "click it," that means select it. Remember that if you have single-clicking turned on, just hover the pointer over (that is, point to) the item to select it. Generally, we are working from the defaults set by Microsoft.

You probably remember that Folder view was introduced with Windows 95 in the form of Windows Explorer, and although it's still in Windows 7 under that name, it's not featured as much as it used to be. This is because the functionality of Windows Explorer can be added to all folder windows (such as Computer) simply by enabling the Show All Folders option (and optionally choosing Automatically Expand to Current Folder) in the Folder Options dialog box under Appearance and Personalization in the Control Panel (see Figure 4.7).

Figure 4.7
The Folder Options dialog box, where you can choose to see more folder information in the navigation pane.

The Folder paradigm affords significant power and flexibility in file and folder control; Microsoft and other software makers have adopted it for other classes of programs. For example, right-click on Computer and choose Manage. The resulting application (Computer Management) uses the same approach, as do many web pages.

The Folder view (call it Windows Explorer, if you want) lets you examine the Control Panel, the LAN, the Internet, your hard disk, or the Recycle Bin—all with a minimum of effort.

To recap, you can get to Windows Explorer by clicking Start, All Programs, Accessories, Windows Explorer.

Figure 4.8 shows the folders that appear on my own computer in Folder view.

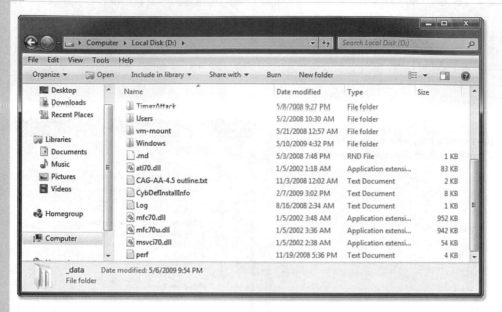

Figure 4.8
The basic
Windows
Explorer screen,
showing the
computer's
major compo-
nents on the left
and the contents
on the right.

Displaying the Contents of Your Computer

When you use Windows Explorer, all the objects constituting your computer appear in the list on the left. Some of those objects have a triangle pointing right to the left of them, which means the object is collapsed; it contains subitems that aren't currently showing. These triangles are visible only if the mouse cursor is in the left Navigation pane; once you move out of the Navigation pane, the triangles fade and are no longer visible.

Click an item in the left pane to see its contents in the right pane. If the item has a white triangle pointing to the right, click it to open the sublevels in the left pane, showing you the relationship of the folders and other items in a tree arrangement. In the figure, you can see that the Documents Library has been opened in this way. Notice that the triangle is no longer white and pointing to the right, but is now black and pointing downward, indicating that the object's display has been expanded. Clicking the black triangle causes that branch to collapse.

If you open a local disk drive or disk across the network, you can quickly get a graphical representation of the disk's folder layout. Then click a folder to see its contents. By right-clicking on disks, folders, or files, you can examine and set properties for them. The straight lines connecting folders indicate how they're related. If you have more folders than can be seen at one time, the window has a scrollbar that you can use to scroll the tree up and down.

Notice that there are two scrollbars—one for the left pane and one for the right. These scroll independently of one another, which can be very useful when you're copying items from one folder or drive to another.

Working with Objects in Folder View

Working with folders and files in this view is simple. As explained previously, you just click an item in the left pane, and its contents appear in the right pane. Choose the view (Large Icons, Small Icons, and so on) for the right pane using the toolbar's More options button, near the top-right corner. In Details view, you can sort the items by clicking the column headings.

When they're displayed, you can drag items to other destinations, such as a local hard disk, a floppy drive, or a networked drive. You can drag and drop files, run programs, open documents that have a program association, and use right-click menu options for various objects. For example, you can right-click files or folders and choose Send To, DVD RW Drive to copy items to a DVD disc. I use the Send To, Mail Recipient option all the time, to send attachments to people via email.

With a typical hard disk containing many files, when its folders are all listed in the left pane, some will be offscreen. Because the two panes have independent scrollbars, dragging items between distant folders is not a problem. Here's the game plan:

1. Be sure the source and destination folders are open and visible in the left pane, even if you have to scroll the pane up and down. For example, a network drive should be expanded, with its folders showing (using and mapping network drives is covered in Chapter 20, "Using a Windows Network").

2. Click the source folder in the left pane. Now its contents appear to the right.

3. Scroll the left pane up or down to expose the destination folder. (Click only the scrollbar, not a folder in the left pane; if you click a folder, it changes the displayed items on the right side.)

4. In the right pane, locate and drag the items over to the left, landing on the destination folder. The folder must be highlighted; otherwise, you've aimed wrong.

This technique suffices most of the time. Sometimes, it's too much of a nuisance to align everything for dragging. In that case, use the cut/copy-and-paste technique discussed earlier in the chapter. Remember, you can copy and paste across your home LAN as well as between your local drives.

Here are a few tips when selecting folders:

- You can select only one folder at a time in the left pane. If you want to select multiple folders, click the parent folder (such as the drive icon) in the left pane and select the folders in the right pane. Use the same techniques described earlier for making multiple selections.

- When you select a folder in the left pane, its name becomes highlighted. This is a reminder of which folder's contents are showing in the right pane.

- You can jump quickly to a folder's name by typing its first letter on the keyboard. If there's more than one folder with the same first letter, each press of the key advances to the next choice.

- The fastest way to collapse all the branches of a given drive is to click that drive's black triangle sign.

- You can quickly rearrange a drive's folder structure in the left pane by dragging folders. You can't drag disk drives, but you can create shortcuts for them (for example, a network drive) by dragging them to, say, the desktop.

- If a folder has subfolders, those appear in the right pane as folder icons. Clicking one of those opens it as though you had clicked that subfolder in the left pane.

- When dragging items to collapsed folders (ones with a plus sign), hovering the pointer over the folder for a second opens it.

- You can use the right-click-drag technique when dragging items if you want the option of clearly choosing Copy, Move, or Create Shortcut when you drop the item on the target.

- To create a new folder, in the left pane, click the folder under which you want to create the new folder. Right-click in the right pane and choose New, Folder.

- Delete a folder by right-clicking it and choosing Delete. You're asked to confirm.

 caution

Although it's powerful, Folder view is also dangerous. It makes accidental rearrangement of your hard disk's folders extremely easy. When selecting folders, be careful to not accidentally drag them. The icons are small, and this is easy to do accidentally, especially in the left pane. A little flick of the wrist and a click of the mouse, and you've dragged one folder on top of another folder. This makes it a subfolder of the target. Remember, the left pane is "live," too. Rearranging the directory tree could make programs and files hard to find and even make some programs not work.

Windows Shortcut Keys

Longtime users of Windows have probably grown accustomed to navigating around the Windows user interface using the keyboard. This especially comes in handy when your mouse or trackball decides to suddenly quit working, and you need to save the document you're working on. On modern computer keyboards, you will see a Windows key that looks like the Microsoft Windows logo—pressing this Windows key once will bring up the Start menu. However, starting with Windows XP, you can use combinations of the Windows key and other keys to perform certain system tasks quickly. Although not an exhaustive list, Table 4.1 shows several Windows key shortcuts that are useful in Windows 7 that might help speed your way through the Windows UI.

Table 4.1 Windows Shortcut Keys

Windows Key Combination	Description
Windows+Shift+left, right arrow	Moves the active window to the left or right monitor in multi-monitor setups
Windows+P	Opens the Projector Settings application to select where the active display is presented (used mainly with laptop and multimonitor computers)
Windows+spacebar	Shows the desktop; all windows become transparent so you can see the desktop behind them
Windows++/− (plus/minus keys)	Zooms in/out
Windows+E	Opens Windows Explorer
Windows+L	Locks the computer
Windows+D	Minimizes all windows and show the desktop
Windows+Tab	Windows Aero task switcher—works like Alt+Tab but shows a preview of the window you are switching to
Windows+F	Opens a search window

As you can see, there are a multitude of Windows key combinations that can make your day-to-day life easier as you're jetting around the Windows interface. A more comprehensive list of Windows shortcut keys can be found in the Windows 7 online help.

Gestures

In Windows 7, Microsoft has introduced an all-new way of interacting with the Windows UI—gestures. While the majority of Windows gestures are used only on a tablet PC (see Chapter 38, "Tablet PC Features," for more information on Tablet PC features), there are three useful gestures that can make working with Windows 7 much easier:

- To quickly maximize a window, grab the title bar of the window by clicking on it, and then quickly drag the mouse so that the pointer touches the top of the screen. The window will grow to fill the entire screen. To return the window to its previous size, simply grab the title bar and drag the window back to the desktop.

- You can make a window fill the entire left or right side of the screen by grabbing the title bar and dragging the window to the left or right edge of the screen, so that the mouse pointer touches the edge of the screen. This is useful if you have two windows that contain similar information (two word processing documents, for example) and you need to compare the contents side by side. As with the maximize gesture just discussed, simply grab the title bar and move the window back to the desktop to restore the window to its previous dimensions. These gestures are called Aero Snap, so named because they easily allow you to "snap" a window to the top or sides of the screen.

- You can reduce desktop clutter by using what has been dubbed the Aero Shake. If you have multiple open windows displayed on the desktop, and you need to have only a single window displayed, you can grab the title bar of the window you want to focus your attention on and shake it back and forth. All other displayed windows will minimize, leaving just the desired window open on the desktop. To restore the minimized windows, perform the Aero Shake again and all the windows magically appear once again.

➡ *For more on gestures and touchscreen shortcuts, **see** Chapter 38.*

The Taskbar, the Start Menu, and Other Tools

The taskbar is the command center for your user environment under Windows 7. With few or no desktop icons after initial setup, everything you do within Windows 7 has to start with the taskbar. The taskbar (refer to Figure 4.1) is host to several other highly useful tools, including the Start menu, the taskband, the open application buttons, and the notification area.

The Start menu is the control center for Windows 7. Most native applications and installed applications have an icon within the Start menu that is used to launch or access them. The Start menu has two columns of access elements.

By default, the Start menu displays the most recently accessed applications. A fresh installation of Windows 7 includes prestocked items in this list, such as Windows Media Player and the Getting Started menu, which walks you through various configuration items, such as adding additional users and personalizing the Windows 7 environment. This leaves room for only a single recently accessed application. These prestocked items will disappear, but if you are impatient you can forcibly remove them one at a time by issuing the Remove from This List command from the right-click pop-up menu.

At the bottom of the left column is All Programs, which is an access point to the rest of the Start menu. Those of you from Windows 9x and above will recognize this as the Programs section of the Start menu. The Start menu's right column lists Documents, Pictures, Music, Games, Computer, Network (optionally), Control Panel, Devices and Printers, Default Programs, and Help and Support.

Below the right column is the Shut Down button and the Shut Down menu, marked by a right arrow. The Shut Down button works exactly as advertised—it shuts down and powers off the computer with no confirmation dialog boxes, other than prompts to close any open files. The Shut Down menu enables you to choose other options for shutting down Windows 7, including Switch User, Log Off, Lock, Restart, Sleep, and Hibernate. Sleep is used to put the computer in a low-power state so you can quickly recover and continue working from where you left off, while Hibernate writes the contents of the computer memory to the hard drive and powers off the computer, so it can be left unattended for longer periods of time without fear that a power failure will wipe out any work you might have in memory at the time. It is important to note that the Hibernate option is available only if Hybrid Sleep is disabled (see Chapter 3 for more information on Hybrid Sleep). Hybrid sleep is enabled by default on desktop machines but not on laptops. The Lock button locks the computer so no one else can access it without the proper password—obviously, your user account will need a password set for this option to do any good.

 tip

Pressing Ctrl+Esc or the Windows key opens the Start menu as though you clicked the Start button. You then can navigate using the arrow keys. Use the Enter key to launch or access the selected item.

Clicking any of the items listed on the Start menu either launches an application or opens a new dialog box or menu. Most of the items on the top level of the Start menu are discussed later in this chapter. Clicking All Programs scrolls to a second page of programs, while leaving the quick links such as Control Panel still visible, which is the same behavior as in Windows Vista.

You can add new items to the Start menu by dragging an item from Computer or Windows Explorer over the Start menu button, then over All Programs, and then to the location where you want to drop it. You can even manipulate the Start menu as a set of files and shortcuts through Computer or Windows Explorer. You need to go to the system root (usually C:, but it could be anything on multi-boot systems) and drill down to \Users\<*username*>\Start Menu\Programs (where <*username*> is the name of the user account whose Start menu you want to modify).

To the far right on the taskbar is the *notification area*. Some services, OS functions, and applications place icons into this area. These icons provide both instant access to functions and settings, as well as status displays. For example, when you're working on a portable system, a battery appears in the notification area indicating how much juice is left. The clock is also located in the notification area.

Notice that the far-right portion of the taskbar, to the right of the clock in the notification area, is blank. Microsoft has done away with the classic Quick Launch bar in Windows 7 and put the Show Desktop button in its place. If you hover over the Show Desktop area of the taskbar, all the currently open windows will "turn to glass" and allow you to see what is currently hidden on the desktop. Never fear, however, as the applications will come back just as quickly once you move the mouse away from the Show Desktop section of the bar. You can also click the Show Desktop button to quickly minimize all open windows (much like the classic behavior of the Show Desktop button), and restore them just as quickly by clicking the button a second time.

Between the Start button and the notification area are the active application buttons. These are grouped by similarity, not by order of launch. Notice that instead of the traditional application buttons you have grown accustomed to since Windows 9x, applications that are running in the Windows 7 GUI are represented by a square icon, with no accompanying window title text. This is a major change from previous Windows versions, but once you get used to it you will see that it is quite superior to the previous methods of organizing the running applications.

As previously mentioned, the Quick Launch bar that has been around since Windows 9x is missing, much to the chagrin of Quick Launch bar enthusiasts everywhere. In Windows 7, Microsoft has replaced the Quick Launch bar functionality with "pinning," which enables you to take an application shortcut and place it permanently on the taskbar. You can then click any of the pinned applications to launch an instance of that application. You can also pin frequently used documents to the pinned applications on the taskbar (how's that for recursion?) for quick launch at any time. To accomplish this, you simply drag a file onto its respective application on the taskbar, and the application file is now pinned to the taskbar application. You can access these pinned applications by right-clicking the pinned application and choosing one of the application files.

With practice, most users find that this is a superior alternative to the Quick Launch bar. There is, however, a way to get the Quick Launch bar back:

1. Right-click an open section of the taskbar and choose Toolbars, New Toolbar.

2. In the Folder: bar at the bottom of the dialog box, enter `%AppData%\Microsoft\Internet Explorer\Quick Launch`.

You'll now find the Quick Launch bar on the far right of the taskbar, and you can move it anywhere.

Each running application has a gray border around the application icon. If you hover over the application icon, you will see thumbnails of each of the windows that particular application has open. Unless you have super-human eyesight, you probably won't be able to read the text in those thumbnails, which can make for an interesting time trying to figure out which of those tiny thumbnails was the email you were just working on. Windows 7 comes to the rescue with an enhancement called Aero Peek. Simply hover over one of the presented thumbnails, and all the other open windows "turn to glass" and the

tip

There might be times when you want to open a file with an application that is not its default—for example, you might want to open a file with a CSV (comma-separated values) extension in Notepad rather than Microsoft Excel. You can do this by holding down the Shift key while you are dragging the file to the desired application on the taskbar. The application file will then be pinned to the selected application.

note

You can reposition the taskbar on the right, left, or top of the screen. Just click any part of the taskbar other than a button and drag it to the edge of your choice. The Taskbar and Start Menu Properties dialog box includes a locking option to prevent the taskbar from being moved accidentally. Be sure to deselect this option before you attempt to relocate the taskbar (right-click the taskbar and clear the check mark next to the Lock the Taskbar option). This can also be accomplished by right-clicking the Start button, choosing Properties, and changing the Taskbar Location on Screen setting on the Taskbar tab.

selected window rises to the foreground so you can see exactly what is in that window. You also have the option of closing any of the application's open windows directly from the thumbnail view.

You can further control and modify the taskbar and Start menu through their Properties dialog boxes.

➥ *For more information on customizing the taskbar and the Start menu, **see** Chapter 23.*

Uninstall or Change Programs

As with Windows Vista, Windows 7 doesn't include an Add or Remove Programs applet. Instead, Windows 7 provides you with the Uninstall or Change a Program applet, which enables you to uninstall, change, or repair a program.

Uninstalling a program is analogous to what we called "removing" a program in earlier versions of Windows. *Changing* a program enables you to make changes to the functionality and features of the program, such as installing Microsoft Access from the Microsoft Office CD if you didn't install that program previously. *Repairing* a program enables you to repair any problems you're having with a program, such as a word processing program not saving files.

You've probably noticed that not all programs show up in the Uninstall or Change a Program applet. They don't appear because only programs that comply with the 32-bit Windows API standard for installation get their filenames and locations recorded in the system database, allowing them to be reliably erased without adversely affecting the operation of Windows. Many older or less-sophisticated applications simply install in their own way and don't bother registering with the OS.

What's more, the built-in uninstaller lets you make changes to applications, such as adding or removing suboptions (assuming that the application supports that feature).

Using the uninstall feature of the applet is simple:

1. Click Start, Control Panel, click Programs, Uninstall a Program.

2. Check the list of installed applications. A typical list appears in Figure 4.9. Note that you can sort the applications by clicking the column heading.

 note

In Windows XP and earlier versions, you could add Windows updates in the Add or Remove Programs applet. In Windows 7, adding and viewing Windows 7 updates is performed in the System and Security section of the Control Panel. You'll learn more about updating Windows 7 in Chapter 22.

 tip

Never attempt to remove an application from your system by deleting its files from the \Program Files folders (or wherever). Actually, "never" might be too strong. Removal through manual deletion should be only a last resort. Always attempt to use the Uninstall or Change a Program applet or the uninstall utility from the application first.

 tip

Some programs, such as Microsoft Office, include service packs and other updates that help keep the programs running in top condition. However, these updates might cause Windows to run slowly and/or otherwise malfunction. If you suspect that a recently installed upgrade is the problem, you can view and uninstall updates by clicking the Uninstall a Program link and following the upcoming instructions starting with step 3.

Figure 4.9
Choosing the
program to
uninstall or
change.

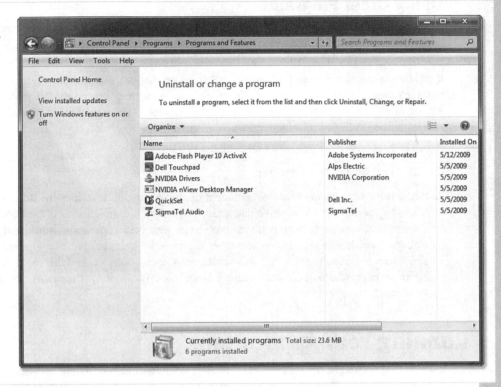

3. Select the program you want to change or uninstall.

4. Click the Uninstall/Change button.

5. Answer any warnings about removing an application, as appropriate.

Some applications (for example, Microsoft Office) prompt you to insert the program CD when you attempt to change or remove the app. These prompts can be annoying, but what can you do? The setup, change, and uninstall programs for some large suites are stored on their CDs, not on your hard disk. Just insert the disc when prompted.

 tip

Obviously, removing an application can't easily be reversed by, say, restoring files from the Recycle Bin because settings from the Start menu and possibly the Registry are deleted.

 note

Incidentally, the Uninstall or Change a Program applet can be run only by users with Administrator credentials on their local computer. Although some applications can be installed or removed by nonadministrators, most require Administrator privilege.

Add New Programs

So how do you install a program on a disc in your CD or DVD drive from the Control Panel in Windows 7? You no longer can as you did with Windows XP and earlier versions of Windows. Nearly all software written for Windows comes with an autoinstall program that runs when you insert the CD or DVD into the appropriate drive. Microsoft obviously believes that adding software from the Control Panel is now superfluous, but if you have a program that won't open the autoinstall program automatically, consult your software installation instructions or search for the autoinstall file on your CD using Computer or Windows Explorer. Autoinstall files usually have the name setup.exe or install.exe.

Using Older Programs

As I said at the beginning of the chapter, Microsoft is constantly moving people toward upgrading to the newest version of Windows. If you still have Windows 3.x, you will be dismayed to learn that Windows 7 64-bit versions will not run DOS and Windows 3.x programs.

If you have programs written for Windows XP or earlier that worked correctly in those older OSs but don't work well in Windows 7, Microsoft was kind enough to include the Program Compatibility Wizard in Windows 7 so you can select and test compatibility settings that could identify the problem(s) and hopefully get your program working again.

Here's how you open the Program Compatibility Wizard:

1. Click Start, Control Panel, Programs.

2. Under the Programs and Features section at the top of the window, click the Run Programs Made for Previous Versions of Windows link. The Program Compatibility Wizard window appears; you can use it to pinpoint the problem(s) with your application. Additionally, Microsoft is making available a free download named Windows XP Compatibility Mode, which enables you to run programs written for Windows XP much more easily under Windows 7. For more information on Windows XP Compatibility Mode, see Appendix A, "Using Virtualization on Windows 7."

Running Your Applications

If you're just upgrading from a previous version of Windows (such as 9x, XP, or Vista), you already know how to run applications, how to switch between them, and how to manage them. But if you are new to Windows OSs, here is a quick how-to guide.

How to Launch Your Apps

Applications are launched under Windows 7 in a number of different ways, as is the case with many other things in Windows. You'll probably end up using the technique that best fits the occasion. To run an application, perform one of the following tasks (ranked in order of ease of use):

- Use the Start button to find the desired application from the resulting menus. Click All Programs if you don't see the one you want.

- Open Computer or Windows Explorer, browse through your folders to find the application's icon, and double-click it.

- Find the application by clicking Start and then typing the application name in the Search box. (The Search method works only for programs installed in a predefined list of folders called the search path, which is discussed in Chapter 29, "Command-Line and Automation Tools.")

- Locate a document that was created with the application in question and double-click it. This runs the application and loads the document into it. With some applications, you can then close the document and open a new one, if you need to.

There are two easy ways to open an existing document in the application that created it:

- Click Start, Documents, and look among the most recently edited documents. Clicking one opens the document in the appropriate application.

- You can also click Start, Recent Items, and look among the most recently edited files if you have customized the Start menu to show Recent Items.

In the name of expediency, we don't cover all these options. When you get the hang of the most common approaches, you'll understand how to use the others. Notice that some of the approaches are "application-centric," whereas others are "document-centric." An application-centric person thinks, "I'll run Word so I can write up that trip expense report." A document-centric person thinks, "I have to work on that company manual. I'll look for it and double-click it."

Running Programs from the Start Button

The most popular way to run your applications is to use the Start button, which is located in the lower-left corner of your screen. When you install a new program, the program's name is usually added somewhere to the Start button's All Programs menu lists. If you've recently used an application, Windows 7 might list it in the recently used list on the top-level Start menu area. Sometimes you'll have to "drill down" a level or two to find a certain program because software makers sometimes like to store their applications under their company names. Then you just find your way to the program's name and choose it, and the program runs.

Note that all selections with an arrow pointing to the right of the name have submenus—that means they open when you click them or hover the pointer over them. Several levels of submenus might exist. For example, to see the System Tools submenu, you have to go through All Programs, Accessories, System Tools.

Often, you'll accidentally open a list that you don't want to look at (say, the Games submenu). Just move the pointer to the one you want and wait a second, or press the Esc key. Each press of Esc closes one level of any open lists. To close all open lists, just click anywhere else on the screen, such as on the desktop or another window. All open Start button lists go away.

 tip

Sometimes, spotting a program in a list is a visual hassle. Press the first letter of the program you're looking for, and the cursor jumps to it. If multiple items start with that letter, each keypress advances one item in the list. Also, pressing the right-arrow key opens a submenu. The Enter key executes the highlighted program. Items in the lists are ordered alphabetically, although folders appear first, in order, with programs after that.

Shortcut Doesn't Work

What do you do if you click a shortcut somewhere in the Start menu and nothing happens or you get an error message? Too much software overhead would be involved for the OS to keep track of all the shortcuts and update them as necessary when the files they point to are moved or deleted. A system that has been in use for some time will certainly have "dead" shortcuts, just as web pages have broken links floating around. When you click a shortcut icon anywhere in the system—be it in the Start menus, on the desktop, or in a folder—and you get an error message about the program file, click OK and let Windows take a stab at solving the problem by searching for the application. If it's found, Windows 7 "heals" the shortcut so that it will work again the next time you use it.

If that doesn't work, try searching by using Start, Search, or typing into the Search box above the Start button. (And recall that you can access the Search window by tapping F3 or Windows+F.) See whether you can track down the runaway application. If you're successful, you're probably better off erasing the bad shortcut and creating a new one that points to the correct location. You can create a new shortcut by right-clicking the app's icon and choosing Create Shortcut. Then drag, copy, or move the shortcut to wherever you want, such as onto the Start button.

Another good trick to help you sort out a bad shortcut or to follow where its trail is leading is to right-click the icon and choose Properties, Find Target.

Remember, moving folders that contain applications (for example, Office might be in C:\Program Files\MSOffice) is a *really* bad idea. Once installed, many programs need to stay where they were put, unless you use a utility program specifically designed for the task. This is because application locations are recorded in the system Registry, and simply moving the program executable files around doesn't update the system Registry.

Running a Program from Computer or Windows Explorer

If you're a power user, chances are good that you'll be sleuthing around on your hard disk using either the Computer approach or Windows Explorer. I certainly have programs floating around on my hard disk that do not appear in my Start button program menus, and I have to execute them directly. In general, the rule for running programs without the Start menu is this: If you can find and display the program's icon, just double-click it. It should run.

 tip

Just as in Windows XP, 2000, and Vista, the differences between Computer and Windows Explorer within Windows 7 are more cosmetic than functional. In fact, simply by changing the default view, you can obtain the same view (that is, the same layout, panes, and details) using either interface. To alter the views, use the Organize toolbar button.

Getting to a program you want is often a little convoluted, but it's not too difficult to grasp. Plus, if you understand the DOS directory tree structure or you've used a Mac, you already know more about Windows 7 than you think. Double-click a drive to open it, and then double-click a directory to open it. Then double-click the program you want to run. Figure 4.10 shows a typical directory listing for Computer.

 tip

Network is a version of the Computer interface that is used to gain access to network resources. Overall, it's used in the same manner as Computer. The only difference is that you must be on a network and someone must grant you access to shared resources on other systems for this tool to be of any use. Thus, we've left the discussion of this tool to Part V, "Networking."

Figure 4.10
A typical directory as shown in Computer.

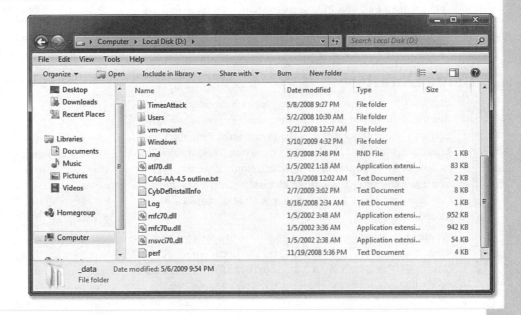

Here are some notes to remember:

- Folders are listed first, followed by files. Double-clicking a folder reveals its contents.

- If you want to see more folders on the screen at once to help in your search, you have several options. You can use the More options button on the toolbar to change view options. The Small

Icons view uses small icons with only the object name. The Medium Icons, Large Icons, and Extra Large Icons views display images extracted from the file objects themselves—these views are most useful for graphic files. The List view displays everything in a column by its object name only. The Details view offers the most comprehensive information about file system objects in a multicolumn display, with object names, object type, size, modified date, comments, and so on. The Tiles view provides an image with the object type and size.

Of course, many of the files you'll find in your folders are *not* programs; they're documents or support files. To easily find the applications, choose the Details view and then click the column head for Type. This sorts the listing by type, making it easy to find applications in the list (which carry an Application label).

Using Libraries

Windows 7 is designed to help you focus on your creative tasks instead of the underlying OS, which supports the tools and files. Part of this includes the Documents, Pictures, and Music Start menu items. These links also appear on most file or browse windows, as well as within Computer and Windows Explorer. These three elements always link you back to a standard location where your personal data files are stored.

Windows 7 introduces the concept of libraries for your personal documents. While the standard My Documents, My Music, My Pictures, and My Videos folders are still listed and accessible under your user folder, Windows 7 gives you the ability to see data from all these directories in one convenient place—the library. Libraries can pull their data from multiple sources, whether that source is a folder on the local hard drive, an external hard drive, or a network location, and presents the files in an easy-to-manipulate interface. For more on libraries and how to configure them, see Chapter 5.

The Documents library is the master folder for all your personal data files. This is the default storage location whenever you save a new document or data file. These libraries are provided to simplify the storage and retrieval of your most intimate file-stored creations. Clicking on one of these Start menu links opens a Computer window to the library specified.

 tip

Pressing Backspace while in any folder window moves you up one level in the directory tree. Also, the Back and Forward buttons work just like they do in a web browser—they move you forward and back through folders you've already visited.

 note

Applications, registered file types, and certain system files do not have their file extensions (a period and three-letter label that follows the filename) displayed by default. "Hidden" system files and directories are invisible, too. This choice was made to prevent cluttering the display with files that perform duties for the OS but not directly for users. It also prevents you from meddling with files that could cripple applications and documents, or even the system at large. Personally, I like seeing as many details about files as possible, so when I first install a system, I change the default settings to show me every file on my system. You can do this through the View tab of the Folder Options applet, accessed through the Control Panel. You can also access the Folder Options applet quickly by typing `folder` in the Start menu Search box.

 tip

Documents is not the same as Recent Items. Recent Items is a quick-access list of the most recently accessed resources. This includes documents, music files, image files, archive files, and even (sometimes) programs.

Pictures

The Pictures library is to Windows 7 what the My Pictures folder was to Windows XP. You can store pictures in this folder and then view the pictures quickly from the Start menu (by clicking Start, Pictures) or from the Favorites Links section in Computer or Windows Explorer. A new installation of Windows 7 includes eight high-quality sample pictures in the Sample Pictures subfolder.

Music

The Music library is to Windows 7 what the My Music folder was to Windows XP. You can store music files in this folder and then listen to the music files quickly from the Start menu (by clicking Start, Music) or from the Favorites Links section in Windows Explorer. A new installation of Windows 7 includes three high-quality sample music files in the Sample Music subfolder.

Using Speech Recognition

Not everyone who uses Windows uses the keyboard. Some people are physically unable to use a keyboard, and others prefer voice commands to typing text whenever possible. With Speech Recognition, Windows 7 accommodates users who want to talk to their computer.

Windows 7 interfaces with a keyboard and mouse (or mouse equivalent) by default. You can set up Speech Recognition by clicking Start, Control Panel, Ease of Access, Speech Recognition. The Speech Recognition window appears (see Figure 4.11).

Figure 4.11
The Speech Recognition window lets you configure your Speech Recognition settings.

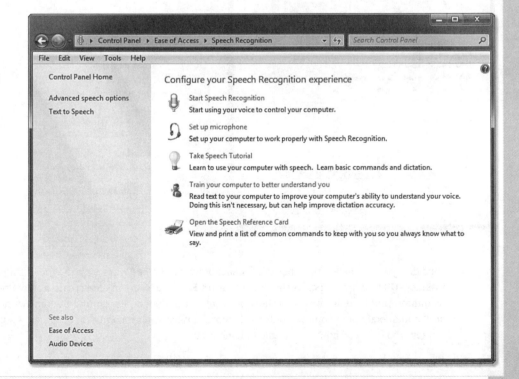

This window contains five links to choose from, but the link you want to click first to set up Speech Recognition is Start Speech Recognition. After you click this link, the Set Up Speech Recognition Wizard appears, enabling you to set up the computer to recognize your voice. Tasks you complete in the wizard include setting up the microphone, taking a speech tutorial, and reading text to your computer to help your computer better translate your voice to text.

You can also view and print the Windows Speech Reference Card that contains a list of common voice commands that Windows 7 understands.

Advanced Speech Options

You can further configure Speech Recognition options by clicking the Advanced Speech Options link in the Speech Recognition window. The Speech Properties window appears with the Speech Recognition tab open, as shown in Figure 4.12.

Figure 4.12
The Speech Properties window Speech Recognition tab.

In this tab, you can select the Microsoft Speech Recognition software for the type of English you're speaking—US English (which is the default) or UK English. You can also create a new Speech Recognition profile, determine whether you want to run Speech Recognition when Windows 7 starts, and specify how your computer will improve its speech-recognition accuracy. As part of that accuracy, you can also adjust your microphone input.

If you prefer Windows to read text aloud through your computer speakers, click the Text to Speech tab (see Figure 4.13).

Figure 4.13
The Speech Properties window Text to Speech tab.

By default, only one voice is available in Windows Vista: Microsoft Anna, which is a pleasant female voice. You can preview Anna's voice by clicking Preview Voice. You can also control Anna's voice speed using the Voice Speed slider bar. Enable Text to Speech by clicking OK.

Help and Support

We haven't yet advanced our computing systems to the level displayed in *Star Trek*, where officers state an action verbally and the action takes place. When you want your computer to do something, you need to tell it what to do. Often you have to explain in great detail at every step exactly what actions to take or not to take. The Windows 7 Help system is designed to help you find out what everything within the environment can and cannot do, as well as teach you how to perform the activity you need for work or play.

You can access the Help system by clicking on the Help and Support item on the top level of the Start menu. The Help system offers a wide range of options, from a search routine, to topic-organized texts, to task-assisting walk-throughs, to Internet-updated dynamic content help (see Figure 4.14). The Help system also includes access to a full index, a history list, and a favorites list. It operates in much the same way as a web browser—using hyperlinks, Back and Forward buttons, and the capability to return to the start of the system using the Home button. When searching for material, you can use Boolean rules to fine-tune your keyword search phrases (AND, OR, NOT, and NEAR). This is definitely a tool that is worth exploring and consulting in times of trouble or confusion.

Figure 4.14
The Windows Help and Support interface.

Exiting Windows Gracefully

When you've finished a Windows 7 session, you should properly shut down or log off to ensure that your work is saved and that no damage is done to the OS. Shall we reiterate? Shutting down properly is very important. You can lose your work or otherwise foul up Windows settings if you don't shut down before turning off your computer. If multiple people share the computer, you should at least log off when you're finished so that others can log on. Logging off protects your work and settings from prying eyes. When you shut down, Windows does some housekeeping, closes all open files, prompts you to save any unsaved work files, and alerts the network that you and your shared resources are no longer available for consultation.

You can always choose to shut down the computer; all or only some of this information might apply to your machine. Newer machines have more shutdown features because they're likely to have advanced power management built in to them via ACPI (Advanced Computer Power Interface).

These are the steps for correctly exiting Windows:

1. Close any programs that you have running. (This can almost always be done from each program's File, Exit menu if the menu bar is active or by clicking the program's close button.) If you forget to close programs before issuing the Logout or Shut Down command, Windows attempts to close them for you. If you haven't saved your work, you're typically prompted to do so. You must close some programs, such as DOS programs, manually. Windows alerts you if it can't automatically close an open program. Quit the DOS program and type **exit** at the DOS prompt, if necessary. If you are just switching user context, your open application's status is saved so you can quickly return to it later.

2. Click Start, and then move the mouse over the right-arrow button to the right of the Shut Down button. You'll see the menu shown in Figure 4.15.

3. Click on the desired option.

Figure 4.15
The Shut Down selection menu.

Consider these points:

■ The Hibernate option records the current state of the system to disk and then shuts down the computer. When the power is turned back on, the system reboots. If you log back in as the same user who initiated the hibernation, the system returns to its exact state at the moment of hibernation.

- If you want to log off, expand the Shut Down menu and select Log Off.

- If you attempt to shut down the computer while another user's desktop is still active (that is, you choose Switch User and at least one other user is still logged on), you'll see a warning message stating that performing a shutdown could result in data loss, along with the options to continue with shutdown (Yes) or abort (No).

- Sleep puts the computer in a suspended state, letting you quickly come right back to where you were working before you suspended the PC. This means you don't have to exit all your applications before turning off your computer. You only have to choose Sleep. This also saves energy because the hard drives, the CPU, the CPU fan, some internal electronics, and possibly the power supply and fan go into a low-power state. If your monitor is Energy Star compliant, it should also go into a frugal state of energy consumption. When you want to start up again, a quick press of the power switch (on some computers, a keypress on the keyboard or a jiggle of the mouse will do) should start up the system right where you left off.

 tip

Logging off clears personal settings from memory and puts the computer in a neutral state, waiting for another user to log on. However, it doesn't bring the system to its knees. Logging off does not stop running services, which can include web services, file sharing, print sharing, UPS support, and scheduled tasks.

- Be sure to press the power button for just a second or so. Anything more than 4 seconds on most modern computers in a Sleep state causes the computer to completely power down.

- Be aware that Sleep holds your system state only as long as the computer has power. In XP, if the power failed, everything stored in the computer's RAM is lost. You'd end up doing a cold boot when the power is restored or, if it's a laptop with a dead battery, when you hook up your AC adapter to your laptop again. The good news is that in Windows 7, Sleep is more intelligent. When the battery level gets too low, the power management system in Windows 7 switches into gear and initiates Hibernation (which we'll discuss next). One of the more interesting features of recent versions of Windows, including Windows 7, is *hibernation*. Like Sleep mode, hibernation lets you pause your work and resume later, without laboriously shutting down and reopening all your applications and files. But unlike Sleep, Hibernate isn't "volatile." If the AC power fails or batteries run flat, it doesn't matter because Hibernate stores the system state—that is, the contents of memory and the status of all hardware devices—on a portion of the hard disk, instead of keeping the system RAM alive in a low-power state. After storing the system state to the hard disk, the computer fully shuts down. When it's restarted, a little internal flag tells the boot loader that the system has been stored on disk, and it's reloaded into memory.

- Hibernation requires as much free hard disk space as you have RAM in your PC. If you have 512MB of RAM, you'll need 512MB of free disk space for hibernation to work. When you choose Hibernate from the Shut Down menu, Windows 7 has to create a fairly large file on disk. In my case, for example, it's 2GB in size. On a 3GHz Intel Pentium 4, the entire process takes about 15 seconds. Restarting takes about the same amount of time. Remember, if you're going to put a laptop running on batteries to sleep for more than a few hours, use Hibernate or just do a complete shutdown, closing your applications and documents. That way, if the batteries run out, you won't lose your work.

Dealing with a Crashed Application or Operating System

Even though Windows 7 is fairly immune to crashing, the applications that run on it are not necessarily so robust. Not to be cynical, but many IS professionals don't consider any version of Windows worth their trouble until at least a service pack or two hit the streets, because they know that bugs tend to be prevalent in first-release software. Still, with an OS as complex as Windows 7, we bet there are a few gotchas lurking.

Forcing Your Computer to Shut Down

If your system is really acting erratically or stuck in some serious way and you've already killed any unresponsive programs, press Ctrl+Alt+Del. This should bring up the Windows 7 options menu. Click the red Shut Down button in the lower-right corner of the screen. If you get this far, there's hope for a graceful exit. You might have to wait a minute or so for the Turn Off command to take effect. If you're prompted to shut down some programs or save documents, do so. Hope for a speedy shutdown. Then reboot.

My point here is that you're going to bump into some unstable behavior from time to time. If you notice that a program isn't responding, you might have a crash on your hands. To gracefully survive a crash, possibly even without losing any of your data, try the following steps:

1. Try pressing Esc. Some programs get stuck in the middle of a process and Esc can sometimes get them back on track. For example, if you accidentally pressed Alt, this activates the menus. A press of Esc gets you out of that loop. If you've opened a menu, two presses of Esc or a click within the application's window might be required to return to normal operation.

2. Windows 7 has greatly improved application-management facilities. In most cases, even after an application has crashed, you should still be able to minimize, maximize, move, resize, and close its window.

3. Can you switch to the app to bring its window up front? First try clicking any portion of the window. If that doesn't work, click its button in the taskbar. Still no? Try using successive presses of Alt+Tab. If you get the window open and responding, try to save any unfinished work in the app and then try to close it by clicking the Close button or selecting File, Exit.

4. If that doesn't work, try right-clicking the program's button in the taskbar and choosing Close from the pop-up menu.

5. If that doesn't work, press Ctrl+Shift+Esc to launch the Task Manager. Notice the list of running applications. Does the one in question say "Not responding" next to it? If so, click it and then click End Task.

6. If Task Manager reports that you don't have sufficient access to terminate the task, you must reboot the system. First, attempt a graceful shutdown using the Shut Down option in the Start

Menu. However, if that fails (that is, it hangs on the hung application or it never seems to complete the shutdown process), you need to resort to power-cycling. When the system reboots, you should be back to normal.

Ctrl+Alt+Del Doesn't Work

If Ctrl+Alt+Del doesn't work, it's time to power-cycle the computer. Press the power switch to turn off the machine. This might require holding in the power button for more than 4 seconds. You could lose some work, but what else are you going to do? Sometimes it happens. This is one good reason for saving your work regularly and looking for options in your programs that perform autosaving. As writers, we set our AutoSave function in Microsoft Word to save every 5 minutes. That way, we can recover from a system crash and lose only up to 5 minutes of work instead of everything.

Incidentally, although it's extremely rare, I've known laptops to not even respond to any form of command or power button when the OS was fully hung. I've even had to remove any AC connection, fully remove the main battery, wait a few seconds, and then reinsert the battery and reboot. Removing the battery is important; otherwise, the battery keeps the computer in the same stuck state, thinking it's just in Sleep mode.

5

MANAGING FILES AND SEARCHING

What's New in Windows Explorer

Chapter 4, "Using the Windows 7 Interface," touched on the two applications that allow you to view and manipulate files, folders, libraries, and other computer information: Computer and Windows Explorer. You may remember that Computer was dubbed My Computer in Windows XP, and both Computer and Windows Explorer are present in Windows 7 with many of the same functions and features as in Vista, XP, and previous versions of Windows. For example, you can use the built-in tools in Computer and Windows Explorer to move, copy, delete, rename, and create new files and other items on your computer.

Indeed, Computer and Windows Explorer have nearly identical interfaces and options. If you're in Windows Explorer, you can open the Computer folder in the Navigation pane to view your computer's media. With the Computer window open, you can view other directories and files.

By default, the Computer folder (or window) opens in the Content pane on the right and shows the current hard drives and removable drives installed on the computer, as shown in Figure 5.1.

 note

Windows Explorer is still hidden away in the Accessories area of the Start menu. This is because Microsoft wants to draw your attention away from how files are managed on the hard drive and to direct your attention to displaying folders and documents within libraries (or collections). Libraries are discussed in more detail in Chapters 3 and 4.

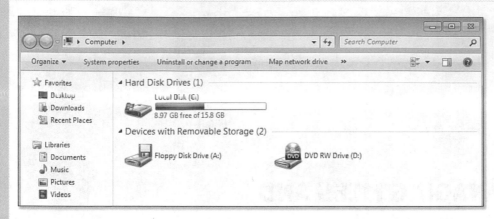

Figure 5.1
The Computer window with the hard drive(s) and removable drive(s) in the Content pane.

However, when you open Windows Explorer, Windows 7 opens the Libraries library and displays the sublibraries within, as shown in Figure 5.2.

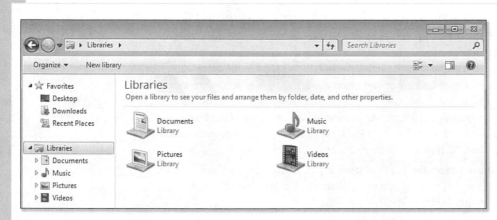

Figure 5.2
The Windows Explorer window with the contents of the Libraries library in the Content pane.

Although Computer and Windows Explorer have many of the same features and are highly similar to their counterparts in Windows Vista, they differ from My Computer and Windows Explorer in older versions of Windows as follows:

- The menu bar at the top of the window is hidden by default and is replaced with features closely aligned with the navigation and search tools in Internet Explorer. These include Back and Forward buttons, a box that shows *breadcrumbs* of where you are in relation to other windows, and the Search box replaces the Search pane in older versions of My Computer/Windows Explorer. (See more about breadcrumbs in the "Buttons, Breadcrumbs, Toolbars, and More" section later in this chapter.)

- The toolbar has been combined with organizational features of the menu bar in older versions of My Computer/Windows Explorer; the options in the toolbar change to reflect the type of information you're viewing in the Content pane so that you can perform tasks more quickly. For example, if you're viewing picture files in your Pictures Library, you may see toolbar options for burning a disc or creating a slideshow, as shown in Figure 5.3. If you're viewing your computer media in the Computer window, you'll see toolbar options to view system properties, uninstall or change a program, map a network drive, and more, as shown in Figure 5.4.

Toolbar options change based on what you are doing with Windows.

Figure 5.3
The toolbar options for the Pictures library in Windows Explorer.

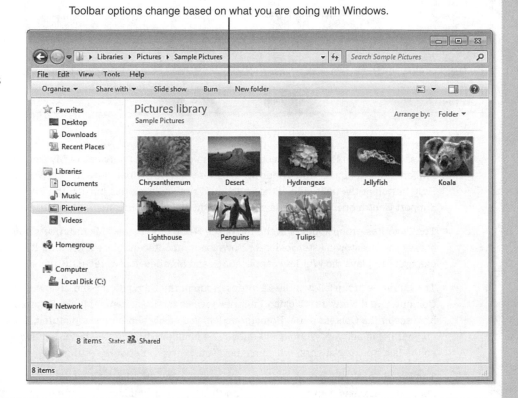

- You now have a wider variety of views when you look at objects in the Computer or Windows Explorer window. You'll learn more about the different views available to you in the "Customizing File and Folder Views" section later in this chapter.

 note

If you have more toolbar options than the toolbar can hold, Windows 7 gives you a clue that more options are available by showing the double-arrow (----)----) button to the right of the rightmost button in the toolbar. Figure 5.4 shows an example of this double-arrow button.

The toolbar options changed to show options specific to working with the Computer window.

Click this button to see more options.

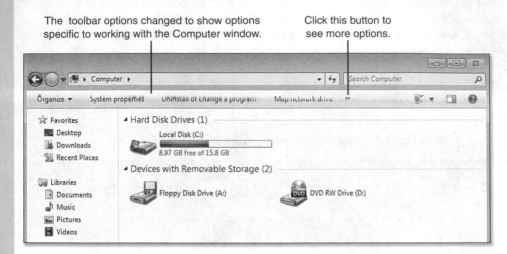

Figure 5.4
The toolbar options for the computer media listed in the Computer window.

- Instead of clicking Help in the menu bar as you did in earlier versions of My Computer/Windows Explorer, the Computer and Windows Explorer window toolbars in Windows 7 include a Get Help button at the right side of the toolbars. When you click this button, the Windows Help and Support Center opens and displays the topic that is most germane to your current situation.

- The Favorites group appears at the top of the Navigation pane. This group lets you quickly access the Desktop, master folder for Downloads, and Recent Places. Clicking Recent Places, for example, displays the Windows applications and libraries you've recently visited.

- The Libraries group follows the Favorites group in the Navigation pane, followed by Homegroup, Computer, and Network. Clicking Libraries reveals the Documents, Music, Pictures, and Videos libraries in the Content pane. Homegroup lets you easily share music, pictures, and documents on your home network. You should already be familiar with the Computer window at this point, so the last item is Network, which enables you to access network settings.

- The Details pane appears at the bottom of the window and displays *metadata*, or information about the information in the computer (in the Computer window) or in the folder (in the Windows Explorer window). See "Viewing Meta-Information" later in this chapter for more information.

The Legacy of WebView

Windows XP included Microsoft's WebView technology that attempted to make your local content integrate as seamlessly as possible with Internet-based content. This integration was designed to offer the benefits of more information displayed within the interface by default and quick access to common activities.

 note

The chapters in Part IV, "Windows 7 and the Internet," cover the ins and outs of getting connected, browsing the Web, using search engines, creating and serving web pages, and using email, newsgroups, and so forth. However, what's relevant here is how the Windows 7 WebView affects how you work with files and folders.

Microsoft ended WebView with Windows XP, but many features of WebView were integrated into Windows Explorer and the Computer folder in Windows Explorer in Vista, and these features have been improved and refined in Windows 7.

Figure 5.5 shows Windows Explorer in WebView, which is the standard view. Classic view, which was an option in Windows Vista and enabled you to use a Windows 2000–like interface, no longer exists in Windows 7. WebView gives you access to some common tasks related to files and folders in the toolbar above the Navigation and Content panes. The Details pane at the bottom of the window displays basic information about a selected item, such as

- The selected item's name and type (such as document, folder, application, library, and so on)

- The date on which it was most recently modified

- Its size and other item-specific information

Access common files and folders tasks here.

Figure 5.5
Windows
Explorer in
WebView
(standard
view).

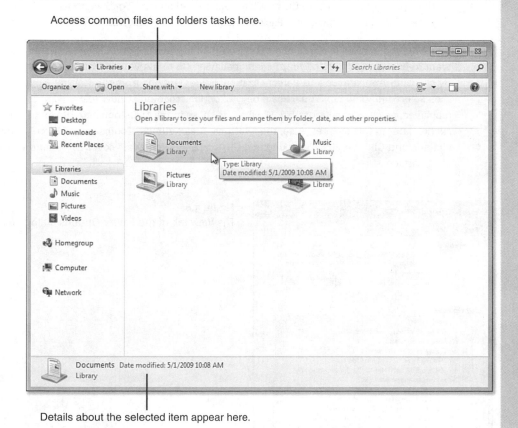

Details about the selected item appear here.

Much of this information also appears in a ToolTip when the mouse cursor is placed over an object, as shown in Figure 5.5.

How WebView Gives Windows 7 a Browser Look and Feel

Some key WebView effects have remained in Windows 7, such as Desktop Gadgets (formerly part of the Windows Sidebar in Vista). Microsoft has worked hard to dovetail the interfaces of Internet Explorer and Computer/Windows Explorer more tightly than ever in Windows 7. Some of the key WebView effects that have remained in Windows 7 include

- Computer and Windows Explorer have Back and Forward buttons, an Address bar, and a Search box similar to Internet Explorer.

- The toolbars in folder and Windows Explorer windows are customizable and have address fields, just like a browser. You can type in a web address and press Enter (or click Go), and the Internet Explorer window appears and displays the content. If you enter a drive letter (C:, for example), its contents are displayed.

- Windows 7 can navigate the contents of compressed archives, such as zipped files, without a third-party utility. Archive files act like compressed folders. You'll learn more about zipping and packing files in "Zipping and Packing Files" later in this chapter.

There are many more features and options in the interface. If you're the controlling type, you might want to fine-tune aspects of your folders' behavior. Go to the Folder Options Control Panel applet by choosing Appearance and Personalization, Folder Options from the Control Panel window, and then select the View tab. You'll see a bevy of options that affect how folders and their contents are displayed, as shown in Figure 5.6. We'll get to those in the "Customizing File and Folder Views" section later in this chapter. Also, the "Buttons, Breadcrumbs, Toolbars, and More" section in this chapter, and Chapter 23, "Tweaking and Customizing Windows," cover even more ways to change the interface.

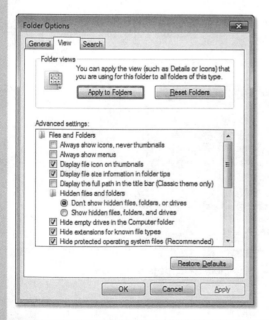

Figure 5.6
The View tab of the Folder Options dialog box.

Buttons, Breadcrumbs, Toolbars, and More

One big improvement introduced in Windows Vista and carried over into Windows 7 is the OS's capability to let you know where you are in relation to parent and child windows. These *breadcrumbs* appear as text and icon representations of folders, windows, and services, as shown in Figure 5.7.

 note

If there are no other child locations underneath the parent location, a right arrow will only appear to the right of the location name if that location has a submenu associated with it. Otherwise, no right arrow will appear next to the location name.

Breadcrumbs show your current location; click any individual breadcrumb to navigate to that location.

Clicking a blank location in the Address bar shows the exact folder you're viewing.

Figure 5.7
Breadcrumbs in the Address bar.

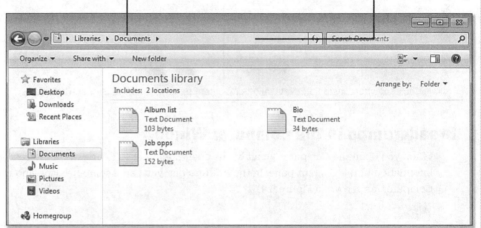

The Address bar displays your current *location*, which is any disk drive, library, folder, or other place where you can store files and folders. As you read the Address bar from left to right, the parent location appears at the far left of the box. Each child location appears to the right of its parent location, and the current location you're in appears without any child locations to its right. For example, in Figure 5.7, the current location is Documents. Each location is followed by a right-facing arrow.

The breadcrumbs that appear depend on the library or folder you're in. What's more, the right arrow not only shows that the next window or service is the child of the current parent or service, but it also lets you select from a menu of related options. Let's take a look at examples of the breadcrumbs you see in the Computer window and Windows Explorer.

 tip

If you want to see the exact folder path you're in instead of the location, click on a blank area in the Address bar. The information in the Address bar changes to the exact path, as shown in Figure 5.8. Return to the location view by clicking on a blank spot in the Navigation or Content pane.

You can also type the exact path in the Address bar to open a specific library or folder instead of using location-based navigation.

The exact folder now appears.

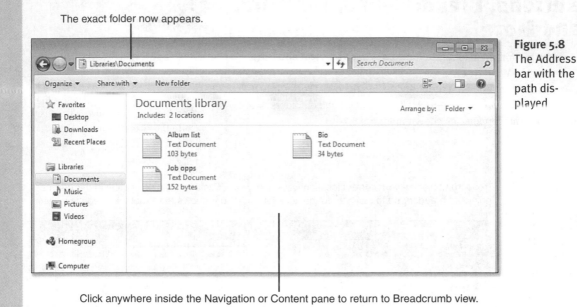

Figure 5.8
The Address bar with the path displayed

Click anywhere inside the Navigation or Content pane to return to Breadcrumb view.

Breadcrumbs in the Computer Window

When you open the Computer window, the open Computer folder displays the computer media information in the Content pane. In the Address bar, you see a computer icon and the location name Computer, as shown in Figure 5.9.

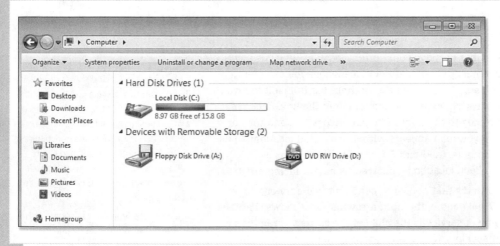

Figure 5.9
The Computer window Address bar.

The home icon appears at the left side of the Address bar, followed by the Computer folder name. In the Computer location, the home icon is a computer. If you double-click the C: drive in the Content pane, the Address bar adds the name of your C: drive—the default name is Local Disk (C:)—to the right side of the Address bar, as shown in Figure 5.10.

Figure 5.10
The Computer window Address bar with the name of the C: drive added.

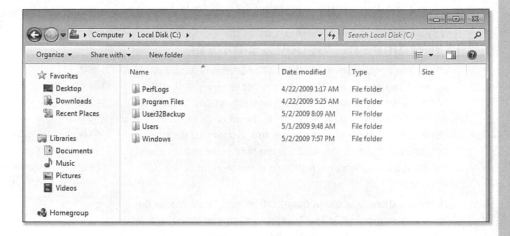

Note that the home icon has changed from a computer to a hard disk. The icon changes to reflect the location type. For example, if you open a folder on the C: drive, the icon in the Address bar changes to an open folder.

If there is a submenu associated with a location in the Address bar, you can open this submenu by clicking the right arrow to the right of each location. When you click the right arrow, the arrow changes to a button and the arrow points down toward the menu, which appears directly underneath the down arrow. Figure 5.11 shows the submenus for the home icon. Clicking on Computer or Local Disk (C:) would show those submenus as well.

Figure 5.11
The submenu for the home location.

Menu options in bold text are locations that are currently open. If you click another location in the menu, the Address bar changes to reflect the new location to which you have moved.

Breadcrumbs in Windows Explorer

When you open Windows Explorer, the Libraries window appears by default, and the Address bar shows you that the Libraries library is your location. The functionality of the Address bar in Windows Explorer is the same as in the Computer window—you can move to a location by clicking on the location name in the Address bar, and you can also open submenus by clicking the right arrow to the right of the location name.

However, there is one significant difference: The Address bar shows your user profile as a location. When you click the right arrow next to the user profile name, a submenu appears that lets you open your Contacts; Desktop files; Downloads, Favorites, Links, and My Documents folders; games and media folders; and searches.

 tip

You can move to different locations in the Address bar in one of two ways:

- Click the location name in the Address bar.
- Click the Back and Forward buttons. If you click the Back button, you go back to the location immediately to the left of the current location in the list. Click the Forward button to go to the current location's child location. If you can't go back and forward any more in the list, the Back and/or Forward buttons will be inactive.

User Profiles

User profiles are files that contain configuration information for each user on your computer. Configuration information includes desktop settings, network connections, and application settings. When you log in to Windows 7 using your account, Windows reads this user profile and configures your desktop, network connections, and application settings so that everything works the way you expect.

A user profile is different from a user account. A user account contains information about what files and folders your account can access, the changes your account can make to your computer, and your user preferences such as your desktop background and color theme.

Windows 7 assigns the same number and type of directories to each user profile. The user profile file also remembers which files go in which directory for that user. For example, if I have my own documents in my Documents library and Lisa has her own documents in her Documents library, I will see only my documents.

Navigating the File System

In Windows 7, the toolbar appears just below the Address bar by default, and changes every time you click on an object in the Computer window or Windows Explorer. These changes reflect what you can do with the file or folder. A menu bar is also available, however, and you must first enable the menu bar as described in "Turning Panes On and Off" later in this chapter.

Figure 5.12 shows two different examples of menu toolbar options available for two different objects. In the first part of Figure 5.12, the Windows Explorer window shows the Music library with the five menu toolbar buttons showing what you can do with the files, including Play All to play all the music files in the library and Burn to burn to a disc.

Figure 5.12
The Music
library menu
toolbar
options.

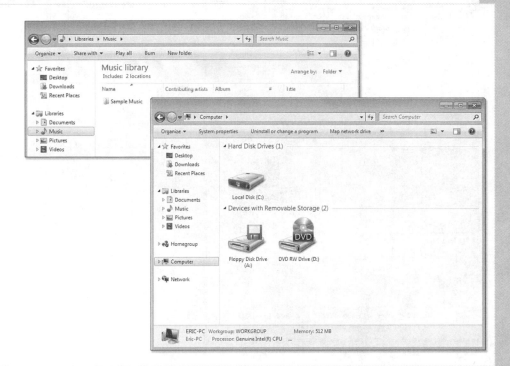

The second part of Figure 5.12 shows the Computer window with the computer's media listed. The menu toolbar buttons are different from those available for the Music library. You can organize the folder's contents, access system properties, uninstall or change a program, or map a network drive. As mentioned previously, the double-arrow (>>) displays to indicate additional options are available. In this case, if you click the double-arrow button to the right of Map Network Drive, you'll see a pop-up menu for opening the Control Panel.

You probably noticed that a few parts of the toolbar never change: the Organize button (on the far left) and Views (Change Your View) button (unlabeled, third from the right). These buttons let you determine how to organize and view the files, folders, and other objects. When you click the Organize button, a menu appears with many of the same options that were available in the File menu in My Computer/Windows Explorer in Windows XP, as shown in Figure 5.13.

When you click the down-arrow button to the right of the Views button, the Views menu appears, as shown in Figure 5.14. This menu shows you the different ways of presenting information in the Content pane of the window. You can select from eight different options using the slider bar, which appears to the left of the selected view type. You will learn more about views in the "Customizing File and Folder Views" section later in this chapter.

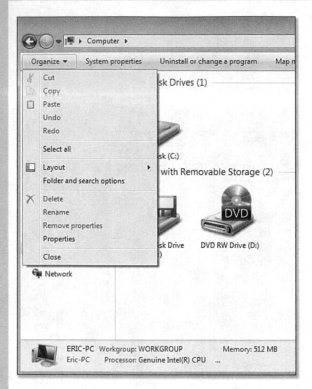

Figure 5.13
The Organize menu.

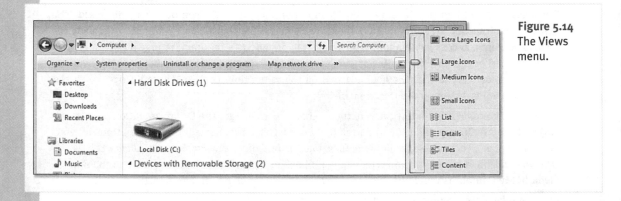

Figure 5.14
The Views menu.

Right-Clicking

Windows makes good use of the right mouse button to access information in Windows Explorer and Computer. Indeed, use of the right mouse button has become so prevalent that even the latest versions of the Mac OS incorporate the right-click to open and manipulate objects on the screen.

In Windows Explorer, right-clicking on a file, folder, or library opens a pop-up menu so that you can work with it in various ways, depending on the object type. You can open a document, folder, or library; share a file or folder with other users in your homegroup; send a document to an email recipient; run a program; install or set up a utility such as a screen saver; play a sound file; and so forth. Figure 5.15 shows a pop-up menu for a music file. To learn more about homegroups, see Chapter 17.

Figure 5.15
The pop-up menu for a music file.

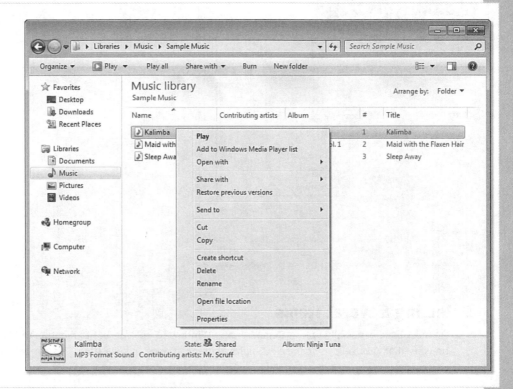

When you right-click on a file or folder, a new button may appear on the menu bar to give you more options. In Figure 5.15, the pop-up menu provides a number of choices, starting with Play at the top of the menu. The Play button also appears in the menu toolbar so that you can click the Play button or click the down-arrow button to the right of the Play button to choose the media player you want to use.

In the Computer window, right-clicking on a computer media icon brings up different options for working with the C: drive, as shown in Figure 5.16. You'll also notice that the Properties button appears on the menu bar (and as an item in the pop-up menu) so you can open the Properties window for the C: drive.

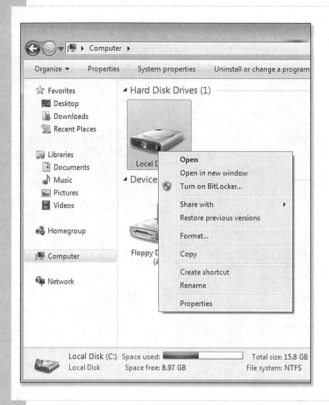

Figure 5.16
The pop up menu for a hard drive,

Selecting Several Items

On most lists, especially within Computer and Windows Explorer, not to mention the file and browser dialog boxes, you can select multiple items at once to save time. The normal rules of selection apply:

- Draw a box around them by clicking and holding over empty space near the first item and then drag across and over the desired selections until all are highlighted and/or contained within the selection box; then release the mouse button.

- Select the first of the items, hold down the Ctrl key, and click to select each additional object you want to work with. Use this technique to select a number of noncontiguous items.

- Select the first of the items, hold down the Shift key, and click the last item. This selects the entire *range* of objects between the starting and ending points.

After several items are selected (they will be highlighted), right-clicking any one of the objects brings up the Cut, Copy, Paste menu. The option you choose applies to *all* the selected items. Also, clicking anywhere outside the selected items deselects them all, and Ctrl-clicking (or pointing) to one selected object deselects that object.

Drag-and-drop support is implemented uniformly across the Windows 7 interface. In general, if you want something placed somewhere else, you can drag it from the source to the destination. For example, you can drag items from the Search results list into a folder or onto the desktop, or you can add a picture attachment to an email you're composing by dragging the picture file into the new email's window. Also, the destination folder does not have to be open in a window. Items dropped onto a closed folder icon are added to that folder. You can also drag and drop items via the taskbar by dragging an item over an application button, pinning it to the application. A pop-up menu appears, enabling you to select the item (such as a music file) and launch the application. You can also drop items into the Start menu to add them to the listings, or drop items over desktop icons to open them with the application onto which you drop the item (assuming the application supports the object's file type). However, you can also use the Cut, Copy, and Paste methods of moving files and folders.

Arranging your screen so you can see both source and destination is graphically and intuitively reassuring because you can see the results of the process. To quickly arrange two windows side by side, pull one window to the far-left side of the screen until the background becomes highlighted, and then release the mouse. The window snaps into place, taking up half the screen. Pull the other window to the right in the same manner, and it then fills the right half of the screen. To show only one window, use Aero Shake by grabbing the window's title bar and jiggling (shaking) it toward the second window a few times. Windows 7 displays the window in the middle of the screen, hiding the second window.

⚠ caution

Don't try moving program files unless you know they have not registered themselves with the OS and they can harmlessly be moved around between folders.

Viewing Meta-Information

A feature in Computer and Windows Explorer that was introduced in Windows Vista is the Details pane, which appears at the bottom of the Computer or Windows Explorer window, as shown in Figure 5.17.

In Windows XP and older versions of Windows, Windows Explorer and My Computer only showed basic information about the selected object in the status bar. This information is called *meta-information*, or information about the information contained in the file. For example, when you clicked on a Microsoft Word file you would see information about the type of file, the date and time the file was saved, and the size of the file, all in small text that was squeezed onto one line in the status bar.

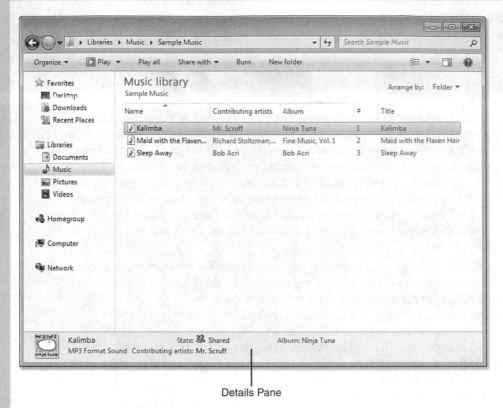

Figure 5.17
The Details
pane at the
bottom of
the window
contains
meta-
information.

Details Pane

As you can see in Figure 5.17, the Details pane provides information about a selected object in a format that's easy to read. Information in the Details pane varies with the type of object you're viewing. In Figure 5.17, you see a music file that includes the following information:

- The icon associated with the file. In this case, it's an album cover.

- The name of the file.

- The program the file is associated with, which is an MP3 audio file.

- The name of the artist(s).

- The album name.

The Details pane is different when you open the Computer window and click the Local Disk (C:) icon. As shown in Figure 5.18, the Details pane shows a bar that denotes the amount of space used on the hard drive, the amount of free space on the drive, the total size of the drive, and the file system used.

 note

If you don't select a file, folder, or other object in the Content pane, the Details pane displays information about the current location. For example, if you haven't selected a file in the Music library, the Details pane shows a folder icon with the number of items in the folder.

Figure 5.18
The Details pane show-ing meta-information for Local Disk (C:).

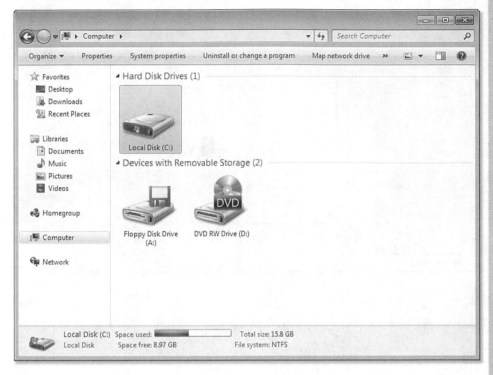

Turning Panes On and Off

Windows Explorer and the Computer window offer several panes, and you can turn each one on and off to suit your needs. Windows Explorer offers four panes, whereas you can view only three panes in the Computer window. Both windows allow you to display and use the menu bar, which is turned off by default.

View the panes you have open by clicking the Organize button in the toolbar and then choosing Layout. The options appear in the flyout menu, as shown in Figure 5.19. The Layout menu displays an icon to the left of each inactive pane name, and a blue box around a check mark signifies that the pane is currently active.

By default, the Computer and Windows Explorer windows display the Navigation and Details panes. In addition, the Library pane is available in Windows Explorer (but not in the Computer win-dow).

The Preview pane is disabled by default. When you select it in the Layout menu, the Preview pane appears at the far right side of the window and shows a thumbnail preview of the file when you click the filename, as shown in Figure 5.20. If the file is a multimedia file, you can play the file in the small window and see whether the file is something you want to play in Windows Media Player or your multimedia player of choice. If there is no file to preview, a message appears in the Preview pane: "Select a file to preview."

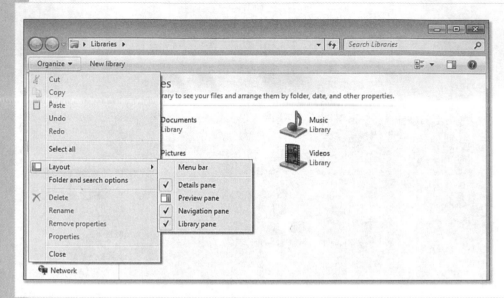

Figure 5.19
The Layout flyout menu in Windows Explorer.

Figure 5.20
The Preview pane with a multimedia file displayed.

When you click Menu Bar in the Layout flyout menu, the menu bar you may be familiar with from earlier versions of Windows appears above the menu toolbar.

This menu bar contains the well-known File, Edit, View, Tools, and Help menu options. Many features in these menus were brought over from Windows XP and Vista, and you can't get to these features without enabling the menu.

Customizing File and Folder Views

When you create a new user profile, Windows 7 automatically creates a personal folder that matches your username and places a number of subfolders within that master folder. These subfolders are categorized by name (including My Documents, My Pictures, and My Music) and allow you to put your files into them. What's more, these subfolders are private; no other user that uses your computer can view or open these subfolders. Yet what Microsoft gives you isn't uniquely you.

Windows 7 offers a wide range of options for customizing how files are displayed through the Computer and Windows Explorer utilities. The full set of options is available from the View menu (accessible when the menu bar is displayed), although you can access many of the options from the toolbar as well. The options on the View menu change slightly based on which window you're viewing (Computer versus Windows Explorer) and whether you're viewing a library or folder.

The most common controls found on the View menu (see Figure 5.21) are

- **Status Bar**—If you miss the status bar at the bottom of the window, use this control to enable the display of this information bar. It shows the number of items in a library or folder, number of items selected, information about menu bar commands as you hover over them, and so on.

- **Views**—This section allows quick change of the view used to display file objects: Extra Large Icons, Large Icons, Medium Icons, Small Icons, List, Details, Tiles, and Content. Content view is new to Windows 7 and displays files and folders in a mixed graphical/stacked arrangement.

- **Arrange By**—This menu item appears in Windows Explorer when folders are displayed in a library and is used to define custom attributes for the selected folder. It defaults to Folder view, but you can change the arrangement of items based on author, date modified, tag, type, or name. The Arrange By options are specific to the type of library or folder selected.

- **Sort By**—This menu allows you to determine the sort order for files and folders. For example, you could group music files by name and show the files in ascending order.

- **Group By**—This menu allows you to group files by a certain criteria, such as the filename, file type, date, and so on.

 note

The Preview pane settings persist regardless of your current location or whether you're using Windows Explorer or the Computer window. For example, if you enable the Preview pane in the Music library and then move to the Documents library, the Preview pane remains visible. Similarly, if you enable the Preview pane while using Windows Explorer, the pane is still available if you open the Computer window.

 tip

A quick way to access the menu bar without going through the Layout menu is to press the Alt key.

- **Choose Details**—This command sets the details that appear in ToolTips, details, and Tile view. The defaults are name, date modified, type, and size. Over 100 options are available, which include attributes, company, file version, owner, and subject.

- **Go To**—This menu is used to navigate back, forward, up one level, or to recently visited locations.

- **Refresh**—This command reloads the display of files and folders.

note

Windows 7 remembers the view type you selected for each folder, but if a view type isn't specified, the default view type is Tiles.

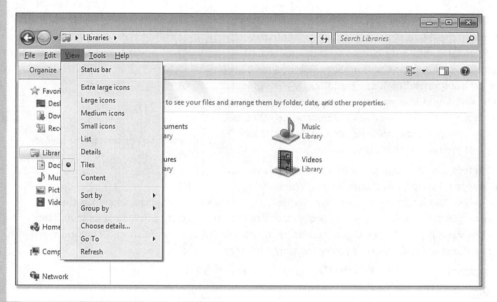

Figure 5.21
The View menu of Windows Explorer.

Setting Folder Options

Folder Options should be seen as more of a superset of controls over all folders on a system, whereas folder customization occurs on an individual or parent and subfolder basis. Folder Options is a Control Panel applet you can access from Computer and Windows Explorer. This applet is used to set a wide range of file system features.

Open the Folder Options dialog box by clicking the Organize button and then clicking Folder and Search Options. The Folder Options dialog box appears as shown in Figure 5.22.

The General tab of the Folder Options dialog box defines whether folders are opened in the same or in a new window, and whether single-clicks or double-clicks are used to open items. You can also configure the Navigation pane to show all folders by default, and/or automatically expand to the current folder. If you make changes to this tab, you can always return to the default by clicking the Restore Defaults button.

Figure 5.22
The Folder Options dialog box.

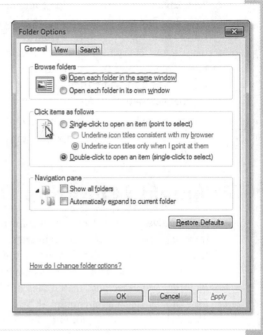

The View tab (see Figure 5.23) perform two major functions—folder view management and advanced settings management. For folder view management, all folders can be reset to their default views, or the currently selected folder's view can be applied to all folders.

Figure 5.23
The View tab of the Folder Options dialog box.

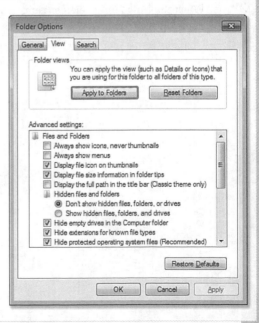

The Advanced Settings section contains a long checklist of settings. One use of this section is to choose what you want the OS to show you and hide from you. For example, if you want to see every file on your system, enable Show Hidden Files, Folders, and Drives and disable Hide Extensions for Known File Types and Hide Protected Operating System Files (Recommended). To return to the defaults, just click the.

The other tab in the Folder Options dialog box is the Search tab, which you learn more about in the section, "Searching," **p.173**.

note

If you've tried to delete a folder that looked empty but an error message states that the folder still contains files, you are probably dealing with hidden files. To see what's not being shown, change the Hidden Files and Folders Advanced setting to Show Hidden Files, Folders, and Drives. You might run into this issue with downloaded applications that must be extracted to a temporary folder before being installed. They sometimes include files premarked as hidden.

Managing Libraries

In Windows 7, libraries provide a convenient mechanism for grouping related content items in ways that make sense to the user. The default libraries group items by type of content, so you'll find document files in Documents, music and related files in Music, photos and images in Pictures, and video and related files in Videos. But there's no reason why you can't create a library for a project that might contain all these file types, and more. Let's take a look at what's involved in creating a library, and adding and removing elements from that library.

Creating a Library

To create a new library, open Windows Explorer to the Library view, then right-click in the left pane and select New, Library in the resulting pop-up menus (see Figure 5.24).

When the New Library element appears in the right pane, give that library a unique and descriptive name. I called mine Win7Project for this book (see Figure 5.25).

Right-click an empty space in the left pane.

Figure 5.24
The right-click technique is a quick
and easy way to create a new library.

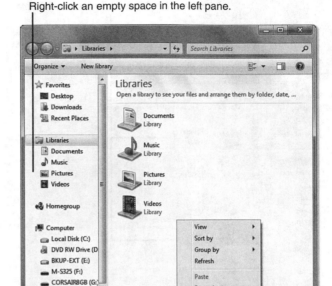

Choose New, Library, and then type a name for the library.

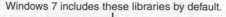

Windows 7 includes these libraries by default.

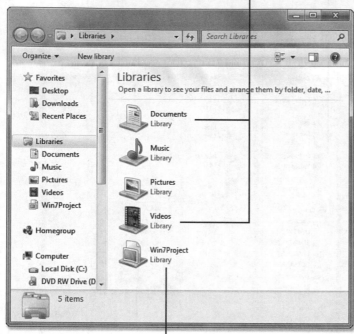

Figure 5.25
A newly created library with a descriptive name.

A new library can be named whatever you like.

Add Elements to a Library

The contents in a library are rooted in a folder on a hard disk somewhere, so the process of populating a new library begins by including an existing folder. You might want to consider creating a new folder for this purpose if you'd prefer to leave your existing folder structure alone.

 note

Windows 7 won't let you include a folder from a removable drive in a library, so don't bother trying this with a folder from a UFD or other removable drive or media.

The easiest way to add elements to a library is to open two instances of Windows Explorer:

1. In one Windows Explorer window, open the source folder that contains the items you want to add to the library.

2. In the other Windows Explorer window, open the target library.

3. Right-click items in the source window and select Copy.

4. Right-click in the library window and select Paste Shortcut to add items to the library without moving them into your base folder. On the other hand, you can drag and drop items if you want to move them into your library folder. The results of both such operations appear in Figure 5.26.

After clicking Paste Shortcut, a shortcut to the item appears in the new library; the original file remains in its original location.

Figure 5.26
To add items to the library, paste those items or paste shortcuts into the library window.

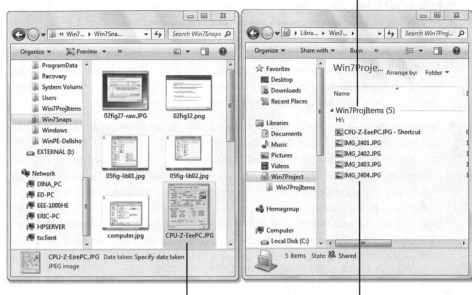

Right-click a source file and select Copy.

These items have been moved to the new library and now reside only in that location.

Remove Elements From a Library

If you've pasted shortcuts into your library, you need only delete the shortcuts to remove their parent items without affecting those items. If you've copied the parents into the library's base folder but have retained originals, you can delete the copies to remove them from the library. If you moved the files from their original folder into the base folder, you must move them back to the original or some other folder to keep them. If you delete them, they will be placed in the Recycle Bin.

Searching

The Search function has been greatly refined in Windows 7 compared to Vista and previous Windows editions. Called Desktop Search (or Search, for short), Windows 7 lets you search for files, folders, email messages, hard drives, PCs, and much more, whether the items are local or remote. You can search from the Search box on the Start menu, or use the familiar Search feature in Computer or Windows Explorer.

In addition, Windows 7 introduces a new technology referred to as federated search, which enables you to use something called a search connector to easily find web-based applications on internal and external sites, right from your Search tool.

Types of Searching

Windows 7 uses two different types of searching:

- **Intermediate searching**—Uses an index to find objects with filenames that you type into the Search box in Windows as well as in the Start menu. Like the index of a book, Windows 7 stores information about files such as the filename, file date, and properties, including words in a document. As you type your search criteria into the Search box, the list of programs changes to show you files that meet that criteria based on what Windows 7 finds in the index. The big advantage to intermediate searching is that it's fast, but it only uses one criteria (the filename), so if you need more information you need deep searching.

- **Deep searching**—Lets you search for different and multiple criteria such as the filename, the date the file was saved, and the location in which the file was saved. You can use Boolean arguments such as AND and OR as well as "greater than" and "less than" to help Windows 7 search for the files you need. For example, you may want to search for a file that was saved before (or less than) a certain date. You can also use wildcards in filenames to search for filenames that contain letters in certain places. For example, if you want to search for files that start with the letter *N* and end with the letter *W*, you would type **N*W** as the filename to search for; the asterisk represents all characters and any number of characters between *N* and *W*. In this case, Windows 7 would also find folders in which a parent folder begins with *N* and the child folder begins with *W*, such as \Notebooks\Work.

Search Feature Variations

The Search feature in Computer and Windows Explorer is not exactly the same as the Search box in the Start menu or the Live Search feature in Internet Explorer 8.

The Search feature in the Start menu searches for programs, Control Panel items, Internet favorites, and websites you have visited that are in your web history, in addition to documents, music, videos, and email messages. When you use the search engine in Internet Explorer 8 (be it the default Live Search or another search engine), that search engine searches the Web, not your computer.

What's more, the Search feature doesn't exist in some Windows 7 components (such as Windows Help and Support) or in many third-party programs, which include older programs such as Microsoft Office 2003.

Changing Search and Indexing Settings

Note while reading this section that we're describing the built-in Windows 7 Search features. Your system might have a different search tool installed, such as Google Desktop Search, Yahoo Widgets, or some other brand—those tools will operate differently. You'll have to refer to those tools' help files or websites to learn how they work. However, you might want to know that you can choose which program will do your searching for you, and even switch back and forth between the programs you want to use as your default. Choose Start, Default Programs, Set Your Default Programs, and you'll see a screen that allows you to change which search tool to use by default.

Windows 7 indexes most common files on your computer, including all the files in your personal folder, your email, your offline files, Internet Explorer History, and the Start menu. Program files and system files are not indexed because Microsoft says those files are rarely searched.

That doesn't mean that Windows 7 won't search nonindexed files. Windows 7 searches filenames and contents in indexed locations and only searches filenames in nonindexed files by default. You can change this default in the Folder Options dialog box from Computer or Windows Explorer.

Open the Folder Options dialog box by clicking the Organize button in the menu toolbar and then clicking Folder and Search Options. In the Folder Options dialog box, click the Search tab, which appears as shown in Figure 5.27.

Figure 5.27
The Search tab of the Folder Options dialog box lets you choose indexing options.

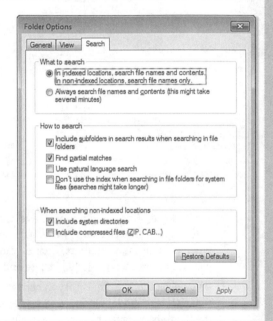

You determine what to search in the What to Search area at the top of the tab. Your other option is to have Windows 7 search filenames and contents in all files. This type of search could be a lot slower than the default, depending on how many files you're searching. When you search nonindexed locations, you can also tell Windows 7 whether you want to include system directories and compressed files at the bottom of the tab.

In the How to Search area in the middle of the tab, the default search parameters are to search in subfolders and to find partial matches. You can also decide how to search, including using natural language search (where you get to ask a question), and turn off the index. If you decide you don't like your changes and want to revert to the defaults, click Restore Defaults.

The Indexing Options applet in the Control Panel also lets you view the state of the index and make changes to the file types and folders you want to index. Open the Indexing Options applet by clicking Start, Control Panel, and then Indexing Options (in Icons view). The Indexing Options window appears as shown in Figure 5.28.

Figure 5.28
The Indexing Options window.

The Indexing Options window shows how many items are indexed and which folder locations have indexed files. You can modify the folder locations by clicking Modify. If you want to really drill down when configuring your index, click Advanced. The Advanced Options dialog box appears so that you can index encrypted files, delete and rebuild your index, and set the index location.

If you click the File Types tab, as shown in Figure 5.29, you can scroll down the list and add and remove files to index categorized by file extension. You can also tell Windows 7 whether you want the file to be indexed by properties only or by properties and file contents. If you don't see the extension in the list, type the file extension in the Add New Extension to List text box at the bottom of the tab and then click Add.

Figure 5.29
The File Types tab in the Advanced Options dialog box.

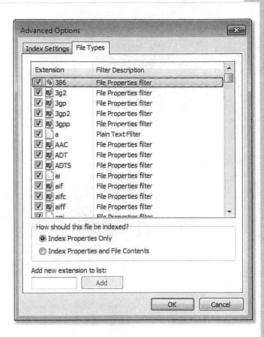

Searching As You Type

You can search for files, folders, movies, and even URLs as you type in the Computer or Windows Explorer window as well as in the Start menu. You do this by typing characters in the Search box; Windows displays the matching results in the Search box.

Searching in Computer or Windows Explorer

Start searching by typing a character in the Search box. After you type the character, Windows automatically searches for items in the current location that match your criteria (see Figure 5.30). As you type more characters in the Search box, Windows 7 refines the search and culls the list of matches until you find the one match you need—or at least narrows it down to only a few matches so you can find the file you need quickly.

 tip

When you type characters in the Search box, you can refine your search by prefacing the search characters with the object criteria name in which you want to search, followed by a colon and then your search criteria. For example, if you want to find a file with a name that starts with *b*, type `filename:b` in the Search box. This searches for all files with a name starting with the letter *b*. Other object criteria names include date and type. You can also use filters, which you'll learn about shortly, to accomplish similar tasks.

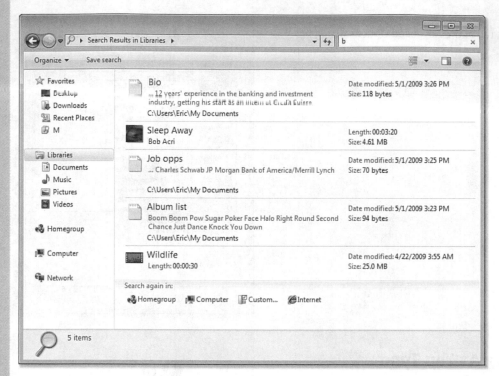

Figure 5.30
The list of search results in Windows Explorer.

You can also refine searches using the Add a Search Filter pane that appears under the Search box when you click in or type in the Search box. (You have to be quick; this tiny window displays for only about five seconds at a time.) Available filters change depending on the library or folder selected in Windows Explorer or the Computer window. For example, with the Music library selected, you can select Album, Artists, Genre, and Length filters. Filter options for the Libraries library include

- **Kind**—The Kind filter includes types of objects, such as calendar, communication, document, email, game, recorded TV, saved search, and many more.

- **Date Modified**—Selecting Date Modified opens a pop-up calendar in which you can select a specific date or a range of dates, or select less-defined date ranges such as A Long Time Ago or Earlier This Year.

- **Type**—The Type filter lists some common file types to search for, such as MP3, MVW, and text document.

- **Name**—The Name filter lets you enter one or more letters of a file or folder name.

Can't Find a Program

If you cannot find programs using the Search box in Windows Explorer, use the Start menu Search box instead. Begin typing **Programs**, and a list of matches will appear above the Search box. Just click the link for Programs and Features. You could also open Control Panel and click Programs and Features directly.

If you know the group where your wayward file resides, you can click one of these filters, and then type your search criteria in the Search box or select it from a pop-up menu. An example of using the Kind filter is shown in Figure 5.31.

Figure 5.31
Using the
Kind filter.

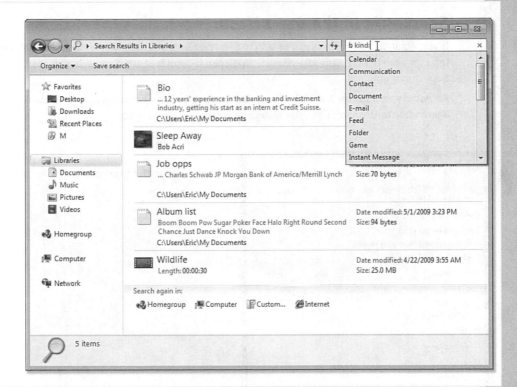

If the search doesn't find any files, folders, or other objects that meet your search criteria, the Content pane in the Computer or Windows Explorer window states, "No items match your search." You can click one of the icons listed under Search Again In to change the location being searched. Or you'll need to erase one or more characters in the Search box, or erase all the characters in the Search box and start over.

 note

When searching in the Computer window, a message bar might appear, prompting you to add C:\ or another drive to the index. When you click the bar, a shortcut menu appears with Add to Index and Modify Index Locations options.

If you want to save the results of your search, click the Save Search button in the toolbar. Windows 7 asks you to name your search before you save it, and after you save the search file the file appears at the bottom of the Favorites list.

Can't Find a File

If after much trying you still can't find the folder or file you're looking for, the problem could be that your search might only be looking at indexed locations—and indexed locations aren't all the locations on your computer. Consider using the Indexing Options window to rebuild your index and include your entire C: drive.

Searching in the Start Menu

If you want to perform a faster search to see what's on your computer that matches your search criteria, or zero in on programs, you can type search criteria in the Search box at the bottom of the Start menu.

As with typing in the Search box in Computer or Windows Explorer, type one character in the Search box and you will see the results as shown in Figure 5.32.

Figure 5.32
The results in the Start menu.

You can open an item in the results list, whether it's a program, multimedia file, picture, document, or other file type, by clicking its link. If your search turns up no matches, the Start menu states, "No items match your search."

 tip

In the Start menu, you can see all results from the Start menu search by clicking the See More Results link at the bottom of the search list. If you have not installed another desktop search engine, this launches your search results in a search window called the Search Explorer, which is essentially Windows Explorer with search-related menu items. If you have changed the default search tool, such as to Google Desktop Search, you'll see a Search Everywhere link rather than a Search More Results link, and the results will appear in that search tool's interface.

Can't Find Files That Belong to Other Users

If your search results aren't returning files that belong to other users on you computer, you should know that Windows 7 only searches your own files to index by default. However, you can add another user's files to your search results by opening the folder that contains the user's files. This is usually in the form of C:\Users*User*, where *User* is the name of the person on your system with the files. (You may need to type the administrator password to get access to these files.) After this folder is open, perform your search, and the files in the directory are included in the search.

Grouping and Stacking

Windows 7 not only comes with more powerful searching tools but more powerful organizational tools as well for sorting and filtering files.

In Details view in Computer or Windows Explorer, the top of the Content pane that displays files in your search results list includes column headings that double as filter controls, enabling you to filter the files in the Content pane. When you hover the mouse pointer over a column heading, a down-arrow button appears on the right. Just click the arrow button to display filter information in a small window underneath the button. Figure 5.33 shows an example.

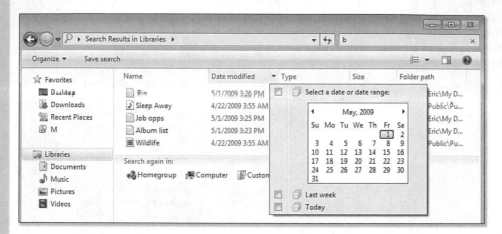

Figure 5.33
The window for filtering files by a specific date.

The filter criteria are available when searching or when simply browsing libraries or folders, and they change depending on the location you're in. Some of the criteria you can sort by include

- Name, in three different categories (A–H, I–P, and Q–Z)

- Date modified, which lets you filter by a specific date you can select from a calendar, as shown in Figure 5.33

- Type, which may include the ability to filter by compressed folders, file folders, documents, images, registration entries, and so on

- Size, which lets you display objects by categories of size, such as Medium (100 KB–1 MB), Large (1–16 MB), Huge (16–128 MB), or Unspecified

Additional criteria may include folder path, contributing artists, album, title, tags, rating, and many more, all with subcriteria that let you focus on specific information you want to see.

These filtering windows also let you use the options described in the "Customizing File and Folder Views" section earlier in this chapter for browsing your files and folders. For example, to view your files in a stacked arrangement, such as pictures taken in a certain month, right-click on a blank area of the Content pane, select Arrange By, and then select Month. Windows 7 takes all these pictures and combines them into stacks based on month, as shown in Figure 5.34.

Stacked files behave like folders, so you can open up the stacked file and see what's inside. So what's the big deal? Stacks are a quick way to collect content that meets your criteria and put them all in one place. And stacks have no physical location on your computer, so they don't take up space on your computer as a folder does—stacks are just another representation of your content based on your filter criteria.

Figure 5.34
Stacked files
organized by
months.

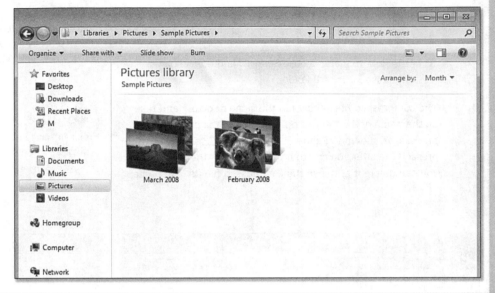

Windows 7 also allows you to group files by the criteria listed by the filter. Just right-click on a blank area of the Content pane, select Group By from the shortcut menu, and select a group criterion. For example, if you group files by name, Computer or Windows Explorer will group all the files by filename starting with the A–H group at the top, followed by the I–P group, and ending with the Q–Z group at the bottom. The grouping filter allows you to get a more granular view of which files belong to a particular group.

Zipping and Packing Files

In the 1980s, as computer networking and sharing files through bulletin board systems became popular, it became important to make files as small as possible because transmission speeds in those days were slower than a snail's pace compared to today's speeds. (Of course, back then we thought 1200bps was blazing speed!)

Today we still send files back and forth through email, and computer server bandwidth has trouble handling it all, so compressing files to their minimum size is as relevant now as it was years ago. In fact, it's become so relevant that Microsoft included built-in compression technology beginning with Windows XP, and compression technology is also included in Windows 7.

One of the most popular compression systems in the 1980s and 1990s was PKZip. Like Xerox and Google, whose brand names became synonymous with the products they perfected, compressing files soon became known as *zipping*. Today Windows 7 still refers to compressed files as zipped files.

Here's how you compress one or more files:

1. Select the file(s) you want to compress.

2. Right-click a selected filename.

3. In the pop-up menu choose Send To and then click Compressed (Zipped) Folder.

The compressed file appears in the same directory and takes on the name of the file you right-clicked in the compression process, as shown in Figure 5.35. Windows 7 selects the compressed file after you create it and highlights the filename so you can delete it and give the compressed file its own name.

 tip

You can add new files to the compressed file by dragging the files to the compressed file.

 note

You can't compress a file when you're viewing a stack. The Send To option doesn't appear on the flyout menu.

Figure 5.35
A compressed, or zipped, file.

After you compress the file, you can extract files by right-clicking the compressed file and then clicking Extract All. A dialog box appears and allows you to select a destination folder for the extracted files.

 note

JPEG files are already compressed, so you won't see much more compression from those files when you place them in a compressed file. The total size of a compressed JPEG file is about the same size of the total size of an uncompressed JPEG file.

File and Folder Security

File and folder security is a necessary part of computing, especially in these days of always-on net-working and multiple users and networks interacting with your computer. Therefore, security is an integral part of Windows 7.

As Windows NT was developed in the 1990s, Microsoft realized that the standard File Allocation Table (FAT) file system could not provide security features users would need, including permissions and editing to restrict user access to specific files. In response, Microsoft developed the NTFS file system. Today Microsoft recommends that computer users running Windows format their hard disks in NTFS primarily because NTFS-formatted files and folders provide better security.

You can access, view, and change security settings for folders and individual files. Here's how:

1. Right-click the file or folder.

2. Click Properties in the menu.

3. Click the Security tab. Figure 5.36 shows the Security tabs for a folder and a file, respectively.

Folder Properties

File Properties

Figure 5.36
Windows offers differ-ent security options for folders and files.

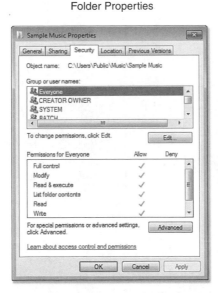
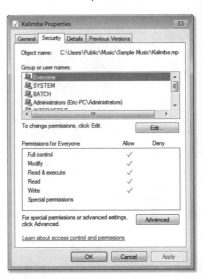

As you can see, there are only minor differences between the Security tab for a folder and the Security tab for a file. You can view the permissions for each group or username by clicking the group or username in the Group or User Names list. Change permissions for the selected group or user by clicking Edit. If you need to set special permissions or advanced settings, click Advanced.

➡ *To learn more about Windows 7 file security and other security features, **see** Chapter 31, "Protecting Your Data from Loss and Theft." You can also learn more about file management options, including file and folder encryption and managing access and control by users and groups, in Chapter 31.*

6

PRINTING

Windows Printing Primer

In most cases, installing and using a printer in Windows 7 is nearly effortless. Just plugging the printer into your computer is usually enough. Installation and setup is automatic and silent. Add ink and paper, and within a few seconds you can start printing from whatever programs you use, without thinking any more about it. It doesn't always go quite this smoothly, though, so we've devoted this chapter to the ins and outs of installing and using a printer in Windows 7.

Windows gives you control over the printing system through the Devices and Printers window, shown in Figure 6.1. To get there, click Start, Devices and Printers.

Figure 6.1 shows icons for four output devices:

- The HP LaserJet printer is shared by another computer on the network. The network cable icon above the letters HP indicates this.

- The Okidata printer is the default printer, as indicated by the check mark. It's also shared to others on the network, as indicated by the tiny icon showing two people, next to the word State. (The default printer check mark supersedes the network or sharing indicators on the printer icon itself, but all the indicators appear next to the word State.)

- The Fax device and XPS Document Writer icons don't represent actual printers, but are options for faxing and creating portable XPS documents directly from within your applications. I'll discuss this more shortly.

 tip

Devices and Printers should appear in your Start menu, but if it doesn't, right-click the Start button and select Properties. Click Customize. Scroll down through the list of available items, and check Devices and Printers.

Figure 6.1
The Devices and Printers window is the starting point for printer setup and management. It's the graphical user interface to the Windows Print Manager.

Initially, the task ribbon shows just two tasks: Add a Device and Add a Printer. If you click one of the printer icons, additional items appear: See What's Printing, Manage Default Printers, Print Server Properties, and Remove Device.

You will probably find that the first time you log on to Windows 7, one or more printer icons are already present. These may include any or all of the following:

- Icons for any printer(s) you have attached to your computer, which were detected by Windows and set up automatically.

- Icons for any printer(s) shared by computers attached to your network. Windows might discover and add these automatically or, on a corporate network, they might be installed for you by your network administrator.

- An icon for Microsoft XPS Document Writer. This is not a printer in the physical sense. XPS is a type of electronic document format comparable to Adobe's Acrobat (PDF) format. It lets any computer view and/or print the document without having to have the application that created it. If you select XPS Document Writer as the "printer" in any of your applications, the program's print function will create an XPS document file that you can then send to other people.

- A Fax icon. If your computer has a modem with fax capability, or if your organization has a network fax server, the Fax printer lets you send faxes directly from your applications without having to first print a hard copy and then feed it through a fax machine or scanner. Instead, you simply select the Fax printer from inside your application and use the normal print function.

In the next section, I'll show you how to add for new printers icons that don't appear automatically. The subsequent sections will tell you how to manage your printers.

Installing and Configuring a Printer

If your printer is already installed and operational at this point, you can skip this section and skim ahead for others that may be of interest. However, if you need to install a new printer, modify or customize your current installation, or add additional printers to your setup, read on.

You might want to add a printer in a few different instances, not all of which are obvious:

- You're connecting a new physical printer directly to your computer (obvious).

- You're connecting a new physical printer to your network (obvious).

- You want to create a formatted print file, usually PostScript file, that can be sent to a print shop (not so obvious).

- You want to set up different printer preference schemes, such as "black and white only" or "photo quality," for a single physical printer, so that you can simply select a printer icon instead of having to manually change your printer settings for each print job (obscure but useful time-saving idea).

The basic game plan for installing and configuring a printer is as follows:

- Read your printer's installation manual and follow the instructions for Windows 7 or, if there are none, the instructions for Windows Vista, XP, or 2000.

- Plug in the printer. Many newer printers are detected when you plug them into the parallel or USB port. Your printer might be found and then configure itself automatically. If it does, you can skip on down to "Printing from Your Applications," later in this chapter.

- If the printer doesn't configure itself, you can run the Add New Printer Wizard (or use a setup program, if one is supplied with your printer). We'll go over this procedure in detail in the next section.

 tip

Before you buy a new piece of hardware, it's always a good idea to check the Windows Compatibility Center on the Web at www.microsoft.com/windows/compatibility. Or, check the device's box, manual, or manufacturer's website to ensure that it's compatible with Windows 7 or Vista. If the device is listed as compatible with XP but not Vista or Windows 7, you *might* be able to use the device's XP software, but it's not guaranteed.

You should know, though, that Windows 7 comes with preinstalled drivers for more printers than are listed in the Windows Compatiblity Center. Before assuming that your old printer isn't supported, go through the manual installation procedure to see if your printer make and model is listed as an installation choice. If it's not, check the manufacturer's website for a downloadable driver.

 tip

Some printer manufacturers ask you to install their driver software *before* you plug in and turn on the printer for the first time. *Heed their advice!* If you plug the printer in first, Windows may install incorrect drivers.

If this happens to you, unplug the printer, delete the printer icon, run the manufacturer's setup program, and follow their instructions from there.

At this point, you should have a functioning printer. You might want to make alterations and customizations to the printer setup, though. For example, you can do the following:

- Right-click the icon for the printer you'll be using most often and select the Default Printer option. This way, your printer will be preselected as the printer of choice when you use the Print function of Windows applications.

- Set job defaults pertaining to paper tray, two-sided printing, scaling, type of paper feed, halftone imaging, printer setup information (such as a PostScript "preamble"), ink color, and paper orientation. These will be the default print settings that every Windows application will start with when you select this printer.

- Check and possibly alter device-specific settings such as DPI (dots per inch) and font substitution.

- Share the printer and specify its share name so that other network users can use your printer.

- If you are on a network and want to control who gets to use your printer, set permissions on the Security tab of the Properties dialog box. (You must have Computer Administrator privileges to do this.)

We'll discuss these topics in the following sections.

 note

You can select a network printer as your default printer even if you move from one network to another (as you might with a laptop that you use at work and at home). Windows 7 is supposed to remember which printer is the default printer on each network you use.

note

Printer security issues such as setting permissions, conducting printer access auditing, and setting ownership are covered in Chapter 20, "Using a Windows Network."

Adding a New Printer

How you go about adding a new printer depends on how you'll be connecting to it:

- If your printer is connected directly to your computer with a USB, parallel, or serial printer cable, you are installing a *local printer*. Installing a local printer is covered in the next section.

- If you want to use a printer that's shared by another computer on your network, you still need to set up a printer icon on your own computer. This is called installing a *network printer*.

  ➡ *For detailed instructions on installing a network printer,* **see** *"Using Printers on the Network,"* **p. 552.**

- A printer that's physically connected to the network wiring itself and not cabled to another computer is called a "local printer on a network port," just to make things confusing. We'll cover the installation of these in Chapter 20 as well. However, if you have a network-attached printer, try the standard Add Printer procedure we describe in the next section. Windows 7 is pretty smart about finding and using networked printers.

Installing a Local Printer

In most cases, Windows 7 will detect and set up a printer that's directly attached to your computer with no help at all. In some cases, it won't do this, and you might have to help. This section will help you in this case. The procedures vary, depending on how the printer is connected to your computer:

- Parallel printer port

- USB

- Network, wireless, or Bluetooth

- Infrared

- Serial port

Here's the basic game plan, which works with most printers. First, you must be logged on using a Computer Administrator account. Just follow these steps:

1. Read the printer's installation instructions specific to Windows 7 or, if there are none, look for Windows Vista, XP, or 2000 instructions. You may be instructed to install software *before* connecting the printer to your computer for the first time. This is especially important if your printer connects via USB.

2. If the printer uses a cable, connect the printer to the appropriate port on your computer according to the printer manufacturer's instructions.

3. Locate the type of connection that your printer uses in the following list as directed:

   - **Parallel port**—Connect the printer to your computer's parallel port. Windows *should* detect and install the printer. If it doesn't, open the Devices and Printers window and select Add a Printer to start the wizard. Click Add a Local Printer. Select Use an Existing Port, and highlight the LPT port number that you used for the printer—this is usually LPT1. If Windows doesn't automatically detect your printer type, follow the steps in the next section, "If the Printer Isn't Found."

   - **USB**—Install any driver programs provided by your manufacturer, and then connect the printer's USB cable to your computer. Windows will detect it and automatically start the Add A Device wizard. Because USB is hot pluggable, you don't need to shut down or restart your computer. Simply follow the instructions onscreen to finish installing the printer.

   - **Network, wireless, or Bluetooth**—If your printer can be directly attached to your network, connect it, and then click Add a Printer in the Devices and Printers window. Select Add a Network, Wireless, or Bluetooth Printer. If Windows finds the printer, select it and click Next. Otherwise, click The Printer That I Want Isn't Listed, and click Next. Enter any required information as prompted.

     If you are using a wireless network or Bluetooth, be sure that your computer's wireless or Bluetooth adapter is turned on and enabled. On some laptops these are switched off by default to conserve power.

- **Infrared**—Be sure your printer is turned on and within range of your computer's infrared eye. Also, make sure that your computer's infrared (IrDA) interface is turned on and enabled in software. Windows should detect the printer automatically and create an icon for it.

- **Serial port**—Some antique laser and daisywheel printers use a serial data connection. (If you're still using one of these, I like you already.) The next section describes how to set up a serial printer.

If Windows can't automatically detect the make and model of your printer, it will ask you to assist in selecting the appropriate type. If you can't find your printer's make and model in the list of choices, see step 5 in the next section.

note

Many new computers have no parallel port. If you have a printer that has only a parallel port connector, but no parallel port on your computer, you can purchase an add-on parallel port card for your computer. Alternatively, you can get a network parallel print server device, or USB-to-parallel printer adapter, and connect to the printer through your network or a USB port.

If the Printer Isn't Found

If your printer isn't found automatically using the options in the preceding section, you have to fake out Plug and Play and go the manual route. To do so, follow these steps:

1. Open the Devices and Printers window by clicking Start, Devices and Printers. At the top of the Devices and Printers window, select Add a Printer.

2. Select Add a Local Printer.

3. Select the port to which the printer is connected. The choices are as follows:

   - **LPT1:, LPT2:, LPT3:**—These are parallel port connections. Most computers have only one parallel port connection, LPT1. The higher-numbered ports will still appear in the list even if your computer doesn't have them—be careful.

   - **COM1: through COM4:**—If you know your printer is of the serial variety, it's probably connected to COM1 or COM2. If COM1 is tied up for use with some other device, such as a modem, use COM2.

   - **File**—If you select this port, when you subsequently print a document, you will be prompted for the name of a file into which the printer commands will be stored. The main use for this option is with a PostScript printer driver, to create a file for submission to a print shop.

   - **BTH001**—This is for printing to a wireless Bluetooth printer if you have one connected to your computer.

   - **XPS**—The XPS port provides another "save to file" function. This port directs print output to an XPS sharable document format file.

   - **Create a New Port**—This is used to make connections to printers that are directly connected to your LAN and are to be controlled by your computer. Its use is covered in Chapter 20.

   After selecting the correct port, click Next.

4. Select the manufacturer and model of your printer in the next dialog box, as shown in Figure 6.2. You can quickly jump to a manufacturer's name by pressing the first letter of the name, such as *H* for HP. Then use the up- and down-arrow keys to home in on the correct one.

Figure 6.2
Choose the make and model of your printer here.

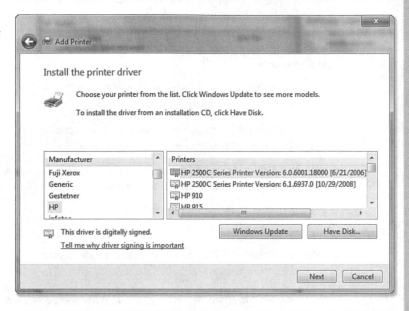

If you can't find the appropriate model, you have three choices:

- If you have an Internet connection, click Windows Update to see if Microsoft has a driver available. This might well work.

- Get the manufacturer's driver on a floppy disk or CD-ROM or download it via the Internet, open or run the downloaded file to expand its files, and then click Have Disk. Locate the driver (look for an INF file, the standard type for driver setup programs) and click OK.

- Choose a similar, compatible model and risk getting less-than-perfect output. This option can often be successful with dot-matrix printers and *older* inkjet and laser printers, but is less likely to work with modern cheap inkjet or laser printers that have no internal "smarts."

➥ *For more information on dealing with unlisted printers, **see** the next section, "What to Do If Your Printer Isn't Listed."*

If the wizard finds that the appropriate driver is already installed on your machine, you can elect to keep it or replace it. It's up to you. If you think the replacement will be better, go for it. By contrast, if no driver is listed on the machine, you may be prompted to install it or insert a disk from the vendor. On the whole, manufacturer-provided drivers tend to be newer and better than the default ones provided with Windows.

When you have selected a printer manufacturer and model, click Next.

5. By default, the printer will be named using its full model name. You can change or shorten this if you wish. Then, click Next.

6. By default, the printer will be shared on your network. The default share name is the printer's name as set in the previous step, but you can modify or shorten the share name if you wish. Some computers have trouble with names longer than 31 characters, so if you intend to share the printer, keep the name short and sweet. To help other users identify the printer, you can also type in a location and a comment.

   If you do not want to share the printer, click Do Not Share This Printer. Then, click Next.

7. If you want this printer to be your default (primary) printer, check Set As the Default Printer.

   Click Next. A User Account Control prompt may appear, confirming that you want to install the driver.

8. If you want be sure the printer is working, click Print a Test Page; otherwise, click Finish.

When you're finished, the icon for the printer appears in your Devices and Printers window.

 note

If the driver software isn't "signed" with digital proof that it came from the manufacturer that it says it came from, Windows may warn you. Permit the software to be installed only if you *know* that it came directly from a reputable manufacturer. If it came from a website other than the manufacturer's, you probably do *not* want to trust it. On a corporate network you may be prevented from installing any unsigned drivers.

➡ *If you want to share the new printer with other users on your network,* **see** *"Sharing Printers," p. 568.*

If you have just set up a printer that's connected to a serial (COM) port, right-click the printer's icon and select Properties. View the Ports tab, highlight the correct COM port line (which should be checked), and click Configure Port. Select the proper data transfer rate in bits per second (baud rate), data bits, parity, stop bits, and flow control. For *most* serial printers, these settings should be 9600, 8, None, 1, and Xon/Xoff, respectively. Finally, click OK to save the changes.

If your printer is set up and working now, you can skip ahead to the section "Changing a Printer's Properties."

What to Do If Your Printer Isn't Listed

If your printer isn't detected with Plug and Play and isn't listed in the printer manufacturer and model selection list discussed in the previous section, you'll have to find a driver elsewhere.

First, your printer probably came with a CD-ROM containing driver software. In the printer manufacturer selection dialog box (refer to Figure 6.2), click Have Disk, and then click Browse to find the Windows 7 driver files for your printer. Select the appropriate INF file and click OK.

If you can't find the disk or if it doesn't contain a Windows 7 driver, don't worry; there's still hope. Windows Vista, XP, and Windows 2000 drivers are compatible, and your disk most likely has drivers for these OSs. Virtually all printers manufactured since the late 1990s have Windows XP– or Windows 2000–compatible drivers, and many earlier printers are supported as well.

The Windows Update button lets Windows download additional printer drivers from Microsoft, and this may well obtain the correct driver for you.

If Windows Update doesn't help, your next step should be to visit the printer manufacturer's website. Check out their Product Support section, and look for a way to locate and download drivers. If you can find an appropriate driver, follow the manufacturer's instructions for downloading it. It will probably come as a compressed or executable file that has to be expanded or run, and this will put the installation files into a folder on your hard drive. You can then use the "Have Disk" feature discussed earlier to point Windows to this folder.

If neither Microsoft nor the manufacturer provides a driver, hope is fading. Still, some off-brand printers or models are designed to be compatible with one of the popular printer types, such as the Apple LaserWriters, HP LaserJets, or one of the Epson series. Also, many printer models are very similar and can use the same driver (with mostly correct results). Check the product manual or manufacturer's website to see if your printer supports an *emulation mode*. This might help you identify an alternative printer model, and you can try its driver.

 tip

Use the Internet to see if other people have run into the same problem and have found a solution. For instance, you might use Google to search for "`Windows 7 printer driver manufacturer model`", substituting in the manufacturer's name and model number. However, don't download a driver from some random site: It could be infected with a virus. Download drivers *only* from a credible corporate or institutional website.

Assuming that you have obtained a printer driver, follow these instructions to install it:

1. If you obtained a driver by downloading it from the Internet, run the downloaded file. This will either install the drivers directly or "expand" or "unzip" a set of files into a location on your hard disk. Take note of the location.

2. Follow steps 1 through 4 in the preceding section.

3. Click the Have Disk button.

4. You're now prompted to insert a disk. Click the Browse button. If you downloaded the driver, locate the folder in which the driver files were expanded or unzipped. If you have a CD, insert the CD, wait a few moments, then browse to the driver files on the CD.

   The wizard is looking for a file with an `.inf` extension, which is the standard file extension the installer setup file provided with all drivers. You may have to hunt around a bit to find a folder with drivers for Windows 7, Vista, or XP.

5. When you have located the folder with INF files, click OK. You might have to choose a printer model from a list if multiple options exist.

6. Continue through the wizard dialog boxes as explained in the previous section.

Changing a Printer's Properties

When you add a printer, the wizard adds an icon for it in the Devices and Printers window, and it's ready to go. At that point, you can start using it, or you can adjust its preferences and properties to suit your taste.

Each printer driver several sets of preference and roperties dialogs, each with enough settings to choke a horse. The basic settings are covered in this chapter, whereas you'll find those relating to network printer sharing in Chapter 20.

Different printers have different features, and your printer's driver will dictate the particular set of options that will be available. Because of the variations possible, the following sections describe only the most general and common options. (In other words, your fancy new printer may have options we've never even heard of.)

As I mentioned, there are several sets of printer properties and preferences, each of which serves a different purpose:

- **Printing Preferences**—These are the default settings that each application will start with when you use the application's Print function. These include paper size, page orientation, and paper source. Although many applications have a Print Setup command that lets you make changes for an individual document, each application starts with the selections made in the printer's Printing Preferences.

    Preferences are *per-user* settings. Each computer user can set his or her own printing preferences.

- **Printer Properties**—These are settings that apply to the printer itself, most of which tell Windows how to communicate with the printer, what capabilities and optional features it has, and so on. Printer properties also include settings that determine the initial printing preferences for each user.

- **Print Server Properties**—These are settings that apply to all printers used by the computer. They include paper size and form definitions.

The three sets of printer settings are described in the following sections.

Printing Preferences

If you find yourself having to change the same page setup settings nearly every time you go to print something, you save can yourself time by changing the setting in the Printing Preferences dialog. These settings are used as the defaults whenever you select a printer in one of your applications.

 note

Each printer has also a Properties dialog box, but on Windows 7, it's of no use because of how the new Devices and Printers window is organized. (The Properties dialog *is* useful for most other devices.) It takes a little getting used to, because in all previous versions of Windows, to configure a printer you would right-click its icon and select Properties. In Windows 7, you must use the other three choices that I just mentioned.

 tip

If the Layout tab is not present, you should be able to set the default page orientation on the Paper/Quality or Effects tabs. If your printer's preferences dialog looks like the one shown in Figure 6.3, as it does on at least some Hewlett-Packard laser printers, you must click on an icon to change the orientation. I have no idea why they'd make such an important setting so unobvious.

Figure 6.3
On some Hewlett-Packard printers, to change the default page orientation, you must click the icon in the right side of the Printing Preferences window.

Click on the page icon to switch between portrait and landscape orientation.

To change your personal printing preferences for a particular printer, click Start, Devices and Printers. Right-click the printer icon and select Printing Preferences. The number of tabs and the choices they offer vary widely from printer to printer. I describe them in general terms in Table 6.1.

Table 6.1 Printing Preferences Tabs

Tab	What It Controls
Layout	Landscape or portrait paper orientation, the number of pages placed on each sheet, and so on.
Paper/Quality	Bin or feed slot to use, type of paper, and so on.
Effects	Page resizing, watermarks, and so on
Finishing	Stapling, duplexing (two-sided printing), collating, binding, and so on.
Advanced	Printer features, color management, and in some cases, paper and layout choices.
Services	Leads to manufacturer web pages and online services.

If you want to change a printer's default preferences for *all* users, view its Printer Properties, as described in the next section, and click Printing Defaults on the Advanced tab. This brings up the Printing Preferences dialog, but the settings serve as the default settings for all users. They can then customize their printing preferences from that starting point.

Printer Properties

To make changes to a printer driver or its physical connection to your computer, or to define some of the default settings that will be supplied to every user, click Start, Devices and Printers. Right-click the printer icon and select Printer Properties. (That's Printer Properties, not just plain Properties.) This displays a dialog like that shown in Figure 6.4.

Figure 6.4
A typical printer's Printer Properties dialog box. The settings available vary among printers. Some have more or fewer tabs.

 tip

Each time you add a printer, Windows creates an icon for it in the Devices and Printers window. Although each is called a printer, it is actually just a "pointer" to the printer, much the way a shortcut represents a document or application on the Windows desktop. A given *physical* printer can have multiple icons, each with different default settings. For example, one could be set to print in landscape orientation on legal-size paper, whereas another printer could default to portrait orientation with letter-size paper. Of course, you can always adjust these settings when you go to print a document, but that can get tedious. If you create multiple printer icons for the same printer, with different, descriptive names, you can choose a setup just by selecting the appropriate printer icon.

A printer's Properties dialog box can have any of several tabs. Table 6.2 shows the general breakdown. Again, the tabs you'll see can vary depending on the capabilities of your printer.

Table 6.2   Printer Properties Tabs

Tab	What It Controls
General	This tab lists the name, location, model number, and features of the printer. From this tab, you can print a test page. You also can click the Preferences button to change your personal printing preferences (the same settings described in the previous section) Some color printers may have settings for paper quality and color control and buttons for maintenance functions on this tab.
Sharing	On this tab, you can alter whether the printer is shared with other network users and what the share name is.
Ports	On this tab, you can select the printer's connection port, add and delete ports, and in some cases configure the physical connection itself. This tab also lets you set up additional ports for network-connected printers.
Advanced	This tab controls time availability, printer priority, driver file changes, spooling options, and advanced printing features such as booklet printing and page ordering. The first two settings are pertinent to larger networks and should be handled by a server administrator. Booklet printing is worth looking into if you do lots of desktop publishing. Using this option, you can print pages laid out for stapling together small pamphlets. The New Driver button on the Advanced tab lets you replace the current driver with a better one, should this be necessary. The Printing Defaults button lets you set the default printing properties supplied to each user. They can then customize them as described in the previous section.
Color Management	On this tab, you can set optional color profiles on color printers, if this capability is supported.
Security	This tab let you control who has access to print, manage printers, or manage documents from this printer.
Device Settings	The settings on this tab vary greatly among printers. For example, you can set paper size in each tray, tell Windows how much RAM is installed in the printer, and substitute fonts.
About	Lists the printer's driver components.
Utilities	This tab, if present, might contain options for inkjet nozzle cleaning, head cleaning, head alignment, and so on.
Bluetooth	This tab, if present, contains information about your Bluetooth printer and connection in case you need to troubleshoot connection problems.

➡ *For more details about printer sharing, printer pooling, and other server-related printing issues,* **see** *Chapter 20.*

Print Server Properties

To define paper sizes or forms, or to change the location of the spooling folder that is used to hold data being sent to the printer, click Start, Devices and Printers. Select any printer icon, and then select Print Server Properties up near the top of the window.

The Print Server Properties dialog box is covered in Chapter 20 because it's mainly a networking topic.

Removing a Printer

You might want to remove a printer setup for several reasons:

- The physical printer has been removed from service.

- You don't want to use a particular network printer anymore.

- You had several definitions of a physical printer using different default settings, and you want to remove one of them.

- You have a nonfunctioning or improperly functioning printer setup and want to remove it and start over by running the Add Printer Wizard.

In any of these cases, the approach is the same:

1. Be sure you are logged on with Administrator privileges.

2. Open the Devices and Printers window.

3. Be sure nothing is in the printer's queue. You have to cancel all jobs in the printer's queue before deleting the printer. If you don't, Windows will try to delete all jobs in the queue for you, but it unfortunately isn't always successful.

4. Right-click the printer icon you want to kill, and choose Remove Device.

5. Windows will ask you to confirm that you want to delete the printer. Click Yes. The printer icon or window disappears from the Devices and Printers window.

Printing from Your Applications

When you print from Windows applications, the internal Print Manager kicks in and spools the print job for you, adding it to the queue for the selected printer. The spooler then feeds the file to the assigned printer(s), coordinating the flow of data and keeping you informed of the progress. Jobs are queued up and listed in the given printer's window, from which their status can be observed; they can be rearranged, deleted, and so forth. All the rights and privileges assigned to you, as the

 tip

The removal process removes only the printer icon in the Devices and Printers window. The related driver files and font files are *not* deleted from your hard disk. Therefore, if you ever want to re-create the printer, you don't have to insert disks or respond to prompts for the location of driver files. On the other hand, if you are having problems with the driver, deleting the icon and then reinstalling the printer won't delete the bad driver. Use the New Driver tool on the Advanced tab of the Properties dialog box to solve the problem in this case.

 tip

As a shortcut, to print a document, in many cases you can simply right-click it in any Windows Explorer view and select Print. The document must have an association linking the filename extension (for example, .doc or .bmp) to an application that handles that file type, and the application has to support printing this way for this to work. Also, you won't have the option of setting printing options. The default settings are used.

user, are applicable, potentially allowing you to alter the queue (as discussed later in this chapter), rearranging, deleting, pausing, or restarting print jobs.

If the application doesn't provide a way to select a specific printer (typically through a Print Setup dialog box), then the default printer is used. You can select a default printer from the Devices and Printers window by right-clicking a printer's icon and choosing Set As Default Printer.

➥ *For more information about file associations, **see** "Setting Folder Options," **p. 168.***

The rest of this chapter deals mostly with how to work with the printer queues of your own workstation printer or of network printers, and how to alter, pause, delete, or restart print jobs.

No Output from Printer

If your print jobs never make it out the other end of the printer, open the Devices and Printers window and work through this checklist:

- First, ask yourself whether you printed to the correct printer. Check to see whether your default printer is the one from which you are expecting output. If you're on a LAN, you can easily switch default printers and then forget that you made the switch.

- Right-click the printer icon and see whether the option Use Printer Online appears. If it does, select this item.

- Check to see whether the printer you've chosen is actually powered up, online, and ready to roll.

- If you're using a network printer, check whether the station serving the printer is powered up and ready to serve print jobs.

- Then check the cabling. Is it tight?

- Does the printer need ink, toner, or paper? Are any error lights or other indicators on the printer itself flashing or otherwise indicating an error, such as a paper jam?

- Are you printing from an MS-DOS application? You may need to use the net use command to redirect an LPT port to your Windows printer. See "Printing from DOS Applications" earlier in this chapter for more information.

- If all else fails, restart Windows. It's sad that we have to suggest this, but it sometimes does bring a zombie printer back to life.

Printer Produces Garbled Text

If your printed pages contain a lot of garbled text or weird symbols, check the following:

- You might have the wrong driver installed. Run the print test page and see whether it works. Open the Devices and Printers window (by choosing Start, Devices and Printers), open the printer's Properties dialog box, and print a test page. If that works, you're halfway home. If it doesn't, try removing the printer and reinstalling it. Right-click the printer icon in the Devices and Printers window and choose Delete. Then add the printer again, and try printing.

- If the printer uses plug-in font cartridges, you also might have the wrong font cartridge installed in the printer, or your text might be formatted with the wrong font.

- Some printers have emulation modes that might conflict with one another. Check the manual. You may think you're printing to a PostScript printer, but the printer could be in an HP emulation mode; in this case, your driver is sending PostScript, and the printer is expecting PCL.

Printing Offline

If your printer is disconnected, you can still queue up documents for printing. You might want to do this while traveling, for instance, if you have a laptop and don't want to drag a 50-pound laser printer along in your carry-on luggage. (It's hard to get them through security.)

If you try this, however, you'll quickly find that the Print Manager will beep, pop up messages to tell you about the missing printer, and otherwise make your life miserable. To silence it, Open the Devices and Printers window. Right-click the printer icon and select See What's Printing. Then, in the queue window's menu, click Printer, Use Printer Offline. The printer's icon will turn a light-gray color to show that it's been set for offline use, and Windows will now quietly and compliantly queue up anything you "print."

Just don't forget that you've done this or nothing will print even when you've reconnected your printer. You'll end up yelling at your unresponsive printer, when it's only doing what it was told. When you've reconnected the printer, repeat those steps and uncheck Use Printer Offline. This is a nifty feature, but available only for local printers, not printers shared by other computers.

Printing from DOS Applications

If you are still using MS-DOS applications, printing is one of the more problematic areas. Many modern inexpensive inkjet and laser printers don't support output from DOS programs because they don't have enough built-in smarts to form the character images by themselves. If you need laser or inkjet output from a DOS application, be sure that any new printer you buy uses a page-description language supported by your application, such as PostScript, HP's PCL, or one of the Epson text formats.

Furthermore, most DOS applications can print only to LPT ports. If you want to use a printer that is on a USB port or is out there somewhere on a LAN, you must share the printer (even if it's just attached to your own computer and you're not using a network), and then issue the command

```
net use lpt2: \\computername\sharename
```

from the Command Prompt window, replacing *computername* with your computer's name and *sharename* with the name you used when you shared the printer. Direct your DOS program to use LPT2. (You can use LPT1, LPT2, or LPT3, but you must select an LPT port number that does not have an associated physical LPT port in your computer.)

➡ *For more information about the* net use *command,* **see** *"Managing Network Resources Using the Command Line," p. 573.*

Working with the Printer Queue

After you or other users on the network have sent print jobs to a given printer, anyone with rights to manage the queue can work with it. If nothing else, it's often useful to observe the queue to check its progress. This way, you can better choose which printer to print to, or whether some intervention is necessary, such as adding more paper.

To view a printer's queue, click Start, Devices and Printers, then double-click the printer's icon. For a local printer this should display the queue window. For network printer, this displays a summary window; double-click See What's Printing to view the queue.

Figure 6.5 shows a sample printer's folder with a print queue and related information. The window displays the status of the printer (in the title bar) and the documents that are queued up, including their sizes, status, owner, pages, date submitted, and so on.

 tip

You can drag a printer's icon from the Printers window to your desktop for easy access.

 tip

When print jobs are pending for a local printer, workstation, an icon appears in the notification area, near the clock. You can hover the mouse pointer over it to see the number of your documents waiting to print. Right-click it and select the printer's name to examine the queue.

Figure 6.5
A printer's queue window showing one print job printing and one pending.

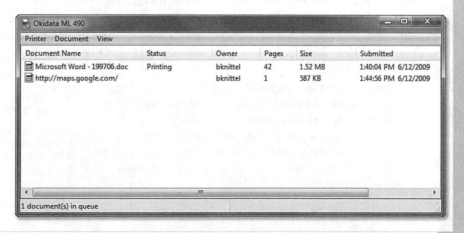

Document Name	Status	Owner	Pages	Size	Submitted
Microsoft Word - 199706.doc	Printing	bknittel	42	1.52 MB	1:40:04 PM 6/12/2009
http://maps.google.com/		bknittel	1	587 KB	1:44:56 PM 6/12/2009

Okidata ML 490

1 document(s) in queue

For network printers, to keep network traffic down to a dull roar, Windows updates the queue display only every so often. If you are printing to a network printer and want to check the current state of affairs, choose View, Refresh, or press F5 to immediately update the queue information.

Deleting a File from the Queue

After sending a document to the queue, you might reconsider printing it, or you might want to reedit the file and print it again later. If so, you can remove the file from the queue. To do so, right-click the document and choose Cancel, or choose Document, Cancel from the menu. The document is then removed from the printer's queue window.

If you're trying to delete the job that's currently printing, you might have some trouble. At the very least, the system might take some time to respond.

And, as mentioned earlier, if you are told that you don't have permission to delete another user's document, click Printer in the queue windows' menu, select Open As Administrator, follow the User Account Control Prompt to enter an Administrator's password, then try again.

 tip

By default, all users can pause, resume, restart, and cancel printing of their own documents. However, to manage documents printed by other users, the printer's owner or the network administrator must give you the Manage Documents permission.

If you find that Windows says you don't have permission to perform some function, such as deleting a document from the queue or changing printer settings, in most cases you can right-click the document or printer and select Run As Administrator to perform the operation with elevated privileges. From the pop-up menu, select the task that you were trying to perform, and try again.

Canceling All Pending Print Jobs on a Given Printer

Assuming you have been given the privilege, you can cancel *all* the print jobs on a printer. In the Devices and Printers window, right-click the printer and choose Cancel All Documents. A confirmation dialog box appears to confirm this action.

If you have a printer's queue window open, you can also select Printer, Cancel All Documents from that window's menu.

Pausing, Resuming, and Restarting the Printing Process

If you need to, you can pause the printing process for a particular printer or even just a single document print job. This capability can be useful in case you have second thoughts about a print job, want to give other jobs a chance to print first, or just want to adjust or quiet the printer for some reason.

To pause a print job, right-click it and choose Pause. Pretty simple. The word Paused then appears on the document's line. The printing might not stop immediately because your printer might have a buffer that holds data in preparation for printing. The printing stops when the buffer is empty. When you're ready to resume printing, right-click the job in question, and choose Resume.

 tip

Pausing a document lets other documents later in the queue proceed to print, essentially moving them ahead in line.

In some situations, you might need to pause all the jobs on your printer so that you can add paper to it, alter the printer settings, or just quiet the printer for a bit while you take a phone call. To pause all jobs, open the printer's queue window and choose Printer, Pause Printing. You have to choose the command again to resume printing, and the check mark on the menu goes away.

Should you need to (because of a paper jam or other botch), you can restart a printing document from the beginning. Just right-click the document and choose Restart.

Advanced Printer Management

Windows 7 comes with a printer management tool that's part of the Windows Management Console system. It's intended primarily for network administrators who sometimes have to manage dozens of printers spread around an office. I won't go into great detail on this tool here because it's fairly self-explanatory, but I'll show you how it works.

To run the tool, click Start, Control Panel, System and Security, Administrative Tools. Then, double-click Print Management. You might need to confirm the User Account Control prompt or enter an Administrator password, because this tool requires elevated privileges.

The left pane lets you choose views that include lists of all the printers installed on the local computer (or on a domain network), all printers that have documents pending, and so on. You can also create custom "filters" to select only printers with specific attributes.

Under the Print Servers section, the local computer is listed, and you can right-click the "Print Servers" title to add the names of other computers on your network (or named print server devices). You can use this feature to build a single panel that lists all your organization's printers. Print servers that you add to this list will remain in the list the next time you run the printer management tool.

XPS Print Output

Windows 7 includes support for a newer document file type called XPS, which stands for XML Paper Specification. This is a file format that represents printed output electronically. The idea is that you can view an XPS file on any computer that has an XPS viewer program, without having to have a copy of the application that created the document. For example, you can view the XPS version of a Microsoft Word document without having to have a copy of Word. If this sounds suspiciously like Adobe's PDF file format, you're right. XPS is Microsoft's attempt to create a universal electronic document format. XPS has some advantages, but PDF is so widely used and understood that we suspect XPS doesn't stand a chance.

In any case, Windows 7 does come with built-in support for XPS. You can generate XPS documents simply by following these steps:

1. Edit and format a document in one of your applications. Be sure to save the document in the application's native format, so that you can come back and change it later. You can't edit an XPS file.

2. Use the application's Print function. Most applications display the standard Windows print dialog. Select the Microsoft XPS Document Writer printer. Click Print.

3. When the Save the File As dialog box appears, select a location and name for the XPS document.

You can now distribute the XPS document to others to view and print as desired.

Windows 7 and Vista have built-in XPS document viewers. On Windows 7 or Vista, just double-click an XPS file to open and view it.

Microsoft has created tools for viewing and creating XPS files on Windows XP, which you can get from www.microsoft.com; just search for `"Get the XPS Viewer"`. This tool requires the .NET Framework, so you may need to download and install that program as well. On other operating systems, you will need to download an XPS viewer program from some other source.

Faxing

If your computer has a fax-capable modem installed, you can use it to send and receive faxes. All Windows 7 editions come with fax software built in.

To send a fax from Windows 7, set up the fax service as described in Chapter 11, "Scanning and Faxing."

Then create a document using your favorite application, click Print, and select Fax as the printer. Windows will ask you for the fax phone number and make the call—no paper is involved. The fax service can even add a cover sheet to your document on the way out. To receive faxes, your modem can be set to answer calls. When a fax arrives, you can view its image onscreen or print it, or even have it printed automatically.

Third-party fax software has more bells and whistles, and can provide fax services for the whole network, but the basic version that comes with Windows will take care of most home and small office users' needs. Windows 7 faxing can't be shared among a number of users on the LAN the same way you can share regular printers, though. If you want to provide a shared fax modem for your LAN, you should look for a third-party product.

We talk more about faxing in Chapter 11.

GADGETS AND OTHER SUPPLIED ACCESSORIES

Using Gadgets

As mentioned in Chapter 1, "Introducing Windows 7," that old monster dubbed Active Desktop back in the Windows 98 days silently slipped away into oblivion and was dropped by Microsoft after we all realized that even the fastest computer could be brought to its knees when a few Active Desktop items were running. Add a weather map, stock sticker, and headline news ticker, and mysteriously, your computer would either lock up entirely or run so slowly that it might as well have. After you rebooted, you'd see a message such as this:

```
Internet Explorer has experienced a problem or error. As a
precaution, your Active Desktop has temporarily been turned
off. To start the Active Desktop again, use the following
troubleshooting tips
```

Remember that? Enabling Active Desktop actually set Internet Explorer to be the system shell. Rather than your desktop essentially being a Windows Explorer folder, it was now much more, tying closely into Internet Explorer. If IE crashed, the house of cards came crashing down, including your interface with the operating system. The problem had to do with Active Desktop being ravenous for system resources. Add more than a couple Active Desktop elements, and the system would starve for resources, disabling other applications you might want to open or have open.

Again the question was raised: Can't we do something useful with all that otherwise barren computer landscape, especially now that screens are wider than they used to be? Apparently we have become enamored with the idea of our laptop computers being even better than video games or movie theaters in some ways. We can isolate ourselves now, with our own personal laptop wide-screen movie theaters. Give me a stack of movies and a pair of headphones, and I'm gone for days, despite my heated complaints about the demise of the taller screens. I mean, what *are* computer makers and Microsoft—and even Apple— thinking? Do engineers think that most of us use computers to watch the latest Hollywood blockbusters that we've illegally downloaded from BitTorrent? No, we're web browsing and writing documents in Office, such as PowerPoint presentations, Word docs, or Excel spreadsheets. These applications beg for taller not wider screens. If you're a writer, good luck finding a laptop with an old-fashioned 4:3 aspect ratio. Everything is now "wide," meaning also not as tall. Translate: more scrolling. (Incidentally, all the figures in this book are captured in 1024×768 resolution, which is a 4:3 ratio.)

But enough of my rant. In any case, we now have a generation of wide screen displays with gobs of extra unemployed pixels to both sides during most of the workday. That being the case, Microsoft was wise to exhume the concept of Active Desktop and give it another go, in the form of gadgets and Windows Sidebar. Gadgets are analogous to the Active Desktop add-ins or applets. If you're familiar with Mac OS X, perhaps you are thinking of Apple's Dashboard and Widgets right about now.

Windows Sidebar *was* the place on Vista's screen (left or right side) where the gadgets typically lodged themselves. As mentioned in Chapter 1, Windows Sidebar has gone away in Windows 7, which is no big loss, since it used to mysteriously disappear from Vista for no good reason. Folks often pulled gadgets onto the desktop as a workaround, and to make them bigger or to show more text, as with a news feed. True, once they were on the desktop, they could become easily obscured by other windows, but the new Windows 7 *desktop peek* feature makes it so easy to check your gadgets and then flip right back to what you were doing that this doesn't matter.

Although Windows Sidebar is gone, the Gadget Gallery that premiered with Vista remains and is now called *Desktop Gadget Gallery*. You reach the Desktop Gadget Gallery by clicking Start and typing **gadget** (which will find Desktop Gadget Gallery) or by right-clicking the desktop and choosing gadgets.

Gadgets have proven to be more stable than their predecessor Active Desktop. They should be, simply because they are built using either DHTML or the Windows Presentation Foundation. Gadgets in general perform well and do not appreciably slow down your computer the way Active Desktop used to. There is a host of third-party gadgets, many of them useful for businesspeople.

Which gadgets you put on your desktop depends on your needs, of course. Typically, you'll add a clock and a calendar,

 note

Actually, `sidebar.exe` is still the application that is responsible for running and displaying gadgets on the desktop. There just is no longer a Windows Sidebar proper.

 note

For gadgets to show on your desktop, you have to turn on Desktop Items from the desktop context menu. Right-click the desktop and choose View/Desktop Items. Note that this is a toggle, so you can also easily hide all your desktop items (including shortcuts, folders, etc.) by using this command.

a CPU and RAM gauge (to see how maxed out your computer is, sort of like having a tachometer in your car), and a notepad. If you work with international money exchanging, or travel frequently, the always up-to-date currency calculator is nice. The RSS feeds gadget connects to Internet Explorer and downloads headlines from your subscribed RSS feeds.

Figure 7.1 shows an example of a gadgets setup using some of the gadgets supplied with Windows 7. I have added a few other gadgets that I downloaded from various places on the Web. One is called Index Monitor, which lets you easily observe and control Window's indexing service.

tip

If you have multiple monitors, you can set which one will display your gadgets. You can put the gadgets on a second monitor and maximize your primary monitor for use with your main applications. As you'll see later, you can even fill up the entire second monitor with gadgets by dragging them there.

Figure 7.1
A typical desktop setup with several gadgets installed, including a local weather and temperature gauge.

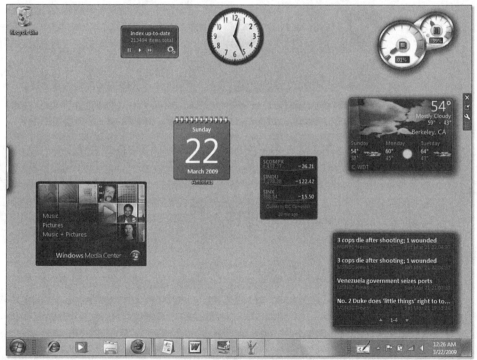

Adding New Gadgets

Microsoft supplies a stock set of gadgets to choose from. Choosing and organizing them is self-explanatory and intuitive after you learn the basics:

1. Right-click anywhere on the desktop and choose Gadgets. A dialog box with available gadgets appears, as shown in Figure 7.2.

Figure 7.2
Adding gadgets to your desktop is done through this dialog box. Use the right and left arrows to scroll through available gadgets.

2. Click Show Details to open the details for any gadget that you click. Depending on the gadget, you might see a useful description. Leave the panel open, and any gadget you click will have its details shown there.

3. Double-click a gadget to add it to your desktop. Alternatively, you can drag it to the desktop and release it where you want it.

I Can't See My Gadgets

If you find that you cannot see the gadgets even though they are turned on, first hover your mouse pointer over the Show Desktop button to display all desktop items, including gadgets. Still not working? Display the desktop, right-click it, and choose View, Show Desktop Items.

But if you want a particular gadget to always be in front of other windows, right-click the gadget and choose Always on Top.

Downloading New Gadgets

Notice that, as with all Explorer windows, there is an as-you-type search box in the upper-right corner to help you find the gadget you are looking for. If you can't find the tool for the job, try searching the Internet:

1. At the bottom of the Add New Gadgets dialog box, click Get More Gadgets Online. This will open a browser window in which you can download new gadgets.

2. To add a gadget from the web page, follow the instructions. The web page changes frequently, so we will not describe it here. Many gadgets have reviews so that you can read before trying.

3. After you decide you want to install or try a particular gadget, click Download. If it's a third-party program (which is likely), you'll see the dialog box shown in Figure 7.3.

Figure 7.3
You'll see a warning like this, even for gadgets posted on Microsoft's website. Make sure you know and trust the creator of the gadget before installing it.

4. So, should you install a foreign gadget? Consider the source. Microsoft no doubt does not post downloadable gadgets that have not been tested and approved. I would not hesitate to install any gadgets found on the Microsoft web pages. Click OK to download the gadget.

5. When downloaded, click Open. You will see a dialog box asking for confirmation, as you see in Figure 7.4.

Figure 7.4
Confirm whether you want to install the downloaded gadget. Clicking Install will launch an automated installation.

6. Click Install and the gadget is installed and added to your desktop automatically.

One gadget I find useful is called Uptime. This gadget allows you to see how much time has passed since you last restarted your computer. Even though Windows 7 is stable, restarting once in a while is a good idea, I keep an eye on this gadget to help me keep track of when to reboot. I have made the mistake of letting my computer run for a month without rebooting, to the point that it began to act weirdly and slow down.

Peeking at Gadgets

If you are working on a document that obscures the gadgets, you might want to pop the gadgets forward to check the time, headlines, or whatever. Simply click or hover over the Desktop Peek button in the lower-right corner of the screen and the desktop and gadgets will pop into view, in front of your document. Then, click the button again and they will all disappear behind the document that was previously open.

Adjusting a Gadget's Settings

If you move the cursor over a gadget, a little control panel for it will pop up. Most gadgets have settings that you can control in this way, as shown in Figure 7.5.

Figure 7.5
Most every gadget has these control buttons for closing them or adjusting settings. These buttons appear only when you hover the mouse pointer over them.

 tip

There are three types of gadgets in the current gadget universe: Windows Desktop gadgets, Windows Live gadgets, and Windows Sideshow gadgets. The Windows Live website offers gadgets that you can install on your Windows Live home page. Those gadgets won't install into Windows 7—they are a different animal. Those are Windows Live gadgets as opposed to Desktop gadgets, and they install into a customized web page and thus only appear in a browser window. Just to confuse matters more, there are also SideShow gadgets. These gadgets are for displaying information on stuff like keyboards, laptop cases, remote controls, cell phones, and the like, without having to open the device.

 note

If you are running a 64-bit version of Windows, you can only use 64-bit gadgets. Some gadgets are written for 32-bit operating systems and will not work on the 64-bit version of Windows 7. Likewise, 64-bit gadgets will not work on a 32-bit operating system.

 tip

Pressing Windows+M minimizes any open windows so that you can view your desktop. Press again and your documents reappear.

Here's how to adjust or close a gadget:

1. To close the gadget, click the X.

2. To adjust the settings for the gadget, click the wrench. (Some gadgets don't have a wrench and adjustment dialog box but may have settings on the gadget itself.) See Figure 7.6 for an example of an adjustment dialog box.

Figure 7.6
Some gadgets let you make adjustments, which will vary from gadget to gadget. This set is for the Slide Show gadget.

3. Adjust settings as necessary, and click OK.

Moving Gadgets Around

Gadgets are flexible and can be moved all around the screen. They can be dragged onto another monitor. To move gadgets:

1. Grab a gadget and drag it to the spot where you want it. To drag the gadget, click and drag the little Move Gadget button that looks like a grid. This shows up when you hover over the gadget. (See Figure 7.5, in which the grid or Move Gadget button is showing.) (With most gadgets, you can drag them from any spot on the gadget, but this is the official spot to drag with to avoid making other changes or clicking links on the gadget.)

2. Drop it where you want it. As you move a gadget around on the desktop, it can obscure another gadget. This is different from how gadgets worked in Windows Sidebar under Vista, where they automatically adjusted to make room for each other in a graphically smooth and groovy way. So you will have to manually position your gadgets. Unfortunately, the View, Auto arrange icons command reached by right-clicking the desktop doesn't arrange gadgets, only icons.

Adding a Gadget More Than Once

There is nothing to prevent you from adding a gadget to the desktop more than once. Want a pile of notepads? Lots of slideshows running at the same time? A passel of stock tickers or news feeds all visible at once? No problem. Just add them, make the adjustments, and position them as you want.

If you deal with businesses or associates in multiple time zones, for example, it would be useful to have multiple clocks on your desktop, one for each time zone. Figure 7.7 shows an example. I named the clocks using the adjustment dialog box for each one.

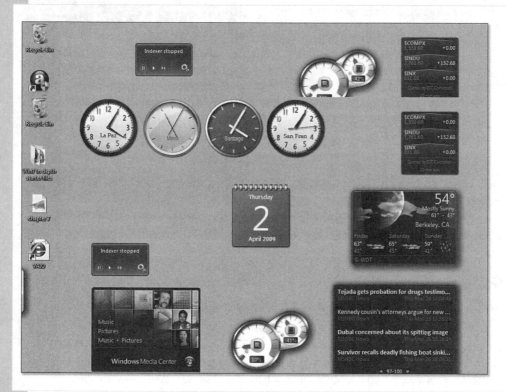

Figure 7.7
Adding gadgets more than once is possible. Here I added four clocks set for different time zones.

Changing Opacity of Gadgets

When you right-click a gadget, the pop-up menu includes an Opacity option, which determines whether you can see through the object. This is a nifty feature, owing once again to the advanced video architecture of Windows 7. What do you do with a transparent gadget? Suppose, for example, that you don't want to have to keep peeking at the desktop to see a clock but you don't want that clock to completely obscure what is behind it, as shown in Figure 7.8. Here's what you do:

1. Set the gadget to always be on the screen by right-clicking it and choosing Always on Top.

2. By default, the gadget is 100% opaque. You want to be able to see through it a bit, so opacity to the rescue. Right-click on the gadget, choose Opacity, and choose the desired level of opacity.

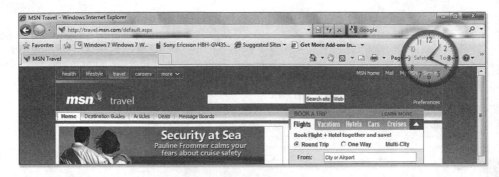

Figure 7.8
Use the Opacity setting to create transparent or semi-transparent gadgets, such as this clock.

Note that even though a gadget is transparent, moving the cursor over the gadget makes it opaque, and you cannot click something behind it. You'll have to move the gadget first.

Removing Gadgets

Gadgets you install will remain active until you close them and will persist on subsequent reboots. Likewise, if you log off and log back on, they will be reloaded.

Gadgets you download will be added to your Desktop Gadget Gallery. They will live there until you right-click them and click Uninstall. This makes it easy to activate and deactivate gadgets and still have them readily available.

As mentioned earlier, you can close an individual gadget by hovering over it and then clicking the X when its tool handle pops up. But for a more comprehensive approach that, among other things, allows you to see all the currently running gadgets and quickly remove selected ones, do this:

1. Click Start and type in **gadgets**. A series of gadget-related tasks appears.

2. Click View List of Running Gadgets. You'll see the View Gadgets dialog box, shown in Figure 7.9.

3. Click the ones you want to stop running and click Remove. Close the box when you're finished.

Even after you remove a gadget, it's not erased from your computer. It's still in the list of available gadgets, and clicking the + (add) button at the top of the Sidebar will reveal it, if you want to use it later. You can safely remove gadgets without fearing that you're obliterating them.

Installed gadgets do not appear in the Control Panel's Programs applet, so you can't remove them from your hard disk that way. You must right-click a gadget in the Desktop Gadget Gallery and choose Uninstall to remove it from your drive.

 tip

The default gadget location is C:\Program Files\Windows Sidebar\ Gadgets. Shared gadgets are located at C:\Program Files (x86)\ Windows Sidebar\Shared Gadgets.

 tip

If you are interested in making your own gadgets go to Google and search for "make build Vista gadgets."

Figure 7.9
Use the View Gadgets dialog box to see what gadgets are currently running and stop them if you want. Stopping a gadget does not uninstall it.

Using the Snipping Tool

The Snipping Tool is an application included in Windows 7, Windows Vista, and Experience Pack for Windows XP Tablet PC Edition 2005. The first time it appeared was as a Tablet PC *powertoy* back in 2002.

No Tablet PC (or any PC for that matter) is complete without the Snipping Tool, which lets you use your mouse or stylus to snip any object on your screen. This program lets you capture portions of the screen (called snips), consisting of an open window, a rectangular area you choose, a freeform area, or the entire screen. You can then annotate snips using your mouse or a tablet stylus, and save them to disk or email them. Files can be saved as images (PNG, GIF, or JPEG image files) or as an HTML page.

To open the snipping tool, go to All Programs and choose Snipping Tool, or type **snip** into the Start Search field.

Using the Snipping Tool is easy and requires only a few clicks of the mouse. When you open the Snipping Tool, your entire screen will fade, a dialog box will appear (shown in Figure 7.10), and your mouse will turn into a pair of scissors. The dialog box offers a few options regarding snipping types that will become useful. Other, smaller options do exist as well in the Options drop-down list. These options refer to the cropping line color and other various tasks.

Figure 7.10
The Snipping Tool dialog box. The screen color level drops a bit when this dialog box appears. Select the area you want snip.

The different types of snips that you can do from the screen are as follows:

- **Rectangular Snip**—This is the most common snip. You take your stylus and make a rectangular box on the screen.

- **Full-Screen Snip**—A snip of the full screen is done quickly and with a tap of the pen or a click of the mouse.

- **Window Snip**—Snip any window that you have open on your screen. Simply select the window that you want, and it will automatically be snipped.

- **Free-form Snip**—Using the pen makes this snip a lot easier to use. This snip gives you any shape—for example, a circle—that you want to make into a snip.

Each snip will be shown in a red frame by default unless you change this setting in the options. This frame lets you see exactly which section you are snipping. The Snipping Tools dialog box will also disappear when selecting your snip. After you have decided how you want to snip the current screen, simply click and hold the mouse while dragging around the snipping areas. With the entire screen faded, the selected snip on the screen will be unfaded and outlined in red (by default), as shown in Figure 7.11.

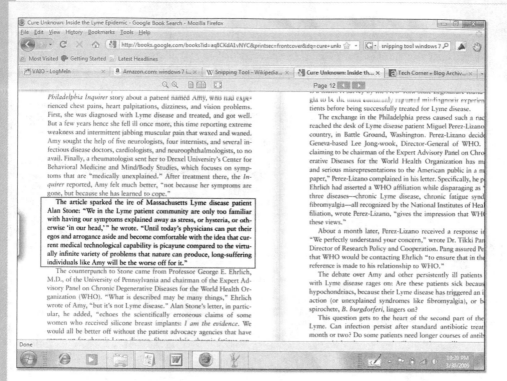

Figure 7.11 Selecting the area using the Snipping Tool.

After you select the area, the snipped area will automatically be sent to a separate window, the Snipping Tool editing window, shown in Figure 7.12. This window will allow you to draw on, erase, highlight, and save the snipped area.

When saving the snip, you are offered a variety of file extensions. You can save the snip as an HTML, PNG, GIF, or JPEG file.

Choose Tools, Options for some goodies. For example, if you choose Include URL Below Snips (HTML only), take a snip of an Internet Explorer page, and save the snip as a Single HTML or MHT file, the URL of the page will be displayed below the snip. This is an excellent way of sending bits of a

 tip

For quick access to the Snipping Tool, assign a shortcut key to it, such as Shift+Ctrl+S. To do this, right-click the shortcut in the Start menu and choose Properties. Click the Shortcut Key box and press any combination. (Some combinations will not register because they are assigned to other functions.)

web page to people without requiring that they view the web page in a browser. Simply paste the snip into an email message. This only works on HTML-formatted web pages, incidentally.

Once a snip is saved, you can reopen the snip with your browser (for HTML files) or your Paint program (for files with picture extensions). You also can copy snips directly from the Snipping Tool window and paste them anywhere as a picture type. This is a great feature if you have to copy a few words out of a document that is in a picture format or PDF. Snipping tools really benefit tablet users because a stylus pen makes snips more precise.

 tip

If you do a lot of partial screen capturing, the Snipping Tool is quite handy. If you are always capturing the whole screen, however, a quicker trick is to press Alt+Print Screen, which will capture the current active window only and send it to the Clipboard. Then switch to your target application (I use Paint, for example, for images in this book) and press Ctrl+V to paste it in.

Figure 7.12
In the Snipping Tools editing window, make the edits you like before saving.

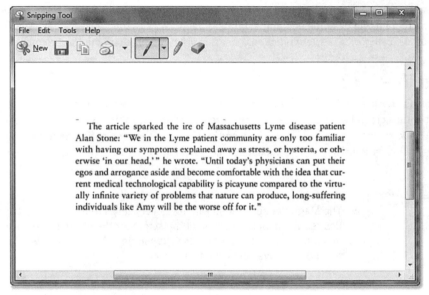

Exploring the Other Accessories

As you likely already know from using Windows in the past, a number of other freebie accessories come with Windows. Some are useful and some end up lying fallow for many PC users who never even know they exist. These little apps have been carried forward from generations of Windows going back to when I started writing about it with Windows 3.0. Because they are so well known by this point, we won't tie up book pages here with the detailed descriptions used in our past books. It will suffice here to briefly tell you what each does. Some of them, such as Calculator, Paint, and WordPad, deserve extra merit here because they were seriously updated for Windows 7.

The following sections provide a brief rundown of each program.

Narrator

This is an Accessibility tool that helps the visually impaired read text on the screen, because the computer reads aloud to you, in a synthesized voice. Obviously, you need speakers or a headset to hear this. Run Narrator by typing **narr** at the Start menu and clicking Narrator. Be careful, because the program will describe every item on the screen, and say the name of every key you press. Fine-tune the categories of events and text that this utility reads aloud via the Preferences menu.

Magnifier

This is an Accessibility tool that helps the visually impaired see a selected portion of the screen or all of the screen better by increasing the size of text and graphics. Simply press the Windows key (or click the Start button) and type **mag** and you will see the application name pop up. Click it. A small application window will appear, as shown in Figure 7.13.

Figure 7.13
The Magnifier application window is very tiny. From here, adjust settings as desired to magnify a portion of the screen or the entire screen, and set the magnification level. You can also choose how the magnification "lens" follows the mouse movements and text cursor.

There are two modes of operation: Full Screen and Lens. The first magnifies the whole screen, and the screen will pan and scan as you move the mouse beyond the edge of the screen. Lens mode will enlarge only the screen area under the mouse as it moves. See Figure 7.14 for an example. We have turned on the Color Inversion option in the Options dialog box for this effect.

Figure 7.14
The Magnifier in Lens mode with Color Inversion turned on.

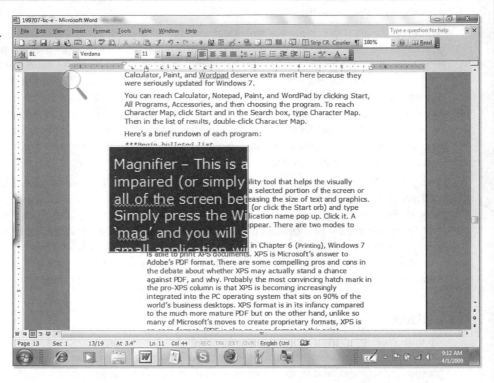

In Lens mode, there is a magnifying glass icon on the screen. Mousing over that will reveal a >> symbol. Click that to reveal the Magnifier window again in order to increase or decrease magnification with the + and – buttons. Click the gear icon to set options. Options include specifying the size of the lens (in height and width) and setting the multiplier for magnification when you click the + or – button. A nice feature for typists is that the magnifier lens can be set to follow the text insertion point.

XPS Viewer

As was discussed in Chapter 6, "Printing," Windows 7 is able to print XPS documents. XPS is Microsoft's answer to Adobe's PDF format. There are some compelling pros and cons in the debate about whether XPS may actually stand a chance against PDF, and why. Probably the most convincing hatch mark in the pro-XPS column is that XPS is becoming increasingly integrated into the PC operating system that sits on 90% of the world's business desktops. XPS format is in its infancy compared to the much more mature PDF, but on the other hand, unlike so many of Microsoft's moves to create proprietary formats, XPS is an open format. (PDF is also an open format at this point, although many people are under the misconception that PDF is a

 tip

With the advent of the little-screened "netbooks" that have become increasingly popular, Magnifier is a timely tool. Screens on netbooks are very small and often sport high resolution (translate: everything on the screen is miniscule!). Everyone who uses a netbook can potentially benefit from using this tool.

proprietary Adobe format.) This should assist XPS in getting a toehold in the otherwise PDF-dominated world of portable documents.

What this means is that you can simply print a document to the Microsoft XPS Document Writer and name the output file. You can then email or otherwise send that file to other computers or users who have the XPS Viewer installed (for XP users it is a download). In Vista, you were able to view XPS documents either in a viewer that was hosted within Internet Explorer 7 or in the supplied XPS Viewer. In Windows 7 the same is true except that the XPS Viewer has been updated. Not as sophisticated as Adobe Reader or Acrobat by far, the XPS Viewer in Windows 7 only allows you to search an XPS document for a word or phrase, zoom in and out, digitally sign documents, and set document permissions. Adobe isn't quaking in its boots yet, but it took over a decade for PDF to mature, so XPS has some catching up to do.

To run the XPS Viewer, click the Start button and type **XPS**. You should see it listed. Alternatively, click All Programs and click XPS Viewer. Of course, because of the file association set up for XPS files, clicking one will open the document in the XPS Viewer. Trying to digitally sign a document will fail unless you own a digital signature. Choose Permissions, Set Permissions, and this will lead you to Windows Live ID and the Windows Rights Management Wizard, where you can sign up for one. This will activate your machine. You can then specify permissions for the file. If you are a viewer of the document, you can see what permissions you have been granted.

Calculator

Up until Windows Vista, Calculator was a quick-and-dirty onscreen version of two traditional pocket calculators: a standard no-brainer calculator (Standard mode) and a more complex scientific calculator (Scientific mode) used by statisticians, engineers, computer programmers, and business professionals. These two modes were good for calculating your lunch bill, a list of inventory items, or the mortgage payment on your office building, but neither sported a running tape that you could use to backtrack through your calculations. Now, in the new version of Calculator that is completely updated for Windows 7, there are additional modes, views, and options. While most users will only require standard calculations, there is the previously available Scientific mode as well as a Statistics mode and a Programmer mode. Calculator will also do unit conversions for you—both date conversions and measurement conversions. For example, you can enter two dates and the application will calculate the number of years, months, weeks, and days between them. Unit conversion is extensive, including options for angle, energy, length, power, pressure, temperature, time, velocity, volume, and weight. Each of these categories has between 5 and 14 different target conversion units. For example, you can convert between foot-pounds/min to watts.

One of the best features of the new Calculator is that it has a larger screen that displays the history of calculi and lets you clear as well as edit them. We have all waited a long time for this. How many times have you been adding a list of numbers and wondered if you made an error in entry? One of the best features of the running "tape" is that you can backtrack and edit your entries after the fact by double-clicking that entry's line on the tape. If you do so, the application will display the original calculation result and the altered result when you press Enter, so you can easily compare them.

Finally, there is a Template mode that offers three calculation templates: Gas Mileage, Lease Estimation, and Mortgage Estimation. Plug in a few variables and click Calculate and you have your result. For example, provide the values for distance and fuel consumption, and your miles per gallon is calculated. With Lease Estimation things are pretty much the same, only there are more fields to fill in: lease value, period of time, number of payments per year, residual value, interest rate, and periodic payment. The same principle applies for Wage and Mortgage Estimation. Figures 7.15 and 7.16 show examples of two Calculator modes and templates.

Figure 7.15
Calculator in Programmer mode with the Template set to Length conversion.

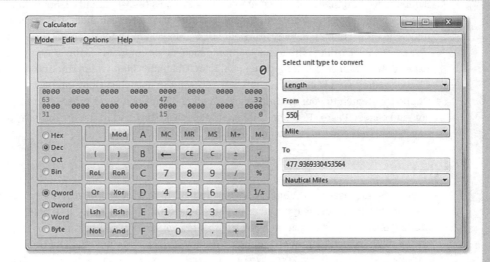

Figure 7.16
Calculator in Scientific mode and Template set to Mortgage Estimation. Notice the running "tape" in the left pane. Double-clicking an entry allows you to edit an entry to correct it or to do a "what if?" adjustment without reentering everything.

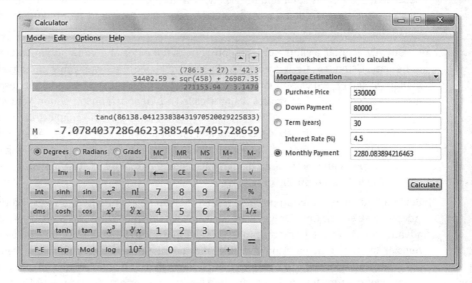

Character Map

Character Map is a utility program that lets you examine every character in a given font and choose and easily insert into your documents special characters, such as trademark (™ and ®) and copyright symbols (©); foreign currency symbols (such as ¥), accented letters, and nonalphabetic symbols (such as fractions, ¾); DOS line-drawing characters (+), items from specialized fonts such as Symbol and Wingdings; or the common arrow symbols (←, →, ↑, and ↓). Some fonts include characters not mapped to the keyboard. Character Map lets you choose them, too, from its graphical display. The Program Map displays Unicode, DOS, and Windows fonts' characters. You can choose the character set, rearrange the items in a font (such as grouping all currency types together) to eliminate hunting, and search for a given character. Character Map works through the Windows Clipboard. You simply choose a character you want to use, click Copy, and it moves onto the Clipboard. Switch to your destination application (typically a word processing file), position the cursor, and choose Paste. To reach Character Map, click Start and in the Search box, type `Character Map`. Then, in the list of results, double-click Character Map.

Paint

This is another perennial Windows accessory that, like Calculator and WordPad, Microsoft finally realized either had to be updated or put out to pasture. With so many free pixel editing programs around, one wonders why it is necessary to keep Paint out of the pasture, but perhaps it's to show off the new "ribbon" interface and help Windows 7 look more unified. The ribbon was introduced and popularized by Office 2007. We personally dislike the ribbon because it uses up increasingly precious vertical screen real estate (as we see more wide screens on laptops and monitors) and because it rearranges itself and messes with what was a good thing—menus and commands that stay put. But alas. The version of ribbon integrated into Paint and WordPad with Windows 7 is called the "Scenic Ribbon."

Essentially, Paint is a simple drawing program that creates and edits bitmapped images in a variety of formats. Using free-form drawing tools, text, and special effects, you can create projects such as invitations, maps, signs, and wallpaper for your desktop, and you can edit images linked into documents created by other programs. Paint is called a *bitmapped image editor*. Your computer's screen is divided into small dots (*pixels* or *pels*) that are controlled by the smallest division of computer information—*bits*. A *bitmap* is a collection of bits of information that creates an image when assigned (*mapped*) to dots on the screen. This bitmap is similar to one of those giant electronic billboards in sports arenas that can display the score, a message, or even a picture by turning on and off specific light bulbs in the grid.

Being a bitmapped drawing program, rather than an object-oriented drawing program such as Adobe Illustrator or CorelDraw, Paint has some significant limitations to keep in mind—also some advantages. After you paint a shape, you can't move it independently. You can use the computer to remove an area of the painting and place it somewhere else—as if you were cutting out a piece of the canvas and pasting it elsewhere. But all the dots in the area get moved, not just the ones in the shape you're interested in. Paint can store output in a variety of formats: BMP, DIB, JPG, TIF, GIF, and PNG.

Paint for Windows 7 is the tenth iteration of Paint included in a Windows OS (originally called Microsoft Windows Paint in Windows 1.0) though it is dubbed version 6.1. (Vista's version was 6.0.) In addition to the new toolbar previously mentioned, including a configurable Quick Access Toolbar (QAT), Paint now also has full PNG alpha channel compatibility. People who work with transparent color channels in PNG files will appreciate this, perhaps eliminating the need for an additional image editing program in their software suites. There are also now 9 brush types instead of 12 (as in the XP and Vista versions) but those brushes are much more expressive. Whereas they used to be just shapes, now they are textures such as waterbrush, crayon, oil brush, highlighter, and pencil. There are now 23 predefined smooth-drawing shapes instead of just 4. Figure 7.17 shows a screenshot of Paint.

Figure 7.17
The new Paint version 6.1 further promotes the Microsoft "ribbon" user interface and adds a few useful and expressive features.

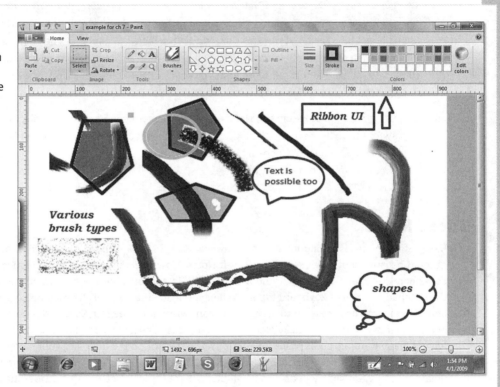

Notepad

Notepad is a simple, no-frills text editor that does no fancy formatting (though it does enable you to change the display font) and is popular for composing "clean" ASCII (.txt) files. I use Notepad to jot down quick notes. You could say Notepad is a *text editor*, whereas WordPad (see the following discussion of WordPad) is a *word processor*. Unlike WordPad, Notepad cannot view or edit Microsoft Word (.doc) or Rich Text Format (.rtf) files. It's a perfect tool to call up whenever you need to view a simple README.TXT file or fine-tune some program code (programmers like this tool). Although they're visually boring and lackluster, text files do have some important advantages over formatted text documents. Most importantly, they are the lowest common denominator for exchanging text between different programs and even between different types of computers. Literally any kind of word processor and many other types of programs, from email tools to databases, can share textual information using simple text files, regardless of computer type or operating system. To be sure your recipients who are using other kinds of computers can read a text email attachment or a text file on a disk, stick with the simple text files such as the ones Notepad creates. Windows recognizes any file with a .txt extension as a text file and opens it in Notepad when you click it.

My Text Is Chopped Off

If you can't see all the text in a Notepad window you must manually turn on word wrap to get the text in a file to wrap around within the window. By default, word wrap is turned off, which can be annoying. The good news is that word wrap is now a persistent setting. After you turn it on and then close Notepad, it should be on the next time you run it. If you need to edit program code, be sure to turn off word wrap, or your program lines will wrap, making editing and analysis of code more confusing.

If you still can't see enough text, Notepad now supports changing the font display. Change the display font from the Format menu. Choosing a monospaced font (for example, Courier) might help you line up columns. Choosing a smaller font and a proportional font (for example, Times) crams more text into the window.

Sticky Notes

Using Sticky Notes is analogous to using physical Post-It Notes. You might take their function for granted because they look like simple Post-It Notes. However, they are quite sophisticated and can be a boon to Tablet users. As of Windows 7, Sticky Notes works with pen input (write directly on the notepad) as well as keyboard typing. When you reach the edge of the note using the stylus, the note will enlarge as necessary to accept your handwriting or drawing. Scratchout gestures have been implemented as well. Sticky Notes can be organized as a stacked pad of notes. So, instead of having many different notes stuck on your physical desk or on the edges of your computer monitor, you have just one little pad and can easily scroll through all the notes. This enables you to write whatever you want and even draw a small picture. Take Sticky Notes into consideration the next time you need to jot down a list of important items, such as a grocery list. Click the Sticky Notes icon on the taskbar to alternate between showing and hiding all your notes.

Another neat feature of Sticky Notes is its capability to record a sound. This sound is stored by the Sticky Note and can be played as many times as you want or need. Little verbal reminders can be a great way to keep you updated. To leave a short verbal reminder, click the red Record dot and Sticky Notes will start recording. Click the stop button when you are done recording or when the time of recording has run out.

To play the sound, click the Play button. The recording will be deleted only when you delete the note or record over the sound.

WordPad

For more capable word processing than Notepad can accomplish, you can use WordPad. Many people think they need to purchase Microsoft Office (which includes Microsoft Word) to do serious word processing, and Microsoft would love you to do so, but it is not necessary. Though it's not Microsoft Word, WordPad works fine for most everyday writing chores. And now with the updated Windows 7 version that includes some tasty additions, this is even truer. As mentioned elsewhere in the book, WordPad also now includes the Scenic Ribbon that debuted with Office 2007, supposedly easing use.

WordPad offers most of the formatting tools people need for typical writing projects, and the price is right. You can edit documents of virtually any length, it supports drag-and-drop editing, and it can accept graphics pasted into it from the Windows Clipboard. WordPad enables you to do standard character formatting of font, style, and size; paragraph formatting of line spacing, indents and margins, bullets, justification, and right and left alignment; adjust tab stops; search and replace; and insert headers and footers. It has pagination control, lets you insert and edit graphics, and has Undo and Print Preview.

 note

To get around the display issue stated above, you can download the free Word Viewer program from Microsoft. Search microsoft.com for Word Viewer. You want the download named "Word Viewer," not "Word Viewer 2003." Also download and install the Microsoft Office Compatibility Pack for Word, Excel, and PowerPoint 2007 File Formats. Together, these two downloads let you open, view, and print any Microsoft Word program with all formatting intact. (There are similar free viewer downloads for Excel and PowerPoint.) With the Word Viewer and the Compatibility Pack installed, you can open, view, and print any Microsoft Word document; you just won't be able to edit or save it.

WordPad doesn't do tables, columns, indexes, or master documents; it also doesn't have outline view or legal line numbering. Go get Word or WordPerfect if you have that level of word processing needs. WordPad can open and save documents in Rich Text Format, text files such as Notepad creates, Unicode, Word for Windows (`.doc` and now `.docx` files from Office 2007), and Windows Write format (`.wri`). WordPad correctly opens even incorrectly named (wrong extension) RTF and Word 6 files if you select the All Documents option in the Files of Type area in the Open dialog box or type the document's full name. If WordPad doesn't detect a file's format, it opens it as a text-only file. Note that if a document contains formatting information created by another application, it will likely appear as garbage characters mixed with the document's normal text.

Adding and Modifying Tab Stops

If you find that Inserting and adjusting tab stops in WordPad is a pain, there is an easier way. You can easily insert and adjust tabs in WordPad by clicking in the ruler area. Choose View, then click the Ruler button to turn on the ruler. Then, click in the ruler area where you want to insert a tab stop. You can drag the cursor left and right to see a vertical rule to align the stop. To kill a tab stop, drag it out of the ruler area into the document.

As of Windows 7 (WordPad 6.1) it is now easier to insert pictures by simply clicking a Picture button on the Home ribbon. See Figure 7.18. However, the more-extensive Insert menu of version 6.0 is gone. In the old WordPad it was possible to easily insert all kinds of object items such as PowerPoint slides, Excel spreadsheets and charts, Word documents (if you had Office installed, obviously), and other OLE objects right into a WordPad document. With WordPad 6.1 your options (at least via the ribbon and menu) are limited to pictures and date/time, although the Paint Drawing button on the ribbon makes it very easy to cook up a graphic right there in your document. Just click the button, do your drawing in Paint, and click the red X to close the Paint window. Your image is dropped into the WordPad document. Resize and reposition as necessary.

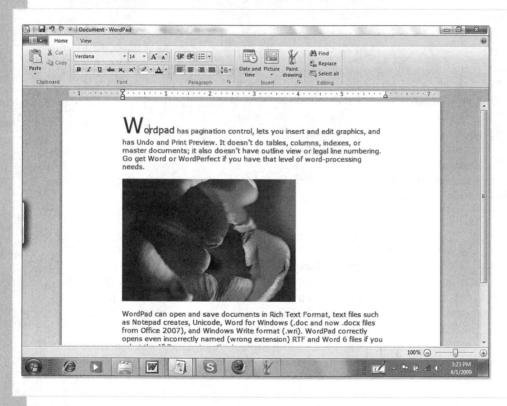

Figure 7.18
WordPad 6.1 features the Scenic Ribbon and makes dropping in or creating pictures easier. But it still has its limitations.

MULTIMEDIA AND IMAGING

IN THIS PART

8	Windows Media Player	231
9	Windows Media Center	251
10	Windows Imaging Tools	277
11	Scanning and Faxing	293
12	Sound Recorder, DVD Maker, and Other Multimedia Tools	313

8

WINDOWS MEDIA PLAYER

Learning the Basics

Windows Media Player (WMP) has grown into a pretty amazing application with multiple personalities. Its talents include playing music and video files from online sources or local drives (including DVDs), playing online radio and TV stations, displaying specialized web pages, organizing your music files (MP3s and WMAs), burning music CDs, copying and syncing to portable MP3 players, and providing a conduit to online media shopping sites. Windows 7 includes an updated version of WMP that sports a refreshed user interface, additional features, and some much-welcomed interoperability. WMP 12 has divided Now Playing and Library views into separate interfaces.

Media Types Compatible with WMP

WMP can play the file types shown in Table 8.1.

Table 8.1 Windows Media Player–Supported File Types

File Type	Filename Extension(s)
Music CD (CD audio)	.cda
Intel Indeo video	.ivf
Audio Interchange File Format (digitized sound)	.aif, .aifc, .aiff
Windows Media (audio and video)	.asf, .asx, .wax, .wm, .wma, .wmd, .wmv, .wvx, .wmp, .wmx, .wpl
Windows Media Center video	.dvr-ms
Windows video and audio	.avi, .wav
QuickTime content*	.mov, .qt
Windows Media Player skins	.wmz, .wms
MPEG (Motion Picture Experts Group) video	.mpeg, .mpg, .m1v, .mp2, .mpa, .mpe, .mp2v, .mp2, .mp4
AU (UNIX audio)	.au, .snd
MP3 (digital audio)	.mp3, .m3u
MIDI (Musical Instrument Digital Interface)	.mid, .midi, .rmi
DVD video	.vob
Advanced Audio Coding	.aac

Formats not supported: RealNetworks (.ra, .rm, .ram), iTunes (.m4p, .acc).

* Only QuickTime files version 2.0 or earlier can be played in WMP. Later versions of QuickTime require the proprietary Apple QuickTime Player.

DVD Playback in Windows 7

Windows 7 versions that include Media Center have native DVD playback capability. If your version of Windows 7 does not contain Media Center and you want to play back DVD video and **.mp2v** files, you must first install a hardware or software DVD decoder on your system. (If you insert a DVD and it doesn't run, it's likely you need an appropriate video coder/decoder, or codec, or the DVD has copyrighted content playback restrictions.) WMP 12 attempts to automatically detect required codecs and provides a download location where applicable.

Installing a decoder is typically a simple software update you can download from the Web. To get a DVD decoder, search the Web for **WinDVD** or **Power DVD**. The decoder will cost you a few bucks, probably around $10. (Although current boxed editions of both players are around $50–$60.)

Getting Around in Windows Media Player 12

WMP 12 has a redesigned user interface, as shown in Figure 8.1, to make it easier for you to manage and enjoy your digital media. The classic menus still exist (hidden by default) but navigational tabs have been replaced by simplified breadcrumb navigation, making managing and viewing your digital media easier than ever. The Now Playing drop-down button is still there, but it's now relocated in the bottom-right corner of the Library view. Now Playing now operates in a separate control window.

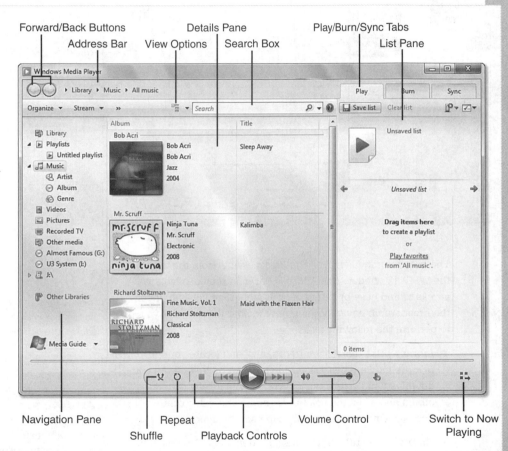

Figure 8.1
The redesigned Windows Media Player user interface is much easier to use.

Navigating Menu Breadcrumbs

The breadcrumbs in WMP 12, shown in Figure 8.2, provide a way to quickly focus on the task you want to perform by giving you efficient access to lower-level categories (for example, Library > Playlists, or Library > Music > Artist).

Breadcrumb Trail

Figure 8.2
New redesigned breadcrumbs in Media Player 12.

The breadcrumb navigation trail is accessible from the top of the WMP 12 window (the Address bar) and provides instant access to and easy browsing of your stored media. Just under the breadcrumb navigation is a new toolbar that enables you to perform the following tasks:

- **Library**—Use this feature to organize and locate your favorite media types you've downloaded or created. As you download and create music, WMP automatically generates album and artist information for audio and video content. You also can view content by type and by genre.

- **No Disc**—The title of this category defaults to No Disc if no media disc is in your CD or DVD-ROM drive; otherwise, it

 tip

Many visualizations are available online for use with WMP 12. A personal favorite of mine called PixelTrip can be obtained from the WMP website at www.wmplugins.com/ ItemDetail.aspx?ItemID=881. *Another excellent visualization* is provided by Brian Spangler and is called TwistedPixel. You can download it from his website for free at www.visolu.com/TwistedPixel.

assumes the name of the volume stored in that drive. WMP analyzes multimedia content stored on disc to obtain album names, movie titles, and associated tracks or chapters.

WMP 12 groups and relocates options for Play, Burn, and Sync to a separate window pane off to the right side, with tabs for each as follows:

- **Play**—Drag and drop items to create a playlist and save or clear playlist entries. WMP 12 also makes audio and video playback easier on remote devices with the Play To icon (placed to the right of Clear List and next to List Options), which remains gray until you connect a media player device. The List options button reveals settings to hide, sort, and save lists, as well as skipped playlist entry options, and help topic access.

- **Burn**—After you download or convert music tracks to WMA format, use this feature to transfer your music mix to writable CDs (CD-R or CD-RW media).

- **Sync**—After you download or convert music tracks to WMA format, use this feature to transfer your music mix to portable audio players designated "Compatible with Windows 7."

Isolated at the bottom-left corner is a button labeled Media Guide. This option enables you to purchase media online or select from a variety of online content.

The menus below each button provide quick access to settings and options relevant to the task of that tab. For instance, as shown in Figure 8.3, the arrow below the Organize button provides the options for managing libraries, sorting media selections, layout options, and quick access to the Options dialog.

 tip

When you copy music, WMP can prevent copied tracks from being played on any other computer to limit distribution and enforce media usage rights for copyright-protected music. If you want to disable this feature so that you can move copied music from one PC to another, choose Organize, Options and select the Rip Music tab. Then uncheck the Copy Protect Music check box under Rip Settings.

 tip

Be sure you fill your CD with all the music you want to play; unlike conventional CD-mastering programs or Windows 7's Copy to CD feature in other parts of the OS, WMP's Copy to CD feature closes the CD (so it no longer can accept data) after you copy your selected music to it, even if you use only a small portion of the CD. Why? Standalone CD players are designed to handle single-session CDs and won't work if you add music later. If you want to create a CD for playback on your computer, use Windows Explorer's Copy to CD feature instead, which will allow you to copy music over several sessions.

 tip

To show the classic menus, right-click an empty area of the taskbar or an empty area around the playback controls and select Show Menu Bar or press Ctrl+M.

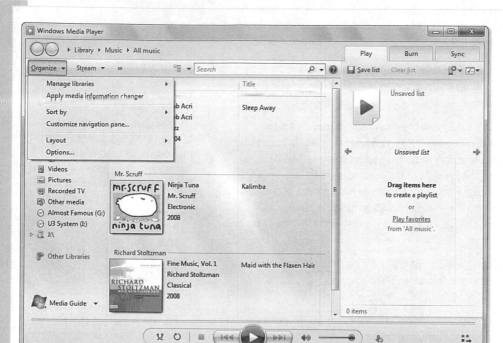

Figure 8.3
New tab menus for accessing options in Windows Media Player 12.

Redesigned Browsing and Searching

The navigation of the Music library is similar to that in Windows Explorer.

You can browse your media by performing the following steps:

 note

For the best browsing and search experience, ensure that the media information is correct and up to date.

1. Click the Library breadcrumb (or the leftmost breadcrumb in the trail) to choose the type of media to browse, as shown in Figure 8.4. Options include Music, Videos, Pictures, Recorded TV, Other Media, and Playlists.

2. Choose the desired view for your media by clicking the arrow next to the media option you've chosen. This includes Artist, Album, All Music, Genre, and more.

3. Narrow the items shown for the chosen category by clicking the arrow on the Address bar, as shown in Figure 8.5.

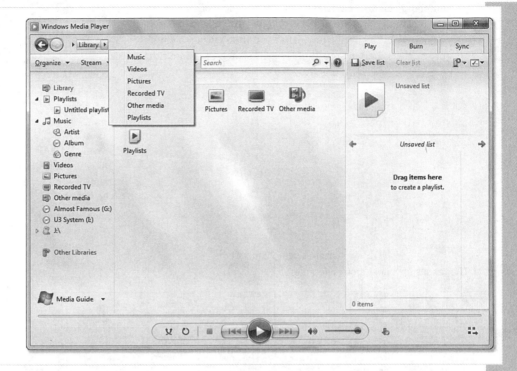

Figure 8.4
Select a media category.

Figure 8.5
Narrow the items shown in the view by using the Address bar.

Searching can also be used to narrow the view of a chosen media category if there are several entries to choose from and you only want a specific few. After you have chosen a category as described in Step 1, enter your search term into the Search box, as shown in Figure 8.6.

tip

You can further arrange the display for a given category by clicking the View Options button placed left of the Search box.

note

To return to a higher level in the current view, click the desired level in the Address bar.

Insert a search query here.

The results of your search appear here.

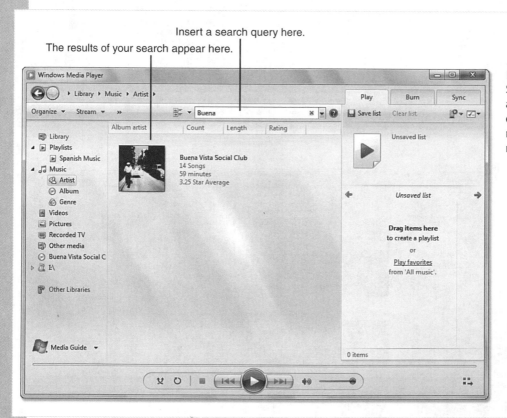

Figure 8.6
Searching is a fast and easy way to narrow your media views.

Playing Audio and Video in WMP 12

There are three options for playing audio and video media in WMP 12. These include audio CDs and video DVDs, media stored on your hard disk, and media accessible over a home network.

Playing an Audio CD or DVD

To play an audio CD or DVD in WMP 12's new Now Playing window, follow these steps:

1. Insert the CD or DVD you want to play into your computer's CD-ROM or DVD-ROM drive. The audio disc will begin playing.

2. Click the icon indicated by three squares and an arrow pointing right, located in the bottom-right corner, as shown in Figure 8.6. This switches to a miniature window with its own controls.

3. While a disk is playing, you can use the Play/Pause, Previous, and Next buttons of the playback controls shown in Figure 8.7 to navigate the songs or chapters on the disk, or you can right-click above the Now Playing window and select Show List to select from any song on the disc.

 tip

To play a DVD in full screen, click the Full Screen option of the right-click context menu shown in Figure 8.7 or press Alt+Enter while the video is playing or paused.

Figure 8.7
Select the CD you want to play from the Now Playing menu.

Playing Media Stored on Your Hard Disk or Network Share

To play an item stored on your hard disk, add it to the library following the instructions in the section "Adding Items from Your Computer to Your Library" later in the chapter. After you add the item to the library, you can select the media you want to view by double-clicking it in the Library view. If you want to add an item to the current playlist, right-click the item and select Add to Playlist. Playlist items can be navigated using the same playback controls described in the previous section.

➡ *To play media shared over your home network, **see** the section "Sharing Media Throughout Your Home," p. 248.*

Getting Music and Video on Your Computer

WMP offers many ways to add media to your media library. These methods include ripping music from CDs to your computer, purchasing media from online stores, and adding media items already stored on your computer to the library.

Ripping Songs from CDs onto Your Computer

The process of copying music from a CD to your computer and converting it to a format that WMP understands is known as *ripping*. Songs ripped using WMP automatically appear in the media library for playing.

To rip music to your computer, complete the following steps:

1. Click the Organize menu on the WMP main window and select Options. The Options dialog box appears.

2. Select the Rip Music tab, shown in Figure 8.8.

3. Choose the desired format and bit rate for the file by adjusting the Audio Quality slider. Also select the desired options from the Format drop-down list. For more information on these options, see "Choosing a File Format" and "Choosing a Bit Rate" later in this section.

 tip

When playing large amounts of media from your library, you may want to have WMP randomly choose the next song to play or shuffle your playback. To do this, click the Turn Shuffle On button shown in Figure 8.1.

 note

For best results when ripping music, make sure your computer is connected to the Internet. When connected to the Internet, WMP retrieves media information for inserted CDs and stores it in the ripped media files. If the media information is incorrect or missing, you can add it or edit it after ripping. In addition, the filenames of the ripped music files can be set to use this media information in different ways. To do this, click the Burn Options icon (the drop-down arrow located in the upper-right corner) on the Burn tab and select More Burn Options. In the Options dialog box, you can change the rip music location by clicking Change in the Rip Music to This Location section. You can change the ripped music filename by clicking File Name in this same section and formatting the filename as desired. I choose to use Track Number followed by the Song Title with a space as the separator. I use this because it results in a very neat Music folder when organized.

Figure 8.8
Change the format and bit rate on the Rip Music tab of the Options dialog box.

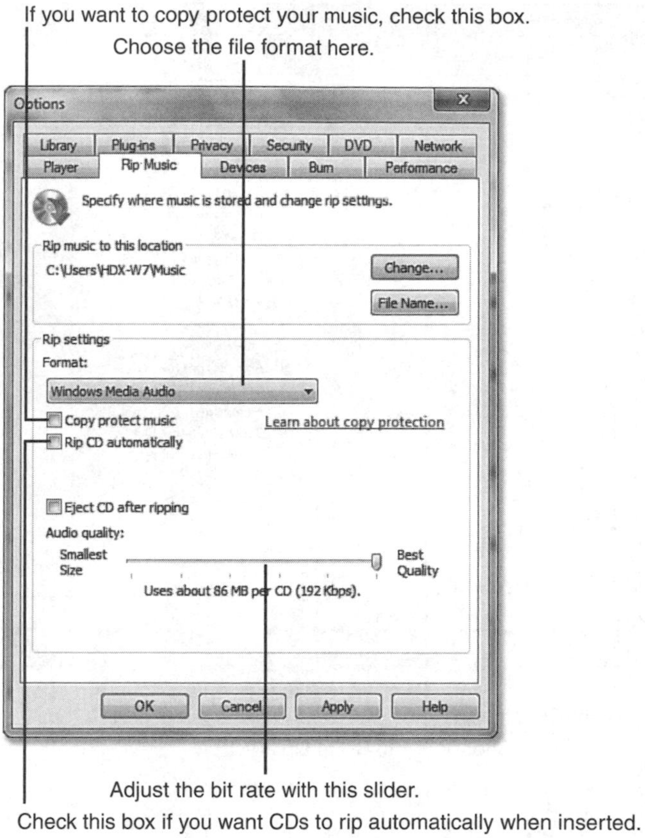

If you want to copy protect your music, check this box.
Choose the file format here.

Adjust the bit rate with this slider.
Check this box if you want CDs to rip automatically when inserted.

4. Insert a CD into the CD-ROM drive and right-click the desired audio disc in the Navigation pane, as shown in Figure 8.9. Select Rip CD to Library.

5. After WMP has started ripping the CD, you may choose to uncheck songs that you do not want WMP to rip to your computer. You can also stop or start by clicking the Rip CD to Library option from the right-click context menu of the CD/DVD drive entry in the Navigation pane, the Rip CD/Stop Rip button that appears next to Create Playlist (when a disc is inserted).

🔍 **note**

WMP 12 can begin ripping automatically when you insert a new CD and the Rip CD Automatically box is checked (disabled by default). Automatic ripping options can be changed by clicking Organize, select Options, and then open the Rip Music tab.

Figure 8.9
The Rip menu used for copying from CDs to your computer.

Right-Click the CD

Choose Rip to CD to Library

Choosing a File Format

By default, WMP 12 uses the Windows Media Audio format. This format offers a balanced combination between sound quality and file size. Other formats are available in the Format drop-down list on the Rip Music tab of the Options dialog box:

- **Windows Media Audio Pro**—Ideal for portable devices because of its higher sound quality at low bit rates

- **Windows Media Audio (Variable Bit Rate)**—Results in smaller file size with the same audio quality

- **Windows Media Audio Lossless**—Provides the best audio quality with the largest file size

- **MP3**—Provides added flexibility with similar audio quality and a slightly larger file size than Windows Media Audio

- **WAV (Lossless)**—Another lossless format, providing added flexibility with high audio quality and large file size

Adding Items from Your Computer to Your Library

By default, WMP searches certain folders on your computer for media files and automatically adds these files to your library. If your media does not appear in the library automatically, it is located in a folder that is not monitored by WMP. To change the folders that are monitored, perform the following steps:

 tip

To add .m4a, .mp4, .m4p, or .aac files from iTunes to your WMP library, you must first convert the files to a compatible format such as Windows Media Audio or MP3. Many software programs convert media files, such as Xilisoft Audio Converter. To find one of these programs, search Google for "`Audio Converter`" and look for one that supports your desired source file type.

1. Right-click the Music entry in the Navigation pane and select Manage Music Library. You may individually configure Music, Videos, Pictures, and Recorded TV.

2. Make your appropriate selection (we've chosen Music for this example).

3. As shown in Figure 8.10, you can Add or Remove monitored folders.

Figure 8.10
Add new libraries with the Music Library Locations dialog box.

Taking Your Music and Video on the Go

WMP provides many ways that make it easier than ever to take your music and video files with you. WMP has built-in functions for burning CDs, synchronizing files to your portable media player, and sharing your media throughout your home network.

Media Player and Windows Compatibility Versus iTunes and iPod

One of the first questions that I am asked is, "Should I get an iPod or another type of MP3 player?" Having used a large number of portable music players in the past, I would recommend one of the excellent, more featured alternative players. If you are choosing a new portable device, the first consideration is the software you currently use for your digital media. If you currently use iTunes for your digital media management and purchasing, you should definitely choose the iPod because it would integrate with your current media system. However, if you currently use WMP or any other PC-based media software, I recommend using WMP in conjunction with a WMP-compatible device.

Of the portable devices I have used, the Creative Zen X-Fi, found at www.creative.com, is by far a superior device. The device has an incredible screen offering 16.7 million colors to view your video as well as extremely crisp audio provided by Creative's patented audio processors. The player also includes the ability to listen or record FM radio and support for free audio and video podcasts from www.zencast.com. Other advantages over the iPod include an expansion slot for Secure Digital (SD) or SDHC memory. The Zen provides a much larger number of formats, which is its main advantage over the iPod, in my opinion. Instead of being limited to a couple of audio and one video format, the Zen offers support for the WMA, MP3, and WAV audio formats as well as MPEG1/2/4-SP, WMV9, Motion-JPEG, DivX, and XviD.

All compatible devices also support the large number of online content providers available through WMP 12 instead of being restricted to only one provider, as iTunes/iPod is, the iTunes Store. For this reason, it is my recommendation to choose WMP 12 and a compatible device over iTunes and the iPod as long as your current media software is not iTunes.

Burning Customized CDs

WMP provides the capability to create customized CDs for playing in your home or car CD player. Before you can burn a CD, you must first have a Windows 7–compatible CD burner and a blank CD-R disc. To burn a custom CD, perform the following steps:

1. Begin by selecting the Burn tab.

2. Click the arrow on the Burn tab and select Audio CD (if not specified by default), as shown in Figure 8.11.

3. Insert a blank CD into your CD burner drive.

note

If you have multiple CD burners, you can change the destination burner by clicking Next Drive in the List pane of the Burn tab, as shown in Figure 8.12.

Figure 8.11
Select Audio CD from the Burn Options menu on the Burn tab.

Figure 8.12
Use the Burn tab to change the destination drive, set up the Burn List, and start the burn.

4. Create the list of songs to burn by dragging items from the Details pane to the Burn List. To remove items from the list, right-click the item and choose Remove from List. You can rearrange items by clicking and dragging the songs to match the order you desire for your CD.

5. Under the Burn tab, choose Start Burn, as shown in Figure 8.12. The current progress can be viewed in the Burn List.

Syncing Files to Your Portable Media Player

The first step to synchronizing your files with your portable media player is to choose a portable device. Many players will work with WMP, but for the best experience, you should look for a device that is branded Certified for Windows 7.

 note

As you add items to the Burn List, you will notice that the time remaining, or free space on the disc, decreases to account for the newly added songs. If you choose more files than can fit on a single CD, you can choose to remove some items or have WMP automatically split the list to burn two CDs.

TiVo "To Go"

TiVo Desktop software (which you can obtain freely from TiVo.com) enables you to publish your PC media collections to your TiVo. TiVo Desktop Plus (which you must purchase) provides transfer capability and also enables you to convert media libraries for playback on iPods, PSPs, and other compatible devices. You must first have a TiVo connected to your home network (see your TiVo manual for how to accomplish this task) with at least one recording transferred from your TiVo DVR to your TiVo Desktop Plus. After you've transferred recordings to your PC you can add them to your WMP Library as described in "Adding Items from Your Computer to Your Library," earlier in this chapter, and sync the files to your device automatically or manually, as described next. See tivo.com/mytivo/howto/gettivoanywhere/howto_transfer_to_ipod_pc.html for more information.

Windows 7 compatibility (that is, "Compatible with Windows 7") carries the assurance that vendor products meet with Microsoft standards (in this case, Windows 7 Media Player) for easy installation and reliable operation. When shopping for your compatible media player, look for the Compatible with Windows 7 logo shown in Figure 8.13.

Figure 8.13
Compatible with Windows 7 branding indicates compatible products and services for the device.

After you have your device, open WMP and connect the device to your computer. WMP gives you the option to choose between Automatic and Manual sync methods when first setting up synchronization. For a description of these methods, see the corresponding section that follows. If you decide later to change the sync method then right-click the media player entry in the Navigation pane and choose Properties. On the Sync tab you can then select or clear the Start Sync When Device Connects check box.

 tip

Due to the healthy rivalry between Microsoft and Apple, iPod users cannot directly synchronize media libraries and playlists using WMP. However, compatibility plug-ins overcome this obstacle, enabling iPod synchrony with WMP. For one such example, see www.mgtek.com/dopisp.

Choosing What Syncs Automatically

If your device is set to sync automatically, the items selected to sync will be updated each time you connect your device to your computer. To select the items that will be synchronized, follow these steps:

1. Click the Sync Options icon on the Sync tab, and select Set Up Sync.

2. In the Device Setup dialog box, shown in Figure 8.14, you can choose the playlists that are synchronized with your device. Using the available playlists, click Add to sync the selected playlist with the device. To stop a playlist from synchronizing, select it in the Playlists to Sync list and click Remove.

tip

To make sure your favorite playlists sync in the event that your device runs out of storage space, use the priority arrows in the Device Setup dialog box to set the priority of the selected playlist. WMP 12 defaults to manual mode when there is insufficient space to synchronize playlists.

Figure 8.14
The Device Setup dialog box allows you to choose the playlists to sync and their priority.

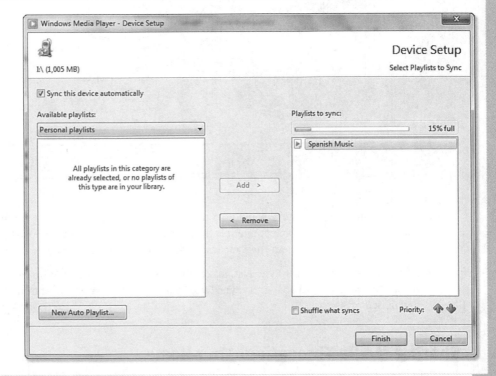

Selecting Item to Sync Manually

If your device is set to sync manually, each time you want to make changes to the files on your device, you must create a list of files to sync. To remove files from your device, navigate the device using the Navigation pane to find your file. Right-click the file and choose Delete. To set up a list of files to sync to the device, perform the following:

1. Select the Sync tab and clear the Sync List by clicking the Clear List button, as shown in Figure 8.15.

Figure 8.15
The Sync tab enables you to manually set up your Sync List for your device.

2. Find your media in your library and drag them to the List pane to add them to the Sync List, as shown in Figure 8.15. To select multiple items, hold down the Ctrl key while selecting your media. To remove items from the Sync List, right-click the item and select Remove from List.

3. After you have set up your Sync List, make sure that all the items will fit on your device by looking at the List pane just above the Sync List. Remove any necessary items from the Sync List and click Start Sync.

Sharing Media Throughout Your Home

Before you begin to set up media sharing throughout your home, you will need to make sure you have all the required equipment. To enable media sharing, you need a home network and a networked digital media player. A networked digital media player, also known as a digital media receiver, is connected to your network and plays the content shared by WMP on your Windows 7 machine. Suitable digital media receivers include other Windows 7 PCs and the Xbox 360, as well as a number of standalone units that can be found by visiting microsoft.com/windows/windowsmedia/devices/default.aspx.

To connect a digital media receiver to your network, you can use an Ethernet cable or a wireless network adapter. Consult the documentation that comes with your device for more information on getting it connected to your home network. If you are connecting another Windows 7 PC as a digital media receiver or setting up a new home network, see Chapter 17, "Creating a Windows Network."

After your device is connected to the network, turn it on and complete any configuration steps that may be needed to finalize the installation. After your device is fully connected and operational, complete the following steps to enable media sharing on your Windows 7 PC with your newly installed digital media receiver:

1. Click the Stream menu and select Turn On Media Streaming With HomeGroup from the drop-down options.

2. In the Media Streaming Options dialog, click the Turn On Media Streaming button, as shown in Figure 8.16.

 tip

To change what library items are shared with new devices by default, open Control Panel, select Networking and Internet, choose HomeGroup, and enable or disable shared library entries. To change what library items are shared with a certain device, click the Choose Media Streaming Options link (under Share Media with My Devices), highlight the appropriate device entry, and click Customize.

Figure 8.16
The Media Streaming Options dialog box is shown if media streaming is currently disabled.

3. Select the types of media you're willing to share among HomeGroup computers (for example, Pictures, Video, Music) and which computers to allow or block, then click OK.

4. The first time through you are given an automatically generated HomeGroup password. Write this down and click Finish.

 caution

Not all shared media will play back on your digital media receiver. Check your device's documentation for information on supported media types. Also note that media obtained from online stores may be supported only if purchased and might not be supported if obtained from a subscription service.

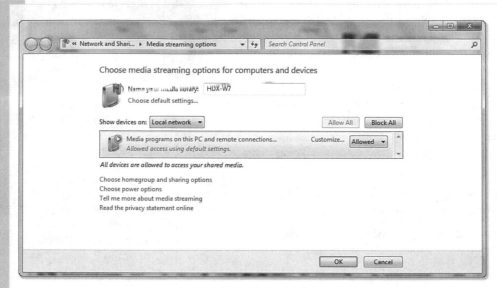

Figure 8.17
The Media Streaming dialog box shown if media streaming is enabled. Notice the addition of the device list.

After you have sharing enabled, you are ready to play your media on your new digital media receiver. For information on how to do this, see the documentation that came with your device. If your digital media receiver is another Windows 7 PC, the shared media will appear in the Navigation pane of WMP 12, as shown in Figure 8.18.

Figure 8.18
Accessible shared media appears in the Navigation pane of WMP. Remote library entries are named after the remote computer's given name and appear after the Other Libraries entry.

9

WINDOWS MEDIA CENTER

Windows Media Center—What's the Hubbub?

Windows Media Center (or *WMC* as I'll refer to it from here on out) is included in Windows 7 Home Premium, Professional, Enterprise, and Ultimate editions. All other versions of Windows 7 do not include the WMC components. WMC is an outgrowth of Microsoft's interest in evolving the common PC into a multimedia entertainment center. Due to specific hardware requirements, which include a TV tuner capture card with built-in MPEG-2 video encoding and decoding, a high-end graphics card with a minimum of 64MB of video memory, DVD recording, a fast processor, and other goodies, WMC is usually purchased as a preloaded component on a new PC.

With the advent of the Windows Anywhere initiative, users without WMC-compatible hardware can purchase the hardware separately, install it, then upgrade the OS to an appropriate version of Windows 7 and enjoy WMC on their PC.

 note

Complete books have been written about Windows Media Center Edition (the predecessor to WMC-equipped versions of Windows Vista), and I expect new books will be written about WMC as well, although I believe that within a week's time of experimentation, a fairly savvy user can discover the ins and outs of WMC on her own. It certainly helps to have a bit of a primer, however, with some tips scattered throughout. That's what this chapter is all about.

WMC adds the capability to do the following with a large TV-like interface using a remote control:

- Display and record TV shows

- Listen to cable, broadcast, and Internet FM radio

- Rip and play music CDs

- Play DVDs

- Manage and display your digital photographs

- Record DVDs

Of course, as you know, you can rip music CDs, play DVDs, and display your digital photographs using Windows Media Player and Windows Photo Gallery, as described elsewhere in this book. WMC essentially puts a new skin on those functions and integrates them with TV viewing and a few other goodies. Windows 7 Media Center includes easier access to IPTV content and TV guides, rich touchscreen capabilities, and a variety of tools for accessing, navigating, and searching through video content.

As we know, Microsoft (often standing on the shoulders of innovative giants) has helped push the industry to new heights, or at least to take a deep breath on the technology ascent, by codifying standards. Whether through fostering cooperation among technology companies or by forcing its own agenda, it doesn't much matter. Progressive standards for such things as data CD recording, sound and video cards, high-resolution color displays, energy conservation, standardized I/O ports, Plug and Play (PnP) interfaces, as well as greater overall computer performance have often been championed by Microsoft. Standards, of course, serve Microsoft because its bread and butter depends on selling OSs that can run reliably on as many brands and models of PCs as possible.

WMC is an exciting milestone in the evolution of PC OSs that began in earnest back when the first spec for a multimedia PC (MPC) was issued by Microsoft. I remember writing, even somewhat wistfully, about the MPC in my earlier Windows books (3.11 and 95). At that time, it was a big deal to include in PCs the now-ubiquitous sound cards and CD-ROM drives. (I recall purchasing my first outboard SCSI-based CD-ROM drive from Toshiba for $600 and change.) The next step (learning from the woefully underpowered MPC spec) was the Entertainment PC 97 spec. The minimum system requirements for the Entertainment PC 97 are a 150MHz Pentium chip, a 256KB Level 2 cache, 32MB of memory, 3D audio, and the Universal Serial Bus. This spec was a subset of the Simply Interactive PC (SIPC) spec, to be technically accurate.

Of course, bloatware applications and the increasing speed demands of the once-gluttonous Windows itself also spurred the demand for quicker PCs. Unfortunately, this comes at some cost to the environment as well as our pocketbooks, as we feel obliged to continuously dispose of older computers and upgrade to newer ones. On the upside of this unceasing speed and size war (the belief that bigger and faster are always better) comes the likes of WMC. Were it not for lightning-fast CPUs, video cards, hard drives, front-side buses, DVD drives, and inexpensive color displays, PCs couldn't begin to tackle exotic, highly data-intensive tasks such as DVD playback and TV recording.

Following on the heels of the popular TiVo digital video recorder (DVR) and competing systems such as ShowStopper

 tip

You'll find a lot of WMC information at www.hack7mc.com/ and www.microsoft.com/windowsxp/using/mce/default.mspx.

(from Panasonic) and ReplayTV (from ReplayTV), the WMC attraction to many is driven primarily by its capability to mimic a DVR. Although, as I mentioned, WMC also gives you MP3, CD, and DVD playback and digital photo slideshows, we could already do those with Windows Media Player and the Windows Picture and Fax viewer, respectively. The only difference in those departments is the delivery medium: WMC lets you control the show from the comfort of your armchair, using a remote control. The show itself plays on your TV or, preferably, through your TV projector in your home theater.

The idea of a computerized house—especially for entertainment delivery—is so appealing that home builders are beginning to build WMC machines, along with in-wall wiring and integrated large plasma screens, into newly built homes. Some developers are doing this on a large-scale basis, in hundreds of homes. This helps housing developers differentiate themselves from the competition.

Speaking of competition, alternative hardware and software packages have been on the market for some time that do all that WMC does, but it's more of a mix-and-match approach to creating a home-entertainment PC. For TV viewing and recording, you have to add hardware such as a TV tuner/video card to your PC, be sure that the sound card and TV tuner work together, and so on. You can record and play back TV and even do text searches through recorded captions, looking for hot words in, say, a newscast. A quick search on the Web reveals a few well-liked products, including

- CyberLink PowerCinema

- SageTV Media Center

- SnapStream Beyond TV

Some of these programs have numerous features that WMC is missing, such as web-based control and media-server capability.

What's New in Windows 7 Media Center?

Microsoft has upped the ante in terms of value-added features for WMC customers new and old alike. Many original features remain intact, but more importantly there are much-needed upgrades to the way existing features function and multimedia collections are accessed, displayed, or navigated. Windows 7 makes multimedia a core component of its operation to include native DVD playback (in other words, no third-party software installation), support for unprotected iTunes music, and support for AVCHD video from popular high-definition (HD) digital camcorders.

The following features cover most of what's new in Windows 7 WMC:

- Start menu improvements include text visibility for enhanced readability and increased icon size for better viewing. WMC is now visually less cluttered than previous versions, the Start menu overlays any currently playing media, and it also recalls the last location strip between sessions instead of resetting to TV and Movies.

- Now Playing features upsized thumbnails, improving visibility over the miniscule proportions of Windows Vista, which irked many users. The thumbnail tile's title is situated for better readability and usability—particularly among international versions of WMC in which foreign languages make for long title displays.

- Music library enhancements further improve user-friendliness, especially with regard to large audio collections. Obscure albums lacking album art are no longer treated to bland blue backgrounds with white text—random color schemes now help those entries visually blend with other artwork within the Music Library gallery.

- Music Now Playing is treated to a much-welcomed makeover. WMC begins music playback at the Now Playing page, but after a while the action items (for example, View Queue, Visualize, Play Pictures, Shuffle, Repeat, Buy Music) fade away into an animated backdrop of scrolling album cover art—a neat visual effect. If you press a remote control button or move the mouse, the action items come back into full view against the backdrop of album covers.

- Content rating is even easier through Rating Shortcuts. Press numeric buttons 1 through 5 on your remote or keyboard to rate music and pictures in real time.

- Turbo Scroll caters to large media collections. Hold down on left or right directional buttons to transition into an abbreviated content listing ordered in alphabetical chunks. Let go on the appropriate letter combination to position the library at an exact location.

- Shared Libraries builds upon the Home Group features of Windows 7 and is common across Music, Pictures, Video, and Recorded TV. You can peruse and enjoy content from a variety of computers on your home network and select among local media collections or browse among remote shared media libraries.

- Ambient Slideshow enhances the Pictures viewing experience. It launches both in screensaver mode and upon invoking the new Play Favorites feature on the Start menu. Ambient Slideshow corresponds directly to the content rating system by playing only the pictures you've rated as 3 stars or higher. Also provided are zooming features, zooming animations, and slideshows within slideshows for enhanced picture viewing experiences.

- Videos library enhancements are purely functional—no cosmetic changes are involved. Like other categories (Pictures, Music, and Recorded TV) it draws upon the Shared Libraries feature for remote and local media collections. H.264 (MPEG-4) playback is supported by default and the Video Play All feature cycles through all entries in a specific category in continuous playback mode. You can also resume previous playback exactly where you left off.

- Integrated TV Pack Enhancements provides additional support for Asian, European, and U.S. TV-viewing customers. Apart from upgrades for foreign audiences, the seek bar is interactive and allows you to select relative positions within playing content. Users that enjoy mouse navigation in WMC can enjoy greater interactivity than before.

Aside from functional improvements, Microsoft has gone to great lengths to improve the visual aspect of WMC. There are lots of subtle behavioral changes and visual improvements that further enhance the WMC customer experience. And with greater availability across a variety of Windows 7 products, WMC is fast becoming a fixture of the modern media-rich lifestyle.

The WMC Hardware

Suffice it to say that WMC machines have considerable hardware requirements. At the very least, a WMC machine has the following:

- A remote infrared (IR) sensor that enables the remote control to communicate with the computer and that also controls the cable or satellite set-top box

- A fast graphics card for smoothly displaying moving images such as video and TV playback

- A TV tuner that captures the television signal from a cable, satellite, or HDTV antenna source

- A hardware encoder that enables you to record TV shows from cable, satellite, or HDTV antenna to your computer's hard disk in real time

- A TV output jack so that you can display WMC content on a TV connected to your computer

- A digital audio output that allows you to integrate digital audio from your computer into an existing home-entertainment system

You can read about Windows Media Center feature set and related information at www.microsoft.com/windows/windows-media-center/default.aspx.

High-Definition TV (HDTV) Requirements

WMC is not limited to watching, or recording, TV in standard-definition TV (SDTV) format. HDTV shows, movies, and DVDs can also be watched or recorded on your computer. Unfortunately, you need different hardware to do so than the average WMC computer has available. So, just what will you need to achieve your goal of watching HD video? Well, at a minimum consider the following:

- **An HD input source**—This can be a cable box, satellite (I have a Hughes HR10-250 with DirectTV HD programming and TiVo software for DVR), or broadcast (over the airwaves) TV with an output your computer TV tuner can use as an HDTV input source.

  A hybrid HDTV tuner can tune and record only one signal (either analog or digital) at any given time. Combo HDTV tuners for the PC can perform both simultaneously. Tuners with High-Definition Multimedia Interface (HDMI), Digital Video Interface (DVI), or YPbPr (analog video signal carried by component video cables) aren't far away, in my opinion.

- **An HDTV tuner for your computer**—If you are purchasing a new Windows 7 computer with WMC, make sure it has an HDTV-compatible tuner. If you are upgrading your existing computer or building your own, look for a new tuner with HD capabilities built in.

- **A powerful video card**—Video memory is used during the overlay process to display the output from your TV tuner. HDTV requires more video memory (than SDTV) to display on your monitor without losing frames. Look for a video card with a minimum of 128MB, with 256MB recommended and 512MB preferred if you plan to use multiple output monitors.

- **A vast amount of storage**—HD video requires an enormous amount of disk storage. Video compression is also a requirement to lower the storage needs to a reasonable, cost-effective solution. To give you an idea for comparison, my TiVo box that uses MPEG-2 video compression and has 500GB of storage can record 515 hours of SDTV but only 77 hours of HDTV. Luckily, terabyte disk drives have recently become available at reasonable cost.

- **An HDTV display**—Although you can watch HDTV on your computer, you really will not get the most out of it without an HDTV display of 40 inches or more to view your HDTV shows.

- **A reasonable budget**—External terabyte disk drives as of this writing cost under $200 for a bare-bones model. Internal drives are available, and you can expect to pay a premium for them. Video cards with 512MB of video memory cost a few hundred dollars. The cost of HDTV displays, fast processors, fast RAM, and so on, all add up.

The New WMC PC Form Factors

As of this writing, no brand-name manufacturers provide complete ready-to-run systems running Windows 7 Media Center. If you can't find what you want in a brand-name system by the time this book reaches your hands, you can have a local computer builder design the perfect system for you. If it meets the minimum requirements for Windows 7 Home Premium, Professional, or Ultimate, it should be upgradable to the latest edition of WMC.

WMC PCs come in a wide variety of form factors that push the outside of the envelope of what we call a PC. They range from boxes that look much like PCs to those that most definitely do not. Figure 9.1 shows an example of several WMC PCs. As you can see, there's a trend to blend the look of the PC with home-entertainment gear such as a stereo receiver. This is becoming the preferred form factor for audiophile types who don't want their WMC machine to take up a lot of space or to look like a computer. This design also allows the computer to be rack-mounted or stacked with other A/V gear.

Due to the miniaturization of large hard disk storage, proliferation DVD writers, and availability bright wide-screen LCDs, another class of WMC-based computer has recently emerged: portables. These power-packed portable entertainment systems come in three flavors—a laptop computer on steroids, a Tablet PC, and a small, dedicated playback-only WMC machine. Figure 9.2 shows a small, dedicated WMC portable tablet device from Samsung. The Qosmio has a TV tuner card in it. However, some WMC laptops do not record TV, owing to the lack of a TV tuner card. Virtually all the small, portable WMC tablet-format devices are playback-only devices as well.

Figure 9.1
WMC PCs take major liberties with the physical appearance of a PC.

Figure 9.2
Laptops can run WMC, too, if they sport the necessary hardware. Dedicated tablet-format WMC machines are also available.

As of this writing, you can find some information about WMC PC hardware at www.microsoft.com/windows/windows-media-center/get-hardware.aspx.

Is Windows Media Center Based on Home or Business Versions?

Good question. I've had some debate with friends and colleagues about this. Media Center Edition (MCE) 2004 was based on Windows XP Professional. It included the capability to join a domain and encrypt the file system. When MCE 2005 came out, these features were no longer available, indicating that the 2005 version was based on the Home version of XP. This inability to join a domain handicapped business users and indicated that Microsoft's primary focus for MCE was the home user. That decision must have generated a lot of negative feedback to Microsoft because the current version of MCE is included in a home version (Windows 7 Home Premium) and a business-capable version (Windows 7 Professional and Ultimate).

Can I Upgrade My Non-WMC PC to a WMC PC?

You might be wondering, "Can I install WMC on my own PC if I have the right hardware?"

You can if you have the right hardware and purchase a copy of Windows 7 Home Premium, Professional, or Ultimate. Each of these versions includes WMC and supports a wide range of hardware. You can purchase any of these versions as upgrades for previous Windows MCE computers; however, you do not need a WMC computer to use these products. You can also purchase a standard version and replace your current OS. Some compatible video/TV cards are as follows:

- AVerMedia AVerTV Combo ATSC/NTSC/QAM Tuner Card

- LEADTEK WinFast HDTV200

- HAUPPAUGE WinTV-HVR-2250 TV Tuner Card

- ASUS My Cinema EHD3-100 Dual Hybrid

- Diamond ATI TV Wonder HD 650 Combo Card

- DViCO FusionHDTV7 Dual Express DUAL HDTV/Analog TV Tuner Card

Microsoft makes a remote control for WMC machines, which I suggest picking up. It has useful keys along the top edge to control movies, skip commercials, and adjust the system volume. Figure 9.3 shows a typical remote.

tip
You'll find a lot of WMC hardware information at the Microsoft Partner Directory at www.microsoft.com/ windows/products/winfamily/ mediacenter/partners/default.mspx.

Figure 9.3
Example of an IR remote control designed for WMC.

If you want to research how to upgrade to WMC or create a homebrew WMC box, you might want to do some web surfing. One such site available at the time of this writing is www.tomshardware.com/ reviews/windows-7-htpc,2159.html.

Basic WMC PC Hookup

If you've had the joy (or job) of setting up a home-entertainment system or home theater, you know how convoluted the wiring can become. Assuming you have mastered the typical scenario with a TV or projector, an A/V switch, multiple video input devices, Dolby 5.1 (or 7.1) sound, and consolidating your remote controls, installing a WMC computer into your A/V arsenal is a relative no-brainer. Figure 9.4 displays a sample of the potpourri of gear you can integrate into a WMC setup.

Leaving out the Cray computer, five digital HD video dishes on the roof, and the four subwoofers you're likely to have accumulated over time if you're a home theater nut, Figure 9.5 shows a typical basic WMC hookup.

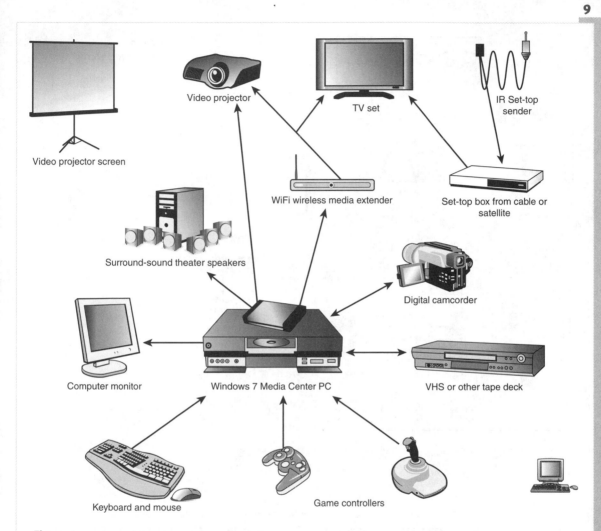

Figure 9.4
A Windows 7 WMC PC can serve as a creativity and entertainment center, integrating a mess of equipment.

Notice in Figure 9.5 that a relationship exists between the cable or satellite box and the infrared blaster that connects to the IR receiver for the WMC remote control. This allows the single remote control to also control the cable/satellite box.

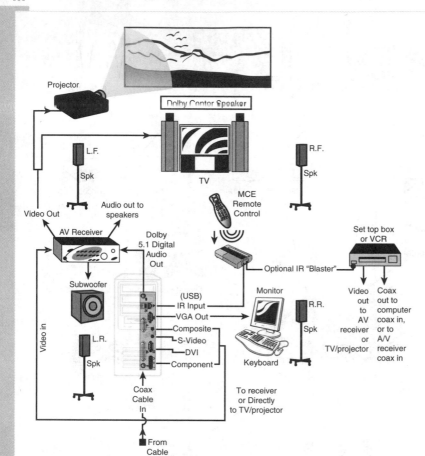

Figure 9.5
A typical WMC wiring diagram.

Also note that, depending on your computer's video card, you have more or fewer options for output to external display hardware (projectors, TV, and computer video displays). Most WMC computers have at least a composite video output with which to drive your TV or projection unit. For the cleanest image, though (especially if you are using a projector), you need a higher-resolution video connection. The next step up is an S-Video output. Obviously, your TV/projector must have an S-Video input for this to work. Moving up from there, many projectors have a VGA input, just like on the back of a computer monitor. I run a long VGA extension cable from my WMC machine to my projector using such a cable. I can run the projector in 1024×768 mode with a nice resolution and even do word processing or web surfing on my 10-foot screen, sitting in an easy chair with a wireless mouse and keyboard.

My TV Tuner Is Not Working

If you have a Media Center tuner that either is not supported by Windows 7 or does not work under Windows 7, you can often resolve the problem by going to your manufacturer's website, downloading the latest Windows 7 driver, and installing it. This worked for me on my Toshiba Satellite with an external USB TV Tuner. If you have supported hardware, but the driver fails to load, you need to determine why. Some helpful troubleshooting device driver suggestions can be found in Chapter 26, "Keeping Windows 7 and Other Software Up to Date."

For the ultimate in clarity, you have to use the DVI as your conduit to the projector. My projector (Sanyo Z2) has a DVI connector, as does my PC. The catch here is that DVI cables are expensive, whereas VGA cables are not, and S-Video and composite video cables are super cheap. Some sites online will sell you DVI cables at a fraction of what they charge at computer stores, though. (An excellent cable source is www.csccable.com.) Keep in mind when considering your connection type that clarity will go from best to worst, in this order: DVI, VGA, component, S-Video, composite.

Media Center Extender

After folks catch on to the idea of WMC computers, they will not want to be trapped in the one entertainment room the computer is directly tethered to. A series of gadgets called the Media Center Extender lets you gain access to PC-based content for any connected (wired or wireless) TV or monitor within the house. To this aim, Microsoft is focusing on a new generation of products that will allow access to digital entertainment, such as live and recorded TV, photos, movies, and music that resides on a Windows 7 Media Center PC from any room in the home.

Since the release of the first version of Media Center in 2004, a variety of hardware makers have released products with Media Center Extender technology embedded in them. This includes many new TVs, set-top boxes, and the Microsoft Xbox 360. Set-top boxes ship with remote controls. These products typically range in price from $100 to $250.

Other manufacturers, incidentally, are working on their own implementations of this grand idea, independently of Microsoft. Onkyo, Sony, InterVideo, Linksys, and HP are some of the manufacturers releasing similar hardware devices and systems, some of which will work with WMC and some of which will be for their own platforms. We're beginning to see many (mostly wireless) schemes for integrating more and more of the home with the computer-based entertainment system.

 tip

Here's a video about how to set up an Xbox 360 as an extender: www.microsoft.com/windowsxp/mediacenter/videos/Xbox360connection.asx.

Here's a good FAQ on Media Center Extenders: www.microsoft.com/windows/products/winfamily/mediacenter/extenderfaq.mspx.

The WMC Functions

As mentioned earlier in this chapter, WMC is simply a program that runs as a shell on top of Windows 7. The program path is %SystemRoot%\ehome\ehshell.exe.

The shell has a large-print GUI that at first suggests it is designed for people with vision disabilities. It is certainly a boon to the visually impaired, but the thinking behind the interface was to make it easier to read on a TV screen. If you've ever used WebTV, you know what I mean—reading normal computer-sized text on a TV set can send you running to the optometrist for a checkup.

note

The "eh" means "electronic home," which is an overarching Microsoft initiative for developing the networked home of the future, based on Microsoft technology.

When you boot a WMC-enabled computer, it comes up looking like any normal Windows PC. Nothing notable happens until you run the WMC program. Your desktop and Start menu sport a little green icon that launches the WMC interface. Then, you see the WMC Start screen. When it appears, maximize the window; it then looks like the screen shown in Figure 9.6.

The number of options on the Start screen varies depending on the hardware in your computer. If you don't have an FM radio function on your TV card, for example, you won't see any radio functions (as is the case here).

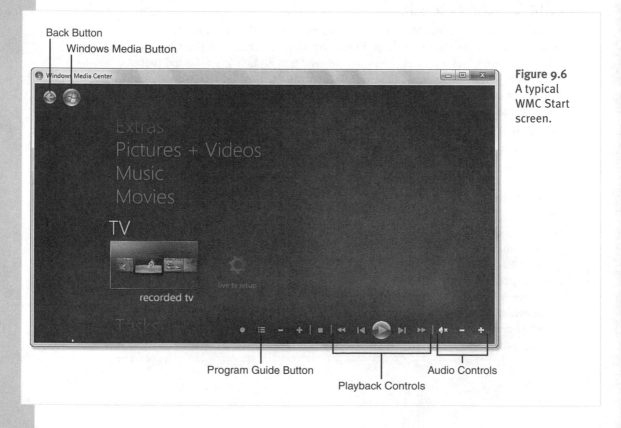

Figure 9.6
A typical WMC Start screen.

The following sections discuss the central features of WMC, but with emphasis on a few tricks for each one instead of telling you how to use them. Their use is actually straightforward, and you really don't need me to explain it to you. Suffice it to say, you engage each function of WMC by scrolling vertically to select the main function, or horizontally to select a subfunction, and then simply clicking the name (or alternatively using the remote control's up and down arrows to highlight the name) and pressing the Select button.

No Video in WMC

If the device driver is loaded and functioning properly and you are still unable to see live or recorded video in WMC, it is time to look at signal-related issues. First, be sure the cables are connected properly. If you have another device, such as a portable TV, you can use to verify that the cables are connected properly and carrying a valid TV signal, do so. That way, you know that the cabling is not an issue. You may also find that the signal is not properly formatted for your TV tuner by using an external device.

If you get a good video signal and you still can't see any video in WMC, perhaps WMC is not properly configured. The best way to test and verify your signal setup is to go to the Start page, select Tasks, Settings, TV, Set Up TV Signal, and then manually configure your TV signal. When you get to the TV Signal Setup dialog box, click the Next button to proceed to the Select Your TV Signal dialog box and let WMC attempt to automatically detect your signal. Failing this, TV Setup will give you the option to let WMC try again or you can choose Let Me Configur My TV Signal Manually. Verify your settings, or change them, to the correct signal provider. Use Cable for a TV signal from a cable set-top box, Satellite for a signal from a satellite provider (Dish, DirecTV, and so on), or Antenna for a public broadcast antenna or coaxial output from any type of signal provider. Then, move on to the Select a Working TV Signal dialog box. This is where you get the opportunity to select your TV Tuner's input signal. If you use a public broadcast (coaxial cable) signal, your input should be on channel 2, 3, or 4, with 3 being the most common. S-Video or composite video are more likely to be used by satellite and cable boxes, but some cable boxes also provide a coaxial output. If you use a cable box with a coaxial output, check the back of the box for a switch to set the channel to output the signal on. Usually, it is set to channel 3 with an alternative of channel 4. If you are unsure of your input channel, a simple test is to just try each input choice one at a time and see whether you get a signal in the preview window. After you obtain a signal, click Next and work your way through the rest of the dialog boxes until you complete the video setup.

For example, my TV tuner has coaxial and composite TV signal inputs. My signal provider is a DirectTV HD DVR with HDMI, composite, and YbPbR outputs. It is designed to provide HD signals to HD devices, but my TV tuner is an SDTV device. When I first connected it using the composite inputs, I could not figure out why I was not getting a picture. I was fairly confident that the cables were okay because I was getting sound. Then it dawned on me that I had my DVR set to provide an HD picture to my HDTV at 1080i. HDTV signals are output only on the HDMI and YbPbR outputs. To get a video signal output on the composite video outputs, I had to reconfigure the DVR to SDTV 480i mode.

Movies

Windows 7 separates the Movies and TV categories in WMC. The Movies library now contains its own subcategories, such as Title, Genre, Year, Parental Rating, Type, and Date Added. Little has changed visually for the Movies library, but it is capable of sharing content from other computers on the network. Out-of-box support for H.264 in Windows 7 includes Media Center Extenders (both stand-alone and integrated implementations) and the XBox 360 in extender mode.

Playback options include the ability to continuously play all videos in a specific gallery. Like slideshows, you can have a nonstop panorama of your favorite memorable moments caught on camera—such as a collection of your favorite vacation videos. Both Movies and TV have the ability to resume playback wherever you previously left off—no more seeking to the place where you were interrupted last time.

TV

Although it's novel that you can use your computer to watch TV, who cares? Personally, I never thought there was much worth watching on the tube anyway. Then again, I never have made a science out of TV program selection the way some people have. So, I end up channel surfing when I have some downtime, missing the beginning of a show I would have liked to see. Or maybe a friend tells me about an excellent program after the fact, when it's too late.

The electronic TV Guide in WMC has made a friend out of TV again and changed my watching habits. The Guide is your online TV programming guide, so you can see what is on TV and perform searches for programs you might want to see, prearrange recordings of upcoming programs, and so forth.

Using the Guide, I'm finding that there *are* some amazing shows from time to time—excellent documentaries, music programs, and old movies, for example. I can cull through two weeks' worth of upcoming programs using keyword searches and hone in on something I'd like to see. For example, recently I ran a keyword search on "music" and landed on a documentary about Joni Mitchell. I also set the DVR to record some weekly series, such as PBS's *Nova* and the daily broadcast of the BBC news. They stack up on my hard drive, and I can watch them whenever I get around to it.

WMC has three advantages over and above a competing service such as TiVo:

- I don't have to pay a monthly subscription charge (or lifetime charge) to access a TV programming guide.

- Nobody is keeping tabs on my viewing habits. (TiVo reports what you watch, and this data is used as input for various marketing databases.) Even if you can opt out of the data collection and the collection is anonymous, many people don't bother. In essence, many TiVo watchers' habits are being studied en masse.

- I don't need to rent or purchase another piece of hardware. I already have my computer, and it's a multifunction machine. It does a lot more than just tune in and play back TV shows.

On the downside, though, TiVo has some features that are more advanced than those offered by WMC. For example, if you have both satellite and cable feeds, TiVo can combine both program guides into a single onscreen grid. And, because TiVo is a simple machine, it's not likely to go haywire just when the Super Bowl is about to begin. A TiVo also has the advantage of being a dedicated device. For example, if your WMC machine is recording the latest episode of *America's Funniest Home Videos*, you're probably not going to be able to effectively play *World of Warcraft*.

Setting Up the Guide

Before you can benefit from the Guide, you have to configure some settings. Go to the Start page and click Tasks, Settings, TV, Guide.

The Guide downloads new data at a time you choose on the Settings screen, keeping the listings up-to-date. It does this in the background while you're doing other work. Your computer has to be on, however.

The Guide displays channel and network information, titles and times of shows, and information about each show. You can drill down to check out an upcoming show to determine whether it's one you've seen, for example. You select a show and then click More Info/Details to do this.

When you're watching live TV, the DVR is at work in the background, even if you're not recording a previously scheduled show. It records what you are watching live, so you can press the Pause button (onscreen, on your keyboard, or on the remote) and go grab a snack. While you're gone, the recording continues, although the playback is paused. This way, when you return, you just press the Play button and you're back in the groove, right where you left off, without missing any of the action. This is possible only because a WMC computer is fast enough to enable the DVR to record one thing and play back another simultaneously. Thus, it's writing to the hard drive and reading from it more or less at the same time.

WMC interleaves the hard disk reads and writes so intelligently that no recorded or played-back frames are dropped. Caching of video data in separate RAM buffers helps make this possible. If you're not taxing the system heavily by doing other highly disk- or CPU-intensive computing in the background, this works flawlessly. WMC is given high priority by the OS by default, and I haven't noticed dropped data, even with a large number of other tasks running.

Owing to this same sleight of hand, you can also record a live show in the background and view a previously recorded one—a nice feature that other DVRs can perform. You cannot, however, watch one live show while recording another live show unless you have multiple TV tuners installed. This is because a TV tuner can tune to only one channel at a given time.

 tip

To program WMC to record an upcoming show, highlight the show in the Guide and press the Record button on the remote or on the keyboard. One press records the individual show. Press it again to record the series.

 tip

If you want to record (and save) a program you're watching live, press the Record button on the remote or keyboard. Otherwise, the program isn't saved to disk.

 tip

We all hate commercials, and DVRs let you skip them quite easily. If your WMC computer has a keyboard, it probably has a Skip Ahead key. So does your remote. This key jumps the playback ahead 29 seconds per press. Because commercials are typically 30 or 60 seconds long, one or two presses skips a commercial. I've gotten good at guessing the right number of presses to skip a spate of commercials in just a couple of seconds. If you get too aggressive, you'll need to back up. Each press of the Replay key on the remote backs you up 7 seconds.

Heavy Disk Consumption in Live TV

Unfortunately, the file format Microsoft originally used for the Vista and XP WMC DVR (DVR-MS) is not very efficient, especially if you use the highest-quality settings. The files appear to be equivalent in size to the digital video files you would import from a DV camcorder. Figure about 3GB for a one-hour show. A half-hour show consumes about 1.5GB. Windows 7 uses a new WTV format (using the .wtv extension), which will not play on Vista and XP machines—but DVR-MS will play in the new WMC. WTV replaces DVR-MS for recorded TV shows for playback on Vista Media Center with TVPack2008 and Windows 7 computers. There's simply no way to utilize WTV files on unsupported machines, and copy protected WTV files can be played only on the machine where they are originally recorded. WTV recordings can also access digital video broadcasting (DVB) subtitles for playback and records all audio streams (that is, audio descriptions), unlike the DVR-MS format.

Microsoft's decision not to use a more compressed file format such as WMV or DivX isn't sensible, in our opinion. Now Microsoft has decided to employ another format that doesn't work outside WMC, WMP, and so on. You can, however, view WTV recordings in Windows Vista's Media Center (and related extenders) with the additional TV Pack.

One hour of Xvid or DivX consumes roughly 350MB—almost a factor of 10 difference! Even normal DVD data is smaller (about 2GB per hour). There are ways to convert Microsoft's format and store it as Xvid or DivX, but the couple of programs that are out there are still in beta stages as of this writing (for example, tvshowexport).

This flaw seriously limits the number of shows you can keep on the hard disk at any one time, especially at the highest-quality setting. You can choose a lower-quality setting as the default for all recordings, but you might not like the results. The four levels of record quality are fair, good, better, and best.

 tip

You can lower the quality level as a global default but still set the quality to a higher level for individual programs you intend to record. Use the Advanced Record settings for the program in question.

Table 9.1 shows the amount of hard disk space used for recording video, as well as the data rate used.

Table 9.1 Hard Disk Consumed Per Hour of Recording

Quality	Per Minute	Per Hour	Data Rate
Fair	20.48MB	1.2GB	2796Kbps
Good	24.06MB	1.41GB	3284Kbps
Better	34.82MB	2.04GB	4754Kbps
Best	45.57MB	2.67GB	6221Kbps

Pictures + Videos

Pictures + Videos is simply a slideshow presenter and video manager. You point the program to the directory (the default is Pictures) containing your digital photos, and you can step through the pictures manually or let the slideshow feature run automatically. Actually, the slideshow effect is quite pleasing because it does a cross-fade and some panning around in a bit of a random way to give a little more professional feel to your slideshow. (Some people call this the "Ken Burns" effect, after the documentary film maker Ken Burns who so often uses old still images in his productions.)

Windows 7 introduces the new Ambient Slideshow that launches as a screensaver when you initiate Play Favorites from the Pictures + Videos menu. All pictures you personally rate 3 stars or higher are pulled into the Ambient Slideshow with zoom in, zoom out, and zooming animation features. It can also play slideshows within a slideshow selection. The animation starts off as a gallery wall of your pictures (see Figure 9.7). The new ratings system places your rated pictures into various buckets that WMC uses to draw its slideshow images from to produce the gallery wall and other effects.

Figure 9.7
View your image collection as a slideshow in WMC.

The Shared category of the Pictures Library inherits the Shared library, which includes images from other computers on the network. You can also create custom slideshows using the Create Slide Show action under the Slide Shows category heading, as shown in Figure 9.8. If you hold down left or right directional arrows on your remote, Turbo Scroll will fast-forward images through the slideshow.

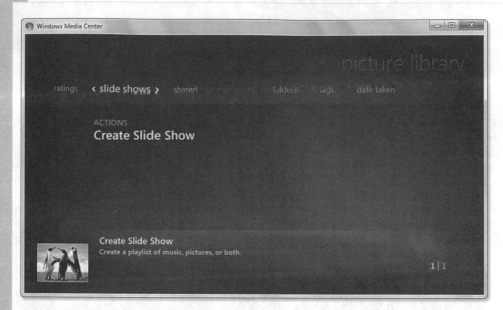

Figure 9.8
Create custom slideshows from your picture collections.

Personally, I have all my photos stored in my external FireWire drive because there are so many of them. So, I have to direct Pictures to find them there. You can do this by adding a folder to watch (Tasks, Settings, Library Setup) or creating a shortcut to the actual source of your files and putting that in Pictures:

1. Arrange Windows Explorer so that you can right-click and drag your photo folder into Pictures.

2. Left-click the relocated photo folder and select Create Shortcut Here from the context menu that appears.

3. When you go to Pictures in WMC, you'll now see a folder there with the name of your photo folder. Open that folder to see the pictures.

When you play your slideshow, it begins at the level of the open folder. If you have your photos arranged in folders, like I do, first drill down into the folder to be included in the slideshow. Photos in the folders below the current level will not be displayed. You can use the remote control or keyboard to step through the slides.

If you just stick in a memory card from your camera, you can view those photos without even loading them onto the hard disk. Just do the following:

1. Insert a memory card.

2. When prompted by AutoPlay, select View Pictures Using Windows Media Center.

3. The Play Slide Show menu appears with the memory card selected. The name varies depending on the type of media inserted. For example, if your pictures are on a memory stick, the media is

called MEMORYSTICK. If you are using an SD memory card, the media is called Microsoft WPD FileSystem driver.

You can add music to your slideshow (and even a playlist consisting of a number of files). This is a nice feature to spice up your slideshows. This way, even if you are boring your audience with endless pictures of your baby, at least they'll have some music to listen to.

Follow these steps:

1. From the WMC Start screen, go to Music and start your music playing first.

2. Return to the WMC Start screen and go to Pictures.

3. Click Tasks, Settings, Pictures to choose whether the song information shows onscreen while songs are being played.

4. Move back a page by clicking the Back button at the top of the WMC window. (It looks like a green left arrow.)

5. Start your slideshow by selecting Slide Show.

 tip

You can print a picture when stepping through images from WMC. When the picture you want to print is onscreen, press the More Info/Details button on the remote control. Then, choose Picture Details. Next, choose Print from the menu and Print once more when prompted to confirm your selection to print the image.

Music

This feature works in conjunction with Windows Media Player. WMC puts its interface (skin) on top of WMP. You can play audio CDs, copy CD tracks to your Music library, or play your library. When playing CDs or files from the library, song and album information (if available) is displayed onscreen. If you use another program—such as iTunes, MusicMatch, or WinAMP—to organize and play your MP3, WMA, or AAC files, you're out of luck unless you also import your files into WMP. But be careful that you don't rearrange your files in WMP and then mess up your song organization in your other player.

For dropping in a CD and playing it straight away, do the following:

1. Run WMC or press Start on the WMC remote.

2. Insert the CD. It should start to play.

3. If you want to copy the CD files into your Music library, select Copy CD.

When your MP3 files are all organized using WMP, run Music. You can play back tunes and view visualizations on your TV or computer monitor. You have to use WMP to create playlists, manage your files, and modify ID3 tags (things like genre, artists' names, and so forth), however.

Click the Visualize button to switch the screen to a series of sometimes-lovely and mesmerizing motion graphics. WMC uses the same visualizations as WMP. You can find and install new ones by searching the Web for "visualization" and downloading ones designed for WMP.

Some Tricks of the Trade

For the most part, using WMC is intuitive. You might need a bit more information in some areas, however, to get the most out of WMC. In this section, we look at a few of these items, such as

- Playing DVDs and other video files

- Viewing TV shows on your HDTV or projector

- Broadcasting TV shows to your TV or projector

- Burning DVDs from recorded TV

- Setting Parental Control ratings

Playing DVDs and Other Video Files

After setting Windows Media Center as the default DVD player, simply inserting a DVD into a DVD-ROM drive should result in Media Center playing the DVD. To go to the DVD menu (where you can change scene selections, change languages, or choose your DVD's special features), press the DVD Menu button on the remote.

You can change the language, closed captioning, and remote control option defaults for all DVD playback in the main settings screen in WMC. (Go to the Start screen and select Tasks, Settings, DVD.)

Viewing TV Shows on Your HDTV or Projector

If you want to watch your recorded or live TV on something other than your computer screen, your computer must, obviously, have an output your TV can accept. I discussed this earlier in the chapter. Most HDTVs and many projectors have DVI or VGA connectors. These are the preferred methods to use to connect the display output of your WMC computer to your HDTV or projector.

The key to obtaining the best picture is to choose an output resolution that corresponds to your HDTV or projector display resolution. HDTV supports 480i/480p at 720×480, 720p at 1280×768, and 1080i/1080p at 1920×1024. If your projector is not an HDTV projector, you need to refer to your documentation to determine the best output resolution (usually 640×480, 800×600, or 1024×768) to use for your VGA connection.

The truly nice feature about using your HDTV, or projector, as the output of your WMC computer is that your HDTV becomes the primary display of your computer. If you use a wireless media center keyboard with built-in trackpad (mouse), you can operate your entire computer from your couch. This opens up many possibilities for family entertainment—from using your WMC computer as a DVR, to playing music from your CD collection, watching DVD movies, playing video games, or even browsing the Internet.

If your WMC computer is in one room and your HDTV or projector is in another room, one easy method to connect them is to use a Microsoft Xbox 360. To connect your WMC computer and Xbox 360, you need the following:

- WMC computer with a wired or wireless network connection

- Microsoft Xbox 360 with a wired connection, or the optional wireless network adapter

- A network hub for a wired connection, or a wireless access point, router, or hub for a wireless network connection

- Optional Xbox 360 Universal remote control

- An SDTV with composite inputs or an HDTV with YPbPr inputs

After you have assembled the required hardware, the next step is to set it up, connect the various cables, and then configure the software. The basic process for a wireless network is as follows:

1. Install the wireless network adapter to the Xbox 360.

2. Connect the Xbox 360 AV HD adapter cable to the Xbox 360, set the Xbox 360 switch to HDTV, and connect the other end of the cable with three RCA male connectors color-coded green, red, and blue to your HDTV YPbPr inputs—green to green, red to red, and blue to blue. Then connect the audio inputs using the other set of color-coded connectors, yellow, red, and white, to your HDTV audio inputs—red to red and white to white. Leave the yellow connector unused.

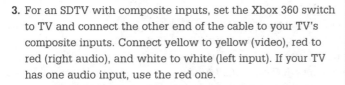

tip

If you have a problem connecting your Xbox 360 to your SDTV/HDTV, check out the Xbox 360 support page at support.xbox.com/support/en/us/xbox360/hardware/console/setup/ConnectToTVList.aspx.

3. For an SDTV with composite inputs, set the Xbox 360 switch to TV and connect the other end of the cable to your TV's composite inputs. Connect yellow to yellow (video), red to red (right audio), and white to white (left input). If your TV has one audio input, use the red one.

4. Set your HDTV to use the YPbPr (component video) inputs. If you use an SDTV, set it to use the composite or monitor input.

note

Optional Xbox AV cables are available with S-Video and VGA connectors.

5. Boot the Xbox 360 and configure the wireless network card to match the settings in your wireless access point, router, or hub.

6. Open WMC and go to Start, Tasks, Add Extender, and step through the Extender Setup Wizard.

At this point, your Xbox 360 should be live and capable of accessing all the content on your WMC PC. You can use the Xbox 360 universal remote, or your WMC remote, to control the displayed Media Center Extender menus.

Broadcasting TV Shows to Your TV or Projector

Getting your TV signal to your TV can be a problem if your WMC computer is not in the same room as your TV or if you do not have a Microsoft Xbox 360. Your cleanest and clearest signal is over a DVI cable, but these are expensive—especially in any significant length. No matter which kind of cable you use (S-Video, composite, component, VGA, or DVI), you'll likely end up drilling holes into your house or apartment, or at least snaking the cable around the room and possibly tacking it around your baseboards. What a hassle.

If you're like me, you'll want a quick-and-dirty solution, at least as proof of concept, until you have that free Saturday to venture into the depths of your crawl space under the house and install the more permanent wiring. So trek down to your local electronics store (for example, RadioShack) and purchase a short-range A/V transmitter/receiver combo designed for this purpose. I bought a set (RCA brand) for about $100. These transmit and receive composite video and accompanying stereo audio. You connect the small transmitter box to the computer's video and audio outputs, and connect the other (receiver) module to the TV or projector. The results, in my case, didn't look too bad, either. I was surprised. Check the specs on the package to see how far it can broadcast, and be sure you can return it if your walls turn out to be too thick; there is metal or some other signal blockage; too much video or audio noise is introduced by your microwave oven; or the TV and computer are too far away from each other for the product to work properly.

That leaves one additional issue: the remote control signal. I have my projector upstairs and my computer downstairs. I wanted to use the WMC remote. So, how was I going to get the IR signal to the IR receiver on my WMC computer? Again, the solution was found at the local electronics store—an IR extender that uses radio frequencies to transmit the IR signal between rooms.

So, I purchased an IR remote control extender. Similar to the A/V transmitter, this gadget has two parts: a transmitter and a receiver. Set up the transmitter near your TV or projection screen. Put the receiver near your WMC machine with its IR blaster pointed toward the WMC IR receiver (what you'd normally point the remote control at). Now, you can use your remote from the comfort of your recliner. It will relay the signal back to the computer.

After you get the IR remote control working and the image coming through to your TV or projector, you might also have to reduce the size of the WMC window on your computer screen if you want to see the entire image on your TV or projector. This can take a little trial and error. The WMC window is completely sizable, just as any window is, and as you resize the window, the video image resizes accordingly.

 tip

Some short-range TV transmitters have an IR relay built in to them, so check that option first. The RCA job I bought did not.

 tip

Don't confuse the IR blaster that comes with the WMC computer with the IR receiver that's typically built in to a little box that has a USB connector on it. Your little WMC remote control receiver box has two mini jacks on the back that you can plug IR blasters into. (A blaster typically has a long, skinny wire and a little IR module on the end.) You can use blasters to change the channel on external devices, such as set-top cable boxes or your VCR. Consult your computer's manual for how to position the blaster on your set-top box or VCR so that your remote control keypresses are passed through to those devices.

I originally made the mistake of thinking these little IR pods were receivers. They are not. Point your remote at them, and they do nothing. All they do is repeat IR signals received by your IR receiver module along to another device. For tips about using the set-top box IR pods, read this URL (despite referencing XP MCE 2005, the setup information still applies): www.microsoft.com/windowsxp/mediacenter/using/setup/settop.mspx.

On my system, I position the WMC window all the way into the upper-left corner of my computer monitor and then drag the window's lower-right corner diagonally until the window fills the projector's (or TV's) image. Because I have my projector in another room, I save myself the hassle of running back and forth between rooms by temporarily connecting a small TV monitor that sits beside my computer. I use that to make this adjustment. Then, I switch the output back to feed the projector.

 tip

If you don't like the WMC video player, the files the WMC DVR creates (they have the extension .dvr-ms and you can find them in the Recorded TV directory on the drive specified in the WMC Recorder settings) can also be played by WMP or other, more feature-rich players, such as BS.player.

Burning DVDs from Recorded TV

An obvious trick you can perform is to create a DVD or VHS tape of shows recorded from TV + Movies. One reason to do so is to keep the shows to watch months or years from now, without tying up hard disk space in the meantime. (Be sure you are aware of copyright laws that pertain to the shows you want to copy, of course.) If your WMC computer includes a recordable DVD drive, you are already capable of creating your first DVD. It's a simple process with WMC. Just follow these steps:

1. Insert a blank recordable DVD in your DVD recorder.

2. Select Recorded TV in the TV category.

3. Select the TV show you want to record.

4. Press Enter on the selected title or right-click to bring up the details window.

5. Press the right-arrow key or click the Actions entry.

6. Under Additional Commands, choose Burn a CD/DVD.

Now that you have recorded your first TV show to DVD, you may have noticed that it recorded everything that occurred during your recording. This usually includes a few minutes of the previous show, commercials, and a few minutes of the following show. That's a lot of extra material that you probably don't want to watch, and it is certainly a lot of storage space you don't want to waste. So, what can you do about it? Quite a bit, actually.

Windows 7 includes Windows Movie Maker. It's a basic application for merging video clips with simple transitions and creating an output file. The output file has several options—from playback on your computer as an AVI file to reducing it in resolution and compressing the file so that you can play it back on any Windows Mobile device, including your Windows Smartphone. It is also possible to burn the output file to DVD using Windows DVD Maker. Windows Movie Maker was included in Vista, but as of Windows 7 it is a download from the Windows Live site.

Some key items to keep in mind with using Windows Movie Maker to edit and publish your recorded TV shows include

- **Storage space and compression**—High-quality video consumes a great deal of storage space on your disk. The WMC file format (DVR-MS) provides good-quality video files, but a long-term storage conversion to a higher compression video format can lower your storage requirements significantly. Storing your files in high-quality DVD format can reduce the file size by two-thirds.

- **Video quality**—The better the quality of the video, the more space it requires on your disk. If you use a recorded TV show in SDTV format, use an output resolution of 720×480 as your highest-quality setting. Broadcast SDTV is as low as 320×240, whereas cable and satellite SDTV can be as high as 720×480. Using an output format higher than the input format generally does not produce a higher-quality video. Instead, it usually just takes up more storage space on the disk.

- **Back up your work**—Editing is a time-consuming process. Make frequent backups of your work in progress to avoid data loss in the event of a computer software/hardware glitch.

- **Output/storage**—Depending on the size of your video, you might output to a video CD (VCD). A VCD cannot store as much data as a DVD but is less expensive. A VCD also makes a good alternative for sending smaller files to relatives. If a file is too large to fit on a VCD, use a DVD. A single-sided DVD can store up to 2 hours of video in standard mode and 1 hour in high-quality mode.

 tip

To dub a show from your WMC machine to a VHS tape, connect the composite video output (or S-Video output of your S-VHS recorder) to the recorder. Then, start playing back the show on the computer. Try a little sample at first, and play the tape back on a TV set to ensure that the entire image is making it onto the tape. On some computers, the entire video image is automatically scaled to fit into the NTSC analog output. On others, you have to manually size and position the playback window, as explained in the previous section.

Setting Parental Control Ratings

You might want to control what kinds of TV, movies, or DVDs are playable on your system. To prevent your children from watching inappropriate TV, follow these steps:

1. From the WMC Start screen, select Tasks, Settings, General, Parental Controls.

2. When prompted, enter your four-digit code using the numeric keypad on the remote or keyboard. If this is the first time you have entered a code, confirm the code when prompted.

3. Select TV Ratings.

4. On the TV Ratings menu, you can make the selections shown in Table 9.2.

5. When finished specifying your ratings, click the Save button.

Table 9.2 TV Parental Controls

Control	Function
Turn on or turn off TV blocking.	Select or clear the check box next to Turn On TV Blocking. When the box is selected, TV programs that exceed the selected rating level are blocked.
Block or unblock unrated TV Programs.	Select or clear the check box next to Block Unrated TV programs. When the box is selected, TV programs that do not have a rating are blocked.
Set the maximum allowed TV rating.	Use the arrow buttons and the CH/PG+ and CH/PG− buttons to select the rating that cannot be exceeded for TV programs.

To prevent your children from seeing X-rated DVDs, follow these steps:

1. From the WMC Start screen, select Tasks, Settings, General, Parental Controls.

2. When prompted, enter your four-digit code using the numeric keypad on the remote or keyboard. If this is the first time you entered your code, confirm the code when prompted.

3. Select Movie/DVD Ratings.

4. On the Movie/DVD Ratings menu, you can make the selections shown in Table 9.3.

5. When you finish specifying your ratings, click the Save button.

Table 9.3   Movie/DVD Parental Controls

Control	Function
Turn on or turn off movie blocking.	Select or clear the check box next to Turn On Movie Blocking. When the box is selected, movies or DVDs that exceed the selected rating level are blocked.
Block or unblock unrated movies.	Select or clear the check box next to Block Unrated Movies. When the box is selected, Movies or DVDs that do not have a rating are blocked.
Set the maximum allowed movie rating.	Use the arrow buttons and the CH/PG+ and CH/PG– buttons to select the rating that cannot be exceeded for movies or DVDs.

Table 9.4 shows the keyboard shortcuts for playing DVDs when you don't have the remote control available or are sitting at your PC.

Table 9.4   DVD Keyboard Shortcuts

To Do This...	Press...
Go to the DVD menu	Ctrl+Shift+M
Play	Ctrl+Shift+P
Pause	Ctrl+P
Stop	Ctrl+Shift+S
Rewind	Ctrl+Shift+B
Fast forward	Ctrl+Shift+F
Skip back	Ctrl+B
Skip forward	Ctrl+F
Go to the previous chapter	Page Down
Go to the next chapter	Page Up
Change the DVD angle	Arrow keys
Change the DVD audio selection	Ctrl+Shift+A
Change the DVD subtitles selection	Ctrl+U

10

WINDOWS IMAGING TOOLS

Image Manipulation in Windows 7

From the earliest versions of Microsoft Windows, there have been tools that helped you manage images on your PC. In the early days, when the technology we enjoy today was not as readily available, these programs were limited to creating a picture on your computer screen and printing it out—very limited, but then again, so was the hardware.

Witness the leap from Windows Vista, just barely two years old, and you can see that Microsoft has further refined the tools built in to Windows 7 to handle this massive influx of digital content. In this chapter, we discuss the ways to get digital images into your computer, how to touch them up so they appear their best, and how to share these pictures with others.

What's Built in to Windows 7 for Photographs?

Like digital photography? Own a scanner? Windows 7 supports the immense popularity of digital photography and scanning with the new Windows Media Libraries. Windows 7 introduces a new centralized location to organize all of your media and has more closely integrated it with Windows Explorer and Windows Media Player.

The Windows Pictures Library can help you have more fun and get more use from your photographs. In the following sections, you'll learn how each of these features works.

Windows Pictures Library

Many Windows 7 options can be accessed through the new Windows Pictures Library included with Windows 7. You can find the Windows Pictures Library, shown in Figure 10.1, by choosing Start, Pictures.

 tip

The new Windows Media Libraries are not real folders, per se. They are special folders that collect, display, and give access to a specific type of media from a centralized locale. You can add to the list of folders being watched for various types of media by clicking the 2 Locations link under the Windows Pictures Library header in the folder listing. By default there are two locations, so you should see something like Includes: 2 Locations.

Figure 10.1
The Windows Pictures Library main screen.

By default, the Windows Pictures Library shows all photos that are in all watched folders, including the current user's Pictures folder. You easily can add individual photos or entire folders of photos.

To add an individual photo to Windows Pictures Library, do the following:

1. Open Windows Pictures Library.

2. Open the folder that contains the photo or video that you want to add to the Windows Pictures Library.

3. Click and drag the photo from the folder that contains the photo to the Windows Pictures Library.

 tip

Microsoft has created Library folders for each type of media—images, videos, and audio. Each and every one of these folders behaves in the same manner, so the information contained in this chapter works with any type of media. That's a good thing, as well, because most digital still cameras are more than capable of taking video. Just make sure your storage card has enough room on it to store a day at Disney!

That's it! After you drag the photo into the Windows Pictures Library, the file is copied to your Pictures folder and appears in the Library.

Importing Files into the Windows Pictures Library from a Media Source

To add all the photos from a specific multimedia storage device, simply connect the device to your computer. These devices are typically your digital still camera or a media card or USB thumb drive. Windows Pictures Library will scan the device and add any photos and movies it finds to the associated libraries (that is, images will go to the Windows Pictures Library, videos will go to the Videos Library, and so on). A folder can be removed just as easily in Windows Explorer, by finding the folder under the Folders selection in the left pane, right-clicking it, and choosing Delete.

Organizing Photos and Movies in Windows Pictures Library

Once you start importing several photographs into Windows Pictures Library, your main gallery view can start to become a little crowded. To alleviate this problem, Windows Pictures Library prompts you to create custom categories called *tags* to better group your media. Windows 7 will ask you to create a tag each time you insert media or import from a camera or other media device. Make the tag as descriptive as possible. If you take a range of different pictures in a set, try using a date and a location description to better organize your media.

Working with Scanners and Cameras

With Windows Vista, Microsoft replaced the functionality of the Scanner and Camera Wizard with the Windows Gallery, which has now been replaced in Windows 7 with the Windows Pictures Library. The Windows Pictures Library allows you to scan images from a scanner, copy images from a digital still camera, or import a movie from a supported video camera. Almost any modern imaging device is supported by Windows Pictures Library. If you have more than one imaging device supported by Windows 7, you can import images from any of them from within the Windows Pictures Library or in the new Windows Media Player.

Using Windows Pictures Library with a Scanner

To start the Windows Pictures Library with your scanner, push the Scan button on your scanner. This will open the new Windows Fax and Scan application (see Figure 10.2). You may also use the image acquisition feature from within your favorite photo editor or paint program. Image acquisition is located in the File menu of most applications.

When the wizard starts, follow this procedure to scan your pictures:

1. On the Choose Scanning Preferences screen, select the profile (which defaults to photo) and select New Scan to prescan your picture with default settings. With some scanners, you might need to press the Scan button on the scanner itself to perform the preview (see Figure 10.2).

Figure 10.2 The New Scan pane, where you can set the scanning options.

2. You can manually adjust the contrast, brightness, and resolution for the scan (I recommend 75dpi for scans you plan to use in slideshows and 150–300dpi for scans you want to print). After this is done, click Scan to acquire the picture from the scanner.

3. When scanning is complete, you will be prompted to tag the picture. This is optional but will make finding your scanned pictures easier after they are imported into Windows Pictures Library. Click OK, and the picture is shown as it is imported into the Photo Library. You can then use the postprocessing commands mentioned elsewhere in the chapter to clean up the picture, if needed.

 tip

If you place only one photo on your scanner, the wizard automatically selects it for you. Adjust the scan boundaries by dragging the corners only if you want to crop the photo during the scan. If you place more than one picture on the scanner, you will need to adjust the scan boundaries manually to scan each photo.

Scanner Not Recognized by Windows Pictures Library

If your scanner was working fine with Windows XP, but you find that Windows 7 will not show it in Windows Pictures Library, there are some things you can try.

The Windows Pictures Library is certainly a convenient way to use your scanner, but it's not the only way. Before you try the scanner again, be sure you install drivers for your scanner that are compatible with Windows 7 or Vista. You might be able to use Windows XP–compatible drivers if you can't get Windows 7 drivers yet. Install the latest drivers available (you might need to restart your computer afterward) and try the wizard again. Windows Update is a great way to get new drivers.

Next, see whether you can use the scanner with its own TWAIN or ISIS driver. If you can, you don't need to use Windows Pictures Library. Remember to use the Scan button on the scanner if it has one; some scanners require you to push this button to start the scanning process.

Contact the scanner vendor for help if you're still unable to use the scanner with either the wizard or its own scanning software.

Finally, you need a way to view and organize your pictures after you've scanned them. Although the Pictures folder has some built-in tricks, third-party software can help you view and locate pictures stored in any folder and on any type of media. Here are a few programs that you should consider:

- **IrfanView (www.irfanview.com)**—IrfanView is one of the oldest and most venerated freeware image viewers and processors available. It works just fine with Windows 7 and even has a nice thumbnail manager for organizing your images outside the Windows libraries system. Go to Options, Properties/Settings, open the Toolbar tab, and select the Grosberg_24 set. It's a lot easier to see in Windows 7.

- **Google's Picasa (www.picasa.com)**—If you're a Google user, then Picasa 3 may just be the answer for you. Not only does it handle images like the old Vista Photo Gallery (just way better), it also lets you manage your albums online and gives you more options to share your pictures.

Using Windows Pictures Library with a Digital Camera

Importing photographs from your digital camera is a simple process. The import process is automatically started when your camera is connected and powered on. You will see a dialog box similar to Figure 10.3 (your camera name will appear at the top of the dialog box). You can begin the import process by selecting the highlighted option, Import Pictures and Videos Using Windows.

Click this option to begin importing
your images from your camera.

Figure 10.3
The AutoPlay menu for a digital camera.

Windows will scan your camera's storage media for any and
all pictures and videos and will ask you to add tags (see
Figure 10.4). Do so and click Import.

Once Windows has completed the import it will open the
Imported Pictures and Videos page for you to review.

Windows offers a default collection of settings that control
how pictures and videos are imported into your computer. You
can change how these settings work before you even complete your first import by clicking the Import Settings link in
the Import Pictures and Videos dialog box to open the Import
Settings dialog box, shown in Figure 10.5. The following are
the options:

■ **Settings For**—Use this menu to select which settings you
will be modifying. In this case, the Cameras and Portable
Devices option should already be selected.

 tip

The first time you connect your digital camera to your computer,
Windows 7 might need to load drivers specifically for your camera. For
most modern cameras, this is a
transparent process that only takes
a few seconds, but it might be a
good idea to have any CDs or DVDs
that came with the camera on hand,
in case specialized drivers are
required. Sony cameras in particular,
which use the proprietary Sony
Memory Stick technology, have
required special drivers be installed.
Windows 7 has a lot more drivers
preinstalled than previous versions
of Windows.

Figure 10.4
The Import Pictures and Videos dialog box enables you to tag photos you are importing.

Figure 10.5
The Import Settings dialog box enables you to modify import settings.

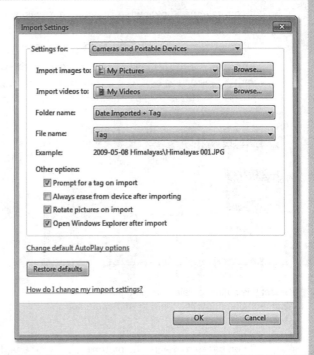

- **Import Images To**—Enables you to choose the top-level folder where the pictures are imported. A subfolder will be created for each import session, depending on the setting of the Folder Name option.

- **Import Videos To**—You may also select a different folder to import videos to, and Windows 7 knows how to tell the files apart.

- **Folder Name**—This option allows you to specify the folder to which the pictures will be imported. As stated, this is a subfolder of the Import Images To option.

- **File Name**—Identify the naming convention used to name the individual pictures. Preserve Folders means use the existing folder arrangement on the card or camera. You would use this option if you have a fancy camera and you organize your photos in your camera, or you had already organized the photos on a CD or DVD or removable camera card or USB flash drive using another program. More likely, you'll want to use the Tag setting.

The next set of options controls how Windows deals with the import process. First, you will want to leave checked the Prompt for a Tag on Import option, because that will help you keep your import sessions organized. The Always Erase from Device After Importing option does allow you to clear your camera after each use, but Windows 7 now knows what images it has already imported, so it will not re-import duplicates over and over again. Choosing this option is generally a good idea unless you have another way to erase the pictures from your camera.

If your camera knows what orientation it was held in when the images were taken, you are also given the option to perform automatic rotation of your images on import. Finally, you can choose whether you prefer Windows Explorer to open following the import.

After you set the options to your liking, click the OK button and click Import in the Import Pictures and Videos dialog box. The wizard displays each picture while it copies the selected pictures and provides a status display onscreen, shown in Figure 10.6.

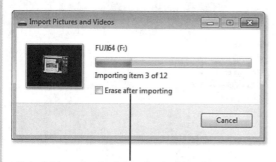

Figure 10.6
The wizard displays the progress of the import task.

Select this option to delete the images from your camera after importing them to your computer.

If you chose to delete the pictures from your imaging device, the wizard will delete them from your camera after it has successfully imported them to your computer and inform you of its progress.

Now the pictures are imported from your digital camera into the Windows Pictures Library. You can view each of the pictures and, if needed, perform some basic manipulation on them in Windows Media Player, as outlined in the next section.

Manipulating Pictures in Windows Media Player

Unless you are a perfect shot every time you click the shutter, there will inevitably be times where the photos you take with your digital camera can use some touching up—anything from removing red eye to cropping out unnecessary portions of the photograph. Despite the fact that versions of Windows prior to Vista did not include this functionality for you (requiring you to purchase third-party software), Windows Media Player contains some tools that allow you to do basic image correction.

To fix a photo using the Touch Up tool, navigate to the photo inside Windows Media Player. Right-click on the image and select the Picture Details option. Now, click the Touch Up option and this will give you the following options to the left of the picture (see Figure 10.7):

Figure 10.7
Fixing a photograph in the Windows Media Center.

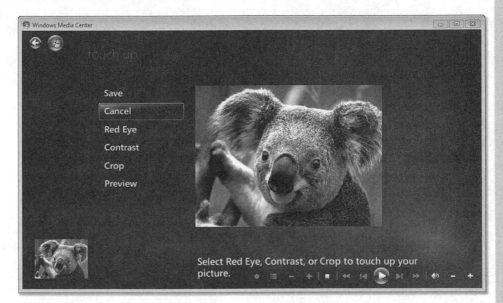

- **Red Eye**—Enables you to select an area of the picture for the wizard to remove "red eye" (caused by the flash bouncing off the retina)

- **Contrast**—Gives you a submenu allowing you to change the brightness and contrast of the picture

- **Crop**—Gives you a highlighted frame within the picture, allowing you to "cut out" unnecessary picture elements

- **Preview**—Allows you to take a closer look at the changes you've made before committing to them

Each of these tools automatically adjusts the aspects of the image for you. If you don't like what Touch Up does, you can cancel the changes by clicking the Cancel button. If you want to save your changes, you will have no choice but to overwrite your existing image.

What's New in Vista Is Old in Windows 7?

It's somewhat difficult to reconcile the fact that Microsoft removed a lot of features from Windows 7 that were just added in Windows Vista, but that's somewhat how Microsoft works. This isn't the first time they figured out another way to handle something and just made the changes. The good news is that you can find the old Photo Gallery refreshed and reinvigorated in the new Windows Live software package, a free download for any Windows user. Windows Live offers you free web calling, email, instant messaging, an expanded word processor that also neatly works with common (and non-Microsoft) blogging tools, the new Movie Maker, and the Photo Gallery application, all tightly integrated with your online Windows Live account.

Don't worry if you only have a Hotmail address or an old, and mostly dead, Passport. It will get you into Windows Live. Just keep in mind that there are other choices available. Google and Yahoo! Both offer a wide range of free and low cost tools which perform the same functions. Just because you're using Windows doesn't mean you are required to use Microsoft software.

Printing Your Masterpiece

Windows 7's Slideshow feature can show you your digital photos immediately. How about instant prints from your digital photos? By printing the photos on your own color printer, you can have pictures as fast as your printer can produce them and get them in a variety of sizes.

You can print photos from either the toolbar in a photo folder or the pull-down menu in a photo folder. To make prints from the digital pictures stored on your computer, simply select the photos you want to print (use Ctrl+click or Shift+click to select individual photos from the folder, or you can use Ctrl+A to select all of them) and click the Print button. This brings up the Print Pictures dialog box, shown in Figure 10.8.

From here, you can modify the options that control how and where the picture is printed. Above the picture you are printing, you can change the printer used, the paper size in the printer, and the print quality used. At the bottom, you can choose how many pictures are to be printed, as well as the option Fit Picture to Frame. If selected, this means that Windows will resize the picture so that it fills up the entire picture size selected on the right side of the window at the expense of cropping out some of the top and/or sides of the photograph. When deselected, it will print the original photograph in its entirety but will leave whitespace at the top and/or sides of the frame, where the photograph does not exactly fit the photograph size selected.

 tip

If you haven't used your inkjet printer for a week or more, or your printouts are of poor quality, click the Utilities tab (if available) and run your printer's head cleaning or nozzle test options with plain paper inserted in your printer (take out the photo paper until you're ready to print a good print). Head and nozzle clogs will ruin your printout and waste expensive photo paper, and most recent printers also offer a cleaning routine on this tab. If your printer doesn't have a menu option for head cleaning, check the instruction manual for the correct method to use. You might need to press buttons on the printer to activate a built-in head-cleaning routine.

Figure 10.8
Options for
printing a pic-
ture.

Along the right side of the Print Pictures window, you will see several options for how the printed photographs will fit on the paper selected. As you choose different finished photograph sizes on the right, the picture preview in the middle of the window will change to reflect how the photos should actually appear on the paper when printed, as reflected in Figure 10.9. If you choose fewer photographs than are available for the layout chosen, Windows will leave blank space on the photo sheet to conserve ink in your printer.

 tip

For best picture quality, it is generally recommended to leave the Fit Picture to Frame option selected. If you want exact control over what is displayed in the picture, use the Edit picture option in Windows Pictures Library.

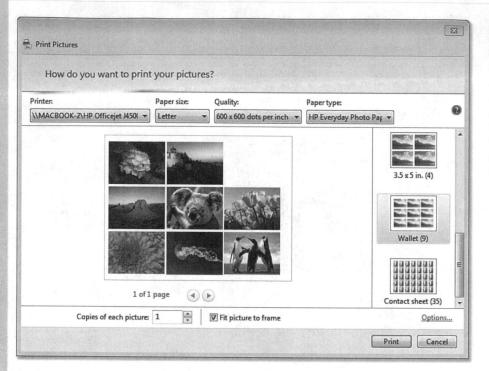

Figure 10.9
We are printing fewer pictures than are available in the format chosen, and thus Windows leaves blank spaces on the sheet.

Poor Print Quality with Digital Photos

If you find that your digital photos look terrific onscreen but are poor quality when printed, there are three major factors that control digital photo quality—any of which could be the culprit:

- Camera settings

- Printer settings

- Paper type

Get any of these wrong, and you won't get the print quality you want.

Your digital camera should be set to its highest quality and resolution settings, especially if it's a 2-megapixel or lower-resolution camera. Highest quality uses less compression to avoid loss of fine detail (more space is used on the flash memory card per picture than with lower quality settings), and highest resolution uses all the pixels to make the picture (again, requiring more space on the flash memory card per picture). If you use your camera to create pictures for use

Continued...

on the Web, the lower quality and resolution settings are fine, but printed pictures need the best quality available. Remember that your monitor needs just 96 dots to make an inch, whereas most inkjet printers put 600 to 1,200 dots into the same inch. So, a picture that's just right to fit on the screen doesn't have enough detail to print well.

Similarly, the printer should be set for the best quality setting that matches the paper type. If you're planning to print "knock-'em-dead" digital masterpieces, be sure to use photo-quality paper and set the printer's options accordingly. Just want a quick snapshot for the refrigerator? Use plain paper and set the printer for plain paper. Mismatch print type and paper type and you're sure to have problems because inkjet printers calculate how much ink to use and how to put it on the paper according to the options you select.

Remember, high-quality printing takes time; several minutes for an 8×10-inch enlargement on photo paper with high quality settings is typical.

If your digital camera is only capable of 2 to 5 megapixels, it's time to upgrade; 7 to 10 megapixel (also called 7–10MP) cameras are as cheap as ever and the storage needed to support those large images is also dirt cheap. You can generally find 8 to 16GB SD, xD, miniSD, or microSD (these sizes also add the term HC, or High Capacity, to the name) cards for as little as $30–$50. It's all the more mind boggling when you realize that an 8GB microSD card, about half the size of a key on a laptop, can be had for as low as $20. So, before you start collecting more low-grade images of your family, take a gander at the $100–$150 offerings in the camera section at your local big box store. Make sure to pick up some storage cards at the same time.

Sharing Your Photos with Others Electronically

Windows Windows Pictures Library supports two methods of sharing your photographs with others without having to print them out—emailing and burning them to CD/DVD. This section touches on the first of these methods. To learn more about creating a CD or DVD with Windows Pictures Library, see the next section "Burning Your Pictures to CD or DVD."

Emailing photographs is straightforward; you select the pictures you want to email and choose E-mail from the toolbar at the top of the window. You are then given the option of resizing the files to a lower resolution to make them smaller and therefore easier to send to someone as an email attachment. The Attach Files dialog box defaults to 1024×768, which is a good standard size—however, you can size them to any resolution from 640×480 to 1280×1024, or choose to leave them at the same resolution as the source. Whichever resolution you choose, the Attach Files dialog box will give you the size in megabytes of the attachments.

 tip

Windows Mail is no longer included in Windows 7. It is a part of the Windows Live software set, which you can download from Microsoft for free. It's now integrated into Windows Live, but it still supports a wide range of email account types and advanced email management functions, including improved handling of email messages that include images. There is additional information on Windows Live in Chapter 15.

After you have decided on a picture resolution, click the Attach button. Windows Pictures Library will then resize each of the pictures and open a new email message in the default email program (which, by default, is Windows Mail) with each of the photos as a separate attachment to the email. All that's left to do is address the email, edit the subject and text, and click Send.

Burning Your Pictures to CD or DVD

There are times where you might think, "Having pictures on the computer is great, and I really like the printed photographs, but how can I keep my pictures in a more permanent format?" If you have a CD-RW or DVD-RW drive in your computer (most modern computers come with one by default), Windows 7 can help you create a photo disc so that you can keep your digital masterpieces safe from the hands of time, or the destructive power of the next big Internet worm.

The integration of Windows Photo Gallery and Windows Explorer as the Windows Libraries in Windows 7 means you can burn files to disc in one convenient place. Fortunately, Windows actually knows which files are images and which are not.

Writing Photos to CD Using Windows Explorer

When Windows 7 detects a supported CD-RW or DVD-RW, it asks you whether you want to write, or more commonly, burn data to it. Your options are to use it as a thumb drive (Read/Write) or as a storage medium (Read Only). Here's how to use it:

1. If you want to copy only some of the pictures in your folder, select the pictures you want to copy and then insert a blank disc into your CD/DVD drive.

2. To copy all photos in the folder to CD, don't select any pictures first. Insert a blank CD or DVD into your CD/DVD drive. When you are done with the Setup Wizard, all items inside of your Windows Pictures Library will have been added to the disc. You will be warned that the disc you inserted does not have enough space to hold all of your media items.

3. You will be prompted to name the disc. Do so and click Next.

4. The pictures are copied to the CD or DVD, depending on the method you selected.

5. If you are having problems making a CD successfully, adjust the speed used by your drive to record data. The easiest way to do this is to open Windows Media Player; click Organize, Options; change to the Burn tab; and change the burn speed to a slower speed (see Figure 10.10).

Your photo folders act as regular folders after they've been copied to the CD. If you want to use the special imaging features, such as Slideshow or photo printing discussed earlier in this chapter, select a file in the folder and choose File, Preview. The picture is loaded into the Windows Photo Viewer, which has buttons for photo printing, slideshows, image rotation, editing, and other imaging options.

Figure 10.10
Selecting a lower burn speed on a CD-RW drive that lacks buffer-underrun protection.

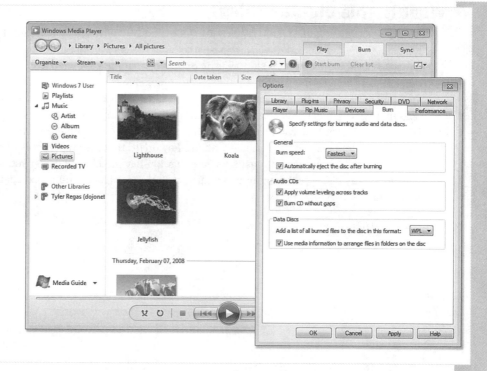

Making CDs and DVDs from Windows Media Player

When you first start Windows Media Player, select the Burn tab. From there you can select the photos you want to burn to recordable media and drag them to the sidebar. When you click the Start Burn button Windows Media Player burns the selected items to disc based on your settings in the Options dialog box.

Which Output Option to Use

Obviously, you must choose the output option that best suits the intended audience. Who is the audience for your photo CD or DVD? Are you sending images to Granddad to play back on his DVD player in the living room, or are you preparing a slideshow for an important business meeting that will be played on a computer? Compatibility is the name of the game when it comes to sharing recordable CDs and DVDs, as you probably know. Target your audience and keep in mind that there are many firmware differences between different brands, models, and vintages of CD and DVD players that determine whether they can play back a disk. Send up a test balloon (send your colleague a couple example disks) and make sure your intended audience can read it. Few things are more disconcerting than having a crowd of people gather to see your show and all you have to share is a blank screen.

What Is This Blu-Ray Thing?

Now that CD-R, CD-RW, DVD-R, DVD+R, DVD-RW, and DVD+RW are all supported standard disc types and very few optical drives are incapable of, at the very least, burning a CD-R, there's only one new place to go: Blu-Ray. Blu-Ray is an optical disc storage technology developed by Sony. The process uses blue lasers, something which was impossible just five years ago, to write huge amounts of data to a disc the same size as your standard CD-R. A single-layer Blu-Ray disc (BD) can hold up to 25GB of data, while a dual-layer BD (which isn't any larger than a single layer) can hold 50GB. A dual-layer DVD can hold up to 8.5GB, so you can see why Blu-Ray is becoming important. Many computers are starting to come with Blu-Ray drives that are still capable of dealing with all of the older disc formats, as well. Just be aware that Blu-Ray media isn't cheap yet, and that if you burn a Blu-Ray disc, you'll want to make sure your recipient has a Blu-Ray–compatible player to play it on.

11

SCANNING AND FAXING

Introducing Windows Fax and Scan

Windows Fax and Scan lets you fax and scan documents with a single application, rather than using the combination of Fax Console and the Scanner and Camera Wizard that you had to use in Windows XP. You can see the application in Figure 11.1.

Windows Fax and Scan uses the following hardware:

- An image scanner for scanning documents or photos

- A fax device such as a modem

You don't need to have both a scanner and a fax modem to take advantage of Windows Fax and Scan. The program does help you use both together, but it can be useful even if you have just one or the other.

 note

Windows Fax and Scan is available on all versions of Windows 7. (This is a big improvement over Vista, where it was provided only with the Business, Enterprise, and Ultimate editions.) If you don't see Windows Fax and Scan in your Start menu, go to the Control Panel, select Programs, and select Turn Windows Features On and Off. You should be able to enable it there.

 note

If your computer has a dial-up (analog) modem, the modem probably includes fax capabilities.

If your computer doesn't have a modem, you can easily install an inexpensive internal or USB external fax modem. If you have Internet-based telephone service, contact your phone service provider to see whether your line can carry fax signals. In a corporate setting, check to see whether your organization uses digital telephone wiring before you try to hook up a dial-up modem. Digital phone lines can damage your modem.

Figure 11.1
Windows Fax and Scan lets you scan and/or fax documents.

The scanner and fax modem can be integrated into an all-in-one unit (print, scan, copy, fax), or you can use separate components. If you have a fax server or a multifunction device on your network, you can also use it with Windows Fax and Scan.

In this chapter, we'll show you how to set up the Windows Faxing service, how to send faxes from Windows Fax and Scan, and finally how to use the program to scan and store email and print documents.

note

Windows Fax and Scan is designed primarily to make it easy to scan, store, and fax documents. Although you certainly can use it to scan pictures, if your primary goal is to scan your photograph library, you're better off using the Windows Photo Gallery tool, which is discussed under "Working with Scanners and Cameras" on page 279.

Preparations for Using Windows Fax and Scan

If your scanner or fax device is not already installed, follow the manufacturer's recommendations to install the fax or scanner hardware before you use Windows Fax and Scan. If you need to install a dial-up modem, you can use the Add a Device applet in Control Panel to install most serial modems or USB modems that don't include special drivers. If your modem or scanner includes a disk with Windows 7 or Vista drivers, install them as directed. Windows XP drivers may be used with some devices if Windows 7 or Vista drivers are not provided by the vendor.

If you are given a choice between installing TWAIN or WIA drivers for your scanner, install WIA (Windows Imaging Architecture) drivers for use with Windows Fax and Scan. This is something to be especially careful of if you have a scanner that came with Windows XP drivers but not Windows 7 or Vista drivers. TWAIN drivers may support more advanced scanner features, such as transparency adapters or dust and scratch removal, found on some models, but they are not compatible with Windows Fax and Scan. Some scanner driver installations install both types of drivers.

➡️ *To learn how to scan images that require TWAIN drivers (such as slides and negatives) and fax them,* **see** *the section "Scanning and Faxing Slides and Transparencies," p. 310.*

Configuring the Fax Service

To set up your system to send and receive faxes with a fax modem, click Start, All Programs, Windows Fax and Scan. Make sure Fax view is selected: click Fax at the bottom of the left pane. Next, click the New Fax button on the toolbar (refer to Figure 11.1). The Fax Setup dialog box appears. The first time you do this, Windows will walk you through the process of setting up the faxing software.

Select Connect to a Fax Modem. On the next screen, enter a name for the modem or keep the default name, Fax Modem. Click Next to continue.

Configuring Fax-Receiving Options

On the next screen, choose how you wish to receive faxes. Your options include the following:

- **Answer Automatically**—Choose this option if you have a dedicated fax line or a single phone line with a distinctive ring detection switch that automatically routes different types of calls to different devices. The fax modem will pick up every incoming call, so don't make this selection if your computer shares your personal phone line.

- **Notify Me**—Choose this option if you have a single phone line but don't have a distinctive ring detection switch. Windows will pop up a notification when the phone line rings, and you'll opt whether to answer it and receive the incoming fax.

 note

If you have an all-in-one device, it most likely will *not* be seen as a fax device by Window Fax and Scan. The Faxing part of Fax and Scan works only with fax modems and Microsoft-compatible network fax servers. To send faxes through your all-in-one device, just select it as a printer. The device *should* be able to scan through Windows Fax and Scan.

 note

You can often get by just plugging in the device and letting Windows find it, but you really should read the manufacturer's installation instructions. In some cases it's necessary to install the supplied software before installing the device for the first time. If you do things out of order and run into trouble, install the software, then go to the Device Manager, find the incorrectly installed device, delete it, and then restart Windows.

If Windows detects your modem but can't find a driver for it, you'll need to download one from the manufacturer's website. Your PC manufacturer also might be able to supply a driver.

 note

You might see a Windows Security Alert indicating that Windows Firewall is blocking Windows Fax and Scan from receiving incoming network connections. If you get this prompt, click Unblock. In most cases, you should leave Private Networks checked and leave Public Networks unchecked.

- **I'll Choose Later**—Choose this option if you want to create a fax right away and prefer to delay setting up receiving faxes until later.

A New Fax dialog box appears. If you don't want to send a fax now, close it.

➡ *To learn how to send faxes,* ***see*** *"Sending Faxes from Windows Fax and Scan," p. 299.*

Setting Up Sender Information

Click Tools, Sender Information to set up the information you want to place on your cover pages and in the top margin of outgoing faxes. You can complete as much or as little (even none) of the dialog box as desired.

Creating a Customized Cover Page

To create a customized cover page, click Tools, Cover Pages. Existing personalized cover pages (if any) are listed. Then,

- To create a new cover page from scratch, click New.

- To customize one of the standard cover pages that are provided by Microsoft, click Copy, select a cover page template, and select Open. Then, highlight the copied entry and click Rename. Give it a new name, but be sure that the name still ends with .cov. Press Enter, and then click Open to personalize the cover page.

- To modify one of your existing cover pages, select it and click Open.

In each case, this opens the Fax Cover Page Editor, shown in Figure 11.2.

Use the Insert menu to place fields and field names as desired, along with simple shapes. Use the Format menu to align objects, adjust spacing, center the page, or change the order of overlapping objects. Use the View menu to show or hide menus and grid lines (grid lines are hidden by default, but can be useful in aligning design elements). Use the File menu to print or save your cover page. Cover pages are saved with the .cov file extension and are saved in your Personal CoverPages folder by default.

 tip

When you insert a field name and associated field, they're selected as a group and they will move as a group. If you want to move one of the components separately, click somewhere in the cover page away from any items. Then, move the desired items.

To move several items at once, hold the Shift key down and click on each of them, and then drag them. You can also click the Select icon (leftmost on the toolbar) and drag a box around the items you want to move.

Figure 11.2
Creating a cover page
with the Fax Cover
Page Editor.

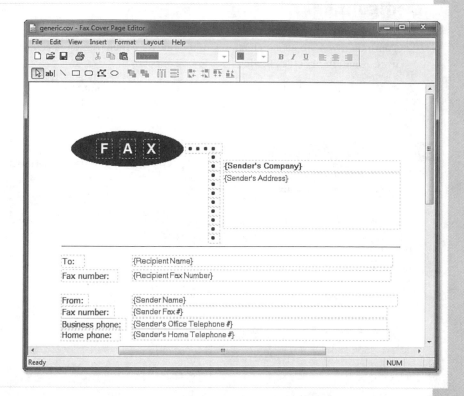

To make your personalized cover page available to all users, you must copy the cover page file to
`\ProgramData\Microsoft\Windows NT\MSFax\Common CoverPages\xx-xx`, where *xx-xx* is a
code that specifies your geographic region and language. Moving the file to there is a bit tricky.
Follow these steps:

1. Create a cover page, and save the cover page file in the default location (your Personal
   CoverPages folder). Test it by sending it in a fax, to be sure that it looks the way you want it to.
   After you're sure that it's correct, proceed to the next step.

2. Click Start, Documents. Dig into Fax, then Personal CoverPages. Locate the cover page file, right-
   click it, and select Cut.

3. Browse to folder `\ProgramData\Microsoft\Windows NT\MSFax\Common Coverpages`. The
   uppermost folder, `ProgramData`, is usually hidden, so you will have to type `\`**ProgramData** into the
   Explorer window's address bar (just type it in where the breadcrumb path list is). Then double-
   click Microsoft, Windows NT, MSFax. Windows will say you don't have permission to view MSFax.
   Click Continue to grant yourself permission, and continue to Common Coverpages, and then into
   the regional folder, which is `en-US` for U.S. English but might be different on your computer.

4. Right-click in the folder's contents pane and select Paste. You will have to go through a User
   Account Control prompt to get permission to paste the file into this folder.

The cover page will now be available to all users on your computer.

Configuring Fax Settings

To configure your computer's fax settings, click Tools, Fax Settings. If prompted by UAC, click
Continue if you are an administrator, or provide an administrator password if you are a standard
user. A multitabbed Fax Settings dialog box appears.

1. Select the General tab (see Figure 11.3) to specify whether the fax service should send, receive,
   or send and receive faxes and how to answer incoming calls.

Figure 11.3
Configuring general fax settings.

2. Click More Options. In the TSID and CSID boxes, enter your fax number and/or company name.
   This information will be displayed on the other person's fax machine when you send or receive a
   fax.

   If you want incoming faxes to be printed automatically, check Print a Copy To and select a
   printer from the drop-down list.

   Click OK to save the information.

3. Click the Tracking tab to adjust how to be notified about the status of a sent or received fax. By
   default, all notifications (which appear as pop-up balloon notes), fax monitor settings, and sound
   options are enabled. Clear check boxes to disable selected notifications.

4. Click the Advanced tab to view or move the location of the Fax Archive folder, disable the ban-
   ner line at the top of sent faxes, adjust redialing settings, and specify when discount long-
   distance rates start and end.

5. Click the Security tab to specify which users and groups can send faxes or manage the fax service and fax documents. By default, everyone can use the fax service. If you want to restrict its use, remove Everyone and add individual users.

6. Click Apply; then click OK to save your changes and close the Fax Settings dialog box.

7. Click Tools, Fax Accounts if you need to add or remove a fax modem or network fax server.

8. Click Tools, Options to bring up a multitabbed Fax Options dialog box. The General tab is used to enable (default) or disable playing a sound when new messages arrive. Click the Receipts tab to configure the sending of email delivery receipts (which can also include a copy of the sent fax). Click the Send tab if you want to enable the inclusion of an original message in a reply. Click Compose to change the default font used for faxes (10-pt. Arial Regular).

 tip

If you regularly send faxes to conventional fax machines (which usually have resolution of no more than 200dpi), a 10-pt. font is a little too small for easy reading. We recommend 12-pt. Arial instead.

Sending Faxes from Windows Fax and Scan

To send a fax with Windows Fax and Scan, click the New Fax button to open the New Fax dialog box, shown in Figure 11.4.

Figure 11.4
You can send a fax by printing to the Fax printer, but you can also create one from scratch by clicking New Fax.

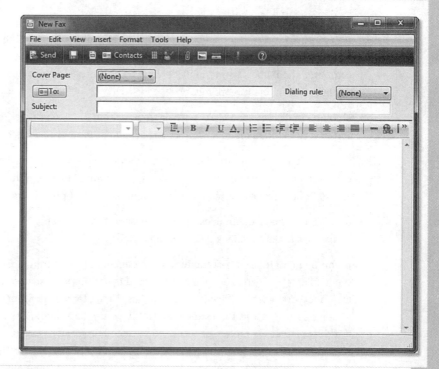

Fax Modem Doesn't Work

If your fax modem doesn't work, check the following:

Test the fax modem: To make sure your modem is working properly, open Control Panel. In the search box, type the word modem, then select Phone and Modem. Enter your location information if it is requested, and click the Modems tab when it appears. Select your modem in the list of Modem devices, then click Properties, and select the Diagnostics tab. Click the Query Modem button to send test commands to the modem.

If the modem does not respond, check the modem listing in Device Manager; for an external modem connected to a serial (COM) port, you should also check the serial port section of Device Manager. If you see problems reported with the modem or the port, view the device's Properties to diagnose the problem.

➡ *For more information on Device Manager, **see** Chapter 25, "Troubleshooting and Repairing Problems."*

If you have an external fax modem: Check the modem's power supply. If your modem is not connected to a working AC adapter, or if the AC adapter is not plugged in to a working AC outlet, your modem will not work. Some external modems have an on/off switch. Make sure the modem is turned on before use.

An external fax modem must be connected to a working COM or USB port. A COM (also known as RS-232 or Serial) port is a 9-pin male D-connector. The cable between the modem and the computer should be secured in place with the thumbscrews provided. Loose cables can cause the fax modem to not work reliably.

If you have disabled the COM ports in your system BIOS, you must reenable them before you can use an external modem. Check your system or motherboard documentation for details.

If you are using a COM-to-USB adapter, make sure the adapter works correctly. Problems with the adapter could cause your modem to appear to malfunction. Frankly, we advise you to use only USB or internal devices if you no longer have COM ports on your system.

If a USB external modem doesn't work, make sure the USB port is working. Attach a USB mouse to the port to check its operation.

If you have an internal fax modem: On a desktop PC, an internal fax modem slides into one of the available PCI expansion slots. If the card is not properly seated in the expansion slot, it may not work reliably. Click Start, right-click Computer, select Manage, and select the Device Manager. Be sure that the modem doesn't have a yellow triangular ! warning icon by its name. If it does, either it's broken or you need to install driver software for it. Try this: Right-click it, select Update Driver Software, and select Search Automatically for Updated Driver Software. If this doesn't work, you may have to search for software on the manufacturer's website.

Selecting Recipients

To send a fax to a recipient not on your Contacts list, enter the fax number or numbers in the To field. If you want to enter more than one recipient, use a semicolon to separate fax numbers. To send a fax to selected recipients on your Contacts list, or to create a new contact, click the To button to open the Select Recipients dialog box.

Can't Fax to Specified Contacts

Windows Fax and Scan can fax only to contacts that have fax numbers in their contact information or to manually entered fax numbers. If you have contacts that do not have fax numbers listed, you will need to enter the fax numbers manually at faxing time or, better still, edit their contact information to supply the fax number.

If the contact has a fax number listed, you might need to add the area code or country code to the number to enable Windows Fax and Scan to make the call. Use the same information as you would provide for a standalone fax machine.

Entering Text

Enter the subject of the fax into the Subject field. If you are using a cover page and want to add notes to the cover page, enter note text into the Cover Page Notes field. The main text entry field is below a text-formatting toolbar (refer to Figure 11.4). Use this toolbar to change font and font size, select from predefined text and paragraph styles, insert bullet points or numbered steps, and align text.

Selecting a Cover Page

Windows Fax and Scan includes four standard cover pages: confident, fyi, generic, and urgent. To use one of these cover pages, or to select from a personal cover page, click the Cover Page pull-down menu and select the desired cover page.

To create your own customized cover pages, see "Creating a Customized Cover Page" earlier in this chapter.

Inserting Images, Text, and Files

To insert an existing image file, place the cursor where you'd like the image to go and click Insert, Picture. You can insert bitmap, JPEG, GIF, or PNG file types. Navigate to the picture location, select the image, and click Open. The picture is imported at the cursor location.

 note

The picture might appear to be too wide for the page, but Windows Fax and Scan scales it to fit on the page.

To insert a file attachment into the fax, click Insert, File Attachment. Navigate to the file and click Open. The file is converted to fax pages when the fax is received by a standard fax machine. (You must have an installed application capable of printing this file.)

To insert text from a TXT or HTML file, place the cursor where you want to make the insertion. Click Insert, Text from File. Navigate to the file and click Open. The text is inserted at the file location.

 tip

After inserting text, use the text-editing tools to delete any unwanted text or change text formatting.

Adding Scanned Pages

To add scanned pages to your fax, place the pages you want to scan into your scanner. Click Insert, Pages from Scanner. The pages are scanned automatically and show as an attachment. If your scanner does not have an automatic document feeder (ADF), remove the first page after scanning it, insert the next page, and repeat the process until all pages have been scanned. Each scanned page is inserted as a TIFF file.

Scanner Doesn't Work

If your scanner doesn't work, check the following:

Test the scanner: To make sure your scanner is working properly, start Windows Photo Gallery, click File, and select Import from Camera or Scanner. Select the scanner, and click Import. The scanner application should appear.

Obtain WIA drivers: If the scanner does not respond, make sure you are using the correct drivers:

Best: Windows 7 or Windows Vista drivers with Windows Image Acquisition (WIA) support
Acceptable: Windows XP drivers with WIA support
Not Acceptable: Windows 7, Vista, or XP drivers with TWAIN support only

Windows Fax and Scan and Windows Photo Gallery use WIA to interface with the scanner. With some types of scanners, the driver CD you receive with the scanner may include only TWAIN drivers. TWAIN drivers can be used through third-party applications' Import menus, but they don't work with WIA applications.

Visit the scanner vendor's website to download and install WIA drivers if your scanner works with its own scanning application but not with Windows Photo Gallery or Windows Fax and Scan. Note that some scanner vendors include both TWAIN and WIA in their default driver installation routine.

Previewing the Fax

After typing and inserting all the information needed into the fax, click View, Preview to see a preview of the fax. Alternatively, click the Preview icon, which is just to the right of the Save icon on the toolbar. Attachments are converted into text or graphics, as appropriate. Figure 11.5 shows a typical fax in Preview mode. Use the Zoom Level pull-down menu to select a magnification for review.

Figure 11.5
Previewing a fax before sending it.

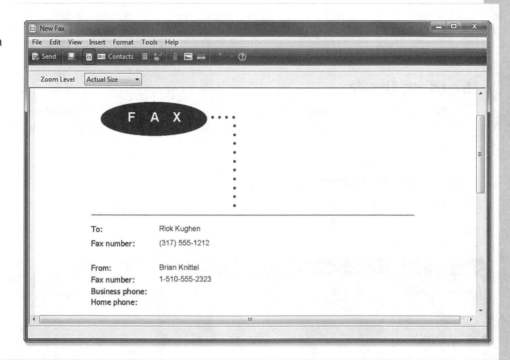

Click View, Preview again, or click the Preview icon again, to return to the normal fax-editing mode.

Setting Up Dialing Rules

If you need to specify a prefix for an outside line, click the Dialing Rule pull-down menu (to the right of the To box; refer to Figure 11.4), and select My Location to use the location information you set up when you installed your modem. If you are dialing from a different location, select New Rule. When the Phone and Modem Options dialog is displayed, click New and provide the necessary information.

Can Fax at Office or Home but Not from Other Sites

If you can fax from your office or home with a particular dialing rule (My Location or a customized location), but you cannot fax from other locations, such as a meeting room or hotel, you should find out what is needed for a dialing rule and create a new one. If you will not be using that location again, you can also specify the phone number manually and add codes such as 9 (outside line) or a comma (each comma adds a one-second pause) as a prefix to the destination fax number.

Sending the Fax

To send the fax, click Send. The fax is placed in the Windows Fax and Scan program's Outbox folder until transmission is complete. After the fax is transmitted, the fax is placed in the Sent Items folder.

Monitoring Outgoing Faxes

After you click Send, a pop-up window (see Figure 11.6) appears, displaying the status of the current fax and previous fax events.

Figure 11.6
The Review Fax Status window appears when you send a fax.

At the end of the fax transmission, a notification is also displayed over the system tray.

Can't Detect a Dial Tone

If the fax modem doesn't detect a dial tone, it can't work. Make sure the RJ-11 telephone cable is properly connected to the fax modem and to the phone jack. Some fax modems use a pair of RJ-11 ports, one for the phone line and one to permit a telephone to piggyback on the modem to share a line when the modem is not in use. Make sure you connect your telephone cables to the correct ports. A good way to start is to unplug the

Continued...

phone cable from your modem and plug it into a regular telephone. Be sure the phone gets a dial tone.

Replace damaged or suspect cables: If you're like us, you probably have a dozen or so unused RJ-11 cables lying around from various telephone, fax machine, and modem installations.

If the fax modem connects to a Y-splitter or other line-sharing device, try disconnecting the line-sharing device and cabling your modem directly into the phone jack. A defective line-sharing device can cause the fax modem to malfunction.

Receiving Faxes

To configure Windows Fax and Scan to receive a fax automatically, select Tools, Fax Settings, and make sure that the option Allow the Device to Receive Fax Calls is enabled (refer to Figure 11.3) and the Automatically Answer After radio button is selected. Specify the number of rings to wait before answering. The computer will now answer any incoming call on the telephone line connected to its modem, just like a standard fax machine.

 note

You can later review, print, or resend any fax you've sent or received. To resend a fax, right-click it in the upper-right pane and select Forward as Fax.

If you configure Windows Fax and Scan to receive a fax automatically, incoming faxes are received and saved to the Inbox automatically. If you configure Windows Fax and Scan to receive faxes manually (refer to Figure 11.3), a notification appears when an incoming call is detected. If the incoming call is from a fax device, click the notification balloon to have the modem pick up and receive the fax.

During the reception, the Review Fax Status window displays the status of the incoming fax. Click Close to close the window after receiving the fax.

Printing Received Faxes Automatically

To print received faxes automatically, click Tools, Fax Settings. On the General tab, click More Options. In the When a Fax Is Received section, open the Print a Copy To pull-down menu and select a printer. When you receive a fax, the fax will automatically be printed on the specified printer.

Scanning Documents with Windows Fax and Scan

To start Windows Fax and Scan, click Start, All Programs, Windows Fax and Scan. When you open Windows Fax and Scan, the program opens to the Fax dialog box, shown previously in Figure 11.1. Click the Scan button in the bottom of the left pane to switch to the Scan view.

You can change the scanner's settings for any individual photo or document, but it helps to predefine the settings you use most frequently as the defaults. So, before you scan your first documents, take a moment to configure the program's scan settings. Click Tools, Scan Settings. The default settings, known as scan profiles, for a typical scanner are shown in Figure 11.7.

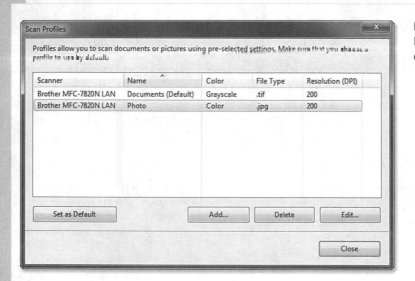

Figure 11.7
Default scan profiles for a typical scanner.

Editing Scan Profile Defaults

The Photo setting is the default scan profile (refer to Figure 11.7). If you plan to scan documents more often than photos, click the Documents profile name (second column), and then click the Set as Default button to make it the default profile. This will set this profile as the one to use with your scanner's "one-button scanning" feature, if it has one.

To edit the default scan resolution or other settings for a profile, select the profile, and then click Edit. Figure 11.8 illustrates the settings for the Documents profile.

From this dialog box, you can select the scanner (if you have more than one installed), the profile name, the paper source (such as flatbed or automatic document feeder [ADF]), the paper size, the color format (black and white, grayscale, or color), the file type (JPEG, BMP, TIFF, or PNG), and the scan resolution, brightness, and color. Make the changes you want to the profile and click Save Profile to replace the current settings with your changes.

Figure 11.8
Editing the
Documents
scan profile.

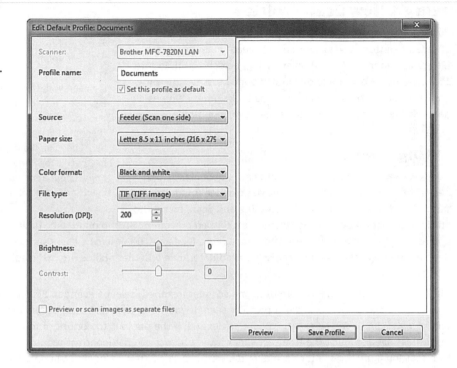

Choosing the Right Settings

What resolution should you use? 300dpi matches the Very Fine (best quality) black-and-white document resolution setting supported by most recent fax machines. However, for most faxing applications, 200dpi is adequate. Use a higher resolution, such as 600dpi, if you are scanning a photo for printing on a high-quality color inkjet or laser printer or for publishing use. See the printer documentation or the publisher's requirements for the recommended dpi. For images that you plan to email or use on a web page, try 75 to 96dpi. This will produce a smaller image that is better suited for displaying on a computer screen.

For color photographs, set the Color Format to Color. For black-and-white pictures or faded documents, set the Color Format to Grayscale. For most typed documents and for pencil or pen-and-ink line drawings, select Black and White.

Under File Type, for color or grayscale scans, the TIFF format produces the best quality but is rather large. If you want to save disk space, use JPEG or PNG. BMP can be used by applications that do not support other file types, but BMP files are also large. For black-and-white scans, use the TIFF format. JPEG is *not* a good choice—it can cause blurriness and weird image distortions in black-and-white scans.

Creating a New Scan Profile

You can create a new profile to give yourself an additional set of default settings to choose from. To create a new scan profile, click Add in the Scan Profiles dialog, box shown in Figure 11.7. The Add New Profile dialog box appears. Enter the profile name, select the paper source, and make other changes as needed. Click Save Profile to save the new scan profile.

Scanning Images

Windows Fax and Scan is best used to scan documents (text and black-and-white drawings), but you can use it to scan pictures. To scan a photo with Windows Fax and Scan, insert the photo into your scanner. If the scanner is a flatbed design, insert the photo face down (photo against the cover glass). If the scanner includes a feeder (ADF) or uses a sheet-fed design, see the documentation or markings on the scanner to determine whether photos are inserted face up or face down.

 tip

The preset resolution for a new scan profile is 200dpi. To match the dpi of current Windows desktops, we recommend 96dpi for viewing or emailing. Use a resolution of at least 200dpi or more for profiles intended for printing or faxing. See the sidebar "Choosing the Right Settings" for specific resolution recommendations for different types of documents and destinations.

Click New Scan. If you have more than one scanner installed, select a scanner. Select the profile desired, and click Preview to see a preview scan. If you wish, click and drag the bounding boxes to the edges of the photo, or crop the photo as desired. If the photo is too bright or too dark, adjust the Brightness slider. Adjust the Contrast slider if the photo is too flat (contrast too low) or too harsh (contrast too high). To see the results of the changes, click Preview again. When you are satisfied with scan quality, click Scan (see Figure 11.9).

➡ *If you are unable to scan, see "Scanner Doesn't Work"*
on page 302.

A scanning progress bar appears, and the scanned image is displayed in the workspace after being saved to disk, as shown in Figure 11.10.

You can select items in the Fax and Scan workspace list and right-click to choose various actions such as View, Print, Send To (for faxing), Rename, and Move to Folder.

 tip

Fax and Scan doesn't let you drag and drop files, which is sort of annoying. It's sometimes easier to work with scanned files using Windows Explorer. You'll find the files under My Documents, inside the Scanned Documents folder.

 ## Slow Scanning Speed

If a USB 2.0-based scanner is very slow, make sure you have connected the scanner to a USB 2.0 (also known as Hi-Speed USB) port. Some front-mounted USB ports support only USB 1.1 speeds. If you have connected the scanner to an external USB hub, try connecting the scanner directly to a USB port on the computer.

Figure 11.9
Preparing to scan a
photo.

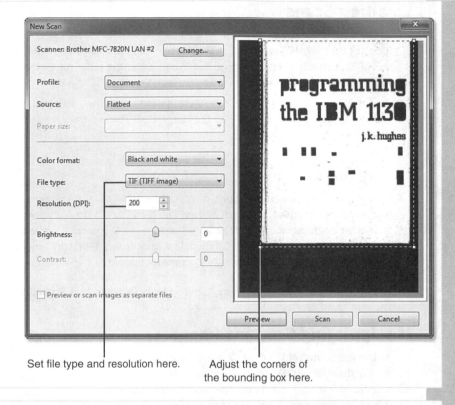

Set file type and resolution here.　　Adjust the corners of
the bounding box here.

Figure 11.10
The scanned
document or
image
appears in
the Windows
Fax and Scan
workspace.

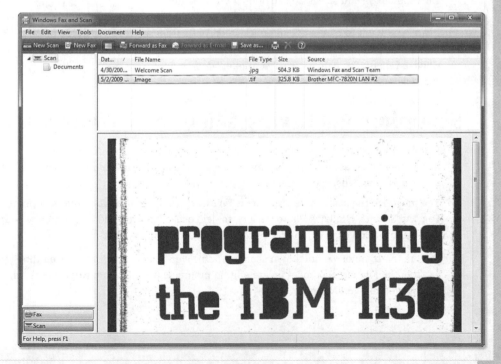

Emailing Scans

If you have a standalone email program (such as Outlook) installed, it's easy to email a scanned document or photo. Just open the Documents folder in Scan view. Select the item you want to email, and click Document, Forward as Email. Enter the recipient(s), message, and other information, and click Send to send the scan.

If you use a web-based email service, you'll have to compose an email and use your email system's Add Attachment feature to upload the image files. You can find them under My Documents inside the folder Scanned Documents.

Faxing Scans

To fax a scanned document or photo without switching to the Fax view, select the item you want to fax and click Document, Forward as Fax. The New Fax dialog box appears. Enter the fax number and other information and click Send to fax the scan. If you want to fax more than one scanned image (or set of images), in the Fax window, click Insert, File Attachment, and locate the additional image(s). You'll find them under My Documents inside the folder Scanned Documents.

➡ *For more information, **see** "Sending Faxes from Windows Fax and Scan," p. 299.*

Manipulating Scanned Images

On a clean install of Windows 7, scanned images are edited by Windows Photo Gallery by default. To edit a scanned image, click Start, Documents, Scanned Documents. Right-click the image and select Edit to open it with the default photo editor. To choose a different photo editor, select the image you want to edit, and right-click Open With. Choose your preferred image editor from the context menu, or click Choose Default Program to select a different program from those listed.

 note

If you edit the image with a program that supports other image file formats, such as Adobe Photoshop or Adobe Photoshop Elements, make sure you save the edited image as a JPEG, TIFF, BMP, or PNG file if you want to be able to use it in Windows Fax and Scan.

Scanning and Faxing Slides and Transparencies

If you work with traditional photos, some of your photos might be slides or negatives rather than prints. Most late-model flatbed scanners, including some all-in-one units, include support for 35mm slides and negatives, and some also support larger sizes.

You must use the scanner vendor's own TWAIN drivers, not the WIA drivers supported by Windows Fax and Scan or Windows Photo Gallery, to gain access to slide and transparency adapters. Thus, if you want to fax a scan of a negative or slide, follow this procedure:

1. Run the scanner vendor's own scan program. This can be run directly from the Start menu, or from the File menu of most image-editing programs (look for an entry such as Import). Be sure to choose the TWAIN driver.

2. Select an appropriate resolution: 600dpi will provide adequate resolution for faxing (although it's too low for printing). Use higher resolution for printing.

3. Save the scanned image to the Scanned Documents folder under Documents.

4. Start Windows Fax and Scan and attach the scanned image to a fax.

5. Send the fax.

SOUND RECORDER, DVD MAKER, AND OTHER MULTIMEDIA TOOLS

Become a Recording Star

As with past versions of Windows, Windows 7 comes with a simple tool to help you create and do basic modification of sound files—Windows Sound Recorder. Although it is admittedly utilitarian in nature, this tool enables you to add audio notations to everything from word processing documents to slideshows and enables you to create slideshows and photo CDs. This chapter covers the functionality of Windows Sound Recorder, the Snipping Tool, and making DVDs, and offers some troubleshooting tips for when things don't come out sounding exactly right.

This chapter also touches on the other multimedia utilities that come with Windows 7. Because many of the accessory programs fall into discrete categories, such as communications, multimedia entertainment, or system tools, look to relevant sections of this book to find coverage of such tools. This chapter covers the more basic, yet still quite useful, tools that don't fit neatly into a pigeonhole.

Windows Sound Recorder

Sound Recorder has been included with Windows since its earliest days. It is not feature rich by any stretch of the imagination—in fact, it enables you only to record an audio file and save it to the hard drive on your computer. Whereas the older version of Sound Recorder enabled you to record an audio file, change the speed of the recorded playback, and do basic editing and conversion of the saved output, this functionality is missing with Windows 7. Sound Recorder can work with files that are in the Windows Media Audio (.wma) format.

To start Sound Recorder, click Start, All Programs, Accessories, Sound Recorder. This gives you the Sound Recorder interface, shown in Figure 12.1

Figure 12.1
The Windows Sound Recorder main interface.

Really only one option is available: Start Recording. Clicking this button enables you to record audio using your PC's microphone. When you have recorded all the information you need, click the Stop Recording button (which appears after a recording is started). When you stop recording, you get a Save As dialog box asking you where to save the recorded output, as shown in Figure 12.2.

Figure 12.2
The Save As dialog box, which defaults to the Documents library.

Here, you need to enter a filename to save the file; you can optionally enter artist and album information by clicking on the function links at the bottom of the Save dialog and entering the desired data (see Figure 12.3). If you enter the artist and album information, you can access this information later inside Windows Media Player and the Documents library.

Figure 12.3
The Save As dialog box, with optional tag information entered.

The file location defaults to the Documents library, but you can change the location where the file is saved by clicking the Documents icon in the sidebar (you might need to click the Browse Folders button) and browsing to the library where you want to save the file.

If you saved the file in the default location, you can click Start, Documents and see the file that you just recorded; if you specified the artist and album information, it is displayed here as well (see Figure 12.4).

Select the sound file.

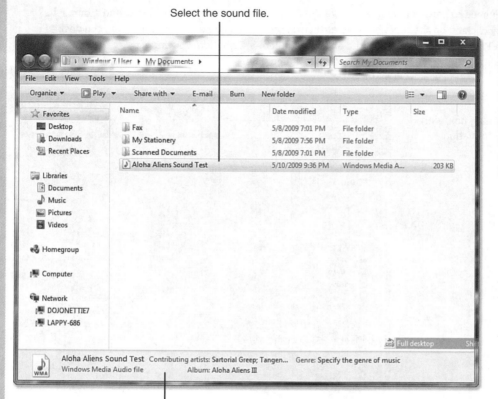

Figure 12.4
An audio file
in the
Documents
library.
Notice the
tag informa-
tion that was
entered ear-
lier.

The tag information appears here.

Volume Control

The Volume Control accessory is basically a no-brainer. It provides a pop-up volume control sport-
ing balance, mute, and other controls for your audio subsystem. Whether you're playing radio stations from the Web, playing CDs from your CD drive, listening to TV (if you have a TV tuner card),
or recording sound files, you need access to these controls from time to time. Of course, if you don't
have a working sound card installed, this accessory isn't available—or, at least, it doesn't do anything. A little-known fact for many people is that this accessory has two sets of controls—one for
recording and one for playback.

1. To open the standard volume controls, simply click the little speaker icon in the notification area
   on the Windows 7 taskbar (see Figure 12.5).

Figure 12.5
The volume mixer, as seen when you click the speaker icon in the notification area.

2. You can alter the system volume setting by dragging the volume slider up or down. You can mute the output by clicking the picture of the speaker at the bottom of the column. If you want to see another volume control, you can select Mixer at the bottom of the column. Figure 12.6 shows the standard volume control.

3. In the Volume Mixer, you typically see two sliders, one for the audio device and one in the Applications group for the system sounds. You might see additional sliders for each running application. These sliders are linked, so adjusting the speaker volume changes the volume level for system sounds. Sometimes, though, you want the alert sounds to be lower than other sounds coming out of your computer, so you can independently control the sliders for each represented application. If you happen to be watching a YouTube video with low audio, you don't want to be blown away by your New Email sound.

 note

The Device slider links all the available sliders together and controls both up and down directions for all sliders. The position of the Device slider also represents the highest volume that any device can be set to. This is important because each Application slider can be set to a volume lower than the one set by the Device slider. Its somewhat confusing described in words, so try it in practice to see it in action.

Figure 12.6
The basic volume control for setting playback volume.

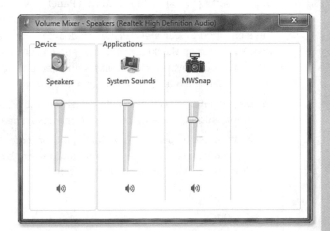

No Sound

What do you do when adjusting the volume control from the notification area icon still doesn't produce any sound?

Various goofs, settings, conflicts, and/or program malfunctions can cause a loss of sound in your projects. As a result, troubleshooting your sound system isn't always easy. One tip is in order here: If you're using a laptop computer, ask yourself whether the sound stopped working after you hibernated or suspended the system. This problem is common on several laptops, and this bug might not have been worked out of Windows 7 for your sound chip set because some parts makers are still working through their transition to Vista drivers. Try rebooting the computer, and see whether the sound comes back to life.

Another thing to look for is a manual volume control on the computer. Many laptops have a control that you can turn or push, often found along the edge of the computer itself. For example, Toshiba has a hardware volume controller on its laptops, and HP has a touch-sensitive slider pad that needs special software to be installed. Such settings override any settings within Windows. If you have a set of powered speakers attached to your computer, make sure they are plugged in to power and are turned on. I often forget to do this and then wonder why I have no sound. For serious problems, you should consult other chapters in this book that deal with the Control Panel and the Device Manager. If none of these remedies works, you might have a bad sound card, or you might need a new device driver.

If you are doing any sound recording, be sure to view the recording controls, too. You can access both the playback and recording level controls as described next.

The controls you see by following these steps are a simplified version of the overall volume settings. To access the detailed volume settings, choose Start, Control Panel, look under Hardware and Sound in the default view and Sound if you have changed to Icon view, Playback; double-click the Speakers entry in the Sound window; and choose the Levels tab. Your sound system's capabilities and default settings determine the format of the volume controls you see. On one of my computers, the controls look like what you see in Figure 12.7.

 tip

To quickly adjust or mute the sound output from your system, or to adjust the master volume level (useful when the phone rings), click the little speaker icon in the notification area, near the clock.

In this window, you can manually adjust the individual levels of the output elements. You can mute individual output elements by clicking the small speaker icon to the right of the volume sliders.

If you are using a sound card with support for more than two speakers, you can also run basic diagnostics and choose the speaker configuration here by clicking the Speakers item in the Playback window and clicking the Configure button.

Figure 12.7
The detailed volume controls.

More options are available to you, as well. Here they are, tab by tab:

- **Playback**—Use this tab to select the output device you are using. In the vast majority of cases, you will have only one option. However, if you have speakers that plug in and USB speakers, you can choose one of them.

- **Recording**—This tab works much like the Playback tab, but for recording devices. Many podcasting microphones use USB to connect instead of the usual input jack.

- **Sounds**—This is the standard Sounds tab that has been included in versions of Windows since time immemorial. You can select from sound themes in the Sound Scheme pull-down and modify which sounds do what and when in the Program Events list. One new thing for Windows 7 is that there are actual themes now—14 new ones plus two more for Ultimate users, to be exact.

- **Communications**—In this new tab, you can actually tell Windows how to deal with the volume if you happen to be using your computer for phone calls. The default is set to decrease the volume by 80%.

Using the Snipping Tool

The Snipping Tool, as you can see in Figure 12.8, is for capturing images of your desktop. Don't underestimate the utility of a screen-capture program. If you ever have an IT guy say he can't help you because he has never seen the error message, use the Snipping Tool to show him your evidence. Granted, you can't always do this because your entire computer might be frozen, but it *will* come in handy.

Figure 12.8

You start the Snipping Tool by going to Start, Snipping Tool (or by choosing Start, All Programs, Accessories, Snipping Tool). You select the type of "snip" you want by clicking the down arrow next to the New button. Your options are

- **Free-form Snip**—Enables you to literally draw around something as if you were cutting it out with scissors. The results will still be rectangular in form, though.

- **Rectangular Snip**—Enables you to drag out a rectangular-shaped area to the size you want. Think of it as precropping an image. Otherwise, you'd have to capture the entire screen and then cut out what you want. This option eliminates the extra steps.

- **Windows Snip**—Enables you to click on a particular window to capture only that window, automatically cutting out the desktop image and anything else, even underlying windows.

- **Full-screen Snip**—Enables you to capture the whole screen in one go.

Once captured, you can draw on or highlight sections of your images and then save them. Click the disk image in the toolbar to open the Save dialog box (or click File, Save). The default location is your Pictures library (covered in detail in Chapter 10). You can save your images in the following file formats:

- **PNG**—The Portable Network Graphics file format is the newest and most accessible file format today. It was developed to replace the GIF file format, which, at the time, was owned by CompuServe. PNGs are generally larger but they can also store more complex amounts of data.

- **GIF**—The classic GIF file format is a very simple file format designed to make images as small as they possibly can be for quicker transfer over the network.

- **JPG**—Also known as JPEG, this file format was designed by the Joint Photographic Experts Group to offer photojournalists a file format that could retain a lot of data but could also be compressed for network deliveries to newspapers around the world. JPG offers a lot of options, including continuously variable compression.

- **MHT**—A Single File HTML format, which is proprietary to Microsoft and really has little use, especially as a file format for screen captures. I'd avoid this unless your intent is to confuse individuals attempting to view images on your computer.

Viewing Your "Snipped" Images

Windows 7 offers a number of ways to view, organize, and work with your images, which are covered in detail in Chapter 10. There are two ways to quickly work with the images you have created using the Snipping Tool—Windows Photo Viewer, and Paint, the Windows classic, which has been updated significantly for the first time since the release of Windows 95 (see Figure 12.9).

Figure 12.9
Viewing your
snipped
image in
Paint.

Aside from receiving a ribbon user interface somewhat like the toolbar system introduced in Microsoft Office 2007, Paint now sports a wide range of rather useful features and supports a number of file formats, including PNG, GIF, and JPG, which were covered earlier in this chapter. Other formats supported by Paint are

- **BMP**—The classic Microsoft Bitmap file format (with either the `.bmp` extension or the rarely used `.dib` extension) is available in monochrome, 4-, 8-, and 24-bit color formats.

- **TIFF**—This format, created by Aldus (those people who made PageMaker), is quite capable of storing a wide range of detailed image data. This makes it well suited for storing fax information, which is why Aldus created it, back when every fax machine maker had its own format. Its extensions are `.tif` and `.tiff`.

The new Paint offers you a load of new features with which you can further edit and manipulate your screen captures.

Recording to DVD

If you have saved a lot of pictures and/or home videos on your computer and now need to prepare a nice presentation, want to send DVDs to your relatives, or just want a nice way to store your media before it completely takes over every kilobyte of storage space, you're covered: Microsoft's DVD Maker program is a simple, fast, and efficient way to create DVDs that will play in most computers and even DVD players.

Unlike versions of Windows before Vista, Windows 7 comes with a DVD-burning application built in to the OS. You can open the DVD burner by choosing Start, All Programs, Windows DVD Maker (see Figure 12.10).

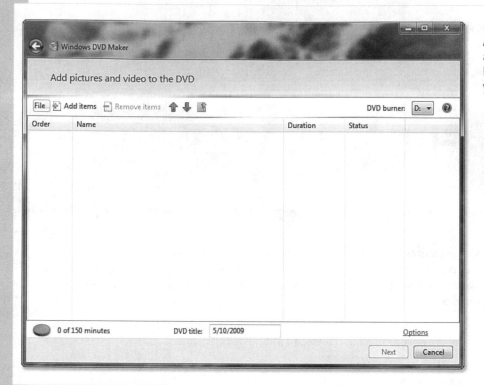

Figure 12.10
Adding pictures and videos to begin making your DVD.

From this screen, you can click Add Items and browse for video files or still photographs. After you select the movie files or pictures, they appear in the main screen in the order in which they will be played on the DVD.

When you have the media elements in the order you prefer, you can change the advanced options for the DVD by clicking the Options link to open the DVD Options dialog box (see Figure 12.11).

The first set of options on the DVD-Video tab controls how you see the video after the DVD is put in the DVD player—whether you start with a menu or start with the video.

 tip

If you want to make a quick slideshow from pictures stored on your computer, click Add Items and Ctrl+click any pictures you want to add. Windows DVD Maker makes a slideshow out of the photos you selected; you can change the order in which the slides are presented in the main screen.

The second set of options controls the aspect ratio for the DVD. Changing this option to 16:9 enables you to create widescreen DVDs suitable for playing on high-end TV sets. If you play a movie that was encoded with the 16:9 aspect ratio on a standard TV set (4:3), the movie will be "letterboxed" (have black bars at the top and bottom of the movie). This is to allow standard TV sets and computer displays to show all the content from a widescreen movie without losing any content.

Recording to DVD **323**

CHAPTER

12

Figure 12.11
Advanced DVD options.

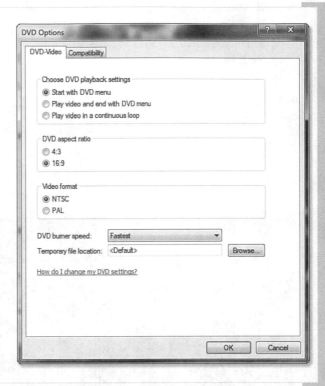

The standard aspect ratio (4:3) allows standard TV screens to use the entire screen for displaying the movie, but on widescreen TVs the movie will be "pillar boxed" (have black bars on either side of the movie). The format you use depends mainly on your source media.

The third set of options enables you to use either the National Television System(s) Committee (NTSC) or Phase-Alternating Line (PAL) format for the video. NTSC video is the format of choice for the Americas as well as some Asian countries; PAL is used most everywhere else. Unless you need to play the movie you're creating on a PAL-compliant DVD player, it's generally best to leave the setting as NTSC.

You can also change the DVD burner speed. This should be set as high as you can without creating "coasters" (DVDs that had a failure during writing, rendering them useless). Another area where you may have problems is with plug-ins or filters that cause compatibility issues with DVD Maker. Under the new Compatibility tab, you can select which filters DVD Maker will use or try to access and, therefore, eliminate that one possible

 note

The more common manner of referring to aspect ratio is either as standard definition (4:3) or high definition (16:9), more commonly known as HD. By the time this book is published, the United States will have passed the deadline for the official move to HDTV. This means that all U.S. broadcasters must send out their signals on the new HD bands. As a point of clarification, most HD content is broadcast or delivered via cable or satellite transmission in 16:9. Most modern laptop and widescreen computer displays have an aspect ratio of 16:10. There are also a number of models of HDTVs that use a 16:10 aspect ratio.

conflict. Of course, the only time you would experience this is if you had installed other DVD authoring software, and if that were the case you likely would not be using DVD Maker.

When you finish on the main pane, click Next. You are presented with the Ready to Burn DVD dialog box, shown in Figure 12.12.

Figure 12.12
The Ready to Burn DVD dialog box, where you can change display options for the movie.

From this dialog box, you can change the style of the menus for the DVD movie, change the text and/or styles for the menu, or modify the settings for the slideshow in the movie. By clicking the Slide Show button in the toolbar, you can add audio to the slideshow or change the other settings for the slideshow (see Figure 12.13).

After you add music to the slideshow, change the length of time between slides, and change the transitions, you can preview the slideshow by clicking the Preview button. When you're satisfied with the show, click the Change Slide Show button.

 tip

If you want to make multiple copies of the same movie, it is best to do it now; by burning multiple copies at once, you bypass the lengthy encoding phase. If you are unable to burn another copy, you can always create copies from the one DVD you did burn. You will require software like Nero Burning ROM or Roxio's Easy DVD Copy 4.

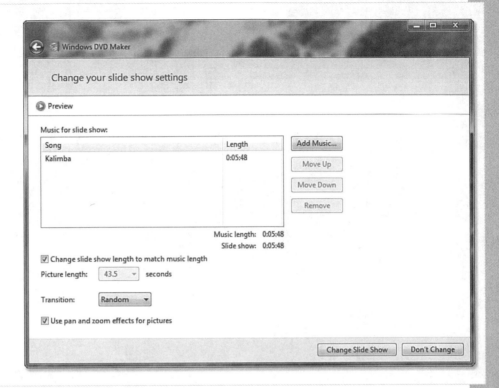

Figure 12.13
Slideshow
options in
Windows DVD
Maker.

When everything is completely ready to go, click the Burn button. If you don't have a blank DVD in the drive, you're prompted to insert one. From here, make a cup of coffee and go to lunch; burning a DVD generally takes much longer than burning a CD, not only because a DVD can hold more data, but primarily because it takes a long time for the software to properly encode your source media to work as a DVD.

The DVD Maker encodes the movie, which is very CPU intensive. After the movie is encoded, DVD Maker burns the DVD, ejects it, and gives you the option to burn another copy of the DVD you just created.

Errors Burning DVDs

I constantly get errors when writing DVDs in Windows DVD Maker, and the DVDs I create don't play in either a standalone DVD player or my computer.

Writing DVD files can sometimes be a tricky and resource-intensive task. Many modern DVD drives have more than enough file cache to prevent buffer underrun errors but, as with CDs, sometimes problems happen. The best way to prevent underrun errors when burning a DVD is to choose a slower burning speed in the DVD Options dialog box of the movie in DVD Maker.

WINDOWS 7 AND THE INTERNET

IN THIS PART

13 Getting Connected   329

14 Using Internet Explorer 8   355

15 Email and Newsgroups with Windows Live Mail   393

16 Troubleshooting Your Internet Connection   417

GETTING CONNECTED

Going Worldwide

Hooking up to the Internet used to be a privilege afforded only to universities and corporations. Now it's actually an essential part of owning and using any PC, and it's available to virtually everyone.

In this chapter, you'll find information about choosing an Internet service provider (ISP), making the connection through a modem or other link, installing and configuring your system, and making your system safe and secure. This chapter tells how to select an Internet connection technology and connect a single computer to the Internet. However, this isn't your only option. You can take any one of several routes:

- If your computer is part of an existing local area network (LAN) with Internet access, you can skip this chapter entirely because Internet access comes as part and parcel of your LAN connection. In fact, if you are part of a corporate LAN, it is probably a violation of your company's security policy to establish your own independent connection. (If it's not, it should be!)

- If you have a LAN for your home or office, you can provide Internet access to all of your computers through one connection. You should read Chapter 19, "Connecting Your Network to the Internet," and decide whether you want to connect your LAN. Use the instructions in this chapter to set up the initial connection; Chapter 19 tells you how to share it with the rest of your workgroup. (If you have two or more computers but haven't yet set up a network to connect them, you should seriously consider doing so. Chapter 17, "Creating a Windows Network," tells how.)

- If you want to use your existing ISP account and connection technology, you can skip the introductory sections of this chapter and go right to "Installing a Modem for Dial-Up Service" or "Installing a Network Adapter for Broadband Service," on **page 345**.

- If you need to make a clean start with the Internet, read on!

Connection Technologies

Not long ago, you had one choice to make for your Internet connection: which brand of modem to buy. Now options abound, and you can choose among several technologies, speeds, and ISP types. A huge technology shift is taking place as high-speed digital (*broadband*) connection services are being deployed worldwide.

Let's take a look at the basic Internet connection technologies that are appropriate for an individual user or workgroup. After describing each one, I'll show you roughly what each costs to set up and use.

Analog Modem

Standard, tried-and-true dial-up modem service requires only a telephone line and a modem in your computer. The downside is that this ties up a telephone line while you're online. Furthermore, if you have call waiting, the "beep" that occurs when someone calls while you're online can make the modem drop its connection. To avoid these hassles, many people order an additional phone line just for the modem, and this adds to the monthly expense.

Dial-up service is adequate for general Web surfing—that is, reading text and viewing pictures. However, you will find it woefully inadequate for viewing video or for voice communication. (In other words, forget about YouTube.)

To use standard dial-up Internet service, you need a modem and a telephone cable. Modems come in internal, external, USB, and PC Card varieties from dozens of manufacturers. Most computers made for home use come with a modem preinstalled. On business computers, they're usually an extra-cost item.

ISDN

Integrated Services Digital Network (ISDN) is a special digital-only telephone service that can carry two independent voice or data conversations over one telephone wire. ISDN service is actually a different type of telephony; you can't plug an ordinary telephone into an ISDN line. ISDN modems can carry data at 64Kbps or 128Kbps, depending on whether you use one or two of its channels to connect to your ISP. Although ISDN Internet service is still available in some areas, I don't recommend it as an Internet connection option. Dial-up is nearly as fast as ISDN. If you need greater speed, and you can't get DSL or cable service, satellite and wireless service are better options.

DSL

Digital Subscriber Line (DSL) service sends a high-speed digital data signal over the same wires your telephone line uses while that line is simultaneously used for standard telephone service. This means that you can get DSL service installed without needing an extra telephone line. The most common DSL service is called *asymmetric*, or *ADSL*, because it receives data at 128Kbps to 6000Kbps but sends at a lower rate. (This is fine because most Web surfing involves sending a very small request and receiving a large amount of data.)

 note

DSL varieties include asymmetric, symmetric, high-speed, and DSL over ISDN, so you might run into the acronyms *SDSL*, *ADSL*, *HDSL*, and *IDSL*, or the collective *xDSL*. For this chapter, these distinctions are unimportant, so I just call it DSL.

DSL has at least one Achilles' heel: Its availability is restricted by your distance from the telephone company's central office, and it isn't available when the distance is more than a couple of miles (as the wires run, not as the crow flies). DSL's reach can be extended by optical fiber lines and special equipment, but this is expensive for the telephone companies to install. DSL might never make it into rural areas.

DSL modems come in two varieties: External units connect to your computer through a network adapter or a USB cable. Internal units plug right in to your computer. If your ISP uses external adapters, before you buy a network adapter, check with your DSL provider, because often one is included in the installation kit. In addition, before you decide to pay extra to get service for multiple computers, read Chapter 19 to see how all your computers can share a single connection.

Cable Modem

Your local television cable company may provide cable modem Internet service, which sends high-speed data signals through the same distribution system it uses to carry high-quality TV signals.

Cable modem service has none of the distance limitations of DSL. One criticism of cable service is that data speeds can drop during high-use times such as the early evening because everyone in a given neighborhood is sharing a single network "pipe." Surveys show, however, that cable subscribers usually get several times the download speed of DSL subscribers.

➥ *For more information on DSL and cable modem service, **see** Chapter 19, which describes these technologies with a focus on using them to connect a LAN to the Internet, but you still might find the information helpful.*

Cable modems generally are external devices that connect to your computer through a network adapter or a USB cable. Before you buy a network adapter, though, check with your ISP; one might be included in the installation kit. Some ISPs charge extra to lease the modem. The price of a cable modem is $30–$60 new and about $1 on eBay, so leasing one from your cable company isn't such a deal. Also, if you have more than one computer and your cable ISP wants to charge you for extra connections, read Chapter 19 to see how all your computers can use a router to share a single connection.

Part IV

Satellite Service

Satellite Internet service uses microwave signals and small (roughly 2-foot-diameter) dish antennas to connect to an orbiting communication satellite. You should consider only *bidirectional* satellite service, which uses the satellite dish for both sending and receiving. Satellite's one advantage is that it's available where DSL and cable haven't yet reached, wherever there's a good view of either the southern sky in the Northern Hemisphere, or the northern sky in the Southern Hemisphere. The disadvantages are many: Installation requires the abilities of both a rocket scientist and a carpenter, the equipment and service plans can be expensive, you'll have to sign a long-term contract to get discounts on installation and equipment, and the system suffers from the same slowdowns that affect cable service. If you download more than your monthly quota allows, you'll likely be punished by having your download speed cut to a crawl for the remainder of the month. Heavy rain or snow can interfere with the signal, so service may be interrupted or degraded during storms. Despite all this, many people beyond the reach of cable and DSL say that satellite service is usually worth the hassle.

Satellite service requires you to purchase a receiving dish antenna, a receiver, and a USB or network adapter to connect the setup to your computer. Your ISP should furnish these devices. For unidirectional satellite service, you also need to have a phone line near your computer.

Installing satellite or wireless modems is not terribly tricky, but the procedure is specific to the type of hardware you're using. Therefore, unfortunately, I have to leave you at the mercy of the manufacturer's instruction manual, and can't provide any specific instructions in this book.

One bit of advice I can give: Installing a satellite dish is difficult, and it's best to hire a professional dish installer for this task. (Our executive editor, Rick Kughen, didn't have the benefit of this sage advice when he installed his, and his conclusion is, "About halfway through the ordeal, I decided that I really wished I had paid the $199 installation fee.") Some satellite providers offer free installation, however, so you might not have to get dirty installing your own or pay big bucks to have someone else do it.

 caution

After your satellite connection is set up, you *must* be sure that Windows Firewall is enabled to protect your computer against hackers. I mention this again later in the chapter. You can read more about firewalls and network security in Chapter 32.

Wireless and Cellular Service

Wireless Internet service is available in most major metropolitan areas and even in some remote areas, through cellular telephone providers. (Our editor, Rick Kughen, notes that he can get wireless Internet service in his rustic fishing village in central Indiana!) Three types of service are available:

- **Fixed-antenna wireless service**—The wireless modem connects to a small whip or dish antenna, and data transfer rates typically are more than 1Mbps using setups with fixed antennae.

- **Wireless modems for laptops**—With this type of service, you connect a small plug-in PC card or USB wireless modem unit to your computer, and the install software provided by your cellular company. The modem as a built-in radio, and it establishes a data connection through the cellular network.

- **Tethered data service through a cell phone**—Some cell phones let you connect a data cable from the phone to your computer. The telephone provides the radio and modem components.

Fixed-antenna wireless is similar to satellite service. You must purchase a receiving antenna, a receiver, and a USB or network adapter to connect the setup to your computer. Your ISP should furnish these devices. You might also have to pay for professional installation. When the network connection is set up, you can use it on a single computer or share it using a router, as I describe in Chapter 19.

The other two options are portable, and serve only a single computer. You may be able to find data plans that let you buy service on a day-by-day basis rather than committing to a long-term service contract. This can be very cost effective when you travel. Since the setup and usage steps are specific to each provider, I can't provide instructions in this chapter.

Choosing a Technology

With all the options potentially available to Windows users for Internet access, making a choice that fits your needs and limitations can become a bit confusing. Research the options that local and national ISPs provide, and then start narrowing them. Table 13.1 summarizes the costs and speeds of several ways for a single computer user to access the Internet (excluding ISDN and wireless service). The prices shown are typical costs for the service in question after applying the usual discounts and special offers.

Table 13.1 Internet Connection Options for the Individual User

Method	Approximate Cost (per Month)	Approximate Setup and Equipment Cost	Time Limits in Hours (per Month)	Availability	Download Speed
Analog modem	$0*–$25	$50	10 to unlimited	Worldwide	33Kbps–56Kbps
DSL	$30 and up	$100	Unlimited	Limited but growing	312Kbps–6Mbps
Cable modem	$30–$50	$100	Unlimited	Limited but growing	1Mbps–10Mbps
Satellite	$50–$150	$200–$800	25 and up	Almost worldwide	400Kbps

* Some ISPs are "free;" I discuss them later in this chapter.

Remember that you have several costs to factor in:

- The cost of hardware required to make the connection

- The cost of installation and setup

- The monthly ISP cost for Internet service

- The cost of telephone lines, if you order a separate line just for Internet access, or the savings you'll get if you can drop one or more phone lines you use for just dial-up service when you upgrade to DSL or cable

- The savings you'll get if you can drop separate dial-up service accounts and extra phone lines for high-speed service that you can share

In addition, if you travel frequently, ask any prospective ISP to tell you if they provide free dial-up or wireless hot-spot Internet service when you're on the road. These costs can add up quickly if you select an ISP that makes you pay extra for this service.

For more information on selecting an Internet technology and to help choose an ISP, check out these sites:

- For information on DSL and cable, see www.dslreports.com.

- For information on satellite service in North and Central America, check out www.starband.com, www.hughesnet.com and www.wildblue.com. In Australia, check www.telstra.com. In Europe, Southern Africa, the Middle East, the Indian subcontinent, and Southeast Asia, see www.intel-sat.com. Satellite services are often resold through regional companies.

- For information on wireless service, see www.mobilebroadbandnetwork.com or contact your area's cellular providers.

Choosing Equipment

You need to purchase equipment that is compatible with the particular type of Internet service you'll be using. Your computer might have come with a modem preinstalled, so, if you will use dial-up service, you might not have to make any decisions. If you will buy new connection hardware, here are some points to consider:

- Most broadband services require specific hardware that your ISP provides (you can sometimes buy a DSL or cable modem independently, but be sure it will be compatible with the equipment your ISP uses). In addition, broadband modems connect via USB or through an Ethernet network adapter. If your service needs a network adapter, and your computer doesn't already have an Ethernet adapter, be sure to get one that's compatible with Windows 7.

- If you will want to share your Internet connection with other computers via a LAN, read Chapter 19 before making any hardware purchases; you'll find information on some special hardware setups.

- Above all, be sure any hardware that you have to plug directly into the computer (modem or LAN adapter) appears in the Windows Compatibility Center list (www.microsoft.com/windows/compatibility). This is important because not every vendor provides Windows 7–compatible drivers for all of their products. Therefore, check the list before you make any purchases.

- For dial-up service, choose a modem that is compatible with the fastest service level your ISP provides. Your ISP should be using V.90 modems for 56Kbps service. If your ISP still uses X2 or K6Flex modems, it's way behind the times. Some ISPs support the V.92 call-waiting protocol. If you have a modem that supports this feature, ask prospective ISPs whether they support it and whether there's an additional charge.

Ordering the Service

Ordering standard dial-up modem Internet service is really quite simple. Just call the ISP, talk to the sales department, and ask the sales representative to mail or fax you instructions for configuring Windows 7. In fact, it's easy enough that they might just talk you through it over the phone.

Ordering cable, DSL, or satellite service is also quite easy because the ISP takes care of all the details. The provider first checks to see whether your neighborhood qualifies for the service. Then a rep calls you back with the news and either sends you a self-installation kit or schedules an installation appointment.

When the service is installed, you're ready to configure your Windows 7 computer. If you're using DSL or cable Internet service, skip ahead to "Installing a Network Adapter for Broadband Service" on **page 345**.

If you're using satellite service, skip ahead to "Satellite Service" on **page 332**.

If you're using dial-up Internet service, continue with the following section.

Installing a Modem for Dial-Up Service

Installing a modem is a pretty painless process these days. Your modem should come with straightforward installation instructions; follow those, and you'll be online in no time.

For an internal modem, you'll pop open your PC's case and insert the modem card into a free expansion slot inside the computer. For an external modem, it's a more simple matter of cabling it to a USB or serial port on your PC. (Don't forget to connect the power supply and turn it on.) A PC card modem simply plugs into your portable computer.

➥ *For more information about installing new hardware,* ***see*** *Chapter 27, "Installing and Replacing Hardware."*

From that point, here's what you need to do.

If your modem is Plug and Play–compatible, Windows 7 should automatically detect it when you turn on your computer and log in. In many cases, Windows already has the required software available and installs it.

If Windows cannot find a set of drivers that matches your brand and model of modem, you might be asked to insert a CD or floppy disk that the modem manufacturer should have provided with your modem.

 note

When you have your modem set up, skip ahead to "Configuring a Dial-Up Internet Connection" on **page 338**.

If you're using an older modem, you might need to add it to the configuration manually by following these steps:

1. Choose Start, Control Panel. In the search box in the upper-right corner, type the word **modem**. Then, click the phrase Phone and Modem.

2. Select the Modems tab, shown in Figure 13.1

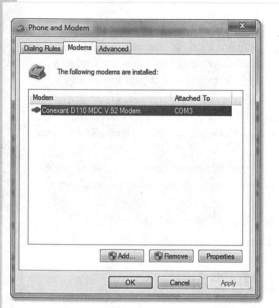

Figure 13.1
The Modems tab identifies the modems currently installed in your system.

3. If Windows has already detected your modem, its name appears in the Modems tab. If the correct modem type is listed, skip to step 8. If the wrong modem type is listed, skip to the next section, "Changing the Modem Type."

   If no modem is listed, click the Add button to run the Add Hardware Wizard.

4. Click Next. Windows locates the COM port and determines the type of modem you have. If this is successful, Windows tells you. In this case, continue with step 7.

5. If Windows detects your modem incorrectly and doesn't offer you the chance to correct the mistake, skip to step 7 and then correct the problem using the instructions in the next section. If you are given the opportunity to correct the problem, click Change and locate the manufacturer and model of your modem in the dialog box. If you find the correct make and model, select them and click OK. If your modem came with a driver disk for Windows 7, click Have Disk and locate the installation file for the modem.

   If your modem isn't listed, try to download the proper driver from Windows Update or from the modem manufacturer (using another computer, of course). You also might try selecting a similar model by the same manufacturer.

6. After you select the modem type, click OK and then Next.

7. Click Finish to complete the installation.

8. Select the Dialing Rules tab.

9. Select My Location and click Edit.

10. Enter the General tab information for your current location, as shown in Figure 13.2.

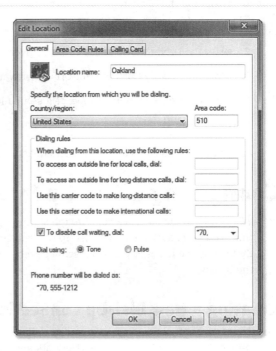

Figure 13.2
In the Edit Location dialog box, you can record the dialing instructions for your current location. The important settings are Country/Region, Area Code, codes for outside lines (if you are on a corporate phone system), and Disable Call Waiting.

11. Enter a name for your location—for example, home, the name of your city, or another name to distinguish the current telephone dialing properties. Set the country, area code, and dialing rules information.

    For example, if your telephone system requires you to dial a 9 to make an outside local call, enter **9** in the box labeled To Access an Outside Line for Local Calls, Dial. Make a corresponding entry for long-distance access.

    If your telephone line has call waiting, check To Disable Call Waiting, Dial and choose the appropriate disable code.

    I assume here that your ISP access number is a local call in the same area code. If this is not the case, you might want to fill in the Area Code Rules tab for the ISP access number. (If you don't know the number yet, don't worry; you can come back and fix it later.)

12. Click OK.

Now your modem is installed and you can continue with "Configuring Your Internet Connection," later in this chapter.

Changing the Modem Type

If Windows incorrectly determines your modem type, you can change it by selecting the appropriate modem in the Modem list (see Figure 13.1) and clicking Properties. Then follow these steps:

1. Select the General tab and click Change Settings.

2. Select the Driver tab and click Update Driver.

3. Select Browse My Computer for Driver Software.

4. Click Browse to locate the proper INF setup file.

5. Click Finish.

Alternatively, you could delete the modem and add it back in manually.

Configuring a Dial-Up Internet Connection

Windows can quickly walk you through setting up the connection from your modem to your ISP. In this section, I show you how to set up the connection the first time, and how to modify it later on if that should be necessary. The subsequent sections tell you how to use the connection to connect to the Internet.

Creating a New Dial-Up Connection

To set up a new connection to your dial-up Internet service, click Start, Control Panel, View Network Status and Tasks (under Network and Internet), and select Set Up a New Connection or Network. Select Connect to the Internet and click Next. Click Dial-Up.

If you already have an account with an Internet Service Provider (ISP), you need to fill in the information provided by your ISP when prompted.

The first field asks for the local access telephone number for your ISP. Enter the local number, optionally preceded by any other codes needed to dial the call. For instance, in the United States, if you enter an area code, you must first enter a 1, then the area code, as shown in Figure 13.3. You can enter parentheses or dashes (-) between the parts of the number, if you want; the modem ignores them.

 note

This step in the Connect to the Internet Wizard doesn't actually deal with the area code correctly. We'll fix it later, under "Adjusting Dial-Up Connection Properties."

Figure 13.3
When prompted, enter the local access number for your ISP.

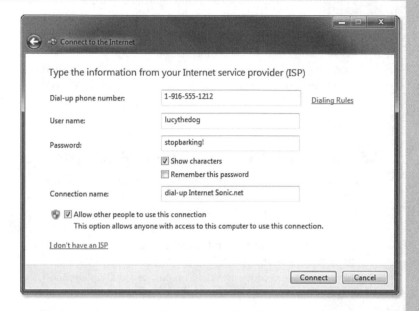

The next two fields ask for your ISP username and password, as shown in Figure 13.3. If you select the Show Characters option, the Password field displays the characters in your password instead of the black circles. This can be useful if you need to verify that you are typing in the correct password.

If you want to have Windows remember the password for your ISP account so you don't need to type it in each time you connect to the Internet, select the Remember This Password option.

The last field asks for a connection name. Type in a name that will help you identify what the connection is used for. The name of your ISP is always good.

The last option, Allow Other People to Use This Connection, is not enabled by default. Select this option if you want the Internet account information to be useable by anyone who uses the computer. Uncheck this if you don't want other users to connect to the Internet with your dial-up account.

 caution

Be sure to use a local number. Your ISP will not help pay your phone bill if you choose a toll number by mistake!

 tip

If you will be traveling, you'll probably accumulate several of these dial-up connections, one for each location you visit, so it would be helpful to add the location to the connection name, as in "Earthlink - Chicago."

Click Connect. Windows 7 immediately dials your ISP. Check to be sure that the connection works before proceeding.

The last step in setting up a dial-up Internet connection is to clean up the new connection's settings such the area code and call waiting control. We'll do that in the next section.

For maximum protection against hackers, I suggest that you read Chapter 32, on network security. At the very least, follow the steps in the next section to be sure that Windows Firewall is enabled. It ought to be enabled by default, but you should check just to be safe.

Adjusting Dial-Up Connection Properties

As configured by the wizard, your dial-up connection is properly set up for most ISPs. However, the wizard doesn't do a good job of setting up the area code and call-waiting settings, so you might want to manually adjust these. You won't likely need to change any of the other settings, but just in case (and because I know you're curious), I walk you through the various settings and properties that are part of a dial-up connection.

To adjust a connection's properties, click the Network icon in the taskbar, as shown in Figure 13.4. This displays all dial-up connections you've configured (see Figure 13.5).

 note

If you have several ISP accounts, ISP access numbers for different cities, or both personal and business dial-up connections, you can add additional connections by repeating the Connect to the Internet Wizard process for each access telephone number or account.

 tip

You can instantly view your list of dial-up connections by clicking the Network icon in the notification area of the taskbar, as described in the next section.

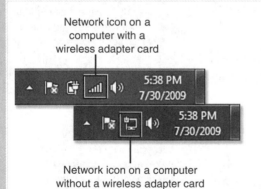

Network icon on a computer with a wireless adapter card

Network icon on a computer without a wireless adapter card

Figure 13.4
Click the Network icon in the taskbar to work with your list of Internet and network connections. On your computer, the icon may appear as shown at the left. If you have a wireless network adapter in your computer, it appears as shown at the right.

Right-click the icon for your dial-up connection and select Properties. You'll see five tabs, shown in Figure 13.6, which I will run through in the order in which they appear. Only a few settings ever need to be changed for an ISP connection:

- The General tab lists modem properties and the ISP telephone number. The following two settings are the most important ones to examine and if necessary, change:

  - If you travel with your computer, check Use Dialing Rules, and be sure that the ISP's area code is set correctly in its own box, and is not entered in the same box as the phone number. Figure 13.6 shows how it should look.

Figure 13.5
The View Available Networks list shows icons for each of your dial-up accounts and high-speed links.

Click the name or icon to make a connection.

- If your telephone line has call waiting service, you must tell Windows to disable call waiting when it dials your ISP.

  To do this, click the Dialing Rules button. Select your current location and click Edit. If the location name is "My Location," change it to the name of your city. Then, at the bottom, check To Disable Call Waiting, Dial: and select the code used by your telephone company. Figure 13.2, earlier in the chapter, shows how this might look. Click OK twice to return to the connection properties dialog.

- If you have multiple modems, you can choose at the top of this tab which one to use for this particular connection. (If you select more than one modem, Windows will attempt to use them simultaneously. Don't do this unless your ISP offers "modem binding" service.)

- Using the Configure button for the modem, you can set the maximum speed used to communicate from the computer to the modem. For *external* modems connected via a COM port, if you don't have a special-purpose high-speed serial port, you might want to reduce this speed from the default 115200 to 57600.

- Using the Alternates button for the telephone number, you can add multiple telephone numbers for your ISP, which will be automatically tried, in turn, if the first doesn't answer.

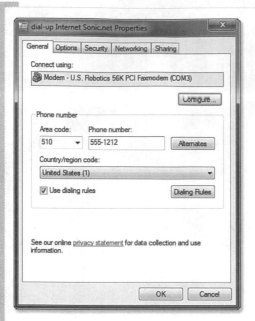

Figure 13.6
A dial-up connection's Properties dialog box lets you change dialing rules, set network parameters, manage the security options, and manage networking and sharing options.

- On the Options tab, you can configure dialing and redialing options.

  - Select the Display Progress While Connecting option to have progress information displayed during the connection process.

  - Select the Prompt for Name and Password, Certificate, etc. option to have Windows 7 prompt you for your dial-up username and password each time you connect. You can also use dial-up networking to log on to your Windows domain. Don't check this option if you use a commercial ISP; that's only for connections to corporate networks.

  - You can select to have Windows 7 prompt you for the phone number of your ISP each time you connect.

  - You can select a time to wait before hanging up the line when no activity occurs. By doing so, if you pay an hourly rate to your ISP, you can help cut costs by having your computer disconnect itself from the Internet if it detects that you've not been using your connection for a set amount of time.

  - To maintain a permanent, or *nailed-up*, dial-up connection, check Redial If Line Is Dropped and set the disconnect time to Never. (Do this only with the consent of your ISP.)

  - The Security tab controls whether your password can be sent in unencrypted form. It's okay to send your ISP password unsecured.

- The Networking tab determines which network components are accessible to the Internet connection. If you're dialing in to a standard ISP, leave File and Printer Sharing unchecked; you'll learn more about that in Chapter 19.

- The Sharing tab allows other network users to connect through your computer's Internet connection. You'll learn more about Internet Connection Sharing in Chapter 19.

Click OK to save your changes.

 tip
If you want to rename a dial-up connection, you have to go about it an odd way: Open the Network and Sharing Center and select Manage Adapter Settings. An icon for your dial-up connection will appear here. Right-click it and select Rename.

Making and Ending a Dial-Up Connection

If you use a dial-up connection with an analog modem, after you've set up an icon for your ISP, making the connection is a snap. You use this same procedure if you use a broadband connection with Point-to-Point Protocol over Ethernet (PPPoE) that requires you to log on:

1. Click the Network icon in your taskbar (refer to Figure 13.4).

2. Select the appropriate connection from the list and click Dial.

3. When Windows displays a connection dialog box (see Figure 13.7). If you previously let Windows remember the password, you can simply skip ahead to step 4.

   Otherwise, enter the password assigned by your ISP. At this point, you can check Save This User Name and Password for the Following Users. Select "Me Only" or, if you want to allow others to connect with your account (or you don't care who uses your account), select Anyone Who Uses This Computer. Then, click Dial.

Figure 13.7
If you previously saved your dial-up password, you can just click Dial to connect. Otherwise, enter your username and password.

4. For a dial-up connection only, check that the phone number is correct, including area code and any required prefix numbers. You might need to click Properties to correct your current location (Dialing From) and/or the Dialing Rules if the prefix or area code isn't correct.

5. Click Dial to make the connection.

Windows then dials your ISP and establishes the connection.

Modem Doesn't Dial ISP

If you attempt to connect to your ISP, but the modem doesn't make an audible attempt to connect, there are several possible solutions:

- Your phone line might not be correctly plugged into the modem. Be sure the phone cable is plugged into the correct jack on the modem.

- The phone line might not be working. Try an extension phone in the same wall jack to see if there's a dial tone.

- The modem might be working, but its speaker volume might be turned down. (This has fooled me more than once!) Some external modems have volume knobs. You can set the volume on an internal modem by opening Control Panel, Hardware and Sound, Device Manager. Expand the Modems option in the tree to view all your modems, right-click the modem in the tree, and select Properties. Select the Modem tab and adjust the volume control.

- The modem might have a hardware problem. Open the modem properties, as described in the previous paragraph. View the Diagnostics tab and click Query Modem. After 5–15 seconds, you should see some entries in the Command/Response list. If an error message appears instead, your modem is not working properly. If it's an external modem, be sure it's powered up. If it's an internal modem, see Chapter 27. Try to update the modem's driver software.

If the connection fails, Windows displays a (usually) sensible message explaining why: There was no dial tone because your modem is unplugged, there was no answer at the ISP or the line is busy, or your user ID and password failed. In the last case, you get three tries to enter the correct information before Windows hangs up the phone.

Modem Dials ISP But the Connection Fails

If you attempt to connect to your ISP, and the modem makes the call, but the Internet connection still fails, Windows should indicate what sort of problem was encountered. You might have typed your account name and password incorrectly. Try one or two more times. If it still doesn't work, a call to your ISP is the best next step. Your ISP might require you to enter the account name information in an unintuitive way. (Earthlink, for example, at one time required you to put ELN\ before your account name.) Your ISP's customer support people can help you straighten this out.

When your connection is made, you should be able to browse websites, check your email, and so on.

Can't Reach Any Websites

If your Internet connection seems to be established correctly, but you can't reach any websites, turn to Chapter 21, Troubleshooting Your Network," for the nitty-gritty details. Troubleshooting connection problems is such a large topic that an entire chapter is devoted to it.

Hanging Up a Dial-Up Connection

When you finish using your Internet connection, click the Network icon in the taskbar, as shown earlier in Figure 13.4. Click the name of your Internet connection, then click Disconnect. Windows will hang up the connection.

Installing a Network Adapter for Broadband Service

If you are going to use cable or DSL Internet service, the following sections should help you get the service installed and working. To start with you will need to connect your computer to your cable or DSL modem. A very few DSL and cable modems use a USB connection and can just be plugged into your computer this way.

However, most DSL and cable service providers require an Ethernet network adapter for use by their modems. Most computers have an Ethernet adapter built in, ready to use. Or, your ISP will supply and install one for you. You won't have to lift a finger. You just need to log in using an Administrator account and supervise while the installer does his or her stuff.

 tip

If a professional installer configures your computer or adds software to it, be sure to take thorough notes of what he or she does. Don't hesitate to ask questions—you have a right to know exactly what the installer is doing. Be sure to test the setup before the installer leaves.

If you want to purchase or install the network adapter yourself, install it according to the manufacturer's instructions. This process will go something like this:

- For an internal adapter in a desktop computer, shut down Windows, unplug the computer, and install the card. Then, power up the computer and log on.

- For a laptop computer, if you have to install a plug-in PCMCIA (PC Card) adapter, you don't need to shut down Windows. Just plug in the card.

The Plug and Play system should take care of the rest for you.

After installation, confirm that the network adapter is installed and functioning by following these steps:

1. Click Start, right-click Computer, and then select Manage.

2. Select the Device Manager in the left pane. The list in the right pane should show only "first-level" items. Under Network Adapters, you should see no items listed with an exclamation mark icon superimposed.

If the network adapter appears and is marked with a yellow exclamation point, follow the network card troubleshooting instructions in Chapter 21, "Troubleshooting Your Network."

If you're using cable Internet service, skip ahead to "Configuring a PPPoE Broadband Connection" on **page 347**.

 caution

When your network adapter is working and connected to your DSL or cable modem, Windows may pop up a box asking you to set a location for the network it has just detected. If you plugged your network adapter directly into your cable or DSL modem, you *must* choose Public as the location, so that Windows knows to block network services that could be abused by hackers.

Installing Filters for DSL Service

For DSL service with self-installation, you will be provided with filters, devices that plug into your telephone jacks and block the DSL signal from reaching your telephones and answering machines. You need to identify every phone jack that is connected to the line your DSL service uses, and install a filter on every jack but the one that plugs into your DSL modem. If you need to plug a phone into the same jack that the DSL modem uses, use a dual jack adapter, with a filter on the side that connects to the phone.

 tip

If a jack is unused, you don't need to plug a filter in it, but it's a good idea to put a label over the jack indicating that it carries the DSL signal. This way you'll remember to add a filter if you ever do plug a phone or other device into this jack.

Alternatively, the service installer might connect your telephone line to a device called a *splitter* outside the house and will install a separate cable to bring the DSL signal to your computer. These devices separate the high-frequency DSL carrier signal from the normal telephone signal.

Now, skip ahead to "Configuring a PPPoE Broadband Connection" on **page 347**.

Configuring a High-Speed Connection

If you're using an Ethernet network adapter to connect your computer to a DSL or cable Internet service, the installer might set up your computer for you. "Self-install" providers give you a set of instructions specific to your service. I can give you a general idea of what's required.

caution

If your broadband service uses a network adapter (that is, an Ethernet adapter) to connect to a cable or DSL modem, you *must* take the following steps to secure your computer from hackers.

1. Click the Network icon in the taskbar and then click Open Network and Sharing Center.

2. Under View Your Active Networks, locate the icon that corresponds to the network adapter that connects to your DSL or cable modem—it's probably labeled Local Area Connection.

   Be sure that the label next to the network's icon says Public Network, *not* Home Network or Work Network. Because the connection hooks up directly to the Internet, it must be designated as a Public network.

   If the label says Home Network or Work Network, click on those words and select Public Network.

3. Now, for additional insurance, at the left, select Change Adapter Settings. Locate the icon for the adapter that goes to your DSL or cable modem. Right-click it and select Properties.

4. Under This Connection Uses the Following Items, uncheck File and Printer Sharing for Microsoft Networks, and uncheck Client for Microsoft Networks.

5. If your ISP requires you to set a specific IP address for the network adapter, highlight Internet Protocol Version 4 (TCP/IPv4) and click Properties. Check Use the Following IP Address, and enter the IP Address, Subnet Mask, and Default Gateway provided by your ISP. You may also be instructed to enter DNS server addresses.

6. Click OK.

After the adapter has been configured and attached to the DSL or cable modem with a network cable, you configure the connection. The procedure you should use depends on whether your ISP uses PPPoE or an always-on connection. The following sections describe these procedures.

Configuring a PPPoE Broadband Connection

Most DSL and some cable Internet providers use a connection scheme called *Point-to-Point Protocol over Ethernet (PPPoE)*. This technology works a lot like a standard dial-up connection, but the "call" takes place through the DSL circuit or TV cable instead of over a voice connection. Windows 7 has PPPoE software built in, but the setup process varies from provider to provider; yours should give you clear instructions.

If you perform the procedure manually, the steps should look like this:

1. Open the Network and Sharing Center window by clicking Start, Control Panel, View Network Status and Tasks.

2. Click Set Up a New Connection or Network. Select Connect to the Internet and click Next. If Windows says you are already connected to the Internet, click Set Up a New Connection Anyway. If Windows asks, "Do you want to use a connection that you already have?," click No, Create A New Connection.

3. Select Broadband (PPPoE).

4. Enter the username and password assigned by your ISP. You might want to check Show Characters before you enter the password, to make sure you enter it correctly.

5. In most cases, you will want to let anyone who uses your computer use your Internet connection. To make this easy, check both Remember This Password and Allow Other People to Use This Connection.

6. Enter your ISP's name and click Connect.

At this point, you're prompted to sign on. Surprisingly, the procedure for signing on and off is exactly the same as for dial-up Internet service. This is described earlier in this chapter under "Making and Ending a Dial-Up Connection," so I won't repeat the instructions here. I will repeat one tip: remember to click the Network icon on the taskbar, shown in Figure 13.4, whenever you want to start or stop your Internet connection.

 note

Some ISPs give you a CD-ROM with installation software that does the next setup procedure for you. I intensely dislike this practice: Who knows what other software—including adware and "customer support" spyware—they're installing? Personally, I lie to them, tell them I'm installing the connection on a Macintosh or Linux computer that can't use their software, and ask for the information needed to perform the setup manually. Sometimes this works, and sometimes it makes life difficult. For instance, one major ISP I've worked with requires you to set up the service account through a special website, so if you want to shun its software, you need Internet access to set up your Internet access.

 note

Installing a network adapter to connect to a broadband modem doesn't give you a LAN—it's just a way of connecting to the modem. If you want to set up a LAN in addition to an Internet connection, see Chapter 17, "Creating a Windows Network," and Chapter 19, "Connecting Your Network to the Internet."

Setting Up Dynamic IP Addressing (DHCP)

In most cases, your ISP will use the DHCP protocol to configure client network adapters. This is the default setting for all new network adapters.

Some ISPs require you to give them the *MAC address* of your network adapter. This is an identification number built into the hardware that uniquely identifies your particular network adapter. To find this number, follow these steps:

1. Open a Command Prompt window by clicking Start, All Programs, Accessories, Command Prompt.

2. Type `ipconfig /all` and press Enter.

3. You might need to scroll back, but find the title that reads something similar to Ethernet Adapter Local Area Connection. Look for the name of the adapter that goes to your broadband modem. This might be Local Area Connection 2, if you've installed an extra adapter. Ignore any entries that mention the word Miniport. If you have multiple adapters and can't tell which is which, unplug the network cable from all but the one that goes to the modem and type the command again.

4. Find the line titled Physical Address. It will be followed by six pairs of numbers and letters, as in 00-03-FF-B9-0E-14. This is the information to give to your ISP.

Alternatively, you might be instructed to set your computer's name to a name that your ISP provides. To do this, follow these steps:

1. Log on using an Administrator account. Click Start, right-click Computer, and select Properties.

2. Under Computer Name, Domain, and Workgroup Setting, click Change Settings. On the Computer Name tab, click the Change button.

3. Enter the computer name as supplied by your ISP, as shown in Figure 13.8.

Figure 13.8
Specify a required computer name in the Computer Name/Domain Changes dialog box.

4. Click More and enter the domain name specified by your ISP, as shown in Figure 13.9.

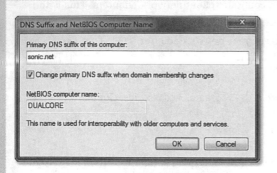

DNS Suffix and NetBIOS Computer Name

Primary DNS suffix of this computer:

sonic.net

☑ Change primary DNS suffix when domain membership changes

NetBIOS computer name:

DUALCORE

This name is used for interoperability with older computers and services.

OK   Cancel

Figure 13.9
Enter the domain name provided by your ISP. This may just be their domain name or it can include an additional location prefix.

When you close all these dialog boxes by clicking OK, you need to let Windows restart. When it restarts, your Internet connection should be up and running.

Setting Up a Fixed IP Address

In some cases, your ISP will require you to set your LAN adapter to a fixed IP address. This might be required with either PPPoE or "always-on" service. To set the address, follow these steps:

1. Log on as a Computer Administrator. Open the Network and Sharing Center window, for example, from Start, Control Panel, View Network Status and Tasks.

2. Under View Your Active Networks, click the connection name, for example, Local Area Connection. In the Status window, select Properties to open the Local Area Connection Properties dialog box.

3. Select the Networking tab, select the Internet Protocol (either Version 6 or Version 4 depending on the IP provided by your ISP), and click the Properties button.

4. Select Use the Following IP Address, and enter the IP address, subnet mask, and default gateway information provided by your ISP, as shown in Figure 13.10.

Figure 13.10
Here you can add the network address, subnet mask, and DNS information supplied by your ISP.

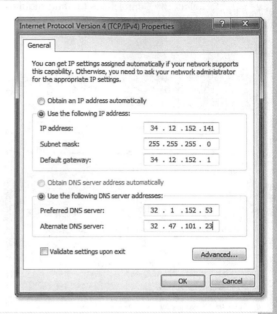

5. Select Use the Following DNS Server Addresses, and enter the two DNS addresses provided by your ISP.

6. Click OK to return to the Local Area Connection Properties dialog box.

When you have completed this procedure, return to the PPPoE setup steps, or, if you have always-on service, open Internet Explorer to test-drive your new connection.

Changing the Default Connection

If you don't establish a connection manually before using an Internet program such as Internet Explorer, Windows dials your ISP automatically when you start these programs. If you don't want Windows to dial automatically, or if you have defined multiple dial-up connections, you can tell Windows which, if any, of the connections you want it to dial automatically.

To change the default settings, follow these steps:

1. Open the Control Panel, select Network and Internet, and click Internet Options. Alternatively, within Internet Explorer, you can choose Tools, Internet Options.

 tip

If you use your computer at work and at home, and have a fixed IP address at home, leave the IP address and DNS settings set to Obtain Automatically for work, and make the fixed IP address entries for home on the Alternate Configuration tab that appears when Obtain Automatically is selected.

When you're entering TCP/IP dotted-decimal numbers such as 1.2.3.4, the spacebar advances the cursor across the periods. This technique is much easier than using the mouse to change fields.

2. Select the Connections tab and highlight the dial-up connection you want to use for Internet browsing (see Figure 13.11).

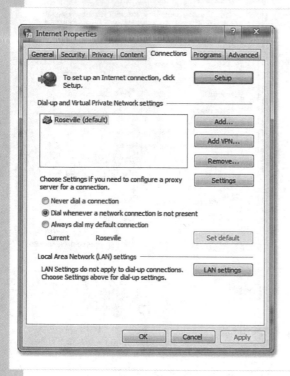

3. If you use a standalone computer or a portable computer that sometimes has Internet access via a LAN, select Dial Whenever a Network Connection Is Not Present.

   If you want to use the modem connection even while you're connected to a LAN, you can select Always Dial My Default Connection.

   Finally, if you don't want Windows to dial automatically and you prefer to make your connection manually, you can choose Never Dial a Connection.

4. If you have actually changed the default dial-up connection, click Set Default.

5. Click OK.

Managing Multiple Internet Connections

Life would be so simple if computers and people just stayed put, but that's not the way the world works anymore. Portable computers now account for more than half of the computers sold in the United States. Managing Internet connections from multiple locations can be a little tricky.

I talk a bit more about the ins and outs of traveling with your computer in Chapter 34, "Wireless Networking," and Chapter 35, "Hitting the Road," where the topics are wireless and remote networking.

The issue comes up with plain Internet connectivity as well, so let me share some tips:

- If you use a LAN Internet connection in the office and a modem connection elsewhere, open the Connections tab of the Internet Properties dialog box and choose Dial Whenever a Network Connection Is Not Present, as I discussed in the previous section, "Changing the Default Connection."

- If you use different LAN connections in different locations, see "Multiple LAN Connections," in Chapter 35.

- If you use a dial-up ISP with different local access numbers in different locations, life is a bit more difficult. It would be great if Windows would let you associate a distinct dial-up number with each dialing location, but it doesn't—dialing locations just adjust the area code and dialing prefixes.

  The solution is to make separate connection icons for each location's access number. After you set up and test one connection, right-click its icon and select Create Copy. Rename the icon using the alternate city in the name; for example, I might name my icons My ISP Berkeley, My ISP Freestone, and so on. Finally, open the Properties dialog box for the new icon and set the appropriate local access number and dialing location.

  In this case, it's best to tell Windows never to automatically dial a connection (as shown earlier in "Changing the Default Connection") because it will not know which of several connections is the right one to use; it might dial a long-distance number without you noticing.

Moving around from one network to another or one ISP to another can also cause major headaches when you try to send email. The reason is that outgoing email has to be sent from your email program to a mail server called an SMTP server. These servers are set up to reject incoming email from any unidentified user who is not directly connected to or dialed up to their own network. For example, if you have an email program that is set up to send email through your company's mail server and you try to send mail from home, your company's server will see that you're connected from a foreign network—that is, your ISP's network—and might reject the message, calling it an "attempt to relay mail."

Likewise, you might experience the same problem if you are set up to send through your ISP's mail server and then try to send mail from a wireless connection at an Internet café.

USING INTERNET EXPLORER 8

What's New in Internet Explorer 8?

If you have used Internet Explorer 5, 6, or 7, then IE8 will be mostly familiar to you. Some of its new features are behind the scenes—not readily apparent, but designed to make IE run more smoothly and reliably than ever. Others are enhancements that you will see, including these:

- The interface is streamlined; the menu and links are no longer visible by default (although you can still activate them, if you want).

- The Search Companion in Internet Explorer 6 is long gone; it was replaced by the Live Search box at the upper-right corner of the window (underneath the Minimize, Maximize, and Close buttons) in IE7 and remains in IE8. The Live Search box makes it faster and easier for you to search for items on the Web.

- The toolbar appears below the Address box, and Internet Explorer presents web pages in tabs. You can open a new page in your current tab, or you can open a new tab and have any number of web pages open at one time, all contained within a single browser window. You just click on tabs to switch between each web page. The Favorites and Add Favorites buttons appear to the left of the tab.

- IE8 introduces the concept of Tab Groups. If you're the type of web surfer who enjoys tabbed browsing, you'll really enjoy Tab Groups that combine and color code related tabs. As you close tabs within a group, the next active tab is shown constantly keeping you within context of the current task.

- The right side of the toolbar contains easily accessible task menus, including the capability to obtain RSS feeds automatically from sites that IE8 recognizes as having them available.

- As with IE6, playback support for Flash and Shockwave files is built into IE8.

- IE8 provides enhanced navigation with Compatibility View. As with all new browser releases, some websites cease to function or render properly, and IE8 addresses this issue to display pages as designed for IE7. No more misaligned text or text boxes and misplaced images. Plus you can specify Compatibility View settings on a per-site basis. Is that cool or what?

- Suggested Sites (off by default and disabled during InPrivate viewing or secure SSL and intranet connections) makes site suggestions based on your viewing habits. IE sends information to Microsoft via a secure connection, where it is stored temporarily per session with a uniquely generated identifier.

 tip

When you open a website, IE8 automatically looks for web feeds that are available on the page. A *web feed* is content that is published frequently by a website. That content can include text, graphics, audio, and video. You may have heard of RSS, or Really Simple Syndication, which is the leading system for creating and delivering web feeds (commonly used for blogs). If IE8 finds a web feed on the page, the Web Feed button changes color from gray (no web feed) to orange (web feed available) so you can download and view and/or listen to the content as well as subscribe to the feed so you can receive new content from the website automatically.

- InPrivate is a new security mode that consists of private browsing, blocking, and subscription. This privacy protection mode does not retain browsing or search histories, site cookies, form data, or login passwords and automatically clears the browser cache.

- Accelerators perform selection-based searches so that users can invoke an online service from any page with a simple mouse gesture. Selecting text and objects reveals access to available Accelerator services, which eliminates the need to cut and paste between web pages.

- Web Slices are updated snippets of an entire page that users can subscribe to based on developer-designated page portions. Web Slices are automatically updated by the browser to present visual representations for websites viewable directly from the Favorites bar in a convenient flyout window.

- AutoComplete in IE8 has changed considerably. Inline AutoComplete is gone, but the Address bar now features domain highlighting for added security. Only the top-level domain is visible in black while the remaining URL is grayed out—a feature that cannot be disabled by users or the sites they visit—to simplify the task of spotting site spoofers. Furthermore, the Address bar is no longer a location for typing URLs: it's a fully fledged search entry tool that scours the Web, visited sites, Favorites, and RSS feeds.

- SmartScreen Filter is an extension of IE7's phishing filter that prevents harmful or imposter sites from duping users. IE8 will produce a prompt reporting that a given site should be avoided, giving the user safe alternative options (visit the home page, previous site, or continue on to the designated-unsafe destination).

- The Favorites bar now replaces the Links bar in both form and function. It hosts content from Web Slices, RSS feeds, documents, and site links. You can view snapshots of pages that developers design specially for this purpose.

- Performance and stability has increased considerably in IE8. The integrated HTML processor, CSS engine, mark-up tree manipulation, and JScript runtime environment have been vastly improved. IE8 also uses a loosely coupled architecture that runs the browser frame and its tabs in separate process spaces so that glitches and hang-ups don't crash everything. ActiveX permissions are designed with greater granularity so that, instead of global disablement, users can now exercise discretion on a per-site basis.

Among the more noticeable and noteworthy IE8 features are Accelerators and Web Slices. Together, these two features enable you to glean information from sites and services without directly visiting them.

An Accelerator delivers data from the Web to your browser in summarized form. Suppose you visit a contact page that displays a physical address: highlight the information, select a maps Accelerator, and the relevant information appears in a pop-up window or new tab, depending on the Accelerator's design. Microsoft Accelerators take advantage of Live Maps, Bing (formerly Live Search), and Windows Live Spaces services. Others are designed specifically for other popular sites and services, including Amazon, eBay, Facebook, and Yahoo.

Web Slices deliver dynamic page content to your browser via the Web from pages you're not even visiting. You can keep up-to-date tabs on changing stock prices or pricing bids without directly accessing financial sites and auction pages. When you visit a site that is capable of delivering Web Slice content, the Web Slice icon (located on the Favorites bar) turns green. As content changes, the title changes to bold. Click the Web Slice, and a flyout window appears to display relevant content. Click the flyout window and IE automatically brings the full page within focus of your browser—or you can just preview data in the drop-down window pane.

note

A Department of Justice Consent Decree has caused some changes in the way that middleware applications are handled. In Windows Vista, you can configure your computer to show only Microsoft middleware applications (Windows Mail, Internet Explorer, and so on), to show only non-Microsoft middleware applications (Mozilla Firefox, Mozilla Sunbird, Eudora, and so forth), or to show some combination of both. Microsoft has removed Windows Mail (along with Photo Gl downloads.

tip

Check out the variety of Microsoft's Accelerator Add-ons Gallery at www.ieaddons.com/en/accelerators. You can find Accelerators for many popular sites and services to improve your browsing results and enhance productivity levels.

Internet Explorer 8 Quick Tour

Web browsers have become so ubiquitous that we assume you are already comfortable with the basics of web browsing. And because many Windows 7 elements such as Windows Explorer, the Control Panel, and Network use the background code of IE7, you are probably already familiar with the location of common toolbar buttons, menus, and other screen elements.

Still, IE8 does have some new features, so we provide an overview of how to use some of them here. This overview will be especially useful if you are switching from an even earlier version of Internet Explorer or another web browser, such as Netscape Navigator.

→ *You must have a connection to the Internet configured on your computer before you can connect to the Web.* **See** *Chapter 13, "Getting Connected."*

You can begin browsing the Internet by launching Internet Explorer from the Start menu, or more conveniently from the Windows 7 taskbar.

If you connect to the Internet via a dial-up connection, you might be prompted to connect. When the connection is established, Internet Explorer probably opens by default to the Windows Bing home page, as shown in Figure 14.1, so you can search the Web. Some PC manufacturers, such as Compaq, customize IE before delivery so that you see their home page instead.

→ *To change the home page so that you see a personal favorite when IE opens,* **see** *Chapter 23, "Tweaking and Customizing Windows."*

Internet Explorer Crashes on Certain Web Pages

You might find that IE8 occasionally fails to properly render a page or appears incompatible with certain page content or site scripting. When visiting a site built for IE7, the browser automatically offers you Compatibility View. You'll know it's in effect because an informative balloon tip appears along with an icon of a broken page that lights up on the right side of the Address bar. To enable this workaround, click the icon to activate Compatibility View; click again to disable it. IE8 remembers this mode for the pages you revisit so you won't have to keep engaging it, but you can also opt out of this feature for certain pages. IE8's Compatibility View only appears upon detection of an incompatible site.

Web pages change frequently, so the page you see will probably look different than Figure 14.1. The general layout of the IE8 window might also be different from what is shown here, although if you have performed a standard installation of Windows 7 and have not done any customizations, it should look like this.

 tip

Want even more space to view web pages? Press F11 to change the view and remove some screen elements to make more room for web documents. If you don't like what you see, press F11 again to toggle back.

In IE7, the Links bar provides users with one-click access to their favorite sites; however, in IE8 this has undergone complete renovation and is now the Favorites bar. Consider creating buttons on the Favorites bar for the web pages you visit most frequently—page links, RSS feeds, Web Slices, and even Microsoft Office documents. To see the Favorites bar (enabled by default), right-click on an empty area of the toolbar and click Favorites from the pop-up menu. The Favorites toolbar appears, as shown in Figure 14.2. Before you customize the Favorites bar, keep these tips in mind:

- The star icon just to the right of the Favorites button adds the current page to the Favorites toolbar.

- The Get More Add-ons button opens a Web Slice where you can explore and obtain IE8 add-ons.

Figure 14.1
Internet Explorer opens with MSN as the default home page; however, you're free to change this to any website you prefer.

- The Suggested Sites Web Slice enables you to receive website suggestions based on your browsing interests. Turn on Suggested Sites so that IE8 can better assist your web surfing habits.

- You can remove unwanted Favorites buttons by right-clicking them and choosing Delete from the menu that appears. Alternatively, you can click the Favorites button and delete Favorites entries in the Favorites management window.

- Make space for more Favorites (and Internet Explorer's toolbar area) by right-clicking the Favorites button and uncheck Lock the Toolbars from the menu that appears. Click the dotted handle on the left side of the toolbar and drag it down to the Tabs level, then reenable the Lock the Toolbars option.

- To create more room, reduce the length of your Address box and move it to share a "line" with another toolbar. (The main toolbar, on the top line, is a good place for the Address box.) Experiment with the placement of all toolbars so that you have as much space as possible to view web pages.

- The easiest way to add a web page to the Favorites bar is to click the star and arrow icon or drag the icon for the page from the Address box and drop it onto the Favorites bar.

Add the current page to your favorites list.

Add the current page to the Favorites toolbar.

Get new add-ons for IE8.

IE8 will suggest sites you might
like based on the pages you visit.

Figure 14.2
The Favorites bar is
a handy place to
store your most fre-
quently visited web-
sites.

You can navigate around the Internet by typing web addresses into the Address box or by clicking
hyperlinks on a page. The mouse pointer changes from an arrow into a hand whenever it is located over
a link. Among the most useful features of the IE8 interface are the Back and Forward buttons. When you
click the Back button, you return to the previously visited page. Clicking Forward moves you ahead once
again. (To move around even faster, Alt+left arrow and Alt+right arrow produce the back and forward
functions; if you have a new mouse, it might also have special Back and Forward buttons on it.)

What Happened to the Website?

If you receive a lot of "Page not available" errors, even on major commercial sites, the most obvious
suggestion is to check your Internet connection. Your server might also be having a temporary problem, or high Internet traffic might be preventing your access. Another thing to consider is whether
the page you are trying to visit is on a secure web server. Click the Tools button in the toolbar, click
Internet Options, and then click the Advanced tab. Scroll down to the group of security settings and
see whether any of the encryption protocols supported by IE are disabled. For example, if you are
trying to visit a page that uses PCT encryption but Use PCT 1.0 is disabled, that page will not open.

Notice that next to both the Back and Forward buttons are downward-pointing arrows. If you have been browsing several web pages, click the Recent Pages button, which is the down-arrow button next to the Forward button. A menu similar to that shown in Figure 14.3 should appear, showing a backward progression of the web pages you have visited. Click a listing to move back several pages simultaneously instead of one at a time.

Browsing in Tabbed Pages

If you open several different pages at once and you don't want multiple Internet Explorer buttons to clog your taskbar, you can view multiple pages from within the IE8 window by creating new tabbed pages and then opening a new website in each page. Tabbed pages have been around for a long time in other web browsers such as Firefox and add-ons to IE such as Avant Browser, but now Microsoft has finally caught up with the times in IE7, thank goodness.

 tip

Type a term in the Address box and IE8 performs a search using your default search engine selection. AutoComplete produces an immediate list of hits drawing from your History and Favorites, all organized categorically. Search terms aren't isolated to word beginnings, either—portions of page titles and URLs are also included. Highlight a list entry and press Enter to visit the page.

If you want IE8 to include RSS feeds, click Tools, open the Internet Options dialog box, and open the Content tab. Under the AutoComplete heading, click the Settings button. Check the box next to Feeds, click OK to accept the changes, and then click OK to close the Internet Options dialog box. That's it!

Click here to go back more than one page at a time.

Figure 14.3
To move back several web pages instead of to the previous one, click the Recent Pages button next to the Forward button.

IE8 introduces the concept of color-coded Tab Groups for at-a-glance visualization of related browser tabs. Though subtle, this improvement can significantly impact your productivity levels by logically grouping related tabs. For example, in IE7 if you write a blog or update page content and preview changes before posting to the Web, the content often appears in a new tab to the far right—far removed from the current working tab. You could easily get confused with multiple open tabs with no visual indication as to how those tabs relate to each other—there was simply no at-a-glance contextual information to distinguish between tabs.

New to IE8, however, are color-coding and grouping options, which eliminate all that guesswork. You can even move tabs between groups by simply dragging the desired tab into a designated group, at which point it assumes the appropriate color coding. Right-click any tab to control the entire group, including closing the group, closing all tabs except those in a given group, and ungrouping select tabs from a chosen group. You can also perform actions to individual tabs. And if you accidentally close the wrong tab or tabs, you can recover by pressing Ctrl+Shift+T. You can also right-click any tab and select Recently Closed Tabs to pick from a list of associated tabs. IE8 has adopted and embraced all the features of competing browsers to ensure it maintains all the best-of-breed options right at home.

New tabs open to present multiple links that allow you to open recently closed tabs, an InPrivate browsing session, and the Accelerator that makes selection-specific searches and page content grabbing easier. Each tab is perfectly isolated to prevent browser crashes when a single page blows up—a previous sore spot for IE browsing. Now you can restore the crashed tab and reload exactly the information when it crashed, including unfinished blog entries, interrupted email correspondence, or interrupted streaming video.

When you open IE8, your home page appears in the default tab. As mentioned earlier, the default home page is MSN, as shown in Figure 14.4.

Figure 14.4
Internet Explorer displays Microsoft's Bing search engine in the Search tab.

The name of the page appears in the tab. Next to the tab is a second, smaller tab. When you click this tab, a new tabbed page appears to the right of the first tab and displays the New Tab page, as shown in Figure 14.5.

The New Tab page provides information about how to get started with tabbed browsing and to learn more about tabs. The tab at the top of the window (with the title "New Tab – Windows Internet Explorer") is raised and appears in a different color, to let you know that the tabbed page is the one you're viewing. Now that the new tabbed page is open, you can open a website in the page by typing the URL in the Address box.

Figure 14.5
The New Tab page provides convenient links to get you going.

A new tabbed page as it first appears.

Click this tab to jump back to your home page.

Type an address here, or select one of your favorites and the new page appears on the new tab.

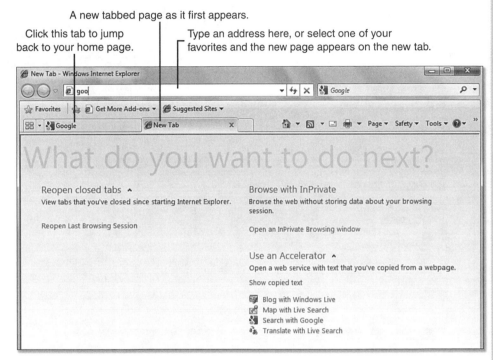

You can create a new tab by clicking the small tab to the right of the new tab you just created. If you want to close your current tab, click the X to the right of the tab title.

Each tab has a set width, and all the tabs must fit between the Add Favorites button and the buttons on the right side of the toolbar. If the page title in the tab is too long to fit in the width of the tab, the title is truncated with ellipses at the right side of the title. You can view the entire name by moving the mouse pointer over the tab; about a half-second later, a pop-up menu appears that displays the full name of the tab. Unless the name of the page is extremely long, the full name appears in the Internet Explorer title bar as well.

 tip

Tabs also have pop-up menus that you can access by right-clicking a tab that has a web page. This pop-up menu lets you close the current tab, close all other tabs except for the current one, refresh the page in the tab, refresh the pages in all tabs, and create a new tab.

When you create more than one tab, two small buttons appear to the left of the first tab. When you click the Quick Tabs button, a list of all your open web pages in tabs appears in the Quick Tabs page, as shown in Figure 14.6.

note

A shortcut for accessing the Quick Tabs page quickly is to press Ctrl+Q.

Click the Quick Tabs button to see all the open tabs.
Click this button to see a list of your tabbed pages in a list view.

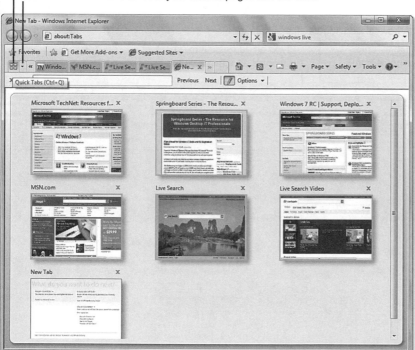

Figure 14.6
The Quick Tabs page is a great jump-off point for your most frequented sites.

The Quick Tabs page shows thumbnails of all the web pages in all the tabs. The page titles and the Close (X) button appear above the thumbnails. Click a thumbnail to open the tab, or click the Close (X) button to close the tab.

You can also view a list of all the tabs in list form by clicking the Tab List button. A list of open tabs appears underneath the button. Open a tab by clicking the tab name in the list; the currently open tab has a check mark to the left of the tab title.

If you close Internet Explorer while you have more than one tab open, a dialog box appears and asks if you want to close all tabs. When you click the Close Tabs button, IE8 closes and

tip

Some other tabbed-browser programs give you more extensive tabbing features, such as setting up favorite groups of websites as related tabs that you can open up all at once—a great feature for doing research on specific topics where you have a load of web pages open at once. Check out Avant Browser or Firefox.

only one tab appears the next time you open IE8. You can click the Show Options button to tell IE8 to reopen all the currently open tabs the next time you open Internet Explorer, and then click the Close Tabs button to close IE8.

Browsing with Enhanced Privacy and Security

The Internet is becoming an increasingly rich connective space where much personal information is given and sometimes taken. Users aren't always aware that when they browse the Internet the websites they visit might be tracking their browsing habits. IE8 safeguards your personal browsing information from other people entrusted with access to your computer and from sites you aren't aware are attempting to pilfer your data.

IE8 includes a series of security and privacy features, one of which is called InPrivate Browsing. An InPrivate session captures all traces of your personal browsing activities—including those deemed Not Safe For Work (NSFW)—and erases those details when you close the browser. All cookies, temporary Internet files, browsing history, form information, submitted usernames, and typed passwords simply vanish. To enable InPrivate Browsing, either click the Safety button in the toolbar and select InPrivate Browsing or press Ctrl+Shift+P.

New malware protections such as the SmartScreen antiphishing filter prevent those most prolific online scams from fooling you into revealing sensitive information to unauthorized parties. SmartScreen warns you when you select a site deemed harmful (for example, known to harbor malware or to be posing as a false front for a financial institution) with a constantly updated database of bad sources.

InPrivate Filtering is designed to deter sites from sharing your browsing habits without your knowledge. InPrivate Filtering enables selective site blockage so that the places you visit cannot harvest your information and pass it along to third parties. A small lock icon with an arrow (at the lower right of the browser window; see Figure 14.5) indicates that InPrivate Filtering is active. To enable InPrivate Filtering, either click the Safety button in the toolbar and select InPrivate Filtering or press Ctrl+Shift+F. You can also access InPrivate Filtering settings from the Safety menu. If InPrivate Filtering blocks from display third-party data that you need, you can specify custom feature settings as a workaround.

Microsoft also includes additional safety features. IE8 blocks common forms of cross-site scripting attacks and provides better protection against malicious ActiveX controls. It also attempts to prevent click-jacking, which is when an attacker places invisible buttons above or below legitimate buttons, thereby duping unsuspecting users into activating malicious code or revealing private information. And unlike previous browsers, IE8 offers the Delete Browsing History screen so you have granular control over cookies and temporary Internet file deletions. To access IE8's improved browsing deletion tools, click the Safety button and choose Delete Browsing History or simply press Ctrl+Shift+Del. If you check the box titled Preserve Favorites Website Data, no information related to your bookmarked sites will be erased.

Adding Sites to Your Favorites

It's very inefficient (not to mention annoying) to type the URL in the Address box every time you want to access your favorite sites. It's also difficult, if not impossible, to remember all your favorites.

Fortunately, IE8 lets you add, save, and categorize your favorites so you can access them in the Favorites pane, which now entirely replaces the Links bar (and all related functionality). The Favorites Bar contains the Favorites button, a quick Add To Favorites button, the Suggested Sites Web slice, and a Get More Add-Ons Web slice.

The process of adding a favorite is fairly simple. Your first step is to browse to the website you want to make one of your favorites. For best results, open the main or index page of the website first. Now try the following:

1. Click the Add to Favorites button in the Favorites Center on the toolbar (the side window that appears when you click the Favorites button), and then click Add to Favorites Bar.

2. In the Add a Favorite dialog box, type the name of the favorite in the Name box, as shown in Figure 14.7. You can also change the name so that you will be able to easily identify the page. Whatever name you enter is shown in your Favorites list.

3. From the Create In list, select the folder where you want to save the favorite. IE8 contains five folders by default: the home (Favorites) directory, Microsoft websites, MSN Websites, and Windows Bing.

4. If you want to create a new folder or subfolder within one of the current folders, click the New Folder button. The Create a Folder window appears, as shown in Figure 14.8.

Figure 14.7
The Add a Favorite dialog box.

Figure 14.8
The Create a Folder window.

5. Type the folder name in the Folder Name box.

6. From the Create In list, select the folder where you want to create the new folder. The default is the home (Favorites) directory.

7. Click Create. The new folder you created appears in the Create In list.

8. Click Add. IE8 adds your favorite to the list.

Now that you've added a favorite to the list, you can view the favorite by opening the Favorites Center pane. Here's how:

1. Click the Favorites button in the toolbar. The Favorites Center pane appears on the left side of the window, as shown in Figure 14.9. Notice that the Favorites Center pane overlaps the web page you're viewing.

Figure 14.9
The Favorites pane keeps your most favored web-sites in order.

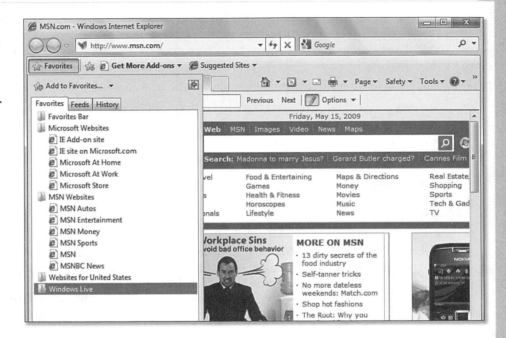

2. Click the folder that contains the favorite. The favorite appears underneath the folder name.

3. Click the favorite name to open the web page in the right pane.

4. Close the Favorites Center pane by clicking the Favorites button.

Using Multimedia Browsing and Downloading

When the Web first debuted as a method for sharing scientific data among physicists, the hypertext format of the data was specifically chosen to enable sharing information in many different formats. For early Internet users, the ability to download pictures and other graphics in conjunction with web pages was both exciting and profound.

Today, web pages containing pictures are the norm. Web developers continue to push the multimedia horizon, with many sites now featuring audio and video. You can even listen to radio stations and watch other broadcasts live over the Web.

In addition to multimedia-rich websites, you'll find that the Web is a good place to download software. You can find many places to download freeware, shareware, and software updates, and sites to purchase and download full versions of programs.

Images

Believe it or not, graphics-rich websites were once controversial. Some people believed that graphics would put too much strain on the bandwidth capacity of the Internet, but those gloom-and-doom predictions have not become a reality. Backbone improvements have helped the Internet keep pace with the ever-growing appetite for multimedia on the Web, and images are now both common and expected.

Internet Explorer supports three basic graphics formats used in web pages:

- **JPEG**—Short for Joint Photographic Experts Group, this format enables pictures to be significantly compressed (reducing download time and bandwidth, but also image quality), so this is often used for photos on web pages.

- **GIF**—Short for Graphics Interchange Format, this format is often used for buttons and other simple icons used on web pages.

- **PNG**—Short for Portable Networking Graphics, this format was developed to help images load faster and keep them looking the same on different platforms.

The exact format used for each image is not apparent when you view the page. Normally, the specific format used is not important unless you plan to copy the graphics and use them for some other purpose. For web use, the formats are essentially interchangeable.

By default, IE8 displays graphics used in web pages. Although the idea of disabling this feature to enable speedier downloads might seem appealing, many web pages now rely so heavily on graphics that they do not include text links. This means you cannot navigate the site without the images. Don't disable this feature unless you deem it absolutely necessary.

 caution

Before you use any graphics you find on the Web, check the website for a copyright statement or other information about terms of use. You should obtain permission before you use any copyrighted material.

Audio and Video

A growing number of websites offer audio or video content in addition to standard text and graphics. When used in conjunction with web content, the terms *audio* and *video* can mean a few different things:

- Basic audio files, such as MIDI music files, that play in the background while you view a web page.

- Video files on websites that download and play automatically or play when you click a Play button.

- Video media that plays using Windows Media Player (WMP).

- Animated GIFs that give the appearance of a video signal but have a significantly reduced bandwidth requirement. They display a series of static GIF frames that simulate video and are often used in logos and those annoying home mortgage ads with someone dancing.

- Flash movies that also appear to be video but are actually vector-based instructions requiring very little bandwidth. "Vector-based" simply means that they have small mathematical descriptions (much the same way fonts do in Windows) that can be manipulated to animate the objects.

- Streaming audio or video that you choose to open and listen to or watch.

You might have noticed that when you visit certain websites, a song starts to play while you read the page. Audio isn't nearly as common as graphics in web pages because some people find it annoying. If you come across a web page that contains a song you would rather not hear, the most obvious solution is to turn down your speaker volume or mute the Windows volume control. If you're listening to music on your computer (such as from a CD or MP3 file) and you don't want to end your entire audio experience by turning off the speakers, see the note.

Likewise, some websites contain video files and animations set to download and play automatically. MPEG and AVI video files are usually very large; if you have restricted bandwidth capacity, you might want to consider disabling them.

 note

To disable audio, video, or other multimedia from automatically downloading when you visit a website, see Chapter 23. By disabling these "features," you also might notice that web pages will load faster. Note that some web pages use media-playback programs that IE settings won't control. For example, if a page has a RealMedia or QuickTime sound or video file in it, automatic playback of those files will commence regardless of IE settings.

Web-based video seems to be improving almost daily, but most broadcasts are still lower in quality than that produced by a plain old television set. Whereas a broadcast TV signal typically delivers about 30 frames per second (fps), typical web-based streaming videos provide just 5–15fps. In contrast to streaming, many sites give you the option of downloading a video clip before playing it. Usually the clip in this format is much larger and of a higher quality than the streaming video. After the entire clip has been downloaded, it can be played and might appear as a high-quality image, depending on how it was produced. Playback typically is in Windows Media Player, QuickTime Player, or RealPlayer. The ranges of file sizes, frame sizes, and compression techniques—all of which affect the quality of the picture—abound. Unlike the TV standard we are all accustomed to, the Web is the wild, wild West of video nonstandards.

➡ *To learn more about using the Windows 7 audio controls, **see** Chapter 12, "Sound Recorder, DVD Maker, and Other Multimedia Tools."*

MPEG, AVI, and WMV Videos

By default, MPEG, AVI, and WMV (Windows Media Video) files are played using Windows Media Player (WMP). Windows Media formats are sort of the new kid on the block and are Microsoft's attempt to be a big player in the Internet multimedia market. Just as movies encoded in Apple's QuickTime format or RealNetworks' RealPlayer format require those companies' proprietary player, Microsoft's proprietary format plays only in the Microsoft player.

➡ *WMP is covered in depth in Chapter 8, "Windows Media Player," but because how you deal with online video is relevant to mastering web browsing, I briefly mention its use in this context. Be sure to check Chapter 8 for more information about WMP.*

Most web pages that feature videos online give you links for RealPlayer, QuickTime, or WMP, and let you choose your preference. Some sites give you links for downloading MPEG or AVI files. These don't stream, so you must first download them. Depending on your connection speed, downloading could take a while because these files tend to be very large. Just be prepared for a long download, especially if using a dial-up connection.

You might notice that WMP opens as soon as you click the link. Earlier versions of WMP (prior to version 8) remained blank until the entire file was downloaded. Now, with some types of files such as WMV files, movies can start playing more quickly even though they are not technically streaming. (See the next section to read about streaming.) Instead, they are doing a progressive download. This is less reliable than streaming, but at least you don't have to wait until the movie is completely downloaded before you start seeing it. The download might stop a few times, though, if your connection speed is slow. QuickTime movies have had this feature for some time; now WMP does, too.

If you click the Media button in the toolbar, a miniature version of WMP opens in the left pane of your IE window, along with links for supposedly interesting media. When you click a web page link for an audio or video file, you are asked whether you want it to play in this tiny Media Player or open in a regular WMP window. The choice is up to you. The advantage of opening in the small window is that it lets you neatly play some tunes, movie trailers, or whatever in the left pane while you continue your web surfing.

Streaming Broadcasts

As mentioned earlier, another type of sound or video that you might play over the Internet is *streaming audio* or *streaming video*. Streaming audio/video is a format in which a signal "plays" over your Internet connection, starting a few seconds after you click, instead of playing from a file that was first downloaded to your hard drive.

When you first click a streaming signal, a portion of the signal is buffered in RAM on your computer. This buffer helps provide a steady feed if connection quality wavers. If the signal is received faster than it can be played, the additional data is buffered. However, if your connection deteriorates significantly, the video might not play smoothly. Streaming broadcasts are not written to the disk, so retrieving the signal later from your own PC will be impossible.

Although the minimum requirement of many streaming audio signals is typically 56Kbps, a quicker connection is desirable. A lower speed delivers a lower-quality broadcast, skipping and jumping of video, or stopping altogether.

Streaming audio signals are often used to play various types of audio signals over the Web. For example, most online music retailers offer you the capability to listen to sample audio tracks from many of the CDs they sell. In addition, you can listen to many radio stations and programs—such as those on National Public Radio (www.npr.org)—over your Internet connection instead of a radio.

A number of information providers use streaming video to send newscasts and other broadcasts across the Web. You can watch news stories online through many news sites, such as www.cnn.com. You'll notice that you can continue to surf the Web while a current audio or video is playing.

MSN (www.msn.com) provides links to a number of online video resources, streaming and other-wise.

To access streaming audio or video signals, you need to have an appropriate plug-in program for IE8, such as RealPlayer from RealNetworks (www.real.com), QuickTime from Apple (www.apple.com/quicktime), or WMP 12, included with Windows 7. After you have downloaded and installed the appropriate streaming player (following the installation instructions provided by the player's publisher), you can access the streaming signals over the Web.

Although WMP can handle many formats, most broadcasts require a specific player. Check the web-site that hosts the streaming media you want to play for specific requirements. Some websites offer a choice of player formats, and often the website will have a convenient link for downloading the necessary freeware. RealPlayer is a common application used for streaming audio, and many streaming video providers use QuickTime. Although the look might be different because of custom "skins" used on flashier sites, the basic functions are similar. If you look closely, you can tell whether it's WMP, RealPlayer, QuickTime, or another player.

Sometimes you need to wait for the file to download; other times it streams right away. QuickTime gives you the choice to download the entire file first so you can avoid glitches when you watch it. Notice that the play slider can go at a different rate than the progress bar, which indicates how much of the file has been downloaded. When it's downloaded, you can easily replay the clip with-out interruption. Note that WMP can be encoded right into a web page, so the video might begin playing when you hit a particular URL.

➥   *To learn about downloading programs from the Web,* **see** *"Downloading Programs," **p. 373**.*

To use a streaming media player, follow these steps:

1. Locate a link to an audio clip or video signal that you want to access, and click it.

2. Your streaming media player should open automatically. RealPlayer, WMP, and QuickTime include standard Play, Pause, and Stop buttons.

3. When you are finished listening to the streaming signal, click the Close (X) button for the player.

MP3 Audio

MP3 is an audio file format whose name refers to files using MPEG Audio Layer 3, an encoding scheme for audio tracks. MP3 files are small (about 1/12 the size of CD audio tracks), but they maintain a high sound quality. A minute of CD-quality MP3 music requires only 1MB of storage space.

Controversy has surrounded MP3 since its introduction. The small size of MP3 files makes it easier for people to slide behind copyright laws, pirate music, and illegally distribute them over the Internet. Authorities are currently working on ways to prevent these actions. However, this has only led to Napster spin-offs that are harder to control and much more difficult to track down or prosecute. It will be interesting to see how the Justice Department handles the impending and unavoidable new age of intellectual property protection.

The bottom line is this: Distributing or downloading MP3 files from any artist without permission is technically a violation of the law. Although some artists (particularly new ones) willingly provide audio tracks for free download as a means of building a fan base, many MP3 sites contain audio files that have been pirated. If you have questions about the legality of MP3 files you find on the Internet, you need to be the judge. Probably the most ethical approach is not to download them, but I don't want to sound like a prude. As I said, it's a brave new world out there in copyright protection. I believe that free music on the Web probably drives the purchase of new CDs and concert ticket sales. I'm a musician myself, and although I would want my music (and my books) protected, I also wouldn't mind more people becoming acquainted with my works—it could pay off in the long run. In any case, you might want to be careful sharing your MP3s of other people's music on the Web because it could be deemed illegal.

The MP3 format has become extremely popular, with tiny portable players (such as the iPod from Apple) available that can store endless hours of music. It is possible to load all your music into your computer and create your very own jukebox. Software for recording and organizing your music is available at www.real.com/player, www.itunes.com, www.winamp.com, and new.music.yahoo.com, to name a few. Many different applications can download MP3 files, including WMP, RealPlayer, and QuickTime. A number of consumer electronics companies are also now producing devices that allow you to play MP3 files away from your computer. Samsung makes a single device (called a Digimax) that functions as three: a digital camera, a PC camera to use for video conferencing, and an MP3 player. A wide variety of MP3 players is available, with varying storage capacities—some units as small as a pen. You can transfer MP3 files to the player's storage via a USB or a parallel or serial port connection.

For a good resource and free downloads, and to learn a bit more about the MP3 format, go to www.mp3.com. After you have downloaded an MP3 file, you can play it using WMP, RealPlayer, QuickTime, or any other MP3-compatible player.

tip

Sound quality is affected not only by your hardware, but also by the player application. Experiment with several different programs to find the one that works best for you.

When you click a web page link for an MP3 file, your default MP3 application will probably open, which might not be the application you want to use. In addition, the MP3 file will be inconveniently saved in IE's cache. You can exercise more control over the process by following these steps:

1. When you see a link for an MP3 file, right-click the link and choose Save Target As.

2. Select the location where you want to save the file download.

3. When the download is complete, open the desired player application manually and choose File, Open to listen to the file. If you click Open in the File Download dialog box, your default MP3 player opens.

 note

Another product called mp3PRO is an audio format that uses half the storage space per minute, allegedly without reducing quality. You can learn more about mp3PRO at www.mp3prozone.com.

Downloading Programs

Although the Web is most often thought of as a source of information and entertainment, it is also an excellent—and often only—place to obtain new software or updates for existing programs.

You can find numerous excellent resources for downloading free or trial versions of software. Good sources are www.tucows.com and http://download.cnet.com/windows/. Follow the specific instructions for installation provided by the software publisher (and offered on most download sites), but when you're downloading, these general rules apply:

- Some websites require you to choose from a number of "mirror sites" for your download. Mirror sites are servers in different parts of the world that have the same files on them. The redundancy prevents traffic jams on a single server when many people access it for the same program downloads. You are asked to select a location that is geographically close to you, but you're usually free to choose any site you want. The closer ones are sometimes faster, but not always. Sometimes I get quicker downloads from a mirror site in another country whose citizens are likely sleeping.

- To begin the download, typically you click a link that says something similar to "Download Now." This should open a dialog box asking you if you want to open or save the file. Choose to save. Select a location that you will remember for saving the download files—it is a good idea to create a Downloads folder. Within the Downloads folder, I create a new subfolder with the name of the program and then switch to that folder and save the program there. This way, all my downloads are organized.

- At the office, check with your network administrator before you install any new software to find out what your company policies are. In fact, if you are in a corporate environment, you probably won't be able to install new programs unless you are one of the lucky few with Administrator privileges. Most corporations limit users installing software, for obvious security reasons.

- Scan all downloads with virus-scanning software before you install them. Pay particular attention to archives and ISO image files, which are often carriers of software viruses regardless of whether or not the software comes from legitimate channels (though there's less likelihood than with peer-to-peer and free hosting sites).

- Many downloads come in a compressed ZIP format. If you download such a file, you can run it easily in Windows 7 because ZIP files are supported without needing to install a ZIP program such as WinZip or TurboZIP. Just double-click the ZIP file, and it will open in a folder window. Then examine the contents. You probably need to double-click the installer or Setup program to begin installing the program into Windows 7.

During the download process, a window appears showing the download progress and the estimated time remaining. The estimates are helpful, but thanks to fluctuating transfer speeds, these estimates also can be extremely unreliable. You might want to watch the window for a moment to see if the estimate changes in your favor. If you can't wait that long, click Cancel and try again later.

In addition to downloading new software, you can download updates to software you already own. Check the manufacturer's website occasionally to see whether new updates, patches, or bug fixes are available (this is especially important for entertainment software).

 tip

Downloads are fastest when Internet traffic is low, such as late at night. If you are given a choice of mirror sites for a download, keep in mind the local time for each site and choose a server located where current traffic is likely to be lower.

 tip

Create a Software folder in your Favorites list, and add to it the manufacturers' websites for software you own. Doing so will make it easier to periodically check for updates.

Protecting Against Bad Downloaded Programs

IE helps protect your computer from potentially malicious software. When you use IE to download a file, a message might appear in the information bar just below the Address box saying this:

> To help protect your security, Internet Explorer blocked this site from downloading files to your computer. Click here for options.

Clicking the information bar opens a drop-down list of options (see Figure 14.10).

Figure 14.10
IE offers to block downloads from pages until you specify otherwise.

If you choose to allow the page to download a program, you'll see another dialog box warning you about downloaded programs and asking whether you want to run the program from its remote location across the Web or save it to your hard disk, as shown in Figure 14.11.

Figure 14.11
If you decide to accept downloads from that page, you'll see another warning and some options at the bottom of the dialog box.

If you choose to run the program from the site rather than save it, you'll likely see the dialog box shown in Figure 14.12. All executable files that are downloaded are checked for publisher information using a scheme called Authenticode. Authenticode checks the digital signature of the file against a database of known good software publishers, and gives you some advice about the file. After being presented with the information, you can make a more informed decision about running the file.

Figure 14.12
If a publisher is not verified, you will be prompted if you try to run the program from the web page.

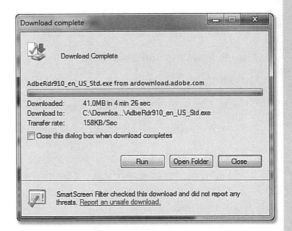

Some program publishers have been "black listed," and Windows 7 prevents them from running in your PC under Windows 7. Executable files with blocked publishers are not allowed to run.

 tip
You can unblock a publisher by using Manage Add-Ons in Internet Explorer. This is explained later in this chapter, in the section "Viewing and Managing Your IE Add-Ons."

Protecting Against "Drive-By" Downloads of IE Add-Ons

A recurring cause of instability in Windows machines is attributable to what's sometimes called "drive-by" downloads from the Web. How many times have you visited a website only to see a pop-up dialog box saying you need to install software for the website to work on your browser? Sometimes it's clearly stated why this is necessary (for playing a video, a proprietary sound file, or Flash animation, for example), and other times, the reason is not so clear. All you know is that you are faced with the decision of letting some (typically) unknown source install software on your computer so you can enjoy the web page, or opting out and moving on. Maybe you assume it can do no harm because it's only an addition to IE and not to your operating system. But because IE is often the back door through which viruses, adware, spyware, Trojan horses, and other malware infect your computer, being cautious at this juncture is extremely important.

These spur-of-the-moment additions that websites can push at you are called *IE add-ons*, and they are typically ActiveX controls (although not all are). ActiveX controls and active script (sometimes called script or JavaScript) are small programs used extensively on the Internet. Without scripts, websites would be much more static and boring. Script and ActiveX controls allow all sorts of animation and other entertaining features on the Internet. Websites become more interactive by offering customized content based on information about your computer, your browser, and so on. Common add-ons include extra toolbars, animated mouse pointers, stock tickers, and pop-up ad blockers.

 tip

IE has its own pop-up blocker. See "Blocking Pop-Ups and Pop-Unders," later in this chapter.

Add-ons can be installed from a variety of locations and in several ways, including these:

- Download and installation while viewing web pages

- User installation via an executable program

- As preinstalled components of the operating system

- As preinstalled add-ons that come with the operating system

A risk of add-ons is that these programs can also be used to collect information from your computer for harmful purposes. After 6 months or a year of surfing the Web with IE, many users don't recall what add-ons they authorized and don't know what those add-ons might be doing to compromise the stability of their systems.

You could unknowingly have many add-ons installed. This can happen if you previously gave permission for all downloads from a particular website, or because the add-on was part of another program that you installed. Some add-ons are installed with Microsoft Windows.

You'll sometimes be given more information about potentially damaging add-ons so you can make an informed decision about installing one. Some add-ons have digital signatures that verify who wrote them. This is called a *certificate*. IE verifies a signature and can tell you if it's valid. If a signature is reported as invalid, you definitely shouldn't trust the publisher as asserting a truthful identity. Allowing installation of ActiveX controls that have invalid signatures obviously is not recommended and introduces additional risk to your computer.

IE blocks file downloads in these circumstances when you are using the default security settings:

- When a file has an invalid signature on its certificate

- When a file has no signature on its certificate

- When you or someone else who uses your computer has blocked the source of the file

Even if an add-on has a legitimate certificate, it doesn't mean the program won't mess up your computer. In the end, it is your decision whether to install an add-on. Make the decision based on whether you know the source to be trustworthy. After installing an add-on, if your system or IE becomes unstable, use the information in the following section to track and remove the add-on.

 note

Certificates provide authoritative proof of identity to establish trust between two parties in an online transaction.

Allowing Add-Ons with Invalid Signatures

Some add-ons are known to be bad; Microsoft has blocked these intentionally. You can't install or run add-ons from blocked publishers on the computer. If you really want to, you can force the use of an add-on that has an invalid signature:

1. In IE, click the Tools button, click Internet Options, and then click the Security tab.

2. In the Security Level for This Zone box, click Custom Level.

3. Scroll down to Download Unsigned ActiveX Controls and choose Enable or Prompt.

Another approach is to unblock a *specific* publisher. This is a safer approach because it doesn't open you up to all invalid signatures. To do this, follow these steps:

1. Click the Tools button, click Manage Add-Ons.

2. Select the publisher you want to unblock and then click Enable (you can also right-click the add-on entry and click Enable from the context menu that appears).

3. Some publishers' add-ons have related add-ons that are affected when you enable or disable them. From the Enable Add-Ons dialog box that appears, select any related add-ons and click Enable.

Viewing and Managing Your IE Add-Ons

You can review all your add-ons, update selected ones, choose ones to remove, and, if you've been having IE crashes, potentially see which one was responsible for your last IE crash. (Crashing can happen if the add-on was poorly built or was created for an earlier version of IE.) You work with your add-ons using the IE Add-On Manager, which even shows some add-ons that were not previously shown and could be very difficult to detect.

To see all add-ons for Internet Explorer, follow these steps:

1. Click the Tools button, and then click Manage Add-Ons. You'll see the Manage Add-Ons window, shown in Figure 14.13.

2. In the Show drop-down list, select the set of add-ons you want to see.

Add-ons are sorted into four groups in the Show list. All add-ons represent a complete list that includes all the add-ons that reside on your computer. Currently loaded add-ons are only those that were needed for the current web page or a recently viewed web page. Choosing Run Without Permission shows add-ons that do not explicitly require permissions to run. Choosing Downloaded Controls lists all browser-based controls (such as Java plug-ins).

Some add-ons can crash your IE session. If you experience a system crash after you've installed an add-on, you have two options:

- **Disable it**—If an add-on causes repeated problems, you can disable the add-on. Click the add-on you want to disable and then click Disable. Some web pages, or IE, might not display properly if an add-on is disabled. It is recommended that you disable an add-on only if it repeatedly causes IE to close. Add-ons can be disabled but not easily removed.

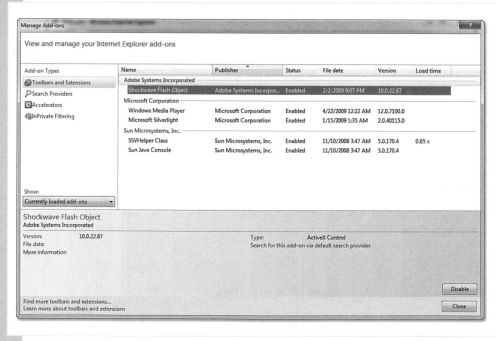

Figure 14.13
The Manage Add-Ons window lets you see and control the IE add-ons you've either wittingly or unwittingly downloaded and installed.

- **Report it**—When prompted, you might want to report the glitch to Microsoft. This is completely anonymous and requires nothing from you but your permission. Microsoft claims the info is used improve its products and to encourage other companies to update and improve theirs.

note

If you disable an add-on and then realize it was needed, click the add-on you want to enable, select the entry in Manage Add-Ons and then click Enable.

Internet Explorer Add-On Crash Detection attempts to detect crashes in IE that are related to an add-on. If IE identifies the faulty add-on, you'll be informed. You then have the option of disabling add-ons to diagnose crashes and improve the overall stability of IE.

Customizing the Browser and Setting Internet Options

One of the most important features of Internet Explorer is the capability to tailor it to your specific needs. Every user sets up IE differently based on programs used, favorite websites, bandwidth capability, security needs, and so on.

You can make most customizations in the Internet Options dialog box, which you can access either through the Control Panel or by clicking the Tools button and then clicking Internet Options. The dialog box contains seven tabs, each holding a number of unique preference settings. Figure 14.14 shows the General tab.

Figure 14.14
On the General tab, you can set general preferences for your home page, browsing history, search settings, tab options, and appearance properties.

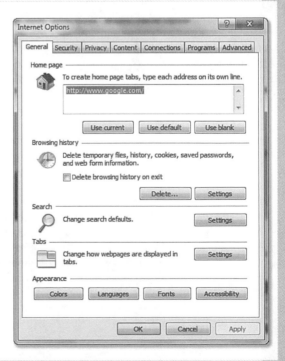

Check each tab in the dialog box to customize your own IE8 settings. Table 14.1 describes some of the key Internet Options settings you can change.

Table 14.1 Important Internet Options

Tab	Option	Description
General	Home Page	The home page is the first page that appears when you open IE. It is probably set to the MSN home page or has been customized by your PC's manufacturer. Consider changing this page to your company's home page or something else you find more useful.
	Browsing History	IE8 maintains a record of the websites you have visited. You can change the length of time these records are kept or clear the history altogether, including all cookies, saved passwords, and web form information. A cookie is a message from a website that IE8 stores on your computer. When you return to that website, IE8 sends the message in the cookie to the site so that it loads more quickly and can also provide customized web searches. If you don't want cookies on your computer, you can delete them.
	Search	You can change the default search provider for IE8.
	Tabs	You can tell IE8 whether you want to have tabbed web pages and how to open pop-ups and links from other programs.
	Appearance (Colors, Fonts, and so on)	You can customize default colors, fonts, and languages, and set accessibility options here.
Security	Zones and Levels	You can set security options for IE8. See "Setting Security and Privacy Preferences," later in this chapter.
Privacy	Settings	This area defines how and when cookies are sent. See "Setting Security and Privacy Preferences," later in this chapter.
	Pop-Up Blocker	You can turn on the pop-up blocker to keep most pop-up windows generated by a website from appearing and annoying you. If you want to see these pop-up windows, you can also turn off the pop-up blocker.
	InPrivate Filtering	You can enable InPrivate Filtering data collection and disable toolbars and extensions when InPrivate Browsing is in effect.
Content	Parental Controls	You can specify time-of-day settings, enforce activity reporting and control access to Web-sites, games, and Internet programs.
	Content Advisor	You can set ratings for each website you visit to control which users can see that content on your computer. See "Controlling Objectionable Content," later in this chapter.

Table 14.1   Continued

Tab	Option	Description
	Certificates	When a web page tries to run a script or install a piece of software on your computer, you can accept certificates from the publisher to authenticate their identity and trustworthiness. See "Setting Security and Privacy Preferences," later in this chapter.
	AutoComplete	You can enable or disable AutoComplete when typing web URLs, email addresses, or form data.
	Feeds and Web Slices	You can specify how often you receive a web feed and updated content from a website.
Connections		You can set up preferences for your Internet connection, whether it be through a dial-up or network connection.
Programs		You can select default programs for various actions. See "Setting Default Mail, News, and HTML Editor Programs," next.
Advanced		You can set various (but obscure) options for browsing, multimedia, web page printing, searches from the Address bar, and security. You can also enable and disable automatic downloading of graphics, videos, audio, and more.

Setting Default Mail, News, and HTML Editor Programs

Windows 7 has consolidated much of this information for setting defaults in the Set Default Programs window, which you can access through the Control Panel. You can also access the default program settings in the Programs tab of the Internet Options dialog box.

The Programs tab still lets you set your preferred HTML editor for editing HTML files. If you have not installed any other Internet-related software packages, such as Microsoft Word, you probably won't have many choices here, but if you use different programs, these options can be useful. Figure 14.15 shows the default program settings you can make on the Programs tab, and Table 14.2 describes the various options you can set.

If you are a web developer, make sure the correct editor is listed here. This will simplify editing during your testing process. The list might include Word, Notepad, FrontPage, or another installed editor.

If you want to view and change Internet programs, click Set Programs. In the Default Programs window, click Set Your Default Programs. The Default Programs window then appears, as shown in Figure 14.16.

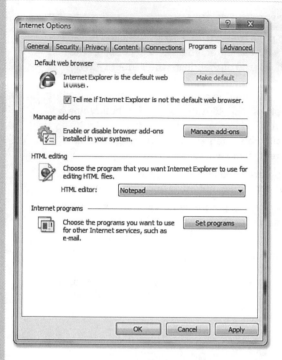

Figure 14.15
On the Programs tab, you can choose the default HTML editor.

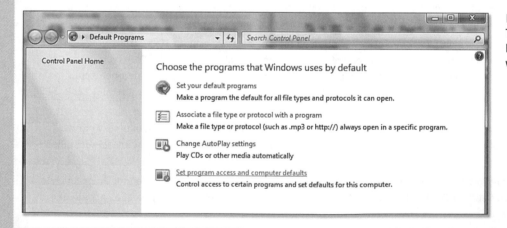

Figure 14.16
The Default Programs window.

The Programs list displays all the IE-related programs you can set. If you haven't installed very many programs, only one option likely will be available in the Programs list. After you click a program in the list, the program description appears to the right of the Programs list. Table 14.2 lists the default Internet programs in Windows 7.

Table 14.2   Default Internet Programs

Program	Description
Internet Explorer	You can set IE8 as the selected program to open all applicable file types and protocols.
Windows Calendar	Windows Calendar is the standard calendar for Windows 7 and the Windows Mail application. However, if you install Microsoft Outlook, Outlook will have a separate calendar file.
Windows Contacts	Windows Contacts is your default address book (and was previously called Address Book).
Paint	This program allows you to create and edit drawings by using a variety of shapes, brushes, and colors.
Windows Disc Image Burner	You can burn a CD and DVD from an ISO disc image file.
Windows Media Center	You can set this program to open DVR files by default. DVR files are the standard format for Windows-recorded video. Windows Media Center is available only in the Home Premium and Ultimate editions of Windows 7.
Windows Media Player	You can set this program to open all popular music and video file types (such as AVI video, MPEG video, and MP3) in WMP.
Windows Photo Gallery	You can choose Windows Photo Gallery to open all applicable image formats, including GIF, JPG, PNG, and TIF.
Windows Search Explorer	You can set this program to quickly search for files and folders anywhere on your computer.
Wordpad	You can create and edit basic text documents with rich formatting and picture options.

You can set the program as the default for all the file types and protocols it can open by clicking the Set This Program As Default button. You can also choose which file types and protocols the selected program opens by default by clicking the Choose Defaults for This Program button.

Email Link Troubles: Changing the Default Email Program

Microsoft ships Windows 7 without a default email client. You can still download and install Windows Mail, but there are also several useful alternative email clients available online. To specify a default email client that you've installed, click the Tools button, click Internet Options to open the Internet Options dialog box, and then select the Programs tab. Click the Set Programs button to open the Control Panel's Default Programs window and click the Set Your Default Programs link. You should be able to select any installed email client (such as Outlook, Windows Mail, Eudora, Mozilla Sunbird, and so on) here.

Setting Security and Privacy Preferences

In many ways, the Web is a safer place than the "real" world, but it does present its own unique dangers. The greatest hazards involve sensitive and private information about you or your company being compromised, or having your computer infected with a software virus. IE8 incorporates a number of security features to protect you from these hazards, and you can customize those features to suit your own needs, browsing habits, and company policies.

Begin by clicking the Tools button and opening the Internet Options dialog box. Click the Security tab. Click Default Level in the lower-right corner of the dialog box to show the slider that allows you to set a security level for each zone, as shown in Figure 14.17.

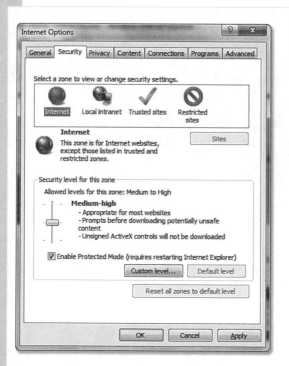

Figure 14.17
On the Security tab, you can customize security settings for various web zones.

You first need to select a zone for which you want to customize settings. Figure 14.17 shows the four zones, described here:

- **Internet**—This zone applies to all resources outside your LAN or intranet.

- **Local Intranet**—This zone applies to pages available on your company's intranet. These pages are usually more trustworthy and can justify less-restrictive settings.

- **Trusted Sites**—You manually designate these sites as trusted. To designate a trusted site, browse to the site, open this dialog box, select the Trusted Sites zone, and click Sites. Here you can add the site to your Trusted Sites zone list. Trusted sites usually allow lighter security.

■ **Restricted Sites**—Designated in the same manner as Trusted Sites, websites listed here are ones you specifically find untrustworthy. They should have the strictest security settings.

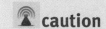 **caution**

Before you designate a web page as trusted, remember that even the most diligently maintained sites can be compromised. Recent "hacker" attacks at websites of the FBI, U.S. Army, and others might make you question the practice of designating any website as "trustworthy."

Each zone has its own security preferences that you can set. The easiest way to set preferences is to choose one of the three basic levels offered in the dialog box. The default level is Medium, and for most web users, this setting works best because it provides a good balance of security and usability. The High setting offers the greatest possible security, but you might find that the level is so restrictive that it's difficult to browse your favorite websites.

In contrast, the Medium and Medium-Low levels make browsing much easier because you aren't presented with dialog boxes and warnings every time a potentially hazardous activity begins. Because these two levels leave too many doors open to virus infection and other dangers, they are not advisable in most situations.

Besides setting a basic security level, you can customize individual settings. First, choose a basic level (such as Medium) and then try these steps:

1. Click Custom Level to open the Security Settings dialog box, shown in Figure 14.18.

2. Browse the list of options and apply custom settings as you see fit.

3. Click OK when you're finished. A Warning dialog box appears, asking whether you really want to apply the changes. Choose Yes.

Figure 14.18
You can scroll through this list to make custom security setting changes.

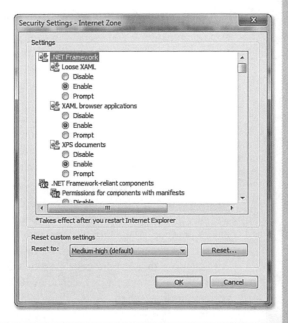

Review the items in the Security Settings dialog box that pertain to ActiveX controls and Java applets. Assess these settings carefully, especially those for ActiveX controls, because of the unique hazards they can present. The ActiveX standard contains loopholes, so unsigned controls can run virtually any OLE-compliant operation on your system. Java, on the other hand, is relatively—but not entirely—secure.

You should also consider your desired level of cookie security. Because cookies are text only, they cannot contain a virus or other harmful content. However, they can contain personal information, such as a record of web pages you have visited, how long you spent at a page, how many times you have visited, personal preferences for a web page, and even user IDs and passwords. For these reasons, many people regard cookies as an invasion of privacy.

You can disable cookies, or you can choose to have IE prompt you every time a site attempts to leave a cookie in your cache. However, keep in mind that some websites make such heavy use of cookies that you could find it difficult—if not impossible—to browse the Web normally.

To set your cookie preferences, click the Tools button, click Internet Options, and then click the Privacy tab. The Settings area enables you to determine how and when cookies are sent. Choose a level you are comfortable with, or click the Advanced button to select the Override Automatic Cookie Handling option and specify whether IE will always accept, block, or prompt you before enabling first-party or third-party cookies. (For more on first- and third-party cookies, see "Getting a Microsoft Live ID," later in this chapter.)

You might want to override your normal cookie settings for certain websites. If so, go to the Websites area of the Privacy tab and click the Edit button. In the text box, enter a complete website address. Then click the Block or Allow button to specify websites for which you want to never or always allow cookies.

Blocking Pop-Ups and Pop-Unders

Pop-up windows are an intrusive means for advertisers on the Web to ensure that you see their plug. We've all seen pop-up windows that appear unexpectedly, sometimes blaring music or flashing to catch our attention. Usually they pop up when you've clicked a link to go to another page. A less intrusive, though a little more insidious, window is called the pop-under window. You don't discover it until you close the window you're looking at. This way, it's harder to tell which site actually spawned the pop-under, so you don't know who to blame.

Many power users have figured out ways to prevent pop-ups, such as by installing the Google toolbar or one of the many add-ins, or installing some other browser, such as Opera, that blocks pop-ups. AOL's browser does this, as does Mozilla's Firefox. Oddly enough, 70% or more of web surfing is done with IE, even though prior versions didn't contain the modern nicety of pop-up blocking. The good news is that IE8 has a pop-up blocker built in.

 tip

You can stop the pop-ups dead in their tracks with this quick solution: turn off Active Scripting (JavaScript). This works because pop-up windows require Active Scripting to launch. Even though other browser functions need Active Scripting, you can surf quite effectively on most sites without it. To turn off Active Scripting, click the Tools button, click Internet Options, select the Security tab, change your Internet security level to High, and click OK. Five quick steps, no pop-ups, and you haven't spent a dime on a blocker or upgraded to the latest version of IE. Of course, using the latest IE is a better idea because of the improved security features and add-in management.

IE's pop-up blocker is turned on by default. When a pop-up window tries to launch, you'll receive notification in the IE yellow information bar (just below the Address box). It will inform you that that a pop-up has been blocked and list steps you can take to show the pop-up, if you want. Click on the information bar to see the options (see Figure 14.19).

Figure 14.19
IE8 blocks pop-ups. When a pop-up is blocked, you can click on the information bar for options.

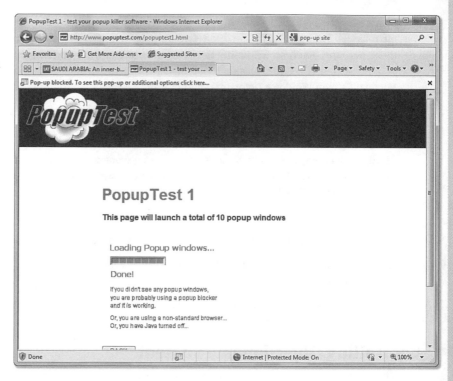

Sometimes it's useful to see blocked pop-ups. Just follow these steps:

1. Click the information bar.

2. From the menu, choose Show Blocked Pop-ups.

Some sites won't work properly with pop-ups disabled, such as shopping sites. If you want to always allow pop-ups from one or more specific sites, you can authorize this by adding those sites to an exception list:

1. Click the Tools button, choose Pop-Up Blocker, and then choose Pop-Up Blocker Settings.

2. In the Pop-Up Blocker Settings window, type the URL of the website, and then click Add.

3. Repeat step 2 for as many sites as you want to add. When you're finished, click Close.

A Few Notes About Pop-Up Exceptions

Sometimes the pop-up blocker won't be able to preclude a pop-up from appearing, for several possible reasons. First, you might have software on your computer that is launching pop-ups. To stop these pop-ups, you have to identify the software and remove it or change its settings. Try installing an adware and spyware sleuthing program such as Spybot Search & Destroy, Ad-Aware, or Microsoft's own Windows Defender (another free real-time monitoring program for blocking pop-ups and spyware).

Second, some pop-ups are written cleverly enough that they can circumnavigate the IE pop-up blocker.

Third, Internet Explorer will not block pop-ups from websites that are in your Local Intranet or Trusted Sites zones. If you want to specifically remove such a site from your trusted zone, you can do that from the IE Settings dialog boxes:

1. In IE, click the Tools button, click Internet Options, and then click Security.

2. Click the zone from which you want to remove a website, and then click Sites.

3. Skip this step unless you chose the Local Intranet zone in the last step. Click Advanced and then go to Step 4.

4. In the Websites box, click the website you want to remove, and then click Remove.

Controlling Objectionable Content

The Web holds the most diverse range of information and content of any library in the world. That diverse range includes a great deal of material that you might deem objectionable, and there is no perfect way of protecting yourself from it—short of never going online. However, IE incorporates two features, called Parental Controls and the Content Advisor, to help you screen out many of the things you or the other people using your computer would rather not see.

Parental Controls

Parental Controls is a new feature, introduced in IE7, that remains in IE8. If your children often use your computer and you don't want them seeing some material on the Web, or even using a certain program, you can set up Parental Controls to block access to those websites.

You must set up a System Recovery Account password before you can use Parental Controls. The System Recovery Account is an administrator account that is built into Windows 7, in case problems arise with your account. You'll learn more about the System Recovery Account for recovery purposes in Chapter 25, "Troubleshooting and Repairing Problems." However, this account password serves a second purpose: You can use the password to disable Parental Controls. Without this password, any user on your computer can disable Parental Controls.

After you set up the System Recovery Account password, click the user picture or name in the list to set up Parental Controls for that user. The User Controls window allows you to enable Parental Controls, as shown in Figure 14.20.

In this window, you can also collect information about the user's activity on your computer; determine the websites, games, and other programs you don't want the user to access; and control how long the user can use the computer.

The Content Advisor

The Content Advisor evaluates web content based on a rating system. The included rating system was originally developed by RSACi (Recreational Software Advisory Council on the Internet) and is now handled by the Internet Content Rating Association (ICRA), but you can add other rating systems, if you want.

Figure 14.20
Set Parental
Controls for
the selected
user in the
User Controls
window.

You must manually enable the Content Advisor, but after it is set up, you can password-protect the Advisor so that only you can adjust the settings. To enable the Content Advisor, open the Internet Options dialog box and do the following:

1. Click the Content tab and click Enable to open the Content Advisor dialog box. (You may be asked to allow this operation via the familiar User Account Control dialog box.)

2. The Content Advisor dialog box contains four tabs, as shown in Figure 14.21. On the Ratings tab, you can move the slider to set a rating level in each of the categories presented.

3. Click the Approved Sites tab. List specific websites here to control access to them. Click Always to make it easily acceptable, or click Never to restrict access.

4. On the General tab, choose whether unrated sites can be viewed. Keep in mind that many objectionable sites will not be rated. You can also set a password to let users view unrated or restricted sites on a case-by-case basis, or you can add another rating system here.

5. Click the Advanced tab. If you plan to use a ratings bureau or PICSRules file that you obtain from the Internet, your ISP, or another source, add it here. Click OK when you're finished.

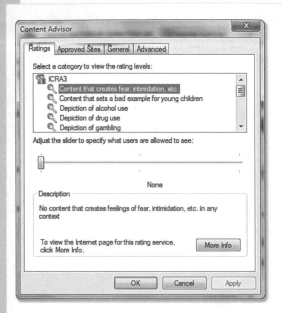

Figure 14.21
On the Ratings tab, you can move the slider to change the rating level.

RSACi and other organizations provide content-rating systems based on the Platform for Internet Content Selection (PICS) system developed by the World Wide Web Consortium, or W3C (www.w3.org/PICS). The systems work by using metatags in the code of a web page. The tags are usually generated by the rating organization after a site developer follows a brief rating procedure. Developers can then place the PICS metatag in the header of their HTML code, where it is identified by IE's Content Advisor when you try to open the page. The tag identifies the types and levels of content contained in the site, and the Content Advisor allows or disallows the site based on the content settings you have chosen. If you want to screen websites using a system other than RSACi's, you must install an appropriate PICSRules file provided by the rating organization.

Of course, rating is voluntary. Developers set the rating levels in the metatags based on their own evaluation of the site content, so you don't get a surefire guarantee that the tag accurately represents the site. RSACi periodically audits rated sites, and web developers generally *try* to rate their sites as accurately as possible. Because it is a voluntary system, providing inaccurate ratings defeats the purpose.

Effectively Searching the Web

You've probably heard that you can find virtually anything on the Web, and if you've spent much time online, you might be left wondering where it all is. Finding information on the Web is a fine art, but IE8 makes the process much simpler than before.

IE7 first streamlined the search approach by dropping the Search Companion found in IE6 and replacing it with the Search box to the right of the Address box, which remains in IE8, as shown in Figure 14.22.

tip

With IE8, you can type your search keywords directly into the Address bar, which will take you to the search results page of your default search engine.

Figure 14.22
The Search box enables you to search for several different kinds of information.

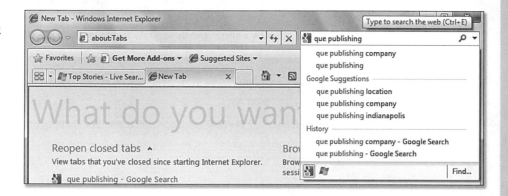

If you haven't typed anything in the Search box, the name of the search engine appears in the box. By default, the search engine name is Bing, Microsoft's search engine. To begin searching, enter a word, phrase, or even question in the Live Search box, and then click the Search button. Your results will appear in the Live Search page, with nine links appearing on each page. If you type a single word—such as "antiques"—the search will probably yield a list of results too big to be useful. Using more words, and more descriptive words, will narrow your search. You probably will get better results by searching for "antique furniture" or "antique French furniture" instead. You can click directly on a search result to link to that site, or you can click Next to see the next 15 results.

To start a new search, type another word, phrase, or question in the Live Search box. If you want to go back to the results from a previous search, click the Back button.

You can also refine and expand your search using the Live Search box. Click the down-arrow button to the right of the Search button to open the Search menu. This menu enables you to modify your search in three ways:

- Find on This Page opens the Find dialog box so you can find a word or phrase in the current web page.

- Find More Providers opens the Add Search Providers to IE8 page on the Microsoft website so you can add a search engine to the Search menu. When you search in the Live Search box, you can open the Search menu and select the search engine you want to use.

- Change Search Defaults opens the Change Search Defaults dialog box so you can set one of the search providers you have added as the default search engine.

When you're finished searching, close the Search Companion. To revisit a previous search, click the History button on the IE toolbar and go to the Search folders. Depending on the search engines you used, you could find information in folders labeled bing.com, search.yahoo.com, and google.com. Another way to find previous search results is by clicking the Search button at the top of the History pane and entering a word to search among the pages you've visited recently.

As helpful as the Search box in IE8 can be, when you've become familiar with the Internet, you are likely to discover your own favorite search engine. You could add it to your Favorites bar for easy access. Many search engines have advanced options that enable you to perform a more directed search.

Try these helpful search engines by entering them directly from a web page:

- www.lycos.com (includes tabbed categories more effective searching)

- www.google.com (includes category links and a drop-down list for refined searches, and Google Groups, which searches newsgroups)

- www.webcrawler.com (combines results from top search engines for combined search power)

15

EMAIL AND NEWSGROUPS WITH WINDOWS LIVE MAIL

Choosing an Email Client

From the start, the Internet has been touted as a means for enhancing human communications, and among the many communication protocols available in the online world, few have had the impact of electronic mail (email). You already know email and Web (its official protocol name is HTTP), but do you remember FidoNet, NNTP, Gopher, UUCP, Archie, Jughead, Veronica, or WAIS? All of these are, in one form or another, antiquated methods of communicating over the Internet. AOL had its own technologies, which weren't compatible with CompuServe's or Prodigy's technologies. Email was the great level playing field which was available to all, so it became the standard we now know.

To fully understand the nature of email, keep in mind that, at its most basic level, it is simply a way for users to send messages to each other over a network. This network could be a local area network (LAN) run by your company using Microsoft Exchange Server software. In this situation, the network server manages all message traffic. The server can also act as a gateway to other servers, allowing you to send mail beyond the LAN. If you have an email account with an Internet service provider (ISP) or other Internet-based service, the provider's server acts as your gateway to other mail servers across the Internet.

Given that email is here to stay, you must decide which email client you plan to use for reading, composing, and sending messages. A number of options are available to you, and which one you ultimately choose will depend not only on your personal preferences but also on professional needs. This choice is made all the more critical because Microsoft has removed Outlook Express from Windows 7. In fact, Windows Mail, MSN Messenger, and Photo Gallery are no longer part of Windows 7. To have access to these programs, you must download the Windows Live Essentials package of applications from Microsoft.

Windows Live Mail is a multifeatured program designed to appeal to a variety of email users, but it isn't for everyone, especially if you work in a corporation that requires tight integration of email with its communications infrastructure (for example, mobile communications devices such as the iPhone, BlackBerry, Palm OS or WebOS, Symbian, and Windows Mobile smartphones). Windows Live Mail can also function as a newsgroup client, making it a "one-stop" program if you routinely communicate via email and use newsgroups.

Windows Live Mail includes some important improvements over its predecessor, Windows Mail from Windows Vista, although it is essentially an update of the same program. One of the most significant additions to Live Mail is the inclusion of a calendaring system, which makes Live Mail more like Outlook than ever before.

 note

While it is neither convenient nor intuitive to have to download it, Windows Live Essentials is an excellent set of programs, and it's free. Windows Live Essentials includes: Messenger for IM, Mail for email, Writer for blogging, Photo Gallery for image management, Movie Maker for making movies, Toolbar for Internet Explorer, and Family Safety to help keep your kids safe.

 tip

If you use a Windows Mobile device as your smartphone, you also have received a copy of Outlook along with your handset. You'll need this copy because ActiveSync, the software that synchronizes your desktop to your handset, won't work with anything else. If you prefer, however, you can still install Windows Live Mail and use it for other email accounts.

Windows Live Mail Quick Tour

Because covering the many different email clients available would be beyond the scope of this book, we will assume that you have chosen Windows Live Mail. You can download it, as well as a series of other helpful applications, for free and it will meet many, if not all, of your email needs.

Getting Windows Live Essentials

Once you have an Internet connection configured and can access websites, go to www.windowslive.com and download Windows Live Essentials for free. The initial download is just the installer (1.08MB). The speed of your Internet connection and the components of Windows Live Essentials you choose will determine how long it takes for the installation. By default, all components are selected (see Figure 15.1) except Movie Maker Beta, for a total of 164MB. If you have Outlook installed, it will also offer you the Outlook Connector and the Office Live Add-in (which requires a free Office Live account). If you choose everything, including Movie Maker Beta, the download is 184MB. If you're still on dial-up, I would start the process before you "close shop" for the night. It should be done by morning.

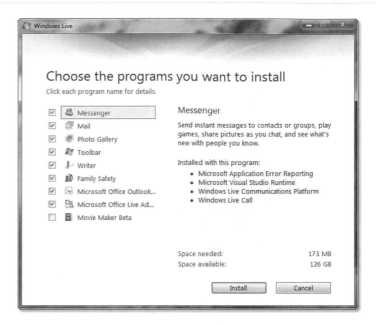

Figure 15.1
Windows Live Essentials program selection screen in the installer application.

Launching Windows Live Mail

After Windows Live Essentials is installed, it will be located in your Start menu. You can launch it by clicking Start, All Programs, Windows Live, and selecting the Windows Live Mail item. Once it's running and you can see its icon on the taskbar, right-click the icon and select Pin This Program to Taskbar so that it will always be available there.

Setting Up an Email Account

Before you can send or receive email, you need to have an email account. Microsoft assumes that when you download Windows Live Essentials you have a Windows Live account. There is also a good possibility that your account has already been set up for you by your ISP. You've likely been using an email account for some time. If that account happens to be from one of the numerous free online providers, all the better.

Wherever you get your email from, Windows Live Mail can likely handle it rather easily. If you have a Hotmail, Messenger or MSN Messenger, Windows Live, Xbox Live, or even an old Passport account, you can log in to Windows Live. If you don't have any of these accounts, you can create one for free at www.windowslive.com. You can sign up for an @live.com or @hotmail.com address or, such as Passport used to allow, you can use your own email address.

When you run Windows Live Mail the first time, the New Account Wizard will run to walk you through setting up access to your account. These steps also work for setting up a second or third account on the same machine:

1. If this is your first time starting Windows Live Mail, skip to step 2. If you have already configured Windows Live Mail for an email account and would like to add another, click the Add Another Email Account link in the sidebar. You'll see the dialog box shown in Figure 15.2.

2. Enter your email address, that account's password, and your display name (for example, Simon LeBon, Eric Idle, or Darth Vader), and then click Next.

note

As you likely know, Windows likes to have default programs for certain tasks. If you use Internet Explorer and then install Firefox, the new application will ask you if you want to make it the default application for web browsing. If you make that change and then go back to IE, it will ask if you want to make it the default again or to just stop asking. Email works the same way. Windows 7 doesn't come with a mail client, so the first one you install becomes the default. Since you're installing Windows Live Mail as part of the Essentials package, Windows Live Mail becomes the default. You can even manage the applications Windows uses as default for various file types and tasks by going to Start, Control Panel, and opening the Default Programs item. Once that opens, click the Set Your Default Programs link.

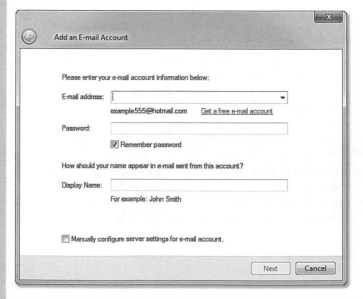

Figure 15.2
Starting the New Account Wizard to set up your email account.

3. If Windows Live Mail recognizes the service provider you have entered, it already knows how to reach those servers and will complete the configuration automatically. In most cases, however, Live Mail can generally figure out your mail server settings by using a kind of "best guess" technology. If it is capable of doing so, click Finish. If not, you will receive the server configuration pages and jump to step 4. You should have this information from your ISP or email service provider (you may also choose to do this manually if you prefer).

 tip

Most ISPs provide this information on their websites. So if you cannot locate the documentation you received when you signed up for service, your easiest option is to visit your ISP's website to find your incoming and outgoing email server names.

4. The next wizard box asks for your incoming mail server type (either POP3, IMAP, or HTTP), the address of your mail server and whatever settings it requires to allow you access, what your username is, and how to connect to the outgoing server (see Figure 15.3) as well as any other settings specified by your provider. Click Next.

Figure 15.3
Enter your mail server details here. This information should have been supplied by your ISP or other email provider.

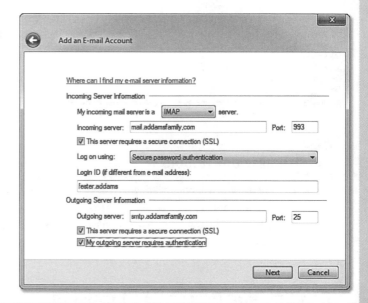

5. If you have successfully configured the account by filling out the dialog box, you will be informed that you have completed the setup. Click Finish. You will know for sure once you click Finish and Windows Live Mail tries to connect to the server (see Figure 15.4).

6. If any settings were not correct, you will not be logged in and you will receive warning dialog boxes alerting you to check your settings again. You can find these settings by right-clicking the account name in the sidebar and selecting Properties.

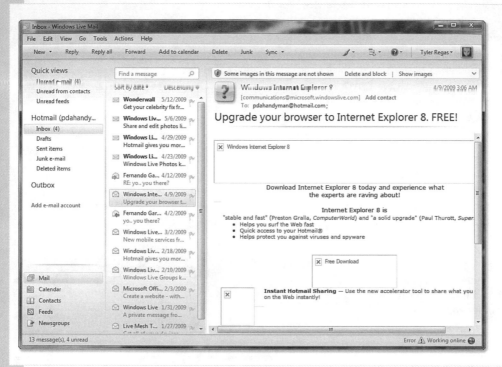

Figure 15.4
Now you can
see your
email.

Password Trouble

If the server will not accept your password, you might've used the wrong letter case. Many
email servers are case sensitive. If the Caps Lock key on your keyboard is on, you might have
entered the password in the wrong case. Sometimes, an inadvertent space can be the culprit
as well.

Reading and Processing Incoming Messages

After you have an account set up, you are ready to begin
downloading and reading mail. To get started, open Windows
Live Mail and go to the Inbox. By default, Windows Live Mail
automatically checks for new mail when it first opens. If your
installation is configured otherwise, click the Sync button on
the toolbar. As your mail is coming in, a dialog box appears
indicating which account is being checked and shows the
progress of the sending and receiving. It will also tell you

 note

Secure Password Authentication (SPA)
is used by some email services to prevent unauthorized users from getting or
sending your email. When you attempt
to receive your mail in Windows Live
Mail, a screen will pop up asking for you
to enter a username and password.
Both Windows Live Mail and MS
Outlook have this feature. Most email
(POP) servers do not use this feature, so
you should probably leave it turned off.

how many messages are being transferred. New messages will then appear in your inbox as well as in the Unread E-mail Quick View folder, as shown in Figure 15.5.

Figure 15.5
The Unread E-mail Quick View has three new messages and is displaying the first message, which was marked unread but now is marked as read because it appears in the viewer pane.

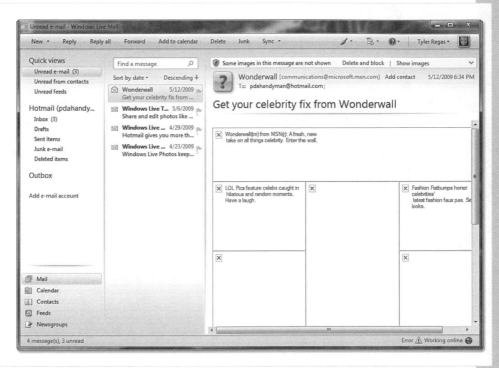

When you reply to a message, you need to be wary of a few things. First, note that if the incoming message was sent to a group of people, clicking the Reply button will send your message to the single person who sent it to you; clicking Reply All will send your message to the entire list of people who received the original message. Although this can be a helpful tool when communicating with a group of people, it could get you in trouble if you think you are writing to a specific person and accidentally click the Reply All button. Before you send any message, make sure the correct person or persons are listed in the To: and Cc: fields. Anyone listed in those two fields will receive a copy of the message as well as a list of the other recipients and their email addresses, so make sure you aren't airing your dirty laundry more publicly than you intended. The section "Creating and Sending New Mail" later in this chapter discusses addressing messages more thoroughly.

The rest of the reply process is straightforward. You just type in your own text and click Send on the toolbar when you are ready to deliver the message. By default, Windows Live Mail automatically places the text of the original message in the reply.

tip

Windows Live Mail does not show the menu bar by default; instead, it shows a small icon on the toolbar that sits between the icon of a paintbrush and a question mark on a small, round disc, all just left of the active email account selector. Just click and you will see Options and other items. You can make the menu bar appear from this menu, as well.

When you're composing your reply, keep in mind these important points:

- Consider editing the quoted text in the reply by cutting it down to the text you actually intend to respond to. Most people don't appreciate reading four pages of quoted text followed at long last by "Me too."

- Include enough of the original text to help the recipient understand exactly what you are replying to. If the recipient doesn't read your reply for several days, he might not remember what the original statements were.

- Breaking up quoted text with your own inserted comments is usually acceptable, but make sure it is obvious which words are yours. Figure 15.6 illustrates this reply technique in a plain text message. Windows Live Mail inserts the > sign before each line of the email you're responding to. In an HTML email (sometimes mistakenly called rich text), a solid vertical bar runs down the left side of the original text, and writing new text between paragraphs doesn't break that bar, so it's difficult to tell what text is newly written. In that case, use colored text or another font (choose Format, Font).

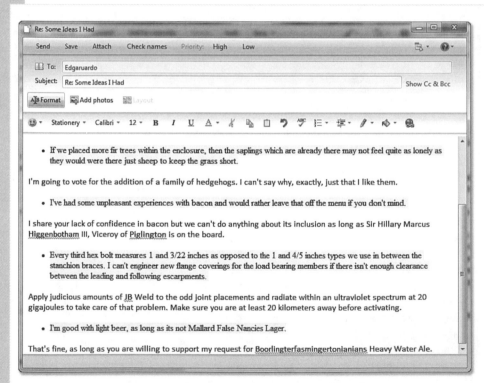

Figure 15.6
Highlighted text and reply text are interspersed throughout the message, but there is little doubt as to who wrote what.

Deleting Messages

How and when messages are deleted depends on what kind of mail server you use. If you receive mail from a POP server, deleted messages remain in the Windows Live Mail Deleted Items folder indefinitely, similar to "deleted" files in the Windows Recycle Bin. You can permanently delete messages by right-clicking the Deleted Items folder and choosing Empty 'Deleted Items' Folder from the shortcut menu that appears.

You can change the way Windows Live Mail handles items in the Deleted Items folder. To do so, choose Tools, Options, and select the Maintenance tab to customize when and how mail messages are deleted. Note that you may need to set Windows Live Mail to show the menubar using the iconic Tools menu in order to see the full Tools menu, as described earlier in this chapter.

If you have an IMAP mail server, deleted messages are moved to an online Deleted Items folder or Trash folder, depending on what it's named on the server itself.

 note

Note that the term "delete" means that the message is removed from the server permanently and that "purge" means that it is removed from the current view and dealt with as determined by any rules you may have in place. For example, if you opt to have deleted messages moved to the Trash folder, it will be marked as deleted from the Inbox, but will appear in the Trash folder after it is purged.

Checking Mail in Multiple Accounts

If you have several mail accounts, but Windows Live Mail doesn't check all of them when you click Sync, open the Properties dialog box for each of your mail accounts. On the General tab is an option labeled Include This Account When Receiving Mail or Synchronizing. Make sure a check mark appears next to this option for each of your mail accounts.

Creating and Sending New Mail

The process of creating and sending new mail is almost as easy as receiving it. To open a New Message composition window, click the New button on the Windows Live Mail toolbar.

Addressing messages properly is important. A single misplaced character, or an extra one, in an email address can send the message to the wrong person or to no one at all. Typical email addresses can look like these:

bob@pearsoneducation.com
rick.kughen@fakeemail.com
bknittel@bogusmailserver.com

 tip

In Outlook Express, you had to install Microsoft Word to have a spell-checking option when composing mail. In Windows Live Mail, spell checking is built in. Click the Check Spelling icon in the toolbar when composing a message (the button with ABC and a red check mark). Adjust your spelling options by going to Tools, Options, and clicking the Spelling tab.

Notice that Windows Live Mail only has the To: address field that appears by default. The To: field is the only required field when sending email; all the others, including the Subject line and even the message body, can be blank. The To: field usually contains the email address of the primary recipient, although it can contain more than one address, as shown in Figure 15.7. Separate multiple addresses with a semicolon (;).

 tip

Some mail servers are case sensitive. If you're not sure whether yours is, just type the whole address in lowercase letters.

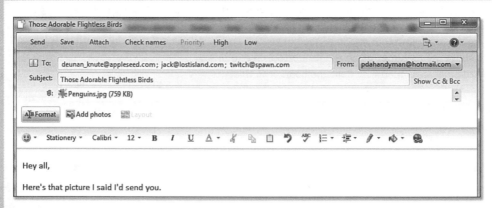

Figure 15.7
A new message with an attachment has been addressed to several people.

To send email to several people, use the Cc: field. Cc: is short for Carbon Copy or, these days when that messy blue paper is nearly extinct, Courtesy Copy. To send to several people without allowing its recipients to see the names or email addresses of others who also received it, enter addresses in the Bcc: field (Blind Carbon/Courtesy Copy). To make the Cc: and Bcc: fields appear, click the link called Show Cc & Bcc at the right end of the Subject field.

When you are finished composing the message, just click Send on the toolbar. If you want to save the message for later editing, and not send it yet, click File, Save. The file is then saved in your Drafts folder, where you can open it again later, edit it, and send it.

 tip

It is a good idea to use the Bcc: field when you are sending an email to a large audience. This hides the addresses from prying eyes and potential spammers who might then pick up the addresses. Use the Cc: line if you are corresponding with a few people on a project and want everyone to be in the loop and be able to see everyone else's address. This also allows any recipient to click Reply All and send a response to the group, whereas Bcc: does not.

Identity Crisis

What do you do if you don't like the name Windows Live Mail uses to identify you in outgoing messages? The name Windows Live Mail uses could be indicative of several things. First, if you have multiple accounts or identities configured in Windows Live Mail, make

Continued...

sure you are selecting the desired account in the From: pull-down menu when you send the messages. You can also open the Accounts dialog box and check the settings for your email address(es). To open the Accounts dialog, you will need to activate the Show Menu Bar option in the Tools menu. The Name field under User Information on the General tab is the name used to identify you on outgoing mail.

Sending and Receiving Attachments

Of the many features that make email a versatile method for communication, perhaps the most useful is the capability to send files along with an email message. You can attach any electronic file stored on disk to an email message in Windows Live Mail and then send it to someone else.

Attaching a file to an outgoing message is easy. In the message composition window, click the Attach button on the toolbar and locate the file you want to send in the Insert Attachment dialog box. After you have selected the file, click Attach. The file attachment should appear in the header information, as shown earlier in Figure 15.7.

 note

Some email accounts do not allow you to send or receive file attachments with messages. Others, particularly HTTP accounts, limit the number and size of attachments allowed. Check with your account provider to find out whether you have this capability. Also, make sure that the recipient has the capability to receive attachments.

Before you send any attached files, consider the bandwidth it will require. Even if you have a fast network or Internet connection, if the recipient connects to the Internet via a dial-up modem, downloading the attachment could take a long time. In general, you should avoid sending any attachments that are larger than 1 or 2MB unless you are sure the recipient's connection can handle them or that the recipient knows in advance that they're about to receive some rather large files. It's best to ask your recipient first. Many mail servers (especially web-based accounts) limit the total amount of space a person can use, and many also set a limit to the size of attachments allowed (often capping the attachment size at 1 or 2MB, though some high-speed servers such as Comcast cap it at 10MB at the time we wrote this).

One more thing: If you or the recipient uses a 56Kbps or slower Internet connection, it is usually a good idea to compress large attachments before you send them. Simply right-click the document(s) you wish to send, choose Send To, and then Compressed (Zipped) Folder. Attach the compressed version to your email.

To open an attachment in a message you receive, right-click the attachment (listed in the header) and choose Save As to save it to disk, or Open to simply open it. If the attachment is a picture file, it often appears in the body of the message as well, depending on the format of the image file.

 tip

Here is a tip that can save you a significant amount of cash. You can view and print Microsoft Word, Excel, PowerPoint, and Visio attachments without having to purchase Microsoft Office. You can't edit the documents, but you can view and print them. All you need to do is download the free Word, Excel, and PowerPoint viewer programs from Microsoft. Go to www.microsoft.com/downloads and search for **Office viewers**.

Guarding Yourself Against Email Viruses

Computer viruses often propagate themselves through email attachments. Hackers seem to get their jollies out of slowing down the Internet or bringing corporate business to a crawl. One way to do this seems to be to target the most popular email programs, such as Outlook and Windows Live Mail's predecessor, Outlook Express. As a result, the bulk of email-borne contagion exists in the form of attachments whose payloads prey on the weaknesses in those two programs. Personally, I think that both these programs are excellent email clients, so I don't suggest changing your email program just to avoid the onslaughts of malicious Internet hackers.

As you might suspect, Microsoft doesn't want to lose customers either, so it makes a point of looking for viruses and posting critical updates to its site for easy download. A good approach is to run a Windows System Update regularly. Automatic Updates are turned on for just this reason.

In addition, security has been improved in Windows Live Mail to specifically combat this problem. By going to Menus, Safety Options, you'll notice a wide range of new options for protecting yourself from malicious email. On the Security tab you will note that Windows Live Mail offers an option to warn you if another program attempts to send a message appearing to be from you. As you may be aware, this is a common way for viruses to spread. I recommend that you keep this option selected.

There is also an option that deals with potential threats from incoming email attachments. If you click the box next to Do Not Allow Attachments to Be Saved or Opened That Could Potentially Be a Virus, you'll be more protected, but your ability to access any attachment to email in Windows Live Mail will be limited. If you're diligent about it, a better way of dealing with the possibility of attachment-borne viruses is to carefully look over your incoming email before opening any attachment, following the tips presented a little later in this section. I've found that when enabling the automatic feature in Windows Live Mail, even the most innocuous attachments are prevented from opening. (You can regain access to these attachments simply by returning to the Security dialog box and deselecting this option.)

Yet another option is to download and use one of many available antivirus programs. A reliable source is www.mcafee.com, and its website is another good place to check for the latest discovered viruses and how to protect your computer from them. I like a freebie called Avast (www.avast.com) and have had good luck with it for several years. AVG also offers a free version of its commercial package. You can find it at http://free.avg.com.

➡ *For help dealing with junk mail and spam and phishing emails, and for information on protecting your computer from viruses, adware, malware, Trojans, and all other manner of invasive mischief,* **see** *Chapter 30, "Protecting Windows from Viruses and Spyware," and Chapter 33, "Protecting Yourself from Fraud and Spam."*

Contrary to popular belief, simply downloading an infected attachment virtually never harms your computer. With few exceptions, it is only if you open an attached executable file that there could be dire consequences. If possible, save the file attachment on a separate disk and then scan it with antivirus software.

Be especially wary of the following:

- Attachments you weren't expecting (even from people you know). If in doubt, write back to the sender and ask whether they intended to send you the attachment. Their computer may have a virus they are unaware of. Ask whether the attachment is safe and whether they've run it on their computer.

- Executable attachments (filenames ending in .exe, .vbs, or .js). Be aware that sometimes filenames are misleading on purpose. For example, you might see an attachment such as party.jpg.vbs. This is not a picture. The final extension (.vbs) is the one that counts.

- Emails with cryptic or odd subjects and messages, such as "I Luv U," "Here's that document you requested," or "CHECK THIS OUT!!!"

- Anything that comes from a source you are unfamiliar with.

Setting Up a Signature

If you use email for much of your personal and business communication, you may like to "sign" outgoing messages with an electronic signature file. These signatures frequently include additional information about you, such as an address, title, phone number, company name, web URL, or a witty quote. Windows Live Mail makes it easy to set up a standard signature that will be included in every message you compose. You can configure your own signature by following these steps:

1. Choose Menus, Options. Click the Signatures tab, shown in Figure 15.8.

Figure 15.8
You can create a standard signature for your outgoing messages here.

2. Click New to begin typing a new signature. Type your signature information.

3. If you have multiple email accounts, click Advanced and select the account or accounts you want this signature to be used with.

4. Place a check mark next to Add Signatures to All Outgoing Messages to enable this feature. Notice that, by default, your signatures will not be added to replies and forwards. Click OK when you're finished.

> **tip**
>
> Consider creating several signatures, with varying levels of personal information. You can then choose a signature in the message window by selecting Tools, Insert Signature in the message composition. If you have more that one signature configured, you will see a menu allowing you to select from the available choices.

Using the Windows Live Mail Contacts

You don't have to communicate via email for long before you mistype someone's address. Suddenly, spelling has become more important than ever before. Your local mail carrier can direct your parcel to you when the label is misspelled, tattered, and torn, but email with a misspelled address just gets bounced back to you or lost in the black hole of the "catch-all," an account designed to receive incorrectly addressed email. Email addresses can also be cryptic and long, and a very rare few are even case sensitive. The Windows Live Contacts list (previously called Address Book in Outlook Express and Windows XP) feature in Windows Live Mail is a big help with all of this.

You can open Contacts in its own window by clicking the Contacts item in the sidebar.

Adding, Editing, and Removing Entries

A foolproof way to add someone to your Contacts is by doing the following:

1. Open a message sent to you by someone you want to add to the Contacts.

2. Click the Add Contact link that appears to the right of the address you want to add to your contacts.

3. An Add a Contact dialog box opens for the entry, as shown in Figure 15.9. Go ahead and fill out as much of the form as you can now. You will save yourself a load of time later.

You also can add someone to your Contacts the old-fashioned way—that is, manually from a business card or other source. In Windows Live Mail, click the Contacts icon to open the Contacts list. Click the New button and the Add a Contact dialog box opens for you to enter information.

To edit a contact later, click again on the Contacts item in the sidebar to open the Contacts list. Select the contact that you want to edit by double-clicking that person's name. The Properties dialog box now opens with a summary of that person's contact information. To change or add information, you need to click one of the other tabs along the side of the dialog box—the information cannot be changed on the Summary tab.

Figure 15.9
Go through all the tabs in the Add a
Contact dialog box and enter any
information about this contact you
feel appropriate.

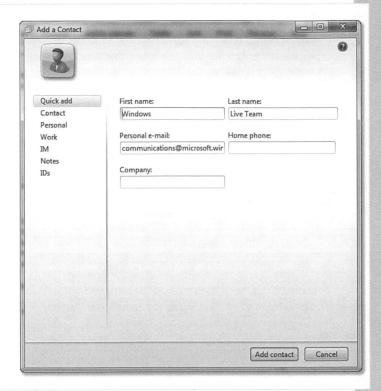

You might find duplicate listings or unwanted contacts in your Contacts. Deleting a contact is simple: Just highlight the entry and click Delete (on the toolbar). Be certain you've selected the correct contact, because this action cannot be undone.

Dealing with Spam

A hot topic in email circles today is the subject of commercial advertisements that are mass delivered via email. This type of unsolicited mail is generally referred to as *spam*, a name attributed in Internet lore to a Monty Python musical skit pertaining to the pink meat product of the same name. This type of mail is so offensive to some people that a few states have even enacted laws against it.

Some groups are also working with the U.S. federal government to ban unsolicited email and place identification requirements on people and organizations who send advertisements via email. Countless antispam organizations exist, with one of the foremost being CAUCE, the Coalition Against Unsolicited Commercial Email (www.cauce.org).

The real problem with spam is that scam operations are rampant and difficult to detect. Spam also has an impact on Internet traffic, requiring a considerable amount of bandwidth that many people feel would be better used for other purposes.

If you have been online for more than an hour, you've almost certainly received some spam yourself. Windows Live Mail has a Junk Mail filter inherited from Outlook that uses massive amounts of data collected by Microsoft's Hotmail service to help differentiate junk mail from real mail. As a default, it is turned on.

Before mail comes into your Inbox, it is analyzed by the Junk Mail filter using the latest information supplied by Microsoft through online updates. It then moves suspected junk mail into the Junk Mail folder for you to examine later. I do recommend that you visually scan the Junk Mail box once a day until you become convinced that it's not eating up real emails that you would otherwise miss.

If an email has been mistaken as spam, right-click it and choose Mark As Not Junk. It will be moved to the Inbox. If you want to prevent the next email from this sender from going into Junk Mail again, right-click the email and choose Add Sender to Safe Sender's List. This puts them in your "white list" of valid senders.

Newsgroups and the Internet

With the overwhelming and still growing popularity of the Web since its inception in the early 1990s, you might easily forget that the Internet was around for more than two decades before the first web page saw the light of a cathode ray tube. Before the inception of the Web, people used the Internet to access newsgroups. Newsgroups began in 1979 as a forum in which UNIX users could communicate with each other, and the concept grew steadily from there into what is now a global assemblage of people sharing information on virtually every topic imaginable.

Originally, news servers exchanged articles using UNIX-to-UNIX Copy Protocol (UUCP), which involves direct modem dial-up over long-distance phone lines. In 1986, the Network News Transport Protocol (NNTP) was released, allowing news to be transported via TCP/IP connection over the Internet. Most modern newsgroups use the NNTP protocol, and it is the only news protocol supported by Windows Live Mail.

Newsgroups are scattered on servers around the world, and the rough network used to carry newsgroup bandwidth is generally referred to as *Usenet*. We're not implying, however, that some authority provides oversight of Usenet. "Usenet is not a democracy" is one of the first statements you will read in virtually any primer or Frequently Asked Questions (FAQ) list on the subject, alluding to the virtual anarchy in which this medium exists. Usenet has become so large and diverse that a simple definition cannot possibly do it justice.

What we can do, however, is roughly describe the types of newsgroups and news servers that you can access using Windows Live Mail. Basically, the administrator of your news server determines which news feeds you will have access to. Feeds are passed along to the server from adjacent servers, providing a decidedly decentralized structure to Usenet. Each server maintains a list of message IDs to ensure that new articles are received at a given server only once. An individual server can control which feeds it propagates, although the interconnectivity of Usenet servers ensures that a lone server has little or no control of the overall distribution. Thus, the authority of a news server is generally limited to what clients (that would be you) can access and what kind of material those clients can post. Likewise, the decentralization of servers means that an article you post may take hours—or even days—to circulate among all other news servers.

A free alternative to commercial news servers is a web-based news service, such as the one created by groups.google.com. An advantage of using a web-based news service is that a search brings back results from many newsgroups, not just one. It's a terrific way to find expert postings on just about anything from open-heart surgery, to child adoption, to what people think of the new car you're considering buying. However, messages are not brought into your news client program (such as Windows Live Mail) for reference offline.

Many folks still use newsgroups and want a decent reader and newsgroup message composer that works more like an email program. It's also noteworthy that Microsoft has rethought newsgroups a bit and has some useful offerings in the way of

> **note**
>
> The terms *newsgroup* and *Usenet* are used almost interchangeably in today's online world, but it is useful to know that *newsgroup* refers to individual groups, whereas *Usenet* refers to the entire network of groups as a whole.

help information on all its products, by way of Microsoft Communities, a set of super newsgroups with new features.

Locating News Servers

Many ISPs and companies provide news server accounts to their Internet users, but you still might find yourself looking for a server on your own. This might be the case even if you have a news account available to you; some service providers censor the news content that is available, and if you want uncensored news, you must rely on a different source.

Censorship, Big Brother, and NNTP Servers

News feeds are censored for a variety of reasons. For example, your company's server might restrict feeds from **alt.**, **rec.**, and **talk.** groups to reduce the number of work hours lost to employee abuse or simply to reduce bandwidth. Many other servers restrict feeds that contain pornographic content for both legal and moral reasons.

Even if your news server provides a relatively unrestricted news feed, you should exercise care when deciding which articles you download from the server. Virtually all servers maintain logs of the activities of each login account. This means that your service provider can track which articles you download, and in most cases these logs can be subpoenaed and used against you in court.

In other words, Big Brother might be watching you download porn, bomb-making instructions, and bootleg copies of the latest Hollywood blockbuster. Be especially paranoid if you access a company news server; hours spent receiving otherwise legal content such as fruitcake recipes, Bill Gates jokes, and the like could still land you in hot water if the boss is monitoring your online activities.

Many news servers are available through virtually any Internet connection, but you'll pay for that connection. Typically, monthly charges for a personal news server account range from $2 to $20 per month and get higher for corporate or higher-bandwidth accounts. If you plan to use newsgroups frequently, you might want to factor in this cost when you're shopping for an ISP. You can find a good list of commercial news servers at http://freenews.maxbaud.net/forfee.html.

However, if you have an Internet connection and simply want a different news server, you can find a list of free news servers available online at http://freenews.maxbaud.net/newspage.html?date= today. The list of free servers can change daily.

Web-based news servers at the time of this writing could be found at http://newsguy.com/news.asp.

Newsgroup Isn't Available on News Server

If a newsgroup you want to access isn't available on your news server, click Reset List in the Newsgroup Subscriptions window. The newsgroup may be new and simply not shown in your current list. If the group still isn't there, try contacting the ISP or other service that hosts the list and ask that service to add it. Often, new groups simply go unnoticed because so many of them are out there. Many news servers are willing to respond to such a request, unless they have a rule restricting or censoring the particular group.

Try paying for an alternative dedicated news server that does carry the newsgroup you're interested in.

Setting Up a Newsgroup Account in Windows Live Mail

Before using newsgroups, you have to set up a news account in Windows Live Mail. Windows Live Mail actually comes with a newsgroup already set up, called Microsoft Communities, but it only has groups that pertain to Microsoft products, so you can write in for support on Windows 7, Office, and any other products. For real newsgroup reading, you have to configure a regular newsgroup account. Before you can configure your news account, you need to obtain a news server address, which should look something like news.domainname.com or possibly nntp.serviceprovider.com.

Your company might also have a news server account with a commercial provider. You can configure multiple server accounts in Windows Live Mail, just as you can set up multiple email accounts.

As mentioned earlier, a news server provides you with news feeds from other news servers. Which feeds are available to you depends on decisions made by your server's administrator. For example, some news servers restrict feeds for all alt. (alternative) newsgroups because some of them contain highly objectionable material.

➡ *If you do not have a news server you can access,* ***see*** *"Locating News Servers," **p. 409**.*

To set up your account in Windows Live Mail, follow these steps:

1. Open Windows Live Mail, and click Newsgroups in the sidebar. Note the presence of the Microsoft Communities account already configured.

2. Click Add Newsgroup Account in the sidebar to open the wizard.

3. Follow the instructions in the wizard for inputting your display name and email address (the wizard might provide this information for you).

4. Type the name of your news (NNTP) server. If you don't know the NNTP server name, contact your ISP or check its web page.

5. (Optional) You might have to log on to your news server with a password. If your ISP says you do, click that option in the box before clicking Next. You'll be prompted to enter your username and password.

6. Click Finish. This finalizes your setup.

Downloading the Newsgroup List

After you have set up the news account, Windows Live Mail's next step is to download a list of newsgroups from the server. This is part of the "subscription" process. First, though, Microsoft asks whether it should search for Microsoft's proprietary Communities technology that helps newsgroups work better. Doing this is your choice, but be aware that it doesn't harm anything to search. When the list is finished downloading, it will look like Figure 15.10. (I sorted this list to show only newsgroups with the word "unix" in it, so your list will look different.)

tip

Although new newsgroups are created daily, the list that has been downloaded to your computer is static and doesn't show new groups. The next time you click a newsgroup server in the left pane, you'll probably see a dialog box telling you that new groups have been added since your last session, giving you the option of updating your list. To make sure you have a current list, right-click on a newsgroup server name in the left pane and choose Reset List.

Figure 15.10
Downloading the list of newsgroups.

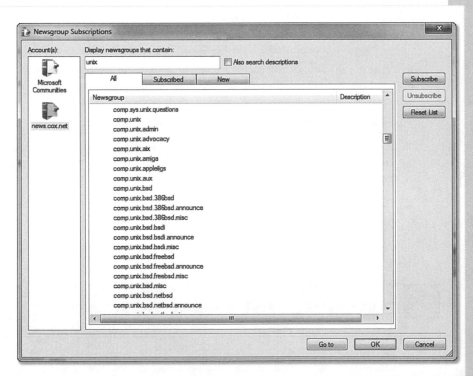

Depending on the size of the list and the speed of your connection, downloading could take several minutes. You might have time to go get another cup of coffee. When the process is finished, the list is downloaded and you are ready to locate and subscribe to newsgroups. If your news server required a password and it was incorrect, you will be prompted again to enter it.

Finding and Reading Newsgroups

Usually, before you can read a newsgroup, you must first subscribe to it. A subscription simply means you've placed a bookmark of sorts in Windows Live Mail for that group, making it easy to return to and follow conversations whenever you are using Windows Live Mail.

Before you can subscribe to a newsgroup, you must find one that piques your interest. Searching for a group in your down-loaded list is fairly simple in Windows Live Mail (refer to Figure 15.10). As you type a word in the Display Newsgroups That Contain field, the list of newsgroups shrinks. You can experiment by typing a keyword you are interested in and pausing after each keystroke.

Newsgroups are usually—but not always—named descriptively. In Figure 15.10, where I used the term "unix," you can see that all the groups listed have that term in its name.

 tip

If you don't find a newsgroup that interests you, try a search at http://groups.google.com or another web source to see whether other groups not currently available on your news server exist. There is no such thing as a "complete" list of newsgroups, so a search of several different resources will yield the best results.

Subscribing to Newsgroups

Windows Live Mail does not require you to subscribe to a group to view its contents. You can sim-ply select a group from the list and click Go To to see messages posted to the group, but you might find it easier to manage the process by simply subscribing anyway. Subscribing to a newsgroup does not require any great level of commitment on your part because you can always unsubscribe with just two mouse clicks.

When you find a newsgroup you want to subscribe to, do the following:

1. Click once on the newsgroup name to select it, and then click the Subscribe button. You may also double-click the newsgroup to subscribe or unsubscribe. Try it. An icon will appear next to the subscribed group names, as shown in Figure 15.11.

2. Click Go To at the bottom of the Newsgroup Subscriptions window. The window closes, and the 300 most recent posts are downloaded to your computer.

Actually, only the message headers are downloaded, and they appear listed in the window. The message contents are not downloaded until you choose to view a specific message.

 ### Some Messages Are Unavailable After Synchronizing

If you synchronize a group but then find that some of the messages you click are unavailable, you should first check that the settings for the group are correct. If the group isn't set to All Messages, and the Synchronize check box isn't checked, this could easily explain the missing message bodies. Another possibility is that the message was removed from the host server sometime after the header list was distributed. It can take up to 72 hours after a message is physically removed before it disappears from the header list.

Continued...

News servers only have so much disk space. To allow them to continually add incoming files to their lists, they must continually discard old files. If your server is missing a few articles, you may "ask" for a repost of the incomplete files, but while the poster is expected to service reasonable repost requests, there is no requirement to do so. Sometimes, a regular poster might not service repost requests at all, but will instead indicate an FTP, ICQ, or IRQ service where you can pick up missing files. And in many cases a repost request will be answered by a person who just happens to have downloaded the same file set and is willing to help support the group.

Finally, if you are doing everything right and your server is not gathering all the articles that were posted, consider informing your ISP's support desk of the problem. It does not do any good to complain to everyone else in the newsgroup if you are not telling the few people who are actually paid to help you. Servers and the connecting routers are sensitive electronic equipment, and their only guarantee is that they will fail at some point. Help your ISP monitor the network.

If your server is poorly connected and misses a lot of articles, as stated previously, consider hiring a dedicated news service as a secondary server.

Figure 15.11
You can select a newsgroup and subscribe to it here. When you click Go To, this window automatically closes.

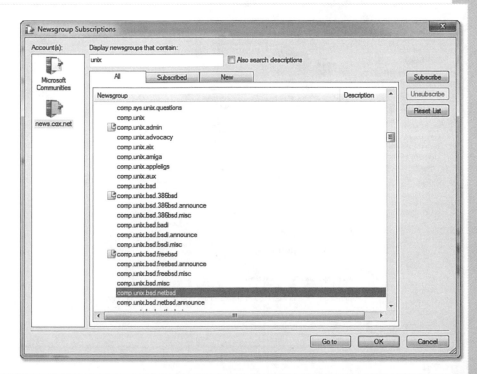

If you decide that you don't want to remain subscribed to a group, unsubscribing is easy. Just right-click the group's listing in the left pane and choose Unsubscribe from the context menu that appears. Alternatively, click the Newsgroups icon in the toolbar, choose the news server in question, and click the Subscribed tab. This will list all the groups you are subscribed to. Click a group, and then click Subscribe or Unsubscribe.

Reading and Posting Messages to a Newsgroup

When you first access a newsgroup, only the first 300 message headers are downloaded. You can download an additional 300 headers by clicking the Headers button in the toolbar.

tip

Turn on and off the Preview pane by clicking View, Layout.

If you want to read a message, just click it and it will appear in the Preview pane. If you are not using the Preview pane, you can double-click a message to open it in a separate message window.

As you peruse the list of messages in the group, you need to understand the concept of *discussion threads*. A thread occurs when someone responds to a message. Others respond to the response, and this conversation becomes its own discussion thread. Messages that are part of a thread have an arrow next to them, and you can click this icon to expand a list of other messages in the thread. Figure 15.12 shows several expanded threads.

Figure 15.12
Threaded messages.

Which Messages Are New?

If you can't tell which messages are new, open the Options dialog box by choosing Menus, Options. On the Read tab, place a check mark next to Mark All Messages As Read When Exiting a Newsgroup.

Posting messages to a newsgroup is simple. Perhaps the easiest way to post is to reply to an existing message. This process works much the same as replying to regular email, except that you must take extra care to ensure that your reply is going to the right place. Notice that the toolbar has a new button—the Reply Group button—as shown in Figure 15.12.

Each reply button serves a unique purpose:

Reply Group	Sends a reply back to the newsgroup itself
Reply	Sends a reply only to the original sender using the email address they set up their account with
Forward	Forwards the message to a third party

 caution

Information posted in newsgroups can be viewed by anyone, and we do mean *anyone*! Never post personal or sensitive information in a newsgroup.

One aspect to watch carefully is that messages you post to a newsgroup are relevant. If the newsgroup is moderated, someone reviews all posts and removes posts deemed inappropriate. Look for a newsgroup FAQ for more information on netiquette (Internet etiquette) and any rules that might apply to the groups you are subscribed to.

 note

The default news message format is Plain Text. You should maintain this setting to ensure that your message can be read by other news readers.

Managing Messages

By default, Windows Live Mail is not configured to delete any messages from your newsgroups. If you would prefer that your newsgroups be cleaned up for you, you can set the option to delete messages from your computer and specify any number of days after you download them. Likewise, you can also set up Windows Live Mail to delete read messages every time you leave the group. You can review these settings by choosing Menus, Options. In the Options dialog box, click the Advanced tab, and then click the Maintenance button. The resulting Maintenance dialog box is shown in Figure 15.13.

Message No Longer Available

If a message you read earlier appears to no longer be available, you may have configured Windows Live Mail to delete read messages a specific number of days after you have downloaded them. To change this option, click the Maintenance button on the Advanced tab of the Options dialog box to open the Maintenance dialog box shown in Figure 15.13.

Figure 15.13
Review your message management settings here.

If you want to maintain a record of the messages in your newsgroup, remove the check mark next to each Delete option. Messages remain in Windows Live Mail indefinitely if you deselect both of these options, but keep in mind that if the group has high traffic, these messages could eventually eat up a lot of disk space.

TROUBLESHOOTING YOUR INTERNET CONNECTION

It's Great When It Works, but...

Browsing the Internet is great fun and very useful. In fact, watch as I instantly transfer millions of dollars from my secret Swiss bank account to... wait a minute, what's a "404 Server Not Found Error"? What's going on? Did the modem disconnect? Is the IRS closing in on me? Help! Where's my money?

If you've used the Internet for any length of time, this scene might seem all too familiar—except for the bit about the Swiss bank account. (A guy can dream, can't he?) Connecting to the Internet and using the Web is an amazingly user-friendly experience, yet we can't escape that it's a staggeringly complex system. If something goes wrong at any step along the way between your fingertips and a server in cyberspace, the whole system comes to a crashing halt. Where do you begin to find and fix the problem?

In this chapter, I'll show you the basic strategies to use when tracking down Internet problems, and I'll briefly discuss some of the diagnostic tools available to help you pinpoint the trouble.

 tip

Experiment with the diagnostic tools that we'll be discussing in this chapter when your network and Internet connection are operating correctly, to learn how the programs work and what output you should expect. This way, if you run into trouble later, you can compare the results to what you saw when things were working.

Before You Run into Trouble

The best tool to have on hand when you're diagnosing Internet problems is information about what you should expect when your connection is *working*. If you collect this information in advance of running into trouble, you'll save yourself a lot of time, trouble, and grief.

For starters, gather the information that your ISP provided when you set up your Internet connection. This might include the following information:

- The customer support telephone number for your ISP.

- The type of service you're using: dial-up modem, DSL, cable modem, satellite, or other type of service.

- For dial-up service, the dial-in telephone number(s) for your area and the URL of the web page that you can use to find other dial-up numbers in other areas.

- For DSL or cable service, the make and model of the DSL or cable modem that you were given.

- The login name and password used to connect to the service. (This usually does not apply to cable Internet service; your provider will tell you if it does.)

- The usernames and passwords used to access the email accounts you have with your ISP.

- The names or IP addresses of any servers provided by your ISP, including outgoing mail (SMTP server), incoming mail (POP3 server), and news reader (NNTP server).

- If your service provides you with a static IP address, you need to know your IP address, your network mask, your gateway address, and two or more DNS server addresses.

I suggest that you collect, type, and print all this information and store the printout in a handy place near your computer. You can use WordPad (click Start, All Programs, Accessories, WordPad) or your favorite word processor. The important part is to *print the information* so it's available even if your computer is acting up. Keep the printout in a manila file folder labeled "Internet Connection Information."

It's also helpful to collect the correct output of the TCP/IP diagnostic programs (whose use I'll describe later in the chapter) and store copies of the output in your file folder for reference. You can use the PrntScrn key to take snapshots of the output and setup windows, and then paste the pictures into a word processing document so you can print it. Again, it really helps to have this information available when trouble occurs—but you have to prepare it in advance.

Here are some things to record:

- The output of the `tracert` command-line program showing the results for a sample website. The `tracert` tool records all the intermediate steps that Internet data passes through between your computer and a site on the Internet. Knowing what the route looks like when things are working can later help you determine whether a problem is in your computer or out on the Internet, beyond your control.

To record this output, open a Command Prompt window (click Start, All Programs, Accessories, Command Prompt) and type this command:

```
tracert www.sonic.net
```

This command might take about 30 seconds to display several lines of text, ending with "Trace complete." If it does run successfully, type this command:

```
tracert www.sonic.net > goodtrace.txt
```

This time, you will not see any output but the command is running. After the same 30 seconds, the command prompt returns. Now type this:

```
notepad goodtrace.txt
```

This is the saved output of the successful `tracert` command, which you can now print and put into your Internet Connection Information folder.

- The output of `ipconfig /all`, run on each of your computers while you're successfully connected to the Internet. `ipconfig` lists all your networking settings, so you can check for mistakes.

  To record this output, type these commands:
  ```
  ipconfig /all > ipconfig.txt
  notepad ipconfig.txt
  ```

  As before, you should print and file the results.

- The Network Hardware and Protocol Configuration dialog boxes in Network Connections, as pictures snapped with PrntScrn. If you have a network or a network adapter that you use for a broadband cable or DSL Internet connection, it's handy to record the setup information in case you need to reenter it later. For example, you might need to do that if you replace your network adapter. To document these settings, follow these steps:

  1. Open WordPad (click Start, All Programs, Accessories, WordPad) or your favorite word processor.

  2. Open the Network Connections window (click Start, Control Panel, View Network Status and Tasks [under Network and Internet], Change Adapter Settings).

  3. Right-click the icon that corresponds to your Internet connection (a dial-up, broadband, or LAN connection, depending on your Internet connection type) and select Properties.

  4. Select the first tab. Press Alt+PrtScrn. Click the cursor in the word processor window, and press Ctrl+V to paste in the picture.

 note

The User Account Control warning might pop up at various points during this procedure. If it does, click Continue, or supply an Administrator account name and password to proceed.

5. Return to the Properties dialog box and select the next tab. Again, press Alt+PrtScrn to capture a picture of the dialog box; then select the word processor and press Ctrl+V to paste in the picture. Repeat this process for every tab in the dialog box.

If the dialog box has a Networking tab that has a list labeled This Connection Uses the Following Items, select each of the items in this list in turn. For each one, if the Properties button is enabled, click it, and if a subsidiary Properties dialog box appears, take pictures of every tab on that box, too. Press Cancel to close it.

6. Close the Connection Properties dialog box. Repeat steps 3 through 5 for any other connection icons in the Network Connections window.

7. Print the word processing document and store it in your file folder.

- The configuration of any routers or network connection equipment. If you have an Internet connection sharing router, it's a *very* good idea to record its correct settings, in case they are accidentally changed or you update or replace the device. You can do this by printing each of its setup screens from your web browser.

- The settings for any dial-up connections used. Many ISPs talk you through their setup process or provide you with "wizard" software that does the work for you, and it's important to record the setup information in case you need to reconstruct it someday. The information you need is the telephone number, login name, and password.

- Diagrams showing network cabling, hubs, routers, and computers. If your 3-year-old is a budding network installer and rewires your computer, it's handy to have a diagram of the correct setup to help you get all the wiring spaghetti back in order.

 tip

In a business setting, documenting your LAN configuration is a "due diligence" issue—it's not optional. Be sure to keep the documentation up to date, too. If you use an outside contractor to set up your business's computers, network, or Internet connection, be sure your contract specifies that good documentation will be provided.

With this documentation at hand, you'll be armed with supportive information if a problem does occur.

Troubleshooting Step by Step

A functioning Internet connection depends on an entire chain of hardware and software components that reaches all the way from your keyboard to a computer that might be halfway around the world. Troubleshooting is a real detective's art, and it's based more on methodical tracking down of potential suspect problems than intuition. If something goes wrong, you have to go through each component, asking "Is *this* the one that's causing the problem?"

Windows 7 comes with network-troubleshooting capabilities that, in *some* cases, can identify and repair problems automatically. If you encounter Internet connection problems—especially problems using high-speed broadband Internet service—try these steps:

1. Click Start, Control Panel, View Network Status and Tasks (under Network and Internet). This displays the Network and Sharing Center. If there is a problem with your Internet connection, Windows displays a red X, as shown in Figure 16.1.

Figure 16.1
Windows displays a red X on the map, showing that your Internet connection is not working.

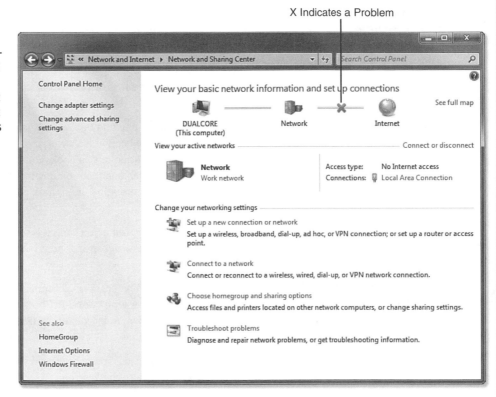

2. Double-click the red X.

3. If Windows displays a message indicating that it might be able to repair the problem, click Repair.

4. If that does not solve the problem, go back to the Network and Sharing Center. At the bottom of the page, click Troubleshoot Problems, and then click Internet Connections. Click Advanced, Run As Administrator, and then click Next. Follow the troubleshooting wizard's prompts from there.

If the wizard's diagnosis is "The DNS server isn't responding," and if you connect to the Internet through a shared connection using a router, this most likely means that your connection sharing router can't connect to the Internet. The problem is either with the router, your cable or DSL modem, or its connection to the Internet. Use Internet Explorer to connect to your sharing router, as described later in the chapter under "Identifying Network Hardware Problems." If you can bring up the router's setup web page, the router is working, so your best bet is to contact your ISP for further assistance.

5. If this does not fix the problem, and if your computer connects to the Internet through a wireless or wired Ethernet connection, go back to the Network and Sharing Center. Click Troubleshoot Problems, and select Network Adapter. Again, click Advanced, Run As Administrator, and then click Next.

If the problem occurred because your computer failed to obtain its network settings from a router, this procedure will often work. In many cases, though, you'll need to locate the problem yourself, using good, old-fashioned Sherlock Holmes–style deductive reasoning. Here's how it goes. Let's assume that you are having trouble using a certain website. It could be that

- You can view some of its pages but not others, or you see text displayed but not the streaming video or sound.

  In this case, you know that your Internet connection itself is fine because something does appear. The problem, then, is that the video or sound application isn't working. You might want to check the index to see whether we discuss the application in this book. You might also check the application's built-in help pages. If the application was one that you downloaded or purchased, check the manufacturer's website for support information or an updated software version.

- Nothing on this particular site is responding. In this case, see if you can view any other website. Try www.google.com, www.quepublishing.com, your ISP's website, or your local newspaper's website.

  If you get a response from even one other website, again, your Internet connection is fine. The problem is most likely with the site you're trying to use or with your ISP. Check to be sure that Internet Explorer isn't set up to block access to the site you're interested in. (See Chapter 14, "Using Internet Explorer 8," for more help on this topic.)

- You can't view any web pages on any site. If this is the case, you know that your Internet connection itself is at fault. This chapter can help you find out what's wrong.

To that end, Figures 16.2 and 16.3 show flowcharts to help direct you to the source of the problem. The first chart is for dial-up connections to an ISP; the second is for broadband or LAN connections. If you're having Internet connection trouble, follow the appropriate flowchart for your type of connection. The endpoints in each flowchart suggest places to look for trouble. I discuss these in the sections that follow.

Figure 16.2
Flowchart for diagnosing dial-up Internet connection problems.

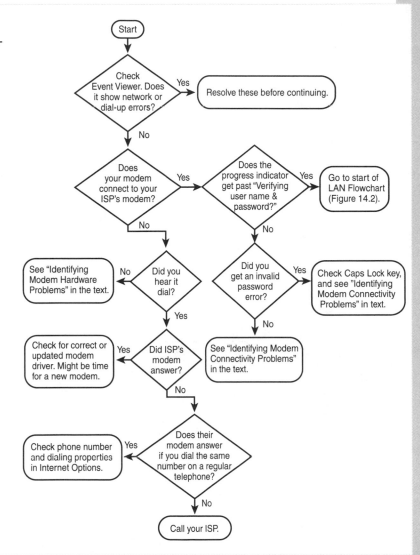

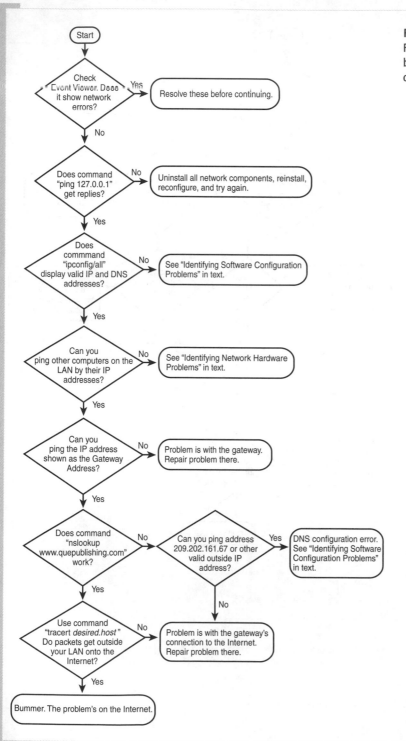

Figure 16.3
Flowchart for diagnosing broad-band or LAN-based Internet connection problems.

Identifying Software Configuration Problems

Software configuration problems can easily be the cause of Internet connection problems, and it's fairly simple to determine that this is the problem—you can't make any Internet connection whatsoever, although the Device Manager says your network card or modem seems to be working correctly. The potential problems depend on the type of Internet connection you use.

Troubleshooting a Dial-Up Connection

If your modem appears to connect to your ISP but you still can't access any web pages or Internet services, here are some steps you can take:

1. In Internet Explorer, select Tools, Internet Options. Select the Connections tab. Be sure you have selected the correct dial-up connection. Select the dial-up connection entry and click Settings. Be sure that Use a Proxy Server for This Connection is not checked. (The exception to this rule is if you are using a third-party connection speed-enhancement program; in this case, the software manufacturer might specify proxy settings.) Close all the Settings dialog boxes.

2. Click the network icon at the bottom-right corner of your screen to display the connection list, as shown in Figure 16.4. Right-click the entry for your dial-up connection and select Properties. Alternatively, click Start, Control Panel, View Network Status and Tasks (under Network and Internet), click Change Adapter Settings, and then right-click the entry for your dial-up connection and select Properties.

   View the Networking tab. Under Components Used by This Connection, only the Internet Protocol Version 4 and Version 6 entries, and possibly QoS Packet Scheduler, should be checked.

3. On the Security tab, look at the Authentication settings. This should be set to Allow These Protocols, with at least the Unencrypted Password and Challenge Handshake Authentication Protocol (CHAP) boxes checked if you're connecting to an ISP, and the Microsoft CHAP box checked as well if you're connecting to your office LAN.

If none of these steps identifies a problem, it's time to call your ISP for assistance. You might have to spend a half hour on hold listening to really bad music, but at this point, it's their job to help you get online, and they should help you cheerfully and expertly. (Otherwise, you should get a new ISP.)

Click to connect or disconnect,
right-click to set Properties

Figure 16.4
The Windows 7 Network Connection taskbar icon provides quick access to a list of network connections. If you have a wireless network connection, the icon will look like a set of stairs.

Click the network icon to
open this pop-up window

Troubleshooting a Cable or DSL Modem Connection

If your computer connects directly to a cable or DSL modem, you might have one or two network cards installed in your computer, depending on whether you're sharing the high-speed connection on your LAN.

To check for the proper settings, follow these steps:

1. In a Command Prompt window (click Start, All Programs, Accessories, Command Prompt), type **ipconfig /all** and press Enter. Be sure that the IP address and DNS information for the network card that connects to your high-speed modem is accurate. Your ISP's tech support people can help you confirm this.

2. If your DSL provider requires you to "sign on" before using the Internet, you'll be using a sort of "dial-up" connection, except that the connection is made digitally over the DSL network. (This is called Point-to-Point Protocol over Ethernet, or PPPoE.) You set up this connection using the Broadband (PPPoE) option, as described in Chapter 13, "Getting Connected."

 note

If you have DSL or cable service but your computer connects to a connection sharing router and the *router* connects to the DSL or cable modem, don't follow these instructions. Instead, see "Identifying Network Hardware Problems" later in this chapter.

If this is the case, and if you use a LAN adapter to connect to your DSL modem, the IP address displayed for the LAN adapter itself will have an IP address that is used only to communicate with your DSL modem. Be sure to check with your ISP to be certain that this computer-to-modem connection is configured correctly; if it's not, you won't be able to make the connection to your ISP.

Use the Connection icon to connect to your ISP. You can get to it quickly by clicking the network icon in the taskbar (as shown in Figure 16.4). Select the name of the connection for your Internet service, and click Connect.

When the logon process has completed, `ipconfig /all` should show a dial-up connection with a different IP address. This is your real, public Internet address for the duration of the connection.

3. If you're sharing your computer's high-speed connection with your home or office LAN using two network cards in your computer, be sure you've enabled sharing on the correct connection. The connection to check as "shared" is the one that connects to your high-speed DSL or cable modem. The LAN-side connection is not the shared connection and should have an IP address of 192.168.0.1. Internet connection sharing is described in Chapter 19, "Connecting Your Network to the Internet."

Troubleshooting a LAN Connection

If you connect to the Internet via a wired or wireless connection on your LAN, the first question is, can you communicate with other computers on your LAN? To test this, you should use the `ping` command.

Open a Command Prompt window (click Start, All Programs, Accessories, Command Prompt) and type the command **ipconfig**. The output of `ipconfig` lists a number called a gateway address. To test the connection to your gateway, type **ping** followed by the gateway address, and then press Enter. For example:

```
ping 192.168.0.1
```

This tests the connection to the computer or router that is sharing its Internet connection. If `ping` says "Request timed out" or "Transmit failed" instead of listing four successful replies, you have a LAN problem that you need to fix first.

If you are using a wireless network connection, be sure your wireless connection is working correctly, that you are connected to the correct wireless network, and that you have the correct network key entered. Chapter 21, "Troubleshooting Your Network," is devoted to LAN troubleshooting.

If you can communicate with other computers on the LAN but not the Internet, can anyone else on your LAN access the

 tip

Windows has a diagnostic and repair function that resets all the software components of a LAN connection, including the DHCP address assignment. This often solves LAN problems. To use it, open the Network Connections page, find your LAN or wireless connection, right-click it, and select Diagnose. If a problem is identified, follow the instructions or select the Reset option.

A quicker path to the Diagnose function is through the network icon on your taskbar (see Figure 16.4). Click the network icon, right-click your connection name, select Status, then click Diagnose.

Internet? If no one can, the problem is in your LAN's connection to the Internet. If your LAN uses Windows' built-in Internet Connection Sharing (ICS), go to the sharing computer and start diagnosing the problem there. Otherwise, follow these steps:

1. Open a Command Prompt window and type **ipconfig /all** to view your TCP/IP settings. The output appears similar to that shown in Listing 16.1. (The Tunnel Adapter entries are not important here and are not shown.)

Listing 16.1   Output from the ipconfig /all **Command**

```
Windows IP Configuration
    Host Name . . . . . . . . . . . . .: MyComputer
    Primary Dns Suffix  . . . . . . . :
    Node Type . . . . . . . . . . . . :  Hybrid
    IP Routing Enabled. . . . . . . . :  No
    WINS Proxy Enabled. . . . . . . . :  No
Ethernet adapter Local Area Connection:
    Connection-specific DNS Suffix  . :
    Description . . . . . . . . . . . :  Intel PCI Fast Ethernet Adapter
    Physical Address. . . . . . . . . :  00-03-FF-D0-CA-5F
    DHCP Enabled. . . . . . . . . . . :  Yes
    Autoconfiguration Enabled . . . . :  Yes
    Link-local IPv6 Address . . . . . :  fe80::8014:cfc7:9a98:cdfe%10(Preferred)
    IPv4 Address. . . . . . . . . . . :  192.168.1.106(Preferred)
    Subnet Mask . . . . . . . . . . . :  255.255.255.0
    Lease Obtained. . . . . . . . . . :  Sunday, July 5, 20097:22:23 PM
    Lease Expires . . . . . . . . . . :  Sunday, July 5, 2009 7:22:22 PM
    Default Gateway . . . . . . . . . :  192.168.1.1
    DHCP Server . . . . . . . . . . . :  192.168.1.1
    DHCPv6 IAID . . . . . . . . . . . :  167773183
    DNS Servers . . . . . . . . . . . :  192.168.1.1
    NetBIOS over Tcpip. . . . . . . . :  Enabled
```

Within the output, check the following:

- The DNS suffix search list and the connection-specific DNS suffix should be set correctly for your ISP's domain name or your company's domain name. (This is helpful but not crucial.) It can also be left blank.

- The IP address should be appropriate for your LAN. If you're using ICS, the number will be 192.168.0.*xxx*. If you're using a hardware connection-sharing device, the number might be different.

- If your IP address appears to be 169.254.*xxx.yyy*, the sharing computer or router was not running when you booted up your computer, or it is no longer set up to share its connection. Get the sharing computer or router restarted and then skip to step 2.

- The default gateway address should be the IP address of your router or sharing computer, usually something similar to 192.168.0.1 or 192.168.1.1.

- The default gateway address and your IP address should be identical for the first few sets of numbers, corresponding to those parts of the subnet mask that are set to 255. That is, both might start with 192.168.0 or 192.168.1.

- If your computer gets its IP address information automatically, DHCP Enabled should be set to Yes. If your computer has its IP address information entered manually, no DHCP server should be listed.

- If you're using connection sharing, the DNS server address will be 192.168.0.1. Otherwise, the DNS server numbers should be those provided by your ISP or network administrator.

- If your computer gets its settings automatically or uses a shared connection, continue with the next two steps.

2. Be sure the master router or sharing computer is running. Then, in the Network Connections window, right-click your Local Area Connection icon and select Diagnose. This might lead you through solving the problem. Alternatively, view the Network and Sharing Center, and select Troubleshoot Problems from the task list. Select Internet Connections, then repeat the process selecting Network Adapter.

3. Repeat the `ipconfig` command and see whether the correct information appears now. If it does, you're all set. If not, the master computer or the router is not supplying the information described previously and needs to be set correctly before you can proceed.

These steps should take care of any software configuration problems. If none of these steps indicates or solves the problem, check that your network or modem hardware is functioning correctly.

Identifying Network Hardware Problems

If you suspect hardware as the source of your Internet connection problems, check the following:

- Log on using an account with Administrator privileges. On the Start menu, right-click Computer and select Manage to open Computer Management. Select Device Manager. Look for any yellow exclamation point (!) icons in the device list. If your network adapter is marked with this trouble indicator, you must solve the hardware problem before continuing. If the device needs an updated driver, see "Updating Drivers" in Chapter 27, "Installing and Replacing Hardware," for more information.

- Also within Computer Management, check the Event Viewer for any potentially informative error messages that might indicate a hardware problem.

- Use `ipconfig` on each of your computers to check that all the computers on your LAN have the same gateway and network mask values, and similar but distinct IP addresses.

- If your LAN has indicator lights on the network cards and hubs, open a Command Prompt window and type

```
ping -t x.x.x.x
```

where $x.x.x.x$ is your network's default gateway address. (This might be something similar to 192.168.0.1.) This forces your computer to transmit data once per second. Confirm that the indicator lights blink on your LAN adapter and the hub, if you have one. This test might point out a cabling problem.

- If your hub or LAN card's indicator doesn't flash, you might have a bad LAN adapter, the wrong driver might be installed, or you might have configured the card incorrectly. You can stop the ping test by pressing Ctrl+C when you're finished checking.

If you use a hardware connection-sharing router for a broadband (DSL or cable) connection, your router might provide further assistance. To access the router, follow these steps:

1. Open a Command Prompt window (click Start, All Programs, Accessories, Command Prompt).

2. Type the command **ipconfig** and press Enter.

3. Note the gateway address. It will be something along the lines of 192.168.0.1.

4. Open Internet Explorer. In the Address bar, type the URL //**192.168.0.1**, but enter the gateway address that you noted in the previous step.

5. You are prompted to enter the administrative username and password for your router. Each manufacturer has a default name and password, which you can find in the router's user's manual. You might also have changed it when you installed it.

6. Most routers have a Status menu item that displays the status of the router's Internet connection. If it says that it can't connect, you might have an incorrect PPPoE username or password entered. Or it might have dropped the connection. In this case, there might be a Connect button you can click, or you might want to just power off and then power on the router.

If you use a dial-up Internet connection, the next section can help you diagnose modem problems.

Identifying Modem Hardware Problems

Modems can have a greater variety of problems than network adapters. You can take a few steps to determine what the problem might be:

1. Before getting too frustrated, check the obvious one more time: Is a functioning telephone line connected to the right socket on the modem? Unless you're using an ISDN modem, it also doesn't hurt to plug in an extension phone and listen as the modem dials and your ISP answers. You must somehow put the extension on the "line" side of the modem, though, because most modems disable the "telephone" jack when dialing. A duplex telephone jack can help with this.

   If dialing was actually taking place but you couldn't hear it, run the Phone and Modem Options (open the Control Panel and click Hardware and Sound; then, click Phone and Modem Options). Select the Modems tab, highlight the modem, and click Properties. Click Change Settings, and then click Continue. Select the Modem tab and move the volume slider up to its rightmost position. Click OK to save the change.

If you have a voicemail system that uses a stutter dial tone to indicate that you have messages waiting, your modem might not dial when the stutter is active. If this is the case, open the Control Panel. In the Search box, type **modem**, then click Phone and Modem. Select the Modems tab. Select your modem and click Properties. Select the Modem tab and disable the Wait for Dial Tone Before Dialing option, as shown in Figure 16.5.

Figure 16.5
Uncheck the Wait for Dial Tone Before Dialing option if your voicemail notification interferes with dialing.

2. If you have an external analog or ISDN modem, be sure that it's plugged in and turned on. When you attempt to make a connection, watch for flickering in the Send Data LEDs. If you don't see flickering, your modem cable might not be installed correctly.

3. Check the Event Viewer for informative error messages that might indicate a hardware problem.

4. In the Start menu, right-click Computer, select Manage, and select Device Manager. Look for any yellow exclamation point (!) icons in the device list; if a modem or port is marked with this trouble indicator, you need to solve the hardware problem before continuing. Double-click the line that's marked with the exclamation point and read the explanation of the problem. If the device needs an updated driver, see "Updating Drivers" in Chapter 27 for more information.

5. On the Options tab of the Dial-Up Connection Properties dialog box, check Prompt for Phone Number and try to make the connection. This shows you the actual number being dialed. Verify that the call-waiting code, outside line-access codes, and area code are correct. These are set on the connection's General tab and in the Phone and Modem Options Control Panel applet (in the Dialing Rules dialog box, select the proper location and click Edit).

 note

If you'd like to learn more about troubleshooting hardware and resolving device conflicts, pick up the latest edition of Scott Mueller's *Upgrading and Repairing PCs*, published by Que.

6. If you have an analog or ISDN modem and dialing is taking place but no connection is made, open Control Panel and type **modem** into the Search box. Click Phone and Modem. Select your modem and click Properties. Click Change Settings. Select the Diagnostics tab and check Append to Log. Close the dialog box and try to make the connection again. Go back to the Properties dialog box and select View Log. This log might indicate what is happening with the modem. Be sure to uncheck Append to Log when you're finished, or the file that stores this information could grow to enormous proportions.

Identifying Modem Connectivity Problems

Modem problems are usually due to incompatibility with your ISP's equipment or to poor telephone line quality. If your modem fails to make a connection or disconnects by itself, you need to look for a few things:

- If the ISP's modem answers but you don't establish a connection, your modem might be incompatible; call your ISP for assistance.

- If your modem disconnects and you are told that there was a problem with your username or password, try to connect again and check these entries carefully. If you try two or three times and still can't connect, contact your ISP for help. Sometimes, ISPs get bought by other companies, and the format of the required sign-on username can change as a result.

- Create and view a log file of modem activity and look for error messages indicating a protocol-negotiation error. Your ISP can assist with this as well.

- If your modem makes screeching sounds for approximately 15 seconds and hangs up, your modem is probably incompatible with the equipment used at your ISP, and you need an updated modem. Before you buy a new one, note that some modems can be updated via software. Check the manufacturer's website for information.

- If your connection works but the modem disconnects after a certain amount of time, there are two possible causes. If your connection was sitting idle, you might have run into the Windows inactivity timer. Click the network icon in the taskbar, right-click the name of your dial-up connection, and select Properties. View the Options tab. Check the entry Idle Time Before Hanging Up. Increase the time or select Never. If this problem recurs, you might enable the modem log and see whether it provides an explanation. Your ISP might also have set up its equipment to disconnect after a certain period of inactivity.

- If you don't think that idle time was the cause, your connection might have been interrupted by call waiting. On the connection's General tab, check Use Dialing Rules, click the Dialing Rules button, and then click Edit. Verify that To Disable Call Waiting is checked, and that the proper call-waiting turn-off setting is selected (for example, *70). Some newer modems can cope with call waiting and even alert you to a call coming in. If you rely on call waiting, it might be time for an upgrade. In this case, however, you're probably better suited switching to a cable or DSL connection, if one is available to you.

- If none of these is the cause, you might simply have a scratchy telephone line or a flagging older modem. This is an annoying problem that is difficult to diagnose. Try changing modems.

If your modem is making contact with your ISP but, despite a solid modem connection, you still can't use the Internet, see the next section for tips on diagnosing Internet connectivity problems.

Troubleshooting Internet Problems with Windows TCP/IP Utilities

If you think you are connected to your ISP but you still can't communicate, you can use some of the command-line tools provided with Windows to trace TCP/IP problems. (TCP/IP is the network language or protocol used by the Internet.)

To run the command-line utilities, open a Command Prompt window with Start, All Programs, Accessories, Command Prompt. Then, type in the commands as I describe them later. If you're not familiar with a particular command-line utility, type the command name followed by / ?, as in this example:

```
ping /?
```

Now, let's go through some of the TCP/IP diagnostic and command-line utilities provided with Windows.

note

If you're a UNIX devotee, you'll find these utilities familiar, if not identical, to their UNIX counterparts. If you're new to TCP/IP networking or debugging, you might find these utilities a little unfriendly. (Welcome to the world of networking.)

ipconfig

ipconfig is one of the most useful command-line utilities provided with Windows because it displays the current IP address information for each of your computer's network adapters and active dial-up connections. On networks that assign addresses automatically, ipconfig can tell you what your computer's IP address is, if you ever need to know it.

After opening a Command Prompt window, the command ipconfig prints the following information (of course the IP, subnet, and gateway information ipconfig provides will be different for your computer, and you might see a dial-up connection listed instead of a LAN adapter):

```
Windows IP Configuration

Ethernet adapter Local Area Connection:
   Connection-specific DNS Suffix  . :
   Link-local IPv6 Address . . . . . : fe80::8014:cfc7:9a98:cdfe%10
   IPv4 Address. . . . . . . . . . . : 192.168.15.106
   Subnet Mask . . . . . . . . . . . : 255.255.255.0
   Default Gateway . . . . . . . . . : 192.168.15.1
```

(You can ignore the Tunnel Adapter information; this is part of the Version 6 Internet Protocol system, which is used only on large, managed corporate networks.)

If you type the command

```
ipconfig /all
```

Windows displays additional information about your network settings, including the information shown in Table 16.1.

Table 16.1 Information Displayed by `ipconfig/all`

Setting	What It Means
Host Name	The name you gave your computer.
Primary DNS Suffix	The Internet domain to which your computer belongs. (You might temporarily belong to others as well while using a dial-up connection.) This might be blank; it is not a problem.
Node Type	The method that Windows uses to locate other computers on your LAN when you use Windows Networking. This usually is Hybrid or Broadcast.
DNS Suffix Search List	Alternative domain names used if you type just part of a hostname and the default domain does not provide a match.
Connection-specific DNS Suffix	The domain name for this particular connection. This is most applicable to dial-up connections.
DHCP Enabled	If set to Yes, this adapter is set to receive its IP address automatically. If set to No, the address was set manually.
DNS Servers	IP addresses of domain name servers.

`ipconfig` displays most of the information that can be set in the Network and Dial-Up Connection Properties dialog box, but it shows their real-world values. This makes it an invaluable "first stop" when troubleshooting any network problem. If you determine that an Internet connection problem lies in your equipment somewhere (because you cannot access any Internet destinations), typing **`ipconfig /all`** can tell you whether your network setup is correct. You need this information at hand before calling your ISP for assistance.

ping

If you try to browse the Internet or share files with other computers on your LAN and get no response, it could be because the other computer isn't receiving your data or isn't responding. After `ipconfig`, `ping` is the most useful tool to determine where your Internet connection or your network has stopped working.

Here's how it works:

1. The `ping` command sends a few packets of data to any computer you specify.

2. The other computer should immediately send these packets back to you.

3. `ping` lets you know whether the packets come back.

Therefore, `ping` tests the low-level communication between two computers. If `ping` works, you know that your network wiring, TCP/IP software, and any routers in between you and the other computer are working. `ping`

 tip

You can type `ping  x.x.x.x`, replacing *x.x.x.x* with the default gateway address or the address of any other operational computer on the Internet or your network (if applicable), and in an instant, you will know whether your dial-up or high-speed modem, computer, network hardware, and cabling are operating properly. If echoes come back, the physical part of your network is functioning properly. If they don't, you can use `tracert` and other tools (explained later in this chapter) to see why.

takes several options that can customize the type and amount of output it reports back to you. Three especially useful variations of these options exist; the first two are

```
C:\> ping hostname
```

where *hostname* is the name of one of the computers on your network, and

```
C:\> ping nnn.nnn.nnn.nnn
```

where *nnn.nnn.nnn.nnn* is a computer's numeric IP address, as discovered by ipconfig. That is, you can ping a computer either by its name or by its IP address. These variations transmit four packets to the host or IP address you specify and tell you whether they return. This command returns the following information:

```
C:\> ping www.mycompany.com
Pinging sumatra.mycompany.com [202.222.132.163] with 32 bytes of data:
Reply from 202.222.132.163: bytes=32 time<10ms TTL=32
Reply from 202.222.132.163: bytes=32 time<10ms TTL=32
Reply from 202.222.132.163: bytes=32 time<10ms TTL=32
Reply from 202.222.132.163: bytes=32 time<10ms TTL=32
```

In this example, the fact that the reply packets came back tells us that the computer can communicate with www.mycompany.com. It also tells us that everything in between my computer and mycompany.com is working.

The third useful variation is to add the -t option. This makes ping run endlessly once per second until you press Ctrl+C. This is especially helpful if you're looking at indicator lights on your network hub, changing cables, and so on. The endless testing lets you just watch the screen to see whether any changes you make cause a difference.

> **note**
>
> It's not uncommon for one packet of the four to be lost; when the Internet gets congested, sometimes ping packets are discarded as unimportant. If any come back, the intervening networks are working. It's also not unusual for the name that appears after "Pinging" to be different from what you typed. Some computers have alternative names.

ping is a great quick test of connectivity to any location. If the ping test fails, use tracert or path-ping to tell you where the problem is. ping is a good, quick tool to use to discover whether an Internet site is alive. (However, some large companies have made their servers not respond to ping tests. For example, ping www.microsoft.com doesn't work ever, even with a good Internet connection. It's not just that Microsoft got tired of being the first site everyone thought of to test their Internet connections; malicious people also can use ping to suck up all of a company's Internet bandwidth.)

tracert

tracert is similar to ping: It sends packets to a remote host and sees whether packets return. However, tracert adds a wrinkle: It checks the connectivity to each individual router in the path between you and the remote host. (Routers are the devices that connect one network to another. The Internet itself is the conglomeration of a few million networks all connected by routers.) If your computer and Internet connection are working but you still can't reach some or all Internet sites, tracert can help you find the blockage.

In the output of tracert, the address it tests first is your local network's gateway (if you connect to the Internet via a high-speed connection or a LAN) or the modem-answering equipment at your

ISP's office (if you're using a dial-up connection). If this first address responds, you know that your modem, LAN, or broadband connection is working. If the connection stops after two or three routers, the problem is in your ISP's network. If the problem occurs farther out, there might be an Internet outage somewhere else in the country.

Here's an example that shows the route between my network and the fictitious web server www.fictitious.net. Typing

```
C:\> tracert www.fictitious.net
```

returns the following:

```
Tracing route to www.fictitious.com [204.179.107.3]
over a maximum of 30 hops:
1    <10 ms   <10 ms   <10 ms   190.mycompany.com [202.201.200.190]
2    <10 ms   <10 ms    10 ms   129.mycompany.com [202.201.200.129]
3     20 ms    20 ms    20 ms   w001.z216112073.sjc-ca.dsl.cnc.net [216.112.73.1]
4     10 ms    10 ms    10 ms   206.83.66.153
5     10 ms    10 ms    10 ms   rt001f0801.sjc-ca.concentric.net [206.83.90.161]
6     10 ms    20 ms    20 ms   us-ca-sjc-core2-f5-0.rtr.concentric.net [205.158.11.133]
7     10 ms    20 ms    10 ms   us-ca-sjc-core1-g4-0-0.rtr.concentric.net [205.158.10.2]
8     10 ms    20 ms    20 ms   us-ca-pa-core1-a9-0d1.rtr.concentric.net [205.158.11.14]
9     10 ms    20 ms    20 ms   ATM2-0-0.br2.pao1.ALTER.NET [137.39.23.189]
10    10 ms    20 ms    20 ms   125.ATM3-0.XR1.PAO1.ALTER.NET [152.63.49.170]
11    10 ms    10 ms    20 ms   289.at-1-0-0.XR3.SCL1.ALTER.NET [152.63.49.98]
12    20 ms    20 ms    20 ms   295.ATM8-0-0.GW2.SCL1.ALTER.NET [152.63.48.113]
13    20 ms    20 ms    20 ms   2250-gw.customer.ALTER.NET [157.130.193.14]
14    41 ms    30 ms    20 ms   www.fictitious.com [204.179.107.3]
Trace complete.
```

You can see that between my computer and this web server, data passes through 13 intermediate routers owned by two ISPs.

I should point out a couple of tracert oddities. First, notice in the example that on the command line I typed www.fictitious.net, but tracert printed www.fictitious.com. That's not unusual. Web servers sometimes have alternative names. tracert starts with a reverse name lookup to find the *canonical* (primary) name for a given IP address.

You might run into another glitch as well. For security reasons, many organizations use firewall software or devices, which block tracert packets at the firewall between their LAN and the Internet. In these instances, tracert will never reach its intended destination, even when regular communications are working correctly. Instead, you'll see an endless list that looks similar to this:

```
14      *        *        *      Request timed out.
15      *        *        *      Request timed out.
16      *        *        *      Request timed out.
```

 tip

As I mentioned at the start of the chapter, when your Internet connection is working, run tracert to trace the path between your computer and a few Internet hosts. Print and save the listings. Someday when you're having Internet problems, you can use these listings as a baseline reference. It's very helpful to know whether packets are stopping in your LAN, in your ISP's network, or beyond when you pick up the phone to yell about it.

This continues up to the `tracert` limit of 30 probes. If this happens, just press Ctrl+C to cancel the test. If `tracert` could reach routers outside your own LAN or PC, your equipment and Internet connection are fine—and that's all you can directly control.

pathping

`pathping` provides the function of `tracert` and adds a more intensive network traffic test. `pathping` performs the route-tracing function faster than `tracert` because it sends only one test packet per hop, compared to `tracert`'s three.

After determining the route, `pathping` does a punishing test of network traffic at each router by sending 100 `ping` packets to each router in the path between you and the host you're testing. It measures the number of lost packets and the average round-trip time for each hop, and it displays the results in a table.

The results tell you which routers are experiencing congestion because they cannot return every echo packet they're sent, and they might take some time to do it. Performing the `pathping` test can take quite awhile. Fortunately, you can cancel the test by pressing Ctrl+C, or you can specify command-line options to shorten the test. A reasonably quick test of the path to a site—say, www.quepublishing.com—can be performed using just 10 queries, instead of the default 100, by using this command:

```
pathping -q 10 www.quepublishing.com
```

You can type

```
pathping /?
```

to get a full description of the command-line options.

route

Most of us have no more than one modem or one LAN adapter through which we make our Internet and other network connections, but Windows networking components are sophisticated enough to handle multiple LAN and dial-up adapters in one computer. When multiple connections are made, Windows has to know which connections to use to speak with another remote computer. For the TCP/IP or Internet Protocol (IP) data, this information comes from the routing table. This table stores lists of IP addresses and subnets (blocks of IP addresses) and also indicates which adapter (or interface) Windows used to reach each of them.

Now, this is getting into some hardcore networking that only a few readers will be interested in. Please don't think that you need to know about this tool; there will be no quiz next Friday. I'm discussing this only to cover the details for those few people who have a complex network setup and need to know how to go to this information. You don't have to worry about routing unless one of the following scenarios is true:

- You use a dial-up connection and a LAN adapter simultaneously.

- You use multiple LAN adapters.

- You use virtual private networking (VPN) connections, as discussed in Chapter 35, "Hitting the Road."

If you have trouble reaching an Internet destination and fall into any of these three categories, type **route print** at the command line. You're shown a table that looks similar to this:

```
===========================================================================
Interface List
 10 ...00 03 ff d0 ca 5f ...... Intel 21140-Based PCI Fast Ethernet Adapter
  1 ......................... Ooftware Loopback Interface 1
 13 ...00 00 00 00 00 00 00 e0  isatap.{3C3E0C23-191B-4E11-9713-97D239EA2995}
 11 ...02 00 54 55 4e 01 ...... Teredo Tunneling Pseudo-Interface
===========================================================================

IPv4 Route Table
===========================================================================
Active Routes:
Network Destination        Netmask          Gateway        Interface  Metric
        0.0.0.0          0.0.0.0      192.168.15.1   192.168.15.106     20
      127.0.0.0        255.0.0.0         On-link         127.0.0.1    306
      127.0.0.1  255.255.255.255         On-link         127.0.0.1    306
127.255.255.255  255.255.255.255         On-link         127.0.0.1    306
   192.168.15.0    255.255.255.0         On-link    192.168.15.106    276
 192.168.15.106  255.255.255.255         On-link    192.168.15.106    276
 192.168.15.255  255.255.255.255         On-link    192.168.15.106    276
      224.0.0.0        240.0.0.0         On-link         127.0.0.1    306
      224.0.0.0        240.0.0.0         On-link    192.168.15.106    276
255.255.255.255  255.255.255.255         On-link         127.0.0.1    306
255.255.255.255  255.255.255.255         On-link    192.168.15.106    276
===========================================================================
Persistent Routes:
  None

IPv6 Route Table
...
```

(You can ignore the IPv6 section for now.)

There's a lot of information here, but for our purpose, we can boil it down to this: The entry for network destination 0.0.0.0 is the effective gateway address for general Internet destinations. This can be different from your LAN's specified default gateway, especially while a dial-up or VPN connection is active. That, in turn, might mean that you can't get to the Internet. If you have multiple LAN adapters, the issues are more complicated. Contact your network administrator for assistance.

Third-Party Utilities

In addition to the utilities provided with Windows, you can use some third-party tools to help diagnose your connection and gather Internet information. I describe three web-based utilities and one commercial software package.

Speed Check

Ever wondered how to find the real-world transfer rate of your Internet connection? Intel Corporation has a nifty web-based program to measure transfer speeds using an Adobe (formerly Shockwave) Flash applet. Check out www.intel.com/Consumer/Game/broadband-speed-test.htm. (Every time I put this URL into print, Intel seems to feel the need to change it. If you get a "Page not found" error, search the Intel site for "broadband speed test.")

You can find other speed test sites at www.dslreports.com. Click Tools and then Speed Tests.

whois Database

Anyone registering an Internet domain name is required to file contact information with a domain registry. This is public information, and you can use it to find out how to contact the owners of a domain whose customers have sent spam mail or with whom you have other concerns.

Finding the registrar for a given domain name can be cumbersome. You can find the registrar information for any .aero, .arpa, .biz, .com, .coop, .edu, .info, .int, .museum, .net, or .org domain via the following web page: www.internic.net/whois.html.

The search results from this page indicate the URL of the whois lookup page for the associated domain registrar. Enter the domain name again on that page, and you should see the contact information.

It's a bit harder to find the registrar associated with two-letter country code domains ending in, for example, .au, .de, .it, and so on. The InterNIC site recommends searching through www.uwhois.com.

You can find the owner of an IP address through a similar lookup at www.arin.net/whois. Enter an IP address to find the owner of the block of IP addresses from which the specific address was allocated. This is usually an ISP or, in some cases, an organization that has had IP addresses assigned to it directly. You might have to visit www.apnic.net or another registry.

Reverse tracert

As I discussed earlier, the tracert program investigates the path that data you send through the Internet takes to reach another location. Interestingly, data coming back to you can take a different path, depending on the way your ISP has set up its own internal network.

It's handy to know the path data takes coming to you. If you record this information while your Internet connection is working and subsequently run into trouble, you can have a friend perform a tracert to you. (You need to give him your IP address, which you can find using the ipconfig command.) If the results differ, you might be able to tell whether the problem is with your computer, your ISP, or the Internet.

You can visit www.traceroute.org for a list of hundreds of web servers that can perform a `tracer-oute` test from their site to you. Don't be surprised if the test results take a while to appear; these tests typically take a minute or longer.

WS_Ping Pro Pack

If you want to be well equipped to handle Internet and general networking problems, you can buy third-party utilities that are much easier to use than the standard ones built into Windows. I like WS_Ping ProPack from Ipswitch Software (www.ipswitch.com). This one utility packs almost all the TCP/IP tools into one graphical interface and adds other features such as `whois` for domain-registration lookups, SNMP probing, and network scanning. The program can be used for free for 30 days, after which the registration fee is $44.95 for a single-user license. I rarely use third-party add-ons such as this, but this particular program is on my "must have" list.

V

NETWORKING

IN THIS PART

17	Creating a Windows Network	443
18	Mix and Match with Old Windows and Macs	487
19	Connecting Your Network to the Internet	515
20	Using a Windows Network	541
21	Troubleshooting Your Network	575

CREATING A WINDOWS NETWORK

Creating or Joining a Network

Not too many years ago, networking was expensive, complicated, and found only in *big* business environments. But networking is for everyone now, in the home or at work. And it's amazingly inexpensive. Even if you have just two computers, for about the cost of a trip to the movies you can set up a network that will let everyone trade music, video, and documents, use the same printer and Internet connection, and back up files, almost effortlessly. And, creating a speedy, useful network isn't nearly as hard or expensive as you might think. Once you've done the planning and shopping, you should be able to get a network up and running in an hour or two.

The Professional and Ultimate versions of Windows 7 have some spiffy features that come into play when they're hooked up to a corporate network with Windows Server, expensive servers, and highly trained technicians. But setting up that sort of network is beyond our scope here.

This chapter tells you how to set up a local area network (LAN) for a small group of users, at home or at work, using *any* edition of Windows 7. This type of LAN is called a *peer-to-peer network* because no one computer has a central role in managing the network.

Now, if you're adding a computer to an existing network, you can skip ahead to the section "Installing Network Adapters." If you're on a corporate network, you probably won't need to handle any of the installation details yourself—your IT department will likely take care of all of this for you, and you can just skip ahead to the next chapter.

If you're setting up a new network, though, read on. This chapter should give you all the information you need.

Planning Your Network

You must plan your network around your own particular needs. What do you expect from a network? The following tasks are some you might want your network to perform:

- Share printers, files, and optical (DVD and CD) drives
- Share an Internet connection
- Receive faxes directly in one computer and print or route them to individuals automatically
- Provide access to a wide area network (WAN) or other remote site
- Provide access to your LAN via a modem or the Internet from remote locations
- Host a website
- Operate a database server
- Play multiuser games

You should make a list of your networking goals. You need to provide adequate capacity to meet these and future needs, but you also don't need to overbuild.

Instant Networking

If your goal is to share printers, files, and maybe an Internet connection among just a few computers that are fairly close together, and you won't need wireless connections, here's a recipe for instant networking. Get the following items at your local computer store, or at an online shop such as www.buy.com. Chain computer or office supply stores are also a good bet if a sale or rebate offer is available.

- One 10/100BASE-T network adapter for each computer that doesn't already have a network interface. These cost $5–$15 for internal PCI cards, and $10–$40 for PCMCIA or USB adapters. (The Buy.com category is Computer & Office, Networking, Wired Networking: Adapters (NICs). Get a featured or sale price internal PCI card for a desktop, or PC Card or USB adapter for a notebook.) But, check before you buy: Most computers these days have a built-in network adapter.

- A 10/100BASE-T switch with four or more ports for $10–$40, or a DSL/cable-sharing router with a built-in four-port switch for $20–$90. (The Buy.com category is Computer & Office, Networking, Wired Networking: Routers or Switches.) I recommend using a router even if you aren't setting up a shared Internet connection.

- One CAT-5 patch cable for each computer. You'll place the switch or router next to one of the computers, so you'll need one 4-foot cable. The other cables need to be long enough to reach from the other computers to the switch. (The Buy.com category is Computer & Office, Networking, Wired Networking: Cables.)

When you have these parts, skip ahead to the "Installing Network Adapters" section, later in this chapter. By the way, I'm not getting a kickback from Buy.com! I've just found that buying from them is a no-brainer. Their prices are low enough that it's hardly worth the time to shop around and, more important, their service is ultra-reliable and fast.

On the other hand, if you want to use wireless networking, need access to large databases, want fast Internet connectivity, or require centralized backup of all workstations, you need to plan and invest more carefully. I discuss some of the issues you should consider in the next section.

Are You Being Served?

If you're planning a network of more than a few computers, you need to make a big decision: whether or not to use Windows Server. The Server versions provide a raft of networking services that Windows 7 doesn't have, but you must learn how to configure and support them.

Table 17.1 lists the primary trade-offs between Windows 7 and Windows Server.

Table 17.1   Primary Differences Between Windows 7 and Windows Server

Network with Windows 7 Only	Network with Windows Server
Allows connections for up to 5 computers for the Home versions of Windows 7, 10 computers for other versions.	Unlimited connections (subject to client licensing fees).
Cost is low.	Requires an extra computer, a copy of Windows Server, and additional fees for Client Access Licenses. The added costs will easily exceed $1,000.
Configuration is simple (relatively, anyway).	Complex to configure and administer.
Each machine must be administered independently.	Administration is centralized.
Rudimentary remote access, connection sharing, and WAN support are provided.	The features are more sophisticated.
Managing file security can be difficult when you have more than one user per computer.	Centralized user management eases the task of managing security.

For me, the 5- or 10-connection limit with Windows 7 is the main dividing line. If you have a network of more than 10 computers, I recommend using at least one copy of Windows Server.

You can certainly use Server with smaller networks, too. Reasons for doing so include these:

- You want to connect your LAN through a WAN or through the Internet to another LAN at another location; that is, you want to join your network to a Server domain somewhere else. This is often the case in a business's branch office.

- You want to support multiple simultaneous remote dial-in or virtual private network (VPN) users. (Of course, you can buy inexpensive VPN routers or software to handle this.)

- You want to exercise strict security controls, restrict your users' ability to change system settings, or use automatic application installation.

 note

If you are running either of the Windows 7 Home editions, your computer will be limited to a maximum of 5 user connections. All other versions support a maximum of 10.

 note

When I talk about Windows Server here, I mean the business Server versions. There is a product called Windows Home Server, but it's meant just to back up files across the network, and it too has a limit of 10 connections.

- You want to take advantage of advanced networking services such as Group Policy, DHCP, DNS, WINS, and so on.

If you decide you need or want Windows Server, you should get a book dedicated to that OS and a big box of Alka-Seltzer before you go any further.

When to Hire a Professional

You've probably heard this old adage: "If you want something done right, do it yourself!" It is true, to a point. Sometimes, though, the benefit of hiring someone else outweighs the pleasure of doing it yourself.

For a home network, you should definitely try to set it up yourself. Call it a learning experience, get friends to help, and, if you run into problems, treat yourself to a truly humbling experience and watch a high-school-aged neighbor get it all working in 15 minutes. As long as you don't have to run wires through the wall or construct your own cables, you should be able to manage this job even with no prior networking experience. When something is called "Plug and Play" now, it really is.

However, the balance tips the other way for a business. If you depend on your computers to get your work done, getting them set up should be your first concern, but keeping them working should be your second, third, and fourth. If you have solid experience in network installation, installing a Windows 7 network will be a snap. But your business is hanging in the balance, and you should consider the cost of computer failure when you're deciding whether it's worth spending money on setup and installation. Hiring a good consultant and/or contractor will give you the following:

- An established relationship. If something goes wrong, you'll already know whom to call, and that person will already know the details of your system.

- A professional installation job.

- The benefit of full-time experience in network and system design without needing to pay a full-time salary.

- Time to spend doing something more productive than installing a network.

If you do want to hire someone, it's important to choose your consultant or contractor very carefully. Here are some tips:

- Ask friends and business associates for referrals before you go to Craigslist or the Yellow Pages.

- Ask a consultant or contractor for references, and check them out.

- Find out what the contractor's guaranteed response time is, if problems or failures occur in the future.

- Be sure that documentation is one of the contractor's "deliverables." You should get written documentation describing your system's installation, setup, and configuration, as well as written procedures for routine maintenance, such as making backups, adding users, and so on.

Even if you do hire someone else to build your network, you should stay involved in the process and understand the choices and decisions that are made.

Choosing a Network and Cabling System

For a simple home or small office network, you can choose among four types of network connections:

- **10/100BASE-T (Fast Ethernet) over high-quality CAT-5 unshielded twisted-pair (UTP) cables**—These cables look like telephone cables, with a fatter version of a telephone modular connector at each end. This networking scheme is dirt cheap and ultra-reliable.

- **1000Mbps (Gigabit) Ethernet over CAT-5E cables**—These cables look like CAT-5 cables, but they are capable of carrying the higher-speed signals required by Gigabit Ethernet. The higher speed is great, and worth the extra cost, if you routinely back up hard disks or copy huge video files over your network. You'll often see Gigabit Ethernet referred to in computer specs as 10/100/1000 Mbps.

- **Phoneline or powerline networking**—You can purchase network adapters that send data signals between your electrical outlets, or between telephone jacks that are wired to the same phone extension. Its popularity is fading due to the rise of...

- **802.11n or -g wireless networking**—Wireless networking sends data over a radio signal, so no cabling is necessary. It's much easier to set up, but it can't be used over long distances, and in some buildings the signal might not go as far as the advertising leads you to believe it will.

For the average small office or home network, any of these four options will provide perfectly adequate performance. In the following sections, I go over each type in a little more detail. Then, I discuss additional network features you might want to consider, such as printing and Internet connectivity.

 tip

If your network is small and/or temporary, you can run network cables along walls and desks. Otherwise, you probably should keep them out of the way and protect them from accidental damage by installing them in the walls of your home or office. As you survey your site and plan your network, consider how the network cabling is to be routed.

Can't Drill Through Walls or Ceilings

If for any reason you are unable to drill through walls or ceilings to install network cables, you can install wires along baseboards, around doors, and so on. It's not as pretty, but because network wiring is low voltage, it's not as risky to do so as it would be with power wiring. (My office has a cable shamefully strung through a skylight, across the ceiling, and into a closet.) You also can use products called wiring channels to conceal the wires that run along baseboards and use rubber guards to protect them where they might be trod upon. You can find these products in the hardware store or in business product catalogs. Of course, you can also consider using a wireless network.

10/100BASE-T Ethernet

10/100BASE-T Ethernet networks use unshielded twisted-pair cabling (commonly called UTP or CAT-5 cable) run from each computer to a device called a switch or router, as shown in Figure 17.1.

The 10/100 part of the name means that the equipment can run at 100Mbps, but it can automatically slow down to 10Mbps if it's connected to older 10BASE-T equipment.

 note

You might have heard these connecting boxes called "hubs." Hubs and switches do the same job of passing data between the network's computers, but hubs use an older technology. All "hubs" made in recent years are actually switches, so I'll use the term switch in this chapter.

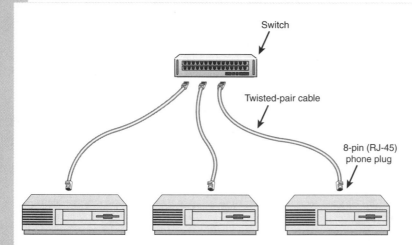

Switch

Twisted-pair cable

8-pin (RJ-45) phone plug

Figure 17.1
A 10/100BASE-T network connects each computer to a switch with UTP cabling. It sounds sophisticated, but remember, you can buy this stuff at most office supply stores. I've even seen it in chain drug stores.

The cables look like telephone cables, and the connectors look like fat versions of telephone modular plugs, but it's a dangerous comparison, because the electrical properties of the cables and connectors are specifically tuned for networking, and ordinary telephone wiring *will not work*.

These networks require that you use cable and connectors designated "CAT-5" or better. They have labels on the wire that state this clearly. CAT-5, CAT-5E, and CAT-6 are all fine. You can buy premade network cables in lengths of 3–50 feet, or you can buy bulk cable and attach the connectors yourself. I discuss this more in the "Installing Network Wiring" section later in this chapter.

A cable is run from each computer to a switch, which is a small connecting box that routes the signals between each computer. You need to get a switch that has at least as many ports (sockets) as you have computers, plus a spare or two. 10/100BASE-T switches cost roughly $5–$10 per port.

 tip

Multiple switches can be connected if your network grows beyond the capacity of your first switch. So, you can add on instead of entirely replacing your original equipment.

 tip

If you have DSL or cable broadband Internet service, see Chapter 19, "Connecting Your Network to the Internet," for some advice about hardware connection-sharing devices before you make any decisions about your network. Some connection-sharing router devices have a built-in switch, sparing you the expense of buying a separate one.

10/100BASE-T network interface cards (NICs) are available for as little as $5 each (if you catch a sale) and are made by companies such as Intel, 3Com, NETGEAR, Farallon, SMC Networks, Kingston Technology, D-Link, Linksys, Boca, and CNet. Most generic brand, cheap-o NICs are based on one of a handful of standard circuit chips, so they'll usually work just fine, even if they're not listed in the Windows Compatibility Center at www.microsoft.com/windows/compatibility.

Overall, 10/100BASE-T networking is as inexpensive as it gets—hooking up three computers should set you back less than $75, maybe much less. It's easy to set up, and it's very reliable. On the down side, though, you do need to run those wires around, and any connectors and wall data jacks need to be CAT-5 certified as well. If you use in-wall wiring, the work should be done by someone with professional-level skills.

1000Mbps Ethernet (Gigabit Ethernet)

Ultra-high-speed Gigabit Ethernet networking is probably overkill for most home and small office networks, but it's making an appearance in the corporate world and in some fields such as medical imaging and digital movie production. Gigabit speed can also help if you back up your hard disk over your network, or copy large video files. The cost is so low now that some new PCs and all Macs now come with 10/100/1000Mbps Ethernet adapters built in as standard equipment.

If you want to use Gigabit Ethernet, you need to use CAT-5E or CAT-6 certified connectors and cabling; CAT-5 gear won't cut it. You should use only commercially manufactured patch cables or professionally installed wiring. Most Gigabit switches can run any port at 10-, 100-, or 1000Mbps, so not all of your computers need to use the more expensive cabling and adapters.

Phoneline and Powerline Networking

HomePNA Alliance devices send network data by transmitting radio signals over your existing telephone wiring, using a network adapter that plugs in to a telephone jack (see Figure 17.2). These devices don't interfere with the normal operation of your telephones; the extra signal just hitchhikes along the wires.

 note

Add-on adapters come in three styles: internal PCI cards for desktop computers; external adapters that you connect with a USB cable; and thin, credit card–sized PCMCIA (PC Card) adapters for laptops. You may not need to add one, though: Many modern computers already have a 10/100 or 10/100/1000 Ethernet adapter built in, with a socket on the back of the computer box.

 tip

Even if you're not going to set up a shared broadband Internet connection, I recommend that you buy an Internet connection sharing router instead of a plain switch, just to get the DHCP service it provides (more on that later in the chapter). On sale, these routers cost no more than a plain switch. In fact, as I wrote this, my newspaper had an ad for a router for $20 with a $20 mail-in rebate.

 note

Most cable/DSL-sharing routers have 10/100Mbps switches built in. Your Gigabit adapters will run at 100Mbps—one-tenth of what you are paying for—if plugged into a 10/100Mbps switch. If you want your computers to communicate with each other at Gigabit speed, but you have a slower connection sharing router, plug your computers into a 10/100/1000Mbps (Gigabit) switch using CAT-6 cables and then connect the switch's "cascade" port to your cable/DSL-sharing router.

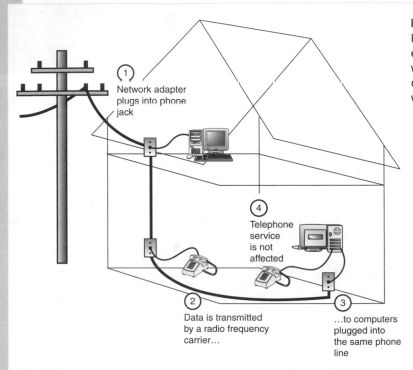

Figure 17.2
Phoneline networking uses existing household telephone wiring to carry a radio frequency signal between networked computers.

① Network adapter plugs into phone jack

④ Telephone service is not affected

② Data is transmitted by a radio frequency carrier...

③ ...to computers plugged into the same phone line

Phoneline networking is intended primarily for home use. The products are relatively inexpensive—about $70 per computer—and don't require you to string cables around the house. However, they have some disadvantages:

- All your adapters must be plugged into the same telephone line. So the same extension must be present at a phone outlet near each of your computers. If you need to call in a wiring contractor to add a phone extension, you haven't saved much over a wired network.

- "Access point" devices, used to link a standard wired-networked computer to your phoneline network, are relatively rare.

 tip

If you use phoneline networking, be certain to get only HomePNA 2.0–compatible adapters or better. This will ensure that your equipment will operate at least at 10Mbps and will work with other manufacturers' products. Don't get any device that connects through your computer's parallel port: It's too slow.

- 10Mbps is fine for sharing an Internet connection or printers, but you'll find that it's too slow to back up a chock-full hard disk over your network—it could take days!

Without a hardware access point, it's difficult to use a hardware Internet Connection Sharing device or to add standard wired computers to your network. However, Windows 7 can manage it in software, if necessary. I discuss this later in this chapter under "Bridging Two Network Types."

HomePlug (HomePlug Powerline Alliance) adapters work in a similar fashion, sending signals through your electrical wiring, and are plugged into a wall socket. These also provide 10Mbps performance, and they are more flexible than the phoneline system because you don't need a phone jack near your computers—just a nearby electrical outlet.

In addition, you can get HomePlug devices called "bridges," which are specifically designed to link a wired network to the powerline network, for about $60—the Linksys Powerline EtherFast 10/100 Bridge is an example. This means you can easily add a shared Internet connection sharing router or mix in wired computers. Figure 17.3 shows how this would look in a typical home network.

Figure 17.3
Typical powerline networking setup, showing HomePlug adapters and bridges.

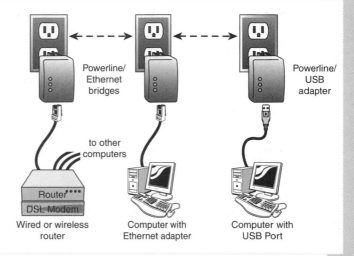

802.11g and 802.11n Wireless Networking

One way to build a network without switches, cables, connectors, drills, swearing, tools, or outside contractors is to go wireless. Blocks of radio frequencies in the 2.4GHz and 5GHz bands are reserved for close-range data communications, and standardized products from cordless telephones to computer networking devices are now available to take advantage of this. Prices have fallen to the point that wireless connectivity is now competitive with wired networks, even before the installation cost savings are factored in.

Today's high-speed 802.11g equipment operates at up to 54Mbps and is compatible with older 802.11b (11Mbps) equipment. Some manufacturers offer Wireless-G equipment that operates at up to 108Mbps. This is great, but you should know that you'll get the speed boost only if you buy all your equipment from the same manufacturer (and even then, you need to read the packaging carefully to see if the double-speed function will work with the particular parts you're buying).

A newer standard for wireless networking called 802.11n recently received of industrywide approval. "Wireless-N," as it's also called, offers even higher speed and greater range than Wireless-G. You may want to check to see if Wireless-N is a good option for your network. If you use it, be wary of buying "Pre-N" equipment, which was based on earlier drafts of the standard.

Most such equipment should work with equipment designed according to the final, official specification, but some might require a software update, and some might not work at all. Check product reviews before you buy!

Wireless-G networking products typically

- Give actual throughput of about half the advertised speed.

- Can transmit data about 100 feet indoors and up to 300 feet outdoors. (Wireless-N should go about 50% farther.)

- Are available for both desktop and laptop computers, in PCI, PCMCIA (PC Card), or USB formats.

- Cost $25–$70 per adapter.

- Can be bridged to a wired LAN through an optional device called an access point, router, bridge, or base unit, costing $20 and up. (That's not a typo: $20, if you catch a good sale. $40 may be more typical without a sale.)

- Usually don't work well between floors of a multistory building.

note

You might also read about 802.11a equipment. "Wireless-A" is used mainly in corporate environments and is much more expensive than the more modern Wireless-G equipment that I recommend.

tip

Whether or not you decide to set up a shared Internet connection, you'll save time and money by using a wireless Internet connection sharing router as your network's access point. A router includes a DHCP server (more on that later) that simplifies setting up your network.

Figure 17.4 shows a typical family of wireless products: a wireless access point (Ethernet bridge), a wireless router that can also share a DSL or Internet connection, an internal wireless network adapter for desktop computers, and a PCMCIA adapter for laptops.

Figure 17.4
Typical wireless networking equipment. Clockwise from upper left: access point, router with Internet Connection Sharing capability, PCI adapter, PCMCIA adapter. (Photo used by permission of D-Link.)

Mixed Networking

If you are updating an existing network or are connecting two separate types of networks, you should consider several things.

If you have some existing 10Mbps-only devices and want to add new 100Mbps devices without upgrading the old, you can buy a new dual-speed (10/100) switch, which connects to each computer at the maximum speed its adapter permits. Read the specifications carefully. You want a switch, or a hub that's labeled "N-way autosensing." Be sure to use CAT-5 certified cables to connect to the 100Mbps devices.

Finally, if you want to mix standard Ethernet and wireless devices on your network, you can use the Bridging feature built into Windows 7, or you can use one of the bridges or access points I mentioned earlier. Adding a wireless router or access point device is by far the best approach; you can read about bridging in the section "Bridging Two Network Types," later in this chapter.

Additional Networking Functions

Besides sharing files between computers, there are several other things that you can do with a network. In the next few sections, I outline some additional features you might want to include in your network.

Printing and Faxing

Shared printers simply need to be connected to their host Windows computers with a standard USB or parallel printer cable. Other computers can then reach the printer through the network. However, If you need to put a printer farther than about 10 feet away from a networked computer, beyond the reach of a standard printer cable, you have three choices:

1. Get a really long cable and take your chances. The electrical signal for a USB or parallel printer connection is not supposed to be extended more then 10 feet, but with parallel cables I've gotten away with 25 feet in the past. Buy a high-quality shielded cable. You might get data errors (bad printed characters) with this approach.

2. Use a network-capable printer and cable it directly to your network switch. Some printers have networking capability built in. For some printers, you can buy an add-on network printer module. Alternatively, you can buy a "print server" module, which connects to the printer's USB or parallel port and to a network cable. Network supply catalogs list myriad such devices. Some of the newer DSL/cable-sharing routers and wireless access points have a print server built in. These are great for small offices.

3. Use a printer-extender device. These devices turn a parallel port signal into a serial data connection, somewhat as a modem does. I don't like these devices because they result in very slow printing.

If several people on your network need to send or receive faxes, you might want to set up a network-based faxing system. Unfortunately, Windows 7 does not let you share your fax modem with other users on your network, as Windows Server does. If you want to share a single fax line with several users on your network, you have to use a third-party solution. The easiest approach is to use a "network-ready" all-in-one printer/scanner/fax unit. If you shop for one of these, be sure that its faxing features are network compatible. There are also third-party software products that can give network users shared access to a fax modem. The former gold standard product was Symantec's WinFax Pro, but it's been discontinued, and most of the products still on the market seem to be oriented toward large corporations. For a small office network, you might consider products such as Snappy Fax Network Server from www.snappysoftware.com or ActFax from www.act-fax.com.

Providing Internet Connectivity

You'll probably want to have Internet access on your LAN. It's far less expensive, and far safer security-wise, to have one connection to the Internet for the entire LAN than to let each user fend for himself or herself.

Windows 7 has a built-in Internet Connection Sharing feature that lets a single computer use a dial-up, cable, or DSL modem and make the connection on behalf of any user on your LAN. You can also use an inexpensive hardware device called a router to make the connection. I strongly prefer the hardware devices over Windows Internet Connection Sharing. This topic is important enough that it gets its own chapter. If you want to share an Internet connection on your network, I recommend that you read Chapter 19 before you buy any equipment.

You should also study Chapter 32, "Protecting Your Network from Hackers and Snoops," and pay close attention to the section titled "Network Security Basics" to build in proper safeguards against hacking and abuse. This is especially important with full-time cable/DSL connections.

Providing Remote Access

You also can provide connectivity to your network from the outside world, either through the Internet or via a modem. This connectivity enables you to access your LAN resources from home or out in the field, with full assurance that your network is safe from outside attacks. Chapter 35, "Hitting the Road" covers dial-up and VPN network access, and Chapter 37 covers Remote Desktop.

If you need to access your network from outside and you aren't planning to have a permanent direct Internet connection, you might want to plan for the installation of a telephone line near one of your Windows 7 computers so that you can set up a dedicated modem line for incoming access.

Installing Network Adapters

If you're installing a new network adapter, follow the manufacturer's instructions for installing the product for Windows 7. If there are instructions for Windows Vista but not Windows 7, the Vista instructions should work. And if there are no instructions at all, just follow these steps:

1. If you have purchased an internal card, shut down Windows, shut off the computer, unplug it, open the case, install the card in an empty slot, close the case, and restart Windows.

If you are adding a PCMCIA or USB adapter, be sure you're logged on with a Computer Administrator account, plug it in while Windows is running, and skip ahead to step 3.

2. When you're back at the Windows login screen, log in as a Computer Administrator. Windows displays the New Hardware Detected dialog box when you log in.

3. In most cases, Windows should already have the software it needs to run your network adapter. If it doesn't, the New Hardware Detected dialog box might instruct you to insert your Windows 7 DVD. If Windows cannot find a suitable driver for your adapter from this DVD, it might ask you to insert a driver disk that your network card's manufacturer should have provided (either a CD-ROM or a floppy disk). It may also offer to go online to get a driver from Windows Update. If you have an Internet connection up at this time, the online option is very useful.

If you are asked, insert the requested disk and click OK. If Windows says that it cannot locate an appropriate device driver, try again, and this time click the Browse button. Locate a folder named Windows 7 or Windows Vista (or some reasonable approximation) and click OK.

4. After Windows has installed the card's driver software, it automatically configures and uses the card. Check the Device Manager, as described in the next section, to see whether the card is installed and functioning. Then you can proceed to "Installing Network Wiring," later in this chapter.

 For more-detailed instructions about installing drivers, **see** *Chapter 27.*

Checking Existing Adapters

If your adapter was already installed when you set up Windows 7, it should be ready to go. Follow these steps to see whether the adapter is already set up:

1. Click Start, right-click Computer, and select Manage.

2. Select Device Manager in the left pane, and open the Network Adapters list in the right pane.

3. Look for an entry for your network card. If it appears and does not have a yellow exclamation point (!) icon to the left of its name, the card is installed and correctly configured. In this case, you can skip ahead to "Installing Network Wiring."

If an entry appears but has a yellow exclamation point icon by its name, the card is not correctly configured.

 tip

If you've never worked inside your computer, jump ahead to Chapter 27, "Installing and Replacing Hardware," for advice and handy tips.

 note

The exact name of the folder containing your device driver varies from vendor to vendor. You might have to poke around a little on the disk to find it.

note

If you see an exclamation point icon in the Network Adapters list, skip ahead to Chapter 25, "Troubleshooting and Repairing Problems," for tips on getting the card to work before you proceed. Here's an additional tip: Network adapters are really inexpensive. If you're having trouble with an old adapter, just go get a new one.

4. If no entry exists for the card, the adapter is not fully plugged into the motherboard, it's broken, or it is not Plug and Play capable. Be sure the card is installed correctly. If the card is broken or not Plug and Play, you should replace it. Check out Chapter 27 for troubleshooting tips.

Installing Multiple Network Adapters

You might want to install multiple network adapters in your computer in these situations:

- You simultaneously connect to two or more different networks with different IP addresses or protocols. You'd use a separate adapter to connect to each network.

- You want to share a broadband cable or DSL Internet connection with your LAN without using a hardware-sharing router. I strongly recommend using a hardware router, as I discuss in Chapter 19, but you can also do it using one adapter to connect to your LAN and another to connect to your cable or DSL modem.

- You have two different network types, such as phoneline and Ethernet, and you want the computers on both LAN types to be able to communicate. You could use a hardware access point, but you could also install both types of adapters in one of your computers and use the Bridging feature to connect the networks. I discuss bridging later in this chapter.

I suggest that you use the following procedure to install multiple adapters:

1. Install, configure, and test the first adapter. (If you're doing this to share an Internet connection, install and configure the one you'll use for the Internet connection first. Be sure you can connect to the Internet before you proceed.)

2. Click Start, Control Panel, Network and Internet, Network and Sharing Center. Click Change Adapter Settings from the Tasks list on the left side of the window. Select the icon named Local Area Connection and choose Rename This Connection in the ribbon bar. (Or right-click the icon and select Rename.) Change the connection's name to something that indicates what it's used for, such as "Connection to Cable Modem" or "Office Ethernet Network."

3. Write the name on a piece of tape or a sticky label and apply it to the back of your computer above the network adapter, or to the edge plate of the network card.

4. Install the second adapter. Configure it and repeat steps 2 and 3 with the new Local Area Connection icon. Name this connection appropriately—for example, "LAN" or "Wireless Net"—and put a tape or paper label on the computer, too.

If you follow these steps, you'll be able to easily distinguish the two connections instead of needing to remember which Local Area Connection icon is which.

Installing Network Wiring

When your network adapters are installed, the next step is to get your computers connected. Installing wiring can be the most difficult task of setting up a network. How you proceed depends on the type of networking adapters you have:

- If you're using wireless adapters, of course, you don't need to worry about wiring. Lucky you. You can just skip ahead to "Installing a Wireless Network," later in this chapter.

- If you're using phoneline networking, plug a standard modular telephone cable into each phoneline network adapter and connect them to the appropriate wall jacks. The adapter must be plugged directly into the wall jack, and then additional devices such as modems, telephones, and answering machines can be connected to the adapter. Remember that each of the phone jacks must be wired to the same telephone line. Then skip ahead to the "Configuring a Peer-to-Peer Network" section, later in the chapter.

- If you're using a powerline networking adapter, follow the manufacturer's installation instructions. If you're using a powerline bridge, plug the bridge into a wall socket and connect it to your computer or other networked device with a CAT-5 patch cable. Follow the manufacturer's instructions for configuring the adapter's security features. You should enable encryption if it's available. Then skip ahead to the "Configuring a Peer-to-Peer Network" section, later in the chapter.

If you're using wired Ethernet adapters, you need to decide how to route your wiring and what type of cables to use. The remainder of this section discusses Ethernet wiring.

Cabling for Ethernet Networks

If your computers are close together, you can use prebuilt patch cables to connect your computers to a switch. (The term *patch cable* originated in the telephone industry—in the old days, switchboard operators used patch cables to connect, or patch, one phone circuit to another.) You can run these cables through the habitable area of your home or office by routing them behind furniture, around partitions, and so on. Just don't put them where they'll be crushed, walked on, tripped over, run over by desk chair wheels, or chewed by pets.

If the cables need to run through walls or stretch long distances, you should consider having them installed inside the walls with plug-in jacks, just like your telephone wiring. I discuss this topic later in this section. Hardware stores sell special cable covers that you can use if you need to run a cable where it's exposed to foot traffic, as well as covers for wires that need to run up walls or over doorways.

 tip

As you install each network card and plug it into the cables running to your switch, you should see a green light come on at the switch and on the network adapter. These lights indicate that the network wiring is correct.

Switch Lights Do Not Come On

If one or more UTP switch link lights do not come on when the associated computers are connected, the problem lies in one of the cables between the computer and the switch. Which one is it? To find out, do the following:

1. Move the computer right next to the switch. You can leave the keyboard, mouse, and monitor behind. Just plug in the computer, turn it on, and use a commercially manufactured or known-to-be-working patch cable to connect the computer to the switch. If the light doesn't come on regardless of which switch connection socket you use, you probably have a bad network card.

2. If you were using any patch cables when you first tried to get the computer connected, test them using the same computer and switch socket. This trick might identify a bad cable.

3. If the LAN card, switch, and patch cables are all working, the problem is in whatever is left, which would be your in-wall wiring. Check the connectors for proper crimping and check that the wire pairs are correctly wired end to end. You might need to use a cable analyzer if you can't spot the problem by eye. These devices cost about $75. You connect a "transmitter" box to one end of your cabling, and a "receiver" to the other. The receiver has four LEDs that blink in a 1-2-3-4 sequence if your wiring is correct.

General Cabling Tips

You can determine how much cable you need by measuring the distance between computers and your switch location(s). Remember to account for vertical distances, too, where cables run from the floor up to a desktop, or go up and over a partition or wall.

Keep in mind the following points:

- I refer to "CAT-5" here, but if you're using 1000Mbps Ethernet, you must use CAT-5E or CAT-6 equipment.

- Existing household telephone wire probably won't work. If the wires inside the cable jacket are red, green, black, and yellow: no way. The jacket must have CAT-5 (or higher) printed on it. It must have color-matched twisted pairs of wires; usually each pair has one wire in a solid color and the other white with colored stripes.

 caution

If you need to run cables through the ceiling space of an office building, you should check with your building management to see whether the ceiling is listed as a plenum or air-conditioning air return. You might be required by law to use certified plenum cable and follow all applicable electrical codes. Plenum cable is specially formulated not to emit toxic smoke in a fire.

- You must use CAT-5-quality wiring and components throughout, and not just the cables. Any jacks, plugs, connectors, terminal blocks, patch cables, and so on also must be CAT-5 certified.

- If you're installing in-wall wiring, follow professional CAT-5 wiring practices throughout. Be sure not to untwist more than half an inch of any pair of wires when attaching cables to connectors. Don't solder or splice the wires.

- When you're installing cables, be gentle. Don't pull, kink, or stretch them. Don't bend them sharply around corners; you should allow at least a 1-inch radius for bends. Don't staple or crimp them. To attach cables to a wall or baseboard, use rigid cable clips that don't squeeze the cable, as shown in Figure 17.5. Your local electronics store or hardware store can sell you the right kind of clips.

- Keep network cables away from AC power wiring and away from electrically noisy devices such as arc welders, diathermy machines, and the like. (I've never actually seen a diathermy machine, but I hear they're trouble.)

> **note**
>
> If you really want to get into the nuts and bolts, so to speak, of pulling your own cable, a good starting point is Frank Derfler and Les Freed's *Practical Network Cabling* (Que, 1999; ISBN 078972247X), which will help you roll up your shirt sleeves and get dirty (literally, if you need to crawl around through your attic or wrestle with dust bunnies under too many desks at the office).

Figure 17.5
Use rigid cable clips or staples that don't squeeze the cable if you nail it to a wall or baseboard.

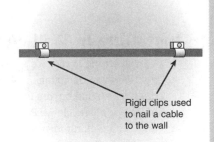

1/4"

Rigid clips used to nail a cable to the wall

Wiring with Patch Cables

If your computers are close together and you can simply run prefabricated cables between your computers and switch, you've got it made. Buy CAT-5 (or better) cables of the appropriate length online or at your local computer store. Just plug (click) them in, and you're finished. Figure 17.1 shows how to connect your computers to the switch.

If you have the desire and patience, you can build custom-length cables from crimp-on connectors and bulk cable stock. Making your own cables requires about $75 worth of tools, though, and more detailed instructions than I can give here. Making just a few cables probably doesn't make buying the tools worthwhile. Factory-assembled cables are also more reliable than homemade ones because the connectors are attached by machine. They're worth the extra few dollars.

For the ambitious or parsimonious reader, Figure 17.6 shows the correct way to order the wires in the connector.

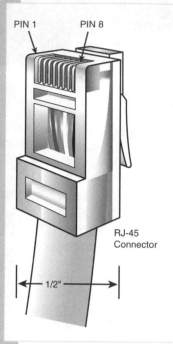

PIN 1   PIN 8

RJ-45
Connector

1/2"

TIA/EIA 568B Standard

PIN	DATA	WIRE COLOR
1	TX+	White/Orange
2	TX–	Orange
3	RX+	White/Green
4	–	Blue
5	–	White/Blue
6	RX–	Green
7	–	White/Brown
8	–	Brown

Figure 17.6
Standard wiring order for UTP network cables.

Installing In-Wall Wiring

In-wall wiring is the most professional and permanent way to go. However, this often involves climbing around in the attic or under a building, drilling through walls, or working in an office telephone closet. Personally, I find it a frustrating task and one I would rather watch someone else do. Hiring someone to get the job done might cost $30–$75 per computer, but you'll get a professional job, and if you consider that the price of network cards has gone down at least this much in the last 10 years, you can pretend that you're getting the wiring thrown in for free.

In-wall wiring is brought out to network-style modular jacks mounted to the baseboard of your wall. These RJ-45 jacks look similar to telephone modular jacks but are wider. You need patch cables to connect the jacks to your computers and switch, as shown in Figure 17.7.

 tip

Look in the Yellow Pages under "Telephone Wiring," and ask the contractors you call whether they have experience with network wiring.

 note

To pick a technical nit here, the modular connector used in networking is really called an 8P8C connector. The "true telephone RJ45" connector is slightly different, and not compatible. If you're buying RJ45 connectors, just make sure that the package says that the connectors are for networking use.

Figure 17.7
Connect your computers and switch to the network jacks using short patch cables.

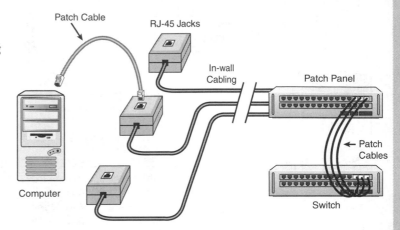

Patch Cable

RJ-45 Jacks

In-wall Cabling

Patch Panel

← Patch Cables

Computer

Switch

Connecting Just Two Computers

If you're making a network of just two computers, you might be able to take a shortcut and eliminate the need for a network switch or additional special hardware. If you want to add on to your network later, you can always add the extra gear then.

If you are connecting two computers, simply run a special cable called an *Ethernet crossover cable* from one computer's network adapter to the other, and you're finished. This special type of cable reverses the send and receive signals between the two ends and eliminates the need for a switch. You can purchase an Ethernet crossover cable from a computer store or network supply shop, or you can make one, as shown in Figure 17.8.

 note

Microsoft is encouraging the use of a special USB Cable for use by the Windows Easy Transfer program, for people who don't have a network. But, you can just as easily (and much less expensively) use an Ethernet crossover cable.

 tip

Be sure that your crossover cable is labeled as such. It won't work to connect a computer to a switch, and you'll go nuts wondering what's wrong if you try. Factory-made models usually have yellow ends. When I make them myself, I draw three rings around each end of the cable with a permanent-ink marker.

If you have a cable that you're not sure about, you can tell what kind of a cable it is by looking at the colors on the little wires inside the clear plastic connectors at the two ends. Considering just the colors on the wires, without regard to whether the colors are solid or striped:

- If you can see that each color is in the exact same position at both ends of the cable, in the arrangement "AABCCBDD," you have a standard Ethernet patch cable.

- If a pair of wires that is together at one end of the cable is split apart at the other end (that is, if one end has the pattern AABCCBDD and the other has BBACCADD) you have an Ethernet crossover cable.

- If the pairs of wire are all split symmetrically around the center of the connector (that is, if the pattern is ABCDDCBA), the cable is a telephone cable and *not* an Ethernet cable. You can't use this type of cable for networking.

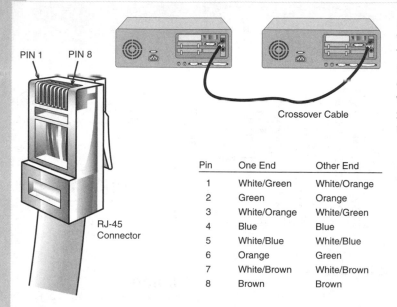

PIN 1   PIN 8

RJ-45
Connector

Figure 17.8
Wiring for a UTP crossover cable. The cable reverses the send and receive wires so that two network cards can be directly connected without a switch. Note that the green pair and orange pair are reversed across the cable.

Crossover Cable

Pin	One End	Other End
1	White/Green	White/Orange
2	Green	Orange
3	White/Orange	White/Green
4	Blue	Blue
5	White/Blue	White/Blue
6	Orange	Green
7	White/Brown	White/Brown
8	Brown	Brown

Connecting Multiple Switches

You might want to use more than one switch to reduce the number of long network cables you need if you have groups of computers in two or more locations. For example, you can connect the computers on each "end" of the network to the nearest switch, and then connect the switch to a main switch. Figure 17.9 shows a typical arrangement using this technique.

If you need to add a computer to your LAN and your switch has no unused connectors, you don't need to replace the switch. You can just add a switch. To add a computer to a fully loaded switch, unplug one cable from the original switch to free up a port. Connect this cable and your new computer to the new switch. Finally, connect the new switch's cascade port to the now free port on the original switch, as shown in Figure 17.10.

 note

A switch's *uplink* or *cascade* port is a connector designed to be connected to another switch or hub. Some switches have a separate connector for this purpose, whereas others make one of the switch's regular ports do double-duty by providing a switch that turns the last switch port into a cascade port. Refer to your switch's manual to see what to do with your particular hardware.

Figure 17.9
You can connect groups of computers with multiple switches to reduce the number of long cables needed. Use the cascade port on the remote switches to connect to the central switch.

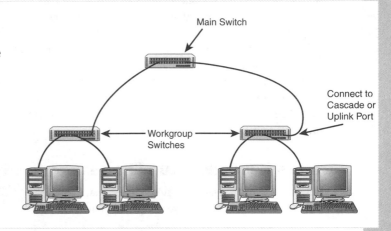

Main Switch

Connect to
Cascade or
Uplink Port

Workgroup
Switches

Figure 17.10
You can expand your network by cascading switches. The instructions included with your switch describe how to connect two switches using a patch cable. Some switches have a dedicated uplink port, whereas others have a switch that turns a regular port into an uplink port.

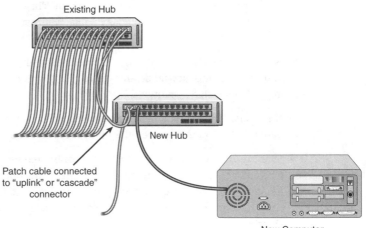

Existing Hub

New Hub

Patch cable connected
to "uplink" or "cascade"
connector

New Computer

Installing a Wireless Network

If you are installing a wireless network, you need to configure wireless security and networking options after installing your network adapters.

You really do have to worry about wireless network security. In my home, I can pick up signals from four separate wireless networks: mine, the house next door's, and two others (I can't tell

 note

This section tells how to set up a wireless network in a home or small office. On a corporate wireless network, your network administrator will most likely be the one to configure the wireless adapter and security settings.

whose they are). It's not uncommon to find that you can receive signals from several neighbors. And people do actually drive around with laptops in their car, looking for free Internet access. To protect against both freeloaders and hackers, one or two protection techniques are used: *encryption*, which scrambles data, and *authentication*, which certifies that a given computer should be allowed to connect to the network. You can use either encryption alone, or both encryption and authentication.

Wireless Network Setup Choices

To be able to distinguish your network's signal from others and to secure your network, you must make the following choices when you set up a wireless network:

- **An SSID (Service Set Identifier)**—A short name that you give your network, up to 32 characters in length. This could be your last name, your company name, your pet's name, or whatever makes sense to you.

- **A security type**—The authentication method that your network uses to determine whether or not a given computer should be allowed to connect. For Windows 7, the choices are as follows, in order of increasing security:

    - **No Authentication (open)**—No authentication is performed; any computer can connect to the network. Networks that use WEP encryption should use this option.

    - **Shared**—All devices on the network are configured with a common passphrase (which is a fancy name for a password). Any device that knows the passphrase is allowed to connect to the network. Due to bugs in the technology, this option actually creates additional security risks and should not be used unless you have to use the WEP encryption option discussed shortly.

    - **802.1X**—An older authentication method that uses a network server, software certificate, or smart card to authenticate computers. This method is used on some corporate networks.

    - **WPA-Personal**—An improved authentication method that uses a passphrase to validate each computer's membership in the network. The passphrase also serves as an encryption key. The WPA encryption scheme has been broken, however, and it's been superceded by WPA2.

    - **WPA2-Personal**—An improved version of WPA-Personal.

    - **WPA-Enterprise**—A version of WPA that uses a network server, smart card, or software certificate to validate network membership, used on corporate networks.

    - **WPA2-Enterprise**—An improved version of WPA-Enterprise.

 caution

If you want to use file and printer sharing on your wireless network, you must make the network secure by assigning a cryptographic "key" to the network. Otherwise, random people will be able to get at your computer.

If you want to set up an "open" wireless hotspot to share your Internet connection with friends, neighbors, or the world, that's great, but you must not use file and printer sharing on the same network. See "Special Notes for Wireless Networking" on page 521 for a safer option.

- **An encryption type**—The encryption method used to secure network data against eavesdropping. The options that are available depend on the security (authentication) type that was selected. The choices, in increasing order of security, are:

  - **None**—No data encryption is performed. This option is available only when the security type is set to No Authentication.

  - **WEP**—Data is encrypted using the WEP protocol, using a 40-, 128-, or 256-bit key. WEP is available only when the Security Type is set to No Authentication, Shared Authentication, or 802.1X. WEP encryption can be broken by a determined hacker.

  - **TKIP**—An encryption method that can be used with any of the WPA security types.

  - **AES**—An improved encryption method that can be used with any of the WPA security types.

- **An encryption key**—The key used to encrypt and decrypt data sent over the network. The different encryption methods use keys of different lengths:

  - For WEP encryption, you must enter a key as a string of 26 hexadecimal digits—that is, the numerals 0 through 9 and the letters A through F. (Windows 7 supports 40- and 128-bit WEP encryption, but 40-bit encryption is not recommended. You can join a 40-bit WEP network but not create a new one.)

    Some earlier versions of Windows let you enter a WEP key as a text phrase, but the text method was not standardized, and was pretty much guaranteed not to work across brands of wireless routers and access points, so it's been abandoned.

  - For WPA or WPA encryption, enter a passphrase, a word, or phrase using any letters or characters, of 8 or more letters—the more the better, up to 63. The passphrase is case sensitive and can contain spaces, but must not begin or end with a space.

  - The encryption key should be kept secret because, with it, someone can connect to your network, and from there get to your data and your shared files.

- **A channel number**—The channel number selects the frequency used to transmit your network's data. In the United States, this is a number between 1 and 11; the numbers might be different in other countries. The most common channels used are 1, 6, and 11. Some wireless routers select a channel automatically, but if you have to choose one, start with channel 6, and change it if other networks interfere with yours.

Why so many different security methods? Because thieves, like rust, never sleep, and it seems that as soon as a new, safer method is standardized, someone figures out a way to break it. WEP stands for Wired-Equivalent Privacy but it turned out to be an overly optimistic name. It was found shortly after its release that a determined interloper can break WEP security in as little as a few hours. WPA (which stands for Wi-Fi Protected Access) has an improved encrypting scheme and is strong enough to prevent most attacks. WPA2 is a further improvement upon that, and it's the best option we have at present. It should deter even the most determined hacker (but I wouldn't want to bet that it would keep the National Security Agency scratching its collective head for too long, if you know what I mean).

Which method should you use? On a corporate network, your network manager will configure your network or will give you setup instructions. On a home or small office network, you're limited by the least-capable of the devices on your network—your weakest link. So, select the best security method that is supported by *all* of your network gear, including any access points or routers.

Here are the options you should consider, in *decreasing* order of security; use the first one that your equipment supports:

- If all of your equipment supports WPA2, use WPA2-Personal security with AES encryption.

- If all of your equipment supports WPA, use WPA-Personal with AES encryption.

- If the best method that is supported by all of your equipment is WEP, use No Authentication (open) security with WEP encryption. Use the 128-bit WEP option; Windows 7 doesn't let you create a 40-bit WEP network.

- If you want to run an open network that anyone can use without any security at all, use No Authentication and no encryption. This is definitely not a good idea if you also have computers that use file or printer sharing on the same network. (We'll talk about that more in Chapter 19.)

Finally, one more bit of nomenclature: If you have a router or access point, you are setting up what is called an *infrastructure network*. Windows 7 has a wizard to help you choose the correct settings. We'll go through this in the next section.

Longer Is Better

The strength of any encryption scheme is measured by the amount of effort, time, and resources an attacker needs to break or decipher the encrypted data. The strength of wireless encryption depends on both the encryption method used (WPA2, WPA, or WEP), and also on the length of the private key that you select when you set up the network. Due to the mathematical techniques used, WPA2 is stronger than WPA, and WPA is much, much stronger than WEP. And for any of these encryption methods, the more binary bits in the key, and the more random that they are, the longer it takes a hacker to guess or determine your key. The bottom line is, you should use the strongest encryption method that is supported by all your wireless equipment, and you should use a long, randomly selected key. Long, random keys can be difficult to

 note

Windows 7, Vista, and XP with Service Pack 3 all have built-in support for WPA2. If your router doesn't support WPA2 or WPA, you might be able to install updated firmware to get it. If you have computers running Windows XP SP2, you can update them to support WPA2 by downloading and installing SP 3, or a hotfix available at support.microsoft.com/kb/893357.

 note

If you don't use a router, but just want to create a wireless network between two or more computers, you are creating an *ad hoc* network. We focus on infrastructure networks in this book because using a router makes it easier to network with wired-in computers and also to share an Internet connection.

 note

Despite its irritating length, if you use WEP security, it's better to use the hexadecimal format. The reason is that the hexadecimal format specifies the actual key, whereas a passphrase must be converted by some software scheme into a hexadecimal key, and for WEP, not every wireless device and OS uses the same scheme. For example, the passphrase abnormalities might turn into one key on a Linksys router and a different key on Windows 7. Thus, you could type the same passphrase into your router and into Windows, and the network would not work. To be safe, use a hexadecimal key.

For WPA security, the passphrase-mangling scheme is part of the standard, so it's fine to use a passphrase; every device will derive they same key from it.

type and impossible to remember, but think of it this way: If you were trying to guess someone's cat's name, which would you stumble across first: Fluffy, or ZGwPEr23?

An encryption key is specified as a hexadecimal number (a number composed of the digits 0 through 9 plus the letters A through F) or as a *passphrase*, which is a word or phrase using any letters or symbols. If you use the passphrase method, Windows mangles the passphrase characters to construct a somewhat longer hexadecimal key. Table 17.2 lists the key lengths that can be selected in Windows 7, along with the lengths of the corresponding hexadecimal number or passphrase.

note

Instead of making up a key or passphrase, an even better idea is to let the Windows Wireless Networking setup wizard make up a random key for you, or find a website that can generate random passwords for you. For example, the tool at www.yellowpipe.com/yis/tools/WEP_key/generator.php generates random WEP keys, and there is a link on that page to a corresponding random WPA key generator.

Table 17.2   WEP/WPA Key Formats

Encryption Strength	Passphrase/Key Format
256-bit WPA or WPA2	8–63 text characters (the more the better!) or 64 hexadecimal digits
104-bit (also called 128-bit) WEP	13 ASCII characters or 26 hexadecimal digits
40-bit (also called 64-bit) WEP	5 ASCII characters (any character) or 10 hexadecimal digits (0–9, A–F)

To enter a WPA2 or WPA key, type in a word, phrase, or random string of characters 8 to 63 characters in length (including spaces), or exactly 64 hexadecimal digits. Most people use the passphrase option. For best security, use a *long* phrase, use mixed upper- and lowercase, and add numeric digits and punctuation to the mix.

To specify a 104-bit WEP key, you could enter 13 ASCII (text) characters, such as the word abnormalities, or a 26-digit hexadecimal number, such as 3F985B1C89E00CDE1234434ED4. You must use the same key on all your computers and on your wireless router or access point, if you have one.

If you are joining an existing wireless network, you have to use the network key that was set by whomever set up that network. If you are creating a new network, use the strongest encryption method and the longest key that is supported by *all* of the devices and computers on your network. This means that if you have even one computer that doesn't support WPA, you need to use WEP, and if you have even one computer that doesn't support 256-bit keys, you have to use a 128-bit key. If you have a

note

Windows 7 and Vista have built-in support for WPA2. If you want to use WPA2 on computers running Windows XP, either install Service Pack 3 or download a hotfix from the Microsoft Support Site at http://support.microsoft.com.

note

Windows 7 will let you connect to an *existing* wireless network that uses 40-bit WEP security, but the wireless network setup wizard will not let you create a *new* network with 40-bit WEP security.

router, access point, or network adapter that doesn't support WPA, it's worth checking to see if you can update its internal software (firmware) or drivers to support this stronger encryption method.

Setting Up a New Wireless Network

If you're setting up a new wireless network using a wireless router or access point, the hardest part of the job is setting up security and Internet access settings in the router itself. There are three ways to configure a new router:

- Using a setup program provided by the router's manufacturer on a CD or DVD. This is usually the quickest and easiest method, since the setup program knows exactly how to configure your router. If you have high-speed Internet service, the setup program may also be able to set up the router to connect to your Internet service at the same time. (The next two options don't do that).

- If your router supports WiFi Protected Setup (WPS), using the Set Up a Network wizard provided with Windows 7. If your router has eight-digit numeric PIN code printed on the bottom, or if it has a pushbutton labeled WPS, you can use this wizard.

- Manually, by connecting to the router using a web browser.

I give general instructions for these three setup methods in the following sections. The manufacturer's instructions might be more detailed.

Whichever method you use, as I mentioned in the previous section, you need to select up to five things to set up a wireless network: an SSID (name), security type, encryption type, encryption key, and possibly a channel number. A setup program or the Set Up a Network Wizard might help you make these selections automatically.

 tip

Before you get started, you might want to check the router manufacturer's website to see if a firmware update is available. (Firmware is the software built into the device.) Update the firmware following the manufacturer's instructions before you start using the network since the update process sometimes blows out any settings you've made in the router, and you'll have to start over as if the router was new. It's still worth doing this, as firmware updates are usually issued only when serious bugs have been found and fixed.

Using the Manufacturer's Setup Program

The easiest way to set up a wireless router is using a program provided by the manufacturer. Connect one of your computers to the wireless router using an Ethernet cable, then run the program from the manufacturer's CD or DVD.

The setup program will typically suggest default settings for the router, which you may change. As I mentioned previously, select WPA2 security unless your router or one or more of your computer's don't support it.

You should write the final settings down, especially the security key. The setup program will then install the settings in the router. When your computers detect the new wireless network, you can connect to it and type in the security key.

If the router doesn't set up Internet service, see "Setting up Internet Service" after I describe the other setup methods.

Using the Set Up a Network Wizard

If your router supports the WiFi Protected Setup (WPS) automatic configuration scheme, Windows 7 can set up the router for you automatically. You'll need the router's 8 digit PIN number to use this method. The PIN might be printed on a label on the bottom of the router, or, you might be able to find out what the PIN is by connecting to the router using a web browser. I'll tell how to do this shortly. Also, this method works only on a router that has all of its factory-default settings and hasn't yet been configured. (If you have a used WPS-capable router, you may be able to use its setup web page to restore its factory default settings.)

To Set Up a Network wizard, follow these steps:

1. Connect your computer to the wireless router using an Ethernet cable, and power up the router. Wait 60 seconds or so before proceeding. If you are prompted to select a network location, choose Home.

2. Click on the Network icon in the taskbar and select Open Network and Sharing Center.

3. Under Change Your Networking Settings, select Set Up a New Connection or Network. Highlight Set Up a New Network and click Next.

4. Wait for your wireless router to appear in the dialog box. When it does, click Next. If it doesn't appear within 90 seconds, it might not be WPS capable, or it may already have been configured. If so, skip ahead to "Configuring Manually," **page 470**.

5. Enter the PIN code printed on your router and click Next. If the PIN is not printed, see if you can get it out of the router. Follow steps 2 through 5 in the section titled "Configuring Manually" to get into the router. See if any of its setup screens display the WPS PIN number. (On a TrendNet router I tested, I found this under Wireless, Wi-Fi Protected Setup).

6. Adjust the network name if you wish, as shown in Figure 17.11.

   If not all of your computers support WPA2 security, click the circular arrow button to expand the advanced settings section. Change the Security Level to WPA-Personal if all computers support that, or WEP if that's the best method supported by all of your computers. You can also select No Security, but I *strongly* recommend against this.

   When the settings are made, click Next.

7. The wizard will configure the router, and will eventually display the security key. Write this down and keep a copy of it in a safe place. (If your location is secure, you can write in on a sticky note and attach it to the router itself).

   I suggest that you also click Print These Network Settings, which displays a WordPad document that lists the security information and also provides instructions on setting up other computers. You should print this document.

8. You have the option of using a USB thumb drive to copy the network settings to other computers. If you want to do this, plug in a removable USB drive, click Copy the Network Profile to a USB Drive, and follow the wizard's instructions. Carry the drive to each of your other computers with wireless adapters, insert it, and run the setupSNK.exe application. Alternatively, just type in the network key manually at each computer.

Change the network name here.

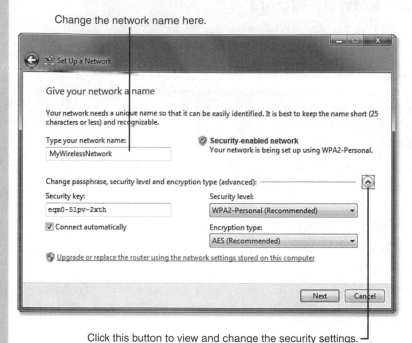

Figure 17.11
The Set Up a Network wizard lets you change the default network name and security settings.

Click this button to view and change the security settings.

When you've followed these steps, your computers can all attach to the wireless network, using the network key that the wizard selected. If you need to set up Internet service as well, see "Setting up Internet Service" after the following section.

Configuring Manually

If you have to configure your router manually, your best bet is to follow the manufacturer's instructions. I can't give you specific instructions here, but I can give a general outline of the process:

1. Connect your computer to the wireless router using an Ethernet cable, and power up the router. Wait 60 seconds or so before proceeding. If you are prompted to select a network location, choose Home.

2. Click Start, All Programs, Accessories, Command Prompt. Type the command **ipconfig** and press Enter.

3. Look for the heading that reads something like "Ethernet Adapter Local Area Connection," and under that, look for the Default Gateway setting. It should be 192.168.0.1, 192.168.1.1, or something like this.

4. Open Internet Explorer, and in the address bar, type / / followed by the Default Gateway numbers (for example, //**192.168.0.1**) and press Enter.

5. Log on to the router using its administrative username and password. In many cases you can leave the username blank and enter `admin` for the password, but this varies by manufacturer. You'll have to read the instruction manual or search the Web to find the default password for your router.

   You may wish to change the default password as your first step. If you do change it, be sure to write the new password down and store it in a secure place.

6. Use the router's web page menus to locate the Wireless configuration page. Enter a network name (SSID), select a security type, and enter a key.

7. Use the appropriate "save settings" button or menu choice, wait 30 seconds and try to have one of your other computers connect to the router using a wireless adapter, following the instructions under "Joining an Existing Wireless Network" on **page 472**.

   When other computers can connect successfully, if the computer you used for setup has a wireless adapter, you can disconnect the Ethernet cable. (Ethernet connections are faster and more reliable than wireless, though, so use wired connections whenever it's convenient to do so.)

When your computers can connect to the wireless router, you can have the router establish an Internet connection for you.

Setting Up Internet Service

Once your wireless network is working and your computers can connect to the wireless router, you will probably want to have the router share a high-speed Internet connection.

If you used the manufacturer's setup program to configure your router, it may have set this up for you already. If you have to set up the Internet side of your router manually, try to follow the manufacturer's instructions. I can give you only general instructions here.

To set up shared Internet service, view to the router's setup web pages by following steps 2 through 5 in the preceding section, "Configuring Manually." Locate the router's Wide Area Network (WAN) or Internet setup web pages. Many routers have button that you can click to run an Internet setup wizard; otherwise, you'll have to set up the connection manually.

In general terms, there are three ways to connect:

■ If your wireless router's WAN (Internet) port is connected to a network that has an Internet connection, chose the router's "direct connection" option.

■ If you use Cable Internet service, most likely you'll select the DHCP option. You may have to enter a specific host name supplied by your cable company. Other cable ISPs key off your network adapter's MAC address, so you may have to call the ISP to inform them of the router's MAC address (which is usually printed on the bottom of the router).

■ If you use DSL service, most likely you'll select the PPPoE option. You'll have to enter a username and password.

Your ISP should help you get the Internet connection working, or at least, they should provide you with the information you need to get it working.

See Chapter 19 for more detailed instructions on connecting your LAN to the Internet.

Joining an Existing Wireless Network

If you are using a wireless connection on a corporate network, your wireless configuration can and should be managed by your network administrators. Your administrator will most likely install a security "certificate" file that will identify your computer as one authorized to use the wireless network. It's also likely that you won't need to—or be able to—change any settings to use the network.

However, if your home or small office wireless network has already been configured and you're just adding a new computer, or if you are taking your computer into someone else's office or home and want to use their wireless network, connect to and use the network by following this manual procedure:

 note

If the network you want to use doesn't appear, it could be because the signal is too weak. Also, some people prevent their router from broadcasting the SSID name over the airwaves. (This doesn't really provide much extra security because hackers can find the network anyway.) If the network you want to use isn't broadcasting its SSID, **see** "Adding a Network Manually" on **page 968**.

1. In the notification area, locate the network icon and click it.

2. Windows displays a list of the names (SSIDs) of the wireless networks that it "hears." Click the network you want to use and then click Connect.

3. Windows determines what type of security the network is using. If the network is encrypted, it prompts you to enter the network key. Enter the passphrase or the 10- or 26-digit hexadecimal key that was used to set up the network to begin with.

4. When the connection has been established, Windows will ask you to select a network location: Home, Work, or Public. It is very important that you make the right selection. See "Choosing Your Network Location" on **page 475** for details.

➥ *We talk more about managing connections to multiple wireless networks in Chapter 34, "Wireless Networking."*

After the wireless connections are made, you can continue setting up the rest of your network, as described in the following sections.

Configuring a Peer-to-Peer Network

When you're sure that the physical connection between your computers is set up correctly, you're ready to configure Windows 7. With today's Plug and Play network cards and with all the needed software built in to Windows, this configuration is a snap.

If your computer is part of a Windows Server domain network, which is often the case in a corporate setting, skip ahead to "Joining a Windows Domain Network."

Configuring the TCP/IP Protocol

After your network adapters are all installed—and, if you're using a wired network, cabled together—you need to ensure that each computer is assigned an *IP address*. This is a number that uniquely identifies each computer on the network. These numbers are assigned in one of the following ways:

- If the network has a computer that uses Windows Internet Connection Sharing to share an Internet connection, if you have a hardware Internet sharing router, or if you are on a corporate LAN running Windows Server, each computer will be assigned an IP address automatically— they're doled out by the Dynamic Host Configuration Protocol (DHCP) service that runs on the sharing computer or in the router. This is why I recommend using a router even if you aren't setting up a shared Internet connection.

  By default, Windows sets up new network adapters to receive an address this way. If your network fits into this category, you don't have to change any settings, and you can just skip ahead to the section "If You Have a Shared Internet Connection."

- Each computer can be given an address manually, which is called a *static address* as opposed to a dynamic (automatic) one. If you are not going to use a router or a shared Internet connection, you should set up static addressing. I tell you how shortly.

- If no static settings are made but no DHCP server exists on the network, Windows automatically assigns IP addresses anyway. Although the network will work, this is not an ideal situation and can slow Windows down. The setup steps I show in the following two sections will let you avoid having IP addresses be assigned this way.

If you're setting up a new computer on an existing network, use whatever scheme the existing computers use; check their settings and follow suit with your new one. Otherwise, use either of the schemes described in the following two sections.

If You Have No Shared Internet Connection

If you're setting up a new network from scratch, and you do not have a connection sharing computer, router, or wireless access point, you should use static addressing. If your computer will be part of an existing network with predetermined IP addresses, your network manager will provide you with the setup information.

Otherwise, for most home and small office networks, the following static address scheme should work fine:

IP Address	192.168.1.1 for your first computer,
	192.168.1.2 for your second computer,
	192.168.1.3 for your third, and so on.
	I strongly suggest that you keep a list of your computers and the addresses that you assign to each of them.
Subnet Mask	255.255.255.0
Default Gateway	(Leave blank)
Preferred DNS Server	(Leave blank)
Alternate DNS Server	(Leave blank)

Follow these steps on each computer to ensure that the network is set up correctly:

1. Log on using a Computer Administrator account. Click Start, Control Panel, View Network Status and Tasks (under Network and Internet), Change Adapter Settings. Right-click the Local Area Connection or Wireless Connection icon that corresponds to your LAN connection and select Properties.

2. Highlight Internet Protocol Version 4 (TCP/IPv4) and click Properties.

3. Change the settings in the Properties dialog box. Figure 17.12 shows an example, but you must use the address values appropriate for your computer and your network.

 tip

If your computer will move back and forth between a network that uses automatic configuration and a network that uses static settings—say, between work and home—select Obtain An IP Address Automatically. A tab named Alternate Configuration will appear. Select the Alternate Configuration tab and configure the static settings. Windows will use these static settings only when a DHCP server is not present.

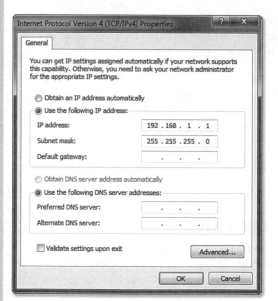

Figure 17.12
Make IP address settings within the Internet Protocol Version 4 (TCP/IPv4) Properties dialog box.

If You Have a Shared Internet Connection

As I mentioned previously, if you plan to share an Internet connection with all the computers on your network, you should read Chapter 19 first. Keep the following tips in mind:

■ If you will use Windows Internet Connection Sharing, first set up the one computer that will be sharing its connection, as described in Chapter 19, then set up networking in your other computers.

 note

If you add a shared Internet connection later, go to every one of your computers, bring up the TCP/IP Properties dialog box shown in Figure 17.12 again, and select Obtain an IP Address Automatically and Obtain DNS Server Address Automatically. Otherwise, the shared connection will not work.

- All the computers, including the one sharing its Internet connection, should have their Local Area Network connection set up to Obtain an IP Address Automatically and Obtain DNS Server Address Automatically (see Figure 17.12).

- If you will use a hardware router, configure the router first, following the manufacturer's instructions. Enable its DHCP feature. If you can, set the starting DHCP IP address to 100 so that numbers from 2 to 99 can be used for computers with static settings. Also, if your ISP has provided you with static IP address settings, be sure to enter your ISP's DNS server addresses in the router's setup screens so it can pass them to the computers that rely on the router for their IP setup.

Now that your new network connection is set up, be sure to assign it the correct network location, as described in the next section. This is a critical part of Windows networking security.

Choosing Your Network Location

When you connect to a new network for the first time, Windows 7 will prompt you to choose a network location. The type of location you select determines the Windows Firewall settings that are applied and the networking features that will be available. As an example, a higher level of security is required when you connect to the Internet in an airport lobby, as opposed to the network in your home. Windows remembers the location setting for each different network to which you connect, so you can be sure that the appropriate level of security is always applied.

The following three network location choices are available:

- **Home**—A Home network is one where you trust the other computers on the network. (That is, you trust the people using the other computers.) File and printer sharing is enabled, as is Network Discovery, which makes your computer visible to other users and makes their computers visible to you. It's possible to join a homegroup, which we'll discuss shortly.

- **Work**—A Work network is like a Home network. Other computers are trusted. File and printer sharing and Network Discovery are enabled. It's not possible to create a homegroup; so, if you are setting up a small office network and want to use the HomeGroup system, feel free to set your computer's location to Home.

- **Public**—A Public network is one where you don't trust the other users or computers on the network. File and printer sharing and Network Discovery are disabled on this network connection.

  Any connection that leads directly to the Internet without a firewall or router in between *must* be designated a Public network to protect your computer from the hackers and bad software "out there." This goes for dial-up Internet as well as Ethernet connections that plug into a cable or DSL modem.

  You should also select Public when you are connecting to any wired or wireless network or Internet service in a hotel, Internet café, airport, dorm, school, and so on, and even an office network belonging to a client, customer, or anyone else whom you don't want poking into your computer.

Here's a good rule of thumb: If you don't need to use file sharing and printer sharing in a given location, select the Public location.

When you move your computer from one network to another, Windows will usually detect the change and prompt you to select a new network location.

To change your network location manually

1. Click Start, Network and Internet, View Network Status and Tasks.

2. Locate the icon for the active network connection and click the Home Network, Work Network, or Public Network label next to the icon.

3. Select the correct network location.

 caution

If you connect to a wireless or wired network that you've never used before and Windows doesn't quickly prompt you to select the network location type, change the location manually, using the following procedure.

Setting Your Computer Identification

After you've configured your network, the next step is to make sure that each of the computers on your network is a member of the same domain or workgroup.

If you are part of a Windows domain-type network, your system administrator will give you the information you need to set your computer identification.

If you are setting up your own network of Windows computers without Windows Server, click Start, right-click Computer, and select Properties. Look at the "Computer Name, Domain, and Workgroup settings" section on each of the computers on your network. Do they each have a different full computer name and the same workgroup name? If so, you're all set.

If not, click Change Settings, click the Network ID button, and prepare to answer the wizard's questions. Click Next on the wizard's first screen. You are asked to select the option that best describes your computer:

 note

Your domain administrator must know about your new computer and create a computer account for it before you try to add your computer to the domain. Refer to Chapter 2, "Installing and Upgrading Windows 7," for more details.

- This Computer Is Part of a Business Network; I Use It to Connect to Other Computers at Work.

- This Computer Is a Home Computer; It's Not Part of a Business Network.

Which one you choose makes a significant difference. If you choose the "Home Computer" option, the wizard sets up your computer for peer-to-peer networking with the workgroup name WORKGROUP and finishes.

 note

If you use the Home Computer option, be sure that all your computers are set up the same way, with the workgroup name WORKGROUP. Otherwise, you'll have trouble working with the other computers on your network.

If you choose the "Business Network" option, Windows configures your computer for a higher standard of security than it will for home use.

The wizard next asks you to choose from one of the following responses:

- My Company Uses a Network With a Domain

- My Company Uses a Network Without a Domain

If you are joining an existing domain network managed by Windows Server, check With a Domain (but you should consult with your network manager first).

Otherwise, if you are building your own network as described in this chapter, select Without a Domain and click Next.

The last question asks for a name for the network workgroup. Leave the default setting WORKGROUP in place.

Click Next and then click Finish to complete the setup. You need to let Windows restart your computer if you changed any of the settings or names.

 caution

You must be sure that every computer on your network uses the same workgroup name if you want them to be able to easily share files and printers.

Configuring Windows Firewall

It is a good idea to check that Windows Firewall is set up correctly; otherwise, you could end up exposed to Internet hacking, or you could find that your network is so locked down that you can't use file and printer sharing. Windows Firewall is discussed in more detail in Chapter 32.

If your Windows 7 computer is connected to a domain network, your network manager can and should configure your computer so that it uses a correctly configured firewall "profile" when you are connected to the corporate network. You won't be able to change these settings. You network manager will also probably configure another "default" profile to protect you when you are disconnected from the corporate network, such as when you are traveling or using your computer at home.

In this section, I assume that you are managing your own computer and that your network is not protected by a professionally installed firewall. Home and small office users should go through this quick checklist of steps to confirm that your network will function safely:

1. Log on using a Computer Administrator account. Click Start, Control Panel, System and Security, Windows Firewall.

2. Click Turn Windows Firewall On or Off. In both the Home or Work (Private) and Public sections, be sure that Turn On Windows Firewall is selected, and that Notify Me When Windows Firewall Blocks a New Program is checked.

   In general, Block All Incoming Connections doesn't need to be checked. You can check it in the Public profile section to get the strongest security, but you might not be able to use some Internet services like FTP (file transfer), telephone, or voice or video chat.

These are the default settings, but it's best to check them to be sure.

Setting Up a Homegroup

Windows 7 has a new networking feature called HomeGroup that can make sharing files, folders, printers, and music/video media very easy. What a homegroup does is let each user decide whether or not to share specific categories of documents, music, video, printers, and so on, or even specific folders and files. Once shared, every user on every computer in the homegroup can see the items, without worrying about passwords or usernames. It's all just there, organized, and easy to get to.

HomeGroup networking works by setting up a password that is used to join each computer to the group. Once a computer has been made a member of the homegroup, any user on any of the member computers can see any of the group's shared folders and printers.

note

If you're wondering why it's "HomeGroup" here and "homegroup" almost everywhere else in this chapter, it's because the genius lawyers at Microsoft want people to use the trademarked word HomeGroup when we talk about the product feature, but to use homegroup when we talk about a group of computers that *use* the feature. Got it?

Is a homegroup right for you? Consider these points to decide whether or not to use this new feature:

- The HomeGroup feature works only with Windows 7 computers. Computers running Windows Vista, XP, Mac OS, Linux, and so on can still use folders and printers shared by computers in the homegroup if you take some additional steps. (I talk about this in Chapter 18 under "Using Windows Vista and XP with a Homegroup," **page 494**.)

- Likewise, Windows 7 computers that aren't members of the homegroup can still access the folders and printers shared by the group's member computers, if you take those same additional steps.

- Within a homegroup, you can't decide individually which other users can see your shared stuff and which users can't. Anybody who can use a computer that's a member of the homegroup can use the content that you decide to share.

  What you *can* control is whether to share your stuff or not, and whether the other users can just view and use your stuff or modify, delete, and add to it.

note

If you have a computer that is part of a domain network when you connect at work, you can still join it to your homegroup at home. You'll be able to use folders and printers shared by other computers in the homegroup, but you won't be able to share any of your computer's folders with the group.

If you don't need to control access on a person-by-person basis, then a homegroup is definitely a convenient thing to set up. If a homegroup isn't right for you, skip ahead to the next section, "Alternatives to Using a Homegroup." (It's easy to change your mind later on, so don't worry too much about this.)

To set up a homegroup, log on to one of your Windows 7 computers and perform the following steps:

1. Click Start, Control Panel, Choose Homegroup and Sharing Options (under Network and Internet).

2. Click Create a Homegroup.

3. Select which types of *your* content you want to share with everyone else in the homegroup, as shown in Figure 17.13. Check Pictures, Documents, Music, and/or Videos to let other users see your files. Check Printers to share your computer's printer(s) with other computers in the home-group. (You can easily change these selections later, as we discuss in Chapter 20, "Using a Windows Network.") When you've made your selections, click Next.

Figure 17.13
Select the types of files you want to share with everyone else in the homegroup. This selection applies only to your own files—other users get to choose for themselves what they want to share.

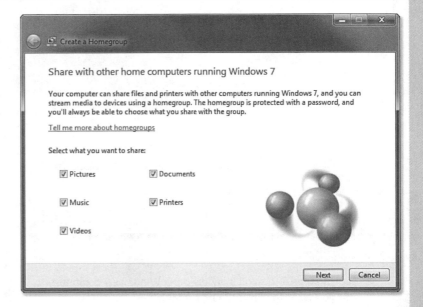

4. Windows will create the homegroup settings, and will display a password as shown in Figure 17.14. You might want to jot it down, as you'll need it to join your other Windows 7 computers to the homegroup. Upper- and lowercase matter, by the way. Click Finish to complete the process.

5. We suggest that you use the random homegroup password that Windows generated for you. You don't have to worry about remembering it, because any member computer can redisplay it for you whenever you want. But if you really want to change it, you can, and now is the time. Click Change the Password, and then when the pop-up box appears, confirm by clicking Change the Password there too. Type in a new password. (Remember that any member computer can view it, so *don't* use your personal password.) Click Next, then Finish.

Now, on to your other computers:

6. You or another computer owner should go to another Windows 7 computer on your network, log on, and click Start, Control Panel, Choose Homegroup and Sharing Options, Join Now.

7. Select the types of files that *this* computer user wants to share with the rest of the homegroup. (And remember, it's easy to come back and change these selections later.) Then, click Next.

8. Enter the homegroup password and click Next. (If you don't have it written down, go to a computer that's already a member, and click Start, Control Panel, Choose Homegroup and Sharing Options, View or Print the Homegroup Password.) Finally, click Finish.

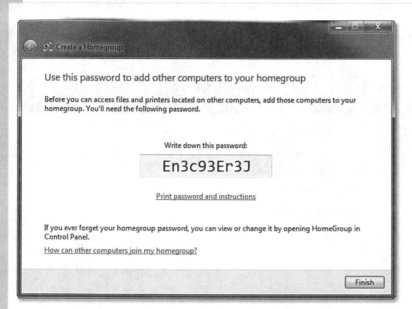

Figure 17.14
The homegroup password consists of a series of letters and numbers that are case sensitive. You'll need it when you join other computers to the homegroup. But don't worry about losing it; Windows can display it for you later on.

Repeat steps 6 through 8 on any other Windows 7 computers that you want to join to the homegroup.

Each user on each computer will have to log on and decide which of their materials they want to share with the homegroup. Until they do, their names won't appear in the Homegroup listing in Windows Explorer. I talk about this in Chapter 20 under "Sharing With a Homegroup," **page 562**.

note

If you have computers running Windows XP, Vista, Mac OS, Linux or other OSs, read Chapter 18 to see how to make it easier to share files and printers with these other OSs.

Alternatives to Using a Homegroup

HomeGroup security gives anyone in the group access to any shared folder or printer. If you need to restrict access to shared folders and printers on a user-by-user basis, or if you have computers that don't run Windows 7, you might not want to set up a homegroup, but instead use the traditional Windows file sharing scheme. There are two ways you can configure traditional sharing:

- If you have OSs other than Windows 7 on your network and you don't need per-user security, you can turn off Password Protected Sharing. To do this, click Start, Control Panel, Choose Homegroup and Sharing Options (under Network and Internet), Change Advanced Sharing Settings, Turn Off Password Protected Sharing.

This makes any shared folder or printer available to anybody who can connect to your network, with no passwords required at all.

If you have computers running Windows XP, Vista, Mac OS, Linux or other OSs, read Chapter 18 for more information on sharing with these OSs.

■ If you need to control in detail which users can use which shared files and folders, leave Password Protected Sharing turned on (which is the same as disabling Simple File Sharing on Windows XP). You will have to set up the same user accounts with the same passwords on each of your computers so that people can access shared folders and printers.

➥ *For more information on Password Protected Sharing, including ways it works differently on Windows 7 than previous versions of Windows, **see** "Configure Passwords and File Sharing," p. 924.*

Wrapping Up

This completes the procedure for setting up Windows networking on one Windows 7 computer. Repeat the procedures on your other computers, and you'll be able to start using your network.

Before you do, though, now that you have a LAN—even if it's just a simple peer-to-peer LAN—you should be worried about network security and hackers. Why? Because you'll certainly be connecting to the Internet, even if only intermittently, and when you do, you risk exposing your network to the entire world. These risks are not as far-fetched as you might think.

Refer to Chapter 32 to find out what risks you'll be exposed to and what you can do to protect your LAN. If you use Internet Connection Sharing or a connection-sharing router, you're in pretty good shape. But in any case, go through Chapter 32 carefully—it is very important.

Then, read Chapter 20 to learn how to get the most out of your Windows network.

Windows 7 has some additional advanced networking features that you might want to take advantage of, and they're covered in other chapters. See Chapter 35 for instructions on enabling incoming access to your computer via dial-up modem or VPN connections. See Chapter 18 for information about networking with Mac, UNIX, Linux, and older versions of Windows, as well as installing advanced networking services.

Joining a Windows Domain Network

This section describes how to add your computer to a domain network run by a version of Windows Server. If you're lucky, your network administrator will take care of this for you. Alternatively, she or he might give you custom-tailored instructions for your network. By all means, use those instructions instead of the generic plan in this section.

 note

Most Windows 7 installations will work "out of the box" without the need to install any additional network components. If your network uses Novell servers, though, your network manager may give you instructions for adding additional client software.

At the very least, your network administrator will give you four pieces of information:

- The name to be given to your computer.

- The domain name for your network.

- Your network logon name and password.

- Any specific configuration information for the Internet Protocol (TCP/IP). In most cases, it is not necessary to make any changes in the default settings.

If your computer was connected to the network when you installed Windows 7 and you entered this information then, your network setup is already complete and you can skip to Chapter 20.

Use the following procedure to make your computer a member of your network domain:

1. Log on to Windows with a Computer Administrator account.

2. Click Start, right-click Computer, and select Properties. Click Change Settings in the Computer Name, Domain, and Workgroup settings section.

3. Click the Network ID button.

4. Select This Computer Is Part of a Business Network; I Use It to Connect to Other Computers at Work, and then click Next.

5. Select My Company Uses a Network with a Domain, and then click Next twice.

6. Enter your network login name, password, and the network domain name, as supplied by your network administrator. Then click Next.

7. You might be asked to enter your computer's name and its domain name. This information will also have been supplied by your network administrator. If you're asked, enter the computer and domain names provided, and then click Next.

   You also might be prompted for a domain Administrator account name and password. If this occurs, the network administrator will have to assist you.

8. You should finally get the message "Welcome to the *xxx* domain." Close the Properties dialog box and allow Windows to restart.

   If an error message appears instead, click Details to view the detailed explanation of the problem. Report this information to your network administrator for resolution. The problem could be in your computer or in the network itself.

When your computer has been joined to the domain and restarted, the Windows 7 Welcome screen no longer appears and you need to use the old-style logon system to sign on. To

note

If your computer is disconnected from the network or you want to install new hardware, you can log on using a local account. Select the computer's name instead of your network domain name, and log on using a local Computer Administrator account.

log on, press Ctrl+Alt+Del and then enter your account name, password, and domain name. You can specify an alternative domain name by entering your username and account together this way: *myaccount@domain*.

Checking Out the Neighborhood

Your network is finally ready to go. After you have configured, connected, and perhaps restarted each of your computers, open Windows Explorer: Click Start, Computer or, alternatively, Start, Documents. (Any Windows Explorer view will work.) Look for the Network item at the left edge of the Window, as shown in Figure 17.15.

Figure 17.15
Windows Explorer has links at the left edge that let you explore your network, and your homegroup, if you have one.

Explore homegroup members here.

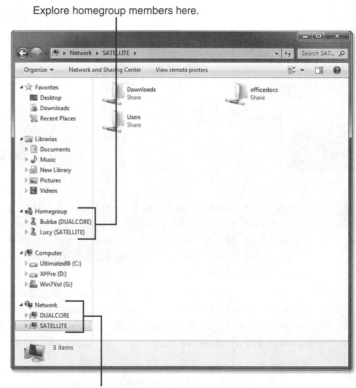

Explore network computers here.

If your network is up and running, and Network Discovery is enabled, you should see one icon for every computer you've connected. Double-click any icon to see what that computer is sharing with the network.

If you set up a homegroup, the Homegroup list will have an entry for each user who has elected to share files. There may be entries for the other users on your own computer, as well as users on other computers. Shared printers *should* already be listed in your Devices and Printers Control Panel applet, automatically, although if you have one or more printers that are not connected via USB cables, you may have to take additional steps to share them.

For more information on using your network and sharing resources, see Chapter 20.

➡ *If you don't see other computers in the Network window, see Chapter 21, "Troubleshooting Your Network."*

Bridging Two Network Types

Windows 7 provides the capability to connect or bridge two different network types through software. This can eliminate the need to buy a hardware device to connect two disparate networks. Figure 17.16 shows an example of what bridging can do. In the figure, one Windows 7 computer serves as a bridge between an Ethernet LAN and a phoneline LAN.

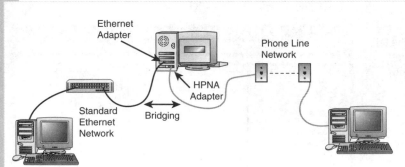

Figure 17.16
Bridging a phoneline and Ethernet network with Windows 7. Computers on either network can communicate as if they were directly connected.

Bridging is similar to routing, but it's more appropriate for small LANs because it's easier to configure and doesn't require different sets of IP addresses on each network segment. Technically, bridging occurs at the physical level of the network protocol stack. Windows forwards network traffic, including broadcasts and packets of all protocol types received on either adapter to the other. In effect, it creates one larger network.

To enable bridging in your Windows 7 computer, install and configure two or more network adapters, as described under "Installing Multiple Network Adapters," earlier in this chapter. However, don't worry about setting up the Internet Protocol (TCP/IP) parameters for either of the adapters yet. Then do the following:

1. View the connection icons by clicking Start, Control Panel, View Network Status and Tasks (under Network and Internet), Change Adapter Settings.

2. Select the icons you want to bridge by clicking on the first, holding down the Ctrl key, and clicking on the second.

3. Right-click one of the icons and select Bridge Connections.

4. A new icon named Network Bridge appears. Select this new icon and, if you want, rename it appropriately—for example, "Ethernet to Phoneline."

5. Double-click the new Network Bridge icon. Select Internet Protocol (TCP/IP) and configure your computer's TCP/IP settings. You must do this because any TCP/IP settings for the original two adapters are lost.

When you've created a bridge, your two network adapters function as one and share one IP address, so Microsoft disables the "network properties" of the individual network adapters. You must configure your computer's network properties with the Network Bridge icon.

Remember that the connection between the two networks depends on the computer with the bridge being powered on.

You can remove the bridge later by right-clicking the Network Bridge icon and clicking Delete.

18

MIX AND MATCH WITH OLD WINDOWS AND MACS

Networking with Other Operating Systems

Most Microsoft online help and websites tell you how well Windows 7 networking works with Windows 7 and Windows Server computers, but these instructions consider only "vanilla" Windows networks. Real-life networks are seldom so simple, even at home. Often networks have a mix of operating systems, and Windows often has to be coaxed into getting along with them.

On a real-life LAN with multiple OSs, it's not enough that computers be capable of coexisting on the same network cable at the same time. They need to actually work *with* each other, or *internetwork*, so that users of these various systems can share files and printers. At best, this sharing should occur without anyone even knowing that alternative platforms are involved. Achieving this kind of seamlessness can range from effortless to excruciating.

Save the Heartache—Buy a Network Appliance

One way to avoid *most* of the hassles of internetworking is to buy a *network appliance*, also called *network-attached storage (NAS)*: a small server computer that "speaks" all the networking languages you need—Windows, UNIX, Macintosh, or whatever. These devices can cost as little as $200 and can put several hundred gigabytes of storage on your network that anyone can access. They tend to be very easy to set up, and a few even provide Internet Connection Sharing, wireless connectivity, an email server, a firewall, and a web server all in the same box. Products for the home and small office are made by Axentra (www.axentra.com), Cisco (www.linksysbycicso.com), D-Link (www.dlink.com), Buffalo Technology (www.buffalotech.com), and several other companies.

Acer, Hewlett-Packard, Niveus, Velocity and others make NAS devices based on a Microsoft software package called Windows Home Server. These products "speak" only SMB, but Macs and Linux can use them, and they provide great backup services for Windows computers.

If you're shopping for such a network appliance, be very careful to check what format it uses on its disks and what maximum file size it supports. Some devices support a maximum file size of only 2GB or 4GB, depending on the disk format and internal software used. Such a device might be okay for storing documents and photos, but it will be incapable of storing complete movies and computer backup files, many of which run 6GB in size or more—often way more. Other devices use proprietary networking drivers and/or proprietary disk formats. Personally, I'd only use a NAS device that uses standard file access protocols (SMB, NFS, and so on) *and* a disk format that can be read by Windows or Linux, so that if the hardware box were to die, I could at least put its hard disk into my desktop computer and extract its contents.

If a network appliance isn't in the cards, you need to get your computers to interoperate directly. This chapter shows you how to get computers running Windows, Mac OS X, UNIX, and Linux to play together nicely.

Some new features have been added to Windows 7 networking, and support for some old features has been removed. With respect to internetworking, this list provides a summary of the most significant changes since Windows Vista and XP:

- Windows 7 behaves differently from previous versions of Windows when Password Protected Sharing is turned off. This is discussed later in the chapter under "Password Protection and Simple File Sharing."

- The NetBEUI network protocol is not available under Windows 7. This could impact you if your network includes computers running Windows XP, 2000, Me, 98, or earlier versions. I'll discuss this in more detail when I talk about networking with older versions of Windows later in this chapter.

- The Link Level Discovery Protocol (LLDP) is relatively new to Windows. LLDP lets Windows 7 eke out a map of the connections between your computers and the other hardware on your network. LLDP support is currently available only for Windows 7, Vista, XP (via a download), Server 2003, and Server 2008. Connections to computers running older versions of Windows will not be diagrammed on the network map. Computers running Linux and Mac OS X probably won't appear, either—LLDP support was not available at the time this book was written, but I suspect that it will eventually be provided in a future Mac or Linux version or update. An Open Source effort to bring LLDP to Linux and the Mac was underway at the time this was written (see http://openlldp.sourceforge.net) and some commercial network mapping applications (such as LANsurveyor at www.solarwinds.com) also have a Mac LLDP responder.

- Microsoft does not provide out-of-the-box support for Novell NetWare (an industrial-strength corporate networking system) with Windows. Novell Corporation has a NetWare client that works on Windows 7, but its installation and use is beyond the scope of this book.

However, although some things change, other things stay the same. You probably won't be surprised to learn that the Network Browser service (the relatively obscure software component responsible for collecting the list of names of the computers on your network, the list upon which the old Network Neighborhood display was based) is still present, and it still doesn't work worth a darn.

In addition to covering internetworking issues, this chapter discusses some of the advanced and optional networking features provided with Windows 7. These features are not needed for "vanilla" Windows networks, but they are used for the more complex networks found in corporate environments.

Internetworking with Windows Vista, XP, and 2000

Windows 7's file and printer sharing services work quite well with Windows Vista, XP, and Windows 2000 Professional. All three OSs were intended from the start to work well with the TCP/IP network protocol favored by Windows 7.

If your network has computers running these older versions of Windows, the differences in OSs show up in these areas:

- **Default networking protocols**—You might have configured older computers to use the NetBIOS or SPX/IPX protocols as the primary networking protocol. Windows 7 and Vista require that you use TCP/IP. And, it's best if you use *only* TCP/IP.

- **LLDP mapping**—By default, Windows XP and Windows 2000 computers did not come with support for LLDP; without LLDP, these computers will appear as "orphans" on the network map display. You can download and install an LLDP add-on for Windows XP, but not for Windows 2000.

- **Password Protected Sharing (Simple File Sharing)**—Windows 7, Vista, XP, and 2000 can provide username/password security for shared files and folders. Windows 7, Vista, and XP also have a "passwordless" option that Windows 2000 doesn't have. You might need to work around this.

- **HomeGroup networking**—Windows 7 lets you join your computers in a homegroup, which simplifies file sharing security. A Windows 7 homegroup member can still share files and printers with older versions of Windows, but there are some subtleties that we explain in this chapter.

We cover these topics in the next four sections.

Setting TCP/IP as the Default Network Protocol

When installed, Windows 2000 and XP were set up to use the TCP/IP network protocol for file and printer sharing. If your network previously included Windows 95, 98, or Me computers, you might have changed the network protocols to simplify internetworking with the older operating systems.

Because Windows 7 and Vista support only TCP/IP, you need to make sure that TCP/IP is enabled on your Windows 2000 and XP computers. Also, Windows networking works much more reliably when every computer on the network has the exact same set of protocols installed. You should ensure that TCP/IP is the *only* installed network protocol.

Follow these steps on all your computers that run Windows 2000 Professional, XP Home Edition, or XP Professional:

 note

These instructions don't apply if your computer is part of a corporate network, especially one that uses Novell NetWare servers. If your computer is connected to a corporate network, your network administrator will make all necessary changes for you.

1. On Windows XP, log on using a Computer Administrator account. On Windows 2000, log on using the Administrator account.

2. On Windows XP, click Start, Control Panel, Network and Internet Connections; then click the Network Connections icon. On Windows 2000, click Start, Settings, Network and Dial-Up Connections.

3. Right-click the Local Area Connection icon and select Properties.

4. Look in the list of installed components and make sure that Internet Protocol (TCP/IP) is listed. If not, click Install, select Protocols, click Add, and select Internet Protocol (TCP/IP). If your network uses manually assigned (static) IP addresses, configure the Internet Protocol entry just as you configured your Windows 7 computers.

5. Look in the list of installed components for the NWLink IPX/SPX or NetBEUI protocols. Select these entries and click Uninstall.

6. Click OK to close the Local Area Connection Properties dialog box.

7. From the menu in the main window (Network Connections on Windows XP, Network and Dial-Up Connections on Windows 2000), select Advanced, Advanced Settings. Select the Adapters and Bindings tab.

8. In the top list, select Local Area Connection. In the lower list, make sure that Internet Protocol (TCP/IP) is checked under both File and Printer Sharing for Microsoft Networks and Client for Microsoft Networks.

9. Click OK to close the dialog box.

After checking all your computers, restart *all* your computers if you had to make changes on *any* of them.

Installing the LLDP Responder for Windows XP

Windows 7 and Vista include a graphical network map feature that's pretty and might even be useful. The problem is that it diagrams only Windows 7 and Vista computers and most, but not all, network hardware devices such as routers, switches, and hubs.

Computers and network appliances that offer Windows file sharing and are part of the same workgroup also show up on the display, but they appear as disconnected icons at the bottom of the map. You can't do anything about this for Windows 2000 computers, but Microsoft did create an add-on to Windows XP called the LLDP Responder for Windows XP that lets XP computers appear on the network wiring diagram.

To download the software, search Microsoft.com or Google for "Link Layer Topology Discovery (LLTD) Responder." You need to install it on each of your XP computers while logged on as a Computer Administrator. After you install it, it starts to work immediately—no configuration steps are needed.

Some Computers Are Missing from the Network Map

If computer names are missing from the network map, the network has elected a browser master that doesn't have all the protocols used by Windows networking computers on your LAN. This is a random selection, so be sure to install and bind the same set of protocols on every workstation in your LAN.

If a Windows XP computer appears but is shown at the bottom of the map, download and install the LLTD Responder for Windows XP. Visit http://support.microsoft.com for downloading instructions.

If you have a network router, hub, switch, or other device that does not appear correctly on the network map, visit the manufacturer's website to see if they can provide a firmware update that includes LLTD support.

Be careful to print copies of any network device's configuration screens before updating its firmware. You might also see if the device includes a "save configuration to disk" option. But don't forgo the screen printouts. Often, after a firmware upgrade, network devices revert to their original factory settings and, in some cases, won't accept previously saved configuration files—you'll need to reconfigure them entirely by hand.

Password Protection and Simple File Sharing

On small Windows networks (that is, networks that aren't managed by a Windows Server computer using the Domain security model), each computer is separately responsible for managing usernames and passwords. Before Windows XP, this made it difficult to securely share files across the network—you had to create accounts for each of your users on every one of your computers, using the same password for each user on each computer.

Windows XP introduced a concept called Simple File Sharing; when enabled, it entirely eliminated security for file sharing. All network access was done in the context of the Guest user account, regardless of the remote user's actual account name. Essentially, anyone with physical access to your network could access any shared file. This made it much easier for other people in your home and office to get to each other's files. (Horrifyingly, it was enabled by default, and there was no Windows Firewall when XP first came out—so everyone on the Internet also could get to your files, until Windows XP Service Pack 2 was released. But I digress.)

Windows 7 and Vista also include Simple File Sharing, although it's now called Password Protected Sharing. And, the effect of disabling and enabling the feature is reversed on the two newer operating systems. Table 18.1 shows the settings and the results.

Table 18.1   File Sharing Settings on Windows 7, Vista, and XP

Windows 7 and Vista: Password Protected Sharing	XP Professional: Simple File Sharing	...Means Account and Password Are
On	Unchecked	Required
Off	Checked	Not required

This setting is not always changeable. In Windows XP Home Edition, Simple File Sharing cannot be turned off. In all other versions of Windows it can be turned on or off, except if the computer is a member of a domain network. In this case, passwords are always required.

Finally, Windows 7 has a new twist in the way that security works when Password Protected Sharing is turned off. On Vista and XP, when passwords are not required, *all* network access uses the Guest account. Thus, anyone on the network can access any file in a shared folder only if the file can be accessed by Guest, or by the user group "Everyone."

But on Windows 7, it works this way: When a remote user attempts to use a folder or file shared by a Windows 7 computer with Password Protected Sharing turned off,

- If the remote user's account matches an account in the Windows 7 computer *and* that account has a password set, that account is used for file access.

- If the remote user's account matches an account in the Windows 7 computer but that account has no password set, then the Guest account is used.

- If the remote user's account matches no account in the Windows 7 computer, the Guest account is used.

This might seem convoluted, but this is actually a very useful change. First of all, this change was necessary to support the new HomeGroup feature. All homegroup member computers use a special, password-protected account named HomeGroupUser$ to access other member computers, and this change lets it work whether Password Protected Sharing is turned on or off. Second, it gives you the *option* of giving designated users additional access privileges, without requiring you to set up a full-blown security scheme.

I know this has probably given you a headache by now. You probably just want to know how to get at the library of pictures stored on your old computer. In the end, it can be pretty easy to decide how to set things up, based on how concerned you need to be about security.

To see how to set up your network, decide which of the following three categories best describes your environment:

1. **My computer is part of a corporate domain network.**

   In this case: Accounts and passwords are always required. Your network administrator sets these up. Use the Security tab on any folder that you share to select the users and groups to which you want to grant access.

2. **Ease of use is my priority, and network security is not a great concern.**

   In this case: Turn off Password Protected Sharing on your Windows 7 and Vista computers, and enable Simple File Sharing on Windows XP Professional computers. This lets anyone on the network access any shared folder.

   Alternatively, you can create an account named, for example, "share" on each of your computers and assign a password to it, using the same password on each computer. When you share folders, be sure that you give Everyone or this "share" account permission to use the folder, as discussed in Chapter 20 under "Sharing Resources." When you want to use a shared folder or printer stored on another computer, Windows will prompt you for a username and password. Enter username *share* and the password you chose for the *share* account.

   In any case, you *must* make sure that a firewall is set up to block File and Printer Sharing access over your Internet connection. Use a connection-sharing router, Windows Firewall, or a third-party firewall program to do this. If you have a wireless network, you *must* enable WPA or WEP security.

   If you have Windows 2000 computers on your network, see if you can get by without sharing any printers or folders from those computers—let them use resources shared by your XP and Windows 7 computers. Otherwise, you must create an account on the Windows 2000 computers—everyone can use a single account (for example, "share," as described previously), or create an account for every user.

3. **Network security is important to me; I want specific control over which users can use which shared files and folders.**

   In this case: Turn on Password Protected Sharing on your Windows 7 and Vista computers, and disable Simple File Sharing on any XP Professional computers. Do not share sensitive resources from any computer that runs Windows XP Home Edition (or do not use XP Home Edition at all). Do not create a homegroup.

   On every computer that does share sensitive folders or printers with the network, you need to create an account for every user who needs access to the shared folders or printers. For each user, be sure to create an account with the same name and the same password as on that user's own computer.

> **note**
>
> If you change your password on any computer, it's a good idea to make the same change on every computer where you have an account. This way, you won't be asked to supply your password whenever you use network resources.

To change the Simple File Sharing setting on Windows XP Professional, follow these steps:

1. Log on as a Computer Administrator.

2. Click Start, My Computer.

3. Press and release the Alt key to display the menu. Select Tools, Folder Options, and then select the View tab.

4. Scroll to the bottom of the Advanced Settings list. Simple File Sharing is the last entry in the list. Check or uncheck the entry as desired.

More discussion of file sharing password arrangements is found in Chapter 17, "Creating a Windows Network," and in Chapter 32, "Protecting Your Network from Hackers and Snoops."

 note

All of these rules about whether a password is required or not are interpreted by the computer that is *sharing* a folder or printer. When any version of Windows *uses* a folder or printer shared by another computer, *that* computer sets the rules for requiring a password. For example, XP Home Edition never requires an account or password when someone wants to use its shared folders, but it can still use password-protected shared resources shared by, say, Windows 7 or even a Windows domain server.

Using Windows Vista and XP with a Homegroup

If you have two or more Windows 7 computers, you can set up a homegroup (as described in Chapter 17) to simplify sharing libraries, folders, and printers. The HomeGroup system is based on regular Windows file sharing, so computers running other operating systems can also participate in your network.

The easiest way to make XP and Vista fit in is to disable password protected sharing on all your computers. (Password protected sharing is discussed in the previous section.) Here are the instructions for doing this on various versions of Windows:

- **Windows 7**—Click Start, Control Panel, View Network Status and Tasks (under Network and Internet), Change Advanced Sharing Settings. Scroll down, select Turn Off Password Protected Sharing, and then click Save Settings.

- **Windows Vista**—Click Start, Control Panel, Set Up File Sharing (under Network and Internet). Click the circular icon to the right of Password Protected sharing, click Turn Off Password Protected Sharing, and then click Apply. You might need to confirm a user account control prompt.

- **Windows XP Professional**—Log on as a computer administrator. Click Start, My Computer. In the menu, select Tools, Folder Options, and then select the View tab. Scroll the list down to the bottom, check Simple File Sharing, and then click OK.

- **Windows XP Home Edition**—No adjustments are necessary.

Now Windows 7 computers will connect to other Windows 7 computers using the special HomeGroupUser$ account, but all other combinations will use the Guest account. This means you need to make sure that resources are shared so that "Everyone" can use them. In particular, the file security settings for the shared folder and its contents must be set so that Everyone has read or read and write permission.

To ensure that this happens, use the following procedures when you're sharing folders on various versions of Windows:

- **Windows 7**—Right-click a folder or library and select Share With, Share with Homegroup (Read) or Share with Homegroup (Read/Write). Then, right-click it again and select Share With, Specific People. Type or select Everyone in the drop-down list, and click Add. If you want other users to be able to change the contents of the folder, next to Everyone, click the word Read in the Permissions column and select Read/Write. Click Share to finish.

- **Windows Vista**—Right-click a folder and select Share. Type or select Everyone in the drop-down list, and click Add. If you want other users to be able to change the contents of the folder, next to Everyone, click the word Reader in the Permissions column and select Contributor. Click Share to finish.

- **Windows XP Professional or Home Edition**—Right-click a folder and select Sharing and Security. Select Sharing This Folder and click Apply. Select the Security tab. Under Group or User Names, if there is an entry for Everyone, select it; otherwise, click Add, type the word **Everyone**, press Enter, and select the entry for Everyone. In the lower section, in the Allow column, Read & Execute, List Folder Contents, and Read should be checked. If you would like to let other network users modify the contents of the folder, check Modify. Click OK to finish.

 caution

If you give Everyone permission to change files, you must be sure that your network is secured. If you have a wireless network, you must have it set up so that it has WEP or WPA security enabled (that is, so that a password or key is required to use the network). If you connect to the Internet, you must be sure that Windows Firewall or a third-party firewall product is set up to block Windows file sharing. If you don't secure your network, "Everyone" means "anyone in the world," and that's a recipe for disaster.

If you want to use passwords to protect access to shared folders, you should leave password-protected sharing turned on. There are two ways in which you can deal with the Windows XP and Vista computers:

- Set up accounts on every computer using the same account name and password for each person, on each computer. This will give you complete control over who has access to which folders shared by Windows 7, Vista, and XP Professional. (Per-user security is not available on folders shared by XP Home.)

- Set up a single account that you'll use for file sharing, perhaps named *share*, on every computer, with the same password on every computer. Use this account when you set the permissions on shared folders, and use this account when Windows asks for an account and password when you connect to another computer.

If you share your printer, it's enough just to enable sharing. By default, all versions of Windows enable Everyone to print to every installed printer, so anyone on the network should be able to print to any shared printer without changing the security settings.

Internetworking with Windows 95, 98, and Me

Internetworking between Windows 7 and Windows 95, 98, or Me requires some additional setup work.

First, Windows computers have difficulty "seeing" each other if you don't have the exact same set of networking protocols installed on every computer on the network. You need to ensure that every Windows 95, 98, and Me computer has the TCP/IP protocol installed, and you also must uninstall the NetBEUI and IPX/SPX protocols from them.

Second, the default password security settings used when Windows 7 is installed make Windows 7 harder for a network hacker (or hardware hacker) to break your Windows 7 passwords. Unless you turn off Password Protected Sharing, you need to change one of Windows 7's security settings. This significantly increases the risk that someone could break into your computer.

If you really must use Windows 95, 98, or Me on your network, you most likely need to change the protocol settings on the older computers, using the following steps. You might be asked to insert your Windows installation CD, unless your computer manufacturer copied its entire contents to your hard drive.

 caution

Microsoft no longer creates security updates for Windows 95, 98, or Me. Furthermore, to be able to access resources shared by Windows 7 from Windows 9x or Me, you might need to reduce Windows 7's security level considerably.

These OSs really should no longer be used. I'm not trying to make more money for Microsoft; it's simply not safe to continue to use these OSs in any situation where Internet access also exists. If you must continue to use these OSs to run specific applications, consider running them within Microsoft Virtual PC or VMware instead, with their networking functions disabled.

1. On your Windows 9x or Me computer, click Start, Control Panel, and then open the Network icon.

2. In the components list, select entries whose names start with "NetBEUI" or "IPX/SPX Compatible Protocol," and click Remove. Repeat for any additional entries.

3. Make sure that Client for Microsoft Networks appears in the list. If it does not, click Add, Client, and select Client for Microsoft Networks. Click OK as necessary to return to the Network control panel dialog box.

4. If your Windows 9x/Me computer is a member of a corporate domain network, view the Access Control tab and select User-Level Access Control. Enter the name of a domain controller computer. (Your network administrator will help with this.)

   On home or small-office networks, view the Access Control tab and make sure that Share-Level Access Control is selected.

5. Click OK to close the dialog boxes. You might be prompted to insert your Windows installation CD if you had to add the Client for Microsoft Networks in step 3.

6. Let Windows restart.

If you need to share printers or folders from your Windows 9x or Me computers for use by computers running Windows 2000, XP, Vista, or 7, do not set a password for the shared folder. These newer versions of Windows cannot supply a password in the way that Windows 9*x* or Me expects. The only security option you have is whether to select Read-Only or Full on the Sharing tab of the folders you select to share. "Full" lets other network users add to, change, or delete files in the shared folder.

You should not expect to be able to access folders or printers shared by computers running Windows 7 from computers running Windows 9*x* or Me, unless you've turned Password Protected Sharing off and use the username Guest. (Windows 9*x*/Me cannot provide valid username and password information to Windows 7 unless you make unacceptably risky changes to Windows 7's password database.)

Internetworking with UNIX and Linux

The UNIX operating system, originally developed in the 1970s at AT&T's Bell Laboratories as a platform for internal software development and as a "workbench" for programmers, is still evolving and growing. Most of the Internet software you're familiar with today was originally developed on UNIX systems, in fact. The Open Source phenomenon (which is by no means new but is certainly resurgent) has also produced no-cost UNIX clones such as NetBSD and Linux. Perhaps hundreds of millions of people use these UNIX-type OSs every day, sometimes without even knowing it. For example, the Apple Mac and iPhone OSs are based on NetBSD, and Linux can be found in home computers, network routers, TiVo digital video recorders, engineering workstations, Internet servers, cell phones, IBM mainframes, laptops for children in the developing world, and space probes.

This section looks at ways to network Windows 7 with UNIX-type OSs. Although many of the examples involve Linux, most of the examples can be translated to almost any UNIX-type OS. And because typing "UNIX-type" is already getting tiresome, from here on, I sometimes write just "UNIX," but I always mean "UNIX and/or Linux and/or Mac OS X."

Samba

Samba is an open source (free) software suite available on most UNIX-like OSs. The Samba server program makes it possible for UNIX computers to share folders and printers that Windows users can access, and the Samba client tools let UNIX users access folders and printers shared by Windows computers. Samba is included with Apple's OS X, which is how Macs get their Windows file sharing capability. The names of the Samba programs start with the letters smb, which stands for Server Message Block. This is the name of the network protocol on which Windows file sharing is based.

 note

You can get more information about Samba and download a version for your UNIX system from www.samba.org. Most Linux distributions include a version of Samba and install it by default. For a good Samba introduction and reference, check out *The Official Samba-3 HOWTO and Reference Guide* (Prentice Hall, 2003, ISBN 0131453556).

Samba Client Tools

To access file services on a Windows server from UNIX, you must know exactly what resources are available from a given host on the network. Samba includes a command-line program called smb-client for just that purpose. This application enables you to list available Windows shares and printers from within UNIX. For example, the command smb-client -L //lombok lists all the folders and printers shared by the computer named lombok.

When you know the name of the desired shared folder, the smbmount command enables you to mount the Windows share on the local (UNIX) file system. The command

smbmount //lombok/shareddocs /mnt/winshare -U brian

mounts the SharedDocs folder shared by computer lombok to the local directory /mnt/winshare. The -U switch tells smb-client what username to use when trying to mount the share. You are prompted for a password.

You also can use a Windows printer from a UNIX client, but the procedure is complex, and is beyond the scope of this chapter. Some Linux distributions include a GUI print configuration tool to simplify the process. In any case I recommend that you read the SMB How-To at http://en.tldp.org/HOWTO/SMB-HOWTO.html.

note

If the Windows computer is running Windows 7 with Password Protected Sharing turned off, you can specify any nonexistent account name to gain access using the Guest account. If you specify a valid account name, you will gain access using this account. This differs from previous versions of Windows where, if Password Protected Sharing is turned off, the Guest account is used no matter what. Password Protected Sharing is discussed earlier in the chapter under "Password Protection and Simple File Sharing."

Samba Server Tools

Samba also includes tools and servers to make your UNIX system look just like a Windows-based network server; this capability lets your Windows computers use files and printers shared by UNIX systems.

The parameters for configuring Samba in a server capacity are contained in the file /etc/smb.conf on the UNIX host. The default file included with Samba has comments for every parameter to explain each one. Configuring the Samba server is beyond the scope of this book. However, I can offer a few pointers:

- Some OSs, such as the Mac OS X, include a GUI tool to configure Samba file sharing. These tools make the job a lot easier.

- If you have to set up file sharing by hand, read the documentation and FAQs for your Samba version before starting the setup procedure. A good place to start is http://en.tldp.org/HOWTO/SMB-HOWTO.html.

- Configure Samba for user-specific passwords with the security option. You need to set up UNIX user accounts for each of your Windows users. Alternatively, you can set up a single UNIX account that all Windows user will share; Windows users need to supply the selected username and password when they use UNIX shares.

- Either way, set encrypt passwords = yes in smb.conf. You also need to set up a user and password file for Samba's use, which is usually specified with the smb.conf entry smb passwd file = /etc/smbpasswd. Your Samba documentation explains how to do this.

- Alternatively, you can use share-level security without a password. This makes Samba behave similar to Windows 7 with Password Protected Sharing turned off. However, in this case, you *must* take care to prevent SMB access to your UNIX computer from the Internet. To be precise, you must be sure that TCP port 445 is blocked.

When you have finished editing the `smb.conf` file, you can test to see that the syntax is correct by using the Samba program `testparm`. `testparm` checks `smb.conf` for internal "correctness" before you actually use it in a production environment.

Printing to UNIX Queues from Windows

You can configure Samba to offer standard Windows shared printer service. As an alternative, Windows 7 has built-in support to send output to UNIX-based printers using the Line Printer Remote (LPR) protocol. You can install a standard Windows printer whose output is directed to a UNIX system and can use this printer just as you would any local or networked Windows printer.

➡ *For instruction on connecting to an LPR-based printer,* **see** *"Using UNIX and LPR Printers," p. 555.*

Printing to Windows Printers from UNIX

You can install software on Windows 7 to let UNIX users print to any local printers shared by your computer. This is the receiving end of the LPR protocol, and it's called Line Printer Daemon (LPD) Print Service.

To install this service, log on as a Computer Administrator and follow these steps:

1. Click Start, Control Panel, Programs, Turn Windows Features On or Off.

2. Scroll through the list of features and open Print and Document Services.

3. Check LPD Print Service, and then click OK.

Carriage Returns and Line Feeds Are Mangled

If you send plain-text files from UNIX machines to Windows printers using `lpr` and Print Services for UNIX and find that carriage returns and line feeds are mangled (for example, line feeds are inserted where just carriage returns were present in text that should have been overprinted), you need to disable the translation of both newlines and carriage returns, or just carriage returns, by adding a value to the Registry.

➡ *For instructions and warnings about using the Registry editor,* **see** *"Using Regedit,"* **p. 812.**

Continued...

Use the Registry editor called Regedit to find the key HKEY_LOCAL_MACHINE\System\ CurrentControlSet\Control\Print\Printers*printername*\PrinterDriverData, where *printername* is the name of the shared printer the UNIX user is using. Then,

1. Select the key PrinterDriverData and choose Edit, New, DWORD Value. Enter the name **Winprint_TextNoTranslation**, and set the value to **1**.

2. To prevent the server from replacing CR with CR+LF but still have it replace LF with CR+LF, add the DWORD value **Winprint_TextNoCRTranslation** with the value 1.

3. After making either of these additions, go to Computer Management, view Services, right-click TCP/IP Print Server, and select Restart.

Some Windows printer drivers do not correctly implement overprinted lines. You might find that thes lines are now correctly stacked on top of each other, but only the text from the top-most line is visible. You might need to use the binary mode flag (-o l) in your lpr command and add a form feed to the end of your file.

If you later decide to undo the Registry change, you can remove the value item or set its value to 0 and then restart the service.

Services for NFS

Windows 7 Ultimate and Enterprise editions come with client support for the network file system (NFS) file sharingsystem used on many UNIX systems. By "client support," I mean that Windows 7 Ultimate and Enterprise editions can use files and folders shared by NFS file servers, but they cannot share files to the network using NFS. It's an optional component and is not installed by default.

To install client support for NFS file resources, follow these steps:

1. Log on as a Computer Administrator.

2. Install Services for NFS by clicking Start, Control Panel, Programs, Turn Windows Features On or Off. Expand the Services for NFS entry and check both Administrative Tools and Client for NFS. Click OK to complete the installation.

3. Click Start, Control Panel, System and Security, Administrative Tools.

4. In the tool list, double-click Services for Network File System (NFS).

This displays the Services for Network File System management tool. The tool is not put together in the usual way. The right pane contains only help information. It's useful, though; click on any of the links to display the Windows Help pages for NFS. The management functions are found in the left pane.

To configure the client, follow these steps:

1. To select the method that NFS should use to map Windows logon names to UNIX logon names, right-click Services for NFS in the left pane and select Properties. If your network provides UNIX name-mapping information through Active Directory, check Active Directory and enter the name of the Windows domain. If a User Name Mapping Service server exists on the network, check Use Name Mapping and enter the hostname of the mapping server. Either way, your network administrator should provide you with this information.

   If you select neither Active Directory nor User Name Mapping, the NFS client will access shares anonymously. The NFS server might restrict or reject anonymous access.

2. To select whether to use "hard" or "soft" mounts, right-click Client for NFS in the left pane and select Properties. This setting determines how many times the client service will attempt to reconnect to a server that goes offline or becomes unreachable. Microsoft recommends using soft mounts, although your network administrator might advise otherwise.

   This Properties dialog box also lets you determine whether the client uses TCP, UDP, or TCP and UDP for NFS access. You should be able to use the default TCP/UDP setting.

3. To set the UNIX access mask that the client should use when creating new files or folders in an NFS share, right-click Client for NFS in the left pane, select Properties, and view the Permissions tab. Check the boxes corresponding to the permissions that you want to grant on new files that you might create. (This setting corresponds to the umask setting in a UNIX shell; the default Client settings correspond to a umask of 755.)

To start or stop the client service, right-click Client for NFS and select Start Service or Stop Service. Normally, it should start immediately on installation and whenever you start Windows.

Subsystem for UNIX-Based Applications

With Windows 7 Ultimate and Enterprise editions, Microsoft offers a free set of tools called the Subsystem for UNIX-based Applications (SUA). SUA provides almost all the utilities you need to seamlessly glue together a network that includes Windows, UNIX, and Linux computers and services.

 note

SUA is available only on Windows 7 Ultimate and Enterprise editions. It is not available on any other Windows 7 versions.

The "Subsystem" part of the name is significant. The Windows NT kernel on which Windows 7 is based was designed to allow direct support of other OS models in addition to Windows. SUA is actually a full-fledged UNIX OS environment that runs *in parallel* to Windows, not "over" it. SUA runs UNIX executable files directly and provides a mostly POSIX-compatible environment with complete case-sensitive filenames, fork() and pthreads support, a single-root file system, and so on.

When the optional Software Development Kit (SDK) component is downloaded and installed, a full UNIX toolkit is available, containing over 300 standard UNIX programs. (About all that's missing is an X Window server.)

To install SUA on Windows 7 Ultimate or Enterprise, follow these steps:

1. Click Start, Control Panel, Programs, Turn Windows Features On or Off, and check Subsystem for UNIX-Based Applications. Click OK to perform the installation.

   If you need to run only a few specific UNIX applications that you already possess, you can stop at this point.

   If you want to install the full complement of UNIX utilities and development tools and/or the X Window System environment, proceed to step 2.

2. Click Start, All Programs, Subsystem for UNIX-Based Applications, and select Download Utilities for Subsystem for UNIX-Based Applications. Download and save the installation package to a temporary location.

3. Right-click the downloaded file and select Run As Administrator. If you want to install the package on only one computer, take note of the temporary file location displayed in the Unzip to Folder field, and then click Unzip. This unzips the files to the temporary folder and automatically runs the setup program. Then proceed to step 4.

   If you want to install the package on several computers, follow these additional steps:

   a. Uncheck the option When Done Unzipping Open Setup.exe.

   b. Create a folder named **SUA SDK Setup** on a network-shared folder.

   c. Set the Unzip to Folder path to this new folder. Then click Unzip to unzip the setup files.

   d. To install the utilities and SDK programs on a given computer, locate and open the SUA SDK Setup folder. Right-click `setup.exe` and select Run As Administrator.

4. Click Next to start the installation wizard. Successive wizard pages ask you to enter your name and organization, and approve the license agreement. In the fourth page, you are asked whether to perform a standard or custom installation. The standard installation installs the base SUA utilities (a set of BSD UNIX programs) and base SDK components (mostly standard include files, libraries, and build utilities).

   If you select custom installation, you can additionally elect to install the SVR-5 utilities (a set of programs deriving from UNIX SVR-5), GNU compilers and utilities, the GNU SDK, Perl, and a Visual Studio debugger add-in. To select a component, click the red X and select Will Be Installed on Local Hard Drive.

   In most cases, you probably want to select the custom installation and install all components.

5. Click Next until you reach the Security Settings page. Here, you can enable `setuid` behavior and case sensitivity for filenames and system objects.

   With `setuid`, you can mark a program so that when anyone runs it, it runs with the security context of the program's owner. In Windows terms, it automatically uses "run as" whenever it's run, and the user doesn't need to enter a password. Case sensitivity lets the Windows file system treat upper- and lowercase letters as distinct; for example, `Note.txt` and `NOTE.TXT` are considered to be different filenames, and both can exist in the same folder. UNIX applications treat them as different files. (However, Windows applications do not and just open a file arbitrarily.)

Both `setuid` and case sensitivity are the norm on UNIX systems. Some UNIX programs require them, but they are foreign concepts to most Windows users, and they have both positive and negative security implications. Microsoft recommends disabling `setuid` unless you are sure that your UNIX applications or daemons (services) require it. Case sensitivity is usually required for correct operation of UNIX software-development tools (makefiles).

For more information, open and read `install.htm`, which was unzipped into the temporary folder or network shared folder in step 3. Also remember that you can change these settings after installation by editing the Windows Registry and rebooting, as noted in `install.htm`.

6. After the installer finishes, if you enabled case sensitivity or `setuid`, restart Windows. When Windows is back up again, log on as a Computer Administrator.

7. Click Start, All Programs, Subsystem for UNIX-Based Applications, Check for Critical Updates. This takes you to a Microsoft web page that lets you check for security updates to the utilities.

Although updates for the UNIX Subsystem itself are delivered through Windows Update and Automatic Updates, security fixes for the downloaded utilities are not. You need to remember to periodically use this menu selection to check for security updates to the utilities.

When the utilities and SDK have been installed, you can start a UNIX shell (Command Prompt window) by clicking Start, All Programs, Subsystem for UNIX-Based Applications, and either C Shell, Korn Shell, or SVR-5 Korn Shell, depending on your preference. The What's New menu item provides information on how SUA differs from the Windows XP Services for UNIX and provides an overview of SUA features.

For detailed help information, click Start, All Programs, Subsystem for UNIX-Based Applications, Help for Subsystem for UNIX-Based Applications. The UNIX `man`, `apropos`, and other standard help programs are available within the UNIX shells.

Internetworking with Macintosh

The Apple Macintosh is arguably *the* computer of choice in the music, graphic arts, design, and publishing worlds. Apple has even moved to the Intel processor platform, and you can run Windows on a Mac, if you want to. But if you're a Mac fan, you probably don't want to.

Although Macs used to live pretty much in a world apart, it's common now for both Macs and Windows computers to need to coexist on the same network. However, Macs normally use a proprietary file sharing system called AppleTalk File Protocol (AFP), while Windows computers use a protocol called Server Message Block (SMB).

To link Macs and PCs on a network, either the Macs must learn to "speak" SMB or the Windows computers must speak AFP. Both solutions are possible. On a corporate network based on Windows Server, your network administrator can install a component called Services for Macintosh (SFM), which speaks AFP to make Windows-based resources visible to Macs, and resources shared by Macs visible to Windows users. The process of installing and configuring SFM is not complicated, but it needs to be done by the administrator of a Windows Server computer; as such, it's beyond the scope of this book.

Microsoft appears to have lost interest in providing support for Mac users in the home and small office. Fortunately, Apple has stepped up and provided Windows-compatible networking support as a standard part of OS X. You can also add Windows networking support to older Mac OS computers.

We cover these options in the next several sections. First, though, let's talk about other issues that come up when Windows and Macs need to work together.

Compatibility Issues

If you share files between Macs and Windows computers on your network, there are some compatibility issues that you should be aware of.

Resource Data Issues

The first issue arises because Mac files actually consist of two separate parts, called *forks*:

- The data fork, which contains data, document text, program code, and so on

- The resource fork, which in applications contains language-specific strings and dialog box layouts for programs, and in documents contains the association information that links a document to the application that created it

The two parts can be read and written to completely independently. It's as if each Mac file is composed of two bundled but separate files.

Windows also supports this concept. On Windows, the separate parts are called *streams* rather than forks. But, for reasons unknown, they're not used for Mac file sharing. When a Mac file is copied to a Windows shared folder, the resource fork data is stored in a separate hidden file. If the Mac file is named `special.doc`, the resource data is put into a file named `._special.doc`. It's invisible unless you enable the display of hidden files in Windows Explorer.

The problem is that if you move, edit, or rename the main document or application file in Windows, the resource file might be left behind or end up with the wrong name. Then, on the Mac side, the Mac will no longer know what application to use to open the document, or, in the case of an application program, the application will not run. Thus, it's best not to store Mac applications on Windows shares if they will be renamed or moved.

Mac Files Have Lost Application Associations

After a Windows user edits a shared file and a Mac user tries to open the file, the Mac Finder may say it can't find the application required to open the document. What happened is that the file's resource fork was stripped out when the file was edited in Windows, so the file's Type and Creator codes are missing. The Mac user should drag and drop the file onto the application's icon or manually locate the application, then resave the file. This will restore the association for future edits.

The Type and Creator codes can also be set using a Mac resource editor. However, resource editing is tricky and best not done unless it's an emergency.

Type and Creator codes are case sensitive. MSWD is not the same as MsWd or mswd. Case can often cause confusion if you must restore the codes after they were stripped on a trip through Windows or DOS.

Filename Compatibility Issues

Mac filenames can have up to 255 characters and can contain any character except the colon (:).

Windows permits filenames up to 256 characters in length but has a longer list of unacceptable characters: the colon (:), backslash (\), forward slash (/), question mark (?), asterisk (*), quotation mark ("), greater-than symbol (>), less-than symbol (<), and pipe symbol (¦).

Therefore, for files that will be shared, it's best to avoid all of these characters when you name files on your Mac.

Multiple-Use Issues

Some Mac applications don't properly install themselves when they're installed into a Windows shared folder. An error occurs when more than one user tries to run the application at the same time.

Application Concurrency Issues

When a Mac application is installed on a shared folder stored on a Windows computer, an "Unable to Open File" error occurs on Macs when more than one Mac user attempts to run the application concurrently.

"Unable to Open File" Error Occurs on Macs

Some Mac programs fail to open their application executable files in the proper file sharing mode. You can patch the problem by using a resource editor program on the Mac:

1. Obtain a copy of ResEdit. In the past we recommended that you download it from ResExcellence (www.resexcellence.com), which was a terrific resource (pun intended) for all things resource related. As of this writing, the site is not active, but we hope that they get their act together to get it back on the air. For novice users, a better resource editor program is File Buddy, from SkyTag Software (www.skytag.com).

2. Start ResEdit or File Buddy. Select File, Get Info. In the dialog box that appears, you can select the application.

3. Put a check in the Shared check box.

4. If you're using ResEdit, quit the application and choose Yes to save the changes. In File Buddy, click OK.

Working with Mac OS X

Mac OS X comes with Windows-compatible networking support built in, via the Samba software mentioned earlier in the chapter. This means that Macs running OS X can connect directly to drives and folders shared by Windows computers. You don't even need to use the command line; the Mac GUI manages the Samba client and server components for you.

note

This section shows you how to use Windows shared files from your Mac, and how to share files from your Mac for use by Windows. To see how to set up file sharing on Windows, see Chapter 20, "Using a Windows Network."

Using Windows Shared Files on the Mac

On OS X 10.5 and later editions, you can easily browse folders shared by Windows computers from any Finder window. In the left pane, under Shared, you can select a Windows computer from the list of detected computers, and then browse into its shared folders, as shown in Figure 18.1. When you select a remote computer, OS X will attempt to connect to the computer using your Mac account's username and password so that it can display a list of available shared folders. If this fails, you can use a different account by clicking the Connect As button that will appear in the upper-right corner of the Finder window.

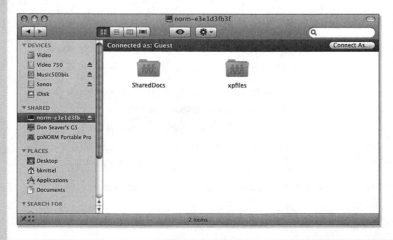

Figure 18.1

The Finder in OS X 10.5 and later lets you easily select and connect to both Mac and Windows computers.

If you are using OS X 10.4 or earlier, or if the Windows computer does not appear in the list of local computers that the Finder displays under Shared, there is an alternative way to connect. Select the Finder and choose Go, Connect to Server. The dialog box shown in Figure 18.2 appears.

You can enter the UNC name of the shared folder directly, in the format smb://*computername*/*sharename*, where *computername* is the name of the Windows computer or its IP address, and *sharename* is the name of the shared folder. For example, the Public folder on a computer named MyVPC-U could be entered as smb://myvpc-u/public, or using the computer's IP address, as something like smb://192.168.0.12/public. Click Connect to proceed.

Figure 18.2
The Connect to Server dialog box lets a Mac OS X computer connect directly to a folder shared by Windows. Enter `smb:` followed by the share's UNC path, or click Browse.

Enter a UNC path

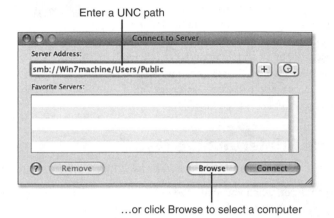

...or click Browse to select a computer

You can click the + button to add the path to the Favorites list.

Click the Browse button to select from a list of detected Mac and Windows computers.

Whichever method you use, when you connect, a login dialog box may appear. If you're connecting to a Windows 7 computer on a home or small office network, the following applies:

- If Password Protected Sharing is enabled, or to access files that are shared only to specified user accounts, choose Connect As Registered User. Enter a username and password that is valid on the Windows 7 computer. (On a home or small office workgroup network, you can ignore the Workgroup or Domain entry, if it appears. Fill in just the Name and Password entries.) You will connect with the file and folder access rights associated with this account.

- If you have disabled Password Protected Sharing, select Connect As Guest; or, enter the username Guest with no password. (Actually, you can enter any *invalid* username, with any password.) This gives you the file and folder access rights granted to Everyone. In most cases, this means that you will have access to the Public folder but no other shared folders, unless the person who shared the other folders explicitly granted rights to Everyone.

If you are connecting to a Windows computer on a Windows domain network, enter a valid domain username and password.

When the Mac has made the network connection, the shared folder is displayed in a Finder window like any other folder.

To disconnect from the network share on OS X 10.5 or later, click the eject button next to the computer's name under Shared in the Finder window. On OS X 10.4, drag the shared folder desktop icon to the trash, or locate it in the Finder and click the Eject button.

Now, recall the point I made earlier about Mac files having two parts, or *forks*. If you copy a file from a Mac to a shared Windows folder, Windows might create an extra hidden file to contain the resource information for the file. The resource file's name will consist of a period and an underscore followed by the name of the main file. Windows users need to move and rename these files together; otherwise, Mac users will receive errors when they try to access the files.

note

When a Mac user opens a Window share, the Finder creates a file named .DS Store and sometimes also one named ._.DS_Store. These hold Mac desktop information. Windows users should ignore these files, just as Mac users should ignore the file desktop.ini.

Using Windows Printers on the Mac

If you are using a Mac, to use a printer that is shared by a Windows computer, follow these steps:

1. On the Windows computer, when you share the printer, be sure to use a share name that's no more than 12 letters long. If you use a longer name, the printer might not appear in the list of printers on the Mac.

2. On the Mac, open System Preferences and select Print & Fax.

3. If the page is locked, click the lock icon and enter an administrator's credentials.

   Click the + button to add a printer.

   On OS X 10.4, at the bottom of the Printer Browser dialog box, click More Printers.

4. At the top of the next Printer Browser dialog box, select Windows (on OS X 10.5 and later) or Windows Printing (on OS X 10.4), and underneath, select the appropriate Windows workgroup name. In the computer list, choose the name of the computer that is sharing the printer you want to use.

5. In the Connect To dialog box, enter a username and password that is valid on the Windows computer. If you turned off Password Protected Sharing on Windows 7, you can select Connect As: Guest, or enter username Guest with no password.

6. Select the desired shared printer in the list. Open the Print Using list (on OS X 10.5 and later), or the Printer Model list (on OS X 10.4), and select the correct printer manufacturer name and model. Finally, click Add.

note

In our testing we found that there could be delays of up to a couple of minutes between printing a document from the Mac and having the Windows printer start up.

This adds the Windows printer to the list of available printers on your Mac.

Using Mac Shared Files on Windows

Mac OS X computers can share folders with Windows computers over the network, thanks to the Samba file server software that is installed as part of OS X.

To enable Windows-compatible file sharing on OS X 10.5 (Leopard), follow these steps:

1. Open System Preferences and select Sharing. If the panel is locked, click the lock icon and enter an administrative password.

2. If File Sharing is not checked, check it. Select folders to share, and for each selected folder, choose the user accounts that can access the share. This much is standard for file sharing on the Macs. The next step lets you use these same folders from Windows computers.

3. Click Options, and check Share Files and Folders Using SMB, as shown in Figure 18.3.

To enable Windows-compatible file sharing on OS X 10.4 (Tiger), follow these steps:

1. Open System Preferences and select Sharing. Check Windows Sharing.

2. Click the Accounts button and check the names of the accounts that you want to permit to be used for Windows Sharing connections.

3. Click Show All and select Accounts.

tip

To save yourself a world of pain, create user accounts on your Mac and Windows computers using the same account names (short names, in Mac parlance) and passwords on both types of computers. From the Windows side, you cannot use or even see a list of the folders or printers shared by the Mac unless you are using a Windows account that matches up with one on the Mac and that has been enabled on the Sharing page.

Figure 18.3
Enable Windows-compatible file sharing from the Options button on the System Preferences Sharing page.

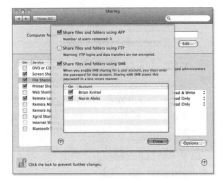

On Windows, you can use Mac shared folders just as you use folders shared from any Windows computer. Macs appear in the list of available computers in the Network folder, and you can open the shared folders from those icons.

You can also specify a Mac shared folder directly using its UNC pathname. By default, OS X 10.5 shares users' Public folders, with share names based on each user's full name. For example, the path to my Public folder might be *computername*\brian knittel's public folder. OS X 10.4 shares users' entire home directories by default, using each users's short name, so on OS 10.4 my home directory's UNC path might be *computername*\bknittel.

note

When you open the Network folder icon for a Mac running OS X 10.4, or use the net view command to view the items shared by a Mac running OS X 10.4, you will see only shared folders and printers that you have permission to use.

Using Mac Shared Printers on Windows

After enabling Windows Sharing in System Preferences, you can share your Mac's printer(s) with Windows users by selecting Show All and then clicking Print and Fax. View the Sharing tab, click Share These Printers with Other Computers, and check the printers that you want to make available to others.

To use a printer shared from a Mac on Windows, follow these steps:

1. Set up accounts on both the Mac and on Windows, using the same account name and the same password on both computers.

2. On the Mac, enable SMB File Sharing on the Mac as described under "Using Mac Shared Files on Windows," earlier in this chapter. Then, enable Printer Sharing on the System Preferences Sharing page. Select at least the printer that you want to use from Windows.

3. Follow the strange procedure that I describe next.

The strange bit is that you must trick Windows into using a PostScript printer driver, no matter what type of printer the Mac is really sharing. The Mac accepts only PostScript printer codes and converts the PostScript to the appropriate codes for its installed printer.

To connect to the Mac printer from Windows, follow these steps:

1. Click Start, Devices and Printers, Add a Printer, Add a Network, Wireless, or Bluetooth Printer.

2. Wait for the desired Mac printer to appear in the list. Double-click it. If requirements 1 or 2 from the previous list aren't met, the printer won't appear.

   It also won't appear if the Mac is on a different subnet than the Windows computer. In this case, click The Printer That I Want Isn't Listed, check Select a Shared Printer by Name, and then enter the printer share name as *ipaddress**sharename*, where *ipaddress* is the IP address of the Mac and *sharename* is the name of the Mac printer.

3. When the message "The server for the printer does not have the correct printer driver installed" appears, click OK.

4. In the Manufacturer list, select HP. In the Printers list, if the Mac printer is a color printer, select HP Color LaserJet 2800 Series PS. If the Mac printer is a black and white printer, select HP LaserJet 2300 Series PS. Then click OK.

Installing Optional Network Components

Windows 7 comes with some networking features or services that are not used in most networks but can be essential in others. I don't cover these features in great detail because your network manager will probably install them for you if they're used on your LAN.

Table 18.2 describes the optional features. Not every component is available on every version of Windows 7.

To enable any of the components, click Start, Control Panel, Programs, Turn Windows Features On or Off. Check the box next to each desired feature, and then click OK.

Table 18.2   Windows 7 Optional Networking Features

Category/Component	Description
Web and Application Services	
Internet Information Services and Internet Information Services Hostable Web Core	IIS is a full-featured web server. IIS can also be used by software developers as a platform for a new generation of peer-to-peer application software, which is why certain IIS components are provided with all versions of Windows 7. If you install an application that requires IIS, the application's installer will most likely configure it for you.
Windows Communication Foundation HTTP Activation	The HTTP Activation system can be used by .NET application software to run services on demand. This component is enabled by the application program(s) as needed. (This selection is located under Microsoft .NET Framework 3.0.)
Microsoft Message Queue (MSMQ) Server	MSMQ Server is a tool used primarily in distributed database applications. It is provided with Windows 7 primarily for use by software developers who are writing and testing such applications.
Subsystem for UNIX-based Applications (SUA)	SUA provides a UNIX-compatible environment and toolkit that can be used to migrate UNIX applications and services to Windows. SUA was discussed earlier in this chapter.
Management and Monitoring Tools	
SNMP Feature	The Simple Network Management Protocol (SNMP) is a remote monitoring and measurement tool used by some network-management systems.
WMI SNMP Provider	This allows Windows Management Instrumentation (WMI) applications to access SNMP data.
Telnet Client	This enables you to connect computers and network devices using a command-line interface. This service has significant network security risks and should not be enabled unless required by a network administrator.
Telnet Server	This enables you or an administrator to log on to your computer remotely using only a command-line interface.
TFTP Client	This can be used to retrieve files from a TFTP server. This tool is used primarily to test network boot servers or to retrieve network device firmware.
Networking Services	
Internet Printing Client	This provides support for network- or Internet-hosted printers or printing services using the Internet Printing Protocol (IPP).
LPD Print Service	This service lets UNIX computers send print output to your Windows computer's shared printers.
LPR Port Monitor	This enables you to send print output to network-connected printers or UNIX servers. (IPP, LPD, and LPR are found in the Print and Document Services list.)
RIP Listener	This service is used to listen for network routing information in large networks. Don't install it unless it's required by your network administrator.

Table 18.2 Continued

Category/Component	Description
Services for NFS	This enables you to use files shared by NFS file servers (typically UNIX file servers).
Simple TCP/IP services	This suite of services performs simple functions for testing purposes, such as echoing data to a remote computer or generating a stream of data. Don't install these services unless you're instructed to do so by a network administrator. Hackers can use them to tie up your network with pointless traffic.
Reliable Multicast Protocol	This network protocol is also called Pragmatic General Multicast, or RFC 3208. It may be required by certain file sharing or multimedia applications that transmit content to large numbers of computers at once.

The Reliable Multicast Protocol is installed using a different procedure from that used to install the other services listed in Table 18.2. If required, it can be installed for a specific network adapter using these steps:

1. Click Start, Control Panel, View Network Status and Tasks (under Network and Internet), Change Adapter Settings.

2. Right-click a network adapter and select Properties.

3. Click Install. Select Protocol, and click Add.

4. Select Reliable Multicast Protocol and click OK.

The Hosts File

If you have an office LAN, especially one with mixed and matched computers, you probably, like me, have a chart of computer names and IP addresses posted on your wall—not just computers, but routers, firewalls, monitored devices, and all manner of devices. Who knows? Soon the espresso machine might be wired in, too.

On a corporate or enterprise LAN, the LAN administrators will probably enter each device into the organization's domain name system (DNS) so that you can type a command such as `ping firewall` instead of needing to type `ping firewall.mycompany.com` or, worse, something like `ping 192.168.56.102`.

On a home or small office LAN, though, you probably don't have your own domain name server. The hosts file is the answer to this annoying situation. You can add entries to the file `\windows\system32\drivers\etc\hosts` to associate names with IP addresses. The Windows domain name lookup software looks first in the hosts file before consulting the network, so you can add entries for your own workgroup's computers and devices, regardless of OS.

The format is simple, but editing it is a bit tricky. The hosts file has become a target for adware hackers, who put fake entries in it to hijack your web browser.

To edit it, click Start, All Programs, Accessories, and right-click Notepad. Select Run As Administrator and confirm the User Account Control prompt. Then, when the Notepad window opens, open `\windows\system32\driver\etc\hosts`.

Add lines to the file, listing IP addresses at the left margin, followed by some whitespace (tabs or spaces), followed by one or more names. You can enter simple names or full domain names. Simple names are assumed to belong to your own domain.

My hosts file looks like this:

```
127.0.0.0 localhost
192.168.56.1 firewall
192.168.56.45 macmini
```

The first entry is the default entry shipped with Windows. `localhost` stands for "my own computer" and is used for internal testing of the network software.

I added the second entry myself to give a name to my network's firewall. I can now configure the firewall by typing `telnet firewall` instead of needing to look up at that sheet on the wall and type a bunch of numbers.

Finally, there's an entry for my Mac computer, `macmini`. This way, I can view its web server's home page from Internet Explorer using `http://macmini` instead of needing to remember its IP address.

This file also serves as a sort of documentation of my network because it records important IP addresses. One thing you must watch out for, though, is that Windows checks this file before using the real DNS system to look up names. If you put a name in your LAN's (or the Internet's) DNS system and the computer's IP address later changes, your hosts file will be incorrect. It's best to use this file only for machines that are in nobody's DNS system.

CONNECTING YOUR NETWORK TO THE INTERNET

It's a Great Time to Connect Your LAN to the Internet

Because you now have your computers tied together with a nifty, inexpensive local area network (LAN), it seems silly that each user should have to use a modem to gain Internet access individually. No worries: You have a host of options for shared Internet connections. You can use a high-speed connection to serve the entire LAN, or you can share a modem connection made from one designated Windows 7 computer. Either way, shared access makes online life simpler *and safer* for everyone on the network.

A shared Internet connection can actually provide better protection against hackers than can an individual connection, because a shared connection has to funnel through a router device or a software service that blocks outside attempts to connect to your computers—except on your terms. This chapter shows you several ways to set up a shared Internet connection.

 note

You should also read Chapter 32, "Protecting Your Network from Hackers and Snoops," for more details on protecting your network from hacking.

Ways to Make the Connection

When you're using a single computer, you use its analog modem or a broadband cable, DSL, or satellite modem to connect to your ISP as needed. When you share your Internet connection on a network, either you designate one computer running Windows 7 (or Vista, or XP) to make the connection or you use an inexpensive hardware device called a *connection-sharing router* or *residential gateway* to serve as a bridge between your network and a dial-up, cable, or DSL modem. Whichever method you choose, the designated computer or router automatically sets up the connection any time anybody on your network needs it.

As an overview, Figure 19.1 shows five ways you can hook up your LAN to an Internet service provider (ISP). Throughout this chapter, we'll refer to these as schemes A through E. They are

A. **Windows Internet Connection Sharing (ICS) with an analog dial-up connection**—In this scenario, the built-in software in Windows automatically dials your ISP from one computer whenever anyone on the LAN wants to connect to the Internet. This is called *demand-dialing*. (By the way, the modem doesn't have to be an external one; it can be an internal modem. I just wanted it to show up in the figure.)

B. **ICS with a broadband DSL or cable modem**—The computer that hosts the shared connection uses a second LAN adapter to connect to a broadband modem. This type of connection might be always-on, or, if your ISP uses a connection-based setup called PPPoE, Windows will establish the link whenever anyone wants to use the Internet.

 *To learn more about PPPoE, **see** "Configuring a High-Speed Connection," **p. 347**.*

C. **Connection-sharing router with a broadband connection**—You can use a small hardware device that can cost as little as $20 to do the same job as ICS. The advantage of this is that you don't have to leave a particular Windows computer turned on for other users to reach the Internet. It is also more secure because a separate device is shielding Windows from the Internet.

D. **Cable service with multiple directly connected computers**—This is the setup that some cable ISPs recommend for a home with more than one computer, but it is a *bad idea*. You can't use this method and also use file and printer sharing. Use schemes B, C, or E instead. See "Special Notes for Cable Service," later in this chapter, for more information.

E. **Routed service with a router**—Some ISPs provide *routed* Internet service through DSL, cable, Frame Relay, or other technologies. There's usually an extra charge for this type of service because it provides a separate public IP address to each computer on the LAN. This has some advantages that I discuss later, but it also incurs a risk of exposing your network to hackers, unless you're vigilant in setting it up.

 note

One disadvantage of schemes A and B is that the one "sharing" computer must be turned on before anyone else can use the Internet connection.

note

Although I really prefer using the shared connection strategies—the first three schemes in Figure 19.1—they have a drawback: It's more difficult to enable incoming access to your computer. In particular, it makes it hard to reach your computer with Remote Desktop, and it can be difficult for someone (tech support personnel, for example) to work with Windows XP users using Remote Assistance. I show you how to make these strategies work at the end of the chapter, under "Making Services Available."

Figure 19.1
Five ways to connect your LAN to the Internet.

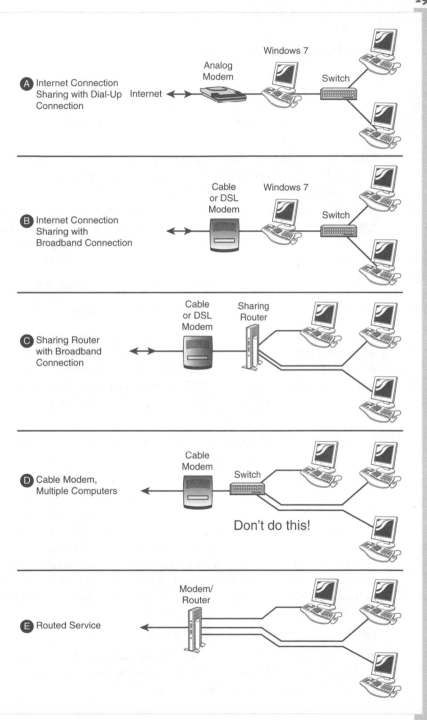

A Internet Connection Sharing with Dial-Up Connection

B Internet Connection Sharing with Broadband Connection

C Sharing Router with Broadband Connection

D Cable Modem, Multiple Computers

E Routed Service

Now let's look at the issues involved in having a single ISP connection serve multiple computers.

Managing IP Addresses

Connecting a LAN to the Internet requires you to delve into some issues about how computers are identified on your LAN and on the Internet. Each computer on your LAN uses a unique network identification number called an *IP address* that is used to route data to the correct computer. As long as the data stays on your LAN, it doesn't matter what numbers are used; your LAN is essentially a private affair.

When you connect to the Internet, though, those random numbers can't be used to direct data to you; your ISP has to assign a *public* IP address to you so that other computers on the Internet can properly route data to your ISP and then to you.

Now, when you establish a solo dial-up connection from your computer to the Internet, this isn't a big problem. When you dial up, your ISP assigns your connection a temporary public IP address. Any computer on the entire Internet can send data to you using this address. When you want to connect a LAN, though, it's not quite as easy. Two approaches are used:

- You can get a valid public IP address for each of your computers.

- You can use *one* public IP address and share it among all the users of your LAN.

The first approach is called *routed* Internet service because your ISP assigns a set of consecutive IP addresses for your LAN—one for each of your computers—and routes all data for these addresses to your site. This is shown in scheme E in Figure 19.1. The second approach uses a technique called *Network Address Translation*, or NAT, in which all the computers on your LAN share one IP address and connection. This is how schemes A through C work.

NAT and Internet Connection Sharing

Microsoft's Internet Connection Sharing system and the popular devices called *residential gateways*, *connection-sharing routers*, or *wireless routers* use NAT to establish all Internet connections using one public IP address. The computer or device running the NAT service mediates all connections between computers on your LAN and the Internet (see Figure 19.2).

NAT works a lot like mail delivery to a large commercial office building, where there's one address for many people. Mail is delivered to the mail room, which sorts it and delivers it internally to the correct recipient. With NAT, you are assigned one public IP address, and all communication between your LAN and the Internet uses this address. The NAT service takes care of changing or translating the IP addresses in data packets from the private, internal IP addresses used on your LAN to the one public address used on the Internet.

Using NAT has several significant consequences:

- You can hook up as many computers on your LAN as you want. Your ISP won't care, or even know, that more than one computer is using the connection. You will save money because you need to pay for only a single-user connection.

Figure 19.2
A NAT device or program carries out all Internet communications using one IP address. NAT keeps track of outgoing data from your LAN to determine where to send responses from the outside.

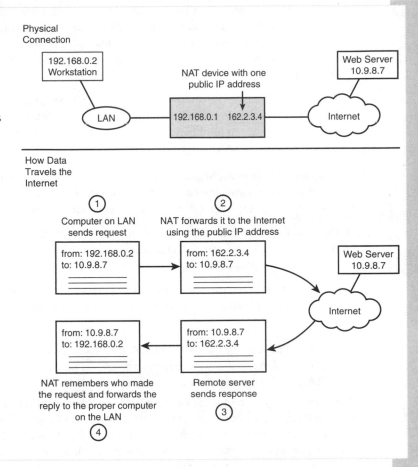

- You can assign IP addresses inside your LAN however you want. In fact, all the NAT setups I've seen provide DHCP, an automatic IP addressing system, so virtually no manual configuration is needed on the computers you add to your LAN. Just plug a computer in, and it's on the Internet.

- If you want to host a website, VPN, or other service on your LAN and make it available from the Internet, you have some additional setup work to do. When you contact a remote website, NAT knows to send the returned data back to you, but when an unsolicited request comes from outside, NAT has to be told where to send the incoming connection. I discuss this later in the chapter.

- NAT serves as an additional firewall to protect your LAN from probing by Internet hackers. Incoming requests, such as those to read your shared folders, are simply ignored if you haven't specifically set up your connection-sharing service to forward requests to a particular computer.

■ Some network services can't be made to work with NAT. For example, you might not be able to use some audio and video chat services. These programs expect that the IP address of the computer on which they're running is a public address. Windows ICS and some hardware-sharing routers can sometimes work around this problem using the Universal Plug and Play (UPnP) protocol, which I'll discuss later in the chapter.

■ A hardware connection sharing router might provide you with better security than Windows ICS because, as special-purpose devices, their software is simpler and less likely to be buggy than Windows. Also, when used with Windows Firewall, you have *two* separate lines of defense against hackers instead of just one.

Starting with Windows 98, Microsoft has provided a NAT service through its ICS feature. It's a built-in part of Windows. Given the choice between using Windows' ICS service and buying an external hardware router, I recommend that you use a router, for two reasons:

■ First, to use ICS, you have to leave one of your Windows computers turned on so that other computers can reach the Internet. Connection-sharing routers have to be left on, too, but they consume very little power compared to what a PC sucks up.

■ More important, connection-sharing routers provide better security than using Windows alone. With the hardware router, a hacker would have to break through the router and *then* break into Windows.

I won't go so far as to say that you shouldn't trust ICS, and later I show you how to hook up your LAN using all of the methods I described earlier. I just put in as my final word on this issue that I use DSL/cable-sharing routers at my own home and office.

If you decide to use a router, look at the products made by Linksys, D-Link, SMC, and Netgear. You can find them at computer stores, office supply stores, and online (check www.buy.com), and on sale you can pick one up for $20 or less. Wireless versions that include an 802.11g or 802.11n wireless networking base station as well as a switch or hub for wired Ethernet connections don't cost that much more—I'm looking at the ads in my Sunday paper right now and see prices ranging from $40 to $60.

More advanced (and expensive) versions include additional features such as a built-in print server or virtual private networking (VPN) service. For example, the D-Link DI-713P Wireless Broadband Router provides NAT (connection sharing), a three-port Ethernet switch, a print server, and a wireless access point, all in one box. But although combination devices might be less expensive when you look at the total cost of getting separate devices, separate units give you more flexibility in where you locate the devices, and if one device fails, you don't lose all the functions at once.

The next section discusses issues that are important to business users. If you're setting up a network for your home, you can skip ahead.

A Warning for Business Users

My enthusiasm notwithstanding, cable and DSL Internet service can give you a painful, bumpy ride. Some DSL ISPs (two that I've used, for example) have gone bankrupt and stranded their customers. Service outages are a fact of life, and I've seen problems stretch out over weeks. Customer support ranges from okay to incredibly bad, installation appointments are routinely missed, and even billing can be a terrible mess. If you ask a provider for a service-level agreement (a guaranteed percentage of uptime and throughput), the likely reply will be hysterical laughter.

So, if your business truly depends on your Internet connection for survival, DSL and cable might not be for you.

It costs a lot more in the short term to set up business-class Internet and networking service, but if you lose business when your connection fails, you probably can't afford the risks that come with consumer-class DSL and cable Internet access.

There are some DSL and cable providers that have products tailored for businesses, and for really serious reliability, you might investigate Frame Relay. Frame Relay is an old technology, with pricing schemes from the pre-Internet era, and it requires equipment that seems expensive by today's standards. However, Frame Relay customers can expect service interruptions of no more than three minutes per month versus perhaps three hours per month with DSL service. If this sounds worthwhile to you, contact a telecommunications consultant or a networking pro for more information.

Special Notes for Wireless Networking

If you're setting up a wireless network, you *must* enable WEP or WPA encryption to protect your network from unexpected use by random strangers. People connecting to your wireless network appear to Windows to be part of your own LAN and are trusted accordingly.

➡ *To learn more about setting up a secure wireless network, **see** "Installing a Wireless Network,"*
   p. 463.

If you really want to provide free access to your broadband connection as a public service, provide it using a second, unsecured wireless router plugged into your network, as shown in Figure 19.3. Use a different channel number and SSID from the ones set up for your own wireless LAN. Set up filtering in this router to prevent Windows file-sharing queries from penetrating into your own network. See "Scheme E—Routed Service Using a Router," later in this chapter, for the list of ports that you must block.

(And remember that someone might use your connection to send spam or attack other networks. If the FBI knocks on your door some day, don't say I didn't warn you.)

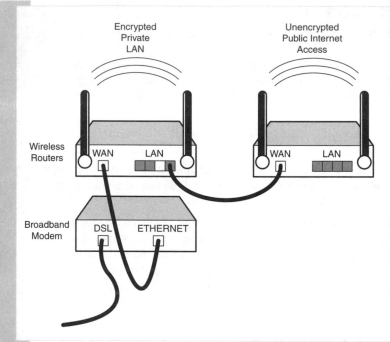

Encrypted Private LAN

Unencrypted Public Internet Access

Wireless Routers

WAN   LAN

WAN   LAN

Broadband Modem

DSL   ETHERNET

Figure 19.3
If you want to provide unsecured, free wireless Internet access to strangers, use a second wireless router to protect your own LAN.

Special Notes for Cable Service

Some cable ISPs can provide you with multiple IP addresses so you can connect multiple computers directly to your cable modem. This is scheme D in Figure 19.1. It's a very simple setup, but I strongly urge you *not* to use this type of service. You can't take advantage of file and printer sharing on such a network.

If you want to take full advantage of having a LAN in your home or office, use scheme C instead: Simply add an inexpensive connection-sharing router—at a cost of less than $40, as I mentioned previously—and you'll get *all* the benefits of a LAN without the risks of a direct connection.

Some cable ISPs don't want you to use a router, but I think it provides superior protection against hacking, and that needs to be your first priority. If your ISP charges extra for multiple connections, you could pay your ISP for the extra connections but use just the one, safe shared connection to provide service to your other computers.

 caution

The "Scheme D" setup requires you to connect your cable modem directly to your LAN, without any firewall protection between the Internet and your computers. If you do this, you *have* to disable file and printer sharing on each computer. In Windows 7 parlance, you must designate your network a Public network. If you don't, you would expose all your computers to a *severe security risk*.

Configuring Your LAN

In the following sections, I describe how to set up each of the connection schemes diagrammed in Figure 19.1. If you're still in the planning stages for your network, you might want to read all the sections to see what's involved; this might help you decide what configuration you want to use. If your LAN is already set up and your Internet service is ready to go now, just skip ahead to the appropriate section.

Scheme A—Windows Internet Connection Sharing with a Dial-Up Connection

This section shows how to set up the Internet connection method illustrated in Figure 19.1, A.

The ICS feature provided with Windows 7 can share modem or broadband connections that require a sign-on procedure. The connection is made automatically whenever any user on the network tries to access the Internet; this is called demand-dialing. The following section describes how to set it up.

Setting Up the Shared Connection

To set up a shared connection, first install and test your modem and ISP information on the computer that will be used to share the connection. To do this, set up a standard dial-up connection using the procedure described in Chapter 13. Be sure that you can access the Internet properly by viewing at least one web page. When you know this is working, follow these steps:

1. Click Start, Control Panel, View Network Status and Tasks (under Network and Internet). Select Change Adapter Settings. Right-click the icon for your ISP connection and select Properties.

2. Select the Sharing tab. Check all the boxes, as shown in Figure 19.4.

3. Select the Options tab. Uncheck Prompt for Name and Password and also Prompt for Phone Number. This allows the connection to start up without user intervention.

4. If you want a dedicated, always-on 24×7 connection, check Redial If Line Is Dropped, set the number of Redial Attempts to 99, set Time Between Redial Attempts to 10 Seconds, and set Idle Time Before Hanging Up to Never. Be aware that if you pay per-minute charges, this can result in an astounding phone bill!

   Usually, though, you'll want a demand-dialing connection. Use these settings: Uncheck Redial If Line Is Dropped. Set the number of Redial Attempts to 10, set Time Between Redial Attempts to 10 Seconds, and set Idle Time Before Hanging Up to 10 Minutes. (I recommend using 10 minutes to start with; you can increase it later if you find that the line disconnects too frequently while you're working.)

note

If your computer has multiple network connections, the Home Networking Connection selection will be present. Open the drop-down list and select the network connection that leads to your network's other computers.

caution

Step 5 is a crucial part of protecting your computer and LAN from hacking over the Internet. Omitting this step could make your computer vulnerable to hacking.

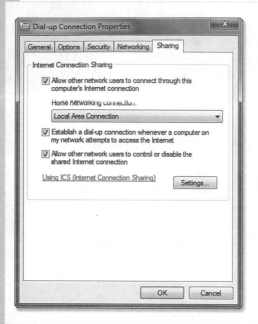

Figure 19.4
On the computer that will share its connection, enable Internet Connection Sharing. Check all the boxes.

5. Select the Networking tab. In the list of components used by the connection, be sure that only Internet Protocol Version 6 (TCP/IPv6), Internet Protocol Version 4 (TCP/IPv4), and QoS Packet Scheduler (if present) are checked, as shown in Figure 19.5. This will prevent file sharing from being exposed to the Internet. The firewall will do that, too, but it doesn't hurt to be extra safe.

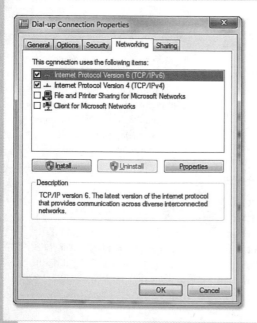

Figure 19.5
Be sure that on your Internet connection, the Client and Sharing components are not checked.

6. Click OK.

7. Restart your computer and try to view any web page (such as www.google.com). Your computer should automatically dial your ISP. If the web page appears, proceed to "Configuring the Rest of the Network." If it doesn't, you'll have to resolve the problem before continuing.

Shared Connection Doesn't Happen

If you attempt to view a web page on a network with a shared connection and no Internet connection is established, first listen to the modem to see whether it's trying to establish the connection. If it is, you might just need to wait a bit and try to view the page again. Sometimes Internet Explorer gives an error message before the modem has had enough time to make the connection.

If the modem is making a connection but web browsing still fails, the dial-up connection on the shared computer might not be set up with a saved and shared password. On that computer, open the Network and Sharing Center, select Connect to a Network, and attempt to make the connection manually. Be sure that you've checked Save This Username and Password and selected Anyone Who Uses This Computer.

Configuring the Rest of the Network

When the shared connection is set up, configuring the rest of your LAN should be easy. On each of your *other* computers (all except the connection-sharing computer), follow these steps:

1. Open Network and Sharing Center and select Change Adapter Settings. Right-click the computer's Local Area Network icon and select Properties. (On versions of Windows other than Windows 7, you might have to use different selections to get to your network adapter's settings; check online help or your copy of the corresponding *Special Edition Using* book.)

2. Select Internet Protocol Version 4 (TCP/IPv4) and then select Properties.

3. Check Obtain an IP Address Automatically and Obtain DNS Server Address Automatically. Then, click OK.

4. Repeat steps 2 and 3 for Internet Protocol Version 6 (TCP/IPv6).

5. When finished, you should be able to open Internet Explorer and view a website. When you try, the connection-sharing computer should dial out for you.

note

When you're using a shared dial-up connection, it takes a while for the dialer to go through its paces if the connection wasn't already up. Before it can finish, you might get an error from IE saying that it can't open the page. If this happens, just wait a few seconds and Refresh (press F5) to try again.

If you are using Windows Internet Connection Sharing or a connection-sharing router that supports Universal Plug and Play (UPnP), the Network window of all the computers on your network should have an icon that represents the shared Internet connection, as shown in Figure 19.6. To display this window, select Network in any Windows Explorer window (Computer, Documents, and so on). Or, open the Network and Sharing Center and double-click the Network icon at the top.

If you are using Windows Internet Connection Sharing, the shared connection will be labeled "Internet Gateway Device." To control a dial-up or PPPoE DSL Internet connection shared by one computer from your other networked computers, right-click this icon and select Enable or Disable. (This works on all

tip

If any of your other networked computers wants to dial an ISP itself, perhaps because it had previously been set up to make its own connection, just delete its dial-up connection icons. In Windows 7, you can do that from the Network and Sharing Center. Select Change Adapter Settings, then delete the now unneeded icon(s).

of the computers except the one that is sharing its connection. On the computer that is sharing its connection, you have to use the Network connection list that appears when you click the Network icon in the taskbar.)

Figure 19.6
The other computers on your network can control a shared connection from their Network window.

Can't Access a Shared Modem Connection from the LAN

When you first start using the Internet, a delay of 30 seconds or so is normal while the dial-up connection is established. But, if the connection doesn't progress after 30 seconds, be sure of the following: The sharing computer was turned on when you booted up your computer, and your computer is set to obtain its IP address automatically.

Try to make the connection from the sharing computer to be sure the modem is connecting properly. If it's not, scan through the troubleshooting notes in Chapter 13 to diagnose the dial-up connection problem.

Can't Access a Shared DSL or Cable Connection from the LAN

If you attempt to view an Internet page from a LAN computer, but your web browser doesn't get past "Looking up host www.*somewhere*.com," be sure that the sharing computer was turned on when you booted up your computer, that the connection to the DSL or cable modem is the one marked as shared, and that your computer is set to obtain its IP address automatically.

Try to view web pages from the sharing computer to be sure the high-speed connection is functioning. If it's not, scan through the troubleshooting notes in Chapter 13, and also go through Chapter 16, "Troubleshooting Your Internet Connection," to diagnose the Internet connectivity problem.

If you are using a connection-sharing router, view the router's built-in Status web page (usually by viewing `http://192.168.0.1` or `http://192.168.1.1` with IE). See if the router has been able to connect to your ISP. You might have entered an incorrect password, or, for cable systems, you might need to "clone" the MAC address of the computer that you originally used to set up the Internet connection.

➡ *If you want to make services available to the Internet, continue with "Making Services Available," later in this chapter.*

Scheme B—Windows Internet Connection Sharing with a Broadband Connection

This section shows how to set up the Internet connection method illustrated in Figure 19.1, B.

The procedure for configuring a shared high-speed cable or DSL Internet connection with Windows ICS is very similar to that for setting up a shared dial-up connection. To prepare, be sure to install and test your DSL or cable connection on the computer you'll use to host the shared connection, as described in Chapter 13. It's essential that you have this working before you proceed to set up your LAN and the shared connection.

Verify that the broadband Internet connection is labeled as a Public network. To do this, follow these steps:

1. Click Start, Control Panel, View Network Status and Tasks (under Network and Internet).

2. If your broadband connection is not active, click Connect to a Network and make the connection.

3. In the Network and Sharing Center window, be sure that your Internet connection's location is labeled "Public Network."

When your broadband connection is configured correctly and is working, follow these steps:

1. Open the Network Connections window by clicking Start, Control Panel, View Network Status and Tasks. Select Change Adapter Settings.

2. Locate the icon that corresponds to your broadband connection.

   If you have cable Internet service, this will probably be a network adapter. Earlier, I suggested that you rename it something like "Internet Connection," or it may still be labeled Local Area Connection. If you use DSL service that requires a username and password to sign on, locate the connection icon that you set up for your ISP; it might be named "Broadband Connection." Right-click this icon and select Properties.

3. Choose the Sharing tab. Check all the boxes, as shown earlier in Figure 19.4.

4. Select the Networking tab. In the list of components used by the connection, be sure that *only* Internet Protocol Version 6 (TCP/IPv6), Internet Protocol Version 4 (TCP/IPv4), and QoS Packet Scheduler, if present, are checked. This will prevent file sharing from being exposed to the Internet. (Windows Firewall will do that, too, but it doesn't hurt to be extra safe.)

5. Click OK.

6. Click Windows Firewall in the Network and Sharing window. Make sure Windows Firewall is On.

7. Restart Windows and try to view any web page (such as www.google.com). If it doesn't appear, you'll have to resolve the problem before proceeding. You should check the appropriate connection icon to be sure it's still configured correctly for your ISP.

Now, follow the instructions under "Configuring the Rest of the Network," on **p. 525**, to set up your other computers.

 tip

If your broadband service uses a LAN adapter instead of USB to connect your computer to the DSL or cable modem, you'll be installing two LAN adapters in this computer: one for the LAN and one for the modem. I suggest that you install them one at a time. Install the one that you'll use for your broadband connection first. From the Network and Sharing Center, select Change Adapter Settings, right-click the network adapter's icon, and rename it DSL Modem Connection or Cable Internet Connection, or some other name that indicates what it's used for, as shown in Figure 19.7. Configure and test the Internet connection. Then install the network adapter that you'll use to connect to your LAN. Rename this connection LAN Connection or leave it as Local Area Connection. This will help you later in the setup process, when you need to know which connection goes to your ISP.

Figure 19.7
Install and
rename your
network
adapters one
at a time,
indicating
what purpose
they'll serve.
"DSL Modem
Connection"
or "LAN
Connection"
is much more
informative
than "Local
Area
Connection
#2."

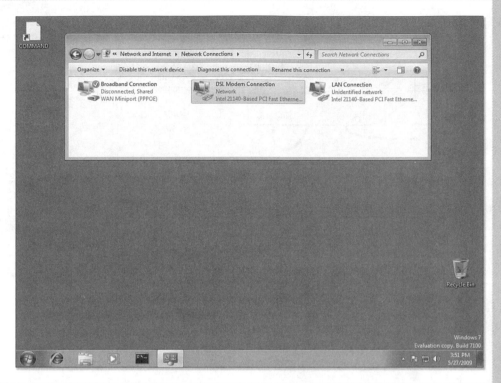

Scheme C—Connection Sharing Router with a Broadband Connection

This section shows how to set up the Internet connection method illustrated in Figure 19.1, C.

Your router's manufacturer will provide instructions for installing and configuring it. If you're using cable or DSL Internet service, you'll connect your broadband modem to the router using a short Ethernet patch cable. Then you'll connect the router to your LAN using one of the two methods shown in Figure 19.8.

If you connect your router to a separate switch (or hub), be sure that the link indicators come on at both the switch and the router. If they don't, you might need to move the switch end of the cable from a regular port to an uplink port or *vice versa*.

You then configure the router, telling it how to contact your ISP and what range of IP addresses to serve up to your LAN. Every device will use a different procedure, so you will have to follow the manufacturer's instructions.

If your ISP uses PPPoE to establish a connection, you need to enable PPPoE and store your logon and password in the router. Most DSL service works this way. If your DSL provider does use PPPoE, you should enable the router's auto-sign-on feature, and you can optionally set up a "keepalive" value that will tell the modem to periodically send network traffic even if you don't, to keep your connection active all the time. (This might violate your service agreement with the DSL provider— better check before you do this.)

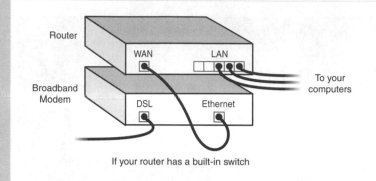

Figure 19.8
Connecting a connection-sharing router to your LAN.

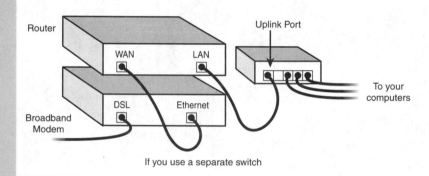

If you use cable Internet service and your ISP didn't provide you with a special hostname that you had to give to your computer, your ISP probably identifies you by your network adapter's MAC (hardware) address. You *might* find that your Internet connection won't work when you set up the router. One of your router's setup pages should show you its MAC address. You can either call your ISP's customer service line and tell them that this is your new adapter's MAC address, or configure the router to "clone" your computer's MAC address—that is, copy the address from the computer you originally used to set up your cable connection. Your router's setup manual should tell you how to do this.

 caution

Be sure to change the factory-supplied password of your router after you install it. (And write the password somewhere in the router's manual, or put it on a sticky label on the bottom of the router.) Also, be sure to disable outside (Internet) access to the router's management screens.

As you are configuring your router, you might want to enable Universal Plug and Play, discussed next in this chapter.

You might also opt for even better hacker protection by having your router filter (block) Microsoft file and printer sharing data. This is usually done on an advanced setup screen labeled Filtering. See "Scheme E—Routed Service Using a Router," later in this chapter, for the list of ports that you must block.

When the router has been set up, go to each of your computers and follow the instructions under "Configuring the Rest of the Network," on **p. 525**.

Using Universal Plug and Play

If you use a hardware connection-sharing router, you might want to consider enabling a feature called Universal Plug and Play (UPnP). UPnP provides a way for software running on your computer to communicate with the router. Specifically, UPnP provides a means for the following:

- The router to tell software on your computer that it is separated from the Internet by NAT. This may let some software—the video and audio parts of most instant messaging programs, in particular—have a better chance of working.

- Software running on the network to tell the router to forward expected incoming connections to the correct computer. Again, Windows Live Messenger is a good example. When the computer on the other end of the connection starts sending data, the router would not know to send it to your computer. UPnP lets UPnP-aware application programs automatically set up forwarding in the router.

- Other types of as-yet-undeveloped hardware devices to announce their presence on the network so that Windows can automatically take advantage of the services they provide.

To use UPnP, you must enable the feature in your router. It's usually disabled by default. If your router doesn't currently support UPnP, you might have to download and install a firmware upgrade from the manufacturer. Most routers now do support UPnP.

Scheme D—Cable Internet with Multiple Computers

This section shows how to set up the Internet connection method illustrated in Figure 19.1, D. As I mentioned earlier in the chapter, you *cannot* safely use file and printer sharing with this setup. Use this setup only if you don't want file and printer sharing and just want to have several computers with Internet access.

In this configuration, follow your ISP's instructions for setting up each computer separately. The only unusual thing here is that the computers plug in to a switch or hub, and the switch or hub plugs in to the cable modem—otherwise, each computer is set up exactly as if it was a separate, standalone computer with cable Internet service.

To verify that the network location is set to Public Network on Windows 7, follow these steps:

1. Click Start, Control Panel, View Network Status and Tasks (under Network and Internet).

2. Check that the label under your network connection is labeled Public Network. If it's not, click the network location label, and select Public Network.

> **caution**
>
> On each Windows 7 and Vista computer, you must set the network location for the connection that goes to your switch and cable modem to Public Network. On Windows XP, be sure that Windows Firewall is enabled, and that file and printer sharing is disabled.

If you later decide that you want to use file and printer sharing, *do not* simply set the network location to Home or Work and enable file and printer sharing. Instead, set up a shared connection using scheme B or C.

Scheme E—Routed Service Using a Router

This section shows how to set up the Internet connection method illustrated in Figure 19.1, E.

Some ISPs will sell you service that provides multiple, fixed IP addresses. This is the case for Frame Relay service and, in some cases, higher-priced business-class DSL service. You should really have a good reason for going this way, beyond just wanting to connect multiple computers—it's not as secure as a single shared connection. Good reasons might be that you want the reliability of Frame Relay service or you need fixed IP addresses to host web, email, or other Internet-based services on several different computers.

For this type of service, if you are using a cable, DSL, satellite, or Frame Relay modem with a built-in router, your ISP will help you configure your network. In this setup, you will be provided with a fixed list of IP addresses, which you'll have to parcel out to your computers. Your ISP should help you install all of this, but I can give you some pointers.

First of all, it is *absolutely essential* that your router be set up to protect your network. You must ensure that at least these three items are taken care of:

1. The router must be set up with filters to prevent Microsoft file-sharing service (NetBIOS and NetBT) packets from entering or leaving your LAN. In technical terms, the router must be set up to block TCP and UDP on port 137, UDP on port 138, and TCP on ports 139 and 445. It should "drop" rather than "reject" packets, if possible. This helps prevent hackers from discovering that these services are present but blocked. Better to let them think they're not there at all.

 tip

I *strongly* urge you to ask your ISP to set up filtering in your router for you, to block all Windows networking services.

2. Be *absolutely* sure to change your router's administrative password from the factory default value to something hard to guess, with uppercase letters, lowercase letters, numbers, and punctuation. Don't let your ISP talk you out of this, but you should let them know what the new password is so they can get into the router from their end, if needed.

3. Disable SNMP access, or change the SNMP read and read-write "community names" to something other than the default. Again, use something with letters, numbers, and punctuation.

Second, either your ISP will set up your router to automatically assign network addresses using DHCP, or you will have to manually set up a fixed IP address for each computer, using the IP address, network mask, gateway address, and DNS server addresses supplied by your ISP.

If you will be making the settings manually, make a list of the names of each of your computers and the IP addresses you want to assign. Follow these steps on each computer that is to get manual settings:

 caution

If your router is not properly configured to filter out NetBIOS traffic, your network will be exposed to hackers. This is absolutely unacceptable. If you're in doubt, have your ISP help you configure the router. Also, after setting things up, visit www.grc.com and use the ShieldsUP pages there to be sure your computers are properly protected. For more information about network security, see Chapter 32.

1. View the Network and Sharing Center.

2. Under View Your Active Networks, right-click Local Area Connection and select Properties.

3. Select the Networking tab, select Internet Protocol Version 4 (TCP/IPv4), and then click Properties.

4. Enter an IP address and the other information provided by your ISP. The required settings are the IP address, subnet mask, default gateway, and DNS server(s).

 note

If your ISP supplies you with Internet Protocol Version 6 (TCP/IPv6) settings, repeat the previous steps, except select Internet Protocol Version 6 (TCP/IPv6) in step 3.

Making Services Available

You might want to make some internal network services available to the outside world through your Internet connection. You would want to do this in these situations:

 caution

Make absolutely sure that Windows Firewall is turned on, to protect your network from hackers. For more information on network security, see Chapter 32.

- You want to host a web server using Internet Information Services (IIS).

- You want to enable incoming VPN access to your LAN so you can securely connect from home or afield.

- You want to enable incoming Remote Desktop access to your computer.

If you have set up routed Internet service with a router (scheme E in Figure 19.1), you don't have to worry about this because your network connection is wide open and doesn't use NAT. As long as the outside users know the IP address of the computer hosting your service—or its DNS name, if you have set up DNS service—you're on the air already.

Otherwise, you have either Windows Firewall, NAT, or both in the way of incoming access. To make specific services accessible, you need to follow one of the sets of specific instructions in the next few sections, depending on the type of Internet connection setup you've used. Skip ahead to the appropriate section.

 note

If you're interested in being able to reach your computer over the Internet using Remote Desktop, see Chapter 37, "Remote Desktop," which is entirely devoted to the subject.

Enabling Access with Internet Connection Sharing

When you are using Microsoft's Internet Connection Sharing feature, you need to execute two steps to provide outside access to a given service supplied by a computer on your network. First, you must tell the connection-sharing system (ICS) which computer on your network is to receive incoming connection requests for a particular service. Then, on the computer that provides the service, you must tell Windows Firewall to let these requests through.

Most server-type functions, such as Remote Desktop and IIS, require manual setup. On the computer that is providing the service itself, you must tell Windows Firewall to allow incoming connections to the service by following these steps:

1. Open the Windows Firewall screen by clicking Windows Firewall in the Network and Sharing Center.

2. Click Advanced Settings. In the left pane, click Inbound Rules. See if the service this computer is providing is already listed with Yes in the Enabled column and Allow in the Action column. If so, you can proceed to configure the computer that is sharing its Internet connection.

3. If the service isn't already listed, click New Rule in the right pane. Click Port, click Next, select TCP or UDP, and enter the specific port number or port number range required by the service, as shown in Figure 19.9. Table 19.1 lists common services, port numbers, and protocols. (For the FTP and DNS services, you have to make two entries.)

4. Click Next and click Allow the Connection.

5. Click Next and leave all three check boxes (Domain, Private, Public) checked.

6. Click Next. For the rule name, enter the name of the service you're enabling, add an optional description, and click Finish.

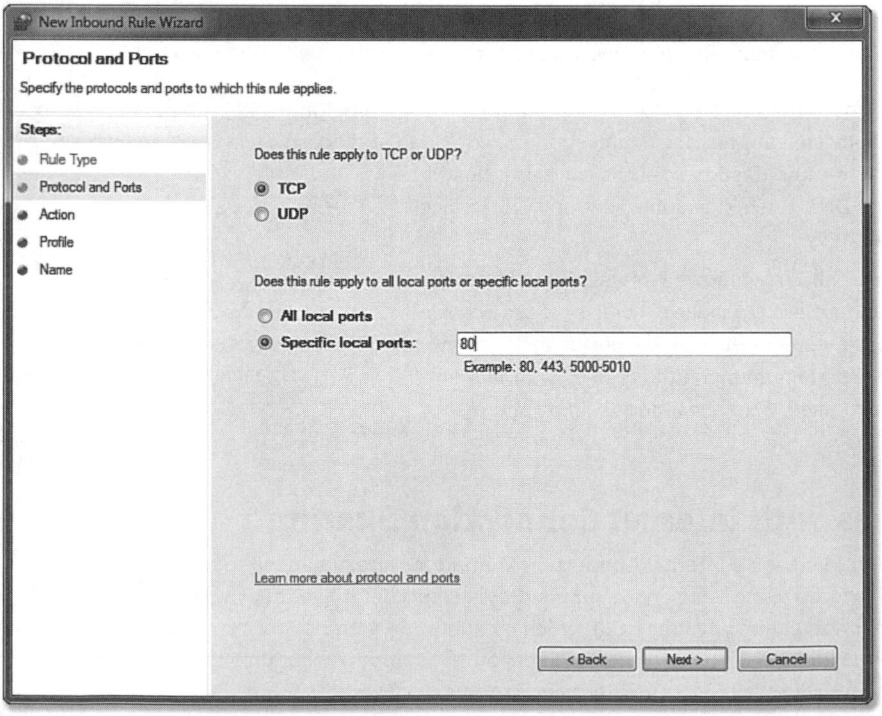

Figure 19.9
Add a service's port number and protocol type to Windows Firewall on the computer that is running the service.

Table 19.1 Common Services and Port Numbers

Service	Protocol	Port
Domain Name Service (DNS)	TCP and UDP	53
FTP Server	TCP	20 and 21
Internet Mail Server (SMTP)	TCP	25
Post-Office Protocol Version 3 (POP3)	TCP	110
Remote Desktop	TCP	3389
Secure Shell (SSH)	TCP	22
Secure Web Server (HTTPS)	TCP	443
Symantec PCAnywhere	TCP	5631
Telnet Server	TCP	23
Web Server (HTTP)	TCP	80

Next, you must instruct the computer that is sharing its Internet connection to forward incoming requests to the designated computer. On the computer that physically connects to the Internet, follow these steps:

1. Click Start, Control Panel, View Network Status and Tasks, and then select Change Adapter Settings.

2. Right-click the icon for the shared Internet connection and select Properties. View the Sharing tab and, in the Internet Connection Sharing section, click Settings.

3. In the Advanced Settings dialog box, shown in Figure 19.10, check the Service entry for each service for which you want to permit access and for which you have servers on your LAN. The most common ones to select are Remote Desktop, FTP Server, and Web Server, if you have set up IIS.

Figure 19.10
The Services tab lets you specify which services are to be forwarded by Internet Connection Sharing.

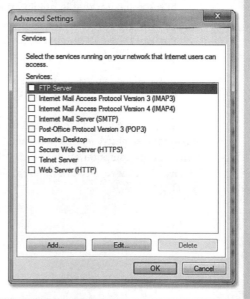

4. When you select a check box, the Service Settings dialog box appears, as shown in Figure 19.11.

Figure 19.11
The Service Settings dialog box lets you specify the name or IP address of the computer that is to handle incoming connections for a particular service.

5. Enter the IP address of the computer that is hosting this service, if your LAN uses fixed IP addresses. If your LAN uses automatically assigned addresses from ICS, you can enter the computer's name, and the software will locate the correct computer. Click OK to save the settings.

6. If the service you want to use isn't listed, you need to find out what TCP and/or UDP ports the service communicates with. You have to search through the service software's documentation or on the Internet to find these port values.

To add an unlisted service, click Add. Enter the name of the service, the IP address or hostname of the computer that is running this service, and the port number, as shown in Figure 19.12. Generally, you'll want to use the same number for the port number the public sees (external port) and the port number used on the LAN (internal port). Check TCP or UDP, and then click OK.

If the service you're adding uses more than one protocol type or port number, you'll have to make multiple entries.

When you've enabled the desired services, incoming requests using the selected service ports will be forwarded to the appropriate computer on your LAN. Windows Firewall will know to let these services through.

 note

If you want to use an incoming VPN connection, you must set it up on the computer that is sharing its Internet connection. ICS can't forward VPN connections to other computers.

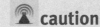 **caution**

With the exception of incoming VPN connection service, I suggest that you don't run any other services on the computer that manages your firewall and/or ICS, especially IIS. There's too great a risk that a security flaw in the service might let hackers compromise the firewall.

Figure 19.12
Enter port information for a new service in this dialog box.

Enabling Access with a Sharing Router

If you use a connection-sharing router on your LAN, you need to follow a somewhat different procedure to enable outside access to services on your network.

You must still open Windows Firewall on the computer(s) providing services, as described in the first six-step procedure in the previous section. Then you must use a manufacturer-specific procedure to set up forwarding for services that you want to expose to the Internet.

One difficulty with these devices is that you must forward services by IP address, not by computer name, and, normally, you set up computers to obtain their IP addresses automatically. This makes the computers moving targets because their IP address could change from day to day.

You have to make special arrangements for the computers on your LAN that you want to use to host services. On your router's setup screens, make a note of the range of IP addresses that it will hand out to computers requesting automatic configuration. Most routers have a place to enter a starting IP address and a maximum number of addresses. For instance, the starting number might be 2, with a limit of 100 addresses. For each computer that will provide an outside service, pick a number between 2 and 254 that is *not* in the range of addresses handed out by the router, and use that as the last number in the computer's IP address. I recommend using address 250 and working downward from there for any other computers that require a static address.

To configure the computer's network address, follow the instructions under "Port Forwarding with a Router" on **page 1019**, with these changes:

- The material in Chapter 37 shows instructions for setting up Remote Desktop, with protocol TCP port 3389. You'll need to use the protocol and port numbers for the service you're enabling.

- Use a static IP address ending with .250 for the first computer you set up to receive incoming connections. Use .249 for the second computer, and work downward from there. Be sure to keep a list of the computers you assign static addresses to, and the addresses you assign.

For services that use TCP/UDP in unpredictable ways, you must use another approach to forwarding on your LAN. Some services, such as Windows Live Messenger, communicate their *private,* internal IP address to the computer on the other end of the connection; when the other computer tries to send data to this private address, it fails. To use these services with a hardware router, you must enable UPnP, as described earlier in the chapter.

Other services use network protocols other than TCP and UDP, and most routers can't be set up to forward them. Incoming Microsoft VPN connections fall into this category. Some routers have built-in support for Microsoft's PPTP protocol. If yours has this support, your router's manual will tell you how to forward VPN connections to a host computer.

Otherwise, to support nonstandard services of this sort, you have to tell the router to forward *all* unrecognized incoming data to one designated computer. In effect, this exposes that computer to the Internet, so it's a fairly significant security risk. In fact, most routers call this targeted computer a DMZ host, referring to the notorious Korean no-man's-land called the Demilitarized Zone and the peculiar danger one faces standing in it.

To enable a DMZ host, you want to use a fixed IP address on the designated computer, as described in the previous section. Use your router's configuration screen to specify this selected IP address as the DMZ host. The configuration screen for my particular router is shown in Figure 19.13; yours might differ.

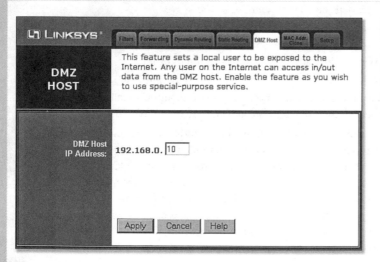

Figure 19.13
Enabling a DMZ host to receive all unrecognized incoming connection requests. This is an option of last resort if you can't forward incoming connections any other way.

Now, designating a DMZ host means that this computer is fully exposed to the Internet, so you must protect it with a firewall of some sort. On this computer, you *must* set its network location to Public Network.

You should also set up filtering in your router to block ports 137–139 and 445. Figure 19.14 shows how this is done on my Linksys router; your router might use a different method.

 tip

It's not a bad idea to enable filtering for these ports even if you're not using a DMZ host. It's *essential* to do this if you set up a DMZ host.

Figure 19.14
Configuring filters to block
Microsoft file-sharing services.

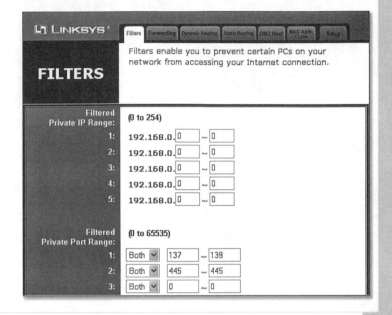

USING A WINDOWS NETWORK

Windows 7 Was Made to Network

Most homes and offices have more than one computer, and you'll quickly find that as days go by, you end up using most or all of them. You'll download a file, and a few days later, when you want to use that file... where is it? You hardly need to ask: If there's a 50/50 chance that the file you want is on your computer rather than some other computer in the home or office, 9 times out of 10 it will be on the other computer. This is not just a fact of life, it's a law of nature. But with a network, you can easily access any file and any printer, on any computer, from your own, short-circuiting the law—for a while, at least. A network also lets everyone in your home or office share printers and an Internet connection, saving you time and money.

In Windows 7, using files and printers on the network is exactly the same as using files and printers on your own hard drive. The "look and feel" are identical. The only new tasks you have to learn are how to find resources shared by others and how to make your own computer's resources available to others on the network. Windows 7 also adds security enhancements that make the process of connecting to and using other resources more secure.

By the way, I'll use the word *resource* frequently in this chapter. When I say *resource*, I mean a shared folder or printer on someone else's computer, which you can access through the LAN or the Internet. *The American Heritage Dictionary* defines a resource as "an available supply that can be drawn upon when needed." That's actually a perfect description of a network resource: It's there for you to use—provided that you can find it and that you have permission.

Windows networks work pretty much the same way whether they're in your home, in a small office, or in a large corporate setting. Big "domain" networks managed by computers running Windows Server software, though, may have some additional features. The following are some notable differences you might see on a domain network:

- The network administrator can set up *roaming profiles* so that your settings, preferences, Documents folder, and so on are centrally stored on the network and are available to you on any computer on your LAN or even at other network sites.

- Active Directory (AD) gives you added search functions to find users and printers on your network. These search functions appear as added icons and menu choices that only AD network computers have.

- The network administrator might use *policy* functions to limit your access to applications, Windows features, and settings. If you are on a domain or AD network and can't find an option I mention in this chapter, ask your network manager if its use has been restricted.

If you are using a home or small office workgroup network, don't feel left out. Because a workgroup typically has fewer than 10 computers, the searching and corporate-style management functions provided by AD simply aren't necessary.

Using Shared Folders in Windows 7

Windows 7 lets you share folders and their contents with other network users. Users within your network can see the folders and, if permission settings allow it, access the files in them just as they would any file on their own hard drive. In this section, I'll show you how to use files and folders shared by other users. Later in the chapter, you'll learn how to share folders on your own computer.

Browsing Through a Homegroup

If your computer is a member of a homegroup, on the left side of any Windows Explorer display (for example, the Computer or Documents window), you'll see the title "Homegroup." Under this are entries for each user's account, on each of the homegroup computers. Anyone who has elected to share materials with the homegroup—and whose computer is turned on—will be listed here.

➡ *If you can't or don't want to use a homegroup, skip ahead to "Browsing a Network's Computers," p. 544. To see how to set up a homegroup for your Windows 7 computers, see "Setting Up a Homegroup," p. 478.*

The homegroup list will include accounts for any additional users on your own computer, as well as the users on other computers. They all show up in this single list. (The account you're using yourself, though, won't be listed.)

You can open these entries to see what files and folders are being shared, as shown in Figure 20.1. It doesn't matter whether the other user's materials are stored on your computer or are on another computer on your network; it works the same way regardless. You can only see materials that the other user elected to share.

Libraries and folders shared by the other users.

Homegroup users are listed here.

Figure 20.1
If your computer is a member of a homegroup, you can view the materials shared by other members of your group from any Windows Explorer display.

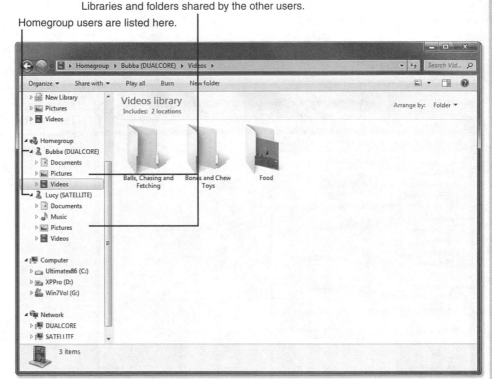

If the other user gave the homegroup permission to make changes to the folder, you'll be able to edit, delete, and rename files and add new files. Otherwise, you'll just be able to view, read, print, and play the files. If you want make changes in this case, just drag a copy from the other user's folder into one of your own folders, or onto your desktop.

To see how you can share *your* files with the group, see "Sharing with a Homegroup" on **page 562**.

 tip

You can bookmark a network computer or a shared folder so that you can easily come back to it later. To do this, browse to locate the computer or folder as just described. Then, in the window's left pane, right-click Favorites and select Add Current Location to Favorites.

Whether you have a homegroup set up or not, you can also browse through files and folders shared by any networked computer using the Network list, described next.

Browsing a Network's Computers

In any Windows Explorer display (for example, the Computer or Documents window), the left pane contains an item titled Network. If you open this item, you'll see icons for every active computer on your network. You'll see a display like the one shown in Figure 20.2.

note

Computers whose workgroup or domain name is different from yours may take longer to appear, but all computers on your computer's same "subnet" should eventually show up. On a corporate network, computers on other subnets and those separated by firewalls may not appear. You can still use their resources, by typing their share names directly in UNC format as described later in the chapter under "Network Power User Topics."

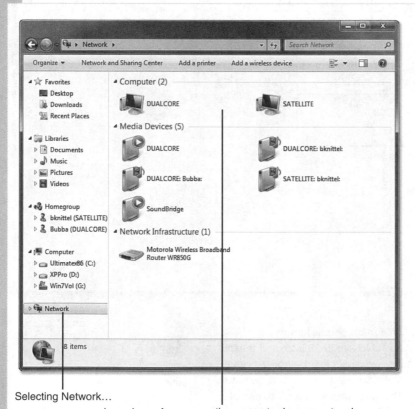

Figure 20.2
The Network display lets you browse through your network's resources.

Selecting Network...

...shows icons for every active computer in your network.

The Network window shows computers with shared folders, shared Media Center libraries, and network hardware. You can browse into any of the folder icons to locate shared files and folders that you want to use.

When you browse into other Windows 7 computers, you will notice that the entire \users folder structure is shared, with the name Users. This folder contains everyone's user profiles and documents, and is shared by default. What preserves everyone's privacy and security is that each user must give other users (or other groups, or everyone) permission to read a folder or file in order for them to even see that it exists. This scheme makes it much simpler to control which items you share, simply by changing the security settings on the files and folders themselves. I'll talk more about this later in the chapter under "Sharing Resources."

In particular, on Windows 7 computers, the Public folder is shared "in place," meaning it's found inside the Users share, and is not shared separately under its own name. The Public Folder Sharing option in the Advanced Sharing Settings window on Windows 7 just controls whether remote users can have access to the Public folder.

When you browse into Windows Vista and XP computers, the Public user profile is shared separately, under the name Public, or Shared Documents. And shared user profiles will be shared individually as separate shares.

Viewing a Shared Folder Directly Using Its UNC Path

If you know the Universal Naming Convention (UNC) pathname of a shared folder on a specific computer, you can instantly view its files by typing the UNC path into the Address box at the top of any Windows Explorer window. You can type a path that includes just the computer name, a computer name followed by a shared folder name, or a longer path that specifies subfolders or a file within the shared folder.

For example, suppose you want to see the folders shared by a computer named "laptop." Open a Windows Explorer window by clicking Start, Computer. Click in the Address box and the "breadcrumb" path will disappear. Then, type **laptop** and press Enter. This will display all of laptop's shared folders, without your having to browse your way there. Likewise, you can see the files shared by a user whose account is named "lucy" on that computer using \\laptop\users\lucy, as shown in Figure 20.3.

I talk more about UNC pathnames later in the chapter, in the section "Understanding the UNC Naming Convention."

tip

It can take time and effort to dig down to the network, so if there is a particular shared file or folder that you use frequently, you might find it helpful to create a shortcut to it. Just hold down the Alt key while you drag the file or folder into your desktop. You can leave the shortcut there, or move it to some other convenient location.

You can also bookmark a networked computer or shared folder. To do this, browse to locate the computer or folder. Then, in the Explorer window's left pane, right-click Favorites and select Add Current Location to Favorites.

Finally, you can also add network location to one of your libraries, as I'll discuss later under "Network Power User Topics."

note

Remember, for all folders shared by Windows Vista, Windows 7, and Windows Server 2008 computers, to even see that a folder or file exists inside a shared folder, you must have permission to read the file or view the folder's contents. In folders shared by other operating systems, you may be able to see the presence of files and folders that you don't have permission to read.

tip

If you're using Windows 7 Professional, Enterprise, or Ultimate editions, you can make a shared folder's contents available even when you're disconnected from the network. For instructions, see "Offline Files" on **page 991**.

You can type a UNC path into the Address box.

The files in the shared folder.

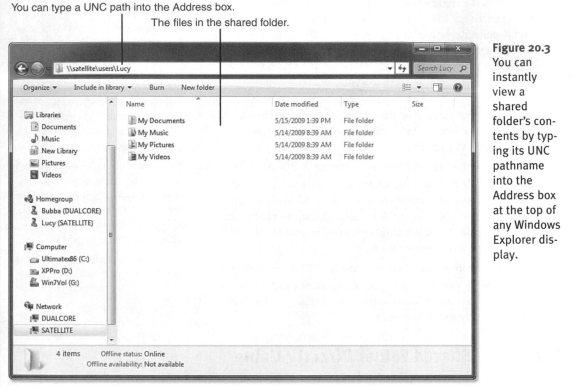

Figure 20.3
You can instantly view a shared folder's contents by typing its UNC pathname into the Address box at the top of any Windows Explorer display.

Searching the Network

If there is a particular file that you'd like to find, but you don't know where it is, browsing through the network isn't a particularly easy way to find it. However, you can quickly locate shared folders and files by name and by content using the Search box at the upper-right corner of any Windows Explorer window.

To begin a search, open any Windows Explorer window, for example, by clicking Start, Computer, or Start, Documents. Then follow the instructions under the next several headings, to find files, computers, or printers.

Searching for Files or Folders

You can search a particular network computer for files and folders by name and by content, using these steps:

1. Open an Explorer window and select Network in the left pane.

2. Expand the Network list, and click the name of a computer.

3. Type all or part of the desired filename, or a word or phrase to be found in the file, in the Search box.

This will locate files and folders within the contents of all shared folders on that computer, but only those that you have permission to view.

➡ *To learn more about searching for files on Windows 7, **see** "Searching," p. 173.*

To perform the same search across several computers, start with one computer, as just described. Then, when the Search Again In ribbon appears across the bottom of the search results listing, click Custom, as illustrated in Figure 20.4. Expand the Network list and check the names of all the computers that you'd like to include in the search (including the one you started with). Click OK to restart the search across all of the selected computers.

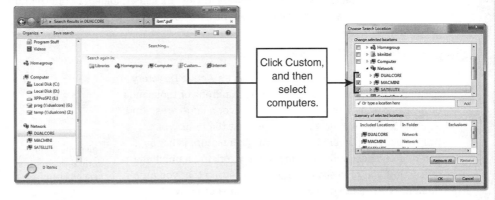

Figure 20.4
To search several computers for a file, select a network computer, start the search, click Custom, and then select the names of all computers to search.

To search all the shared libraries in a homegroup, the steps are similar:

1. Open an Explorer window and select Homegroup in the left pane.

2. Type all or part of the desired filename, or a word or phrase to be found in the file, in the Search box.

This will search all of the libraries shared by *other* users in the homegroup, but it won't search your own libraries (and it can't search the libraries in any computer that isn't turned on and connected to the network). To add your own libraries to the search, when the Search Again In ribbon appears at the bottom of the search results listing, click Custom. Check Libraries *and* Homegroup, then click OK.

You can use the Custom option to chose any number of specific locations that you'd like to search. In the Homegroup and Network categories, you can open the lists under these titles and select just particular users and specific categories of files. The "Computer" entry is useful, because it searches all drives attached to your computer. Just remember that every time you select Custom, you have to select *all* of the locations you'd like to include in the search.

On an Active Directory network, the domain administrator can choose to list, or *publish*, some shared folders in the directory; they might contain important resources that the company wants to make widely accessible and easy to find. See "Searching Active Directory," later in the chapter, for more information. If you are trying to find a particular shared folder but it has not been explicitly published in the directory, you're out of luck; there's no other way to find it besides browsing through the network's computers or searching specific computers as described earlier in this section.

Searching for Computers

To search for a computer by name, select the word Network in the Explorer window's left pane and type all or part of a computer name in the Search box. Windows will display an icon for each matching computer.

You can explore any of the listed computers to view its shared folders or printers; if you delve into the shared folders, you can open or copy the available files as you find them.

Searching for Printers

Searching for printers is possible only on an Active Directory network. In a large corporate network, hundreds or thousands of network printers might be scattered over a large area. Find Printers lets an AD network user find just the right type of printer using a powerful query form. This feature is handy if you're a business traveler using the network in an unfamiliar office, or if you're in such a large office setting that you aren't familiar with all the printing resources on your network.

To search AD for a printer, open any Windows Explorer view and select Network in the left pane. Click Search Active Directory and select Printers in the Find drop-down list. You can leave the scope set to Entire Directory, or you can select a subdomain next to the word In.

You can search for printers in three ways: by name and location, by printer capabilities, or by more advanced attributes. To find all the printers in the directory, leave the form blank, as shown in Figure 20.5, and click Find Now.

 tip

View the entire directory the first time you use Find Printers. This will give you an idea of how location and printer names are organized in your company. If too many names are listed, you can click Clear All to clear the search listing and then restrict your search using a location name that makes sense for your network. For example, if your company has put floor and room numbers such as "10-123" in the Location column, you could restrict your search to printers on the 10th floor by searching for "10-" in Location.

Figure 20.5
You can search Active Directory for a printer based on location or capabilities (features) that you require.

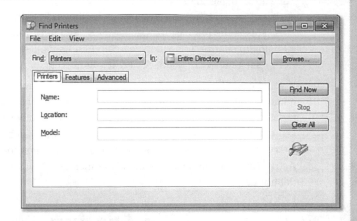

Searching Active Directory

Active Directory contains information on many more objects than just users, computers, and printers. It includes shared folders, organizational units, policy settings, certificate templates, containers (business groupings), foreign security principals, remote storage services, RPC services (used for advanced client/server software applications), and trusted domains. It can also contain information for other objects defined by your own organization. Most of this information is used only by domain administrators to configure Windows networks over vast distances; however, you can search for anything and can specify your qualifications based on more than 100 different criteria.

To make an AD search, select Network in the left pane of a Windows Explorer view and select Search Active Directory. The AD search tool appears, as shown in Figure 20.6. To start, select one of several search categories in the Find drop-down list. You can use a quick form-based search for any of the most useful objects, similar to the forms you may have seen if you have ever searched for users.

Figure 20.6
Using the Active Directory search tool, you can use a simplified form for any of several categories of directory objects, or you can use the Advanced tab to construct queries using any of the available fields.

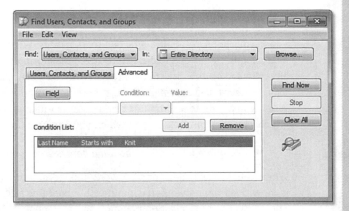

You can also use the Advanced tab to build specific queries such as "Last Name Starts with *xxx*," as shown in Figure 20.6. This is the full-blown search system, and here you have 53 fields to choose from when searching for users, everything from Assistant to ZIP Code: A to Z, if you need it.

If you choose Find: Custom Search, you have the whole gamut of fields in the entire catalog of ADobjects to choose from, and in the Advanced tab, you can enter Lightweight Directory Access Protocol (LDAP) queries directly for submission to the AD service. This is the native query syntax for Active Directory, and it's available here mostly for system debugging.

 note

Strangely, in Custom Search, any qualifiers set in the form-based search are applied along with a manually entered LDAP query; you should be sure to clear the form if you are going to enter an LDAP query directly.

note

For a brief introduction to LDAP queries, you might visit technet.microsoft.com and search for "LDAP Query Basics."

Security and File Sharing

As the preceding note says, Windows 7 computers only let network users see the presence of files and folders that they actually have permission to use, based in most cases on their username and password. It's worth explaining just how that permission is determined. It's not that difficult a topic, but it's complicated by the fact that there are several different ways that permissions are calculated by Windows networking, depending on settings and the versions of Windows you encounter. In the following discussion, I refer to "files," but the issues are the same for both the files and folders inside any shared folder.

There are two levels of security involved when Windows grants a user access to a file over a network: permission settings on the file itself, which would apply if the user logged on at the computer directly, and "network permissions," which can add additional *restrictions* when the file is accessed over the network, but can't grant any additional *permissions* that a user wouldn't have if he or she tried to access the file while logged in directly to the computer. I'll explain why this is done shortly. Let's look at file permissions first.

File Permissions and Networking

File permissions determine who can read, modify, write to, or delete a file or folder based on their user account. Files and folders stored on a disk formatted with the NTFS file system (which is always used on the disk that contains Windows 7) can have these permission settings set on a user-by-user basis as well as by membership in groups like "Administrators" or even "Everyone." When you log on to a computer using your username and password, these settings determine which files you can look at, and which you can change.

➡ *For more information about file permissions,* ***see*** *"NTFS File Permissions," **p. 903**.*

When you access a file over a network, this permission system still applies. What can get confusing is, how does the networked computer that contains a file you want to use determine who you are? The answer to that question depends on the version of Windows and some settings. Here are several scenarios you might encounter. Go down through the list to find the first scenario that describes your situation, and stop there. In the following discussion, "the network computer" refers to a computer on the network that has a file you want to use, and "you" and "your computer" are trying to get to the file.

- If your computer and the network computer are members of a domain network, your user account is recognized by all computers on the network. You'll get access to the file based on the permissions granted to your account, and to groups to which you belong.

- If your computer and the networked computer are members of a homegroup, and if you left enabled the Advanced Sharing setting Let Windows Manage the Workgroup Connections, as it is by default, your computer will connect to all other homegroup computers using the built-in user account HomeGroupUser$. The member computers all know the HomeGroupUser$ account's password, so homegroup access works regardless of how your user accounts are set up. Whenever you share a library, folder, or file with your homegroup, Windows sets permissions on that library, folder, or file so that the HomeGroupUser$ account has Read and/or Write access. In this way, all users in the homegroup get the same access rights to the shared resources.

- If the network computer runs Windows 7 or Vista with Password Protected Sharing turned on, or XP Professional with Simple File Sharing disabled, or Windows Server in a domain that your computer is not a member of, the network computer will see whether it has an account set up with the same name and password as on your own computer. If so, it will grant you access to files based on rights set for your account. If the account or password doesn't match, your computer will prompt you to enter an account name or password that *is* valid on the network computer.

- If both your computer and the network computer run Windows 7, and the network computer has Password Protected Sharing turned off, a rule unique to Windows 7 applies:

  - If the network computer has an account with the same name as your account, and that account has a password set, you will be given access to a file based on privileges set for your account and groups you belong to.

  - If the network computer doesn't have an account with the same name as yours, or if your account on that computer has no password set, files will be accessed via the Guest account. Basically, you will only be able to access files readable or writable by group Everyone.

- The last scenario is that the network computer runs Windows 7 or Vista with Password Protected Sharing turned off, or XP Home Edition or XP Professional with Simple File Sharing turned on, and your computer isn't running Windows 7. In this case, the network computer grants access using the Guest account in all cases. Basically, you'll only be able to use files that are readable and/or writable by Everyone or Guest.

Phew! I know this looks like a big mess, but it actually boils down to just two alternatives: A network computer either will use a specific account to access files, in which case you can get to the files that this account can see, or will use the Guest account, in which case you only can get to files that are marked as usable by Everyone or Guest.

Another point to remember is that files stored on removable media typically don't use the NTFS format, and don't have any per-user permission settings. Floppy disks and flash media formatted with the FAT or ExFAT file systems are readable and writable by everyone, and CD/DVD-ROMs are readable by everyone who connects to the computer. Network permissions, described next, do apply.

Network Permissions

The preceding permission scheme applies equally to files accessed over the network and files accessed directly by logging in to a computer. When you share a folder or drive through the network, though, you can assign privileges, again based on user accounts that act like a filter for the file permissions that we just discussed. A network user gets only the privileges that are listed in *both* file permissions *and* network permissions. Figure 20.7 shows how this works.

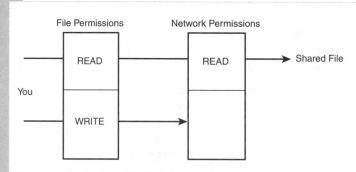

Figure 20.7
You only get access rights that are given to you both through file permissions and through network permissions.

Another way to look at this is, a network user *loses* any permissions that are *omitted* from the network permission list. This can be used in complex ways, but mostly only two situations are used:

- If you share a folder and set its network privilege list to give Read access, but not Write access, to Everyone, then users get Read access *if* their user account gives them permission, but *nobody* gets to modify its files over the network.

- If you set the network permissions so that Everyone has both Read and Write permissions, then users get exactly what they'd get if they tried to use the file while logged on directly; no more, no less.

These are the two ways Windows sets up network permissions when you share folders using the techniques that I describe later in the chapter.

Using Printers on the Network

Whether you're part of a large corporation or a small workgroup, or even if you're a home user with just two computers, network printing is a great time and money saver. Why connect a printer to each computer when it will spend most of its time idle? By not having to buy a printer for each user, you can spend the money you save more constructively on faster, higher-quality, and more interesting printers. You might add a color photo-quality printer or a transparency maker to give your network users more output choices.

Because the software comes with Windows 7, and you can hook computers together for about the cost of a movie ticket, printer sharing alone is a good enough reason to install a network.

The best part is that, from the user's standpoint, using a network printer is no different from using a local printer. Everything you learned about printing in Chapter 6, "Printing," applies to network printers; the only difference is in the one-time step of adding the printer to Windows. Later in the chapter, I describe how to share a printer attached to your computer; right now, let's look at using a printer that has already been shared elsewhere on the network.

Windows can directly attach to printers shared by any computer that supports Microsoft Networking services, whether it's running Windows 7, Vista, XP, 2000, NT, 98, or 95; Windows for Workgroups; OS/2, or even the Samba service from UNIX. Windows can also connect to networked printers that use the LPR or other TCP/IP protocols.

Using a Shared Printer

To use a shared printer, you have to set up an icon for the printer in your Devices and Printers window. The easiest way to do this is to browse or search your network for shared printers, following these steps:

1. Click Start, Computer. (Actually, any Windows Explorer window will work: Computer, Documents, and so on.)

2. In the left pane, click Network. Locate the computer that is sharing the printer you want to use. (On a large network, you can use the Search box to help find it.) Double-click the computer icon.

3. Double-click the icon for the printer you wish to use.

4. Windows will try to get the printer's driver software from the computer that is sharing the printer. Click Install Driver if you trust the owner of the other computer. Windows may also automatically locate and install a driver, if the driver software is "signed" (that is, certified as having come directly from the stated manufacturer without any modification). Click Cancel if you can't trust the other computer; in this case use the procedure that immediately follows this one, so that you can select your own driver software.

 tip

If you will use this printer most or all of the time, open Devices and Printers, right-click the printer's icon, and select Set As Default Printer.

You might want to verify that you can actually use the printer and that its output is correct. To do so, open Devices and Printers, right-click the printer icon, and select Printer Properties. Click Print a Test Page to ensure that the network printer is working correctly.

That's all there is to it. You can now use this printer just like any other Windows printer, so the printer-management discussion in Chapter 6 applies to network printers, too. The only difference is that the remote computer's administrator might not

 note

You might find that you *do* have access to the printer's Printer Properties dialog box. Don't make any changes without the permission of the printer's owner. It's considered bad form to change the hardware setup of someone else's printer without permission.

have given you management privileges for the printer, so you might not be able to change the printer's properties, or delete print jobs created by other users.

An alternative way to add a printer is with the Add Printer Wizard, using these steps:

1. Click Start, Devices and Printers, Add a Printer.

2. Select Add a Network, Wireless or Bluetooth Printer.

3. Windows 7 displays a list of printers that it knows about, such as ones that it finds shared within the same workgroup. If the printer you want to use is listed, select it, then click Next, and proceed with step 5.

4. If the printer that you want to connect to isn't listed, click (drumroll, please) The Printer That I Want Isn't Listed.

   You're then presented with another dialog box, where you can type the location and name of the printer to which you want to connect. If you know its network name already, click Select a Shared Printer by Name and enter the share name into the Name box in UNC format—for example, \\san\LaserJet. Click Next to finish installing the printer. If you don't know the name, click Browse, and you'll be able to dig into your network to find the printer. The Network window that appears has a functioning Search box in its upper-right corner. The search function works only when you've selected a computer name in the left pane. (And if you search for a printer by name, if results appear, be sure to select only a result that is shown with a shared printer icon.)

5. After you've identified the shared printer, click Next. Select the printer's manufacturer and model number from the displayed lists. If the printer model isn't listed, click Windows Update to see if the driver can be downloaded. Otherwise, follow the steps under "What to Do If Your Printer Isn't Listed" on **page 194**.

6. Click Next when you have selected your printer model. Then, follow any additional instructions to finish setting up the printer.

Again, as noted previously, you can now use this printer like any other Windows printer, and if you will use it most or all of the time, you may want to make it your default printer.

Using Printers over the Internet with IPP

The Internet Printing Protocol (IPP) permits you to send output to printers over the Internet. Some companies and service bureaus provide this sort of service. If you need to connect to an IPP-based printer, follow these steps:

1. Click Start, Control Panel, Programs, Turn Windows Features On or Off. Click the + sign next to Print and Document Services. Check Internet Printing Client if it's not already checked, then click OK. You only need to perform this step once.

2. Click Start, Devices and Printers, Add a Printer.

3. Select Add a Network, Wireless or Bluetooth Printer, then immediately click The Printer That I Want Isn't Listed.

4. Click Select a Shared Printer by Name, enter the URL supplied by the print service provider, then click Next.

5. You might be prompted to select the printer manufacturer and model number. The print service provider will tell you which model to select.

6. You might also be prompted to enter a username and password, which will also be supplied by the service provider. By default, Windows will use your current logon name, domain, and password.

When the new printer icon is installed, you have a fully functional Windows printer. You can view the pending jobs and set your print and page preferences as usual, as long as you're connected to the Internet (or the LAN, in a service establishment).

 tip

If you use a printing service while traveling, remember to delete the printer from your Printers folder when you leave town; you don't want to accidentally send a report to Katmandu after you've returned to Kalamazoo.

Using UNIX and LPR Printers

In the UNIX world, most shared printers use a protocol called LPR/LPD.

➡ *For more information about UNIX printing,* ***see*** *"Internetworking with UNIX and Linux," p. 497.*

The LPR protocol is used outside UNIX, too. Manufacturers such as Hewlett-Packard make direct network-connected printers that accept the LPR protocol, and many companies sell small LPR-based print server devices that can attach to your printer

 note

If you have a UNIX background, you might be happy to know that the familiar lpr and lpq utilities are available as command-line programs in Windows 7 once LPR support has been installed. Read on in this section to find instructions for installing LPR support.

as well. You can connect one of these printers to your LAN, configure its TCP/IP settings to match your LAN, and immediately print without running a cable from a computer to the printer. This way, you can place a printer in a more convenient place than can be reached by a 10-foot printer cable. Better yet, you can use these networked printers without requiring a Windows computer to be left turned on to manage it.

To have Windows send output to an LPR print queue or device, follow these steps:

1. Click Start, Control Panel, Programs, Turn Windows Features On or Off. Click the + sign next to Print and Document Services. Check LPR Port Monitor if it's not already checked, then click OK. You only need to perform this step once.

2. Click Start, Devices and Printers, Add a Printer.

3. Click Local Printer. (You're right, it doesn't make sense that you have to select Local, not Network.)

4. Select Create a New Port, and set the type to LPR Port. Click Next.

5. In the Add LPR Compatible Printer dialog box, enter the IP address or hostname of the UNIX or print server, and the name of the print queue on that server.

6. Select the manufacturer and printer model. (If the appropriate driver is not listed, you might be able to get it by clicking Windows Update.) Then, click Next to proceed with the printer installation.

Because an LPR printer is considered a local printer, you can share it with others on your network as a regular Windows shared printer. Alternatively, they can connect to it directly, as you did.

> **note**
>
> If you enter the wrong IP address, hostname, or print queue name, right-click the printer's icon and select Printer Properties. Select the Ports tab, highlight the LPR port, and click Delete Port. Click Add Port, and enter the correct information. When the new port has been added, check the check box next to its name.

Using Other Network-Connected Printers

Windows 7 can use other types of network-connected printers as well. Some printer models come with a built-in network connection, and others have a network adapter option. You can also buy network printer servers, which are small boxes with a network connector and one to three printer-connection ports. These devices let you locate printers in a convenient area, which doesn't need to be near a computer.

The installation procedures for various printer and server models vary. Your networked printer or print server has specific installation instructions. You have a choice about how the printer will be shared on your network:

- You can install the network-to-printer connection software on *one* of your Windows computers and then use standard Windows printer sharing to make the printer available to the other computers on your network.

- You can install the printer's connection software on *each* of your computers.

With the first method, you guarantee that print jobs will be run first come, first served (or you can set priorities for print jobs, if you want) because one computer will provide a single queue for the printer. Another plus is that you have to do the software setup only once; it's much easier to set up the additional workstations to use the standard Windows shared printer. The one computer must be left on for others to use the printer, however.

With the second method, each computer contacts the printer independently, so there could be contention for the printer. However, no computers need to be left on because each workstation contacts the printer directly.

You can use either method. The first one is simplest and is best suited for a busy office. The second method is probably more convenient for home networks and small offices.

Network Power User Topics

This section presents some Windows networking techniques that can let you get the most out of your network. You can scan through this section for any tips that might be helpful in your home or office.

Backing Up Your Computer over the Network

You can back up the contents of your hard disk, or attached external drives on your computer, to another computer's hard disk over the network. On all Windows 7 versions except Starter and Home Basic, you can back up to a shared network folder using the built-in Windows Backup program, as discussed under "The All New Backup and Restore" on **page 863**.

You can also back up files over the network using command-line tools. I give an example of this at the end of this chapter, under "Managing Network Resources Using the Command Line" on **page 573**.

Finally, most third-party back up program let you back up to a network location.

Adding a Network Folder to a Library

You can actually link other people's shared folders right into one of your own libraries, so that their content appears along with your own, although doing so is not quite as simple as you might hope. You have to use the following procedure:

1. View your library, for example, the Documents library.

2. At the top where it says "Includes:" and the number of locations, click the word Locations, then click Add.

3. In the Include Folder in Documents window, locate the folder you want to add, from one of two places:

   - If the folder you want to add belongs to another user on your own computer, select Computer in the left pane, then drill down into the drive on which Windows is installed, then into the Users folder, then into the other user's profile folder, until you locate the folder you want to add.

   - If the folder you want to add is on another computer, select Network in the left pane, double-click the computer's name, then double-click the shared folder. (To get to a folder shared by one of the computer's users, the shared folder is named Users.) Then, drill down to the folder you want to add to your library.

 note

Don't dig into the Homegroup list. Most of the items listed in the Homegroup list are libraries. You need to locate the actual folder that went into the other user's library, in one of the two locations just mentioned.

4. When you have located the desired folder, click it, then click Include Folder.

Be aware, though, that if you add a folder from another computer to one of your own libraries, Windows may take a long time to display your library when the other computer is not running and connected to the network.

Sharing and Using an Entire Drive

Shared folders don't have to be subfolders. Computer owners can share the *root folder* of a disk drive, making the entire drive available over the network. This is especially useful with DVD, CD, floppy, and USB disk drives. For example, if an entire CD-ROM drive is shared, you can access the data CD in it from any computer on the network.

Just so you know, Windows automatically shares your entire hard drive with the special name C$. (Any other hard drives would also be shared as D$, E$, and so on.) These shares don't show up when you browse the network—the dollar sign at the end tells Windows to keep the name hidden. Oddly enough, they don't appear if you view the drive's Sharing properties either. You can only see them if you type "net share" at the command prompt. And, you can't use these shares on a home/small office workgroup network; they can be accessed only by the "true" Administrator account on a domain network.

But, you can get around this by sharing the root (top level) folder of one of your drives using a share name of your own choosing. For example, you could right-click your DVD drive in the Computer window, and share the drive using the name dvd, using the instructions for sharing a folder found later in the chapter. Then, on another computer, you can map a drive letter to the shared disc, using the instructions under "Mapping Drive Letters," also found later in this chapter.

 tip

You can use this technique to install software on a computer that has no working CD/DVD drive but does have a working network connection. Just put the CD into a computer that does have a working drive, and share that drive.

Understanding the UNC Naming Convention

For more complex networks, you should have some background in the way that files and folders are named on a network. File and folder shares are accessed via Universal Naming Convention (UNC) names with Windows 7, just as in previous versions of Windows.

Virtually the only difference you'll notice between local and networked files is in their names. Each computer on your network has a name, and every folder or printer that is offered up for shared use on the network must be given a share name as well. For example, if I want to give officemates the use of my business documents, I might create a folder on my hard disk named C:\business related documents and give that folder the share name of docs.

 note

It might seem confusing to use a different name for the share name than for the folder. The reason for this is that whereas folder names can be very long and can contain spaces, if your network has Linux or Mac computers on it, it's best if your share names are limited to 12 characters or less and have no spaces. Think of it as a "nickname."

My computer is named Ambon, so other users can use this folder by its network name, \\ambon\docs.

To continue the preceding example, I might specify the location of a particular file on my hard drive with a drive and pathname, like this:

```
C:\business related documents\roofing bids.xls
```

A user on another computer can refer to this same file using a syntax called the *Universal Naming Convention*, or *UNC*:

```
\\ambon\docs\roofing bids.xls
```

The double backslash indicates that `ambon` is the name of a computer on the LAN instead of the name of a folder on the hard disk. `docs` is the share name of the folder, and everything past that specifies the path and file relative to that shared folder.

If the computer whose files you want to use is on a corporate LAN using Active Directory or is part of a distant company network, you can also specify the remote computer name more completely, as in the following:

`\\ambon.mycompany.com\docs\roofing bids.xls`

Or, if you know only the remote computer's IP network address (such as when you're connecting to the remote computer with Dial-Up Networking), you can even use a notation like this:

`\\192.168.0.10\docs\roofing bids.xls`

No matter which way you specify the remote computer, Windows finds it and locates its shared folder `docs`.

 note

Elsewhere in this chapter, I use UNC names such as `\\server\folder` as a generic sort of name. By `server`, I mean the name of the computer that's sharing `folder`. It doesn't have to be a Windows Server, it can be any computer on your network. You need to use your network's actual computer names and shared folder names.

Shared printers are also given share names and are specified by their UNC path. For example, if I share my HP LaserJet 4V printer, I might give it the share name `HPLaser`, and it will be known on the network as `\\ambon\HPLaser`. Here, it's not a folder, but rather a printer, and Windows keeps track of the type of resource.

Mapping Drive Letters

If you frequently use the same shared network folder, you can make it a "permanent houseguest" of your computer by *mapping* the network folder to an unused drive letter on your computer—one of the letters after your hard drive's usual `C:` and the CD-ROM drive's usual `D:`. You can give the shared folder `\\server\shared` the drive letter `X:`, for example, so that it appears that your computer has a new disk drive `X:`, whose contents are those of the shared folder.

Mapping gives you several benefits:

- The mapped drive appears along with your computer's other real, physical drives in the Computer view for quick browsing, opening, and saving of files.

- Access to the shared folder is faster because Windows maintains an open connection to the sharing computer.

- MS-DOS applications can use the shared folder through its assigned letter. Most legacy DOS applications can't accept UNC-formatted names such as `\\server\shared\subfolder\file`, but they can use a path such as `I:\subfolder\file`.

- If you need to, you can map a shared folder using an alternative username and password to gain access rights that you might not have with your current Windows login name.

To map a drive, follow these steps:

1. Open any Windows Explorer window. Press and release the Alt key to display the menu. Then click Tools, Map Network Drive.

2. Select an unused drive letter from the drop-down list, as shown in Figure 20.8. If possible, pick a drive letter that has some association for you with the resource you'll be using: E for Editorial, S for Sales—whatever makes sense to you.

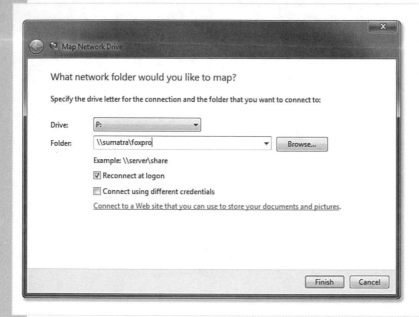

Figure 20.8
You can select any unused drive letter to use for the drive mapping.

3. Select the name of the shared folder you want to assign to the drive letter. You can type the UNC-formatted name, if you know it already—for example, `\\servername\sharename`.

Alternatively, you can click Browse to poke through your network's resources and select the shared folder, as described earlier in this chapter. Find and select the desired shared folder, then click OK.

4. You have two options:

- If you want this mapping to reappear every time you log in, check Reconnect at Logon. If you don't check this box, the mapping will disappear when you log off.

- If your current Windows username and password don't give you sufficient permissions to use the shared resource, or if your username won't be recognized at the other computer because your account name is different there, select Connect Using a Different Username. (This works only if usernames are actually used on the networked computer. If it always grants access via the Guest account, as discussed under "File Permissions and Networking" earlier in this chapter, it doesn't matter what account information you supply.)

note

You must use the same username for *all* connections to a given computer. If you have other drive letters already mapped to the other computer with your original username, you have to unmap those drives before you can make a drive mapping with a different username.

5. Click Finish.

6. If you selected Connect Using a Different Username, Windows will display a prompt for a username and password. Enter them, then click OK.

After you map a drive letter, the drive appears in your Computer list along with your local disk drives. You might notice a couple of funny things with these drives:

- If you haven't accessed the network drive for 20 minutes or so, it might turn gray, indicating that the network connection to the remote computer has been disconnected. When you use the drive again, it will reconnect and turn black.

- If the remote computer (or you) really goes offline, a red X appears through the drive.

 tip

If you're using Windows 7 Professional, Enterprise, or Ultimate editions, you can make the drive's contents available even when you're disconnected from the network. For instructions, see "Offline Files" on **page 991**.

Mapping a Drive to a Subfolder

When you're setting up a mapped drive and you browse to find a shared folder, you may notice that Windows lets you delve into the shared folders themselves. If you drill down into a subfolder and select it as the location to use in mapping a drive letter, you'll find that the mapped drive starts at the subfolder. That is, the subfolder becomes the mapped drive's "root directory," and you can't explore upward into the shared folder that contains it. You can map a drive letter to a subfolder using the GUI method described in the preceding section, or using the net use command-line utility described later.

Mapping a subfolder can be a good thing because it makes any program that uses the mapped drive letter see just that subfolder as the drive's root directory.

 tip

This feature is most useful for administrators in setting up scripts to map drives based on a user's login name. For example, mail might be stored in subfolders of \\server\mail according to username. Mapping drive M: to the folder \\server\mail\%username% would let users get at their mail (directly) via drive M: and discourage users from poking around in other people's mail folders.

Once administrators have configured the drive mapping, users can configure their mail programs to get mail from drive M:, and the same configuration will work for everyone.

Sharing Resources

On a large corporate LAN, most important network resources, shared folders, and printers are set up and tightly controlled by network managers. You might not be able to share resources from your own computer, although in many companies you can, and it's useful to know how to do this so that you can easily give co-workers access to files that you use in common.

On the other hand, on a home or office workgroup network, any Computer Administrator user can set up and manage file and printer sharing.

Before you decide to share resources, you should give some thought to just what you want to share, how you want to organize it, and who should have permission to see, use, or change files you've published in the shared folders.

You can elect to share your files with others in several different ways:

- If your computer is part of a homegroup, you can store files you'd like to share in one of your libraries, and share your libraries with the homegroup

- You can move files to a folder under \Users\Public, which is called the Public user profile folder. Here, anyone can access them automatically without your having to do anything else but enable sharing the Public folder, as described shortly.

- You can elect to share any folder anywhere within your own user profile; the files or folders can reside anywhere within your own profile folder found under \Users on the hard disk.

- You can create new, separate folders on your hard disk and share them under their own share names.

In the past, it was more common to create separate folders and share them independently. To some extent this makes it easier for other users to locate shared folders, since each folder has its own name. Starting with Windows 7, Microsoft suggests "sharing in place," using any of the first three methods. These are easier to set up, but it's perhaps a bit harder on people who want to use shared materials, since it all has to be found within the single shared Users folder. Any of the methods are acceptable, though; it really just depends on how you prefer to organize your files.

The next sections describe how to share folders these various ways.

Sharing with a Homegroup

If your computer is a member of a homegroup, you can share the entire contents of any of your libraries so that the other members of the homegroup can see and use files in your libraries, but not change them. Use the following procedure:

1. Click the network icon in the taskbar and select Open Network and Sharing Center, or click Start, Control Panel, View Network Status and Tasks (under Network and Internet).

2. Click Choose Homegroup and Sharing Options.

3. Check the libraries that you want to share, and uncheck any that you don't want to share, as shown in Figure 20.9. Click Save Changes when you're done.

This method shares libraries *read-only*: All other homegroup members can see, view, play, and print any of the files in your shared libraries, but they can't change, delete, rename, or add to them.

Figure 20.9
You can change your mind about sharing or not sharing your libraries and printers with the homegroup at any time.

Setting Permissions for HomeGroup Sharing

If you want to let other users change the files in one of your libraries, or if you want to enable or prevent access to a specific library, folder, or individual file, use this procedure:

1. Locate the library, folder, or file in Windows Explorer, right-click its icon, and select Share With.

2. Select one of these choices:

   - **Nobody**—Keeps everyone else out of the library, file, or folder.

   - **Homegroup (Read)**—Lets everyone else in the home-group read, but not change, rename, delete, or add to the file(s).

   - **Homegroup (Read/Write)**—Lets all other homegroup users not only view, but make changes to the selected library, folder, or file. This includes adding new files, deleting files, and so on.

   - **Specific People**—Enables you to choose access levels for individual users. This may not work quite as you might guess, as I'll explain next.

 note

The first time you share a new folder, use one of the two Share With Homegroup options. This makes the folder appear in the Homegroup listing on everyone else's computer. *Then*, if you want to customize access for specific people, right-click again and select Share With Specific People to make adjustments.

Editing Permissions for Specific People

The fourth choice, Specific People, lets you set permissions for yourself, for the homegroup, for Everyone, and for individual user accounts, using the permissions list shown in the File Sharing dialog box, shown in Figure 20.10.

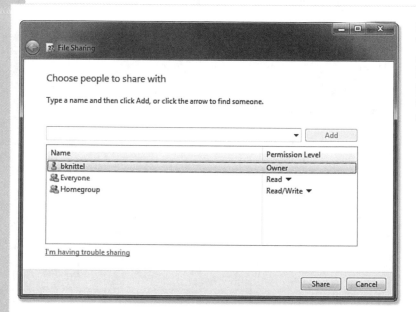

Figure 20.10
You can control the type of access to a shared library, folder, or file that is granted to your homegroup, and in some cases to specific user accounts.

Any entries that you add for individual users *won't* apply when other users in your homegroup try to use the shared resource, because member computers always use a common built-in account. Entries for individual users only affect access from computers that aren't members of the home-group, and from computers not running Windows 7. And whether a specific account will be used or the Guest account will be used depends on that complex list of situations I provided under "File Permissions and Networking" earlier in this chapter.

If you have computers on your network that run older versions of Windows, and thus can't be members of the homegroup, you can give their users easy access to your shared files in either of two ways:

- You can turn off Password Protected Sharing on your computer. Then, add Everyone to the permission list. The other computers will get access to the files this way.

- If you want to leave Password Protected Sharing turned on on your computer, either create accounts for each of the other computers' users on your computer, using their account names and passwords, or create a single user account named, for example, "sharing" on your computer, assign a password to it, and have all of the other users use this account when they connect over the network. Add this account to the permissions list, and grant it Read or Read/Write access.

To change the permissions granted to a user or group listed in the File Sharing dialog box, shown in Figure 20.10, change the entry in the Permission Level column to Read, Read/Write, or Remove, which removes the entry from the list. To add a new entry, select a name from the drop-down list next to the Add button, then click the Add button. You can then change the new entry's Permission Level.

Your account is listed as the file's or folder's owner, and you can't change this entry.

➡ *To see how to set up a homegroup for your Windows 7 computers,* **see** *"Setting Up a Homegroup," p. 478.*

 note

If you add Everyone to the list, the permissions you give to it will set the minimum access level granted to, well, everyone. Specifically, if you grant Everyone Read/Write access, this trumps any other settings in the list. *Anyone* will be able to change the files.

Sharing the Public Profile Folder

There is a very simple way to share files and folders with other users without using a homegroup, which makes this a simple solution if your network includes computers running older versions of Windows.

The trick is to use the folder named `\Users\Public` on the drive that contains Windows. If you enable Public Folder Sharing, this folder will be readable and writable by everyone on the network.

To enable sharing the Public folder, follow these steps:

1. Click the network icon in the taskbar and select Open Network and Sharing Center; or click Start, Control Panel, View Network Status and Tasks (under Network and Internet).

2. Click Change Advanced Sharing Options.

3. Locate Public Folder Sharing, and select Turn On Sharing. Then click Save Changes.

This makes the folder available to anyone who can connect to your computer over the network. Next, you must make it possible for people to connect. You can do this in either of two ways:

 tip

In previous versions of Windows, the public folder was listed in the [My] Computer display as "Shared Documents." It's not this easy to get to in Windows 7, so if you use this sharing method, you might want to create a shortcut to `\Users\Public` on your desktop for easy access.

■ Leave Password Protected Sharing turned on. Each of the other users on the network will need an account on your computer. You can create individual accounts, or you can create a single account, set a password on it, and have all the other users use that name and password when they go to use your computer's shared folder `Users\Public`. (The folder's full UNC name is `\\computername\Users\Public`, with the actual name of your computer substituted in place of *computername*.)

■ In the Change Advanced Sharing Options screen, turn Password Protected Sharing off. Now, literally anyone who can connect to your network will be able to read and write files in your computer's shared folder `Users\Public`.

 caution

If you use this second option, be careful only to let trustworthy people connect to your network. If you have a wireless network, you *must* have WEP or WPA security enabled on it.

Once the Public folder has been shared, you must move or copy files or folders that you want to share into the Public folder structure.

Sharing Your Own Folders

To share a folder that's inside your user profile (for example, a folder inside your Documents folder), without sharing an entire library, just right-click the folder or file in any Windows Explorer view and select Share With.

The entire \Users directory structure is shared by default on Windows 7, so all that's necessary is to let Windows change your file's or folder's permissions so that network users can see it. This is called "sharing in place." Just follow the steps:

1. Locate your file or folder in Windows Explorer. Right-click it and select Share With.

2. If the Homegroup options appear, select one of the two Homegroup options, as outlined previously under "Setting Permissions for HomeGroup Sharing." This makes the folder appear in everyone else's Homegroup listing. If you want to customize access to the folder, right-click it again, select Share With, Specific People, and proceed as described under "Editing Permissions for Specific People."

   If the Homegroup options don't appear, select Specific People, and proceed as described under "Editing Permissions for Specific People."

If you later want to stop sharing this file or folder, right-click and select Sharing With, Nobody.

Sharing Folders Independently

To share a folder that isn't inside your user profile folder, follow these steps:

1. Locate the folder in Windows Explorer, or to share an entire drive, select the name of the CD-ROM, floppy, USB, or hard drive from the Computer view.

2. Right-click the folder's or drive's icon and choose Share With.

3. If the Homegroup options appear, proceed as outlined previously under "Setting Permissions for HomeGroup Sharing." (Be sure to select one of the two Homegroup options first, even if you intend to customize access to specific users).

   If the only option is Advanced Sharing, select it and skip to step 4.

   If the Specific People option is available, and you are okay with having the folder's share name exactly match the folder's actual name, select Specific People and proceed as described under "Editing Permissions for Specific People."

   Otherwise, press Esc to remove the menu, right-click the folder's or drive's icon, select Properties, and select the Sharing tab

4. If you are okay with having the folder's share name exactly match its actual name, click the Share button, then proceed as described under "Editing Permissions for Specific People."

5. Click Advanced Sharing. Click Share This Folder, and correct the share name as desired.

6. You can enter a comment that will appear when people browse to this folder over the network, if you wish.

7. To set permissions, you could click the Permissions button and edit the network access permissions using an interface similar to the one for editing NTFS file permissions. (If you do, recall the discussion under "Security and File Sharing" earlier in this chapter. The permissions you would set here only serve to filter file access permissions set on the Security tab.)

In Windows 7, it's easier to avoid the Permissions button; just click OK to create the share, then click the Share button to change or add to the permissions. With this method, Windows will adjust both network *and* file permissions to match your selections. It's a lot easier, and it's sure to give you the results you want.

8. Click OK to close the dialog box.

If you later want to stop sharing the folder or drive, follow these steps:

1. Locate the folder or drive in Windows Explorer. Right-click it and select Properties.

2. Select the Sharing tab, and click Advanced Sharing.

3. Uncheck Share This Folder, then click OK.

Alternatively, you can locate the folder, right-click it, and select Share With, Nobody. However, this not only removes the share, it may also remove file permission changes.

 tip

You can prevent other users from seeing your shared folder when they browse the network by adding a dollar sign to the end of the share name, as in `mystuff$`. They must know to type this name to use the shared folder. This technique alone does *not* prevent anyone from seeing your files if they know the share name.

note

If you are canceling sharing of an entire drive, you may notice that in Windows 7, the administrative share `C$`, `D$`, and so on is not listed. You can safely uncheck Share This Folder and the administrative share will not be canceled.

File Is in Use by Another User

If you go to edit a file in a folder you've shared on the network, and receive an error message indicating that the file is in use by another user, you can find out which remote user has the file open by using the Shared Folder tool in Computer Management, as I describe later in this chapter under "Monitoring Use of Your Shared Folders."

You can wait for the remote user to finish using your file, or you can ask that person to quit. Only in a dire emergency should you use the Shared Folder tool to disconnect the remote user or close the file. The only reasons I can think of to do this are that the remote user's computer has crashed but your computer thinks the connection is still established, or that the remote user is an intruder.

Sharing Printers

You can share any of your "local" printers so that other people on the network can use it. A "local" printer is any printer that is directly cabled to your computer, or to which you connected via the network using LPR or other direct network protocols.

To be sure that printer sharing is enabled, do the following. You should only need to do this once.

1. Click the network icon in the taskbar and select Open Network and Sharing Center; or click Start, Control Panel, View Network Status and Tasks (under Network and Internet).

2. Look to see what type of network you're attached to. If your network is labeled Public Network, and you really are connected to a public network (for example, in a café, hotel, or school), you should *not* enable file and printer sharing—this would expose your computer to hackers. If the label says Public Network but you really are on a safe, protected home or office network, click the Public Network label and change it to Home or Work, as appropriate.

3. At the left, click Change Advanced Sharing Settings.

4. Under File and Printer Sharing, make sure Turn On File and Printer Sharing is selected. If it isn't, select it and click Save Changes; otherwise, click Cancel. This will take you back to the Network and Sharing Center.

5. If your computer is part of a homegroup, click Choose Homegroup and Sharing Options. If Printers isn't checked, check it and click Save Changes; otherwise click Cancel.

6. Close the Network and Sharing Center window.

Now you can share any printer that is attached to your computer. To share a printer, follow these steps:

1. Click Start, Devices and Printers.

2. Right-click a printer that you'd like to share and select Printer Properties. This is near the middle of the right-click menu; you don't want the last entry labeled just "Properties."

3. Select the Sharing tab.

4. If Share This Printer isn't already checked, check it. Windows will fill in a share name for the printer, as shown in Figure 20.11. If you like, you can shorten or simplify it.

5. Click OK.

Other people on your network can now use your printer, by following the instructions earlier in the chapter under "Using Shared Printers."

In most cases, that's all you need to do. In some cases you might wish to change some the advanced settings described in the next few sections, but these are optional.

Figure 20.11
Enabling sharing for a printer.

Setting Printer Permissions

If you have a workgroup network and have disabled Password Protected Sharing, or if you have set up a homegroup, you don't need to worry about setting permissions for printers: anyone can use your shared printer. If you're on a domain network, or have chosen to use detailed user-level permissions on your workgroup network, you can control access to your shared printers with security attributes that can be assigned to users or groups, as shown in Figure 20.12 and described next:

Permission	Lets User or Group...
Print	Send output to the printer.
Manage this printer	Change printer configuration settings, and share or unshare a printer.
Manage documents	For the CREATOR OWNER entry, this permission lets a user suspend or delete his or her own print jobs. For other users and groups, this permission lets the user cancel or suspend *other* users' print jobs.
Special permissions	Don't bother with this entry; it just controls whether a user can change the permission settings.

You don't have to change any of the default permission settings, unless you want to restrict the use of the printer to just specific users on your network. If this is the case, open Devices and Printers, right-click the printer whose settings you want to change, and select Printer Properties. View the Security tab. Select group Everyone, and click Remove. Then, click Add to add specific users or groups, and give them Print permission. (You could also give someone Manage This Printer or Manage Documents, if you really do want to let them change the printer's settings or delete other users' print jobs.)

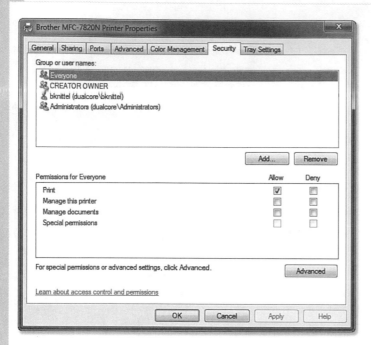

Figure 20.12
The Security tab lets you assign printer-management permissions for users, groups, and the creator of each print job.

Don't change the CREATOR OWNER entry, however. It should have the Manage Documents permission checked so that a user can delete his or her own print jobs from the queue.

Changing the Location of the Spool Directory

When jobs are queued up to print, Windows stores the data it has prepared for the printer in a folder on the computer that's sharing the printer. Data for your own print jobs and for any network users will all end up on your hard drive temporarily. If the drive holding your Windows folder is getting full and you'd rather house this print data on another drive, you can change the location of the spool directory.

To change the location of the Windows print spooler folder, follow these steps:

1. Open the Devices and Printers window.

2. Click on any printer, then, in the upper task menu, click Print Server Properties.

3. Select the Advanced tab, and click Change Advanced Settings.

4. Enter a new location for the Spool Folder and click OK.

Printer Pooling

If your network involves heavy-duty printing, you might find that your printers are the bottleneck in getting your work done. One solution is to get faster printers, and another is to add multiple printers. But, if you have two printers shared separately, you'll have to choose one for your printing, and you'll almost certainly encounter bank-line syndrome: The other line always seems to move faster.

The way around this problem is to use printer pooling. You can set up one printer queue that sends its output to two or more printers. The documents line up in one list, and the printers take jobs from the front of the line, first come, first served.

To set up pooled printers, follow these steps:

1. Buy identical printers—at least, they must be identical from the software point of view.

2. Set up and test one printer, and configure network sharing for it.

3. Install the extra printer(s) on the same computer as the first. If you use network-connected printers, you need to add the necessary additional network ports.

4. View the printer's Properties dialog box and select the Ports tab. Mark Enable Printer Pooling and mark the ports for the additional printers.

That's all there is to it; Windows passes print jobs to as many printers as you select on the Ports tab.

Managing Your Network

When you select Network in the left pane of any Windows Explorer view, the top of the window lists some tasks that can help you manage your network:

- **Network and Sharing Center**—Opens the Network and Sharing Center window, which you can use to make new network connections, and also change the Home, Work, or Public label for your current network.

- **Add a Printer**—Opens a wizard to connect to a printer, either a locally attached or a networked printer.

- **Add a Wireless Device**—Opens a wizard to assist in adding a wireless device such as a wireless printer or network card.

Additional tasks related to using a network can be performed from within the Network and Sharing Center:

- **Set Up a New Connection or Network**—Starts a wizard to connect to other types of networks, for example, to define a connection to a corporate network via modem or over the Internet.

- **Connect to a Network**—Displays a list of active and defined network connections. This can be used, for example, to actually connect to another network via dial-up or VPN networking.

- **Choose Homegroup and Sharing Options**—Lets you join or leave a homegroup, and control what libraries are shared with the group. The tasks you can perform from here are described shortly.

- **Change Advanced Sharing Settings**—Lets you control networking services and select whether or not passwords are required on your network, as discussed in Chapter 17.

- **Troubleshoot Problems**—Lets you start troubleshooters to investigate and repair common network problems.

If you select Choose Homegroup and Sharing Options, you can perform several tasks to work with your homegroup. If you aren't currently a member of a homegroup, you'll be able to create one, provided that your network location is set to Home Network. If you are member of a homegroup already, there are several actions you can select:

- **View or Print the Homegroup Password**—Click this to redisplay the password that other computers need to join your homegroup.

- **Change the Password**—Click to select your own password for your homegroup. We suggest that you keep the random one that Windows generates for you, but you can change it if you like. If you do want to change it, it's best to do so before you join other computers to the group. And *don't* change it to your own user account password or one you use for, say, your online banking, since anyone who uses a member computer can view this password.

- **Leave the Homegroup**—Click to remove your computer from the group.

- **Change Advanced Sharing Settings**—Click to change networking features such as Password Protected Sharing. For more information about this setting, see "Using Windows Vista and XP with a Homegroup" on **page 494**, and "Security and File Sharing" on **page 550**.

- **Start the HomeGroup Troubleshooter**—Click if you encounter problems connecting to other homegroup users or computers.

In addition, Windows provides tools that you can use to monitor the use of the files you're sharing, and command-line tools that you can use to manage network resources that you use and share.

Monitoring Use of Your Shared Folders

If you've shared folders on your LAN, you might want to know who's using them. For example, you might need to know this information if someone were editing a file in your shared folder. If you tried to edit the same file, you'd be told by your word processor that the file was "in use by another." But by whom?

The Computer Management tool can help you. Open the Start menu, right-click Computer, select Manage, and open the Shared Folders item in the left pane. The Sessions and Open Files sections can show you who is using your shared folders, and which files they currently have open. In an emergency, you can right-click and disconnect a user or close an open file with the Delete key. (This is a drastic measure and is sure to mess up the remote user, so use it only when absolutely necessary.)

Managing Network Resources Using the Command Line

If you find yourself repeating certain network and file operations day after day, it makes sense to try to automate the processes. You might get so used to the graphical interface that you forget the command line, but it's still there, and you can perform drive mappings and printer selections with the command line almost as easily as from the GUI.

The `net` command comes to us virtually unchanged since the original PC network software developed by Microsoft and IBM debuted in 1984. There are so many variations of the `net` command that I think of them as separate commands: `net view`, `net use`, `net` *whatever*. Each `net` command contains a word that selects a subcommand or operation type.

Interestingly, the `net` command not only can manage and explore your network, it also can start and stop Windows services and create user accounts and groups. You can get online help listing all the `net` subcommands by typing `net /?`, and get detailed help by typing `net` *command* `/?`, where *command* is any one of the `net` subcommands.

The most common use of the `net` command is to map network folders to drive letters, and network printers to LPT ports for use by MS-DOS programs, using the `net use` format. Net use makes and disconnects drive mappings, and establishes printer redirection for command-line programs. The basic command is as follows:

net use *drive* sharename

The following example maps drive letter Q to the shared folder \\abalone\book:

```
net use q: \\abalone\book
```

You can't replace the shared folder attached to an already mapped drive, so you should try to delete a previous mapping before trying to make a new one:

```
net use q: /delete
net use q: \\abalone\book
```

 tip

If the drive mapping didn't exist beforehand, the `/delete` command will print an error message. That's fine if you're typing commands directly in the Command Prompt window. If you perform drive mapping in a batch file, the error message would be disconcerting. You can prevent it from appearing by issuing the command this way:

```
net use q: /delete >nul 2>nul
```

NUL is a special filename to Windows; it's basically a black hole for data.

Here is an example of a batch file that performs a simple computer-to-computer backup of some important files. Let's say I want to back up the folder C:\book, and all of its subfolders, from my computer to a shared folder on another computer named abalone. I could put the following commands into a file named backup_book.bat:

```
@echo off
net use q: /delete 1>nul 2>nul
net use q: \\abalone\book
xcopy c:\book q: /e /r /c /y
net use q: /delete
```

net use also maps network printers to the legacy DOS printer devices LPT1, LPT2, and LPT3. The only way to redirect DOS program output to a network printer is through net use.

The following command directs DOS application LPT1 printer output to the network printer:

```
net use lpt1: \\server\printername
```

The following command cancels it:

```
net use lpt1: /delete
```

TROUBLESHOOTING YOUR NETWORK

When Good Networks Go Bad

As part of my software consulting work, I end up doing a fair bit of network support for my clients. And every time I get a call from a client with a network problem, I cringe. I never know whether it's going to take 10 minutes or a week to fix. Sometimes the problem isn't so bad; I've fixed more than one "broken" computer by turning it on. If such an easy fix doesn't present itself immediately, though, a bit of a cold sweat breaks out on my forehead. The problem could be anything. How do you even start to find a nasty problem in the maze of cards, wires, drivers, and hidden, inexplicable system services? And it's difficult enough debugging the stuff that belongs there. What if viruses, adware, or rootkits are messing up the works?

Well, if you work for a corporation with a network support staff, of course, the answer to any of these questions is "Call the Help Desk!" or "Call Bob!" or call whoever or whatever is responsible for network problems in your organization, and then take a refreshing walk around the block while someone else sweats over your network. It's great if you can get that kind of support. If you want to or have to go it alone, though, the good news is that some tools provided with Windows can help you find the problem. After discussing troubleshooting in general, this chapter shows you how to use these tools.

In reading this chapter, you probably won't find the solution to any particular network problem you're having. I can't really help you solve any one specific problem here, but I can show you some of the tools available to help you identify the source of a problem you might have.

Getting Started

I've spent many years helping clients and friends with hardware, software, and network problems. One thing I've noticed is that the most common—and most frustrating—way people report a problem is to say "I can't..." or "The computer won't..." Unfortunately, knowing what *doesn't* happen isn't helpful at all. I always have to ask "What happens when you *try*?" The answer to that question usually gets me well on the way to solving the problem. The original report usually leaves out important error messages and symptoms that can identify the problem. So, start by trying to express whatever problem you're having in terms of what *is* happening, not what isn't. You'll move from "I can't log on at the bank" to something like "The bank's website says my password is invalid" or "Windows says that I don't have any network connections." This leads from the vague toward something that you can grapple with.

Extending that principle, as you work on a problem, pay as much attention to what *does* work as to what doesn't. Knowing what isn't broken lets you eliminate whole categories of problems. For example, check to see whether a problem affects just one computer or all the computers on your local area network (LAN). If other computers can manage the task that one computer is having trouble with, you know that the problem is located *in that one computer*, or in its connection to the others.

The following are some other questions I always ask:

- Does the problem occur all the time or just sometimes?

- Can you reproduce the problem consistently? If you can define a procedure to reproduce the problem, can you reduce it to the shortest, most direct procedure possible?

- Has the system ever worked, even once? If so, when did it stop working, and what happened just before that? What changed?

These questions can help you determine whether the problem is fundamental (for example, due to a nonfunctioning network card) or interactive (that is, due to a conflict with other users, with new software, or confined to a particular subsystem of the network). You might be able to spot the problem right off the bat if you look at the scene this way. If you can't, you can use some tools to help narrow down the problem.

Generally, network problems fall into one or more of these categories:

- Application software

- Network clients

- Name-resolving services

- Network protocols

- Addressing and network configuration

- Driver software

- Network cards and hardware configuration

- Wiring/hubs

If you can determine which category a problem falls in, you're halfway to finding the culprit. At that point, diagnostic tools and good, old-fashioned deductive reasoning come into play.

You might be able to eliminate one or more categories right away. For example, if your computer can communicate with some other computers but not all of them, and your network uses a central hub, you can deduce that at least your computer's network card and the wiring from your computer to the hub are working properly.

Windows comes with some diagnostic tools to help you narrow down further the cause of a network problem. In the rest of this chapter, I outline these tools and suggest how to use them.

 tip

You might also peruse Chapter 16, "Troubleshooting Your Internet Connection," for tips on diagnosing network problems specific to the Internet (TCP/IP) protocol.

Diagnostic Tools

Each diagnostic tool described in this section serves to test the operation of one or more of the categories mentioned in the preceding section. The tools are discussed in roughly the order you should try them.

Some tools can be used to find problems in any of the many networking components. These tools quickly identify many problems.

The Network and Sharing Center

The Network and Sharing Center is the first place to start diagnosing a network problem because it can quickly take you to Windows network troubleshooters, status displays, and network settings. It can also display a network map that shows whether your computer can communicate with any other computers on your LAN using the Windows file and printer sharing client services. If at least one other computer is visible and online, you can be pretty sure that your computer's network card and cabling are okay.

There are several ways to bring up the Network and Sharing Center:

- Click the small network icon located in the right corner of the taskbar near the time of day. At the bottom of the pop-up, click Open Network and Sharing Center.

- Click Start, Control Panel, View Network Status and Tasks (under Network and Internet).

- Click Start, Computer. At the bottom left, click Network. Then, at the top click Network and Sharing Center.

Use whichever method is convenient. This brings up the window shown in Figure 21.1. The little map at the top of the window shows your current network status. A broken line or red X indicates that you have no functioning network or Internet connection.

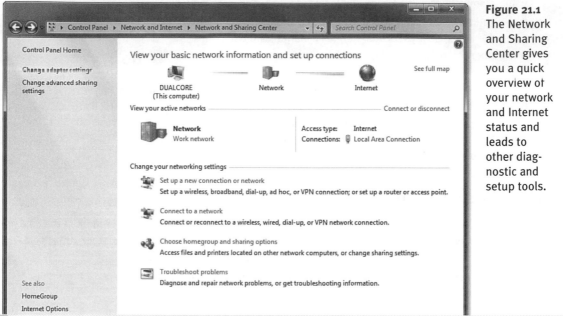

Figure 21.1
The Network and Sharing Center gives you a quick overview of your network and Internet status and leads to other diagnostic and setup tools.

Under View Your Active Networks, Windows displays information about any active network and/or direct Internet connections. For example, in Figure 21.1, you can see that I am attached to a LAN, through the Local Area Connection network adapter. Its network location is Home Network, which means that file and printer sharing are allowed and that a homegroup can be used.

➥ *If you want to use the HomeGroup feature, your network location must be "Home Network." For more information, **see** "Setting Up a Homegroup," p. 478.*

This window leads to several other useful tools:

- To see whether various networking features are turned on or off, click Change Advanced Sharing Settings.

- To let Windows try to diagnose your network problem, click Troubleshoot Problems. Then select a troubleshooter for the particular problem you're having (see "Network Diagnostics," later in the chapter, for a description of the troubleshooters).

- To check or modify the settings for one of your network adapters, click Change Adapter Settings.

- To check or change your homegroup settings, click Choose Homegroup and Sharing Options.

- To see if your computer can find other computers on your network, click See Full Map.

If you're having problems with file and printer sharing, the first thing to check is the Network Map.

Network Map

To view the Network Map, open the Network and Sharing Center as described in the previous section. Then, click See Full Map. The window that appears should look something like Figure 21.2, except that the names of the computers on your network will be different. My network also includes a router (gateway) device, which also appears in this display because its Universal Plug and Play (UPnP) feature has been enabled.

Figure 21.2
The Network Map shows other computers your computer knows about. The actual connections may or may not be shown.

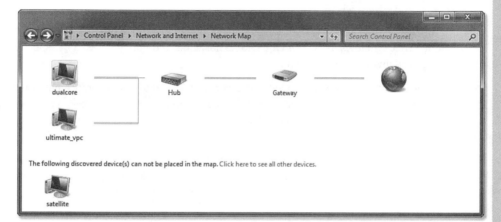

If you see at least one other computer besides your own displayed here, your computer's network cabling, network adapter, and drivers are working correctly. In addition, both your computer and the computers shown are both running the Network Discovery service and/or file sharing. (To turn on Network Discovery, go back to the Network and Sharing Center and click Change Advanced Sharing Settings.)

If other computers don't appear, and you know that Network Discovery is turned on and that Windows Firewall is open, it's possible that the network browser function, which is a behind-the-scenes service that Windows uses to locate other computers, is not working. This is a common problem. To investigate it, try these procedures:

> ### note
>
> If you have a computer that Windows says "cannot be placed on the map," it might be running a Windows version prior to Vista, running some other OS, or connected to your OS through a more complex network.

- Wait 20 minutes and press the F5 key. Other computers may appear this time.

- Check each of the computers in your workgroup and make sure that each computer is set to use the same workgroup name and that each computer has the same set of network protocols installed. In particular, because Windows 7 supports only TCP/IP, any computers running Windows 98 or Me must be reconfigured to use only TCP/IP and not IPX/SPX or NetBEUI.

> ➡ *For more information about networking with older versions of Windows,* ***see*** *"Networking with Other Operating Systems," **p. 487**.*

Now, click the Back arrow to return to the Network and Sharing Center. Next, look at the label under your network connection in the middle View Your Active Networks section. The network type label should say Work Network or Home Network. If it says Public Network, file and printer sharing should not be available because this would be risky in a public setting with other unknown computers. You can change it from Public to Home or Work *if* you trust the other computers on your network.

➥ *For more information,* **see** *"Choosing Your Network Location," p. 475.*

If you are having trouble with file and printer sharing with some or all of your other computers, and this screen didn't identify the problem, click Change Advanced Sharing Settings. This displays settings that Windows uses with Work/Home networks and Public networks, respectively. The settings are divided into two parts:

- **Home/Work**—Used for network connections that lead to home or office networks. A network can be a home or work network even if it provides Internet access, as long as a router or firewall is placed between the network and the Internet, and as long as you trust all the computers plugged in to the network.

- **Public**—Used for network connections that lead to a public network. A public network could be a direct Internet connection (for example, a connection that plugged in directly to a DSL or cable modem), or a network in a public place such as a hotel or café, where you do not trust the other computers.

Actually, though, this control panel is somewhat misleading. Only the first two settings are different for Home/Work and Public networks: Network Discovery and File and Printer Sharing. The remaining settings are location-independent; that is, they apply to all network locations. The default settings are listed in Tables 21.1 and 21.2.

Table 21.1 Location-Dependent Advanced Sharing Settings

Setting	Default Setting Home/Work	Public	Description
Network Discovery	On	Off	When off, other computers will not appear on the network map and your computer will not appear on other computers' maps.
File and Printer Sharing	On	Off	When off, *your* computer will not share its files and/or printers with other computers. You can still use files and printers shared by *other* computers.

Table 21.2   Location-Independent Advanced Sharing Settings

Setting	Default Setting	Description
Public Folder Sharing	On	When off, the Public user folder will not be shared. When On, it is shared and anyone can store or change files in it.
Media Streaming	On	Media Streaming settings are based on computer names rather than network location.
File Sharing Connections	128-bit	By default, encrypted network connections use a strong key.
Password Protected Sharing	On	When on, other users must have a user account and password to use shared files and printers that are not accessed via a homegroup. When off, other users who don't have an account on your computer, or who have an account with no password, will be granted access to shared files and printers via the Guest account. (For more information, see "Configure Passwords and File Sharing" **p. 924**.
HomeGroup Connections	Windows	By default, Windows manages the user account and password used for HomeGroup sharing. For more information see "Setting Up a Homegroup," page 478.

Network Diagnostics

Windows 7 features a network repair tool called Network Diagnostics that is said (by Microsoft) to be capable of recognizing and diagnosing more than 100 network problems. I'm skeptical of claims like this, but, on the other hand, it takes only a few seconds to let Network Diagnostics examine your network and offer whatever advice it can, so it's absolutely worth a crack.

To run the Network Diagnostics tool, open the Network and Sharing Center as described on page 577. Click Troubleshoot Problems. Then, select one of the network troubleshooters:

- **Internet Connections**—Select this if you are having a problem reaching the Internet or just a particular website.

- **Shared Folders**—Select this if you can't access a network shared folder whose name you know.

- **HomeGroup**—Select this if you are having problems accessing a homegroup.

- **Network Adapter**—Select this if you are having general problems accessing the Internet and/or network resources.

- **Incoming Connections**—Select this if other computers can't connect to your computer's shared files or to other programs or services that you want to make available on your computer (for example, Remote Desktop, a web server, and so on).

- **Connection to a Workplace Using DirectAccess**—Select this if you can't access your corporate network over the Internet via the DirectAccess virtual private networking feature.

Windows will display a box that says "Identifying the problem..." and will then display a results window that explains what was found to be wrong, what Windows did about it (if anything), what the outcome was, and where to go for more assistance.

If the diagnostics tool doesn't solve your network problem, check Windows Firewall to be sure it isn't blocking a desired network service.

tip

Whichever troubleshooter(s) you use, if the word Advanced appears on the first screen, click it and select Run As Administrator, and also check Apply Repairs Automatically.

note

The troubleshooters aren't good at determining that nothing is actually wrong with their particular area of concern. If a troubleshooter says that it can't find the problem, don't assume that there *is* a problem with that specific topic. There might not be one. Just try another troubleshooter.

Windows Firewall

Another configuration setting that could prevent file and printer sharing from working correctly is Windows Firewall. To ensure that file and printer sharing isn't blocked, open the Windows Firewall window by clicking Start, Control Panel, System and Security, Windows Firewall. Windows Firewall is much improved in Windows 7, and can filter network activity based on the type of network to which you're attached. So, in Windows 7, for both Home or Work (Private) networks and for Public networks, the Windows Firewall State should be On, and Incoming Connections should be set to Block All Connections to Programs That Are Not on the List of Allowed Programs.

Click Allow a Program or Feature Through Windows Firewall to view the settings. File and Printer Sharing should be checked, but *not* in the Public column. Core Networking should be checked in both columns.

➡ *For more information about configuring the firewall,* ***see*** *"Configuring Windows Firewall,"* ***p. 937.***

If the firewall settings appear to be correct, the next step is to check Windows Event Viewer, to see whether Windows has left a record of any network problems there.

Event Viewer

Event Viewer another important diagnostic tool and one of the first to check because Windows often silently records useful information about problems with hardware and software in an Event Log. To check, open the Event Viewer: Click Start, right-click Computer, select Manage, and then select the Event Viewer system tool. Start with Custom Views, Administrative Events. This provides a view of all significant management events from all of the various Windows events logs (and there are a lot of them!).

If nothing useful appears there, select Windows Logs, and examine the System, Application, and Security logs in turn. Finally, open Applications and Services Logs, Microsoft, Windows, and under any of the network-related categories, view the Operational and Admin logs.

Event Viewer displays Event Log entries, most recent first, on the right (see Figure 21.3).

Figure 21.3
Event Viewer might display important diagnostic information when you have network problems.

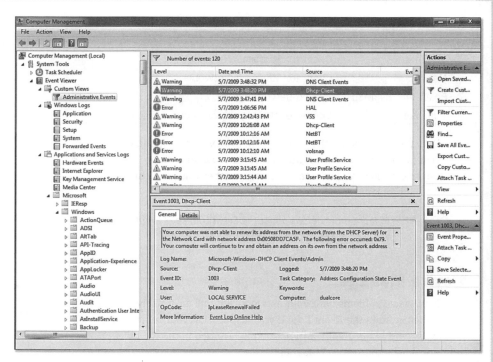

Log entries for serious errors are displayed with a red X in a circle; warnings appear with a yellow ! in a triangle. Informational entries (marked with a blue *i*) usually don't relate to problems. Double-click any error or warning entries in the log to view the detailed description and any associated data recorded with the entry. The Warning entry in Figure 21.3 indicates that my computer couldn't acquire a network address in a reasonable amount of time. It turns out that my router had come unplugged.

These messages are usually significant and informative to help diagnose network problems; they might indicate that a network card is malfunctioning, that a domain controller for authentication or a DHCP server for configuration can't be found, and so on. The Source column in the error log indicates which Windows component or service recorded the event. These names are usually fairly cryptic. Table 21.32 lists a few of the more common nonobvious ones.

Table 21.3 Network Sources of Event Log Entries

Source	Description
Application Popup	Can come from any system utility; these warning messages are usually significant.
Atapi	IDE hard disk/CD-ROM controller
Browser, bowser	Name resolution system for Client for Microsoft Networks
Dhcp-Client	Network address assignment service client
DNS Client Events	Network name lookup client
Dnsapi	DNS client component
Dnscache	DNS client component
MrxSmb	Client for Microsoft Networks
NetBT	Client for Microsoft Networks
RasClient, RasMan	Dial-up networking
Time Service	Computer clock synchronization service

If you're at a loss to solve the problem even with the information given, check the configuration of the indicated component, or remove and reinstall it to see whether you can clear up the problem.

➥ *To learn more details about the Event Log, **see** "Event Viewer," **p. 655.***

Device Manager

Hardware problems with your network card will most likely be recorded in the Event Log. If you suspect that your network card is the culprit, and nothing is recorded in the Event Log, check the Device Manager.

To use it, click Start, right-click Computer, select Manage, and choose the Device Manager system tool. Any devices with detectable hardware problems or configuration conflicts appear with a yellow ! icon when you display the Device Manager. If no yellow icons appear, you don't have a *detected* hardware problem. This doesn't mean that you don't have a problem, but the odds are slim that your network card is the problem.

If devices are shown with ! icons, double-click the device name to see the Windows explanation of the device status and any problems. A device that you've told Windows not to use (disabled) will have a red X on it; this is generally not a problem.

 tip

A problem with one network system usually causes other problems. Therefore, the oldest error message in a closely timed sequence of errors is *usually* the most significant, with subsequent errors just a result of the first failure. Because the Event Log is ordered most-recent-first, you might get the most useful information down a bit from the top of the list.

 tip

The real cause of your problem might reveal itself at system startup time rather than when you observe the problem. Reboot your system and note the time. Then reproduce the problem. Check the Event Log for messages starting at the reboot time.

➥ *For more detailed instructions and tips on device troubleshooting, **see** Chapter 25, "Troubleshooting and Repairing Problems."*

Testing Network Cables

If your computer can't communicate with any other computer on your LAN, and the Device Manager doesn't indicate a faulty network card, you *might* have a wiring problem. Wiring problems can be the most difficult to solve because it's difficult to prove that data is leaving one computer but not arriving at another. The `ping` program, discussed later in this chapter, can help with this problem.

➥ *To learn how you can use the `ping` command to diagnose Internet-related problems, as opposed to LAN problems, **see** "ping," p. 434.*

If your computer is not properly wired into the LAN or is connected through a wireless network, in many cases, Windows displays an offline icon right on the system tray and indicates that your network card is disconnected. It might not, though, so you shouldn't take a lack of this kind of message to mean that no wiring problems exist.

If your network uses UTP cabling plugged in to a hub, there's usually a green LED indicator on each network card and at each port on the hub. Be sure that the lights are on at each end of your network cable and those for the other computers on your LAN.

You also can use inexpensive (about $75) cable test devices that check for continuity and correct pin-to-pin wiring order for UTP wiring. They come as a set of two boxes. One gets plugged in to each end of a given cable run, and a set of blinking lights tells you whether all four wire pairs are connected and in the correct order. (If you install your own network cabling and/or make your own patch cables,.)

 note

If you really want to get into the guts of your network cabling or are planning a major installation and want to learn more details so that you can oversee a professional installation, I recommend that you read *Networking with Microsoft Windows Vista* by Paul McFedries, published by Que.

Checking Network Configuration

If hardware isn't at fault, you might have a fundamental network configuration problem. Often the Event Log or Device Manager gives these problems away, but if they don't, you can use another batch of tools to check the computer's network configuration.

ipconfig

If your computer can't communicate with others on your LAN, after you check the Event Log and Device Manager, use the `ipconfig` command-line utility to see whether your computer has a valid IP address. Check other computers on the LAN, too, to ensure that they do as well.

In the Command Prompt window (which you open by choosing Start, All Programs, Accessories, Command Prompt), type the following command:

```
ipconfig /all
```

The results should look something like this:

```
Windows IP Configuration
    Host Name . . . . . . . . . . . . : myvpc-hb
    Primary Dns Suffix  . . . . . . . : mycompany.com
    Node Type . . . . . . . . . . . . : Hybrid
    IP Routing Enabled. . . . . . . . : Yes
    WINS Proxy Enabled. . . . . . . . : No

Ethernet adapter Local Area Connection:
    Connection-specific DNS Suffix  . :
    Description . . . . . . . . . . . : Intel 21140-Based PCI Fast Ethernet Adapter
    Physical Address. . . . . . . . . : 00-03-FF-DD-CA-5F
    DHCP Enabled. . . . . . . . . . . : Yes
    Autoconfiguration Enabled . . . . : Yes
    Link-local IPv6 Address . . . . . : fe80::ed10:dff9:693c:803d%8(Preferred)
    IPv4 Address. . . . . . . . . . . : 192.168.15.108(Preferred)
    Subnet Mask . . . . . . . . . . . : 255.255.255.0
    Lease Obtained. . . . . . . . . . : Friday, October 20, 2006 5:55:11 PM
    Lease Expires . . . . . . . . . . : Friday, October 27, 2006 5:55:23 PM
    Default Gateway . . . . . . . . . : 192.168.15.1
    DHCP Server . . . . . . . . . . . : 192.168.15.1
    DHCPv6 IAID . . . . . . . . . . . : 201327615
    DNS Servers . . . . . . . . . . . : 192.168.15.1
    NetBIOS over Tcpip. . . . . . . . : Enabled
```

(Unless you're troubleshooting IPv6 Teredo connections, ignore the parts that mention Tunnel Adapters.)

The most important items to look for are the following:

- **Host Name**—This should be set to the desired name for each computer. If you can correspond with some computers but not others, be sure that the ones that don't work are turned on and correctly named. Make sure you don't have two computers with the same name, and that none of the computer names is the same as the workgroup name.

- **IP Address**—This should be set appropriately for your network. If your LAN uses Internet Connection Sharing (ICS), the address will be a number in the range 192.168.0.1 through 192.168.0.254. If your LAN uses DHCP for automatic configuration, your network manager can tell you whether the IP address is correct. Networks with cable/DSL sharing routers *usually* use numbers starting with 192.168.x where x is a number from 0 to 15.

  If your IP address starts with the numbers 169.254, your computer is set for automatic configuration but no DHCP server was found, so Windows has chosen an IP address by itself. This is fine if your LAN uses this automatic configuration system; perhaps you've just connected a few computers so you can share files and printers. However, if you expected to get Internet access through your network—that is, if you use ICS or a hardware Internet connection router, or you have a more complex network with a DHCP server—this is a serious problem. Restart the connecting sharing computer or the router, and then restart your computer and try again.

- **Network Mask**—This is usually 255.255.255.0, but other settings are possible. All computers on the same LAN should have the same network mask.

Each computer on the same LAN should have a similar valid IP address and the same network mask. If they don't, check your network configuration. The built-in Windows Repair function may also be used to help fix problems with DHCP based (automatic) IP address assignment.

note

To learn more about IP addressing, network masks, and configuration, visit http://support.microsoft.com and search for article number 164015, "Understanding TCP/IP Addressing and Subnetting Basics."

Computer

You can check computer's identification and workgroup or domain membership setup from the Computer window. To do so, click Start, Computer. Look at the bottom of the screen for the computer name and domain or workgroup name, as shown in Figure 21.4.

Figure 21.4
Your computer's name and workgroup or domain membership are displayed at the bottom of the Computer window.

Computer Name | Workgroup or Domain Name
Workgroup/Domain Indicator

On a Windows Workgroup network, the workgroup name should be the same on all computers on your workgroup LAN. All of the computer names *must* be different from each other.

On a Windows domain network, you should see your computer's name displayed as part of a Windows domain name (for example, my computer named myvpc-hb would be called myvpc-hb.mycompany.com on a domain network) and the domain name. Your domain name might not include .com. It might say .local instead or use a different ending. In any case, be sure that your computer is actually a domain member. If the word "Workgroup" appears instead, your computer is not a domain member and will not be able to use domain logins or some domain resources.

> **note**
>
> None of your computers can use the workgroup or domain name as its computer name. For example, if your workgroup is MSHOME, you can't also name a computer MSHOME. If you find this on one of your computers, change that computer's name.

Network Connections

You can manually check all installed network protocols and services and their configuration by viewing Network Connections and viewing the properties for Local Area Connection. To view this screen, click Start, Control Panel, View Network Status and Tasks (under Network and Internet), Change Adapter Settings. Then, right-click your Local Area Connection icon (or the appropriate wireless connection icon) and select Properties.

Confirm that each required protocol is installed and correctly configured. In general, the settings on each computer on your LAN should match, except that the IP address differs (usually only in the last of its four dot-separated numbers). If your LAN uses automatic IP address configuration, use the ipconfig command, described earlier, to check the settings.

Testing Network Connectivity

A few tools can help you determine whether the network can send data between computers; these tools test the network protocols as well as low-level network hardware layers.

ping

Ping is a fundamental tool for testing TCP/IP network connectivity. Because most networks today use the Internet (TCP/IP) protocol for file and printer sharing services, as well as for Internet access, most Windows users can use the ping test to confirm that their network cabling, hardware, and the TCP/IP protocol are all functioning correctly. Ping sends several data packets to a specified computer and waits for the other computer to send the packets back. By default, it sends four packets and prints the results of the four tests.

To see whether the network can carry data between a pair of computers, use the ipconfig command (described previously) to find the IP address of the two computers. Then, on one computer, open a Command Prompt window by choosing Start, All Programs, Accessories, Command Prompt.

Next, type the following command:

```
ping 127.0.0.1
```

This command tests the networking software of the computer itself by sending packets to the special internal IP address 127.0.0.1. This test has the computer send data to itself. It should print the following:

```
Reply from 127.0.0.1: bytes=32 time<10ms TTL=128
Reply from 127.0.0.1: bytes=32 time<10ms TTL=128
Reply from 127.0.0.1: bytes=32 time<10ms TTL=128
Reply from 127.0.0.1: bytes=32 time<10ms TTL=128
```

If it doesn't, the TCP/IP protocol itself is incorrectly installed or configured; check the computer's IP address configuration, or, if that seems correct, remove and reinstall the Internet Protocol from Local Area Connection in Network Connections. (I have to say, in more than 15 years of working with PC networks, I've never seen this test fail.)

If your computer can send data to itself, try another computer on your LAN. Find its IP address by running `ipconfig` on that computer and then issue the `ping` command again on the first computer, as in this example:

```
ping 192.168.0.23
```

Of course, you should use the other computer's real IP address in place of 192.168.0.23. You should get four replies as before:

```
Reply from 192.168.0.23: bytes=32 time<10ms TTL=32
Reply from 192.168.0.23: bytes=32 time<10ms TTL=32
Reply from 192.168.0.23: bytes=32 time<10ms TTL=32
Reply from 192.168.0.23: bytes=32 time<10ms TTL=32
```

These replies indicate that you have successfully sent data to the other machine and received it back.

If, on the other hand, the `ping` command returns `Request timed out`, the packets either didn't make it to the other computer or were not returned. In either case, you have a problem with your cabling, network adapter, or the TCP/IP protocol setup.

You can use `ping` to determine which computers can send to which other computers on your LAN or across wide area networks (WANs) or the Internet. Ping works when given a computer's IP address or its network name.

 note

If you enter a computer name, and `ping` can't determine the computer's IP address, the problem isn't necessarily a wiring problem—it could be that the DNS or WINS name lookup system is not working correctly. Try using an IP address with `ping` in this case to help determine what the problem really is.

Diagnosing File and Printer Sharing Problems

If the tests in the previous sections don't point to a problem—that is, if basic network connectivity is fine but you're still having problems with file or printer sharing—the next step depends on whether you have a workgroup or domain-type network.

If you're on a domain network, it's time to call your network administrator for assistance. They've had more training and experience in network troubleshooting than I can impart in the space allowed here.

If you're on a home or small office workgroup network, there are a few things you might try. Here are some tips:

- Did you make sure that file sharing is enabled on each of your computers?

- Do your Windows 7 and Vista computers have a network location setting of Home or Work? The Public setting blocks file sharing.

  On Windows XP, there is no network location setting. Instead, open Windows Firewall and make sure that File and Printer Sharing is checked.

- If you use Internet Connection Sharing, restart the computer that's sharing your Internet connection and wait a minute or two after it's booted up. Then, restart your other computers. This may help. The ICS computer needs to be up and running *before* any other computers on your LAN start up.

- If you don't see other computers in the Network Map window, wait 10 to 20 minutes (really), and then select View, Refresh or press F5. Sometimes it takes up to 20 minutes for the list of online computers to be updated.

- If you can see the folders shared by another computer but can't move any files into them, or edit files in them, then your network is fine—you just have a permissions problem. On the computer that is sharing the folder, be sure that the folder is shared so that remote visitors can change files. For more information, **see** "Using Shared Folders in Windows 7," **p. 542**.

  If the sharing computer has password-protected sharing enabled (or, on XP, Simple File Sharing turned off), the owner of the other computer should check to see that your user account has permission to read and/or modify the files in the shared folder. In the folder or files' Security properties, check to see that your user account is listed or that the group you're in, such as Users or Everyone, has the necessary permissions. File permissions are discussed on page 903 under "NTFS File Permissions."

  In Windows 7, Password Protected Sharing works differently than it did on Vista and XP (where the feature was called Simple File Sharing). If you can't access a file over the network that you know you could access if you were logged on directly at the sharing computer, that computer might be using the Guest account to access the file, not yours. For more information, see "Configure Passwords and File Sharing" on page 924.

  One way you can tell whether this feature is causing your problem is to log on at the sharing computer, right-click [My] Computer and select Manage. At the left, open the Shared Folders item and select Sessions. Try to access the problem file or folder from across the network. You should see an entry for the networked computer. If the username is Guest, you will only be able to read or write files that group Everyone can read or write. As I mentioned previously, see page 924 for a discussion about the way Password Protected Sharing works in various situations.

VI

MAINTAINING WINDOWS 7

IN THIS PART

22	Windows Management and Maintenance	**593**
23	Tweaking and Customizing Windows	**679**
24	Managing Hard Disks	**709**
25	Troubleshooting and Repairing Problems	**737**
26	Keeping Windows 7 and Other Software Up to Date	**757**
27	Installing and Replacing Hardware	**779**
28	Editing the Registry	**805**
29	Command-Line and Automation Tools	**821**

22

WINDOWS MANAGEMENT AND MAINTENANCE

Windows 7 incorporates the most powerful set of management and diagnostic utilities yet seen in a desktop version of Windows. Although Windows 7 offers many new and improved tools, they work in (mostly) familiar ways. In Windows 7, there's as much emphasis on helping you use familiar tools in better ways as on the creation of new tools. The emphasis on a new and improved interface for a mix of familiar and new tools begins with the Control Panel, which is where many (although not all) management and maintenance tasks are performed.

In addition to the Control Panel, however, Windows 7's management and diagnostic tools can also be found in the following locations:

- Computer Management
- System tools
- Administrative tools
- Task Manager
- Command-line programs
- Maintenance
- Registry editor

In this chapter, we give you a tour of all of these management

 note

In a few cases, a Start menu item and a Control Panel item point to the same utility. For example, Administrative Tools and Getting Started can be launched from the Start menu or from Control Panel. In these and other cases, the same utilities are launched regardless of how you start them.

tools, except command line programs, which are discussed in Chapter 29, and the Registry editor, which is the sole topic of Chapter 28, "Editing the Registry." Many of the other tools we show you are discussed in more detail in other chapters; we point this out as we go.

The Windows 7 Control Panel

Just as with previous Windows versions, the Control Panel is the central location for making systemwide modifications to everything from accessibility options to user profiles. Windows 7 includes the third generation of Category view, first introduced in Windows XP. In Windows XP, Category view was merely annoying, while in Windows Vista, Microsoft somehow found a way to make it—in addition—disorienting, obtuse, and nearly incomprehensible. How did Microsoft do this time? While the Windows 7 Control Panel is still organized as a very wordy web page as in Windows Vista, with links to access virtually every individual Control Panel applet from one or more (mostly) logical categories that also include shortcuts to the most commonly used utilities, it does have one advantage over its Windows Vista and Windows XP predecessors: you can switch between Category view and individual shortcuts (Small Icons view or Large Icons view) at any time using a pull-down menu (refer to Figure 22.1). To help you make sense of and navigate through this "new and improved" Category view, see Tables 22.1–22.8 in the next section.

As with previous versions of Control Panel, some items are simply a shortcut to operations you can perform in other ways. For example, you can adjust display and audio properties settings by right-clicking the desktop and selecting Personalize, or you can use the Appearance and Personalization category in the Control Panel. However, the Control Panel is also the home of applets that are not available elsewhere, such as iSCSI Initiator and Parental Controls.

As with previous versions, the preference settings you make via the Control Panel applets are stored in the Registry. Some are systemwide, whereas others are made on a per-user basis and go into effect the next time you log in.

Keep in mind that you must have Administrator-level access to modify many of the settings in the Control Panel. User-level settings such as display appearances are not a big deal. However, systemwide settings such as the addition and removal of hardware are governed by system security settings, and you must have the requisite permissions to successfully make modifications. Depending upon the settings you use for User Account Control (UAC), you might see the UAC dialog box appear when you select options marked with the Windows 7 security shield. Administrators using the

 tip

By default, the Control Panel displays as a window when you click Start and select Control Panel. However, you can also configure the Control Panel to display as a flyout menu from the Start menu (a huge time-saver if you ask us). To make this your default setting, right-click the Start menu and select Properties. In the dialog box that appears, click Customize; then select the Display As a Menu radio button under the Control Panel in the list of Start menu items. Control Panel items are displayed individually, as in Small Icons or Large Icons views (previously known as Classic view).

If you use a particular applet a lot, you can drag it into the Start menu or the taskbar for even faster access. Dragging an applet to the Start menu or taskbar doesn't actually move the applet. Instead, it creates a shortcut.

Windows 7 default settings for UAC will see the UAC dialog box far less often than with Windows Vista. However, if you are a standard user, not an administrator, you can expect to see the UAC dialog box appear about as often in Windows 7 as in Windows Vista.

➡ *For more information on User Account Control,* ***see*** *"User Account Control," p. 84.*

Not all Control Panel settings are discussed in detail in this chapter. Because a few Control Panel options pertain to other topics, such as networking or printing, or fall under the umbrella of system management, performance tweaking, or system applications, you'll find them in later chapters. Table 22.10, in the next section, lists each applet and where to look in this book for additional coverage when relevant.. Also, I won't bore you by covering each and every option in the dialog boxes. Many settings are intuitively obvious.

Breaking Down Category View

Although Windows 7, like Windows Vista, defaults to Category view, the categories and their contents are somewhat different in Windows 7 than in its predecessor.

There are eight standard categories in Category view on any computer running Windows 7 (settings formerly in a separate Mobile category have been folded into other categories). Virtually every Control Panel applet in Windows 7 can be accessed from one or more categories.

Tables 22.1 through 22.8 list the tasks for each category. These are listed in the order of appearance, from top left to bottom right, not alphabetically. Clicking any of the categories takes you to another dialog box showing those tasks.

In the Control Panel screens, items featuring the Windows 7 Security shield indicate that the item is protected by User Account Control; with the default UAC settings, standard users must provide a password from an Administrator account to open these items.

 tip

Although the Control Panel's Small Icons and Large Icons views offer more than four dozen icons, you may find that you use just a few of them frequently. To make it even easier to get to your favorites, you can add to the Jump List on the taskbar shortcuts to your favorite Control Panel icon or categories.

To use the shortcut, right-click the Control Panel icon on the taskbar and select the icon you want to open. It sure beats clicking through several menus.

 note

If you need to access a Control Panel option that's available only in Large Icons or Small Icons view, or if you just plain prefer to view individual icons, open the Control Panel and click Large Icons or Small Icons (see Figure 22.1).

 note

The items listed in Tables 22.1 through 22.10 include every item in every edition of Windows 7. If you have the Home Starter, Home Premium, Professional or Enterprise edition, your Control Panel might not have every item listed here.

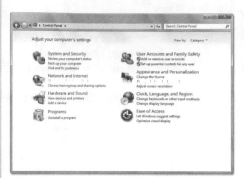

Figure 22.1
The Control Panel in the default Category view (left) and the Small Icons view (right). You can also choose Large Icons view (not shown).

Table 22.1   System and Security Category

Applet or Subcategory	Tasks
Action Center	Reports security and maintenance problems and offers solutions
Windows Firewall	Configures Windows Firewall
System	Displays processor speed, Windows Experience Index, remote access, and other system properties
Windows Update	Configures delivery and installation of updates to Windows and other Microsoft applications
Power Options	Manages power settings for laptop and desktop systems
Backup and Restore	File backup/restore services; Enterprise, Professional and Ultimate versions also offer Complete PC (disaster recovery) backup/restore
BitLocker Drive Encryption	Full-disk encryption for internal and external hard disks and USB flash memory drives (Ultimate, Enterprise editions only)
Administrative Tools	Tools for managing advanced features and diagnosing system problems

Table 22.2   Network and Internet Category

Applet or Subcategory	Tasks
Network and Sharing Center	Displays and configures network status
HomeGroup	Configures HomeGroup and sharing options
Internet Options	Configures security, connection, and other settings for Internet Explorer 8 and other Microsoft applications

Table 22.3   Hardware and Sound Category

Applet or Subcategory	Tasks
Devices and Printers	Adds and configures devices, printers, and faxes
AutoPlay	Configures AutoPlay settings for supported devices
Sound	Configures audio hardware and system sounds
Power Options	Configures power plans, power buttons
Display	Adjusts resolution, visual effects, display settings, and multiple monitor support

Table 22.4   Programs Category

Applet or Subcategory	Tasks
Programs and Features	Installs, enables, and removes Windows features and applications
Default Programs	Configures startup and default programs and file types
Desktop Gadgets	Adds and configures desktop gadgets

Table 22.5   User Accounts and Family Safety Category

Applet or Subcategory	Tasks
User Accounts	Creates and configures user accounts and passwords
Parental Controls	Configures parental controls and displays reports
Windows CardSpace	Creates and configures Information Cards for logging in to password-protected sites
Credential Manager	Manages Windows credentials for logging on to Windows and websites

Table 22.6   Appearance and Personalization Category

Applet or Subcategory	Tasks
Personalization	Configures visual effects, display settings, and sound effects
Display	Configures screen font size, display settings, resolution, and ClearType settings
Desktop Gadgets	Configures and installs desktop gadgets (replaces Windows Vista's Sidebar)
Taskbar and Start Menu	Configures appearance of taskbar and Start menu
Ease of Access Center	Configures user interface for users with limited vision or hearing
Folder Options	Configures folder settings
Fonts	Views, installs, and removes fonts

Table 22.7   Clock, Language, and Region Category

Applet or Subcategory	Tasks
Date and Time	Sets date, time, time zone; adds additional clocks; configures time synchronization
Region and Language	Selects default language, location, keyboard settings

Table 22.8   Ease of Access Category

Applet or Subcategory	Tasks
Ease of Access Center	Configures user interface for users with limited vision or hearing
Speech Recognition Options	Configures speech recognition and microphone

Virtually every Control Panel applet visible in Large Icons view or Small Icons views can be accessed from one or more categories. However, a few can be accessed only from Large Icons or Small Icons view. Applets are listed and cross-referenced to their respective categories in Table 22.9.

Table 22.9   Control Panel Applets and Categories

Applet	Also Found in This Category
Action Center	System and Security
Administrative Tools	System and Security
AutoPlay	Hardware and Sound
Backup and Restore	System and Security
BitLocker Drive Encryption	System and Security
Color Management	Hardware and Sound
Credential Manager	User Accounts and Family Safety
Date and Time	Clock, Language, and Region
Default Programs	Programs
Desktop Gadgets	Programs; Appearance and Personalization
Device Manager	System and Security, Hardware and Sound
Devices and Printers	Hardware and Sound
Display	Hardware and Sound; Appearance and Personalization
Ease of Access Center	Appearance and Personalization; Ease of Access
Folder Options	Appearance and Personalization
Fonts	Appearance and Personalization
Getting Started	—
HomeGroup	Network and Internet
Indexing Options	System and Security

Table 22.9   Continued

Applet	Also Found in This Category
Internet Options	Network and Internet
Keyboard	Hardware and Sound
Location and Other Sensors	—
Mouse	Hardware and Sound
Network and Sharing Center	Network and Internet
Notification Area Icons	Appearance and Personalization (submenu)
Parental Controls	User Accounts and Family Safety
Pen and Input Devices	Hardware and Sound
Performance Information and Tools	System and Security
Personalization	Appearance and Personalization
Phone and Modem	—
Power Options	System and Security; Hardware and Sound
Programs and Features	Programs
Recovery	Action Center (submenu)
Region and Language	Clock, Language, and Region
RemoteApp and Desktop Connections	—
Sound	Hardware and Sound
Speech Recognition	Ease of Access
Sync Center	Network and Internet
System	System and Security
Tablet PC Settings	Hardware and Sound
Taskbar and Start Menu	Appearance and Personalization
Troubleshooting	Action Center (submenu)
User Accounts	User Accounts and Family Safety
Windows CardSpace	User Accounts and Family Safety
Windows Defender	—
Windows Firewall	System and Security
Windows Mobility Center	Hardware and Sound
Windows Update	System and Security

You can use either Category view or the individual Large Icons view or Small Icons view to access virtually every feature of the Control Panel. From the home view of Control Panel, select the view you prefer from the View By menu in the upper-right corner.

More Than One Way to Skin a Cat

As with previous versions of Windows, there are usually several ways to get to the same place. For example, if you right-click Computer on the Start menu and select Properties, you get the System control panel, just as if you went through Control Panel under System and Security. This is fine; you'll eventually decide that one way or the other is easier for you to remember and faster to use.

However, one thing that you might find confusing about Windows 7 is that to improve security, functions that require Administrator privileges have been separated from functions that don't. Features that used to live together in the same Control Panel applet or dialog in previous versions of Windows might not be together on Windows 7, or worse, access to them might be blocked if you don't get to the Control Panel item in just the right way. (This is the "disorienting" part that we mentioned earlier.) We've done our best to tell you about these issues throughout this book, which leads us to this important advice: When you need to change a Windows setting that you know exists but can't seem to find, look it up by name in the index of this book. Chances are that the index will point you to specific instructions for finding the setting on Windows 7.

What Should You Use?

Working with the Control Panel in Category view simplifies access to both commonly and less-commonly used configuration controls. However, some applets are referenced by more than one category. Consequently, to provide an exhaustive discussion of the applets, this chapter focuses on reviewing each applet as listed in Large Icons/Small Icons views. If you want to use Category view, refer to Tables 22.1 to 22.9.

Table 22.10 shows a list of all the standard Control Panel applets and what they accomplish. Your Control Panel may include other applets that are installed by other products from Microsoft and third parties.

Table 22.10   Control Panel Applets

Applet	Function
Action Center	Displays condition of security and maintenance settings, including Windows Firewall, antivirus, antimalware, Windows Backup, Windows Update, Reliability Monitor, and others.
Administrative Tools	Provides shortcuts to these administrative tools: Component Services, Computer Management, Data Sources (ODBC) settings, Event Viewer, iSCSI Initiator, Local Security Policy, Performance Monitor, Print Management, Services, System Configuration, Task Scheduler, Windows Firewall with Advanced Security, Windows Memory Diagnostics, and Windows PowerShell Modules. These tools are discussed later in this chapter.
AutoPlay	Configures AutoPlay options for different types of storage media and multimedia files.

Table 22.10 Continued

Applet	Function
Backup and Restore	Provides file backup and restore and system restore, and the recovery disc maker. See Chapter 31, "Protecting Your Data from Loss and Theft," and Chapter 25, "Troubleshooting and Repairing Problems," for details.
BitLocker Drive Encryption	Configures and manages full-drive encryption (Enterprise, Ultimate, and Professional only). See Chapter 31 for details.
Color Management	Configures color management settings for displays and printers.
Credential Manager	Stores credentials used for Windows login as well as those used for other servers and websites.
Date and Time	Sets the current date, time, and time zone for the computer. It can also synchronize system time with an Internet time server.
Default Programs	Configures default file types for installed programs. Associates file types with a particular program. Also configures program access and computer defaults and provides access to AutoPlay options.
Desktop Gadgets	Manages and configures the "new" Desktop Gadgets feature (an updated version of the Windows Vista Sidebar). Also used to download additional gadgets. See Chapter 7 for details.
Device Manager	Configures hardware devices and drivers. Also displays usage of hardware resources such as interrupt requests (IRQs), direct memory access (DMA) channels, I/O port addresses, and memory addresses.
Devices and Printers	Manages and installs many types of devices and printers, including monitors, digital cameras and imaging devices, mice, keyboards, and others. Replaces the Add Hardware, Printers, and Scanners and Cameras applets in previous versions of Windows. For more information, see Chapter 6, Chapter 10, and Chapter 11.
Display	Sets color calibration, screen font size, resolution, ClearType, and other display settings. See Chapter 23 for details.
Ease of Access Center	Configures accessibility tools, such as Magnifier, Narrator, On-Screen Keyboard, High Contrast display, and others.
Folder Options	Sets systemwide folder view options, file associations, and indexing.
Fonts	Adds and deletes typefaces, and displays examples of system-installed typefaces for screen display and printer output. Includes improved preview and new character search options.
Getting Started	Provides shortcuts to common tasks for new Windows 7 users, including personalization, transferring files and settings from another computer, setting up a homegroup, configuring Windows Update, downloading Windows Live Essentials, configuring Windows Backup, adding new users, and changing screen font size.

Table 22.10 Continued

Applet	Function
HomeGroup	Configures and manages the new HomeGroup feature, which enables easy and secure network sharing between computers running Windows 7. HomeGroup settings are covered in detail in Chapter 17.
Indexing Options	Configures what locations are indexed and how indexing is performed. Indexing is covered under "Changing Search and Indexing Settings" on page 174.
Internet Options	Sets Internet Explorer options. For details, see Chapter 14.
Keyboard	Sets key repeat rate, cursor blink rate, language of your keyboard, keyboard type, and drivers, and includes keyboard troubleshooting wizards.
Location and Other Sensors	Manages the new Windows 7 support for GPS, weather, and other types of sensors.
Mouse	Configures mouse properties such as motion speed, double-click, button orientation, cursor shapes, and other proprietary settings dependent on your mouse driver.
Network and Sharing Center	Manages all network connections, including LAN, dial-up WAN, and VPN. Configures networking components (clients, services, and protocols) and file/folder devices. These connections are covered throughout Part V, "Networking," and Part VIII, "Windows on the Move,"
Notification Area Icons	Configures when icons in the notification area are displayed. New in Windows 7.
Parental Controls	Configures user-based restrictions on computer use, gameplay, and program access.
Performance Information and Tools	Displays Windows Experience Index and provides access to performance configuration options.
Personalization	Configures window and desktop appearance, screen savers, audio sound schemes, mouse pointers, desktop themes, and display settings. For details, see Chapter 23.
Phone and Modem	Adds, removes, and sets the properties of the modem(s) connected to your system. Using this applet, you can declare dialing rules (long-distance numbers, call waiting, credit card calling, and so on). You also can add and remove telephony drivers. This applet is discussed in Chapter 13.
Power Options	Configures power settings ("power plans"), power and sleep buttons, and other power management issues. See Chapter 35 for laptop-specific recommendations. Basic power options are discussed in this chapter.
Programs and Features	Uninstalls and changes installed programs. Enables or disables Windows features. Tracks installed Windows updates.

Table 22.10   Continued

Applet	Function
Recovery	Provides access to System Restore, as well as troubleshooters, program uninstallers, and file restore from backup. See Chapter 25 for more information.
Region and Language	Sets how Windows displays times, dates, numbers, and currency through region/country settings and language preferences.
RemoteApp and Desktop Connections	Manages remote connections to your workplace provided by Windows Server 2008 R2.
Sound	Configures audio devices or changes sound scheme. For details, see Chapter 23.
Speech Recognition	Configures speech recognition. For details, see Chapter 4.
Sync Center	Configures sync partnerships such as Offline Files and others. File synchronization is covered in Chapter 35.
System	Examines and changes your identification (workgroup name, domain name, computer name) and installed devices. Displays amount of RAM available to Windows, type of processor, and processor speed. Using this applet, you can add, disable, and remove specific devices using the Device Manager; configure remote access; set up user profiles; set environment variables; configure visual effects, performance, and Data Execution Protection (DEP); configure Windows Update settings; and set emergency startup options.
Tablet PC Settings	Configures settings for Tablet PC displays and handwriting recognition. For more information, see Chapter 38.
Taskbar and Start Menu	Sets the properties for the taskbar and Start menu. For details, see Chapter 4 and Chapter 23.
Troubleshooting	Provides troubleshooters for Programs, Hardware and Sound, Network and Internet, Appearance and Personalization, System and Security features, and Remote Assistance. See Chapter 25 for more information.
User Accounts	Adds, deletes, or configures users. Enables you to assign groups, manage passwords, and set logon mode. Basic user setup is covered in Chapter 3.
Windows CardSpace	Sets up and manages credentials for logging in to secure websites, such as online stores and e-banking.
Windows Defender	Configures and manages integrated antispyware utility. To learn more about Windows Defender, see Chapter 30.
Windows Firewall	Enables you to turn on, turn off, and fine-tune the firewall that protects your computer from uninvited invasion from the Internet. To learn more about Windows Firewall, see Chapter 32.

Table 22.10 Continued

Applet	Function
Windows Mobility Center	Provides one-click access to audio, power scheme, display brightness, wireless and external display configuration, Sync Center settings, and external presentation display features. To learn more about Windows Mobility Center, see Chapter 35.
Windows Update	Configures how you receive updates to Windows and other Microsoft applications, such as Office. To learn more about Windows Update , see Chapter 26.

The following sections cover significant applets not covered in other chapters in alphabetical order.

Action Center

Action Center provides one-stop access to information and alerts for system security and maintenance features in Windows 7. Action Center (see Figure 22.2) displays two major sections: Security and Maintenance. A red bar next to either section indicates issues you need to deal with, and a solution button you can click to solve the problem.

Get more information about other settings.

The red bar indicates an item that needs your attention.

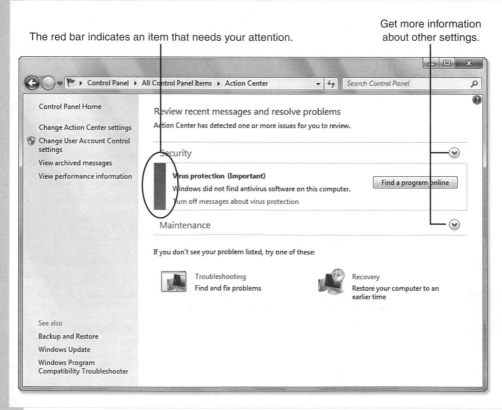

Figure 22.2
Action Center reports that this system needs antivirus software.

To get more information about other settings, click the down arrow next to each section. Figure 22.3 shows the settings in the Security section, and Figure 22.4 shows the settings in the Maintenance section.

Figure 22.3
Security settings monitored by Action Center.

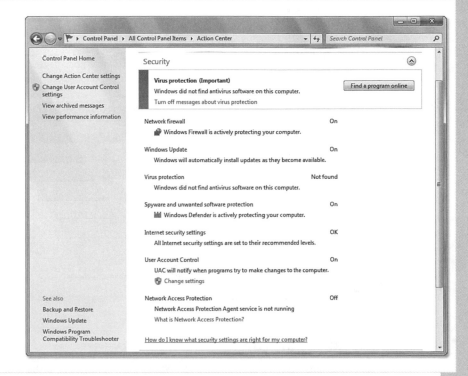

Security features monitored by Action Center include: the firewall (Windows Firewall or a compatible third-party firewall), Windows Update, virus protection, spyware protection, Internet security, UAC, and network access protection. As with earlier Windows versions, antivirus software is not included. Network Access Protection (NAP) is provided by some corporate networks to automatically update clients before they connect to the network.

The Maintenance section provides access to Reliability Monitor and monitors backup, Windows Update, and system maintenance features.

You can also launch troubleshooters and System Restore from Action Center. Click the Change Action Center link in the task pane to disable warnings for selected settings if desired (for example, if you are already getting security messages from a system suite).

It's important to realize that Action Center provides access to features it monitors only if the feature is disabled or missing (as with the missing antivirus program message shown in Figure 22.2). If you need to make changes to the components that Action Center monitors, go to the appropriate part of the Control Panel to make those changes.

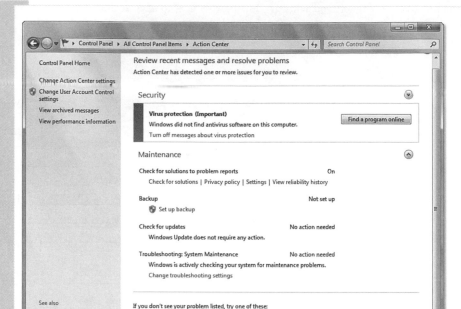

Figure 22.4
Maintenance settings monitored by Action Center.

Reliability Monitor

Reliability Monitor, which was introduced in Windows Vista as part of the Performance and Reliability Monitor applet, is now launched by clicking View Reliability History from the Action Center's Maintenance section. (You have to expand the Maintenance section in order to see View Reliability History, under Check for Solutions to Problem Reports.) Figure 22.5 displays a typical Reliability Monitor report. To see the details of a problem report, click a column in the graph, then click View Technical Details in the list in the bottom part of the window

In addition to tracking failures in four areas (applications, hardware, Windows, and miscellaneous), Reliability Monitor also tracks software installs and uninstalls (including both drivers and applications) and captures version information for drivers and applications. It also calculates a reliability index. A yellow triangle with a ! symbol indicates a failed application or driver install, whereas a red circle with an X symbol indicates other types of failures.

 tip

Use Reliability Monitor to look for patterns indicating problems with your system. For example, a pattern of frequent display driver crashes suggests you should change display driver versions.

Icons indicate warnings and other types of failures.

Click a column...

Figure 22.5
The details of a busy day
as recorded by
Reliability Monitor.

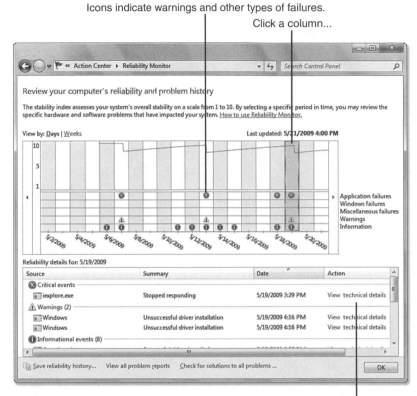

...then click the corresponding
View Technical Details link.

AutoPlay

AutoPlay isn't new to Windows 7. Its ancestor, Autorun, has been used to automatically start programs from a CD or DVD drive since Windows 95. In Windows XP, AutoPlay was extended to USB drives and other types of removable-media drives. AutoPlay is found in the Hardware and Sound category of the Control Panel and is also available in Classic view.

Windows 7 follows the lead of Windows Vista in how AutoPlay is configured. Rather than being configured on a drive-by-drive basis through the AutoPlay tab in a drive's Properties dialog box as in Windows XP, Windows 7's AutoPlay applet (see Figure 22.6) permits you to configure AutoPlay defaults for different types of media and multimedia files on a global basis.

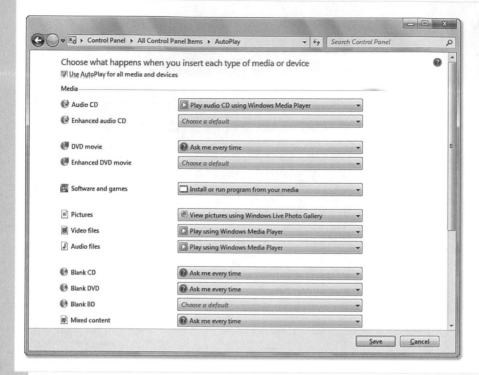

Figure 22.6
Using the AutoPlay applet to configure global settings for automatically recognizing media and file types.

Unlike Windows XP's AutoPlay, which was primarily designed for photos, music, and video files, Windows 7's AutoPlay also includes support for various types of CD and DVD movie discs, including HD DVD, Blu-ray Disc movies, DVD-Audio, Video CD, and Super Video CD. This is made possible in part by Windows Media Player 12's built-in support for DVD video and also enables you to use specialized players for certain types of video discs if you want.

AutoPlay also includes support for devices you connect to your system, as well as built-in devices. As in Windows XP and Vista, the exact programs available for any media or media file type vary according to the programs installed. You can also disable AutoPlay for particular media or media file types or globally.

Windows 7's AutoPlay is safer than in its predecessors in two important ways:

■ Autorun.inf files on non-optical removable media drives (such as USB flash memory drives) are ignored by AutoPlay, so that users cannot be tricked into running malware from the drive.

■ If the media contains one or more programs, AutoPlay indicates that the programs will be run from the media.

Color Management

The Color Management dialog is designed to help you configure your displays, printers, and scanners to produce more accurate color. Color Management helps your display and printer to produce matching colors and photo editing programs to create or edit images that are optimized for web, print, or display purposes.

Color Management uses files known as color profiles to achieve these goals. Color profiles are provided by display, graphics software, and printer vendors, and you can also create your own by using calibration software.

Color Management has three tabs: Devices, All Profiles, and Advanced. Use the Devices tab to determine what (if any) color profile is in use for your displays, printers, and scanners. Use the All Profiles tab to display the color profiles installed on your system. Use the Advanced tab to select the color profile to use for various types of images and to calibrate your monitor.

Date and Time

Date and Time is a simple applet you're sure to have used in the past to adjust the system date and time. That is, it adjusts the hardware clock in the computer, which is maintained by a battery on the motherboard. The system date and time are used for myriad purposes, including date- and time-stamping the files you create and modify, stamping email, controlling the Task Scheduler program for automatic application running, and so on. Date and Time is found in the Clock, Language, and Region category of the Control Panel and is also available in Small Icons/Large Icons views.

 note

The Date and Time applet doesn't change the format of the date and time, only the actual date and time stored on your computer's clock. To change formats, see the description of the Region and Language applet later in this chapter.

When you're a member of a Microsoft network domain, you should never need to set the clock. It is kept synchronized to the domain controller (Windows 2000 Server, Windows Server 2003, or Windows Server 2008). Many network services, including authentication protocols and replication, require exact or close synchronization of all systems within the network.

If your system is part of a workgroup or just a standalone system, you can sync your clocks with an Internet time server. The Date and Time applet includes a third tab for doing just that. However, this capability is not available on domain clients. The ability to sync with an Internet time server through the Date and Time applet is reserved for workgroup members, standalone systems, and domain controllers.

The Date and Time applet can also be accessed by clicking the clock and selecting Change Date and Time Settings or right-clicking over the clock and selecting Adjust Date/Time. To set the date and time, follow these steps:

1. Run the Date and Time applet.

2. Click Change Date and Time.

3. Alter the time and date by typing in the corrections or by clicking the arrows. The trick is to click directly on the hours, minutes, seconds, or AM/PM area first, and then use the little arrows to the right of them to set the correct value. So, to adjust the a.m. or p.m., click AM or PM, and then click the little up or down arrow. After setting the month and year, you can click the day in the displayed calendar. Click OK.

4. Click the Change Time Zone button to adjust the zone. Why? It's good practice to have your time zone set correctly for programs such as client managers, faxing programs, time synchronizing programs, or phone dialing programs. They may need to figure out where you are in relation to others and what the time differential is. Also, if you want your computer's clock to be adjusted automatically when daylight saving time changes, be sure the Automatically Adjust Clock for Daylight Saving Changes check box is selected. Click OK.

5. Click the Internet Time tab. Click Change Settings. On this tab, you can enable clock synchronization with an Internet time server. Five known time servers are provided in the pull-down list, but you can type in others. If you want to force a sync, click the Update Now button.

6. Click OK to save changes and close the applet.

 tip

You can also adjust the time and date using the `time` and `date` commands from a command prompt. For example, open a Command Prompt window (click Start, All Programs, Accessories, Command Prompt), type **time**, and press Enter. This command displays the current time and a prompt to enter the new time, as shown here:

```
The current time is:
21:39:31.78
Enter the new time:
```

Enter the new time, or press Enter to leave the time as it is. The same process applies to the date. Type **date** and press Enter. The current date is displayed with a prompt to enter the new date, as shown here:

```
The current date is: Fri
09/29/2006
Enter the new date: (mm-dd-yy)
```

Dealing with Daylight Saving Time

If your system's BIOS is also configured to automatically adjust for daylight saving time (DST), you may find that your system's clock is set incorrectly when the time changes twice a year, because both the BIOS and Windows make the adjustment. You should disable your system BIOS's DST adjustment and use Windows' instead. There are two reasons:

First, it's easier to configure time zones and settings from within Windows than from within the BIOS setup program.

Second, starting in 2007, DST in the United States begins the second Sunday of March and ends on the first Sunday of November. A Windows update or the built-in Internet time synchronization feature will enable your system to know when DST starts and ends. If you leave your computer's BIOS in charge of adjusting for DST, you will need to install a BIOS update—assuming that your PC's manufacturer is keeping up with U.S. law on this topic. Wherever you live, keep in mind that Microsoft issues updates on a regular basis for time-zone changes around the world, so keeping your PC's BIOS out of the time-zone adjusting business makes good sense everywhere.

When Internet synchronization is enabled, your clock is reset to match the time servers once each week. Internet synchronization should be configured only on systems with an active Internet connection. Clock synchronization does not initiate a dial-up connection. Plus, if there is a firewall or proxy server between your client and the Internet, the clock synchronization packets may be blocked.

Additional Clocks

Are you an eBay user? Do you need to know what time it is at headquarters? Whatever your reason for keeping an eye on other time zones, you can use the Additional Clocks tab to display up to two additional clocks.

Select the time zone (eBay runs on Pacific time, by the way) and provide a descriptive name to replace the default Clock 1 or Clock 2, and click Apply, then OK. When you hover your mouse over the date and time display in the notification area, the additional clocks are displayed along with the primary clock.

Default Programs

Default Programs can be found in the Programs category of the Control Panel, is also available in Large Icons and Small Icons views, and can also be opened directly from the Start menu's right pane. It enables you to choose the default program you prefer for a particular file type, associate a file type with a particular program, change AutoPlay settings (see "AutoPlay" earlier in this chapter for details), and specify which programs are the defaults for web browsing, email, playing media, instant messaging, and providing Java Virtual Machine (JVM) support.

Set Your Default Programs

Select this option, and your default programs for web browsing, photo viewing, media playback, and so forth are displayed in the left pane. Select a program from the list, and select from two options listed in the right pane:

- **Set This Program as Default**—Choose this option to use the selected program as the default for all file types and protocols it can open.

- **Choose Defaults for This Program**—Choose this option to specify which file types and programs the application will open by default.

We recommend the second option. When you select it, each file and protocol type you can choose from is listed, along with the current default. To change all items listed to default to the selected program, click the Select All check box. To change only selected options, click the empty check box next to each item you want to change. Click Save to complete the process.

Set Associations

The Set Associations dialog box provides an easy way to change file associations from a single dialog box, rather than requiring you to right-click a file, select Open With, and choose a program. Set Associations lists the file extensions supported by applications on your system and the current default. Click a file extension to select it, click Change Program, and select the program from the list of recommended programs, or click Browse to find the program you prefer. Select the program and click OK to finish the process.

Set Program Access and Computer Defaults

Select this option, and you can select from up to four different configurations for web browsing, email, and other common activities:

- Computer Manufacturer (available only on installations preinstalled by the computer manufacturer)

- Microsoft Windows

- Non-Microsoft

- Custom

For maximum flexibility, choose Custom. In the Custom configuration, you can specify not only default programs but also whether to permit or deny access to non-Microsoft alternatives to the default web browser, email, media player, IM, and JVM programs on your system, such as Firefox or Opera web browsers, Thunderbird or Eudora email clients, AOL or Trillian IM clients, and so forth. Credit the existence of this feature to antitrust litigation against Microsoft for embedding IE and other technologies into the OS. In other words, this applet enables Windows 7 to play nicely with other vendors' products.

Device Manager

The Device Manager is so important in keeping your system working properly that it can be accessed from two different categories: System and Security and Hardware and Sound. When the Device Manager is launched, you are presented with a category list of the devices installed in the system (see Figure 22.7). When there are no problems, the display is a bit bland (but in this case, bland is good). To see the individual devices, expand any of the listed categories. Then, to access a device's Properties dialog box, just double-click it.

The Device Manager serves several functions, the foremost of which is to aid in the resolution of hardware problems. When any device fails to function as expected, it will be highlighted with a yellow triangle or a down arrow. The yellow triangle indicates a warning or a possible problem, such as a driver that has not been loaded or an Unknown Device (see Figure 22.7). A down arrow indicates a disabled device, device conflict, or other serious error. When the Device Manager is launched and a device has an outstanding issue, its category will be expanded so that you can easily see the warning or error icon.

When a device's Properties dialog box is opened, the General tab displays basic information about the device, plus details on the device's current status. In most cases, the status report will point out exactly what is preventing the device from functioning normally. You may correct the issue on your own, or if you need help or guidance, click the Troubleshoot button on the General tab for a wizard or further guidance. This button has various labels, according to the problem you have. For example, if you have a driver problem, the button is called Reinstall Driver. If you have a resource problem, the button is called Check for Solutions. If the device is enabled, the button is called Enable Device, and so forth.

Figure 22.7
The Device
Manager dis-
playing an
unknown
device.

Click an arrow to expand a category.

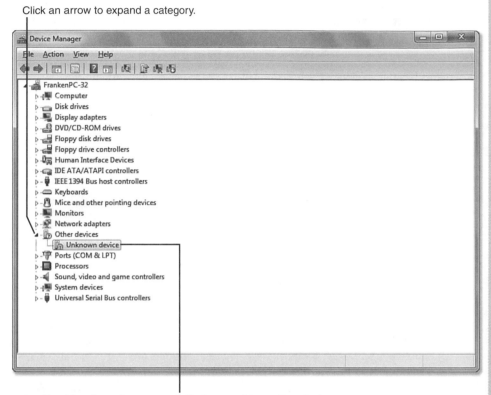

A yellow triangle or down arrow indicates a problem with a device.

Depending on the device, there can be many other tabs in addition to the General tab. In most cases, you'll see a Driver tab, and almost as frequently you'll see a Resources tab. The Driver tab offers details about the currently installed driver for this device and enables you to update, roll back, or uninstall the driver.

Device driver rollback, just as in Windows XP and Vista, removes the current driver and restores the previous driver (assuming there was one). The ability to remove the current or newly installed driver and return to the previously used driver is often a lifesaver. I can't remember how many times I've had to remove a new driver and then had to go through the process of reinstalling the hardware just to get the old driver back. The Roll Back Driver button performs this operation with a simple click. No muss, no fuss.

The Resources tab specifies the system resources to which the device is assigned. These include IRQ, I/O ranges, DMA, and more. On Plug and Play (PnP) devices, you can switch the settings from automatic to either a predefined configuration set or a fully customized setting. For some PnP cards, the settings on the Resources tab are read-only. In such cases, the settings are configured by the system BIOS and by the expansion slot the card is plugged into. See your system or motherboard documentation to determine how to change BIOS settings, or to determine which IRQ is assigned to a particular slot.

The Details tab, added as a standard feature to the Device Manager in Windows XP SP2, provides access to a huge list of technical details about your device. It defaults to displaying the device description (the same one you see on the main Device Manager window), but you can also view approximately 25 arcane technical details such as the Device Instance ID, Enumerator, and so on. Some devices may list additional information. A few of the most useful ways to use this tab include

- Use the Hardware IDs and Compatible IDs selection to determine the PnP information used to install the device.

- Use the Manufacturer selection to determine the manufacturer of the device.

- Use the Power Capabilities selection to determine the device's support for various power management states.

Access the Advanced tab found on some devices to configure special settings used by that device. The Power tab on USB root and generic hubs can help you determine whether a particular hub has enough power for a particular USB device. The Power Management tab found on some devices enables you to control whether the computer can turn off a device to save power and whether the device can wake the computer from standby.

For any other tabs that may appear in a device's Properties dialog box, be sure to consult the device's user manual.

From the main Device Manager view, you can perform a few helpful actions:

- Change views between devices by type, devices by connection, resources by type (IRQ, DMA, I/O port address, and memory), and resources by connection (USB ports, legacy ports, and so forth)

- Force a scan for hardware changes

- Show hidden devices

Understanding and Resolving Hardware Conflicts

Windows, together with its Plug-and-Play technology, has grown far better at detecting and preventing hardware conflicts over the past few years. Still, system conflicts do arise, especially when you're using legacy hardware, such as integrated serial and parallel ports.

Historically, configuration and installation problems were due to incorrect settings on ISA cards or integrated ports. If two

 tip

Some devices are hidden from view in the Device Manager. Hidden devices include non-PnP devices and devices that have been physically removed from the computer but have not had their drivers uninstalled. To see hidden devices in the Device Manager list, choose View, Show Hidden Devices. A check mark should appear on the menu, indicating that hidden devices are showing. Click it again to hide them.

 note

Windows 7 no longer supports the ISA bus, which has been with us in some form since the first IBM PC of 1981. So, don't bother trying to run Windows 7 on a motherboard with ISA cards. Legacy ports such as PS/2 mouse and keyboard ports, serial ports, and parallel ports, which were originally serviced by the ISA bus, are now serviced by a separate legacy I/O controller on the motherboard or a legacy I/O controller component in the I/O controller hub or South Bridge component of the chipset.

cards or ports were configured to use the same IRQ, base I/O port address, DMA, or base memory address, a conflict would occur. Thanks to PnP support for legacy ports, PCI, PCI Express, and AGP cards, resource conflicts are almost unheard of in recent years.

Hardware uses four major resources:

- IRQs

- DMA

- I/O port addresses

- DMA channel

tip

By default, the Device Manager displays Devices by Type. To see IRQ and other hardware resources in use in the Device Manager, click View, Resources by Type.

You can view the resources used by a particular device, and, depending upon the specific device and motherboard design, there are various ways to solve the rare conflicts that might occur.

IRQs

PC architecture includes a means for a piece of hardware to quickly gain the attention of the CPU through a message called an *interrupt request*, or *IRQ*. An IRQ is sent directly from hardware to the CPU, which then services the request accordingly. A common example occurs when data comes in to your system's modem or LAN card. The modem or LAN card triggers the predetermined IRQ, and the CPU then begins to execute the program code that is appropriate for handling that interrupt. In fact, a part of the OS called the *interrupt handler* is responsible for making it so.

note

You may see IRQs from 80 to 190 assigned to the Microsoft ACPI-Compliant System when you view IRQ assignments in the Device Manager or with System Information (MSInfo32).

Most systems suitable for use with Windows 7 feature an Advanced Programmable Interrupt Controller (APIC). APIC permits PCI, AGP, and PCI Express cards and non-legacy integrated devices (such as USB ports and SATA host adapters) to use IRQ settings above 15 (often called PCI IRQs). APIC is enabled through the system BIOS. Figure 22.8 shows a typical Windows 7 system with multiple devices assigned to PCI IRQs.

As shown in Figure 22.8, IRQ sharing is enabled automatically by Windows 7 when the system supports it. In some cases, however, some motherboards might not permit IRQs to be shared, even by PCI devices.

tip

If you no longer use legacy ports, disable them in the system BIOS. By disabling legacy ports, you enable the IRQs and other hardware resources used by serial, parallel, or PS/2 mouse ports to be available for PCI, PCI Express, and AGP devices, including integrated devices. On some systems, it may also be necessary to open the PnP/PCI dialog box in the system BIOS and assign the IRQs formerly used by legacy ports to be available for PnP/PCI devices.

If you find yourself short on IRQs or if you have two devices attempting to use the same IRQ and creating a conflict, try moving the PCI or PCI Express card to another slot. On some machines, each PCI slot's PCI Interrupt (A through D) is mapped to an ISA-type IRQ (numbers up to 15). By simply moving a card to a neighboring slot, you may get your hardware working. Note that PCI, PCI Express, and AGP slots all use PCI interrupts, and that some systems assign the same PCI interrupt to two slots, or to a slot and an integrated device. See your system or motherboard manual for details.

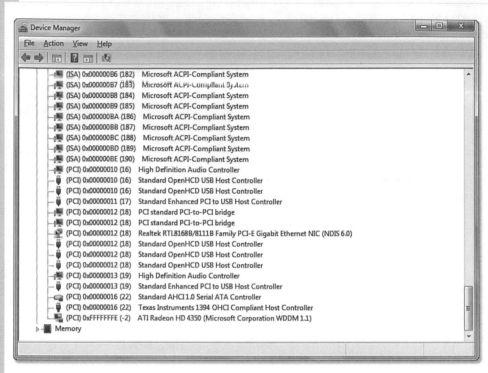

Figure 22.8
IRQ sharing
enables this
PC to use PCI
IRQ 22 for
IEEE-1394
host con-
trollers and a
Serial ATA
host adapter.

DMA Channels

A typical PC has eight DMA channels, labeled 0 to 7 (DMA 4 is used as a cascade controller between DMA channels 0–3 and 5–7). DMA channels are used for rapidly transferring data between memory and peripherals without the help of the CPU. In current systems, DMA channels are used only by parallel ports in enhanced capabilities port (ECP) or enhanced capabilities port/enhanced parallel port (ECP/EPP) modes.

Although recent EIDE hard drives use a variation of DMA called Ultra DMA (UDMA) for fast data transfer, DMA transfers performed by PCI-based devices don't use specific DMA channels. The only time a PCI device ever needs to use a DMA channel is if it's emulating an ISA device that uses one, such as a PCI-based sound card emulating an ISA-based sound card.

I/O Port Assignments

In PC architecture, I/O ports are mapped into system memory and, therefore, are accessed by the CPU using memory addresses. As you might expect, each device that uses an I/O port must have a different port address, or data intended for one device will end up at another. However, if a device must use a bridge to communicate with the rest of the system, the device and the bridge might use the same I/O address range (see Figure 22.9).

Check out the I/O folder off the Hardware Resources node in Computer Management, as shown in Figure 22.9, to see a sample list of I/O addresses and assignments. As you can see, this folder contains quite a few assignments. Note that the addresses are in standard memory-mapping parlance—hexadecimal.

note

A common source of I/O contention occurs among video cards, SCSI devices, and network cards. However, most devices can use a choice of several I/O port address ranges to avoid conflicts.

Figure 22.9
Typical I/O assignments in a Windows 7 machine are numerous. Notice the scrollbar. Only about half the assignments are visible in this figure.

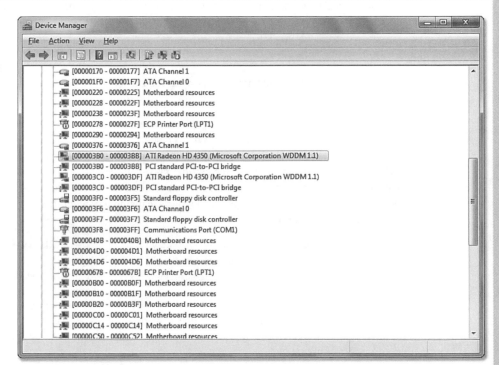

Memory Addresses

Similar to the I/O port address, the base memory address is the beginning memory address that some cards or motherboard hardware use to communicate with the CPU. Sometimes, this setting is called the *RAM starting address* (or *start address*).

If you open Computer Management and go to System Information, Hardware Resources, Memory, you'll see memory addresses such as the following:

```
0xA0000-0xBFFFF    PCI bus
```

This address means the memory area between A0000 and BFFFF is assigned to the PCI bus. (The 0x indicates that it is a hexadecimal address.) PnP configuration enables the system to place devices that need memory addresses in nonconflicting areas. Sometimes, memory address references in hardware documentation omit the last zero (A000).

Solving Resource Conflicts

Although PCI, AGP, and PCI Express cards and integrated devices are designed to share IRQs, you may see a resource conflict when you attempt to install a legacy port, such as a serial (communications) or parallel (LPT) port.

When a hardware conflict is detected, it's reported by the wizard at the end of the device installation process.

If you cannot select a nonconflicting setting with the device you're installing, you have a few options:

- Change the settings for the conflicting device with the Device Manager, as discussed later in this chapter.

- If the device you are attempting to install is an integrated legacy port, restart the system and select different settings in the BIOS setup. With a modern system, select Auto as the setting, which will enable the BIOS or Windows 7 to select a nonconflicting setting. If you must choose a particular IRQ or other hardware resource setting, make sure you don't choose a setting used by another port or card. For example, it's easy in most systems to choose the same IRQ and I/O port address range for both serial (communications) ports, causing a conflict. Be sure you choose different IRQs for each serial port.

- In some cases, particularly with legacy ports, you may not be able to resolve a conflict and will need to disable the conflicting device on one of the cards with the Device Manager.

If you have a resource conflict, what should you do? Most drivers don't have resources that can be reassigned. Others have an option button called Reinstall Driver that's useful if the system thinks that would solve a nonfunctioning-device problem. Most PCI, PCI Express, and AGP cards (as well as integrated ports such as USB, FireWire, and PATA/SATA) don't permit their resources to be reassigned because they obtain their resource settings from Windows or from the system BIOS. Some systems allocate resources depending on which slot you use for a particular card.

However, you can usually reassign resources for legacy ports like serial (COM) and parallel (LPT) ports. To reassign a resource, open the Device Manager, open the Properties dialog box for the device, and click the Resources tab. To select a different resource, uncheck the Use Automatic Settings box and choose Change Setting.

caution

In general, be cautious about configuring resource settings manually. When you change settings manually, the settings become fixed, and Windows 7's built-in device contention resolution is less likely to work. Also, if you install too many devices with manually configured settings, you might not be able to install new PnP devices because none will be available. In the worst-case scenario, the system might not even boot if conflicts occur with primary hardware devices, such as hard disk controllers or video cards. If you decide to use manual configuration, make sure you know what you're doing and have the specs for the hardware in question at hand.

To select an alternative setting on most systems, clear the Use Automatic Settings check box; then click Change Setting to change the settings. If the system displays an error message, use the Setting Based On scroll box to try a different Basic configuration.

On some older systems, you might be able to click the resource shown in the Resource Settings window and change it directly.

In an attempt to prevent folks from inadvertently doing damage, the Resources tab keeps an eye on what you're doing. If you attempt to reassign to a resource that is already in use using either method, you'll be warned about the conflict. Keep trying configurations until the conflicting device listing is clear. Then, click OK and restart your computer if prompted.

 caution

Notice the Setting Based On drop-down list on the Resources tab. It lists the hardware configurations in which the currently selected device is enabled. If you choose a hardware configuration other than the default, and you change any resource settings, resource conflicts may occur when you use the default hardware configuration. Resource conflicts can disable your hardware and cause your computer to malfunction or to be inoperable.

Devices and Printers

Devices and Printers (Figure 22.10) is a new Windows setup and management tool that you can reach from the Hardware and Sound category of Control Panel. You can also reach it from the Start Menu. It enables you to manage devices such as mice, game controllers, displays, keyboards, external storage devices, printers, scanners, faxes and multifunction devices from a single interface.

Figure 22.10
The Devices and Printers window.

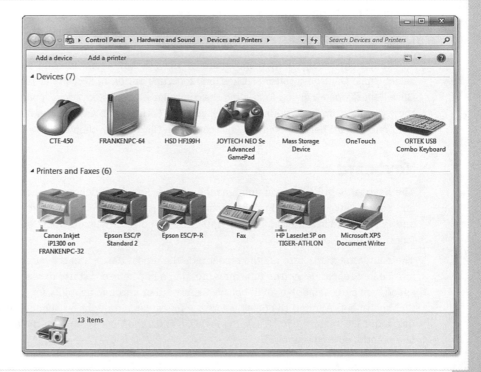

To manage a device other than a printer or fax, right-click it to select a troubleshooter, the device's properties sheet, to create a shortcut to the device, or to choose from device-specific configuration tasks.

In the following sections, we'll show you how to use Devices and Printers to manage devices such as mice, keyboards, and game controllers. Printer and multifunction printer management is covered in Chapter 6, while fax, scanner, and multifunction fax and scan device management are covered in Chapter 11.

Game Controllers

If you're serious about playing games on your computer, you need a game controller, such as a joystick, flightstick, gamepad, driving wheel, and other hardware devices designed specifically for the games of your choice. If you're an extreme gamer, the type of controller you need can vary greatly with the types of games you play. Game controllers have reached the point at which serious flight simulator enthusiasts hook up a flightstick, throttle, and separate rudder foot pedals to more accurately simulate the flying experience. Sports gamers usually go for handheld digital gamepads for fast response times. And fans of racing games just aren't getting the full experience without a force feedback steering wheel with its own set of foot pedals for the gas and break (and possibly even a clutch).

This book doesn't cover gaming to any extent, but if you are a gamer, and you buy a game controller, it likely comes with an installation program. If not, Windows 7 may detect it automatically, or you may need to run the Add Device applet available through the Devices and Printers menu in the Hardware and Sound category. In most cases, USB devices have no-brainer installations. Just plug it in and you are good to go.

To manage the settings for a game controller, right-click the controller in Devices and Printers and select Game Controller Settings. Click the Properties button to access the Test and Settings tabs. Click Test to open a dialog for testing the controller's buttons, joysticks, pedals, or other features. If the controllers are not working properly, click the Settings tab and click the Calibrate button. The Calibrate wizard helps you set up your controller. Click Apply, then OK, to save changes.

Keyboard

The Keyboard applet lets you fine-tune the way the keyboard behaves, check the keyboard driver, and perform some keyboard troubleshooting. Start it by right-clicking the keyboard icon in Devices and Printers and selecting Keyboard Properties, or select Keyboard from Control Panel's Small Icons or Large Icons views.

The main attractions here are the repeat rate, the repeat delay, and the cursor blink rate. By altering the key-repeat delay (the time after pressing a key before it starts to repeat) and the repeat speed, you can calm down an ill-behaved keyboard or improve usability for someone with a mobility impairment. Altering the delay before the repeat sets in might be helpful if you use applications that require extensive use of, say, the Page Up and Page Down, Enter, or the arrow keys (perhaps in a point-of-sale situation).

You also might want to change the cursor blink rate if the standard blinking cursor annoys you for some reason. You can even stop it altogether (the setting is None). I prefer a nonblinking one myself.

The defaults for these keyboard settings are adequate for most users and keyboards.

If you need to check keyboard properties, including the keyboard driver in use, click the Hardware tab and then click Properties. The Device Manager entry for the keyboard opens.

Mouse

It's almost impossible to use a modern computer without a mouse or equivalent pointing device. To make sure your mouse is working to your satisfaction, use the Control Panel's Mouse applet (see Figure 22.11) to fine-tune its operation. From Devices and Printers, right-click the mouse icon and select Mouse Properties, or open Mouse from the Large Icons or Small Icons views of Control Panel.

Figure 22.11
Setting mouse properties can help you get your work done more efficiently, though the defaults usually work fine without modification.

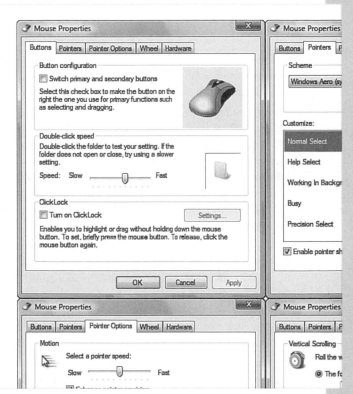

Available settings include

- Left/right button reversal

- Double-click speed

- ClickLock

- Look of the pointers

- Pointer scheme

- Pointer speed

- Enhance pointer precision

- Snap to the default button of dialog boxes

- Display pointer trails and length

- Hide pointer while typing

- Show location of pointer when Ctrl is pressed

- Set wheel scroll to number of lines or screen at a time

- Troubleshooting

- Access device properties (same controls as through the Device Manager)

The options vary based on pointing device type, and sometimes you are supplied with even fancier options if your pointing device comes with a custom driver. For example, the Synaptics touchpads let you scroll a window by sliding your finger down the right side of the trackpad.

Poor lefties never get a fair shake in life, what with all the right-handed scissors and tools around. Well, they get one here (except for some types of weird, ergonomically shaped mouse devices that don't work well in the left hand). If you're left-handed, you can move the mouse to the left side of the keyboard and then reverse the function of the buttons on the Buttons tab of the Mouse applet. Right-clicks then become left-clicks.

On the same tab, you can set the double-click speed. A middle-range setting is appropriate for most folks. Double-click the folder icon to try out the new double-click speed. The folder opens or closes if the double-click registered. If you're not faring well, adjust the slider, and then try again. You don't have to click Apply to test the slider settings. Just moving the slider instantly affects the mouse's double-click speed.

 tip

If all else fails and you just can't find a double-click speed to suit your needs or abilities, forget double-clicks altogether. Instead, click an icon or any selectable object in the Windows 7 environment. A single-click usually will highlight the option. Think of this as getting the object's attention. Then press Enter on the keyboard to launch, open, or execute the selected object.

As you know, the pointer cursor changes based on the task at hand. For example, when you're editing text, it becomes an I-beam. You can customize your cursors for the fun of it or to increase visibility. You can even install animated cursors to amuse yourself while you wait for some process to complete. Just as with icons and screen savers, the Web is littered with Windows cursors, if you want to collect a few thousand. Windows 7 comes with enough to keep me happy, organized into schemes. You can change individual cursors or change a set of them in one fell swoop by using the *cursor schemes*.

Like color schemes and sound schemes, cursor schemes are collections of cursor shapes. When you select a scheme, all the cursors in the scheme go into effect at once. You can choose from approximately 20 canned schemes.

You can change individual cursors in a scheme, if you want. To change a cursor assignment, click a cursor in the list. Then click Browse. The default location is …\windows\cursors. Animated cursors move for you in the Browse box (a thoughtful feature). After you custom-tailor a set of cursors to your liking, you can save the scheme for later recall. Click Save As and name it.

Windows 7 supports both the now-traditional scrolling wheel and the newer horizontal tilting mouse wheel with the Wheel tab. Use this tab to adjust how both types of wheels operate.

 note

Use one of the Extra Large cursor schemes if you have trouble seeing the pointer. Also, some of the schemes change the pointer into things that don't resemble pointers and can make selecting or clicking small objects difficult because the pointer's hotspot is difficult to locate. Sometimes, the cursor is distracting and can obscure the item you want to select or click.

Ease of Access Center

The Windows 7 Ease of Access Center is similar to the Windows Vista version, and, unlike the Windows XP Accessibility Center it replaces, is designed to be easy enough to enable users with visual or hearing impairments to set up their own systems, not merely use a system that has already been customized by another user for easier operation. The Ease of Access Center is found in two Control Panel categories: Appearance and Personalization and Ease of Access, and is also listed in the Large Icons/Small Icons views.

After you open the Ease of Access Center (see Figure 22.12), Windows 7's text-to-speech tool reads the top of the dialog box to the user and then highlights each of the tools (Magnifier, Narrator, On-Screen Keyboard, and High Contrast) in turn. To open a tool, all the user has to do is press the spacebar when the tool is highlighted.

To use other Ease of Access settings, scroll down the list and select from the following:

- **Use the Computer Without a Display**—Offers options including Narrator, Audio Description of videos, text-to-speech setup, disabling of unnecessary animations, and adjusting how long Windows dialog boxes stay open.

- **Make the Computer Easier to See**—Specifies how to turn on High Contrast displays, enable Narrator and Audio Description, adjust text and icon sizes, turn on Magnifier, increase the thickness of the focus rectangle and blinking cursor, and disable background images and unnecessary animations.

- **Use the Computer Without a Mouse or Keyboard**—Offers the On-Screen Keyboard and the Speech Recognition dialog box.

- **Make the Mouse Easier to Use**—Adjusts the mouse cursor size and color, enables Mouse Keys, and enables hover to switch to a window option.

- **Make the Keyboard Easier to Use**—Turns on the user's choice of Mouse Keys, Sticky Keys, Toggle Keys, or Filter Keys. See "Accessibility Keyboard Settings" later in this chapter for details.

- **Use Text or Visual Alternatives for Sounds**—Configures Sound Sentry, which can flash the active caption bar, active window, or the desktop to notify a user of a warning; offers option to enable text captions for spoken dialog boxes when available.

- **Make It Easier to Focus on Tasks**—Configures accessibility keyboard settings, Narrator, and removal of background images.

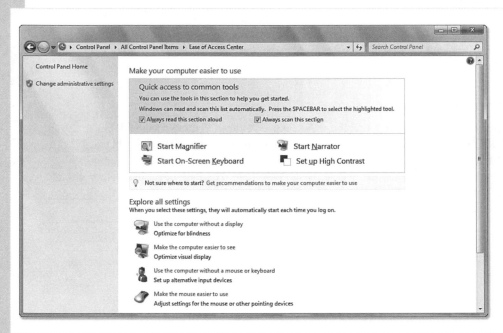

Figure 22.12
The Ease of Access Center talks users through selecting common accessibility tools.

You can use many combinations of Ease of Access features to help make the computer use easier.

Ease of Access Keyboard Settings

The keyboard settings are intended to deal with such problems as accidentally repeating keys or pressing combinations of keys. These options fall into three categories: Sticky Keys, Filter Keys, and Toggle Keys.

Sticky Keys are settings that, in effect, stay "down" when you press them once. They are good for controlling the function of the Alt, Ctrl, and Shift Keys if you have trouble pressing two keys at the same time. To use them, set the Sticky Keys option on; then choose the suboptions as you see fit. For some users, the shortcut of pressing the Shift key five times is a good way to activate Sticky Keys. If you turn on this activation method, note that pressing the Shift key five times again turns off Sticky Keys. This trick isn't explained clearly in the dialog boxes. Also, if you choose the Press

Modifier Key Twice to Lock option, that means you press, for example, Shift twice to lock it. You can then press Shift twice again to unlock it.

Filter Keys let you "filter" (remove) accidental repeated keystrokes if you have trouble pressing a key cleanly once and letting it up. This feature prevents you from typing multiple keystrokes. The shortcut key for turning on this feature works like the one for Sticky Keys; it's a toggle. If you hold down the right Shift key for eight seconds, a Filter Keys dialog box appears. Click Yes to enable Filter Keys.

The Toggle Keys option, when turned on, sounds a high-pitched tone when Caps Lock, Scroll Lock, or Num Lock keys are activated and a low-pitched tone when they're turned off again.

Each of these three keyboard features can be used independently or together. Note that a slowdown in performance occurs

 tip

Filter Keys, when activated, can make it seem that your keyboard has ceased working unless you are very deliberate with keypresses. You have to press a key and keep it down for several seconds for the key to register. If you activate this setting and want to turn it off, the easiest solution is to use the mouse to open the Control Panel (via the taskbar), run the Ease of Access applet, turn off Filter Keys, and click Apply or OK.

at the keyboard if sounds are used, because the sound is generated by playing a WAV file that briefly eats up your system resources. Processing of keypresses doesn't commence until after the keyboard sound finishes, which can result in jerky performance.

When Sticky Keys or Filter Keys are turned on, a symbol appears in the notification area. The Sticky Keys feature is indicated by three small boxes with a fourth larger box above them, representative of the Ctrl, Alt, and Shift keys. The Filter Keys feature is represented by the stopwatch, which is representative of the different key timing that goes into effect when the option is enabled.

Ease of Access Sound Settings

The two Ease of Access sound settings—Sound Sentry and ShowSounds—are useful for those with hearing impairments, or for computer users working in a noisy environment, such as a factory floor or flight deck. Instead of playing a sound when an error message or other event that causes a sound occurs, some type of visual display appears onscreen.

With Sound Sentry, a portion of the normal Windows screen blinks. With ShowSounds turned on, a text caption or special icon will pop up over a window or dialog box when a sound is played. The information in the pop-up window will inform you of the sound played and whether the audio clue is a warning, error, and so on.

If you choose Sound Sentry, you have a choice of the visual warning to use. The options are offered in a pull-down list, which includes the Flash Active Caption Bar, Flash Active Windows, and Flash Desktop. Typically, you'll want the window of the application or at least its title bar to flash. Don't make the desktop flash because it won't indicate which program is producing the warning.

 tip

Some programs are finicky about the sound options, especially ShowSounds. If they're not programmed correctly, they don't display a sound. Think of it like closed captioning for TV. Not all shows have it.

Ease of Access Display Settings

Special display settings increase the screen contrast by altering the display scheme. Using this applet actually is just an easy way to set the display color scheme and font selection for easier reading, just as you could do from the Personalization applet, as discussed in Chapter 23. The big plus of setting the contrast here is that you can quickly call it up with a shortcut key combination when you need it. Simply press Left+Alt, Left+Shift, Prnt Scrn, and the settings go into effect. I have found this feature useful for when my eyes are tired or in imperfect lighting situations. Figure 22.13 compares the normal appearance of the Ease of Access Center with Aero enabled to the High Contrast White version, which as a byproduct also sets the appearance of buttons and toolbars to Windows Classic.

Figure 22.13
Windows Aero (left) compared to High Contrast White (right).

Standard Aero Theme　　　　　　　　High-Contrast Theme

A fourth option, Mouse Keys, enables users who have problems using a mouse to use the numeric keypad to emulate the mouse. Mouse Keys can be configured to run all the time, or only when needed by pressing the left Alt+Left Shift+Num Lock keys at the same time. Mouse Keys also offers options to accelerate the mouse pointer and adjust the mouse pointer speed. When Mouse Keys is active, it displays a mouse icon in the notification area.

 tip

You get to select which predefined color scheme (both Windows provided and ones you've created through the Display applet) will be used as the High Contrast scheme. It's easier to observe the look of the schemes using the Personalization applet than in the Ease of Access Center applet. Do it there, and then decide which one you like best. Then come back to the Ease of Access dialog and make your choice.

Accessibility Mouse Settings

Using the Mouse Keys setting, you can control the mouse with the keypad if you have problems controlling your mouse's movements. This feature can bail you out if your mouse dies for some reason, too, or if you simply don't like using the mouse. As is covered in Chapter 4, you can execute many Windows and Windows application commands using the keyboard shortcut keys. But sometimes an application still responds only to mouse movements and clicks. Graphics programs are a case in point. When you use this Accessibility option, your arrow keys do double duty, acting like pointer control keys.

To use this option, simply turn on Mouse Keys from one of the dialog boxes that offer it and apply the change. Then, to activate the keys, press Left+Alt, Left+Shift, and Num Lock at the same time. The notification area should show a mouse icon. If the icon has a red line through it, Mouse Keys is disabled, so press the Num Lock key to enable it.

Now you can move the pointer around the screen using the arrow keys on the numeric keypad. If you're using a laptop, you'll have to consult its manual to determine how to activate the numeric keypad, or look for an Fn key and contrasting-color keyboard markings for the numeric keypad that take effect only when Fn+Num Lock is pressed first. The normal arrow keys won't cut it.

Use the Pointer Speed sliders if you need to adjust the speed settings for the arrow keys. Turn on the Ctrl and Shift options for speeding up or slowing down the mouse, assuming you can press two keys simultaneously. This setting really speeds things up.

If you adjust the configuration on the Settings dialog box, you have to click OK and then click Apply before the changes register. Then, you can go back and adjust as necessary.

Fonts

The first version of Windows to include a unified system for displaying and printing text across all Windows applications and printers was Windows 3.0. This was an attempt to catch up to the Macintosh, whose integrated support for PostScript font and graphics rendering gave it a big lead over earlier versions of Microsoft Windows. When Microsoft Windows 3.1 was introduced along with a new scalable font technology known as TrueType, Windows users had font capabilities on a par with the Mac. With the development of OpenType by Adobe and Microsoft, which integrates PostScript and TrueType support into a single font format, publishing and graphics users have never had it so good.

Windows 7 follows in this tradition, using the same TrueType and OpenType font outline technologies supported natively by Windows XP and Windows 2000. However, the font previewing and management tools in Windows 7 are better than those in either Windows XP or Windows Vista.

Fonts 101

The Fonts folder can be accessed from the Appearance and Personalization category of the Control Panel and is also available in Large Icons and Small Icons views. Use the Fonts folder to view fonts, preview fonts, print font samples, and access special characters.

The word *font*, as used in Windows, refers to a typeface. Those people in typesetting circles believe the term is misused in PC jargon, and you should be calling, say, Arial a typeface. But, oh well. There goes the language (again). Fonts are specified by size as well as by name. The size of a font is measured in *points*. A point is 1/72 of an inch.

Note that all fonts except some raster fonts (see the following Tip) are scalable to any size needed. Technically, the OpenType and TrueType fonts installed on a Windows system are font outlines: Windows scales the font outline as needed for display and for printing. Although you can content yourself with picking a standard font size from a menu in Microsoft Word, CorelDraw, or Adobe Photoshop, you can enter any size you want in the Font menu or dialog box for a TrueType or OpenType font. If you need a 131.76 point font, you've got it! And, you can see it onscreen.

Windows 7 includes about 130 font families, most of which are OpenType fonts. (A few TrueType fonts are included in that number, as are a small number of fonts.) A font family might include only a single style, or several styles (Roman, Italic, Bold, and so on). If you have installed Microsoft or third-party office suite or graphics packages, you may have additional fonts installed.

 tip

To determine whether a font is OpenType or TrueType, open a font family icon, then double-click one of the typefaces to see a sample. The font sample dialog box indicates the type of font.

As you can see from Figure 22.14, the Fonts folder in Windows 7 is nothing like its predecessors: you now see a preview of the Roman (standard weight) typeface in a font family, and you also see fonts designed for languages different from your currently selected language. These fonts, shown in gray, are hidden—they will not show up in font menus.

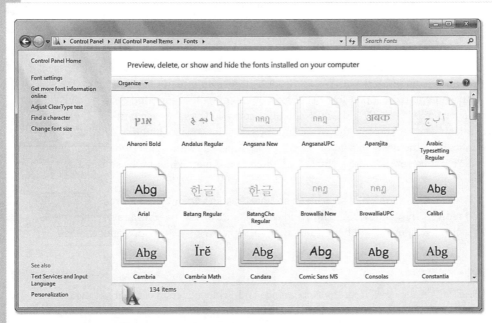

Figure 22.14
The default Large Icons view of the Fonts folder. Fonts in gray are hidden from view in applications' Fonts menu.

Figure 22.15 shows a typical preview of a font family that includes multiple styles. As you can see, Windows 7 has uncluttered the Fonts folder by grouping styles together in the main fonts folder and showing you the different styles only when you select a family.

Figure 22.15
The Arial fonts family as installed in Windows 7 has five members (Black, Bold, Bold Italic, Italic, and Regular).

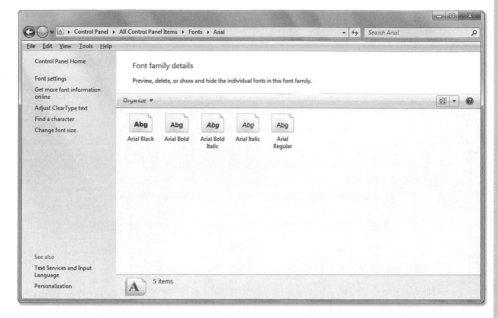

Font Types

The two primary categories of fonts are *serif* and *sans-serif* designs. Serifs are the little embellishments (often called "feet") that extend from the main *strokes* of the character. Serifs often are added to improve readability. As the name implies, sans-serif fonts lack these embellishments, making for a cleaner look. Sans-serif fonts tend to work well for headlines, whereas serif fonts are traditionally used for body text. Combining one serif and one sans-serif font in this way will look good together, but two sans-serif fonts or two serif fonts will clash. Times New Roman is a serif font, whereas Arial is a sans-serif font. The body text (the part you're reading now) of this book is a serif font; the headings in this book are sans-serif fonts.

The next major classification of fonts has to do with the spacing between characters. In *monospaced* fonts such as Courier New, every character occupies the same amount of horizontal line space. For example, *l* and *W* get the same amount of linear space.

By contrast, *proportionally spaced* fonts give differing amounts of line space, depending on the character. A *W* gets more space than an *l* or an *i*. The body text in this book uses proportionally spaced fonts, making it easier to read. The advantage of using

 tip

Aligning text in emails can be tricky. Although numbers in most proportionally spaced fonts are monospaced, each press of the spacebar when a proportional font is in use moves the cursor only a small increment. Even if you use tabs to align text, different email clients may interpret tabs differently or might use a proportional font and replace tabs with spaces, throwing off alignment. To help align columns of text in emails, send email in HTML-based (rich-text) format if the receiver can handle it, or attach a document in a common format, such as Microsoft Word that contains properly aligned text.

See Chapter 15, "Email and Newsgroups with Windows Live Mail," for more details about HTML mail.

monospaced fonts is that they allow you to easily align columns of text or numbers when you're using a simple word processor such as Notepad or sending email. You can use the spacebar to align the items in the columns, as you would on a typewriter.

Two other categories of fonts (after headline and body text) are ornamental and nonalphabetic symbols. *Ornamental* (sometimes called *display*) fonts have limited application. They are often fun in the short term, or for a one-shot deal such as a poster or a gag. They often attract attention but are too highly stylized to be suitable for body text, and they can distract the readers' attention from your message. Windows 7 doesn't include ornamental fonts, although it includes a few script fonts (which mimic handwriting). You should use ornamental fonts sparingly and only when you want to set a special mood.

Symbol or pi fonts contain special symbols such as musical notes, map symbols, or decorations instead of letters, numbers, and punctuation marks. Good examples are Symbol, Zapf Dingbats, WingDings, and WebDings (the last two are included in Windows 7).

➡ *To learn more about symbol and other nonkeyboard characters,* **see** *"Character Map," p. 667.*

Font and Font Information Sources

The Microsoft Typography website (www.microsoft.com/typography/default.mspx) provides a wealth of information about fonts, including tools, utilities, and links. Click the Font Foundry List link (under Resources) to find a list of all commercial, freeware, and shareware type foundries.

Some of my favorite commercial font foundries include

- **Adobe Systems** (www.adobe.com/type/index.html)—Features low-cost font libraries for educators and the Adobe Font Folio collection of more than 2,200 typefaces.

- **Bitstream** (bitstream.com; sales at new.myfonts.com)—This site also features WhatTheFont, a font identification service.

- **Monotype Imaging** (www.fonts.com)—Home of many Windows fonts, including Times New Roman and Arial.

Save money and find some unusual fonts with these low-cost font sources:

- **BuyFonts** (www.buyfonts.com)—Starter and professional fonts (for Windows only)

- **The Scriptorium** (www.fontcraft.com)—Features a huge variety of historic and specialized fonts

You can also find a lot of low-cost or free fonts online or in CD collections at retail stores.

Font Substitutions

In a perfect world, everyone working with a particular document would already have the correct fonts necessary to view and print it just as the originator intended. Unless you use only the basic fonts that every version of Windows from 3.1 to the present has included as standard (Arial, Courier New, and Times New Roman) or embed the fonts you use in a document (a feature not all applications or all fonts support), mismatches between installed fonts on the system used to create the document and on the target system are likely to happen.

To enable a document created with missing fonts to display and print in a reasonable facsimile of the original, font substitution features in applications and printer drivers are used. For example, in Microsoft Word, to determine whether font substitutions are taking place, choose Tools, Options, Compatibility, Font Substitutions. Some applications, such as CorelDraw, display a warning dialog box and provide the opportunity to select a substitute font if you open a file that contains fonts not present on your system.

Another kind of font substitution pertains only to PostScript printers. Because PostScript printers have internal fonts, printing is faster using them than forcing Windows to download a similar font file into the PostScript rasterizer and then commence printing. For example, the Windows Arial font and the PostScript Helvetica font are virtually identical. So, you can tell your PostScript printer driver to use only the Helvetica font in the printer whenever you print a document formatted with Arial. Likewise, Times can be substituted for Windows's Times New Roman.

A font substitution table is responsible for setting the relationship of the screen and printer fonts. In Windows 7, you can find this table on the Device Settings tab of a printer's Properties dialog box.

Font Installation and Management

In Windows 7, font management is performed by right-clicking any empty space in the Fonts folder and selecting from the View, Sort By, or Group By options. You can view, sort, and group by the following default categories: font name, font style, hide/show, designed for (alphabets), category (text, symbol/pictograph, display), designer/foundry, embeddability, and font type (OpenType, TrueType, Raster). You can view all of this information at once in the Details view, and you can add additional sort options, such as size, collection, and others. Unfortunately, Windows 7 does not offer the helpful List Fonts by Similarity feature found in Windows XP.

Windows 7 uses a new method for installing fonts. To install the font, right-click the font file in Windows Explorer and select Install. If prompted, provide the necessary UAC credentials, and the font is installed into the Fonts folder.

To remove fonts from your system, open the Fonts folder, right-click the font family or the individual style, and choose Delete. The fonts are removed permanently from your system.

 tip

Although Windows 7 font management is (mostly) better than its predecessors, if you're serious about using fonts to make your documents and websites look better, you need better font-management tools than the Fonts folder. Here are a few possibilities; check with these and other vendors for versions that are compatible with Windows 7:

- **FontAgent Pro**—Insider Software; www.fontagentpro.com
- **Printer's Apprentice**—Lose Your Mind Development; www.loseyourmind.com
- **Suitcase for Windows**—Extensis a division of Celartern, Inc.; www.extensis.com
- **Typograf**—Neuber Software; www.neuber.com/typograph/index.html

Notification Area Icons

For years, the icons in the notification area (previously known as the system tray) have been a frustration: If the software vendor responsible for the icon didn't provide a way to enable or disable the icon, you were stuck with it. While Windows XP and Windows Vista added the option to click an arrow to display/hide inactive icons, users who have wanted to control individual icon behavior have been looking for a solution. Now, Windows 7's new Notification Area Icons applet (see Figure 22.16) enables you to manage those icons.

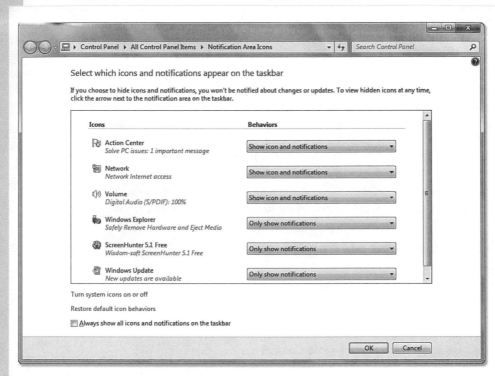

Figure 22.16
Setting the notification area icon options for a Windows 7 system with Microsoft and third-party icons.

For each icon displayed, you can choose from three options:

- Show icon and notifications
- Hide icon and notifications
- Only show notifications

You can keep or override the default behavior for each icon, and you can manage both standard Windows applets and icons provided by third-party programs (such as the Wisdom-soft ScreenHunter program shown in Figure 22.16).

Performance Information and Tools

Performance Information and Tools combines the Windows Experience Index (an updated version of the computer performance rating system introduced by Windows Vista) with easier access to a wide variety of performance-adjusting settings used in previous Windows versions. The principle behind Performance Information and Tools is to help you determine how well your system runs

Windows 7 and to make it as easy as possible to tweak your system for better performance. It is available from the System and Security category of Control Panel, or in Large Icons or Small Icons view.

The Windows Experience Index

When you open Performance Information and Tools, the first item you're likely to notice on the main dialog box is the Windows Experience Index (WEI) base score and component ratings (see Figure 22.17).

Figure 22.17
The Windows Experience Index includes scores from five different subsystems, but the lowest score determines your system's rating.

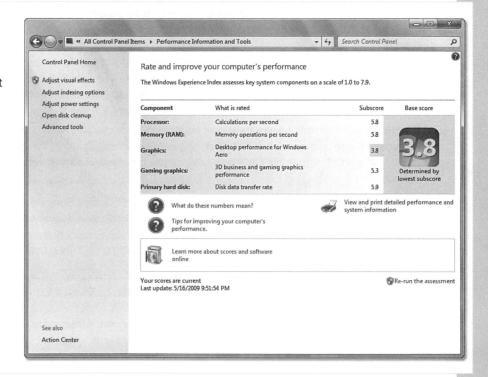

Five subsystems are evaluated to provide the basis for determining the WEI:

- Your processor's calculations per second (CPU)

- Memory operations per second (RAM)

- Desktop performance for Windows Aero (Aero)

- 3D business and gaming graphics performance (3D)

- Your primary hard disk's data transfer rate (HD)

Each item is scored, and the lowest score (note—*not* an average) is used to calculate the computer's WEI. This might seem like an odd method to use, but the advantage is that it helps you determine what part of your system is the principle performance bottleneck. For example, in examining the system shown in Figure 22.18, note that the lowest scores (3.8 and 5.3) are related to the graphics card. By upgrading the graphics card to one with a more powerful GPU, the system's WEI should increase. The other scores are 5.8 or higher, indicating satisfactory performance

Interpreting the Windows Experience Index

How important is the WEI base score (the lowest of the subsystem scores) to your satisfaction with Windows 7? According to Microsoft, computers with base scores of 2 or less will satisfactorily perform basic tasks such as office productivity or web surfing but are probably not powerful enough to run Windows Aero or advanced multimedia features. Computers with a base score of 3 can run Windows Aero but may not be powerful enough to run high-end features such as Aero across multiple displays or display HDTV. Computers with a base score of 4 or higher can use all features. Systems with higher scores will perform better in 3D gaming. The highest score, 7.9, was achieved by the fastest-performing computers available when Windows 7 was released.

If you previously used Windows Vista, you might recall that the highest WEI score was 5.9. By increasing the maximum score to 7.9, Microsoft provides more headroom for today's faster subsystems. Microsoft's Engineering Windows 7 blog points out changes in WEI ratings of hard disks and graphics:

- Hard disks with poor write cache flush performance will receive lower disk scores compared to the same hardware measured under Windows Vista's WEI. Most conventional hard disks with properly operating write flush cache are expected to score in the 5.0–5.9 range. Extending the scoring range up to 7.9 provides headroom for SSDs and faster conventional drives.

- Graphics performance is affected by the DirectX version supported by the GPU, the driver version used, and GPU performance. For example, if you have a DirectX 9.0–compliant graphics card using WDDM 1.1, your maximum score is 5.9. Higher scores are only possible with DirectX 10.*x*–compliant graphics cards that perform at about the same frame rate as in DirectX 9 mode. For mainstream DirectX 10 gaming, you will want a card with a WEI subsystem index of 5.0 or higher.

More Light on Windows 7's WEI

The TechARP website www.techarp.com/showarticle.aspx?artno=622 points out additional system components that affect your WEI score in Windows 7:

- Processor scores are determined by a combination of design and performance. For example, mainstream quad-core processors will typically score in the 7.0+ range, while dual-core processors will typically score in the 4.8–6.5 range.

- Memory scores are determined by memory size and performance. For example, the maximum score a system with less than 3GB of RAM can receive is 5.5, while a system running 64-bit Windows 7 with less than 4GB of RAM will top out at 5.9. Systems utilizing dual-channel memory will score higher than systems using the same memory size in a single-channel mode.

The easiest way to improve the WEI in a major way is to upgrade one or more of the major subsystems it rates. For example, replacing the video card can boost scores for Aero and for 3D graphics. Adding more RAM can boost memory scores. Upgrading to a faster processor can boost processor scores. Upgrading to a hard disk with a larger buffer, faster rotation rate, or both, can increase hard disk performance. Some upgrades, such as RAM and CPU, will boost performance in multiple areas.

If you decide to upgrade your system, look at the following factors:

- **Integrated video**—If you can replace integrated video with a PCI Express (PCI-E) or AGP video card that uses a GPU listed on the Windows 7–compatible GPU list, you can significantly improve your Aero and 3D scores. Look for a unit with at least 128MB of RAM if you are primarily concerned about business graphics, or a unit with 512MB or more of RAM for 3D gaming. The latest nVidia GPUs have model numbers in the GTX 2*xx* series, whereas the latest ATI GPUs have model numbers in the HD 4*xxx* series. Higher model numbers generally indicate better performance, but see the manufacturers' websites for details.

- **Processor**—Economy processors such as the AMD Sempron, Intel Celeron, or Intel Pentium Dual-Core have slower core clock speeds, slower front side bus connections to memory, and smaller L2 cache sizes than their full-performance counterparts (AMD Phenom, 64FX, 64 X2 or Intel Core 2 Duo, Core 2 Quad). However, a processor upgrade might also require a motherboard and memory module upgrade as well. Look at other upgrades first to improve your system's base and subsystem scores.

- **Memory (RAM)**—Windows 7 runs best with at least 1GB of RAM available to Windows. Many so-called "1GB" systems, particularly laptops, actually share 128MB of RAM or more with the integrated graphics subsystem. Thus, for best system performance, consider upgrading systems that use shared video memory to 2GB or more of system memory.

To determine the amount of memory actually available to Windows, type **DXDIAG** into the Instant Desktop Search box and press Enter. This runs DirectX Diagnostics. The System dialog box indicates the amount of memory available to Windows in Windows 7.

The System Properties dialog box in Windows 7 now shows total system memory, including memory set aside for graphics memory. The difference between these amounts in Windows 7 is the amount of RAM used for shared video (graphics) memory.

- **Hard disk drives**—The best hard disks for desktop computers feature spin rates (RPM) of 7,200 to 10,000 and 16MB or larger buffer sizes. If your hard disk has a lower spin rate, smaller buffer size, or both, it's limiting the performance of your system. If you're considering a hard disk upgrade, keep in mind that new Serial ATA (SATA) drives are generally faster and larger than traditional PATA (ATA/IDE) drives. However, some older systems may have limited or no support for SATA drives. Laptop drives tend to feature lower spin rates, smaller buffer sizes, and smaller capacities than desktop drives.

 tip

When you display your system's WEI, you may see specific advice that a particular program, process, or setting is slowing down your system. Use this information to go directly to the best task to help improve performance. For example, if a startup program is causing system problems, you'll be advised to use the Manage Startup Programs task.

Click the link Tips for Improving Your Computer's Performance on the Performance Information and Tools page to learn about the tools provided in the Tasks list on the left side. Each of these tools is discussed in the following sections.

Adjust Visual Effects

When you select Adjust Visual Effects from the Tasks list of Performance Information and Tools, you open the Visual Effects tab of the Performance Options dialog box (see Figure 22.18). This tab provides options to allow Windows to manage effects, adjust for best appearance, or adjust for best performance, or choose your own custom settings.

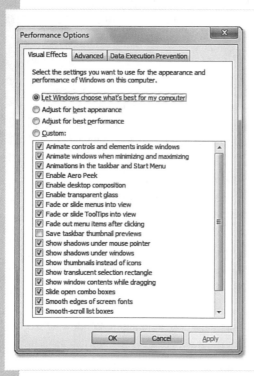

Figure 22.18
The Visual Effects tab of the Performance Options dialog box.

When you select the first three options, Windows 7 selects the appropriate settings. Click Custom, or clear an effects checkbox or click an empty checkbox after selecting any of the other options, and the Custom option is selected. You can enable or disable a long list of effects. These effects include animate resizing of windows, fade ToolTips, show shadows under menus, and use visual styles on windows and buttons.

Unless your system is low on physical RAM or uses integrated video or a PCI (not PCI Express or AGP) video card, there is little need to modify the default settings for these controls in

 tip

Keep in mind that you can also boost your visual performance more significantly by switching from Aero to Windows 7 Basic. By ditching the 3D and transparency effects in Aero, your system will display windows faster.

respect to performance. However, if you think no shadows or no animation looks better, you can customize the look and feel of the user environment all you want.

Adjust Indexing Options

One of the most important "behind the scenes" features in Windows 7 is the integrated indexing feature. It enables you to find a file in just seconds with Instant Desktop Search and zero in on the media you want to play in Windows Media Player, to give just two examples of how indexing makes life in Windows 7 land easier and more fun.

When you click the Adjust Indexing Options task in the Tasks list of Performance Information and Tools, you open the Indexing Options dialog box (see Figure 22.19). The top of the dialog box lists the number of items indexed and the locations that are indexed. Click Modify to specify what to index; use this option to enable or disable indexing of system or other drive folders. Click Advanced (and provide Administrator-level credentials as required) to repair or rebuild indexes (Index Settings tab) or to adjust how indexing takes place for each file extension registered on the system (File Types tab). Files containing readable text (.doc, .xls, and similar extensions) are indexed by name and contents, whereas other types of files are indexed by name only. If you have a low-performance system, you can speed it up by disabling indexing.

Figure 22.19
The Indexing Options dialog.

Other Performance Options

Selecting the Adjust Power Settings task in the Tasks lists opens the Power Options dialog box, discussed later in this chapter in the "Power Options" section. Selecting the Open Disk Cleanup task opens the Disk Cleanup utility. For details, see Chapter 24.

Advanced Tools

Click the Advanced Tools task in Performance Information and Tools to open the Advanced Tools window (see Figure 22.20), which provides specific suggestions for improving system performance and links to nine different tools you can use to fine-tune performance.

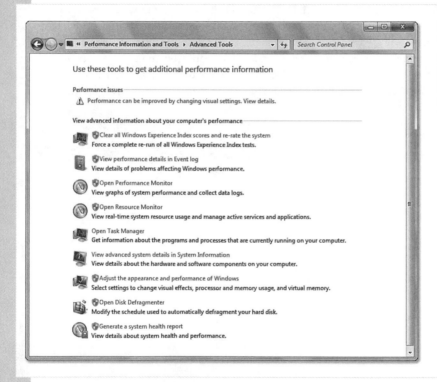

Figure 22.20
The Advanced Tools window for a system whose performance can be improved by changing visual settings.

Click each item under the Performance Issues category to open a pop-up window with specific recommendations for improving performance.

Table 22.11 lists the advanced performance information tasks and where they are discussed in this book.

Table 22.11   Advanced Performance Information Tasks

Task	Opens	For More Information
Clear all Windows Experience Index scores and re-rate the system	Windows Experience Index tests	"Performance Information and Tools," p. 632
View performance details in Event log	Microsoft Management Console Event Viewer	"Computer Management," p. 652
Open Performance Monitor	Performance Monitor	"Performance Monitor," p. 639
Open Resource Monitor	Resource Monitor	"Resource Monitor," p. 641
Open Task Manager	Task Manager	"Task Manager," p. 672
View advanced system details in System Information	Information summary page	"System Information," p. 670
Adjust the appearance and performance of Windows	Visual Effects and Advanced tabs of the Performance Options dialog box	"Adjust Visual Effects," p. 636 and "Adjust Advanced Performance Options," p. 650
Open Disk Defragmenter	Disk Defragmenter	"Disk Defragmenter," p. 730
Generate a system health report	Performance Monitor, System Diagnostics Report	"System Diagnostics Report," p. 641

Performance Monitor

Performance Monitor provides Windows 7 users with a one-stop solution for tracking system performance. Performance Monitor opens to the Performance Monitor Overview and System Summary (see Figure 22.21), which provides a real-time overview of CPU, disk, network, and memory subsystem performance.

For an even more detailed and customizable look at system performance data, click the Performance Monitor node on the left. Performance Monitor permits you to choose from dozens of performance counters ranging from .NET to iSCSI, TCPv4 and -v6, WMI objects, and many others. You can monitor local or network computers with Performance Monitor, and you can view information in line, bar, or report modes. Right-click the counter area to add, edit, or remove counters; save the current image; or view properties (see Figure 22.22).

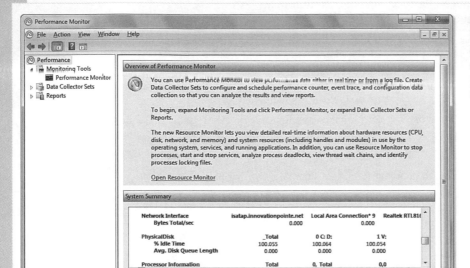

Figure 22.21
Performance Monitor provides an overview of system performance and reporting tools.

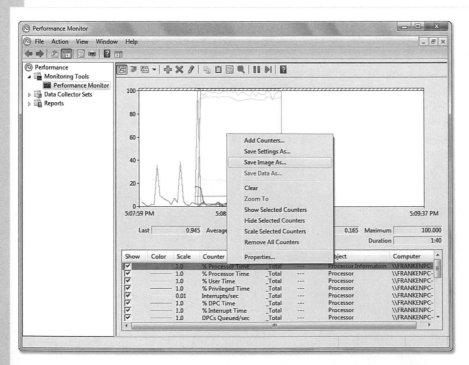

Figure 22.22
Preparing to save the current Performance Monitor counters as an image.

Resource Monitor

To see a real-time graphical view of processes, CPU, disk, memory, and network activity, start the Resource Monitor from the Advanced Tools window (refer to Figure 22.20). Resource Monitor's display (see Figure 22.23) is somewhat reminiscent of the Performance tab in Windows XP's Task Manager, but the Overview tab provides four gauges, instead of two as in Windows XP's Performance tab, and provides detailed information for each monitored process. To filter for a particular process, click its check box.

Figure 22.23
Using Resource Monitor to track detailed use of CPU, disk, network, and memory usage.

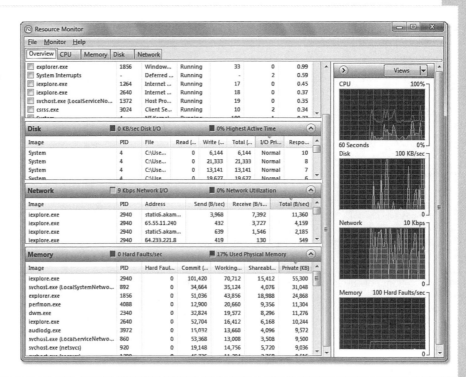

System Diagnostics Report

When you click Generate a System Health Report in the Advanced Tools window (refer to Figure 22.20), Windows 7 uses Resource and Performance Monitor to scan the system and display a System Diagnostics Report. A typical example is shown in Figure 22.24. The report includes information on system diagnostics, software configuration, hardware configuration, and CPU, network, disk, and memory subsystems, and concludes with a summary of the system and the files used to create the report.

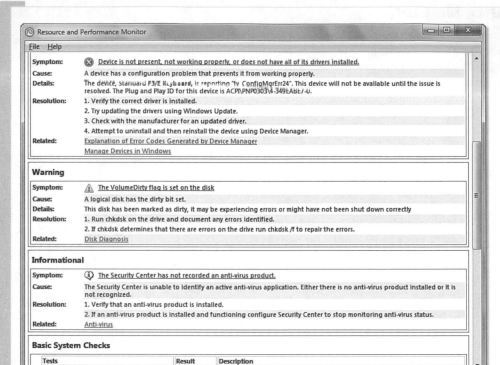

Figure 22.24
A portion of a typical System Diagnostics Report.

Some of the system components tracked by the System Diagnostics Report include disabled devices; device driver and other hardware problems; antivirus and firewall protection status; resource usage; system services; startup programs; SMART disk status; Windows Experience Index score; network interfaces; and CPU, hard disk network, and memory performance.

Power Options

Although the Power Options icon is familiar to Windows XP users, the Windows 7 version of this fundamental Control Panel utility has gone through some significant changes. On the main page of this dialog box, three different power plans (known as power schemes in Windows XP and earlier versions of Windows) are listed: Balanced, Power Saver, and High Performance. The Balanced power plan strikes a happy medium between performance and energy savings on a desktop, or between performance and battery life on a portable system. Power Saver saves a lot of energy (provides a long battery life) but does so by reducing performance and dimming the screen on a portable system. High Performance maximizes system speed but uses a lot of energy on a desktop and provides a short battery life on a portable system. You can access Power Options through the Hardware and Sound category, or in Large Icons or Small Icons view.

➥ *To learn more about power settings on laptops and Tablet PCs,* **see** *"Getting the Most Out of Your Battery," p. 974.*

Programs and Features

Programs and Features performs most of the same tasks for Windows 7 that the Add or Remove Programs applet performed for Windows XP. However, there is no provision for installing programs with Programs and Features. Because this feature was hardly used in Add or Remove Programs, its absence in Programs and Features is no great loss. The major functions of Programs and Features include

- Changing or uninstalling existing programs

- Viewing installed updates

- Enabling or disabling Windows features

Programs and Features is available from the Programs category of Control Panel and is also available in Large or Small Icons view.

Uninstall or Change a Program

You may occasionally have programs on your system that don't show up in the Uninstall or Change a Program listing you see when you open Programs and Features (see Figure 22.25). Only programs that comply with the 32- or 64-bit Windows API standards for installation have their filenames and locations recorded in the system database, allowing them to be reliably removed without adversely affecting the operation of Windows. Many older or less-sophisticated applications simply install in their own way and don't bother registering with the operating system. These programs, which are increasingly rare today, must be removed manually.

What's more, the built-in uninstaller lets you make changes to applications, such as adding or removing suboptions (assuming the application supports that feature).

Use of the uninstall feature of the applet is simple:

 tip

Never attempt to remove an application from your system by deleting its files from the \Program Files folders (or wherever). Actually, "never" may be too strong. Removal through manual deletion should only be done as a last resort. Always attempt to use the Programs and Features applet or the uninstall utility from the application first. Contact the vendor for help if you cannot uninstall the application. In a few cases, it might be necessary to go into the system Registry to remove pieces of an application.

1. Open the Programs category, then Programs and Features applet from the Control Panel.

2. Check the list of installed applications. A typical list is shown in Figure 22.25. To sort applications by criteria such as size or date of installation, click the appropriate column head. You can use this information to find space-hogging programs you don't use.

3. Select the program you want to change or uninstall.

4. Click the Uninstall or Change button above the program listing. Note that program listings marked as (Remove Only) don't offer Change as an option.

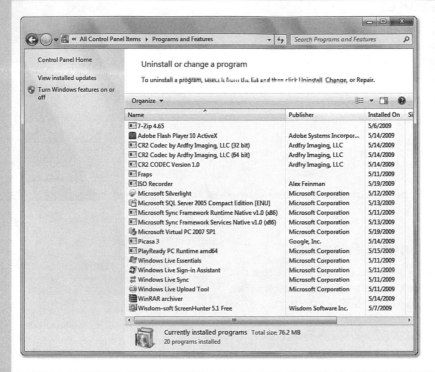

Figure 22.25
The main window of the Programs and Features applet lists programs that can be uninstalled or changed.

5. Answer any warnings about removing an application as appropriate.

6. At the end of the process, the selected program is removed from your system and from the list of installed applications. Depending on the program you uninstalled, you may need to restart your system.

Some applications (for example, Microsoft Office) prompt you to insert the program CD when you attempt to change or remove the app. These prompts can be annoying, but what can you do? The setup, change, and uninstall programs for some large suites are stored on their CDs, not on your hard disk. So, just insert the disc when prompted.

View Installed Updates

To see updates for Microsoft Windows 7, Microsoft Office applications, and other applications that receive updates through Windows Update, click View Installed Updates in the Tasks list of Programs and Features. All installed program (but not driver) updates are shown. Figure 22.26 shows a typical listing.

 tip
Obviously, removing an application can't easily be reversed by, say, restoring files from the Recycle Bin, because shortcuts on the Start menu and Registry settings are also deleted.

 note
Incidentally, Add or Remove Programs can be run only by users with Administrator credentials on their local computer. Although some applications can be installed or removed by nonadministrators, most do require Administrator privileges.

Figure 22.26
Viewing updates for Microsoft Windows 7.

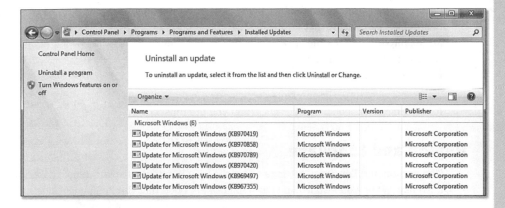

If you determine that an installed update is not working correctly, select it and click Uninstall. (Note that some updates cannot be uninstalled.)

Turn Windows Features On or Off

In addition to managing add-on products and applications through the Programs and Features applet, you can also enable and disable Windows 7 features. Click the link in the Programs and Features Tasks list to open the Windows Features dialog box, shown in Figure 22.27.

> **note**
>
> To view updates for separate programs bundled with Windows 7, such as Windows Defender and Windows Media Player, or hardware driver updates, open the Windows Update icon in the Control Panel's Large Icons or Small Icons view.

Generally, you should need to add features only if you are configuring Windows 7 for specialized situations. For example, if you need to manage a remote client with Telnet, you should add the Telnet client. To learn more about a feature, hover your mouse over the feature to see a brief explanation.

Figure 22.27
Preparing to configure Windows features.

An empty check box indicates that the feature is turned off. A check mark in a box indicates that the feature is turned on. Shaded boxes indicate that only some features are turned on. For example, note that the only active parts of Print and Document Services on this system are the Internet Printing Client and Windows Fax and Scan.

To enable a feature, click an empty check box. To disable a feature, clear a check box. Click OK when you are finished.

note

Enabling or disabling a feature doesn't change the size of your Windows 7 installation; it merely changes whether you can use the feature.

Region and Language

The Region and Language settings affect the way Windows displays times, dates, numbers, and currency. When you install Windows, chances are good that the Region settings are already set for your locale. This is certainly true if you purchase a computer with Windows 7 preinstalled on it from a vendor in your country or area. The Region and Language applet is found in the Clock, Language, and Region category and is also available in Large Icons or Small Icons view.

Running this applet from the Control Panel displays the dialog box you see in Figure 22.28. To change the settings, simply click the appropriate tab, and then click the drop-down list box for the setting in question. Examples of the current settings are shown in each section, so you don't need to change them unless they look wrong. The predefined standards are organized by language and then by country. If you can't find a standard to your liking, you can always create a customized format by clicking the Additional Settings button, which opens the Customize Format multi-tabbed dialog.

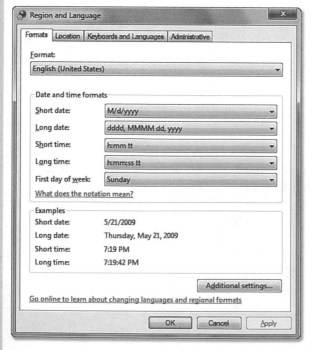

Figure 22.28
Making changes to the Region and Language settings affects the display of date, time, and currency in Windows applications that use the internal Windows settings for such functions.

System

The System Properties dialog box has long been perhaps the single most important part of the Control Panel for determining what's going on inside your system. Windows 7 has drastically remodeled the look and features of this Properties dialog box in the System applet (see Figure 22.29 to better show you what's "under the hood." Access System from the System and Security category, from Large Icons or Small Icons view, or by right-clicking Computer and selecting Properties.

Figure 22.29
The System applet in Windows 7 makes it easier than ever to view important information about your system's hardware, network settings, and performance.

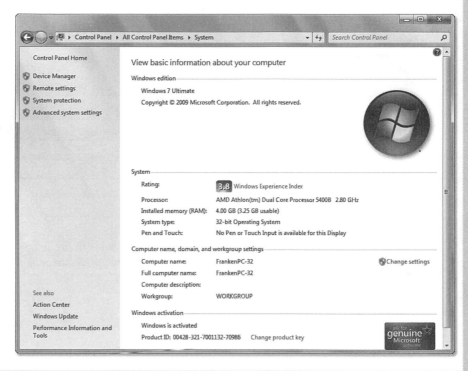

The top of the main System window shows the Windows 7 edition in use. The System section shows the Windows Experience Index, processor and RAM information, and operating system type (32 bit or 64 bit).

Unlike in Windows XP and earlier versions, which made you dig through tabs to find the computer name, domain, and workgroup settings, they're out front in this version. If you can't connect to other computers, workgroup or domain name problems are often the culprit. Click the Change Settings button at the right to change this information.

Is your version of Windows activated? Look at the Windows Activation section of the dialog box to find out. If you need to change the product key, click the Change Product Key button.

The Tasks list provides access to other System functions. See "Device Manager" earlier in this chapter to learn more about this task. The other tasks are discussed in the following sections.

Remote Settings

Click Remote Settings in System's Tasks list to open the Remote tab of the System Properties dialog box (see Figure 22.30). Use this tab to configure both Remote Assistance (top) and Remote Desktop (bottom) connections to your computer.

 tip

Virtually all "Windows 7-capable" systems on the market can run the 64-bit (x64) version of Windows 7, which enables you to use more than 3GB of RAM and create larger files. Should you? Install the x64 version only if can obtain x64 drivers for your hardware and verify that your favorite programs can run under x64 versions. Although x64 support is much more widespread today than it was a couple of years ago, some hardware and programs still support only the 32-bit version. Digital photography fans in particular should note that 64-bit RAW codecs (necessary to preview RAW files in Windows) are not yet available for some digital cameras, or might be available only from third-party vendors.

Figure 22.30
Use the Remote tab to configure Remote Assistance and to permit, deny, or configure Remote Desktop connections.

➥ *To learn more about Remote Assistance and Remote Desktop,* **see** *Chapter 36, "Meetings, Conferencing, and Collaboration," and Chapter 37, "Remote Desktop," respectively.*

System Protection

Click System Protection in the System window's Tasks list to open the System Protection tab (see Figure 22.31) of the System Properties dialog box. This tab is used to view and create restore points that can be used by System Restore and to launch System Restore. It also lets you select which drives to protect using System Restore.

➥ *To learn more about System Restore,* **see** *Chapter 25, "Troubleshooting and Repairing Problems."*

> **🔍 note**
>
> Network Level Authentication (NLA) is the more secure type of Remote Desktop connection. Windows 7 includes NLA support. If you want to connect a Windows XP client to a Windows 7 client running Remote Desktop with NLA enabled, you must download and install the Terminal Services Client (Remote Desktop Connection v6) on the Windows XP system. The Windows XP system must be running Service Pack 2 or 3. You can also install this update on a Windows Server 2003 with Service Pack 1.

Figure 22.31
Use the System Protection tab to manage System Restore.

Advanced System Settings

Click Advanced System Settings in the System window's Tasks list to open the Advanced tab of the System Properties dialog box. It has four buttons. Three of these buttons, described next, are labeled Settings and are contained within the Performance, User Profiles, and Startup and Recovery sections. The fourth button is Environment Variables, discussed in the upcoming "Environment Variables" section.

- The Settings button under the User Profiles heading opens the User Profiles dialog box. This interface is used to manage local and roaming profiles stored on the local computer. User Profiles are discussed in Chapter 3.

- The Settings button under the Startup and Recovery heading opens the Startup and Recovery dialog box. This interface is used to configure multibooting actions and how system failures are handled. If you have installed Windows 7 in a multiboot configuration with an earlier version of Windows, you can specify whether to run Windows 7 or the earlier version as the default. You can also specify how long to wait before starting the default OS (30 seconds is the preset value) and whether to specify a time for displaying recovery options. By default, Windows 7 writes an event to the system log in case of system failure and restarts the system automatically. Clear check boxes to disable either or both of these features. During a system failure, Windows 7 also automatically creates a kernel memory dump called MEMORY.DMP in the root folder of the system drive (normally C:). Other debugging operations include no memory dump, a small memory dump (64KB), or a complete memory dump. By default, a memory dump overwrites the previous one unless you disable this feature by clearing the Overwrite check box.

  ➡ *To learn more about multiboot configurations,* **see** *Chapter 2, "Installing and Upgrading Windows 7."*

- The Settings button under the Performance heading opens the Performance Options dialog box. The settings for Visual Effects tab are discussed in "Adjust Visual Effects," earlier in this chapter.

Adjust Advanced Performance Options

Click the Advanced tab in the Performance Options dialog to view or change processor scheduling or virtual memory settings. By default, processor scheduling is configured to provide best performance for programs. If you are configuring a system used primarily to perform services such as printer spooling, click Background Services.

To change the location and size of the paging file, click Change in the Virtual Memory section of the Advanced tab. This opens the Virtual Memory dialog. By default, Windows 7 automatically selects the location and size of the paging file. To select size or location manually, clear the Automatically Manage Paging File Size for All Drives checkbox. You can then select which drive (or drives) you want to use for paging. To disable the paging file on any drive, click No Paging File, and click Yes on the warning dialog that appears. To set up a system managed paging file on a different drive, click the drive and select System Managed Size. To set up up a custom paging file on any drive, click the drive, click Custom Size, and enter the values for minimum and maximum size. Click OK to continue. You will be prompted to restart your system if you change any of page file settings.

Data Execution Prevention (DEP)

The Data Execution Prevention tab of the Performance Options dialog box (see Figure 22.32) configures settings that prevent malicious applications from executing programs in protected areas of RAM. Protected areas of RAM, supposedly reserved for the OS and other programs that are running, can potentially be invaded by malware, which then tries to load and execute itself in the legitimate memory space.

> ### tip
>
> Generally, there's little benefit to changing the location of the paging file unless you have two or more physical hard disks and the non-system physical hard disk is faster than the system hard disk, or if the system hard disk has limited space (less than 15% of its capacity available).

Figure 22.32
Use the Data Execution Prevention tab to manage DEP.

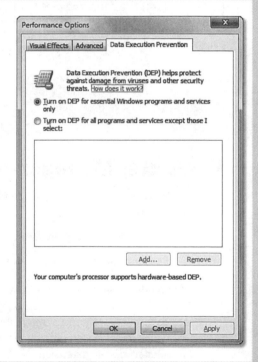

➡ *To learn more about DEP,* ***see*** *"Data Execution Prevention," **p. 857**.*

Environment Variables

The Environment Variables button on the Advanced tab of the System Properties dialog box opens the Environment Variables dialog box. This interface is used to define user and system variables.

These include TEMP and TMP, which point to storage locations where Windows can create temporary files. It also defines the PATH, which is the list of folders into which Windows looks to find programs and software components. In most cases, you should not need to edit the system variables, although we do discuss "Setting the PATH Environment Variable" on page 827. For more information about environment variables, see "Setting Environment Variables," p. 825.

Windows Directory Is Overflowing

If the storage volume where your main Windows directory resides is becoming full, you can perform three operations to improve performance and keep the risk of insufficient drive space to a minimum. First, move the paging file to a different volume on a different hard drive (see "Adjust Advanced Performance Options," in this chapter for details on this). Second, define the **TEMP** and **TMP** variables to point to a **\Temp** folder you create on a different volume on a different hard drive. Third, through Internet Options, define a location for the temporary Internet files within the alternate **\Temp** folder. After rebooting, the new locations will be in use. However, you may need to delete the old files from the previous temporary file location (typically **\Users \<*username*>\AppData\Local\Microsoft\Windows\Temporary Internet Files**). Don't forget to change permissions on the new **\Temp** folder to permit access by the group Users. See Chapter 31 to learn how to set NTFS file permissions for a specified file or folder.

Using a different hard disk for the paging file and temporary files, particularly if it's connected to a different ATA/IDE host adapter than the system hard disk or uses the SATA interface, will provide better performance than using a different partition on the system hard disk.

Computer Management

The Computer Management window includes an important set of management tools that you can reach two ways:

- From the Start menu, right-click Computer, select Manage.

- From Administrative Tools, select Computer Management.

Either method opens the Microsoft Management Console (MMC), a UAC-protected feature in Windows 7. MMC (see Figure 22.33) provides one-stop access to the major system management features in Windows 7 and, through its use of snap-in extensions, additional management tasks as well. When you start Computer Management, Windows 7 launches MMC and installs the Computer Management snap-in extension.

Computer Management provides easy access to the following tasks:

- Managing local users and groups

- Managing shared devices and drives

- Checking system event logs containing information such as logon times and application errors

- Seeing which remote users are logged in to the system

- Viewing currently running system services, starting and stopping them, and setting automatic startup times for them

- Managing server applications and services such as the Indexing service and web services

Figure 22.33
Computer Management (MMC) with some nodes expanded.

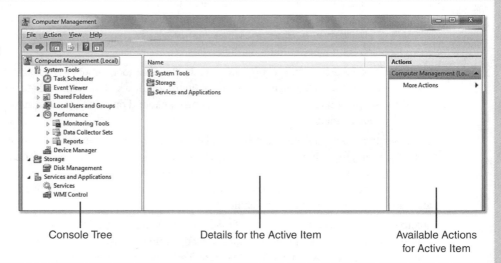

Console Tree   Details for the Active Item   Available Actions for Active Item

The Computer Management tool looks similar to the familiar Windows Explorer. It uses a three-pane view, with the *console tree* (for navigation and tool selection) in the left pane, details of the active item shown in the center pane, and actions that can be performed on the selected item in the right pane.

Items in the tree are called *nodes* (akin to folders in Explorer). The three nodes in Computer Management are as follows:

- System Tools

- Storage

- Services and Applications

The System Tools section of Computer Management contains the following tools:

- **Task Scheduler**—A utility program for automating execution of programs. This tool is discussed in detail in Chapter 29.

- **Event Viewer**—Used to view the event details contained in the Application, Security, and System logs. This tool is discussed shortly.

- **Shared Folders**—Used to manage shared folders and remote users accessing shared folders. This is discussed later in this chapter.

- **Local Users and Groups**—Used to manage local user accounts and groups. This tool is discussed in Chapter 3.

- **Performance**—This item opens the Performance Monitor tool that was discussed under "Performance Monitor" on page 639.

- **Device Manager**—This tool was discussed earlier in this chapter on page 612.

The Storage section contains the Disk Management tool, which is used to define new drives as Basic or Dynamic, create/delete/manage partitions and volumes, format, assign drive letters, and so on. This tool is discussed in Chapter 24. The Storage section might also contain additional tools if you've installed third-party storage hardware or software tools.

The Services and Applications section contains the Services tool, which is discussed later in this chapter, and WMI Control, which is used to configure Windows Management settings, a topic beyond the scope of this book. Additional tools may be found on some systems, depending on enabled Windows features.

As you would expect, you can conduct administrative chores by selecting a tool in the console tree and then clicking items in the center pane. When you select an item in the center pane, views and actions (right pane) change as appropriate for that item, typically displaying attributes of the item or tool you selected. For example, the Local Users and Groups branch can display the names and properties of all the users on the machine.

Explore with the interface to uncover all that is available from these three "little" nodes in the left pane. However, avoid making any changes or modifications (where possible) unless you know what effects your alterations will have. You'll be surprised. Open each node by clicking the right arrow. If you use the default Detail view, some helpful information about various items in the right pane is displayed along with the items in most cases.

By default, you manage the local computer. To manage a remote computer (assuming you have permission), right-click the topmost item in the tree—Computer Management (Local)—and choose Connect to Another Computer.

Experienced system managers may want to go to Computer Management and dig through submenus themselves, but the Administrative Tools window, as we've already seen (refer to Figure 23.32), provides shortcuts to the most significant features of the MMC, most of which will be discussed in the following sections.

Task Scheduler

Task Scheduler can be run from the Administrative Tools window in Control Panel, the System Tools node in Computer Management, or from the Start menu (All Programs, Accessories, System Tools, Task Scheduler). Using Task Scheduler, you can set up any program or script (or even open a document) to be run automatically at predetermined times. This utility is very useful for running system maintenance programs or your own scripts and programs when you can't be around to execute them manually.

➡ *To learn more about Task Scheduler,* **see** *"Task Scheduler," p. 839.*

Event Viewer

Event Viewer is an administrative application used to view the log files that record hardware, software, and system problems and security events. You can think of an "event" as any occurrence of significance to the OS. Logs are useful because, like a seismograph in earthquake country or a black box in an airplane, they provide a historical record of when events occurred. For example, you can see when services were started, stopped, paused, and resumed; when hardware failed to start properly; when a user attempted to access protected files, or when a user attempted to remove a printer over which the user doesn't have control. The logs report the level of danger to the system, as you can see in Figure 22.34. Event Viewer can be accessed directly from the Administrative Tools window or from the Event Viewer section of the MMC. It is protected by UAC and contains four nodes:

- Custom Views

- Windows Logs

- Applications and Services Logs

- Subscriptions

Figure 22.34
The Overview and Summary feature of Event Viewer.

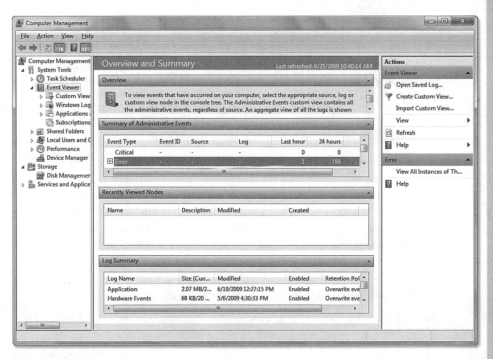

The logging features built in to Windows 7 record all types of events, including many that never trigger an error message but can inform you of various problems or potential problems with your system's configuration.

Types of Log Files

Windows 7 generates five primary logs (files) in its Windows Logs category. These logs are explained in Table 22.12.

Table 22.12 Windows Log Files

Type of Log	Description
Application log	Contains events logged by applications or programs. For example, a database program might record a file error in the Application log. The program developer decides which events to record.
Security log	Can record security events such as valid and invalid logon attempts, as well as events related to resource use such as creating, opening, or deleting files. An administrator can specify which events are recorded in the Security log. For example, if you have enabled logon auditing, attempts to log on to the system are recorded in the Security log.
Setup log	Contains entries pertaining to the installation and activation of updates for Windows 7 and its components.
System log	Contains numerous entries pertaining to system events such as booting up, shutting down, loading drivers, and errors with hardware conflicts. For example, the failure of a driver or other system component to load during startup is recorded in the System log. The event types logged by system components are predetermined by Windows 7 and cannot be altered by the user or administrator.
Forwarded events	Contains entries pertaining to events forwarded to another computer that has subscribed to these events. Use this feature to monitor events on a remote computer by configuring the monitoring computer to subscribe to events on the remote computer, and by configuring the remote computer to forward events to the monitoring computer.

Windows 7 also generates many additional logs in other categories. Under the Custom Views node, the Administrative Events log file displays errors and warnings derived from the Application and System logs. It's a convenient way to view problems in a single location. Under the Application and Services Logs node, Windows 7 includes many empty log files (DFS Replication, Hardware Events, Internet Explorer, Key Management Services, and Media Center), which can be enabled by using the Windows Event Collector Utility (`wecutil.exe`) to subscribe to the appropriate event. Open the Microsoft and Windows nodes to view logs of many Windows 7 features.

Now that you have a basic understanding, let's consider Event Viewer, an application that displays each of the log files and also lets you do the following:

- Apply sorting, searching, and filtering that make it easier to look for specific events

- Control settings that affect future log entries, such as maximum log size and the time old entries should be deleted

note

Only a user with Administrative privileges can work with the Security log. Any user can view the Application and System logs, however.

- Clear all log entries to start a log from scratch

- Archive logs on disk for later examination and load those files when needed

Overview and Summary

When you open Event Viewer, it opens an Overview and Summary of administrative events (shown earlier in Figure 22.35). You might want to switch Event Viewer to full-screen mode and drag the dividers between panes, to see all the details at once.

The Overview and Summary displays five categories, listed in order from most serious to least serious:

- Critical

- Error

- Warning

- Information

- Audit Success

To help you more quickly determine any trouble spots in your system, each category totals up events in the last hour, last 24 hours, last 7 days, and a grand total. On the system shown in Figure 22.35, one error event has taken place in the last hour, but 188 error events have been logged in the last 24 hours. To expand a category, click the plus (+) sign next to the category name.

Viewing Event Details

To view the details of a particular event, double-click it. Figure 22.35 displays the details for an Error event.

The General tab displays an overview of the log entry. To see the log entry in its native XML format, click the Details tab. XML View is selected by default. To return to the previous view, use the back (left arrow) button at the top of the Event Viewer dialog box.

Event Viewer Actions

Windows 7's Event Viewer makes actions easy to use by displaying them in the Actions pane on the right side of the dialog box at all times. By using the Actions pane, you can create or import custom views, connect to another computer to view its events, view all instances of a particular problem or event, view event properties, save events, and filter the current log.

Click to return to previous view.

Scroll to see a complete list of error events.

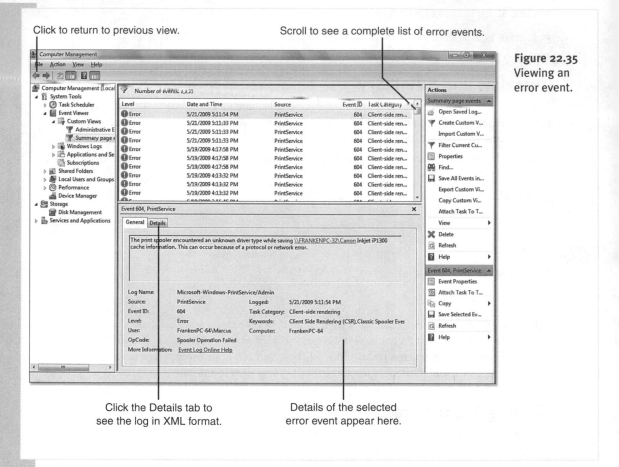

Figure 22.35
Viewing an
error event.

Click the Details tab to
see the log in XML format.

Details of the selected
error event appear here.

Shared Folders

The Shared Folders node (see Figure 22.36) includes three nodes:

- **Shares**—Allows you to manage the properties of each shared resource. For example, you can alter the access rights for a shared resource so that certain users have read-only access. You can also change share permissions for a resource in the Properties dialog box of any shared resource by right-clicking the resource and clicking Properties.

- **Sessions**—Allows you to see which users are connected to a share and, optionally, disconnect them.

- **Open Files**—Allows you to see which files and resources are open on a share. You also can close files that are open.

Figure 22.36
The Shared
Folders sec-
tion of the
MMC, dis-
playing a file
opened by
another user
via Windows
7's new
HomeGroup
feature.

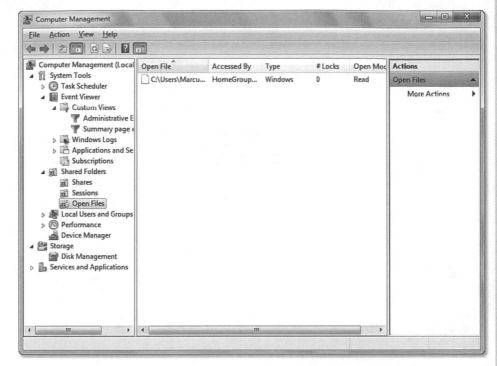

Services

Windows 7 is highly modular. Many of the inner housekeeping chores of the OS are broken down into services that can be added, removed, started, and stopped at any time, without requiring a reboot. A typical Windows 7 system has 60 or more services running at any one time. When Computer Management is open, you can view Services in use by expanding the Services and Applications node and clicking Services. You can also use the Services shortcut in Administrative Tools, the Component Services shortcut in Administrative Tools, or by opening Task Manager and viewing the Services tab.

Use the Services dialog in Computer Management to view all installed services and their status (Automatic, Manual, or Stopped). Use this tool to start and stop services. Figure 22.37 shows a typical Services listing. To start, stop, pause, or restart a service, you can use the context menu or the VCR-like buttons on the toolbar. For deeper control of a service, such as to declare what automatic recovery steps should be taken in the case of the service crashing, which hardware profiles it should run in, and more, right-click the service and select Properties.

Start, stop, pause, or restart a service.

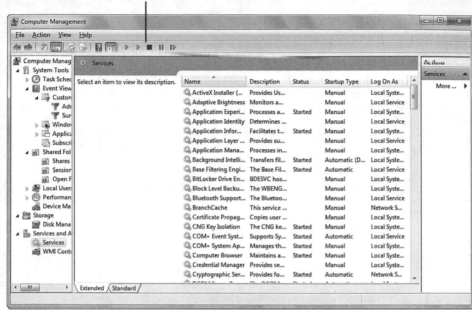

Figure 22.37
The Services
dialog in the
MMC.

Within the Properties dialog box, you'll find controls to set a service's startup type (Automatic, Manual, or Disabled), start, stop, pause, and resume buttons, and a startup parameters field. You also can set the account under which the service is executed (Log On tab), define how a service recovers from failures—for example, restart, run a program, or reboot the system (Recovery tab), and view a list of service, program, and driver dependencies (Dependencies tab).

Administrative Tools

The Administrative Tools icon in the Control Panel's Large Icons or Small Icons view (it's also located in the System and Security category) is not a single program; rather, as the name implies, it provides a convenient way to access a variety of specialized tools you can use to manage more technical aspects of your Windows 7 system.

The Administrative Tools are listed in Table 22.13. Several of the items are discussed elsewhere, as noted in the Table. The remaining items are discussed in the following sections.

 note

You might find websites suggesting that you can speed up your computer by disabling a bunch of Windows services. We don't recommend that you do this. Microsoft has made Windows 7 do a *very* good job of keeping services out of your way, especially during startup and shutdown, so we suggest leaving the default set of services alone.

 tip

For easy access, you can also customize the Start Menu so that Administrative tools appears in it. To do this, right-click Start, select Properties, Customize. Scroll down the list and under System Administrative Tools, select Display on the All Programs Menu.

Table 22.13 Administrative Tools

Administrative Tool	Remarks
Component Services	This tool lets you manage COM+/DCOM objects and is primarily for software developers.
Computer Management	See "Computer Management," p. 655.
Data Sources (ODBC)	This tool is used by program developers and network database integrators. Its use is beyond the scope of this book.
Event Viewer	See "Event Viewer" on page 652.
iSCSI Initiator	iSCSI Initiator lets your computer to connect to network-attached storage.
Local Security Policy	See "Tightening Local Security Policy," p. 934.
Performance Monitor	See "Performance Monitor" on page 639.
Print Management	This tool lets you manage printers and print servers.
Services	The Services tool lets you manage the software services that work behind the scenes in Windows.
System Configuration	System Configuration lets you manage programs that run when Windows starts or when you log on.
Task Scheduler	See "Task Scheduler," p. 839.
Windows Firewall with Advanced Security	See "Advanced Settings," p. 941.
Windows Memory Diagnostics	See "Windows Memory Diagnostics Tool," p. 745.
Windows PowerShell Modules	See "Windows PowerShell," p. 837. PowerShell is an enormous topic and is covered in detail in *Windows PowerShell 2.0 Unleashed*, published by Sams.

Figure 22.38 shows a typical view of the Administrative Tools window on a Windows 7 Ultimate system. Home Premium and Home Basic versions of Windows 7 do not include the Local Security Policy and Print Management tools.

In the following sections, I discuss the Administrative Tools that aren't covered elsewhere (as indicated in Table 22.13).

Component Services

Component Services (Figure 22.39) provides an extremely detailed view of COM+ Applications and DCOM Config, while also listing Running Processes, and Distributed Transaction Coordinator transactions and statistics. To see more information about the items listed in the COM+ and DCOM Config categories, right-click each item and select Properties.

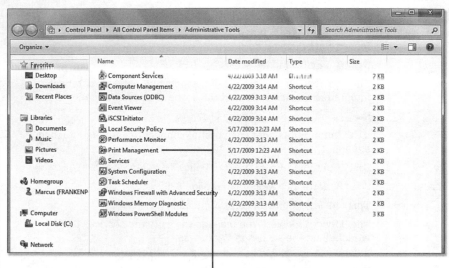

Figure 22.38
The Administrative
Tools window.

Home Premium and Home Basic don't include the
Local Security Policy and Print Management tools.

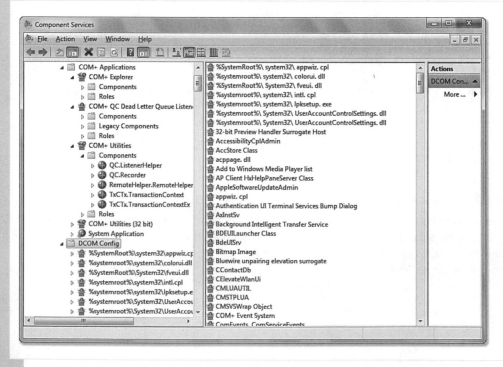

Figure 22.39
Component
Services
(MMC) with
some nodes
expanded.

The General tab of the properties sheet for items in the COM+ category lists the DLL file used by the application, its CLSID and application number; the Transactions tab lists the transaction setting for the program; the Security tab lists the authorization settings and roles used for the item; the Activation tab displays the activation context and object pooling settings used by the item; the Concurrency tab displays the synchronization support and threading model used by the item; the Advanced tab lists other settings such as IIS support.

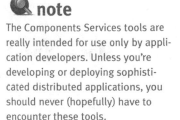

note

The Components Services tools are really intended for use only by application developers. Unless you're developing or deploying sophisticated distributed applications, you should never (hopefully) have to encounter these tools.

The General tab of the properties sheet for items in the DCOM Config category lists the application name, Application ID. Application type, and local path. The Location tab can be used to run the application on the local computer, remotely, or where the data for the application is located. The Security tab lists the launch and activation, access, and configuration permissions. The Endpoints lists the DCOM protocols and endpoints used by the application. The Identity tab is used to specify the user or system account used to run the program.

For more information on managing COM+ and DCOM applications, open the Help menu, select Help Topics, and open the Component Services Administration node. For convenience, the Component Services window also includes entries for the Event Viewer and Services management tools.

iSCSI Initiator

iSCSI Initiator lets your computer connect to and use iSCSI devices such as disk and tape drives, optical drives, storage libraries, and other devices over a corporate IP network. This type of network is often referred to as a storage area network (SAN). When you run iSCSI Initiator, you must provide Administrator-level credentials unless UAC has been disabled.

When you start iSCSI Initiator on a system that uses Windows 7 Firewall, you see a dialog box asking to unblock this service so that it can connect with an Internet storage name service. Click Yes. You may also be prompted to enable iSCSI Initiator to start automatically when the system starts. You should also click Yes on this dialog box if you plan to use iSCSI devices at all times. Otherwise, you must manually start iSCSI Initiator.

The iSCSI Initiator Properties dialog box has six tabs:

- **General**—Opens automatically when you start iSCSI Initiator and shows the current name of the initiator. Click Change to rename the initiator. If your iSCSI connection uses mutual CHAP authentication, click Secret to set up a CHAP secret. To set up IPsec tunneling, click Set Up.

- **Discovery**—Use to set up Target portals (a target is an iSCSI device) and iSNS servers. Get the IP addresses, port numbers, and DNS names from your SAN or network administrator.

- **Targets**—Use to log on to iSCSI targets and display their details. To automatically log on to a target when you restart your computer, click the Automatically Restore This Connection When the Computer Starts check box.

- **Favorite Targets**—Lists automatically logged-in targets.

- **Volumes and Devices**—Use to autoconfigure Favorite Targets or to specify the programs or services that use a particular target.

- **RADIUS**—If your SAN uses RADIUS authentication services, use this tab to specify RADIUS servers and to specify RADIUS login credentials (also known as RADIUS secrets).

Print Management

The Print Management shortcut in Administrative Tools opens the MMC Print Management snap-in. It enables you to control all the printers on your system from a single management window, which can be a great convenience if you're a network manager, or even a home user with multiple printers. Custom filters show printers with jobs, printers that are not ready, printer drivers, and other information.

➥   *To learn more about the Print Management tool,* ***see*** *"Advanced Printer Management," **p. 205**.*

System Configuration

Use the System Configuration utility (`msconfig.exe`) to disable or enable startup programs, adjust boot options, enable or disable startup services, and run various reporting and diagnostic tools.

System Configuration can be run from the Administrative Tools window, or by using the Run command in the Start menu. (Select Start, All Programs, Accessories, Run, type **msconfig**, and click OK.)

System Configuration opens to the General tab. By default, Normal startup is selected. Normal startup runs all device drivers and services. Other options include

- **Diagnostic startup**—Runs basic devices and services only; equivalent to starting the system in Safe Mode

- **Selective startup**—Starts the system with an option to disable all system services, all startup items, or both

To adjust boot options with the built-in boot configuration data (BCD) editor, click the Boot tab (see Figure 22.40). The options on the Boot tab match the options available when you press F8 at startup and display the Advanced boot configuration menu. To boot the system to the Safe Mode GUI, click the Safe Boot check box and select Minimal. Other options include Alternative Shell (boots to the command prompt without network support); Active Directory Repair (boots to the Windows GUI and runs critical system services and Active Directory); and Network (boots to Safe Mode GUI with network services enabled).

Other options you can select include No GUI Boot (disables the Windows splash screen); Boot Log (creates a boot log of startup activities stored as a `ntbtlog.txt` file in the default `SystemRoot` folder, usually `C:\`; Base Video (starts Windows GUI using standard VGA drivers); OS Boot Information (lists driver names as drivers are installed during boot).

Generally, these options are used for diagnostics, but if you want to make a particular combination of settings permanent (until you change them again), click the Make All Boot Settings Permanent check box.

Figure 22.40
The Boot tab of System
Configuration.

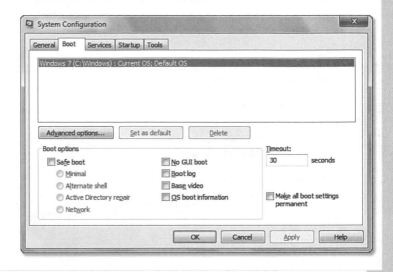

Click the Advanced Options button if you need to specify the number of processors, lock PCI settings, detect the HAL used by the system, or configure a serial (COM), USB, or 1394 port for remote debugging.

The Services tab is used to disable or enable Microsoft and third-party services (note that some Microsoft services cannot be disabled), whereas the Startup tab (see Figure 22.41) is used to disable or enable startup programs. Note that the Startup tab lists the date a particular startup program was disabled, if applicable.

Figure 22.41
The Startup tab of System
Configuration.

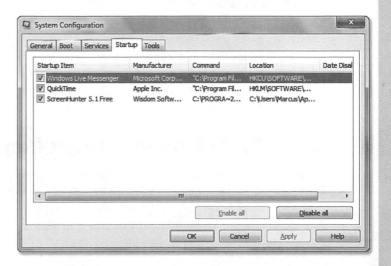

The Tools tab is used to launch various reporting and diagnostic tools found in the `\Windows\System32` folder, including the following:

- About Windows
- Change UAC Settings
- Action Center
- Windows Troubleshooting
- Computer Management
- System Information
- Event Viewer
- Programs
- System Properties
- Internet Options
- Internet Protocol Configuration
- Performance Monitor
- Task Manager
- Command Prompt
- Registry Editor
- Remote Assistance
- System Restore

The command line for each command is shown when you select the command, making it easy to create batch or script commands to run combinations of these tools. To start a tool, select it and click Launch.

 tip

The Autoruns for Windows tool, available from Microsoft's Sysinternals website at `live.sysinternals.com`, provides a much better and more detailed way to view and control startup programs than MSConfig does.

For a comprehensive database of startup programs and a useful discussion of Autoruns and other programs used to determine what's happening at startup, see www.pacs-portal.co.uk/startup_index.htm.

 tip

To copy the command for a particular tool, select the tool, highlight the command string in the Selected Command window, and press Ctrl+C. To paste the command string into a text editor or other program in the Windows GUI, use Edit, Paste, or Ctrl+V. To paste the command string into the command-prompt environment, right-click the Command Prompt window and select Paste.

System Tools Folder in Start Menu

Some of the most frequently used tools to manage your system can be accessed from the System Tools folder in the Start menu. To open the System Tools folder, click Start, All Programs, Accessories, System Tools.

Table 22.14 shows the most frequently used system tools and where each is covered in this book.

Table 22.14 System Tools and Where Each Is Covered in This Book

System Tool	More Information
Character Map	"Character Map," **p. 667**
Computer	"What's New in Windows Explorer," **p. 149**
Control Panel	"The Windows 7 Control Panel," this chapter, **p. 594**
Disk Cleanup	"Disk Cleanup," **p. 724**
Disk Defragmenter	"Disk Defragmenter," **p. 730**
Internet Explorer (No Add-ons)	Chapter 14, "Using Internet Explorer 8"
Private Character Editor	"Private Character Editor," **p. 670**
System Information	"System Information," **p. 740**
System Restore	"System Restore," **p. 740**
Task Scheduler	Chapter 29, "Command-Line and Automation Tools"
Windows Easy Transfer	"Windows Easy Transfer," **p. 101**

Character Map

Character Map is a utility program that lets you examine every character in a given font and choose and easily insert into your documents special characters, such as trademark (™ and ®) and copyright symbols (©), currency symbols (such as ¥) and accented letters, nonalphabetic symbols (such as fractions, ¾), DOS line-drawing characters (+), items from specialized fonts such as Symbol and Wingdings, or the common arrow symbols (←, →, ↑, and ↓). Some fonts include characters not mapped to the keyboard. Character Map lets you choose them, too, from its graphical display. The Program Map displays Unicode, DOS, and Windows fonts' characters.

By clicking the Advanced View check box, you can also choose the character set, rearrange the items in a font (such as grouping all currency types together) to eliminate hunting, and search for a given character.

Character Map works through the Windows Clipboard. You simply choose a character you want to use and click Copy, and it moves onto the Clipboard. Switch to your destination application (typically, a word processing file), position the cursor, and choose Paste.

Using Character Map

To run Character Map, follow these steps:

1. Choose Start, All Programs, Accessories, System Tools, Character Map.

2. Choose the font you want to work with from the Font list.

3. By default, the Character Set is Unicode. This means all the characters necessary for most of the world's languages are displayed. To narrow down the selection, click the Advanced View check box and choose a language from the Character Set drop-down list.

4. To examine an individual character, click a character box, and hold down the mouse button to magnify it. You can accomplish the same thing with the keyboard by moving to the character using the arrow keys.

5. Double-click a character to select it, transferring it to the Characters to Copy box. Alternatively, after you've highlighted a character, you can click the Select button or press Alt+S to place it in the Characters to Copy box. You can keep adding characters to the Characters to Copy box if you want to paste several into your document at once.

6. Click the Copy button to place everything from the Characters to Copy box onto the Windows Clipboard.

7. Switch to your destination application, and use the Paste command (typically on the application's Edit menu) to insert the characters into your document. In some cases, you might then have to select the inserted characters and format them in the correct font, or the characters won't appear as you expected. You can, of course, change the size and style as you want.

 tip

If you know the Unicode number of the item to which you want to jump, type it into the Go to Unicode field. The display scrolls as necessary, and the desired character is then highlighted, ready for copying.

Choosing from a Unicode Subrange

A useful feature of Character Map lets you choose a Unicode subrange. Unicode was designed intelligently with characters grouped in sets. You can choose a subset of a font's characters to help you locate a specific symbol. To check out this feature, open the Group By drop-down list and choose Unicode Subrange. When you choose this option, a box like the one shown in Figure 22.42 pops up.

Click the subgroup that you think will contain the character you're looking for. Good examples are currency or arrows. Make sure to open the Group By list again and choose All when you want to see all the characters again.

Entering Alternative Characters from the Keyboard

At the bottom right side of the Character Map dialog box is a line that reads Keystroke.

For nonkeyboard keys (typically, in English, anything past the ~ character), clicking a character reveals a code on this line—for example, Alt+1060. This line tells you the code you can enter from the keyboard to quickly pop this character into a document. Of course, you must be using the font in question. For example, say you want to enter the registered trademark symbol (®) into a Windows application document. Note that with a standard text font such as Arial or Times New Roman selected in Character Map, the program lists the keystrokes for this symbol as Alt+0174. Here's how to enter the character from the keyboard:

1. Press Num Lock to turn on the numeric keypad on your keyboard. (The Num Lock light should be on.)

Figure 22.42
Choosing a subset of
a font from which to
select a character.

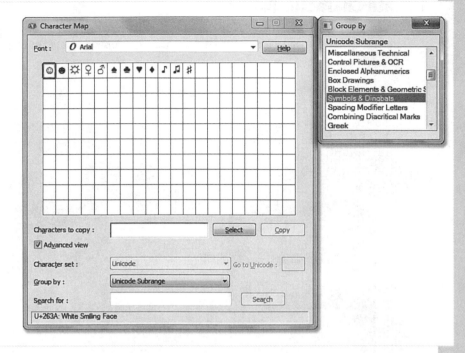

2. Press and hold down Alt, and type the **0**, **1**, **7**, and **4** keys
individually, in succession, on the number pad. (You must
use the number pad keys, not the standard number keys. On
a laptop, you must activate the number pad using whatever
special function key arrangement your laptop uses.) When
you release the Alt key, the registered trademark symbol
should appear in the document.

 tip

Not all programs accept input this way.
If this approach doesn't work with a
program, you'll have to resort to the
standard means of putting characters
into the Clipboard explained previously.

Wrong Characters Displayed When Pasting Characters from Character Map

Are characters pasted from the Character Map appearing in the wrong font?

When you paste a character from Character Map, the application you are pasting the character into might not recognize that the character is coming from a different font. In such cases, the character is mapped to the equivalent character in the current font. For example, if you copied the Pencil (0x21) character from the Wingdings OpenType font but pasted it into a program that uses the Nyala font by default, such as Windows 7 Paint, the character would change into the equivalent character in the other font (in Nyala's case, an exclamation mark). To fix this problem, select the characters you pasted from Character Map and select the correct font in the Font menu of the destination program.

Private Character Editor

If you can't find a character, the new Private Character Editor (see Figure 22.43) enables you to create one, assign it to selected or all fonts, and access it through Character Map.

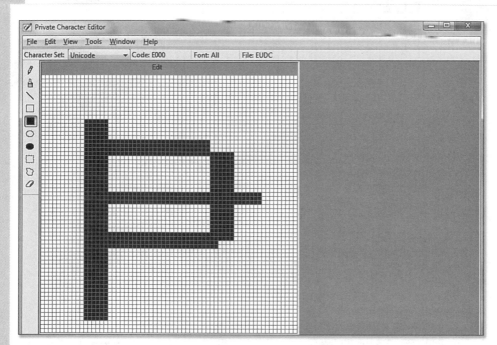

Figure 22.43
Creating a new character with the Private Character Editor.

System Information

System Information is a simple but elegant tool. Opening this tool displays detailed information about your system, its hardware resources, components, and software environment. It brings together information that's normally scattered across the main System dialog box, the Device Manager, and a myriad of other places.

To start System Information, launch it from the Tools tab of System Configuration, or enter msinfo32 in the Start button's Search menu.

Use System Information to help you determine the best configuration for a legacy device, track down software problems, or determine the components in an unfamiliar system.

The top level, labeled System Summary, shows you basic information about your computer, OS revision number, CPU, RAM, virtual memory, page file size, BIOS revision, and so on (see Figure 22.44).

Three nodes appear in the left pane of System Information:

- **Hardware Resources**—Displays hardware-specific settings, such as DMA, IRQs, I/O addresses, and memory addresses. The Conflicts/Sharing node identifies devices that are sharing resources or are in conflict. The Forced Hardware node indicates devices that are manually configured to share settings. This information can help you identify problems with a device.

Figure 22.44
See a summary of your system properties easily from the System Summary node.

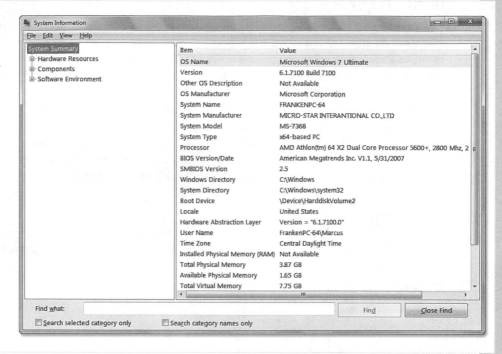

- **Components**—Provides a truly powerful view of all the major devices in your system. Open any subfolder and click an item. In a few seconds, information pertaining to the item is displayed, such as drive IDs, modem settings, and video display settings. In some cases, you can also see driver details. Check the folder called Problem Devices to see a list of all devices not loading or initializing properly.

- **Software Environment**—Acts like a super Task Manager. It displays details of 12 categories of software settings. You can see the system drivers, certified drivers, environmental variables, print jobs, network connections, running tasks, loaded modules, services, program groups, startup programs, OLE registration, and Windows error reporting.

Additional Tools

Besides the standard Control Panel, Computer Management, Administrative Tools and System Tools categories, there are several other important tools that you can use to manage and maintain Windows. I'll cover these additional tools in the following sections.

> **tip**
> Ever wonder why some darned program starts up when you boot, even though it's not in your Start Menu's Startup folder? It's probably hiding somewhere else. To find it, open System Information, travel down the path from System Summary, Software Environment, Startup Programs, and take a look. I found Adobe Photo Downloader, iTunes Helper, and Picasa Media Detector there (to name just three). To disable unwanted programs from running at startup, see the documentation for the programs, or use the MSConfig System Configuration Utility's Startup tab to disable or enable startup items. Before you disable a startup program, though, make sure you really don't need it. To learn more about startup programs, see the database of startup programs at www.pacs-portal.co.uk/

Task Manager

The Task Manager is one tool you're bound to use frequently, perhaps more than any other. Whenever an application crashes, you believe you're running some suspect process that you want to kill, or you want to check on the state of system resources (for example, RAM usage), you can use the Task Manager. Even as nothing more than an educational tool, the Task Manager is informative.

The fastest way to bring up the Task Manager in Windows 7 is to press Ctrl+Shift+Esc or to right-click over an empty area on the taskbar and select Task Manager from the pop-up menu. The Task Manager displays the last-used view by default; the first time you run it, it opens to the Applications tab (see Figure 22.45). However, if you want to find out in detail what's happening inside your system, select the Processes tab, which we'll discuss shortly.

Figure 22.45
The Task Manager shows you which applications are running and lets you terminate hung programs.

The Task Manager in Windows 7 has six tabs, up from five in Windows XP, but it does not include the Shut Down menu found in the Windows XP version. The six tabs are described next, in turn.

Applications Tab

Click the Applications tab to see a list of the programs currently running on the computer. Not a lot of information is displayed—only the application name and the status (running or not responding). However, this tab does provide a more complete report than you'll get by glancing at the taskbar buttons or via the dialog box you see if you press Alt+Tab.

You can sort the list by clicking the column heads. If an application has multiple documents open, the application appears only once in the list, probably with the name of the document that is foremost at the time (has the focus). Some applications don't comply with this single-document interface (SDI) approach, listing each new document as a separate application. Some examples of non-SDI applications are Microsoft Office programs such as Word, Excel, and PowerPoint.

From this list, you can kill a hung application. If an application has hung, it is probably reported in the list as Not Responding (although this is not always true). Click the End Task button to terminate the task. If a document is open and unsaved, and if, for some unexpected reason, the program responds gracefully to Windows' attempt to shut it down (which is unlikely), you might see a dialog box asking whether you want to save the document. More likely, Windows 7 will just ask for confirmation to kill the application.

The Task Manager Is Stalled

If the Task Manager seems stuck (it doesn't reflect newly opened or closed applications), it could be that you've inadvertently paused the Task Manager. Choose View, Update Speed, and then choose any setting other than Paused. Another approach, if you want to keep it paused, is to choose View, Refresh Now.

Patience, Grasshopper

Before you give an application its last rites, pause for a bit. In general, it's not a good idea to kill an application if you can avoid doing so. Terminating an application can cause instability in the OS (even though it shouldn't in most cases because of the kernel design). Or, at the least, you can lose data. Try "jiggling" the application in various ways, in hopes of being able to close it gracefully first. Switch to it and back a few times. Give it a little time. Maybe even do some work in another application for a few minutes, or take a trip to the water cooler. Try pressing Esc while the application is open, or, if you notice that one program seems to stop responding when another program is open, close the other program first.

When executing some macros in Word, for example, I noticed that one of my macros hangs for no apparent reason. It seems to crash Word. So, I killed it from the Task Manager, losing some work. I later realized the solution was to press Esc, which terminated the macro. Having slow network connections and attempting to link to nonexistent web pages, printers, or removable media can also cause apparent hangs. Try opening a CD or DVD drive door, removing a network cable, or performing some other trick to break a loop a program might be in before resorting to killing the program from the Task Manager. This is especially true if you've been working on a document and you might potentially lose data.

Some applications will so intensely perform calculations that the Task Manager will list them as Not Responding. If you suspect this, give the program 5 minutes or so to complete its thinking; I've learned the hard way to be patient with some applications.

Notice that you can also switch to an application in the list or run a new one. Just double-click the application you want to switch to (or click Switch To). Similarly, to run a new application, click New Task (Run), and enter the executable name or use the Browse dialog box to find it.

Sending the Task Manager to the Background

If the Task Manager doesn't drop into the background when you click another program, choose Options and uncheck the Always on Top setting..

Processes Tab

Whereas the Application tab displays only the full-fledged applications you're running, the Processes tab, shown in Figure 22.46, shows *all* running processes, including programs (for example, Virtual PC), services (for example, Event Log), or subsystems. In addition to just listing active processes, Windows 7 displays the user or security context (that is, the user, service, or system object under which the process is executing) for each process. Also, by default, the percentage of CPU utilization and memory utilization in bytes is listed. You can change the displayed information through the View, Select Columns command.

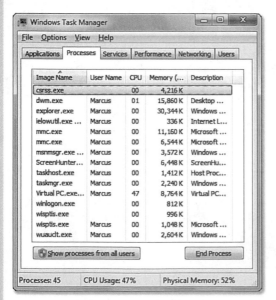

Figure 22.46
The Task Manager's Processes tab shows you which processes are running and lets you terminate hung processes.

 tip

If, for some reason, the Task Manager can't seem to kill off a program that you started, try logging off and then back on. If it's still there or if you don't want to log off, try this procedure:

1. Click Start, All Programs, Accessories.

2. Right-click Command Prompt and select Run As Administrator. Confirm the User Account Control dialog box.

3. Type the command `taskkill /f /im program.exe` but enter the program's actual name as it's displayed in the Processes tab in place of `program.exe`. Do not use this method to try to kill a system service. Instead, use the Services tab.

Almost any listed process can be terminated by selecting it and then clicking the End Process button. There are some system-level processes that even an administrator doesn't have sufficient privileges to kill.

You might also discover at times that an application will fail to be killed, typically due to a programming error or a memory glitch. In those cases, you should reboot the system. You might find that sometimes a hung application also will prevent a normal shutdown. If your attempt to reboot fails, you'll have to resort to manually turning the power off and then back on. Hopefully, you saved often and didn't lose too much work.

Altering the Priority of a Task

In the beginning, all tasks are created equal. Well, most of them, at least. All the processes under your user account's security context will have Normal priority by default. Most kernel or system processes will have High priority. You might want to increase or decrease the priority of a process, though changing the priority typically isn't necessary. To do so, right-click the task and choose the new priority through the Set Priority submenu.

You can assign six priority levels to processes: Realtime, High, AboveNormal, Normal, BelowNormal, and Low. Realtime is restricted for use by administrators. You should keep away from High because it can interfere with essential OS operations (especially if you have several user processes set to High).

Services Tab

The Services tab separates services from other memory-resident processes. Use it to quickly determine the services installed on your system and which ones are currently running. It lists services by name, description, status, and group. Right-click a service to stop or start it.

Performance Tab

The Performance tab of the Task Manager indicates important conditions of your OS. It shows a dynamic overview of your computer's performance, including CPU usage, memory usage, and totals of handles, threads, and processes (see Figure 22.47).

 tip

At the bottom of the Processes tab is a button labeled Show Processes from All Users. If you click this, you can see not just the processes under your user account and those of the system but also those of other active users. Plus, when displayed, you can also terminate them using the End Process button. This button is protected by UAC.

 caution

Avoid altering the priority of any task listed with a username of SYSTEM. This indicates the process is in use by the kernel. Altering the execution priority of such processes can render your system nonfunctional. Fortunately, process priority settings are not preserved across a reboot, so if you do change something and the system stops responding, you can reboot and return to normal. In some cases, raising the priority of an application can improve its performance. However, increase the priority in single steps instead of automatically setting it to the maximum. Throwing another top-priority application into the mix of kernel-level activities can render the system dead, too.

 tip

If you have a multiprocessor or multicore computer and you want to assign a task to a given processor, right-click the process and choose the Set Affinity command. Choosing this command guarantees that the process receives CPU time only from the CPU you choose.

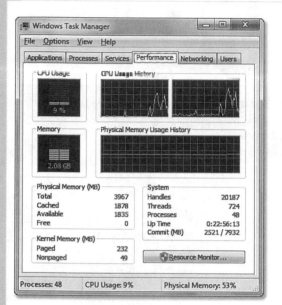

Figure 22.47
The Performance tab displays some interesting statistics and a chart of CPU and physical memory usage over time.

From the Performance tab, the View menu includes CPU History and Show Kernel Times. The former command is used to show different graphs for each CPU (only useful on multiple-CPU systems). The latter command sets the display to show kernel activity in red and user activity in green on the CPU and memory usage. If your system has two or more CPUs or a dual- or quad-core CPU, you will see a separate CPU gauge for each physical CPU or CPU core. (How cool is that?)

Although CPU usage is interesting, the most important of these numbers is memory usage. You can easily check in the Physical Memory area to see how much memory is installed in your system, how much is available for use by applications before disk caching begins, and how much the system is using for caching.

> **note**
>
> *System cache* is the total current swap and RAM area allocated for system operations. When your computer has to go to a disk cache to access information, it significantly slows down overall system performance, which is why having more system RAM is almost always better.

The Kernel Memory area reports the memory in use strictly by the OS for running the OS internals. Nonpaged kernel memory is available only to the OS. This memory is in physical RAM and can't be paged out to the hard disk because the OS always needs fast access to it, and it needs to be highly protected. Paged memory can be used by other programs when necessary.

In the System section, you can see the number of handles, threads, and processes. Handles are tokens or pointers that let the OS uniquely identify a resource, such as a file or Registry key, so that a program can access it. A thread represents a single subprocess. An increasing number of programs are multithreaded, running multiple subprocesses at the same time. Multithreading applications are designed to run better on multiprocessor or multicore processors such as the AMD Phenom and Athlon 64 X2, Intel Core 2 Duo and Core 2 Quad, and others.

Most of these size reports are of use only to programmers. However, the charts can offer strong, telltale signs of system overstressing. If you see, for example, that your page file usage is consistently nearing the top of its range, you are running too many programs. If the CPU is topped out most of the time, you also could be in trouble. Perhaps you have a background task running that is consuming way too much CPU time. An example could be a background program doing statistical analysis or data gathering.

 note

When the Task Manager is running, even if minimized, a green box appears in the notification area, indicating CPU usage. It's a miniature bar graph.

Networking Tab

The Networking tab displays a bandwidth consumption history graph. As network operations occur, this graph will plot the levels of usage. If the system has two network adapters, you can determine which one is active, and separate graphs show activity on each adapter.

 tip

If you really want to dig into the internal operation of Windows, its services and applications, download the Process Monitor and Process Explorer tools that I discuss in the last section of this chapter, "Third-Party Tools."

Users Tab

The Users tab shows a list of all active users on this system or connected via the network. From here, you can disconnect a network user, log off a local user, or send a user a text message. The Users tab will be visible only if you are not participating in a Windows 2000/Windows Server 2003 Active Directory–based network or have not disabled Fast User Switching if participating in a workgroup.

Third-Party Tools

Finally, I'd like to point you to some third-party tools that I've found to be indispensable in managing and maintaining Windows computers. I don't have room to describe them in detail, but you may want to visit the listed websites to read more about them.

- **ProcExp**—Process Explorer is an expanded version of the Task Manager that lets you really dig into the list of programs and services running on Windows. Three really cool things it can do that the Task Manager can't are tell you what network connections a program has, tell you what Windows services a given program is hosting, and let you see the text strings within the program file. These can really help when you're tracking down malware or any a suspicious program. Get it from www.sysinternals.com.

- **AutoRuns**—This is a Sysinternals program that gives you total control over the programs that Windows runs automatically. These include not just the programs that windows runs on startup and when you log on, but services, print monitors, Explorer add-ons and other types of programs that can run without your knowing about it.

- **Tweak-7**—This program available from www.tweakvi.com lets you adjust a whole slew of Windows settings that aren't available in the Control Panel.

- **Vista Boot Pro**—This inexpensive program (originally developed for Windows Vista) lets you easily manage Windows 7's boot menu. It's an indispensible tool if you've set up a multi-boot system. Available from www.vistabootpro.org.

By the way, the Sysinternals programs that I listed were developed by Windows whizzes Mark Russinovich and Bryce Cogswell, who are now employed by Microsoft. These tools are free, and you can download them from www.sysinternals.com, or get more detailed information at technet.microsoft.com/en-us/sysinternals/default.aspx. I mentioned only two Sysinternals tools here, but there are over 75 of them in all, covering a wide range of Windows management and diagnostic topics.

 tip

If you need instant access to one of the SysInternals tools, visit `live.sysinternals.com`. Click the desired .exe file name, and when your browser asks you want to do with the file, choose Run.

TWEAKING AND CUSTOMIZING WINDOWS

GUI: To Tweak or Not to Tweak

Tweaking the GUI doesn't mean anything lascivious. This chapter describes the graphical user interface and some interesting, useful, and fun stuff you can do with it—changes to help increase your computing efficiency and perhaps even make your computer more fun to use.

As you know, the GUI is the translator that interprets human input into commands the computer can interpret. It's also responsible for displaying output from computer programs and the OS so you can understand the results. The Windows 7 GUI is set up with factory defaults that 90 percent of users will never touch, despite its being highly programmable and easily modifiable through the Control Panel, Folder Options, Properties dialog boxes, and so on. If you're a GUI hacker (you know who you are) and all you want to do is get your work done, well, more power to you because you're the one who's going to get the pay raise. But playing with the GUI can be fun.

Most folks won't modify their GUIs, but it's a shame they don't. Often, not even knowing there is recourse, users develop headaches from screen flicker, come down with eyestrain from tiny screen fonts, or live with color schemes they detest. They can usually rectify these problems with little effort, and have some fun choosing from hundreds of desktop themes, screen savers, wallpaper images, and so on. Likewise, means for managing zip archives, altering the right-click Send To options, and handling numerous other functions users have to deal with every day often take just a few clicks, a quick download, a Registry hack, or a setting change.

Screen Fonts Too Small

There are a couple of ways to fix screen fonts that are too small to read easily. The most common one is to decrease the screen resolution. However, on LCD monitors, as explained earlier, this is not the optimum solution. Leave the screen resolution on an LCD (including laptops) at the native resolution for the screen (check the manual); then tell Windows 7 to use a larger font. To increase the font size (up to 200%) of icons, the taskbar, menus, and other common Windows elements, do the following:

1. Right-click on the desktop and choose Personalize.

2. Click Display.

3. Select the Medium or Larger setting in the main pane, or click Set Custom Text Size (DPI) in the Tasks list.

Some of this chapter deals with standard display options. Other portions deal with deeper GUI tweaks and tricks. Just skim for the part that interests you.

➥ *This chapter only briefly covers multimonitor support because it's related more to hardware upgrades than the GUI. For coverage of multiple monitors, **see** "Installing and Using Multiple Monitors," p. 790.*

Start Menu Pizzazz!

The default Start menu of Windows 7 is similar to the Windows Vista version, and much improved over Windows XP and the old Windows 2000 style. For those of you who prefer the Windows 2000 menu—called the Classic Start menu—and want to keep using it, you're out of luck. Microsoft didn't include the option to switch to the Classic Start menu style in Windows 7 like it did in Vista and XP. But, if you're willing to give the new look and feel a solid go, there are many nifty improvements you can take advantage of and even customize.

Tweaking the Start Menu

Tweaking the Start menu involves a right-click over the Start button (orb) to select the Properties command from the pop-up menu. This reveals the Taskbar and Start Menu Properties dialog box. The Start Menu tab is selected by default rather than the first tab—Taskbar—because you're checking the Start menu's properties.

Click the Customize button to open the Customize Start Menu dialog box, shown in Figure 23.1, which displays more than 50 options. The Customize Start Menu dialog box essentially lets you control how links, menus, and icons look and behave on the Start menu. Some of the options are

■ Include items on the Start menu: Computer (enabled by default), Connect To, Control Panel (enabled by default), Default Programs (enabled by default), Devices and Printers (enabled by default), Documents (enabled by default), Downloads, Favorites Menu, Games (enabled by default), Help (enabled by default), Homegroup, Music (enabled by default), Network, Personal Folder (enabled by default), Pictures (enabled by default), Recent Items, Recorded TV, Run Command, Videos.

- Enable context menus and dragging and dropping.

- Highlight newly installed programs (enabled by default).

- Enable flyout menus for items such as Computer, Control Panel, Documents, Music, and Pictures when you click (or hover) on them, or treat those items as links and open a separate window showing the item's contents. (See "Cascading Elements from the Start Menu" later in this chapter.)

- Search other files and libraries, selecting to search with (default) or without public folders. When entering as-you-type searches from the Start menu, Windows 7 will include public folders rather than just the files for the currently logged-in user.

- Search for programs and the Control Panel when performing as-you-type searches.

- Sort the All Programs menu by name automatically, which keeps the menu organized alphabetically.

- Display Administrative Tools, such as Event Viewer and Task Scheduler, on the Start menu.

- Choose between large (default) and small icons.

- Set the number of recently accessed applications to be displayed (the default is 10).

- Set the number of recent items to display in jump lists (the default is 10).

Figure 23.1
The Customize Start Menu dialog box.

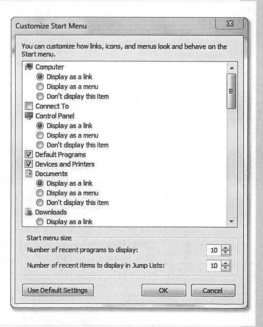

Back on the Start Menu tab, you can select which action to take when the Power button is clicked. Your options are Switch User, Log Off, Lock, Restart, Sleep, Hibernate, and Shut Down (default).

Finally, you have two Privacy choices:

- **Store and Display Recently Opened Programs in the Start Menu**—Turn this off if you don't want prying eyes to see which programs you worked with in the recent past.

- **Store and Display Recently Opened Items in the Start Menu and the Taskbar**—Turn this off if you don't want others to see which items you worked with recently. These items are associated with jump lists on the Start menu, as described in Chapter 3, "The First Hour."

With a bit of experimentation, you'll find the combination of features that best suits your preferred Start menu population and function.

Tweaking the Taskbar

The taskbar itself has configurable options; these are contained on the Taskbar tab of the Taskbar and Start Menu Properties dialog box. You can lock the taskbar so that stray mouse actions won't alter its placement or configuration, auto-hide it to maximize the desktop area, use small icons as the default, set it to appear along any edge of the screen, and combine buttons by default or only when the taskbar is full.

You'll probably recall many of these controls from previous Windows OSs. In addition, there is automatic grouping of similar taskbar items as in Vista and XP. And if you have Aero turned on, you will see thumbnails of apps and docs when you mouse over a taskbar button.

As you probably know, and as mentioned in Chapter 4, task buttons on the taskbar are listed from left to right in their order of launch, up to a point. The default setting is to group buttons by similarity, which creates a stacked button representing similar programs. For example, if three Word documents are open, they appear as a single stacked button. The same applies if Windows Explorer and the Computer window are both open, or if Control Panel, Devices and Printers, and Default Programs are open simultaneously. Just hover your mouse pointer over the stacked button to display a pop-list of applications or documents it represents, and then choose one you want to jump to.

 tip

If you want to return your Start menu settings to the factory defaults, there's a shortcut. Just open the Customize Start Menu dialog box as previously described and click Use Default Settings.

 tip

Technically, almost everything on your Start menu can be found in C:\ProgramData\Microsoft\Windows\Start Menu\Programs.

What doesn't appear in this location is in the folder under Users, for example:

C:\Users\Eve\AppData\Roaming\Microsoft\Windows\Start Menu

You can modify those locations if you want to add shortcuts to or remove shortcuts from your Start menu. Remember, the Start menu is just a collection of shortcuts to programs and documents, not the actual files themselves.

 note

Auto-Hide is inherited from previous Windows versions and gives you more available screen real estate by causing the taskbar to appear only if you mouse down to the bottom of the screen.

Hide Notification Area Icons and Notifications

If you're experienced with previous Windows OSs you might be familiar with how quickly the notification area (called the system tray in XP, immediately to the left of the digital clock at the bottom of the screen) can fill up with icons. Some systems have had more than a dozen. Windows 7 manages its notification area intelligently by allowing inactive icons to be hidden. Plus, instead of displaying a long stream of active icons, only three or so are displayed along with an up arrow, which you can click to access the hidden icons. By clicking the Customize button in the Taskbar and Start Menu Properties dialog box, you can customize which icons and notifications are hidden or displayed.

Reposition the Taskbar

As with previous versions of Windows, you can still drag the taskbar to any edge of your desktop: top, bottom, or sides. You can also still expand the thickness of the taskbar to allow multiple rows of task buttons. Just hover the mouse pointer near the edge of the taskbar so that it turns into a double arrow, and drag it up, down, or sideways.

 tip

If you can't get the taskbar to resize or move, it's locked. Right-click an empty part of the bar (not on a button or Quick Launch shortcut) and select Lock the Taskbar to uncheck it.

Display Properties

The launching point for altering your GUI display settings is the Personalization window. From there you can reach a multitude of GUI settings, mostly affecting visual effects rather than GUI functionality:

- Themes for GUI elements

- Desktop background

- Window color

- Sound effects

- Screen saver settings

- Desktop icons

- Pointer and cursor shapes and sizes

- Special GUI effects such as Aero and window animations

You can most easily reach the display properties by right-clicking the desktop and choosing Personalize. Figure 23.2 shows the resulting Personalization window. This is a greatly redesigned window compared to the Windows Vista and XP counterparts.

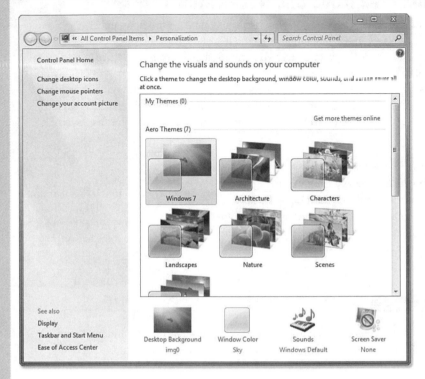

Figure 23.2
You can alter a multitude of display attributes from the desktop Personalization window.

Notice that the Tasks list includes Change Desktop Icons, Change Mouse Pointers, and Change Your Account Picture for easy, one-click access to the related dialog boxes. Clicking the Display link near the bottom of the Tasks list lets you modify advanced properties such as resolution, color calibration, hardware acceleration, refresh rates, and relative and custom text sizes.

The following sections briefly describe various primary options, which are in order of appearance in the Personalization window, starting with the main pane.

Themes

A theme is a background plus a set of sounds, icons, and other elements to help you personalize your computer with one click. Windows 7 includes several themes in the Personalization window (see Figure 23.3), such as the default Windows 7 (Aero) theme and a handful of other Aero themes for your choosing, all of which offer bold, stunning images and pleasing color palettes.

🔍 **note**

You also can get to the display properties from Control Panel. Click Start, Control Panel, Appearance and Personalization, Personalization.

🔍 **note**

Earlier in the chapter, we discussed the Classic Start menu style and mentioned it had been removed from Windows 7. The Windows Classic theme is different from the Start menu style. The Classic theme gives you a general Windows 2000 look and feel across the desktop, windows, and dialog boxes; however, you don't get the old Windows 2000 Start menu look and functionality.

Figure 23.3
You can choose an overarching desktop theme of visuals and sounds using this window.

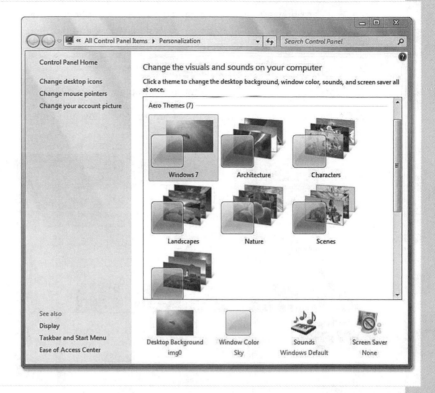

Scrolling through the list of themes, you'll find the Basic and High Contrast Themes section. If you prefer the look of Windows 2000 and older versions, you can go retro by selecting the Windows Classic theme. High Contrast themes are helpful for the visually challenged.

If you make changes to desktop colors or other GUI attributes such as those described in this chapter, you can save that theme to disk so you can later reload it. (Themes are stored in files with a .theme suffix.) Just click the Save Theme link and give it a name. The modified theme will appear in the My Themes section near the top of the Personalization window.

 tip

Click the Get More Themes Online link to go to a Microsoft Windows website where you can download and safely install extra themes. You should exercise caution when downloading themes from non-Microsoft sources on the Web because these files modify critical system settings and could wreak havoc on a machine if they are not designed properly. Also, you face significant virus risks.

Desktop Background

The desktop is used to express your inner personality. It's one of the few places where you can actually customize the otherwise impersonal personal computer. Hanging some wallpaper (such as a picture of your kids, your car, a sunset, and so forth) on your desktop gives the environment a more custom feeling. Microsoft includes dozens of options for you to goof around with. These include some stunning photographs, small tiles repeated across and down your screen, or solid colors. You can choose from a few supplied photos or supply your own, such as from your digital camera. Gone are the old desktop patterns, such as bricks and bamboo, that were available in previous Windows versions.

To personalize your desktop, follow these steps:

1. Right-click on an empty spot on the desktop and choose Personalize.

2. Click Desktop Background. You see the window shown in Figure 23.4.

Figure 23.4
Use this Desktop Background window to personalize your desktop with photos and colors.

3. Click one of the images you like or search for another one. From the Picture Location drop-down list, choose Windows Desktop Backgrounds, Pictures Library, Top Rated Photos, or Solid Colors.

Windows Desktop Backgrounds are high-quality images designed to scale well and look good on any screen. Pictures Library lets you choose from photos in the Public Pictures folder on your computer, which is a shared folder that anyone using your computer (locally or on the LAN) can see. Top Rated Photos points to a folder supplied with Windows 7 that includes some additional photos for you to play with.

 tip

By the way, if you don't want a pretty picture (or you need to hide the image of the sultry pin-up before your spouse returns), you can select Solid Colors in the Picture Location drop-down list. Then, choose a solid color of your liking from the resulting palette.

You can also use a personal photo. If you keep your stockpile of photos organized elsewhere, just click the Browse button, locate the correct folder, and choose your image. Acceptable photo formats are JPG, JPEG, BMP, DIB, TIF, and PNG images.

In addition to files already on your local system (or accessible over your LAN), you can grab any image from a website by right-clicking it and selecting Set as Background from the pop up menu.

If you want to add some variety to your desktop, configure your desktop background as a slideshow. Just select more than one image for your desktop background, and then select a number of seconds, minutes, or hours in the Change Picture Every drop-down list.

caution

Remember, most images on the Web are copyrighted by the owner of the site. Using an image without permission is stealing. We recommend that you only use images provided expressly for desktop background use, or that you obtain permission first before using images not specifically offered as desktop backgrounds.

Making a Picture Fit Your Desktop

If an image is too small to fill up your desktop, you can always set the Picture Position control to Stretch. Other options in the Picture Position control list include Fill (default), Fit, Tile, and Center. Fit takes a picture smaller than your screen resolution and enlarges it so that it fills the screen lengthwise. Conversely, it takes a picture larger than the screen and shrinks it. Stretching can distort the picture or cause it to pixelate, so if you want it to look good, make sure to shoot the picture at, or convert it to, a size roughly matching the resolution setting of your display and then choose the Center option. If the image is larger than the screen's resolution, stretching actually shrinks the image to fully fit on the desktop.

If you choose Center and the image is larger than the screen, you can see only the center portion of the image that fits within your display. The Tile choice repeats the photo in its full size, numerous times on the screen. This works only with small images because, just as with the Center command, large images will not even fully fit on the screen once. So shrink the image's size using an image or photo program. For example, right-click the image in question, choose Open With, and then choose a graphics program such as Paint (use the Resize command in the Image group on the Ribbon). Experiment with resizing the picture to, say, 300×400 pixels. Always save the file under a different name first so that you don't mess up the original, which is in a higher resolution that you may want to keep.

Stretched a Bit Thin

If a desktop image looks blocky, either use a larger image or turn off the Fit setting. See the Control Panel, Appearance and Personalization, Personalization, Desktop Background, Picture Position option.

Window Color and Appearance

To customize your desktop even further, use the Window Color link near the bottom of the Personalization window to access the Window Color and Appearance feature. From this link, what you see will vary greatly depending on whether you are running in Aero mode or the older, less flashy Windows Basic (non-Aero) mode. Figure 23.5 shows both boxes.

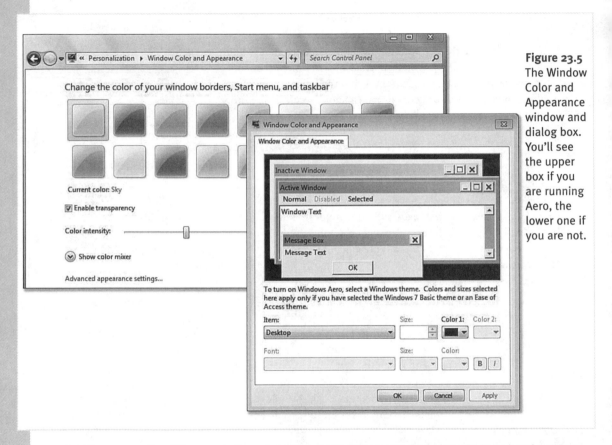

Figure 23.5
The Window Color and Appearance window and dialog box. You'll see the upper box if you are running Aero, the lower one if you are not.

As you can see, the difference in these interfaces is like that between a butterfly (Aero) and a caterpillar (non-Aero). Let's explore the Aero approach first and then the non-Aero.

Aero Mode

In Aero's Window Color and Appearance window, simply click a color button and the scheme will change. Microsoft has made it easy to choose color schemes this way, without putting you through the hassle of applying a specific color to each GUI element (title bars, document workspace, scrollbars, and so on) or choosing schemes by names that don't mean much to you, such as Wheat. (You can still assign individual colors if you want to by clicking the Advanced Appearance Settings link.) The effects of choosing a color button are immediately displayed across all open windows and applications when you click on it. Drag the Transparency slider to alter how translucent your window borders, title bar, and other elements will be. This effect is also instantly applied across the interface. Very slick.

Want to adjust the exact color hue, saturation, and brightness? Click the Show Color Mixer button. Three sliders show up. Adjust as you please. (Saturation means how pure the color is, by the way.)

Non-Aero (Basic) Mode

High Contrast (helpful for the visually challenged) or Windows Basic looks can be achieved by returning to the Personalization window and selecting a non-Aero theme from the Basic and High Contrast Themes section. If you prefer the look of Windows 2000 and older versions, select Windows Classic in the theme list.

Click Window Color to open the Window Color and Appearance dialog box (see Figure 23.6). You can alter the color settings, component size, and fonts of each individual component of a windowed display for most non-Aero themes. Careful—you can do some serious mischief here, creating some egregious color schemes to attract the fashion police or the scorn of a co-worker who passes by your desk frequently. Or you can design or choose schemes that improve readability on screens (or eyes) with certain limitations.

Figure 23.6
The Window Color and Appearance dialog box lets you control the color and font size of specific window elements.

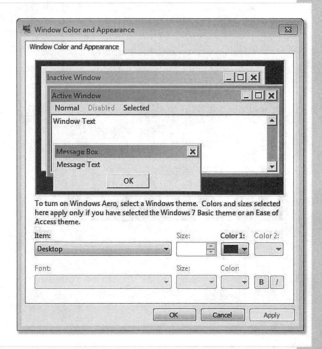

To change the settings, use the various pull-down lists or click on a window element in the preview area, such as the Active Window title bar. Then you can click Color 1 or Color 2 and assign colors from the color picker. In some cases, two colors are assignable because some elements (for example, title bars) transition from one color to another.

When using the color picker, clicking the Other button opens the Color dialog box (see Figure 23.7). You work with two color mix controls here. One is the *luminosity bar* (which looks like a triangle arrow pointing left), and the other is the *color refiner cursor* (which looks like a set of crosshairs).

Just drag these cursors one at a time until the color in the Color/Solid box is the shade you want. As you do so, the numbers in the Hue/Sat/Lum and Red/Green/Blue boxes below the color refiner change.

 tip

If you spend considerable time creating a color, component, and font styling, be sure to save it as a theme and give it a unique name (for example, Laura's Theme). You do this by clicking OK in the Window Color and Appearance dialog box and then, in the Personalization window, choosing Save Theme. Otherwise, if you switch to another view, even for a second, you'll lose all of your previous settings.

- *Luminosity* is the amount of brightness in the color.

- *Hue* is the actual shade or color. All colors are composed of red, green, and blue.

- *Saturation* is the degree of purity of the color; it is decreased by adding gray to the color and increased by subtracting gray.

You also can type in the numbers if you want, but using the cursors is easier. When you like the color, you can save a color for future use by clicking Add to Custom Colors.

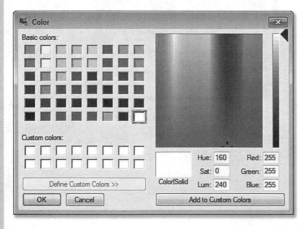

Figure 23.7
The Color dialog box lets you fine-tune colors assigned to various Windows elements.

Sounds

The Sounds link in the Personalization window associates Windows events with sounds. Windows 7 comes with tons of sound files, a big improvement over the measly assemblage of WAV files supplied with some earlier versions of Windows. In fact, just as with the color schemes, you can create and save sound schemes by using the Sound applet; you can set up and save personalized schemes to suit your mood. Microsoft supplies a fairly rich variety of sounds for your auditory pleasure.

Despite the diverse selection, you can still use sounds you've put together using the Sound Recorder. For example, you could record a sound file that says "New Mail" and link it to that action if you don't always notice the generic "new mail" sound when your messages arrive.

If you want to get fancy, you can record from a disc or tape recorder rather than from a microphone. This way, you can sample bits and pieces from your favorite artists by popping the audio disc into the computer and tapping directly into it rather than by sticking a microphone up in front of your boom box and accidentally recording the telephone when it rings. Just check out the Volume Control applet, and figure out which slider on the mixer panel controls the input volume of the disc. Then, use the Sound Recorder applet to make the recording. I have a few good ones, such as James Brown's incomparable "Ow!" for an error message sound.

 tip

Make sure that WAV files you intend for system sounds aren't too large. Sound files *can* be super large, especially if they are recorded in 16-bit stereo. As a rule, keep the size to a minimum for system sounds because it takes a few seconds for a larger sound to load and play.

You assign sounds to specific Windows "events" like this:

1. Right-click the desktop and choose Personalize.

2. Click Sounds. You'll see the dialog box shown in Figure 23.8.

Figure 23.8
The Sound dialog box, Sounds tab. Change system sounds from here.

The Program Events section lists the events that can have sounds associated with them. Several classes of events are listed on a typical computer, such as New Mail Notification, the Windows User Account Control warning, Windows Logon, Exit Windows, Low Battery Alarm, and so on. As you purchase and install new programs in the future, those programs may add their own events to your list. An event with a speaker icon already has a sound associated with it. You can click it and then click the Test button to hear the sound. The sound file associated with the event appears in the Sounds list at the bottom of the Sound dialog box.

3. Click any event in the Program Events list for which you want to assign a sound or change the assigned sound.

4. Open the drop-down Sounds list and choose the WAV file you want to use for that event. These names are for the various classes of dialog boxes that Windows displays from time to time. The sounds you're most likely to hear often will be Asterisk (Windows error), Critical Stop, Default Beep, Exclamation, Windows Logon, Windows Logoff, and Windows Explorer Blocked Pop-up Window. You might want to start by assigning sounds to them and then add others as you feel like it.

5. Repeat these steps for each item you want to assign or reassign a sound to. Then click OK to close the dialog box.

 tip

The default folder for sounds is \windows\media. If you have a WAV file stored in another folder and want to assign it to an event, use the Browse button in the Sound dialog box to locate it. You don't have to move your sound files to the \windows\media folder for it to work. However, if you reassign sounds regularly, you'll find that the process is easier if you move your WAV files into the media folder first.

At the top of the list of available sounds is an option called (None), which has the obvious effect: No sound will occur for that event. Assigning all events to (None) effectively silences your computer for use in a library or other silent setting. You can also silence all sounds easily by choosing No Sounds from the Sound Scheme drop-down list.

In the same way that the Window Color and Appearance dialog box (non-Aero mode theme) lets you save color schemes, the Sounds applet lets you save sound schemes. You can set up goofy sounds for your humorous moods and somber ones for those gloomy days. The ones supplied with Windows 7 are pretty decent, actually, and considering the amount of work required to set up your own schemes, you'll probably make out best just trying a scheme to see if you like it. To choose an existing sound scheme, just use the Sound Scheme drop-down list and select one.

You can set up your own sound schemes by assigning or reassigning individual sounds, as already explained. But unless you *save* the scheme with the Save As button, it'll be lost the next time you change to a new one. So, the moral is that after you get your favorite sounds assigned to system events, save the scheme. Then, you can call it up any time you want.

The Playback and Recording Tabs

In Figure 23.8, notice that in addition to the Sounds tab, there are also Playback and Recording tabs. Here, you can declare the default hardware you want to use for audio playback and recording. Most systems offer minimal choices in these departments because typical computers have only a single sound system.

Both tabs include Configure and Properties buttons for your sound hardware, which depend on your sound system's chipset. Some offer options to adjust bass and treble; expanded stereo (sort of a wider sound based on adjustment of the "phase" of the signal going to the amplifier); sample-rate conversion options; equalization optimization based on the kind of speakers you have; amplitude gain or reduction; and hardware acceleration. (Use full acceleration if you're a gamer because it affects DirectSound used in some games.)

Clicking the Recording tab, then on a microphone icon (Mic), and then clicking Configure opens the Speech Recognition window. From here, you can start using speech recognition, set up your mic, take a tutorial about how to use recognition, train your computer to better understand your voice, and open and print a Speech Reference Card (a cheat sheet of commands).

The Communications Tab

New to Windows 7 is the Communications tab, which you use to adjust the volume of system sounds while you're using the computer as a phone. On this tab you can select to mute all sounds, reduce the volume by 80% or 50%, or do nothing if Windows detects communication over the PC.

Screen Savers

We all know what screen savers are. In the Personalization window, you can click on Screen Saver, and you'll see the dialog box shown in Figure 23.9.

Figure 23.9
The Screen Saver Settings dialog box.

You can choose from several supplied screen savers and perhaps others you have installed from other sources. In the old days when phosphors would "burn," screen savers prevented a ghost of an image from being burned into the screen for all time, no matter what was being displayed. Most modern CRTs don't actually need a screen saver because the phosphors are more durable; LCD monitors use liquid crystal cells, not phosphors.

So, what good is a screen saver nowadays, you ask? Well, some monitor/card combinations go into low-power states when the screen is blanked, so if you choose Blank Screen, there could be some advantage.

Because far too many people leave their computers on all the time (it's not really true that they will last longer that way), efforts have been made by power regulators and electronics manufacturers to devise computer energy-conservation schemes. Some screen savers will turn off the video card instead of displaying cute graphics. And, of course, some screen savers are fun to watch. Windows 7 comes with a handful of screen savers, such as 3D Text, Blank, Bubbles, Mystify, Photos, and Ribbons. All but Blank and Photos are in 3D.

 tip

Interested in space exploration? Think life might exist on other planets? If you want to become part of the largest global experiment in massive parallel processing, you can download the SETI@home screen saver to harness your computer's otherwise wasted CPU cycles to sift through signals from outer space, searching for signs of intelligent life out there. (Go to http://setiathome. ssl.berkeley.edu if you're interested in participating.)

Some screen savers are mindless; others are more interesting. Some, such as 3D Text, have additional options such as font, size, and color. You can check out each one as the spirit moves you. Just highlight it in the Screen Saver drop-down list and click Preview, or watch what happens in the little preview monitor. If you do a full-screen preview, don't move the mouse until you're ready to stop the preview or it will stop even before it gets started. If a particular screen saver has configuration elements, click the Settings button.

You can also create a personalized screen saver by displaying selected pictures and videos as a slideshow. Here is how to create your own slideshow as a screen saver for your Windows 7 desktop:

1. In the Screen Saver Settings dialog box, open the Screen Saver drop-down list and select Photos.

2. Click Settings to choose the pictures and videos you want in your slideshow and other options. After you make your changes, click Save and then OK.

Note that there are two more settings in the Screen Saver Settings dialog box:

- **Wait *x* minutes**—After the number of minutes you set here, the screen saver will begin. The smallest value is 1 minute. The largest is 9,999 minutes.

- **On Resume, Display Logon Screen**—A screen saver often comes on after you leave your desk for a while. As a safety precaution, in case you forget to log off or lock the computer (via Start, Lock) before leaving, it is a good idea to require that you provide your logon password when you return to your desk and touch a key or move the mouse.

If you're looking to find the actual screen-saver files on your hard drive, they have an `.scr` extension and are stored in the windows\system32 folder. In your Windows 7 system, they might be hidden. In Windows Explorer, click Organize, Folder and Search Options, and then click the View tab. In the Advanced Settings list, select the Show Hidden Files, Folders, and Drives radio button, and uncheck the Hide Extensions for Known File Types option. Click OK to close the dialog box. You should be able to see the SCR files in windows\system32 at this point.

note

You must have a video card that's compatible with Direct3D to use the 3D screen savers in Windows 7. The OS will display a message to this effect in the Screen Saver Settings dialog box if you attempt to select a 3D screen saver without the proper card installed.

Double-clicking a screen saver runs it. Right-clicking and choosing Install adds it to your screen saver list. If you run it, just press a key or click the mouse to stop it.

The Web is littered with screen savers. The following are some reliable sources:

- **Screensaver.com**—www.screensaver.com

- **Softpedia**—www.softpedia.com

Between those two sources alone, you have access to more than 2,500 screen savers. Plus, many of the screen savers designed for previous versions of Windows will work on Windows 7.

In addition to selecting the screen saver du jour, you should also define the length of time the system must be idle before the screen saver is launched, as well as whether to display the logon screen or return to the desktop when the system is resumed (that is, when the keyboard or mouse is activated by a user).

If you are working from a portable system or are an energy conservationist, the Screen Saver Settings dialog box also offers quick access to the power saving properties of Windows 7. Click the Change Power Settings link to open the Power Options window, which was discussed in Chapter 22, "Windows Management and Maintenance."

tip

You can uninstall screen savers you install, but you cannot uninstall the screen savers that come with Windows 7.

➥ *Power settings for laptops offer several power plans to choose from.* **See** *"Getting the Most Out of Your Battery," p. 974.*

Setting Desktop Icons

You might want to change which basic system icons are always included on your desktop. Here's how:

1. Open the Personalization window.

2. In the Tasks list, click Change Desktop Icons.

You can turn on or off five common shortcut icons to appear on the desktop:

- Computer
- User's Files
- Network
- Recycle Bin
- Control Panel

You can also manage the icons used for these desktop shortcuts using the Change Icon and Restore Default buttons. You can also uncheck the Allow Themes to Change Desktop Icons check box, if you want your desktop icons to remain static.

note

Change Mouse Pointers is the next link in the Personalization window. However, we don't discuss it here because it's covered in Chapter 22.

Account Picture

You can change the picture associated with your Windows user account that appears on the Welcome screen and your Start menu. Just click on the Change Your Account Picture in the Personalization window Tasks list. In the Change Your Picture window that appears, click one of the thumbnails, and then click Change Picture. You can also click the Browse for More Pictures link, and then locate and select a different image (including one of your own).

Display Settings

The Display link in the Tasks list of the Personalization window opens the Display window, shown in Figure 23.10. From here, you can increase the size of text and other elements of most windows by selecting the Medium – 125% or Larger – 150% radio button.

The options listed in the Tasks list let you tweak the video driver's most basic settings—screen resolution (desktop size), brightness, and color quality. You can configure other display settings (covered next), connect to a projector, adjust the ClearType text, and set custom text size up to 200%.

note

Screen fonts are smoothed using the standard Windows method or using ClearType (the default). ClearType often improves the visibility range on older LCD displays.

Figure 23.10
The Display window.

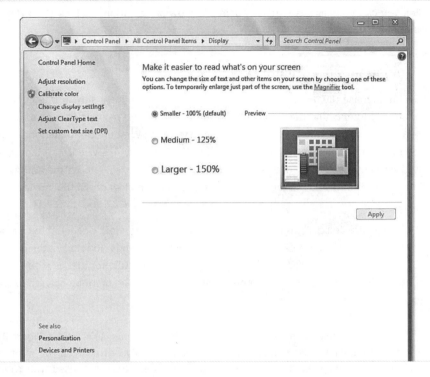

The Screen Resolution Window

Click the Change Display Settings link in the Tasks list of the Display window to open the Screen Resolution window. In this window you can select a display if you are using multiple monitors, change resolution settings, and connect to an external projector, among other tasks.

Windows 7 allows you to display the same desktop view on two or more monitors. On a notebook PC, you can display the desktop on both the built-in LCD panel and an external monitor. On desktop PCs, you need multiple video cards or a single card with dual outputs to use multiple monitors. You can also set up multiple screens such that each one is displaying different information, thus enlarging your overall desktop area (called *extended desktop*). This is covered in detail in Chapter 27, "Installing and Replacing Hardware."

When you plug in a modern monitor, Windows usually detects it and sets the correct resolution, refresh rate, orientation, and color depth for it. Most newer monitors and projectors support Extended Display Identification Data (EDID), a standard video data format that transmits this information to the computer when you plug them in.

The Resolution setting makes resizing your desktop a breeze. Many of us want to cram as much on the screen as possible without going blind. This setting lets you experiment and even change resolution on-the-fly to best display whatever you're working on. Some jobs, such as working with large spreadsheets, databases, CAD, or typesetting, are much more efficient with more data displayed on the screen. Because higher resolutions require a trade-off in clarity and make onscreen objects smaller, you can minimize eyestrain by going to a lower resolution, such as 1024×768 pixels. (A *pixel* is essentially one dot on the screen.)

Moving in Slow Motion

If you increase the resolution and find that the screen updates slowly when you drag windows around, you may find that running in True Color at a high resolution, such as 1280×1024, can result in response delays, especially if you have Show Window Contents While Dragging turned on (in the Performance Options dialog box). When you move a window, it moves jerkily across the screen. If you play videos such as Windows Media Video, QuickTime, MPEG, or RealPlayer movies, you'll also notice these higher color depths can slow down the movies or make them play jerkily.

Unless you're doing high-resolution photographic-quality work or something similar, you don't need the high-resolution 24-bit or 32-bit color depth settings. Right-click the desktop and select Screen Resolution. Click Advanced Settings, and on the Adapter tab, click the List All Modes button. Try reducing the color depth a notch (such as to 24- or 16-bit color if you have those options) and enjoy the speed increase.

To change the resolution, open the Resolution list. A slider appears, as shown in Figure 23.11. Move the slider to the resolution you want, and then click OK or Apply. You are asked if you want to keep the changes. The good thing about the no-reboot video subsystem, first introduced with Windows 98, is that the driver settings should revert within 15 seconds unless you accept them. So, if the screen goes blank or otherwise goes bananas, click Revert or just wait. It should return to the previous setting.

Where Did Those Icons Go?

If after changing the screen resolution, desktop items move off the edge of the screen and some windows can't be closed, it's possible that you switched to a lower resolution from a higher one. Theoretically, Windows is good about relocating desktop icons, but some applications might not do the same. For example, the small AOL Instant Messenger dialog box can be off the edge of the screen somewhere, and when it is, you can't get to it. Closing and rerunning the program doesn't help.

One trick is to switch to the application by pressing Alt+Tab. Then press Alt+spacebar and press M. This key combination invokes the Move command for the window. Then you can use the arrow keys on the keyboard to move the window (typically to the left and/or up). When you have the title bar of the window in view, press Enter. If this trick doesn't work, switch back to the previous higher resolution, reposition the application window in question closer to the upper-left corner of the screen, and then switch back to the lower resolution. It might help to remember that your screen is always decreased or increased in size starting from the lower-right corner and moving up or down diagonally.

Figure 23.11
Adjusting the resolution setting in Windows 7.

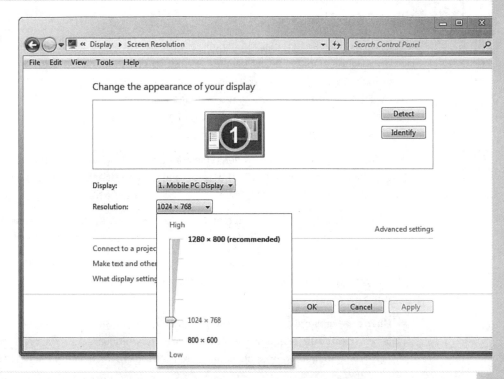

Stick with Native Resolution

All laptops, notebooks, and almost all desktop computers have LCD monitors these days. Unlike their somewhat more-versatile yet clunky and energy-hungry CRT-based progenitors, these space-saving displays are optimized for one resolution, called their *native* resolution. On LCDs, it's recommended you don't change the setting from the native (sometimes called *suggested*) resolution. Although choosing a lower resolution will result in making screen elements larger (and thus easier for some people to see), it will also produce a blockier, fuzzier display. This effect is mitigated somewhat on more intelligent displays by engineering that provides antialiasing. Trying a higher resolution than the native one typically will not work. There is a discrete number of pixels on the display, and these are of a predetermined size.

Trying to jam more pixels on the screen, if it works at all, does so by creating a "virtual" screen that is larger than the actual one. This will require you to pan and scroll the screen image. Check the computer's or monitor's manual if you're in doubt about which external monitor resolutions are supported.

What Does That Say?

If you want to use an external TV monitor, but the output text is illegible, it's important to note that displaying computer output on a TV monitor can be problematic. TV sets (as opposed to professional TV monitors) often overscan, pushing the edges of the image off the edge of the screen. The following are a few points to remember when you're using a TV or video projector, whether you're doing presentations, playing games, or giving your eyes a break by moving your focal plane back a bit:

- If your computer and TV or video projector have HDMI (High-Definition Multimedia Interface) or DVI (Digital Video Interface) connectors, use those for the best image quality. Use "S" (Super VHS) inputs if other connectors are not available.

- Use the Detect button in the Screen Resolution window (right-click the desktop and select Screen Resolution) to let Windows 7 automatically detect the output device.

- If you cannot get a decent screen image or if it's blank, restart in Safe Mode and try updating your video card or TV tuner driver. Still no luck? Uninstall the driver and then re-install it in Safe Mode.

- Check the tabs in your adapter and monitor Advanced Settings dialog box for buttons that let you center the image on the TV. It's most likely off center or needs resizing when you first try it. Some drivers, such as those from ATI, have advanced properties for fine-tuning a TV display.

- Your application may have a "zoom" control for easily increasing the size of text onscreen, without the hassle of reformatting the entire document. Microsoft Office tools such as Excel and Word, for example, have such a feature. Try bumping up the zoom size to increase legibility.

Exploring Advanced Display Settings

The Advanced Settings link in the Screen Resolution window opens the monitor and adapter Properties dialog box. This dialog box has four tabs—Adapter, Monitor, Troubleshoot, and Color Management.

The Adapter tab displays information about the video card and offers access to update, roll back, disable, and uninstall the video driver through the Properties button. (Click the Resources tab in the Properties dialog box if you want to fine-tune the configuration of the driver.) The List All Modes button is used to view the color, resolution, and refresh rate combinations supported by this video adapter.

Uh-Oh! My Monitor Died

What do you do if you change your resolution or refresh rate, and now the screen is blank? Normally, you shouldn't have this problem because Windows 7 asks you to confirm that a screen resolution works properly and switches back to the previous resolution if you don't confirm. If you changed color depth and resolution, and the system is stuck with a blank screen, you can reboot, press F8 during boot, and choose Safe Mode. Right-click the desktop, choose Screen Resolution, and reset the properties to what the computer was running at before the change. Be sure to reset both the screen resolution and the color depth (click Advanced Settings, List All Modes). In the worst-case scenario, start with 800×600 and 16-bit color. Then reboot normally. After you've rebooted successfully, right-click the desktop, choose Screen Resolution, and increase the settings one step at a time. Don't change resolution and color depth at the same time, though. Increase one first and then the other, rebooting in between changes.

Note that some motherboards reserve F8 for a boot selection menu, which would prevent the preceding approach from working. If that is the case on your PC, reboot and press F6 to display advanced boot options. Then choose appropriately from the resulting menu.

The Monitor tab offers access to update, roll back, disable, and uninstall the monitor driver (Properties button), and to set the screen refresh rate. Use the screen refresh rate with caution because it can damage older monitors or render your desktop unviewable. Higher refresh rates reduce the flickering of the display. You can also select a color depth setting at the bottom of this tab.

Blurry Images in LCD

Unlike CRTs, LCDs do not benefit from higher refresh rates. Don't try to use anything above a 60Hz refresh rate for an LCD monitor. Also, check the LCD monitor's internal settings (check its manual) for a "phase adjustment" or focus adjustment to help clear up fuzziness on small text.

The Troubleshoot tab is used to set the hardware acceleration rate, anywhere between None and Full. Basically, this indicates how much video processing is offloaded to the video adapter instead of being performed by Windows 7 on the CPU. The more you can offload processing to the video card, the more smoothly your system will function. If you have problems with jitters or lockups, you may need to reduce the amount of hardware acceleration, if that option is not grayed out. (Some cards won't let you change this setting, or you won't have the privilege level necessary unless you are an administrator.)

The Color Management tab is used to set the color profile used to manage colors for your adapter and monitor. If you are performing high-end image processing, you may want to investigate this feature in the Windows 7 Resource Kit.

Fine-Tuning Display Settings

To fine-tune display settings beyond just the resolution, click the Advanced Settings link in the Screen Resolution window, and then click the List All Modes button. Assuming that Windows 7 has properly identified your video display card and that the correct driver is installed, the List All Modes dialog box (see Figure 23.12) should include all the legitimate options your card is capable of. Your color depth options, such as 256 Colors, High Color 32 bit, True Color 16 bit, and so on, are limited by the amount of video RAM on the card and the resolution you choose. The higher the resolution, the more memory is used for pixel addressing, limiting the pixel depth (number of colors that can be displayed per pixel). With many modern cards, this limitation is no biggie, and it's likely that many Windows 7 users will not have to worry about it except possibly in cases when they have large monitors displaying 1600×1200 (or higher) and want 32-bit color *and* a high refresh rate. All modern color monitors for PCs, however, are capable of displaying 16 million colors, which is dubbed True Color.

 tip

Contrary to some advertising accompanying flat-panel monitors, LCDs don't give a hoot about high refresh speed. In fact, they don't like high speeds. LCDs use a completely different technology, typically with a transistor for each pixel. The dots don't have to be refreshed as they do in a CRT. If you notice a blurry display on a desktop LCD screen, it's probably because the refresh rate is set too high (such as to 75Hz). Lowering it to 59 or 60Hz should resolve the problem. This advice applies only to LCDs attached to analog display cards. Some outboard LCD monitors are driven by their own digital adapter cards, and refresh settings don't affect those cards.

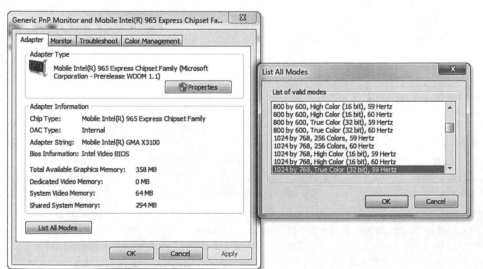

Figure 23.12
The List All Modes dialog box.

If you are experiencing any problems with your video system, from pop-up errors blaming the video system, to a flickering display, to even trouble resetting the resolution and color, click the Advanced Settings link in the Screen Resolution window and then the Troubleshoot tab. There may be some useful information there, depending on your monitor.

 caution

If you specify a refresh rate that is too high for your monitor, it could damage the monitor. Also, trying to expand the desktop area to a larger size might not work. You just get a mess on the screen. If you have this problem, try using a setting with a lower refresh rate, such as 60Hz or "interlaced." The image may flicker a bit more, but at least it will be visible.

Reducing Screen Flicker

If your CRT monitor is flickering, you can change the refresh rate to fix the problem. Increase the refresh rate of the display subsystem to at least 70Hz by right-clicking the desktop, choosing Screen Resolution, and clicking Advanced Settings. In the Properties dialog box, click the Monitor tab, and then open the Screen Refresh Rate drop-down list.

Note that this applies *only* to older, CRT-style monitors, not thin, flat-panel LCD monitors. Most LCDs should be run at 60Hz for the clearest image.

Miscellaneous GUI Tips

Windows 7 offers many new features and capabilities. But you don't have to settle for the out-of-the-box defaults; you can customize to your heart's content. In the following sections, we provide you with several tips to help you soup up your Windows 7 installation.

Single- or Double-Click?

If you find that you accidentally run programs or open documents when you are certain that you didn't double-click anything, you probably have Single-Click selection turned on. As a result, one click (or tap, if you're using a touchpad) runs the program or opens the document that is highlighted. Change to Double-Click selection mode by opening a folder window; choosing Organize, Folder and Search Options; and selecting Double Click to Open an Item.

Fonts Preview Trick

If you've ever tried to see what a font looks like before you printed it, you know how frustrating it can be. But, getting a preview of a font is now easier than ever before. Just open the Fonts applet through Control Panel, Appearance and Personalization, click any listed font, and click Preview. A font sampling window opens, displaying details about the font, a sample of most characters, and several sizes of characters (see Figure 23.13).

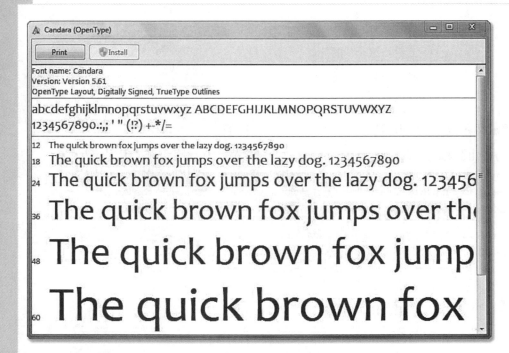

Figure 23.13
A font sampling window.

Which Windows Are You Using?

If you're dual- or multibooting between Windows 7 (using the Windows Classic theme) and other Windows products, you may sometimes wonder which OS you're running at any given time because the GUIs of the post-Windows 95 OSs are often quite similar. Yes, you'll see a few giveaways, such as Computer versus My Computer, but if you're using the Windows Classic theme, the clues can be subtle.

To determine what's running, use these techniques to remind yourself:

- Execute `winver` from the Run command or from the Command Prompt window to open a dialog box that displays the OS name, version and build, and applied Service Packs.

- Click Start and right-click Computer. From the menu that appears, click Properties. The first set of information in the System applet indicates the version of Windows you're currently using. You can also access the System applet from Control Panel, System and Security.

Limiting Flip 3D

If your computer does not have a high video performance rating and you have Aero turned on, using Flip 3D might be a bit slow if you have many apps and documents open at once. This can be particularly true if your windows have active video running because that consumes significant video display chip bandwidth.

One solution is to limit the number of mini-pages that Flip 3D displays when you press Ctrl+Windows+Tab.

tip

Only attempt this if you know how to edit the Registry. Chapter 28, "Editing the Registry," details Registry editing.

1. Ensure you have Windows Aero enabled already. If you have Windows Classic or another non-Aero theme running, right-click the desktop, select Personalize, and then change to the Windows 7 (Aero) theme.

2. Go to Start, All Programs, Accessories, Command Prompt.

3. Type **regedit** and click OK.

4. Navigate your way to HKEY_CURRENT_USER\Software\Microsoft\Windows\DWM.

5. In the right pane, right-click an empty area, point to New, and select DWORD (32-bit) Value. Name it **Max3DWindows**. Right-click Max3DWindows and select Modify. Depending on your type of graphics card, your best bet is to base the value of this DWORD on the Windows Experience Index (see Chapter 22). If your computer has a rating of 1 to 2, set the Registry value as 3. If your rating is set to 3, you can have your Registry value set to 5. If your computer has a rating of 4 or 5, you can have anything over 10 as the Registry value and it will still run smoothly.

note

To access the Windows Experience Index, click Start, right-click Computer, select Properties, and choose Windows Experience Index (or choose System Rating Is Not Available and then click Rate This Computer).

6. Set the value and then click OK. Close the Registry Editor.

7. Restart your computer for the changes to take effect.

More Visual Effects

There is another hidden location for Windows 7 GUI settings somewhat akin to those provided by Tweak UI, a utility that gives you access to hidden Windows settings. For this semisecret list, follow these steps:

1. Open Control Panel.

2. Choose System and Security, System.

3. Click Performance Information and Tools in the Tasks list.

4. Click Advanced Tools in the Tasks list.

5. Click Adjust the Appearance and Performance of Windows. (The UAC dialog box might appear.)

You will see the Performance Options dialog box shown in Figure 23.14.

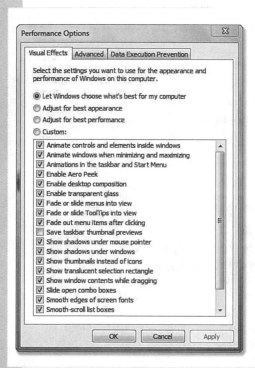

Figure 23.14
A treasure trove of UI and performance settings.

Have a ball making changes. Use care when adjusting the performance settings (processor scheduling and virtual memory). You don't want to slow down your foreground processing unless you don't mind waiting for response from your apps and input devices (keyboard and mouse). Letting Windows 7 handle stuff like virtual memory paging size (Advanced tab) and DEP (Data Execution Prevention tab) is generally the best way to go.

Administrator Tools Not Showing Up

Windows 7 is designed as an end-user OS. Thus, most of the system-level management tools are not made readily accessible by being placed in plain sight on the Start menu. Instead, they are contained within a subfolder of the Control Panel known as Administrative Tools. Open Control Panel, click System and Security, Administrative Tools to open a folder containing these management tools.

To gain access to Administrative Tools from the Start menu, right-click the Start menu and select Properties. In the Taskbar and Start Menu Properties dialog box, click Customize on the Start Menu tab. Scroll down to the bottom of the list, and in the System Administrative Tools section, select the Display on the All Programs Menu and the Start Menu radio button. Click OK.

Cascading Elements from the Start Menu

Cascading is the ability to expand certain folders right off the Start menu. These expanded menus are also called *flyout menus*. The native Windows 7 interface can be configured to add cascading menus to the Computer, Control Panel, Documents, Downloads, Games, Music, Personal Folder, Pictures, Recorded TV, and Videos items on the Start menu. This is the same feature discussed earlier in the chapter to gain direct Start menu access to Administrative Tools.

The process is simple:

1. Right-click the Start button and select Properties from the pop-up menu to open the Properties for the Start menu.

2. Select the Start Menu tab and click Customize.

3. Scroll down the list of Start menu items and change the settings for the desired items to Display as a Menu.

The menu item(s) now have a right-facing arrow by their names in the Start menu. When you click the menu item, a flyout menu appears.

Configuring the Recycle Bin

The Recycle Bin holds recently deleted files to provide you with a reasonable opportunity to recover them. As discussed in Chapter 4, "Using the Windows 7 User Interface," the Recycle Bin holds the last deleted files that fit within its size restriction. That restriction, by default, is 10% for drives up to 40GB; for larger drives, the maximum is 4GB plus 5% of the capacity. However, you can customize the Recycle Bin for your specific needs.

The Recycle Bin's Properties dialog box (accessed by right-clicking over the icon and then selecting Properties) displays available space for each partition/volume on the system. If you've never deleted a file by mistake and don't think you ever will, you can elect to delete files immediately without storing them in the Recycle Bin. It's better, however, to allow the Recycle Bin to catch your deleted files, even if that means lowering the maximum amount of allocated disk space. A final control in this dialog box enables a deletion confirmation dialog box—it's recommended you leave this enabled as a safety measure.

Keep in mind that files moved to the Recycle Bin are not actually deleted. Instead, their path information is removed from the normal interfaces and moved into the Recycle Bin. Deleted files still remain on the drive exactly where they were before the deletion operation. This means they take up space on the drive. So, if you leave the default percentage setting on a 160GB hard drive, you can have up to 12GB of deleted files still sitting on the drive, slowing down the drive's seek time.

24

MANAGING HARD DISKS

The Nature of Hard Disks

For many users and system administrators, intelligent hard disk management forms the core of efficient system management. Until solid-state drive (SSD) technology becomes truly affordable, we're stuck with the problems and limitations created by a crude system of motors, spinning platters, and delicate parts, such as read/write heads floating microns above a flying surface that can be easily ruined by particles as small as those found in a puff of cigarette smoke.

Perhaps someday, hard disks will be relics of the past, useful only for industrial art or bookends flanking tech books on a shelf. (They'll make good doorstops, too.) Until that time, we're stuck with the peculiar vagaries of hard disks. The good news is that high-capacity drives are cheap and plentiful.

No doubt the majority of Windows 7 users will never set up RAID arrays, multiple-booting arrangements, or dynamic disks; use encryption; or do any remote disk administration. Perhaps they will perform occasional disk cleanups and defragmenting, or learn to share folders over the network. These tasks are enough to get them by. Yet with a bit more knowledge from reading this chapter, you can learn how extensive Windows 7's hard disk configuration capabilities really are.

 note

RAID is short for *Redundant Array of Independent (or Inexpensive) Disks*. In this hard disk scheme, two or more drives are connected for higher fault tolerance and performance. RAID arrangements are used frequently on servers, but aren't generally necessary for personal or client computers.

Windows 7 File and Storage Systems

Windows 7 supports two types of storage models: basic disks and dynamic storage. Windows 2000, Windows XP Professional, and Windows Vista also support dynamic storage. When you prepare a hard disk for use, you can choose between these storage models. The following sections explain how they differ and when to use each type.

Basic Disks

The traditional storage model of disk structure uses partition tables. Each hard drive can hold up to four *primary partitions* or up to three primary partitions and one *extended (secondary) partition*. Within this extended partition, you can create logical drives. The total number of primary partitions and logical drives cannot exceed 32 per hard drive. This disk structure is understood and can be accessed by MS-DOS, all versions of Windows NT, as well as Windows 2000, XP, Vista, and Windows 7. When viewed in Disk Management, a disk drive prepared in this fashion is known as a basic disk.

The annoyances and limitations of this partition table methodology are artifacts of Microsoft operating systems, incidentally, not something imposed by hard disks themselves or their manufacturers. Some other OSs don't suffer the same peculiarities.

The major reasons to continue using basic storage include

- Support for all versions of Windows that can read the file system used on the drives. For example, if you need to support dual-booting with Windows XP Home Edition and Windows 7, you must use a file system that both OSs support. XP Home does not support dynamic disks, so you must use basic disks.

- Support for multiboot configurations. Dynamic disks don't use boot loaders, so you cannot select between OSs; therefore, you cannot use this type of storage as your only drive in a multiboot configuration.

You can convert basic to dynamic disks without data loss, but to convert a dynamic disk back to a basic disk using the Windows 7 Disk Management tool, you must delete the disk structure (and, of course, the data).

note

Storage types are separate from the file systems they contain. Both basic and dynamic disks can contain any combination of FAT16, FAT32, NTFS v4, NTFS v5, and NTFS v6 partitions or volumes. All drives are either basic or dynamic. You might occasionally run across a format called exFAT, but it works only on USB flash drives (UFDs) and isn't relevant to hard disks.

tip

If you need to convert a dynamic disk to a basic disk without data loss, use Avanquest Software's Partition Commander Professional 10 (www.avanquest.com).

Dynamic Storage

With dynamic storage, the restraints of primary and extended partitions are gone. Under this storage model, free space on a hard drive is divided into volumes instead of partitions; these volumes can be noncontiguous and can span one or more disks. In addition, volumes on a dynamic disk can be configured as simple, spanned, mirrored, striped, or RAID-5, as described next. Basic storage partitions can be configured only as simple partitions, unless they are remnants from a previous OS retained during an upgrade.

- **Simple volume**—Uses free space available on a single disk. This space can be a single contiguous region or multiple concatenated regions. Under the basic storage model, each partition or logical drive is assigned a separate and distinct drive letter, and functions as a distinct region of disk space. Dynamic storage can be configured to see multiple regions of a disk as a single volume, accessed with a single assigned drive letter.

- **Spanned volume**—Extends the concept of a simple volume across multiple disks (up to a maximum of 32). All joined regions on these disks are seen as a single volume to programs accessing them. However, if a single unit in a spanned volume fails, the entire set is lost.

- **Mirrored volume**—A volume in which data from one disk is mirrored or duplicated on a second disk. This process provides for data redundancy, often called *fault tolerance.* If one disk fails, the data can be accessed from the second disk. A mirrored volume cannot be spanned; each volume must be contained on a single disk. Programs see only one volume, and Windows ensures that both disks are kept in sync. *Mirroring* is also known as *RAID-1.*

- **Striped volume**—A volume in which data is stored across two or more physical disks. When data is written to a striped volume space, it is allocated alternately and evenly to each of the physical disks. A striped volume cannot be mirrored or spanned via Windows 7. (It is possible on hardware-based RAID.) *Striping*, often termed *RAID-0*, is used to increase storage system throughput. If a single unit in a striped volume fails, the entire set is lost.

- **RAID-5 volume**—A fault-tolerant version of a striped volume. When data is written to a RAID-5 volume, it is striped across an array of three or more disks, and a parity value is added. If a hard disk belonging to a RAID-5 volume fails, the remaining drives can re-create the data using this parity value. Note the difference here between a mirrored volume and a RAID-5 volume.

 note

A mirrored volume contains two disks; if either one fails, the OS goes to the other for data access.

A RAID-5 volume contains three or more disks, any of which can fail without the system halting. The OS then reconstructs the missing data from the information contained on the remaining disks.

 caution

Converting a hard disk to dynamic storage is a one-way process unless you use a third-party utility such as Partition Commander Professional 10. To change a dynamic disk back to a basic disk using the Windows 7 Disk Management tool, you must delete all volumes before converting the drive back to basic storage. Also note that dynamic disks can be read by Windows 7, Windows Vista, Windows XP Pro, Windows Server 2003, Windows Server 2008, and all versions of Windows 2000. Windows XP Home, Windows NT, Windows 98/SE/Me, and all earlier versions of Windows cannot access dynamic storage volumes.

When you change the boot disk to dynamic, you can no longer multiboot into another OS because the familiar boot loader screen disappears. Only one installation of Windows can own a set of dynamic disks, so if you are planning to use dynamic disks as your RAID solution on a multiboot computer, think about investing in a hardware-based (SCSI or SATA) RAID solution.

What are the advantages of dynamic storage?

- First and foremost, noncontiguous regions of multiple disks can be linked so that they appear as one large region of disk space to any program. By linking them, you can increase the size of a disk volume on-the-fly, without reformatting or having to deal with multiple drive letters.

- Second, and perhaps more important, from an administrator's point of view, disk and volume management can be performed without restarting the OS.

However, on a multiboot system, OSs other than Windows 7, Windows Vista, Windows 2000 (Server and Professional), Windows XP Professional, Windows Server 2003, and Windows Server 2008 cannot see dynamic storage drives. Unlike NTFS, which applies to only the formatted partition, dynamic storage affects the entire hard drive. So if you plan to use dynamic storage, plan ahead and keep other OSs on different hard drives. In addition, you must ensure that the boot drive is a basic storage drive so that the boot menu will function.

Organizational Strategies

Although the disk systems described in the preceding section are interesting, especially to power users and system administrators who have multiple drives available, most Windows 7 users set up their systems with standard partitions (that is, basic storage) and the NTFS file format. But what about other file systems? How should you organize multiple disks? What about preparing your disks, and what kinds of strategies should you consider?

If you're not going to stick with the straight and narrow of running only NTFS on your hard disk, consider following these alternative strategies and rules:

- Whenever possible, create a separate partition for your data files. This tip has particular relevance to users who test new software or OSs. If you store your data on a separate partition, reinstalling an OS is a simple matter of formatting your system partition and starting from scratch. Although you still need to reinstall your programs, using a separate data partition ensures that you didn't miss a data file somewhere along the line. It also makes backups simple and straightforward. You can image your system partition; you then need to update this image only when you add a new device or software program (see the next paragraph). Data backups can be run on a daily or weekly basis (determined by how often your data changes) and can be set to run on your data partition. Even if you use Windows 7's much-improved backup software, it's still easier to make backups if you separate your OS and applications from your data.

- Use the Windows 7 Backup and Restore utility to create an image of your system. Just click the Create a System Image link in the Tasks list. Having such an image is worth its weight in gold if you like to "tinker" with your system and program configurations. When you have your OS set up, your principal applications installed, and everything tweaked and configured to perfection, you can create an image of your system on a separate drive or partition. If you need to reinstall your OS for whatever reason, the complete process—from beginning to end—should take no more than 20 minutes. When you add, delete, or reconfigure a program, or make changes to the hardware configuration of your disk subsystem, be sure to update your disk image.

- The easiest way to maintain a disk image is to buy a separate hard disk just for image storage. A 500GB external hard disk is appropriate for most image storage needs, but smaller and larger sizes are available.

- Many of today's PCs use Serial ATA (SATA) and/or SCSI host adapters exclusively, whereas older systems use ATA/IDE host adapters. Some "tweeners" offer one ATA/IDE host adapter with four or more SATA adapters. If you have two ATA/IDE drives (a hard disk and a DVD drive), you should not put both of them on the same host adapter. DVD drives transfer data at slower rates than hard disks, slowing down OS and application installations as well as backups to CD or DVD media. With second-generation, high-capacity SATA drives selling for very reasonable prices, it's time to bite the bullet and switch to SATA. The disk-installation utilities provided by many drive vendors can copy your entire existing IDE drive to a new SATA drive during the installation process.

Disk Management

Now that we've covered the essentials of basic and dynamic disks, and tips for optimizing and organizing storage, this section focuses on managing your computer's disks.

The Disk Management utility (shown in Figure 24.1) is responsible for the creation, deletion, alteration, and maintenance of storage volumes in a system. This tool is located within the Computer Management interface of Administrative Tools (accessed through Start, Control Panel, System and Security, Administrative Tools, Computer Management, Disk Management). It is protected by User Account Control. Another access method is right-clicking Computer and choosing Manage. Using the Disk Management utility, you also can assign the drive letters used by your DVD and hard disk drives.

As discussed in Chapter 22, "Windows Management and Maintenance," this single interface lets you manage both local and remote computers using the various administration utilities shown in the left pane. Using this interface, I'll show you shortly how to perform different procedures on your existing and new hard disks. The process is quite simple for most of the operations because you will be presented with a wizard to complete them.

 tip

If the Administrative Tools menu selection is not displayed on the Start menu, right-click the Start menu button and select Properties, click Customize, scroll down to the System Administrative Tools items, and then select the Display on the All Programs Menu and the Start Menu radio button.

If you enable the Control Panel to act as a menu, you can access Administrative Tools through it off the Start menu as well.

 tip

You can change the way specific types of volumes are displayed in Disk Management. To do this, click View, Settings. From there, you can select the color you want to use to represent any of the various disk states shown by Disk Management. By selecting the Scaling tab from the Settings dialog box, you can also change the way in which Disk Management shows the scaling of each disk. This capability is particularly useful if you want the scale display to be more representative of the actual physical sizes of your disks.

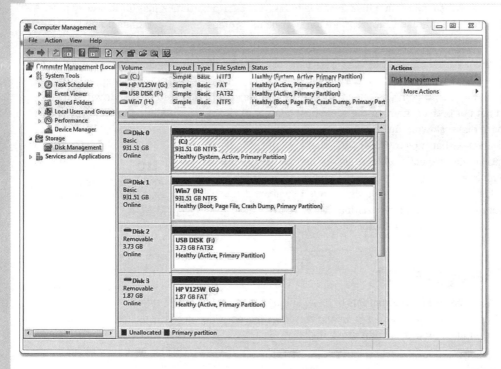

Figure 24.1
The Disk Management tool is part of Computer Management.

Most operations on disks can be performed by right-clicking the disk or volume you want to affect. As usual, you are presented with a context-sensitive menu from which you can perform any actions relating to the volume or disk you click. From the graphical layout in the Disk Management utility, you can also see what is going on with your disks at any given time. As always, you can select the Help option from within any right-click context menu or the menu bar along the top of the window to get an explanation of the operations available to you.

Assigning Drive Letters and Joining Volumes

Windows automatically assigns letters to the drives. However, this assignment might not suit your system; for example, you might have already mapped a network drive to the same letter that Windows assigns to a new drive.

Using Disk Management, you can easily assign logical drive letters to your hard disks and removable drives such as DVD or Iomega REV. You can't change the drive letter of your boot drive (usually the C: drive), but you can change any of the others.

To change the letter, right-click the disk volume or drive in the bottom-right pane of Disk Management, and select Change

caution

Many MS-DOS-based and Windows-based programs make references to a specific drive letter (for example, environment variables). If you modify the drive letter of a drive with these programs installed, they might not function correctly.

Drive Letter and Paths. A dialog box appears, listing the current drive letter assignment. Click Change. Under Assign the Following Drive Letter, choose the desired new letter. Click OK and confirm that you really do want to make the change.

In addition to or instead of assigning a drive letter to a disk drive or partition, you can "graft" the disk volume onto another. Windows lets you specify a folder that will become the mount point for the new drive. For example, let's assume you create a folder named C:\TEMP, and you want it to have a lot of drive space. You could install a new hard drive and, instead of assigning it a drive letter, tell Windows to access it through C:\TEMP. Your C:\TEMP files and subfolders are then stored on the alternate drive.

Grafting Versus Dynamic Disks

Assigning mount points is different from what happens when you aggregate dynamic disks into one large volume. Although dynamic disks and regular (basic) disks both support the use of mount points, dynamic disks can create one large, apparently contiguous disk space. Mount points graft subsequently added drives at a folder, similar to grafting two trees by tying together a branch from each tree. Figure 24.2 illustrates the differences between the two approaches.

 tip

By using a mount point, you can add space to the folders under the mount point folder using an available drive. This is a good way to add space in a controlled fashion for a specific purpose, such as to store scratch files or web page images.

 note

You can graft new volumes or disks onto a folder only on an NTFS-formatted drive. The new volume can have any format, however.

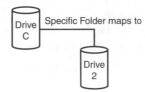
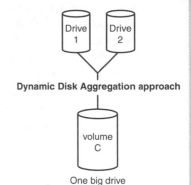

Figure 24.2
You can join drives two different ways: using mount points or using dynamic disk aggregation.

Mount Point approach

One regular drive with a large folder at mount point

Dynamic Disk Aggregation approach

One big drive

In Figure 24.3, I've grafted a hard disk containing digital photos (J:) into the mount point on drive C:\Users\Marcus_S\Pictures\More Pix.

note

If the folder you specify as the mount point already contains files, these are inaccessible as long as the drive-to-path mapping exists because that folder is now remapped into the new location. The original files reappear if you delete the drive path. Therefore, it's usually a good idea to create a new folder as a mount point or delete all the contents of an existing folder before establishing the mount point.

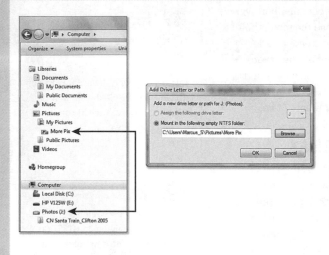

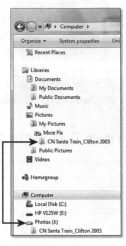

Figure 24.3
Assigning a partition or volume to a folder rather than a drive letter joins the volume to an existing volume. The contents of the added volume appear as subdirectories of the mount point folder.

Even if you have several hard drives and DVD drives, you can graft them all together onto your C: drive, making it appear as one big file system. It's a great management concept: You can add space to your file system by attaching new disk volumes directly into the original folder structure. (UNIX users are probably smirking at this point because the UNIX OS has worked this way since it was written in the 1970s.)

If you mount a drive and assign it a drive letter, you can access it through both pathways.

To graft a disk volume to an existing file system, follow these steps:

1. Create the folder that is to serve as the mount point for the new drive or volume.

2. Highlight the new drive or volume in Disk Management.

3. Right-click, select Change Drive Letter and Paths, and click Add.

4. Select Mount in the Following Empty NTFS Folder.

5. Enter the folder's pathname, or click Browse to locate it.

6. Click OK to save the path.

7. Click OK to close the dialog box.

tip

When Windows Explorer shows you free disk space on the original drive, it measures only the space on the physical drive, not space on any grafted drives. You'll actually have more space than you think because files on the grafted folders are stored on another volume. If you want, you can also assign a drive letter to the added volume so that you can view and monitor its free space directly.

Alternatively, you can use the command prompt, change to the folder in the grafted volume, and use the DIR command, which lists free space on the actual current volume.

You can assign a given drive or volume to only one drive letter but to an arbitrary number of paths. (It's a little strange to see the same files appear in several different places, so we recommend that you not go nuts with this feature.)

By the way, this "grafting" technique works with both basic and dynamic NTFS disks. Only Windows dynamic disks can be "grown" by changing their partition size on the fly. If you use a basic-formatted disk, as most users do, the grafting trick is a good one to know.

Dynamic Disk Management

If you are using only Windows 7 on a system, upgrading your storage devices to dynamic disks is usually the best way to go because of the many advantages of the dynamic disk storage system. Remember, though, that you can't boot into or read your dynamic disks from any other OS after you upgrade them. You can upgrade a disk through Disk Management, right-clicking the drive's icon in the bottom pane (click the part of the graphical display that reads "Disk 0," "Disk 1," and so on, not on the volume), and choosing Convert to Dynamic Disk. Then, choose the disk and click OK. Next, just select the disk to convert from the list that appears and click Convert.

If you don't have the option of upgrading to dynamic disks, one of two possible issues might be the cause. First, the disks might have already been upgraded to dynamic disks. Second, the disk might not be a hard drive, but rather a CD, DVD, or removable media device.

Extending a Disk

One of the cool options available in Disk Management is the option to extend the volume on a dynamic storage drive. Extending is actually another way of "stretching" a simple volume to a specified size when unallocated space is present on the disk. Sometimes, you might want to rearrange the way you've set up your disks, so this option can come in handy.

 tip

If you're running out of room on your C: drive, decide whether it makes sense in your situation to add lots of space to just one folder (for example, Documents). If it does, install and format a new hard drive, and assign it a letter. Copy the original folder to the new drive; then add a path to the new hard drive using the name of the original folder. This way, you can preserve your original data and have room for

 tip

Another good time to use this feature is when you've backed up application data onto a CD or DVD disc. If you want to use the backed-up data in an emergency, you can add a path for your DVD drive to make its files appear in the original data location your application expects. That way, you can use the data off the media without restoring it to disk or reconfiguring your application. Later, you can delete the path to regain access to the "real" folder.

 caution

As you learned earlier in this chapter, dynamic disks cannot be changed back to basic disks using Windows 7's Disk Management without completely destroying any partitions and reformatting the disk, so back up all data first. When you're ready, right-click the volume and select Delete Volume.

From there, you can re-create your simple volume by right-clicking a disk and going through the applicable steps.

To perform the actual extend operation on a disk, you need to have an area of the disk that is unallocated. From there, right-click an existing partition and select Extend Volume to bring up the Extend Volume Wizard. The wizard enables you to specify the size you want to extend the volume to. Finishing the operation leaves you with a disk that is now larger than before. This operation is not limited to volumes that are mounted as drive letters; you can also perform this task on volumes that are mounted into directories.

note

You can also extend a basic volume; however, it must be raw (not format-ted with a file system) or formatted with NTFS.

When Disk Management extends a disk, it is actually creating a new partition and mapping it to the same drive letter as the partition to be extended. It is, in effect, a spanned volume. Although this approach is a bit different from the traditional method performed by disk utilities, such as PartitionMagic, the upside of the Disk Management approach is that you can extend your disk with-out needing to wait for the volume to be resized and data to be shuffled around. The Disk Management approach happens very quickly, without even rebooting your system.

Shrinking a Disk

Windows 7 supports shrinking a basic or dynamic disk volume as well as extending it. When you shrink a volume, the space removed from the volume becomes unallocated space. You can use it for another volume or save it for a future multibooting OS. To shrink a volume, right-click it and select Shrink Volume. The system calculates the amount of space that can be removed, and you can use all or part of this amount.

caution

If you shrink your system's boot vol-ume, you cannot extend it (unless you want to connect your system's hard disk to another system running Windows 7). Before you shrink a boot volume, be sure you calculate how much room you'll need for future data, programs, and updates to Windows 7.

Creating a Spanned Volume

A spanned volume is a volume in which the disk space spans multiple partitions and disks. Using a spanned volume is a handy way of turning a couple of small disks into one large disk, mounted under one drive letter or folder. Simple volumes can also be extended using spanned volumes, as shown in the previous section. Spanned volumes can be created only on dynamic disks. A spanned volume basically is the same as an extended volume, except that the former adds drive space from other hard drives and the latter adds drive space from the same drive.

Creating a spanned volume is just a matter of right-clicking an empty partition and selecting New Spanned Volume, which starts the New Spanned Volume Wizard. This wizard enables you to select which disks to include in your spanned volume from the Available box and click Add. They then appear in the Selected box (see Figure 24.4). At this point, you also can select the amount of space to use for each disk. The total size of your spanned volume is the cumulative total of the space you select on each disk. After clicking Next, you are prompted to assign a drive letter or drive path (mount point) for the new spanned volume. Click Next. Choose whether to format the new volume and, if you choose to do so, select a file system and allocation unit size, enter a volume label, and choose whether to enable file and folder compression. Click Next. In the summary screen, if no changes are necessary, click Finish to create the spanned volume.

Figure 24.4
Selecting disks to create a new spanned volume.

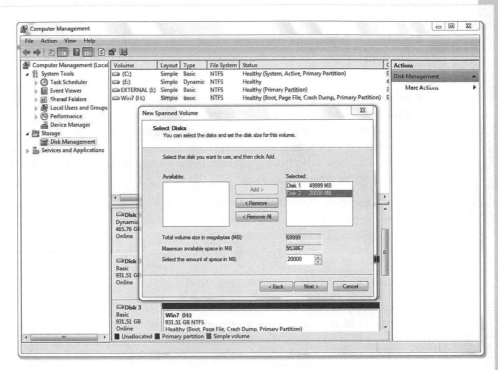

Creating a Striped Volume

One of the procedures you can perform with Disk Management is to create a striped volume. Creating such a volume is often desirable simply because of the ease of administration and the substantial gain in speed. To create a striped volume, you must have more than one disk. For the definition of a striped volume, see "Dynamic Storage," earlier in this chapter.

When you're creating a striped volume, you are creating partitions of the same size across two or more disks. Bear this point in mind as you plan your implementation because you need to have the same amount of space available on each disk that you want to use for your set.

To create a striped volume, follow these steps:

1. Right-click one of the disks to be used in the striped volume set, and select New Striped Volume. The New Striped Volume Wizard starts. Click Next.

2. Select the disks you want to include as part of a striped volume. The wizard automatically selects the first free disk as the first in the striped volume. You can select the remaining disk(s) from the left column and add them to the right column for the set. When you are done adding disks, click Next.

 note

Notice that the wizard automatically sets the size for all selected disks to the largest amount of free space that is equally available on each disk.

3. You are prompted to assign a drive letter or drive path for the new striped set. Choose from the following three options:

- **Assign the Following Drive Letter**—This option assigns your set one drive letter, as with any normal drive. Selecting this option is the most common method of mounting a striped set, and it suffices for most purposes.

- **Mount in the Following Empty NTFS Folder**—By mounting a striped set to a folder, you are effectively creating a mount point within another disk. The mount point isn't actually on another disk, in the physical sense. The folder you use just has the amount of storage equal to the size of your striped set. This approach is more closely related to the UNIX approach, in which the actual drive letter is not used but the folder is referred to as the mount point. (Mount points were discussed earlier in this chapter.)

- **Do Not Assign a Drive Letter or Drive Path**—This option creates the striped set and leaves it for you to allocate later, using either of the two methods mentioned previously.

4. Click Next.

5. Select the volume format options and click Next.

6. When you are presented with a summary of the actions to be performed by the wizard, click the Finish button so your new striped volume will be created and mounted under the path you chose in step 3.

 note

In Windows Explorer, notice that the icon for the folder mount point shows up as a hard disk. This icon appears simply so that you can differentiate between a mounted folder and a plain folder.

RAID and Dynamic Disk Information Storage

When a basic disk is made a member of a mirror, stripe, or RAID set, it's marked (or "signed") with a tiny, hidden partition at the end of the disk drive. This partition tells Windows that the disk is a member of a fault-tolerant disk set. The information about the configuration itself—for example, whether a given disk is the primary or secondary disk in a mirror set—is stored in the Registry. If you think about it, you can see that this is not a great place to store this kind of information: If a disk is damaged, Windows might not be capable of reading the Registry to find the configuration information. That's why you were always exhorted to update your Emergency Boot Disks when you made changes in the old Windows NT Disk Management; the disk configuration was stored on the emergency disks, too.

For dynamic disks, Windows creates a 4MB partition at the end of each disk drive in which it stores all the configuration information for all the dynamic drives in your computer. This redundant information helps Windows reconstruct a picture of the whole system if any drives are damaged or replaced, and it's another good reason to use dynamic disks over basic ones when you're building a Windows 7 system.

Creating and Attaching VHDs

New to Windows 7 is the capability to create and attach (or mount) virtual hard disks (VHDs) and treat them like a removable disk without the need to use virtualization software such as Microsoft Virtual Server or Virtual PC. A VHD is a type of file that contains everything a physical drive offers—file system, structure, and so on. You can load nearly any type of operating system into a virtual disk, and load multiple virtual disks on a single physical host. Virtual disks can help you save money and effort as an alternative to installing multiple hardware drives in a computer. Regardless of the ability to create and use VHDs directly in Windows 7, you can also run Virtual PC if you want.

Creating a VHD

To create a VHD in Windows 7, follow these steps:

1. Open the Disk Management window.

2. Click the Action menu item, and click Create VHD. The Create and Attach Virtual Hard Disk dialog box opens.

3. Click Browse and navigate to the folder that will hold your VHD file.

4. Enter a name for the VHD in the File Name text box, and then click Save.

5. You can control the size of the VHD by entering a maximum size in the Virtual Hard Disk Size box and selecting MB, GB, or TB from the drop-down list.

6. Finally, you can select the size of the virtual disk, either fixed (default) or dynamically expanding (see Figure 24.5). A fixed size VHD file doesn't increase or decrease in size regardless of the data it holds. A dynamically expanding VHD file starts small and grows as the amount of the data it holds increases, but only to the maximum specified size.

7. When you're finished, click OK. Your VHD file is created.

Figure 24.5
Creating a new VHD file from the Disk Management tool in Windows 7.

To initialize your new VHD, follow these steps:

1. Right-click the new unallocated VHD disk number (on the left) in the Disk Management utility and select Initialize Disk.

2. In the Initialize Disk dialog box, select a partition style—MBR (Master Boot Record) or GPT (GUID Partition Table). Use the GPT partition style if your disk is larger than 2TB or is on an Itanium-based computer, but be aware that this partition might not work with all previous Windows versions.

3. Click OK.

4. To create a volume, right-click the new unallocated disk (with the hatched background) in Disk Management and select New Simple Volume.

5. The New Simple Volume Wizard starts and walks you through volume creation, including the selection of the file system (NTFS or FAT32). When you're finished, the new VHD is attached and ready for use.

Attaching an Existing VHD

To attach an existing VHD, such as a demo VHD file you download from the Microsoft Download Center, follow these steps:

1. Select Action, Attach VHD. The Attach Virtual Hard Disk dialog box prompts you for the location of the VHD file.

2. Locate the file and highlight it.

3. Click Open, and then click OK.

For basic information about virtual machine technology and Windows 7, refer to the "Taking the Virtual Machine Approach" section in Chapter 2. For details about working with VHDs in Windows 7, read the "Frequently Asked Questions: Virtual Hard Disks in Windows 7" TechNet article at http://technet.microsoft.com/en-us/library/dd440865(WS.10).aspx.

Convert from FAT to NTFS

Aside from managing drive volumes in the Disk Management utility, you can also change a partition's file system using a built-in Windows 7 tool. *Convert* is a command-line program that converts an existing FAT16 or FAT32 partition to NTFS.

The command-line syntax for the Convert program is as follows:

```
CONVERT volume /FS:NTFS [/V]
```

 caution

This conversion process is a one-way street. The only way to revert an NTFS partition back to a FAT partition with the native tools is to reformat the drive. To revert and not lose your data, you have to use a program such as PartitionMagic (from Symantec; www.symantec.com) or Partition Commander Professional 10 (www.avanquest.com).

The arguments are as follows:

`volume`	Specifies the drive letter (followed by a colon), mount point, or volume name
`/FS:NTFS`	Specifies that the volume should be converted to NTFS
`/V`	Specifies that Convert should be run in Verbose mode

Considering the work the Convert program has to do, it's surprisingly fast, even on a well-populated disk.

Windows 7 Disk Maintenance Tools

As you've learned in previous sections, the Disk Management utility provides all the essential tools for creating, sizing, converting, and deleting drives and partitions. There are, however, other disk maintenance tools in Windows 7 that help you keep disks clean and healthy. We cover many of the most frequently used tools of this type throughout this section.

You'll find that several disk maintenance tools are available through a drive's Properties dialog box. To reach the dialog box, right-click a drive in the Computer window and select Properties. Figure 24.6 shows the properties for both an NTFS drive and a FAT drive. Notice the difference in the number of tabs—NTFS has more options because of its support for security and quota management.

Figure 24.6
Properties tabs for NTFS and FAT volumes.

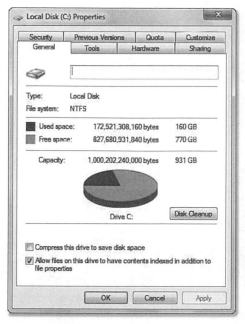
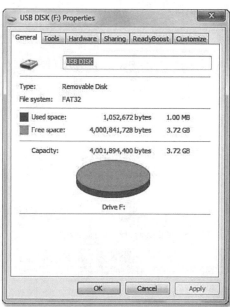

The following sections explain how to use many of the disk maintenance tools included in Windows 7.

Disk Cleanup

In the course of daily use, Windows 7 generates thousands of temporary files to aid in system operation. These files are critical to the operation of the programs that use them. However, as most people are well aware, temporary files have a habit of being much more persistent than their name implies. And over the course of time, these files add up and consume large amounts of valuable disk space. The Disk Cleanup utility provides you with a safe and reliable way to delete these temporary files from all their various hiding spots and thus free up disk space on your hard drive.

To access this utility, do the following:

1. Start Disk Cleanup from the General tab of a drive's Properties dialog box; from the Accessories, System Tools folder; or from the Performance Information and Tools applet in Control Panel, among other methods.

2. Specify which drive you want to clean up (if you have more than one drive installed). Disk Cleanup calculates your disk space, searching for files that can be safely deleted or compressed. The details of this analysis are then displayed in a dialog box similar to the one shown in Figure 24.7.

Figure 24.7
A Disk Cleanup analysis report.

3. If you agree with the items Disk Cleanup has chosen for deletion, click Clean Up System Files.

Understanding Disk Cleanup Options

Near the top of the Disk Cleanup dialog box is the total amount of disk space you can free on this drive by accepting the selected recommendations listed shortly. You can exclude or include file groups from the cleanup process by removing or placing a check mark in front of the types listed. When you select an entry, you see a description of which files that group contains and what their purpose is. By selecting a group and then clicking the View Files button, you can see in the resulting folder window exactly which files are slated for death. Use this option if you have any doubts about a group of files, where they reside, or what they do.

The following file groupings might be listed:

- **Downloaded Program Files**—These files are ActiveX controls and Java applets used by web pages you have visited. If you delete them, they will be reloaded the next time you visit the pages.

- **Temporary Internet Files**—This one is a biggie. Every time you access a web page, your browser stores or caches the various elements of that page on the hard disk. When you revisit a page, any elements that have not changed since your last visit are reloaded from the hard disk instead of the site itself, to speed the rendering process. Deleting these temporary Internet files frees the largest amount of disk space of any of the group lists. However, if you use a modem to access the Internet, you will notice longer rendering times the next time you return to one of your favorite sites.

- **Offline Webpages**—These files are web pages you've visited that are stored on your PC so you can access them when you're not online. Deleting offline web pages doesn't affect your personalized settings for web pages.

 note

Agreeing to delete temporary Internet files does not delete your *cookies* (personalized settings for websites), so don't worry about needing to re-enter user ID information or other such information for sites you frequently visit. Cookies and temporary Internet files are stored by default in *x:*\Users\ *<username>*\AppData\Local\ Microsoft\Windows\Temporary Internet Files (where *x:* is the volume the system is installed on).

If you're concerned about web-surfing privacy, including electronic commerce and banking or confidential business matters, you should delete temporary Internet files frequently.

- **Recycle Bin**—Clearing this folder is the same as manually clearing your Recycle Bin. It is a good idea to have a quick look at the files stored there before choosing this option. Select this option and click the View Files button under the group description; a folder window then opens, listing the contents.

- **Temporary Files**—Similar to cached web pages, when you connect to a network location and access a read-only file, a temporary copy is sometimes stored on your hard drive. Clearing these temporary copies does not erase the files you explicitly marked as available for offline use, so this is a safe choice.

- **Offline Files**—If you use the Windows 7 Sync Center (see Chapter 35, "Hitting the Road"), selected files and folders from a network connection are stored locally for access while you are disconnected. Do not delete these files unless you're sure you can work without the local copies. You'll lose any changes you made to offline files if you delete them here, so don't make this choice without synchronizing first.

- **Thumbnails**—Thumbnails are generated automatically by Windows 7 for picture, video, and document files. Deleting thumbnails forces Windows 7 to re-create thumbnails when you open a folder.

- **Per User Archived Windows Error Reporting**—Windows Error Reports are used when reporting errors and checking for solutions.

After running Disk Cleanup initially, a tab named More Options appears in the Disk Cleanup dialog box. The Programs and Features Clean Up button opens the Uninstall or Change a Program window, so you can uninstall programs you no longer use.

You can use the System Restore Clean Up button to delete all but the most recent restore points. This might free up a significant amount of drive space, but it will eliminate your capability to roll back to previous states of the system, and it also eliminates file shadow copies and older system images that are part of restore points. Use this option only if you are desperate for additional space on your drive, because deleting this information could prevent you from recovering from a system problem later. (See Chapter 25, "Troubleshooting and Repairing Problems," for information on System Restore.)

 tip

Running Disk Cleanup weekly can do wonders to improve a system's performance, especially if you are using a hard disk that has less than 25% of its space available at any given time. The first time you run it, the program might take quite a while to run, but with regular exercise, this program speeds up because the disk stays cleaner. Once a month—after you check the contents of the individual folder groups carefully—you should empty all folders of all temporary files.

Using Internet Explorer's Cache Cleanup

If you would prefer not to use the Disk Cleanup utility, you can choose a second option for clearing out those disk-hogging cached Internet files.

To access it, open Control Panel, Network and Internet, Internet Options. On the General tab of the Internet Properties dialog box, you will find a section titled Browsing History (see Figure 24.8).

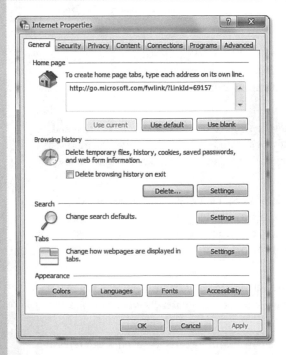

Figure 24.8
The Internet Properties dialog box lets you control most aspects of Internet browsing.

The Delete button opens a Delete Browsing History dialog box (see Figure 24.9). Here you can selectively delete temporary Internet files, cookies, history, form data, passwords, or InPrivate Filtering data. The Preserve Favorites Website Data option at the top of the dialog box helps you ensure your Favorites list is preserved, regardless of other files you choose to delete.

Figure 24.9
The Delete Browsing History dialog box lets you selectively delete categories of files used for Internet browsing.

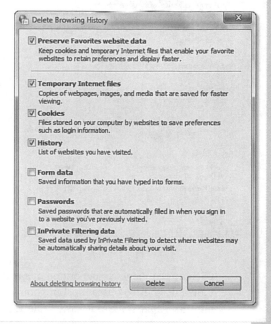

Clicking the Settings button in the Browsing History section of the Internet Properties dialog box opens the Temporary Internet Files and History Settings dialog box (see Figure 24.10). You can configure options for how often cached files are checked against their original counterparts, how much disk space these cached files are allowed to take up, and in which folder they are stored.

When the disk space setting is exceeded, files are removed on a "first in, first out" basis; that is, the oldest files are deleted to create space for newer ones.

Clicking the Move Folder button lets you specify a location where these temporary files will be stored. You can, for example, change this path to a temporary folder or a drive with lots of free space. (The authors of this book usually redirect Internet Explorer to deposit its temporary Internet files into a \temp folder we've created on one of our drives.) If you do a lot of web surfing, you'll want to map this temp location to a fast volume that is not on the same physical hard drive as your main Windows partition.

 tip

Changing the location for the storage of temporary Internet files is especially a good idea if the system is a client on a domain network and roaming profiles are in use. By storing the temporary files outside your profile, it will take less time to log in and log out, plus your profile will consume less space on the network server.

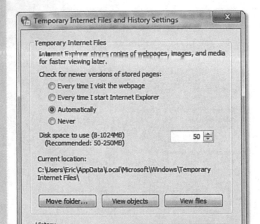

Figure 24.10
The Temporary Internet Files and History Settings dialog box.

Clicking the View Objects button opens the Downloaded Program Files folder, and clicking the View Files button opens the Temporary Internet Files folder. You can also control how many days Internet Explorer saves items in your History folder from this dialog box.

Detecting and Repairing Disk Errors

NTFS was introduced and billed as a "robust and self-healing" file system, as opposed to FAT, which is not. All in all, we have to agree with Microsoft on this one. We have yet to see an NTFS partition go "sour" in any way, shape, or form. We've had NTFS partitions that would not boot and key system files that would not run, but for the most part, these errors were self-inflicted and usually brought on by playing with fire.

The disk repair program in Windows 7's GUI is called Error Checking. These are the command-line versions (stored in the %SystemRoot%\System32 folder):

- chkntfs.exe—Works with NTFS volumes and drives

- chkdsk.exe—Works with FAT/FAT32 partitions and drives

For a description of how each works, just add the normal /? switch or see Windows online help. The available commands enable you to turn automatic checking on and off, and repair a "dirty" (improperly shut down) drive at bootup.

Error Checking reviews the file system for errors and the drive for bad sectors (bad spots). To run the program, do the following:

1. In Computer or Windows Explorer, right-click the drive you want to check.

2. On the context menu, choose Properties.

3. Click the Tools tab.

4. In the Error-Checking section, click Check Now. A dialog box appears, as shown in Figure 24.11.

Figure 24.11
Checking a disk for errors in the file system.

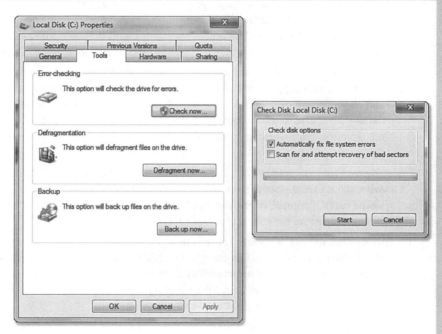

The meaning of the options is as follows:

■ **Automatically Fix File System Errors**—If file directory errors (for example, lost clusters, files without end-of-file markers, and so on) are found, this option specifies whether the program should fix them.

■ **Scan for and Attempt Recovery of Bad Sectors**—This option specifies whether the program should attempt to locate bad sectors, mark them as bad, and recover data from them by writing it in a known, good area of the disk. If you select this option, you do not need to select Automatically Fix File System Errors; Windows fixes any errors on the disk.

 tip

If your volume is formatted as NTFS, Windows automatically logs all file transactions, replaces bad clusters, and stores copies of key information for all files on the NTFS volume.

You can run the error check with neither of the option boxes turned on, and you are not required to close all open files and programs. However, if you check either of the boxes, you are told that Windows can't check the disk while it's in use. You are given the option of deferring the check until the time you restart your system.

Disk Defragmenter

When an OS stores data on a hard disk, it places that information in the first available "hole" it can find that isn't already occupied by another file. However, if the disk already contains several other files, that location might not be large enough for the complete file. When this happens, the OS places as much of the file as it can in the space available and then searches for another open hole for the balance of the file. This process continues until the entire file has been written to disk. Any files that are not written to a contiguous disk location are considered "fragmented."

The problem with fragmentation is that it slows down the rate at which your hard disk can retrieve information and supply it to the requesting program. Hard disks remain largely mechanical devices and are governed by the laws of physics. To access files stored on a disk, the drive must physically move a small arm to the correct location on a spinning platter. These movements are measured in milliseconds, but milliseconds add up, especially when a file is spread over a hundred unique locations.

Fragmentation is not always a bad thing. If an OS had to find a contiguous section of disk space for every file it stored, your system would slow down as your drive filled up. Eventually, your system would reach a point at which the disk still had ample free space, but none of this space would be in contiguous blocks big enough to hold a file.

Disk Defragmenter addresses this fragmentation problem by reorganizing all the files on your hard disk so that they are stored as complete units on a single area of the disk. To do so, it identifies any remaining free areas, moves small files there to open up more space, and uses this newly opened space to consolidate larger files. This shuffling process repeats until all the files are moved around in this manner and the entire disk is defragmented.

In Windows 7, unlike Windows XP, the Disk Defragmenter process is automated. You configure when it takes place, and it does the rest.

Configuring Defrag

The fastest way to open Disk Defragmenter is to click Start, type **disk** in the Search box, and select Disk Defragmenter from the results list. You can also open Disk Defragmenter from All Programs, Accessories, System Tools, Disk Defragmenter. By default, Disk Defragmenter (Figure 24.12) runs on a weekly schedule. Click Configure Schedule to specify a frequency (daily, weekly, monthly), a day of the week, a time, and which disks to defragment if your system has two or more disks. To defragment your hard disk immediately, click Defragment Disk.

Figure 24.12
The Disk Defragmenter window in Windows 7 can schedule a defragmentation session or run the utility immediately.

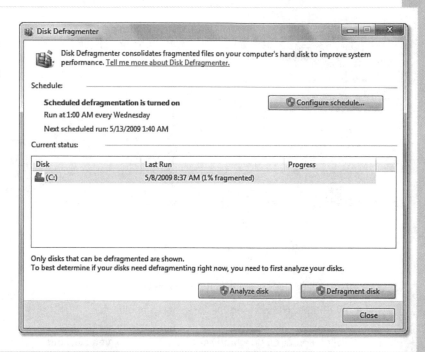

Compression: How It Works, How to Use It

Windows 7 ships with built-in provisions for file compression that is implemented via NTFS. File compression works by encoding data to take up less storage space. Digital data is compressed by finding repeatable patterns of binary 0s and 1s. The more patterns found, the more the data can be compressed. Text can generally be compressed to approximately 40% of its original size and graphics files from 20% to 90%. Some files (namely EXE files) compress very little because of the lack of repeating data patterns within the program. The amount of compression depends entirely on the type of file and compression algorithm used.

Compressing a file or folder in Windows is a simple process:

1. Open Windows Explorer and select the file or folder you want to compress.

2. Right-click and select Properties from the context menu.

3. Click the Advanced button at the bottom of the Properties dialog box.

4. In the Advanced Attributes dialog box that appears, check the Compress Contents to Save Disk Space box (refer to Figure 24.13).

5. Click OK, and you are prompted to choose whether you want to compress files and folders (if you're compressing a folder) recursively. Doing so is generally desirable and a safe bet.

Figure 24.13
Compressing a folder with Windows 7

Two caveats are in order with compression:

- A file or folder can be compressed or encrypted, but not both. These options are mutually exclusive.

- By default, compressed files are shown in blue and encrypted files are shown in green. If you choose Control Panel, Folder Options and select the View tab, you can find an option to display compressed and encrypted files or folders in an alternate color.

➡ *To learn more about file encryption on NTFS volumes, see Chapter 31, "Protecting Your Data from Loss and Theft."*

Use compression only when expressly needed. Compression causes significant performance reduction if a sizeable number of commonly accessed files are compressed, due to the CPU processing required to decompress them for use.

Third-Party Management Tools

Table 24.1 provides a list of tools that you should not be without if you are serious about hard disk tweaking, backup, and recovery. By searching on the Web, you can easily find any of these popular programs. To determine which versions of a particular tool are compatible with Windows 7, contact the software vendor.

 caution

When using compression, keep in mind some disk space requirements. If you try to compress a volume that's running extremely low on free space, you might see this error message:

```
Compression Error
File Manager/Explorer cannot
change compress attributes for:
"path\filename"
```

This error message indicates that the system needs additional free space to perform compression. The system is not designed to manipulate the data in place on the disk. Additional space is needed to buffer the user data and to possibly hold additional file system metadata. The amount of additional free space required depends on the cluster size, file size, and available space.

Table 24.1   Third-Party Disk Management Tools

Type of Program	Vendor	Product Name
Data Recovery	Ontrack	EasyRecovery DataRecovery
	Iolo	Search and Recover
	Diskeeper	Undelete
Disk Management	Acronis	Acronis Disk Director Suite 10
	Symantec	PartitionMagic
	Avanquest Software	Partition Commander
Professional Compression (Zip file)	ConeXware	PowerArchiver
	WinZip International LLC	WinZip
	PKWare	PKZip for Windows
	FileStream, Inc.	TurboZIP
	Info-Zip	Info-Zip
	Win.rar GmbH	WinRAR

Hard Disk Troubleshooting

If you work with computers long enough, you will face some form of hard disk problem. It's not a matter of *if*; it's a matter of *when*. The laws of statistics apply to everyone and everything—and that includes hard drives. In the following sections, when I speak of hard drive problems, I'm not referring to a software program that is acting petulantly or a DLL that has been overwritten by a poorly designed installation routine. I'm talking about the inability to access a critical file, a hard drive that will not boot, or one of those cryptic "Fatal Error—Cannot access hard disk" messages that cause the blood to drain from the face of even the hardiest administrator.

These sections are not meant to be comprehensive—full books have been written on solving hardware problems, and thousands of individual chapters have been written about hard drives and the multitude of problems they can exhibit. These sections will give you some tried-and-true starting points if your hard drive starts to give you grief.

Hard drive problems range from file system structures that have been twisted out of shape to catastrophic, dead-in-the-water hard drive failures. And as any seasoned administrator will tell you, the catastrophic failures are the easy ones to diagnose and fix. More often than not, the inconsistent "What the heck?" problems are the real "head-scratchers."

To keep it simple, let's begin with the most important factor in troubleshooting problems of all shapes and sizes—be it a car that will not start or a computer that will not boot. And that is....

Take the Mental Approach First

I come from a long line of tradesmen who made a living getting their hands dirty and solving mechanical problems. As a writer and computer consultant, I rarely get my hands dirty anymore, but I have discovered that the principles of problem solving that I learned when I was young are the same across all fields. You need to be methodical, and if you are going to make assumptions, they had better be good ones; otherwise, you just might steer yourself down the wrong garden path.

The very first step to take when you have a disk access problem is to stop, sit down, and think. Although this advice might seem obvious, it is seldom realized in practice. People experience what they conclude is a hard drive problem, open their case, and start ripping out components when, in fact, they have a file system problem that could have been easily resolved by running Error Checking on their drive. Similarly, others start reinstalling OSs when the problem is not software, but a failing CMOS battery or a loose cable that is causing the motherboard to lose sight of the hard drive.

None of this exposition is meant to imply that I'm smarter or better at diagnosing problems than the next guy, and in the end, I might come to the same conclusion as the person who leapt in and started ripping his case apart. What separates us, in my humble opinion, is that the steps I use to solve a problem today will apply equally well to a completely different problem I encounter a week from now.

So when you have a hard drive problem—or what you think is a hard drive problem—before you pick up a DVD or a screwdriver, get yourself a cup of coffee and take a few minutes to get a clear picture of the nature of the problem in front of you. The following are some questions you might want to ask yourself:

- When did the problem start?

- What was I doing when I first noticed the problem?

- Is the problem consistent? If so, how? If not, what is missing from the puzzle?

This last point bears some elaboration. Computers, as a whole, are extraordinarily consistent devices. Input goes in here; output comes out over there. In the case of hard drives, you lay out structures on them, and the OS uses these structures to tell programs where their data is located. When you have inconsistencies, one of two forces is at work:

- You're not seeing or you're overlooking something.

- You could have more than one problem on your hands.

The key to this forced reflection is to have a "plan" before you react. And the cornerstone of that plan must be to do no further harm, and to figure out what the problem is without complicating matters further.

After you've pondered and had a cup of coffee, the next highly recommended tools to pick up are a notepad and a pencil. Begin by jotting down some notes on what happened, what you think the problem is, and what might be a good course of action to solve that problem. Use your notepad to reason out the problem; more often than not, eliminating a piece of flawed logic with an eraser is easier than restoring all the programs to your hard drive.

Problems and Solutions

Hard drive problems fall into two general categories:

- Hardware
- File structure

Hardware related problems involve the hard drive itself, cabling, power, connections, or the motherboard.

File structure problems involve the tracks and partitions on the hard disk, the boot records, or the files the OS uses to initialize itself.

If you power up your computer and the BIOS cannot find the attached hard drive, chances are, you have a hardware problem. On the other hand, if the BIOS finds and recognizes your hard drive but fails to boot, you likely have a file structure problem. Note the "chances are" and "likely" qualifiers in these sentences. As you read through the following scenarios, bear in mind the complications that can be brought on by compounded problems. In other words, file structure problems and hardware problems can sometimes overlap. For example, a damaged master boot record (MBR) might be the result of a failing hard drive; repairing the MBR might fix a consequence of the problem, but not the problem itself.

System Starts but Cannot Find the Hard Drive

If the computer fires up (the BIOS information appears and the floppy drive is accessed, but nothing more), you have some sleuthing to do. Follow these steps:

1. Turn off the computer, open it, and check the cables. Are the power and data cables attached to the drive? On SATA drives, be sure the SATA data and power cables are firmly attached to the drive. First-generation SATA drives don't use locking mechanisms on these cables, and they can be easily removed. If you recently installed a new piece of hardware or were mucking around inside your computer case, it's very possible that you unintentionally jiggled a connection loose. If you use an ATA/IDE drive, be sure pin 1 (marked as a red or speckled stripe on the edge of the cable) is lined up with pin 1 on the hard disk and motherboard. If you use only 80-wire cables, the cable is keyed, so it can't be installed wrong. However, older, 40-wire cables (often used on CD and DVD drives) are not always keyed.

2. Check the settings on the drive to be sure they are correct. If you have a SCSI drive, check the ID number and termination, per the instruction manual for the drive. If you have an ATA/IDE drive, check the master/slave settings and channel assignment. If you have two devices on the same ATA/IDE channel, both set to master or both set to slave, there will be a conflict. You can have only one master and one slave per ATA/IDE channel. You typically change the setting by using a little jumper block on the back of the hard drive, next to the data and power connectors (ditto for ATA/IDE-based DVD drives). Many recent systems use the CSEL or Cable Select setting for both drives. When used with an 80-wire 40-pin cable, the blue end of the cable plugs into the motherboard, the drive on the middle of the cable (gray connector) is slave, and the drive on the far end of the cable (black connector) is master. Note that many Western Digital hard disks do not use a jumper block if they are the only drive on the cable.

3. Check the BIOS settings by pressing the appropriate key during POST (Power-On Self Test) and having the computer autodetect the drive type. Be sure the drive is listed and recognized. If you have just upgraded to SATA hard disks, be sure the SATA host adapters on the motherboard are enabled in the system BIOS. On many systems, SATA functions are disabled by default. If you use an SATA host adapter card, or if the SATA ports on your motherboard use a third-party chip rather than being controlled by the motherboard chipset, you will need to install the appropriate third-party driver file before you can use SATA drives.

 tip

Most modern PCs and BIOSs autodetect the hard drive that's connected to the data cable after the drive gets power. You no longer need to enter all the explicit information about the drive, such as the number of heads, the sectors, the landing zone, and so on. Just set the BIOS to Autodetect.

Hard Drive Initializes but Will Not Boot

Windows 7 makes it easier than ever to repair a system that will not start or will not load Windows 7. These features are useful if some of your system files become corrupt or are accidentally erased, or if you have installed software or device drivers that cause your system to not work properly. However, these features are used more to restore a system with a damaged Registry or destroyed system files than to resolve hard drive–specific problems. If you've already tried the actions listed in this section, to no avail, flip over to Chapter 25 for details on numerous other recovery techniques that might be of benefit to you. Be sure to check out Startup Repair, Safe Mode (in the "Boot Options" section), and System Restore.

Editing the Boot Sequence

Windows 7 doesn't use the `boot.ini` file familiar from Windows NT, Windows 2000, and Windows XP installations. Instead, Windows 7 uses the method of determining boot settings known as a boot configuration database (BCD) store. BCD is compatible with both traditional BIOS firmware and the new Extensible Firmware Interface (EFI). EFI firmware will eventually replace BIOS firmware in new systems and also supports dual-boot installations with older Windows versions. You can make simple changes to the boot sequence (such as specifying whether Windows 7 or an older version of Windows is the default OS) with the System Configuration tool MSConfig (see Chapter 22 for details). However, you can also use the command-line `bcdedit` tool to edit the boot configuration, with Administrator permissions. To learn more about `bcdedit`, see the "Editing Windows 7 Boot Menu Entries" section in Chapter 2. You should also read the article "Boot Configuration Data Editor Frequently Asked Questions," available from http://technet. microsoft.com/en-us/library/cc721886(WS.10).aspx.

TROUBLESHOOTING AND REPAIRING PROBLEMS

Troubleshooting 101

Inevitably, the only time you'll ever have a problem with your computer system is the exact moment when it's not convenient—or, more specifically, the moment when any delay would be severely detrimental to your work or life schedule. Fortunately, the designers of Windows 7 have learned from the problems experienced by previous Windows versions, including Windows Vista and Windows XP. Windows 7 is designed to be the most stable version yet *and* the easiest to fix.

In this chapter, we discuss many of the fault-tolerant features of Windows 7, along with specific tools you can employ to resolve problems.

For example, if you're having a problem with a device (look for the yellow triangle with an exclamation point or the down-arrow over the device icon in Device Manager), open its Properties dialog box in Device Manager and follow the suggested solution on the General tab. It might run a troubleshooter, update or reinstall drivers, or start the device.

 tip

Search http://technet.microsoft.com for **Windows 7: Troubleshooting and Support** to get dozens of links. To find help on a specific problem, search on that topic and then follow the links. You can also open the Troubleshooting Control Panel applet or search for **Troubleshooting** in the Help and Support Center. In addition, the Program Compatibility Wizard (described in detail in Chapter 26) helps you resolve problems with programs that don't run properly.

Easy Repair Options at Boot Time

If you cannot start your Windows 7 system, don't panic. Windows 7 makes the startup repair process easy and transparent to the user—a big change from repairing startup problems with Windows XP and previous versions of Windows.

If you cannot start your system from the hard disk, insert your Windows 7 installation media and use it as a boot device. After selecting the language, time and currency formats, and the keyboard-input method on the opening screen, click Next. On the following screen, select Repair Your Computer. The system searches for recovery options.

The System Recovery Options screen appears. It should find your Windows installation, which it identifies by partition size and drive letter. You're presented with these options:

- Use Recovery Tools that Can Help Fix Problems Starting Windows. Select an Operating System to Repair.

- Restore Your Computer Using a System Image that You Created Earlier.

The first option gives you access to the full set of System Recovery tools; the second option enables you to restore your computer from a system image, if you created one before losing the ability to start Windows. You'll use the first option most of the time when troubleshooting Windows 7 startup problems.

 note

You can also click the Load Drivers button in the System Recovery Options screen to load a hardware driver. You're prompted to insert the installation media for the device and select the driver from the media.

Using System Recovery

Ensure the Use Recovery Tools that Can Help Fix Problems Starting Windows option is selected in the System Recovery Options screen, and that Windows 7 is highlighted in the Operating System column, and click Next. The Choose a Recovery Tool screen appears (see Figure 25.1) with the System Recovery Options menu displayed.

System Recovery tools include these:

- Startup Repair

- System Restore

- System Image Recovery

- Windows Memory Diagnostic

- Command Prompt

Each of these repair options is discussed in this chapter.

 note

You can use the system repair disc maker built into Windows 7, which enables you to create a bootable system disc in case of emergencies and run the repair tools discussed in the following sections. Just go to Backup and Restore in Control Panel and click Create a System Repair Disc in the Tasks list.

If you can't access the system repair disc maker and are using a preinstalled edition of Windows 7, ask your hardware vendor how to access the Repair Your Computer feature. A vendor might include a special boot disc with a system or provide you with instructions on how to make a boot disc that contains the files necessary to repair your installation.

Figure 25.1
The Choose a Recovery Tool screen provides you with a variety of repair options if your system cannot start normally.

Startup Repair

Typically, the easiest repair to try when you have a system that won't boot is the Startup Repair option, shown at the top of the System Recovery Options menu in Figure 25.1. When you select Startup Repair, Windows performs a series of tests to determine the problem and then performs repairs.

The resulting Startup Repair screen displays two links. If you are curious about what Windows did, click the View Diagnostic and Repair Details link to open the Startup Repair dialog box. Scroll through the dialog box to satisfy yourself with the solution. In this example (see Figure 25.2), OS files were missing and the partition table was repaired. Click Close to return to the

 note

Windows 7 can perform several rounds of startup repairs before it gives up. So, if you restart your system after performing a startup repair and you still have problems, rerun the Startup Repair procedure to fix additional problems. Repeat until your system starts properly, or until Windows 7 is unable to perform additional repairs. See other portions of this chapter for additional suggestions.

main Startup Repair screen. Click the View Advanced Options for System Recovery and Support link to return to the System Recovery Options menu, or click Finish to restart your system. Don't boot from the DVD; your system should start up normally.

Figure 25.2
Startup Repair found the problem (missing OS files) and repaired it, enabling the system to start normally.

Startup Repair

Diagnosis and repair details:

Root cause found:

No OS files found on disk.

Repair action: Partition table repair
Result: Completed successfully. Error code = 0x0
Time taken = 4640 ms

Close

System Restore

System Restore enables you to restore the computer to a previously saved state, so you can "roll back" your computer to the way it was working before your cat jumped on the keyboard, or before you installed that stupid program or device driver that crashed your system. Here's how it works.

Performing a system restore does not affect personal files, such as documents, Internet favorites, or email. It simply reverses system-configuration changes and removes installed files to return the system to a stored state. System Restore automatically monitors your system for changes. Periodically, easily identifiable restoration points are created. Plus, you can create your own restoration points manually.

Unlike Windows XP, which requires you to start the system in Safe Mode before you can run System Restore, Windows 7 offers System Restore on its System Recovery Options menu (refer to Figure 25.2).

Configuring System Restore

Before you can use can use the System Restore option, you need to have configured System Restore and saved at least one restore point. System Restore has two control interfaces. One is the System Protection tab of the System Properties dialog box. Open it by clicking the System Protection task in the Tasks list of the System applet in the Control Panel. (It's protected by User Account Control.) The other control interface is the System Restore utility itself, accessed through Start, All Programs, Accessories, System Tools, System Restore.

System Restore is enabled or disabled for all drives in the computer via the System Protection tab (see Figure 25.3) of the System Properties dialog box. It is enabled by default for the system drive.

Click the Configure button to open the System Protection dialog box for the selected hard disk. In the Restore Settings section, the Restore System Settings and Previous Versions of Files option is selected by default if System Protection is currently enabled. You can change the default to Only Restore Previous Versions of Files. This configuration disables System Restore, enabling you to only use the Shadow Copy function of Windows 7 to restore single documents to a previous version. The Turn Off System Protection option deletes all restore points for that disk. You cannot restore the disk until you turn on System Protection again and create at least one restore point for that disk.

note

Each time you modify and save a document such as in Microsoft Word, the Volume Shadow Copy Service (VSS) saves a copy of the previous version. This is referred to as a shadow copy. You can restore previous versions by right-clicking a document in Windows Explorer, selecting Properties, and clicking the Previous Versions tab. However, you may have to first enable VSS through the Services (services.msc) utility.

tip

Unless you're very low on hard disk space or have another reason to disable System Protection, leave the Restore System Settings and Previous Versions of Files default option selected.

Figure 25.3
The System Protection tab of the System
Properties dialog box in Windows 7.

System Restore is enabled by default on the system drive.

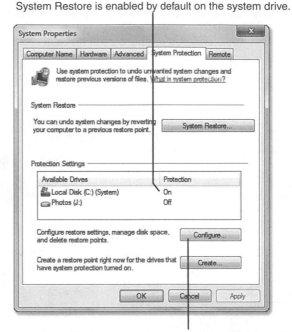

To enable System Restore on the selected disk, click Configure.

The System Restore drive configuration in Windows 7 permits you to adjust how much of the hard disk (or partition) can be used for System Restore files. This option is also available in Windows XP but not in Windows Vista. Although the slider bar in the Disk Space Usage section of the System Protection dialog box allows you to use the entire disk capacity, by default System Restore uses up to 5% of a disk's capacity or a maximum of 10GB on hard disks over 64GB, and uses a maximum of 3% of disk space on drives or partitions less than 64GB in size. We can only speculate that the slider enables allocating so much file space for Volume Shadow Copy storage to permit users to override defaults on drives where there's lots of file volatility and they wish to keep many previous versions, or where shadow copies themselves are quite large.

You can also delete all restore points for the selected hard disk from within the System Protection dialog box by clicking the Delete button. The number of restore points retained by System Restore depends on the amount of drive space allocated to System Restore, as well as the rate and significance of changes to the system.

Creating Restore Points

Windows 7 creates restore points automatically whenever any one of several specific events occurs:

- When a program is installed using InstallShield or Windows Installer
- Automatic updates via Windows Update

- Any restore operation

- Every seven days if no other restore points were created within that time period

As Figure 25.4 shows, these factors can result in a lot of restore points being created in a short amount of time.

Choose a restore point from this list.

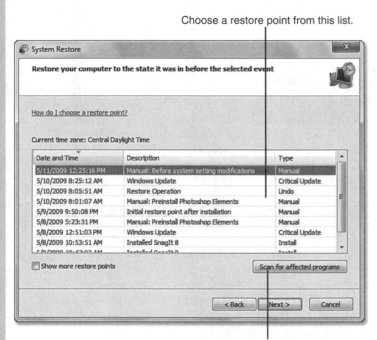

Figure 25.4
Various types of restore points on a typical system.

Click here to see what might be affected
if you use the selected restore point.

Keep in mind that not all program installations use InstallShield or Windows Installer. Thus, you should always manually create a restore point before you install applications.

To manually create a restore point, open the System Protection tab in the Systems Properties dialog box and click Create (refer to Figure 25.3). Enter a descriptive name for the restore point and click Create. The date and time are added automatically. A progress bar appears while the restore is being created; click Close when prompted to complete the process.

Creating a restore point at any restore operation enables you to reverse a restoration. Thus, if after a successful restoration you are not pleased with the outcome, you can reverse the restoration. The system automatically removes any failed or incomplete restoration operations.

System Restore does not replace the uninstallation process for removing an application. System Restore monitors and protects only against changes to the OS; it does not track the addition of new files to the system. Use the Programs and Features applet in Control Panel or a vendor-provided uninstall routine to remove applications.

Restoring Your System to an Earlier Time

You can restore your system to an earlier time by running System Restore from the System Recovery Options menu when you boot from the Windows 7 DVD (see Figure 25.1, earlier in this chapter) or by running System Restore from the System Protection tab or the System Tools menu. From the opening menu, click Next to continue.

Select a restore point from the list in the System Restore window (refer to Figure 25.4). By default, only the last 5 days' worth of restore points are listed. To select an older restore point, click the Show More Restore Points check box. To view a list of all program, driver, and patch changes that might be affected when returning to a certain restore point, click the Scan for Affected Programs button. Click Close to return to the list of restore points. After selecting a restore point, click Next to continue.

If you have more than one drive with System Restore enabled, select which drive(s) to restore. The system drive is always selected. Click Next to continue, if applicable, and then click Finish. Click Yes to confirm that you want to restore your system. A progress bar appears while System Restore prepares your system, and then your system restarts.

At the end of the process, a dialog box appears, indicating that your system has been restored to the date and time of the restore point you selected.

System Image Recovery

System Image Recovery is the counterpart to the Create a System Image function in Windows 7 (described in Chapter 31, "Protecting Your Data from Loss and Theft"). After making an image backup of your system, System Image Recovery enables you to perform a "bare metal" restoration from the System Recovery Options menu.

To restore your system from an image, start your system from the Windows 7 DVD. If you're restoring from an external hard disk that contains your system image, ensure it is connected. (If you backed up to DVD, have the media ready.) In the initial screen, select the language, time and currency formats, and the keyboard-input method, and then click Next. In the next screen, click Repair Your Computer. In the System Recovery Options screen, select the Restore Your Computer Using a System Image that You Created Earlier option, and click Next.

The Select a System Image Backup screen appears, as shown in Figure 25.5. By default, the most current image backup is listed. To restore from this backup, click Next. To choose an earlier backup, select the Select a System Image option, click Next, and then select it from the list.

 caution

When we say "bare metal," we mean it. All your data, files, and programs installed since the drive was imaged—everything—ends up in the big bit bucket in the sky. Be sure you want to perform a complete system restore before you run the System Image Recovery. And be ready to kiss goodbye everything you placed on your drive after it was imaged.

You'll rest better if you run the built-in Windows Backup and Restore utility (or a good third-party file backup program) regularly in addition to creating a system image. If you do, you can restore your data files after you run System Image Recovery and get back to work.

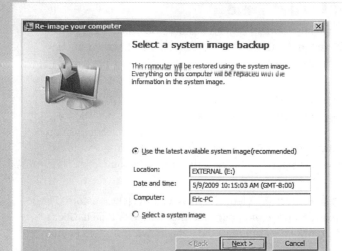

Figure 25.5
Preparing to restore the most recent system image.

The Choose Additional Restore Options screen appears. If you are installing to an unformatted hard disk or to a hard disk that is larger than your original, the Format and Repartition Disks check box shown in Figure 25.6 will be available. Select it and click Next to prepare your hard disk for use. When you're ready to continue the restore operation, click Next to view a summary of the restoration settings. If no changes are necessary, click Finish. The restoration process starts immediately if you are restoring from a hard disk connected to the system. If you are restoring from CD, DVD, or other media, insert the media as requested.

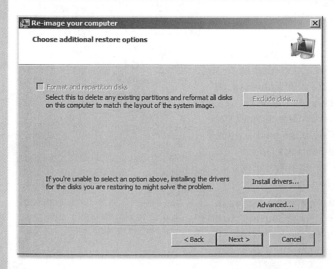

Figure 25.6
Click the check box, if available, to repartition your hard disk to match the layout of the original backup.

When the restoration is finished, the system restarts normally. To get the system back to its most recent configuration, restore file backups made with the Windows 7 Backup and Restore utility or other backup software.

➥ *For complete information about Windows backup and restore options, see Chapter 31, "Protecting Your Data from Loss and Theft."*

Windows Memory Diagnostic

If any recent version of Windows had a motto, it could very well be, "It's the RAM, stupid!" All kidding aside, if your system's memory is hosed, so is Windows. The Windows Memory Diagnostics Tool is designed to help you get help for a sick system.

The Windows Memory Diagnostics Tool can be run from the Administrative Tools window in the Control Panel (see Chapter 22, "Windows Management and Maintenance," for details), from the System Recovery Options menu, or from the Windows Boot Manager. If you run it from the Administrative Tools window, it is protected by UAC, and you can choose to restart your system immediately for testing or to schedule testing the next time you restart your system.

Regardless of how you start it, the Windows Memory Diagnostics Tool (see Figure 25.7) runs before the Windows 7 GUI starts.

 caution

Do not restore to a hard disk that might still have salvageable data, even if your Windows installation no longer boots. Instead, buy a new hard disk or use one that does not contain any needed data, and use it as the restore target.

You can use programs such as Ontrack EasyRecovery DataRecovery on a working system to recover data from your crashed system hard disk, even if its file system is no longer functioning. However, the capability of any program to recover data depends upon the data areas not being overwritten. If you restore your backup over what's left of your original installation, you wipe out at least some of the data that remains.

Figure 25.7
The Windows Memory Diagnostics Tool performing a memory test.

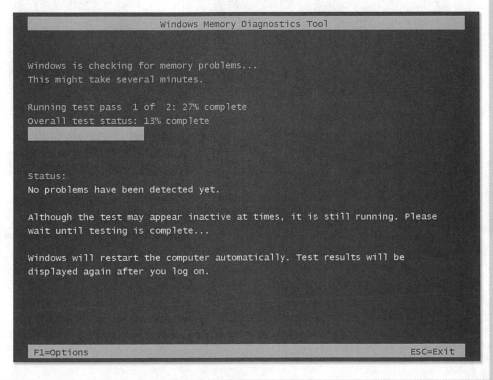

```
                         Windows Memory Diagnostics Tool

Windows is checking for memory problems...
This might take several minutes.

Running test pass  1 of  2: 27% complete
Overall test status: 13% complete


Status:
No problems have been detected yet.

Although the test may appear inactive at times, it is still running. Please
wait until testing is complete...

Windows will restart the computer automatically. Test results will be
displayed again after you log on.




F1=Options                                                         ESC=Exit
```

To adjust the number of test passes (the default is two), to specify how thorough a test to perform, or to configure other options, press the F1 key to display the Options dialog box, shown in Figure 25.8. You can configure three items:

- **Test Mix**—Basic (quick test, usually finished in about 5 minutes), Standard (adds tests to Basic), or Extended (adds tests to Standard)

- **Cache**—Default (some test with cache on, some with cache off; doesn't change settings), On (turns on memory cache for all tests), Off (disables memory cache for all tests)

- **Pass Count**—0–99 (select 0 for infinite test passes; press Esc to cancel)

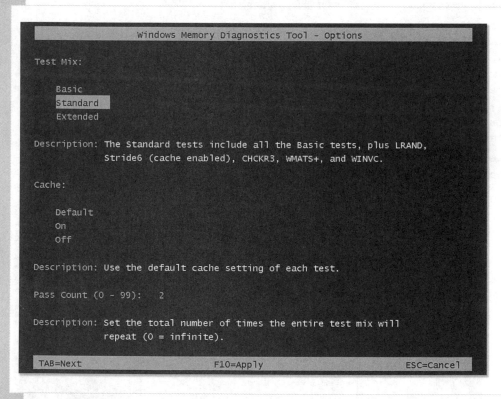

Figure 25.8
The Windows Memory Diagnostics Tool – Options screen.

Press Tab to move between menu items, press F10 to apply changes, or press Esc to cancel any changes and begin running the tests. In the test progress screen, pressing Esc stops the tests and restarts the system.

Command Prompt

The Command Prompt option in the Choose a Recovery Tool screen (refer to Figure 25.1) opens a command-prompt interface with all the power of the command prompt environment, instead of the limited features of the Recovery Console used in Windows XP. You can run disk management, copy, delete, and other commands, just as you would from within the Windows 7 GUI. For more information about command-prompt utilities, see Chapter 29, "Command-Line and Automation Tools."

Using Regedit to Repair a System That Won't Start

Another handy Startup Repair feature in Windows 7 is the capability to run the Registry editor (Regedit) from the Command Prompt window. If you cannot start your system because of driver or service problems or other Registry-related issues, you can use Regedit to work on your system and repair problems.

To start Regedit from the Choose a Recovery Tool screen in the System Recovery Options dialog box (refer to Figure 25.1), click Command Prompt. When the command prompt window opens, type **regedit** and press Enter.

Before making any changes with Regedit, export the current Registry with File, Export so that you have a backup copy, in case of problems. By default, Export saves only the current branch. To export the entire Registry, select All in the lower-left corner of the Export Registry File dialog box. Provide a name for the exported Registry, such as the computer name and current date, and click Save. You can use USB flash memory drives and other types of storage to save the exported Registry. However, you should not save it to the hard disk, especially if you suspect that you might need to perform data recovery operations on it later. (You don't want to overwrite any recoverable data.)

Sometimes, services running at startup crash, preventing a system from starting. Here's how to use Regedit to disable these services:

1. Select the key HKEY_LOCAL_MACHINE.

2. Browse into the System key, and then the CurrentControlSet subkey if it's displayed.

caution

If you need help running Regedit, see Chapter 28, "Editing the Registry." Don't tinker with the Registry unless you know what you're doing. And if you do tinker with it, make a backup first. Improper editing of the Registry can result in a dead computer.

3. Browse into the services key and look for the likely offending service. Most service keys have a value named Start, with one of the following values:

   - 0   Boot driver loaded by Ntldr (Boot)

   - 1   Driver loaded at kernel initialization by Windows 7 (System)

   - 2   Driver loaded at system startup by Session Manager or Service Controller (Auto Load)

   - 3   Driver or service loaded manually from Services, Control Panel, and so on (Load on Demand)

   - 4   Driver or service that is not running or started (Disabled)

Services with a Start value of 0 or 1 are used to boot Windows, and you shouldn't touch them. Services with a Start value of 2 start about the same time as the Login dialog box appears in Windows. If your Windows system boots and then promptly crashes without your help, try setting the Start value of any suspected service(s) to 3 or 4. Be sure to write down the names of the services and their original Start values before you change anything.

4. Exit Regedit.

5. Type **exit** and press Enter to close the Command Prompt window.

6. Remove the Windows 7 DVD and click Restart to restart your system normally.

7. If your system restarts correctly, you're finished!

You might need to repeat this process a few times, disabling a different service or two each time. In some previous versions of Windows, this procedure required installing a parallel copy of Windows and some loading of the old installation's Registry into the new system's Registry editor, but thanks to the integration of Regedit into the souped-up Command Prompt in the System Recovery Options menu, that's not necessary in Windows 7.

Boot Options

If you are able to start your system but it doesn't run properly, Windows 7 offers several alternate boot methods that can be used to bypass a problem or boot into a reduced environment so that you can solve the problem. For example, if you've recently installed a new device driver that caused a serious system failure (you can't complete the boot process), you can use a boot option to boot without that driver. (This is called the "Last Known Good Configuration," to be exact.)

The boot options of Windows 7 are accessed during the early stages of system startup. If you have more than one OS on your system, the Windows Boot Manager displays; you have until the counter reaches zero to press F8. If you have only Windows 7 on your computer, you'll see a message about pressing F8 after the computer's own Power-On Self Test and the display of the graphical booting screen. You have only a few seconds, so keep your finger over the F8 button and press it when the message appears.

Pressing F8 at the correct moment reveals the Advanced Boot Options menu, which contains several boot options, listed in Table 25.1.

 tip

If you can boot but a device isn't working after you just installed a new driver, see Chapter 27, "Installing and Replacing Hardware."

 note

Some systems and motherboards include a boot menu that uses the F8 key to select a boot drive. If your system includes this feature, check the documentation to determine which keys to press to display the Windows Boot Manager. For example, some motherboards require that you press F11, or F6 and then F8, to display the Windows Boot Manager. You can also try pressing the space-bar after the BIOS loads to access the Windows Boot Manager.

Table 25.1   Advanced Boot Options

Option	Description
Repair Your Computer	Runs the Repair Your Computer scans, as described earlier in this chapter.
Safe Mode	Starts Windows 7 using only basic files and drivers (mouse, except serial mouse devices; monitor; keyboard; mass storage; basic video; default system services; and no network connections).
Safe Mode with Networking	Starts Windows 7 using only basic files and drivers, plus network connections.
Safe Mode with Command Prompt	Starts Windows 7 using only basic files and drivers. After you log on, the command prompt is displayed instead of the Windows desktop.
Enable Boot Logging	Starts Windows 7 while logging all the drivers and services that were loaded (or not loaded) by the system to a file. This file, called ntbtlog.txt, is located in the %windir% directory. Safe Mode, Safe Mode with Networking, and Safe Mode with Command Prompt add to the boot log a list of all the drivers and services that are loaded. The boot log is useful in determining the exact cause of system startup problems.
Enable Low-Resolution Video	Starts Windows 7 using the basic VGA driver. This (640×480) mode is useful when you have installed a new driver for your video card that is causing Windows 7 to hang or start and lock up halfway into the initialization process. The basic video driver is always used when you start Windows 7 in Safe Mode (Safe Mode, Safe Mode with Networking, or Safe Mode with Command Prompt).
Last Known Good Configuration (advanced)	Starts Windows 7 using the Registry configuration information that Windows saved at the last shutdown. Use this option only if you strongly suspect that a program has written incorrect or damaging information to the Registry. The Last Known Good Configuration does not solve problems caused by corrupted or missing drivers or files. Also, any changes made since the last successful startup are lost. If this option does not help, start your system with the Windows 7 DVD and run System Restore from the Startup Recovery Options menu. Select a recent restore point to reset your system's configuration.
Directory Services Restore Mode	Valid only for domain controllers.
Debugging Mode	Starts Windows 7 while sending debug information through a serial or USB cable to another computer.
Disable Automatic Restart on System Failure	Windows 7 can be configured to restart the system automatically if a STOP error occurs. This behavior can make it difficult to determine the cause. Use this option to disable automatic restart; the STOP error stays onscreen, so you can record the error and research a solution.

Table 25.1   Continued

Option	Description
Disable Driver Signature Enforcement	Windows 7 can be configured to prevent the installation of unsigned device drivers. However, in some cases, an unsigned device driver might be the only way to get a system running again. Use this option to enable you to install and use unsigned device drivers if your configuration normally blocks them.
Start Windows Normally	Boots the system without altering the normal boot operation. Use this option to return to normal booting after you've made any other selection from the Advanced Boot Options menu. Selecting this option causes the normal boot to occur immediately; you are not returned to the boot menu.

After you've made a selection from the Advanced Boot Options menu, the system boots using the startup option you selected. If you want to run the Windows Memory Diagnostics Tool before starting your system with Windows 7, press the Esc key to display the Windows Boot Manager.

If you installed Windows 7 as a dual-boot with an older version of Windows, the Windows Boot Manager displays both options. Use the up and down arrow keys to highlight the version of Windows you want to boot, and press Enter.

Whether you have a dual-boot installation or only Windows 7 installed, the Windows Memory Diagnostic option appears in the Tools menu on the Windows Boot Manager screen. To boot Windows 7 after running the Windows Memory Diagnostics Tool, press the Tab key to highlight Windows Memory Diagnostic and press Enter.

Using Safe Mode, you can start your system with a minimal set of device drivers and services. For example, if a newly installed device driver or software is preventing your computer from starting, you might start your computer in Safe Mode and then remove the software or device driver from your system. Safe Mode does not work in all circumstances, especially if your system files are corrupted or missing, or your hard disk is damaged or has failed.

 tip

If a symptom does not reappear when you start in Safe Mode, you can eliminate the default settings and minimum device drivers as possible causes.

In general, if you've just performed some operation that caused a system failure, the best first reboot action is to use the Last Known Good Configuration. If that fails to resolve the issue, use Safe Mode. If the problem is specific to the video drivers (or you suspect that it is), you might want to use Enable Low-Resolution Video instead of Safe Mode. If you've just recently changed video drivers or the video card itself, you might want to use the Enable Low-Resolution Video mode if things don't act normally during the reboot.

When you are able to access the system through Safe Mode, you need to resolve the issue that is causing the boot problem. In most cases, this requires you to reverse your last system alteration, application install, driver update, and so on. If your system stops booting properly and you did not make any changes, you should probably call Microsoft tech support; they might help track down the culprit and get things back on track.

If none of these boot options results in a repaired system or enables you to boot the system, you mightneed to reinstall the operating system.

As a Last Resort

You can reinstall Windows 7 over a damaged Windows 7 installation. Doing so might be time-consuming, but reinstalling is useful if other repair attempts do not solve your problem.

You should attempt an upgrade install first. (Start the installation by booting your system and starting the install from within Windows.) If this works, you will have repaired your OS and retained your installed applications and most system configuration settings.

If upgrading fails, you must perform a fresh (custom) install, which means you have to reinstall all your applications and remake all your settings changes. Unless you format the drive, your data files remain unaffected by the upgrade or fresh install process.

However, it is always a best practice to back up your data. See Chapter 31 to learn how to use the new backup features in Windows 7. Keep in mind that if your system fails to boot, you can't get access to the Windows Backup and Restore tool to create a backup. Although you can copy data from your system (assuming the hard disk is still readable), you won't be able to get back to work until you re-create your work environment.

 tip

If you do a fresh install, Windows 7 will try to preserve your documents and settings by creating a folder called `Windows.old` that contains the old Windows installation. After the installation is complete, check in this folder for the folders that belong to each user and retrieve files from those folders.

 note

If the lost data files were encrypted under NTFS, you need a *recovery key* to gain access to them. See Chapter 31 for information about EFS recovery keys.

More on Recovering Data

If you need to recover data, there are ways to reclaim your data from the hard drive. These techniques assume that the files or folders you want to reclaim did not use NTFS encryption. First, if you have a dual-boot system, look for the `\Users\` folder on the boot drive. Drill down until you find the files you want. Keep in mind that all subfolders of users are hidden except for `Public`. (The "Recovering Data from the System Recovery Options Menu" section at the end of this chapter offers details for finding user files.) Of course, this assumes that the OS you boot into can read the file system that your user files are stored under. Second, you can try to connect the drive to another computer that boots an OS that is capable of reading the volumes and folders in question. Then, go looking for the files. Find them and copy them where you'd like.

If you still can't access your data, you might have to use (and pay for) a data recovery service to rescue your hard disk. Ontrack Data Recovery offers this type of service, in addition to many other companies that may be in your local area.

Using Problem Reports and Solutions

Many versions of Windows have offered assistance in the form of troubleshooters. For example, in Windows XP, you could choose from the following 12 troubleshooters that would walk you through solutions to common problems:

- Games and Multimedia Troubleshooter

- Display Troubleshooter

- Sound Troubleshooter

- DVD Troubleshooter

- Internet Connection Sharing Troubleshooter

- Modem Troubleshooter

- Home and Small Office Network Troubleshooter

- Hardware Troubleshooter

- Input Device Troubleshooter (keyboard, mouse, camera, scanner)

- Drives and Network Adapters Troubleshooter

- USB Troubleshooter

- Printing Troubleshooter

These troubleshooters often didn't solve your problems, though they at least walked you through a logical train of investigation for your malady, possibly leading you to a conclusion or avenue of thought you hadn't previously tried.

Troubleshooters still exist in Windows 7, but they offer more intuitive, detailed assistance. When Windows 7 detects a problem, you are asked if you want help with it. If your problem doesn't trigger a dialog box, open the Troubleshooting applet in Control Panel. The main Troubleshooting screen is shown in Figure 25.9.

Windows 7 groups troubleshooters into categories for your convenience. Each category offers links to tasks that help you fix common computer problems. If you don't see your specific problem/task displayed, you can click a solution category, such as Programs, if that's the area in which you're experiencing a problem. Windows 7 checks the Microsoft website for solution packs to problems with your computer.

Click View All in the Tasks list of the Troubleshooting tool to display a long list of the troubleshooters available in Windows 7.

Click View History in the Tasks list to display a list of detected problems. Figure 25.9 shows a typical listing. Note that problems are listed by product and in newest-to-oldest chronological order.

To clear the Troubleshooting History list, click the Clear History button in the toolbar just above the Name column of the history list.

 note

You should not clear the Troubleshooting History list if you have unresolved problems. If you do, you may not be notified when solutions are discovered.

Click View History to see
a list of detected problems.

Use Remote Assistance to allow a
friend or tech support pro to help.

Click to clear the
troubleshooting history.

Figure 25.9
The Trouble-
shooting tool
in Windows 7.

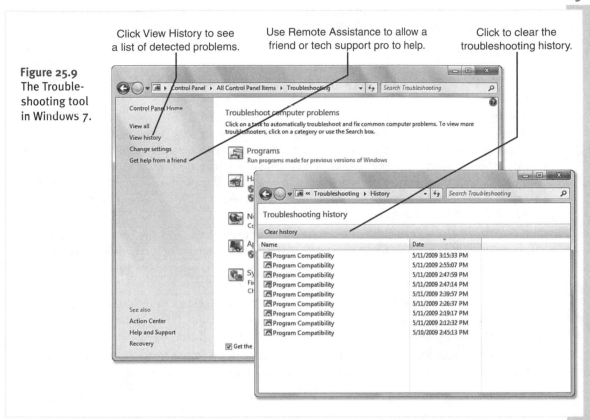

By default, Windows 7 automatically checks for solutions when problems are detected. To change this behavior, click Change Settings in the Tasks list of the Troubleshooting window, click the Off radio button in the Computer Maintenance section, and click OK. You can still run troubleshooters manually at this point, but it's recommended you leave this setting on to let Windows 7 do the work for you.

New to Windows 7 is the Get Help from a Friend link in the Tasks list of the Troubleshooting window. This opens a window that lets you invite a person to connect via Remote Assistance to help you with your computer problem. Just click the Invite Someone to Help You button, which opens a Windows Remote Assistance window in which you can save the invitation as a file you attach to an email, send an email invitation (Windows 7 opens your email client, if it's compatible), or use Easy Connect. Remote Assistance is described in Chapter 36, "Meetings, Conferencing, and Collaboration."

Black Magic of Troubleshooting

It often seems like many professional technophiles have some sort of black magic they use when resolving problems. If you blink, you miss whatever they do to get the system back in working order. It's often as if you are working with a Technomage (for you *Babylon 5* fans).

Yes, it is true that some of our skills in resolving problems seem like hocus pocus. But in reality, it's a mixture of experience and knowledge, both of which you can gain with time and effort.

In our experience, most computer problems are physical in nature—that is, some component is not connected properly or has become damaged. Of the remaining 5% or so, more than 4.99% of computer problems are caused directly by the user—whether through deliberate or accidental activity. User-caused problems are typically configuration changes, installation of new drivers, or deletion of important files and folders.

When troubleshooting a problem on your system, try to mentally walk backward through whatever actions you've performed on the system over the last few days or weeks. In many cases, you might remember installing some downloaded application or changing some Control Panel setting that you meant to uninstall or reverse but never got around to doing. If the brainstorming fails to highlight any suspects, check for physical issues. Is everything powered on? Are cooling fans still spinning? Are all the right cables still firmly connected?

If you don't discover anything obvious physically, try a power-off reboot. The power-off reboot resets all hardware devices and, in many cases, resolves the problem (if it was device related). If possible, shut down the system gracefully. Then keep the power off for about 10 seconds before switching the system back on. You'll be amazed by how often this works.

Your next steps should include a walk-through of the Event Viewer and any other types of log files you can find. Let the problem guide you in this process. For example, if the video system is failing, you probably don't need to look through the security logs.

Problems are sometimes unique and may require a different resolution from any other problem you've tackled in the past. However, the following are some general guidelines:

- Try only one change at a time.

- Reboot twice after each change.

- Test each change for success.

- Try the least-invasive change first.

- Keep a log of your changes. You might need to undo them to produce a result, or you might need to use the resolution process again in the future.

- Consult vendor websites for possible solutions if the problem seems to be specific to one device or software component.

- Be patient and take your time.

- After a few attempts at possible solutions, step back and re-evaluate before continuing.

- If you get frustrated, take a break. Anger and frustration are counterproductive when you need to be thinking clearly.

- Try to undo any recent changes to the system, including new hardware or software patches. You can use System Restore to undo driver or application changes, even if you can't start the system.

- Review areas of the system that caused problems in the past.

- Try to repeat the failure; knowing where, how, or why the failure occurs can lead to a solution.

Troubleshooting is both an art and a science. You need organized patience and outrageous ingenuity. Plus, knowing where to look stuff up never hurts. Keep in mind that the entire Internet is waiting at your fingertips and mouse clicks. Search http://groups.google.com as well the regular Web. Be precise in your search techniques to help find the exact messages you need to read. The Microsoft Knowledge Base is extremely helpful, too. In addition, lots of helpful information is included within the Help and Support system of Windows 7 and the Windows 7 Resource Kit. If all else fails, contact Microsoft technical support over the phone. (See http://support.microsoft.com for email, chat, and phone support.) In most cases, if the troubleshooting techniques in this book don't resolve the issue, it is usually beyond the end user to correct.

Not all the troubleshooting techniques applicable to Windows 7 are discussed within this one chapter. As you've no doubt noticed, we've been discussing troubleshooting throughout much of this book. So before you throw your hands up in frustration that your questions are not answered or your problem is not resolved in this chapter, check out the chapter that is dedicated to the specific subject elsewhere in this book.

Recovering Data from the System Recovery Options Menu

If you decide that the only solution to a totally fouled-up Windows 7 installation is to wipe out the hard disk and start over, and if you discover that you don't have an up-to-date backup of critical data, you can use the Command Prompt option in the System Recovery Options menu (refer to Figure 25.1) to save your data before wiping out your system.

Start by changing to the drive letter containing your Windows system. Don't assume it's the C: drive—for example, on a system that has been partitioned to use BitLocker, the Windows system drive might show up as the D: drive (even though you refer to it as the C: drive during normal operations).

Change to the Users folder:

```
cd\users
```

For this example, let's assume you need to retrieve files that belong to a user called Smith. Use the command cd smith to change to the Smith folder.

The most important user data folders are generally Contacts, Documents, and Favorites. Copy each folder to the target drive using ROBOCOPY (a souped-up version of the venerable XCOPY utility). For example, to copy Smith's Documents folder to a folder on the F: drive called Documents (along with any subfolders), use this command:

 tip

If you perform the dir command, you might see only the Public folder, because all user folders are hidden. Use the command **dir** /**ah**/**p** to view the hidden user folders.

```
ROBOCOPY C:\Users\Smith\Documents\ F:\Documents\ /s
```

Use similar commands to copy Contacts, Favorites, Pictures, and other folders that contain irreplaceable data.

When you're finished, type **exit** and press Enter to close the Command Prompt window. Remove the media or shut down the system, and disconnect the hard disk you used for copying the data.

Go to another system, insert the media or connect the drive, and retrieve the information. If you stored it to a network share, log in to the network share to retrieve the information. You might need to use the Folder Options applet (in Small Icons or Large Icons view) in the Control Panel to enable the display of hidden files and folders to view and access the files from the other system.

 caution

If you decide to use CD or DVD media instead of an external hard disk, USB flash drive, or network share to copy the data, be sure you know what drive letter has been assigned in System Recovery Options Command Prompt mode. It might be D:, E:, or some other letter (and not necessarily the drive letter it normally has). Here's how to tell: Insert a blank disc and type **dir x:** (substitute the drive letter you think is correct for **x**). You see an "incorrect function" error message if you entered the incorrect drive letter. When you format the media, make sure it says that the old file system is RAW and the new file system is UDF before you continue the format. If you don't pay attention to these details, you could format your Windows system drive by mistake.

KEEPING WINDOWS 7 AND OTHER SOFTWARE UP TO DATE

Introducing Updates

Windows 7 is an ever-evolving operating system that requires new updates and maintenance constantly. These updates benefit your computer and render it more secure and stable. Microsoft facilitates the process of keeping your computer system up to date via Windows Update. This built-in tool downloads the most current updates, fixups, hotfixes, drivers, and so on for your system and then commences an installation. Updating has never been so easy and so visual.

Over a period of time, your system will accumulate many updates and newly formed software that Microsoft supplies. As you probably know, Microsoft sometimes gathers a mess of these into one package or compilation and releases it as a service pack.

Later in this chapter, we discuss how to install and remove software applications, including issues of running older programs. As mentioned in Chapter 1, "Introducing Windows 7," older (16-bit) software that you have been using for years will have compatibility errors with 64-bit Windows 7, and you'll learn more about these 64-bit compatibility issues later in this chapter. Also included is a description of side-by-side installations in Windows 7, and how the OS uses virtual registries to run different versions of the same software on a PC.

Understanding Windows Live

Some users confuse Windows Update with Windows Live, but they're two different animals. The Windows Live suite of applications available from http://home.live.com (requires a Live login) extends the online communications capabilities of Windows 7, Windows Vista, Windows XP, and Microsoft Office. It includes email, IM, search, social networking, photo management and publishing, home movie editing, blogging, event planning, online file storage, and family safety applications.

To customize the Windows 7 Gadgets, Windows Live Messenger, or Windows Live Toolbar, visit http://gallery.live.com. To use Windows Live features on a mobile device, visit http://home.mobile.live.com/Home.mvc. To use free and low-cost web-based and email business and marketing tools, visit http://smallbusiness.officelive.com.

Windows Update

Windows Update is an important built-in online tool that ensures your system gets all the latest software additions and bug fixes. Unlike the Windows Update version in Windows XP, Windows 7 supplies users an integrated update system that does not require the user to go to the Microsoft update website. Instead of opening a web browser, the new version of Windows Update opens in the same existing window.

Windows Update has been made to be seamless to its users. Let's say a newly installed update requires a restart while you are in the process of doing important work. You can postpone that restart easily without any disruptions. Also a great feature to Windows Update is the way it handles updates for already running programs. If Windows Update has an update that needs to be installed on an already running program or service, Windows will safely stop the program or service, install the update, and then restart it. This doesn't apply to every program, such as Microsoft Office applications or games, but it does cover antivirus software running continuously in the background and similar programs.

Windows Automatic Updates

Windows users all know how important critical updates are to a system. Windows Update downloads and installs updates automatically by default, guaranteeing your computer acquires all the newest important updates. The tool runs at a scheduled time daily, although you can change the setting to check once a week (which isn't recommended). Windows Update's default setting is to install important (critical and highest-priority) updates first, and then recommended updates. The tool lets you choose whether to install other updates that pertain to your computer but are optional, such as a driver update for your network adapter.

 note

The Windows Update technology is robust. Among other things, system administrators can use it to control updating many machines across a network.

Upon installing Windows 7, Windows Update is configured to

check for updates daily at 3:00 a.m. If you open the Windows Update tool and click Change Settings in the Tasks list, you'll see a prominent green shield icon with a check mark alongside a menu item recommending you leave automatic updates turned on (the default). Selecting Never Check for Updates (Not Recommended) from the drop-down list displays a red shield with an X in the middle.

With automatic updates enabled, information about your computer will be uploaded to the Microsoft Windows Update Database. Then security patches, critical updates, office updates, drivers, and operating system service packs will be automatically downloaded and installed to your computer. If you decide to deactivate automatic updates, you will be bugged incessantly about it, so why fight a good thing? We believe this is good thinking on Microsoft's part.

Allowing Windows to download and install updates automatically keeps your system current without having to remember to initiate an update check. It does not matter whether you have a broadband or dial-up connection. Windows Update downloads just the files you need, or just the parts of the files you need, thereby keeping the downloads as small and fast moving as possible. The system is made additionally efficient by ensuring the system downloads and installs the most crucial updates before less-important patches. So when the next virus outbreak hits, Windows users will immediately be protected. To additionally make the most of your connect time, if you disconnect from the Internet before your updates are finished, nothing is lost.

Letting Windows automatically update can sometimes cause your computer to automatically reboot by itself—a few important updates require a restart to successfully install. That means if you leave Windows Update at its default settings, you could potentially lose unsaved work. For example, say you leave your computer to automatically update at 3:00 a.m. every day, and the previous night you worked on important Word documents and left your computer on. While those important documents are open on your computer (and unsaved), Windows downloads and installs an update that requires a restart. Windows will restart automatically, which could cause you to lose your work. This default selection might not be the best choice for you, and you might want to change these settings.

Be aware that it is still possible that an update could damage your system. Windows Update creates a restore point for your system before installing the available updates. If a problem does occur, you can always roll back a system to its state before the update (see "Installing and Removing Software," later in this chapter).

 note

In Windows 7, you must be logged on as an Administrator, or provide an Administrator password in the User Account Control (UAC) dialog box that appears, to install components or modify Windows Update automatic settings.

 note

Windows does not use your name, address, email address, or any information that can be used to identify you or contact you.

 caution

With Windows 7, keep in mind that with automatic updating turned on, Windows might restart your computer automatically after installing updates. Always save data and close programs if this option is activated. Otherwise, change how Windows controls automatic updates!

To alleviate this type of problem Windows 7 supports *hotpatching*, which enables Windows 7 to install most system updates without rebooting. This is a welcome feature, especially if you like the convenience of automatic updates but dislike having backups, remote access, or other tasks disrupted by system reboots after updates are installed.

Windows Update Applet and Functions

As you can see from Figure 26.1, the user has different options for updating her system. On the main Windows Update applet, you can see the basic settings applied, the last time the system was updated, and what kind of updates (for Windows only). On the left side of the window is a list of options that the user can select.

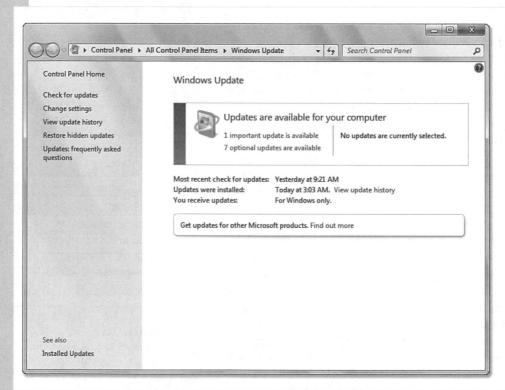

Figure 26.1
The Windows Update applet.

Manually Install Updates Using Windows Update

The process to manually update Windows is easy and user friendly. By manually updating your system, you can obtain various critical and noncritical updates. To use Windows Update manually, follow these steps:

 tip

Another way of getting to the Windows Update page is to click Start, All Programs, Windows Update.

1. Click Start, Control Panel, System and Security, Windows Update.

2. In the Windows Update window, click Check for Updates in the Tasks list. Windows Update will then look for all possible updates.

3. After a list of updates appears, you can select and install the updates you want. If you don't install Important updates at this time, they will be installed during the next scheduled automatic update.

Manually updating your system allows you to decide which updates you want and lets you know which updates you need.

Updates Do Not Install Properly

If one or more of your Windows Updates did not install properly, or the program failed to install and/or produces an error, check the following:

- Is there enough free disk space on your computer? An update will not install if there is insufficient free space for it to install on. Free up space on your system and reinstall the update.

- Did you accidentally cancel an update while it was installing? If the update was not fully downloaded, run Windows Update again. If the update was downloaded but not installed, simply go back and reinstall the update.

- Was the Microsoft Software License Terms accepted? If an error code was created about licensing, review the error code and select Try Again. When the licensing agreement opens it will ask you to review the license and agree to the terms.

- If none of the preceding solutions works, review the error code that was created and search online for more help.

Other Windows Update Settings

You can also hide an update if you do not want to install it. If Windows consistently asks you to install an update and you have no desire to, just hide the update. To hide an update, right-click the update you want to hide and select Hide Update from the shortcut menu. Hiding an update is helpful because you essentially filter the list to display only those updates you're interested in. If you want to see hidden updates again, click Restore Hidden Update in the Tasks list of the Windows Update applet. To install an update, it must not be hidden. If an update is hidden and you do want to install it, restore the update first and then install.

Can't Find Hidden Update

You occasionally won't be able to locate an update you unhid. The likely cause is that a newer update that addressed that problem has already been installed. Windows 7 will check whether a newer update has already been installed before it will allow you to install the older update.

Also, after every update, you can view the installed updates by clicking View Update History, which visually shows you all updates that were installed (or attempted), whether the update installation was successful, the priority of the update, and the date of installation.

Windows Update also allows you to change certain settings pertaining to updating. By clicking Change Settings, you will see options for Windows automatic updating, recommended updates, and which users can install them (see Figure 26.2).

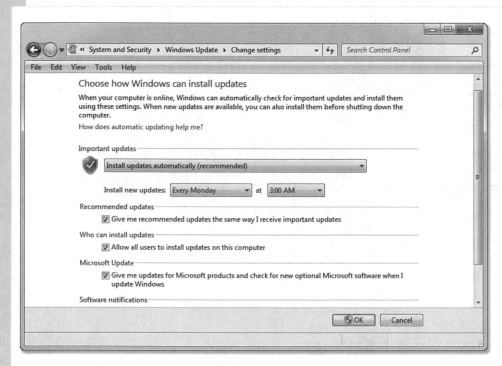

Figure 26.2
Change Settings window in Windows Update.

The Important Updates section offers four drop-down menu items that affect automatic updates. The default setting is to install updates automatically at a set time. You may change this setting if you want to (1) choose which updates to install or (2) choose the updates before downloading. The ability to selectively install updates is valuable. Without choosing one of these options, Windows may automatically restart your system, in which case open or unsaved files could be damaged or lost. If you're the type of user who always reads and responds to system messages, consider changing to one of these settings—automatic updates are important to your system, but you do not want them to ruin your important work. The last option, Never Check for Updates, is strongly discouraged by Microsoft.

When would you use the fourth option, to turn off updates altogether? In general, we'd rule that out as an intelligent option, with two exceptions:

- If you have a computer that is almost always off the Internet or a LAN, is "mission critical" (has to be up and running), and rarely if ever has new software (including email) added to it, this is a potential candidate. When we get such a dedicated system running, we don't have much interest in tempting fate with software or system upgrades.

- If you're running and maintaining PCs in a corporate setting. These PCs *are* connected to the Internet and probably on a corporate network. You want to rigorously test updates before you install them across the corporation's PCs because Microsoft patches and updates can sometimes break your applications' features in subtle ways.

> **note**
>
> All updates that pertain to maintenance and support for Microsoft products are free.

New to Windows 7 is the Allow All Users to Install Updates on this Computer option, which is selected by default. Previous versions of Windows required the user to be logged on as Administrator to manually install updates. This new option lets standard users install all updates, including optional updates, without prompting for administrative credentials. We recommend leaving this option selected on standalone computers.

Finally, the Change Settings window also includes a Microsoft Update check box that enables you to receive updates for Microsoft products and check for new optional Microsoft software when you update Windows.

Viewing and Changing Installed Updates

As stated previously, some updates can cause system problems. By viewing which updates are installed on your computer you can repair critical updates and remove optional updates (see Figure 26.3).

Figure 26.3
Viewing installed updates.

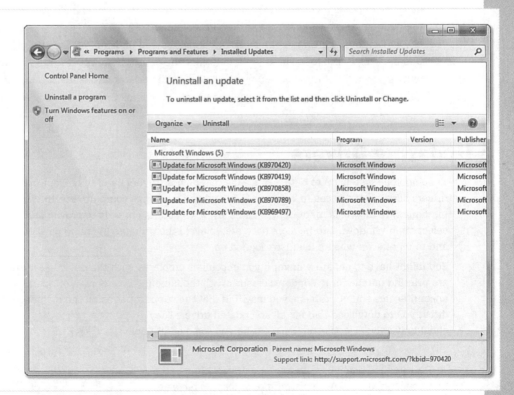

To repair or uninstall an update, follow these steps:

1. Click Start, Control Panel, Programs, Programs and Features, View Installed Updates.

2. Under Programs and Features select View Installed Updates.

3. A list of all updates displays. Click the update you want to change.

4. After selecting an update, you will see various details in the middle of the window. Also, on the top toolbar there will be an option to uninstall (see Figure 26.3). Uninstalling asks for an administrative confirmation before uninstalling.

Can't Uninstall Current Update

If your current update is not uninstalling or Windows 7 reports that the update cannot be uninstalled or produces an error upon uninstalling, the problem might be that Microsoft is not allowing you remove that particular update.

If an update is an Important update and applies to the security of the OS, you cannot install it. Otherwise, if you're on a network, make sure your computer is actually connected to the network. Uninstalling an update requires your computer to be connected to a network due to the Group Policy. Group Policy is a network administrative tool that will manage all settings for users and other computers.

If an update that you uninstalled keeps automatically installing on your computer, then the automatic updating feature in Windows could be the culprit. If you have Windows Update set to update automatically, you may experience this problem. To solve it, you do not have to shut off or change the setting to automatic updating. Instead of disabling features, uninstall the update, click Check for Updates, and then click the appropriate Updates are Available link. This will display a list of updates you may install and the update that keeps automatically installing. For the update you do not want installed, simply right-click the update and select Hide Update.

Updating Drivers

Keeping your system up to date also means that device drivers need to be kept up to date. Updated drivers allow your devices to work properly and will maximize compatibility. In Windows 7, updating hardware drivers is made simple and easy. Microsoft has greatly improved automatic driver selection in Windows 7 to be more accurate, to avoid the prompts plaguing past Windows versions, and to work even when a user isn't logged on.

You might have to update a driver if you encounter problems with the device—for example, if there are printing glitches or if Windows crashes with the famous "Blue Screen of Death." If you encounter this sort of problem, you may find that the support pages on the manufacturer's website direct you to download and install an updated driver. They should give you clear instructions, but here is some additional advice:

- Do you have permission to upgrade drivers? It is necessary to be logged in as Administrator or at least to have an Administrator password when prompted by a UAC box to update drivers.

tip

You might want to try running Windows Update and see whether Microsoft lists updated device drivers for your system.

- Is it really the latest driver? Check the manufacturer's site and the Microsoft site to see what you can find.

- Does the "new" driver work with Windows 7? Make sure that the new driver is for Windows 7 because other drivers for other versions of Windows might not be compatible.

Using Device Manager to Update Drivers

After you've downloaded new driver, it is time to install using the Update Driver Software window. To access the Update Driver Software window, follow these steps:

1. Click Start, Control Panel, Hardware and Sound, Device Manager. (If you are not logged in with Administrator privileges, the Device Manager box will not open without additional input.) You can also type **device manager** in the Start Search box and select it from the results list.

2. In Device Manager, locate the device, right-click it, and choose Update Driver Software.

The Update Driver Software window gives you two choices, as shown in Figure 26.4.

tip

Windows 7 lets administrators set up in a Driver Store drivers that standard users can install when needed, even without administrative privilege. Windows 7 also gives standard users the flexibility needed to install permitted classes of devices even if drivers aren't already in the Driver Store on the local machine. To give standard users this privilege, open the Group Policy Editor (gpedit.msc) and navigate to Computer Configuration, Administrative Templates, System, Driver Installation, Allow Non-Administrators to Install Drivers for These Devices. For more details about the Driver Store and User Access Control, search Microsoft TechNet at http://technet.microsoft.com/en-us/default.aspx.

Figure 26.4
The Update Driver Software window with the list of options.

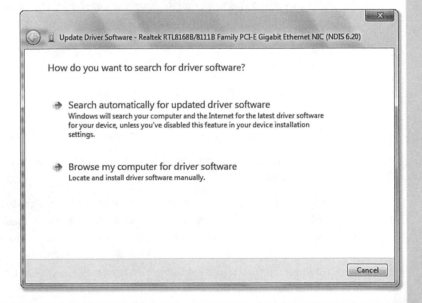

■ **Search Automatically for Updated Driver Software**—Gives permission to Windows to search and locate any drivers on your computer and on the Internet. After Windows searches your computer and the Internet for drivers, if it finds a new driver, it automatically installs it. If no new drivers are found, Windows tells you that your current driver is the most up to date.

■ **Browse My Computer for Driver Software**—If you've already downloaded the driver or want to use a specific driver, enables you to choose to browse and locate that selected driver. When you choose to find the driver by yourself, Windows again gives you options. The first option is to manually locate the driver. To locate the driver you can either type in the location or click Browse. The second option is to choose a driver from a list of device drivers on the computer. When selecting to choose the driver from the list, a selection of device drivers is generated. You can decide which driver you want and install it.

 tip

Downloadable drivers are usually stored in compressed form on the manufacturer's website. If the file is an EXE (executable) file, you will need to open it before you can use its contents; opening it might also install the driver for you. If the driver is in a ZIP archive file, you will need to uncompress it. Fortunately, Windows 7 can uncompress ZIP files for you. You won't need to download a separate unzipping utility.

Windows Update Driver Settings

When installing a new device to your system, Windows 7 will usually automatically install drivers seamlessly. After installing these drivers, Windows 7 continually looks for newer drivers online by using Windows Update. These driver checks and updates happen without you even knowing about them. But in Windows 7 these settings can be changed. To alter these settings, follow these steps:

1. Click Start, Control Panel, System and Security.

2. Select System and click the Change Settings link located in the lower-right side of the page.

3. The System Properties dialog box opens; click the Hardware tab.

4. On the Hardware tab, open Device Installation Settings, and then click No, Let Me Choose What to Do.

You can choose from three settings to instruct Windows Update how to update your drivers (see Figure 26.5). The default and recommended setting is to allow Windows Update to automatically install updated drivers. Another option is to have Windows Update install a driver if the driver software isn't found on your computer. Finally, you can choose to never allow Windows Update to install driver software, which means you must manually update drivers in the future.

Continued...

Figure 26.5
Device Installation
Settings window.

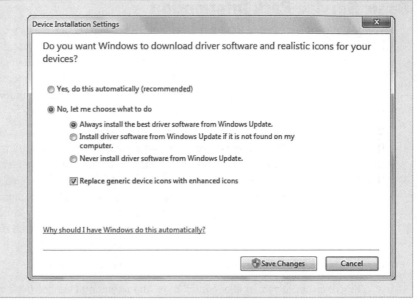

Service Packs

Windows 7 is part of Microsoft's "New Technology" or NT family of OSs, along with Windows Vista, XP, NT, 2000 Professional, the various flavors of Windows 2000 Server, and Windows Server 2003. These OSs were designed from the ground up for stability, reliability, and security. To keep them in tip-top shape, Microsoft releases a constant stream of software updates as follows:

- **Important updates**—Fixes for bugs that are so severe or involve such serious security risks that you really *have* to install them. As you know, Windows 7 can automatically download and install these, or at least download and offer to install them, so you don't miss out. Important updates can be listed by using Windows Update.

- **Recommended updates**—These are not security fixes but are updates to accessory programs such as Messenger and Media Player, new desktop themes, and the like. Recommended updates can be listed by using Windows Update.

- **Hotfixes**—Bug fixes that affect a small enough group of users that Microsoft doesn't send them out to everyone. Instead, you have to hunt for them by searching online, or hear about them from Microsoft's Tech Support department. They're not widely advertised because if you're running into a serious-enough problem, you'll go looking for the solution, and hotfixes tend to be released in a hurry without extensive testing, so they sometimes cause new problems of their own. Hotfix users tend to be corporate IT people whose job it is to stay on top of these things.

 tip

Windows hotfixes are available from the Microsoft Download Center at www.microsoft.com/downloads. On the same web page, you can sign up for the Microsoft Download Notifications service, which sends you a weekly email listing downloads in the categories you choose.

Basic Service Pack Information

Periodically—it's supposed to be every 12 months but in practice it's less often—Microsoft gathers all the important updates, recommended updates, and hotfixes, tests them extensively, and releases them as a service pack (SP). Some service packs are a complete, cumulative set of fixes and additions made since the initial release of an OS, whereas others are incremental and can depend on the installation of a prior service pack. You can obtain service packs on media (discs) or download them from the Microsoft Download Center.

You might wonder whether you really need to install service packs, because you probably install the important updates that Windows 7 downloads and informs you of from time to time. The answer is emphatically *yes*, for two reasons. First, service packs fix those annoying but minor bugs that you may not even realize are there—that odd crash every other week, or that weird sound that Media Player makes once in a while. Service packs can also include numerous performance improvements and new features. Second, application programs will eventually appear that require a certain service pack level to run correctly. Windows evolves, so you need to keep up. Those two reasons alone are enough to warrant installing any service pack.

Here are some other things that you should know about service packs:

- They're either incremental or cumulative. An incremental service pack usually requires the installation of a previous service pack, if applicable. A cumulative service pack includes the old service pack(s) and more.

- Starting about the same time that Microsoft releases a service pack to the public, new computers purchased from major vendors should come with the service pack preinstalled. (At least, it should be an option. If you're buying a new computer, ask for the latest version.) To check the current service pack level of your Windows 7 computer, open your System Information screen.

- Shortly after Microsoft releases a service pack to the public, retail versions of the OS will include the service pack. If you are shopping for additional copies of an OS for upgrading existing PCs or for installation on new PCs, be sure to buy versions that include the latest service pack. A sticker or note on the package indicates whether a service pack is incorporated.

- It's likely the procedure for installation of previous service packs will be similar for subsequent service packs as well.

 note

In a corporate environment, your IT department will most likely control the installation of service packs.

Installation of Service Packs

There is a variety of ways to install a service pack, as presented in the following list:

- **Windows Automatic Updates**—If your computer was set up to automatically download important updates, and you spend enough time connected to the Internet, a service pack will be downloaded automatically. All of the required service pack files will have already been downloaded by the time you get the notification to install them.

- **Windows Manual Update**—If the automatic updates feature is not enabled, you can install a service pack from the Windows Update window. Windows Update will download from Microsoft just those service pack components needed for your computer, saving some download time over the "standalone" method. However, if you have more than a few computers to update, you'll save time by using the standalone method.

- **Standalone**—The standalone method is the traditional service pack format. It's a compressed file that contains all of the updated files. If you have multiple computers to update, and Internet access is difficult or slow, perhaps the standalone method is the one to use.

Before installation of a service pack, follow these guidelines:

- If you use Fast User Switching, be sure all users are logged off. Then, log on as an Administrator. Close any running applications.

- We recommend you perform a full backup of the files you keep on your computer using Backup and Restore.

  ➥ *To learn more about the Windows 7 Backup and Restore feature,* **see** *"The All New Backup and Restore," p. 863.*

- Check the websites of the manufacturers of your computer, your application software, and your antispyware and antivirus packages for updates or special instructions regarding the service pack. Some programs may need to be updated to work with the new service pack. For a list of programs with known compatibility issues with Windows 7 service packs, search the Microsoft Knowledge Base available at http://support.microsoft.com.

- If you suspect your computer may have viruses, spyware, adware, or other pestilential software, take steps to remove it *before* installing the service pack. These programs can cause serious networking and Internet connection problems after installation, and without a functioning Internet connection you may not be able to download the necessary clean-up tools. See Chapter 30, "Protecting Windows from Viruses and Spyware," for details.

- Disable any real-time virus scanners; they can slow down and possibly interfere with the installation. Disconnect from the Internet first if you do this.

- You will need free space on your hard drive for installation.

After following these suggested guidelines, you will be ready to install your service pack.

Installing and Removing Software

Microsoft went the extra mile in working with software (and hardware) developers to ensure a high level of compatibility with Windows 7. The result is a streamlined, user-friendly installation process for thousands of software applications, without the glitches experienced when Windows Vista was released.

As you know, installation of new programs is usually as simple as inserting a media disc into the drive. The autorun program on most application discs does the rest. Or, when it doesn't, you can run the Setup file on the disc, and the rest is automatic. Ditto for programs you download from the Internet. The following section explains how to install software in these different ways.

note

If you are using a Standard user account, you will likely be prompted for an Administrator password when you try to add or remove software programs. If you are logged in as an Administrator, you will be prompted to click Accept or OK for the same procedures.

Installation via CD or DVD

Installing software from a disc is user friendly and easy. Here is what you do:

1. Insert the disc into your computer.

2. Follow the onscreen instructions.

3. Most programs will automatically try to start and begin the installation wizard. If this program automatically tries to install, you will be presented an AutoPlay dialog box that asks whether you want to run the installation wizard.

4. Some programs do not automatically run an installation wizard. In this case, check to see whether the disc comes with instructions or any information for installation. If the installation disc does not come with any instructions, open the disc to view its files. Try to find an `install.exe` or `setup.exe` (executable) file, and open that file. This should start the installation wizard and install the rest of the components.

5. The User Account Control dialog box appears, prompting for administrator confirmation that this install is allowed.

6. Enter a password, if prompted, and select Yes to the confirmation, and the software installation will begin.

Problem Installing from Disc

If you have inserted a disc into the drive but it is not installing, first make sure that you are installing the software correctly.

If there is still a problem with the install, check the disc to see if there are any scratches or blemishes that could create a problem. Scratches on discs can be a major problem and can make the disc reader fail to read the disc correctly. If the disc is okay, check your disc reader. If your disc drive is broken or is faulty, take your computer to a local computer technician.

Installation via Downloaded Program

Installing a program that was downloaded from the Internet is just as easy as installing a program from a disc. Before installing a program, do the following:

- Make sure you trust the publisher of the software.

- Scan the file for viruses. Sometimes antivirus programs can find harmful viruses that can disrupt your system.

- Beware, some programs contain spyware and other software that can be annoying or even harmful.

After you are prepared for installation of your software, follow these steps:

1. Open your web browser and determine where the software is located online.

2. After you find your software, you will be presented two choices: to open and run the program now or to run at a later time.

3. If you want to install your software immediately, click the link to the software. Select Run or Open and follow the instructions.

4. If you want to save the software and install later, click the link and select Save. When you are ready to install this program, find the file on your computer and double-click it.

 note

Sometimes, software can be downloaded as a ZIP or another type of compressed file. In this case, download and save the software on your computer, then right-click the file and select Unzip to uncompress. Windows 7 has a built-in function to uncompress ZIP files.

Viewing and Changing Programs

In Windows 7, you can monitor and change software that is currently installed on your computer. Windows 7 provides a helpful way to show you what software is on your computer.

As you can see in Figure 26.6, you can view information about all installed programs, including how many programs there are, who the publisher of each program is, when a program was installed, and how much space a program takes up. You can easily organize and change views however you please to better fit your preferences.

By clicking any of the installed programs on the list, you can view a program's detailed information in the lower part of the applet. This can help you see what version of the program is installed and allow you to check whether the program is up to date.

On the left side of the window, Windows 7 gives you a few options. The first link lets you view installed updates; these are all the Microsoft updates your system contains.

➡ *To learn more about how to view and change Windows updates,* **see** *"Viewing and Changing Installed Updates," p. 763.*

Also on the left side of the Programs and Features window is a Turn Windows Features On or Off link, which is described in detail in the next section.

Click here to see currently
installed Windows updates.   Click here to toggle Windows features on and off.

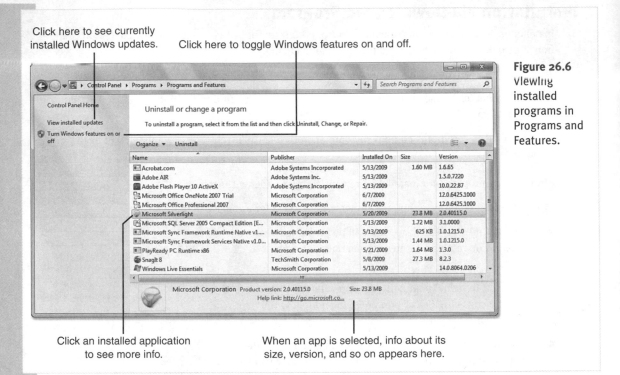

Figure 26.6
Viewing
installed
programs in
Programs and
Features.

Click an installed application
to see more info.

When an app is selected, info about its
size, version, and so on appears here.

Uninstalling Software

As you know, many programs come with their own installation (Setup) programs that handle all the
details of installation, such as file copying, making Registry additions, making file associations, and
adding items to the Start menu. An ever-growing number of applications even provide their own
uninstall routine, which appears as a unique icon within their Start menu folder. But sometimes
programs do not come with built-in uninstallers, or you just want Windows to handle these uninstalls.

Most modern applications are written in compliance with the
Microsoft Windows standards for installation and removal.
Thus, you see them in your installed applications list in the
Programs and Features applet. This list is mainly the result of
the PC software industry's response to kvetching from users
and critics about tenacious programs that are difficult to root
out after they're installed. Some ambitious programs spread
themselves out all over your hard disk like oil on your garage
floor with no easy way of reversing the process. Users complained about the loss of precious disk space, unexplained
system slowdowns, and so forth.

 tip

Never attempt to remove an application from your system by deleting its
files from the \Program Files folders
(or wherever). Actually, "never" may
be too strong. Removal through
manual deletion should only be a
last resort. Always attempt to use
the Programs and Features applet or
the uninstall utility from the application first.

To uninstall software, follow these steps:

1. Click Start, Control Panel, Programs, Programs and Features.

2. Select the program you want uninstalled or changed.

3. Click the Uninstall button on the toolbar.

4. The Programs and Features dialog box appears, asking if you're sure you want to uninstall the program. Click Yes.

5. UAC will ask for administrator confirmation if this uninstall is correct. Enter the password, if necessary, and select Yes to the confirmation. The software will uninstall automatically.

Uninstalling a Program

If the program you want to uninstall doesn't appear in Programs and Features, check its All Programs listing to see if it comes with its own Uninstall program. You can also search for more information about the product. Programs usually come with ReadMe notes or have extra information online.

Also with Programs and Features, you can turn on or off any Windows feature, as shown in Figure 26.7. Turning off a feature can customize Windows 7 for you. For example, if you are running Windows 7 on your desktop and only use a mouse and keyboard for input devices, you can turn off the Tablet PC Components. You do have the option to turn on any feature that is available as well. It is up to you which functions you want to use.

Figure 26.7
Windows features can be turned on or off.

PART

VI

Enabling and disabling features is easy and self-explanatory. Click the Turn Windows Features On or Off link in the Tasks list. If you want to turn on a feature, select the check box next to it to fill in the box. If you do not want a feature, just click the check box to clear it. If you do want to turn off a feature, make sure that you know what you are turning off.

 note

Turning off a feature does not uninstall it completely off your computer as in Windows XP. Instead, it keeps the feature on your hard drive to give you the later option of turning it on. This allows you to turn on and off any feature quickly but does not free up any space on your hard disk.

Compatibility Issues in 64-Bit Version

Windows 7 64-bit is a unique OS that targets and utilizes 64-bit processors. It offers the main benefit of breaking the 4GB RAM limitation, enabling your system to run applications faster than 32-bit environments, and run a lot of applications simultaneously without any noticeable slowdown.

With these great benefits comes a downside. Windows 7 64-bit has some compatibility issues and other limitations. Old 16-bit applications, legacy installer applications and 16-bit DOS, and even 32-bit drivers (you must install x64-bit drivers) are not supported in Windows 7 64-bit.

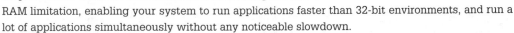

Upgrade Issues with 64-Bit Windows 7

If you are planning to *upgrade* to the 64-bit version of Windows 7, remember you can upgrade only from 64-bit Windows Vista. Also, you can only upgrade your 32-bit Windows Vista system to 32-bit Windows 7. If you have the capability to install the 64-bit version of Windows 7 and you have 32-bit Windows Vista previously installed, you must complete a new clean install. (If you're running Windows XP, you can get an upgrade license to Windows 7, but you must perform a clean install.) Thus, all applications must comply with the new 64-bit application standards. And, of course, you must have a compatible 64-bit CPU in your machine. Most recent desktop CPUs from AMD and Intel support 64-bit versions of Windows 7. To determine whether a particular processor model can run in 64-bit (x64) mode, check the processor's specification sheet at the processor vendor's website.

Windows 7 incorporates Registry redirection and file redirection that is responsible for all the OS's applications compatibilities. However, 64-bit Windows 7 does not incorporate this feature, and many legacy applications will not run or install.

Other Program Compatibility Issues

While running Windows 7, you might decide to install an older program or game. However, Windows 7 might not install the program or might not run the program correctly once installed. Windows 7 sports a new version of the Program Compatibility Wizard to help work around this kind of incompatibility.

The Program Compatibility Wizard is designed to change the compatibility of a certain program and allow that program to work in Windows 7. To open and use this wizard, follow these instructions:

1. Click Start, Control Panel and type **Program Compatibility** in the Search box at the top of the screen.

2. In the results pane, click the Run Programs Made for Previous Versions of Windows link.

3. Control Panel starts the Program Compatibility Wizard. If you're not logged in as Administrator, click Advanced, click Run As Administrator, enter the password, and then click Next.

4. Windows 7 scans your computer for potentially incompatible programs and displays a list (see Figure 26.8). Select your desired program and click Next.

Figure 26.8
The Program Compatibility Wizard displays a list of programs you can troubleshoot.

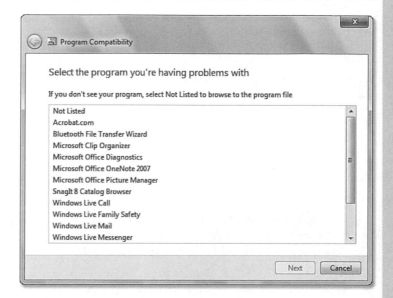

5. In the Select Troubleshooting Option screen, click Troubleshoot Program.

6. The wizard presents a list of problems you might have encountered (see Figure 26.9). Select The Program Worked in Earlier Versions of Windows But Won't Install or Run Now. You can also select any of the other options listed, which might include problems displaying the program or getting permissions. Click Next.

 tip

If your program doesn't appear in the list, click Not Listed, click Next, and then click Browse to locate the program on your hard disk, external drive, or CD or DVD.

7. The wizard asks you what prior version of Windows supported the program. Make a selection and click Next.

8. You have chosen all the basic options, so the wizard now asks you to test the program to make sure that it works correctly. Click Start the Program, and then return to the wizard and click Next.

9. After testing is completed, you are asked whether you want to save these settings, change the current settings, or report the problem to Microsoft and check for a solution online.

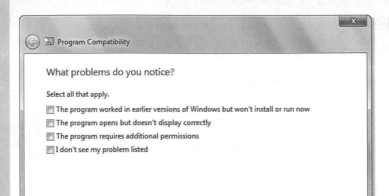

Figure 26.9
The Program Compatibility Wizard displays a list of problems you might have encountered with a specific program.

A new feature in Windows 7 Professional, Ultimate, and Enterprise editions is the capability to run legacy programs in Windows XP Mode. This is a virtual environment within Windows 7 that runs Windows XP with SP 3, enabling you to run all those Windows XP–based programs you can't live without.

You can learn more about Windows XP Mode by visiting www.microsoft.com/windows/virtual-pc/features/default.aspx. Windows XP Mode is also covered in the "The Virtual Machine Approach" section in Chapter 2 and in Appendix A.

Side-by-Side Installs and Virtual Registries

Windows 98 Second Edition provided a feature called *side-by-side DLLs*. This feature allowed a developer to use the version of DLLs required by a particular program without overwriting system DLLs (those stored in the \Windows\System folder). This feature worked *only* on Windows 98SE and only if the program developer took advantage of the feature.

Windows 2000 introduced Windows File Protection, which restored system files automatically if they were overwritten by an application when you installed it or ran it. This protected Windows from crashing but didn't do anything about a program that needed a particular system file version to run.

Side-by-side installs enable users to install multiple versions of the same product on the same computer. For example, suppose Microsoft just released a new version of Office. You want to run a trial version of the new Office suite to learn about new features and test drive it, but you don't want to uninstall the current, well-oiled version. However, multiple programs that use a different version of the same DLL sometimes cause complications—"DLL Hell." When programs use the wrong DLL files, they crash and can take the whole OS down with them.

Windows XP Professional provided a way to handle DLL Hell. It was called *Fusion.* Fusion allowed programs to install whatever system files (DLLs and others) they needed and redirect any files that would replace system files to the program's own folder. When such a program was run, Fusion created a memory-protected virtual machine to run the program with its own DLLs. The end result was that even if two or more programs were running at the same time, using different versions of DLL or other system files that would "break" the system in past versions of Windows, both programs would run properly. No other programs could touch the area of memory granted to each program. Nor could that program or other programs gain access to the area of memory in which the basics of the OS were running.

Windows 7 and Windows Vista contain a different method from the Windows XP solution. Instead of a single Registry, they use a virtual registry that contains multiple DLLs. A virtualized application registry eliminates any conflicts between software. So, if you want to have two versions of Microsoft Office available on the same computer, for example, the virtual registry lets you run them without conflicts.

Virtual registries also have one other important aspect. Because Windows 7 can create and use virtual registries for data, Microsoft applied this concept to users who do not have Administrator privileges. By using virtual registries, nonadministrative guests can use a virtual registry and will not disrupt the main Registry. Usually, only administrators have the rights that allow one to install software that writes to the Registry. But now nonadministrators can install software and other various programs onto the system without causing any harm. Windows 7 will continue to run and display all software installed but will not experience any permanent effect from the data on the virtual registry.

➡ *To learn more about the Windows 7 Registry, **see** Chapter 28, "Editing the Registry."*

 note

Windows Vista introduced virtual folders, which help users get data quickly and easily. This technology has been replaced with libraries in Windows 7. To learn how to use libraries and save searches, see Chapter 5, "Managing Files and Searching."

INSTALLING AND REPLACING HARDWARE

Upgrading Your Hardware

No matter how high the performance of your computer, sooner or later it will start to slow down as newer programs demanding faster hardware show up on your desktop. Chances are performance demands will exceed your computer's capabilities before you or your company is ready to pop for a replacement computer. This chapter will help you make the hardware changes—large or small—you need to get the most work and useful life out of your computer. We'll discuss how to upgrade and install hardware, add a second monitor, connect new and old hard drives, and add memory.

The single most helpful thing you can do to make your Windows 7 computer run at peak speed is to give it enough system memory (or *RAM*, short for *random access memory*). Just as a reminder, your computer uses two types of memory: hard disk space and RAM. RAM holds Windows and the programs you're actually using, and Windows 7 wants more RAM than Windows XP, but is happy with what works for Vista (if not even slightly less). As discussed in the early chapters of this book, Windows 7 can run with as little as 512MB of RAM and an 800MHz CPU, but it will run a bit slowly, and you'll find the experience somewhat unpleasant. Memory is inexpensive these days, and boosting your RAM to at least 1GB will make a huge difference. I discuss adding RAM and upgrading CPUs later in this chapter.

Now, if you're already running Windows 7 on a full-bore, state-of-the-art system, and your computer has a fast video accelerator, a couple of gigs of fast memory, and fast SATA disks, there isn't much more you can do to optimize its hardware. You might just adjust the page file sizes and certainly convert all your partitions to NTFS (which is a requirement for Windows 7), or you might add a ReadyBoost device (more on this later in this chapter). Some of the settings you can make are discussed in Chapter 22, "Windows Management and Maintenance;" Chapter 23, "Tweaking and Customizing Windows;" and Chapter 24, "Managing Hard Disks."

By the same token, if you're doing common, everyday tasks such as word processing, and you're already satisfied with the performance of your computer as a whole, you probably don't need to worry about performance boosters. Your system is probably running just fine, and the time you'd spend trying to fine-tune it might be better spent doing whatever it is you use your computer for (like earning a living).

 tip

This chapter just scratches the surface of the ins and outs of hardware installation and updates. If you want all the details, and I mean *all* the details, get a copy of the best-selling book *Upgrading and Repairing PCs*, by Scott Mueller, published by Que.

If you're anywhere between these two extremes, however, you may want to look at the tune-ups and hardware upgrades we'll discuss in this chapter.

ReadyBoost

Microsoft introduced ReadyBoost as part of Windows Vista. Essentially, it allowed users to allocate all or part of any single USB flash drive (which Microsoft abbreviates as UFD) or a Secure Digital (SD, SDHC, or mini-SD) memory card as an extension to cache memory available in system RAM. In Windows 7 several notable changes are introduced, including

- Vista limited ReadyBoost space to a maximum of 4GB (which is all that 32-bit operating systems can handle anyway) for both 32- and 64-bit versions. In Windows 7, 64-bit versions can allocate up to 128GB for a ReadyBoost cache.

- Vista limited eligible memory devices to UFDs and SD cards; Windows 7 works with those devices plus Compact Flash (CF), all forms of MemoryStick (MS, MS Duo, MS Pro, and so on), and most other memory cards as well. As with Vista versions, devices must meet minimum speed requirements (12.8 Mbps read/write speeds) for use as ReadyBoost cache devices.

- Vista limited ReadyBoost to a single memory device; in Windows 7 you can allocate ReadyBoost cache on multiple memory devices at the same time. When spread across multiple devices performance might not be as fast as when ReadyBoost cache comes from a single device, however.

To allocate space on a memory device for ReadyBoost, right-click the drive icon in Windows Explorer, and then click the ReadyBoost tab in its Properties dialog box. Figure 27.1 shows two different UFDs in use on an x64 Windows 7 machine; the Properties dialog box on the left comes from an NTFS-formatted UFD (NTFS or exFAT are required to create a ReadyBoost cache file greater than 4GB in size), while the box on the right is from a FAT-32 formatted UFD (mixing and matching works fine).

Figure 27.1
In Windows 7, ReadyBoost cache works with multiple devices, where not all formats need be identical.

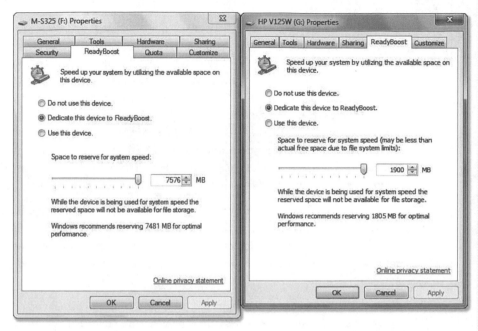

BIOS Settings

Windows 7 depends on proper BIOS settings to enable it to detect and use hardware correctly. At a minimum, your drives should be properly configured in the system BIOS, and your CPU type and speed should be properly set (either in the BIOS or on the motherboard, depending on the system). Thanks to some clever work by Microsoft's engineers, Windows 7 boots faster than other 32-bit versions of Windows, but you can improve boot speed further with these tips:

- Set up your BIOS boot order to start with drive C: so that you can skip the floppy stepper motor test.

- Disable floppy drive seek.

- Turn off any Quick Power-On Self Tests. Some BIOSs have such an option that enables a quicker bootup by skipping some of the internal diagnostics that would usually take place on startup. It makes bootup faster but also leaves you susceptible to errors; some problems will not be detected at startup.

Altered BIOS Settings Prevent Computer from Booting

Today's computer BIOSs include enough arcane settings that it's possible to alter one in a way that prevents proper booting. Before you mess with advanced CMOS settings (not just simple things such as time, date, boot order, power settings, ports, and so on), read the manual for the computer or motherboard. If you decide to change anything, record the old value before making the change. When in doubt, don't alter advanced CMOS settings that affect how the chipset works, whether and where BIOS and video shadowing is used, and so on. By design, default settings from the motherboard maker work under most situations and OSs. Because Windows is the most popular PC OS, you can bet it has been tested and configured for Windows 9x, NT, 2000, XP, Vista, or Windows 7 (unless your motherboard is very old).

That said, what do you do if you've changed something in the CMOS and the computer won't boot? You can try the computer's or motherboard's manual or website for information about Windows 7 settings. If you find nothing, reset all settings to their factory defaults. Most CMOS setups have a Set to Default or similar command you can issue. This should get you out of most any jam.

Using the Set to Default option might also be a good course to take if you make CMOS settings that prevent your computer from booting and you can't remember how to undo those changes. Default settings are usually conservative enough to work under most circumstances. The BIOS in some systems may also have a Fail-Safe Defaults option that sets your BIOS to its most conservative settings.

If what you've done has changed the hard disk Type, or if you manually entered the number of sectors, tracks, platters, and so on, and now it won't boot, use the Auto Detect Hard Disk BIOS setting to discover and enter those numbers automatically. (This is known as *drive autotyping*.)

Upgrading Your Hard Disk

One of the most effective improvements you can make to a system is to get a faster or larger hard drive, or add another drive. SCSI hard disks used to seriously one-up IDE drives, but the new breed of Ultra DMA EIDE drives (which I call Old MacDonald Disks—EIEIO!) and Serial ATA (SATA) drives are speedy and much cheaper than SCSI. An EIDE bus supports four drives (two each on the primary and secondary channels) and is almost always built in to your motherboard. Adding an optical (usually a DVD±RW or a Blu-ray) drive claims one, leaving you with a maximum of three EIDE hard drives unless you install a separate add-on EIDE host adapter or have a motherboard with RAID support. The EIDE spec tops out at 133MBps. SATA supports one drive per channel, but the latest SATA II systems can reach top transfer speeds of 300MBps. Because optical drives also come with SATA connections these days, many new systems skip EIDE in favor of SATA.

The following are some essential considerations for upgrading your hard disk system:

- Don't put a hard drive and an optical drive on the same channel unless you must. (Put the hard drive on the primary IDE1 channel and the optical drive on the secondary IDE2 channel.) On some computers, the IDE channel negotiates down to the slowest device on a channel, slowing down a hard disk's effective transfer rate. Be sure that the hard drive containing Windows is designated as the Primary Master drive.

- Defragment the hard disk with the Defragmenter utility, which you can reach through Computer. Right-click the drive, select Properties, Tools tab, Defragment Now. Do this every week (or run Defrag and set up a schedule so it runs weekly), and the process will take just a few minutes. But, if you wait months before you try this the first time, be prepared to wait a long time for your system to finish. You can also purchase third-party defragmenting programs that do a more thorough job. For more about defragmenting, see Chapter 24.

- Get a faster disk drive (and possibly controller if necessary to support the drive): Upgrade from standard Parallel ATA (PATA) to SATA drives if possible. If you have slower (4,200- or 5,400RPM) drives, upgrade to quicker ones such as the increasingly popular 7,200RPM or 10,000RPM drives. The faster spin rate bumps up system performance more than you might expect. Purchase drives with as large a cache buffer as you can afford. Drive technology is quickly outdated, so do some web reading before purchase.

> **⊛ tip**
>
> Many recent motherboards feature onboard IDE and even SATA RAID, which can perform either mirroring (which makes an immediate backup copy of one drive to another) or striping (which treats both drives as part of a single drive for speed). Although the RAID features on these motherboards don't support RAID 5, the safest (and most expensive!) form of RAID, they work well and are much less expensive than any SCSI form of RAID. Just remember that mirroring gives you extra reliability at the expense of speed because everything has to be written twice, and striping with only two disks gives you extra speed at the expense of reliability—if one hard disk fails, you lose everything. You can now find external terabyte boxes with multiple drives in them that can be set up for striping or mirroring (RAID 0 or 1) at amazingly affordable prices.

Adding RAM

Perhaps the most cost-effective upgrade you can make to any Windows-based system is to add RAM. This one is a no-brainer: If your disk pauses and thrashes each time you switch between running applications or documents, you need more RAM. Although Microsoft says Windows 7 can run with as little as 512MB of RAM, we found that this results in barely acceptable behavior. At least Microsoft was realistic about it this time around. Microsoft had claimed XP could run with 64MB, but that was a stretch. Running with 64MB caused intolerably slow performance. Windows 7's published minimum is 512MB, but if you run memory-intensive applications and want decent performance, you'll want to up it to 1GB, if not 2.

Windows automatically recognizes newly added RAM and adapts internal settings, such as when to swap to disk, to take best advantage of any RAM you throw its way. Upgrade to at least 1GB of RAM if you can afford it, especially if your system uses the economical synchronous dynamic RAM

(SDRAM) or double-data-rate (DDR) SDRAM dual in-line memory modules (DIMMs). Memory prices fluctuate constantly, but these days 2GB DIMMs sell for about $25. This is a cost-effective upgrade indeed. But be sure to get the right memory for your motherboard. A huge variety of memory technologies are out there. At the time this was written, common technologies included SDRAM, Rambus DRAM (RDRAM), DDR, DDR2, and DDR3. Memory speeds range from 100MHz (labeled PC100) to 2200MHz (labeled DDR3-2200). Also, there are error-correction code (ECC) and non-error-correcting RAM varieties (desktop and notebook PCs use non-ECC RAM).

 tip

For more about RAM developments and technology, go to http://en.wikipedia.org/wiki/Random_access_memory.

To find out what type of memory you need, check with your computer manufacturer or the manual that came with your computer or motherboard. Get the fastest compatible memory that your CPU can use and that your motherboard supports. You can get RAM that's rated faster than you currently need, but you won't gain any speed advantage—just a greater likelihood of being able to reuse the memory if you later upgrade your motherboard. Here's a website with some good information about RAM and even possibly what kind your computer uses: www.pcbuyerbeware.co.uk/RAM.htm.

The maximum amount of RAM you can use depends on your computer's hardware and the version of Windows 7 you are using. The following table lists the version and maximum amounts. Many last-generation computers cannot use more than 4GB of memory, and that's all that 32-bit versions of Windows can address, even if you could plug it in without a BIOS upgrade. Check with the computer or motherboard manufacturer's data sheets or website to figure out whether you have to flash upgrade the system board BIOS to support more than 4GB of RAM.

Version	RAM Maximum
All 32-bit Windows 7 versions	4GB
64-bit Home Basic	8GB
64-bit Home Premium	16GB
64-bit all other versions	128GB+

Adding Hardware

One of the tasks that is most common for anyone responsible for configuring and maintaining PCs is adding and removing hardware. The Control Panel contains an applet designed for that purpose, called Devices and Printers (accessible from Control Panel's Hardware and Sound category). You can use it if the OS doesn't automatically recognize that you swiped something or added something new, whether it's a peripheral such as a printer or an internal device such as a DVD-ROM, additional hard disk, or whatever.

If you're a hardware maven, you might visit Devices and Printers occasionally, but only if you work with non–Plug and Play (PnP) hardware. PnP hardware installation is usually

 tip

Microsoft has changed its nomenclature with Windows 7. What used to be called the Windows Compatibility List or Hardware Compatibility List (also abbreviated HCL) is now called the Windows Logo'd Products List. If you want to make life easy for yourself, before you purchase hardware for your Windows 7 system, check the lists on the Microsoft site (look for Windows 7 items at https://winqual.microsoft.com/hcl/default.aspx. Or when looking on a box in a store or online, it should have a "Certified for Windows 7" or "Windows 7" logo on it.

effortless because Windows 7 is good at detection and should install items fairly automatically, along with any necessary device drivers that tell Windows how to access the new hardware. With non-PnP devices now nearly obsolete, you'll only need to mess with this on rare occasions, if at all.

If you've purchased a board or other hardware add-in, you should first read the supplied manual for details about installation procedures. Installation tips and an install program may be supplied with the hardware. However, if no instructions are included, keep reading to find out how to physically install the hardware.

If you're installing an internal device, you'll have to shut down your computer before you open the case. I suggest that you also unplug it because most modern PCs actually keep part of the system powered up even when it appears to be off. Before inserting a card, you should discharge any potential electrostatic charge differential between you and the computer by touching the chassis of the computer with your hand. Using an antistatic wrist strap also is a good idea. Then insert the card, RAM, and so on.

When the device is installed, power your PC back up, log on with a Computer Administrator account, and wait a minute or so. In most cases, the Add Hardware Wizard automatically detects and sets up the new device. If you must run this wizard, type **hdwwiz** in the Start menu search box (it's no longer listed in Control Panel).

If you're adding a USB or FireWire device, plugging in an Ethernet cable, or a digital camera card, you don't need to shut down before plugging in or inserting the new device, but you should close any programs you have running, just in case the installation process hangs the computer. The computer itself (as opposed to applications) doesn't hang often in NT-based systems such as XP, Vista, and Windows 7, so BSODs (blue screens of death) are more rare, but they can happen. Save your work and close your applications before you plug in the new device.

For non-PnP hardware, or for PnP stuff that isn't detected or doesn't install automatically for some reason, you can try this:

1. Type **hdwwiz** in the Start menu search box to launch the Add Hardware Wizard.

2. The wizard starts by advising you to use a CD if one came with your hardware. This is good advice. If you don't have a CD, you can move ahead and use the wizard.

note

Always check the installation instructions before you install the new hardware. In some cases, the instructions tell you to install some software *before* you install the new hardware. If they do, follow this advice! I have made the mistake of ignoring this and finding out that a driver has to be removed and reinstalled in the correct order to work correctly.

tip

You might be tempted to move some adapter cards plugged in to your motherboard from one slot to another, but don't do this unless you really must. Each PCI adapter's configuration information is tied to the slot into which it's plugged. When you restart your computer, the PnP system will interpret the move as your having removed an existing device and installed a new one, and this can cause headaches. In some cases, you'll even be asked to reinsert the driver disks for the device you moved, and you may have to reconfigure its software settings. (From personal experience, I can tell you that moving a modem gives Symantec PCAnywhere fits.) If you must swap slots, don't change or mess with them all at once. Change one and reboot, and then change another. Windows 7 is better about contention and remapping resources than previous Windows versions were.

3. Click Next, and the wizard asks whether you want it to search for the new hardware and figure out what it is (and try to find a driver for it), or whether you want to specify it yourself. Go for the search. If you're lucky, it will work, and you're home free. If a new device is found that doesn't require any user configuration, a help balloon appears onscreen near the system tray, supplying the details of what was located.

 tip

Another way to force a scan of legacy hardware is to open the Device Manager, right-click the computer name at the top of the list, and choose Add Legacy Hardware.

4. If nothing is found, the wizard asks you to manually select the hardware you wish to install from a list. Assuming you know what to choose, click Next. You'll now see a list like the one in Figure 27.2.

5. Choose the correct category and click Next. Depending on the item, you'll next see a different dialog box. For example, for a modem, the wizard offers an option to detect and install it. For most other items, it prompts you for the make and model.

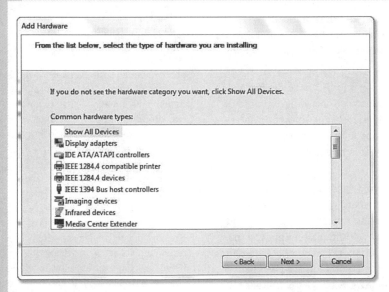

Figure 27.2
When a new PnP device isn't found, you see this dialog box. Choose the right category and click Next.

6. Choose the correct make and model. If you don't see a category that matches your hardware, click Back and then select Show All Devices. It will take a minute for the list to be populated. The box will then show every manufacturer and the devices each manufacturer sells. With some sleuthing, you may be able to find the hardware you wish to install.

 note

Windows 7 64-bit cannot use legacy hardware as XP, Vista, and 32-bit Windows 7 can. All 64-bit drivers must be digitally signed by Microsoft, or they are not allowed to install.

Be sure you choose the exact name and model number/name for the item you're installing. You might be prompted to insert your Windows 7 DVD so that the appropriate driver file(s) can be loaded. If your hardware came with a driver disk, use the Have Disk button to install the driver directly from the manufacturer's driver disk or downloaded file.

Early in the wizard's steps, you can specify the hardware and skip the legacy scan. This option saves time and, in some cases, is a surer path to installing new hardware. It also lets you install a device later if you want to. The wizard doesn't bother to authenticate the existence of the hardware; it simply installs a new driver.

If a device plugs in to an external serial, parallel, or SCSI port, you might want to connect it, turn it on, and restart your system to install it. Some of these devices can't be installed via the Add Hardware Wizard if they're not present when the system starts up.

As mentioned previously, you can also use the Devices and Printers applet to install hardware. To add a network or wireless device of some kind, for example, click Start, Devices and Printers, and then click Add a Device. This triggers a device scan on your PC, and if Windows 7 finds something suitable, it will trigger the device installation at that point. Likewise, to add a printer you can click Add a Printer at the end of the preceding sequence. Then you will see options to add a locally or network-attached print device instead. After that, you'll install any necessary drivers and the process will complete.

Providing Drivers for Hardware Not in the List

If the hardware you're attempting to install isn't on the device list, this might be because one or more of the following is true:

- The hardware is newer than Windows 7 itself.

- The hardware is old, and Microsoft did not include its driver.

- The hardware must be configured using a special setup program supplied with the device.

In such cases, you must obtain a driver from the manufacturer's website (or Microsoft's; check both) and have it at hand in some form (UFD, optical media, or on a hard drive somewhere acces-

 tip

In some cases, you can adjust settings after hardware is installed and possibly adjust the hardware to match. (Some legacy cards have switches or software adjustments that can be made to them to control the I/O port, DMA address, and so forth.) You might be told which settings to use to avoid conflicts with other hardware in the system.

If, for some reason, you don't want to use the settings that the wizard suggests, you can use your own settings and configure them manually. You can do so from the Add Hardware Wizard or via the Device Manager. See Chapter 22 for details on adjusting hardware resources and dealing with resource contention. This is much less of a problem than it once was, now that virtually all modern PC hardware conforms to the Plug and Play spec.

 tip

Use the System applet or the Computer Management Device Manager Console, not the Add Hardware Wizard, to fine-tune device settings, such as IRQ and port selections, update devices and drivers, and remove hardware. Use the Add Hardware Wizard only to add or troubleshoot hardware.

Here's a quick way to access Device Manager: Click Start, type **Device** into the search box, and then select Device Manager from the results list. That's it!

sible). If the manufacturer supplies a setup disk, forget my advice, and follow the manufacturer's instructions. However, if the manufacturer supplies a driver disk and no instructions, follow these steps:

1. Run the Add Hardware Wizard and click Next.

2. Select Install the Hardware That I Manually Select from a List and click Next.

3. Select the appropriate device category and click Next.

4. Click the Have Disk button. Enter the location of the driver. (You can enter any path, such as a local directory or a network path.) Typically, you insert a UFD or optical disk. If you download the driver software from a website, save it on your hard drive. In either case, you can use the Browse button if you don't know the exact path or drive. If you do use the Browse option, look for a directory where an INF file appears in the dialog box.

 tip

If you're not sure which ports and interrupts are already taken, type `system information` in the Search box, then check Hardware Resources to identify available IRQs, DMA, and so on.

5. Assuming the wizard finds a suitable driver file, choose the desired hardware item from the ensuing dialog box and then follow the onscreen directions.

New Hardware Doesn't Work

If you've added some hardware but it doesn't work, try these troubleshooting steps, in this order:

1. Try the troubleshooters included in the Help system, assuming the hardware fits into one of the neatly packaged categories. Open them through the Help and Support page: Click Start, Help and Support, then type in the name or category for the device you're working with.

2. Try rebooting Windows 7.

3. Use System Information and the Device Manager to check resources assigned to the hardware to be sure there are no conflicts. Check the hardware manual to determine whether you should be setting DIP switches or jumpers to avoid conflicts if the device isn't PnP compatible.

4. Open the Device Manager, locate the device entry, and press the Delete key to delete it. Then, power down, remove the device, and restart Windows.

5. Power down again, reconnect the hardware (run the Add Hardware Wizard, also known as `hdwwiz`, if the hardware isn't detected at bootup), and configure as necessary.

6. Check Google; search to see if anyone else has posted about the problem and its solution.

Continued...

7. Check the manufacturer's website. If it has a "Knowledge Base," search that.

8. If you purchased the hardware from a local store, contact it for assistance.

9. Contact the manufacturer via email or phone.

About Windows 7 Drivers

Most Windows Vista drivers work in Windows 7, so if you can't find a driver specifically for Windows 7, try a Vista driver instead. Vista and Windows 7 use a common driver model, so this is perfectly safe most of the time. If a driver you load in Windows 7 crashes (for example, a graphics driver), it simply restarts (after the screen goes black temporarily). In a few moments, you're back up and running.

The user-mode driver model employed in Windows 7 and Vista is called the User-Mode Driver Framework (UMDF), and is part of Microsoft's newest driver model, the Windows Driver Foundation (WDF). A user-mode driver is typically used for devices that plug in to a USB or FireWire bus, such as digital cameras, PDAs, and mass storage devices. This also allows drivers that typically require a system reboot (video card drivers, for example) to install or update without forcing a reboot. For more about user-mode drivers, read http://en.wikipedia.org/wiki/User_Mode_Driver_Framework.

Not all Windows 7 drivers are installed in user mode. Some drivers do need to be installed in the kernel (this model is used in Windows XP and prior versions of Windows). For extra protection, to prevent flaky or bogus drivers from being installed into Windows 7, Microsoft is cracking down, but only for x64-based Windows 7 (that is, 64-bit) versions. Kernel-mode drivers on x64-bit versions of Windows 7 must be digitally signed, which means they have to be tested and given Microsoft's seal of approval. Even the Administrator account cannot install unsigned kernel-mode drivers. User-mode drivers may still be installed without a digital signature, however.

Removing Hardware

Before unplugging a USB, FireWire, or PCMCIA (PC Card) device, tell Windows 7 to stop using it. This prevents data loss caused by unplugging the device before Windows 7 has finished saving all its data. To stop these devices, click the Safely Remove Hardware icon (it's one of the hidden icons available through the up arrow in the notification area). Unplug the device or card only after Windows informs you it is safe to do so.

For the most part, you can remove other hardware simply by shutting your computer off, unplugging it, and removing the unwanted devices. When Windows restarts, it recognizes that the device is missing and can carry on without problems. As a shortcut when you don't want to power down completely, you can hibernate the computer and remove the item. Sometimes, this can prevent a computer from resuming properly though, so be cautious and save your work before you try this method. Test it, and if it works, you can disconnect this item during hibernation in the future, knowing that Windows 7 detects the change upon resuming.

If you want to completely delete a driver for an unneeded device, use the Device Manager. Double-click the device whose driver you wish to remove. This opens its properties dialog box. Click Uninstall Driver. Delete the drivers *before* uninstalling the hardware; otherwise, the device won't appear in the Device Manager's list of installed devices.

➡ *For details about the Device Manager, see "Device Manager," p. 612.*

Installing and Using Multiple Monitors

Chapter 23 discussed briefly the procedure for setting up multiple monitors. In this section, we explain a few of the more convoluted details and issues that can occur when installing additional monitors.

As you know, Windows 7 supports multiple monitors, a great feature first developed for Windows 98. You can run up to ten monitors with Windows 7, but normally, you will use no more than two or three. Using multiple monitors lets you view a large amount of information at a glance. Use one screen for video editing, web design, or graphics and another for toolbars. Leave a web or email display up at all times while you use another monitor for current tasks. Stretch huge spreadsheets across both screens.

Here are some rules and tips about using multiple monitors:

- Some laptops support attaching an external monitor and can display different views on the internal LCD screen and on the external monitor. This feature is called DualView, and if your laptop supports it, your user's manual will show you how to enable it. You can ignore this section's instructions on installing a device adapter and just follow the instructions to set Display properties to use a second monitor.

- Because most computers have no more than one or two PCI slots open, if you want to max out your video system, look into one of the multimonitor video cards available from Matrox, ATI, and various other vendors. From a single slot, you can drive four monitors with these cards. With only two slots, you can drive four to eight monitors. Multimonitor video cards are available for both AGP and PCI slots. Today, most modern graphics cards will drive two monitors without requiring additional hardware of any kind.

- The latest video interface kid on the block, dubbed PCI Express (PCIe) will be at the center of PC graphics for the foreseeable future. The old video champ, AGP, is on its way out. PCIe offers double the bandwidth of AGP 8x. PCI Express X16 slots have peak bandwidth levels of 4.0 GBps (up to 8.0 GBps bidirectional), compared to 2.1 GBps for AGP 8x. PCIe usually support two displays, but some quad-link versions that support four displays are also available. Look for one

 tip

If a USB controller doesn't install properly, especially if the controller doesn't show up in the Device Manager, the problem might lie in your system BIOS. Most BIOSs include a setting to enable or disable USB ports. Shut down and restart. Do whatever your computer requires for you to check BIOS settings during system startup (usually pressing the Del or Esc key from the initial boot screen). Then, enter BIOS setup and enable USB support.

When that is done, if a USB controller still doesn't appear in the Device Manager, it's possible the computer's BIOS might be outdated. Check with the computer or motherboard manufacturer for an update that supports USB under Windows 7.

(be sure your system can accept it) if high performance (such as video or high-end production work) is your aim.

- Many multimonitor arrangements consist of two cards. Today, that usually means dual PCI-e graphics cards.

- If you mix AGP and PCI, older BIOSs sometimes have a strange habit of forcing one or the other to become the "primary" display. This is the display that Windows first boots on and the one you use to log on. You might be annoyed if your better monitor or better card isn't the primary display, because most programs are initially displayed on the primary monitor when you launch them. Therefore, you might want to flash upgrade your BIOS if the maker of your computer or motherboard indicates that an upgrade will improve multimonitor support on your computer by letting you decide which monitor or card should be the primary display.

- Upon connecting a second monitor, you should be prompted with a dialog box that asks you whether you want to use a mirror arrangement or an extended desktop arrangement. With some luck, this wizard will be all you need to fiddle with. If not and you're unhappy with the default choice of primary display, you can adjust it with Display properties once both displays are running.

- If you update an older system to Windows 7, the OS always needs a VGA device, which becomes the primary display. The BIOS detects the VGA device based on slot order, unless the BIOS offers an option to choose which device to treat as the VGA device. Check your BIOS settings to see whether any special settings might affect multimonitor displays, such as whether the AGP or PCI card defaults to primary, or the PCI slot order. Slot 1 is usually the slot nearest the power supply connector.

- The design of the card itself, not the monitor, enables it to operate with multiple monitors on Windows 7. Don't expect any vendors to add multimonitor support simply by implementing a driver update. Either a card supports multiple monitors or it doesn't.

- Most laptops these days support mirror and extended view modes. How well they do depends on their video card and the amount of video RAM. Note: There is a key combo on most laptops that turns the output to the external monitor off or on. Typically, it is the FN key (lower-left corner of the keyboard) combined with another key such as F4 or F5. Look closely at the little icons on your laptop's keytops. You may have to press a combination a few times to get to the desired setup (such as laptop screen on and external screen on, or just one screen on).

- On older motherboards with onboard I/O such as sound, modem, and LAN, you may have difficulties with multimonitor configurations, especially if devices share an IRQ with a particular PCI slot. You might want to disable any onboard devices you're not using, to free up resources for additional video cards to use instead.

 tip

Microsoft doesn't provide many specifics about which video cards/chipsets work in multimonitor mode, perhaps because BIOS and motherboard issues affect the results different users obtain from the same video cards. The Realtime Soft website contains a searchable database of thousands of working combinations and links to other multimonitor resources, including Realtime Soft's own UltraMon multimonitor utility. Check it out at www.realtimesoft.com/multimon.

- Just because a set of cards supports multimonitoring under a previous version of Windows (even Windows XP) doesn't mean it works under Windows 7. Windows 7 has stricter hardware requirements as part of its strategy to increase reliability (that said, if it works with Vista it probably also works with Windows 7).

These steps detail a likely installation scenario for a secondary display adapter for use with multiple monitors. It's possible that it will be much simpler for your system. I have included details step by step mostly for those who run Windows 7 on older systems and add a second display card. With newer systems, such as laptops with dual-monitor video display chipsets, you simply plug in an external monitor and turn it on, Windows detects it, walks you through a wizard, and you're done.

1. Boot up your system into Windows 7, and plug in the second monitor. Or you can right-click a blank area of your desktop. From the resulting pop-up menu, select Properties.

2. Go to the Settings tab. Confirm that your primary display adapter is listed correctly. (That is, if you have an ATI Rage Pro, ATI Rage Pro should be listed under Display.) Your display adapter *should not* be listed as plain-old "VGA," or multimonitoring will not work. If this is the case, you need to find and install correct Windows 7 drivers or consult your graphics card manufacturer's website.

3. After you confirm that the right drivers are loaded for your display adapter and that you are in a compatible color depth, shut down and then power off your system.

4. Disconnect the power cable leading to the back of your system and remove the case cover. Confirm that you have an available PCI slot. Before inserting your secondary display adapter, disable its VGA mode, if necessary, by adjusting a jumper block or DIP switch on the card. Newer cards use the software driver or BIOS settings to enable or disable VGA mode.

Can't Select the Primary Display

It can sometimes be tricky to force Windows 7 to use a particular video display card as the secondary display. It usually defaults to one card and grays out Primary on the other one. If a display card isn't disabled from running in VGA mode, the computer runs the card's power-on self test (POST). When that happens, Windows 7 assigns it primary display status; if the other card's VGA mode can't be disabled, you cannot use the secondary card. Most users will want to keep their first video card as the primary display, so they need to know how to prevent this unwanted POST from occurring.

Generally, dual-display works best and easiest with a multihead graphics card, available in PCIe as well as older AGP and PCI designs. However, many setups use a mix of one AGP and one PCI, or one AGP and one PCIe. This doesn't guarantee that the faster video card will wind up being your primary display. You may need to set the system BIOS option for default video to PCI to enable an AGP+PCI dual display, or to AGP for an AGP+PCIe dual display, to work properly.

Continued...

If your video card uses a jumper block or switch to disable VGA mode, this option makes it easier to use the card as a secondary card because only the primary card needs VGA mode. VGA mode is used for the system's POST and to display startup options before the Windows GUI gets initialized.

Many desktop systems with onboard video automatically disable the onboard video when you install any video card (PCI, AGP, or PCIe), which makes it necessary to install two video cards (or a multimonitor video card) to obtain multimonitor support.

Generally, you can't tell whether a secondary card will work until after you boot Windows 7 with the secondary card in place. Then, the system detects the card and installs the drivers, and the system tries to initialize the card. If the card gets initialized successfully, you should see the Windows desktop on both screens.

If the secondary monitor's screen stays black, check the Device Manager listing for the video card. If the card is listed with a yellow exclamation mark, it's not working properly. A Code 10 error on the card's properties dialog box General tab indicates the card was unable to start.

Restart the system, change the default display setting in the BIOS, and retry it. If necessary, try the card in a different slot.

Something else to try is to right-click an open space on the desktop and choose Personalize, Display, and then right-click the icon for the monitor that you want to make Primary and choose Primary.

5. Insert your secondary display adapter, secure it properly with a screw, reassemble your system, and reconnect the power. Next, connect a second monitor to the secondary display adapter.

6. Turn on both the monitors and power up the system. Allow the system to boot into Windows 7.

7. After you log in, Windows 7 detects your new display adapter and may bring up the Add New Hardware Wizard. Confirm that it detects the correct display adapter and, when prompted, tell Windows 7 to search for a suitable driver. Then click Next.

8. Windows 7 then finds information on the display adapter. When you are prompted, insert your Windows 7 installation CD, or browse to the driver file for your adapter, and click OK.

9. Windows 7 then copies files. When the process is completed, click Finish. Windows 7 then also detects your secondary monitor (if it is a PnP monitor). When prompted, click Finish again.

10. After all appropriate drivers are installed, and your secondary monitor is connected and turned on, a wizard should pop up asking how you want to use the newly connected monitor: either as a mirror (repeating what is on the primary

 note

All this detection may occur without intervention on your part, and a balloon may appear on the taskbar announcing that your new hardware is ready to be used.

monitor) or for an extended desktop area (meaning you can move your mouse across both monitors). Answer accordingly. If you don't see the wizard, right-click a blank portion of your desktop and select Personalize. Then choose Display. You will notice that two Monitor icons now appear in the center window of the display applet, representing your two monitors (see Figure 27.3). Click the Monitor icon labeled 2, and it becomes highlighted in blue.

11. Under the Change the Appearance of Your Displays heading, your secondary display should be visible. In the Multiple Displays pull-down list, select Extend These Displays, and then click Apply. Click Keep Changes to make this change permanent.

12. While the Monitor icon labeled 2 is highlighted, you adjust the resolution and orientation for the new monitor.

13. To change the way your monitors are positioned, click and drag the Monitor icons around. (Note that displays must touch along one edge.) When you find a desirable position, release the mouse button, and then click Apply, and the Monitor icon is aligned adjacent to the other Monitor icon. Also note that wherever the two displays meet is the location your mouse cursor can pass from one display to the next. That's why a horizontal alignment is preferred for a standard desktop arrangement (see Figure 27.3).

note

You can set up Windows 7 with more than one secondary display, up to a maximum of nine additional displays. To do so, just select another supported secondary display adapter with VGA disabled and repeat the preceding steps with another monitor attached to the additional secondary adapter, or attach more than one monitor to either (or both) of your display adapters.

Figure 27.3
A system running dual monitors.

After you finish these steps, you can drag items across your screen onto alternate monitors. Better yet, you can resize a window to stretch it across more than one monitor. Things get a little weird at the gap, though. You have to get used to the idea of the mouse cursor jumping from one screen into the next.

Installing a UPS

Although Windows 7 contains a backup utility you can use to protect your data, and you may use a network drive that's backed up every night for your data, or a mirror drive, blackouts and power outages (and the data loss they cause) can happen anywhere, any time. In addition to regular backups, in mission-critical settings, you should be concerned about keeping power going to your PC during its normal operation.

➡ *Managing backups is discussed in the section "The All New Backup and Restore" p. 863. "Backing Up the Registry" is covered on p. 809.*

 tip

If you're not sure which monitor is which, click the Identify button, shown in Figure 27.3, to display a large number on all screens.

 tip

If you don't have enough open slots to install all extra adapter(s) needed for multiple monitors, look into quad-link video adapter cards that support four monitors (most modern cards support two these days). You can also buy USB monitor adapters if you prefer.

A battery backup unit (also called a *UPS*, which is short for *uninterruptible power supply*) provides battery power to your system for as long as an hour, which is more than enough time for you to save your data and shut down your system. A UPS plugs into the wall (and can act as a surge suppressor), and your computer and monitor plug in to outlets on the rear of the UPS.

Electronic circuitry in the UPS continually monitors AC line voltage; should that voltage rise above or dip below predefined limits or fail entirely, the UPS takes over, powering the computer with its built-in battery and cutting off the computer from the AC wall outlet.

As you might imagine, preventing data loss requires the system's response time to be very fast. As soon as AC power gets flaky, the UPS has to take over within a few milliseconds, at most. Many (but not all) UPS models feature a serial (COM) or USB cable, which attaches to an appropriate port on your system. This cable sends signals to your computer to inform it when the battery backup has taken over and tells it to start the shutdown process; some units may also broadcast a warning message over the network to other computers. Such units are often called *intelligent UPSs*.

Windows 2000 and XP had a function called Windows 2000 UPS Services. This was a service that monitored a serial port for a warning signal from a UPS. If the UPS signaled that a power irregularity had occurred and power was about to go down, an event or series of events could be triggered. Typical events were such things as running a program or sending out an alert to all users or admins on a server

 tip

If the UPS you purchase (or already own) doesn't come with Windows 7–specific drivers for shutdown and warning features, contact the vendor for a software update.

about impending doom. The message could alert users to save their work and power down their computers, for example.

Well, this service was removed in Windows Vista, and is likewise missing in Windows 7. What we have now is effectively what laptop computers have—a power profile that includes battery settings. It's not different—it just works on a desktop PC. You can read about laptop power profiles in Chapter 35, "Hitting the Road," but I tell you a little about how to drill down into the power management settings here. Then later in this chapter ("Choosing a UPS" and "Installing and Configuring UPS"), you can find some tips to ponder when purchasing or setting up a UPS.

If your UPS doesn't have provisions for automatic shutdown, its alarm will notify you when the power fails. Shut down the computer yourself after saving any open files, grab a flashlight, and relax until the power comes back on.

Ideally, all workstations assigned to serious tasks (what work isn't serious?) should have UPS protection of some kind. Although it's true that well-designed programs such as Microsoft Office have autobackup options that help to restore files in progress if the power goes out, they are not always reliable. Crashes and weird performance of applications and OSs are enough to worry about, without adding power losses to the mix. And if power fails during a disk write, you might have a rude awakening, because the hard disk's file system could be corrupted, which is far worse than losing a file or two. Luckily, with NTFS and previous versions (see the section "Recovering Previous Versions of a File" in Chapter 31) and other Windows 7 hard disk features, this is less of a specter than it used to be, but still....

My advice is that you guard against power outages, power spikes, and line noise, at all reasonable cost. With the ever-increasing power and plummeting cost of notebook computers, one of the most economically sensible solutions is to purchase notebook computers instead of desktop computers, especially for users who change locations frequently. They take up little space, are easier to configure because the hardware complement cannot be easily altered, and have UPSs built in. When the power fails, the battery takes over.

If you use Windows 7 systems as servers, you'll certainly want UPS support on those, as discussed in Part V of this book. In place of Windows 2000 UPS Services mentioned previously, today's USB-based UPS systems often come with proprietary programs that sit on top of the capable innards of the built-in Windows 7 event monitor and can work all kinds of magic, signaling users, broadcasting messages about prob-

 tip

When using laptops, be sure your batteries are working. Over time, they can lose their capacity to hold a charge. You should cycle them once in a while to see how long they last. If necessary, replace them. Also, set up the power options on all laptops to save to disk (hibernate) in case of impending power loss. You'll typically want to set hibernation to kick in when 5% to 10% of battery power remains, to ensure that the hard disk can start up (if sleeping) and write system state onto disk.

lems or status, and so on, as the battery begins to run down. Users can be warned to save their work and shut down (assuming they are running on a power source that is also functional, of course).

In addition to protecting your hardware investment from the ravages of lightning storms and line spikes, a UPS confers the added advantage of alerting a remote administrator of impending server or workstation shutdowns so that appropriate measures can be taken.

Choosing a UPS

Before shelling out any hard-earned dough for UPS systems, check to see which ones work with Windows 7. Consult the Windows Logo'd Products List on the Microsoft site. Also, consider these questions:

- Do you want a separate UPS for every workstation, or one larger UPS that can power a number of computers from a single location?

- Which kind of UPS do you need? There are three levels of UPS: standby, line interactive, and online. *Standby* is the cheapest. The power to the computer comes from the AC line just as it normally does, but if the power drops or sags, the batteries take over. There is typically a surge protector filter in the circuit to protect your computer. *Line interactive* UPS units can handle temporary voltage sags without sapping the batteries, using clever electronics to stabilize voltage levels. This keeps your batteries topped up and ready in case of an outage. *Online* UPS systems constantly convert AC to DC, filter and clean up the signal, and then convert it back to AC. The result is super-clean power without spikes or sags. Batteries take over, of course, immediately in all three types, if there is a power loss.

- What UPS capacity does each computer need? The answer depends on the power draw of the computer itself, the size of the monitor, and whether you want peripherals to run off the battery, too. To protect your network fully, you should also install a UPS on network devices such as routers, hubs, bridges, modems, telephones, printers, and other network equipment. Check the real-world specs for the UPS. Its capacity is also determined by how long you want the UPS to operate after a complete power outage. If you just want enough time for you or another user to save work, a relatively small UPS will do. If you want to get through a day's work doing stock trades, you'll need a hefty unit. UPS units are rated in VA (volt-amperes) and watts. You should either measure your equipment's actual power draw or select a UPS with a wattage rating that significantly exceeds the wattage rating on your gear. You'll also want to know how long the UPSs can run at the wattage your system draws. Read the vendor's battery life specifications carefully, and consider the typical length for power outages in your area. Also, compare warranties on units. You will have to replace the batteries every couple of years. How expensive is that? Are the batteries user replaceable?

- Get a unit with an alarm: You want one that is smart enough to interact with a PC and network to emit alerts or other messages.

- What software support do you want? Do you need to keep a log of UPS activity during the day for later analysis? What about utilities that test the UPS on a regular basis to ensure it's working?

 tip

Network hardware and modems should be powered by the UPS, but printers should not. Laser printers, in particular, draw so much power that the actual runtime for a given UPS unit will be just a fraction of what it would be if the laser printer were left out of the UPS circuit. Because systems can store print jobs as temporary files until a printer is available to take them, there's no need to waste precious battery power to keep a printer running through a blackout.

Installing and Configuring a UPS

If you plan to use a UPS that doesn't support signaling to the computer via a data cable, you needn't worry about the following settings because they won't make any difference. Simply plug your PC into the UPS and then plug the UPS into a wall outlet. Do your work at the computer. One day you'll notice that all lights in the room go off, but the computer stays on. That's your moment of grace. Save your work and shut down or hibernate the PC.

If your UPS is smarter (and it should be), simply install it according to the manufacturer's instructions. Typically, you connect the UPS to the power source, the computer to the UPS, and the USB between the UPS and the computer. After successful installation, you'll have a battery icon in your system tray near the clock, just like on a laptop.

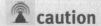 **caution**

If by chance your UPS is a serial-cable unit, be aware that normal serial cables do not work to connect a UPS to a Windows 7 machine. UPS serial cables, even between models from the same manufacturer, use different pin assignments. It's best to use the cable supplied by the UPS maker.

Now all you have to do is tell your system what to do during various cases of battery failure. Your system will constantly monitor the condition of the battery, just as a laptop does. So, if the AC power fails, presumably the UPS switches on, and your PC keeps running. Then, the power profile you use comes into play. Here's how to fine-tune your profile:

1. Click Start, Control Panel, Hardware and Sound, Power Options.

2. Under Select a Power Plan, choose the power plan you want. Under that plan, click Change Plan Settings.

3. In the next dialog box, click Change Advanced Power Settings. You'll see the dialog box shown in Figure 27.4.

Figure 27.4
Here you can set the UPS and system behavior for cases of power outage.

4. Click the + next to the Low Battery Action and the Critical Battery Action and set what you want your PC to do when the power gets low. I suggest Hibernate, not Sleep, because Sleep will keep only your data intact as long as battery power is available. Shut Down is the next best option, but not very good, because if you are not present, unsaved work may be lost when the system shuts down.

5. Set the Low Battery Notification to On for both Plugged In and On Battery. This way, if the battery level is getting low (perhaps due to a worn-out or defective battery), you'll be notified.

6. Set the Low Battery Action for Plugged In, too, to be extra cautious. For example, you might want the computer to notify you that the power is low and then hibernate or shut down.

7. Set the Low Battery Level and the Critical Battery Level after considering your computer's power needs and the capacity of your power supply. I like to play it safe and set Critical to 10% and have the computer hibernate at that point. Then I can wait out the blackout, replace the UPS or battery if necessary, and start back up right where I left off. It takes a few minutes to hibernate sometimes, so make sure you have enough energy in your battery to keep everything working during the wind-down.

Testing Your UPS Configuration

Testing your UPS configuration from time to time is wise, to make sure you aren't left powerless when a real emergency occurs. Follow these steps:

1. Close any open documents or programs.

2. Simulate a power failure by disconnecting the power to the UPS device. After disconnecting the power to the UPS device, check that the computer and peripherals connected to the UPS device continue operating and a warning message appears onscreen.

3. Wait until the UPS battery reaches a low level, at which point a system shutdown should occur.

4. Restore power to the UPS device.

How Do Upgrades Affect a Windows 7 License?

When you install any version of Windows, you must click to approve its End User Licensing Agreement (EULA). Though most people breeze right past this step, the EULA is a legal and binding contract between you and Microsoft. When you sign (or click) the EULA while installing Windows 7, and when your copy of Windows 7 is activated online, a snapshot of your computer system is made (no personal data is recorded, Microsoft claims) and sent to Microsoft to identify your system, matching it with the unique serial number encoded in that particular copy of the software.

Code internal to Windows 7 that you never see unless there is trouble, called Software Protection Platform (SPP), checks your system for authenticity of Microsoft software and alerts Microsoft if it finds inauthentic (pirated) software. SPP's purpose is to help Microsoft crack down on software privacy, and (they say) to help protect you by ensuring that your Microsoft product is authentic. SPP can get upset and nag you if it detects pirated software or other EULA infractions.

In Vista, this capability was branded Windows Genuine Advantage (WGA). In Windows 7 this facility is renamed Windows Activation Technology (WAT). Whereas the first major version of Vista (before Service Pack 1 was released) could actually cripple the OS if it wasn't activated or if indications of piracy were found, subsequent versions of WGA lost this capability, and replaced it with a "nag facility" that sets your screen background to black and nags you to get right with Microsoft, and does so every hour on the hour until you fix the problem (which usually means supplying a valid license key obtained from Microsoft in some form or fashion).

The upshot of WAT (and the WGA technology that remains in synch with that from Vista SP1) is exactly this:

- If you buy a PC with Windows 7 already installed, you have fewer rights of reinstallation. You are not supposed to move Windows over to another machine, and it would be difficult to do so because you typically don't have an install DVD anyway.

- Retail copies of Windows cost much more than OEM copies, for a reason. You can move them around between computers as you upgrade to better machines. If you buy a full retail version, you can put it on another computer and reactivate the new one. Keep in mind, however, that this is legal *only if* you uninstall it from the previous computer. You are supposed to format the system hard disk in the old computer. Microsoft should give you an uninstall utility so you don't have to wipe the hard disk, but they don't. Personally, I think this is because they don't really expect the average small business or home user to do this. Microsoft is simply trying to prevent a PC clone manufacturer from duplicating one copy of Windows on hundreds or thousands of PCs.

Upgrading Hardware in the Same Box and Complying with EULA

Because this chapter deals with upgrading hardware rather than complete computer replacement, the real question is: How do EULA and SPP rules apply to upgrades? How much hardware can you upgrade before SPP starts nagging you through the WAT facility?

In the original version of Windows Vista, SPP worked this way: The hardware in your system was recorded when you activated Windows, as already mentioned. If you changed too many items (most notably, your motherboard and hard disk drive), system functionality was slowly reduced. Over time, portions of the OS were crippled and you'd be running in Reduced Functionality Mode (RFM). At first, there would only be subtle events, such as updates or Aero not working, but eventually the desktop would go black, Windows Explorer wouldn't work, and all you could do is browse the Internet.

Thankfully, this is no longer the case. Because of WAT and a kinder, gentler approach to dealing with activation or potential piracy, you'll simply have to put up with hourly nag sessions and a black desktop background.

What triggers the need to reactivate Windows? As intended, each hardware component gets a relative weight, and from that WGA determines whether your copy of Windows 7 needs reactivation. The weight and the number of changes is apparently a guarded secret. If you upgrade too much at once, WAT decides that your PC is new, and things can get messy.

The actual algorithm that Microsoft uses is not disclosed, but we do know the weighting of components is as follows, from highest to lowest:

1. Motherboard (and CPU)

2. Hard drive

3. Network interface card (NIC)

4. Graphics card

5. RAM

If you just add a new hard disk or add new RAM, there is no issue. If you create an image of your Windows 7 installation on another hard disk and swap that hard disk into the system and boot from it, or if you replace all your RAM and reboot, WAT gets triggered and checks to see whether you must reactivate Windows 7.

In theory, chances that you'll get stung by any of this are not great. It was widely expected that the only users who'd need to worry about reactivation would be users who'd buy a preinstalled system, image the hard disk or try to move the hard disk to a newer, faster computer, or perform a motherboard upgrade using a preinstalled copy of Windows 7.

Unfortunately, in practice users have been forced to reactivate after relatively modest hardware changes. In one Vista example, a user who changed from a DirectX 9– to a DirectX 10–compatible graphics card had to reactivate his installation. But wait, it got worse: Another Vista user had to reactivate Windows after upgrading to a newer version of the Intel Matrix Storage driver for his motherboard. Essentially, WGA mistook a driver upgrade for a significant hardware upgrade. Users who missed the three-day reactivation window (it's easy to do) found themselves needing to make a phone call to reactivate. Users who were hearing-impaired found that difficult to do.

Meanwhile, users of bogus Windows 7 and Vista copies have used activation bypasses such as the Grace Timer or OEM BIOS exploits to run Windows without interference from WAT (WGA in Vista). Essentially, in the original version of Windows Vista, Windows made it way too difficult for legitimate users to cope with systems that could not be activated normally or needed to be reactivated. This led to the proliferation of usable (but illegal) workarounds. Thankfully, WAT brings those days to an end, as SP1 did for Vista.

Upgrading and Optimizing Your Computer

Here are several tips I've learned over the years that can help save you hours of hardware headaches.

Keep an Eye on Hardware Compatibility

If you've been accustomed to thumbing your nose at Microsoft's Hardware Compatibility List (HCL)—renamed Windows Logo'd Products List for Windows 7—because you've been using

 note

Some "legacy" hardware technologies no longer supported include EISA buses, game ports, Roland MPU-401 MIDI interface, AMD K6/2+ Mobile Processors, Mobile Pentium II, and Mobile Pentium III SpeedStep. ISAPnP (ISA Plug and Play) is disabled by default. Startup Hardware Profiles also have been removed.

Windows 9x, it's time to reform your behavior. In a pinch, Windows 9x could use older Windows drivers and could even load MS-DOS device drivers to make older hardware work correctly. Windows 7, like other NT-based versions of Windows, has done away with AUTOEXEC.BAT and CONFIG.SYS, so you can't use DOS-based drivers anymore. And, although Windows 7 can use some Windows 2000 and XP drivers in an emergency, you're much better off with drivers made especially for Windows 7 or Vista. You can view the online version of the Windows Logo'd Products List by visiting the Microsoft website.

 tip

Hardware failures, power failures, and human error can prevent Windows 7 from starting successfully. Recovery is easier if you know the configuration of each computer and its history and if you back up critical system files before tweaking your Windows 7 configuration.

A good hedge against this problem is to create a technical reference library for all your hardware and software documentation. Your reference library should include the history of software changes and upgrades for each machine, as well as hardware settings like those described here.

Sleuthing Out Conflicts

When you're hunting down potential IRQ, memory, and I/O conflicts, use the Device Manager to help out. Yes, Computer Management, System Information, Hardware Resources, and Conflicts Sharing can show you potential conflicts, so those are good places to look, too. But let me share a trick that you can use with the Device Manager that isn't readily apparent.

Normally, the class of devices called Hidden Devices isn't shown. To show them, open the Device Manager (either via Control Panel, System, or from Computer Management). Then, on the View menu, click Show Hidden Devices. A checkmark next to Show Hidden Devices indicates that hidden devices are showing. Click it again to clear the checkmark. Hidden devices include non-PnP devices (devices with older Windows 2000 device drivers) and devices that have been physically removed from the computer but have not had their drivers uninstalled.

Optimizing Your Computer for Windows 7

Optimizing your computer for Windows 7 is actually quite easy. I'm very impressed with the capability of this OS to keep on chugging. It doesn't cough or die easily if you mind your manners.

- If you buy new stuff for an upgrade, consider only hardware that's on the tested products list and the Windows Logo'd Products List (https://winqual.microsoft.com/hcl/).

- When you buy a new machine, get it with Windows 7 preinstalled and from a reputable maker with decent technical support, not just a reputable dealer. The dealer might not be able to solve complex technical problems. Brand-name manufacturers such as Dell, HP, Gateway, Lenovo, Acer, MSI, and so on have teams of engineers devoted to testing new OSs and ironing out kinks in their hardware, with help from engineers at Microsoft.

- If you love to upgrade and experiment, more power to you. I used to build PCs from scratch, even soldering them together from parts. Then again, you can also build your own car. (I used to just about do that myself, too.) Or you can buy it preassembled from some company in Detroit or Japan. It really isn't worth spending much time fiddling with PC hardware unless you assemble systems for some specific purpose. Given amazingly low prices for computers these days, don't waste your time. And don't cut corners in configuring a new machine, either. For an extra $50, you can get goodies such as a modem, network card, and faster video card thrown in. Add more bells and whistles up front and save yourself some hassle down the road.

- Run Windows Update frequently or set it to run itself.

- Schedule hard disk defragmentation (see Chapter 24) and make sure you have a decent amount of free space on your drives, especially your boot drive. Remember that Windows 7's defragmenter requires at least 15% empty space on each drive you want to defragment.

- Get an extra external hard disk of equal size or larger than your computer's internal hard disk. Use an automated backup program, such as the File and Folder Backup built into Windows 7, to automatically back up your important stuff on a frequent basis. (Mine runs every night.) Disks are cheap these days, and your time, contacts lists, emails, and documents are valuable!

EDITING THE REGISTRY

What Is the Registry?

The Windows Registry is a database in which Windows and application programs store all manner of configuration settings, startup information, hardware settings, user preferences, file locations, license and registration information, last-viewed file lists, and so on. In addition, the Registry stores the associations between file types and the applications that use them. For example, the Registry holds the information that tells Windows to use Media Player when you click on an MPG movie file. In the early days of DOS and Windows, programs stored this kind of information in a random collection of hundreds of files scattered all over your hard disk. Thankfully, those days are only a dim memory.

 tip

If you're already familiar with the Registry, you might want to skip ahead to the section "New Registry Features."

How the Registry Is Organized

The Registry is organized a lot like the files and folders on a hard disk. Just as a hard disk can contain partitions, the Registry contains separate sections called *top-level keys*. In each section is a list of named entries, called *keys*, which correspond to the folders on a hard disk. And just as a folder can contain files and more nested folders, a Registry key can contain *values*, which hold information such as numbers or text strings, and more nested keys. Even the way that file folders and Registry keys are described is similar: a folder might be named \Users\brian\chapter28, and a Registry key might be named \HKEY_CURRENT_USER\Software\Microsoft.

The two main "top-level" keys are as follows:

- HKEY_LOCAL_MACHINE contains all the hardware and machine-specific setup information for your computer.

- HKEY_USERS contains a key for each user account created on the computer, including the accounts used only internally by Windows services.

  The keys under HKEY_USERS are mostly named using long numeric strings that are the user account's Security Identifier (SID) number. Usually, not all accounts' keys are visible at the same time. Each account's key is loaded into the Registry when the user logs on and is unloaded a short time after the user logs out. Each user's key contains his or her personal Windows and application settings and preferences.

The Registry Editor displays three other sections that look like they are separate top-level keys but that are actually views of information inside HKEY_LOCAL_MACHINE or HKEY_USERS:

- HKEY_CURRENT_USER is a shortcut to the subsection of HKEY_USERS that corresponds to the currently logged-on user. That is, when *you* run the Registry Editor, HKEY_CURRENT_USER shows *your* Windows and application preferences and settings.

- HKEY_CURRENT_CONFIG is a shortcut to HKEY_LOCAL_MACHINE\System\CurrentControlSet\ Hardware Profiles\Current and contains hardware and device settings specific to the hardware profile used when Windows was started.

- HKEY_CLASSES_ROOT stores file associations, the information that Windows uses to link file types to applications, and a huge amount of setup information for Windows software components. It's actually a combined view of the contents of two other Registry sections: HKEY_LOCAL_MACHINE\Software\Classes, which holds settings that are made for all users, and HKEY_CURRENT_USER\Software\Classes, which holds personal settings made just by the current user. If the same value is defined in both HKEY_CURRENT_USER\... and HKEY_LOCAL_MACHINE\..., the HKEY_CURRENT_USER value is used.

New Registry Features

Windows Vista introduced some new features to the Registry: virtualization and 64/32–bit reflection. These features are also present, although somewhat changed in Windows 7, and this section gives you a brief tour. The features are called Registry virtualization, redirection and reflection. This topic is pretty gnarly and obscure, so on your first read, you might want to skip ahead to the section titled "Backing Up and Restoring the Registry."

Registry Virtualization

On Windows 7 and Vista, if an older application attempts to store information to HKEY_LOCAL_ MACHINE\Software*xxx**yyy* but doesn't have permission to change that key, the information will actually be stored in HKEY_CURRENT_USER\Software\CLASSES\VirtualStore\MACHINE\

Software*xxx**yyy*. This is called *Registry virtualization*. Applications that the user runs will still "see" the information as if it was in the intended location. As a result, applications that aren't aware of the new, tighter restrictions on HKEY_LOCAL_MACHINE will run without a hitch, although their settings will be per-user instead of machinewide.

You need to know this so you can check the alternative locations when you're investigating problems with Registry settings in your system.

If you change an application program's preference setting that should apply to all users of the program, but it affects only you, and the setting isn't changed when other users run the application, most likely the configuration setting is stored in a Registry key under HKEY_LOCAL_MACHINE that isn't writeable by you. When you make the change, Windows virtualizes the Registry value, and only your account sees the change.

To fix this, first try to contact the software manufacturer for a workaround. If none exists, try this:

1. Locate the Registry key in which the setting is being saved. Either search the Registry for the setting value or use a Registry change-monitoring tool such as Registrar Registry Manager, or procmon from sysinternals.com, to see where the application saves your setting.

2. As an Administrator, locate the key in the left pane of the Registry Editor, right-click it, and select Permissions. Select the Users entry and check Full Control.

3. Using your account, locate the virtualized copy of the key under HKEY_CLASES_ROOT\ VirtualStore and delete it.

4. Run the application and change the setting again.

After this, everyone should share the same copy of the setting.

Virtualization doesn't occur under some circumstances. In those cases, the application simply is allowed to fail in its attempt to make changes to HKEY_LOCAL_MACHINE. These circumstances are listed here:

- If User Account Control is disabled.

- If virtualization is disabled by your network administrator, using Group Policy on a Windows domain network.

- If the application is a 64-bit application.

- If the application program has a *manifest*, a block of data inside the application or in a separate file that describes advanced security settings. Almost all the applications that come with Windows—including Notepad; the command-prompt interpreter, cmd.exe; and the Registry Editor—have manifests, so almost all Windows utilities do not see virtualized Registry settings.

- If a key is marked with a special flag that indicates that it is not to be redirected. HKEY_LOCAL_MACHINE\Software\Microsoft\Windows\CurrentVersion\Run is marked this way so that a virus that attempts to set itself up to run at logon via this key won't be capable of doing so. The command-line utility REG can modify the virtualization flag. Type **REG FLAGS /?** at the command-line prompt for more information.

Virtualization is seen as a stopgap measure and will be unnecessary when most applications either store information in HKEY_CURRENT_USER or explicitly set less restrictive permissions on their keys in HKEY_LOCAL_MACHINE when they're installed.

Registry Redirection and Reflection

The 64-bit versions of Windows support running 32-bit Windows applications. This presents a problem because many Windows subcomponents are present in both 32- and 64-bit versions, and information about them (such as program filenames) is stored in the Registry under keys whose names were determined before Microsoft considered the need to distinguish between the two flavors. To manage this, Windows stores information for 32-bit components in an alternate location and feeds the stored information to 32-bit applications when they ask for values from the original location. This is called *Registry redirection*. The information for 32-bit applications is actually redirected to HKEY_LOCAL_MACHINE\Software\WOW6432Node. When a 32-bit application requests information from a redirected key using the original location, it is fed information from below WOW6432Node.

 note

You must close the 64-bit version of the Registry Editor before you can open the 32-bit version, and *vice versa*, unless you start the second instance of the Registry Editor with the -m command-line argument.

When working with the Registry on a 64-bit system, you need to know to look under WOW6432Node when looking for setup information for 32-bit components.

Alternatively, you can use the 32-bit version of regedit; this presents all information in the standard locations seen by 32-bit applications. When you run regedit from the command line, you get the 64-bit version. However, if you run %systemroot%\syswow64\regedit.exe, you get the 32-bit version and can edit the values seen by 32-bit applications.

So that the 32-bit and 64-bit versions of components and applications can communicate, some settings and values that these components store in the registry are copied to *both* locations. This is called *Registry reflection*.

Reflection was used in several sections of the Registry in Windows Vista, but in Windows 7, only two keys are subject to reflection:

```
HKEY_LOCAL_MACHINE\Software\Classes\CLSID
HKEY_LOCAL_MACHINE\Software\Classes\Interface
```

For more information on reflection, see Microsoft Knowledge Base article 305097 at http://support.microsoft.com/kb/305097. Also, search msdn.microsoft.com for the article titled "Removal of Windows Registry Reflection."

Backing Up and Restoring the Registry

Because the Registry is now the *one* place where all the Windows hardware and software settings are stored, it's also the one thing that Windows absolutely needs to run. If you have to use the Registry Editor to manually change Registry settings, we strongly suggest that you back up your Registry *before* you make any changes.

Backing Up the Registry

You can back up the Registry several ways. In order of preference, these are using a third-party Registry-backup program, backing up the entire hard disk using a third-party program or Complete PC Backup, using System Restore, and using the Registry Editor to save a key to a text file.

I suggest that you use a third-party disk-backup solution to back up the Registry files every time you back up your hard disk. Before you install a piece of new hardware or a significant software package, do a full disk backup, including the Registry. Before you manually edit the Registry for other purposes, back up the Registry by any of the means discussed in the next few sections.

Backing Up with Third-Party Registry-Backup Software

There are third-party programs specifically designed to back up and restore the Registry. For example, SuperWin's WinRescue program (www.superwin.com) not only can back up and restore the Registry, but also can defragment the Registry's files and work magic to revive a nonbootable Windows system. (There is a version called WinRescue Vista that you should use if no Windows 7–specific version has been released.) There is also a free tool called ERUNT, which you can download from www.larshederer.homepage.t-online.de/erunt.

These programs come with instructions on backing up, restoring, repairing, and maintaining the Registry.

Backing Up the Hard Disk

You can save the Registry by performing a backup of the entire contents of the hard disk on which Windows resides. On the Windows 7 Home versions, you'll have to use a third-party disk backup program to back up the entire hard disk. On Windows 7 Professional, Enterprise, and Ultimate editions, the Complete PC Backup program can do this for you, or you can use a third-party program.

As an alternative to doing a full disk backup, most third-party disk-backup programs made for Windows 7 include an option to back up the system portion of the Registry. If you use this option, be sure to include all user profiles (everything under \User) so that personal Registry sections are saved as well.

Check your backup software's manual for instructions on saving Registry and system information when you back up. I suggest that you always include the Registry in your backups.

 caution

The backup programs provided with Windows 7 do not provide a good means of backing up the Registry as insurance against accidents. Windows Backup can perform only full-volume backups, which can take a long time. System Restore backs up only HKEY_LOCAL_MACHINE, not your own HKEY_CURRENT_USER data. It's okay to use only if you're modifying just HKEY_LOCAL_MACHINE settings.

Backing Up with System Restore

If you will be changing only entries under HKEY_LOCAL_MACHINE, you can create a restore point to back up a copy of this part of the Registry. To create a restore point, follow these steps:

1. Click Start. Right-click Computer and select Properties. Then, at the left, select System Protection. (Alternatively, type **sysdm.cpl** in a Command Prompt window, and then select the System Protection tab.)

2. Be sure that the disk volume that contains Windows is checked, and click Create.

3. Enter a description for the restore point, such as **Before changing Registry**, and then click Create.

Then, edit the Registry as described later in this chapter.

Backing Up with the Registry Editor

The Registry Editor has a mechanism to export a set of Registry keys and values to a text file. If you can't or won't use a more comprehensive backup system before you manually edit the Registry, at least use this editor to select and back up the key that contains all the subkeys and values you plan to modify. Remember, though, that Regedit cannot remove entries you added that were not in the Registry before the backup!

To back up a key and its subkeys and values, follow these steps:

1. To run Regedit, click Start, and type **regedit** in the Search box.

2. When Regedit appears under Programs in the search results, select it and press Enter. (Alternatively, type **regedit** in a Command Prompt window.)

3. Locate and select the key you plan to modify, or a key containing all the keys you plan to modify, in the left pane.

4. Select File, Export.

5. Choose a location and filename to use to store the Registry keys. I usually use the desktop for temporary files like this, so that I'll see them and delete them later.

6. Select All Files from the Save As Type list, and enter a name (possibly with an extension other than .reg—for example, **before.sav**).

7. Click Save. The chosen key or keys are then saved as a text file.

Restoring the Registry

If you've made Registry changes that cause problems, you can try to remember each and every change you made, re-enter the original information, delete any keys you added, and thus undo the changes manually. Good luck! If you were diligent and made a backup before you started, however, you can simply restore the backup and have confidence that the recovery is complete and accurate.

Signs of Registry Problems

Registry corruption can take two forms: Either the Registry's database files can be damaged by an errant disk operation, or information can be mangled by a buggy program or an overzealous `regedit` user. No matter what the cause, the result can be a system that won't run or one that reboots itself over and over.

These could be other signs of Registry corruption or errors:

- Drivers aren't loaded, or they give errors while Windows is booting.

- Software complains about components that aren't registered or cannot be located.

- Undesirable programs attempt to run when you log in.

- Windows does not boot, or it starts up only in Safe mode.

If you made a Registry backup using a third-party disk or Registry backup tool, use the instructions that came with your product to restore the Registry. If you created a restore point or used Regedit, follow the steps described in the following sections.

Restoring the Registry from a Restore Point

If you created a restore point before modifying the Registry, you can back out the change by following these steps:

1. Click Start. Right-click Computer and select Properties. At the left, select System Protection. Then, click the System Restore button. (Alternatively, type **rstrui** in a Command Prompt window.)

2. Locate the restore point you created. Select it and click Next; then click Finish. Windows will restart.

If the Registry problem is severe enough that Windows can't boot or get to the System Restore function, you can perform a system restore from the system recovery tools on your Windows setup DVD. See "Using System Recovery" on **page 738** for instructions for performing a system restore this way.

Restoring the Registry from Regedit

If a Registry editing session has gone awry and you need to restore the Registry from a key you saved from within Regedit, follow these steps:

1. In Regedit, select File, Import.

2. Select All Files from the Files of Type list.

3. Locate the file you used to back up the Registry key or keys—for example, `before.reg`.

4. Select Open.

The saved Registry keys are then imported, replacing any changes or deletions. However, any keys or values you've added to the Registry are not removed. If they are the cause of the problem, this restore will *not* help.

If the Registry problems persist, you can try a rather drastic measure: You can use Regedit to delete the key or keys that were changed and then import the backup file again. This time, any added keys or values are removed. I suggest that you try this approach only with keys related to add-on software, *not* for any of the Microsoft software or hardware keys.

 tip

If you encounter what you think are Registry problems with add-on software, your best bet is to uninstall the software, if possible, and reinstall it before attempting *any* Registry restores or repairs.

Using Regedit

Most people never need to edit the Registry by hand because most Registry keys are set by the software that uses them. However, you might need to edit the Registry by hand if you're directed by a technical support person who's helping you fix a problem, or when you're following a published procedure to make an adjustment for which there is no Control Panel setting.

In the latter case, before going any further, I need to say this one last time, to make it absolutely clear: Unless you're quite certain that you can't make a mistake, back up the Registry (or at least the section you want to change) before making any changes.

The next few sections cover the basics of the Registry Editor.

Viewing the Registry

The Registry Editor doesn't have a Start menu item. The easiest way to run it is to type **regedit** into the Search field on the Start menu. When `regedit` appears in the results pane under Programs, take one of the following actions, depending on your needs:

- If you are logged on as an Administrator, press Enter or click `regedit`. When the User Account Control dialog box appears, click Continue. The Registry Editor will run with full elevated privileges.

- If you are not logged on as an Administrator but need to change settings in only the HKEY_CURRENT_USER section of the Registry, press Enter or click `regedit`. The Registry Editor will run with reduced privileges, and you will not be able to change systemwide settings.

 note

The reason for these complicated variations is that malicious programs and email attachments can easily abuse the Registry Editor, so it's subject to UAC restrictions. The Registry Editor must be running in elevated mode to modify Registry keys that are secured to be changeable only by the Administrator. By the way, there is no indication in the Registry Editor's title bar to tell whether it's running with elevated privileges—you just have to remember.

- If you are not logged on as an Administrator but need to change systemwide settings in HKEY_LOCAL_MACHINE, right-click `regedit` and select Run as Administrator. Enter an Administrator account's username and password. The Registry Editor will then run with full elevated privileges.

Regedit displays a two-pane display much like Windows Explorer, as shown in Figure 28.1. The top-level keys, which are listed below Computer, can be expanded just like drives and folders in Explorer. In the pane on the right are the values for each key. The name of the currently selected key appears in the status bar.

Figure 28.1
The Regedit screen shows keys on the left and values on the right.

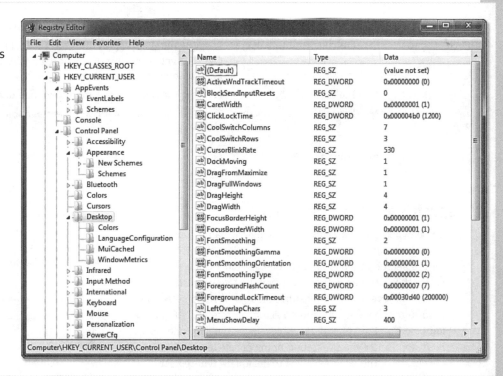

Values have names, just as the files in a folder do, and it's in the values that configuration information is finally stored. Each key has a (Default) value, which is the value of the key itself, and any number of named values. For example, Figure 28.1 shows the key HKEY_CURRENT_USER\Control Panel\Desktop. The value of HKEY_CURRENT_USER\Control Panel\Desktop itself is undefined (blank), and the value HKEY_CURRENT_USER\Control Panel\Desktop\DragFullWindows is 1.

Registry values have a data type, which is usually one of the types shown in Table 28.1. The Registry Editor display lists values by their technical names.

Table 28.1 Data Types Supported by Regedit

Technical Name	"Friendly" Name	Description
REG_SZ	String value	Textual information, a simple string of letters.
REG_BINARY	Binary value	Binary data, displayed as an arbitrary number of hexadecimal digits.
REG_DWORD	DWORD (32-bit) value	A single number displayed in hexadecimal or decimal.
REG_QWORD	QWORD (64-bit) value	A single number displayed in hexadecimal or decimal. QWORD values are used primarily by 64-bit Windows applications.
REG_MULTI_SZ	Multistring value	A string that can contain more than one line of text.
REG_EXPAND_SZ	Expandable string value	Text that can contain environment variables (such as %TEMP%).

Other data types, such as REG_DWORD_BIG_ENDIAN and REG_RESOURCE_LIST, exist, but they are obscure and rare and can't be edited with Regedit.

Searching in the Registry

You can search for a Registry entry by key name, value name, or the contents of a value string. First, select a starting point for the search in the left pane. You can select Computer to select the entire Registry, or you can limit your search to one of the top-level keys or any subordinate key. Next, select Edit, Find from the menu and enter a search string in the Find dialog box. The Find feature is not case sensitive, so it doesn't matter whether you use upper- or lowercase letters. You can check any of the Look At boxes to designate where in the Registry you expect to find the desired text: in the name of a key, in the name of a value, or in the data, the value itself.

Check Match Whole String Only to search only for items whose whole name or value is the desired string.

Click Find Next to start the search. The Regedit display indicates the first match to your string; by pressing F3, you can repeat the search to look for other instances.

Also remember that Windows 7 might store information in some places you are not familiar with, as discussed previously under "New Registry Features."

Editing Keys and Values

Regedit has no Save or Undo menu items. Changes to the Registry happen *immediately* and *permanently*. Additions, deletions, and changes are for real. This is the reason for all the warnings to back up before you poke into the Registry.

 note

When I search the Registry, most of the time, I check all the Look At boxes but not Match Whole String Only.

 tip

The search function has two limitations:

- You can't enter a backslash (\) in the search string when looking for a key or value name; Regedit won't complain, but it won't find anything, either.

- You can't search for the initial HKEY_*xxx* part of a key name. That's not actually part of the name; it's just the section of the Registry in which the key resides.

For example, to find a key named HKEY_CLASSES_ROOT\MIDFile\shell\Play\Command, you can't type all that in and have Find jump right to the key. If you already know the full pathname of a key, use the left pane of Regedit to browse for the key directly.

Adding a Value

To add a value to a key, select the key in the left pane and choose Edit, New. Select the type of value to add; you can select any of the supported Registry data types, which are listed by the "friendly" names shown previously in Table 28.1. The instructions you're following indicate which type of value to add. A new value entry then appears in the right pane.

Type the new value's name and press Enter to edit the value:

- For string values, enter the text of the desired string.

- For DWORD values, choose Decimal or Hexadecimal, and enter the desired value in the chosen format.

- For binary values, enter pairs of hexadecimal characters as instructed. (You'll never be asked to do this, I promise.)

Changing a Value

If you want to change a value, double-click it in the right pane to bring up the Edit Value dialog box. Alternatively, right-click it and select Modify. Then make the desired change and click OK.

That is all you will likely ever need to do with Regedit. However, in the extremely unlikely case that you want to delete a value or add or remove a key, the following sections can help see you through these processes.

 note

Many of the keys that control Windows itself have access restrictions and can be modified only by an Administrator.

Deleting a Value

If you've added a Registry value in the hope of fixing some problem and found that the change wasn't needed, or if you're instructed to delete a value by a Microsoft Knowledge Base article or other special procedure, you can delete the entry by viewing its key and locating the value on the right pane.

Select the value and choose Edit, Delete from the menu, or right-click and select Delete from the context menu. Confirm by clicking OK.

 caution

There is no Undo command in the Registry Editor—when you delete a value, it's gone for good. Be sure you've made a Registry backup before editing or deleting Registry keys and values.

Adding or Deleting a Key

Keys must be added as subkeys of existing keys; you can't create a new top-level key. To add a key, select an existing key in the left pane and select Edit, New, Key from the menu. Alternatively, right-click the existing key and select New, Key from the context menu. A new key appears in the left pane, where you can edit its name. Press Enter after you enter the name.

You can delete a key by selecting it in the left pane and choosing Edit, Delete from the menu, or by right-clicking it and selecting Delete from the context menu. Click OK to confirm that you intend to delete the key. Deleting a key deletes its values *and all its subkeys* as well, so without the protection of Undo (or a Registry Recycling Bin), this action is serious.

Renaming a Key

As you have probably guessed, the pattern for renaming a key follows the Explorer model exactly: Choose the key in the left pane and select Edit, Rename, or right-click the key and select Rename. Finally, enter a new name and press Enter.

caution

Don't attempt to rename keys without a *very good* reason—for example, because you mistyped the name of the key you were adding. If Windows can't find specific Registry keys it needs, Windows might not boot or operate correctly.

Using Copy Key Name

As you have probably noticed by now, the names of Registry keys can be quite long, tortuous things. The Registry Editor offers a bit of help to finger-fatigued Registry Editors (and authors): Choosing Edit, Copy Key Name puts the name of the currently selected key into the Clipboard so you can paste it elsewhere if you need to.

Editing Registry Entries for Another User

As an administrator, you might find it necessary to edit HKEY_USER entries for another user. For example, a startup program in HKEY_CURRENT_USER\Software\Windows\CurrentVersion\Run might be causing such trouble that the user can't log on. If you can't log on as that user, you can edit his HKEY_CURRENT_USER Registry keys in another way:

1. Log on as an Administrator and run Regedit.

2. Select the HKEY_USERS window.

3. Highlight the top-level key HKEY_USERS.

4. Select File, Load Hive.

5. Browse to the profile folder for the desired user. For a local user account, this is in \Users*username*. (For a Windows Server domain, look in the folder used for user profiles on the domain controller.) The folder name of this folder might have the computer name or a domain name attached. For example, on one computer, my profile folder name is bknittel.java.

6. Type the filename **NTUSER.DAT**. (The file will most likely not appear in the Browse dialog box because it's *super hidden*: marked with both the Hidden and System attributes.) Then click Open.

7. A dialog box appears, asking you to enter a name for the hive. HKEY_USERS normally loads user hives with a long numeric name, so I suggest that you type the user's logon name. Click OK. The user's Registry data is then loaded and can be edited, as shown in Figure 28.2.

Figure 28.2
An offline
user's
Registry hive
is now
loaded and
can be
edited.

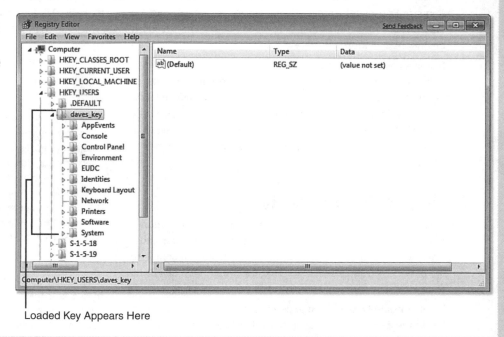

Loaded Key Appears Here

8. When you're finished editing, unload the hive. Select the key you added under HKEY_USERS (for example, daves_key in Figure 28.2), and select File, Unload Hive. Confirm by clicking Yes on the warning dialog box.

Editing Registry Entries for Another Windows Installation

If you need to retrieve Registry entries from an installation of Windows installed on another hard disk or partition, you can load any of that installation's hive files for editing or exporting.

To edit the other installation's Registry, you need to locate its hive files. They are usually found in the locations shown in Table 28.2.

Table 28.2 Usual Location of Hive Files

Key	Default Location and Hive File
HKEY_LOCAL_MACHINE\SAM	\windows\system32\config\sam
HKEY_LOCAL_MACHINE\Security	\windows\system32\config\security
HKEY_LOCAL_MACHINE\Software	\windows\system32\config\software
HKEY_LOCAL_MACHINE\System	\windows\system32\config\system
HKEY_LOCAL_MACHINE\Components	\windows\system32\config\components
HKEY_USERS\.Default	\windows\system32\config\default

To edit another Windows installation's Registry, use the technique I described under "Editing Registry Entries for Another User," but instead of locating a user's NTUSER.DAT file, locate the desired hive file on the other hard drive or partition. Unload it after you've exported or corrected the desired information.

In some cases, you will find that you cannot view or modify keys loaded from another installation. This occurs if the keys are protected with security attributes that list specific users or groups defined in the other installation. In this case, you need to first take ownership of the keys and then add yourself as a user who is authorized to read or change the keys. The next section describes this.

Editing Registry Security

Just as files and folders in an NTFS-formatted disk partition have security attributes to control access based on user and group identity, Registry keys and values also have a complete set of Access Control attributes that determine who has rights to read, write, and modify each entry.

If you absolutely must change permissions or auditing controls, locate the desired key or value, right-click it, and select Permissions. The Permissions dialog box looks just like the comparable dialog box for files and folders (see Figure 28.3), and lets you set read, write, and modify rights for specific groups and users. You'll find a corresponding set of audit settings.

note

You rarely should have to modify Registry security settings, but it does happen. The usual case is that an incorrectly designed program places information in a subkey of HKEY_LOCAL_MACHINE\Software that is intended to be shared and modified by all users running the program. Because Windows does not permit standard users to modify any keys in HKEY_LOCAL_MACHINE\ Software by default, the program might malfunction. Modifying permissions so that standard users can edit the shared key is sometimes necessary to fix the problem. Microsoft also sometimes recommends modifying Registry security in emergency security bulletins.

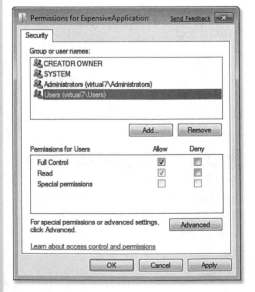

Figure 28.3
Registry key permissions control which users or groups are allowed to see or modify the Registry key and its values.

In most cases, a software vendor supplies precise instructions for making changes necessary to work around an application problem. Here, I describe a general procedure to make a given key readable and writeable by all users. You might do this to make a key capable of sharing information between users, or to repair an alternate Windows installation, as mentioned in the previous section. To set more generous permissions, follow these steps:

1. Locate and select the key in the left pane.

2. Right-click it and select Permissions.

3. Select the Users entry in the top Group or User Names section. If Users is not listed, click Add, type **Users**, and click OK.

4. In the lower section, check Full Control and then click Apply. If this is successful, click OK.

5. If you are unable to make the changes even though you're running the Registry Editor as an Administrator, click Advanced and select the Owner tab.

6. If the Current Owner is listed as unknown, select Administrators in the lower list and click OK.

7. Click OK to close the Advanced Security Settings dialog box, and return to Step 3.

This is a risky procedure because it could result in another user or application being unable to access its own Registry keys. Use this as a procedure of last resort.

Other Registry Tools

There are some third party tools that you can use to edit the registry and adjust Windows features. Here are four of the more popular utilities.

X-Setup Pro

X-Setup Pro by Xteq offers nearly 1,700 settings and tweaks using a slick graphical Explorer-like interface. It includes wizards for some of the more complex tasks, such as mapping file types to Explorer icons. One of its niftiest features is its capability to record a series of changes to a log file that it can then play back on other computers. The cost is $20. You can download it from www. x-setup.net.

Registry Toolkit

Registry Toolkit is a shareware Registry Editor made by Funduc software, with a nifty search-and-replace system. You can scan the Registry, changing all occurrences of one string to another, which is something most other Windows Registry Editors can't do. Its user interface isn't very comfortable or slick, but if you need to manage a lot of identical changes in the Registry, this is one cool tool. It's free to try, $25 to register, at www.funduc.com.

Registrar Registry Manager

Registrar Registry Manager is a powerful Registry-editing tool produced by Resplendence Software Projects (www.resplendence.com), with a drag-and-drop interface. It includes a Registry backup, restore, and defragmentation tool, a Registry-compare tool, an undo capability, and many more features. The full version costs € 45 (about $63), and there is a free "lite" version.

Tweak-7

Tweak-7 from Totalidea Software, available at www.totalidea.com, combines tweaking tools with additional enhancements and plug-ins. The cost is $39.99 for one computer, with multiple-license discounts available.

Registry Privileges and Policies

On Windows corporate "domain"-type networks, administrators can use the *policy* system to restrict users' ability to change their computer configuration. When you log on using a Domain user account, the policy system downloads and installs Registry settings prepared by system administrators. These Registry settings not only can help automate the setup of networking and other components, but can also restrict your ability to (mis)manage your computer.

Here's how it works: Windows looks at a boatload of Registry entries to determine what features to make available to you. For example, one value determines whether the Start menu is allowed to display the Run item; another makes the Control Panel hide the Power Management settings. Most of these values normally don't appear in the Registry at all, but they can be installed there by the policy system, and Windows security settings prevent users from changing or deleting them.

➡ *On a computer that's a member of a Windows Domain network, the policy system is called Group Policy. On a standalone computer, it's called Local Security Policy. Local Security Policy is described in more detail under "Tightening Local Security Policy" on* **page 934.**

COMMAND-LINE AND AUTOMATION TOOLS

Command-Line Tools

Despite the ease of use of the Windows graphical user interface, the command-line interface remains a useful way to perform many maintenance, configuration, and diagnostic tasks. Many of the most important diagnostic tools such as `ping`, `tracert`, and `nslookup` are available only from the command line, unless you purchase third-party graphical add-ons to perform these functions. And although the term "batch file" might bring back uncomfortable memories of the old MS-DOS days, batch files and program scripts are still powerful tools that provide a useful way to encapsulate common management functions. Together, command-line utilities, batch files, and scripts based on Windows Script Host provide a complete set of building blocks from which you can build high-level utilities for repetitive or complex tasks.

 tip

In this book, I only have room to show you how to set up and configure the command-line environment. For much more detail, tutorials, examples, and many helpful tips on using command-line tools, check out Brian's book *Windows 7 and Vista Guide to Scripting, Automation, and Command Line Tools*, published by Que.

The Windows 7 Command Prompt Environment

To open a Command Prompt window in which you can type commands and review output, as shown in Figure 29.1, click Start, All Programs, Accessories, Command Prompt. Alternately, click Start and type **cmd** in the Search box. Then, when cmd.exe has been located, press Enter.

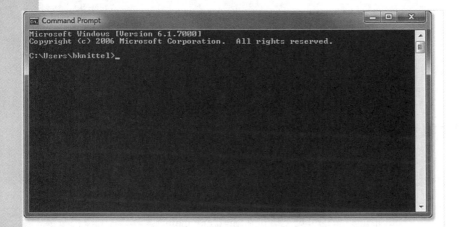

Figure 29.1
The Command Prompt window is the gateway to a world of powerful Windows management tools.

The main difference between a standard Windows application and a command-line program—which in Windows is technically called a *console program*—is that it doesn't use a graphical display or pull-down menus. Instead, you type commands into the Command Prompt window to tell Windows to do something, and the programs type information back to you. Each command line starts with the name of the program that you want to run, followed by additional information called *arguments*. Arguments tell the program what specifically you want to do.

When you type a command line, Windows searches a list of folders called the *search path* for a file whose name starts with the program name you typed and whose name ends with any of several extensions such as .exe, .bat, and .vbs. The most common program extensions are listed in Table 29.1. Windows examines the file to see what type of program it is, and then runs it. It's then the program's job to interpret any arguments you typed after the program name.

 tip

If you plan on using the Command Prompt window regularly, pin it to the taskbar for quick access. Right-click the Command Prompt window icon in the taskbar and select Pin This Program to Taskbar.

 tip

You can also open a Command Prompt window from Windows Explorer. Hold the Shift key down, right-click a folder name, and select Open Command Window Here. The window will open with the selected folder as the default folder.

Table 29.1 Typical Executable Program Extensions

Extension	Program Type
.bat, .cmd	Batch file
.com	Archaic MS-DOS program
.exe	Windows GUI program, console program, or MS-DOS program (Windows determines which by examining the contents of the file)
.js	Script file written in the JavaScript language
.msc	Microsoft Management Console snap-in
.vbs	Script file written in the VBScript language

The search path is defined by a list of folder names in the PATH environment variable, and the complete list of extensions that Windows looks for is defined in the PATHEXT environment variable. The default search path includes the following folders:

```
C:\Windows\system32
C:\Windows
C:\Windows\System32\Wbem
C:\Windows\System32\WindowsPowerShell\v1.0
```

This means that any program file, batch file, or script stored in any of these folders can be run simply by typing its name. You can start both Windows programs and command-line programs in this way. For example, you just have to type **notepad** to start the Notepad accessory.

If you create your own batch files, scripts, or programs, it's a good idea to create a separate folder to store them in, and to put that folder in the search path. I'll show you how to do so later in this chapter, under "Setting the PATH Environment Variable."

Running Commands with Elevated Privileges

Some command-line programs require elevated privileges (via User Account Control) to do their job correctly. To run a command-line program with elevated privileges, you must run it from a Command Prompt window that is itself "elevated."

To open an elevated Command Prompt window, click Start, All Programs, Accessories. Then right-click Command Prompt and select Run As Administrator. Or, if you have the Command Prompt icon pinned to your taskbar, there are two quick ways to open an elevated prompt:

- Right-click the icon, right-click the Command Prompt label in the Jump List pop-up, and then select Run As Administrator.

- Hold down the Shift+Ctrl keys and click the icon.

 caution

Be *very* careful when using an elevated Command Prompt window. Any commands you start from within this window will run with elevated privileges from the get-go, and you will receive no further UAC prompts when you start them. This includes Windows GUI programs—for example, if you type the command optionalfeatures, you will get the Turn Windows Features On or Off dialog box, and you will not have to confirm anything before it starts.

To be safe, do not use an elevated Command Prompt window for general-purpose work. Use it only to accomplish a specific task that requires elevated privileges; then close it.

If you want, you can set a Command Prompt shortcut or pinned taskbar icon so that it is elevated by default. Right-click the icon and select Properties. On the Shortcut tab, click the Advanced button, and check Run As Administrator. Be sure to rename the shortcut so that it's clear that it opens an elevated prompt.

Learning About Command-Line Programs

How do you know what programs are available and how to use them? For that, you have to turn to documentation about the command-line environment. For some reason, Microsoft no longer provides this in the Help and Support system, but you can search online, and some programs can be told to display their own usage information. To show you what's available, we have posted a list of all the programs included with Windows 7 at www.helpwin7.com. And you might want to check out Brian's book *Windows 7 and Vista Guide to Scripting, Automation, and Command Line Tools*. For a general online listing, perform this Google search, and then locate the A–Z listing for Windows Server 2008 or Windows Server 2003. Most of the programs listed there are available on Windows 7.

```
site:microsoft.com command line a-z windows server
```

To get additional information on a command that interests you, try the following sources, in the order listed. I'll use the `rasdial` command in the examples that follow, but you can use the same technique with any command that interests you.

- A majority of command-line commands will print help information if you add /? to the command line. For example, to get information for the `rasdial` command, type **rasdial /?**.

- If the command prints so much text that it scrolls out of view, use one of the following techniques to read it all:

  - Use the Command Prompt window's scrollbars to back up.

  - Press F3 to recall the command line, add ¦ **more** to the end of the line, and press Enter. This will "pipe" the help listing through the `more` command, which displays it one screenful at a time. Press Enter after reading each screen.

- Type the command **help rasdial**. If too much text prints, use the techniques just listed to manage the overflow.

- Open Internet Explorer and type **rasdial** in the Search window. You might also try the Google search `site:microsoft.com rasdial`.

Not every one of those information sources will work for every command, but at least one should lead you to an explanation of what the command does and what its command-line options are, and provide some examples of its use. The command-line options for Windows 7, Vista, XP, and Server 2003 and Server 2008 are pretty much the same, so if you can't find any Windows 7–specific information, documentation for the other versions should be okay to use.

Cutting and Pasting in the Command Prompt Window

Although you will usually use output redirection to store the output from command-line programs in files, you can also use cut and paste to move text into or out of a Command Prompt window.

To paste text into the window at the cursor location, click the window's System Menu (the upper-left corner) and select Edit, Paste. It's easier to do this without the mouse: just press Alt+Spacebar and type E P.

To copy text from the window to the Clipboard, click the window's System Menu and select Edit, Mark. Alternatively, type Alt+Spacebar E M. Use the mouse to highlight a rectangular area of the screen, and then press Enter. This copies the text to the Clipboard.

By default, the mouse does not select text until you use the Mark sequence. This makes it easier to use MS-DOS programs that are mouse-aware. If you seldom use the mouse with MS-DOS applications, click the System Menu (or press Alt+Spacebar), select Defaults, and check Quick Edit. When Quick Edit is enabled, you can use the mouse to mark text for copying to the Clipboard without having to type Alt+Spacebar E M first.

Setting Environment Variables

Using environment variables is one of the ways that Windows communicates information such as the location of system files and folders—as set up on your particular computer—to programs. Environment variables indicate where temporary files are stored, what folders contain Windows program files, and other settings that affect program operation and system performance. In addition, they can be used in batch files to temporarily hold information about the job at hand.

In Windows 7, the initial environment variables that are defined when every Command Prompt window is first opened are set up using the GUI shown in Figure 29.2.

Figure 29.2
Examining the environment variables for the current user (top) and for all users of the system (bottom). The per-user list adds to or overrides the systemwide list.

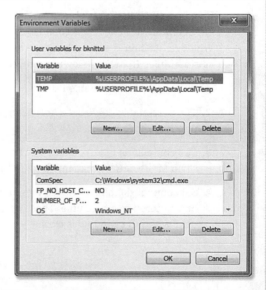

Notice that this dialog box has two sections, System Variables and User Variables. The lower, System Variables section defines the environment variables set up for every user account. The upper, User Variables section defines additional default environment variables just for the current user account. These add to or override the variables set up in the systemwide list.

To open this dialog box, if you are a computer administrator user, use either of these two methods:

- If you have a Command Prompt window open, type the command **start sysdm.cpl** and press Enter. You might need to confirm a UAC prompt. Then, select the Advanced tab, and click the Environment Variables button.

- Alternatively, click Start, right-click Computer, and select Properties. Select Advanced System Settings. You might need to confirm a UAC prompt. Then, click the Environment Variables button.

You can now edit both the upper User Variables (personal settings) and lower System Variables (systemwide settings) lists.

If you are not a computer administrator user, it's a bit trickier. Use either of these two procedures:

- To edit the systemwide settings, you can use either of the preceding methods, but you'll have to supply an administrator password. *Don't* change the upper (personal) part of the dialog box— you will be changing settings for the wrong account.

- To edit your own personal environment variable list, you must use the following method: Click Start, Control Panel, User Accounts and Family Safety, User Accounts. In the task list at the left side, click Change My Environment Variables. You will be able to edit only the upper (personal) environment variable list.

After you have the dialog box open, you can create new variables, delete variables, or highlight and edit existing variables using the corresponding buttons.

If you need to alter a variable, you must understand what happens if there's a conflict between environment variables defined in both the System Variables and User Variables lists. As a rule, Windows examines several locations for definitions, and the last definition seen wins. Windows sets variables from the following sources, in this order:

1. The systemwide variable list.

2. The personal variable list. (At this step, the PATH variable is treated specially. See the next section for details.)

3. Set commands in autoexec.nt. (This applies only for MS-DOS or Windows 3.*x* applications. See "The MS-DOS Environment" later in the chapter for more information.)

4. Subsequent definitions issued by set commands typed in a Command Prompt window or encountered in a batch file. These changes apply only to that particular window and will disappear when the window is closed.

Setting the PATH Environment Variable

If you write batch files or scripts, it's useful to put them into one folder, and to add this folder name to the PATH variable, so that you can run your batch files and scripts simply by typing their names.

Because mis-editing the PATH variable can prevent Windows from finding applications it needs to run, Windows gives the "personal" PATH definition special treatment:

- For the PATH variable, the User Variables definition is *added to* the end of (appended to) the System Variables definition.

- For all other environment variables, a User Variables definition *overrides* a System Variables definition.

In other words, you can enter your own personal folder(s) into the User Variables definition of PATH without worrying about copying or messing up the system definitions.

To create a folder for your own scripts and batch files, use one of these two procedures:

- If you want to use the scripts and batch files only for your own use, create a folder, and put the full path to the folder into your "personal" PATH variable. For example, create a folder named `c:\scripts`.

  Then, add a PATH variable to the upper part of the Environment Variables dialog box (refer to Figure 29.2) with the value `c:\scripts`. If you need to add more than one folder to your personal PATH, put a semicolon (;) between each folder name.

- If you want to create scripts and batch files that can be used by anyone who uses your computer, create a folder and be sure that its permissions are set so that all users can read it.

  For example, create a folder named `c:\scripts`. Right-click the folder, select Properties, and select the Security tab. If `Users` does not appear under Group or User Names, click Edit, then Add, and add "Users" to the list. Be sure that the Read & Execute permission setting is checked.

  → *To learn more about editing file and folder permissions,* **see** *"NTFS File Permissions,"* **p. 903**.

  Then, carefully edit the PATH variable in the lower part of the Environment Variables dialog box (shown in Figure 29.2). Add a semicolon (;) to the end of the existing text, and then add the folder name `c:\scripts`.

Your folder now will be part of the PATH when you open a new Command Prompt window.

The MS-DOS Environment

If you still use MS-DOS programs, you'll be glad to know that the 32-bit versions of Windows 7 still support MS-DOS programs.

Windows 7 and all other versions of Windows based on Windows NT run MS-DOS applications inside a program called ntvdm, which stands for *Windows NT Virtual DOS Machine*. Ntvdm is also used by the Windows 3.*x* support environment. It simulates the environment that DOS programs expect and makes them work correctly under Windows.

Ntvdm runs automatically when you attempt to start an MS-DOS or 16-bit Windows program. You don't have to take any special steps to activate it, but you can tune it in several ways by doing the following:

- Configure user variables in the Environment Variables dialog box, as discussed in the section "Setting Environment Variables" earlier in the chapter.

- Make selections from the DOS window's control menu.

- Make settings in the Properties dialog box for a shortcut to the DOS application.

- Set up custom autoexec.nt and config.nt configuration files so that you can address special memory, driver, or environment variable requirements a DOS program might have.

- Enter environment-altering commands at the command prompt.

I discuss these settings in the next several sections.

> *For more information about virtual PCs,* ***see*** *"Taking the Virtual Machine Approach,"* ***p. 72.***

> *For more information about The Virtual XP system,* ***see*** *Appendix A,* ***"*** *Using Virtualization on Windows 7."*

 note

The MS-DOS and 16-bit Windows subsystems are not provided with the 64-bit versions of Windows. If you use a 64-bit version of Windows 7 and still need to run MS-DOS or Windows 3.1 applications, you can download and install the free Microsoft Virtual PC program from microsoft.com, or use VMWare from www.vmware.com. With either of these programs, you can set up a "virtual" computer, install a copy of MS-DOS, Windows 3.1, or any subsequent version of Windows, and run your older applications inside the simulated environment.

Be sure to install Virtual PC's "Guest Extensions" inside the hosted operating system—these provide important enhancements. For example, they allow you to cut and paste between programs running inside and outside the virtual computer. This isn't quite as effortless as the built-in support provided by 32-bit versions of Windows, but it works very well.

If you have Windows 7 Professional, Ultimate, or Enterprise edition, you might also be able to use MS-DOS applications installed in the Virtual XP system, which is a free download you can get from Microsoft.

MS-DOS App Says Too Many Files Open

If you run an MS-DOS application and it gives an error message saying there are too many files open, you must modify `config.nt` (or create a custom config file). You should change the line that reads, for example, `files = 40` to a larger number; for example, `files = 100`. See "Customizing Autoexec.nt and Config.nt," later in this chapter, for instructions on modifying `config.nt`.

MS-DOS Application Displays Strange Characters

If your older MS-DOS application displays lots of strange characters on the screen, especially the combination ◊[, your program expected the support of a display driver called ansi.sys. You need to add the following line to your `config.nt` file, using the instructions under "Customizing Autoexec.nt and Config.nt" later in the chapter:

```
device=ansi.sys
```

Editing Advanced Settings for a DOS Application

If you're experiencing difficulties while running a specific DOS program, you can fine-tune the VDM environment for the particular application, allowing it to run more smoothly, or in some cases simply allowing it to run at all. DOS property settings can affect many aspects of an application's operation, such as (but not limited to) the following:

- The drive and folder (directory) selected as the default when an application starts
- Full-screen or windowed operation upon launch
- Conventional memory usage
- Expanded or extended memory usage
- The application's multitasking priority level
- The application's shortcut keys
- Foreground and background processing

To edit these properties for a DOS program, do the following:

1. Find the program file or a shortcut to it.
2. Right-click and choose Properties.

 note

If the program is stored on an NTFS-formatted partition, the standard Security tab will also be listed in the Properties dialog box.

Poke through each tab, and use the ? (question mark) button for help on the settings. Educational and game programs will most often require you to adjust the Memory and Compatibility settings.

Customizing autoexec.nt and config.nt

You can choose to further configure the MS-DOS and Windows 3.x environment by modifying Windows 7's equivalent of the old CONFIG.SYS and AUTOEXEC.BAT files. These files are called config.nt and autoexec.nt and are used to configure each DOS VDM when it starts up. Just remember:

- The files CONFIG.SYS and AUTOEXEC.BAT in your hard drive's root folder are completely ignored by Windows 7. If they're there at all, it's only to fool *really* old applications that won't run unless they see that these files exist.

- The files config.nt and autoexec.nt in \windows\system32 are used, but only when Windows needs to start up an MS-DOS or Windows 3.x application. Any change to these files will take effect the next time you start the application—you don't need to restart Windows.

The standard settings in config.nt as set up when Windows is installed are shown in the following listing. The REM comments have been removed for brevity. (If you upgraded your computer from an earlier version of Windows, your config.nt file might be different because the installer might have retained some of your previous operating system's settings.)

```
dos=high, umb
device=%SystemRoot%\system32\himem.sys
files=40
```

You can edit the config.nt and autoexec.nt files with a simple text editor such as Notepad. They're protected files, however, so you must run an elevated version of Notepad, using this procedure:

1. Click Start, All Programs, Accessories.

2. Right-click Notepad and select Run As Administrator.

3. Confirm the UAC prompt, or enter an Administrator password as requested. (Alternately, you can just type **notepad** in an elevated Command Prompt window).

4. Click File, Open, and browse to \windows\system32. Select autoexec.nt or config.nt as desired.

 tip

The Screen tab's Usage options determine whether the application initially comes up windowed or full screen. You still can toggle between views by pressing Alt+Enter. Of course, in full-screen display, the mouse is surrendered to the application. When you use a mouse with a windowed application, the mouse works within the window on its menus, and with Windows when you move the mouse back to the Windows desktop. No DOS-based mouse driver is needed. Mouse support is provided automatically.

 tip

On my computers, I always change the files setting to files=100 and add the line device=%SystemRoot%\system32\ansi.sys.

For more information about ansi.sys, see the next section.

Most of the settings used in MS-DOS 6 still work in `config.nt`, with some changes as noted in Table 29.2.

Table 29.2 Enhanced Settings for `config.nt`

Command	Description
`device=`	Installs loadable device drivers. Drivers that attempt to address hardware directly likely won't work; however, you can load display drivers such as `ANSI.SYS` and memory managers such as `EMM.SYS` and `HIMEM.SYS`.
`dosonly`	Allows only DOS programs to be loaded from a `COMMAND.COM` prompt. Windows and UNIX programs won't run.
`echoconfig`	Tells the VDM to print `CONFIG` and `AUTOEXEC` commands as they are executed from the files.
`files=`	Sets the maximum number of open files. I recommend setting this to 100.
`ntcmdprompt`	Replaces the `COMMAND.COM` interpreter with the 32-bit Windows command interpreter, `cmd.exe`. After you load a TSR or when you shell out of an application to DOS, you will get `cmd.exe` instead, from which you have the added benefits of the full 32-bit interpreter.

If you want, you can create customized copies of `config.nt` and/or `autoexec.nt` and use them just with specific DOS programs. To do this:

1. Use an elevated copy of Notepad to create the new setting file(s) with different names. For example, you might save a modified `config.nt` as `config_wordperfect.nt`.

2. Locate the MS-DOS program's `.exe` or `.com` file icon in Windows Explorer.

3. Right-click the icon and select Properties. Select the Program tab, and click the Advanced button. Enter the path to your customized config file.

 tip

Editing these files properly is no piece of cake. I suggest you have at hand a good DOS reference, such as Que's *Special Edition Using DOS 6.22*, Third Edition. It's out of print, but you can get a used copy at www.abebooks.com, among other places.

Issues with DOSKEY and ANSI.SYS

Two of the most common enhancements used on MS-DOS computers were DOSKEY and ANSI.SYS. DOSKEY provided enhanced command-line editing: for example, the use of the up and down arrow keys to recall previous commands. ANSI.SYS gave DOS applications a way to easily control the position and color of text output onto the screen.

ANSI.SYS can be made available for MS-DOS programs simply by adding the line `device=ansi.sys` to `config.nt` (or an alternate config file). Unfortunately, *no* ANSI cursor support is provided for 32-bit Windows character mode (console) applications.

 note

If you make changes to `autoexec.nt` or `config.nt` after having run an MS-DOS program from a Command Prompt window, you must close the Command Prompt window and open a new one for the MS-DOS subsystem to reload and take on the new configuration.

Conversely, DOSKEY—which has been enhanced significantly from the old DOS days—functions only in the 32-bit Windows console environment, and even if you attempt to load it in `autoexec.nt`, it does not function within the MS-DOS COMMAND.COM shell.

Batch Files

Although Windows Script Host is the most powerful tool for creating your own helpful programs, it's also useful to know how to use the batch file language. Batch files let you take advantage of the hundreds of command-line programs supplied with Windows.

A batch file, at the simplest level, is just a list of command prompt commands that have been typed into a file whose extension is `.bat` or `.cmd`. When you enter the name of a batch file at the command prompt, Windows looks for a file with this name in the current directory and in the folders of the PATH environment variable. Windows treats each line in the batch file as a command, and runs them one after the other as if you'd typed the commands by hand. At this simplest level, then, a batch file can be a big help if you find yourself typing the same commands over and over.

Beyond this, there are several commands that you can use to write rudimentary "programs" within a batch file, so that it can take different actions depending on what you type on the command line, or depending on the results of the commands it executes. These "programming" commands have been greatly improved since the MS-DOS days, so writing useful batch files on Windows 7 is much easier than writing them was in the old days. In particular, the IF and FOR statements have been greatly extended. You can prompt the user for input. It's possible to manipulate strings and filenames and perform arithmetic calculations. You can create subroutines within a single batch file. And there's more.

Unfortunately, I don't have room to provide coverage of batch file programming in this book, but I do in *Windows 7 and Vista Guide to Scripting, Automation, and Command Line Tools*, published by Que.

And some Microsoft documentation is available online. After reading this chapter, go to www.microsoft.com and search for these phrases:

```
Command Shell Overview
Environment Variables
Using Batch Parameters
Using Batch Files
Using Command Redirection Operators
Cmd
Command-Line Reference
```

Then, open a Command Prompt window and type the commands

```
help cmd
help set
help for
help if
```

and so on.

Batch File Tips

Table 29.3 lists several short batch files that I put on every computer that I use. These short command scripts let me edit files, change the path, view a folder with Explorer, and so on, simply by typing a couple of letters followed by a folder or filename. They don't involve fancy programming, but they save me a significant amount of time when I'm working with the Command Prompt window.

If you create a c:\scripts folder and add it to the PATH, as I discussed earlier under "Setting the PATH Environment Variable," you might want to create these same batch files in that folder for your own use.

 tip

To learn how to get the most from the batch files and the command line, get Brian's book *Windows 7 and Vista Guide to Scripting, Automation, and Command Line Tools*.

Table 29.3   Useful Tiny Batch Files

Filename	Contents and Purpose

ap.bat	`@echo off`
	`for %%p in (%path%) do if /%%p/ == /%1/ exit /b`
	`set path="%1";%path%`
	
	Adds the named folder to the PATH if it is not already listed. (This lasts only as long as the Command Prompt window is open.)
	Example: `ap c:\test`

bye.bat	`@logout` Logs off Windows. Example: `bye`
e.bat	`@if /%1/ == // (explorer /e,.) else explorer /e,%1` Opens Windows Explorer in Folder mode to view the named directory, or the current directory if no path is entered on the command line. Example: `e d:`
h.bat	`@cd /d %userprofile%` Changes the current directory to your user profile (home) directory. Example: `h`
n.bat	`@start notepad "%1"` Edits the named file with Notepad. Example: `n test.bat`
s.bat	`@cd /d c:\scripts` Makes c:\scripts the current directory, when you want to add or edit batch files and scripts. Example: `s`

Windows Script Host

In the last decade or so, Microsoft has worked diligently to provide ways for programmers to gain access to the internal functions of commercial applications such as Word and Excel and of Windows itself. The approach is based on a technology called the Component Object Model, or COM, which lets a properly designed program share its data and functional capabilities with other programs—any other programs, written in any other programming language. If you've ever written macros for Word or Excel, you've worked with scripting and COM. One product of these efforts is Windows Script Host, or WSH, which provides a fast and easy way to write your own management and utility programs. Scripts have an advantage over batch files in that they can perform complex calculations and can manipulate text information in powerful ways because you write them in a full-featured programming language.

Scripts can massage, digest, and manipulate text files and data, view and change Windows settings, and take advantage of Windows services through COM objects provided as a standard part of Windows. In addition, if you have COM-enabled applications such as WordPerfect, Microsoft Word, or Excel installed, scripts can even enlist these applications to present information in tidy, formatted documents and charts.

Windows comes with support for two different scripting languages:

- **VBScript**—Nearly identical to the Visual Basic for Applications (VBA) macro language used in Word and Excel.

- **JScript**—Microsoft's version of the JavaScript language, which is widely used to make web pages interactive. (JavaScript, by the way, is not the same thing as Java. Java is another programming language altogether.)

In addition, you can download and install scripting support for other languages. If you have a UNIX or Linux background, for example, you might want to use the Perl, Python, or TCL scripting languages. You can get free WSH-compatible versions of these languages at www.activestate.com.

If you are already versed in one of the scripting languages I've mentioned, by all means, use it. If you don't already know a scripting language, VBScript is probably the best one to start with because you can also use it to write macros for Microsoft's desktop applications. I'll use VBScript in the examples in this section.

Creating Scripts

Just like batch files, scripts are stored as plain text files, which you can edit with Notepad or any other text file editor. To create a script file, choose a descriptive name, something like WorkSummaryReport perhaps, and add the extension that corresponds to the language you'll be using. A script written in the VBScript language must have its filename end with .vbs.

As an example, I'll write a script that I'll call hello.vbs. If you want to try it yourself, the steps are

1. Open a Command Prompt window by clicking Start, All Programs, Accessories, Command Prompt.

2. The Command Prompt window opens on the default directory \users*your_user_name*. If you want to create the script in another folder, you will need to type in a cd command to change directories. (As I suggested earlier in this chapter, you might want to put your scripts into folder C:\scripts, and add that folder to the PATH.) But for the purposes of this example, we'll skip that and use the default directory.

3. Type the command **notepad hello.vbs**. When Notepad asks whether you want to create a new file, click Yes.

4. Type in the text

   wscript.echo "Hello, this message comes from a script"

5. Save the script by selecting File, Save. You can leave the Notepad window open, or close it with File, Exit.

6. Bring the Command Prompt window to the foreground.

7. Type **hello** and press Enter.

If everything works, you see the dialog box shown in Figure 29.3. Click OK to close the dialog box.

Figure 29.3
The sample script displays a simple text message.

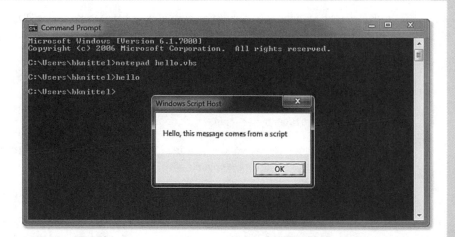

WSH can display its results in a window, as you just saw, or it can display results in the console window, as do most command-line programs. As you saw in the previous sample, the default is to display information in a window because the default interpreter for scripts is wscript. It's usually best to change the default so that the default mode is the text-based console output method. To do this, type this command:

cscript //H:cscript //nologo //s

(Notice that the slashes are doubled-up in this command.) Now, type the command **hello** again. This time the script's output should display within the Command Prompt window.

Some Sample Scripts

I don't have room here to give you even an introductory course in VBScript programming. As I mentioned, that's a topic that can fill an entire book. What I can do is give you some examples of how WSH can be used to perform useful tasks and to manage Windows.

Disk and Network Management

WSH comes with tools to examine and modify drives, folders, and files. Here is an example of a VBScript script that performs a reasonably useful task:

```
set fso = CreateObject("Scripting.FileSystemObject")
set drivelist = fso.Drives
for each drv in drivelist
    if drv.IsReady then
        wscript.echo "Drive", drv.DriveLetter, "has", drv.FreeSpace, "bytes free"
    end if
next
```

It displays the amount of free space on each of your computer's drives. Type this script into a file named freespace.vbs in your batch file directory, and then type the command-line command **freespace**. On my computer this prints the following:

```
Drive C: has 15866540032 bytes free
Drive D: has 27937067008 bytes free
Drive F: has 335872000 bytes free
Drive H: has 460791808 bytes free
```

WSH can also work with networking features. The following VBScript script displays your computer's current network drive mappings:

```
set wshNetwork = CreateObject("WScript.Network") ' create the helper object

set maps = wshNetwork.EnumNetworkDrives    ' collection describes mapped drives
for i = 0 to maps.Length-2 step 2          ' step through collection by twos
    wscript.echo "Drive", maps.item(i), "is mapped to", maps.item(i+1)
next
```

Windows Management Instrumentation

Windows Management Instrumentation (WMI) is a system service that provides access to virtually every aspect of a Windows computer system, from the hardware components up to the highest-level system services. For some components, WMI provides information only. Other components can be changed, and thus, as its name implies, WMI can be used to manage the system. You can use

WMI to start and stop system services, monitor and stop applications, create drive mappings, share folders, and, with the appropriate updated WMI drivers installed, even manage system services such as Internet Information Services, Microsoft Exchange, and the Domain Name Service on Windows Server.

The following script lists the status of each system service installed on your computer. This script file can be named showservices.vbs. (The underscore at the end of some of the lines are part of the script.)

```
set services = GetObject"winmgmts:{impersonationlevel=impersonate," &_
        "authenticationlevel=pkt}!" &_
        "/root/CIMV2:Win32_Service")     ' get services WMI info

for each svc in services.Instances_      ' display information for each service
    wscript.echo svc.name, "State:", svc.State, "Startup:", svc.StartMode
next
```

On my computer, the first few lines of output from this script look like this:

```
AeLookupSvc State: Stopped Startup: Manual
ALG State: Stopped Startup: Manual
AppIDSvc State: Stopped Startup: Manual
Appinfo State: Running Startup: Manual
AppMgmt State: Stopped Startup: Manual
```

Remember, too, that as command-line programs, you can redirect the output of these scripts into a file. The command

```
showservices >listing.txt
```

puts the service list into file listing.txt, just as if showservices was a native Windows executable program.

Windows PowerShell

Microsoft has developed a new command-line environment called Windows PowerShell (WPS), which is installed as a standard accessory starting with Windows 7. WPS in many ways looks and acts like the familiar Command Prompt window, but it's actually a very strange animal, and it gives you access to some very powerful programming tools. I don't have room in this book to teach you much about it, but I will describe how it differs from batch file and scripts, and I'll point you to resources that will help you learn more.

I used the word "strange." Can a computer program be strange? Definitely! For one thing, most Windows PowerShell commands (which are properly called *cmdlets*) generate streams of *objects*, not text. Objects are computer representations of real-world things. They have *properties* that describe attributes of the things they represent, and *methods* that let you manipulate the things. For example, an object that represents a specific file on your hard disk might have properties like Name, Size, and LastWriteTime, and methods like Delete, Edit, and Open. Windows PowerShell works with objects in a new, unusual, and ultimately very powerful way.

Now, if you type `dir` in a regular Command Prompt window, the command shell interprets `dir` and generates a bunch of text listing the current folder's files by name. The `dir` command is programmed very specifically to print information about files in text form. That's all it can do.

In WPS, you can type `dir` and this will also print out a list of filenames, but something completely different is happening behind the scenes. In WPS, `dir` is a shortcut for the `Get-Childitem` cmdlet, which in its simplest use generates a stream of `File` objects; each object represents one of the files in a folder, and each object has properties and methods (for example, `name` and `size`). When an object (of any sort) lands in the WPS prompt window, WPS prints out a line of text listing the object's most important properties. For a `File` object, this includes the file's name, size, and the date it was created. So, when you type `dir`, WPS produces a stream of `File` objects and they end up as a nice, tabular listing of files.

The end result is the same as in the old Command Prompt environment, but it's happening in a general, more abstract way. The cmdlet doesn't know about or care about text or formatting: it simply spits out a bunch of `File` objects. And the WPS window will turn *any* list of objects into a nice tabular listing. Files, user accounts, hard drives, Windows services; whatever object a cmdlet throws into the WPS window turns into a nice text listing.

In addition, WPS includes a full-scale object-oriented programming language and has access to Microsoft's .NET programming platform, which means WPS scripts can perform complex computations and communicate with other computers and networked ("cloud") services.

WPS even lets you do complex things with objects without programming. You can use the familiar ¦ pipe symbol to direct streams of objects from one cmdlet to another, and this lets you do very complex, specific things with tools that are separately very simple and general-purpose in nature. For example, the following command will delete all files in the current folder that are more than 6 months old:

```
dir | where-object {$_.LastWriteTime -lt (get-date).addmonths(-6)} | remove-item
```

It looks complex at first, but it's not so bad. This command line strings three separate cmdlets together:

- `dir`—Spits out a list of all the `File` objects in the current directory. Here, they don't land in the WPS command window, so they don't make a text listing. Instead, the pipe (`|`) symbol instructs WPS to pass the objects to the next command.

- `where-object`—Passes just some of the objects through, based on the "filtering" condition inside the curly brackets. In this example, it passes through only those files that have not been changed for more than six months (that is, whose `LastWriteTime` value is less than the date/time six months back). So, objects representing just the old files are piped to the next command.

- `remove-item`—Deletes the hard disk files corresponding to each of the file objects it receives.

 caution

Don't just open a WPS window and type this command to see whether it works! You'll most likely delete a bunch of important files from your Windows profile folder. If you want to see whether it works, type just the first two parts of the command:

```
dir | where-object {$_.Last-
WriteTime -lt (get-date).
addmonths(-6)}
```

This will print out a list of the selected files but will not delete them.

As I said earlier, you're not limited just to using commands that you type into the WPS window. WPS has a full-scale programming language with variables, loops, subroutines, user-defined objects, and so on. You can use these at the command prompt or in script files. You also can create shortcuts (called *aliases)* for commonly used commands and scripts to make typing easier, and a bunch of aliases are predefined for you.

For more information about WPS, check out Brian's book *Windows 7 and Vista Guide to Scripting, Automation, and Command Line Tools* or *Windows PowerShell 2.0 Unleashed.*

Task Scheduler

Windows Task Scheduler lets you specify programs to be run automatically at specified dates and times and on certain events like system startup, users logging on, or even the occurrence of any event that can be logged in the Event Viewer.

By itself, the Task Schedule service does not significantly affect system performance, although the tasks it runs can. However, you can instruct it not to start specified tasks when the system is busy. You might want to do this, for example, if a particular task generates a lot of disk activity.

What kinds of tasks would you run with Task Scheduler? As I mentioned, the tasks need to run without user interaction. So, they are typically maintenance tasks such as defragmenting the hard disk, cleaning out temporary files, and so on. Windows uses Task Scheduler for this very purpose, and you'll notice that there are several pre-installed scheduled tasks set up when Windows is installed to do this very sort of thing. Task Scheduler can also watch for the occurrence of any event that can be recorded in the Event Log.

Task Scheduler is especially useful with batch files and scripts, because these scheduled programs can usually be designed to run without any user interaction. It's truly the ultimate automation tool because you don't even have to be there when it's working!

There are two types of tasks you can create in Task Scheduler:

- **Basic tasks**—Designed to be run using the current user's account, and support a single triggering event or time.

- **Tasks**—Can be run using any specified user account, and can be configured to run whether the user is logged in or not. Tasks can also be run in Windows XP or Windows

 note

When Task Scheduler runs a task as a different user than the one currently logged on, the logged-on user cannot see or interact with the program. Be sure that scheduled tasks can operate without user input and exit cleanly when they've done their work. And keep in mind that once an application or service is running, even if it was launched through a scheduled task, it will affect system performance just as if you started it manually.

 note

Obviously, the computer has to be alive to run a task, so if you expect to do a disk cleanup at 4:00 a.m., be sure to leave the computer on. If a scheduled task is missed because the computer was turned off, Windows will perform the task the next time the computer is started, but the task will now be running while you're using the computer, which is probably what you were trying to avoid by having it run at night.

Server 2003 compatibility mode, and can be configured to run with higher than normal priority if necessary.

To create a Basic task in Task Scheduler, follow these steps:

1. Open Task Scheduler as discussed earlier in this section. Task Scheduler displays in the top center pane a summary list of tasks that started and/or completed during the last 24 hours, and displays a list of active tasks below that. (Here, "active" means "defined and enabled to run at the specified time or event." It doesn't necessarily mean "actively running right now.")

2. The Add Actions pane is located on the right side. Click Create Basic Task. The Create Basic Task Wizard opens.

3. Enter the name of the task and a description. Enter whatever you want, to remind you of what the tasks does. Click Next to continue.

4. On the Task Trigger screen, select when to run the task. You can choose daily, weekly, monthly, or one time; when the computer starts, when you log on, or when a specific event is logged.

   You can use the When a Specific Event Is Logged option to trigger the task when a specific Event Log entry is recorded. For example, you could use this to perform some sort of notification if a disk error event occurs. You'll need to enter the event's numeric ID number.

    tip

   To find an event's ID number, find an occurrence of the event in the Windows Event Log.

5. Click Next.

6. Specify applicable time options, such as time of day, as required. Click Next.

7. Select what you want the task to do (open a program, send an email, or display a message). Click Next to continue.

8. If you selected Start a Program, use Browse to locate the program, batch file, or script. (For Windows applications, browse in the \Windows or \Windows\system32 folders. For third-party applications, search in the subfolders of the \Program Files folder. For scripts you've written yourself, browse to the folder in which you've stored the script or batch file.) Then provide any necessary command-line switches or settings, and if you want to specify a default drive and folder for the program, enter the path to the desired folder.

   If you selected Send an Email, enter the information for sender, receiver, SMTP email server, message, and so forth.

   If you selected Display a Message, enter the message title and message text. Then, click Next.

9. Review the task on the Summary screen (see Figure 29.4). If you want to set advanced options such as idle time, what to do if the computer is running on batteries, and what to do after the task completes, check Open Advanced Properties for This Task When I Click Finish. Click Finish to complete the task.

Figure 29.4
Completing the
configuration of a
basic task.

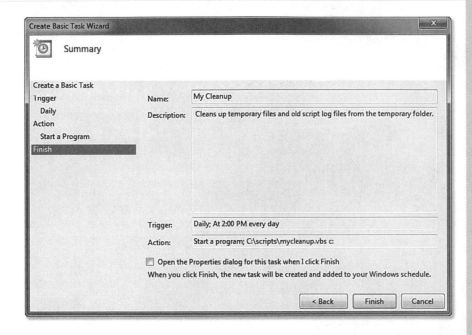

For more advanced scheduling, use the Create Task selection. The Create Task interface uses a multi-tabbed interface instead of a wizard. The General tab includes security options, while the Triggers tab permits you to specify multiple triggers for a task (the task will be performed whenever *any* of the triggers occurs). The Actions tab supports multiple actions in a task, the Conditions tab includes options to configure idle time, power, and network connection requirements, and the Settings tab supports conditions for running and stopping a task. Use Create Task, rather than Create Basic Task, when you need these additional settings in your task.

VII

SECURITY

IN THIS PART

30	Protecting Windows from Viruses and Spyware	845
31	Protecting Your Data from Loss and Theft	863
32	Protecting Your Network from Hackers and Snoops	913
33	Protecting Yourself from Fraud and Spam	945

30

PROTECTING WINDOWS FROM VIRUSES AND SPYWARE

Malicious Software: Ignorance Is Not Bliss

Hackers and computer viruses have long been popularized in movies and the media. Although the term *hacker* has been affectionately used to describe particularly dedicated and skilled computer geeks, it is also used in negative context to describe those who abuse that knowledge for criminal activity. As high-speed Internet connections and personal computers proliferate, these so-called "black hat" hackers continue to amass an impressive arsenal of tools. These tools may be placed into a few major categories according to their primary characteristics. All of the descriptive terms, some of which you've no doubt heard in reference to computers, such as *virus*, *worm*, or *spyware*, all fall under the single category called *malware*: software designed to do bad things.

It's important to understand the differences between the major types of malware because the computer industry is still evolving to fight these threats. At this time, there is no single silver bullet that solves all problems. The computer user who understands the fundamentals of malware is in a better position to make informed decisions and avoid potentially disastrous consequences. This chapter explains the major threat categories and how, when configured properly, Windows 7 can effectively arm you better than ever against malware.

Viruses Past and Present

Not so long ago, computer viruses were a joke among computer professionals. Viruses were a scapegoat on which the uninitiated or uninformed systems administrator could blame irreproducible or incomprehensible computer problems. The word itself maintained a level of mystique, describing little-understood software that spread almost magically unseen. Respected security experts contended that viruses were mostly hype and paranoia, and certainly the least of our worries. Of course, that was during a time when the main exposure to malicious data was confined to what could be put on a magnetic disk. As long as pervasive connectivity and complex networks remained confined to the cognoscenti, computer viruses were not a major concern.

We reached the tipping point sometime in the early 1990s, when several well-known technology companies stepped up to provide virus protection for the masses. The mainstream media heralded the disk-mangling doom of the Michelangelo virus, which was expected to strike each March 6th thereafter in a tawdry birthday celebration of its Renaissance master namesake. (It's also my, Robert Cowart's, birthday, and I am disappointed yearly not yet to have a virus named after me in retaliation for all my books about Microsoft Windows.) On that fateful date, with no warning, the Michelangelo virus began destroying data on the hard disk. The system locked up, the hard disk light stayed on, and, upon restart, victims discovered that disk was irrevocably erased. As it turned out, Michelangelo made a much better news story than it did a computer virus. Although forecasted to impact millions of computers, it affected relatively few.

As technology increased in complexity, so did opportunities for virus writers. Virus construction kits provided simpler power tools for evildoers, as did Microsoft Office with its macro technology. David L. Smith wrote the Melissa macro virus, which duped users into opening a malicious Microsoft Word email attachment. When opened, the macro used Microsoft Outlook to send copies of itself to 50 people in the address book. It was an effective method of propagation that in 1999 clogged email systems around the world. Melissa and subsequent variants of email macro viruses showed that one did not have to be a formidable programmer to elicit formidable mayhem. They also illustrated the defining characteristic of a computer virus that differentiates it from benign programs: the capability to self-replicate. Melissa used a combination of human and technological manipulation to accomplish its mission, but other forms of viruses spread even more effectively.

Worms: "Look, Ma! No Hands!"

Systems that house large databases often contain key financial or business-critical information. SQL Slammer is a computer virus that infected tens of thousands of database systems in 10 minutes. It did this so quickly because it required no human interaction, aside from its initial launch, to propagate. Viruses that can move quickly between networks and carry out their mission automatically are referred to as *worms*. Each computer infected with SQL Slammer blasted network packets to thousands of random computer addresses every second. Each packet carried with it the potential to create another infected computer, which would in turn instantly spew viral packets at an equally furious pace. Owing to the resulting network clog, bank ATMs, airline check-in systems, and Seattle's 911 emergency networks were all temporarily knocked out.

Even so, SQL Slammer was a mere shadow of what it could have been. It did not directly deliver any malicious payload, steal any information, or destroy any data, but it certainly could have.

Worms are the most dreaded form of viruses because they spread so rapidly and have the potential to do incredible damage in a short period of time. More elaborate and sophisticated viruses continue to develop, and some experts believe the worst is yet to come.

Spyware

More often than not, if your Internet-connected computer has become sluggish, peppered with pop-up ads, and is in a general state of malaise, it's because spyware has crept onto your computer. Installed without consent, spyware can perform a range of unauthorized functions including track visited websites, force pop-up advertisements, and even capture keystrokes. Passwords, credit card numbers, and any personal information typed can all be captured on a computer that has the worst type of spyware installed.

Unlike viruses, spyware does not actively reproduce, nor does it traverse networks the way worms do. Aside from plain and simple information theft and forced advertisements, it can apply a vast array of creative implements to inconspicuously do outright bad, or at least ethically questionable, things.

Spyware can be installed on a computer in several ways. Downloading and installing any number of ostensibly harmless components, such as weather trackers, toolbars, or games, can install spyware. The term *Trojan horse* is often used to describe a kind of malicious software that masquerades as something else to get inside your computer. In some cases, innocently clicking a dancing monkey or visiting the wrong website can exploit a security vulnerability and install a Trojan.

Once installed, spyware has an uncanny knack for begetting spyware, inviting unwelcome spyware kin, and dragging a computer to its knees. Fortunately, there are plenty of ways to prevent spyware from infiltrating a computer in the first place, and lots of tools to remove it should it find its way onto your system.

Rootkits and Beyond

As if viruses, worms, and spyware are not enough, they really aren't the worst that can happen to a computer. Good hackers have known for a long time that the best way to infiltrate a system is to do it in such a way that nobody can possibly know they were there. Historically, they used a "kit" of utilities for getting the highest level of access on UNIX systems. Because that level of access is called "root," such tools are called rootkits.

Currently, most of the wonderful security programs that we use to keep our computers safe rely on core Windows components to ferret out unsavory software. These core components provide information about files, applications, and processes, and keep track of what's going on inside the computer. But what if these core components were wrong? What if they had been tampered with or replaced with malicious components that hid information from the antimalware programs, and even Windows itself? Rootkits attempt and often succeed at this feat, acting as a mole in the trusted parts of the OS. They operate below the radar of traditional security programs and are especially troublesome for antimalware writers, who must develop fresh approaches to deal with them. There are ways to detect rootkits, though, and Windows 7 has the built-in security technology to help do that.

What's next? Without question, the human mind's boundless creativity and perseverance will generate additional problems and threats. Antimalware strategists must be weary after years of reactive solutions, going back and forth in a perpetual game of cat-and-mouse. Although the one-upsmanship between malware writers and their rivals might never end, the good guys have shifted toward a more holistic strategy, developing technologies that fight not just some specific type of malware, but combat malware tactics in general. Windows 7 possesses several such features, some passive, and others that must be enabled to be used to maximum advantage.

Antimalware Strategy: Defense in Depth

So far, no one solution has been developed that solves all computer security problems. To date, the best strategy for protecting information systems is to use layers of defense to stop attackers. Although security technologies can be complex, the strategy behind them is simple: Give attackers as little as possible to target, and protect what must be exposed with multiple layers of security. Even if one layer is defeated, another will likely block the attack.

Think of a medieval castle on a hilltop. Tall watchtowers provide visibility in every direction. A massive outer wall surrounds the castle, as does a foul moat. Attack options are limited and grim because there are so many layers of defense to counter. The castle's archers, catapults, and other defenses make even approaching the wall a daunting task, while the moat protects against undermining the castle walls. But even if one were to somehow penetrate the outer defenses, concentric inner walls, protected by all manner of vicious implements, stand ready to deliver more punishment. And then, if the inner walls are breached, the innermost keep must be stormed, which will be defended most fiercely by its inhabitants.

Defense in depth is not a new security strategy, but it is an effective one. Besieging a castle was a formidable task. Eventually, of course, new technology in the form of gunpowder rendered these defenses obsolete. Such is the nature of an arms race.

Windows Action Center

The easiest way to get a high-level security overview of your computer's own defense-in-depth strategy is to check the Control Panel's Action Center, shown in Figure 30.1. It monitors the state of the main security components on the system: Network Firewall, Windows Update, Virus Protection, Spyware and Other Unwanted Software Protection, Internet Security Settings, User Account Control, and Network Access Protection. If there are any security concerns, a yellow or red vertical bar appears alongside a message in the content pane to indicate the importance of the issue, along with a red indicator (for high-priority issues) on the flag icon for this utility in the notification area on the taskbar.

If you see such an indicator, click the flag in the notification area to open a flyout menu. You can either click the appropriate link to resolve the issue in one step, or select Open Action Center to view all message details and take appropriate actions. Common reasons for indicators include outdated virus definitions, security updates to apply, or a firewall disabled, perhaps for troubleshooting purposes.

 note

Action Center also enables you to monitor maintenance issues related to problem report solutions, Windows Backup, Windows Update (also covered in the main Security category), and troubleshooting.

These yellow and red bars alert you to items that need attention.

Figure 30.1
Action
Center
alerts the
user to
security
and main-
tenance
issues.

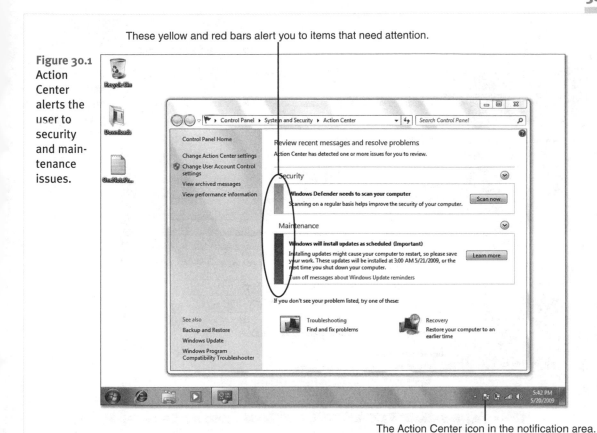

The Action Center icon in the notification area.

Microsoft graciously enables several of the main security cate-
gories right out of the box. With no action on your part,
Network Firewall, Windows Update, Spyware and Other
Unwanted Software Protection, Internet Security Settings, and
User Account Control all show an On or OK status (see Figure
30.2).

 note

If the list of categories isn't displayed, click the arrow to the right of
the main Security category in the
Action Center window.

Clicking the arrow toggles the
display of the Security items.

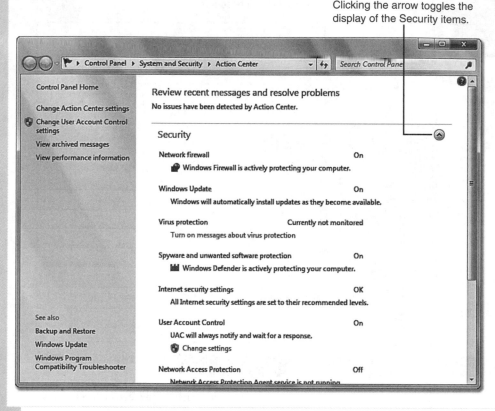

Figure 30.2
Action Center
displays a
list of
security
items.

One section, however, might be red even on a brand-new PC.
Although it is a universally recommended component, and
you'd be remiss to get on the Internet without one, no
antivirus protection is included with Windows 7. Spyware protection is present in the form of Windows Defender, but you
must procure your own antivirus product.

If you buy Windows 7 on a new PC, the manufacturer may
bundle antivirus software, improved firewalls, or some spyware solution besides Windows Defender. You can monitor
these programs in Action Center as well.

Choosing and Installing an Antivirus Client

Antivirus software works primarily by comparing the contents
of the computer with a list of known viruses (virus definitions)

 tip

Software vendors sometimes bundle
security software, including antivirus
and firewall products, that can install
on top of the existing Windows solutions. Overlapping security programs
that perform the same function, when
installed at the same time, can cause
conflicts and unpredictable results.
You don't want two firewall programs,
for example, operating concurrently.
You can select which firewall to run in
Action Center or, if you choose to use
the built-in Windows Firewall, simply
uninstall the secondary firewall using
Programs and Features in Control
Panel.

to see whether any part of a computer is infected. It does this in two different ways. The first is by scheduling recurring scans, daily or perhaps weekly at a time of your choosing, during which the program plods through all endangered areas of the computer. If any viruses are found, they can be cleaned, deleted, or rendered inert, effectively stopping the virus from spreading. Several prominent companies offer antivirus scans of this type for free on their websites. This cleaning approach works magnificently in some cases. In other cases, after a computer is compromised, cleaning a virus is like trying to push a bullet back into a gun.

Viruses are best detected and defeated before they infect and damage a computer, which is why web-based scans alone are not enough. Real-time protection is the second major feature of modern antivirus programs, and the one that's worth money. With real-time protection, computer activity is constantly monitored. Whenever a file is read, opened, or modified, it is checked against the list of known viruses. With this level of protection, a virus can be identified and stopped before it can spread or cause any damage, and that is a valuable service indeed.

Most modern antivirus programs provide both scheduled scans and real-time protection, but both features are only as good as the list of known viruses they can identify. Virus writers are an active bunch, and using an antivirus program with an outdated list is not much better than running nothing at all.

When a new virus is detected in the wild, antivirus vendors race to identify and capture its unique signature. Only then can the vendor's virus definition lists be updated and distributed to customers, so in addition to the quality of the software itself, the experience and knowledge of the response team is of paramount importance. Good antivirus vendors deliver timely and effective virus definition updates, so seek a vendor with a proven record of responsiveness. The heavyweights in the industry are McAfee, Symantec, and Trend Micro, but a number of well-respected smaller vendors do a fine job, some of whose products might be a better alternative.

If you subscribe to a high-speed Internet service, it's likely that your provider will supply you with an antivirus program free of charge. Although ISPs are in general an outstanding bunch, their generosity is far from altruistic. ISPs provide free antivirus programs because if they don't, unprotected systems can bog down their networks, erode trust in their service, and cause a string of headaches. Many hackers first go for easy targets, and an unprotected system on a public network is soon mincemeat or, worse, can be used as a launching pad for further attacks.

If your ISP provides free antivirus protection, the ISP usually has done the homework to select a reputable vendor and can often provide some level of support for that product. You may cross the margin of diminishing utility by paying more for a different antivirus program, so unless you have a specific need, try your ISP's recommended antivirus software if you don't already have some installed.

If your computer manufacturer offers none, and your ISP doesn't either, you might need to buy antivirus software yourself. This might seem challenging at first glance because there are so many features to consider and product lines change frequently. For advice on antivirus software, consult reputable periodicals

 tip

The antivirus business is a 2 billion dollar market, where the initial cost of a software product is quickly outweighed by costs for recurring subscription services for updates. When selecting a product, consider yearly subscription costs over the expected life of your computer. Multiyear subscriptions may provide valuable discounts, but as competition increases, subscription prices may drop.

such as *PC World* or *PC Magazine*, both of which maintain up-to-date information on their websites. You might also want to check out Virus Bulletin at www.virusbtn.com.

It's great when viruses are stopped before they get a chance to take root, but sometimes they're uncovered only after the damage is done. The primary job of your antivirus software is to detect and prevent viruses. Most programs can clean and repair simple infections, but more complex and destructive viruses require separate, specifically designed removal tools. If you're not careful, even if a virus is successfully cleaned, re-infection can occur the second you lift your finger from the mouse button. Regardless of which software protects your computer, here are the steps to break the cycle and get rid of a virus effectively:

 tip

We get no kickbacks for unsolicited advertising in our books (too bad), but we're occasionally moved to give tips to readers about products we like a lot. One of these is Avast! antivirus. For individual users, the price is right—it's free. What's more, it's easy to use, doesn't drag down my system speed as some other antivirus programs do, and it's a real-time virus scanner that protects against malicious code cloaked inside IMs, emails, web browsing, network communications, P2P transfers, web pages, and downloads. For more information, visit www.avast.com.

1. Manually run Windows Update to fix any new security vulnerabilities in Windows. To be thorough, also check vendors' websites for updates to any additional software you may have installed. Remember, if you remove a virus but remain vulnerable to a relapse, you might be in for a long day.

2. Update your virus definitions to detect the latest threats. Most antivirus software uses definition files that become stale quickly. Don't bring a knife to a gun fight.

3. Run a virus scan to find and eliminate any viruses. If you clean or quarantine a virus this way, run a follow-up scan to make sure it's truly dispatched. If not, at least you have identified the name of the threat and can proceed to the next step.

4. Visit your antivirus vendor's website and search for the identified threat. Most likely they have instructions and tools to help remove the virus from your computer. After a removal attempt, run another scan to confirm success. If needed, a general web search can often reveal alternative methods of treatment.

If all else fails, the fifth step to virus removal is tried and true: reinstall Windows from scratch. Make sure to delete and re-create the hard disk partitions during the install, and pat yourself on the back for having a recent backup of your critical data.

➡ *For detailed instructions on reinstalling Windows 7 from scratch,* **see** *Chapter 2, "Installing and Upgrading Windows 7."*

Windows Defender for Spyware Protection

Mark Twain famously said, "There are lies, damned lies, and statistics." No matter whose statistics you believe, reports and personal experiences indicate that most if not the vast majority of Internet-connected systems have some form of spyware installed. It's a big enough problem that Microsoft has included antispyware capabilities in the box with Windows 7. Windows Defender evolved from Microsoft's 2005 free beta release of Microsoft AntiSpyware and is built with technology gained from Microsoft's acquisition of Giant Company Software, Inc. Spyware protection is its chief focus, but as the name implies, Windows Defender does not limit itself exclusively to spyware protection and takes on the remainder of malware that antivirus programs can leave untreated.

After spyware gets onto a system, it can be difficult to remove. Let's assume you have a cousin named Heather who, after admittedly visiting suspicious links on MySpace, is convinced something bad has happened to her computer. Performance has degraded noticeably. Pop-ups abound. Like many, Heather is an avid fan of toolbars and neat programs that do wonderfully cute things. They have cute names such as BearShare and Bonzi Buddy, and at first seem to make the computer more fun than it ever deserved to be.

If her suspicion is correct and the system is indeed infested with spyware, it could take a seasoned computer expert many, many hours to be *almost* certain that the system was rid of malware. "Almost certain" because, once a computer is compromised, it's difficult to know with absolute certainty that it is clean unless drastic measures are taken. Even after scouring the system with a variety of antispyware tools, intermediate-level system cleaners, and ultimately the more advanced power tools, it's difficult to be convinced that a previously compromised system is truly clean because, just as layered defenses are so effective at preventing malware, layered deception can be equally effective at hiding it. A more efficient and effective route in severe cases may be to reinstall from scratch. Not a quick or easy fix.

As with viruses, by far the best way to prevent spyware is to stop it before it gets into the system, and Windows Defender monitors several system locations that are the main targets. It does its best to scan for rootkits, keystroke loggers, and other threats that do not fall into the worm or virus category. Along with real-time protection, Windows Defender provides the capability to periodically scan the computer, at a time and frequency you select, against the list of known spyware agents.

A quick scan of the usual suspect areas is the default configuration, designed for optimal performance and daily use, whereas a full scan exhaustively covers every file and process on the computer. A full scan may result in slow performance while it runs, so is intended to run only occasionally, or when you think spyware may be lurking. To ensure up-to-date scanning capability, Windows Defender automatically checks for updated spyware definitions before each scheduled scan and downloads them if needed. For both real-time protection and scheduled scans, spyware alerts are classified as severe, high, medium, low, or unknown.

Each alert level is subject to finely granular control, including whether to automatically remove detected spyware. Because false positives are a risk, Windows creates a restore point before each automatic spyware removal to enable recovery if needed. The sensitivity and scope of real-time protection can be fine-tuned in even greater detail or disabled altogether. Windows Defender resides in Control Panel (icon view). Its behavior is highly configurable through the Options section of its Tools menu, shown in Figure 30.3. Thankfully, default options should suit most users, although there's enough flexibility to please discriminating tastes.

 note

Real-time protection comes from nine software agents that protect different parts of the system. It's smart to leave all of them on, but each can be disabled independently. That way, compatibility or other issues with a single agent can be addressed while the rest stay active. The Options section shown in Figure 30.3 includes a Real-time Protection link to get details on each agent.

Arcane tweaks aside, the method for rooting out spyware is fairly straightforward in most cases. Click Control Panel, Windows Defender, and then the Scan menu button to perform a quick scan. If you have a healthy level of paranoia, which does *not* mean they're not after you, click the down arrow next to the Scan button and select Full Scan.

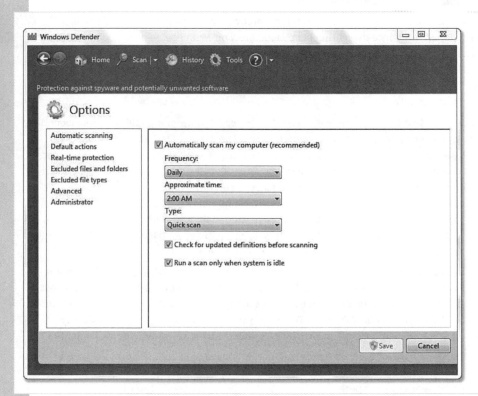

Figure 30.3
Windows Defender's real-time protection allows fine-tuning.

When the scan completes, Windows Defender will either report that it finds no problems, as shown in Figure 30.4, or enumerate all potentially unwanted software it finds. At that point, if you've had enough of this spyware nonsense and just want it gone, click Remove All. To control exactly what will be removed and what will stay, peruse the Review Items section. It includes detailed information on each item detected, and relevant links to Microsoft's online Malicious Software Encyclopedia if applicable. After you've removed the unwanted software, or quarantine it if you'd rather put it in the penalty box and investigate further, you can verify a clean bill of health with a follow-up scan.

For those of you who enjoyed the Software Explorer feature in previous versions of Windows Defender, you won't find it in the latest version that's bundled with Windows 7. Microsoft streamlined Windows Defender to act mainly as a malware scanner and removal program (its original purpose) rather than the more comprehensive tool that it had become. To get a detailed, consolidated view of software running on your computer, or a more detailed way to check up on suspicious software (such as the lack of a digital signature), use AppLocker or a third-party anti-malware tool.

Figure 30.4
Looking for
unwanted software
with Windows
Defender.

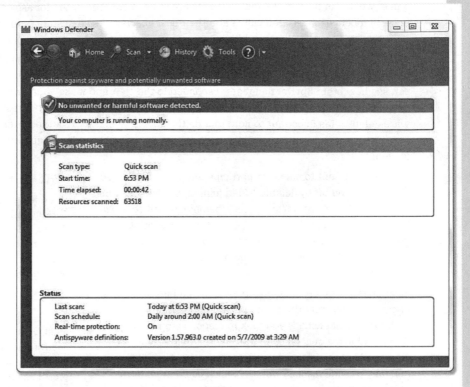

Download Process Explorer

Malware is not usually digitally signed because its authors are not often interested in being identified. However, programs that are set to auto-start can also provide clues about persistent malware, which prefers to restart automatically when the computer is rebooted. For advanced malware detection and removal tools, including those that report on digital signatures, few sources can match the Sysinternals website, a widely respected provider of free Windows power tools.

The reigning champion of its ilk is Process Explorer, available for download at www.microsoft.com/sysinternals. Microsoft bought Sysinternals and hired the brains behind it, software gurus Mark Russinovich and Bryce Cogswell. Unlike antivirus programs, which can interfere with each other, it's safe (and recommended) to use multiple antispyware programs. In addition to Windows Defender and Process Explorer, we also recommend SpywareBlaster, available at www.javacoolsoftware.com.

One interesting feature of Windows Defender is its use of Microsoft SpyNet. There is strength in numbers, and SpyNet leans on the collective wisdom of all participating users to inform decisions about installing unknown or suspicious software. In the television quiz show *Who Wants to Be a Millionaire*, contestants are asked to answer multiple-choice trivia questions for cash. Once per game, when stumped, contestants may choose to "Ask the Audience" for assistance. Studio audience members each electronically enter their best answer; the contestant is instantaneously presented with a graph indicating which answers are most favored by the audience.

SpyNet works much like "Ask the Audience," but instead of cash, you're playing for the safety of your computer. When Windows Defender detects suspicious changes that it has yet to classify, you can see how other SpyNet members responded to the alert and make your own informed choice about how to proceed. Not quite as exciting as a quiz show, perhaps, but a fresh approach to spyware defense. It's important to note that on the television show, "Ask the Audience" is a mixed bag. The audience is often correct on pop culture or general knowledge questions, but sometimes it is wrong.

It's also important to note that participation in SpyNet is elective and turned off by default. When joining, participants must select either Basic or Advanced membership, which controls how much information will be sent to Microsoft about the potential spyware on your computer. Sending information of this kind involves a degree of trust and is not appropriate for everyone.

Essentially, Basic membership sends detailed information about files, complete URLs, and possibly search terms, in addition to what actions you took in response to the potential threat and some general computer information. Advanced membership can contain personal information from file paths and may provide memory dumps, which could provide valuable information to Microsoft engineers but could also contain the most sensitive data on your computer.

For detailed information about what kind of information is sent based on membership type, and how Microsoft promises to protect your privacy, a link to the Windows Defender Privacy Statement Online is provided in the Microsoft SpyNet section of Windows Defender.

Personal Firewalls: A Layer of Protection from Worms

Because worms spread across networks without user interaction, antivirus programs that seek to prevent users from launching viruses do not apply. Defense against worms demands a layered defense, where the first layer is a good network firewall.

➡ *For a more detailed discussion about Windows Firewall, see "Windows Firewall," p. 920.*

 note

As evidenced by the layout of the Security heading in the Action Center, there is often one program to block spyware, another to fight viruses, and yet another to provide a network firewall on a single PC. The industry trend is toward convergence. Many antivirus programs now use their scanning technology to identify and remove spyware, and some include a personal firewall as well. Some packages even include rootkit and phishing protection in some form. (See Chapter 32 for details on phishing.) In coming years, we might see the evolution of an Integrated Security Client rather than a grab-bag of specialized applications, or at least more cohesive suites of products.

Comprehensive PC management services, which include malware defense, are another interesting development. In May 2006, Microsoft launched Windows Live OneCare, an attempt at a more holistic approach to PC management including malware protection, preventative maintenance, backups, and tech support. In the second half of 2009, a new offering called Microsoft Security Essentials (MSE) takes over this job.

Automatic Updates: Remove the Side Doors

In conjunction with antivirus, antispyware, and personal firewall software, automatic updates are a critical part of a solid security strategy because they shut down avenues of attack as soon as they are discovered. Malware often relies on flaws found in software to work. These flaws are akin to open side doors to your home that, hopefully, nobody knows about. There they stand as an open invitation for malware to walk in. Automatic updates don't just shut the door; they usually remove the door entirely and put a permanent wall in its place. You can enable and configure automatic updates in the Security section in Action Center. If daily updates at 3:00 a.m. do not suit you, adjust the time and frequency as you like.

➡ *For a detailed discussion of the important automatic update technologies in Windows 7,* **see** *"Windows 7 and Keeping Up to Date," p. 757.*

Data Execution Prevention

The infamous Internet Worm, launched in 1988 by then Cornell University student Robert Morris, was the first worm to publicly demonstrate the risk of buffer overflow attacks. It infected thousands of systems on the Internet, frustrating military and university researchers at the time. Modern malware writers continue to exploit the same type of vulnerability on a much larger scale. The Internet has grown exponentially, connecting banks, corporations, government agencies, and private homes. The recent generation of worms, such as MS Blaster and Sasser, have attracted mass media attention because they delayed British Airways flights and affected networks from public hospitals in Hong Kong to the Sydney train system—all made possible by a single category of security vulnerability.

Buffers are fixed-length memory locations used to hold data. They can be adjacent to other memory locations also used to hold data. If a program attempts to write more data into the buffer than will fit, the remaining data can overflow into the adjacent memory location and overwrite its previous contents with malicious code. It is an esoteric task that requires a high degree of skill, but if the malicious code can then be *executed*, what was once a fine, upstanding member of the computer community is now, potentially, a minion of evil.

The effects of buffer overflow exploits can be dramatic and complex, though the root cause, and effective remedies, have been known for some time. It's possible to write and compile computer programs in ways that check and prevent these errors, but traditional software engineering tools and practices have failed to address the problem for decades.

New programming tools and conscientious coding can thwart buffer overflow attacks, but because rebuilding all existing computer code is impractical, techniques have been developed to mitigate the risk. Executable space protection techniques, as implemented through Microsoft's Data Execution Prevention (DEP), disallow code execution in areas of memory where it is not expected, and significantly reduce the threat of buffer overflow attacks. It's technology with a proven track record of success. Several critical exploits have already been proven to fail on DEP-enabled systems—but not all DEP is created equally.

Modern processors from both AMD and Intel include hardware-based DEP technology. Windows 7 can take full advantage of this important security feature, but it will not do so by itself. As installed,

DEP is enabled only for core Windows components. To take full advantage of DEP for non-Windows programs, you must find the Data Execution Prevention menu, nestled deep in the user interface, and turn on DEP for all programs. Microsoft did not enable this setting because some programs do not work with DEP enabled. This should not deter you from taking full advantage of DEP because, as shown in Figure 30.5, there is an exception list, and the trouble is worth the extra security.

To enable DEP, follow these steps:

1. Select Start, Control Panel, System and Security.

2. Choose System, Advanced System Settings.

3. On the Advanced tab of the Performance Options dialog box, click Settings (under Performance), and then select the Data Execution Prevention tab.

4. Select the Turn on DEP for All Programs and Services radio button.

5. Click OK. In the System Properties dialog box that prompts you to restart your computer, click OK.

6. Close any remaining dialog boxes and windows, and then restart your computer.

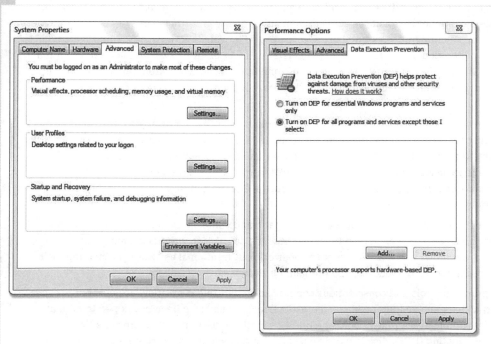

Figure 30.5
Enable DEP for all programs and services.

Hardware DEP takes advantage of the processor's inherent security features. Even if your computer lacks an AMD processor with NX (No Execute) or an Intel processor with XD (Execute Disabled) features, Windows 7 can still provide some level of buffer overflow protection using software DEP. Although not as good as hardware DEP, software DEP has proven effective against real-world exploits. It can protect the exception-handling processes in Windows and provides better protection when programs are built specifically to support software DEP.

> **note**
>
> In addition to DEP, Windows 7 uses address space layout randomization (ASLR) to combat malicious code execution. Without ASLR, key OS components load in predictable locations that are more easily targeted. Randomizing the location of executable images adds a new level of difficulty for would-be exploiters but not for you. This protection activates and selects new random locations automatically at startup.

User Account Control Options

Experienced computer professionals know it is bad juju to perform casual work on a system using a full-fledged administrator account because it is far too easy to blow things up. Instead, they create two different accounts for themselves: a limited-access standard user account with enough power to get daily tasks done but restricted enough to keep them out of serious trouble, and a second, unrestricted administrator account for use only when they need to perform serious tasks.

This best practice, however, didn't reduce the aggravation factor of the User Account Control (UAC) feature introduced in Windows Vista. Designed as a safety mechanism, Vista prompted you for permission to perform system changes, install software, and so on, to help avoid accidents or prevent hackers from accessing your system. Standard users were frequently prompted for permission; administrators received fewer prompts but at a still-annoying rate. And you had two basic choices: leave it on or throw caution to the wind by turning it off.

In Windows 7, you have four sets of options, which vary slightly depending on whether you're logged on as a standard user or administrator. The following are options for an administrator account, unless noted otherwise:

- Always notify me when programs try to install software or make changes to the computer, or when I make changes to Windows settings. (This is the same as Windows Vista UAC turned on, and is the default for a standard user account.)

- Notify me only when programs try to install software or make changes to my computer, and don't notify me when I make changes to Windows settings. (This is the default for an administrator account in Windows 7. This and the next option are new to Windows 7.)

- Notify me only when programs try to make changes to my computer (do not dim my desktop), and don't notify me when I make changes to Windows settings. (Dimming the desktop is a big visible red flag for most users, so going without it is risky.)

- Never notify me of installations or changes. (This is just like disabling UAC in Windows Vista.)

If you elect the third or fourth option, you might also be interested in dog-earing the section of this book on re-installing Windows.

➥ *For information on installing Windows, **see** "Performing a New Installation of Windows 7," p. 50. To get details about UAC, **see** "User Account Control," p. 84.*

You can also use the Local Security Policy console to control whether prompts appear. When using a standard user account, for example, if a task is attempted that requires administrator-level access, the user can either be prompted to enter administrator account credentials or be flat-out denied. The default approach in this case is to prompt the user for credentials so that an over-the-shoulder parent or system administrator can authorize privileged actions. If you would prefer that such requests simply be denied, you can use the Local Security Policy console (click Start, and then type `secpol.msc` in the Search box) to change the setting highlighted in Figure 30.6. See Local Policies, Security Options for this setting.

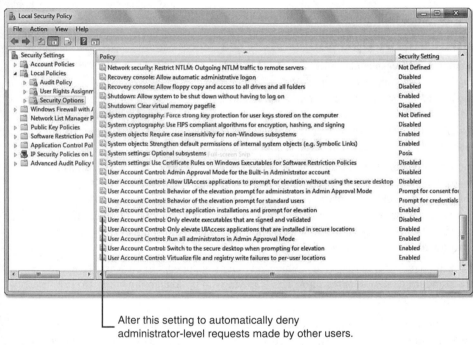

Figure 30.6
Use the Local Security Policy console to change UAC settings.

Alter this setting to automatically deny
administrator-level requests made by other users.

Service Hardening

In addition to security improvements that can be configured, several improvements in Windows 7 might go unnoticed to all but software developers, including malware writers. Microsoft adheres more closely to the well-known security Principle of Least Privilege, which means that people or things should have access only to what they need, and nothing more. It's a sound idea that, had it been followed more closely in earlier version of Windows, would have prevented numerous security exploits.

Core Windows programs, called *services*, have in the past been favorite targets because many of them are always running, often with a wide scope of access to the system. When a service could be compromised, it provided many avenues for further exploration and exploitation. This time around, Microsoft limits access for services to only what the services need. For example, a service's capability to write to the disk or Registry is based strictly on the requirements of the service. This is a real security improvement, which will continue to pay unsung dividends as long as Windows 7 exists.

Internet Explorer 8 Malware Protection

Internet Explorer 8 has several new features specifically designed to increase security. First, tab isolation means that if a website or add-on crashes in Internet Explorer, only the current tab is affected: the browser remains stable and other tabs are unaffected. Internet Explorer also includes crash recovery, which automatically reloads all open tabs and restores connections to their respective sites.

Internet Explorer 8 adds an InPrivate feature to browsing, accessed by selecting Safety, InPrivate Browsing on the command bar. This opens a browser session that records no information, including searches or web page visits. Likewise, InPrivate Filtering turns off any website's capability to track and record your online activities. Deletion of browsing history has been enhanced to preserve or remove cookies and temporary Internet files as you see fit.

Internet Explorer 8 also adds improved techniques to protect you online. The SmartScreen Filter checks a database of dangerous or questionable websites and warns you if you attempt to visit one. It will also warn you if you attempt to download software that is potentially unsafe.

In addition, Internet Explorer 8 includes a cross-site scripting (XSS) filter that can detect malicious code running on compromised websites, to protect you from unwanted information disclosure, cookie theft, account or identity theft, and so on. This new filter stops most such attacks as soon as they begin. Internet Explorer 8 also turns DEP on by default.

> ➥ *For a discussion of more security enhancements in Internet Explorer,* **see** *"Phishing (Fishing) for Information," p. 945.*

> **🔍 note**
>
> Some features of Windows 7 are available only if you have a 64-bit processor and purchase the 64-bit version of Windows 7. The 64-bit version requires digitally signed kernel-mode drivers, the core software that controls various devices on a PC. Iffy drivers have long been a source of computer crashes and instability. Malicious drivers can open a path for kernel-mode rootkits, which are difficult to detect. The desire to ensure that drivers come only from reputable sources is intended to improve stability and security. It may also help prevent installation of sneaky drivers that do things such as circumvent audio or video copy protection.

Avoiding Malware

Taking a minimalist approach to installing software on your computer goes a long way toward avoiding malware. It also saves space, avoids bogging down your PC, and can make the computer simpler and easier to use. That doesn't mean you must forego all the software gadgetry that makes computers useful and fun, but it does require a more judicious attitude on installing software. As with many areas in life, when it comes to installing software from the Internet, installing a CD purchased at the dollar store, or downloading content from a peer-to-peer program, less is more.

Whenever seemingly innocuous software is installed, be it a toolbar, cute purple gorilla, weather program, or anything at all, you are potentially transferring full ownership of your computer to somebody else. One would expect that before such a transition of ownership, the previous owner would ceremoniously sign a title or perform some similar ritual, but clicking OK is usually all it takes.

The best way to prevent an unintentional computer donation is to follow this rule: NEVER install software from a source you don't trust. Once installed, malware can and will take major liberties with your computer. Malware writers go to amazingly creative and destructive lengths to achieve their goals—whether to profit by directing you to ads, theft of personal information, or worse. If your computer gets infected with malware and runs slowly, it might be busy doing lots of work in the background on someone else's behalf. Computer criminals have been known to control an army of thousands, or more than a million, compromised computers and then extort money from online businesses by threatening to use their army of "zombies" to barrage a commercial website, shutting it down for hours or days. It's a credible threat.

You'll find many long lists of things you can to do avoid malware and keep your computer from becoming a zombie. Here are three essential things to remember to protect your Windows 7 computer:

- Install an antivirus program with real-time protection.
- Keep all elements under the Security heading in Action Center set to On.
- Only install software from sources you trust.

31

PROTECTING YOUR DATA FROM LOSS AND THEFT

The All New Backup and Restore

After years of providing slow backup and restore programs that ignored the widespread availability of rewriteable DVD and CD drives, Microsoft made its first big turnaround in Windows Vista with the introduction of the Backup and Restore Center (which is just called Backup and Restore in Windows 7). Although the features and functions of the Backup and Restore Center wildly vary by Vista edition, all Windows 7 editions provide a consistent, fast, and easy-to-use File and Folder Backup Wizard (occasionally referred to as SafeDocs backup) that supports rewriteable CD and DVD drives, as well as external USB and FireWire hard disks, internal hard disks, and shared network folders. However, the network backup option is not available in Windows 7 Home versions.

Users accustomed to Windows Vista's Backup and Restore Center will appreciate the new features, functions, and format of the new Windows Backup applet. You'll also instantly recognize subtle differences to the updated interface in Windows 7 Backup and Restore, which appears nothing like the original. The new Backup and Restore utilizes the same simple design principles but adds granular control over the files and folders you back up, giving you greater flexibility than ever before.

Improvements in the Backup and Restore Features in Windows 7

Windows Backup is structured differently in Windows 7 than in previous versions. The Volume Shadow Copy Service (VSS) is still present and maintains a historic timeline of file and folder changes (called shadow copies), so that you can revert back to previous file and folder states in case either becomes corrupted or damaged. System Restore, the convenient "undo" button for unwanted file and folder changes, is now divided into two parts: Restore My Files (for the current user) and Restore All Users' Files (for everyone else on the system). Windows Backup also enables you to duplicate data for all users, and you're given greater control over individual files and folders.

By default, your backups are created on a regular schedule, but you're free to specify a custom schedule to better suit your usage needs. Windows backup keeps track of your backup preferences, so that whenever a file or folder is added or changed, it becomes incorporated into the scheduled backup. System Image backup (formerly Complete PC Backup) creates an exact duplicate of your working drive, so you can restore to "bare metal" operation whenever your system becomes damaged by malicious software or misbehaving users. Unlike file and folder backups, this is a complete and total restoration where all of your current applications, system settings, and files are replaced.

All Windows 7 versions support file and folder backup with the following options:

- Capability to back up to and restore from network shares

- Scheduled incremental file and folder backup

- Previous versions, which permits the user to revert to the previous version of a file or folder

- System Image Backup, which makes an image backup of a complete system and permits a "bare-metal" restore to the same hard disk, same-size replacement hard disk, or larger replacement hard disk

Table 31.1 lists the backup and restore features supported by each Windows 7 edition.

> **note**
>
> Restore Previous Versions depends upon System Protection restore points (the same restore points used for System Restore). By default, System Protection is disabled for the system drive (usually, the C: drive). It must also be enabled manually for other hard disk drives. If you configure your system to store documents, photos, and other types of files on a different drive, then be sure to enable System Protection for that drive. See Chapter 25, "Troubleshooting and Repairing Problems," for further details.

Table 31.1   Backup and Restore Features

Windows 7 Edition	File and Folder Backup	File and Folder Backup to Network Share	Scheduled File and Folder Backup	Previous Versions	System Image Backup*
Home Basic	Yes	No	Yes	Yes	Yes
Home Premium	Yes	No	Yes	Yes	Yes
Professional	Yes	Yes	Yes	Yes	Yes
Enterprise	Yes	Yes	Yes	Yes	Yes
Ultimate	Yes	Yes	Yes	Yes	Yes

*Backup and Restore's system image tool does not support backing up to network shares under Windows 7 Home versions.

Figure 31.1 shows the all new Backup and Restore applet as it appears in Windows 7.

Figure 31.1
The Backup and Restore applet is simpler than ever before.

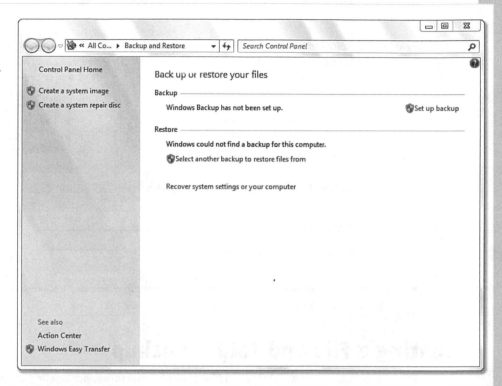

Although the Backup and Restore interface is the same in Home Basic and Home Premium, Home Premium has two additional backup capabilities:

- Home Premium can back up to a network share, whereas Home Basic can back up only to local devices.

- Home Premium's file backup runs on a schedule, whereas Home Basic's file backup runs manually.

 note
You must be an Administrator or provide Administrator-level credentials to perform backups.

File and Folder Backups Versus System Images

File and folder backups differ from System Image and System Restore image backups in several ways:

- You can restore individual files directly from a file and folder backup.

- File and folder backups are designed to protect an individual user's data files, favorites, and settings (including email messages), but not the operating system.

- System images can be used to restore a system from a "bare metal" hard disk but are not designed to permit the restoration of individual files and folders.

Because of the differences in how filo and folder backups, system images, and System Restore image backups work, your best backup strategy on systems that support system image and System Restore backups is to do the following:

1. Create a system image after configuring your system.

2. Set up automatic file and folder backups on a schedule that works for you.

By following this procedure, you can recover from a system crash by

1. Restoring a system image and System Restore image backup.

2. Restoring file and folder backups.

➥ *To learn how to restore a system image backup from the Windows 7 Recovery environment (System Recovery Options),* **see** *Chapter 25.*

 tip

If you need to restore a file from a system image, you can mount the VHD backup file created by Backup and Restore in Microsoft's Disk Management snap-in on the Computer Management and retrieve individual files and folders, or you can use the command-line wbadmin tool. See "Using Disk Management with System Images," in this chapter, **p. 882.**

Creating a File and Folder Backup

Windows 7 has vastly improved the native file and folder backup application and process. Backup and Restore is not set up by default, and you must first configure your backup preferences before proceeding, as follows:

1. Click the Set Up Backup button, shown in Figure 31.1, to get started. Windows Backup launches the Set Up Backup Wizard to guide you through each step.

2. In the next dialog box, select the location where you want to store the backup (see Figure 31.2). You're given the choice of using a disk drive partition, rewriteable CD or DVD drive or hard disk, or a network share (Windows 7 Professional, Ultimate, and Enterprise only).

3. Choose the appropriate backup target. If you select a network share (Windows 7 Professional, Ultimate, and Enterprise only), you must log in to the network share if prompted, even if you are selecting a Public folder and Public Folder Sharing is turned on.

 tip

If you want to use network shares as backup destinations, set up the user(s) and password(s) on the network destination before you start the backup process.

Figure 31.2
Selecting a destination drive or network share for the file backup.

Select the local hard drive or rewritable CD/DVD drive that will store your backup.

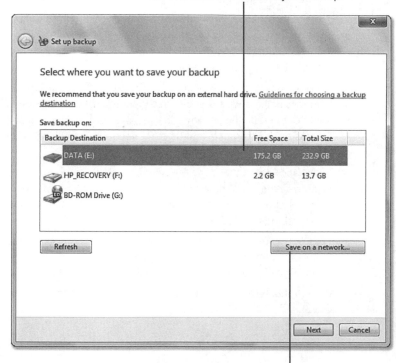

Set up backup

Select where you want to save your backup

We recommend that you save your backup on an external hard drive. Guidelines for choosing a backup destination

Save backup on:

Backup Destination	Free Space	Total Size
DATA (E:)	175.2 GB	232.9 GB
HP_RECOVERY (F:)	2.2 GB	13.7 GB
BD-ROM Drive (G:)		

Refresh   Save on a network...

Next   Cancel

Click here to store your backup on a network share.

4. By default, Windows Backup's Set Up Backup Wizard backs up a wide range of user-created files (see Figure 31.3). The Set Up Backup Wizard enables you to selectively backup libraries, folders, and drives with the Let Me Choose option. There is also an option to include a system image of your drives, which is enabled by default and can be disabled with the Let Me Choose option.

To avoid backing up a particular category, clear the check box.

 note

Use this feature to create backups of specific categories of files by clearing the check boxes for all but a particular category.

Not Everything Gets Backed Up

It's important to realize that the Set Up Backup Wizard does not back up several types of files (and one type of file system), depending upon whether you are using original Windows:

- **Hard disks that use the FAT file system (including FAT32)**—If you are using Windows 7 as a dual-boot with another OS that uses FAT drives, any data on those drives must be backed up with another backup program.

- **Encrypted files using the Encrypted File System (EFS)**—These files are not backed up by the Windows Backup Wizard in original Windows Vista (SP 1). However, in Windows 7, EFS files are backed up by the Windows Backup Wizard. This is a welcome improvement for Professional, Enterprise, and Ultimate users (Home editions don't support EFS). Encrypted file and folder names are displayed in green.

- **Web-based email that is not stored on your hard disk**—Your Hotmail, Yahoo! Mail, or Gmail email won't be backed up until you download it. Microsoft no longer includes a native email client, but you can obtain Windows Live Mail (or another third-party client) to access these or other web-based email services.

- **Files in the Recycle Bin**—If you think you might want these files, get them out of the Recycle Bin. As an alternative, consider dragging files you don't want (at least, in their current locations) into a folder you create called Junk inside your Documents library or other user folders.

- **User Profile Settings**—The Set Up Backup Wizard is for files, not for your digital identity.

 note

The amount of space required for a full system image backup depends on the amount of data you're duplicating. Windows keeps track of files that have been added or modified since your last backup and updates the existing image to save space. Microsoft recommends that you utilize a 200GB external storage device for creating system images, for two reasons: ample space and separate storage. Don't keep system images on the same drive as the original system, because failures can complicate recovery in that situation.

Be sure to note what files are not backed up by
default, and check them if you want them backed up.

Check the items you want to back up.

Figure 31.3
Clear check boxes to skip
backups of listed file types.

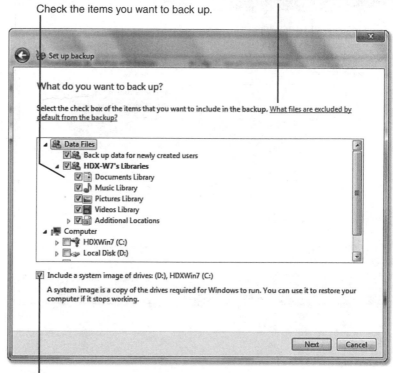

Remove the check here if you don't want to create a system image.

5. Windows Backup then lets you review your backup settings,
as shown in Figure 31.4.

6. Select a schedule by clicking the Change Schedule link to
open the Set Up Backup scheduling options dialog as shown
in Figure 31.5, and then click OK when you're done. Click the
Save Settings and Exit button to begin copying your data to
the designated backup target.

7. A progress dialog box displays the progress of the backup.
At the end of the backup, a dialog box appears indicating
whether the backup was successful. Click Close.

> 🔖 **note**
>
> The Windows Backup schedule can
> be manually specified by clicking the
> Change Schedule link at the Review
> Your Backup Settings prompt of the
> Set Up Backup Wizard. Otherwise, it
> will default to On Demand, which
> means backups occur only when you
> manually invoke the Windows
> Backup program.

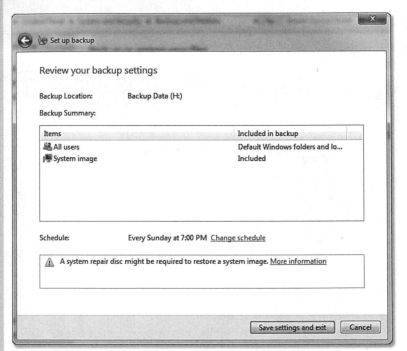

Figure 31.4
The Set Up Backup utility lets you review your settings.

If you choose not to schedule backups to run at a set time, backups will be made only when you manually choose to back up.

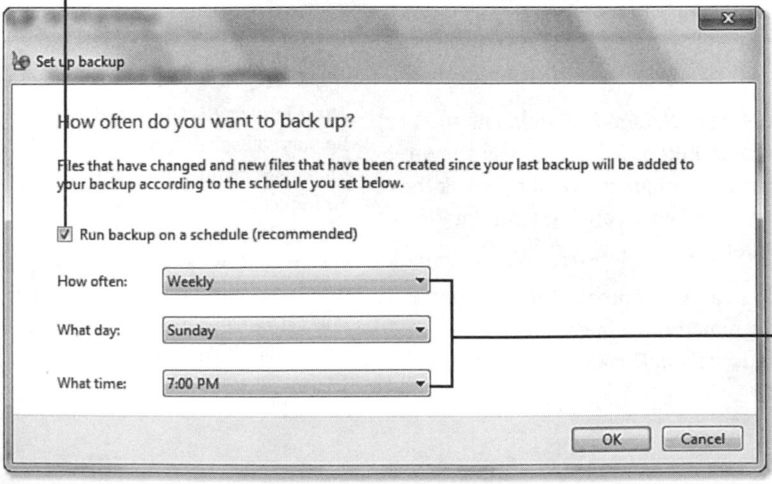

Figure 31.5
The Set Up Backup scheduler helps you automate your backups.

Set backups to run on days and times when you're less likely to be using your computer, and back up at least once a week.

Working with Removable Media During Backups

You can use removable-media drives such as Iomega REV or DVD-recordable drives with either Windows Backup or system image backups (Windows Backup can also use CDs). You must format each disc (unless it's already formatted), and if you use CDs or DVDs with the scheduled backup, the backup will fail if the medium is not in place when the backup starts.

If you use DVDs for system images, you'll probably be using a handful of DVDs for your backup. Instead, consider dedicating an external USB hard disk for backups. You can use the same hard disk for both Windows Backup and system image files, provided that it is large enough to accommodate both.

If you use CDs or DVDs for backups, you will see dialog boxes similar to the following during the backup process when it's time to insert the medium:

- **Label and Insert a Blank Disk**—A dialog box displays the label format to use: *computername, date, time, disk #*. Click OK.

- **Are You Sure You Want to Format This Disk?**—You'll see this dialog box unless you previously formatted or used the CD or DVD. Click Format.

 tip

To save time during the process, click the empty Don't Ask Again for This Backup check box. When this box is checked, unformatted media is formatted automatically.

A format process bar appears, and the backup continues until it's time for the next disc. If you use any type of supported DVD or CD-R, the format should take less than a minute. A CD-RW might take much longer. I recommend using DVDs instead of CDs to save time and disc swaps, but external hard disks make for faster and easier backups.

How Backups Created with Windows Backup Are Stored

Windows 7 uses an entirely different method to catalog, format, and store Windows Backup data than was used in previous editions. You can no longer directly access backup data; instead, you must go through the Restore Files Wizard of the Backup and Restore console. From here, you can select Browse for Files or Browse for Folders and view backup contents through a Windows Explorer interface.

Figure 31.6 shows the internal structure of a Windows Backup archive, as shown in Windows Explorer. The first-level folder is the computer name, followed by nested folders listing the backup set name and date. The actual backup file is listed next, along with a catalog folder.

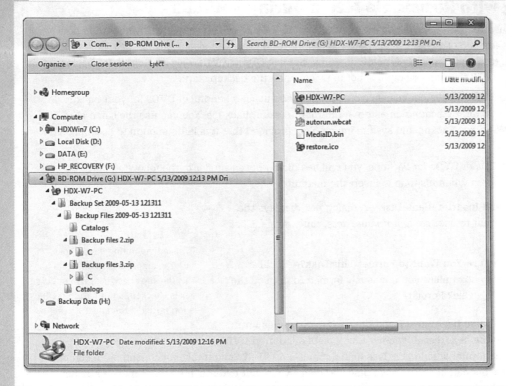

Figure 31.6
The folder structure of a typical archive created with Windows Backup.

Restoring Data from a File and Folder Backup

To restore data files from your backup, click Restore My Files from the Backup and Restore applet, which appears only when a valid backup file exists. The Restore My Files dialog box prompts you to select whether you want to restore the most recent backup or an earlier backup and permits you to make specific file and folder selections.

Restoring the Current User's Data

Select Restore Files and choose whether to restore files from the latest backup or an earlier backup. Click Next to continue. In the next dialog box, click

- Browse for Files to specify individual files to restore

- Browse for Folders to specify folders to restore, or

- Search to specify search terms to locate items to restore

The backup catalog stored with the backup (refer to Figure 31.6) enables you to navigate your backup as you would use Windows Explorer to navigate a drive. After you navigate to the appropriate location and select Add Files or Add Folders, the files or folders are listed (see Figure 31.7). Click Next to continue.

Figure 31.7
Selecting a folder to restore with Restore Files.

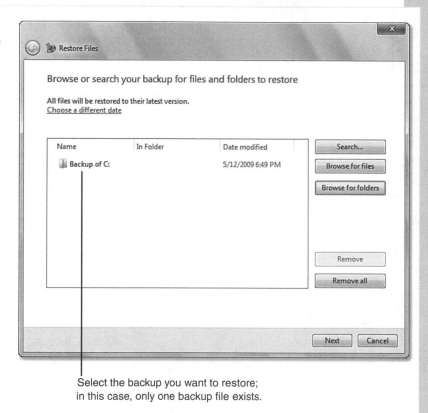

Select the backup you want to restore; in this case, only one backup file exists.

Specify where to save the restored files (see Figure 31.8). By default, the files are returned to their original location. However, you can also use the Browse button to specify a particular location (a helpful feature for testing a backup). If you select the option to choose a location, you can also specify whether to restore the files to their original subfolder and whether to create a subfolder for the drive letter. After specifying options, click Restore.

If the backup drive or removable medium is not already present, connect the backup drive or insert the appropriate medium when prompted. Click OK to continue the restore. At the end of the process, a dialog box appears indicating whether the restore was successful. Click Finish to close the dialog box.

If you choose another location... …you will need to click Browse to choose a new place to store your backup.

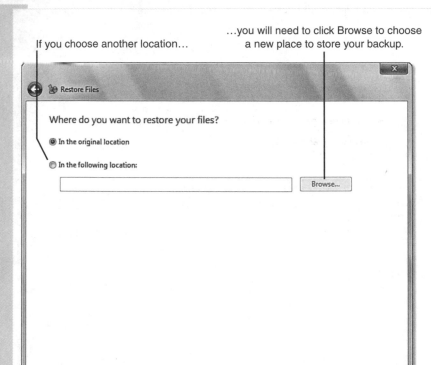

Figure 31.8
Preparing to restore a folder with Restore Files.

USB Backup Device Not Recognized

If a USB-based hard disk or other backup device is not recognized, try a different port. On some systems, you can control the number of active USB ports in the system BIOS/CMOS setup. Thus, it's possible that a port that's physically present might be disabled.

If you plug the drive in to a front-mounted USB port and it is not recognized, try a port on the rear of the system. Front-mounted USB ports must be connected to the motherboard, and some motherboards might not have the connections needed to support front-mounted ports, the connections on the port might be disabled, or the ports might be miswired.

Finally, make sure Group Policy options are not preventing USB drives from working. If your company has standardized on a particular brand and model of USB external hard disk, a Group Policy setting can be created to permit those drives to work, while blocking unauthorized models.

Continued...

If the drive plugs in to a USB port and works, but runs very slowly, a USB 2.0 (Hi-Speed USB) port might be configured as a USB 1.1 port in the system BIOS/CMOS program, or the system might have a mixture of USB 1.1 and USB 2.0 ports. Use only USB 2.0 ports for best performance (USB 2.0 runs at 480Mbps, while USB 1.1 runs at a top speed of 12Mbps). You will normally see a warning that you have plugged a Hi-Speed USB device into a low-speed port, but if USB warnings are disabled, you won't see such a warning.

The process is quick and easy because the backup catalog on the system is used to select the files or folders to restore. If the backup catalog is lost, the files can still be restored by using the Advanced Restore option (next section).

 note

If you click Stop Restore after the system has started copying files to your system, the files that already have been restored remain on the system.

Not Enough Room for Backup on Target Drive

The Windows 7 system image and Windows Backup Wizards are easy to use for basic backup and restore, but if you use advanced options such as network shares or restores from a different system, the potential for problems increases. Make sure users check the target location for adequate space for a backup. If a drive has only a bit more space than the backup requires, the backup might fail or might run very slowly, especially if the drive has not been defragmented lately. Defragment the target drive before using it for backup storage. On a network drive, verify that the user has Read/Write access to the drive. If storage quotas are in use, verify that the user has been provided with an adequate amount of storage on the network drive.

Performing an Advanced Restore

The Advanced Restore option available in Professional, Enterprise, and Ultimate editions supports restoring all users' data or data from a different computer. It can also be used to restore data from the same computer if the backup catalogs were lost. To perform an Advanced Restore, follow these steps:

1. Click the Restore All Users' Files link on the Backup and Restore dialog box. This link is located below the Restore My Files button, both of which do not appear until a valid backup file exists.

2. The Restore Files (Advanced) dialog box opens, shown in Figure 31.9, presenting you with several options.

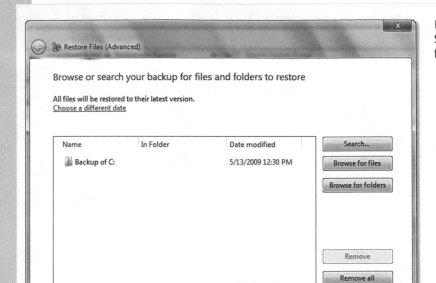

Figure 31.9
Selecting a backup source
for an advanced restore.

3. Click the Choose a Different Date link to open the Restore Files history dialog and select whether to restore files from the latest backup, a previous backup, or a backup from a different computer. Choose Search to search for a restore file by a given keyword. You can also separately browse for files and folders. Click Next to continue.

4. Specify the location of the backup (see Figure 31.10). To enable the system to detect the backup source, be sure to insert the backup medium or connect the backup hard disk. Click Restore to continue, then click Finish on the next dialog box.

Backup Hardware Not Working

The easiest way to determine whether your backup hardware (hard disk or CD/DVD drive) is failing or has failed is to swap the unit for another unit. During the writing of this chapter, I had a number of problems working with rewriteable DVDs during backups. I swapped drives with another system, and the problems went away. The result: I now have a dead DVD rewriter on my junk shelf.

If the problem happens only after an update to Windows, try using System Restore to revert your system to its condition before the update. Use the drive's properties sheet in the Device Manager to roll back to a previous driver version if you suspect that an updated device driver isn't working as well as the old driver.

Figure 31.10
Specifying an alternative destination for an advanced restore from a different drive path.

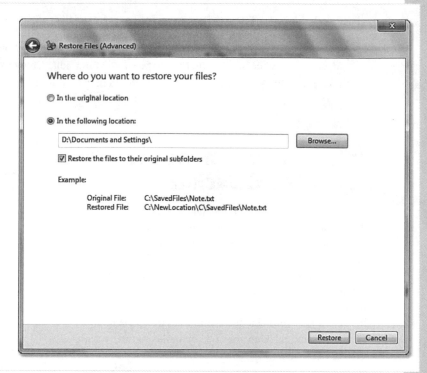

> **Restore Files (Advanced)**
>
> Where do you want to restore your files?
>
> ○ In the original location
>
> ● In the following location:
>
> D:\Documents and Settings\   [Browse...]
>
> ☑ Restore the files to their original subfolders
>
> Example:
>
> Original File: C:\SavedFiles\Note.txt
> Restored File: C:\NewLocation\C\SavedFiles\Note.txt
>
> [Restore] [Cancel]

If you are restoring data from a different computer, the original user account might not match any user on your computer. In such cases, a Missing User Account dialog box appears. You have two options for restoring the data:

- Create a user with the same name on your system before continuing.

- Click the check box to restore files without reassigning security permissions.

Follow the option that makes the most sense in your situation, and click Continue. The restoration begins immediately. Swap media, if prompted. Click Finish at the end of the restoration process.

 note

If the files are being transferred to a computer that will be used by the owner of the original files, create a user with the same name so the files can have that user's permissions. However, if file ownership is not important, click the check box and assign the files to a particular owner later.

It would be a good idea to test your backup before things go wrong. Create a new folder and restore selected files or folders to it. If they restore correctly, you know your backup works. If not, you've discovered a problem before it's too late.

Can't Locate File to Restore from a Multidisc Backup Setup

If the user needs to restore a multidisc (CD or DVD) file backup from a different computer, insert the last backup disc first when prompted for media. This ensures that the catalog will be read properly. Because file backups are stored in separate ZIP files of no more than 200MB each, each disc can be restored separately.

Creating a System Image (Complete PC Backup)

You should create a system image backup as soon as you have installed Windows 7 and configured it to your liking. By doing so, you create a baseline configuration that you can return to in case of a major system crash. From this base configuration you may then add later backup data from your personal collection (documents, pictures, and so forth). We recommend you create a complete system image when you first configure your computer, and then every six months afterward, and back up your personal files regularly with Windows Backup.

To create a system image and System Restore image backup, click the Create a system image link from the Backup and Restore control panel (refer to Figure 31.1). Select the location for the backup—a hard disk, DVD or to a network location (see Figure 31.11). Click Next. Choose the appropriate files and folders to back up from the What Do You Want to Back Up? window and click Next. Review the backup location, the amount of space needed on the target drive, and the drive to be backed up, and click the Save Settings and Exit button to begin (refer to Figure 31.4).

If you back up to an external hard disk (my recommendation for reliability and easy restoration), just sit back and watch the progress bar.

 note

A system image file is stored as a virtual hard disk (VHD) image of the entire disk, excluding some files such as the page file, hibernation file, and so on. For subsequent backups, system images use the persistent VSS mechanism to retain a snapshot of the initial VHD image, and then do a block-by-block image update of the VHD. The VHD now has the most recent disk image, and the shadow copy presents the earlier image (that is, Windows retains the original versions of all changed blocks). System image backups can keep quite a few backups of previous versions this way, depending upon available disk space. In each case, the disk image copy is performed on a temporary VSS snapshot of the live hard disk.

 tip

Before you start the system image process, insert the medium or connect the external drive (and make sure Windows 7 recognizes it). Backup and Restore's system image process ignores empty removable media or optical drives, and can use removable hard disks only if they are formatted using the NTFS file system.

Figure 31.11
Specify where Windows
Backup should save the sys-
tem image.

If you use DVDs, follow the prompts to label and format the
medium when it is inserted. After the medium is formatted, the
backup process continues. When a backup to DVD is complete,
you are prompted to insert each disc to verify the backup. This
feature is designed to protect you against backup failures
caused by scratched or otherwise defective media.

When you store a system image on a hard disk, the backup is
not compressed. However, DVD backups are compressed. The
backup is stored in a folder called `WindowsImageBackup`.

If you decide to create another system image in the future, you
can use the same target drive, and Windows will back up only
the files that have changed since the original image backup.

 tip

Click the Don't Ask Again for This
Backup option to avoid being asked
to format your medium each time.
You can also format your media in
advance with Windows Explorer to
avoid backup failures if one or more
of your discs fail to format correctly.
DVDs are formatted using the widely
supported UDF disk format.

WBADMIN Command-Line System Backup and Restore

To use a network share or to use other advanced system image and System Restore options, including scripted restores, use the command-line backup tool WBADMIN. Originally developed for

Windows Server, WBADMIN provides many options for backing up and restoring a system image. You can also use WBADMIN to restore files from an image backup.

- Use the WBADMIN START BACKUP command to start a backup.

    Usage:

    ```
    WBADMIN START BACKUP
        [-backupTarget:{<BackupDestinationVolume> ¦ <TargetNetworkShare>}]
         [-include:VolumesToInclude]
        [-allCritical]
        [-user:<UserName>]
        [-password:<Password>]
        [-noInheritAcl]
        [-noVerify]
        [-vssFull ¦ -vssCopy]
        [-quiet]
    ```

    Runs a backup immediately using the specified options:

-backupTarget	Storage location for this backup. Requires drive letter or UNC path to shared network folder.
-include	Comma-delimited list of volume drive letters, volume mount points, or GUID-based volume names to include in backup. Should be used when -backupTarget is specified.
-noVerify	If specified, backups written to removable media such as DVD will not be verified. By default, backups written to such media will be verified for errors.
-quiet	Runs the command with no user prompts.

- Example:

    ```
    WBADMIN START BACKUP -backupTarget:e: -
    include:e:,d:\mountpoint,\\?\Volume{cc566d14-44a0-11d9-9d93-
    806e6f6e6963}\
    ```

- Use the WBADMIN GET command to list items in a backup set.

    Usage:

    ```
    WBADMIN GET ITEMS
        -version:VersionIdentifier
        [-backupTarget:{VolumeName ¦ NetworkSharePath}]
        [-machine:BackupMachineName]
    ```

    Lists items contained in the backup based on the options specified:

-version	Version identifier of the backup in MM/DD/YYYY-HH:MM format, as listed by WBADMIN GET VERSIONS.
-backupTarget	Specifies the storage location that contains the backups for which you want the details. Useful when the backups are stored in a different location from the normal location for backups of this computer.

-machine   Specifies the name of the computer for which you want the details. Useful when multiple computers have been backed up to the same location. Should be used when -backupTarget is specified.

Example:

```
WBADMIN GET ITEMS -version:03/31/2005-09:00
```

- Use the WBADMIN STOP command to stop a backup.

Usage:

```
WBADMIN STOP JOB [-quiet]
```

Cancels currently running backup or recovery. Canceled jobs cannot be restarted.

-quiet   Runs the command with no user prompts.

- Use the WBADMIN START RECOVERY command to restore files, volumes, or apps.

Usage:

```
WBADMIN START RECOVERY
    -version:VersionIdentifier
    -items:VolumesToRecover¦AppsToRecover¦FilesOrFoldersToRecover
    -itemtype:{Volume ¦ App ¦ File}
    [-backupTarget:{VolumeHostingBackup ¦ NetworkShareHostingBackup}]
    [-machine:BackupMachineName]
    [-recoveryTarget:TargetVolumeForRecovery ¦ TargetPathForRecovery]
    [-recursive]
    [-overwrite:{Overwrite ¦ CreateCopy ¦ Skip}]
    [-notrestoreacl]
    [-quiet]
```

Runs a recovery immediately based on the options specified:

-version   Version identifier in MM/DD/YYYY-HH:MM format of backup to recover from, as listed by WBADMIN GET VERSIONS.

-items   Comma-delimited list of items to recover. If itemtype is Volume, can be only a single volume. If itemtype is App, can be only a single application. If itemtype is File, can be files or directories, but should be part of the same volume and should be under the same parent.

-itemtype   Type of items to recover. Must be Volume, App, or File.

-backupTarget   Drive letter or shared network folder path of the backup. Useful when the backup to use for recovery is different from the location where backups of this computer are usually stored.

-machine   The computer whose backup you want to use for recovery. Useful when multiple computers were backed up to the same location. Should be used when -backupTarget is specified.

-recoveryTarget   Drive letter of volume to restore to. Useful if the volume to restore to is different from the volume that was backed up.

-recursive	Valid only when recovering files. Recursively recovers files under the specified path. By default, only files that reside directly under the specified folders will be recovered.
-overwrite	Valid only when recovering files. Specifies the action to take when a file being recovered already exists in the same location. Skip causes recovery to skip the existing file and continue with recovery of the next file. CreateCopy causes recovery to create a copy of the existing file; the existing file will not be modified. Overwrite causes recovery to overwrite the existing file with the file from the backup.
-notrestoreacl	Valid only when recovering files. Does not restore the security ACLs of files being recovered from backup. By default, the security ACLs would be restored. Default is true.
-quiet	Runs the command with no user prompts.

Examples:

```
WBADMIN START RECOVERY -version:03/31/2005-09:00 -itemType:Volume -items:d:
WBADMIN START RECOVERY -version:03/31/2005-09:00 -itemType:App -items:SQL
WBADMIN START RECOVERY -version:03/31/2005-09:00 -itemType:File -items:d:\folder
-recursive
```

Remarks: To view a list of items available to recover from a specific version, use WBADMIN GET ITEMS. When the itemtype is App, you can use ADExtended to recover all the related data needed for Active Directory.

Using Disk Management with System Images

As you learned in the previous section, WBADMIN (the command-line counterpart to Windows Backup) can be used to create both system images and System Restore backups. It can also restore backup images or select files and folders. However, because WBADMIN works from the command line and features a complex syntax, it can be a challenging tool to use for restoring individual files and folders from a backup image.

You can also individually view the contents of your backup images by opening the Restore Files Wizard and browsing for individual files or folders. However, there is a new option for managing the VHD images created by Windows Backup: Disk Management. As part of the Computer Management console, Disk Management is an administrative tool for managing and modifying your disk drives and partitions. To mount and browse your VHD backup images with Disk Management, perform the following steps:

1. Click the Start icon, right-click Computer, and click Manage. Supply administrative credentials if prompted.

2. In the left window pane under Computer Management, select Storage and then Disk Management. Once selected, the options for Disk Management are enabled under the Action menu item.

3. Choose Action, Attach VHD.

4. Browse to the appropriate backup file location, select a suitable entry, click Open, and then click OK.

5. Disk Management creates an attachment point with the next available drive letter. You can begin accessing files and folders in the backup image by using Windows Explorer.

When you are finished browsing the image, you can detach the VHD backup file by right-clicking the drive entry and choosing Detach VHD, as shown in Figure 31.12.

Figure 31.12
Detaching VHD backup images with Disk Management.

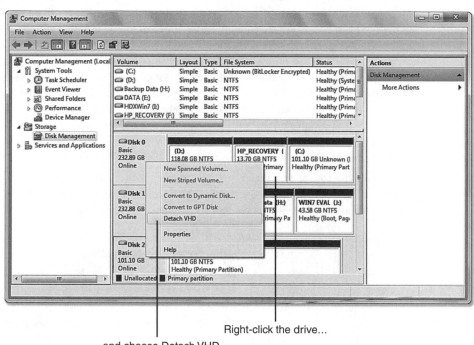

Right-click the drive...

...and choose Detach VHD.

Restoring a System Image

You should restore a system image only in drastic circumstances, such as a complete system failure. Basically, if Windows won't start and you've already tried everything else *and* you've made a system image, it's time to restore it. A complete PC restore (or system image) sets your system to its exact condition at the time of backup. Unlike System Restore, which leaves current data files behind although it resets the Windows Registry to the specified earlier time, a complete PC restore formats your hard disk, wiping out any remaining information and replacing it with whatever you backed up. It's not called a "bare metal" restore for nothing!

To restore a system image from within Windows Backup and Restore, click the Recover System Settings link, and then click the Open System Restore button from the Recovery control panel

 note

After you restore a system image, restore all the file and folder backups available to bring your system as close to its prefailure condition as possible.

applet. This will launch the System Restore Wizard. However, if you need to restore your system from outside the Windows GUI, use the Windows Recovery Environment, which is accessed by booting from the Windows DVD and selecting Repair Your Computer.

➡ *To learn more about restoring a system image,* ***see*** *Chapter 25.*

Encrypted File System (EFS)

If you need to protect files on your system from being read by unauthorized users, you can use the Encrypted File System (EFS) feature that works independently of the NTFS permissions. Note that Windows 7 Home Basic, Home Premium, and Starter Edition do not fully support EFS (search Windows Help and Support for information on using EFS data with these versions). When a file is encrypted, the data stored on the hard disk is scrambled in a very secure way. Encryption is transparent to the user who encrypted the file; you do not have to "decrypt" an encrypted file before you can use it. You can work with an encrypted file just as you would any other file; you can open and change the file as necessary. However, any other user or an intruder who tries to access your encrypted files is prevented from doing so. Only the original owner and the computer's designated recovery agent can get into encrypted files. Anyone else receives an "Access Denied" message when trying to open or copy your encrypted file.

Folders can be marked as encrypted, too. This means that any file created in or copied to an encrypted folder is automatically encrypted. The folder itself isn't encrypted, though; anyone with the proper file access permissions can see the names of the files in it.

EFS Encryption for NTFS Volumes Only

EFS encryption protects the files only while they reside on the NTFS volume. When they are accessed for use by an application, they are decrypted by the file system drivers. This means that files that are encrypted on the drive are not encrypted in memory while being used by an application. This also means that transferring files over the network is done without encryption. Any file action that performs a copy (which includes moves across partitions or volumes) inherits the settings of its new container. In other words, if the new container is not encrypted, the new file will not be encrypted, either, even if it was encrypted in its previous location. If you back up EFS-protected files, they are stored on the backup media in their normal form, not as encrypted. EFS protects files only on the hard drive, nowhere else. Use EFS only when expressly needed. EFS causes significant performance reduction if a significant number of commonly accessed files are encrypted, due to the CPU processing required to decrypt them for use.

You encrypt or decrypt a folder or file by setting the encryption property for the folder or file just as you set any other attribute (such as read-only, compressed, or hidden), through a file or folder's Advanced Attributes dialog box (see Figure 31.13). Right-click the desired file or folder, choose Properties, and from the General tab click the Advanced button to open the Advanced Attributes dialog box.

 note

EFS is not supported in Home versions of Windows 7, so this option will be grayed out in the Advanced Attributes dialog box.

Figure 31.13
Setting encryption for a specific folder.

Select to Encrypt Data

After you set the option to encrypt a folder and click OK in a folder's Properties dialog box, you are prompted to confirm the attribute change. From this dialog box, you can set the option to encrypt all the subfolders and files within the folder you are encrypting. Once all folders, subfolders, and files are encrypted an Encrypted File System dialog box appears reminding you to back up your file encryption certificate and key. You're given three options: Back Up Now (Recommended), Back Up Later, or Never Back Up. We suggest you take care of this now so you never have to worry about it later. Back Up Now takes you to the Certificate Export Wizard, which gives you step-by-step instructions.

Unable to Encrypt Files or Folders

If you are unable to use EFS on a particular drive, make sure that it is not compressed and that the drive uses the NTFS file system. Compressed files and folders are displayed in blue; encrypted (EFS) files and folders are displayed in green in Windows Explorer. A file on an NTFS drive can be encrypted or compressed (or neither), but not both. To check the file system used by a drive, right-click the drive in Computer, select Properties, and view the General tab. A FAT or FAT32 drive must be converted to NTFS to support encryption or compression. Keep in mind that Home editions (and Starter) of Windows 7 do not support EFS, although they do use NTFS as their native file system.

It is recommended that you encrypt at the folder level rather than mark individual files, so that new files added to the folder will also be encrypted. This point is crucial because most editing programs write a new copy of the file each time you save changes and then delete the original. If the folder containing an encrypted file isn't marked for encryption, too, editing an encrypted file results in your saving an unencrypted version.

How File Encryption Works

As a kid, you probably played around with simple codes and ciphers in which you exchanged the letters of a message: *D* for *A*, *E* for *B*, and so on. You might look at this as the process of "adding three" to each letter in your message. Each letter gets bumped to the third-next letter in the alphabet. To decode a message, you subtracted three from every letter to get the original message. In this code, you could say that the "key" is the number 3. Anyone who knew the technique and possessed the key could read and write these secret messages.

Although this example is very simplistic, it illustrates the basic idea of numeric encryption. The cryptographic system used by Windows for EFS also uses a numeric technique, but it's extremely complex and uses a key that is 128 digits long. Such a large number means many possible choices, and that means it would take someone a very long time to guess a key and read an encrypted file.

When you mark a file for encryption, Windows randomly generates such a large number, called a unique file encryption key (FEK), which is used to scramble the contents of just that one file. This unique key is itself scrambled with your own personal file encryption key, an even longer number stored in the Windows Certificate database. The encrypted unique key is then stored along with the file.

When you're logged in and try to open an encrypted file, Windows retrieves your personal key, decodes the unique key, and uses that key to decode the contents of the file as it's read off the hard disk.

The reason for the two-step process is to let Windows use a different and unique key for each file. Using different keys provides added security. Even if an attacker managed to guess the key to one file, he or she would have to start fresh to find the key to other files. Yet your personal key can unscramble the unique key to any file you've encrypted. It's a valuable thing, this key, and I'll tell you how to back it up in a certificate file for safekeeping.

As a backup in case your personal key gets lost, Windows lets each computer or domain administrator designate recovery agents, users who are allowed to decode other people's encrypted files. Windows also encrypts the unique FEK for each of the recovery agents. It, too, is stored along with the file, and anyone who possesses a recovery key can also read your encrypted files. You'll learn about the benefits and risks of this system in "Protecting and Recovering Encrypted Files," later in this chapter.

You can use EFS to keep your documents safe from intruders who might gain unauthorized physical access to your sensitive stored data (by stealing your laptop, for example).

Encrypting Offline Files

Offline files are stored local copies of network files provided so that you may work with certain types of information when you're offline or disconnected from the network. These files are not encrypted by default, but you can enable a new feature in Windows 7 that provides this added safety measure.

File encryption provides another level of access protection that—like EFS—operates independently of NTFS permissions. This safeguards your files in the event your drive is removed or the entire system is stolen. You should especially encrypt offline files if you suspect they will contain confidential, private, or sensitive information.

You can enable encryption of offline files by clicking the Encrypt button on the Encryption tab of the Offline Files dialog box, shown in Figure 31.14. To encrypt offline files, you must first enable offline files on the General tab of a given folder or launch Manage Offline Files from the Start menu using the Search box.

Figure 31.14
Setting encryption for offline files and data.

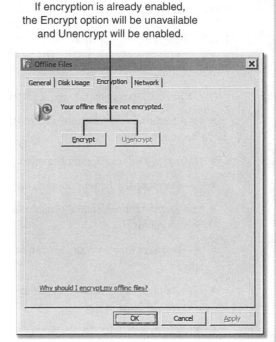

If encryption is already enabled, the Encrypt option will be unavailable and Unencrypt will be enabled.

When encryption is enabled, the Encrypt button will be grayed out and only the Unencrypt button will be active.

Using CIPHER

You also can encrypt or decrypt a file or folder using the command-line program CIPHER and the following syntax. If you've previously used CIPHER on a Windows XP system, keep in mind that the syntax that CIPHER uses in both Windows Vista and Windows 7 is almost entirely new. Several existing parameters have been removed (/F, /I, and /Q), many new parameters have been added (/B, /C, /W, /X, /Y, /ADDUSER, /REKEY, and /REMOVEUSER), and, by default, CIPHER runs even if an error is encountered, unless you use the new /B parameter. In Windows XP, CIPHER stopped on error.

The following is not an exhaustive list of the CIPHER syntax; execute **CIPHER** /? at a command prompt for the complete list of parameters and syntax.

```
CIPHER [/E ¦ /D ¦ /C]
       [/S:directory] [/B] [/H] [pathname [...]]
CIPHER /K
CIPHER /R:filename [/SMARTCARD]
CIPHER /U [/N]
CIPHER /W:directory
CIPHER /X[:efsfile] [filename]
CIPHER /Y
CIPHER /ADDUSER [/CERTHASH:hash ¦ /CERTFILE:filename]
       [/S:directory] [/B] [/H] [pathname [...]]
CIPHER /REMOVEUSER /CERTHASH:hash
       [/S:directory] [/B] [/H] [pathname [...]]
CIPHER /REKEY [pathname [...]]
```

The arguments (parameters) are as follows:

- /B Abort if an error is encountered. By default, CIPHER continues executing even if errors are encountered (new option).

- /C Displays information on the encrypted file (new option).

- /D—Decrypts the folder and halts any further encryption on that folder until reactivated.

- /E—Encrypts the specified directories. Directories are marked so that files added afterward will be encrypted.

- /H—Displays files with the hidden or system attributes. These files are omitted by default (new option).

- /K—Creates a new certificate and key for use with EFS. If this option is chosen, all other options are ignored (new option).

- /N—Works only with /U. Prevents keys from being updated. This is used to find all the encrypted files on the local drives (new option).

- /R—Generates an EFS recovery agent key and certificate, and then writes them to a PFX file (containing the certificate and private key) and a CER file (containing only the certificate). An administrator can add the contents of the CER file to the EFS recovery policy to create the recovery agent for users and can import the PFX file to recover individual files. If SMARTCARD is specified, it writes the recovery key and certificate to a smart card. A CER file is generated (containing only the certificate). No PFX file is generated.

- /S—Performs the specified operation on directories in the given directory and all subdirectories.

- /U—Tries to touch all the encrypted files on local drives. This updates the user's file encryption key or recovery agent's key to the current ones if they are changed. This option does not work with other options except /N.

- /W—Removes data from available unused disk space on the entire volume. If this option is chosen, all other options are ignored. The directory specified can be anywhere in a local volume. If it is a mount point or points to a directory in another volume, the data on that volume will be removed (new option).

- /X—Backs up the EFS certificate and keys into file *filename*. If efsfile is provided, the current user's certificate(s) used to encrypt the file will be backed up. Otherwise, the user's current EFS certificate and keys will be backed up (new option).

- /Y—Displays your current EFS certificate thumbnail on the local PC (new option).

- /ADDUSER—Adds a user to the specified encrypted file(s). If CERTHASH is provided, CIPHER will search for a certificate with this SHA1 hash. If CERTFILE is provided, CIPHER will extract the certificate from the file (new option).

- /REKEY—Updates the specified encrypted file(s) to use the configured EFS current key (new option).

- /REMOVEUSER—Removes a user from the specified file(s). CERTHASH must be the SHA1 hash of the certificate to remove (new option).

- directory—A directory path.

- filename—A filename without extensions.

- pathname—Specifies a pattern, file, or directory.

- efsfile—An encrypted file path.

Used without parameters, CIPHER displays the encryption state of the current directory and any files it contains. You can use multiple directory names and wildcards. You must put spaces between multiple parameters.

CIPHER Produces Unexpected Results

Although using encryption (EFS) via the right-click menu works the same way as in previous NT-based versions of Windows, changes in the CIPHER command-line encryption tool can cause problems, particularly for users who are accustomed to how CIPHER worked in Windows XP. As with wbadmin, some practice time with noncritical files is a good idea.

Rules for Using Encrypted Files

When you work with encrypted files and folders, keep in mind the following points:

- Only files and folders on NTFS volumes can be encrypted.

- You cannot encrypt files or folders that are compressed. Compression and encryption are mutually exclusive file attributes. If you want to encrypt a compressed file or folder, you must decompress it first.

- Only the user who encrypted the file and the designated recovery agent(s) can open it. (You'll learn more about recovery agents shortly.)

- If you encrypt a file in a shared directory, it is inaccessible to others.

- Windows 7 displays encrypted files and folders in green (compressed files and folders are displayed in blue).

- Encrypted files become decrypted if you copy or move the file to a volume or partition that is not formatted with NTFS.

- You should use Cut and Paste to move files into an encrypted folder. If you use the drag-and-drop method to move files, they are not automatically encrypted in the new folder.

- System files cannot be encrypted.

- Encrypting folders or files does not protect them against being deleted, moved, or renamed. Anyone with the appropriate permission level can manipulate encrypted folders or files. (These users just can't open them.)

- Temporary files, which are created by some programs when documents are edited, are also encrypted as long as all the files are on an NTFS volume and in an encrypted folder. I recommend that you encrypt the Temp folder on your hard disk for this reason. Encrypting your original files keeps them safe from prying eyes, but programs often leave behind temp files—usually in the Temp folder—and these files remain vulnerable.

- The page file (used for virtual memory) can be encrypted in Windows 7 through Group Policy settings. You can also configure the Local Security Policy to clear the page file when you shut down the system. Just enable the Shutdown: Clear Virtual Memory Pagefile policy under the Local Policies, Security Option section.

- On a domain network, you can encrypt or decrypt files and folders located on a remote computer that has been enabled for remote encryption. Check with your system administrator to see whether your company's servers support this capability. Keep in mind, however, that opening an encrypted file over a network still exposes the contents of that file while it is being transmitted. A network administrator should implement a security protocol such as IPSec to safeguard data during transmission.

- You should encrypt folders instead of individual files so that if a program creates temporary files and/or saves new copies during editing, they will be encrypted as well.

- Encrypted files, like compressed folders, perform more slowly than unencrypted ones. If you want maximum performance when folders or files in the folders are being used extensively (for example, by database programs), think twice before encrypting them. You might want to perform benchmark tests using encrypted and unencrypted folders with similar data to determine whether your system can handle the performance hit.

Suggested Folders to Encrypt

I recommend that you encrypt the following folders:

- Encrypt the Documents library if you save most of your documents there. Encrypting this folder ensures that any personal documents saved there are automatically encrypted. However, a better alternative would be to create a subfolder under Documents library for personal files and encrypt just this folder. This approach relieves you from having to track which files are encrypted and which are not.

- Encrypt your Temp folder so that any temporary files created by programs are automatically encrypted.

Protecting and Recovering Encrypted Files

Encrypted files are supposed to be very secure; only the user who creates an encrypted file can unscramble it. But this security hangs on your own personal file encryption key, which is stored in the Windows Certificate database (see the sidebar "How File Encryption Works," earlier in this chapter). Where would you be if you accidentally deleted your file encryption certificate, or if your user account was deleted from the system? Could the secret recipe for Aunt Dottie's zucchini fritters be lost forever this way? Probably not. EFS has a "back door" that lets designated recovery agents open any encrypted file.

The availability of this back door is both good news and bad news. The good news is that encrypted files can be recovered when necessary. The bad news is that this capability opens a potential security risk, and you need to be sure you take measures to protect yourself against it.

> **⚠ caution**
>
> If someone steals your laptop computer or gains physical access to your desktop computer, it's possible that even with all of Windows 7's file access security and file encryption, that person can gain access to your files. How? A trick allows this to happen, and you should guard against it. Here's how it works: By reinstalling the OS from a DVD drive, a thief can set up himself or herself as the system administrator. If the default file recovery certificate is still on the computer at this point, the intruder can view encrypted files. To guard against this situation, you should export the file recovery certificate to a floppy disk or other drive and remove it from the computer. I show you how in the next section.
>
> Another method you can use is to configure your system to use BitLocker full drive encryption (available on Windows 7 Ultimate and Enterprise editions). To learn more about BitLocker, see "BitLocker Disk Encryption," later in this chapter.

Securing the Recovery Certificate

Your capability to recover encrypted files hinges on two factors:

- Being listed by the Windows Local or Group Security Policy as a designated recovery agent

- Possessing the file recovery certificate that holds the recovery key data

With a few dirty tricks, it's possible for someone who steals your computer to get himself or herself in as an administrator and pose as the recovery agent. If you really want to ensure the privacy of your files with EFS, you have to save the file recovery certificate on a floppy disk or other removable medium and remove the certificate from your computer.

To back up and remove the recovery certificate, do the following:

1. Click the Start button and type **mmc** in the Search box.

2. When the Console appears, select File, Add/Remove Snap-In.

3. When the Add or Remove Snap-Ins dialog box appears, double-click Certificates, select My User Account, then click Finish.

4. Click OK.

5. In the left pane, expand the Certificates – Current User, Personal, Certificates.

6. In the middle pane, you should see a certificate listed with its Intended Purposes shown as Encrypting File System, as shown in Figure 31.15. If this certificate is not present and you're on a domain network, your domain administrator has done this job for you and you don't need to proceed any further.

7. Right-click the EFS certificate entry and select All Tasks, Export to launch the Certificate Export Wizard.

8. Click Next and then select Yes, Export the Private Key, and click Next.

9. Select Personal Information Exchange and click Next.

10. Enter a password twice to protect this key. (You must remember this password!)

11. Specify a path and filename to be used to save the key. If your system has a floppy drive, insert a blank, formatted floppy disk and type the path and filename, such as a:\recovery.pfx (not case sensitive). Otherwise, you can insert a writeable CD or DVD (recommended) or a USB flash memory drive (not recommended for permanent storage) and type the path and filename. If you use CD or DVD media, click Next and then Finish. A dialog box appears stating that the export was successful; click OK.

12. Click Finish.

note

Unless User Account Control (UAC) has been disabled, you must be an Administrator or provide Administrator-level credentials to back up the recovery certificate.

caution

You should back up and delete the Administrator's recovery certificate (that's the procedure you just performed), but don't delete Administrator as the recovery agent from the Local Security Policy. Leave the Local Security Policy alone. If you delete the entries there, you'll disable EFS.

Figure 31.15
The EFS certificate manager stores keys and certificates to an external location for safekeeping.

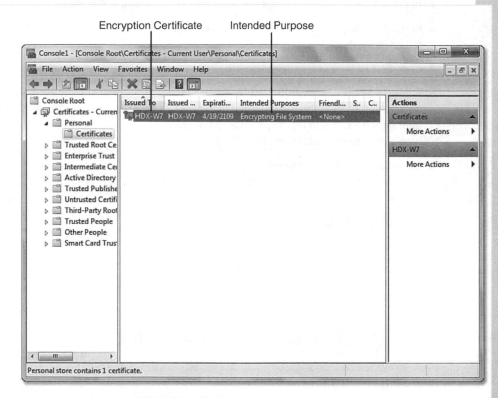

Protecting Your Own File Encryption Certificate

If your user account is lost or you accidentally delete your own file encryption certificate some day, you might lose access to your own files. The recovery agent could still help, but you can protect yourself by exporting your own personal EFS certificate. Basically, follow the same procedure as for the local administrator while logged in as a user. Just be sure to have at least one encrypted file before starting the process. Once complete, label the disk **EFS for *UUU* on *XXX***, where *UUU* is your user account name and *XXX* is your computer name. Store it in a safe place.

Recovering Encrypted Files on Your Own Computer

If your user account is deleted or you end up reinstalling Windows from scratch, you'll lose access to your encrypted files because the Encryption database will be lost. You can log on as Administrator and reinstall the encrypted file recovery certificate, or you can log on as yourself and reinstall your file encryption certificate to get the files back with the following procedure:

1. Open the Microsoft Management Console (MMC), select File, and select Add/Remove Snap-In. Next, highlight the Certificates snap-in and click Add. Select My User Account and click Finish. Finally, click Close and then click OK.

2. In the left pane, expand Certificates – Current User, Personal, Certificates.

3. In the Actions pane, click More Actions and select All Tasks, Import to start the Certificate Import Wizard.

4. Click Next.

5. Enter the name of the certificate file—for example, `a:\recovery.pfx`. Otherwise, you can click Browse and navigate to the drive and folder containing the certificate. To see it, select Personal Information Exchange (`*.pfx`, `*.p12`) as the certificate type. Select it and click Open. Click Next.

6. Enter the password for the certificate, and check Mark the Private Key as Exportable. Click Next twice, and then click Finish.

7. Click OK on the status box.

You should now be able to access the encrypted files. I suggest that you remove the Encrypted check mark from these files. Log on again as the Normal user of these files, and re-encrypt them if you want.

 note

If you use a migration utility to move EFS-encrypted files and folders from a Windows XP system to a Windows 7 system, be sure to export your EFS certificate from the Windows XP system and import it to the Windows 7 system as described here. Otherwise, you will not be able to access your files.

Disk Organization for Data Safety

RAID arrays are no longer exotic. Most late-model desktop computers have provision for RAID 0 or RAID 1 arrays, and many systems have four or more SATA host adapters, making RAID 0+1 arrays possible. Which are the safest types of RAID arrays in common use?

RAID 5 provides maximum safety. With RAID 5, which requires the use of three or more hard disks in a single array, you can rebuild the contents of the array even if one drive fails. RAID 5 sets aside space on each drive for the information needed to rebuild the array in case of drive failure. However, RAID 5 is not yet implemented in desktop computers' onboard host adapters. You must purchase a RAID 5 host adapter and compatible SATA or SCSI hard disks.

RAID 0+1 combines data striping (for performance) and mirroring (for safety). It requires four drives and is supported on many recent desktop computers. It provides a high level of data safety against failures and is inexpensive to implement with SATA or ATA/IDE (PATA) drives.

RAID 1 mirrors the contents of one drive to a second hard disk. It is supported on many desktop systems that are up to several years old, through either a motherboard RAID host adapter chip or the motherboard's integrated chipset. It is inexpensive to implement with SATA or IDE drives.

RAID 0 stripes data across two drives to improve read/write performance. If either drive fails, the array is wiped out. Thus, RAID 0 actually has no redundancy. It should be used only on drives that do not contain data.

To learn more about implementing RAID arrays in Windows, see Chapter 24, "Managing Hard Disks."

BitLocker Disk Encryption

With the widely reported loss or theft of laptops containing sensitive personal and financial information in the last year, hundreds of thousands of people have been forced to change credit card information and worry about identity theft. Thus, the time is ripe for a new approach to protecting hard disk contents from unauthorized use: BitLocker.

BitLocker, available on Enterprise and Ultimate editions, encrypts the entire system hard disk. Originally known as Secure Startup, BitLocker stops unauthorized access, even if the hard disk is moved to a different computer.

Encrypted Files Can Be at Risk on a Sleeping Computer

It's been known that a thief can get around BitLocker's protection if he steals your computer while it's suspended (sleeping) or powered up. To truly protect your computer, you must completely shut it down when you finish using it (or at least invoke hibernation), and don't let it out of your sight for at least 10 minutes after shutdown. This time frame is especially important because Princeton University researchers have discovered that memory chips can be frozen with "canned air," preserving their contents for retrieval, even after the system has been turned off. See http://citp.princeton.edu/memory for details.

Following these procedures is especially important with laptops because the default action when you close the lid or click the little power button on the Start menu is "suspend." You must instead click the options arrow and select Shut Down. When you power up the computer, it should display the black BitLocker protection screen. If it goes directly to Windows, your computer was not protected!

For greater protection, you can use the Power Options applet in the Control Panel (available directly in Small Icons or Large Icons view) to change the default actions for closing the lid or pushing the power button to shut down. You should also use file encryption to further protect any sensitive files on your hard drive.

BitLocker System Requirements

BitLocker in Windows Vista requires that your hard disk have a second partition of at least 1.5GB that is used for the BitLocker encryption tools. You must also have a way to provide credentials to permit the system to recognize you as the authorized user, such as a Trusted Platform Module (TPM) microchip and BIOS or, for systems that lack onboard TPM 1.2 support, a USB flash memory drive.

Customers that didn't deploy Windows Vista with the required two-partition configuration found that enabling BitLocker was entirely too cumbersome. Windows 7 automatically creates the necessary disk partitions during installation and now includes the ability to right-click a drive to enable BitLocker protection. BitLocker also adds a supportive Data Recovery Agent (DRA) for all protected volumes, allowing IT administrators to dictate that all such volumes are appropriately encrypted.

Unable to Use BitLocker

If you are unable to use BitLocker, check the following:

- Is the hard disk properly partitioned? The hard disk must have a 1.5GB primary partition and a separate system partition for Windows (it can be any size above the minimum requirements for Windows 7). You cannot enable BitLocker on a system with a single hard disk partition.

- If the system has a TPM chip, is the feature enabled in the system BIOS? If it is, check with the system or motherboard vendor for a BIOS upgrade.

- If the system does not have a TPM chip, follow the procedure to enable BitLocker in the Group Policy Object Editor.

- If you get the error message `BitLocker could not be enabled. The system firmware failed to enable clearing of system memory on reboot` after restarting your system during the BitLocker setup process, it means that BitLocker has determined your system does not clear out memory during the reboot process. Hackers could analyze the contents of memory for the BitLocker encryption key and use it to bypass BitLocker encryption.

  To enable your system to run BitLocker, contact your system vendor for a BIOS upgrade that includes the clearing of system memory upon reboot option. If this option is not available, you cannot run BitLocker on the system.

BitLocker To Go

Windows 7 introduces a subset of the BitLocker Drive Encryption technology with BitLocker To Go, which extends BitLocker Drive Encryption to USB storage devices. Designated USB drives can be passphrase-protected with controllable length and complexity, and IT administrators can set user policies to apply BitLocker To Go protection on removable drives before they are made usable.

Microsoft permits Windows XP SP3, Windows Vista SP1, and Windows Vista SP2 users to read BitLocker To Go devices using the passphrase. Plugging a BitLocker To Go encrypted USB storage device into Windows 2000 or Windows XP SP2 computers shows an inaccessible unformatted volume.

To encrypt your removable USB media with BitLocker To Go, follow these steps:

1. Open the System and Security category in Control Panel and click BitLocker Drive Encryption.

2. Locate the desired drive entry and click Turn On BitLocker.

3. Choose either a password or smartcard to unlock the drive. For simplicity, we recommend using a reasonably long passphrase—something memorable (to you) but not easily guessable (to others). Enter it twice and click Next.

4. Determine where to store the recovery key. You're given the option of saving it to a file (recommended) or printing the key (not recommended). We suggest you save the key to a file that will be kept on a separate storage volume from the USB drive and the computer itself. Save the key and then click Next.

5. The last dialog box gives you a final option to cancel out of this process. Click Start Encrypting and wait for the process to finish, which takes longer for large storage volumes.

Once the USB storage volume is encrypted, you can unlock and utilize it using the passphrase you entered earlier. Every time the USB drive is inserted, the BitLocker Drive Encryption password dialog box appears. Should you forget the passphrase, BitLocker To Go's recovery key method enables you to access the storage volume. Remember not to leave this recovery key accessible to anyone but yourself, because otherwise the passphrase is ineffective in safeguarding your protected files and data.

Enabling the TPM

The easiest way to use BitLocker is to use your computer's TPM microchip (if it has one). To determine whether your system supports TPM 1.2 and to learn how to enable this feature in the system BIOS, see your system's documentation. A lot of 2006 and newer laptops have onboard TPM 1.2, but older laptops (and most desktops) don't support it.

After you enable TPM in the system BIOS, use the TPM Management Console (`tpm.msc`) to turn on TPM support in Windows (use the Turn On the TPM Security Hardware dialog box) and set up a TPM password (use the Create the TPM Owner Password dialog box). A TPM password is saved as *computer_name*`.tpm`. Thus, if your computer is named WildThing, the password is stored as `WildThing.tpm`.

 tip

Be sure to print your TPM password using the Print option and save it to a location you can access later, such as a CD or DVD.

If your system doesn't support TPM, you can still use BitLocker. However, to use BitLocker without a TPM, you must use a USB flash memory drive to store your credentials, and it must be plugged into the system to permit the system to boot. You must also enable BitLocker Drive Encryption with the Group Policy Object Editor:

1. Click Start, All Programs, Accessories, Run.

2. Type `gpedit.msc` and click OK to open the Group Policy Editor. Click Continue or provide Administrator-level credentials (if prompted by UAC) to continue.

3. Open Computer Configuration, Administrative Templates, Windows Components, BitLocker Drive Encryption, Operating System Drives: Require Additional Authentication at Startup.

4. Select Enabled. Under Options, verify that the option Allow BitLocker Without a Compatible TPM is checked (see Figure 31.16).

5. Click Apply, then OK.

6. Close the Group Policy Object Editor.

Make sure this is checked.

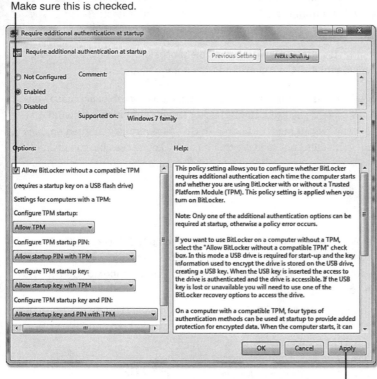

Figure 31.16
Enabling BitLocker support on a system that does not have a compatible TPM.

After choosing to allow BitLocker without a compatible TPM, click Apply.

Encrypting the Drive with BitLocker

To start the encryption process, open the BitLocker Drive Encryption applet in the Control Panel (via either the System and Security category or the BitLocker Drive Encryption entry in Small Icons or Large Icons view) and select Turn on BitLocker next to the appropriate drive entry (if there are several). The BitLocker Drive Encryption Wizard walks you through the paces of setting up necessary drive layout. It starts by establishing space on an existing drive partition or unallocated space on the existing partition. There are really only two quick steps: drive preparation and drive encryption. Upon reboot, the system drive goes through a lengthy encryption process that takes longer for larger drives than for smaller-capacity volumes.

If your system has a TPM, you can choose either to use the TPM chip along with your logon password to access an encrypted BitLocker volume or to assign a PIN that is used along with the TPM. If your system does not have a TPM, you must use a Startup USB key. Make sure you have a USB flash drive available to use for BitLocker key storage. The BitLocker Drive Encryption Wizard provides three options for TPM-enabled systems, and a single option for those without—Require a Startup Key at Every Startup. This is where your Startup USB drive comes into play. You'll also be asked where to store the recovery key, which can also go to the flash drive. Finally, a BitLocker system check ensures that everything is functioning properly, which requires a restart with the drive key plugged in.

When you create the BitLocker volume, you must create a recovery key password, in case BitLocker enters a locked state. If you lose the password, you can be locked out of your data; be sure to save the password to an accessible location and print it for safekeeping. Note that this is not the same as the TPM management password discussed in the previous section.

If you choose to store the recovery key password on a USB drive or in a folder, it is stored in a plain text file. The name of the file matches the administrative password ID: four hex digits, followed by three groups of two hex digits, followed by six hex digits:

aabbccdd-ee-ff-gg-001122334455.txt

The password recovery key file contains the name of the disk volume, the drive letter, and the date of encryption, as well as the password itself, which is stored as eight groups of six digits each:

000000-111111-22222-333333-444444-555555-666666-777777

Recovery keys can be stored on Active Directory servers for systems that are members of a domain.

After you store and print the recovery key password, BitLocker performs a system check to ensure that the recovery and encryption keys can be read before it begins the encryption process. If you use a USB device to enable BitLocker, insert it when prompted. After the system check is performed successfully, BitLocker restarts your system and encrypts your system drive. During the encryption process, an icon in the notification area appears. Hover your mouse over the icon or double-click it to see encryption progress. You can pause encryption if necessary, but you can use your computer normally while encryption progresses. When you start your system, you must provide the appropriate credentials (entering the PIN when prompted or inserting the USB flash drive before starting the system or when prompted). Otherwise, the system will not boot.

In Windows 7, after BitLocker encrypts the system volume and you restart your system, you can encrypt any other volumes on the system drive. To encrypt additional volumes, open the BitLocker Disk Encryption tool in Control Panel and turn the encryption status from Off to On for other system drives you want to encrypt.

➡ *If you are unable to use BitLocker,* **see** *the "Unable to Use BitLocker" troubleshooting note, p. 896.*

BitLocker Drive Encryption Recovery

If you do not provide the appropriate credentials when you attempt to boot a BitLocker-encrypted volume, you are prompted to press the Enter key to enter into the Windows BitLocker Drive Encryption Password Entry dialog box. The drive label, system drive letter, BitLocker encryption date, and key filename are provided so you can locate the correct recovery key password.

Instead of using the normal 1–9 keys on the keyboard, use F1–F9 for digits 1–9, and F10 for 0. If you use the normal 1–9 keys, the password will not work. As soon as you correctly enter the recovery key password, the system starts normally.

How BitLocker Protects Your Information

During normal use, a BitLocker-encrypted volume appears as a normal drive using the NTFS file system, and you can use EFS or disk compression on individual files and folders as with any normal NTFS volume.

However, if you attempt to bypass BitLocker security by booting the system from a Windows DVD and using the Recovery Environment, BitLocker Drive Encryption Recovery will prompt you to provide the password from removable media or by entering it. When you provide the password, you can access the volume for repair or data-recovery processes.

 note

Backups made of a BitLocker-encrypted drive with Windows system image or other backup utilities are not encrypted. Keep them in a safe place.

Once data is transferred from a BitLocker-encrypted drive to any other nonencrypted storage media, it is no longer encrypted.

If you cancel the recovery process, the Recovery Environment will continue, but you will not be able to access the drive without providing the recovery password.

If you attempt to access the drive from the Recovery Console command prompt, you will see this message: "This volume is locked by BitLocker Drive Encryption. Return to the control panel to unlock volume."

If you connect a BitLocker-encrypted volume to another computer running Windows and attempt to access its contents, the volume shows up as a drive letter in Windows Explorer with a size of 0MB, no disk label, and no file system.

If you connect a BitLocker-encrypted volume to another computer running Windows XP or other operating systems, the file system is listed as RAW (unformatted). Third-party data-recovery programs are unable to determine the file system or other information about the drive. The drive can be formatted, but its contents cannot be accessed.

BitLocker prevents access to the drive by unauthorized Windows systems, and prevents other OSs from detecting the file system. BitLocker does this by encrypting the drive with a full volume encryption key using AES encryption, and then encrypting that key with a volume master key, also using AES encryption. The volume master key is unlocked when you provide the proper credentials at boot time, and it, in turn, unlocks the full volume encryption key that is used by a file system driver to decrypt the volume. In recovery mode, the recovery password (eight groups of six digits) unlocks the volume.

 note

By default, BitLocker's AES encryption method uses a 128-bit key and uses the Diffuser algorithm, which protects against ciphertext manipulation key-cracking methods while providing excellent performance. Through the Group Policy Object Editor, you can select other options, including 128-bit without Diffuser, 256-bit with Diffuser, and 256-bit without Diffuser. To select other options, open Computer Components, Administrative Templates, Windows Components, BitLocker Drive Encryption, Configure Encryption Method. Click the Enabled radio button, and select the desired encryption method. Click Apply, then OK.

Differences Between BitLocker and EFS Encryption

Although EFS encryption is familiar to many Windows users because of previous experience with Windows 2000, Windows XP, and Windows Vista, it may be useful to review the differences:

- In the initial version of Windows Vista, BitLocker secures the entire system volume, but not other volumes (drive letters) on a system, while EFS encryption can be used on any volume formatted with NTFS. However, Windows Vista SP1's version of BitLocker can secure additional volumes on the system drive at the user's option.

- BitLocker uses a TPM chip or a USB flash memory drive to provide credentials, while EFS uses a personal certificate stored as part of the OS to provide credentials.

- Neither EFS nor BitLocker encryption protects files once they have been copied to another drive. However, when EFS files are transferred via a file migration program, they retain their encryption attributes, and the original user's EFS certificate must be exported from the source system and imported to the target system to enable encrypted files to be opened on the target system.

 note

Use the Windows command-line utility robocopy.exe with the /EFSRAW option to migrate EFS-encrypted files from Windows to another system.

- EFS encryption is retained when files are backed up, but BitLocker volume encryption is not retained on a backup of a BitLocker volume.

- EFS encryption can be used by Windows editions that do not support BitLocker, and on systems that are not compatible with BitLocker.

- BitLocker encryption cannot protect files on systems in Sleep or Hibernate mode, although EFS encryption can protect files on systems in these modes provided that the user has configured the system to request a strong password when waking up the system.

As you can see, BitLocker and EFS are complementary security features. You can use EFS to protect files on removable hard disks that are not secured with BitLocker, but you can use BitLocker to prevent anyone from using a stolen laptop or desktop computer.

Recovering Previous Versions of a File

Windows 7 Professional, Enterprise, and Ultimate editions enable you to restore a previous version of a file. This is handy if a data file has been edited and the changes are not an improvement, or if a user who intended to save a new version of a file with File, Save As accidentally clicked File, Save instead and overwrote the previous version.

There are two sources for previous versions:

- Backup copies (created with the Windows Backup Wizard)

- Shadow copies (created as part of a volume restore point)

 tip

Although Previous Versions can be a lifesaver, it's no replacement for making backup copies of important files or saving different versions of a file in progress. The last-available previous version might be days or weeks old in some cases, so you might need to reconstruct changes you performed on the current version. In such cases, you may want to use the Open or Copy option, rather than the Restore option, with the most recent previous version.

If you use a drive other than the system drive for data, be sure to enable restore points (System Protection) on that drive if you want shadow copies. A drive without restore points cannot provide shadow copies. In such cases, only backup copies (if they exist) will be available as previous versions. System Restore uses up to 15% of each NTFS drive of at least 1GB in size for restore points. On systems with limited disk space, Windows 7 removes older restore points, which can also cause shadow copies to be lost. If you upgrade to Windows 7 on a system with limited disk space, all existing restore points will be removed and replaced with a single restore point. See KB945681, available at http://support.microsoft.com.

If you have overwritten a file and want to retrieve a previous version, right-click the file and select Properties. Click the Previous Versions tab to see what backup or shadow copies may exist (see Figure 31.17).

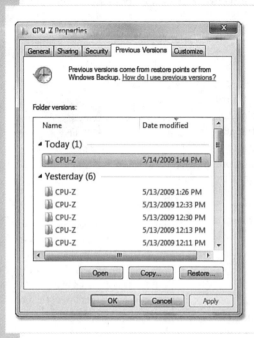

Figure 31.17
Viewing the previous version of a file

If more than one previous version exists, select the one you want to use, and choose from the following options:

- **Open**—The previous version is opened by the default application for the file type. The current version is retained.

- **Copy**—The previous version is copied to the destination you specify.

- **Restore**—The previous version replaces the current version. After selecting this option, you must click Restore to confirm the operation.

Be CAREFUL When Dual Booting

If you use Windows XP and Windows 7 in a dual-boot configuration and Windows XP mounts drives that contain Windows 7 system restore points, Windows 7 will delete those restore points the next time Windows 7 is booted. When the restore points are deleted, any shadow copies contained there are also deleted.

If you use a dual-boot XP/Windows 7 configuration, don't mount Windows 7 drives with Window XP. To prevent Windows 7 drives from being mounted by Windows XP, use the techniques described in KB926185, available at http://support.microsoft.com. (Though this KB is based on Vista and Server 2008, the information still applies to Windows 7.) These methods include creating a new Registry subkey in Windows XP, which prevents XP from mounting the specified drive letter, or using BitLocker on the Ultimate or Enterprise editions of Windows 7 to prevent XP from mounting encrypted drives.

NTFS File Permissions

All versions of Windows 7 use the NTFS (NT File System) directory structure, including Home Basic and Home Premium. NTFS enables you to assign control of who is permitted to access files and folders on a per-user or per-group basis. NTFS permissions can be used to control access for either local folders or network shares.

Windows XP Home Edition and Professional supported installation on disks formatted with the FAT32 file system or the NTFS file system. Many users of XP did use NTFS formatted disks, either by choice or because their computer manufacturers set their computer up that way. The user-based file permission system was in effect, but usually without the users even knowing it—on XP Home Edition, NTFS permission settings were hidden from the user, and on XP Professional, you had to disable Simple File Sharing to see them.

On the other hand with Windows 7 NTFS is mandatory for installation (and also restoration), and the security settings are available to see and modify on *all* versions of Windows 7. Therefore, all Windows 7 users should understand how NTFS file permissions work.

To display or modify NTFS permissions, select a file or folder in Computer or Windows Explorer, right-click Properties, and select the Security tab. You can use the NTFS Permissions dialog box to designate a folder to restrict access toc both network and local users.

In the top part of the Security tab is the list of users or user groups with access to the file or folder. You can select any of the names in the list to view their associated permissions in the bottom half of the tab.

To add users to a file's or folder's permissions list, follow these steps:

1. Right-click the file or folder in explorer and choose Properties, then open the Security tab.

2. Under the Group or User Names list, click the Edit button. The Permissions dialog box opens to a new Security tab.

3. Under the Group or User Names list, click the Add button. The Select Users or Groups dialog box appears.

4. Enter the desired username(s) into the input box provided. You can check your names against the computer's user accounts by clicking the Check Names button. Hint: Use full names like "Bob Cowart" instead of just "Bob." Click OK.

5. With the newly added user account(s) highlighted in the Group or User Names list, select the desired permissions. You can choose to allow or deny a variety of actions for a given user or group. Click Apply and then click OK.

6. Click OK again to close the Properties dialog box.

The permission properties can each be granted or revoked individually. The permissions and their properties are listed in Table 31.2.

Table 31.2 NTFS File Permission Settings and Their Functions

Permission	Properties
Full Control	Gives all the rights listed below, plus lets the user change the file's security and ownership settings.
Modify	Allows a user to modify a file's contents or delete a file.
Read & Execute	Allows a user to read a file's contents and/or run an executable file as a program.
List Folder Contents	Allows a user to view the contents of the folder.
Read	Allows a user to read a file's contents only.
Write	Allows a user to create a new file, or write data in an existing file, but not read a file's contents. For a folder, allows users to add new files to the folder but not view the folder's contents.

Note that each permission has both Allow and Deny check boxes. To get access to a given resource, a user must be explicitly listed with Allow checked or must belong to a listed group that has Allow checked, and must not be listed with Deny access or belong to any group with Deny marked. Deny preempts Allow.

All these permissions are additive. In other words, Read and Write can both be checked to combine the properties of both. Full Control could be marked Allow but Write marked Deny to give all access rights except writing. (This permission would be strange but possible.)

The most productive use of NTFS file permissions is to assign most rights by group membership. One exception is with user home directories or profile directories, to which you usually grant access only to the Administrators group and the individual owner.

Editing NTFS file permissions is protected by UAC (unless you've disabled it). So, expect to see a lot of prompts to Continue (if you're an Administrator) or to provide an Administrator password (if you're a standard user) when you perform these operations.

 tip

If you edit Permissions, before you click OK or Apply, click the Advanced button and view the Effective Permissions tab, as discussed later in this chapter. Enter a few usernames to see that the permissions work out as you expect. If they do, only then should you click OK.

Administrator Can't Delete File or Folder

You might encounter files or folders that can't be deleted even by the Administrator account. They don't have the Read-Only attribute set, but Windows informs you that access is denied.

Sometimes a file or, more often, a folder is set with access controls such that even Administrator can't access or delete it. To erase such a file or folder, take ownership of it as described earlier in this chapter. Give Administrator full access rights. Use the Advanced Security button to view Advanced Permissions, and check Replace Permission Entries on All Child Objects. Click OK or Apply (then click OK), and then try to delete the folder again.

Inheritance of Permissions

Normally, permissions are assigned to a folder (or drive), and all the folders and files within it *inherit* the permissions of the top-level folder. This makes it possible for you to set permissions on just one object (folder), managing possibly hundreds of other files and folders contained within. If necessary, explicit permissions can be set on a file or subfolder to add to or override the inherited permissions. Permissions displayed in the Security tab will be grayed out if they have been inherited from a containing folder.

You can view or change the inheritance setting for a file or folder by clicking the Advanced button on the Security tab. In Figure 31.18, the folder has a check in Include Inheritable Permissions from This Object's Parent.

Figure 31.18
The Advanced Permissions dialog box lets you control the inheritance of permissions and set detailed permissions for user and groups.

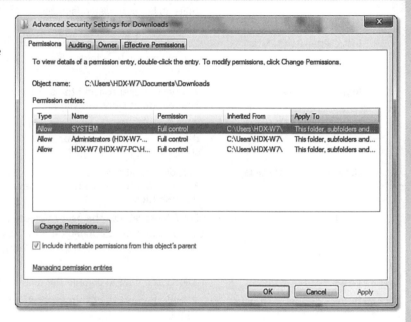

To change inheritance settings, click Change Permissions. You can then uncheck the Include Inheritable Permissions from This Object's Parent box. If you uncheck the box, Windows gives you the option of starting with a blank permissions list (Remove) or keeping a copy of the settings it had before (Copy). In either case, the item now has its own independent list of access rights, which you can edit at will.

When you change permissions on a folder, you may want to cancel any manually added permissions set on the files and folders it contains. Checking the Replace All Child Object Permissions With Inheritable Permissions From This Object option will reset the permissions on all files in this folder and in subfolders, and will force all subfolders to inherit permissions from this folder.

 caution

Changing the permissions of the root folder of the drive containing Windows may make your system unusable. It's best not to mess with the permissions of your boot (usually C:) drive.

Advanced Security Settings

If you edit access permissions in the Advanced Security Settings dialog box, you can exercise more "fine-grained" control over permissions. It's rarely necessary, but for your reference, Table 31.3 lists the available permission settings.

Table 31.3 NTFS Advanced File Permission Settings and Their Functions

Permission	Properties
Traverse Folder/Execute File	For folders, this special permission allows a user the right to move through a folder to which he or she doesn't have List Folder access, to reach a file or folder to which he or she does have access. For files, this permission allows the running of applications. (This permission is necessary only if the user wasn't granted the Group Policy Bypass Traverse Checking.)
List Folder/Read Data	For folders, allows the user to view the names of files or subfolders inside a folder. For files, allows the user to read the data in a file.
Read Attributes	Allows the user to view the attributes of the file or folder (that is, Hidden, Read-Only, or System).
Read Extended Attributes	Allows the user to view extended attributes of files or folders as defined by another program. (These attributes vary depending on the program.)
Create Files/Write Data	For folders, allows the user to create new files inside the folder. For files, allows the user to add new data or overwrite data inside existing files.
Create Folders/Append Data	For folders, allows the user to create new subfolders. For files, allows the user to append data to the end of an existing file. This permission does not pertain to deleting or overwriting existing data.
Write Attributes	Allows the user to change the attributes of the file or folder.
Write Extended Attributes	Allows the user to change the extended attributes of a file or folder.
Delete Subfolders and Files	For a folder, allows the user to delete subfolders and their contents. This permission applies even if the Delete permission has not been expressly granted on the individual subfolders or their files.
Delete	Allows or denies the user the ability to delete the file. Even if Delete is denied, a user can still delete a file if he or she has Delete Subfolders and Files permission on the parent folder.
Read Permissions	Allows the user to view the file's or folder's permissions assigned to a file or folder.
Change Permissions	Allows the user to change the file's or folder's permissions.
Take Ownership	Allows the user to take ownership of a file or folder.

Viewing Effective Permissions

The Effective Permissions tab of the Advanced Security Settings dialog box lets you enter a username and see what privileges the user will have as a result of the current security settings on the file or folder, as shown in Figure 31.19.

Figure 31.19
Effective Permissions shows you how edited Permissions settings will work before they're actually applied to the file.

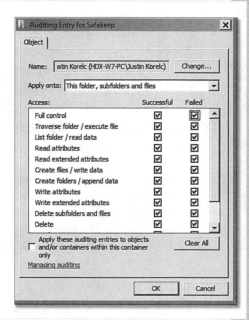

This dialog box displays the effective permissions *as edited*, before they are applied to the file folder. This lets you verify that the permissions you have set operate as desired before committing them to the file by clicking OK or Apply.

Access Auditing

The Advanced Security Settings dialog box provides a way for you (if you are an Administrator) to monitor access to files and folders through the Event Log. The Auditing tab lets you specify users and access types to monitor, and decide whether to record log entries for successful access, failure to access, or both. Auditing can be set for the use of each access attribute that you can set with Permissions: List Folder, Write Data, and so on.

Auditing is useful in several situations:

- To determine what files and folders an errant application program is attempting to use

- To monitor users for attempts to circumvent security

- To keep a record of access to important documents

To enable auditing, locate the folder or file you want to monitor, view the Security tab of its Properties dialog box, click Advanced, view the Auditing tab, click Continue, and click Add. On the Object tab of the Auditing Entry dialog box, select a specific user or group (or Everyone), click OK, and check the desired events to audit from the Access options, and click OK again. You can prevent a new audit setting from propagating into subfolders by checking Apply These Auditing Entries to Objects and/or Containers Within This Container Only. You can enable the resetting of audit properties of all subfolders and files by checking Replace All Existing Auditing Inheritable Auditing Entries on All Descendants With Inheritable Auditing Entries From This Object on the Auditing tab of the Advanced Security Settings dialog box.

An entry is made in the Security Event log for each audited access, so be careful if you are enabling auditing on the entire hard drive!

Taking Ownership of Files

Sometimes files or folders have security attributes set so stringently that even Administrator can't read or modify them. Usually this occurs when the file has permissions set only for its owner and not the usual list: Owner, Administrator, System. This can occur when a user account is deleted. It can also happen when you have reinstalled Windows or are using a disk drive taken from another Windows computer. Whatever the cause, the symptom is that even an Administrator user is not able to access the files in some folder. If you absolutely need to access such files, you can take ownership of the file or folder, and then assign permissions to read and write as appropriate. To take ownership of a file or folder:

1. Log on as Administrator.

2. Right-click the file or folder in Explorer and choose Properties.

3. View the Security tab and click Advanced.

4. View the Owner tab, and click Edit.

5. Select Administrator (the user) or Administrators (the group) from the list. You may want to check the Replace Owner on Subcontainers and Objects box to change subfolders as well.

6. Click OK.

7. Add privileges as necessary to grant access to the desired user(s).

Assigning Permissions to Groups

It's common in an office environment to want shared folders that are accessible by some users and not by others. For instance, you may wish to put payroll information in a shared folder and grant access only to certain administrative employees. In a school environment, you might want some folders that are accessible only by teachers, and others accessible only by members of a particular class. At home, you might want to prevent the children from getting access to the parent's folder. The best practice in this case is to create local *user groups*, which are collections of users that can be given privileges that carry over to the group's members. You can add the group and assign permissions for specific folders and files without having to list each of the qualified users separately.

Another benefit is that you can add and remove users from the group later on without having to modify the settings of the various folders.

To create local user groups, follow these steps:

1. Right-click Computer, click Manage, and open Local Users and Groups; or, on a domain computer, click the Advanced button on the Advanced tab of the User Accounts Control Panel applet.

2. Right-click the Groups entry in the left pane and select New Group.

3. Enter a name for the new group, such as Accounting.

4. Click Add and select users to add to the group.

5. Click create, and then click Close.

To grant the group permissions to specific folders:

1. Right-click the folder or file in Windows Explorer and select Security.

2. On the Security tab and click Edit, and then click Add.

3. Select the group name (on a domain computer you may select domain groups or local groups by selecting Location and choosing a domain name or the local computer name).

4. Click OK, and then check the appropriate permissions for the group to have under Permissions.

5. If Everyone or other groups are listed as having rights to this folder, you may want to select the group(s) and uncheck any undesired privileges. If the entry is grayed out, the privileges are inherited from a containing folder. In this case, when you're finished applying group permissions for this folder go back to the Folder Permissions dialog box and select Advanced, select the desired group, click the Change Permissions button, uncheck Include Inheritable Permissions From This Object's Parent, and click Remove. Click Apply, then click OK. After that, you can remove the permission entries you don't want.

6. **Important:** Before you click OK to commit the changes, use the Effective Permissions tab in the Advanced Security Settings dialog box to check the effective rights of a few different users to be sure that the rights are what you intend. Be sure that Administrator has at least taken ownership privileges.

note

You cannot create local user groups with Windows Home Basic, Home Premium (or Starter Edition) using the local Users and Groups tool. If you're a hard-core Windows hacker, you *can* use the command-line technique explained in the tip at the end of this section. This applies equally to Windows 7 and Windows Vista computers.

tip

On Windows 7 Home versions, if you're willing to work with the command-line interface, you *can* create local groups. Open a Command Prompt window and type the command **net localgroup** *groupname* /**add**, but in place of *groupname* type the name of the group you'd like to create. Then, to add a user to the group, type the command **net localgroup** *groupname username* /**add** and again, in place of *groupname*, type the name of the group you created, and in place of *username*, type the name of a user on your computer. Repeat this command as necessary to add other users. The same command with /delete at the end instead of /add removes a user from the group.

A User Has Access to a Restricted Object

A user in the Users local group has access to an object that the Users local group is not assigned permissions for.

Check to see whether the user belongs to any other groups that have been assigned permissions. Remember that permissions accumulate through groups. If necessary, you can remove groups from those listed as having access to the file, or you can list specific users and/or groups and check the Deny boxes to remove access rights.

Securing Your Printers

If you have a printer that uses expensive paper or ink, and are concerned that guests, kids, or unauthorized persons might use your printer, you should know that printers can be secured in the same way that access is controlled for files and folders: through user and group privileges. In the case of printers, the privileges allow users to add jobs to the printer, delete other people's jobs, and so on.

On a domain network, the network manager usually takes care of this. And on a workgroup it's generally not important to restrict access to printers. If you are using Simple File Sharing, it's not even possible to set up specific printer access privileges.

If you decide to, however, you can set printer access permissions by right-clicking a printer in your Printers folder and selecting Properties. The Security tab resembles the Security tab for files and folders, and can be modified in the same way.

Security Policy Configuration Options

USB flash memory drives are becoming ubiquitous. I carry one around most of the time for quick and easy file transfers, and they've found their way onto many keychains and even a few ballpoint pens and Swiss army knife models. Although USB flash memory drives are handy for data transfer, for improving Windows performance with ReadyBoost, and as a method for providing BitLocker credentials, they are a two-edged sword: They can also be used to steal confidential data, even from systems that use BitLocker or EFS encryption. After all, these encryption methods block unauthorized users from gaining access to data, but they can't stop the authorized user from walking off with data.

In the past, institutions have used fairly crude methods for blocking access by USB devices, even to the point of literally gluing USB ports closed. However, in an era in which parallel, serial, and PS2 devices have been relegated to the boneyard by USB devices, more intelligent management of USB device security is needed. In Windows 7, you can use various Group Policy settings, including the following, to prevent removable-media drives, including USB flash memory drives, from being used to snatch data, while still permitting legitimate uses for printing, input devices, and so forth:

- Removable Disks Deny Write Access

- All Removable Storage Classes Deny Write Access

You can also block installation of unapproved devices, such as USB flash memory drives, or permit only installation of approved devices. For details, see "Step-By-Step Guide to Controlling Device Installation and Usage with Group Policy," at the Microsoft TechNet website.

Third-Party Disc-Backup Tools

Although Windows 7 breaks new ground for Microsoft in its support for both image and file/folder backups, you might still prefer to use third-party backup tools, for the following reasons:

- **Support for existing backup file types**—If you want to be able to access existing backups with Windows 7, you need to use a version of your existing backup software that works with Windows 7. Consult your backup software vendor for specific recommendations.

- **Capability to extract files from an image backup without scripting**—The most recent versions of leading image-backup programs such as Acronis True Image and Symantec Norton Ghost also support individual file/folder restoration from an easy-to-use GUI. Windows 7's system image can be used for file/folder restoration only through the use of the wbadmin command-line tool.

- **Support for advanced backup options such as compression, splitting of a backup into smaller files, password protection, and others**—If you want these or other advanced options, you must use a third-party backup program.

- **Support for tape backups and tape libraries**—Windows 7's backup features do not include support for tape backups and tape libraries, although many third-party backup programs support tape as well as external drives, network shares, and CD or DVD backups.

Because of the extensive changes Windows 7 makes to the structure of user file storage and how the OS works, you will probably need to upgrade existing backup programs to versions made especially for Windows 7. Contact your backup vendor for details.

32

PROTECTING YOUR NETWORK
FROM HACKERS AND SNOOPS

It's a Cold, Cruel World

You might be considering connecting your office or home network to the Internet, or you might have done so already. Connecting will probably be a bit more work than you expect (even with, or due to, my advice), but the achievement will be gratifying. After you make just a few keystrokes, a friend in Italy will be able to log on to your network. Millions of potential customers can reach you. You'll be one with the world.

I don't want to spoil your day, but the cruel fact is that, besides your customers, friends, mother, and curious, benign strangers, your computer and your LAN will be exposed to pranksters, hackers, spammers, information bandits, thieves, and a variety of other bottom-feeders and bad guys who, like anyone else, can probe, prod, and test your system. Will your network be up to the task?

By this point in the book, you are aware that network design is foremost a task of planning. It's especially true in this case: *Before* you connect to the Internet, you must plan for security, whether you have a single computer or a large local area network (LAN).

Explaining everything that you can and should do would be impossible. In this chapter, I give you an idea of what net-

 note

You should know this: Even if you don't have a network, but have just one computer that is only occasionally connected to the Internet by modem, you're still at risk. The material in this chapter applies to almost everyone!

work security entails. I talk about the types of risks you'll be exposed to and the means people use to minimize this exposure; then I end with some tips and to-do lists. If you want to have a network or security consultant take care of implementation for you, that's great. This chapter gives you the background to understand what the consultant is doing. If you want to go it on your own, consider this chapter to be a survey course, with your assignment to continue to research, write, and implement a security plan.

Who Would Be Interested in My Computer?

Most of us don't give security risks a second thought. After all, who is a data thief going to target: me or the Pentagon? Who'd be interested in my computer? Well, the sad truth is that thousands of people out there would be delighted to find that they could connect to *your* computer. They might be looking for your credit card information, passwords for computers and websites, or a way to get to other computers on your LAN. Even more, they would love to find that they could install software on your computer that they could then use to send spam and probe other people's computers. They might even use your computer to launch attacks against corporate or governmental networks. *Don't doubt that this could happen to you.* Much of the spam you receive is sent from home computers that have been taken over by criminals through the conduit of an unsecured Internet connection. The problem has gotten so bad in the past few years that, starting with Windows XP Service Pack 2, when you install Windows software, Microsoft enables the strictest network security settings by default instead of requiring you to take explicit steps to enable them. There were just too many Windows computers—perhaps millions—with no protection whatsoever. And with the advent of high-speed, always-on Internet connections, the risks are increasing because computers stay connected and exposed for longer periods of time.

In this chapter, I explain a bit about how network attacks and defenses work. I tell you ways to prevent and prepare for recovery from a hacker attack. And most importantly, I show you what to do to make your Windows 7 system secure.

To make matters worse, in a business environment, security risks can come from *inside* a network environment as well as from outside. Inside, you might be subject to highly sophisticated eavesdropping techniques or even simple theft. But inside...I know of a company whose entire customer

 tip

This chapter gives you a good background on the ways that the "bad guys" can get into your computer and cause damage. If you don't want to read about this, skip ahead to "Specific Configuration Steps for Windows 7" later in the chapter. If even that's too much, I can give you the short version in one paragraph:

Windows 7 has better security than any previous version of Windows right out of the box. *Don't* turn off User Account Control, Windows Firewall, or Windows Defender, no matter what anyone else tells you. *Do* back up your hard disk frequently. If you do that, and make no changes to Microsoft's default security settings, you'll be better off than 95% of the people out there.

 note

If your computer is connected to a Windows domain-type network, your network administrators probably have taken care of all this for you. In fact, you might not even be able to make any changes in your computer's network or security settings. If this is the case, you might find it frustrating, but it's in the best interest of your organization.

Even if you're not too interested in this topic and don't read any other part of this chapter, you should read and carry out the steps in the section "Specific Configuration Steps for Windows 7."

list and confidential pricing database walked out the door one night with the receptionist, whose significant other worked for the competition. The theft was easy; any employee could read and print any file on the company's network. Computer Security is a real and serious issue. And it only helps to think about it *before* things go wrong.

Types of Attack

Before I talk about how to defend your computer against attack, let's briefly go through the types of attacks you're facing. Hackers can work their way into your computer and network using several methods. Here are some of them:

- **Password cracking**—Given a user account name, so-called "cracking" software can tirelessly try dictionary words, proper names, and random combinations in the hope of guessing a correct password. If your passwords aren't complex (that is, if they're not composed of upper- and lowercase letters, numbers, and punctuation characters), this doesn't take long to accomplish. If you make your computer(s) accessible over the Internet via Remote Desktop or if you run a public FTP, web, or email server, I can *promise* you that you will be the target of this sort of attack.

- **Address spoofing**—If you've seen the caller ID service used on telephones, you know that it can be used to screen calls: You answer the phone only if you recognize the caller. But what if telemarketers could make the device say "Mom's calling"? There's an analogy to this in networking. Hackers can send "spoofed" network commands into a network with a trusted IP address.

- **Impersonation**—By tricking Internet routers and the domain name registry system, hackers can have Internet or network data traffic routed to their own computers instead of the legitimate website server. With a fake website in operation, they can collect credit card numbers and other valuable data. This type of attack is on the rise due to recently discovered vulnerabilities in the Internet's basic infrastructure.

- **Eavesdropping**—Wiretaps on your telephone or network cable, or monitoring of the radio emissions from your computer and monitor, can let the more sophisticated hackers and spies see what you're seeing and record what you're typing. This sounds like KGB/CIA-type stuff, but wireless networks, which are everywhere these days, are extremely vulnerable to eavesdropping.

- **Exploits**—It's a given that complex software has bugs. Some bugs make programs fail in such a way that part of the program itself gets replaced by data from the user. Exploiting this sort of bug, hackers can run their own programs on your computer. It sounds farfetched and unlikely, but exploits in Microsoft's products alone are reported about once a week. The hacker community usually hears about them a few weeks before anyone else does, so even on the most up-to-date copy of Windows, there are a few exploits available for use.

- **Back doors**—Some software developers put special features into programs intended for their use only, usually to help in debugging. These back doors sometimes circumvent security features. Hackers discover and trade information on these and are only too happy to use the Internet to see if they work on your computer.

- **Open doors**—All the attack methods I described previously involve direct and malicious actions to try to break into your system. But this isn't always necessary: Sometimes, a computer can be left open in such a way that it just offers itself to the public. Just as leaving your front door wide open might invite burglary, leaving a computer unsecured by passwords and without proper controls on network access allows hackers to read and write your files by the simplest means. Password Protected Sharing, which I discuss later in the chapter, mitigates this risk somewhat.

- **Viruses and Trojan horses**—The ancient Greeks came up with the idea 3,200 years ago, and the Trojan horse trick is still alive and well today. Shareware programs used to be the favored way to distribute disguised attack software, but today email attachments are the favored method. Most email providers automatically strip out obviously executable email attachments, so the current trend is for viruses to send their payloads in ZIP file attachments. File and music sharing programs, Registry cleanup tools, and other "free" software utilities are another great source of unwanted add-ons commonly called spyware, adware, and malware. You may also hear the term "rootkit," which refers to a virus that burrows so deeply into the operating system that it can prevent you from detecting its presence when you list files or active running programs.

- **Social engineering**—A more subtle approach than brute-force hacking is to simply call or email someone who has useful information and ask for it. One variation on this approach is called *phishing*, where the criminals send email that purports to come from a bank or other service provider, saying there was some sort of account glitch and asking the user to reply with his or her password and Social Security number so the glitch can be fixed. P. T. Barnum said there's a sucker born every minute. Sadly, this works out to 1,440 suckers per day, or more than half a million per year, and it's not too hard to reach a lot of them with one bulk email.

- **Denial of service (DoS)**—Not every hacker is interested in your credit cards or business secrets. Some are just plain vandals, and it's enough for them to know that you can't get your work done. They might erase your hard drive or, more subtly, crash your server or tie up your Internet connection with a torrent of meaningless data. In any case, you're inconvenienced.

- **Identity theft**—Hackers often attempt to steal personal information, such as your name, date of birth, address, credit card, and Social Security number. Armed with this, they can proceed to open credit card and bank accounts, redirect your mail, obtain services, purchase goods, obtain employment, and so on, all without your knowledge. This is one of the most vicious attacks and can have a profound effect on victims. Computers can expose you to identity theft in several ways: You might provide personal information to a phishing scheme or to an unscrupulous online seller yourself. Hackers could break into your computer or that of an online seller and steal your information stored there. Or, criminals could tap into your home or business network, a wireless network in a public space, or even the wiring at an Internet service provider and capture unencrypted information flowing through the network there.

If all this makes you nervous about hooking your LAN up to the Internet, I've done my job well. Before you pull the plug, though, read on.

Your Lines of Defense

Making your computer and network completely impervious to all these forms of attack is quite impossible, if for no other reason than that there is always a human element that you cannot control, and there are always bugs and exploits not yet anticipated.

You *can* do a great deal, however, if you plan ahead. Furthermore, as new software introduces new features and risks, and as existing flaws are identified and repaired, you have to keep on top of things to maintain your defenses. The most important part of the process is that you spend some time thinking about security.

The following sections delve into the four main lines of computer defense:

- Preparation

- Active defense

- Testing, logging, and monitoring

- Disaster planning

You can omit any of these measures, of course, if you weigh what you have at risk against what these efforts will cost you, and decide that the benefit isn't worth the effort.

What I'm describing sounds like a lot of work, and it can be if you take full-fledged measures in a business environment. Nevertheless, even if you're a home user, I encourage you to consider each of the following steps and to put them into effect with as much diligence as you can muster.

Preparation: Network Security Basics

Preparation involves eliminating unnecessary sources of risk before they can be attacked. You should take the following steps:

- Invest time in planning and policies. If you want to be really diligent about security, for each of the strategies I describe in this chapter, outline how you plan to implement each one.

- Structure your network to restrict unauthorized access. Do you really need to allow users to use their own modems to connect to the Internet? Do you want to permit access from the Internet directly into your network, indirectly via a virtual private network (VPN), or not at all? Eliminating points of access reduces risk but also convenience. You have to decide where to strike the balance.

- If you're concerned about unauthorized in-house access to your computers, be sure that every user account is set up with a good password—one with letters and numbers and punctuation. Unauthorized network access is less of a problem with Password Protected Sharing because *all* network users are treated the same, but you must ensure that an effective firewall is in place between your LAN and the Internet. I show you how to use Windows Firewall later in this chapter.

- Install only needed services. The less network software you have installed, the less you'll have to maintain through updates, and the fewer potential openings you'll offer to attackers. For example, don't install SMTP or Internet Information Services (IIS) unless you really need them. Don't install the optional Simple TCP Services network service; it provides no useful function, only archaic services that make great DOS attack targets

- Use software known to be secure and (relatively) bug-free. Use the Windows Automatic Updates feature. Update your software promptly when fixes become available. Be *very* wary of shareware and freeware, unless you can be sure of its pedigree and safety.

- Properly configure your computers, file systems, software, and user accounts to maintain appropriate access control. I discuss this in detail later in the chapter.

- Hide from the outside world as much information about your systems as possible. Don't give hackers any assistance by revealing user account or computer names, if you can help it. For example, if you set up your own Internet domain, put as little information into DNS as you can get away with. Don't install SNMP unless you need it, and be sure to block it at your Internet firewall.

Security is partly a technical issue and partly a matter of organizational policy. No matter how you've configured your computers and network, one user with a modem and a lack of responsibility can open a door into the best-protected network.

You should decide which security-related issues you want to leave to your users' discretion and which you want to mandate as a matter of policy. On a Windows domain network, the operating system enforces some of these points, but if you don't have a domain server, you might need to rely on communication and trust alone. The following are some issues to ponder:

 tip

The most important program to keep up-to-date is Windows 7 itself. I suggest that you keep up-to-date on Windows 7 bugs and fixes through the Automatic Updates feature *and* through independent watchdogs. Configure Windows to notify you of critical updates. Subscribe to the security bulletin mailing lists at www.microsoft.com/security and www.sans.org.

If you use IIS to host a website, pay particular attention to announcements regarding Internet Explorer and IIS. Internet Explorer and IIS together account for the lion's share of Windows security problems.

- Do you trust users to create and protect their own shared folders, or should this be done by management only?

- Do you want to let users run a web server, an FTP server, or other network services, each of which provides benefits but also increases risk?

- Are your users allowed to create simple alphabetic passwords without numbers or punctuation?

- Are users allowed to send and receive personal email from the network?

- Are users allowed to install software they obtain themselves?

- Are users allowed to share access to their desktops with Remote Desktop, Remote Assistance, GoToMyPC, LogMeIn, VNC, PCAnywhere, or other remote-control software?

Make public your management and personnel policies regarding network security and appropriate use of computer resources.

If your own users don't respect the integrity of your network, you don't stand a chance against the outside world. A crucial part of any effective security strategy is making up the rules in advance and ensuring that everyone knows them.

Active Defense

Active defense means actively resisting known methods of attack. Active defenses include these:

- Firewalls and gateways to block dangerous or inappropriate Internet traffic as it passes between your network and the Internet at large

- Encryption and authentication to limit access based on some sort of credentials (such as a password)

- Efforts to keep up-to-date on security and risks, especially with respect to Windows 7

When your network is in place, your next job is to configure it to restrict access as much as possible. This task involves blocking network traffic that is known to be dangerous and configuring network protocols to use the most secure communications protocols possible.

Firewalls and NAT (Connection-Sharing) Devices

Using a firewall is an effective way to secure your network. From the viewpoint of design and maintenance, it is also the most efficient tool because you can focus your efforts on one critical place, the interface between your internal network and the Internet.

A firewall is a program or piece of hardware that intercepts all data that passes between two networks—for example, between your computer or LAN and the Internet. The firewall inspects each incoming and outgoing data packet and permits only certain packets to pass. Generally, a firewall is set up to permit traffic for safe protocols such as those used for email and web browsing. It blocks packets that carry file-sharing or computer administration commands.

Network Address Translation (NAT), the technology behind Internet Connection Sharing and connection-sharing routers, insulates your network from the Internet by funneling all of your LAN's network traffic through one IP address—the Internet analog of a telephone number. Like an office's switchboard operator, NAT lets all your computers place outgoing connections at will, but it intercepts all incoming connection attempts. If an incoming data request was anticipated, it's forwarded to one of your computers, but all other incoming network requests are rejected or ignored. Microsoft's Internet Connection Sharing and hardware Internet Connection Sharing routers all use a NAT scheme.

➡ *To learn more about this topic,* **see** *"NAT and Internet Connection Sharing,"* **p. 518.**

The use of either NAT or a firewall, or both, can protect your network by letting you specify exactly how much of your network's resources you expose to the Internet.

Windows Firewall

One of Windows 7's features is the built-in Windows Firewall software.

Windows Firewall is enabled, or attached, on any network adapter or dial-up connection that directly connects to the Internet. Its purpose is to block any traffic that carries networking-related data, so it prevents computers on the Internet from accessing your shared files, Remote Desktop, Remote Administration, and other "sensitive" functions.

Window Firewall by default blocks all attempts by other computers to reach your computer, except in response to communications that you initiate yourself. For example, if you try to view a web page, your computer starts the process by connecting to a web server out on the Internet. Windows Firewall knows that the returning data is in response to your request, so it allows the reply to return to your computer. However, someone "out there" who tries to view your shared files will be rebuffed. Any unsolicited, incoming connection will simply be ignored.

This type of network haughtiness is generally a good thing, except that it would also prevent you from sharing your computer with people that you do want to share with. For example, it would block file and printer sharing, Remote Assistance, and other desirable services. So, Windows Firewall can make *exceptions* that permit incoming connections from other computers on a case-by-case basis. By that, I mean that it can differentiate connections based on the software involved (which is discerned by the connection's *port number*), and by the remote computer's *network address*, which lets Windows know whether the request comes from a computer on your own network or from a computer "out there" on the Internet. And starting with Windows 7, Windows Firewall uses a third criterion for judging incoming requests: the "public" or "private" label attached to the network adapter through which the request comes. This is a *huge* improvement over Windows XP and Vista.

Here's why: When you're at home, the other computers on your network share a common network address scheme (just as most telephone numbers in a neighborhood start with the same area code and prefix digits). Those computers can be trusted to share your files and printers. However, if you take your computer to a hotel or coffee shop, the computers on your local network should *not* be trusted, even though they will share the same network addressing scheme. With prior versions of Windows, you had to reconfigure Windows Firewall every time you moved your computer from one network to another, so that you didn't inadvertently expose your shared files to unknown people.

As you may know, when you connect your computer to a network for the first time, Windows 7 asks you whether the network is private or public. As you might guess, a public network is one where you don't trust the other connected computers. This would be an appropriate choice in a coffee shop or hotel, or for a connection from your computer directly to a DSL or cable modem. A private network is one where you trust the other computers that are directly attached. This network might connect to the Internet through a router, but you

 note

Windows Firewall has the advantage that it can permit incoming connections for programs such as Remote Assistance. On the other hand, it's part of the very operating system it's trying to protect, and if either Windows 7 *or* Windows Firewall gets compromised, your computer's a goner.

If I had the choice between using Windows Firewall, or an external firewall device—such as a commercial firewall server or a connection-sharing router with filter rules—I'd use the external firewall. But Windows Firewall is *definitely* better than no firewall at all.

can still consider it private, because your local trusted computers can be distinguished by sharing a common network address.

Windows Firewall is enabled by default when you install Windows 7. You can also enable or disable it manually by selecting the Change Settings task on the Windows Firewall window. (I tell you how to do this later in the chapter, under "Specific Configuration Steps for Windows 7.") You also can tell Windows Firewall whether you want it to permit incoming requests for specific services. If you have a web server installed in your computer, for example, you need to tell Windows Firewall to permit incoming HTTP data.

Packet Filtering

If you use a hardware Internet Connection Sharing router (also called a residential gateway) or a full-fledged network router for your Internet service, you can instruct it to block data that carries services you don't want exposed to the Internet. This is called *packet filtering*. You can set this up in addition to NAT, to provide extra protection.

Filtering works like this: Each Internet data packet contains identifying numbers that indicate the protocol type (such as TCP or UDP) and the IP address for the source and destination computers. Some protocols also have an additional number called a port, which identifies the program that is to receive the packet. The WWW service, for example, expects TCP protocol packets addressed to port 80. A domain name server listens for UDP packets on port 53.

A packet that arrives at the firewall from either side is examined; then it is either passed on or discarded, according to a set of rules that lists the protocols and ports permitted or prohibited for each direction. A prohibited packet can be dropped silently, or the router can reject the packet with an error message returned to the sender indicating that the requested network service is unavailable. If possible, specify the silent treatment. (Why tell hackers that a desired service is present, even if it's unavailable to them?) Some routers can also make a log entry or send an alert indicating that an unwanted connection was attempted.

 note

For a good introduction to firewalls, identity theft, and Internet security in general, I recommend *Windows Lockdown! Your XP and Vista Guide Against Hacks, Attacks, and Other Internet Mayhem* (Que, 2008; ISBN 0-7897-3672-1), *Is It Safe?* (Que, 2008, ISBN 0-7897-3782-5), and *The Truth About Identity Theft* (FT Press, 2008, ISBN 0-7897-3793-9).

Configuring routers for filtering is beyond the scope of this book, but Table 32.1 lists some relevant protocols and ports. If your router lets you block incoming requests separately from outgoing requests, you should block incoming requests for all the services listed, unless you are *sure* you want to enable access to them. If you have a basic gateway router that doesn't provide separate incoming and outgoing filters, you probably want to filter only those services that I've marked with an asterisk (*).

Table 32.1 Services That You Might Want to Block

Protocol	Port	Associated Service
TCP	20–21	FTP—File Transfer Protocol.
TCP	22	SSH—Secure Shell protocol, an encrypted version of Telnet.
TCP *	23	Telnet—Clear-text passwords are sent by this remote terminal service, which also is used to configure routers.

Table 32.1   Continued

Protocol	Port	Associated Service
TCP	53	DNS—Domain name service. Block TCP mode "zone" transfers, which reveal machine names.
TCP+UDP	67	BOOTP—Bootstrap protocol (similar to DHCP). Unnecessary.
TCP+UDP	69	TFTP—Trivial File Transfer Protocol. No security.
TCP	110	POP3—Post Office Protocol.
UDP *TCP TCP+UDP *	137–139	NetBIOS—These ports are used by Microsoft File Sharing.
UDP *	161–2	SNMP—Simple Network Monitoring Protocol. Reveals too much information and can be used to reconfigure the router.
TCP *	445	SMB—Windows File Sharing can use port 445 as well as ports 137–139.
TCP	515	LPD—UNIX printer-sharing protocol supported by Windows.
UDP, TCP	1900, 5000	Universal Plug and Play—Can be used to reconfigure routers.

As I said, if you use a hardware router to connect to the Internet, I can't show you the specifics for your device. I can give you a couple of examples, though. My Linksys cable/DSL–sharing router uses a web browser for configuration, and there's a page for setting up filters, as shown in Figure 32.1. In this figure, I've blocked the ports for Microsoft file-sharing services.

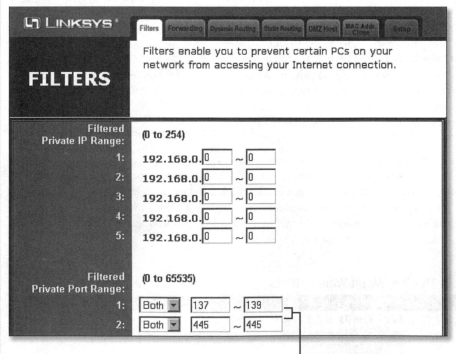

Figure 32.1
Configuring packet filters in a typical Internet Connection Sharing router.

Settings to filter ports 137-139 and 445

If you use routed DSL Internet service, your ISP might have provided a router manufactured by Flowpoint, Netopia, or another manufacturer.

These are complex devices, and your ISP will help you set up yours. Insist that your ISP install filters for ports 137, 138, 139, and 445, at the very least.

Using NAT or Internet Connection Sharing

By either name, Network Address Translation (NAT) has two big security benefits. First, it can be used to hide an entire network behind one IP address. Then, while it transparently passes connections from you out to the Internet, it rejects all incoming connection attempts except those that you explicitly direct to waiting servers inside your LAN. Packet filtering isn't absolutely necessary with NAT, although it can't hurt to add it.

> *To learn more about NAT,* ***see*** *"NAT and Internet Connection Sharing," p. 518.*

You learned how to configure Windows Internet Connection Sharing in Chapter 19, "Connecting Your Network to the Internet," so I won't repeat that information here.

If you have built a network with another type of router or connection-sharing device, you must follow the manufacturer's instructions or get help from your ISP to set it up.

> **⚠ caution**
>
> Microsoft's Internet Connection Sharing (ICS) blocks incoming access to other computers on the LAN, but unless Windows Firewall is also enabled, it does *not* protect the computer that is sharing the Internet connection. If you use ICS, you *must* enable Windows Firewall on the same connection, or you must use a third-party software firewall application.

Add-On Firewall Products for Windows

Commercial products called *personal firewalls are* designed for use on PCs. These types of products, Norton Internet Security 2009 (www.symantec.com) for instance, range in price from free to about $60. Now that Windows includes an integral firewall, add-on products might no longer be necessary, and I don't think that it's worth paying for a software firewall program for Windows. Windows Firewall is good enough, it's free, and it's built in. It's *far* more important that you keep Windows and all of your add-on applications up-to-date, and use Windows Defender or a third-party antivirus/antispyware program.

Secure Your Router

If you use a router for your Internet connection and rely on it to provide network protection, you *must* make it require a secure password. If your router doesn't require a password, *anyone* can connect to it across the Internet and delete the filters you've set up. (As configured by the manufacturers and ISPs, most connection-sharing routers *do not* require a password, although they typically won't accept configuration commands from the Internet, but only from your own network.)

To lock down your router, you have to follow procedures for your specific router. You'll want to do the following:

- Change the router's administrative password to a combination of letters, numbers, and punctuation. Be sure to write it down somewhere, and keep it in a secure place. (I usually write the password on a sticky label and attach it to the bottom of the router.)

- Change the SNMP read-only and read-write community names (which are, in effect, passwords) to a secret word or a very long random string of random characters; or better yet, follow the next recommendation.

- Prohibit write access via SNMP or disable SNMP entirely.

- Change all Telnet login passwords, whether administrative or informational.

If you don't want to attempt to lock down your router, your ISP should do it for you. If your ISP supplied your router and you change the password yourself, be sure to give the new password to your ISP.

Configure Passwords and File Sharing

Windows 7 supports password-protected and passwordless file sharing. Before I explain this, I need to give you some background. In the original Windows NT workgroup network security model, when you attempted to use a network resource shared by another computer, Windows would see if your username and password matched an account on that remote computer. One of four things would happen:

- If the username and password exactly matched an account defined on the remote computer, you got that user's privileges on the remote machine for reading and writing files.

- If the username matched but the password didn't, you were prompted to enter the correct password.

- If the username didn't match any predefined account, or if you failed to supply the correct password, you got the privileges accorded to the Guest account, *if* the Guest account was enabled.

- If the Guest account was disabled—and it usually was—you were denied access.

The problem with this system is that it required you to create user accounts on each computer you wanted to reach over the network. Multiply, say, 5 users times 5 computers, and you had 25 user accounts to configure. What a pain! (People pay big bucks for a Windows Server–based domain network to eliminate this very hassle.) Because it was so much trouble, people usually enabled the Guest account.

Windows 7 has a new feature called the HomeGroup that provides a way around the headaches of managing lots of user accounts and passwords. When you make a Windows 7 computer a member of a homegroup, it uses a built-in user account named HomeGroupUser$ when it accesses shared resources on other computers in the group. The member computers all have this same account name set up, with the same password (which is derived from the homegroup's password in some way), so that all member computers can use any shared resource. When you share a library, folder, or printer with the homegroup, Windows gives the user account HomeGroupUser$ permission to read, or to read and write the files in that folder. It's a simple, convenient scheme, but only Windows 7 computers can take advantage of it.

On Windows 7, another way to avoid password headaches is to entirely disable the use of passwords for network resources. If you disable Password Protected Sharing, the contents of the Public folder and all other shared folders are accessible to everyone on the network, even if they don't have a user account and password on your computer, and regardless of the operating system they're using. This is ideal if you want to share everything in your Public folder and do not need to set sharing permissions for individuals.

From a security perspective, only a few folders are accessible when Password Protected Sharing is disabled, and although anybody with access to the network can access them, the damage an intruder can do is limited to stealing or modifying just the files in a few folders that are known to be public.

If you do disable Password Protected Sharing, it's *crucial* that you have a firewall in place. Otherwise, everyone on the Internet will have the same rights in your shared folders as you. (That's one of the reasons for Windows Firewall, and why Windows is so adamant about either installing Windows Firewall or disabling file sharing.)

By default, Windows 7 has Password Protected Sharing enabled, which limits access to the Public folder and all other shared folders to users with a user account and password on your computer.

If you want to make the Public folder accessible to everyone on your network without having to create for each person an account on every computer, you have four choices:

- If you are on a home or small office network and you have only (or mostly) Windows 7 computers, you can enable the HomeGroup networking feature, as discussed in Chapter 17.

- You can set up accounts for every user on your computer, so that everyone will access the shared folder using their own account. You'll need to be sure that everyone uses the same password on every computer.

- You can create a special user account, for example, named "share," and give people you trust the password to this account. Everyone can use this same username and password to access the shared folder on your computer.

- You can disable Password Protected Sharing. To do this, click Start, Control Panel, Network and Internet, Network and Sharing Center, Homegroup and Sharing Options, Advanced Sharing Options. Under Password Protected Sharing, click Turn Off Password Protected Sharing, and click Apply.

 note

When you disable Password Protected Sharing, you get what was called Simple File Sharing on Windows XP, but with a twist: On XP, when Simple File Sharing was in effect, every network accessed shared resources using the Guest account, no matter what username and password they supplied. On Windows 7, if the remote user's username matches an account on the Windows 7 computer and the account has a password set, they'll be able to access the shared resources using that account's privileges. The Guest account is used only when the remote user's account doesn't match one on the Windows 7 computer, or if the matching account has no password.

If your computer is a member of a Windows domain network, you cannot disable Password Protected Sharing.

Set Up Restrictive Access Controls

Possibly the most important and difficult step you can take is to limit access to shared files, folders, and printers. You can use the guidelines shown in Table 32.2 to help organize a security review of every machine on your network.

Table 32.2   Restricting Access Controls

Access Point	Controls
File Sharing	Don't share your computers' entire hard drives. Share only folders that need to be shared, and, if possible, choose only folders within your Documents folder (for simplicity). Use Password Protected Sharing.
Passwords	Set up *all* accounts to require passwords. You can configure your computers to require long passwords if you want to enforce good internal security. I show you how to do this later in the chapter.
Partitions	If you install IIS and want to make a website or FTP site available to the Internet, set up a separate NTFS partition on your hard drive *just* for website files.
Access Control	Don't disable User Account Control. In fact, even with UAC in place, it's best not to use Administrator or any other Computer Administrator account for your day-to-day work. Instead, create a Standard user account for yourself, and type in an Administrator password when you're prompted to.
FTP	If you install a public FTP server, do not let FTP share a FAT-formatted drive or partition. In addition, you must prevent anonymous FTP users from writing to your hard drive.
SMTP	Configuring an email system is beyond the scope of this book. But if you operate an email server, consider storing incoming mail in a separate partition, to avoid getting overrun with too much mail. Also, you *must* prohibit "relaying" from outside SMTP servers to outside domains, lest your server be used as a spam relay site.
HTTP (Web)	Don't enable both Script/Execute permission and Write permission on the same folder. Enabling both permissions would permit outside users to install and run arbitrary programs on your computer. You should manually install any needed scripts or CGI programs. (The FrontPage extensions can publish scripts to protected directories, but they perform strong user authentication before doing so.)
SNMP	This network-monitoring option is a useful tool for large networks, but it also poses a security risk. If installed, it could be used to modify your computer's network settings and, at the very least, will happily reveal the names of all the user accounts on your computer. Don't install SNMP unless you need it, and if you do, change the "community name" from public to something confidential and difficult to guess. Block SNMP traffic through your Internet connection with filtering.

Testing, Logging, and Monitoring

Testing, logging, and monitoring involve testing your defense strategies and detecting breaches. It's tedious, but who would you rather have be the first to find out that your system is hackable: you or "them?" Your testing steps should include these:

- Testing your defenses before you connect to the Internet

- Detecting and recording suspicious activity on the network and in application software

You can't second-guess what 100 million potential "visitors" might do to your computer or network, but you should at least be sure that all your roadblocks stop the traffic you were expecting them to stop.

Test Your Defenses

Some companies hire expert hackers to attempt to break into their networks. You can do this, too, or you can try to be your own hacker. Before you connect to the Internet, and periodically thereafter, try to break into your own system. Find its weaknesses.

Go through each of your defenses and each of the security policy changes you made, and try each of the things you thought they should prevent.

First, connect to the Internet, visit www.grc.com, and view the ShieldsUP page. (Its author, Steve Gibson, is a very bright guy and has lots of interesting things to say, but be forewarned that some of it is a bit hyperbolic.) This website attempts to connect to Microsoft Networking and TCP/IP services on your computer to see whether any are accessible from the outside world. Click the File Sharing and Common Ports buttons to see whether this testing system exposes any vulnerabilities. Don't worry if the only test your computer fails is the `ping` test. This is a great tool!

 note

If you're on a corporate network, contact your network manager before trying this. If your company uses intrusion monitoring, this probe might set off alarms and get you in hot water.

As a second test, find out what your public IP address is. If you use a dial-up connection or Internet Connection Sharing, go to the computer that actually connects to the Internet, open a Command Prompt window, and type **ipconfig**. Write down the IP address of your actual Internet connection (this number will change every time you dial in, by the way). If you use a sharing router, you need to get the actual IP address from your router's Status page—your computer won't know. Or, try whatismyipaddress.com (no joke!).

Then enlist the help of a friend or go to a computer that is *not* on your site but out on the Internet. Open Windows Explorer (*not* Internet Explorer) and, in the Address box, type *1.2.3.4*, but in place of *1.2.3.4*, type the IP address that you recorded earlier. This attempts to connect to your computer for file sharing. You should not be able to see any shared folders, and you shouldn't even be prompted for a username and/or password. If you have more than one public IP address, test *all* of them.

Shared Folders Are Visible to the Internet

When you use Internet Explorer to try to view your computer from outside on the Internet, and you are prompted for a username and password, or shared folders are visible, Microsoft file sharing services are being exposed to the Internet. If you have a shared connection to the Internet, you need to enable Windows Firewall or enable filtering on your Internet connection. At the very least, you must block TCP/UDP ports 137–139 and 445. Don't leave this unfixed.

If you have several computers connected to a cable modem with just a hub and no connection-sharing router, you should read Chapter 19 for alternative ways to share your cable Internet connection.

If you have installed a web or FTP server, attempt to view any protected pages *without* using the correct username or password. With FTP, try using the login name **anonymous** and the password **guest**. Try to copy files to the FTP site while connected as anonymous—you shouldn't be able to.

Sensitive Web Pages or FTP Folders Are Visible to the Internet

When you access your self-hosted website from the Internet using a web browser or anonymous FTP and can view folders that you thought were private and protected, be sure that the shared folders are not on a FAT-formatted disk partition. FAT disks don't support user-level file protection. Share only folders from NTFS-formatted disks.

Then, check the folder's NTFS permissions to be sure that anonymous access is not permitted. Locate the folders in Windows Explorer on the computer running IIS. View the folders' Securities Properties tab. Be sure that none of the following users or groups is granted access to the folder: Everyone, IUSR_*XXXX* (where *XXXX* is your computer name), IUSR, or IIS_IUSRS. On the folders you wish to protect, grant read and write privileges only to authorized users. In the IIS management console, you can also explicitly disable anonymous access to the website's or a specific folder.

Use network-testing utilities to attempt to connect to any of the network services you think you have blocked, such as SNMP.

Network Services Are Not Being Blocked

If you can connect to your computer across the Internet with remote administration tools such as the Registry editor, with SNMP viewers, or with other tools that use network services, network services are not being blocked

Look up the protocol type (for example, UDP or TCP) and port numbers of the unblocked services, and configure filters in your router to block these services. Your ISP might be able to help you with this problem. You also might have disabled Windows Firewall by mistake.

Attempt to use Telnet to connect to your router, if you have one. If you are prompted for a login, try the factory default login name and password listed in the router's manual. If you've blocked Telnet with a packet filter setting, you should not be prompted for a password. If you are prompted, be sure the factory default password does not work, because you should have changed it.

Port-scanning tools are available to perform many of these tests automatically. For an example, see the ShieldsUP web page at www.grc.com. I caution you to use this sort of tool in addition to, not instead of, the other tests I listed here.

Monitor Suspicious Activity

If you use Windows Firewall, you can configure it to keep a record of rejected connection attempts. Log on using a Computer Administrator–type account. Choose Start, All Programs, Administrative Tools, Windows Firewall with Advanced Security. In the left pane, right-click Windows Firewall with Advanced Security and select Properties. Select one of the available profile tabs (Private Profile, in most cases) and click the Customize button within the Logging area to get to the window shown in Figure 32.2. Enable logging of dropped packets. You can enable this setting for all profiles if you wish.

Inspect the log file periodically by viewing it with Notepad.

 note

If you use a dial-up connection, the firewall log is less useful. It will accrue lots of entries caused by packets left over from connections made by the dial-up customer who had your temporary IP address before you got it. They'll continue to arrive for a while, just as junk mail does after a tenant moves out.

Figure 32.2
Enable logging to see what Windows Firewall is turning away.

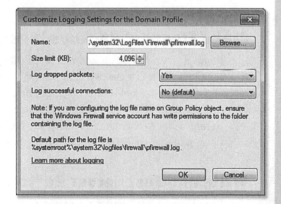

Disaster Planning: Preparation for Recovery After an Attack

Disaster planning should be a key part of your security strategy. The old saying "Hope for the best and prepare for the worst" certainly applies to network security. Murphy's law predicts that if you don't have a way to recover from a network or security disaster, you'll soon need one. If you're prepared, you can recover quickly and may even be able to learn something useful from the experience. Here are some suggestions to help you prepare for the worst:

- Make permanent, archived "baseline" backups of exposed computers *before* they're connected to the Internet and anytime system software is changed.

- Make frequent backups once online.

- Prepare written, thorough, and *tested* computer restore procedures.

- Write and maintain documentation of your software and network configuration.

- Prepare an incident plan.

A little planning now will go a long way toward helping you through this situation. The key is having a good backup of all critical software. Each of the points discussed in the preceding list is covered in more detail in the following sections.

Make a Baseline Backup Before You Go Online

You should make a permanent "baseline" backup of your computer before you connect with the Internet for the first time so that you know it doesn't have any virus infections. Make this backup onto a removable disk or tape that can be kept separate from your computer, and keep this backup permanently. You can use it as a starting point for recovery if your system is compromised.

➥   *To learn more about making backups,* **see** *"The All New Backup and Restore," **p. 863**.*

Make Frequent Backups When You're Online

I hate to sound like a broken record on this point, but you should have a backup plan and stick to it. Make backups at some sensible interval and always after a session of extensive or significant changes (for example, after installing new software or adding users). In a business setting, you might want to have your backup program schedule a backup every day automatically. (You *do* have to remember to change the backup media, even if the backups are automatic.) In a business setting, backup media should be rotated offsite to prevent against loss from theft or fire.

Write and Test Server Restore Procedures

I can tell you from personal experience that the only feeling more sickening than losing your system is finding out that the backups you've been diligently making are unreadable. Whatever your backup scheme is, be sure it works!

This step is difficult to take, but I urge you to try to completely rebuild a system after an imaginary break-in or disk failure. Use a sacrificial computer, of course, not your main computer, and allow yourself a whole day for this exercise. Go through all the steps: Reformat hard disks, reinstall Windows or use the Complete PC Restore feature, reinstall tape software (if necessary), and restore the most recent backups. You will find this a very enlightening experience, well worth the cost in time and effort. Finding the problem with your system *before* you need the backups is much better than finding it afterward.

Also be sure to document the whole restoration process so that you can repeat it later. After a disaster, you'll be under considerable stress, so you might forget a step or make a mistake. Having a clear, written, tested procedure goes a long way toward making the recovery process easier and more likely to succeed.

Write and Maintain Documentation

It's in your own best interest to maintain a log of all software installed on your computers, along with software settings, hardware types and settings, configuration choices, network address information, and so on. (Do you vaguely remember some sort of ordeal when you installed your wireless router last year? How *did* you resolve that problem, anyway?)

In businesses, this information is often part of the "oral tradition," but a written record is an important insurance policy against loss due to memory lapses or personnel changes. Record all installation and configuration details.

> **tip**
>
> Windows has no utilities to print the configuration settings for software and network systems. I use Alt+PrntScrn to record the configurations for each program and network component, and then paste the images into WordPad or Microsoft Word.

Then *print a copy* of this documentation so you'll be able to refer to it if your computer crashes.

Make a library of software DVDs and CD-ROMs, repair disks, startup disks, utility disks, backup disks, tapes, manuals, and notebooks that record your configurations and observations. Keep them together in one place and locked up, if possible.

Prepare an Incident Plan

A system crash, virus infection, or network intrusion is a highly stressful event. A written plan of action made now will help you keep a clear head when things go wrong. The actual event probably won't go as you imagined, but at least you'll have some good first steps to follow while you get your wits about you.

If you know a break-in has been successful, you must take immediate action. First, disconnect your network from the Internet. Then find out what happened.

Unless you have an exact understanding of what happened and can fix the problem, you should clean out your system entirely. This means that you should reformat your hard drive, install Windows and all applications from CDs/DVDs or pristine disks, and make a clean start. Then you can look at recent backups to see whether you have any you know aren't compromised, restore them, and then go on.

But most of all, have a plan. The following are some steps to include in your incident plan:

- Write down exactly how to properly shut down computers and servers.

- Make a list of people to notify, including company officials, your computer support staff, your ISP, an incident response team, your therapist, and anyone else who will be involved in dealing with the aftermath.

- If you had a hacker break-in, check www.first.org to see whether you are eligible for assistance from one of the many FIRST response teams around the world. The FIRST (Forum of Incident

Response and Security Teams) Secretariat can tell you which agencies might best be able to help you in the event of a security incident; call 301-975-3359.

- The CERT-CC (Computer Emergency Response Team Coordination Center) might also be able to help you, or at least get information from your break-in to help protect others. Check www.cert.org. In an emergency, call 412-268-7090.

- You can find a great deal of general information on effective incident response planning at www.cert.org. CERT offers training seminars, libraries, security (bug) advisories, and technical tips as well.

Specific Configuration Steps for Windows 7

Many of the points I've mentioned in this chapter so far are general, conceptual ideas that should be helpful in planning a security strategy, but perhaps not specific enough to directly implement. The following sections provide some specific instructions to tighten security on your Windows 7 computer or LAN. These instructions are for a single Windows 7 computer or a workgroup without a Windows Server. Windows Server offers more powerful and integrated security tools than are available with Windows 7 alone (and happily for you, it's the domain administrator's job to set it all up).

Windows 7's Security Features

Right out of the box, Windows 7 has better security tools built in than any previous version of Windows. If you do nothing else but let these tools do their job, you'll be better off than most people, and certainly far better off than anyone running Windows 98 or XP. These are the built-in security features:

- **User Account Control** —UAC makes sure that programs don't have the ability to change important Windows settings without your giving your approval. This helps prevent virus programs from taking over your computer and disabling your computer's other security features.

- **Protected Mode Internet Explorer**—Internet Explorer is the primary gateway for bad software to get into your computer. You don't even have to deliberately install the bad stuff or go to shady websites to get it—hackers take over well-known, legitimate websites and modify the sites' pages so that just viewing them pulls virus and Trojan horse software into your computer. This risk is so great that Internet Explorer was modified to run with such low privileges that these bad programs can't do any damage.

- **Windows Firewall**—Windows Firewall blocks other computers on the Internet from connecting to your computer.

- **Windows Defender** —Defender is an antispyware program that scans your hard disk and monitors your Internet downloads for certain categories of malicious software. It's not a full antivirus program, but it does help.

These features are all good at their jobs. The best bit of security advice I can give you is this: *Do not disable any of them.* In particular, don't disable UAC. If you find that any of the security features cause some problems with one of your applications, fix the problem *just for that application*, instead of disabling the security feature outright. For example, if you have a program that doesn't work well under UAC, use the Run As Administrator setting on that application's shortcut to let *just that program* bypass UAC.

If you just follow that advice, you'll be in pretty good shape. If you want to ratchet up your defenses another notch or two, read on.

If You Have a Standalone Windows 7 Computer

If you have a standalone system without a LAN, you need to take only a few steps to be sure you're safe when browsing the Internet:

- Enable Macro Virus Protection in your Microsoft Office applications.

- Be sure that Windows Defender is turned on and up-to-date. Or, install a third-party antivirus/antispyware program.

- When you connect to the Internet, be sure to stay connected long enough for Windows Update to download needed updates.

- Be very wary of viruses and Trojan horses in email attachments and downloaded software. Install a virus scan program, and discard unsolicited email with attachments without opening it. If you use Outlook or Windows Mail, you can disable the preview pane that automatically displays email. Several viruses have exploited this open-without-asking feature.

- Keep your system up-to-date with Windows Update, service packs, application software updates, and virus scanner updates. Check for updates every couple weeks, at the very least.

- If you use Microsoft Office or other Microsoft applications, go to the Windows Update web page and select Microsoft Update. This will let Update automatically download updates and security fixes for Office as well as Windows.

 note

Unfortunately, the Windows Automatic Updates pop-up appears only when you are logged in using a Computer Administrator account. Unless you've configured Windows Automatic Updates to alllow all users to install updates, or to automatically install the updates, you need to log on as an administrator at least once every week or two to see if anything new has been downloaded.

- Make the Security Policy changes I suggest later in this chapter under "Tightening Local Security Policy."

- Use strong passwords on each of your accounts, including the Administrator account. For all passwords, use uppercase letters *and* lowercase letters *and* numbers *and* punctuation; don't use your name or other simple words.

- Be absolutely certain that Windows Firewall is enabled on all network and dial-up connections to the Internet.

If You Have a LAN

If your computer is connected to others through a LAN, follow the suggestions from the list in the preceding section. Make the Security Policy changes on *each* computer.

In addition, if you use a wireless network, you *must* use encryption to protect your network. Otherwise, thanks to passwordless file sharing, random people passing by could have the same access to your shared files as you do. Use WPA2 encryption if all of your computers and routers support it; otherwise, see whether you can use WPA. Use WEP only if you have devices that don't support WPA.

Keep Up-to-Date

New bugs in major operating systems and applications software are found every week, and patches and updates are issued almost as frequently. Even Microsoft's own public servers have been taken out by virus software.

Software manufacturers, including Microsoft, have recently become quite forthcoming with information about security risks, bugs, and the like. It wasn't always the case; they mostly figured that if they kept the problems a secret, fewer bad guys would find out about them, so their customers would be better off (and it saved them the embarrassment of admitting the seriousness of their bugs). Information is shared so quickly among the bad guys now that it has become essential for companies to inform users of security problems as soon as a defensive strategy can be devised.

You can subscribe to the Microsoft Email Updates security bulletin service at www.microsoft.com/security. The following are some other places to check out:

> www.sans.org
> www.cert.org
> www.first.org
> www.cerias.purdue.edu/coast
> www.greatcircle.com
> Usenet newsgroups: comp.security.*, comp.risks

Some of these sites point you toward security-related mailing lists. You should subscribe to Microsoft Security Advisor Bulletins at least. Forewarned is forearmed.

Tightening Local Security Policy

You should set your machine's own (local) security policy whether you have a standalone computer or are on a LAN. The Local Security Policy lets Windows enforce some commonsense security rules, such as requiring a password of a certain minimum length or requiring users to change their passwords after a certain number of days.

 note

Local Security Policy settings are not available on Windows 7 Home versions.

If your computer is part of a Windows domain-type network, your Local Security Policy settings will likely be superseded by policies set by your domain administrator, but you should set them anyway so that you're protected if your domain administrator doesn't specify a so-called global policy.

To configure Local Security Policy, log in as a Computer Administrator and choose Start, All Programs, Administrative Tools, Local Security Policy. (If Administrative Tools doesn't appear on the menu, the Administrative Tools Control Panel applet can get you there. You can also customize the Start menu to display Administrative Tools.)

A familiar Explorer view then appears, with several main security policy categories in the left pane, as shown in Figure 32.3. I list several policy items you might want to change.

Figure 32.3
The Local
Policy Editor
lets you
tighten secu-
rity by
restricting
unsafe con-
figuration
options.

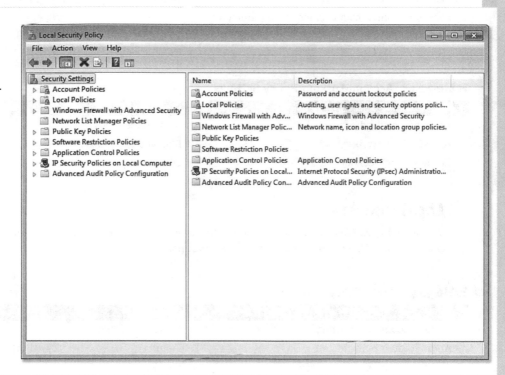

To change the settings, select the policy categories from the left pane and double-click one of the policy names listed in the right pane. A Properties dialog box will appear in which you can change the setting.

You don't need to change all the policies; I list the important ones in the following sections.

Account Policies

Account policies can be used to enforce long, difficult, frequently changed passwords and make it hard for users to recycle the same passwords when forced to change. You should lock out accounts that fail several login attempts, locally or over the LAN. In the Local Security Policy window's left pane, open the list under Account Policy, then select Password Policy or Account Policy to see the available settings. Table 32.3 shows the recommended altered Password Policy settings, and Table 32.4 shows the options at your disposal for locking out an account.

Table 32.3   Password Policy Settings

Password Policy	Local Setting
Enforce password history	10 passwords remembered
Maximum password age	70 days
Minimum password age	1 day
Minimum password length	8 characters
Passwords must meet complexity requirements	Enabled
Store password using reversible encryption	Disabled

Table 32.4   Account Lockout Policy Settings

Account Lockout Policy	Local Setting
Account lockout duration	30 minutes
Account lockout threshold	5 invalid logon attempts
Reset account lockout counter after	30 minutes

Local Policies

You should have Windows make an entry in the Event Log whenever someone oversteps his or her bounds. Table 32.5 shows the recommended audit policy changes.

Table 32.5   Audit Policy Settings

Audit Policy	Local Setting
Audit account logon events	Failure
Audit account management	Failure
Audit directory service access	Failure
Audit logon events	Failure
Audit policy change	Success, Failure
Audit system events	Failure

No changes are necessary in the User Rights assignments section, but you might want to view these entries to see what sorts of permission restrictions Windows uses.

Finally, go through the security options, as listed in Table 32.6. Security options are used to restrict what users can do with system options.

 note

If you're interested in how Windows regulates the operation of your computer, take a look at the settings under User Rights Assignment and Security Options. You'll probably never need to change any of these settings, but these two sections are the heart of Windows' security controls.

Table 32.6 Security Options Settings

Security Option	Local Setting
Interactive logon: Message text for users attempting to log on	You can display a sort of "Posted: No Trespassing" warning with this entry.
Devices: Prevent users from installing printer drivers	Disabled by default. If you want to prevent users from installing potentially untested printer and hardware drivers, check out the options for these settings.
Audit: Shut down system immediately if unable to log security audits	A common hacker trick is to fill up audit logs with junk messages and then break in. If you want, you can have Windows shut down when the Security Event Log fills. The downside is that it makes your security system a denial-of-service risk.

When you log out and back in, the new restrictive security policies will take effect.

Configuring Windows Firewall

The purpose of Windows Firewall is to examine all incoming network data, looking for attempts to connect to your computer. Windows Firewall maintains a list of networking services for which incoming connections should be permitted, within a given range of network addresses. For example, by default, on a private network, Windows Firewall permits file-sharing connections only from computers on the same "subnet" or LAN as your computer. Attempts by users outside your immediate network to contact your computer are rebuffed. This prevents Internet users from examining your shared files. (Outgoing requests, attempts by your computer to connect to others, are not restricted.)

Windows Firewall also monitors application programs and system services that announce their willingness to receive connections through the network. These are compared against a list of authorized programs. If an unexpected program sets itself up to receive incoming network connections, Windows Firewall displays a pop-up message similar to the one shown in Figure 32.4, giving you the opportunity to either prevent the program from receiving any network traffic (Cancel) or add the program to the authorized list (Allow Access). This gives you a chance to prevent "spyware" and Trojan horses from doing their dirty work. Firewall-aware programs such as Windows Messenger automatically instruct Windows Firewall to unblock their data connections.

If you don't recognize the program listed in a Windows Firewall pop-up, click Cancel. This is a break from the way Windows programs usually work: Cancel here doesn't mean "don't do anything now." In this case it actually does make an entry in the firewall's program list, and the entry is set up to block the program.

 note

You might ask, why don't the spyware programs do the same thing? Good question. They will certainly try. However, UAC ensures that unless you give them permission, they won't have the privileges necessary to open up the firewall. Most application setup programs are run with elevated privileges, so they do have the opportunity to configure Windows Firewall as part of the setup process. You will be shown a UAC prompt before such a setup program runs.

Figure 32.4
Windows Firewall displays a pop-up message if an unauthorized program asks to receive network connections.

As I mentioned previously in this chapter, on Windows 7, Windows Firewall has separate settings for each application based on whether your computer is connected to a public or private network. In most cases, it's best to allow a program to receive connections on private networks, but not public. This is certainly the case for file and printer sharing and Windows management functions. The exceptions to this principle would be programs that are meant to work with other Internet users, such as chat or telephony programs.

note

On a corporate network, your network manager might enforce or prevent the use of Windows Firewall, and may restrict your capability to change its settings while your computer is connected to the network.

The remainder of this section discusses the various setup options for Windows Firewall.

Enabling and Disabling Windows Firewall

To configure Windows Firewall, click Start, Control Panel, System and Security, Windows Firewall (or, if you happen to have a Command Prompt window open, just type **start firewall.cpl**). The current settings are listed in the right pane, as shown in Figure 32.5.

In Windows 7, it should not ever be necessary to change the firewall's default settings. However, if you do have to make a change, click one of the left pane tasks, which are described in turn in the followingv sections.

Figure 32.5
Windows
Firewall dis-
plays its cur-
rent status in
the right
pane. To con-
figure it, click
a task in the
left pane.

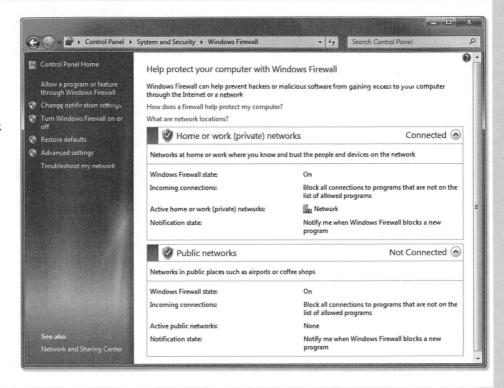

Allow a Program or Feature Through Windows Firewall

If you use a program that has to receive incoming network connections, its setup program should configure Windows Firewall to permit incoming connections; or failing that, the first time you run it you should see a pop-up notification like that shown in Figure 32.4. If you handle that pop-up incorrectly, or want to change the setting, select the Allow a Program or Feature Through Windows Firewall task to bring up the dialog box shown in Figure 32.6. Then, click Change Settings.

To disable a program's connections, find it in the list and uncheck the box to the *left* of its name.

To enable a program's connections, find it in the list and check the box to the left of its name. Then, check either or both of the boxes to the right, to permit it to receive connections through a private network and/or public network.

To make a new entry for a specific program, so that it can receive connections, click Allow Another Program. Then, click Browse and locate the program file (.exe file), and click OK. Click Add, then review the Home/Work (Private) and Public check boxes to make sure that they are set correctly.

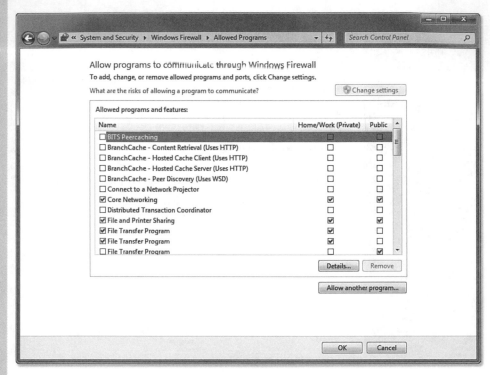

Figure 32.6
The Allowed Programs and Features list lets you list programs and network features (ports) that should be able to receive incoming connections. Here's a feature that's new in Windows 7: Connections can be accepted or blocked based on whether they are received through a private or public network connection.

To open the firewall for a program or service by its network port number, you'll have to use the Advanced Settings task, which is discussed shortly.

Change Notification Settings, Turn Windows Firewall On or Off

Both of these tasks bring up the same screen, shown in Figure 32.7. From there, you can turn Windows Firewall on or off. You can also check a box that blocks *all* incoming connections regardless of any entries in the Allowed Programs and Features list. (This corresponds to the Block All Incoming Connections and Don't Allow Exceptions check boxes in Windows Vista and XP, respectively.) Finally, you can enable or disable the pop-up that occurs when a new program wants to receive incoming connections. If you disable notification, newly discovered programs will be blocked silently.

In previous versions of Windows, it was necessary to disable all firewall exceptions when you brought your computer to a public location, but on Windows 7, as I mentioned previously, this is no longer necessary.

Figure 32.7
The Change
Notification
Settings task
lets you turn
Windows
Firewall on or
off and con-
figure its
pop-up noti-
fication.

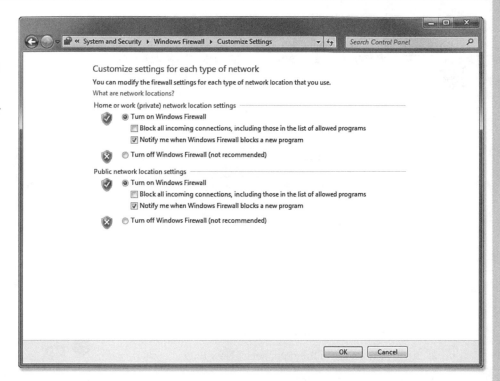

Restore Defaults

This task restores Windows Firewall to its default settings, and clears out any additions you've
made to the Exceptions list. This may cause networking applications such as instant messenger
programs and remote control programs like VNC to stop working until you reinstall them, but it will
re-secure your computer and restore the functioning of standard services like file and print sharing.

Advanced Settings

This task brings up the Windows Firewall with Advanced Security Administrative program, shown
in Figure 32.8. You will need to use this program if you want to open the firewall for a network service based on its port number, because the basic firewall "Allowed Programs and Features" list
does not let you do this on Windows 7. To open an exception for a TCP or UDP network port, follow
these steps:

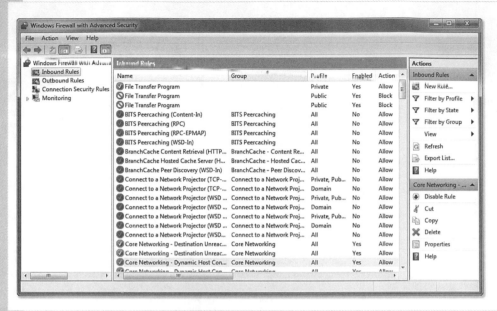

Figure 32.8
The Windows
Firewall with
Advanced
Security pro-
gram lets you
open excep-
tions for a
network ser-
vice based
on a port
number.

1. In the left pane, click Inbound Rules.

2. In the Actions list to the right, select New Rule.

3. Select Port, and click Next.

4. Select TCP or UDP, and select Specific Local Ports. Enter
   the port number or a port number range, then click Next.
   (To open an exception for both TCP and UDP, you must
   enter two separate rules).

5. Select Allow the Connection and click Next.

6. Select the types of networks from which the connection
   should be accepted: Domain (corporate), Private, and/or
   Public. Click Next.

7. Enter a name and description for the network service, and
   click Next.

You can also use this tool to open an exception for a protocol
other than TCP or UDP, and you can filter based on the remote
IP address and port number; I won't describe this other than
to suggest that at step 3, select Custom. It can also provide
outbound connection filtering, but that is out of the scope of
this book and is rarely necessary.

 tip

Are you curious to know what programs
and services on your computer are listening for incoming network connections?
Just follow these convoluted steps:

1. Click Start, and, in the Search box,
   type **cmd**.

2. In the search results, right-click
   cmd.exe and select Run As Administrator. Confirm the UAC prompt.

3. When the command prompt window
   opens, type the command **netstat
   -ab ¦ more**. (This might take quite
   a long time to run.) A list of open
   ports is listed along with the names
   of the programs that are using them.

An even better way to view this information is to download and run the program
at http://live.sysinternals.com/
tcpview.exe.

If you don't recognize a program's name,
use Google to see if it's discussed on any
web pages; this might help you determine whether it's a legitimate Windows
program or some sort of malware.

Windows Live Messenger Can't Send Files

When you attempt to send someone a file using Windows Live Messenger, what actually happens is that the other person's copy of Windows Messenger contacts your computer to pick up the file. If Windows Firewall blocks incoming Windows Messenger data, the other person's copy of Messenger will not be able to retrieve the file. Check the Windows Firewall configuration dialog box to ensure that Windows Live Messenger is listed and that the boxes are checked in both the Home/Work and Public columns.

Also, if you are using a connection-sharing router, enable Universal Plug and Play (UPnP) on the router so that Messenger can tell it how to route incoming file-transfer connections.

More About Security

This chapter just barely scratched the surface of what there is to know and do about network security. Lots of great books have been published on the topic, and I've mentioned several of them in this chapter.

You also can get lots of information on the Web. First, www.sans.org and www.cert.org are great places to start looking into the security community. Steve Gibson has plenty to say about security at www.grc.com—it's educational and entertaining.

Finally, you might look into additional measures you can take to protect your computer and your network. You can configure networks in many ways. For example, it's common to keep public web or email servers separate from the rest of your LAN. For additional security, you even can buy or build special-purpose firewall routers to place between your LAN and the Internet. One nifty way to do this is shown at http://pigtail.net/LRP/index.html.

In any case, I'm glad you're interested enough in security to have read this far in the chapter.

PROTECTING YOURSELF FROM FRAUD AND SPAM

Phishing (Fishing) for Information

At one time, obtaining a free Internet access account was as simple as using a program to generate a fake credit card number and then filling out an AOL application with false information. By the time AOL figured out the credit card number was no good, quite a bit of free online access could be had. This reproachable practice ended when AOL fixed the problem, at which time even more reproachable practices ensued. A perpetrator would use specially designed programs to send a barrage of instant messages to subscribers, posing as an AOL representative, and lure them into providing personal account information. The use of diffuse targets, social engineering, and technology, all used together to steal information, is the essence of phishing.

This particular method of stealing information has become more prevalent in recent years and, by most accounts, is highly successful. Studies done on human susceptibility to specific, concocted phishing scams have varied greatly in results, from as few as 3% to as great as 70% being susceptible. But if even one in a hundred falls prey, the number of potential victims is alarming.

Live Phish: A Real-World Example

The recent vein of phishing email typically claims to come from a pervasive online service such as eBay, a financial institution, or any commercial service you can imagine. The typical example tends to report that some questionable account activity has taken place and require that you click a web link to attend to this matter immediately. Most certainly, this involves divulging personal information, and the criminals hope that, in your haste to rectify the problem, you share enough to be useful. Figure 33.1 shows an example that I found in my inbox recently.

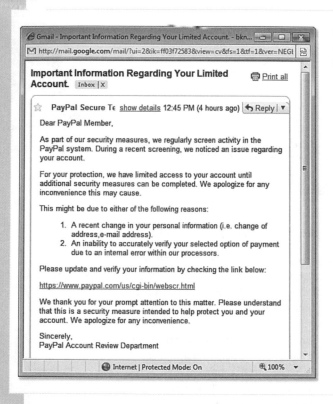

Figure 33.1
Phishing email from...well, it's not really from PayPal.

On the surface, it appears that someone has changed my account without authorization, and PayPal has appropriately sent notification to my email address.

What tips us off that this is a fake? Not much—this is one of the better efforts. It doesn't have the usual obvious misspellings or peculiar language (one of my favorites being "We apologies for any inconvinience this may caused you.") that would never get out the door of a responsible financial corporation. It *is* odd that the email is addressed to just "brian," not my full name, which the real PayPal would know.

The main clues that this email is not really from PayPal lie in the web link. At first glance, the link does appear to be a legitimate PayPal link. But it doesn't matter what *any* blue underlined link says, because the text you see is just an arbitrary description of the underlying actual URL, which is where the link directs you. Before you click a link in any email that

 caution

This fraudulent email is a prime example of a phishing lure, whose aim is to trick you into clicking a web link and divulging your banking password. In other cases, criminals have exploited bugs in web browsers, including Microsoft's Internet Explorer, to create websites that actively push viruses and spyware into visitors' computers. In these cases, just clicking on the email's link causes you damage. So, when you get this sort of email, it's best to check it out before clicking any links, and if it's a fraud, stop before visiting the site.

seems even the least bit suspicious, look to see where the link takes you. There are three ways to find out, but only two can be trusted:

- Hover the mouse over the link, and look in the status bar in the lower-left part of the browser. A URL might be displayed there. However, this text can be easily forged! *Don't trust the status bar display.* Instead,

- Right-click the link and select Properties. If the link is too long to fit in two lines, you might not see it entirely, but if you click and drag over the link, it will scroll to display the entire link. Alternatively,

- Right-click the link, select Copy Shortcut, and paste the copied text into Notepad or Word.

In my sample phishing email, I found that the real link is

`http://203.45.16.221/paypal.ca/us/cgi-bin/webscr.html`

which brings up a big red flag. The use of a numeric address rather than the expected paypal.com name tells us that the computer is most likely a hijacked PC or business server. And notice that the link uses the insecure http: prefix rather than the secure https: that we saw in the original email. So finally, this phishing email has given itself away as a fraud; but some are not so easy to spot. Consider this URL:

`http://www.paypalcom.nz/index.html`

It looks pretty good, but you need to know how to read URLs to know how to spot a fake. Start at the *end* of the domain name and work backward. In this case, the domain name ends with .nz, for New Zealand. PayPal isn't based in New Zealand. The next name working backward is paypalcom, which is all one word, so it's not at all the same thing as paypal.com. It *might* look familiar, but this URL is not related to PayPal, and it's a fraud.

 note

If any of these methods displays something like onclick(); rather than a recognizable URL, the link's target is determined by script programming inside the email, and you can't easily or reliably determine where it leads. In this case, treat the email as very suspicious.

 tip

The commonly recognized site names that end with suffixes such as .com, .org, and .gov should be immediately preceded by the core organization name and immediately followed by a slash (if anything). For example, good URLs include

http://www.mybanksite.com

http://accounts.mybanksite.com/ mainpage.asp

Potential phishing URLs include

http://www.myba.nksite.com/

http://www.mybanksite.com. elsewhere.com/

http://www.mybanksite.com.*xx*/, where *xx* is not your country code

http://202.12.29.20/mybanksite.com/

Although the astute observer might not fall for this particular email, it's highly possible that a bleary-eyed, unsuspecting computer user who has not yet had morning coffee might miss its warning signs. This is where Internet Explorer 8's SmartScreen Filter comes in. Figure 33.2 shows what is presented when the link is clicked.

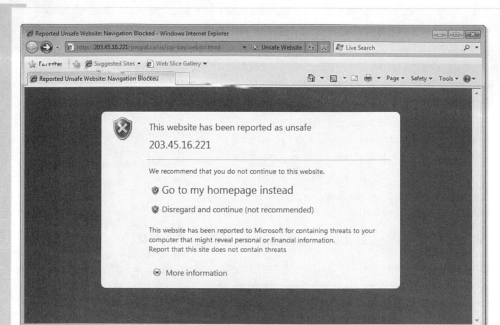

Figure 33.2
The Internet
Explorer
SmartScreen
Filter at
work.

When IE's SmartScreen Filter is enabled, Internet Explorer sends every URL you click to Microsoft for screening against a list of known fraudulent or virus-infested websites. In the case of this phishing email, Internet Explorer 8 has communicated in no uncertain terms that it is a known dangerous site. It provides the option to continue to the web page, if desired, but it explicitly states that clicking the link to proceed is absolutely not recommended.

To use the SmartScreen Filter, click the Safety menu on the IE toolbar, select SmartScreen Filter, and then select Turn On SmartScreen Filter, as shown in Figure 33.3. Be sure that the Turn On SmartScreen Filter button is selected. When the filter is enabled, as I said, every URL you view is sent to Microsoft for checking against a list of known bad sites. This list is built up by feedback from users (and presumably verified by Microsoft staff). In fact, when a site is under investigation, Internet Explorer might prompt you to "vote" on your feeling about the site's safety. And in any case, you can report errors back to Microsoft. If you find that the filter fails to flag a site that you feel is fraudulent, click Safety, SmartScreen Filter, Report Unsafe Website. If it flags a site that you feel is not fraudulent, click the link Report That This Site Does Not Contain Threats in the warning page itself.

 note

Does SmartScreen slow down your web surfing? Not by much, if at all. When you browse to a website, Internet Explorer starts downloading the site's content, and it sends the URL to the SmartScreen servers at the same time. The amount of information sent is very small, and IE continues to download content while SmartScreen is checking. If the response from SmartScreen is delayed, IE may still decide—based on its analysis of the web page content itself—to go ahead and display the page, so you don't have to worry that if Microsoft's servers go down, you'll be stuck.

Figure 33.3
Internet
Explorer's
Safety button
lets you
invoke the
SmartScreen
Filter.

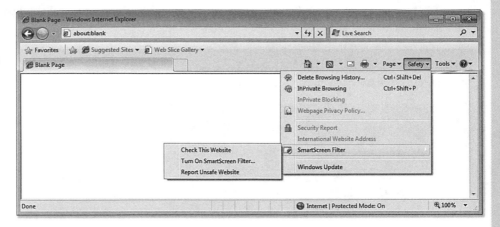

Sacrificing Privacy for Security

If you feel that this feature sounds good but also a little bit creepy, I agree with you. On the one hand, it's nice to have this sort of protection available, because a lot of people just don't have the time to sort out where every email link leads. On the other hand, the filter doesn't just monitor links from fraudulent emails; it communicates data about every web page you visit and every web search you perform. Microsoft states that the information is transmitted in encrypted form and that it has "taken steps to help ensure that no personally identifiable information is retained or used for purposes other than improving online safety"—that is, neither your IP address nor your URLs are archived.

However, in the United States at least, the national security environment is such that (a) it's conceivable that your data could still be captured and scanned by, oh, say, a large government agency with a huge secret budget, and (b) it would be illegal for Microsoft to tell you that this was occurring, if they even knew. Personally, I'll leave SmartScreen Filter turned on. I'm just suggesting that you treat corporate privacy policies as skeptically as you do emails from random banks.

More Help from Internet Explorer

In addition to the SmartScreen Filter, Microsoft has improved a bit upon the venerable Gold Lock. Once stuck discreetly at the bottom of the browser, the new and improved Gold Lock is bigger, better, and more prominently placed right next to the URL it describes. The lock still signifies that the site you are currently browsing is using encryption to protect your session. You can view the site's certificate information by clicking the lock bar (see Figure 33.4), and it will show up against a red background if there is anything odd about the site's certificate. It

 caution

Internet Explorer's SmartScreen Filter tries to make educated guesses about the validity of URLs, but in reality, it's only as good as Microsoft's list of known phishing sites. *Don't rely on it entirely!* Be very skeptical. If you suspect that an email allegedly from one of your financial institutions or organizations is not legitimate, *don't click*. Instead, visit the organization's website directly, by typing its URL yourself, or call your bank and ask if the email is legitimate.

also highlights sites with Extended Validation (previously High Assurance SSL) certificates in green for those sites that have submitted to the more rigorous identification process and paid for the new certificate type.

Green shading indicates greater certainty of the site being legitimate.

Validated name of website owner

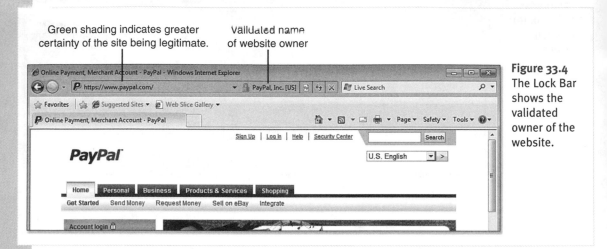

Figure 33.4
The Lock Bar shows the validated owner of the website.

In previous versions of IE, hackers used to be able to hide the true URL being visited in a number of ways, which could mask the fact that you were directed to a suspicious site. Now there will always be a URL bar in every window, so that kind of misdirection will be easier to spot.

Finally, the new browser makes it much easier to clean up your personal information trail. If you were meticulous about cleaning up your personal information before, you had to painstakingly navigate to different areas of Windows to clean temporary Internet files, clear the history, erase autocomplete, delete cookies, and so on. Now, you have two options:

- Click Safety, InPrivate Browsing to start a browsing session where no history or cookies are retained.

- To clean up after the fact, click Tools, Delete Browsing History to clean out information about sites you visited without InPrivate Browsing turned on.

> ### ▲ caution
>
> On the other hand, IE and the web in general now support something that will make bad URLs harder to spot: internationalized domain names (IDNs). Until recently, you had to worry about only your native alphabet or character set in the URL bar, but now you can get international character sets that could look similar to something in your native language yet be a different site entirely. Would you think it was safe to visit http://www.päypal.com? Use a keen eye to watch for accent marks and umlauts!

Use these tools whenever you are using a computer in a public place or are shopping for secret presents.

Two-Way Authentication

Authentication is the process of proving that you are who you claim to be. The frequent use of bogus websites demonstrates the need not only for the users to prove their identity to a site, but also for a site to prove its identity to the users. One way to accomplish this type of two-way authentication is for the user to choose a secret symbol, such as a small picture of a tropical sunset, which is known only between the user and the site. Henceforth, whenever that user visits the site, that tropical sunset picture is displayed alongside the rest of the site information. A malicious site replica will not know which symbol to produce, so even if a user is tricked into visiting one, it will be clear that the site is not authentic. Sounds like an improvement, and it is. Many financial institutions are using this system now, and you may already have seen it in action.

The system works by placing a unique signature on the user's computer. When the customer visits the site and provides a valid account, the site verifies that the computer is the right one. If it is, the picture of the sunset (for example) is displayed along with the password prompt. The customer will recognize the picture, know it's the right site, and type in the password. Nice plan. But what if you are at a computer that you don't usually use? In that case, in addition to your username and password, you have to provide the answer to another security question before the site displays the secret symbol.

Two-Factor Authentication

The most pervasive example of single-factor authentication is having a password to prove that you are who you say you are. Two-factor authentication involves both something you know and something you have. A password or PIN is something you know. Something you have can come in many different forms but is usually either an electronic token of some sort or a biological property, such as your fingerprint or retina, that can be used to identify you. Using two factors to prove who you are is much better than using a password alone because whereas a password can be electronically stolen, obtaining both a password and a unique physical device—or a finger, for that matter—is substantially more difficult.

One challenge with two-factor authentication is that the computer must be capable of validating the "something you have." That usually means extra, specialized hardware. For example, to scan your finger for authentication, the computer must be equipped with a fingerprint reader. To use a special electronic token, you need a piece of equipment that can validate the token. When you consider that some institutions have millions of customers, the cost of extra hardware adds up.

Windows 7 includes built-in support for new and better two-factor security devices such as biometric readers, so hopefully the use of this sort of equipment will increase.

Identity-Management Software

Because no centralized or standard system exists for managing usernames and passwords across different websites, users are forced to improvise solutions for managing their various electronic identities. The most rudimentary solutions to this problem involve using the same or similar usernames and passwords for different sites, using usernames and passwords based on some type of mnemonic system, or even cutting and pasting the information from a Word document.

All these solutions leave much to be desired and become unwieldy as the number of identities increases. Identity is a tricky subject. Just ask any philosopher or information systems architect. The computer industry is still wrestling with this problem. Several solutions are on the table, some of which are relatively simple and direct, and others that attempt to address the system as a whole.

A detailed discussion about the identity problem in the information systems world is way too big for this chapter, but satisfying workarounds available today run independently on Windows 7. Password-management programs keep track of all your various usernames and passwords, and store them in a safe, encrypted format. They often have browser-integrated features that, with your permission, automatically fill in your credentials by site. These programs help circumvent keystroke loggers because there are no keystrokes. If you were ever in the habit of clicking the Remember My Password on This Computer check box at any number of websites, that bad habit can be alleviated by using a password manager. Programs such as Roboform and Login King all provide one-click logons and enable you to use diverse and more complex usernames and passwords because you don't have to remember them. It's nice to know that with so many people focused on making life difficult with malware, innovative and pragmatic software developers are making life on the Web easier.

Fighting Spam

Email users of the world are no doubt nostalgic for a time when Spam was just a tasty pork product. Now it is the scourge of email systems throughout the world, as unsolicited email messages from an ever-increasing number of junk-mail senders congest mail systems and take up space on our computers. Spam is such a problem because, on the scale of subversive electronic activities, it is fairly easy to do, fairly difficult to be caught, and very inexpensive for the sender. Despite ridiculously low response rates, spammers continue to dupe shady advertisers into paying for it.

While the most important cost involved with spam is in human time—time spent reading, deleting, and devising ways to fight it—there's actually a huge environmental cost as well: To filter out the estimated 62 trillion junk emails sent in 2008, computers burned through enough electricity to power 2.4 million homes for the year, leading to 17 million metric tons of CO_2 emissions.

Thankfully, antispam technology continues to get better, and there are several practical things you can do to both make spam less of a nuisance and reduce the risk that it will lead to even more serious problems, such as email-borne viruses or information theft.

To avoid spam, it helps to understand a bit about how you get targeted in the first place. Spammers generally find email addresses by harvesting them from public sources, such as message boards or web pages. They buy them from website operators who aren't above selling email addresses they've collected from visitors, registration pages, or guestbooks. They may distribute virus software that steals email address books from victims' computers. They also use special programs called spambots to methodically crawl the Web for email addresses wherever they might be. Then, because they're not above scamming their own customers, they pad their lists with a huge percentage of email addresses they just make up using common names and domain suffixes. Because little cost or penalty is associated with sending spam to the wrong email address, spammers trade and compile enormous email lists, with many incorrect and probably some legitimate addresses as well. If

 tip

To make it more challenging for spam tools to guess an email address, use uncommon combinations instead of common naming conventions. Although it's less intuitive than john_doe@myemail.com, using initials and meaningful (to you) combinations of numbers, such as jhdo213@myemail.com, makes you a more difficult spam target.

your email address ends up on one of these lists, it will probably stay there, so the best defense is to keep your email address off the list in the first place.

Protect Your Email Address

The best way to avoid getting on spammers' lists is to share your email address only when necessary and only with the trusted few. One of the simplest ways that information is inadvertently shared is bad email etiquette. When a single email is sent to multiple people, it's best to use the Bcc field and keep the names out of the To and Cc lines. The exception to this rule is when you are on a private network, such as a corporate email system, where the email will not generally travel over the Internet unprotected.

Another way to reduce spam is to use multiple email addresses for different purposes. One email address could be a primary address for trusted friends or merchants, and another could be for sites that are less familiar, or for times you need to register with a site for a one-time use. Keeping one address for important communications and another for "junk email" not only is effective at reducing spam, but also can help protect you in other ways. In the phishing example earlier in this chapter, an email arrived from PayPal at my junk email address, yet I knew I had provided PayPal with my trusted email address, so it was a clear red flag. This works even better if you have yet more-specific email addresses for important lines of communication. Free email address services abound. Many of them have good spam-filtering capabilities, so they make good choices for a junk email address.

Better yet, some email systems let you add a suffix to your email address. For example, if my address is brian@myisp.com, I can also use brian+paypal@myisp.com and brian+amazon@myisp.com; in fact, I can use brian+*anything*@myisp.com. If you have such a service, make up a distinct email address every time you register your email address on a website. Then, if one of these appears in a spam list, you can block just that address and never be bothered by it again. (And send a nastygram to the website owner while you're at it.)

Use Spam Filtering

Despite good faith and antispam tactics, an email address *will* eventually receive some spam. Spammers might be innovative, but equally innovative people are at work preventing spam from taking valuable time away from your life. Spam filters analyze email and relegate spam to a "junk mail" folder or the like. They use various methods, including some similar to other antimalware programs, to detect and get rid of spam before it hits your inbox. All online email service providers, such as Yahoo Mail, Gmail, Hotmail, and so on, provide free spam filtering as a matter of their own survival as much as for good customer service.

 note

Here's an unsolicited plug: In my experience, the spam filtering provided by Google's Gmail and the related Google Apps mail service is absolutely amazing, filtering out about 99.98% of the 1,000 or so spams targeted at my email address each day. About 900 of these are refused outright—that is, the Gmail email server recognizes that the email sender is a virus or known spam program, and won't even allow it into my mailbox. Of the remainder, all but about two or three per day are automatically categorized as spam and filed accordingly.

In the past year, only about 30 legitimate emails were incorrectly categorized as spam, and only one was a "personal" email; the rest were legal, bulk mailings from companies that I've done business with. That's an incredible success rate and it's far better than any of the other online email services I use.

Filtering spam at the server level is actually more effective than filtering it in your own computer, because servers will typically receive the same spam email for thousands of customers at once, giving it a higher profile.

Windows Live Mail, a free download that is discussed in Chapter 15, has a built-in junk mail filter itself and some powerful tools for dealing with spam. Most other third-party email programs offer spam filtering as well.

Many aftermarket spam filters also are available as add-on software, where it inserts itself between your email program and the Internet. There are even some plug-in hardware devices that protect from spam at the network level.

Avoid Spammers' Tricks

Spammers have hundreds or maybe thousands of tricks up their grimy sleeves to bypass filters. Still, there are plenty of simple things to do to limit exposure and reduce junk email in its various forms.

Some spammers appear repentantly courteous. That is, they have violated your inbox by being there uninvited, but now that they have your attention, please don't be offended, because you can simply click this link to opt out of receiving any more spam from them. Honest.

Do not reply to spam that claims to provide an "opt out" link. Often, by clicking the link in an attempt to stop receiving spam, you are confirming that your email address is good, and your spam level likely will increase. In fact, it's a good idea to never respond to spam, especially to buy anything. Although it is possible some well-intentioned but ill-advised vendors are using spam to sell legitimate products, all purveyors of spam are suspect simply because of the insidious nature of the communication: unsolicited, unauthorized, unwelcome, and often illegal. Avoid spam like the plague it is. If you suspect an email message is spam, you're probably right. Don't opt out. Don't even open it; just delete it.

Read the terms of use and privacy policies when you register with a website, to make sure they will not sell or share your information. Often at the end of the form are preselected check boxes indicating that you'd love to receive email from them, their sponsors, their affiliates, and so on. Clicking those boxes is considered opting in and permits them to legally bombard you with spam. Many spammers disregard the law anyway, but it's never a good idea to give them carte blanche with your inbox.

The right way for an upstanding website to manage an email list is called "confirmed opt-in," and you've probably used it before. Good citizens of the Internet will not start sending email to you until they have confirmed, by receiving email from your email address, that you actually want it. Without such confirmation, anyone could type your email address into a hundred different Send Me Mail forms, some of which are perhaps distasteful, and every day you'd have an inbox full of junk. This is such an important premise that, in general, if it's not a confirmed opt-in, it might as well be spam.

Junk email can come from the most unlikely sources. Well-intentioned relatives bent on protecting their loved ones from syringes on movie seats, international kidney thieves, or cancer-causing agents in shampoo are responsible for spam that's hard to avoid because, although it might be tempting, you don't want to filter *everything* from them. If you are one of those who likes to be in close contact through email, sharing the trials and tribulations of life with your loved ones by forwarding electronic messages, there is help for you. Instead of forwarding something, consider writing an original heartfelt message to be treasured and appreciated. And if you must forward a tantalizing or tender tidbit, before others spend time reading the message, take a moment to search and make sure it's true. Whatever you do, never send chain mail; it will not bring good luck or take it away, but it will turn you into a spammer.

note

Several Internet sites have evolved to fight electronic chain letters, spam, and especially urban legends that compel so many people to send massive amounts of ultimately groundless email. Snopes.com has emerged as an excellent source to determine whether an email is fact or fiction. Use it often. Your friends and relatives will thank you.

Take Action Against Email Abuse

So far, this chapter has taken the Aikido route to spam and fraud defense: avoidance and being "like water." Among our many techniques, we sidestep dangerous links, make email addresses slippery to spambots, and use identity management software to leave would-be keyloggers with a sieve-fisted find. These are useful defensive techniques, but sometimes a more offensive approach to vanquishing online foes is more effective and satisfying. With enough complaints on file, and if they haven't bought off an unscrupulous service provider, spammers can be identified and their "license to spam" revoked. Once discovered, phishing sites can be quickly put out of business. Many commercial Internet sites provide readily available tools to report suspicious activity. Ebay and PayPal request that you forward suspected fake emails to spoof@ebay.com or spoof@paypal.com, respectively. They will quickly take appropriate action. Responsible sites display security or fraud-related links on the front page, so it's easy to find their preferred mode of communication. If you suspect a phishing scam, take a moment to find the right email address and report it. You may save someone else a lot of heartache, and will validate your own "sleuthiness." If you stumble upon a suspected phishing site with Internet Explorer, you can click Report This Site in the Tools menu to aid other Phishing Filter users.

Reporting spam can be easy, too. Free email services used with a web browser often provide a "report spam" button that can automatically notify the provider to take action. If you prefer to use a separate email program, such as Windows Mail, there are a plethora of add-ons that can help report and eliminate most spam. Some of the most interesting and effective ones use collaborative networks. Like the free email services that have potentially millions of users, these add-ons are based on the premise that humans can filter spam better than any algorithm alone. When a number of users identify a particular message as spam, the other members of the network can be spared the trouble. It's a successful strategy used by companies like Cloudmark, and there are other successful strategies as the field continues to evolve to provide convenient, active ways to fight spam.

On the other hand, there are not-quite-so-convenient yet more active ways for those who desire to "get medieval" on spammers. With a little practice, it's not difficult to track down email headers using publicly available Internet resources. You can often identify the service provider whose network was used to send spam, and they can opt to shut down the spammer's Internet access if enough complaints are received. Additionally, the Federal Trade Commission encourages you to forward spam to spam@uce.gov. The FTC may not respond to individual complaints, but in true democratic fashion, they will tally the votes and go after the worst spammers.

VIII

WINDOWS ON THE MOVE

IN THIS PART

34	Wireless Networking	959
35	Hitting the Road	971
36	Meetings, Conferencing, and Collaboration	999
37	Remote Desktop	1013
38	Tablet PC Features	1029

34

WIRELESS NETWORKING

Wireless Networking in Windows 7

Wireless networks are everywhere. From home to work to just about everywhere on the road, it seems like you can fire up a wireless-capable device and get connected no matter where you are. Wireless networks are popular for several reasons, including low costs to get started and, more important, ease of configuration and use.

With the rapid growth of wireless networking has come evolving standards. The 802.11 series of standards was implemented in wireless hardware and software to ensure interoperability among vendors. However, that hasn't stopped wireless hardware vendors from extending their hardware with proprietary add-ons. One thing is certain: The standards that define wireless networking will continue to evolve. The current state-of-the-art standard 802.11n was an important step forward for wireless performance and reliability, and we're we're sure that network industry gurus are hard at work at whatever's coming next.

Microsoft recognized the popularity of wireless networks among its users. This recognition translates directly into a much improved and enhanced wireless networking experience in Windows 7. Wireless networking is now part of the native networking stack in Windows: Drivers have been updated and improved, and tools such as the Network Diagnostics Framework help in troubleshooting when things go wrong. Microsoft has even taken steps to reduce some of the security problems inherent in wireless networking.

Types of Wireless Networks

Most wireless networks use a wireless router, base station, or access point. These are called *infrastructure networks*; all communications on the network are between the computers and the access point. You can also tie a group of computers together without an access point, and this is called an *ad hoc network*. In this type of network, the computers talk directly to each other. A common scenario for using an ad hoc network is where a group of business people connect together at a conference table in order to share files and information.

This chapter shows you how to use infrastructure networks that have already been set up. We also discuss creating an ad hoc network for quick file sharing between a group of computers at, for example, a meeting.

➡ *For information on setting up a new wireless network for your home or office, **see** "Installing a Wireless Network" on **p. 463**.*

Take Care When You Share

Wireless networking is just another network connection type as far as Windows is concerned, so file and printer sharing is also available. Other wireless users can work with your shared folders, files, and printers, just as if you and they were connected to a wired network. This might be just what you want in your home or office, but at a public location or when using an unsecured, unencrypted wireless network, everyone else who connects to the network, whether you know and trust them or not, might also be able to get to your same shared folders, files, and printers.

To prevent random, unknown people from seeing your shared resources, Windows 7's Network Location feature helps to keep track of the relative safety of various networks to which your computer connects, and enables and disables services based on the type of network. The three predefined location types are domain network, public network, and private network. In more detail, the standard types are as follows:

- **Public network**—A network where other computers and users can't be trusted. The Public network location should be selected for any network link that is directly connected to the Internet without an intervening router or hardware firewall, a network in a café, airport, university or other public location, or a home or office that you are visiting. When you designate a network as a Public network, Windows file and printer sharing is blocked to protect your computer.

- **Home network** or **work network**—A network that is trusted to be secure. If the network has an Internet connection, you know it to be protected by an external firewall or a connection sharing router. You trust the users and the other computers on the network to access files and printers shared by your computer (with or without a password, depending on the Password Protected Sharing setting in

 note

If you need to change the location, just click on the displayed location name displayed in the Network and Sharing Center.

Windows can take up to a couple of minutes to prompt you after you've connected to a new network for the first time. For whatever reason, you can't hurry the process along. During this time, it will treat the network as a public network, and nothing will happen if you click on the location name to try to change it. Just wait for Windows to prompt you.

the Network and Sharing Center window). Examples of Private networks are home or business networks managed by you or someone you trust.

 caution

Be sure to select the appropriate network location when Windows prompts you after you've connected to a new network. If in doubt, select Public. You can always change it to a less restrictive setting later if you find that you can't use the network services you need.

- **Domain network**—A network that is managed by one or more computers running a Windows Server OS. This is a trusted network, and the security of the network and its member computers is managed by network administrators.

The first time you connect to a given network, Windows will prompt you to select the appropriate network location. You can view the current setting through the Network and Sharing Center. On Domain networks, this location is automatically set but it can be changed for other types of networks through the Network and Sharing Center.

Several settings that affect the security of the computer are changed automatically by Windows 7 when you connect to these various types of networks. On Domain networks, Group Policy configures the settings for network discovery and file and printer Sharing alike. When you connect to a Public network, Windows disables network discovery and file and printer sharing.

After connecting, you can change these default settings, but you really should *not* enable file and printer sharing when you're connected to a network that might contain computers that are unknown to you or are not under your control.

Joining a Wireless Network

Windows 7's new "View Available Networks" pop-up list makes connecting to a wireless network easier than ever. This section shows you how to connect to wireless networks in some common—but distinctly different—scenarios.

In the Corporate Environment

Wireless networks in a business setting are frequently configured using automated means. For large enterprises, your computer will be preloaded with a certificate, a sort of digital fingerprint that identifies your computer as being authorized to use the corporate network, and the wireless network will be configured for you. Wireless network clients can now be configured via Group Policy ("Via Group Policy" is short for "By other people, and there's nothing you can do about it") and through the command line by using new netsh commands for wireless adapters.

At Home or the Small Office

A wireless network at home or in a small office usually doesn't have the same configuration needs as in a large enterprise setting, and home users and small offices usually don't have domain controllers and Group Policy infrastructures at their disposal. Wireless network configuration is usually done manually in these environments, first by purchasing and obtaining an access point, then by configuring that access point, and finally by configuring one or more wireless client computers to connect to the wireless network.

When you first plug a Windows-compatible wireless adapter into the computer (or if your computer has an adapter built in), you can begin the process of connecting to a wireless network.

When you are not currently connected to a wireless network, but your wireless adapter can receive signals from one more networks, Windows may pop up a notification box letting you know that a connection is available. Alternatively, you can click the network icon in the taskbar, over near the clock, and Windows will display a list of available wireless networks, as shown in Figure 34.1.

 tip

Always be sure to change the default management password on any access points or routers that you purchase. Even if it means writing the password on a piece of paper and taping it to the bottom of the device, this is still more secure than leaving the default password in place.

Network icon

Figure 34.1
Click the network icon in the taskbar to open the View Available Networks popup window. Then, select the wireless network you wish to use.

To begin the process of connecting, click on a network name, and then click Connect.

If the network is secured, Windows will prompt your for the network's security key or passphrase, which you must obtain from the network's owner. By default, Windows will display the letters and/or numbers you enter so that you can see that you're typing them correctly. If you're concerned that someone might be peeking over your shoulder, check Hide Characters. Click OK, and the connection will be completed.

Windows will save the settings you entered for this network as a *profile*, which will let you reconnect to this network the next time you start Windows at the same site. You can change these settings, as described later in this chapter under "Managing Wireless Network Connections."

Windows Is Unable to Find Any Networks

If you are using a laptop and the list of available wireless networks is empty, check to see whether your laptop has an on/off switch for the wireless adapter (this is put there to let you save battery power when you're not using the network). Be sure the switch is turned on, and then click the Refresh icon in the upper-right corner of the View Available Networks pop-up window. This usually solves the problem!

Also, be sure the wireless network adapter is enabled in software. Click the network icon in the taskbar, select Open Network and Sharing Center, Change Adapter Settings, and see if the wireless network connection icon is labeled "Disabled." If so, right-click it and select Enable.

If that's not it, there is a chance that your computer isn't within range of any wireless access point. I've been in hotel rooms where the wireless signal is almost nonexistent in one room but excellent in a nearby room. Radio interference is just one of the causes of weak or no signal when connecting to a wireless network. Unfortunately, there is little that can be done about this problem aside from moving closer to the access point or, in the case of interference, removing the source of the interference.

➡ *Once you're connected, you can configure file and printer sharing from the Network and Sharing Center. For more information on sharing files and folders,* **see** *"Sharing Resources,"* **p. 561.**

In Someone Else's Office

When you're away from home or the home office, you might find yourself connecting to another person's wireless network. A common scenario is where you visit someone's office and need to access files on their network, or people on that network need to access files on your computer.

When connecting to a someone else's network, it's important to make sure that you're not inadvertently sharing files and folders that you don't want to share. Refer to Chapter 20 for additional information on sharing files safely. You should be sure that your network location is set correctly to protect your computer from being explored by other users:

1. Click the network icon in the taskbar, and then select Open Network and Sharing Center.

2. Note the network location type, which is displayed under the name of the network in the View Your Active Networks section. Click the location name to change it. Your options are as follows:

   ■ If the people at the new network won't need to access files that are located on your computer, set your network location to Public so that Windows disables file sharing entirely. You can still access shared files on their computers.

■ If you need to let others use files or printers shared by your computer, select the Work location. If you want to require others to have an account on your computer in order to access files you're sharing, be sure Password Protected Sharing is enabled: Click Change Advanced Sharing Settings, scroll down, and select Turn On Password Protected Sharing.

At a Public Hot Spot

Public wireless network hot spots (also called WiFi hot spots) are quite helpful when you're on the road and need to check email, get travel information, or just surf the Web. But public hot spots can also be places for would-be attackers to find easy victims.

One path for attack at a public hot spot is through files that client computers accidentally share. Be sure that the network location on your computer is set to Public, which will disable file sharing:

1. Click the network icon in the taskbar and select Open Network and Sharing Center.

2. Note the network location type, which is displayed under the name of the network in the View Your Active Networks section. If it doesn't say Public, click the location name and select Public.

On open, unsecured public hot spots, it's quite common to have eavesdroppers listening to other people's wireless traffic. Even if the network is secured with encryption, it's possible for an eavesdropper to listen to traffic by using software to break the encryption scheme—it can take them mere minutes to break WEP encryption, for example.

So, at a public location, you should be *very* careful when you use websites that display sensitive information or that require you to enter a password. It's best if the website uses the https: URL prefix, so that even if someone was eavesdropping on the network they couldn't see your passwords or data.

 tip

On a public wireless network, it's best to avoid using an email program that uses the POP or SMTP server protocols, and to avoid using FTP (File Transfer Protocol) with a username and password, unless you are certain that the client programs use an encrypted connection.

 ### Unable to Connect to Wireless Network

Sometimes, when you attempt to connect to a wireless network, you are not asked to enter a key, or the connection never completes.

For several reasons, you might not be able to connect to a wireless network even though Windows says that the network is otherwise in range and available. With anything from poor signal strength, an incorrectly typed encryption key, to problems with the wireless access point or DHCP server, the range of problems that can arise when connecting to a wireless network seems limitless.

The View Available Networks list that pops up when you click the taskbar's network icon indicates signal strength next to each wireless network, as a series of green bars. If all or most of the bars are gray, the signal might be too weak at your location to use.

Continued...

In the case of an incorrect security key, Windows won't be able to connect, and it won't be entirely sure why it can't. If you are establishing a connection to the network for the first time, a dialog box will report the vague diagnosis "possible security key mismatch." The thing to do if this happens is to try again until you're sure that you're entering the key correctly.

On a previously successful, established connection profile, you won't see a dialog box, but instead the connection's status will be reported as "limited access" (meaning, really, no access at all, but Windows is hanging on to some sort of unwarranted optimism). The network's owner may have changed the security key. To fix this, right-click the icon in the list of available connections, select Properties, check Show Characters, and correct the security type, encryption type, and security key.

Ad Hoc Networks and Meetings

Earlier in the chapter, I discussed joining a wireless infrastructure network, where computers with wireless adapters communicate with each other, and possibly also with wired networks and the Internet, through a base station called an access point or a wireless router.

Another use of wireless networking, called ad hoc networking, involves two or more computers with wireless connections that can communicate directly with each other without an access point or router.

You can set up an ad hoc wireless network between two or more Windows computers so that you can share files without requiring any additional hardware. This can be handy at a meeting, in a conference room, at home, or when working with a client—anywhere that you want to connect computers to share files and printers.

One computer needs to "create" the network. Then, any others can join it using the standard connection process described in the previous section "Joining a Wireless Network." To create an ad hoc network on Windows 7, follow these steps:

1. Click the network icon in the taskbar and select Open Network and Sharing Center.

2. Click Set Up a New Connection or Network, scroll down and select Set Up a Wireless Ad Hoc (Computer-to-Computer) Network, and then click Next twice.

3. Choose and type in a name for your new network. This name will appear in the list of available connections on other computers.

4. Select a security type. If *all* the computers that need to join the network support WPA2 (Windows 7, Vista, and XP SP3 certainly do), select WPA2-Personal; otherwise select WEP, or if you want no security at all, select No Authentication. (However, because you're almost surely setting up this network to share files, using no security means *anyone* could connect and possibly see the shared files—it's dangerous!)

5. If you selected WPA2 or WEP, enter a security key. For comments about selecting a key, see "Longer Is Better" on page 466.

6. If you might want to reconstruct this network again, at a future meeting perhaps, or if want to you use this as your permanent office or home network, check Save This Network. Finally, click Next.

7. When the setup wizard has finished, click Close. The network will start functioning once other users locate it and connect to it.

To connect to this new ad hoc network, other users can have their OS display a list of available networks and locate the one you created; or, if you elected to save the network profile in step 6, you can give them the setup profile using a removable USB (flash) drive, described shortly under "Copying Wireless Profiles to Other Computers."

To terminate an ad hoc network, click the taskbar's network icon, select the ad hoc network, and click Disconnect.

Managing Wireless Network Connections

If you travel and connect to different networks, you will soon collect a list of several preferred (preconfigured) networks.

When Windows is not currently connected to any wireless network, Windows scans through this list of preferred networks in order and automatically connects to the first one that is in range. In most cases, you will only be within range of one of the networks you want to use, and this system will work without any adjustments. Windows will automatically connect to a network that you have previously selected, and will ignore any other networks that are in range.

Changing Wireless Settings

If you have to change the security information for an existing wireless connection, find the connection's name using one of these methods:

- Click the network icon. If the connection is in range, it will appear in the list of available connections.

- If the wireless network is not listed, click Open Network and Sharing Center, Manage Wireless Networks. The network should be listed here.

Right-click the network name and select Properties. You can change the security type and security key in the Properties dialog box.

Switching Between Wireless Networks

If you are in an area that has several wireless networks to choose from, you may notice that Windows always connects to *your* network and doesn't bother you with the others (unless yours goes offline for some reason). The reason is that once you successfully connect to a new network,

Windows remembers the network's details as a "profile," which is a collection of settings for a given network. By default, Windows searches this list of wireless profiles and automatically connects to the first one that it finds is available. This lets you move from place to place, while Windows automatically connects to whatever network is appropriate.

However, if you find that your computer is in range of more than one of the networks you actually use, you may have to manually instruct Windows as to which one you wish to use, because given a 50/50 chance of picking the wrong one, 9 times out of 10 it will.

To deal with this, you can manually switch networks: View the list of available networks by clicking the network icon in the taskbar. Click on the active network and click Disconnect. Click on the desired network and click Connect.

This will take care of things until you leave the area and then return. If you want to make the network preference permanent, you need to prioritize your wireless connections as described in the following section.

Prioritizing Wireless Network Connections

If you routinely work in an area where your computer can receive signals from several networks that you actually use, you can tell Windows which one to use in preference to the others.

To prioritize your wireless network profiles, follow these steps:

1. Click the network icon in the taskbar and click Open the Network and Sharing Center.

2. Select Manage Wireless Networks, to see the window shown in Figure 34.2.

Figure 34.2
Manage Wireless Networks lets you prioritize, rename, delete, reconfigure, or copy wireless network profiles.

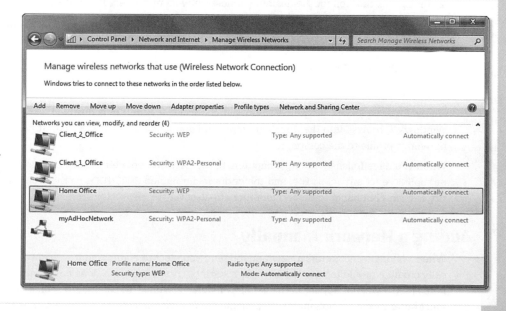

3. Right-click a wireless network that you prefer to use when other listed networks are also available. Then, select Move Up. Repeat this until the entry is above the entries for other networks that are available in the same location.

By default, Windows will "stick" with one connection until it goes out of range. If you have a preferred network that you want to use whenever it becomes available, even if another network is connected, prioritize that network higher than the others. Then, for each of the others in turn, right-click the network profile, select Properties, and check Connect to a More Preferred Network if Available. If you have networks that you use occasionally but do not wish to use automatically, right-click the network profile, select Properties, and uncheck Connect Automatically when This Network Is in Range.

 tip

The names shown in the list of network profiles are the networks' SSID names by default, but you can change the names to something more meaningful to you. A network might have the SSID "evelyn," for example, but "Home Wireless" might be more informative. To rename a network profile, right-click its entry and select Rename. The taskbar network icon's View Available Networks list will display the new name, too.

Copying Wireless Profiles to Other Computers

If you have created a regular or ad hoc wireless network profile on your computer, you can easily copy the profile to other computers so that they can access the wireless network without anyone having to type in the security key again. To copy a wireless profile, follow these steps:

1. Click the network icon in the taskbar, click Open the Network and Sharing Center, and then click Manage Wireless Networks.

2. Right-click the icon for the desired wireless network and select Properties.

3. Click Copy This Network Profile to a USB Flash Drive. Insert a USB drive and Windows will copy a program named setupSNK.exe and some supporting files to the drive.

4. When the wizard has finished, remove the USB drive.

Now, you can take this drive and insert it in other Windows 7, Vista, or XP computers. If AutoRun is enabled, the setupSNK program will run automatically. If AutoRun is disabled, as it is by default on Windows 7, browse into the drive's contents and double-click setupSNK.exe. It will add the ad hoc network's profile to the computer.

When you have finished adding computers to the network, delete from the USB drive setupSNK.exe, autorun.inf, and the entire folder named SMRTNTKY, so that your network's security key isn't left hanging around for others to discover.

Adding a Network Manually

When Windows encounters a new network and you elect to connect to it, Windows will automatically create a profile to save the network's settings. A network that does not broadcast its network name (SSID) will not appear in the list of available networks. To connect to such a network, you must enter its connection information manually. You can also create a profile manually in advance of first encountering a network. To create a new profile, follow these steps:

1. Click the network icon in the taskbar and click Open Network and Sharing Center.

2. Select Set Up a New Connection or Network, and then select Manually Connect to a Wireless Network.

3. Enter the network's name (SSID), set the security type, and enter the key, if required.

4. For a network that broadcast its SSID (a network whose name will appear automatically in the available network list), you can check Start This Connection Automatically.

   For a network that does not broadcast its SSID (a choice the network's owner made in a futile attempt to hide his network from hackers), Windows may display the network in the list of available connections *if* it overhears the network in action. This might or might not happen. So, for such a network, check Connect Even If the Network Is Not Broadcasting. This network will now always appear in the list of (potentially) available connections. You should *not* also check Start This Connection Automatically. If you do, *your* computer will frequently broadcast the name of the network it's looking for, which makes you vulnerable to being tricked.

5. Click Next, and then click Close to save the new profile.

To later connect to a network with a hidden SSID, open the list of available networks, click the name of the "hidden" network, and click Connect.

Deleting Network Profiles

To remove wireless network profiles—to unclutter the list after traveling or so that Windows will not automatically connect to them in the future—follow these steps:

1. Click the network icon in the taskbar and click Open Network and Sharing Center.

2. Click Manage Wireless Networks.

3. Select an unwanted profile, and click Remove.

HITTING THE ROAD

Windows Unplugged: Mobile and Remote Computing

Some people predict that some day, a global Internet will cover every inch of Earth's surface, giving us an always-on, always-available stream of data they call the "Evernet." We're not quite there yet, but today the Internet is available in pretty much any city you might visit, and it has become easy to stay in touch with home while you're traveling.

Windows 7 supports you when you're away from home or the office with some pretty spiffy portability and networking features, including these features that are covered in other chapters:

- Wireless networking support lets Windows 7 stay connected when you're on the go. This was covered in Chapter 34, "Wireless Networking."

- Windows 7 makes it easier to use a portable or laptop computer to make business or school presentations. Presentations are covered in Chapter 36, "Meetings, Conferencing, and Collaboration."

- Windows 7 has a nifty Remote Desktop feature that lets you use your own computer from somewhere else, over the Internet. This is covered in Chapter 37, "Remote Desktop."

This chapter covers several other Windows 7 features, which are mostly related to mobile (portable, laptop, notebook, or tablet) computers:

- For laptops, the Windows Mobility Center puts a bunch of important settings in one window so you can manage your computer's display, power consumption, and networking features.

- Dial-up and VPN networking let you access a remote network when you're traveling, and you can even set up remote access to your own home or office network.

- The Offline Files feature lets you automatically keep up-to-date personal copies of files that are stored on network folders, so you really can "take it with you."

Let's start with the Mobility Center.

Managing Mobile Computers

Mobile computers (which I also call laptops, notebooks, or portables) are no longer an expensive perk provided only to jet-setting executives. They're now standard equipment for most people who work at least part time out of their office, and consumers now buy more portable computers than desktops for home and personal use. Consequently, portables have become powerful and inexpensive, and support for their special needs by Windows has grown considerably.

Windows Mobility Center

If you have a mobile computer (that is, a notebook, portable, tablet, or laptop computer), you'll find that Windows 7 provides a tool called Windows Mobility Center and a special control panel that desktop computers don't have. To open the Mobility Center, shown in Figure 35.1, click Start, All Programs, Accessories, Windows Mobility Center.

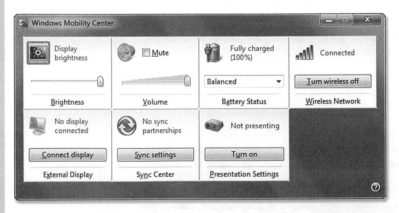

Figure 35.1
Windows Mobility Center is found in the Accessories menu.

The Mobility Center is designed to bring together in one window most of the settings that you'll want to change while using your computer remotely. The settings pertain mostly to power management, so you can make your laptop's battery last as long as possible, and display management, because many people use their laptops to make business and school presentations. Your computer's Mobility Center may display some or all of the following controls:

 tip

You can bring up the Mobility Center by pressing Windows+X. If you use the Mobility Center a lot, you can open it, right-click its icon in the taskbar, and select Pin This Program to Taskbar so that it is easily accessible.

- **Brightness**—The slider lets you increase or decrease your screen's backlight brightness. A lower setting should make your computer run longer on its battery charge. Windows remembers separate brightness settings for battery and AC-powered operation, stores them as part of a power profile, and resets the brightness when the power status changes. You can fine-tune the setting with this control.

- **Volume**—The slider controls your computer's speaker volume and the Mute check box lets you instantly shut the sound off. This may be useful, for example, if you're in a meeting and someone keeps sending you noisy IM pop-ups.

- **Battery Status**—The icon shows you whether you are running on AC or battery-only power. (The power plug in the icon shown in Figure 35.1 indicates that the computer is on AC power.) The battery icon and the text tell you the battery's charge level. The drop-down list lets you select a power profile. Power profiles let you choose a balance between lower power consumption and greater performance. We'll discuss power profiles in more detail in the next section, "Getting the Most Out of Your Battery."

- **Wireless Network**—The icon shows whether you have an active wireless network connection, and the button can enable or disable your computer's wireless adapter to conserve power or gain privacy. If your laptop has a physical switch that turns the wireless adapter on and off, it's likely that both the switch and this setting have to be turned on for the wireless adapter to work.

- **Screen Rotation**—On tablet PCs, this control lets you switch the display between portrait (taller than wide) and landscape (wider than tall) orientation. Generally, in portrait orientation it's easier to read documents, and in landscape it's easier to watch movies.

- **External Display**—When an external display monitor or projector has been connected to your computer's external display connector, this control lets you choose to turn the external display off, have the display mirror what's on your laptop's screen, or treat the display as an extension of your built-in display desktop space. This lets you control what attendees see when you're making a presentation. We'll discuss External Display in more detail in Chapter 36.

- **Sync Center**—The Sync Center is used to copy files to or from an external device like a Windows Mobile handheld device, or to update copies of network server files that you've obtained using the Offline Files feature. We'll discuss Sync Center later in this chapter, under "Offline Files."

- **Presentation Settings**—When you turn Presentation Settings on, Windows suppresses some behaviors that could disrupt your presentation. We'll discuss Presentation Settings in Chapter 36.

 note

Your computer manufacturer may have added additional controls not listed here.

In addition, the Hardware and Sound Control Panel window has some sections that are especially helpful to know about if you have a mobile PC. Some of the settings you might want to remember are as follows:

- **Power Options**—Lets you select a power profile. We'll discuss this in the next section.

- **Change What the Power Buttons Do** (under Power Options)—Lets you choose whether the computer shuts down or goes into Sleep, Hybrid Sleep, or Hibernate mode when you press your portable computer's power button or close its lid while it's running. We'll discuss this in the next section, too.

- **Adjust Settings Before Giving a Presentation**—Lets you specify types of interruptions that you want to prevent during presentations. This will be discussed in more detail in Chapter 36.

Getting the Most Out of Your Battery

The central processor unit (CPU) chip and graphical processor unit (GPU) chip can be the two biggest energy guzzlers in a computer, but in most cases, they spend little of their time actually working. For example, as I type this chapter, my computer's CPU takes less than a millisecond to react to each keystroke and update the display. The CPU and display processor might be occupied with useful work much less than 0.1% of the time. Laptop processors take advantage of the relatively long lulls by slowing their processing speed or *clock speed* way down between bursts of activity, and this significantly reduces power consumption.

Additionally, laptops can conserve energy by dimming the backlight lamp that illuminates the display, and by turning off hardware devices like the disk drive, DVD or CD drive, network adapter, and modem when they are not actively being used—even the devices' interface electronics can be shut down.

Of course, when you're watching a movie (which requires a lot of processor effort to decode the DVD's data into millions of pixels per second) or performing heavy-duty calculations, power consumption can go way up.

On Windows 7, you can adjust how Windows manages hardware power consumption, and how fast the processor is allowed to run, by creating power profiles, which are collections of settings that can be applied in different situations. Out of the box, Windows 7 enables you to choose between three profiles:

- **Balanced**—Select this profile to strike a fair balance between power savings and performance. You'll still get full processing power when it's needed.

- **Power Saver**—Select this profile when you want to extend the battery life as long as possible, even if it noticeably slows the processor and eliminates some graphical effects.

- **High Performance**— Select this profile when you want maximum speed even when your computer is running on battery power. (This option might be hidden until you click the arrow next to Show Additional Plans.)

To view the power profiles, click Start, Control Panel, Hardware and Sound, Power Options. This will display the Select a Power Plan screen, which lets you select the profile you want to use at any given time.

 note

If you have a scenario that's begging for its own profile, you can add a new one to this list. To do so, view the Power Options control panel and click Create a Power Plan in the left pane.

To select what settings are put into effect by each profile, click the phrase Change Plan Settings next to a profile name. This displays the window shown in Figure 35.2. Here, you can select how long Windows should wait before darkening the screen and putting the computer to sleep when idle, under AC power, and battery power. You can use the slider at the bottom to adjust the screen brightness for battery-powered operation.

If you rarely stop while you are actually working, but tend to leave for a while when you do stop, you might gain additional battery life by reducing the time before turning off the display or shutting down when on battery power. Dimming the display can help, too, if you're not working outdoors.

To really change the speed versus power compromise, click Change Advanced Power Settings to get the dialog box shown in Figure 35.3. Here, you can change quite a number of power-related delays and rates. Each setting has two values: one to use when on AC power, and another to use when on battery power. Start by clicking Change Settings That Are Currently Unavailable to gain access to the entire list of settings.

Figure 35.2
On the Edit Plan Settings page, you can adjust various power-saving timers.

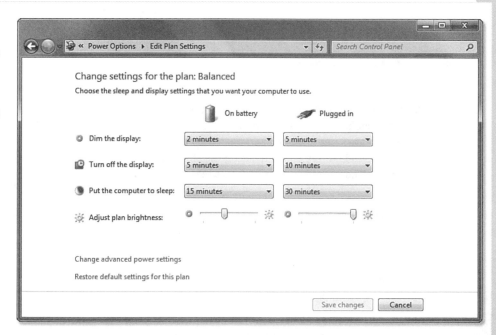

If you really do love tweaking, you might want to look at some of the more interesting advanced settings:

- **Hard Disk**—Set the time that the disk is allowed to spin after being used. The default time on battery is 3 minutes. If your usage pattern usually spins the disk right back up just after it shuts down, you might increase this time.

- **Wireless Adapter Settings**—You can choose any of four settings, from Maximum Performance to Maximum Power Saving (and presumably slower and less reliable data transfer). If your wireless access point is nearby, Maximum Power Saving might help extend battery life.

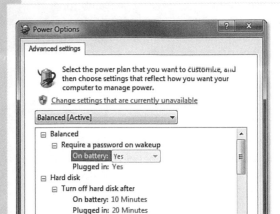

Figure 35.3
The Power Options Advanced Settings dialog box lets you adjust power management settings for a large number of specific devices.

- **Sleep**—Hybrid Sleep is a mode in which Windows will wake the computer up after a certain time in Sleep mode (the Hibernate After time) and perform a full hibernate. You can extend battery life by reducing the Hibernate After time. The trade-off is that Windows takes longer to start up after hibernating.

- **Processor Power Management**—You can set the lowest and highest processor states (speeds), in terms of % of maximum speed. Setting a low minimum speed increases battery life without costing much in performance. Reducing the maximum speed helps battery life but also takes a bite out of performance.

- **Multimedia Settings**—If you use Windows Media Sharing, this setting can prevent Windows from going to sleep while it's sharing media. Sleep cuts off your remote players.

- **Battery**—You can select the battery percentage levels at which Windows takes action to warn you about power loss or shutdown, and what actions to take at low and critically low power levels. You should not select Sleep as the Critical Battery Action, because Windows might not be able to keep system RAM alive when the battery level falls even further.

 note

When Hybrid Sleep is enabled (the default setting), the shutdown options on the Start menu and in the Change What the Power Buttons Do control panel applet list Sleep as a choice but not Hibernate, because hibernating is automatic in this case. If you want to manually control when Windows sleeps and when it hibernates, you must disable Hybrid Sleep. Then, the Start menu's shutdown button and the power button setup applet will offer Hibernate as an option. If you disable Hybrid Sleep, you must remember to manually shut down or hibernate your computer if you're not going to be using it for an extended time.

VPN and Dial-Up Networking

Windows can connect to a remote Windows network via a modem or via a protected connection that's routed through the Internet called a virtual private network (VPN). Using these services, all file sharing, printing, and directory services are available just as if you were directly connected (albeit much slower in some cases). Just connect, open shared folders, transfer files, and use email as if you were "there," and then disconnect when you're finished.

The receiving end of a VPN or a Dial-Up Networking connection is usually handled by the Remote Access Services (RAS) provided by Windows Server or third-party remote connection devices manufactured by networking companies such as Cisco and Lucent. But Windows 7 (as well as Vista and XP Professional) comes with a stripped-down version of RAS so you can set up your own Windows computer to receive a single incoming modem or VPN connection. You can use this, for example, to get access to your office computer and LAN from home, provided that your company's security policies permit this.

You learn how to allow incoming connections later in the chapter.

Virtual Private Networking

Most of us are familiar with using a modem to connect a computer to the Internet. Establishing a dial-up networking or VPN connection is no different; the remote network is just a bit smaller than the Internet.

Virtual private networking deserves a bit more explanation. In a nutshell, a VPN lets you connect to a remote network in a secure way. A VPN creates what is effectively a *tunnel* between your computer and a remote network, a tunnel that can pass data freely and securely through potentially hostile intermediate territory like the Internet. Authorized data is encapsulated in special packets that are passed through your computer's firewall and the remote network's firewall, and is inspected by a VPN server before being released to the protected network.

Figure 35.4 illustrates the concept, showing a VPN connection between a computer out on the Internet and a server on a protected network. The computer sends data (1) through a VPN connection that encapsulates it (2) and transmits it over the Internet (3). A firewall (4) passes VPN packets but blocks all others. The VPN server verifies the authenticity of the data, extracts it (5), and transmits the original packet (6) on to the desired remote server. The encapsulation process allows for encryption of your data, and allows "private" IP addresses to be used as the endpoints of the network connection.

VPN connections work like dial-up connections. After you have an Internet connection established (via modem or a dedicated service), Windows establishes the link between your computer and a VPN server on the remote network. After it's connected, in effect, you are a part of the distant LAN. The connection won't be as fast as a direct LAN connection, but a VPN can be very useful for copying files and securely accessing Remote Desktop connections.

 note

Several companies manufacture VPN software and hardware solutions, some of which are faster and provide better management tools than Microsoft's VPN system. If your organization uses a VPN product purchased from a company such as Juniper Networks or Cisco Systems, you'll have to follow their instructions for installing and using their VPN software.

Windows Server and Windows 7 come with VPN software built in. In the next section, I describe how to use Microsoft's VPN system.

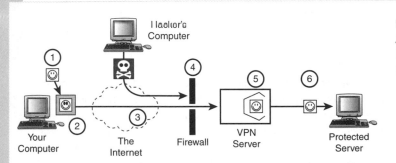

Figure 35.4
A virtual private network encapsulates and encrypts data that is passed over the Internet.

Setting Up a VPN or Dial-Up Networking Connection

To create a VPN or dial-up connection to a remote network or computer, you need a working Internet connection or modem, respectively. You learned how to install both of these in Chapter 13, "Getting Connected," so if you haven't done so already, start there to install and configure your modem and Internet connection.

You also must get or confirm the information shown in Table 35.1 from the remote network's or computer's manager.

Table 35.1   Information Needed for a VPN or RAS Dial-Up Connection

Information	Reason
For Dial-Up	
Telephone number	You must know the receiving modem's telephone number, including area code.
Modem compatibility	You must confirm that your modem is compatible with the modems used by the remote network; check which modem protocols are supported (V.90, V.32, and so on).
For VPN	
VPN server	You need either the hostname or IP address of the remote VPN server computer.
For Either	
Protocols in use	The remote network must support TCP/IP. Windows 7 does not support networking with the IPX/SPX or NetBEUI protocol.
TCP/IP configuration	You should confirm that the Remote Access Server assigns TCP/IP information automatically (dynamically) via DHCP. Usually, the answer is yes.
Mail servers	You might need to obtain the IP addresses or names of SMTP, POP, Exchange, Lotus Notes, or Microsoft Mail servers if you want to use these applications while connected to the remote network.
User ID and password	You must be ready to supply a username and password to the remote server. If you're calling into a Windows workstation or server, use the same Windows username and password you use on that remote network.

Armed with this information, you're ready to create a connection to the remote network. To do so, follow these steps:

1. Click Start, Control Panel, Network and Internet, Network and Sharing Center. Alternatively, click the network icon in the taskbar (near the time of day), and select Open Network and Sharing Center.

2. Under Change Your Networking Setting, select Set Up a New Connection or Network.

3. Select Connect to a Workplace and click Next.

4. Select No, Create a New Connection and click Next.

5. For a VPN connection, select Use My Internet Connection (VPN). For a dial-up connection, select Dial Directly.

6. If you are setting up a VPN connection, enter the hostname or the IP address of the remote VPN server.

   If you are setting up a dial-up connection, enter the telephone number of the remote computer, including area code, in the appropriate format. For telephone numbers in the North American Numbering Plan, the format is (###) ###-####, where # represents a digit. Then click Dialing Rules to double-check that your current location and area code are set correctly. Change it if necessary, and click OK.

7. Change the Destination Name from "Dial-up Connection" or "VPN Connection" to something meaningful to you, such as "Dial-up office network" or "VPN to Big Client."

8. If you want to make the connection available to other users of your computer, check Allow Other People to Use This Connection. If your network uses Smart Card authentication (your network administrator will tell you so), check Use a Smart Card. You will usually not need to check either of these.

9. Check Don't Connect Now; Just Set It Up So I Can Use It Later. Then click Next.

10. Enter the username and password that you use when logging on to the remote computer, or use the name and password assigned by your network administrator. If this is a Windows domain logon, enter the domain name in the Domain (Optional) field. You can check Show Characters if you want to be sure that you typed the password correctly.

    If you want to have Windows remember the password so that you can connect without having to type it every time, check Remember This Password. However, if earlier you checked Allow Other People to Use This Connection, this

 tip

Windows 7 makes it easy to establish network connections. As I just mentioned, you can open the Network Connections pop-up from the Network and Sharing Center. But you can also bring it up these ways:

- Click the network icon in the taskbar. This is the easiest way.

- You customize your Start menu to display the Connect To selection. Then, click Start, Connect To.

would let others connect using your network credentials, so think carefully whether you want to allow that.

11. Click Create, then click Close.

Now, in the Network and Sharing Center window, click Connect to A Network. This opens the Network Connections pop-up window. There should now be an entry for the new connection. Before you use it, you should view and check its properties settings, as described in the next section.

Setting a VPN or Dial-Up Connection's Properties

To edit the properties of a VPN or dial-up connection, open the Network Connections pop-up window as discussed in the preceding paragraph, right-click a connection, and select Properties.

A connection's properties dialog has five tabs and a heap o' parameters. Most of the time, the default settings will work correctly, but you might need to change some of them. I've listed the most important parameters in Table 35.2.

 note

In most cases, the remote network will be a corporate network, so the connection's Network Location should be Work. This was set when you used the Connect to a Workplace option to create the connection; the Connect to the Internet option makes a Public network connection. You shouldn't need to change this setting, but if you do, oddly enough, you can't change it until *after* you've established the connection. If you need to change the network location to Home (so that you can use a homegroup) or Public (to disable file sharing), establish the connection, then open the Network and Sharing Center. Click on the word Work under the established connection, then select a different location.

Table 35.2   Important Dial-Up Connection Properties

Tab	Property	Description
General (VPN)	Host Name or IP Address	Contact information for the VPN server.
	Dial Another Connection First	Check this box and select a dial-up or PPPoE connection if you need to establish an Internet connection before attempting the VPN connection.
General (Dial-up)	Area Code, Phone Number, Country/Region Code	Set the appropriate dialing information here. If the remote server has more than one phone number (or more than one hunt group), you can click Alternates to specify alternate telephone numbers.
	Use Dialing Rules	Check to have Windows determine when to dial prefixes and area codes. If you want to use this, enter the area code and phone number in their separate fields. This feature is useful if you will be calling the same number from several locations with different dialing properties.

Table 35.2 Continued

Tab	Property	Description
Options	Prompt for Name and Password	Check to have Windows allow you to change previously stored credentials.
	Use Windows Logon Domain	Check if you are connecting to a Windows Server computer.
	Redialing Options	You can change these settings to change how Windows deals with busy signals and dropped connections, and what to do if you leave the connection unused for a long time.
Security		Your network administrator may instruct you to change these settings; otherwise the default settings should work. Be sure to leave Data Encryption set to Require Encryption.
	Automatically Use My Windows Logon Name and Password	Check this box if your Windows 7 account uses the same logon name and password (and domain, if you are on a domain network) that you need to enter on the remote network, *and* if you want to let connections be made without your having to reenter your password.
Networking		Usually, all protocols and services should be checked except File and Printer Sharing, which should be disabled so remote network users cannot use your computer's shared folders and printers. If you really do want to let the remote network's users see your shares, check File and Printer Sharing.
	Internet Protocol Version 4 (TCP/IP)	Normally, a Remote Access Server automatically assigns your connection the proper IP and DNS addresses. In the very unlikely event that the network administrator tells you that you must set TCP/IP parameters yourself, select Internet Protocol Version 4 (TCP/IP) from the Components list, and click Properties. Enter the required IP address and DNS addresses there.

Gateway Settings

If you are connecting to small network that has only one subnet (a range of network addresses), and if you want to browse the Internet while you're also using the dial-up or VPN connection, you can change the connection's gateway setting so that Windows won't route connections to Internet hosts through the VPN or dial-up connection—this will speed up web browsing considerably. To change the gateway setting

1. Open the Network and Sharing Center. Click Change Adapter Settings. Right-click the VPN or dial-up connection and select Properties.

2. Select the Networking tab, select Internet Protocol Version 4, and choose Properties. Then click the Advanced button.

3. Uncheck Use Default Gateway on Remote Network.

You can make this change on more complex networks as well, but you'll have to add routing information so that Windows knows which network addresses must be reached through the VPN connection and which are reached directly on the Internet. I explain how to make routing entries later in the chapter under "Advanced Routing for Remote Networks."

After you've finished making any needed changes to the connection's options, click OK. You can now double-click the icon to start the connection process. Or, just click the connection's name in the View Network Connections pop-up window.

VPN Connection Fails Without Certificate

If you receive the message "Unable to negotiate the encryption you requested without a certificate" when you attempt to make a VPN connection, you are trying to connect to a VPN server with a higher level of encryption than your computer or the other computer is configured to carry out. Contact your network administrator to get the appropriate certificate installed.

Managing Dial-Up Connections from Multiple Locations

As you've seen already, Windows lets you enter your current telephone area code and dialing prefix requirements so that when you're making modem calls, Windows uses the customs and prefixes appropriate for your local phone system. This capability is great if you use a portable computer. For example, at home, you might be in area code 415. At the office, you might be in area code 707 and have to dial 9 to get an outside telephone line. When you're visiting Indianapolis, you're in area code 317 and might need to use a telephone company calling card when making long-distance calls.

Windows offers great support for these variations by letting you define "locations," each with a separate local area code and dialing rules. As long as you've told Windows your current location, it will automatically apply the correct set of rules when making a dial-up connection.

 tip

Set up and test the first access number you need. Then when you need to add a new access number, use this trick to copy the original connection's settings: View the Network and Sharing Center, select Change Adapter Settings, right-click the original dial-up connection icon, and select Create Copy. Rename the new icon, and change its telephone number. I name my icons based on the location of the local number: Office-Berkeley, Office-Seattle, and so on.

When you travel and want to make a dial-up connection, select the appropriate dial-up icon and set your current Dialing Rules location before you click Dial.

➥ *For instructions on establishing locations and dialing rules,* **see** *"Adjusting Dial-Up Connection Properties,"* **p. 340.**

However, if you use an ISP with access points in various cities, or your company has different access numbers in various regions, you'll find that this "locations" system does not let you associate a different dial-up number with each location. It would be great if it did, but no such luck.

If you use different "local" dial-up numbers for the various locations you visit with your computer, set up a separate Network Connections icon for each access number and use the appropriate icon when making a connection at each location.

Establishing a VPN or Dial-Up Connection

Making a remote network dial-up or VPN connection is no more difficult than connecting to the Internet.

Check Your Current Location

If you're making a dial-up connection and you've changed area codes or phone systems since the last time you made a modem connection, check your location setting by following these steps before dialing into the network:

1. Open the Control Panel and type the word **modem** in the Search box. Then click Set Up Dialing Rules.

2. Check your current location in the list of configured dialing locations on the Dialing Rules tab.

3. Click OK to close the dialog box.

Windows should now use the correct area code and dialing prefixes.

Make the Connection

To connect to a remote network, follow these steps:

1. Click the network icon in your taskbar, or, alternatively, click Start, Control Panel, Network and Internet, Connect to a Network. Then, click on the name of the connection you wish to establish, and click Connect.

2. Windows will open the View Network Connections popup box, as shown in Figure 35.5. Enter your login name, password, and Windows domain name (if appropriate). You can also select Properties to adjust the connection's telephone number or dialing properties. The Dialing From choice appears only if you checked Use Dialing Rules and have defined more than one dialing location.

 tip

If you travel, you'll find that having your Internet Options set to dial a particular connection automatically is not a great idea. It would dial the chosen connection no matter where you were (and remember, if there's a 50-50 chance of things going wrong, 9 times out of 10 they will). So, if you travel with your computer, you might want to open Internet Explorer and click Tools, Internet Options. Select the Connections tab and choose Never Dial a Connection. This way, you won't be blindsided by an inadvertent call to Indiana while you're in India.

Figure 35.5
In the View Network Connections popup box, enter your user-name and password for the remote network.

3. Click Connect or Dial. Windows shows you the progress of your connection as it dials or contacts the remote server through the Internet, verifies your username and password, and registers your computer on the remote network.

If the connection fails, unless you dialed the wrong number, you'll most likely get a reasonable explanation: The password or account name was invalid, the remote system is not accepting calls, and so on. If you entered an incorrect username or password, you are usually given two more chances to reenter the information before the other end hangs up on you.

 tip

If you're connecting to a remote Windows Server domain, if the Domain box doesn't appear, enter **domain\username** or **username@domain** in the User Name field.

If the connection completes successfully, and you hover your mouse over the taskbar's network icon, a small balloon will appear showing the active network connection. If you click on the network icon, you'll see the dial-up or VPN connection in the list of active connections. To disconnect, just click the name, then click Disconnect.

You can now use the remote network's resources, as discussed next.

VPN Connection Fails with Error Number 720 or 629

If you are trying to make a VPN connection to a computer you set up to receive incoming connections, and the connection fails with error 720 or 629, most likely the computer that you are using to establish the connection has an active LAN connection in the same network address range as the computer to which you're connecting—even though the networks aren't physically attached. It's just an unfortunate coincidence. You must fix this at the VPN host computer. Right-click the Incoming Connections icon and select Properties. Select the Networking tab, highlight Internet Protocol Version 4, and select Properties. Uncheck Allow Callers to Access My Local Area Network, and check Select IP Addresses. Set the From value to **192.168.111.2** and the To value to **192.168.111.20**.

Using Remote Network Resources

When you're connected, you can use network resources exactly as if you were on the network. The Network folder, shared folders, and network printers all function as if you were directly connected.

The following are some tips for effective remote networking by modem:

- Don't try to run application software that is installed on the remote network itself. Starting it could take quite a long time! (However, if you have previously connected directly to the network, and the Offline Files system is in use, you might have a cached copy of the application on your hard disk. Your network manager will set this up for you if it's a reasonable thing to use.)

- If you get disconnected while using a remote network, it's annoying to have to stop what you're doing and reconnect. You can tell Windows to automatically reconnect if you're disconnected while you're working. To do this, open the View Network Connections popup by clicking on the taskbar network icon. Right-click the dial-up connection and select Properties. Select the Options tab, and check Redial If Line Is Dropped. Then click OK.

- You can place shortcuts to network folders on your desktop or in other folders for quick access.

- If the remote LAN has Internet access, you should be able to browse the Internet while you're connected to the LAN. You don't need to disconnect and switch to your ISP. You might need to make a change in your personal email program, though, as noted in the next section.

 tip

If you get disconnected while you are editing a document that was originally stored on the remote network, I suggest that you immediately use Save As to save it on your local hard disk the moment you notice that the connection has been disrupted. Then, when the connection is reestablished, save it back to its original location. This will help you avoid losing your work.

Email and Network Connections

If you use your computer with remote LANs as well as the Internet, or if you use different ISPs in different situations, you might need to be careful with the email programs you use. Most email programs don't make it easy for you to associate different mail servers with different connections.

Although most email servers allow you to *retrieve* your mail from anywhere on the Internet, most are very picky about whom they let *send* email. Generally, to use an SMTP server to send mail out, you must be using a computer whose IP address is known by the server as belonging to its network. You can usually send mail out only through the server that serves your current connection.

See if your favorite email program can configure separate "identities," each with associated incoming and outgoing servers. If you send mail, be sure you're using the identity that's set up to use the outgoing (SMTP) server that belongs to your current ISP, VPN, or dial-up connection.

Monitoring and Ending a VPN or Dial-Up Connection

To check the status of a dial-up or VPN connection, click the network icon in the taskbar, right-click the connection name, and select Status. This will display a dialog box showing the number of bytes sent and received.

To end a connection, click the network icon in the taskbar, click the connection name, then click Disconnect. Poof! It's gone.

Advanced Routing for Remote Networks

As I discussed previously, if you use dial-up or Virtual Private Networking to connect to a remote network with more than one subnet, you usually must let Windows set the default gateway to be the remote network. Otherwise Windows won't know which network hosts must be reached through the VPN or dial-up connection and which can be reached through your Internet connection. Unfortunately, all your Internet traffic will travel through the tunnel, too, slowing you down. The remote network might not even permit outgoing Internet access.

The alternative is to disable the use of the default gateway (as described previously under "Gateway Settings"), and then manually add routes to all subnets known to belong to the private network. To make these changes, you have to work in a Command Prompt window with elevated privileges: click Start, All Programs, Accessories. Right-click Command Prompt and select Run As Administrator. Then confirm the UAC prompt.

To add information about remote network subnets, use the *route* command, which looks like this:

route add *subnet* **mask** *netmask gateway*

The *subnet* and *netmask* arguments are the addresses for additional networks that can be reached through the gateway address *gateway*. To add a route, you must know the IP address and mask information for each remote subnet and your gateway address on the VPN.

You must get the subnet information from the network administrator on the remote end. You can find the gateway address from your own computer. Connect to the remote VPN and type **ipconfig** in the Command Prompt window. One of the connections printed should be labeled PPP Adapter,

SSTP Adapter, or L2TP Adapter. Note the gateway IP address listed. This address can be used as the gateway address to send packets destined for all subnets on the remote network.

Suppose you're connecting to a dial-up networking host through a connection named Client Net and you find these connection addresses:

```
PPP adapter Client Net:
    IP Address. . . . . . . 192.168.5.226
    Subnet Mask . . . . . . 255.255.255.255
    Default Gateway . . . . 192.168.5.226
```

Now suppose you know that there are two other subnets on the remote network: 192.168.10.0 mask 255.255.255.0 and 192.168.15.0 mask 255.255.255.0. You can reach these two networks by typing two route commands:

```
route add 192.168.10.0 mask 255.255.255.0 192.168.5.226
route add 192.168.15.0 mask 255.255.255.0 192.168.5.226
```

Each route command ends with the IP address of the remote gateway address (it's called the *next hop*).

Check your work by typing **route print** and looking at its output. In the IPv4 Route Table section, you should see only one destination labeled 0.0.0.0; if you see two, you forgot to disable the use of the default gateway on the remote network. Verify that the two routes you added are shown.

To avoid having to type all this every time, you can use another neat trick. You can put a rasphone command and route commands in a batch file, like this:

```
@echo off
rasphone -d "Client Net "
route add 192.168.10.0 mask 255.255.255.0 192.168.005.225
route add 192.168.15.0 mask 255.255.255.0 192.168.005.225
```

The rasphone command pops up the connection dialer. When the connection is made, the two routes will be added, and you're all set. With this setup, you'll need the network administrator to give you the real RAS gateway address of the remote VPN server to use as the "next hop" of the route commands. With a shortcut to this batch file, you can connect and set up the routes with just a click.

When you disconnect the VPN connection, Windows removes the added routes automatically.

Incoming VPN and Dial-Up Access

Windows 7 has a stripped-down Remote Access Server (RAS) built in, and you can use it to connect to your computer by modem, or through the Internet, from another location using any computer running Windows 7, Vista, XP, or 2000. After you're connected, you can access your computer's shared files and printers just as you can on your home or office network. This incoming dial-up and VPN feature is available even on the

 note

Setting up your computer to receive Microsoft VPN connections is fairly complex, as you can see from the following instructions. If you want to make VPN connections to your own computer, you might want to check out Hamachi, an alternative "zero configuration" VPN system, available at www.logmeinhamachi.com.

Home versions of Windows 7. To use this feature, your computer must have a modem and/or a dedicated, always-on Internet connection. At most, one remote user can connect at a time.

Setting up a modem to receive calls is straightforward: Just connect your modem to a phone line, and you can dial in from anywhere. Setting up an incoming Internet (VPN) connection is substantially more difficult because you need an always-on Internet connection, whose external IP address you know and can reach from the Internet at large. We talk about ways to establish an Internet hostname using static addressing or dynamic DNS providers in Chapter 37, so I won't repeat that discussion here. Besides a discoverable IP address, you will also have to configure your Internet router or Windows Internet Connection sharing service to forward VPN data through the firewall to the computer that you're going to set up to receive VPN connections. We'll discuss this in more detail shortly, under "Enabling Incoming VPN Connections with NAT."

The process for enabling VPN access is the same as for enabling dial-in access. Let's walk through that process now.

Setting Up VPN and Dial-Up Access

To enable VPN or dial-up access, follow these steps:

1. Open the Network and Sharing Center, and then click Change Adapter Settings.

2. If the standard menu bar (File, Edit, View, Tools, Advanced, Help) isn't displayed, press and release the Alt key. Then click File, New Incoming Connection, and confirm the UAC prompt.

3. Select the user accounts that will be permitted to access your computer remotely. This step is very important: Check only the names of those users to whom you really want and need to give access. The fewer accounts you enable, the less likely that someone might accidentally break into your computer.

4. After selecting users, click Next. Then select the means that you will use for remote access. Check Through the Internet to enable incoming VPN connections, and/or

note

Windows Firewall doesn't have to be told to permit incoming VPN connections, because it knows to let them in.

caution

Permitting remote access opens up security risks. Before you enable incoming access on a computer at work, be sure that your company permits it. In some companies, you could be fired for violating the security policies.

note

The Add Someone button lets you create a username and password so that someone can connect remotely but not log on directly at the computer. The user will only be able to use network resources available to Everyone. You can only delete such an account using the Computer Management Local Users and Groups tool.

caution

Under no circumstances should you enable Guest, HomeGroupUser$, IIS_USR, or a name that looks like IUSR_*xxx*, or IWAM_*xxx* for remote access. Check only the names of users who need access and who have good (long, complex) passwords.

Through a Dial-Up Modem to enable dial-up access. If you enable dial-up access, you must also select the modem that is to be used. Then click Next.

5. Windows displays a list of network protocols and services that will be made available to the dial-up connection. Select the Internet Protocol Version 4 (TCP/IP) entry, and click Properties. Uncheck Allow Callers to Access My Local Area Network, and then click OK.

6. Make sure that Internet Protocol Version 4 (TCP/IP) is checked and that Internet Protocol Version 6 (TCP/IP) is unchecked. Then click Allow Access. When the final window appears, click Close.

When the incoming connection information has been entered, a new Incoming Connection icon appears in your Network Connections window.

When someone connects to your computer, a second icon appears in the Network Connections folder showing their username, as shown in Figure 35.6. If necessary you can right-click this to disconnect them.

note

If you enable dial-up access, the selected modem will answer all incoming calls on its telephone line.

note

Incoming connections could also be set up to allow remote computers to access other computers on your network, but this requires expertise in TCP/IP addressing and routing issues that are beyond the scope of this book.

Figure 35.6
Incoming connections can be monitored in the Network Connections window.

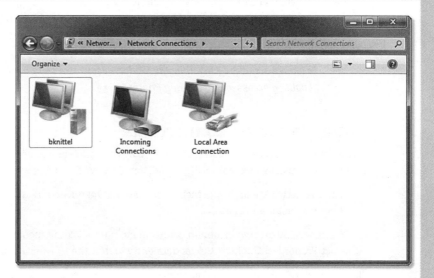

Enabling Incoming VPN Connections with NAT

Microsoft's Internet Connection Sharing (ICS) and DSL/cable sharing routers use an IP-addressing trick called Network Address Translation (NAT) to serve an entire LAN with only one public IP address. Thus incoming connections, as from a VPN client to a VPN host, have to be directed to a single host computer on the internal network.

If you use a shared Internet connection, only one computer can be designated as the recipient of incoming VPN connections. If you use Microsoft's ICS, that one computer should be the one sharing its connection. It will receive and properly handle VPN requests.

If you use a hardware sharing router, the VPN server can be any computer you want to designate. Your router must be set up to forward the following packet types to the designated computer:

> TCP port 1723
> GRE (protocol 47. This is not the same as port 47!)

Unfortunately, many inexpensive commercial DSL/cable connection sharing routers don't have a way to explicitly forward GRE packets. There are several ways around this:

- Some routers know about Microsoft's Point-to-Point Tunneling Protocol (PPTP) and you can specify the computer that is to receive incoming VPN connections.

- If you enable Universal Plug and Play (UPnP) on your router, Windows can tell the router to forward incoming VPN connections. UPnP is discussed in Chapter 19, "Connecting Your Network to the Internet."

- If neither of these options is available, you may designate the VPN computer as a DMZ host so that it receives *all* unrecognized incoming packets. This is relatively dangerous, however.

 caution

If you designate a computer as a DMZ host, that computer can be vulnerable to hacker attacks. You *must* enable Windows Firewall on this computer's network connection, and you *must* designate its network location as Public. You must also configure your router to block Microsoft File Sharing packets, at the very least. Set up filtering to block TCP and UDP ports 137 through 139 and port 445.

➡ *To learn more about forwarding network requests on a shared Internet connection,* **see** *"Enabling Access with a Sharing Router,"* **p. 537.**

Disabling Incoming Connections

To disable incoming dial-up connections so that your modem will not answer the phone whenever it rings, or to disable incoming VPN connections, follow these steps:

1. Click the network icon in the taskbar and select Open Network and Sharing Center. Then, click Change Adapter Settings.

2. To temporarily disable incoming connections, right-click the Incoming Connections icon and select Properties. Uncheck the modem entry and/or the VPN entry, and click OK.

3. To completely disable incoming connections, right-click the Incoming Connections icon and select Delete.

Offline Files

You might recognize the "Offline" problem: If you have a portable computer that you sometimes use with your office network, and sometimes use out in the field, you probably make copies of important "online" documents—documents stored on the network server—on your laptop. But, if you make changes to one of your "offline" copies, the network's copy will be out of date. Likewise, if someone updates the original on the network, your copy will be out of date. And, trying to remember where the originals came from and who has the most recent version of a given file is a painful job. I admit that more than once I've accidentally overwritten a file I'd worked on with an older copy, or worse, overwritten somebody's work, because I wasn't paying attention to the files' date and time stamps.

Windows 7 has a solution to this housekeeping problem: Offline Files and the Sync Center. Here's the skinny: When you use a network folder and tell Windows to make it available for offline use, Windows stashes away a copy (*caches*) the folder's files somewhere on your hard drive, but all you see is the original network folder on your screen. When you disconnect, the shared file folder remains on your screen, with its files intact. You can still add, delete, and edit the files. Meanwhile, network users can do the same with the original copies. When you reconnect later, Windows will set everything right again thanks to a program called the Sync Center.

 note

Offline Files are available only on Windows 7 Professional, Enterprise, and Ultimate editions. The Sync Center is present on Windows 7 Home versions, though, because it can also work with handheld devices such as PDAs and cell phones. If your version of Windows 7 doesn't support Offline Files (or even if it does), you should know about Microsoft's Sync Toy tool, which is a free program you can download from Microsoft.com (search for `Synctoy`; you want version 2.0 or later). Sync Toy can do a pretty good job of copying new and updated files back and forth between a network location and a folder on your portable computer. It's not quite as seamless as Offline Files, but it can do just as good a job.

You'll find that the Offline Files system really works and is more powerful than it seems at first glance. The following are some of the potential applications:

- Maintaining an up-to-date copy of a set of shared files on both a server (or desktop computer) and a remote or portable computer. If you keep a project's files in an offline file, Windows keeps the copies up-to-date on all your computers.

- "Pushing" application software or data from a network to a portable computer. If software or data is kept in an offline file, your portable computer can update itself whenever you connect or dock to the LAN.

- Automatically backing up important files from your computer to an alternative location. Your computer can connect to a dial-up or network computer on a timer and refresh your offline files and folders automatically.

It's very easy to make folders available offline, as you'll see in the next section.

Identifying Files and Folders for Offline Use

You can mark specific files, subfolders, or even entire shared folders from a "remote" server for offline use.

While you're connected to the remote network, view the desired items in Windows Explorer. If you've mapped a drive letter to the shared folder, you can select the mapped drive under Computer as well.

When you find the mapped drive, file, folder, or folders you want to use while offline, select it (or them), right-click, and select Always Available Offline. Be cautious about marking entire shared drives or folders available offline, though, unless you're sure how much data they contain, and you're sure you want it all. You could end up with gigabytes of stuff you don't need.

 note

The server I'm talking about might be in the next room, which isn't very "remote" at all, but that's what I'll call it for simplicity's sake. In this section, a "remote" server refers to some other computer that you access via networking.

 note

Before you mark a folder for offline use, check to make sure that you don't have any of its files open in Word, Excel, or so on. Open files can't be copied.

Can't Make File Available Offline

If Always Available Offline isn't displayed as an option when you right-click a file or folder, several things could be wrong. You must be using Windows 7 Professional, Enterprise, or Ultimate edition—the Home versions don't have it. Also, the option isn't available on network locations you've added to the Network list in Windows Explorer. To make an entire shared folder available offline, view the computer's entry under Network and right-click the folder there, or map a drive letter to the shared folder and right-click the drive letter.

The feature might also be disabled. To check, click Start, All Programs, Accessories, Sync Center. Click Manage Offline Files, and view the General tab. If there is a button labeled Enable Offline Files, click it. Another cause could be that your network manager might have disabled Offline Files via group policy—in this case you're out of luck.

Files of This Type Cannot Be Made Available Offline

If you mark files or folders for offline use, you might receive the error Files of This Type Cannot Be Made Available Offline. Some file types (for example, Microsoft Access MDB database files) usually should not be available offline because such files usually are used by multiple LAN users simultaneously, and there's no way to reconcile changes made by offline and online users. Your network manager might have designated one or more files as being unavailable for offline for this reason. Ask your network manager to check Group Policy entry Computer Configuration\Administrative Templates\Network\Offline Files\Files not cached.

The first time you mark a file or folder for offline use, Windows copies it, and all its contents, from the network location to a hidden folder on your hard drive. This may take a while if there is a lot to copy or if your network connection is slow. If any files cannot be copied, you can click the Sync Center link to see their names and the reasons for the problem.

When the file, folder, or folders have been copied, you will be able to use the network folders whether you're connected to the network or not.

Using Files While Offline

When you've marked a file, folder, or mapped network drive as Always Available Offline, a small green Sync Center icon appears on each folder and file icon to show that it's been marked as available, as shown in Figure 35.7.

 note

The most common reason a file can't be copied is that it is open and in use by an application. If this is the case for any of your files, close the application and perform another sync, as discussed later in this section. Another common problem is that `thumbs.db`, a hidden file Windows creates in folders that contain pictures, is sometimes in use by Windows Explorer and can't be copied. You can ignore problems with `thumbs.db`— right-click the file's name in the Sync Results window and select Ignore.

caution

If the files that you're copying from your network contain sensitive information, you may want to ask Windows to encrypt the copies stored on your computer. To see how to do this, skip ahead to "Managing and Encrypting Offline Files" later in this chapter.

Figure 35.7
When a folder or network drive is Always Available Offline, a Sync Center icon is displayed on each icon.

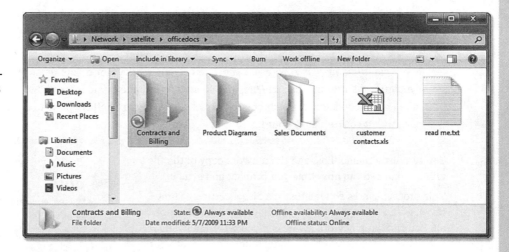

Notice that when you select the item, two new buttons are displayed in the Explorer window:

- **Sync**—Click this button after you've been disconnected from the network and have reconnected. This will reconcile any changes you have made to your copy of the files and changes others made to the originals on the network.

- **Work Offline**—You can click this button to disconnect this shared folder from the network (other network connections remain intact), so that you can make changes to files locally, without actually changing the network copies, and later sync them to the network.

Now, if you disconnect from the network or use the Work Offline button, offline files and folders will remain in the Explorer display.

While offline, you can add new files, delete files, or edit files in a folder that you marked Always Available Offline. If you had mapped a drive letter to the network folder, the drive letter still functions.

 tip

If your network or VPN connection is unreliable, you may find that your applications sometimes hang when you're trying to save your work to a network folder. If this happens to you frequently, the Work Offline button is your new best friend. With it you can *force* Windows to use a local, cached copy of a document while you edit it, then sync it back up after you've saved your changes. Here's how to do it: Locate a network folder in Windows Explorer. Mark it Make Available Offline. Open the folder, and click the Work Offline button. Edit the file(s) you need to edit, then click Work Online. This should run the Sync Center, and copy your changes back to the network.

 note

Folders and/or files that were not marked Always Available Offline will disappear from the display when you disconnect from the network.

Offline Files Are Missing

If you can't find files or folders you know you clearly marked for offline use, you might not have synchronized after marking the file, its folder, or a containing folder for offline use. The solution is to go back online and synchronize. Then check the Sync Conflicts page to see if Windows says that it couldn't copy your file for some reason.

You can also rename files, and the network copy of the file will be renamed the next time you connect and sync up.

This process works so well that it's disconcerting at first because the effect is... well, because there is no effect at all. You can happily work away as if you were really still connected to the network. The only difference is that your changes won't be visible to others on the network until you reconnect.

 note

In most cases, you cannot rename folders while offline.

On some corporate networks, you should be able to rename "redirected" folders if your network administrator has enabled this feature. In general, though, it's best not to try to rename an offline folder while you're offline.

When you do reconnect, you should synchronize your offline files and folders with the network folders so that both sets will be up to date.

Sync Center

You can synchronize files anytime you are connected to the network that contains the original shared folder, whether you connect by LAN, modem, or VPN. You can start a synchronization in any of several ways:

> **⚠ caution**
>
> If you delete a file from a network folder, while you are either offline or online, it will be deleted from your computer immediately and permanently. Deleted network files are *not* saved in the Recycle Bin.

- Click Start, All Programs, Accessories, Sync Center. Then click Sync All.

- Right-click a specific shared file or folder and select Sync.

- Click the Sync button in Windows Explorer.

- If you have a portable computer, click the Sync button in the Windows Mobility Center window.

Synchronization can also occur automatically

- When you reconnect to the network and Windows is idle.

- When you click Work Online in the folder view.

- When you log on and off.

- At specified times and days of the week. For a scheduled synchronization, Windows can even automatically make a dial-up connection.

The Sync Center has the job of reconciling changes made to the online and offline copies of the files.

Reconciling Changes

The Sync Center will automatically copy new or changed files from your computer to the network, and vice versa. However, three situations exist in which it will need some help:

- If both you and another user have changed the same file, you'll have to pick which version to keep.

- If you deleted a file while you were disconnected, you'll have to decide if you want to also delete the network's copy.

- If a network user deleted a file while you were disconnected, you'll have to confirm that you want to delete your copy.

If any problems occur while syncing files, the Sync Center icon in the notification area on your taskbar will display a yellow warning triangle. Double-click the Sync Center icon to display the Sync Center, then click View Sync Conflicts in the tasks list. This displays the Conflicts page, as shown in Figure 35.8.

Double-click the first listed file. This displays an explanation of why Sync Center can't update the file, and you see a selection of choices to resolve the issue. For example, if both you and a network user modified the same file while you were disconnected, the dialog box will look like the one shown in Figure 35.9.

Continue through the conflict list to resolve each problem.

 caution

If the sync process fails because a file is in use, you should repeat the synchronization when no one is editing files in the shared folder; otherwise, you might lose changes to some files.

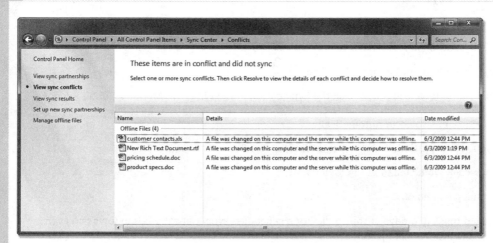

Figure 35.8
The Sync Conflicts page lists files that cannot be reconciled without help.

Figure 35.9
When two users have modified the same file, you can choose to keep one or both versions. The selected version(s) will be copied to your computer and the network.

Managing and Encrypting Offline Files

To manage the Offline Files feature, open the Sync Center with Start, All Programs, Accessories, Sync Center. In the left pane, click Manage Offline Files. The following are tabs on this dialog box:

- **General**—Here you can enable or disable the Offline Files feature entirely. You can also see a list of all files that have been copied to your hard disk for offline use.

- **Disk Usage**—This tab lets you monitor or limit the amount of disk space used by offline file copies.

- **Encryption**—Here you can select to encrypt the network files that are stored on your hard disk. This makes them safe from theft should your computer fall into the wrong hands.

- **Network**—If Windows detects that you have a slow (dial-up, for instance) network connection, Windows can automatically elect to work with offline copies and will sync them up periodically while you continue to work.

Finally, remember that you can uncheck Make Available Offline on a file or folder anytime to remove it from the cached file list. This will delete the cached copies of the files in that folder.

Making Your Shared Folders Available for Offline Use by Others

When you've marked a network file for offline use, Windows makes a copy of the file on your hard disk. While you're connected to the network, it would be faster to use the local copy to access the file; this could really save time, for example, if you are running an application from a network folder. On the other hand, this would not be appropriate for files that change frequently or for database files that are used by multiple users concurrently.

Windows has to know whether or not it's appropriate to serve up the cached copy for online use, and it leaves the choice up to the person who shares the network folder. So, when you share folders on your computer, you can specify the way Windows will make this folder available for offline use by others.

Normally, Windows will not give users a cached file when the network copy is available. It's useful to change the default settings when you are sharing a folder that has "read-only" documents that don't change often, and application programs. In this case, you may be able to give users faster access by following these steps:

1. Use Explorer or Computer to locate the folder you're sharing. Right-click it and select Properties.

2. View the Sharing tab. Click the Advanced Sharing button. If Share This Folder is not checked, check it now.

3. Click the Caching button.

4. Select one of the following caching options:

    - **Only the files and programs that users specify are available offline**—Lets users make the choice of whether or not to make the folder contents available offline. This is the default setting.

- **No files or programs from the share are available offline**—Prevents users from making the folder contents available offline.

- **All files and programs that users open from the share are automatically available offline**—Makes other computers automatically make the contents of any file opened from the folder available for use offline. Furthermore, even while connected, if the user runs an application program from the network folder, their computer will use their cached copy for speedier performance. This is automatic for Windows 7 and Vista computers. Check Optimized for Performance to let Windows XP computers do this as well.

5. Click OK to close the Offline Settings dialog box, and then click OK to close the Advanced Sharing dialog box.

The amount of disk space allocated to "automatically" available offline files is limited to an amount set on the Disk Usage tab in the Sync Center's Manage Offline Files dialog box.

Multiple LAN Connections

Most desktop computers sit where they are installed, gathering dust until they're obsolete, and they participate in only one LAN. But portable computer users often carry their computers from office to office, docking or plugging in to several LANs. Although Windows 7 makes it very easy for you to manage different dial-up and VPN connections, it's difficult to manage connections to different LANs if the network configuration settings are manually set.

IP settings are the difficult ones. If your computer and network are both set up to use DHCP for automatic TCP/IP configuration, you won't encounter any problems; your computer will absorb the local information each time you connect.

If your TCP/IP settings are set manually, things aren't so simple. Microsoft has come up with a partial solution called Alternate Configuration. You can configure your computer for automatic IP address assignment on most networks and manual assignment on one. The way this works is that Windows looks for a DHCP server when it boots up, and if it doesn't find one it uses the Alternate Configuration. This can be a static IP address, or the default setting "Automatic Private IP Address," whereby Windows chooses a random address in the 169.254 subnet.

This means that your computer can automatically adjust itself to multiple networks, at most one of which requires manual IP address settings.

To set up Alternate Configuration, open the Network and Sharing Center, select Change Adapter Settings, right-click your LAN icon and select Properties, and double-click Internet Protocol Version 4 (TCP/IP). Be sure the General tab uses the Obtain an IP Address Automatically setting—if not, this discussion doesn't apply to your computer. View the Alternate Configuration tab and choose User Configured to enter the static LAN's information.

If you need to commute between multiple networks that require manual configuration, you'll have to change the General settings each time you connect to a different network. I suggest that you stick a 3-by-5-inch card with the settings for each network in your laptop carrying case for handy reference.

MEETINGS, CONFERENCING, AND COLLABORATION

Windows 7 Plays Well with Others

Today's computers are no longer seen as tools used in isolation. They've become portals through which people can communicate and work just as easily from across the globe as from across the room. Business users and students are increasingly relying on computers to make presentations and give reports (making them at least more colorful, if not more interesting).

In this chapter, we'll cover several Windows 7 features that make it easier for you to work with others:

- When you use your laptop or tablet computer to display a business or class presentation, the Presentation Settings feature lets you tell Windows 7 not to disrupt your presentation with messages, noises, or the screen saver.

- If you use a laptop computer, the External Display tool makes it easy to control an external monitor or a projector.

- If you need help with your computer, or if you want to demonstrate some computer task or application to others using their computer, Remote Assistance may be just what you need.

We'll start by looking at Windows 7's support for making presentations.

Making Presentations with a Mobile Computer

If you use a mobile (laptop or tablet) computer, Windows 7 has two features that make giving presentations smoother and easier. The features are Presentation Settings and External Display, part of the Windows Mobility Center discussed in Chapter 35, "Hitting the Road." External Display lets you manage an external monitor or a projector, and Presentation Settings keeps Windows from interrupting your presentation.

Adjusting Presentation Settings

One of Windows Vista's more thoughtful additions was the Presentation Settings feature in Windows Mobility Center, and it's available in Windows 7, too. When you indicate that you are making a presentation, Windows takes steps to keep itself out of your way. It can make the following accommodations:

- Display a screen background chosen to minimize distraction or promote your company logo.

- Disable the screen saver, so that if you leave the computer alone for a few minutes, your audience isn't treated to an animated aquarium or a slide show that includes pictures of you getting dressed up for a Halloween party in really bad drag.

- Disable pop-up notifications and reminders from Windows services.

- Set the speaker volume so that you aren't bothered by sounds associated with events like mouse clicks, Window resizing, and the like.

- Disable automatic shutdown so that your computer won't go to sleep while you're talking. (There is unfortunately no corresponding setting for the audience.)

 note

Presentation Settings and the Windows Mobility Center are available only if you are using a mobile (laptop or tablet) computer. However, there is a Registry hack you can use to enable it on a desktop computer.

To use the Presentation Settings, first select the accommodations you'd like Windows to make. To do this, click Start, Control Panel, Hardware and Sound, and then click Adjust Settings Before Giving a Presentation, found under the Windows Mobility Center heading. The Presentation Settings dialog box appears, as shown in Figure 36.1.

Set the check boxes next to the desired accommodations, and preselect the sound volume and desktop background if desired.

If you use a certain external monitor or projector whenever you give presentations, you can instruct Windows to invoke Presentation Settings automatically whenever the display is connected. To do this, attach the display(s), click Connected Displays, and check I Always Give a Presentation When I Use This Display Configuration.

Save your presentation Settings Preferences by clicking OK.

Figure 36.1
Presentation Settings lets you keep Windows quiet during a presentation.

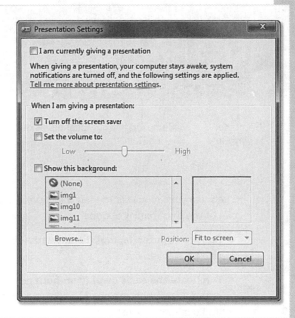

Now, whenever you are making a presentation, open the Windows Mobility Center by pressing Windows+X, or by clicking Start, All Programs, Accessories, Windows Mobility Center. Then, in the Presentation Settings tile, click Turn On.

Controlling External Display

The External Display tile on Windows Mobility Center lets you control what appears on any connected external display or monitor attached to your laptop or tablet computer.

> **tip**
> If you use the Mobility Center a lot, that Windows+X hotkey shortcut will save you a lot of time and clicking! You could also pin a shortcut to Windows Mobility Center in your taskbar to make it easily accessible.

To start, attach your external monitor or projector, or connect to a network-attached projector as described in the next section. Then, press Windows+P to bring up the External Display selection pop-up, shown in Figure 36.2. Alternatively, open the Windows Mobility Center as discussed in the previous section, then click the Connect Display or Disconnect Display button in the External Display tile.

The External Display pop-up lets you choose how to use the added screen real estate.

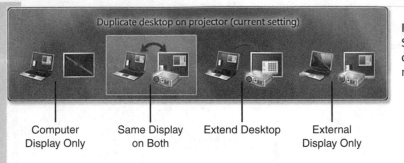

Duplicate desktop on projector (current setting)

Computer Display Only | Same Display on Both | Extend Desktop | External Display Only

Figure 36.2
Select whether to extend or duplicate your desktop on the new display.

Then use your mouse or the left and right arrow keys to select one of the four display options:

- **Show computer (laptop) display only**—External display will be blacked out.

- **Duplicate the same display on both monitors**—This option is useful if you need to see your own presentation and can't see the external display.

- **Extend the desktop across the computer and external displays**—This option is useful if you want to make a presentation on the big screen and view your own notes or other programs on your laptop display. (This sounds good in theory, but for some reason, in practice, I've found that doing this is a lot like trying to rub my tummy and pat my head at the same time.)

- **Use external display only**—The computer display will be blacked out.

Click one of the icons or press Enter to save the setting. You can press Windows+P to change it at any time.

➥ *To learn about Windows 7's other accessories for mobile computers, **see** "Windows Mobility Center," p. 972.*

➥ *For more information about managing external displays, **see** "Installing and Using Multiple Monitors," p. 790.*

 note

If you select the Duplicate option, your screen's resolution might be reduced. Windows will use the highest reasonable screen resolution supported by both monitors. If both displays don't have the same shape, the external display might look pinched or stretched. If this happens, right-click the desktop, select Screen Resolution, and adjust the resolution slider to find a more acceptable setting. Click Apply after making each adjustment. You'll have to find a compromise because you can't select different resolutions for the two monitors when the Duplicate setting is in effect.

Later, when you disconnect the external display, Windows 7 should automatically reset your laptop's screen resolution to its original setting. If it doesn't, right-click the desktop, select Personalize, Screen Resolution, and move the Resolution slider to the laptop display's native resolution—usually the topmost position.

Connecting to Network Projectors

Windows 7 includes support for connecting to video projectors that are reached over a network, rather than requiring them to be attached directly to your computer. Network-attached projectors are becoming a more common feature in corporate conference rooms that are also outfitted with wireless or Ethernet network ports.

To use a network attached projector, follow these steps:

1. Ensure that you have an active wireless or wired connection to the network that leads to the projector.

2. Click Start, All Programs, Accessories, Connect to a Network Projector.

3. If Windows asks for permission to allow the network projector to communicate through Windows Firewall, click Yes. You might need to confirm a User Account Control (UAC) prompt.

4. Click Search for a Projector. If the projector appears in the list of available devices, select its name and click Connect. If the projector can't be found, click the Back button (the left arrow in the upper-left corner of the window), and click Enter the Projector Address. Type in the projector's network path, as provided by your network administrator. Enter the projector's password, if a password is required. Then click Connect.

Next, follow any additional prompts to direct your presentation output to the connected projector. You can press Windows+P to change the way your laptop and the external display are configured, as discussed in the previous section.

Remote Assistance

Remote Assistance lets two people work collaboratively on one Windows computer—one at the computer and one remotely, over the Internet. Remote Assistance is designed to let a person get technical assistance from someone else at a remote location. It's not so much a "let's all work together" tool as a "let me help you with this" tool. In fact, some computer manufacturers advertise that they'll use Remote Assistance to help you with your computer after you purchase it.

Remote Assistance is based on the same technology as the Remote Desktop feature we'll discuss in Chapter 37, "Remote Desktop." There are some similarities, and several significant differences, between the two:

- Remote Assistance is available on all versions of Windows 7 and XP, whereas Remote Desktop is available only on the higher-end Windows versions: Windows 7 Professional, Enterprise, and Ultimate, Windows Vista Business, Enterprise, and Ultimate, and Windows XP Professional.

- With Remote Assistance, both the local and remote users see the same screen at the same time, and both can move the mouse, type on the keyboard, and so forth. With Remote Desktop, when a remote user is working, the computer's monitor displays just the Welcome screen.

- Remote Assistance doesn't make the local computer's hard drives available, nor does it transmit sound, as Remote Desktop does.

- Remote Assistance connections can't be made *ad lib*. One Windows user must invite another through email or Windows Live Messenger. Or one user can offer assistance to another using Messenger. In any case, the procedure requires the simultaneous cooperation of users at both ends of the connection.

- Remote Assistance allows you to use a text chat window or voice chat while the desktop session is active.

 note

To take advantage of the new, more reliable connection method, both you and the person who is helping you—or the person you are helping—must be using Windows 7 or Windows Vista, *and* you must change a setting, as described in the next section. Any user running Windows Vista should have Vista Service Pack 1 installed, or any later service pack.

A big plus with Remote Assistance on Windows 7 and Windows Vista is that it should work even if you are using a shared Internet connection. This is a big improvement over Remote Assistance on Windows XP, which rarely worked over a shared connection. The reason is that on Windows 7 and Vista, Remote Assistance uses Internet Protocol Version 6 and Teredo tunneling to safely pass data through Internet connection sharing routers and firewalls.

Enabling Remote Assistance

Remote Assistance is usually enabled by default when you install Windows, but before you try to use it to get help, you should confirm that it is enabled. Furthermore, if you want to use the new, more reliable connection method to work with another Windows 7 or Vista user, you must change a setting by following these steps:

1. Click Start, right-click Computer, and select Properties.

2. In the Tasks list on the left, click Remote Settings. If a UAC prompt appears, click Continue, or enter an Administrator password, as requested.

3. Check to be sure that Allow Remote Assistance Connections to This Computer is checked. If it isn't, check it.

4. Click the Advanced button.

5. If you use an Internet connection sharing router, check Create Invitations That Can Only Be Used from Computers Running Windows Vista or Later. You will only be able to invite other Windows 7 or Vista users to help you, not XP users, but at least it will work.

   You can also change the number of hours that an invitation to help remains active.

6. Click OK to save your changes.

Requesting Remote Assistance

To invite a friend or colleague to work with you on your computer, first contact your friend and confirm that she is ready to work with you.

 note

You and your friend must both have a working Internet connection to use Remote Assistance.

Then, follow these steps:

1. If the other person is using Windows 7, skip to step 2.

   If the other person is using Windows Vista, use the instructions in the previous section to check the box labeled Create Invitations That Can Only Be Used from Computers Running Windows Vista or Later.

   If the other person is using Windows XP, use the instructions in the previous section to *uncheck* the box labeled Create Invitations That Can Only Be Used from Computers Running Windows Vista or Later.

2. Select Start, All Programs, Maintenance, Windows Remote Assistance, and then click Invite Someone You Trust to Help You.

3. Windows needs to send an "invitation" to your friend. Use one of these four methods:

   - If the other person is using Windows 7, click Use Easy Connect.

   - If you are chatting with your friend using Windows Live Messenger, start a chat session with your friend and click Actions, Request Remote Assistance. When they accept your request, Windows will pop up a password, as described in step 4. You can give them this password over the phone or through the Chat window. Your friend should type the password using uppercase letters.

   - If you have a standalone email program installed in your computer, select Use Email to Send an Invitation.

   - Otherwise, if you use a web-based email program, select Save This Invitation As a File. Select a location to save the invitation file, and make note of it. You'll have to send this file as an email attachment later on, or get the file to your friend some other way.

4. Windows will display a password composed of 12 letters and digits. The password is shown with three groups of letters shaded in different colors to make it easier to read; the shading isn't important. Write the password down and give it to the person who you are inviting to help. It's probably best *not* to put this password into the email, but to give it to them over the phone.

5. If you selected Use Easy Connect, just wait for your friend to start up Remote Assistance (using the steps in the next section) and type in the password you gave to her.

   If you selected Use Email to Send an Invitation, your selected email program will pop up with an email ready to address and send. Enter your friend's email address and send the email. The

 note

If your friend is using Windows XP and you are using an Internet connection sharing router, or if you are on a business network that uses a firewall, the odds of your friend's computer being able to connect to yours are fairly slim. If you can, try to enable Universal Plug and Play (UPnP) in your router before you issue the Remote Assistance request. That might help. However, you're probably better off trying one of the third-party tools I mention later in the chapter.

 note

If your friend uses Windows Vista or XP, tell them to be sure to type the password in uppercase, which is easiest by first pressing the Caps Lock key.

important part is the attachment, which is a file named something along the lines of `Invitation.MsRcIncident`. Don't delete the attachment!

If you selected Save This Invitation as a File, use your web-based email system to send the invitation file you created in step 4 to your friend as an attachment. The file has a name along the lines of `Invitation.MsRcIncident`. Alternatively, get the invitation file to your fiend by other means, such as a flash drive or a network folder.

6. Windows will display a window that says Waiting for an Incoming Connection. Leave this window alone until your friend receives the invitation and responds.

If you sent your request via Windows Live Messenger, you should get a response within a few seconds. If you sent the request by email, it could be some time before the other party receives and reads it.

When your friend responds to your request for assistance, a dialog box will appear on your screen, asking if it's okay for her to connect. Click Yes, and after a short while—perhaps a minute or so—a window will appear with which you can control the Remote Assistance session, as shown in Figure 36.3.

note

If you use a dial-up Internet connection or a DSL service that requires you to sign on, your Internet IP address changes every time you connect. The Remote Assistance invitation uses this address to tell the other person's computer how to contact you, so it will work only if you stay connected from the time you send the invitation to the time your friend responds. If you have a fixed (static) IP address, this won't be a problem.

Figure 36.3
When your Remote Assistant has connected, use this window to chat and control the connection.

At this point, your friend can see your screen and can watch what you do with it, but she can't actually do anything with your computer. She first has to ask to take control, and you have to consent. Then, either of you can type, move the mouse, and otherwise poke around and use your computer.

When a friend asks to take control of your computer, a request will pop up on your screen. If she's just going to work with a normal Windows application such as Word, just click Yes to let her take control. However, if she needs to manage Windows itself, you have to decide who is going to handle the UAC prompts that might appear. By default, your friend won't be able to see or respond to them. You have two options:

- If you want to respond to any UAC prompts yourself, just click Yes to let her connect. If she performs an action that requires security confirmation, his screen will go black for a moment, and you'll have to respond to the UAC prompt.

note

If you don't completely trust the person who's helping you, make this setting change right away: Click Settings, check Use ESC Key to Stop Sharing Control, and then click OK. This way, after you've given the person control, if you don't like what they're doing, you can press the Esc key, and they'll immediately be locked out. Unfortunately, if they press Esc while they're working, the same thing will happen, so you'll have to grant them access again. This can get irritating, but it does let you control what they're doing.

- If you want to let her change Windows settings without your intervention, check Allow *Username* to Respond to User Account Control Prompts, then click Yes. You will be asked to confirm a UAC prompt yourself at this point.

Now your friend should be able to work your keyboard and mouse, and help you.

The Windows Remote Assistance toolbar has a few other features that you will find useful:

- If you want a moment of privacy, perhaps to read email or look at a sensitive file, click Pause. This will black out the other person's view of your screen without disconnecting that person. Click Continue to restore the view.

- To communicate with your friend via text messaging, click Chat. The Remote Assistance toolbar will enlarge. Type your comments into the lower box on the window and press Enter (or click Send), and your friend will see what you type. You'll see your friend's responses in the upper part of the window. Click the Chat button again to shrink the toolbar back to its original size.

- To take control away from your friend, click Stop Sharing. Your friend will still be able to see your screen, but can only watch. He has to request control again to do anything.

When you're finished, click Disconnect to end the Remote Assistance session.

Responding to an Assistance Request

On Windows 7, there are several ways your friend can invite you to provide Remote Assistance: using Easy Connect, Windows Live Messenger, or an invitation email or file. Use one of the following procedures to respond to their request.

Responding with Easy Connect

If both you and your friend are using Windows 7 (or some future version), you can use the new Easy Connect method. Your friend will use Easy Connect to invite you. To respond, follow these steps:

1. Select Start, All Programs, Maintenance, Windows Remote Assistance, Help Someone Who Has Invited You.

2. Select Use Easy Connect.

> **note**
>
> If you don't have Administrator privileges on your computer, you won't be able to give your friend permission to perform administrative actions that require a UAC confirmation, either. There are two ways to work around this.
>
> If the remote user knows an Administrator password and will tell you what it is, check Allow *Username* to Respond to User Account Control Prompts and click Yes. When the prompt appears, select the account and enter the password he gave you.
>
> The second workaround requires some advance setup before you need to use Remote Assistance. An Administrator has to perform these steps: Click Start, All Programs, Administrative Tools, Local Security Policy. Under Local Policies, Security Options, enable User Account Control: Allow UIAccess Applications to Prompt for Elevation Without Using the Secure Desktop. Then restart Windows (on a corporate network, this option can be enabled through Group Policy). With this option enabled, the remote user will be able to respond to UAC prompts even if you don't know an Administrator password.

3. Type in the password they gave you. It consists of 12 letters and numbers and is not case sensitive (upper- and lowercase don't matter). Then, press Enter.

When the connection is established, skip ahead to "Working with Remote Assistance."

Responding Through Windows Live Messenger

If you and your friend are both chatting with Windows Live Messenger, your friend's invitation will appear in a pop-up window. Just click Accept to begin the connection, follow the instructions, and skip ahead to "Working with Remote Assistance."

Responding to an Invitation Email or File

Your friend might send you an email with an attachment containing an invitation file named something like Invitation.MsRcIncident. Alternatively, they might send you the file through a network or a portable drive.

To accept an email invitation, open the message's attachment. (How you do that depends on your email program. If you use web-based email, you might have to download the attachment separately.) Opening the attachment should activate the Remote Assistance connection. If you receive the invitation as a file, just double-click to open the file in Windows Explorer.

You will be asked to enter the password associated with the invitation. The person who invited you will have to tell you what it is.

 note

If your friend is using Windows Vista or XP, you must type the password exactly as they did—upper- and lowercase matter. If your friend is using Windows 7, the password consists of 12 letters and numbers. Upper- and lowercase don't matter.

 note

If Windows is unable to establish a connection to the person who invited you, ask her what operating system she's using. If it's XP and it doesn't work the first time, the chances that it's ever going to work are slim. If she's using Windows 7, ask her to check the box labeled Create Invitations That Can Only Be Used from Computers Running Windows 7 or Later, as described in the "Enabling Remote Assistance" section earlier in this chapter. Then have her send you a new invitation.

Working with Remote Assistance

After you've responded to the assistance invitation, it can take more than a minute for the required software to load and for the other user's desktop to appear on your screen, as shown in Figure 36.4.

Across the top is a menu of controls. The choices are

- **Request Control**—Click to begin using the other computer's mouse and keyboard. The remote user will have to grant permission. After you have control of the other computer, both of you can use your mouse and keyboard.

- **Actual Size**—Click to make the size of the Remote Assistance window exactly match the other person's screen. You might have to scroll around to see all of his or her desktop. This choice alternates with Fit to Screen.

- **Fit to Screen**—Click to shrink the view of the other computer's screen so that it fits perfectly in your Remote Assistance window. You won't have to use the scrollbars to see the far corners anymore but the text might be tiny. Maximize your Remote Assistance window to improve the display.

- **Chat**—Click to open a text chat panel in the left side of the Remote Assistance window. Type your messages into the small box at the bottom of the Chat area.

- **Settings**—Click to turn off the recording of the remote session that Windows makes by default.

- **Help**—Click to display online help for Remote Assistance.

Click here to control the other computer with your keyboard and mouse.

Figure 36.4
The Remote
Assistance
screen has a
control panel
at the top
and a view of
the remote
user's screen
underneath.
Click Request
Control if you
want to
manipulate
the remote
computer.

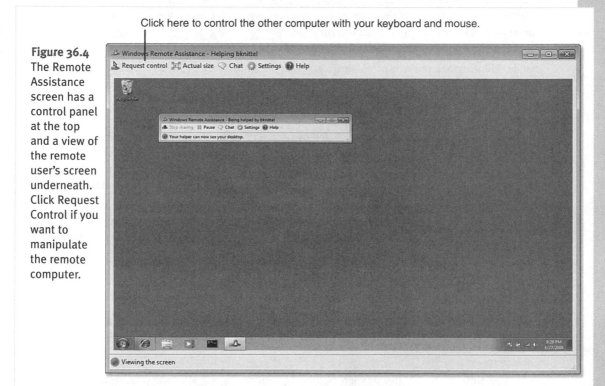

If your friend clicks the Stop Sharing button, you'll lose control of the remote screen. Just click Request Control again to ask for permission to resume working.

Using Third-Party Tools

If you want to help someone with Remote Assistance but can't get it to work, there are several third-party tools that are as good as or better than Remote Assistance (and Remote Desktop), and most of them work even when Remote Assistance and Remote Desktop won't. I talk more about these tools in Chapter 37 under "Third-Party Remote Control Tools" (page 1027), so I won't repeat that discussion here. Here, I'll just mention that the free version of LogMeIn (http://secure. logmein.com) has saved the day for many of my friends and clients.

You might also try one of the online meeting tools described in the next section. They're typically designed to let a group of people work together on a common project, but most of them could also let two people work together to solve a problem with Windows.

Online Meeting Tools

Many previous versions of Windows included collaboration tools that were designed to let several people work together on the same Windows desktop, with the same applications, even when separated by great distances. These tools let two or more people, say, edit a Word file or construct a PowerPoint presentation, as a collaborative effort.

Remote Assistance, described in the previous section, is a fine tool for this purpose for just two people. But previous versions of Windows included programs better suited to the task, such as NetMeeting and Windows Meeting Space, both of which let more than two people work together... and both of which are now "retired" and are not provided with Windows 7.

Microsoft does have a free replacement program called SharedView, which you can search for and download from microsoft.com. It can be used by people running Windows 7, Vista, and XP. The person who initiates a SharedView meeting can share his or her desktop, or individual applications, with other users, and can delegate control of the keyboard and mouse to any of the participants. The program also includes a tool that lets you copy documents and other files back and forth between participants.

Table 36.1 lists some additional alternatives, third-party tools that you might want to investigate. There are numerous tools, and more are appearing all the time, so you might want to supplement this table with some Google searching.

Table 36.1   Third-Party Collaboration Tools

Program and URL	Comments
Adobe Acrobat Connect www.adobe.com/products/ acrobatconnect	$39/month for up to 15 participants. Can include videoconferencing.
Central Desktop www.centraldesktop.com	Bewildering variety of pricing schemes. For free, you can have two meetings with five participants each.
Dimdim www.dimdim.com	Based on Adobe's Flash Player, so most people already have the software. Free version for up to 20 participants.
GoToMeeting www.gotomeeting.com	Includes voice conferencing. 30-day free trial. After that, it's $49/month (less for an annual license) for up to 15 participants.
WebEx MeetMeNow www.meetmenow. webex.com	$49/month for up to 10 participants. Includes voice conferencing by telephone.

Table 36.1 Continued

Program and URL	Comments
Live Meeting office.microsoft.com/ livemeeting	$4.58 per user per month and up. (Who came up with $4.58?)
Microsoft SharedView www.microsoft.com	A free download from Microsoft; connects up to 15 participants. This is a replacement for NetMeeting and Windows Meeting Space. Search Microsoft's site for "SharedView."
Mikogo www.mikogo.com	Free conferencing for up to 10 participants. There is a Mac version as well.
Vyew vyew.com	Free version has advertising and up to 20 participants. You can pay to increase participants and reduce the amount of advertising. Weird, yes, but the software looks good and there are Mac and Linux clients.
Yugma www.yugma.com	Free version "broadcasts" your desktop; $15/month paid version required to share keyboard and mouse control.

REMOTE DESKTOP

Using Your Computer Remotely

Windows 7 Professional, Enterprise, and Ultimate editions (as well as the comparable Windows Vista and XP versions) have a spiffy feature called Remote Desktop that lets you connect to and use your computer from another location. You can see your computer's screen, move the mouse and type on the keyboard, open files, and even print, just as if you were really sitting in front of your own computer. The neat part is that you can do this from just about any computer, as long as it's running some version of Windows or Mac OS X.

Figure 37.1 shows how this works.

This is just what you need when you're out of town and need to read a file you left on the computer back home, or if you want to read your office email from home. I've been using this feature since it appeared in Windows XP Professional, and I love it.

You also can use the Remote Desktop Client program to attach to computers running Windows Server computers to access applications or for administration and mainte-nance.

 note

You don't have to be miles away to take advantage of Remote Desktop, either. You can also use it to access other computers in your home or office, using your local area network (LAN). For instance, you can use it to start a lengthy computing or printing job on someone else's computer without leaving your own desk.

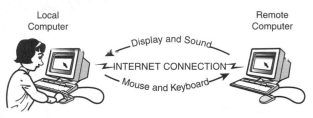

Local
Computer

Remote
Computer

Display and Sound

INTERNET CONNECTION

Mouse and Keyboard

Figure 37.1
You can use any computer running Windows or Macintosh OS X to connect to and control your computer.

This chapter consists of two parts. The first part shows you how to set up your computer so that you can access it remotely. The second part shows you how to connect to another computer using the Remote Desktop Client.

On the other hand, the Remote Desktop Client, which is the application you use to connect to a remote computer and which is discussed in the second part of the chapter, is included with all Windows versions. It also can be downloaded for Mac OS X.

Third-party programs such as LapLink Everywhere, PCAnywhere, VNC, and Timbuktu, and web-based services such as LogMeIn and GoToMyPC, also provide this type of remote access capability, as I'll discuss at the end of the chapter. Some of these products have more sophisticated features, and they can be easier to set up, but Remote Desktop is built into Windows and it's essentially free (well, it's free after you've paid for Windows).

Remote Desktop is a scaled-down version of Windows Terminal Services, a component of the Windows Server versions that lets multiple users run programs on one central server. By "scaled down," I mean that only one person is allowed to connect to Windows 7 at a time, either remotely or with the regular monitor and keyboard. So if you connect remotely, the local user is temporarily kicked out to the Welcome screen. And if a local user logs on while you're connected remotely, *you'll* be disconnected. You won't lose your work—you can reconnect later—but the bottom line is that only one person at a time is allowed to use a Windows 7 computer.

 note

The Remote Desktop Service, which lets you connect to your own computer from another computer, is available only on Windows 7 Professional, Enterprise, and Ultimate Editions, the comparable versions of Vista, and Windows XP Professional. If you have one of the Home versions of Windows, the part of this chapter that talks about setting up access to your own computer does not apply to your version of Windows. If you want to access your "home" computer remotely, look into the third-party programs mentioned at the end of the chapter.

 note

Why would you set up your computer to host Remote Desktop connections when the third-party software can be easier to set up? One reason is that Remote Desktop transfers sound and supports multiple monitors. Another reason is that the online services require you to trust the third parties not to monitor or probe your computer over their connections. With Remote Desktop, the connection is direct to your computer and you control it completely.

Setting Up Access to Your Own Computer

This first half of the chapter tells you how to set up remote access to your own computer. If you want to use the Remote Desktop Connection client to access another computer, skip ahead to "Connecting to Other Computers with Remote Desktop," later in the chapter.

Across a LAN (that is, between computers in your home or office), Remote Desktop Connection works right "out of the box"—you just have to enable the feature.

However, if you want to use Remote Desktop to reach your computer over the Internet, you have to set up several other things in advance.

This procedure might sound complex as you read it, but it really isn't that bad. Let's go through the process step by step. You can go about this in other ways, of course, but what I give you here is a procedure that's suitable for a home user with Windows 7 Ultimate edition or a small-office user with the Professional version.

And, again, let me remind you that there are web-based programs that do much the same thing as Remote Desktop. Several of them are free, and most of them require very little setup work—in particular, they completely bypass the networking issues that we'll discuss shortly. If the instructions in this section sound too difficult, or if the setup doesn't work for you, check out the section "Third-Party Remote Control Tools" at the end of the chapter.

 caution

If your computer is part of a corporate network, check with your network administrators before attempting to make any changes to the Remote Desktop settings. It might be a violation of company policy for you to do so. In fact, in all likelihood, these settings will be locked down and you won't be able to change them anyway. If this is the case, if it's allowed at all, your network admins will have to set up Remote Desktop access for you.

Enabling Remote Desktop Access to Your Computer

To be sure that incoming Remote Desktop connections are enabled on your computer, follow these steps:

1. Click Start, right-click Computer, and select Properties.

2. At the left, click Remote Settings and, if necessary, confirm the User Account Control prompt.

3. Select Allow Connections from Computers Running Any Version of Remote Desktop. (The "more secure" version works only on corporate networks using IPSec security.)

4. By default, all Administrator-level accounts will be allowed to connect to the computer. If you want to grant Remote Desktop access to any Limited users, click Select Users, Add, Advanced, Find Now, and then locate the desired name in the Search Results section. Double-click the name. To add another name, click Advanced and Find Now again.

5. Click OK to close all the dialog boxes.

If your computer is set to go to sleep when it sits unused for a while, and you want the computer to be available for incoming connections at any time, you'll have to disable automatic sleep. To do this, click Start, Control Panel, Hardware and Sound, Change When the Computer Sleeps, and for Put the Computer to Sleep, select Never. Then click Save Changes.

At this point, check to be sure that Remote Desktop has been set up correctly: Click Start, Control Panel, System and Security, and Allow a Program Through Windows Firewall. Find Remote Desktop in the Exceptions list (you might need to scroll down), and be sure it's checked under both Home/Work and Public. If it isn't, click Change Settings, and then check the boxes. If you are using a third-party firewall, be sure to configure it to permit incoming Remote Desktop connections on TCP port 3389.

If you just want to use Remote Desktop within your home or office network, you're finished and can skip ahead to the "Connecting to Other Computers with Remote Desktop" section. However, if you want to reach your computer through the Internet, you have more work to do.

note

A password must be set on a user's account before that user can connect to the computer remotely.

caution

Be sure that every user account that can be reached via Remote Desktop (that is, every Administrator account and any Limited accounts that you entered in step 4) has a strong password. This means a password with uppercase letters *and* lowercase letters *and* one or more numbers *and* punctuation, and at least eight characters in length.

Establishing 24×7 Access

Because you won't be there at your home or office to turn on your computer and establish an Internet connection, you have to set things up so that your computer and connection are always working.

First, you need to get to the BIOS setup screen. Restart Windows and wait for the screen to go black. Press the BIOS setup hotkey. The screen tells you what to press; it's usually the Delete or F2 key. Then, look for the Power Management settings. Find an entry titled AC Power Recovery, or something similar. Some computers have an option labeled Last Setting, which turns the computer on only if it was already on when the power failed. If it's available, that's the one to use. Otherwise, select the setting that turns your computer on whenever the AC power comes on. Then save the BIOS settings and restart Windows.

Besides a 24×7 computer, you need a 24×7 Internet connection. If you have cable Internet service or a type of DSL service that does not require you to enter a username or password, you already have an always-on Internet connection and can skip ahead to the next section. Otherwise:

- See if your DSL provider can upgrade your service to provide a static IP address and always-on service. This *might* be inexpensive enough to make it worthwhile.

- Use a hardware connection-sharing router. If you don't have a router already, buying one is a worthwhile investment. They cost between $0 (after rebate) and $75, and can also provide wireless networking capability for your home or office. Chapter 19, "Connecting Your Network to the Internet," tells how to set up a router for DSL service. Be sure to enable the router's "keepalive" feature so that your connection is kept going all the time.

- If you use the Broadband connection sharing feature built in to Windows, you can add a third-party program to force Windows to keep the connection open all the time. The DynDNS Updater program (which I'll discuss later) can do this for you.

Next, you must make sure you can locate your computer from out on the Internet.

Setting Up Dynamic DNS

All Internet connections are established on the basis of a number called an *IP address*, which is to your Internet connection as your telephone number is to your phone. When you're somewhere else, you'll need a way to let Windows find your home computer's IP address so that Remote Desktop can establish a connection back to it.

The solution to this problem is to use a free dynamic domain name service (DDNS). You'll use the service to give your computer a name, like `lucythedog.homedns.org`. Add-on software in your computer will keep the service updated whenever your computer's address changes.

 note

Many DDNS providers exist, many of which offer free services. You can find them easily enough by doing a Google search for "free DDNS service." Here I give you step-by-step instructions for setting up service with DynDNS.com because it's free and it's directly supported by many hardware connection-sharing routers.

To set up dynamic DNS service at DynDNS.com, follow these steps:

1. Got to www.dyndns.com in Internet Explorer. Click Create Account. Make up a username and password, and enter these along with your email address in the registration form. Be sure to jot down the username and password.

2. Read and acknowledge the terms of service, and click Create Account. (You're allowed only one free account, but you can use it to register several computers, if you want.) Follow the instructions to activate your account and sign on.

3. At the top click Services, click Dynamic DNS, and then click the Get Started button.

4. Enter a hostname that you can easily remember, and select a domain name from the pull-down list. Under the IP Address box, click Use Auto Detected IP Address. Click Create Host. If someone else has claimed the name you chose, change the name or domain and try again until you succeed. Be sure to write down the hostname and domain name that you eventually select.

5. Click Next, and then click Activate Services.

Next, set up a DNS client program so that changes to your IP address are sent to DynDNS.com. Do this on the computer that you're enabling for Remote Desktop access:

1. Log on as a Computer Administrator. Open Internet Explorer and go to www.dyndns.com/support. Click Download Now.

2. Run the downloaded program `DynUpSetup.exe`. Click Yes to run the downloaded program.

3. Step through the installation screens, using the default settings except this important one: On the Install as a Service page, check Install the DynDNS Updater as a Windows Service.

   At the last screen, click Finish, and the Updater program will start.

4. When prompted, enter the DynDNS.com username and password you created previously. This should automatically download the hostname you set up.

 note

If you use a hardware sharing router, your router might have DDNS support built in, which means you can skip this part. Check your router's setup screen to see if it has DDNS support, and if so, set it up to use your DDNS service.

5. Check the box next to the hostname you set up and click OK. In a short time, perhaps 30 seconds later, a balloon pop-up should tell you that the Updater synchronized your IP address with the DynDNS.com service.

To be sure that it's working, click Start, All Programs, Accessories, Command Prompt, and type the command **ping** followed by the hostname and domain name you chose for your computer; for example, ping mycomputer.homedns.org. Press Enter and be sure that the command finds your IP address, and doesn't print "Could not find host."

Now your registered hostname will always point to your computer, even when your IP address changes. After a change, it might take up to an hour for the update to occur, but changes should be infrequent.

Configuring Port Forwarding

The last setup step is to make sure that incoming Remote Desktop connections from the Internet make it to the right computer. If your computer connects directly to your cable or DSL modem, you can skip this step. Otherwise, you have to instruct your sharing computer or router to forward Remote Desktop data through to your computer. To be precise, you have to set up your sharing computer or router to forward incoming requests on TCP port 3389 to the computer you want to reach by Remote Desktop.

The procedure depends on whether you are using the ICS service built into Windows or a hardware-sharing router. Use one of the procedures described in the next two sections.

Port Forwarding with Internet Connection Sharing

If you use the built-in Windows ICS service to share an Internet connection on one computer with the rest of your LAN, the forwarding procedure is pretty straightforward using these steps:

1. Go to the computer that is sharing its connection (whether or not it's the one that you want to reach via Remote Desktop) and log on as an Administrator.

2. View the Properties dialog box for the local area connection that corresponds to the Internet connection itself. On Windows 7, click Start, Control Panel, Network and Internet, Network and Sharing Center. In the Tasks list, select Manage Network Connections.

3. Locate the connection that goes to your Internet service. This might be a broadband icon if you use DSL service, or a local area connection icon for cable service. It should have the word *Shared* next to it. Right-click the icon, select Properties, and view the Sharing tab.

4. Click Settings and, under Services, check Remote Desktop. In the Service Settings dialog box, enter the name of the computer that you want to make available via Remote Desktop and click OK.

5. When you're finished, click OK to close all the dialog boxes.

Now you should be able to reach your computer from anywhere on the Internet using the hostname that you set up on DynDNS.com.

Port Forwarding with a Router

If you are using a hardware connection-sharing router, setup is a bit more difficult but is worthwhile. First, because your router doesn't know your computers by their names, you have to set up a fixed IP address on the computer that you will be using via Remote Desktop, using these steps:

1. Click Start, All Programs, Accessories, Command Prompt.

2. Type the command **ipconfig /all** and press Enter. Locate the Local Area Connection part of the printout, which will look something like this:

```
Ethernet adapter Local Area Connection:

        Connection-specific DNS Suffix  . : somewhere.com
        Description . . . . . . . . . . . : NVIDIA nForce Networking Controller
        Physical Address. . . . . . . . . : 00-53-8F-D2-CA-5F
        Dhcp Enabled. . . . . . . . . . . : Yes
        Autoconfiguration Enabled . . . . : Yes
        IP Address. . . . . . . . . . . . : 192.168.0.102
        Subnet Mask . . . . . . . . . . . : 255.255.255.0
        Default Gateway . . . . . . . . . : 192.168.0.1
        DHCP Server . . . . . . . . . . . : 192.168.0.1
        DNS Servers . . . . . . . . . . . : 200.123.45.6
                                            200.123.67.8
```

The important information is bold. (On your computer, the numbers will be different—use your numbers, not these!)

If the entry Dhcp Enabled says No, you don't have to change anything here. Just note the IP Address entry, skip steps 3 through 9, and configure your router.

3. Click Start, Control Panel, Network and Internet, Network and Sharing Center, Manage Adapter Settings.

4. Right-click your Local Area Connection icon and select Properties.

5. Select the Internet Protocol Version 4 (TCP/IPv4) entry and click Properties.

6. Check Use the Following IP Address. Enter the first three parts of your original IP address exactly as you see it in your Command Prompt window, but replace the last part with **250**. For example, on *my* computer, I'd enter 192.168.0.250. The first three sets of digits might be different on your network.

7. For the subnet mask and default gateway, enter the same numbers that were displayed in the Command Prompt window.

8. Check Use the Following DNS Server Addresses. Enter the one or two DNS Server addresses that were displayed in the Command Prompt window.

9. Click OK.

(If you need to set up any other computers with a fixed IP address, use the same procedure but use addresses ending in .249, .248, .247, and so on, counting backward from .250.)

Now you have to instruct your router to forward Remote Desktop connections to this computer. You need to use the router's setup screen to enable its Port Forwarding feature, which some routers call Virtual Server or Applications and Gaming. There, you need to enter the fixed IP address that you assigned to your computer and tell the router to forward connections on TCP port 3389 to this address. Every router uses a slightly different scheme, but Figure 37.2 shows a typical router. If a range of port numbers is required, or if external and internal numbers are entered separately, enter **3389** in all fields.

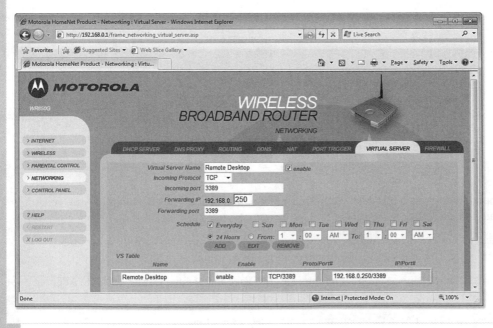

Figure 37.2
Use your router's setup system to forward TCP port 3389 to your computer.

➡ *To learn more about forwarding network requests on a shared Internet connection,* **see** *"Enabling Access with a Sharing Router," **p. 537.***

Now you should be able to reach your computer from anywhere on the Internet, using the hostname that you set up on DynDNS.com.

Connecting to Other Computers with Remote Desktop

To establish a connection to another computer using the Remote Desktop system, you need a copy of the Remote Desktop Client, which is also sometimes called the Terminal Services Client. You can get this program in several ways:

- It's preinstalled on all Windows 7 and Vista computers, on all editions. Select Start, All Programs, Accessories, Remote Desktop Connection.

- It's preinstalled on all Windows XP computers, on all editions. Select Start, All Programs, Accessories, Communications, Remote Desktop Connection. The version that came with XP lacks support for multiple monitors and plug-and-play devices. You can upgrade the version on XP by downloading and installing the new version, as described in the next paragraph.

- You can download it from http://www.microsoft.com/download. Search for "Remote Desktop Connection" and get the latest version available for your operating system. There are versions for Windows and Mac OS X.

Two Monitors Are Better Than One

If your local computer has two or more monitors, you might be able to use them both for the remote connection.

If the remote computer is running Windows 7, when you start the Remote Desktop Client, click the Options button, select the Display tab, and select Use All of My Monitors for the Remote Session. When you connect to the remote computer, set the Display size to Full Screen. (This works only with the Remote Desktop Connection client version 7.0 or higher, as provided with Windows 7 or downloaded from microsoft.com.)

If the remote computer is running Windows Vista *and* both of your monitors have the same height (that is, have the same vertical resolution) *and* are aligned side by side, follow this procedure: click Start and, in the Windows Search box, type `mstsc /span`. Press Enter. When you connect to the remote computer, set the Display size to Full Screen. (This works only with Remote Desktop Connection client version 6.1 or higher, as provided with Windows Vista and 7 or downloaded from microsoft.com. If this does work well for you, you can create a shortcut containing this command.)

When you run the Remote Desktop Client, you'll see the Remote Desktop Connection dialog box, shown in Figure 37.3.

Figure 37.3
The Remote Desktop Connection dialog box enables you to configure the connection and select the remote computer to use.

Enter the IP address or registered DNS name of the computer you want to use. If you have set up a DDNS hostname, as described in the first part of this chapter, the name might look something like `mycomputer.homedns.org`. If you're connecting to a computer on your own network, it's enough just to type its computer name.

At this point, you can select options that control how the remote connection is made, how large a window to use, and so on.

Connection Options

In the Remote Desktop Connection dialog box, you can set several connection options. In most cases, you can use the default settings and simply click Connect to start the connection, but several of the options can be quite useful.

To view the option categories, click the Options button. The dialog box expands to show six pages of settings, which you can select by clicking on the tab names across the top. You will rarely need to adjust any of these settings. However, some situations might require you to change settings before making a Remote Desktop connection. Table 37.1 lists these situations.

Table 37.1 Some Reasons to Change Remote Desktop Settings

Situation	Setting Change
You always connect across the Internet and/or your remote computer is not on a secure corporate LAN.	On the Advanced tab, set Authentication Options to Connect and Don't Warn Me.
You are using a dial-up Internet connection.	On the Experience tab, change the Connection Speed to Modem (56K). On the Local Resources tab, click Settings and set audio playback to Do Not Play.
The remote computer has an Internet connection with a slow upload speed.	Most home Internet service has a fast download speed, but uploads slowly, often less than 500Kbps. If you're connecting to a computer that has a slow upload speed and the screen updates sluggishly, disconnect, and on the Experience tab, set the Performance setting to Broadband. Then try again.

Table 37.1 Continued

Situation	Setting Change
You need to work with the local and remote screens simultaneously.	On the Display tab, change the resolution to a size smaller than your local screen, perhaps 800×600.
You need to see as much of the remote computer's screen as possible.	On the Display tab, change the resolution to Full Screen. If the remote computer runs Windows 7 and you have multiple monitors on your local computer, check Use All My Monitors for the Remote Session.
You need to be able to print from the applications on the remote computer and get the printouts where you are working.	On the Local Resources tab, check Printers.
You don't need to print while connected.	On the Local Resources tab, uncheck Printers.
You want remote applications to be able to access files on the computer where you are working.	On the Local Resources tab, click More, expand the Drives list, and then click the boxes next to the drive letter(s) that you want to be made visible to the remote computer.
You need to use an application that uses a device attached to a COM port (for example, a Palm Pilot) or other local device.	On the Local Resources tab, click More, and then check Ports.

The Full Screen setting is very useful if you have serious work to do on the remote computer because it gives you the maximum amount of desktop space on which to work. Although the resulting connection will fill your local computer's screen, you can still switch back and forth between remote and local work, as I describe in the next section.

When you have made the necessary settings, you might want to save them as the default settings for future connections. To do this, select the General tab and click Save.

Finally, after you have made any necessary option settings, click Connect to begin the connection. Windows prompts you to enter your username and password before it establishes the connection.

The program prompts you to enter a username and password. Type the username and password you use on the *remote* computer, the one to which you're connecting. Entering the password is optional and, in most cases, not entering it here is safer. Let the remote system prompt you for your password.

 tip

If you routinely make connections to different computers using different settings, you can set up Remote Desktop Connection files with the computer name and all options preset. To do this, make the settings, click Save As, and select a file name. You can create shortcuts to the saved files and put them on your desktop, put them in your Start menu, or pin them to your taskbar.

 note

If you are connecting to a Windows Server Domain computer, by default, you use your domain logon. If you need to specify a local machine account, enter your username in the form *machinename\username*, as in mycomputer\Administrator.

If you want the logon name and password to be stored (relatively securely) in the local computer so that future connections can be automatic, enter the password and check Remember My Credentials.

Finally, click OK to begin the connection.

caution

Do not check Remember My Credentials if you are using a computer that is not your own or is not secure, because otherwise anyone who has access to the account will be able to connect to the same remote computer using your logon.

Logon Is Denied

If the remote computer connects but will not let you sign on, the account you tried to use might have a blank password or might be a Standard account that was not entered as an account authorized to connect remotely. See "Enabling Remote Desktop Access to Your Computer," earlier in the chapter, for instructions on authorizing accounts. An account must have a password set before you can use it remotely, even if it's authorized.

If Network Level Authentication is being used and the connection to the remote computer does not use the IPSec network security protocol, you might get a warning that the remote computer's identity cannot be validated. (Thus, you could end up giving your password to a counterfeit computer.) In most cases, this is not a problem, so you can click Yes. You can also check Don't Prompt Me Again for Connections to This Computer, or you can use the Advanced tab in the connection options, as described earlier, to prevent this warning from reoccurring.

Using the Remote Connection

When you're logged on, you'll see the remote computer's desktop, as shown in Figure 37.4, and can use it as if you were actually sitting in front of it. In a full-screen connection, the title bar at the top of the screen tells you that you're viewing the remote computer's screen. The title bar might slide up out of view, but you can hover the mouse near the top of the screen to bring it back. You can also click the Minimize button to hide the remote screen, or click the Maximize button to switch between a windowed or full screen view.

The keyboard, mouse, display, and sound (unless you disabled it) should be fully functional. It all works quite well—it can even be difficult to remember which computer you're actually using!

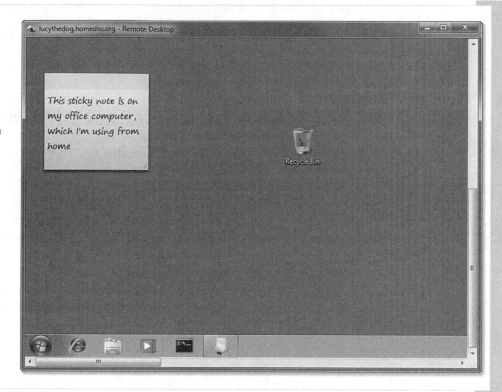

Figure 37.4
The remote computer's desktop appears in a window on your computer. You can also make it take over the entire screen.

This sticky note is on my office computer, which I'm using from home

Recycle Bin

If you elected to connect the local computer's disk drives in the connection options dialog box, the local computer's drives appear in Windows Explorer view. Access to these drives is fairly slow and annoying. Still, you can take advantage of this to copy files between the local and remote computers.

In addition, any printers attached to your local computer will appear as choices if you print from applications on the remote computer, as long as a compatible printer driver is available on the *remote* computer. Printers might not work if you are connecting from a Mac or a computer that is running an older version of Windows.

Keyboard Shortcuts

While you're connected, you might want to use keyboard shortcuts such as Alt+Tab to switch between applications. This can confuse Windows, which won't know whether to switch applications on the local computer or the remote computer. You can

tip
If the computer to which you're connecting has more than one monitor or a larger monitor than the one you're currently using, when you start an application, its window might not be visible. The problem is that when the application was last used, its window was placed on a secondary monitor and its position is now completely off the Remote Desktop screen. To make it visible, hover the mouse over the program's icon in the taskbar. When the preview window appears, right-click it and select Move (or Restore, then Move). Then press and hold the arrow keys to slide the window into view. Press Enter when it's visible, then finish positioning it with your mouse.

specify where special key combinations should be interpreted on the connection options Local Resources tab, as I described earlier, or you can use alternate key combinations to ensure that the desired actions take place on the remote computer. Table 37.2 shows the alternate keyboard shortcuts. Personally, I prefer to use these alternate shortcuts.

Table 37.2 Some Remote Desktop Keyboard Shortcuts

Use These Keys:	To Transmit This to the Remote Computer:
Alt+PgUp, Alt+PgDn	Alt+Tab (switch programs)
Alt+End	Ctrl+Alt+Del (open task monitor)
Alt+Home	(Displays the Start menu)
Ctrl+Alt+Break	Alt+Enter (toggle Full Screen)
Ctrl+Alt+Plus on numeric pad	Alt+PrntScrn (print screen to Clipboard)

When you've finished using the remote computer, click Start. (Yes, our friends who use Apple computers make fun of Windows because of this, but what can we do?)

On the Start menu, you can click Log Off, which will log out of and end the remote session, or you can disconnect leaving yourself logged on with applications running. To disconnect, click the arrow next to the Log Off button and select Disconnect, as shown in Figure 37.5. You can later reconnect via Remote Desktop or by signing on at the remote computer itself.

Click the Arrow to Select Disconnect
Log Off

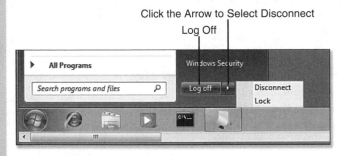

Figure 37.5
Use the Logout or Disconnect choices to end your remote session. Disconnect leaves you logged in on the remote computer.

I use Remote Desktop to use my work computer from home, and I've found that I save a lot of time by never logging off entirely. When I finish at work, I just press Windows+L to switch out to the Welcome screen. Then I can reconnect from home and pick up where I left off without waiting for all those darn startup programs to get going. Likewise, at home, when I'm finished, I simply disconnect, so I never actually log off.

> **One User at a Time**
>
> Windows 7 permits only one person to use each computer. If you attempt to connect to a computer with Remote Desktop while another user is logged on, you have the choice of disconnecting yourself or forcing that user off. If Fast User Switching is enabled, the other user is switched out to the Welcome screen; otherwise, the user is summarily logged off. This is somewhat brutal; the other user might lose work in progress.
>
> If you log on using the same username as the local user, though, you simply take over the desktop without forcing a logoff.
>
> If someone else logs on to the remote computer while you're connected from afar, your session is disconnected. Again, if Fast User Switching is enabled, you can simply reconnect later and pick up where you left off. Otherwise, the same deal applies: If it is a different user, your applications shut down.

If you're using Remote Desktop to use your own computer, this probably won't matter to you because you'll probably never see what happens on the other screen. But if you use Remote Desktop to work on someone else's computer, let that person know what will happen before starting; otherwise, the two of you could get into a tussle, repeatedly kicking the other person off the computer, with neither of you knowing that the other person is there trying to get something done.

Third-Party Remote Control Tools

There are several third-party remote control tools that you might want to consider. A bunch of web-based products have emerged that work very well. Many of them have free versions, and most have some advantages over Remote Desktop: They work with any version of Windows, and they require almost no setup, even if you have a router on your Internet connection. Here are some products to check out:

- **LogMeIn**—Available in free and Pro versions. Pro gets you file transfer, sound, and printing. Mac and Windows versions are available. No network setup is necessary. Find information at www.logmein.com. (I use this program myself to assist several of my clients.)

- **TeamViewer**—Available free for personal, noncommercial use, TeamViewer requires no network setup and can even make your LAN available to the remote client computer through a built-in VPN service. Both Windows and Mac clients and hosts are available. Check out www.teamviewer.com.

- **I'm InTouch**—Another no-network-setup remote access product. The remote client is Java based, so you could access your PC from your Blackberry. How cool is that? Check out www.01com.com.

- **BeAnywhere**—Another subscription-based remote access product, requiring no network setup. Check it out at www.beanywhere.com.

- **LapLink Everywhere** (formerly Carbon Copy)—Requires no network setup. Clients are available for Palms and PocketPCs as well as PCs. Information at www.laplink.com.

- **GoToMyPC**—A commercial subscription-based product that offers remote access through any web browser. Information at www.gotomypc.com.

- **Radmin**—A low-cost remote control program. Information at www.radmin.com. Requires network setup.

- **Symantec PCAnywhere**—One of the original remote control programs. You can connect via modem, LAN, or Internet. It suffers from feature bloat, some long-standing bugs, and Symantec's general disinterest in providing support to individuals, as opposed to big corporate customers; but overall, it's a solid, industrial-strength product. Its file transfer feature is useful. Available from www.symantec.com and most software resellers. Requires network setup.

- **VNC**—An open-source program initially developed by AT&T. A big plus for VNC is that both host and client programs are available for virtually every OS. There are a few VNC versions available, with TightVNC and RealVNC the most popular. At the time this was written, TightVNC and the free version of RealVNC do not work on Windows 7 or Vista as a host. For information, check www.tightvnc.com and www.realvnc.com. Requires network setup.

note

All these products let you access a computer via the Internet. The ones that require network setup can also access a computer across a LAN or corporate network. If you want to access a remote computer via a dial-up modem, though, you must use one of the old-school programs, such as Symantec PCAnywhere. Alternatively, you can set up an incoming dial-up networking connection for your computer, and use Remote Desktop or a network-based remote control program, such as VNC.

TABLET PC FEATURES

Importance of Handwriting

Nowadays, the old "pencil and paper" approach to creating documents has certainly gone the way of the dinosaur. If you're like me, without a keyboard you're lost. I can barely remember how to sign my name on a check. The use of electronic file editing has almost totally put an end to basic handwriting. But what about the times you have to write in longhand? We need longhand when taking basic notes at home or at a business meeting, developing a quick graph or sketch, or even jotting down a shopping list. With these thoughts in mind, how can we connect the digital world with the analog world?

One way has been through Pocket PCs —those little PDAs that sport handwriting recognition and turn your scribbles into text. I use one daily, and it's pretty amazing how good the recognition is. Still, it's just a little PDA, not a full-blown computer. I can scribble into Pocket Word or Pocket Excel, which is pretty cool, but the screen is small, and I mostly use it for email, contacts, and organizing my calendar. But while the PDA was evolving in the foreground and capturing our attention as it merged with cell phones, the Tablet PC was quietly climbing out of the water onto dry land and growing legs.

History of Tablet PCs

Believe it or not, the technology behind Tablet PCs goes back to 1888, with a U.S. Patent granted to Elisha Gray for a device that electronically captured handwriting with a stylus. There have been a handful of patents awarded to inventors who dreamed of an "electronic tablet" with magical computing powers that could interpret handwriting and do useful work with the input. With the advent of powerful portable computers, the idea of a fully functional tablet-style PC crystallized as a specific focus for computer engineers and a select group of computer users ever since the 1980s. In the '80s, due to availability of miniaturized CPUs and their computational capabilities, handwriting recognition began taking strides as a developing technology. Numerous companies developed basic handwriting recognizers that could interpret simple text and numbers.

A decade later, in 1991, the pen was seen as a major competitor to the standard mouse. At this time, Microsoft developed Windows for Pen Computing, an elementary pen extension for Windows 3.1. Figure 38.1 shows some examples of different kinds of tablets that were pioneers in Tablet PC history.

Figure 38.1
From left to right, Fujitsu Stylistic 3500 Tablet PC and the Newton MessagePad 2000.

Around 1993, the Apple Newton was released, stuffed with handwriting recognition technology claimed by Apple to be truly workable. Although the Newton was clever and innovative in many ways, and filled a void between the PDA and the laptop, its handwriting recognition was flawed too, and it soon fell prey to critical reviews.

During the early '90s, pen-based computers from EO, GRiD, Samsung, NEC, Fujitsu, NCR, TelePad, and others arrived and then quietly sank into the sunset with little fanfare. Tablet PCs languished for the rest of the decade but were not giving up the ghost yet. In 2000 at Comdex, keynote speaker Microsoft CEO Bill Gates excitedly presented a webpad and reintroduced the Tablet PC almost as a new technology. Those in the know could see this was hype, but Gates did spark a new flurry of interest in the technology. Pen computing trudged along its evolutionary timeline adding bits and pieces and dropping vestigial ones. Now pen-based XP, Vista, and now Windows 7 computers are readily available and they actually work. The moniker *Tablet PC* actually started sticking in the popular trade press as of about 2005, despite the fact that it was in 2001 that Gates and company office christened the term and created a standard for the Tablet PC that specifies the hardware and software components. As you would expect, a bona fide Tablet PC must run a Microsoft operating system.

Tablet PCs come in two varieties, the *slate* and the *convertible*, as shown in Figure 38.2. The slate Tablet PC is a basic no-frills tablet that requires you use handwriting because there is no keyboard. By contrast, the convertible Tablet PC has both a keyboard *and* a pen. By having a laptop with a keyboard, you can, if a proficient typist, enter basic documents quickly and easily. But then by converting that laptop into a flat slate (either by removing the keyboard or rotating and flipping the screen down on top of the keyboard), you are then fully pen-enabled. Windows 7 employs the full functions of the Tablet PC. A variety of programs and functions are at your pen (or finger) tip.

Slates and convertibles subdivide further into two subcategories, based on screen type. Some screens only accept stylus (pen) input while others allow you to interact with the screen using touch as well as the stylus. The screen input driver is smart enough to know whether you are touching the screen with the stylus or with your finger, and behaves accordingly.

Some of the new breed of tiny "netbook" computers are now beginning to sport tablet-like features such as touch screens, finger and pen input, and convertible (rotate-and-flip) screens. In fact, touch has become so central to many devices such as iPhones, PDAs, and even all-in-one desktop PCs such as HP's TouchSmart desktop PCs that we are certain to soon be seeing tablet-like features on many more computers. In this chapter, we'll discuss the benefits of owning a Tablet PC, and learn the basics of using one.

Figure 38.2
HP tx2500 convertible Table PC with Motion Computing LE1700WT slate Table PC to its right.

Using Speech Recognition with a Tablet PC

Of course, because a Tablet PC is a fully functioning XP, Vista, or Windows 7 machine, it can run speech recognition software such as Nuance Dragon NaturallySpeacking, IBM ViaVoice, or the excellent voice recognition system built in to Windows 7 called Speech Recognition. So if you hate to type, and you don't even want to use a pen much, I suggest you purchase a quality headset and benefit from this technology. With a Windows 7 tablet and the built-in Speech Recognition program, you can dictate text, write emails, surf the Net, switch between tasks, click items on the screen and even enter spreadsheet data. Bob uses Speech Recognition a lot, and even used it to write chapters in this book. We cover this technology briefly in Chapter 4, "Using the Windows 7 User Interface," but not in depth. (Sorry, we didn't have room in the book.)

When you run Speech Recognition the first time, it will walk you through setting up your microphone and then runs a tutorial that introduces you to the essentials of running Speech Recognition. The *most* important thing to know, however (and I had to learn the hard way), is that the internal sound card in most laptops are noisy and do a terrible job with a regular analog microphone (the kind with a 3.5mm headphone plug on the cord). If you try the Speech Recognition and recognition is poor, this is probably the culprit. You'll need at least a run-of-the-mill USB headset, or better yet a good analog headset designed for voice recognition and a USB "pod" to plug that into. The pod is a noise cancellation analog-to-digital converter designed for speech recognition. Good ones are made by Andrea Electronics and VXI. Go to www.sayican.com or http://speechrec-solutions.com/ to get started finding a good mic. There is a wealth of information on headsets at the second link.

Be sure to read up on some of the voice recognition sites about how to maximize accuracy by additional training of your system, how to position your mic relative to your mouth, and how to add new words and exceptions to your Speech Recognition dictionary. Also, be sure to see Chapter 4 for details on setting advanced speech options.

Who Needs a Tablet?

Is a Tablet PC in your future? Possibly. Some would argue that a Tablet PC is for everyone, whereas others are too addicted to the keyboard to let it go. However, even being a keyboard fan myself, as a writer, after I got get used to touching the screen instead of pointing with the mouse, I may never go back because this approach is so much more direct and intuitive. I have been using one for a year or so now, and find myself touching regular laptop and desktop screens to choose dialog box options or move the insertion point in a document, reflexively. I am surprised when it doesn't work!

Tablet functions are easy to use and great for work, school, or personal use. Because they are so portable, almost like a sheet of paper, and because you can easily draw pictures, diagrams, and maps, as well as write longhand text that translates into typed text, a Tablet PC can replace scratch paper, Post-It notes, and other desk-cluttering trivia. Eliminate that mess and invest in a Tablet PC. With Windows 7, a Tablet PC can be an efficient means of staying organized.

What Does a Windows 7 Tablet PC Have That Regular PCs Don't?

The most obvious answer to this question is that Tablet Windows 7 enables you to use handwriting on your computer. Using a pen both as a mouse and for writing increases your computer options. The Handwriting Recognizer can distinguish your handwriting and transform that writing into typed text. The Handwriting Recognizer in Windows 7 adds some very nice features over that in Vista, including Asian language recognition, mathematical equation recognition, and much easier input correction.

With Windows 7, users who have a Tablet PC get extra fun goodies as well. These include special software and hardware that a normal PC does not have. A few basic extras include

- A stylus pen (or simply "stylus"), shown in Figure 38.3, that acts like a mouse and keyboard. Use the stylus to click and accomplish other functions just like a mouse. A stylus has many improved functions over a mouse, discussed later in this chapter.

Figure 38.3
Wacom stylus pen with multiple functionalities.

- Pressure-sensitive touch screens that offer more than a normal monitor. The Tablet PC screen recognizes how hard you push and displays that as a lighter or darker line.

- A swivel screen, in the case of convertible Tablet PCs such as shown in Figure 38.2. This swivel screen can be rotated and closed flat to cover the keyboard and provide a full-layout tablet.

- Buttons on the edge of the screen that are available when a convertible screen covers the keyboard, typically for options such as rotating the screen image, opening the Mobility Center (Tools menu for laptops), or playing a DVD.

- New software that can only be fully utilized by using a pen or finger.

What's New in Tablet Windows 7?

All the existing items for tablets in the previous XP and Vista OS versions are included in Windows 7, and then some. (If you are upgrading to Windows 7 from Vista, not all of these will be new, but if you skipped Vista and joined the party coming from XP, you will mark a few more of these items as "new" in Windows 7):

- **Enhanced stylus graphics**—New visual effects are added in Windows 7 that XP did not have. As you can see when using Windows 7, your computer will recognize the stylus and create a new pointer for your pen. Clicking has also been enhanced to present a ripple effect and a halo for right-clicks.

- **Pen flicks**—Increasing your usage yet again with great added functionality, pen flicks improve how you browse online and how you can edit documents. Flicks are powerful and convenient and can be customized.

- **Better handwriting recognition**—Windows 7 improved the Recognizer so that it is more capable of accurately recognizing different handwriting styles. No longer will you have to comply with a standard writing style. Why change your style when you can just change how Windows 7 understands it? Recognition can "learn" how you write based on your corrections, and also can predict what you are trying to write, based on sentences you have written before.

- **Improved Tablet Input Panel**—There are several improvements to the Tablet Input Panel that make handwriting sentences much easier. In Vista the handwriting recognition results are shown under the area where you write, in text bubbles. To verify correct recognition you need to look down at the bubbles, which might even be hidden by your hand. To correct an error, you tap on a bubble to bring up a secondary window for correction. In Windows 7, after you write a word and lift the pen, recognition occurs and your writing is replaced by the perfectly formed word in a script-like font. The size of the type automatically approximates your writing size. Furthermore, there are new gestures that make it easy and intuitive to enter, correct, insert, and split words and delete text using the pen. Significant improvements were made to handwriting recognition on the four East Asian languages Windows 7 supports: Traditional Chinese, Simplified Chinese, Korean, and Japanese.

- **Math Input Panel**—The new Math Input Panel (MIP) recognizes even complex mathematical notation (high-school and college level) for easy insertion into programs such as Word. See Figure 38.4.

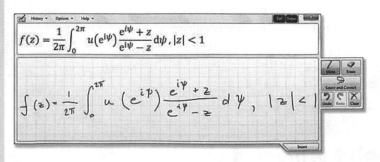

Figure 38.4
Math Input Panel is new in Windows 7. It can easily transform your math scribbles into typeset equations.

$$f(z) = \frac{1}{2\pi} \int_0^{2\pi} u(e^{i\psi}) \frac{e^{i\psi} + z}{e^{i\psi} - z} d\psi, |z| < 1$$

- **Multitouch capabilities**—With a tablet or monitor that supports it, Windows 7 will do nifty multitouch tricks that were first made popular with the iPhone. Microsoft throws in a few gee-whiz apps to show this off, including a virtual piano program, a mapping and directions program, and a touch-aware version of Paint. Vista added Tablet PC support for Business, Enterprise, Home Premium, and Ultimate Editions. Tablet Windows 7 builds on this platform with support for multitouch, a way to use visual gestures on touch screens to instruct Windows 7 what to do, and how to behave. To better understand this capability, watch this Microsoft video demo at http://video.msn.com/video.aspx?vid=8700c7ff-546f-4e1d-85f7-65659dd1f14f.

- The Windows taskbar has seen its most significant revision since its introduction in Windows 95. The taskbar is 10 pixels taller than in Windows Vista to accommodate touch screen input and a new, larger default icon size.

These are but a few improvements that Microsoft created in Windows 7. Later in this chapter, you see in depth what Windows 7 has done with the Tablet PC.

Choosing a Tablet PC

Choosing a Tablet PC can be difficult for new buyers. Everyone has his own distinct likes and dislikes of certain PC styles and layouts. Add to that the quirks of a tablet, and the choice becomes a conundrum. Here are two things to consider when looking for a Tablet PC:

- Most stores do not have Tablet PCs displayed because of the fragility of the swivel screen of the convertible type. Lately, a few stores—Best Buy, for example—have let you touch one before you buy it. Go to these stores and play around with the Tablet to see whether a Tablet PC is for you.

- Tablets come in two different types, and it's your choice which one to buy. Beware that most slate Tablet PCs are not sold in local stores. If having a keyboard is a must for you, but you like the lighter weight and size of the slates (for example, Motion Computing makes a nice small one), consider a fold-up Bluetooth or infrared (IR) keyboard made for PDAs. If the tablet you want has Bluetooth or IR, you can carry a keyboard in your pocket.

Using Your Tablet PC—Differences and Similarities of Functions

Using a Tablet PC can be very different from using a regular PC, depending on the type. With slate design Tablet PCs, you are required to use only the pen for every function (unless you are using voice input). After you become accustomed to a slate Tablet PC, you will not miss a keyboard. If you do miss a keyboard, you can obtain an external one and plug it in via USB or wirelessly with Bluetooth, as I mentioned.

Convertible Tablet PCs are just like a normal laptop but with the added feature of the stylus pen. Unlike slate Tablet PCs, convertibles have a built-in keyboard. One downfall to the built-in keyboard is that it will add more weight and bulk to the computer.

Either design of Tablet PC comes with a stylus and all the tablet functions. Using a pen on the screen is no different from using a mouse—you simply point and click, but in this case, a click is done with the pressure of the pen or a switch on the side of the pen. It could be argued that using a pen is actually faster and more immediately intuitive. Pens vary somewhat in their design but often are set up to cause a left-click when you press the screen and a right-click when you click the button on the pen's side. A right-click also results from pressing the pen (or finger) on the screen and holding it down for a second or two. This typically brings up the context menu of the item being clicked.

As icing on the cake, Windows 7's tablet features include some shortcuts called *flicks* and *gestures* that make tablet computing even more efficient. As mentioned in Chapter 4, Windows 7 has some mouse gestures as well that work on non-tablets. For example, when you drag a window's title bar to the top of the screen and release it, the window maximizes. But on a tablet, there are gestures for things such as going "back" or "forward" between web pages, or for scrolling pages of a document.

Input Methods Using the Input Panel

As with a Pocket PC (if you have used one), Tablet PCs offer a variety of ways to input data and text. In Windows XP Tablet Edition, Microsoft introduced three new ways for a user to input text and phrases. This was refined in Vista. Now in Windows 7, the newest iteration of the *Input Panel* simplifies input matters further.

The basic Input Panel contains a variety of functions and extras. The Input Panel lets you choose where to dock it—it can be docked anywhere on the screen. When you are not using the Input Panel, it will quietly minimize where you docked it and be ready for you to use whenever you click it. This is a bit like the taskbar on any XP, Vista, or Windows 7 computer when set to auto-hide. The Input Panel usually hides itself behind the left or right side of the screen, with only its edge (tab) showing. Tapping the tab causes the Input Panel to slide out onto the screen. You can open the Input Panel without having to go to the tab on the side of the screen, however. Simply hold the stylus over a text box or text area, and a little Tablet Panel icon will show next to your stylus. Clicking this icon will open a floating Input Panel for you to quickly and easily input text. Figure 38.5 illustrates the basic Input Panel. As you can see, it has a nicely sized text frame for you to write in. Windows 7 gives you a large enough text frame to input a decent-sized sentence. As you near the end of the line, another blank line appears below it, so you can keep writing if you want to, before clicking the Insert button to paste the text into whatever app, window, or text field you are using.

The Windows 7 Input Panel has some flashy new features that you might not be able to use, but they are worth mentioning. Specifically, it can recognize mathematical equations and has support for several Asian languages (more on this later in the chapter).

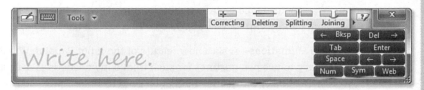

Figure 38.5
The Tablet Input Panel has many new features and abilities.

Writing Methods Using the Input Panel

In Figure 38.5, you can see two different boxes on the top left of the Input Panel. These boxes are the two ways that you can input your handwriting and transform that into typed text. (Previous versions of the Input Panel also had a Character Pad for entering individual letters, much like filling in a printed government form or writing in "graffiti" on a PDA, but this option was moved to an option on the Tools menu.) Briefly, the boxes work as follows:

- **Writing Pad**—The left button presents a free-form-based writing field. You can write longhand or print full words and sentences, and Windows 7 will do its best to transform that into text. Windows 7 will recognize words fairly well even without training and will display each word right in the Input Panel after you lift the pen. It is pretty magical to watch this happen. Suddenly you have excellent handwriting. If a certain word you wrote is not recognized correctly, you can click that word on the Writing Pad and edit it. The word opens up as separate letters in what is called the Character Pad (see Figure 38.6). In the Character Pad, you see a slot for each character. If a character is wrong, simply write over it with the desired character until it is correct. You can use the strikeout, split, and join gestures, too. (See the last item in this list, "Gesture Animations.") Suggested words appear in small print above the Character Pad. Tap a word to select it. Click the x to close the Character Pad and accept the current spelling. The Character Pad also features Smart Corrections. All you have to do is start correcting the word from the left and it starts suggesting words that match. Keep updating until you get the word you want, then close the Character Pad by clicking the little x.

- **Onscreen Keyboard**—Windows 7 incorporates a standard onscreen QWERTY keyboard to fit your needs for using a stylus or finger, if your tablet has touch input ability. This includes all the basic keys situated in the same spot as a normal keyboard. On-Screen Keyboard is a handy tool that will help you with such things as creating a certain password or ID name that may likely include a mix of letters and numbers. With a dual-mode screen, pressing the edge of the docked input panel with your finger will bring out the larger, finger keyboard. Pressing on the tab with a stylus brings out a smaller keyboard for use with a pen. However, the new Windows 7 keyboard can be resized to as large as the entire screen, so you can even do touch typing on it. There is no tactile feedback, but it is still pretty cool. Size the keyboard by dragging its lower-right corner. The keyboard has an intelligent visual feedback scheme to let you know which key you pressed (the key you pressed has a glow fadeout after you release it). Also, the keyboard supports multi-touch, so you can type faster without dropping keys and can press two keys at once (for example, Shift+ a key, Ctrl+ a key, and so on). Your screen has to be multitouch capable, though.

- **Gesture animations**—A slick new feature of the Input Panel in Windows 7 is the inclusion of a set of easy-to-use pen gestures for such frequently needed tasks as splitting words and joining words. Tap one of the gesture animation buttons to see how each gesture works. A little video animation will play, illustrating exactly how to move the pen and what the effect is. Use each of the gestures on the Writing Pad to get the hang of them. These new Input Panel gestures are a godsend while handwriting.

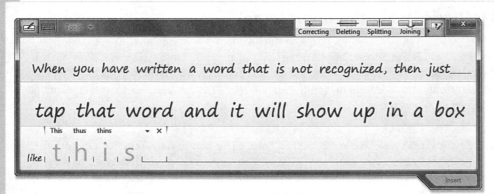

Figure 38.6
Multiple lines open up as you write, and tapping on a word lets you respell it.

Notice that in Figure 38.5 there are buttons on the right side of the Input Panel in freeform-writing mode, whereas in Figure 38.6 there are not. When you first open the Input Panel, these buttons appear so that you can easily enter web addresses, symbols, or numbers. Very handy. Tap the Num, Sym, or Web buttons to see the additional, related keys that pop up. Once you start writing with the stylus rather than tapping these buttons, they vanish to make room for writing.

 tip

A Tablet Input Panel icon can be inserted into your taskbar. Just right-click the taskbar and click Toolbars, Tablet PC Input Panel.

Using the Stylus Pen

The stylus is an essential tool for tablet use and will likely never leave your computer. (If it does, you're up the creek, because it's essential to tablet use, unless you have a touch screen. Some tablets come with a string that you can use to leash your stylus to the tablet with. I suggest using it.) Even with touch capability, a stylus is essential for certain chores that require exactitude. Briefly, here's how it works.

Windows 7 detects that you are using a pen automatically and will change the cursor from an arrow to a small dot when you are writing or pointing and clicking icons, buttons, and other interface items. With some styli, simply pointing at an object such as a menu choice will highlight it, equivalent to dragging the mouse pointer over an item (or hovering over it). That is, you do not actually have to touch the screen.

Pen Cursor Problem

If your pen cursor is off-center, you will quickly find that clicking the onscreen items you want will be difficult. The Tablet PC stylus pen needs to be recalibrated after a period of time. To recalibrate the pen, go to Control Panel, Hardware and Sound, Tablet PC Settings and on the Display tab click Calibrate.

Windows 7 detects pen clicks and will display a neat ripple effect. One tap on the screen with the stylus will create one ripple and represents an onscreen (left) click. So, one ripple equals one click and two ripples equal a double-click. Now if that weren't neat enough, Windows 7 incorporated an even neater right-click.

As you know, the right-click on a mouse is a highly needed function. Most styli incorporate this right-click as a button on the side of the actual pen. If you press this button and tap on the screen, the result is a right-click. Windows 7 will automatically recognize the pen and the right-click and will open the right-click menu. You will also see a lighted halo at the spot you right-clicked. As mentioned before, pressing the stylus to the screen and holding it still for a second or two will result in a larger circle appearing. When you release, the right-click menu appears.

Windows 7 utilizes not only the front of the stylus but also the back end. When writing a note, you may want to delete a small mistake in your text. Instead of clicking the onscreen eraser, erasing with the stylus, and then clicking on the pen button again to continue writing, you can just flip your pen backward and erase. The end of the stylus (shown in Figure 38.3) serves as an onscreen eraser, just like on a real pencil. Windows 7 and apps will often recognize the back end of the pen as the eraser—very slick and intuitive.

Input Panel Options

The Input Panel has a Tools drop-down menu that opens a world of options if you drill down a bit by opening the Options dialog box. But let's look at the menu itself, first.

You can toggle the Input Panel between individual character entry and longhand writing. These differences were explained briefly a bit earlier. Next, you can choose to personalize handwriting recognition (described later in this chapter). Finally, you can declare where you want the Input Panel to dock (also described later in this chapter). There was a Help menu on the Vista version of the Input Panel but that has now been integrated into the Tools menu.

Regarding docking styles, you have a few options. *Docking* simply means where the Input Panel will hang out on the screen once you open it. You can dock it at the top or bottom of the screen, or have it float on the screen. Floating the Input Panel is great when you want to write small, quick text, such as a username and password. Most tablet users will agree that docking on the bottom of the screen is the best strategy, because it not only allows you to write but also is least invasive of other documents that are likely to be on your screen. If you choose to float the Input Panel, its width is manually adjustable. If you dock at top or bottom, it extends fully across the screen.

Choosing Tools, Options opens a complex dialog box with six tabs. Some of those settings are covered later in this chapter. They are all worth exploring.

Gestures and Pen Flicks

Gestures and pen flicks are basic stylus options that let you write and browse even faster and easier. Gestures are quick scribbles with the stylus that effectively scratch out text, or enter the keyboard keys of Backspace, Delete, Space, and Enter. Using pen flicks makes scrolling through documents and browsing the Internet easy. With pen flicks, you can scroll up and down and go back and forward in your current web browser with just a few quick motions of the pen.

Scratch-Out Gestures

The most important gesture of all the tablet stylus options is the Scratch-out gesture. With a Tablet PC, you will be doing a lot of writing with the stylus, and sometimes you will misspell words and make mistakes. Instead of using the back end of the pen to erase an entire word, you can use a Scratch-out. Simply draw a line through the words you want to erase, preferably draw the line from right to left. You can scratch out not only words but also entire sentences.

Pen Flicks

The stylus pen enables you to view and scroll through documents and web pages easier than you can with a touchpad. With a stylus, you are free to touch anywhere on the screen with the pen and instantly click where you need to go. Windows 7 now makes browsing even faster with the introduction of pen flicks.

Pen flicks are common actions that can be done using the stylus pen. For example, suppose you are browsing the Internet and want to go back a page. You could click the Back button once or scroll through the list of web pages you visited to get there. A faster way is to just touch the screen at any spot with the pen and flick the pen toward the left direction. With one flick of the wrist, you will automatically go back to the previous web page.

Conversely, flicking to the right moves forward, analogous to clicking the Forward button on the browser toolbar.

If you think going back and forward is simple, scrolling up and down in a web page is just as easy. Scrolling in a web page using the stylus used to require you to hold your pen on the scrollbar on the screen just as you would do with a mouse. With pen flicks, instead of holding the scrollbar, you can flick up or down to scroll in the respective direction.

To see the list of flicks, make adjustments, and practice using flicks, open Control Panel, Pen and Touch. Or click Start and enter **Flicks**. Then choose Set Flicks to Perform Certain Tasks. Read more about customizing flicks at the end of this chapter.

 tip

Flicking is a little tricky at first. To use pen flicks correctly, you may need to practice. Windows 7 supplies a pen flick trainer, located in the Tablet PC folder under All Programs, Tablet PC. Also, if flicks are not working correctly, perhaps they are turned off. Check the Pen and Touch dialog box's Flicks tab and, if necessary, turn them on.

With a Flick of the Wrist

After using your Tablet PC long enough, you can become proficient at using pen flicks. If you haven't already customized your pen flicks, here is a great tip to make your friends envious.

Windows 7 incorporates a 3-D Windows Switcher called Flip 3-D that is a great visual substitution for the Alt+Tab method. With the following trick, you can trigger Flip 3-D using only the pen:

1. Open the Pen and Touch dialog box and go to the Flicks tab.

2. Make sure that flicks are enabled and that Navigational Flicks and Editing Flicks are enabled.

3. Select Customize to open the Customize Flicks window.

4. Assign one direction of your flicks to be interpreted as the keypress Ctrl+Windows+Tab. Be sure that you add the Ctrl key there, because if you don't, the Window Switcher will not stay open.

5. After using the assigned flick to open Flip 3-D, you can rotate between the slides of the Windows Switcher by using the same flick. Each flick advances one slide. Then simply tap the slide you want to open.

Handwriting Recognition

Just as with the Speech Recognition feature, we have found the Handwriting Recognition feature in Windows 7 to be very good, even without training. Training will always improve your success, however. When you first start using your Tablet PC in Windows 7, it is possible that it may not recognize certain words or phrases correctly. This can be a software issue, or, as with a few of us, your handwriting just stinks. This can easily be solved by using the Handwriting Recognition tool that allows you to teach the Recognizer how you write. Because everyone has a distinct handwriting style, teaching Windows 7 how to recognize your style can help it better read and understand what you are writing. Windows 7 also uses the system Indexer data as a source of clues to help it predict which words you regularly use. (The System Indexer regularly sifts through all your hard disk files and creates an index of all the words in them so you can quickly find files, emails, photos, and so on.)

To teach Windows 7 about your handwriting, use the Handwriting Personalization window (see Figure 38.7).

The Handwriting Personalization window will ask you to demonstrate your handwriting to allow Windows 7 to understand your handwriting better. To open the Handwriting Personalization window, follow these steps:

1. Click the Start button and type **Handwriting** in the search box.

2. Select Personalize Handwriting Recognition. (You can also get to Personalize Handwriting Recognition from the Tools menu of the Input Panel.)

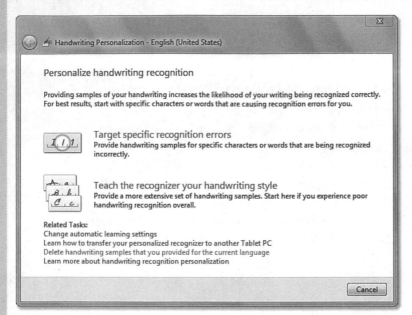

Figure 38.7
Handwriting personalization.

Specific Handwriting Recognition Errors

With the Handwriting Personalization window open, you are given two options. The first option is to target specific handwriting errors that constantly occur. The second option is to allow Windows 7 to better learn how you write.

Automatic correction of common errors in Windows 7's Handwriting Recognition can save you time. Constantly fixing that one word that is always misrecognized can be really annoying. You can force the Recognizer to correct those mistakes and improve how it reads your handwriting with the Handwriting Recognition tool.

Teach the Recognizer Your Style

Teaching the Recognizer how you write can improve its accuracy significantly, especially if your handwriting is sloppy. This process lets you keep your current handwriting style and changes how Windows 7 reads it. If you have trained a speech recognition program to understand your vocal patterns, you'll be familiar with the concept. There are two basic ways that you can change the Recognizer to improve its capability to understand your writing:

- **Numbers, Symbols, and Letters Recognition**—Teach the Recognizer how to read your handwriting by individual words and numbers. The Handwriting Personalization applet will ask you to write the entire alphabet in caps and lowercase, and write all numbers from zero to nine. This way of teaching the Recognizer is basic and quick.

■ **Sentences Recognition**—When using this option, you will be asked to write a variety of sentences so that the Recognizer can get better recognition of your style and sentence compilation. Beware, though, Windows 7 will want you to write a total of 50 sentences for it to fully understand your handwriting. But instead of writing all 50 right away, you can save and do this incrementally. Spend the time to finish this setting. It will save you a lot of time correcting words later.

AutoComplete

The AutoComplete function for tablets is the same as the AutoComplete function used on a regular PC, such as in Internet Explorer or Office. Windows will suggest what word or URL you are typing and give you the option to select it without typing the entire word or URL. With the Tablet Input Panel, you have the same power with your stylus.

Most people log in to an email account or type a URL in their browser everyday. Browsers commonly use the AutoComplete function due to the length of the URL. The stylus input works the same way as if you were typing that URL on your keyboard.

To write a URL in your browser, open the Tablet Input Panel and select the address line. Instead of a keyboard, you are left with the option of handwriting the URL in the Tablet Input Panel. While you are writing the URL into the text field, Windows creates a list of suggestions for you, based on recent entries you have made. Choose one of the suggestions if it is what you are writing. The same will be true with email addresses and filenames.

AutoComplete can be turned off from the Options dialog box if you find it annoying.

Similar to AutoComplete is Predictive Text. This anticipates what you're trying to type or write, based on what you've entered so far. Keep your eye peeled for suggestions that show up near the Input Panel. Tap the one you want to insert into the input area.

note

You might have noticed that if you highlight a phrase such as a URL and then open the Input Panel, the word will appear in the Input Panel. If only small changes are needed, you can enter them in that Character Pad. This helps decrease the amount of writing that you have to do.

note

Windows 7 Tablet Edition includes two tools quite useful for the tablet operating edition: Sticky Notes and the Snipping Tool. These two tools are covered in Chapter 7.

Windows Journal

If you like to keep notes or even a diary, this is the program for you. Windows Journal looks like a basic sheet of paper but on your tablet (see Figure 38.8). You can write anything you want, draw graphs and charts, or just doodle. You can insert pictures, drag items around, add or remove empty space on the page, convert handwriting to typed text, and even search through your handwritten notes using a Find command that does handwriting recognition. It's a pretty spiffy program whose price is right (free) and is a fun way to show off your tablet. It's a great brainstorming tool while in a meeting, while riding on a bus, or in place of the proverbial back of a napkin.

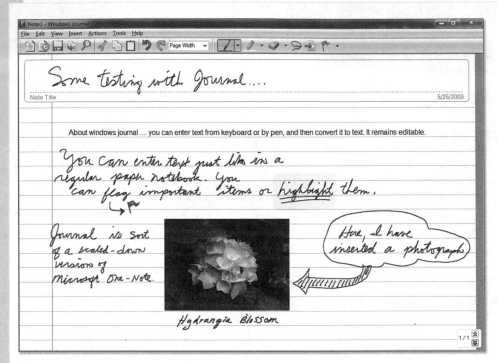

Figure 38.8
Windows
Journal.

At first blush, Windows Journal might look like Microsoft Word. True, it is similar, but the primary difference is that you can use handwriting instead of just plain text. You can easily change the colors of the pens or the highlighters if you take notes. Actually, Journal is more like a little brother to Microsoft One Note, which is the ultimate tablet-centric tool, particularly popular among students.

When you first open Windows Journal, you may wonder why the page is so small. Not a problem. You can easily change the page size via File, Page Setup.

Two options in particular are worth checking out:

- Convert Selection to E-mail

- Convert Handwriting to Text

Both of these options are useful. After scribbling up a set of notes, you may want to consider converting it to text so that you can place it in a Word or other text-based document. To do so, follow these steps:

1. Complete the handwritten text that you want converted.

2. Select the Lasso tool and select all the text that you want converted. The Lasso tool has a weird pivot system that is at first awkward to use. Instead of the red dots being the selector of the text, the Lasso tool uses the white dotted line that comes from the focus point. Also, if the white

dotted line selects about 70% more of the handwriting, it figures out what you are trying to select and will select all of that content.

3. After you select the text you want converted, select Actions in the toolbar and then select Convert Handwriting to Text.

4. A new window appears asking you whether the words that it recognized are correct. You can then change any words that are incorrect.

Converting handwriting to text is a useful function that you will do a lot. You can also convert your text to an email if you want. Follow the preceding steps, but at step 3, click Convert Selection to E-mail. This will open the same window and send the data to your profile mail account.

Tweaking Your Tablet PC Settings

In this section, I will briefly discuss the most important tablet, pen, and touch settings you should know about if you are going to use a tablet with Windows 7.

Tablet PC Settings Dialog Box

The Tablet PC Settings dialog box, shown on the left in Figure 38.9, is a primary applet that offers many handwriting and display settings. It is the central location to adjust tablet settings, including those for the Input Panel. This applet is easily accessible from the classic view Control Panel (click Tablet PC Settings), or from the Category view by going to Control Panel, Hardware and Sound, Tablet PC Settings.

Figure 38.9
From these two dialog boxes, you can make the most signifi-cant settings for a Tablet PC.

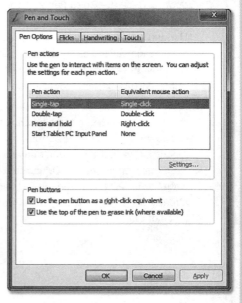

The first thing you will want to do is configure your screen so that Windows 7 knows that you have a pen and/or touch screen. Click the Display tab, then click Setup in the Configure section and follow the prompts.

Next, you should calibrate the screen for accuracy; otherwise, your pen and finger will be clicking things on the screen that you do not intend them to. Having the pointer uncalibrated can cause annoying pen misbehavior such as the inability to grab the scrollbar. Again, on the Display tab, Click Calibrate and follow the prompts. If you have a dual-mode screen (pen and touch), you will do the calibration for each mode. Note that, compared to Vista and XP, calibration now involves more steps, presumably making it more accurate, through redundancy of taps of the screen and averaging the data points. From time to time, you will have to recalibrate your stylus with your tablet. Every few months, take the time to recalibrate your pen (and touch).

Are you left-handed? If so, you have not been forgotten. Click the Other tab of the Tablet PC Settings dialog box and choose Left Handed. As a result of your choosing Left-Handed or Right-Handed, the Tablet Input Panel will either appear on the left or right side of the screen.

The next option worth futzing with is the Buttons tab. Most tablets come with a set of buttons on the side or next to the screen. These buttons perform certain shortcut actions such as rotating the display or bringing up the Mobility settings, and can save you pen strokes or taps. Take the time to set each button to what you want. Setting a button to a function such as opening Windows Journal can be a huge benefit. Obviously, you'll want to set your buttons to launch programs or execute functions that you use most frequently. If the software driver for your buttons is missing, or your PC is not a bona fide tablet, you will not have this tab.

As we said previously in this chapter, Handwriting Recognition is an important tool when writing text. Windows 7 has a great capacity to learn how to recognize your handwriting style. Tweaking the Handwriting settings will be well worth a little toil if you expect to be using the pen to any degree. Click the Go to Pen and Touch link (or click Start and type **Pen** and the link will appear in the search results). This brings up the dialog box you see in the right side of Figure 38.9. Click the Handwriting tab, and you can turn off the Recognizer and turn off automatic learning. Windows 7 keeps each setting on by default, and we recommend that you not change them. Keep the default settings unless you have a personal vendetta against the Handwriting Recognizer. Let your computer learn to better recognize your handwriting over time. Your efficiency will increase markedly.

At the bottom of the Tablet PC Settings dialog box (Buttons tab) there is a link for setting the order in which the screen rotates when you press the rotate button on your tablet. This can be useful to cut down the number of button presses required to switch between portrait and landscape screen modes. Note that if you don't have a rotate button, you can go to Control Panel, Display, Screen Resolution and open the Orientation drop-down list and rotate the screen that way. If you have a slate Tablet PC (no keyboard), choose Portrait or Portrait (flipped) mode as the default if it isn't already selected. Portrait gives more of a "paper" feel, as the layout of the screen is more like a piece of paper.

Screen Does Not Change Layout for Convertibles

If your convertible Tablet PC does not go into tablet mode when you rotate the screen, it could be that your rotation program (a small app that controls the layout of the Table PC display when the screen is physically rotated) failed to initialize. Follow these steps to change the layout of your Tablet PC:

1. Open the Control Panel.

2. Click Hardware and Sound (if in Category view).

3. Click Windows Mobility Center.

4. Click Rotate Screen. Each time you press this button, the screen rotates 90 degrees.

When changing the layout of the screen to portrait using the above method, when you want to revert back to landscape, you must follow the preceding steps again. Using the preceding method is a manual way of rotating the display. To fix the automatic rotation utility program, try reinstalling the program or checking online for a newer version of the software.

In portrait layout, Word documents and full-page items will be easier to read and will require less scrolling. The only time I would suggest you change to Landscape is when you are watching a full-screen movie or slideshow. Most convertible Tablet PCs come with a swivel screen that changes the layout when rotating and closing. When typing on the physical keyboard with a convertible Tablet PC, the screen must be in Landscape mode if you want to read what you are writing. On some models, you can change to Portrait orientation while typing on the keyboard, but do you want to have to cock your head 90 degrees to the side the entire time? (This setting could be useful, however, if you stood the computer on its side and used an external USB or Bluetooth keyboard. I have done this when I really wanted to type and also had a vertical page orientation.)

Aside from the left- and right-handed options, the links on the Other tab are just basic links to the Pen and Touch options and the Tablet PC Panel options. Windows 7 incorporated these links in this menu just to give you quick access to those settings.

Pen and Touch Dialog Box

The Pen and Touch dialog box (shown on the right in Figure 38.9) has four tabs, listed next. Most of the options on these tabs are fine left with the default settings. The option you'll most likely want to change is the touch pointer option on the Touch tab, if you have a touch-enabled screen.

- **Pen Options tab**—Gives you options for how the pen interacts with the screen. Changing how the stylus implements such functions as a right-click can better help you customize your tablet. Other options here let you turn off the right-click equivalent and the back-end eraser. Most likely, you will never want to change these settings. Clicking Settings lets you set such things as how fast a double-tap has to be in order to register, and "spatial tolerance," which is how far away the second tap can be from the point of the first one and still be interpreted as a double-click. (These choices are also on the Touch tab, where they are applicable to touching.)

- **Flicks tab**—If you are new to using pen flicks, leave these settings alone. After a bit of practice, you will be efficient in using pen flicks. You can increase the range of your pen flick usage by changing your settings in the Customize Flicks dialog box, shown in Figure 38.10, which offers additional flicks that can do basic functions such as undo, delete, copy, and paste. You also can add a custom flick, assigning a flick to trigger any key or key combination you choose.

Pen Flicks Not Working

If you find that Pen Flicks will not work at all or only works very scarcely, make sure that pen flicks are turned on. Refer to the "Pen Flicks" section earlier in this chapter.

If pen flicks are turned on, you might just be having a problem implementing a flick. Go to the pen flicks training in the Pen and Touch applet in Control Panel, and click Practice using flicks (at the bottom of the dialog box). This will guide you in how to successfully use pen flicks.

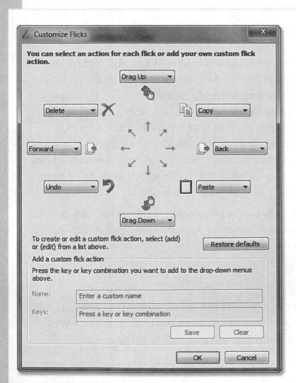

Figure 38.10
Customizing pen flicks.

- **Handwriting tab**—These options were covered briefly in the section, "Handwriting Recognition."

- **Touch tab**—This tab will appear if your tablet has a touch-sensitive screen. There are quite a few options here, if you drill down. On the first level, you can turn off touch altogether. If you do that, touching the screen will not register. Only the pen will. This could be useful if you want to prevent accidental modifications to data or graphics by accidental touches (for example, if you are using a graphics editing program such as Photoshop). Turning on the Touch Pointer results in the appearance of a small image of a computer mouse on the screen wherever you touch the screen with your finger. If you are new to using touch, I suggest turning this on, at least for a while. The advantage is that it helps you aim the pointer more accurately, and it has left and right mouse buttons on it. With time and experience, you may find this little assistant unnecessary and can ditch it. Right-clicks can be performed using "touch and hold" just as with the pen. Simply touch a spot on the screen and hold your position for a second or two, until the large circle appears, and then release, after which the context menu appears. When the Touch Pointer is turned on, you scoot the touch pointer around the screen as it if were the real deal—push on the body of it. Click the buttons by tapping on it. The Advanced Options buttons give you transparency, size, and tracking speed choices.

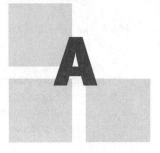

USING VIRTUALIZATION ON WINDOWS 7

As mentioned in Chapter 2, a virtual machine (VM) program simulates the hardware functions of a PC within a process running on another PC. Virtualization is a handy way for individuals and organizations to run multiple operating systems without having to set up dual- or multi-boot environments or purchasing additional hardware. IT departments use virtualization to test software updates and patches before rolling them out to end users, and developers use virtualization when creating new software programs. End users most commonly use virtualization to run older Windows operating systems and applications that require such operating systems on newer versions of Windows. (This is where Windows 7 XP Mode usually comes into play, as described later in this appendix.)

In general, Windows 7 behaves more or less the same with virtualization software as did earlier versions of Windows. You can run Virtual PC 2007 on Windows 7, and create and manage virtual machines using that program. You can also use other packages that are compatible with Windows Vista or Windows 7, including various VMware versions, VirtualBox, and so forth.

 note

Windows 7 introduces a new version of Virtual PC. While you can run Virtual PC 2007 on Windows 7 and use it to run existing VMs you may have set up using that program on Windows XP or Vista, you can't use Virtual PC 2007 to host the free VM that Microsoft supplies for its Windows XP Mode. See the next section for details.

In keeping with other usage scenarios, Windows 7 appears to be more stable and less resource-hungry when running VMs than Vista. As we researched this book, we also couldn't help but notice that Microsoft Virtual PC—which sets up only single-core VMs, no matter how many cores your host PC may possess—runs much faster and better on Windows 7 than it does on Windows Vista.

Windows XP Mode in Windows 7

The Windows 7 Professional, Enterprise, and Ultimate licenses enable users to install and use Windows XP Mode, a free set of downloads from Microsoft that provides an updated version of Virtual PC and a prefabricated virtual hard disk (VHD) for Windows XP SP3, with all the licensing information necessary to run and use this guest operating system on Windows 7. Visit the Microsoft Download Center at www.microsoft.com/downloads/en/default.aspx and search on **Windows XP Mode** to find the version that's right for your PC.

Windows XP Mode, also known as Virtual Windows XP, lets you install and run software in a VM that runs Windows XP SP3 as its guest OS—remember, the XP runtime environment supports 16-bit Windows on Windows for much older Windows applications, and offers a range of compatibility modes to support programs written for older Windows versions. Windows 7 is 32-bit (or 32- and 64-bit) only, depending on which version you use. XP Mode offers a way for users to continue using older Windows applications that may not have worked with Vista, and that definitely don't work with Windows 7. To use them on a Windows 7 machine, you must first install Microsoft Virtual PC, then Windows XP Mode, and then finally install those applications inside the Windows VM that Windows XP Mode makes available.

 note

If you already have Microsoft Virtual PC 2007 installed on your Windows 7 PC, you must uninstall this version before downloading and installing the various Windows XP Mode components (which include a newer version of Microsoft Virtual PC). Otherwise, you will neither be able to install nor be able to use Windows XP Mode. Also, this new Microsoft Virtual PC software requires processor-based virtualization support, which means it might not work on older Intel or AMD CPUs.

Installing Microsoft Virtual PC

If you visit the Microsoft Virtual PC home page at www.microsoft.com/windows/virtual-pc, you will find links to download the latest version of that program. The version that supports Windows XP Mode also offers easy, one-click install and setup for Windows XP Mode, plus one-click launch for Windows XP Mode applications using virtualized icons. It also offers USB support, which means you can plug a USB drive into the host machine, and it will be recognized and read inside the Windows XP VM (a big improvement over previous versions, which didn't recognize any drives except the optical disk and whatever virtual hard disks you may have set up for any given VM).

 tip

You don't want to run any version of Virtual PC on a machine with less than 2GB of RAM, and 3GB or more of total RAM is better still. Each VM you create, even for Windows XP, needs at least 512MB of RAM to operate, and 1GB or more is likewise better. As I worked on this book, I used a test machine with 8GB of RAM so that I could run two or three XP, Vista, or Windows 7 VMs in parallel.

Once you download the program, it's trivially easy to install. Simply double-click the Microsoft Update Standalone Package (MSU) file, follow the prompts through the rest of the installation process, and then reboot your computer when prompted. There are no gotchas along the way, and it shouldn't take more than 5 minutes on most PCs.

Installing Windows XP Mode

You can also download Windows XP Mode files from the Virtual PC home page if you like. This comes in the form of a Microsoft Installer (MSI) file that only runs on Windows 7 Professional, Enterprise, or Ultimate licenses. Here's a pictorial review of the installation process:

> **note**
>
> Remember, Virtual Windows XP and Windows XP Mode refer to the same program.

1. Double-click the MSI file. In the welcome screen that appears, click Next.

2. Specify a target directory for the install (the default appears in Figure A.1). Click Next. Click Yes or enter administrative credentials in the User Account Control window if prompted for permission to continue.

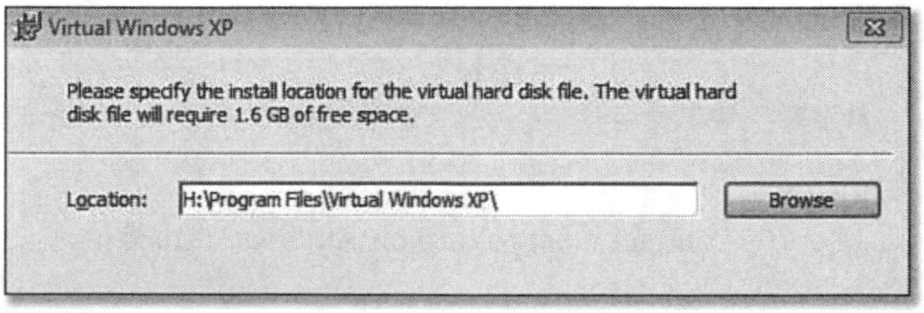

Figure A.1
By default, Virtual Windows XP files go under Program Files.

> **Virtual Windows XP**
>
> Please specify the install location for the virtual hard disk file. The virtual hard disk file will require 1.6 GB of free space.
>
> Location: H:\Program Files\Virtual Windows XP\   Browse

The install process begins and works through a sequence of activities that lasts 5 to 10 minutes. Figure A.2 shows the initial Status window, but you will also see status updates about copying files, updating the Registry, and so forth, as the install process progresses.

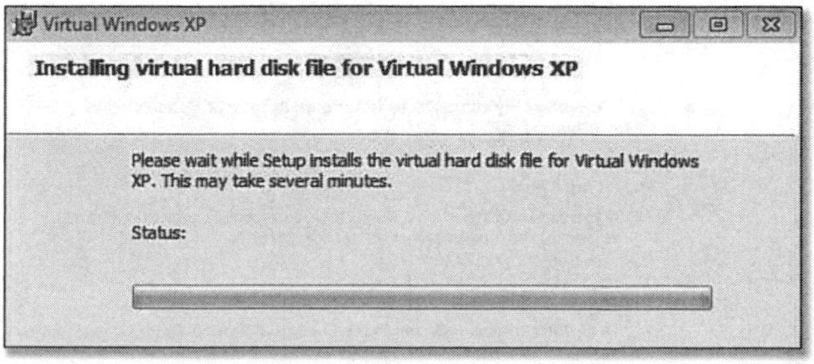

Figure A.2
At the outset, the progress bar is empty, but it fills up as installation proceeds.

> **Virtual Windows XP**
>
> **Installing virtual hard disk file for Virtual Windows XP**
>
> Please wait while Setup installs the virtual hard disk file for Virtual Windows XP. This may take several minutes.
>
> Status:

When the sequence of activities ends, the Windows XP Mode installation completes. Click Finish.

3. Accept the Virtual Windows XP License Agreement. Click Next.

4. Establish a password for the default User account that the ongoing setup script establishes on your behalf (see Figure A.3). Click Next.

Figure A.3
Enter a password twice to secure the default User account.

5. You can elect to turn on Automatic Updates (recommended) or leave them off (see Figure A.4). Click Next.

Figure A.4
Turn on Automatic Updates in the Help Protect Your Computer screen.

6. Provide a name and location for the Windows XP Mode virtual machine. (By default, it appears in the logged-on user's My Virtual Machines folder inside the Documents library.)

7. The Windows XP Mode VM starts. This involves a sequence of activities that includes startup, setup for first use, update downloads and installs, OS startup, and enabling integration features. It can take 2 or more minutes to complete. Finally, you'll see the familiar XP desktop inside a Virtual Windows XP VM (see Figure A.5). You're done with the OS portion of the install.

Figure A.5
A typical
Windows XP
desktop
inside a
Virtual PC
window on
Windows 7.

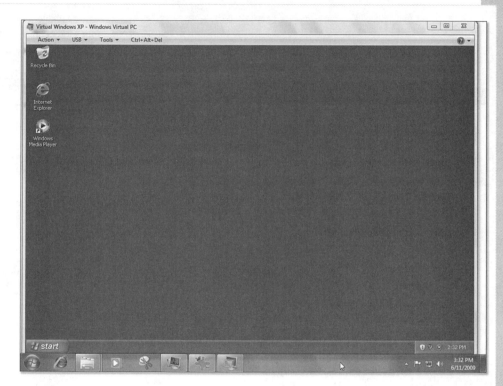

8. Your usual OS completion steps should occur next. At a minimum, this means installing antivirus and antispyware software. But you wouldn't install this VM without also wanting to install a Windows application, as covered in the next section.

Installing Applications into the XP VM

When you're inside the Windows XP VM, you can interact with that virtual desktop just as if it were a real desktop. To install an application, open its installer file on your virtual hard disk, optical, or USB drive inside the VM. Follow your usual installation maneuvers.

Just for grins, I set up a copy of my son's "Alphabet Express" software, a vintage 2001 Windows application. It ran perfectly inside Windows XP Mode, but Figure A.6 shows what the application compatibility window for that program looks like. (To access this control, right-click the EXE file and select the Compatibility tab.) It shows Windows 2000 chosen as a specific compatibility mode, with other selections listed as well.

 tip

If you are an IT professional, you can customize the VHD for Windows XP Mode to include applications your users will want to run within that environment. In fact, you can set up as many VHDs as you like, and make them available for users to grab from servers on an as-needed basis.

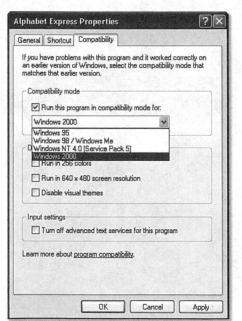

Figure A.6
A Windows 2000 application gets the matching compatibility mode selection.

INDEX

3D screen savers, 695

8P8C connectors, networking, 460

10/100BASE-T Ethernet networks, 448–449
costs, 449
NICs (network interface cards), 449
switches, 448

10/100BASE-T switches, 444

32-bit versions, Windows 7, 39

64-bit gadgets, 212

64-bit processors, software compatibility issues, 774

64-bit versions, Windows 7, 39

802.11g wireless networking, 451–452

802.11n wireless networking, 447, 451–452

1000Mbps Ethernet (Gigabit Ethernet) networks, 449

A

About tab (printer properties dialog box), 199

Accelerators (IE), 27, 356–357
Add-ons Gallery, 357

access auditing, permissions, 907–908

access controls, restrictive configuration, 926

access permissions. *See* permissions

accessibility
display settings, 626
Internet, 330
changing default connections, 349, 352
choosing, 334
connection configuration, 342, 347–349
DSL (Digital Subscriber Line), 331
modem installation, 345
satellite service, 332
troubleshooting, 345
wireless access, 332
keyboard settings, 624–625
mouse settings, 626–627
sound settings, 625

accessories, 220
Calculator, 222–223
Character Map, 224
Magnifier, 220–221
Narrator, 220
new features, 31–32
Notepad, 225–226
Paint, 224–225
Snipping Tool, 216–219
Sticky Notes, 226
WordPad, 227–228
XPS Viewer, 221–222

account picture, setting, 696

accounts
Administrator accounts, 89, 904
policies, local settings, 935–936
Standard user accounts, 770

accounts (email), configuring, Windows Live Mail, 395–398

accounts (newsgroups), configuring, Windows Live Mail, 410–411

Acronis True Image, 911

ActFax, 454

Action Center, 36, 600, 604–606
Reliability Monitor, 606–607

Action Center (Windows), 848–850
balloon notifications, 117

actions, Event Viewer, 657

active defenses (attacks), 919
access controls, restricting, 926
firewall configuration, 919–921
NAT device configuration, 919, 923
packet filtering, 921–923
passwords versus passwordless file sharing, 924–925
routers, locking down, 923–924

Active Desktop, 207–208

ActiveSync, 394

ad hoc networks, 466, 960

ad hoc wireless networks, creating, 965–966

Ad-Aware, 388

adapters (network)
existing network adapters, checking, 455
installing, 454–455
multiple, 456
motherboards, moving, 785

Add Hardware applet, 784–787
Device Manager,
compared, 787
System applet,
compared, 787

**Add Hardware Wizard,
785–786**

**Add or Remove Programs
applet (Control Panel),
application removal, 135**

Add Printer Wizard, 554

add-ons, Internet Explorer
allowing with invalid
signatures, 377
crash detection, 379
managing, 377–379
protecting against, 376–377
viewing, 377–379

adding
gadgets, multiple times, 214
wireless networks profiles,
manually, 968–969

**Additional Clocks tab (Date
and Time), 610**

Address bar
Computer window, 156–157
IE (Internet Explorer), 356
Windows Explorer, 155–156

Address box (IE), 361

**address space layout
randomization (ASLR), 859**

address spoofing, 915

**Adjust Indexing Options
(Performance Information
and Tools), 637**

**Adjust Settings Before Giving
a Presentation (Hardware
and Sound Control Panel
window), 974**

**Adjust Visual Effects option
(Performance Information
and Tools), 636**

**Administrative Tools (Control
Panel), 600, 660–662**
accessing, 706
Component Services,
662–663

iSCSI Initiator, 663–664
System Configuration,
664–666

Administrator accounts, 89
files, inability to delete, 904
folders, inability to
delete, 904

Adobe Acrobat Connect, 1010

**Adobe Photoshop, scans,
editing, 310**

Adobe Systems, fonts, 630

**ADSL (Asymmetric Digital
Subscriber Line), 331**

**Advanced Boot Options menu
(Boot Manager), 748**

**Advanced Programmable
Interrupt Controllers
(APICs), 615**

**Advanced Restore (Backup
and Restore Center), 875–878**

**Advanced Security
Administrative program
(Windows Firewall), 941–943**

**advanced settings, DOS
applications, editing,
829–830**

**Advanced Settings link
(Screen Resolution
window), 700**

**Advanced System Settings
option (System
Properties), 650**

**Advanced tab (Internet
Options), 381**

**Advanced tab (Performance
Options), 650–651**

**Advanced tab (printer
properties dialog box), 199**

**Advanced Tools option
(Performance Information
and Tools), 638–642**

advertisements
pop-ups, blocking, 386–387
skipping, Windows Media
Center, 265

**Aero desktop environment,
21–22, 131–133**
color schemes, 688–689
putting items on, 123
shortcuts, creating, 124

Aero Peek, 133

Aero Shake, 131

Aero Snap, 21–22

Aero Themes, 22

AGP video cards, 790

**air-conditioning air returns,
cabling, 458**

**aligning text, email
messages, 629**

**All Programs command (Start
menu), 132**

**all-in-one devices, Windows
Fax and Scan, preparing, 295**

**always-on connections
(broadband),
configuring, 349, 351**

**Ambient Slideshow
(WMC), 254, 267**

**AMD K6/2+ Mobile
Processors, 801**

**analog headsets, Speech
Recognition, 1032**

**analog modems,
installing, 345**

**analysis reports, Disk Cleanup
utility, 724**

ANSI.SYS, 831–832

**Answer Automatically
fax-receiving option
(Windows Fax and
Scan), 295**

antivirus software, 850–852

Anytime Upgrade, 17

ap.bat file, 833

**APICs (Advanced
Programmable Interrupt
Controllers), 615**

**Appearance and
Personalization applet
(Control Panel), 684**

Appearance and Personalization view (Category view), 597

Apple Newton, 1030

AppleTalk File Protocol (AFP), 503

applets. *See* Control Panel

application concurrency issues, Macintosh internetworking, 505

Application log (Event Viewer), 656

application partitions, data partitions, separating from, 712

applications. *See also* software
crashes, handling and troubleshooting, 147–148
DOS applications
editing advance settings, 829–830
printing from, 202–203
downloading, Internet Explorer, 373–379
launching, 136
Computer, 140
Start button, 137
Windows Explorer, 140
malware, protecting against, 374–375
new features, 37
removing from computer (Add or Remove Programs applet), 135
third-party management tools, 677–678
uninstalling, 643–644

Applications tab (Task Manager), 672–674

AppLocker, 26

architecture backgrounds, 22

arguments, 822

Arrange By command (View menu), 167

ASLR (address space layout randomization), 859

aspect ratios, 323

assigning
drive letters, 714–717
permissions
restricted objects, 910
to user groups, 908–909

associations, file types, 805

attaching VHDs (virtual hard disks), 722

attachments
opening, Windows Live Mail, 403
sending, Windows Live Mail, 403
virus prevention, Windows Live Mail, 404–405

attacks (networks)
address spoofing, 915
back doors, 915
defense measures, 917
active defenses, 919–926
preparations, 917–919
DoS (Denial of Service), 916
eavesdropping, 915
email hoaxes, 916
exploits, 915
identity theft, 916
impersonation, 915
open doors, 916
password cracking, 915
social engineering, 916
Trojan horses, 916
viruses, 916

audio
CDs, ripping, 240–242
configuring, 625
Internet Explorer
downloading, 373–379
supported formats, 368–373
playing, WMP (Windows Media Player), 239–240
streaming audio, playing, 370–371

audio files
creating, Sound Recorder, 691–692
sharing, home networking, 248–250
WMP libraries, adding to, 243

audits
permissions, 907–908
policies, local settings, 936–937

authentication, wireless networks, 464

Auto-Hide, 682

AutoComplete
Internet Explorer, 356, 361, 381
Tablet PCs, 1043

Autodetect, BIOS, 736

autoexec.nt, customizing, 830–831

automatic synchronization, WMP (Windows Media Player), 247

automatic updates, 857
Windows Update, 758–759

Automatic Updates feature, 918

automatically installing service packs, 768

AutoPlay, 29, 36, 600, 607–608

Avast! Antivirus software, 852

AVI files, playing, Internet Explorer, 370

B

Back button, 83

back door attacks, 915

backgrounds, desktop, 22
setting, 685–687
solid backgrounds, 686
stretching, 687

Backup and Restore Center, 601, 712, 863–865

Advanced Restore, 875–878

Complete PC backups
creating, 878–879
restoring, 883–884
with WBADMIN command-line tool, 879–882

features, 864

file and folder backups
Complete PC backups versus, 865–866
creating, 866–870
restoring, 872–877

removable media for backups, 871–872

VSS (Volume Shadow Copy Service), 864

backup folders, excluding/including, 30

backups

Backup and Restore Center, 601, 712, 863–865
Advance Restore, 875–878
Complete PC backups, 878–884
creating file and folder backups, 866–870
features, 864
file and folder backups versus Complete PC backups, 865–866
removable media for backups, 871–872
restoring file and folder backups, 872–877
VSS (Volume Shadow Copy Service), 864
WBADMIN command-line tool, 879–882

baseline backups, 930

computers over networks, 557

creating from System Recovery Options menu, 755–756

EFS (Encrypted File System), 868

FAT file system, 868

frequent, security disaster planning, 930

full system image backups, disk space, 868

multi-disc backups, finding files in, 878

network drives, 29

of recovery certificates, 892–893

Recycle Bin, 868

Registry, 809
hard disk, 809
Regedit, 810
system restore, 810
third-party utilities, 809

Set Up Backup scheduler, 870

Set Up Backup utility, 870

target drives, troubleshooting, 875

third-party backup tools, 911

to network shares, 866

troubleshooting, 876–878

UPS (uninterruptible power supply)
choosing, 797
configuring, 798–799
installing, 795–799
line interactive UPS, 797
online UPS, 797
printers, 797
serial cables, 798
standby UPS, 797
testing, 799

user profiles and, 868

web-based email, 868

Windows Backup schedule, 869

Balanced power usage profile, 974

balloon notifications, initial logon process, 117

bare metal restorations, System Image Recovery, 743–745

baseline backups, security disaster planning, 930

Basic (non-Aero) mode, color schemes, 689–690

basic hard disks, 710. *See also* **hard disks**

dynamic hard disks, converting to, 710–711

basic tasks (Task Scheduler), creating, 840–841

Basic visual palette, 118

batch files, 832–833

batteries (laptops)

cycling, 796

mobile computing, 974–976

power usage profiles, 974
creating, 975
viewing, 974–976

Battery setting (Power Options Advanced Settings), 976

Battery Status icon (Mobility Center), 973

Bcc field (email messages), 402

BCD (boot configuration database), editing, 736

bcdedit tool, 736

binary value data type, 813

Bing.com, 357

BIOS

Autodetect, 736

configuring, 781–782

DST (daylight saving time), configuring for, 610

EFI (Extensible Firmware Interface), compared, 736

troubleshooting, 782

USB controllers, port settings, 790

BitLocker, 110, 601, 895

EFS (Encrypted File System) versus, 900–901

encryption process, 898–900

full drive encryption, 886

recovery process, 899

system requirements, 895

TPM (Trusted Platform Module), enabling, 897–898
troubleshooting, 896

BitLocker to Go, 26, 896–897

bitmapped image editors, Paint, 224

bitmaps, 224

Bitstream, fonts, 630

"black hat" hackers, 845

bloatware applications, 252

blockages, Windows Firewall, checking for, 582

blocking network services
packet filtering, 921–922
troubleshooting, 928

Blu-Ray, 292

Bluetooth tab (printer properties dialog box), 199

BMP (Bitmap) files, 321

boot configuration database (BCD), editing, 736

Boot Manager (Windows), 748–751
Advanced Boot Options menu, 748
changes to, 67

boot process
BCD (boot configuration database), editing, 736
repair options, 738–739
troubleshooting, 736, 748–751
Windows Boot Manager, 748–751

breadcrumbs
Computer window, 156–158
Windows Explorer, 155, 158
WMP (Windows Media Player), 233–236

bridging network types, 484–485

Brightness slider (Mobility Center), 973

broadband Internet connections, 330
always-on configuration, 349, 351
configuring, 347–349
DSL, 516
Internet Connection Sharing (ICS), configuring, 527–529
network adapters, installing for, 345–346
PPPoE configuration, 347

Browse dialog box, 122

browsing
shared folders, 544–545
homegroups, 542–544
UNC (Universal Naming Convention), 545–546
tabbed pages, Internet Explorer, 361–364
WMP (Windows Media Player), 236–238

Browsing History (IE), configuring, 380

Burn tab (WMP), 235

burning
CDs, customized CDs, 244–246
images to DVD, 325

BuyFonts.com, 630

bye.bat file, 833

C

cable modems
high-speed connections, configuring, 347–351
installing, 345
Internet connections, troubleshooting, 426–427

cable service, 516
inability to access on LANs, 527
Internet connections on LANs, 521–522
multiple computers, configuring LANs, 531

cabling systems (networks), 447, 457–458
10/100BASE-T Ethernet, 448–449
802.11g/n wireless networking, 451–452
1000Mbps Ethernet (Gigabit Ethernet), 449
Ethernet crossover cables, 461–462
fax machines, 453–454
installing, 457–463
mixed networking, 453
multiple switches, 462–463
patch cables, 457, 459–460
phoneline networking, 449–450
powerline networking, 451
printers, 453–454
running, 447
testing, 585
updating, 453

caches, 991
cleanup, Internet Explorer, 726–728

Calculator, 222–223

Calendar, Internet Explorer, 383

calibration, Tablet PC screens, 1046

cameras (digital), Windows Pictures Library, 281–284

captioning, enabling, 625

cartoon character backgrounds, 22

cascade ports, switches, 462–463

cascading elements, Start menu, 707

CAT-5 patch cables, 444
10/100BASE-T Ethernet, 448–449

Category View (Control Panel), 82, 595–599
Appearance and Personalization category, 597

Clock, Language, and Region category, 598

Ease of Access category, 598

Hardware and Sound category, 597

Network and Internet category, 596

Program category, 597

System and Maintenance category, 596

User Accounts and Family Safety category, 597

CAUCE (Coalition Against Unsolicited Commercial Email), 407

Cc field (email messages), 402

CDs

backups on, 871–872

customized CDs, burning, 244–246

pictures, burning to, 290–292

playing, WMP (Windows Media Player), 239

ripping, 240–242

software, installing via, 770

cellular service, Internet connections, 332–333

censorship issues, news servers, 409

certificates

Internet Explorer, accepting, 381

recovery certificates

exporting, 886

securing, 887–893

VPNs (virtual private networks)

connection failures, 982

Error Number 629/720, 985

Change Permissions advanced NTFS permission, 906

Change Settings window (Windows Update), 762

Change What the Power Buttons Do (Hardware and Sound Control Panel window), 973

Character Map, 224

troubleshooting, 660

Character Map (System Tools folder), 667–669

child locations, 155

Choose Details command (View menu), 168

CIPHER command-line tool, 887–889

clicks, stylus pen, 1039

client tools, Samba, 497–498

Clock, Language, and Region view (Category view), 598

clock speed, laptops, 974

CMOS (complimentary metal oxide semiconductor), troubleshooting, 782

code base, Windows 7, 14

Cogswell, Bryce, 855

Color dialog box, 690

Color Management (Control Panel), 601, 609

Color Management tab (printer properties dialog box), 199

Color Management tab (Screen Resolution window), 701

color refiner cursor, 690

color schemes, High Contrast White, 626

colors, 690

command prompt, 746

creating backups from, 755–756

Command Prompt window, 822–823

cut and paste, 825

elevated privilege commands, running, 823–824

environment variables, setting, 825–827

opening, 822

taskbar, pinning to, 822

command-line, network resources, managing, 573–574

command-line tools, 821, 824

TCP/IP diagnostic tools

ipconfig, 433–434

pathping, 437

ping command, 434–435

route, 437–438

tracert, 435–437

commands

command-line tools, 821, 824

elevated privileges, running, 823–824

commercials, skipping, Windows Media Center, 265

Compatibility Center (Windows 7), 50

compatibility issues, software, 774–776

Compatibility View, Internet Explorer, 356

Complete PC backups

creating, 878–882

file and folder backups versus, 865–866

restoring, 883–884

Component Services (Administrative Tools), 662–663

compression

downloadable drivers, 766

files, 183–184, 731–732

JPEG files, 184

folders, 731–732

Computer Administrator accounts, 89

computer identification

checking, 587–588

networks, configuring, 476–477

Computer Management window, 652–654
Disk Management utility, 713–723
Event Viewer, 655
actions, 657
log files, 656–657
Overview and Summary, 657
viewing event details, 657–658
nodes, 653
Services, 659–660
Shared Folders, 658–659
Task Scheduler, 654

Computer window, 149–150
Address bar, 156–157
breadcrumbs, 156–158
meta-information, viewing, 163–165
Network, compared, 139
panes, toggling, 165–167
programs, running from, 140
searching, 173–174
configuring, 174–177
deep searching, 174
grouping and stacking, 181–183
intermediate searching, 174
troubleshooting, 179
while typing, 177–181

computers
backing up, networks, 557
networks, searching for, 548
upgrading, 50

config.nt, customizing, 830–831

configuration
audio, 625
BIOS, 781–782
DST (daylight saving time), 610
computer identification, networks, 476–477
dial-up Internet connections, 338–343
Disk Defragmenter, 730–731

email accounts, Windows Live Mail, 395–398
gadgets, 212–213
homegroups, 478–480
indexing, 174–177
Internet connections
broadband connections, 347–351
dial-up connections, 342
manually, 339–340
Internet Explorer, 98–100, 379–390
Content Advisor, 389–390
default programs, 381–383
Parental Controls, 388–389
Pop-Up Blocker, 386–387
privacy, 384–386
security, 384–386
keyboards, 625
LANs, documenting, 420
Last Known Good Configuration, 748
monitors, 697–700
networks
checking, 581–582
troubleshooting, 585–588
new features, 16–17
peer-to-peer networks, 472
network locations, 475–476
TCP/IP protocol, 473–475
printers, 189, 196–200
RAS (Remote Access Services) dial-up networking, 978–987
connection properties, 980–982
gateway settings, 981–982
multiple location management, 982–983
Recycle Bin, 707
searches, 174–177
System Configuration (Administrative Tools), 664–666
System Restore, 740–741

Tablet PCs, 1045–1049
Pen and Touch dialog box, 1047–1049
Tablet PC Settings dialog box, 1045–1047
UPS (uninterruptible power supply), 798–799
user accounts, 88–92
visual effects, 636
VPNs (virtual private networks), 978–987
connection properties, 980–982
gateway settings, 981–982
Windows Explorer, 98–100
Windows Fax and Scan, 295, 305–306
cover pages, 296–297
fax receiving options, 295–296
fax settings, 298–299
sender information, 296
Windows Firewall, 477, 937–938
wireless networks, 464–466, 468–471, 966
Internet service, 471
manually, 470–471
manufacturer's setup program, 468
Set Up a Network Wizard, 469–470

conflicts, HCL (Hardware Compatibility List), 802

Connect to Server dialog box, 507

connection properties, VPNs (virtual private networks), setting, 980–982

connection-sharing routers, 516–518

connections
Internet, 329–330
cellular service, 332–333
changing default connections, 349–352
choosing, 334
configuring, 342, 347–349

dial-up settings, 420
DSL (Digital Subscriber
  Line), 331
flowcharts, 422–423
ipconfig tool, 419,
  433–434
ISP information, 418
LAN connections,
  427–429
methodology, 420–422
modems, 345, 426–433
network cabling
  diagrams, 420
Network Connections,
  419–420
network hardware
  problems, 429–433
pathping command, 437
ping command, 434–435
reverse tracert, 439–440
route command, 437–438
router configuration, 420
satellite service, 332
software configuration
  problems, 425–429
Speed Check, 439
TCP/IP diagnostic tools,
  433–438
third-party utilities,
  439–440
tracert, 435–437
tracert tool, 418
troubleshooting, 345,
  417–420
whois database, 439
wireless access, 332
WS_Ping Pro Pack, 440
LANs (local area networks),
  multiple connections, 998
networks, checking, 588
RAS (Remote Access
  Services) dial-up
  networking
  advanced routing,
    986–987
  current location
    checks, 983
  email connections, 986
  ending, 986
  establishing, 983–985
  monitoring, 986

VPNs (virtual private
  networks), 977–978
  advanced routing,
    986–987
  certificates, 982
  email connections, 986
  ending, 986
  Error Number
    629/720, 985
  establishing, 983–986
  monitoring, 986
  monitoring
    connections, 986
wireless networks
  configuring, 966
  copying profiles, 968
  corporate
    environments, 961
  deleting profiles, 969
  home offices, 961–963
  manually adding profiles,
    968–969
  preferred wireless
    networks, 966
  prioritizing, 967–968
  public hot spots,
    964–965
  small offices, 961–963
  someone else's office,
    963–964
  switching between,
    966–967

**connections properties,
dial-up networking, sitting,
980–982**

**Connections tab (Internet
Options), 381**

**connectivity, networks,
troubleshooting, 588–589**

**connectors, 1000Mbps
Ethernet (Gigabit
Ethernet), 449**

console programs, 822

**Contacts (Windows Live
Mail), 406**
  entries
    adding, 406–407
    deleting, 407
    editing, 406

Content Advisor (IE), 380
  configuring, 389–390

**Content tab (Internet
Options), 380–381**

**context menus, right-click
context menus, 124 126**

Control Panel, 594–595
  accessing, 600
  Action Center, 600, 604–606
    Reliability Monitor,
      606–607
  Add Hardware applet,
    784–787
  Administrative Tools, 600,
    660–662
    Component Services,
      662–663
    iSCSI Initiator, 663–664
    System Configuration,
      664–666
  Appearance and
    Personalization applet, 684
  applets
    Add or Remove
      Programs, 135
    cross-references, 598
  AutoPlay, 600, 607–608
  Backup and Restore, 601
  BitLocker, 601
  Category View, 82, 595–599
  Color Management,
    601, 609
  Credential Manager, 601
  Date and Time, 601,
    609–611
    Additional Clocks
      tab, 610
  default display, 594
  Default Programs, 601, 611
    Set Associations
      option, 611
    Set Program Access and
      Computer Defaults
      option, 612
    setting, 611
  Desktop Gadgets, 601
  Device Manager, 601,
    612–614
    DMA channels, 616

hardware conflict resolution, 614–615
I/O port assignments, 616–617
IRQs (interrupt requests), 615–616
memory addresses, 617–618
resource conflict resolution, 618–619
Devices and Printers, 601, 619–620
Display, 601
Ease of Access Center, 601, 623–624
display settings, 626
keyboard settings, 624–625
mouse settings, 626–627
sound settings, 625
Event Viewer, 655
actions, 657
log files, 656–657
Overview and Summary, 657
viewing event details, 657–658
Folder Options, 168–170, 601
Fonts, 601, 627–631
Getting Started, 601
HomeGroup, 602
Indexing Options, 602
Internet Options, 379–386, 602
Keyboard, 602, 620–621
Large Icons view, 595–604
Location and Other Sensors, 602
Mouse, 602, 621–623
Network and Sharing Center, 602
Notification Area Icons, 602, 631–632
Parental Controls, 602
Performance Information and Tools, 602, 632, 638
Adjust Indexing Options, 637

Adjust Visual Effects, 636
Advanced Tools, 638–642
WEI, 633–636
Personalization, 602
Phone and Modem, 602
Phone and Modem Options, property settings, 430–431
phrases, 82
Power Options, 33, 602, 642
Programs and Features, 602, 643–646
uninstalling programs, 772–774
Recovery, 603
Region and Language, 603, 646
RemoteApp and Desktop Connections, 603
shortcuts, creating, 595
Small Icons view, 595–604
Sound, 603
Speech Recognition, 603
Sync Center, 603
System, 603
System and Security window, 82
System Properties, 647–648, 650–651
Advanced System Settings option, 650
Environment Variables button, 651–652
Remote Settings option, 648–649
System Protection option, 649
Tablet PC Settings, 603
Task Scheduler, 654
Taskbar and Start Menu, 603
Troubleshooting, 603
Troubleshooting applet, 752–753
User Accounts, 603
View By drop-down list, 83
Windows CardSpace, 603
Windows Defender, 603
Windows Firewall, 603

Windows Mobility Center, 604
Windows Update, 604
Convert utility, 722
command-line syntax, 722
FAT16/32 partitions, converting to NTFS, 722–723
converting handwriting to text, 1044
convertible Tablet PCs, 1031, 1036. *See also* **Tablet PCs**
fragility, 1035
swivel screens, 1033
troubleshooting, screen layout, 1047
cookies, deleting
Disk Cleanup utility, 725
Internet Explorer, 365
Copy Key Name command (Regedit), 816
corporate environments, wireless networks, joining, 961
corporate networks, 41–42
Cover Page Editor (Windows Fax and Scan), 296
cover pages (faxes)
customizing, 296–297
selecting, 301
CPUs (central processing units)
minimum requirements, 44
upgrading, 45
crashes
applications, troubleshooting, 147–148
Ctrl+Alt+Del keystroke, troubleshooting, 148
handling, 147
Internet Explorer
add-ons, 379
troubleshooting, 358
Create Files/Write Data advanced NTFS permission, 892, 906

Create Folders/Append Data advanced NTFS permission, 893, 906

Creative Zen X-Fi portable media players, 244

Credential Manager, 601

Critical updates, downloading, 94

cross-references, Control Panel, 598

CRT-based monitors
LCD monitors, compared, 699
screen flicker, troubleshooting, 703

cryptographic keys, 464

CSV (comma-separated values) extension, 133

Ctrl+Alt+Del keystroke, troubleshooting, 148

cumulative service packs, 768

cursor schemes, mouse, 622

Customize Start Menu dialog box, 680–682

customized CDs, burning, 244–246

cut and paste, Command Prompt window, 825

D

data, transferring between computers, Windows Easy Transfer, 101–104

data encapsulation, VPNs (virtual private networks), 977

Data Execution Prevention (DEP), 651, 857–859

data partitions, application partitions, separating from, 712

data recovery, 751
System Recovery Options menu, 755–756

data security, new features, 29–30

data types, Regedit, 813

Date and Time, Additional Clocks tab, 610

Date and Time (Control Panel), 601, 609–611

daylight saving time (DST), BIOS configuration for, 610

DDR SDRAM modules (RAM), 783

Debugging Mode advanced boot option, 749

decoders (DVD), installing, 232

deep searching, Windows Explorer, 174

default home page, Internet Explorer, changing, 359

default Internet connections, changing, 349–352

default programs, 396
Internet Explorer, setting, 381

Default Programs (Control Panel), 601, 611
Set Associations option, 611
Set Program Access and Computer Defaults option, 612
setting, 611

default settings
Start menu, returning to, 682
Windows Firewall, restoring, 941

Defender (Windows), 852–856, 932

defragmentation, hard disks, 783
Disk Defragmenter, 730–731
scheduling, 803

Delete advanced NTFS permission, 906

Delete Browsing History screen (IE), 365, 727

Delete Subfolders and Files advanced NTFS permission, 906

deleting
browsing history, Internet Explorer, 365
Contacts entries, 407
cookies, Disk Cleanup utility, 725
drivers, 789–790
elements, libraries, 173
Error Reports, Disk Cleanup utility, 725
files
Disk Cleanup utility, 725
Internet Explorer, 726–728
Recycle Bin, 121
troubleshooting, 904
incoming messages, Windows Live Mail, 401
offline files, Disk Cleanup utility, 725
offline web pages, Disk Cleanup utility, 725
printers, 200
restore points, Disk Cleanup utility, 726
software, 769–774
suboptions, 134
temporary Internet files
Disk Cleanup utility, 725
Internet Explorer, 365
thumbnails, Disk Cleanup utility, 725
wireless network profiles, 969

demand-dialing, Internet Connection Sharing (ICS), 516
configuring, 523–526

Denial of Service (DoS) attacks, 916

DEP (Data Execution Prevention), 857–859

Department of Justice (DOJ), Microsoft consent decree, middleware applications, 357

Derfler, Frank, 459

desktop, 118, 123
Active Desktop, 207–208
arranging, 163
backgrounds, 22
  setting, 685–687
  solid backgrounds, 686
  stretching, 687
extended desktop, 697
gadgets, 212
  adding, 209–210
  *adding multiple
   times, 214*
  moving, 213
  opacity, 214–215
  removing, 215–216
icons
  setting, 695–696
  troubleshooting, 698–699
images
  capturing, 319–320
  viewing, 320–321
items, drag-and-drop
  support, 163
new features, 22
shortcuts,
  troubleshooting, 138
Snipping Tool, 216–219

**desktop environment (Aero),
21–22, 131–133**
color schemes, 688–689
putting items on, 123
shortcuts, creating, 124

**Desktop Gadget Gallery, 119,
208–209, 601**
gadgets
  adding, 209–210
  configuring, 212–213
  downloading, 211–212
  opacity, 214–215
  peeking, 212
  removing, 215–216

desktop peek, 208

Details pane
meta-information, viewing,
  163–165
Windows Explorer, 152

Details view (Computer), 140

**detecting hard disk errors,
728–730**

device drivers
downloadable drivers,
  compression, 766
updating, 764–767
Windows Update, driver
  settings, 766

**Device Installation Settings
window (Windows
Update), 767**

**Device Manager, 295, 584, 601,
612–614**
Add Hardware applet,
  compared, 787
devices, removing, 789–790
DMA channels, 616
drivers, updating, 765–767
hardware conflicts,
  resolving, 614–615
I/O port assignments,
  616–617
IRQs (interrupt requests),
  615–616
legacy hardware, scanning
  for, 786
memory addresses, 617–618
resource conflicts, resolving,
  618–619
Update Driver Software
  window, 765

**Device Settings tab (printer
properties dialog box), 199**

Device Setup dialog box, 247

Device slider, 317

**device= command
(config.nt), 831**

devices
drivers, providing, 787–789
hidden devices, HCL
  (Hardware Compatibility
  List) conflicts, 802
non-PnP devices, installing,
  785–787
optimization, 802–803
PnP (Plug and Play) devices,
  installing, 784–787
removing, 789–790

**Devices and Printers window,
83–84, 187–189, 601, 619–620**
game controllers, 620
local printers, adding,
  192–195
printers
  *configuring, 189–190,
   196–200*
  installing, 189–190
  *multiple default
   settings, 198*
  *queue management,
   203–205*
  removing, 200
shared printers, icon
  setup, 553
Start menu, placing in, 187

**DHCP (Dynamic Host
Configuration Protocol), 473**
configuring, 349
dynamic IP addressing,
  configuring, 349

diagnostic tools
Computer Management
  Event Viewer, 655–658
  Services, 659–660
  Shared Folders, 658–659
  Task Scheduler, 654
Control Panel, 594–595
  Action Center, 604–607
  *Administrative Tools,
   660–666*
  AutoPlay, 607–608
  Category view, 595–599
  Color Management, 609
  Date and Time, 609–611
  default display, 594
  *Default Programs,
   611–612*
  *Device Manager,
   612–619*
  *Devices and Printers,
   619–623*
  *Ease of Access Center,
   623–627*
  Fonts, 627–631
  *Large Icons view,
   600–604*
  *Notification Area Icons,
   631–632*

Performance Information
and Tools, 632–642
Power Options, 642
Programs and Features,
643–646
Region and
Language, 646
shortcuts, 595
Small Icons view,
600–604
System Properties,
647–652
MMC (Microsoft
Management Console),
653–654
System Tools folder, 666
Character Map, 667–669
Private Character
Editor, 670
System Information,
670–671
Task Manager, 672, 675
Applications tab,
672–674
Networking tab, 677
Performance tab,
675–677
Processes tab, 674–675
Services tab, 675
Users tab, 677
third-party diagnostic tools,
677–678

**diagnostic tools. See specific
diagnostic tools**

dial-up connections (Internet)
configuring, 338–343
hanging up, 349–352
modems
digital telephone
wiring, 293
installing, 335–338
troubleshooting
flowcharts, 422–423
ISP dialing process,
344–345
software
configuration, 425

dial-up networking
offline files, 991
encrypting, 997

identifying for use,
992–993
managing, 997
synchronizing, 995–998
troubleshooting, 992–995
using, 993–995
RAS (Remote Access
Services), 977
advanced routing,
986–987
configuring, 978–987
connection properties,
980–982
current location
checks, 983
email connections, 986
ending connections, 986
establishing connections,
983–985
gateway settings,
981–982
incoming access,
987–990
monitoring
connections, 986
multiple location
management, 982–983
shared folders, availability,
997–998
Sync Center, 991

**dial-up settings, Internet
connections,
troubleshooting, 420**

**dialing rules, fax devices,
configuring, 303–304**

dialog boxes
clicking Yes, 88
Color, 690
Connect to Server, 507
Customize Start Menu
dialog box, 680–682
Delete Browsing
History, 727
Device Setup, 247
Edit Location, 337
Fax Options, 299
Fax Setup, 295
Folder Options, 168–170
Help Protect Your Computer
and Improve Windows
Automatically, 57

Internet Properties, 726
Internet Protocol Version 4
(TCP/IPv4) Properties, 474
List All Modes, 702
Media Streaming, 250
Media Streaming
Options, 240
Music Library
Locations, 243
Network Hardware, 419
New Fax, 299
Open, 122
Pen and Touch, 1040,
1047–1049
Performance Options,
650–651
Power Options Advanced
Settings, 975–976
Print Setup, 201
Printer Properties, 198, 553
Properties, 123–125, 420,
723–730
Disk Cleanup utility,
724–728
Disk Defragmenter,
730–731
Error Checking utility,
728–730
Protocol Configuration, 419
Recycle Bin Properties,
121, 707
Review Your Time and Date
Settings, 57
Save, 122
Scan Profiles, 308
Screen Saver Settings,
693–695
Snipping Tool, 216–219
Software License Terms, 53
Sound, 691
System Properties,
647–652, 741
System Protection, 740
Tablet PC Settings,
1045–1047
tabs, 122
Taskbar and Start Menu
Properties, 682
Type Your Windows Product
Key, 56
UAC, 594
View Gadget, 216

View Options, 127
Which Type of Installation
Do You Want?, 53–55
Window Color and
Appearance, 688–690

**digital audio output, Windows
Media Center, 255**

**digital cameras, Windows
Pictures Library, 281–284**

**Digital Living Network
Alliance (DLNA) devices, 38**

digital photographs. *See*
photographs

**digital telephone wiring,
dial-up modems, 293**

Dimdim, 1010

**DIMMs (dual in-line memory
modules), 784**

DirectAccess, 26

**directories, hidden
directories, 140**

**Directory Services Restore
Mode advanced boot
option, 749**

directory structure, 105–107
junction points, 108
symbolic links, 108
virtualization, 108–109

**directory trees, folders,
navigating, 140**

**Disable Automatic Restart on
System Failure advanced
boot option, 749**

**Disable Driver Signature
Enforcement advanced boot
option, 750**

disabling
features, 773–774
updates, Windows Update,
762–763

**disaster planning, network
security, 929–930**
baseline backup
creation, 930
documentation,
maintaining, 931

frequent backup
creation, 930
incident plan development,
931–932
restore procedures, 930–931
restore procedures,
maintaining, 931

**discussion threads,
newsgroups, 414**

Disk Cleanup utility, 724–728
analysis reports, 724
file groupings, 725
restore points, deleting, 726
running weekly, 726

Disk Defragmenter, 730–731

**Disk Management utility,
713–723, 882–883**
drive letters, assigning,
714–717
dynamic disk
management, 717
hard disks
extending, *717–718*
shrinking, *718*
spanned volumes,
creating, 718
striped volumes, creating,
719–720
VHDs (virtual hard disks)
attaching, *722*
creating, *721–722*
volumes
displaying, *713*
joining, *714–717*

disks. *See* **hard disks**

**disparate networks, bridging,
484–485**

Display (Control Panel), 601

**display adapters, multiple
monitors, 792**

display fonts, 630

display properties
account picture, setting, 696
backgrounds
setting, *685–687*
solid backgrounds, *686*
stretching, *687*

color schemes
Aero mode, 688–689
Basic mode, 689–690
setting, 688–690
customizing, 683–703
desktop icons, setting,
695–696
modifying, 696–703
screen fonts,
previewing, 704
screen savers, setting,
693–695
sounds, setting, 690–693
themes, setting, 684–685

**Display window, display
properties, setting, 696–697**

displays
accessibility settings, 626
multiple displays
installing, 790–795
troubleshooting, 792–793
Tablet PCs
calibrating, 1046
*touch-sensitive
displays, 1049*

DLLs (dynamic link libraries)
DLL Hell, handling, 777
side-by-side DLLs, 776–777
virtual registry, 777

**DLNA (Digital Living Network
Alliance) devices, 38**

DMA channels, 616

documentation
LAN configurations, 420
maintaining for disaster
planning, 931

documents
libraries, 19–20
scanning, 305–306

Documents library, 140

**domain networks, joining,
481–483**

**domain wireless
networks, 961**

**DOS applications, printing
from, 202–203**

DoS (Denial of Service) attacks, 916

DOSKEY, 831–832

dosonly command (config.nt), 831

double-clicks, stylus pen, 1039

downloadable drivers, compression, 766

downloaded program files, deleting, Disk Cleanup utility, 725

downloaded software, installing, 771

downloading
drive-by downloads, avoiding, 376–379
gadgets, 211–212
programs, Internet Explorer, 373–379
QuickTime, 371
RealPlayer, 371
themes, 685
Virtual PC, 1052
Windows Live Essentials, 394–395
Windows Live Mail, 394
Windows XP Mode, 1053–1055

drag-and-drop support, 163

dragging, Taskbar, 683

drive autotyping, 782

drive letters, assigning, 714–717

drive mapping, 573

drive-by downloads, Internet Explorer, avoiding, 376–379

Driver Store drivers, 765

drivers
downloadable drivers, compression, 766
Driver Store drivers, 765
hardware
providing, 787–789
removing, 789–790
searching for, 787–789
kernel-mode drivers, 789

local printers, searching for, 194–195
modems, 295
printers, property sheet, 196–200
UMDF (User-Mode Driver Framework), 789
updating, 764–767
user-mode drivers, 789
WDF (Windows Driver Foundation), 789
WIA drivers, obtaining, 302
Windows Update, driver settings, 766

DSL (Digital Subscriber Line), 331
ADSL (Asymmetric Digital Subscriber Line), 331
filters, installing for, 346
high-speed connections, configuring, 347–351
inability to access on LANs, 527
Internet connections on LANs, 521
network adapters, installing for, 345–346

DSL modems, Internet connections, troubleshooting, 426–427

DSL/cable-sharing routers, 444

DST (daylight saving time), BIOS configuration for, 610

dual in-line memory modules (DIMMs), 784

dual-boot configurations, 891, 902

dual-computer connections, Ethernet crossover cables, 461–462

DualView, laptops, 790

DVD decoders, installing, 232

DVD Maker, 321–325

DVDs
backups on, 871–872
Full Screen option, 239
pictures, burning to, 290–292

playing
troubleshooting, 232
WMP (Windows Media Player), 239
recording to, 325
DVD Maker, 321–325
software, installing via, 770

DVRs. *See* Windows Media Center

dynamic disk aggregation, hard disks, joining, 715–717

dynamic hard disks, 710–712. *See also* hard disks
advantages, 711–712
basic hard disks, converting to, 710
converting to, 711
disk management, 713–718
drive letters, assigning, 714–717
images, creating, 712–713
mirrored volumes, 711
organizational strategies, 712–713
RAID information storage, 720
RAID-5 volumes, 711
simple volumes, 711
spanned volumes, 711
striped volumes, 711
upgrading to, 717
volumes, joining, 714–717

Dynamic Host Configuration Protocol (DHCP), 473

dynamic IP addressing, configuring, 349

E

e.bat file, 833

Ease of Access Center, 601, 623–624
display settings, 626
keyboard settings, 624–625
mouse settings, 626–627
sound settings, 625

Ease of Access view (Category view), 598

Easy Connect, assistance requests, responding to, 1007

Easy Transfer Wizard, 50

eavesdropping, 915

echoconfig command (config.nt), 831

EDID (Extended Display Identification Data), 697

Edit Location dialog box, 337

editing
  advanced settings, DOS applications, 829–830
  BCD (boot configuration database), 736
  Contacts entries, 406
  default scan profiles, 306
  Registry
    entries, separate Windows installations, 817–818
    keys, 814–817
    Regedit, 747–748
    Registrar Registry Manager, 820
    Registry Toolkit, 819
    security attributes, 818–819
    Tweak-7, 820
    X-Setup Pro, 819
  scans, 310

effective permissions, viewing, 907

EFI (Extensible Firmware Interface) firmware, 736

EFS (Encrypted File System), 868, 884–886
  BitLocker versus, 900–901
  CIPHER command-line tool, 887–889
  folder recommendations for, 891
  offline files, 886–887
  restoring encrypted files, 893
  rules for usage, 889–890
  securing encrypted files, 891, 893
  troubleshooting, 885

eh (electronic home), 262

EISA buses, 801

email, 393
  client program, selecting, 393–394
  hoaxes, 916
  ISPs (Internet service providers), 393
  Microsoft E-Mail Updates Service, 934
  Outlook, 394
  photographs, sharing, 289–290
  scans, 310
  Windows Live Mail, 394
    addressing new messages, 402
    configuring accounts, 395–398
    Contacts, 406
    creating new messages, 401–402
    deleting incoming messages, 401
    downloading, 394
    launching, 395–396
    opening attachments, 403
    reading incoming messages, 398–399
    replying to incoming messages, 399–400
    sending attachments, 403
    sending new messages, 402–403
    signature setup, 405–406
    virus prevention, 404–405

email messages, text, aligning, 629

Emergency Boot Disks, updating, 720

emptying Recycle Bin, 725

emulation
  PC emulation, 73
  WOW64 emulation layer, 39

emulation mode, printers, 195

Enable Boot Logging advanced boot option, 749

Enable Low-Resolution Video advanced boot option, 749

enabling Windows Firewall, exceptions, 942

encapsulation, VPNs (virtual private networks), 977

Encrypted File System (EFS), 885–886
  BitLocker versus, 900–901
  CIPHER command-line tool, 887–889
  folder recommendations for, 891
  restoring encrypted files, 893
  rules for usage, 889–890
  securing encrypted files, 891, 893
  troubleshooting, 885

encrypted files, sleeping computers, risks, 891, 895

encryption, 885–886
  BitLocker, 895
    EFS (Encrypted File System) versus, 900–901
    enabling TPM (Trusted Platform Module), 897–898
    encryption process, 898–900
    full drive encryption, 886
    recovery process, 899
    system requirements, 895
    troubleshooting, 896
  BitLocker to Go, 896–897
  EFS (Encrypted File System), 884–886
    CIPHER command-line tool, 887–889
    folder recommendations for, 891
    offline files, 886–887
    restoring encrypted files, 893

How can we make this index more useful? Email us at indexes@quepublishing.com

rules for usage, 889–890
securing encrypted files,
891, 893
troubleshooting, 885
keys, 886
numeric encryption, 886
offline files, 997
passphrases, 466–467
wireless networks, 464,
466–467

**End User Licensing
Agreements (EULAs).** *See*
**EULAs (End User License
Agreements)**

entries (Contacts)
adding, 406–407
deleting, 407
editing, 406

entries (Registry)
editing for separate
Windows installations,
817–818
searching, 814

environment variables
PATH environment variable,
setting, 827
setting, 825–827

**Environment Variables option
(System Properties), 651–652**

**Error Checking utility,
728–730**

**Error Number 629/720
connection failures,
troubleshooting, 985**

**Error Reports, deleting, Disk
Cleanup utility, 725**

**errors, hard disk errors,
detecting and repairing,
728–730**

**Ethernet crossover cables,
two-computer connections,
461–462**

**Ethernet networks, cabling,
457–458**

**EULAs (End User Licensing
Agreements), 53**
hardware upgrades,
799–801

Event Viewer, 655
actions, 657
event details, viewing,
657–658
log entry sources, 583–584
log files, 656–657
networks, troubleshooting,
582–583
Overview and
Summary, 657

events
details, viewing, 657–658
ID numbers, locating, 840
sounds, associating with,
690–693

"Evernet," 971

**exceptions, Windows
Firewall, enabling, 942**

**executable programs,
extensions, 822**

**existing wireless networks,
joining, 472**

exiting Windows 7
Sleep, 146

**expandable string value data
type, 813**

exploits, 915

Explorer (Windows), 81
Address bar, 155–156
breadcrumbs, 81, 155, 158
Details pane, 152
Favorites group, 152
file system
navigating, 158–167
right-clicking, 161–162
selecting multiple items,
162–163
viewing
meta-information,
163–165
file views, customizing,
167–168
files
security, 185
zipping and packing,
183–184
folder views, customizing,
167–170
folders, security, 185

Get Help button, 152
indexing, configuring,
174–177
Layout flyout menu, 166
Libraries folder, 150
Libraries group, 152
location, 149
menu bar, 150
new features, 149–154
panes, toggling, 165–167
searching, 173–174
configuring, 174–177
deep searching, 174
grouping and stacking,
181–183
intermediate
searching, 174
troubleshooting, 179
while typing, 177–181
toolbar, 151–152
user profiles, 158
View menu, 167–168
views, 151–154
WebView, 152–154

exporting
recovery certificates, 886
Registry, 747

extended desktop, 697

**Extended Display
Identification Data
(EDID), 697**

**extended partitions, hard
disks, 710**

**extended view mode,
laptops, 791**

extending hard disks, 717–718

**Extensible Firmware Interface
(EFI) firmware, 736**

**extensions, executable
programs, 822**

**exterior televisions, output,
troubleshooting, 700**

**External Display control
(Mobility Center), 973**

**external fax modems,
testing, 300**

**external hard disks,
purchasing, 803**

external keyboards, slate Tablet PCs, 1035

external routers, 520

Extra Large Icons view (Computer), 140

F

F11 key, Internet Explorer, 358

FAT file system, backups, 868

FAT volumes, Properties tab, 723

FAT16 partitions, NTFS partitions, converting to, 722–723

FAT32 partitions, NTFS partitions, converting to, 722–723

fault tolerance, 711

favorite websites, Internet Explorer, adding, 365–367

Favorites bar (IE), 357, 360
  buttons
    creating, 358–359
    deleting, 359
  expanding, 359

Favorites group, Windows Explorer, 152

Fax and Scan, 293–294
  adding scanned pages to faxes, 302
  configuration, 295
    cover pages, 296–297
    fax receiving options, 295–296
    fax settings, 298–299
    sender information, 296
  configuring, 305–306
  dialing rules, 303–304
  emailing scans, 310
  enabling, 293
  fax devices, preparing, 294–295
  faxing scans, 310
  manipulating scanned images, 310

monitoring outgoing faxes, 304–305
  previewing faxes, 303
  printing faxes
    automatically, 305
  receiving faxes, 305
  scan profiles
    creating, 308
    editing default, 306
  scanning images, 308
  sending faxes, 299–304
  slides, faxing and scanning, 310–311
  transparencies, faxing and scanning, 310–311
  troubleshooting, 300
  Windows Firewall, Unblock option, 295

fax devices
  dialing rules, configuring, 303–304
  preparing, Windows Fax and Scan, 294–295
  shared printers, cabling, 453–454

fax modems, testing, 300

Fax Options dialog box, 299

fax receiving options (Windows Fax and Scan), configuring, 295–296

fax service (Windows Fax and Scan), 293–294
  adding scanned pages to faxes, 302
  configuration, 295
    cover pages, 296–297
    fax receiving options, 295–296
    fax settings, 298–299
    sender information, 296
  dialing rules, 303–304
  enabling, 293
  faxing scans, 310
  hardware requirements, 293
  monitoring outgoing faxes, 304–305
  preparations, 294–295
  previewing faxes, 303

printing faxes
  automatically, 305
  receiving faxes, 305
  scanning pictures, 294
  sending faxes, 299–302, 304
  slides, faxing and scanning, 310–311
  transparencies, faxing and scanning, 310–311
  troubleshooting, 300

Fax Setup dialog box, 295

fax signals, telephone lines, confirming, 293

faxes
  cover pages
    customizing, 296–297
    selecting, 301
  files, inserting, 301–302
  fonts, 299
  images, inserting, 301–302
  monitoring outgoing, 304–305
  previewing, 303
  printing automatically, 305
  receiving, 305
  recipients, selecting, 301
  resolution, 307
  scanned pages, adding, 302, 310
  sending, 299–302, 304
  slides, 310–311
  text faxes, inserting, 301–302
  transparencies, 310–311

features
  allowing, Windows Firewall, 939–940
  disabling, 773–774
  toggling, 645–646

feeds, news servers, censorship of, 409

FEK (file encryption key), 886

file and folder backups
  Complete PC backups versus, 865–866
  creating, 866–870
  restoring, 872–877

file corruption, Registry, signs, 811

File dialog box, 122

file encryption, 885–886. *See also* EFS (Encrypted File System)

file encryption key (FEK), 886

file formats, ripping, choosing, 242

file groupings, Disk Cleanup utility, 725

file ownership, taking, 908

file permissions (NTFS), 903–904
  advanced settings, 906
  assigning to groups, 908–909
  auditing, 907–908
  inheritance, 905
  taking ownership of files, 908
  viewing effective permissions, 907

file sharing
  access controls, setting, 926
  internetworking with Windows XP/2000/Vista, 491–494
  Macintosh OS X, 506–509
  passwords versus passwordless file sharing, 924–925
  security, 550–552
  troubleshooting, 589–590
  wireless networks
    cryptographic keys, 464
    security, 960–961

file system
  meta-information, viewing, 163–165
  navigating, 158–167
    right-clicking, 161–162
    selecting multiple items, 162–163

file types
  associations, 805
  WMP (Windows Media Player), 232

filename compatibility issues, Macintosh internetworking, 505

files
  AppleTalk File Protocol (AFP), 503
  batch files, 832–833
  compressing, 731–732
  deleting
    Disk Cleanup utility, 725
    Internet Explorer, 726–728
  deletion problems with Administrator account, 904
  downloaded program files, deleting, 725
  EFS (Encrypted File System), 868
  encryption, 884–886
    CIPHER command-line tool, 887–889
    EFS (Encrypted File System) versus BitLocker, 900–901
    folder recommendation, 891
    offline files, 886–887
    restoring encrypted files, 893
    rules for usage, 889–890
    securing encrypted files, 891–893
    troubleshooting, 885
  faxes, inserting, 301–302
  filtering, 181–183
  finding in multi-disc backups, 878
  hive files, Registry, 817–818
  In Use by Another User error message, 567
  JPEG files, compressing, 184
  libraries, 19–20
    adding to, 172–173
    managing, 170–173
    removing from, 173
  managing, third-party tools, 732
  meta-information, viewing, 163–165

  multiple files, selecting, 162–163
  networks, searching for, 546–548
  offline files, 991
    deleting, 725
    encrypting, 997
    identifying for use, 992–993
    managing, 997
    synchronizing, 995–998
    troubleshooting, 992–995
    using, 993–995
  offline webpages, deleting, 725
  packing, 183–184
  previous versions, restoring, 901–902
  program files, moving, 163
  right-clicking, 161–162
  searching, 173–174
    configuring, 174–177
    deep searching, 174
    grouping and stacking, 181–183
    intermediate searching, 174
    troubleshooting, 179
    while typing, 177–181
  security, 185
  shared folders, availability, 997–998
  sharing, 561–565
  structural problems, troubleshooting, 735–736
  temporary files, deleting, 725
  temporary Internet files, deleting, 725
  thumbnails, deleting, 725
  views, customizing, 167–168
  WAV files
    size considerations, 691
    storing, 692
  Windows Pictures Library, 279
  zipping, 183–184

Files and Settings Transfer Wizard, 16

files= command (config.nt), 831

Filter Keys, 625

filtering files, 181–183

filters
DSL services, installing for, 346
routers, 532

Finder (Mac OS X), 506

Firewall. *See* **Windows Firewall**

firewalls, 856
configuring, 919–921
function of, 919–921
multiple active profiles, 26
personal firewalls, 923
Windows Firewall, 920–921, 932
Advanced Security Administrative program, 941–943
allowing features, 939–940
allowing programs, 939–940
configuring, 477, 937–938
disabling, 938–939
enabling, 938–939
inadvertent blockage checks, 582
logging, 929
notification settings, 940–941
restoring to default settings, 941
satellite connections, 332
turning off, 940–941

FIRST (Forum of Incident Response and Security Teams), 931

fixed IP addresses, configuring, 349, 351

flicks (Tablet PCs), 1034–1036, 1040–1041
customizing, 1048
Flip 3-D, triggering, 1041
troubleshooting, 1048

Flip 3-D
limiting, 705
triggering, pen flicks, 1041

flowcharts, Internet connections, troubleshooting, 422–423

flyout menus, 126, 707

Folder Options (Control Panel), 168–170, 601
View tab, 154

folder sharing, wireless networks, security, 960–961

Folder view, 127

Folder view (Windows Explorer), 129–130

folders
Administrative Tools folder, accessing, 706
compressing, 731–732
deletion problems with Administrator account, 904
directory tree, navigating, 140
encryption, 884
recommendations for, 891
filtering, 181–183
libraries, 172–173
multiple folders, selecting, 162–163
networks, searching for, 546–548
offline folders
encrypting, 997
managing, 997
synchronizing, 995–998
permissions, inheritance of, 905
Program Files folder, removing programs from, 134
Public folder, sharing, 565
right-clicking, 161–162
searching, 173–174
configuring, 174–177
deep searching, 174
grouping and stacking, 181–183
intermediate searching, 174
troubleshooting, 179
while typing, 177–181
security, 185
selecting, 129
shared folders, 542
availability, 997–998
browsing, 542–546
monitoring use, 572
sharing, 561–567
user profile folder, directory structure, 104–109
symbolic links, 108
viewing, Windows Explorer, 129
views, customizing, 167–170
virtual folders, 777
Windows.old, 751

fonts, 627–630
Character Map, 224
families, 628
faxes, 299
information sources, 630
installing, 631
monospaced fonts, 629
OpenType fonts, 628
ornamental fonts, 630
points, 627
proportionally spaced fonts, 629
screen fonts
previewing, 704
resizing, 680
smoothing, 696
strokes, 629
substitutions, 630–631
types, 629

Fonts (Control Panel), 601, 627–631

Fonts folder, 628

forced shutdowns, 148

forks, 504

Forwarded events log (Event Viewer), 656

forwarding non-standard services to DMZ hosts (routers), 537–539

frames per second (fps), video, 369

free-form snips (Snipping Tool), 217, 320

Freed, Les, 459

FreeNews.net, free news servers listings, 409

frequent backups, security disaster planning, 930

FTP folders, visibility of, 928

Fujitsu Stylistic 3500 Tablet PC, 1030

Full Control NTFS permission, 891, 904

Full Screen option (WMP), 239

full system image backups, disk space, 868

full-screen snips (Snipping Tool), 217, 320

Fusion, DLL Hell, handling, 777

G

gadgets, 24, 119, 207–208
  64-bit gadgets, 212
  adding multiple times, 214
  configuring, 212–213
  desktop, adding, 209–210
  Desktop Gadget Gallery, 208–209
  downloading, 211–212
  improvements, 24–25
  moving, 213
  opacity, changing, 214–215
  peeking, 212
  removing, 215–216
  Windows Desktop gadgets, 212
  Windows Live gadgets, 212
  Windows Sideshow gadgets, 212

game controllers, 620

game ports, 801

garbled text, printers, troubleshooting, 202

Gates, Bill, 1030

gateway settings
  dial-up networking, setting, 981–982
  VPNs (virtual private networks), setting, 981–982

gateways, residential gateways, 518

General tab (Internet Options), 379–381

General tab (printer properties dialog box), 199

gestures, Tablet PCs, 131, 1036–1040
  Scratch-out gesture, 1040

Get Help button, Windows Explorer, 152

Getting Started (Control Panel), 601

Giant Company Software, Inc., 853

Gibson, Steve, 927

GIF (Graphics Interchange Format) graphics format, 320, 368

Gmail, spam filter, 953

Go To command (View menu), 168

Google, 392
  Gmail spam filter, 953

grafting hard disks, 715–717

graphical user interface (GUI). See interface

graphics file formats, 368

graphics cards, Windows Media Center, 255

Gray, Elisha, 1029

Group By command (View menu), 167

grouping searches, 181–183

groups, user groups
  assigning permissions to, 908–909
  restricted objects permissions, 910

GUI (graphical user interface)
  account picture, setting, 696
  Administrative Tools folder, accessing, 706
  backgrounds
    setting, 685–687
    solid backgrounds, 686
    stretching, 687
  color schemes
    Aero mode, 688–689
    Basic mode, 689–690
    setting, 688–690
  desktop icons, setting, 695–696
  display properties
    customizing, 683–703
    modifying, 696–703
    screen resolution, 697–700
  exterior televisions, output, 700
  Flip 3D, limiting, 705
  modifying, 679–680
  Recycle bin, configuring, 707
  screen fonts, previewing, 704
  screen savers, setting, 693–695
  sounds, associating with events, 690–693
  Start menu
    cascading elements, 707
    customizing, 680–683
  Taskbar, customizing, 682–683
  themes, setting, 684–685
  visual effects tools, 705–706
  Windows operating system, determining, 704

Guide (WMC), setting up, 264–265

H

h.bat file, 833

hackers, 845
  attacks, 915

handedness, Tablet PCs, specifying, 1046

handwriting
converting to text, 1044
importance of, 1029

handwriting recognition, 1030
evolution, 1030
Tablet PCs, 1034

Handwriting Recognition (Tablet PCs), 1033, 1041–1043, 1046
Handwriting Personalization window, 1041–1042
Numbers, Symbols, and Letters Recognition, 1042
Sentences Recognition, 1043

hanging up dial-up connections, 349, 352

hard disk media files, playing, WMP (Windows Media Player), 240

Hard Disk setting (Power Options Advanced Settings), 975

hard disks
backing up, 809
basic disks, 710
defragmentation
Disk Defragmenter, 730–731
scheduling, 803
disk management, 713
Convert utility, 722
Disk Cleanup utility, 724–728
Disk Defragmenter, 730–731
Disk Management utility, 713–723
dynamic disk management, 717
Error Checking utility, 728–730
Properties dialog box, 723–730
third-party tools, 732
drive letters, assigning, 714–717

dynamic disks, 710–712
advantages, 711–712
converting to, 711
converting to basic hard disks, 710
mirrored volumes, 711
RAID information storage, 720
RAID-5 volumes, 711
simple volumes, 711
spanned volumes, 711
striped volumes, 711
upgrading to, 717
encryption with BitLocker, 895
EFS (Encrypted File System) versus, 900–901
enabling TPM (Trusted Platform Module), 897–898
encryption process, 898–900
recovery process, 899
system requirements, 895
troubleshooting, 896
encryption with BitLocker to Go, 896–897
errors, detecting and repairing, 728–730
extending, 717–718
external hard disks, purchasing, 803
FAT16/32 partitions, converting to NTFS, 722–723
file compression, 731–732
grafting, 715–717
IDE channels, 783
images, creating, 712–713
joining, 715–717
managing, WSH (Windows Script Host), 836
minimum requirements, 44
organizational strategies, 712–713
PATA (Parallel ATA) hard disks, 783
RAID (Redundant Array of Independent Disks), 709, 894

recommended specifications, 44
SATA (Serial ATA) drives, 713, 782–783
SCSI hard disks, 782
shared hard disks, enabling, 557–558
shrinking, 718
spanned volumes, creating, 718
striped volumes, creating, 719–720
subfolders, mapping to, 561
troubleshooting, 733
boot process, 736
file structure problems, 735–736
hardware problems, 735–736
strategies, 733–734
unrecognized disks, 735–736
Ultra DMA EIDE drives, 782
upgrading, 782–783
VHDs (virtual hard disks), 721–722
volumes, joining, 714–717

hardware
Compatibility Center, 50
drivers
providing, 787–789
WDF (Windows Driver Foundation), 789
hard disk problems, troubleshooting, 735–736
hard disks, defragmenting, 783
HCL (Hardware Compatibility List), 50
installation methods, 784–787
installing, troubleshooting, 788–789
Internet configuration problems, troubleshooting, 429–433
legacy hardware
non-support, 801
scanning for, 786

minimum requirements, Windows Fax and Scan, 293

monitors, multiple installation, 790–795

motherboards
adapter cards, 785
RAM compatibility, 784

network adapters
checking existing, 455
installing, 454–455
multiple installation, 456

networks, cabling systems, 447–454

non-PnP hardware, installing, 785–787

optimization, 802–803

PnP (Plug and Play) hardware, installing, 784–787

printers
configuring, 189, 196–200
installing, 189–195
removing, 200
troubleshooting, 201–202

removing, 789–790

upgrading, 779–780
BIOS settings, 781–782
EULA (End User Licensing Agreement), 799–801
hard disks, 782–783
HCL (Hardware Compatibility List), 801–803
page file sizes, 780
RAM (random access memory), 779, 783–784
ReadyBoost, 780–781
SPP (Software Protection Program), 799

UPS (uninterruptible power supply)
choosing, 797
configuring, 798–799
installing, 795–799
intelligent UPS, 795
line interactive UPS, 797
online UPS, 797

printers, 797
serial cables, 798
standby UPS, 797
testing, 799

Windows Fax and Scan, preparing, 294–295

Windows Logo'd Products List, 784

Hardware and Sound category (Category view), 597

Hardware and Sound Control Panel window (Mobility Center), 973–974

Hardware Compatibility List (HCL). See HCL (Hardware Compatibility List)

hardware conflicts, resolving
Device Manager, 614–615
DMA channels, 616
I/O port assignments, 616–617
IRQs (interrupt requests), 615–616
memory addresses, 617–618

hardware DVD decoders, installing, 232

hardware encoders, Windows Media Center, 255

HCL (Hardware Compatibility List), 50, 784
compliance, 801–803
conflicts, 802
hidden devices, 802
NICs, 449

HD (high definition) aspect ratio, 323

headsets, Speech Recognition, 1032

hearing impairments, sound settings, 625

Help and Support, 141, 143–144

Help Protect Your Computer and Improve Windows Automatically dialog box, 57

hexadecimal format (WEP), 466

hibernation power option (laptops), 796

hidden devices, HCL (Hardware Compatibility List), conflicts, 802

hidden icons, Notification Area, 683

hiding updates, Windows Update, 761

High Contrast White color scheme, 626

high definition (HD) aspect ratio, 323

High Performance power usage profile, 974

high-speed connections, configuring, 347–349, 351

history, Internet Explorer, deleting, 365

hive files, Registry, 817–818

HKEY_CLASSES_ROOT top-level key (Registry), 806

HKEY_CURRENT_CONFIG top-level key (Registry), 806

HKEY_CURRENT_USER top-level key (Registry), 806

HKEY_LOCAL_MACHINE top-level key (Registry), 806

HKEY_USERS top-level key (Registry), 806

home networking, sharing media files, 248–250

Home networks, 475

home pages, Internet Explorer
changing, 359
setting, 380

home theater systems. See Windows Media Center

home wireless networks, 960
joining, 961–963

HomeGroup, 478–481, 602

homegroups, 20–21
  alternatives to, 480–481
  configuring, 478–480
  permissions, setting,
    563–565
  shared folders, browsing,
    542–544
  sharing, 35
  sharing resources with,
    562–565
  Windows Vista, setting up
    for, 494–495
  Windows XP, setting up for,
    494–495

**HomePlug Powerline Alliance
  adapters, phoneline
  networking, 451**

**HomePNA Alliance devices,
  phoneline networking,
  449–450**

**host names, ipconfig
  command, 586**

**hosts file (networking),
  512–513**

hosts files, 512–513

**hot spots, wireless networks,
  joining, 964–965**

hotfixes, 767

hotpatching, 759

**HP tx2500 convertible Tablet
  PCs, 1031**

**HTML editors, Internet
  Explorer, setting, 381–383**

**hubs, non-working lights,
  troubleshooting, 458**

hues, colors, 690

Hybrid Sleep, 100

Hybrid Sleep mode, 976

I

**I'll Choose Later fax-receiving
  option (Windows Fax and
  Scan), 296**

I/O port assignments, 616–617

icons
  desktop
    setting, 695–696
    troubleshooting, 698–699
  Network, 966
  Notification Area, 683
  printer icons, 188
  taskbar, 17–18
    organizing, 96

**ICRA (Internet Content Rating
  Association), 389**

**ICS (Internet Connection
  Sharing), 923, 989**

**ID numbers, events,
  locating, 840**

IDE channels, hard disks, 783

**IDE drives, SATA (Serial ATA)
  drives, switching to, 713**

identity theft, 916

**IDNs (internationalized
  domain names), 950**

IE (Internet Explorer). *See*
  Internet Explorer

**IIS (Internet Information
  Services), 511**

images
  backgrounds,
    stretching, 687
  burning to CD/DVD,
    290–292
  burning to DVD, 325
  desktop images
    capturing, 319–320
    viewing, 320–321
  faxes, inserting, 301–302
  fixing, Windows Media
    Player, 284–286
  GIF (Graphics Interchange
    Format), 368
  hard disks, creating,
    712–713
  Internet Explorer, supported
    formats, 368
  JPEG (Joint Photographic
    Experts Group), 368
  PNG (Portable Networking
    Graphics), 368

  printing, 286–289
  scanning, 308
  sharing electronically,
    289–290
  Windows Pictures
    Library, 278
    adding to, 278–279
    digital cameras, 281–284
    importing to, 279
    organizing, 279
    scanners, 279–281

impersonation, 915

important updates, 767

**Important updates,
  downloading, 94**

**In Use by Another User error
  message, file errors, 567**

**in-wall wiring, installing,
  460–461**

**incident plans, disaster plan-
  ning, developing, 931–932**

incoming access
  RAS (Remote Access
    Services) dial-up
    networking, 987–990
  VPNs (virtual private
    networks), 987–990

incoming messages
  deleting, Windows Live
    Mail, 401
  reading, Windows Live
    Mail, 398–399
  replying to, Windows Live
    Mail, 399–400

**incremental service
  packs, 768**

**indexing, Windows Explorer,
  configuring, 174–177**

**Indexing Options (Control
  Panel), 602**

**Information Bar for Pop-Ups
  (IE), 387**

infrared printer ports, 192

**infrastructure networks,
  466, 960**

**inheritance, permissions,
  891, 905**

InPrivate Browsing (IE),
28, 365

InPrivate Filtering (IE),
365, 380

InPrivate mode (IE), 356

Input Panel (Tablet PCs),
1036–1037
  Options dialog box, 1039
  writing methods, 1037–1038

installation
  applications on Windows
    XP VM, 1055–1056
  DSL filters, 346
  fonts, 631
  LLDP responder for
    Windows XP, 491
  modems, 345
  monitors, multiple monitors,
    790–795
  network adapters, 345,
    454–455
    broadband Internet
      connections, 345–346
    multiple installation, 456
  network wiring, 457–463
    Ethernet crossover
      cables, 461–462
    in-wall wiring, 460–461
    multiple switches,
      462–463
  networks
    professional installation,
      446–447
    wireless networks,
      463–472
  new features, 16–17
  optional network
    components, 510–512
  PnP (Plug and Play)
    hardware, 784–787
  Printers, 189
    local printers, 191–195
    shared printers, 556
  service packs, 768–769
  software, 769–770
    side-by-side installation,
      776–777
    via CD/DVD, 770
    via downloads, 771

SUA (Subsystem for
  UNIX-based
  Applications), 502
updates, Windows Update,
  760–761
UPS (uninterruptible power
  supply), 795–799
Virtual PC, 1052–1053
Windows 7,
  reinstallation, 751
Windows XP Mode,
  1053–1055
wireless networks, 463–472

Integrated TV Pack
Enhancements (WMC), 254

intelligent UPS, 795

interface
  account picture, setting, 696
  Administrative Tools folder,
    accessing, 706
  Aero desktop environment
    Aero Peek, 133
    dialog boxes, 122–123
    gestures, 131
    Help and Support,
      143–144
    libraries, 140–141
    putting items on, 123
    Quick Launch bar, 133
    shortcut keys, 130–131
    shortcuts, 124
  backgrounds
    setting, 685–687
    solid backgrounds, 686
    stretching, 687
  color schemes
    Aero mode, 688–689
    Basic mode, 689–690
    setting, 688–690
  desktop icons, setting,
    695–696
  display properties
    customizing, 683–703
    modifying, 696–703
    screen resolution,
      697–700
  exterior televisions,
    output, 700
  Flip 3D, limiting, 705

logon process, Welcome
  screen, 117
  modifying, 679–680
  new features, 17–23, 25
  Recycle bin,
    configuring, 707
  screen fonts,
    previewing, 704
  screen savers, setting,
    693–695
  sounds, associating with
    events, 690–693
  Start menu
    cascading elements, 707
    customizing, 680–683
  taskbar, 135
    customizing, 682–683
  themes, personalizing,
    684–685
  visual effects tools, 705–706
  Windows Explorer, file
    management, 129
  Windows Media Center, 252
  Windows operating system,
    determining, 704
  WMP (Windows Media
    Player), 233–238

interfaces. *See* **UIs (user**
interfaces)

intermediate searching,
Windows Explorer, 174

internal fax modems,
testing, 300

internationalized domain
names (IDNs), 950

Internet
  ISPs (Internet Service
    Providers), choosing, 334
  modems, installing, 345
  printers
    IPP (Internet Printing
      Protocol), 554–555
    LPR/LPD protocol
      (UNIX), 555–556

Internet Connection Sharing
(ICS), 454, 923, 989
  broadband DSL, 516
  broadband scheme, 527–529

demand dialing, 516
dial-up scheme, 523–526
function of, 923
outside network access,
   enabling, 533–537
residential gateways,
   518–520
versus external routers, 520
Internet connections, 330
broadband, 330
cellular service, 332–333
changing default
   connections, 349, 352
configuring, 342, 347–349
configuring manually,
   339–340
dial-up
   hanging up, 349, 352
   ISP problems, 344–345
DSL (Digital Subscriber
   Line), 331
high-speed, configuring,
   347–351
Internet Explorer, 381
LANs, 515–518
   cable service, 516,
     521–522
   configuring, 523–532
   connection sharing
     routers, 516
   DSL service, 521
   Internet Connection
     Sharing (ICS), 516,
     523–529
   IP address management,
     518–520
   overview, 516
   routed service, 516
   wireless, 521–522
satellite service, 332
shared DSL/cable service,
   inability to access on
   LANs, 527
shared modems, inability to
   access on LANs, 527
troubleshooting, 345,
   417–420
   dial-up settings, 420
   flowcharts, 422–423

ipconfig tool, 419,
   433–434
ISP information, 418
LAN connections,
   427–429
methodology, 420–422
modems, 426–427,
   430–433
network cabling
   diagrams, 420
Network Connections,
   419–420
network hardware
   problems, 429–433
pathping command, 437
ping command, 434–435
reverse tracert, 439–440
route command, 437–438
router configuration, 420
software configuration
   problems, 425–429
Speed Check, 439
TCP/IP diagnostic tools,
   433–438
third-party utilities,
   439–440
tracert, 435–437
tracert tool, 418
whois database, 439
WS_Ping Pro Pack, 440
wireless access, 332
**Internet Content Rating
Association (ICRA), 389**
**Internet downloads, installing
software from, 771**
Internet Explorer
Accelerators, 27, 356–357
   Add-ons Gallery, 357
add-ons
   allowing with invalid
     signatures, 377
   crash detection, 379
   managing, 377–379
   protecting against,
     376–377
   viewing, 377–379
Address bar, 356
Address box, 361
appearance,
   customizing, 380

AutoComplete, 356,
   361, 381
browsing history
   configuring, 380
   deleting, 365
cache cleanup, 726–728
certificates, accepting, 381
Compatibility View, 356
configuring, 98–100,
   379–390
connections, setting, 381
Content Advisor, 380
   configuring, 389–390
cookies, deleting, 365
crash recovery, 28
default home page,
   changing, 359
default mail program,
   setting, 381–383
default news reader,
   setting, 381–383
default programs,
   setting, 381
default search provider,
   setting, 380
drive-by downloads,
   avoiding, 376–379
favorites, adding, 365–367
Favorites bar, 357, 360
   button creation, 358–359
   button deletion, 359
   expanding, 359
home page, setting, 380
HTML editor, setting,
   381–383
Information Bar for
   Pop-Ups, 387
InPrivate Browsing, 28, 365
InPrivate Filtering, 365, 380
InPrivate mode, 356
launching, 358
Live Search box, 355
malware, protecting
   against, 374–375, 861
multimedia browsing, 367
   audio, 368–373
   graphics, 368
   streaming broadcasts,
     370–371
   video, 368–373

new features, 27–28,
355–357
page views, enlarging, 358
Paint, 383
parental controls, 380
configuring, 388–389
pop-up blocker
configuring, 386–387
enabling, 380
privacy settings,
configuring, 365, 384–386
programs
downloading, 373–379
setting default, 381–383
protected mode, 932
Safety button, 949
Search box, 391–392
security, 365
configuring, 384–386
web zones, 384
SmartScreen Filter, 356, 365,
947–949
Suggested Sites, 356
tab grouping, 28
Tab Groups, 355, 361–364
New Tab Page, 363
Quick Tabs Page, 364
tabbed web pages,
enabling, 380
temporary Internet files,
deleting, 365
troubleshooting
crashes, 358
email links, 383
Page not available
errors, 360
web pages, navigating, 361
Web Slices, 27, 356–357, 381
Windows Calendar, 383
Windows Contacts, 383
Windows Disc Image
Burner, 383
Windows Media Center, 383
Windows Media Player, 383
Windows Photo Gallery, 383
Windows Search
Explorer, 383
Wordpad, 383
Internet Information Services
(IIS), 511

Internet Options (Control
Panel), 379–381, 602
Advanced tab, 381
Connections tab, 381
Content tab, 380–381
General tab, 379–381
Privacy tab, 380
Programs tab, 381–383
Security tab, 380, 384–386
Internet Options, General
tab, 380
Internet Printing Client, 511
Internet Properties dialog
box, 726
Internet Protocol Version 4
(TCP/IPv4) Properties dialog
box, 474
Internet search engines, 392
Internet services, wireless
networks, configuring, 471
Internet transfer monitor
(Speed Check), 439
internetworking, 487–488. *See*
***also* networking**
Linux, 497
NFS (network file
system), 500–501
Macintosh, 503
AppleTalk File Protocol
(AFP), 503
application concurrency
issues, 505
applications, lost file
associations, 504
filename compatibility
issues, 505
Mac OS X, 506–510
Macintosh printers, 510
Macintosh shared files,
508–509
multiple use issues, 505
resource data issues, 504
Windows printers, 508
Windows shared files,
506–508
optional network
components, installing,
510–512

UNIX, 497
mangled line
feed/carriage returns,
499–500
NFS (network file
system), 500–501
Samba, 497–500
SUA (Subsystem for
UNIX-based
Applications), 501–503
Windows 95/98/ME,
496–497
with other operating
systems, 488
with Windows
XP/2000/Vista, 489,
494–495
installing LLDP
responder for Windows
XP, 491
password protection and
simple file sharing,
491–494
TCP/IP as default
network protocol, 490
interrupt handlers, 615
interrupt requests (IRQs),
615–616
invalid signatures, add-ons,
allowing, 377
IP address ranges, ipconfig
command, 586
IP addresses, 587
computers, assignment
of, 473
fixed, configuring, 349, 351
LANs, Internet connections,
managing, 518–520
Network Address
Translation (NAT),
518–520
public IP addresses, 518
ipconfig tool
hardware Internet
configuration problems,
troubleshooting, 430–433
host names, 586

Internet connections, troubleshooting, 419, 433–434

IP address ranges, 586

LAN connections, testing, 427–429

modems, troubleshooting, 426–427

network masks, 587

networks, troubleshooting, 585–586

Output from the ipconfig /all Command listing (16.1), 428–429

iPods

compatibility media players, compared, 244

WMP (Windows Media Player), synchronization, 246

IrfanView.com, 281

IRQs (interrupt requests), 615–616

[iniI]Is It Safe?[ffo], 921

ISAPnP (ISA Plug and Play), 801

iSCSI Initiator (Administrative Tools), 663–664

ISPs (Internet Service Providers)

accounts, manually configuring, 339–340

choosing, 334

dial-up process, troubleshooting, 344–345

documentation, obtaining, 397

email, 393

information, 418

installation software, 348

news servers, 409

troubleshooting, 345

items

drag-and-drop support, 163

multiple items, selecting, 162–163

properties, 124

right-clicking, 161–162

Start menu, adding to, 132

viewing, Folder view, 129–130

iTunes, 244

J

joining

domain networks, 481–483

hard disks

dynamic disk aggregation, 715–717

mount points, 715–717

volumes, 714–717

wireless networks, 472, 961

corporate environments, 961

home networks, 961–963

public hot spots, 964–965

small offices, 961–963

someone else's office, 963–964

JPEG (Joint Photographic Experts Group) graphics format, 320, 368

compressing, 184

JScript, 834

Jump List, 18–19

Start menu, 79–80

taskbar, 96–97

adding to, 595

junction points, user profile folder, 108

junk email. *See* spam

K

kernel-mode drivers, 789

Keyboard (Control Panel), 602, 620–621

keyboard shortcuts, 130–131

Remote Desktop, 1027

keyboards

accessibility settings, 624–625

configuring, Ease of Access Center, 625

external keyboards, slate Tablet PCs, 1035

Filter Keys, 625

keys (encryption), 886

wireless networks, 466–467

keys (Registry), 805

adding, 815–816

Copy Key Name command, 816

deleting, 815–816

editing, 814–816

editing for other users, 816–817

renaming, 816

values, 815

Kughen, Rick, 332

L

LAN adapters, 528

landscape backgrounds, 22

Landscape mode (Tablet PCs), 1047

languages, setting, 646

LANs (local area networks). *See also* networks

cabling systems, 447

10/100BASE-T Ethernet, 448–449

802.11g/n wireless networking, 451–452

1000Mbps Ethernet (Gigabit Ethernet), 449

fax machines, 453–454

mixed networking, 453

phoneline networking, 449–450

powerline networking, 451

printers, 453–454

running, 447

computer setup, security guidelines, 934

configuration, documenting, 420

connections, multiple
connections, 998
Internet connection
problems,
troubleshooting,
427–420
routed service, 516
Internet Connection
Sharing, 454
Internet connections,
515–518
cable service, 516,
521, 522
cable service with
multiple computers, 531
configuring, 523–532
connection sharing
routers, 516
DSL service, 521
inability to access shared
DSL/cable service, 527
inability to access shared
modems, 527
Internet Connection
Sharing (ICS), 516,
523–529
IP address management,
518–520
overview, 516
routed services, 532
shared routers with
broadband scheme,
529–530
shared routers with
dial-up scheme,
529–530
wireless, 521–522
LAN adapters, 528
network adapters
checking existing, 455
installing, 454–455
multiple installation, 456
outside access,
enabling, 533
planning, 444–445
professional installation,
446–447
servers, 445–446
remote access, providing,
454

wiring
Ethernet crossover
cables, 461–462
in-wall wiring, 460–461
installing, 457–463
multiple switches,
462–463

LapLink Everywhere, 1028

LapLink PCMover, 100

laptop computers, Windows
Media Center, 256–257

laptops
batteries
cycling, 796
optimization, 974–976
DualView, 790
extended view mode, 791
mirror mode, 791
Mobility Center, 972
controls, 972–973
Hardware and Sound
Control Panel window,
973–974
launching, 972
power options, 796
power usage profiles, 974
creating, 975
viewing, 974–976
processors, clock
speeds, 974
remote computing
dial-up networking,
977–990
LANs (local area
networks), 998
offline files, 991–998
Sync Center, 991
VPNs (virtual private
networks), 977–990

Large Icons view
(Computer), 140

Large Icons view (Control
Panel), 595–604

laser printers, UPS
(uninterruptable power
supply), 797

Last Known Good
Configuration, 748–749

launching
applications, 136
Computer, 140
Start button, 137
Windows Explorer, 140
Internet Explorer, 358
Mobility Center, 972
Windows Live Mail,
395–396

Layout flyout menu, Windows
Explorer, 166

LCD monitors
blurry images,
troubleshooting, 701
CRT-based monitors,
compared, 699
refresh rate, 702

LDAP queries, 550

LE1700WT slate Table
PCs, 1031

legacy hardware
non-support, 801
scanning for, 786

libraries, 19–20, 140, 149
creating, 170–172
Documents, 140
elements
adding to, 172–173
removing, 173
managing, 170–173
multiple folders, selecting,
162–163
Music, 141
toolbar, 159
Pictures, 140
right-clicking, 161–162
searching, 173–174
configuring, 174–177
deep searching, 174
grouping and stacking,
181–183
intermediate
searching, 174
troubleshooting, 179
while typing, 177–181
shared folders, adding
to, 557
Windows Media Center,
Movies library, 264

Windows Pictures Library, 278
  adding pictures to, 278–279
  burning pictures to CD/DVD, 290–292
  digital cameras, 281–284
  importing files to, 279
  organizing, 279
  printing, 286–289
  scanners, 279–281
  sharing pictures electronically, 289–290
WMP (Windows Media Player), adding items to, 243

Libraries folder, 150

Libraries group, Windows Explorer, 152

licensing, EULA (End User Licensing Agreement), hardware upgrades, 799–801

line interactive UPS (uninterruptible power supply), 797

Link Level Discovery Protocol (LLDP), 488

links, IE Favorites bar, 358–359

Linux
  internetworking, 497
    NFS (network file system), 500–501
    Samba, 497–500
  Samba
    client tools, 497–498
    server tools, 498–500

List All Modes dialog box, 702

List Folder Contents NTFS permission, 891, 904

List Folder/Read Data advanced NTFS permission, 891, 906

List view (Computer), 140

listings, Output from the ipconfig /all Command (16.1), 428–429

Live Maps, 357

Live Search box (IE), 355, 391

LLDP (Link Level Discovery Protocol), 488

LLDP mapping, 489

LLDP responder, installing for Windows XP, 491

local account policies, configuring, 935–936

local area networks (LANs). See LANs (local area networks)

local audit policies, configuring, 936–937

local password policies, configuring, 935–936

Local Policy Editor
  account policies, configuring, 935–936
  audit policies, configuring, 936–937
  password policies, configuring, 935–936
  security policies, configuring, 934–935

local printers
  connections
    infrared port, 192
    parallel port, 191
    serial port, 192
  emulation mode, 195
  installing, 191–192
    troubleshooting, 192–195

local security policies, configuring, 934–935

local user groups, 908. See also user groups
  creating, 909

locating news servers, 409

Location and Other Sensors (Control Panel), 602

locking down. See securing

log files, Event Viewer, 656–657

logging, Windows Firewall, enabling, 929

logging off, shutdowns, compared, 146

LogMeIn, 1010

logoff process, 100

logon process, 117

LPD Print Service, 511

LPR Port Monitor, 511

LPR-based computers, networks, configuring on, 555–556

luminosity (color), 690

luminosity bar, 690

Lycos, 392

M

MAC addresses, 349

Macintosh
  applications, lost file associations, 504
  internetworking, 503
    AppleTalk File Protocol (AFP), 503
    application concurrency issues, 505
    filename compatibility issues, 505
    Mac OS X, 506–510
    Macintosh printers, 510
    Macintosh shared files, 508–509
    multiple use issues, 505
    resource data issues, 504
    Windows printers, 508
    Windows shared files, 506–508

Magnifier, 220–221

mail program, Internet Explorer, setting, 381–383

malware, 845
  avoiding, 862
  preventing, 848
    antivirus software, 850–852

automatic updates, 857
DEP (Data Execution
Prevention), 857–859
firewalls, 856
Internet Explorer, 861
service hardening,
860–861
UAC (User Account
Control), 859–860
Windows Action Center,
848–850
Windows Defender,
852–856
protecting against, Internet
Explorer, 374–375
rootkits, 847–848
spyware, 847
viruses, 846
worms, 846–847

**Manage Accounts screen,
89–90**

**Management Instrumentation.
See WMI (Windows
Management
Instrumentation)**

management tools
Computer Management
Event Viewer, 655–658
Services, 659–660
Shared Folders, 658–659
Task Scheduler, 654
Control Panel, 594–595
Action Center, 600,
604–607
Administrative Tools,
600, 660–666
AutoPlay, 600, 607–608
Backup and Restore, 601
BitLocker, 601
Category view, 595–596,
598–599
Color Management,
601, 609
Credential Manager, 601
Date and Time, 601,
609–611
default display, 594
Default Programs, 601,
611–612

Desktop Gadgets, 601
Device Manager, 601,
612–619
Devices and Printers,
601, 619–620
Display, 601
Ease of Access Center,
601, 623–627
Folder Options, 601
Fonts, 601, 627–631
Getting Started, 601
HomeGroup, 602
Indexing Options, 602
Internet Options, 602
Keyboard, 602, 620–621
Large Icons view,
600–604
Location and Other
Sensors, 602
Mouse, 602, 621–623
Network and Sharing
Center, 602
Notification Area Icons,
602, 631–632
Parental Controls, 602
Performance Information
and Tools, 602,
632–642
Personalization, 602
Phone and Modem, 602
Power Options, 602, 642
Programs and Features,
602, 643–646
Recovery, 603
Region and Language,
603, 646
RemoteApp and Desktop
Connections, 603
shortcuts, 595
Small Icons view,
600–604
Sound, 603
Speech Recognition, 603
Sync Center, 603
System, 603
System Properties,
647–652
Tablet PC Settings, 603
Taskbar and Start
Menu, 603

Troubleshooting, 603
User Accounts, 603
Windows
CardSpace, 603
Windows Defender, 603
Windows Firewall, 603
Windows Mobility
Center, 604
Windows Update, 604
MMC (Microsoft
Management Console),
653–654
Programs and Features, 602
Recovery, 603
Region and Language, 603
RemoteApp and Desktop
Connections, 603
Sound, 603
Speech Recognition, 603
Sync Center, 603
System, 603
System Tools folder, 666
Character Map, 667–669
Private Character
Editor, 670
System Information,
670–671
Tablet PC Settings, 603
Task Manager, 672, 675
Applications tab,
672–674
Networking tab, 677
Performance tab,
675–677
Processes tab, 674–675
Services tab, 675
Users tab, 677
Taskbar and Start
Menu, 603
third-party management
tools, 677–678
Troubleshooting, 603
User Accounts, 603
Windows CardSpace, 603
Windows Defender, 603
Windows Firewall, 603
Windows Mobility
Center, 604
Windows Update, 604

managing IE add-ons, 377–379

manually adding wireless network profiles, 968–969

manually configuring wireless networks, 470–471

manually installing service packs, 769

manually installing updates, Windows Update, 760–761

manually synchronizing portable media players, WMP (Windows Media Player), 247–248

manufacturer's setup program, wireless networks, configuring, 468

mapping hard drives to subfolders, 561

Math Input panel, 32

Math Input Panel (Tablet PCs), 1034

Max, Peter, 22

maximizing windows, gestures, 131

maximum requirements, RAM (random access memory), 784

McAfee antivirus software, 851

McFedries, Paul, 585

Media Center. *See* Windows Media Center

media files, sharing, home networking, 248–250

Media Libraries, 278

Media Player. *See* WMP (Windows Media Player)

Media Streaming dialog box, 250

Media Streaming Options dialog box, 249

Medium Icons view (Computer), 140

Melissa virus, 846

memory, 779
hard disk space, 779
RAM (random access memory), 779
cost fluctuations, 784
DIMMs (dual in-line memory modules), 784
maximum requirements, 784
minimum requirements, 783
SDRAM (synchronous dynamic RAM), 783
upgrading, 779, 783–784
troubleshooting, Windows Memory Diagnostic tool, 745–746

memory addresses, 617–618

memory-mapped I/O, 617

menu bars, Windows Explorer, 150

menu breadcrumbs, WMP (Windows Media Player), 233–236

menus
flyout menus, 126, 707
Organize, 160
right-click context menus, 124–126
View, 160
Windows Explorer, 167–168

messages (email)
addressing, 402
attachments, 403–405
creating, 401–402
incoming messages
deleting, 401
reading, 398–399
replying to, 399–400
new messages
addressing, 402
creating, 401–402
sending, 402–403
newsgroups
availability after syn-chronization, 412–413
news indicator, marking, 415

sending, Windows Live Mail, 402–403
signatures, setting up, 405–406

meta-information, 163

metadata, 152

MHT files, 320

Michelangelo virus, 846

microphones, Speech Recognition, 1032

Microsoft Corporation, Department of Justice (DOJ) consent decree, middleware applications, 357

Microsoft Download Center
hotfixes, 767
service packs, obtaining, 768

Microsoft Download Notifications service, 767

Microsoft Knowledge Base, 755

Microsoft Management Console (MMC), 653–654

Microsoft SharedView, 1011

Microsoft SpyNet, 855

Microsoft technical support
contacting, 755
OS desupport dates, 116

Microsoft Typography website, 630

middleware applications, Department of Justice (DOJ) decree, 357

migration utility EFS files, moving, 894

minimizing windows, gestures, 131

minimum requirements
hardware, Windows 7, 44–45
RAM (random access memory), 783
Virtual PC, 1052

mirror mode, laptops, 791

mirrored volumes, dynamic hard disks, 711

mirroring RAID, 783

missing hard disks, troubleshooting, 735–736

Mitchell, Joni, 264

mixed networking, 453

MMC (Microsoft Management Console), 653–654

mobile computing, 972
  battery optimization, 974–976
  dial-up networking, RAS (Remote Access Services), 977
  LANs (local area networks), multiple connections, 998
  Mobility Center
    controls, 972–973
    Hardware and Sound Control Panel window, 973–974
    launching, 972
  offline files, 991
    encrypting, 997
    identifying for use, 992–993
    managing, 997
    synchronizing, 995–998
    troubleshooting, 992–995
    using, 993–995
  RAS (Remote Access Services) dial-up networking
    advanced routing, 986–987
    configuring, 978–987
    connection properties, 980–982
    current location checks, 983
    email connections, 986
    ending connections, 986
    establishing connections, 983–985
    gateway settings, 981–982

incoming access, 987–990
monitoring connections, 986
multiple location management, 982–983
shared folders, availability, 997–998
Sync Center, 991
VPNs (virtual private networks), 977
  advanced routing, 986–987
  configuring, 978–987
  connection process, 977–978
  connection properties, 980–982
  data encapsulation, 977
  email connections, 986
  ending connections, 986
  establishing connections, 983–985
  gateway settings, 981–982
  incoming access, 987–990
  monitoring connections, 986
  RAS (Remote Access Services), 977
  tunnels, 977

Mobile Pentium II/III SpeedStep, 801

Mobility Center (Windows), 972
  controls, 972–973
  Hardware and Sound Control Panel window, 973–974
  launching, 972
  Presentation Settings, 973
  Sync Center, 973
  Wireless Network icon, 973

modems
  connectivity problems, troubleshooting, 432–433
  dial-up modems, digital telephone wiring, 293
  dial-up process, troubleshooting, 344–345

drivers, 295
fax modems, testing, 300
hardware problems, troubleshooting, 430–432
installing, 345
Internet connection problems, troubleshooting, 426–427

Modify NTFS permission, 891, 904

modular connectors, networking, 460

Mojave market campaign, 11

Monitor tab (Screen Resolution window), 701

monitoring
  dial-up networks, connections, 986
  networks, suspicious activities, 929
  outgoing faxes, 304–305
  software, 771
  VPN (virtual private networks), connections, 986

monitors
  blank monitors, troubleshooting, 701
  blurry images, troubleshooting, 701
  configuring, 697–700
  desktop item movement, troubleshooting, 698–699
  exterior televisions, output, 700
  LCD monitors, 699
    refresh rates, 702
  multiple monitors
    installing, 790–795
    laptops, 790
    secondary display adapters, 792
    troubleshooting, 791–793
    video cards, 790–791
  refresh rates, 703
  screen flicker, reducing, 703
  slow motion, troubleshooting, 698
  video cards, quad-link video adapter cards, 795

monospaced fonts, 629

Monotype Imaging, fonts, 630

Morris, Robert, 857

motherboards
adapter cards, moving, 785
RAID, 783
RAM, compatibility, 784

mount points, hard disks, joining, 715–717

mouse
accessibility settings, 626–627
Single-Click setting, 703

Mouse (Control Panel), 602, 621–623

Movies library (WMC), 264

moving gadgets, 213

MP3 files, 242
playing, Internet Explorer, 372–373

MP3 players. *See* portable media players

MPEG files, playing, Internet Explorer, 370

MS-DOS, 828
ANSI.SYS, 831–832
autoexec.nt, customizing, 830–831
config.nt, customizing, 830–831
desupport, 116
DOS applications, editing advanced settings, 829–830
DOSKEY, 831–832

MSConfig, 736

MSMQ (Microsft Message Queue) Server, 511

MSN streaming broadcasts, 371

Mueller, Scott, 50, 431, 780

multi-disc backups, finding files in, 878

multimedia. *See also* Windows Media Center
Internet Explorer, 367
audio, 368–373
downloading, 373–379
graphics, 368
streaming broadcasts, 370–371
video, 368–373

Multimedia Settings setting (Power Options Advanced Settings), 976

multiple accounts, Windows Live Mail, checking, 401

multiple connections, LANs (local area networks), 998

multiple default settings, printers, 198

multiple items, selecting, 162–163

multiple locations, dial-up networks, managing, 982–983

multiple monitors
installing, 790–795
laptops, DualView, 790
secondary display adapters, 792
troubleshooting, 791–793
video cards, 790–791

multiple switches, installing, 462–463

multiple use issues, Macintosh internetworking, 505

multistring value data type, 813

multitouch capabilities, Tablet PCs, 1035

music. *See also* audio and CDs
slideshows, adding to, 269

Music library, 141, 159, 253

Music Library Locations dialog box, 243

Music Now Playing (WMC), 254

N

n.bat file, 833

names, user accounts, changing, 90

naming shared printers, 554

Narrator, 220

NAT (Network Address Translation), 518, 919
devices
configuring, 919, 923
function of, 919, 923
incoming VPN connections, enabling, 989–990
Internet Connection Sharing (NCS), 518–520

nature backgrounds, 22

navigation, web pages, Internet Explorer, 361

Navigation pane (WMP), 250

Nero Burning ROM, 324

NetBEUI network protocol, 488

NetBIOS traffic, filtering, 532

"netbook" computers, 1031

Network, Computer, compared, 139

network adapters, 449
10/100BASE-T, 444
broadband Internet connections, installing for, 345–346
existing network adapters, checking, 455
high-speed connections, configuring, 347–351
HomePlug Powerline Alliance, 451
HomePNA Alliance, 449–450
installing, 345, 454–455
multiple, 456

Network Address Translation (NAT). *See* NAT (Network Address Translation)

Network and Internet category (Category view), 596

Network and Sharing Center, 33–34, 571–572, 577–578, 602, 960–961, 982

network appliances, 488

network cables, testing, 585

network cabling diagrams, Internet connections, troubleshooting, 420

network cards, internal PCI cards, 444

Network Connection taskbar icon, 426

Network Connections, Internet connections, troubleshooting, 419–420

Network Diagnostics tool, network configuration, troubleshooting, 581–582

network drives, backing up, 29

network file system (NFS). See NFS (network file system)

Network Hardware dialog box, 419

network icon, 962, 966

Network Location feature, 960

network locations, peer-to-peer networks, configuring, 475–476

Network Map, 34, 579–581

network masks, 587
    ipconfig command, 587

Network News Transport Protocol (NNTP), 408

network services
    inability to block, 928
    packet filtering, blocking, 921–922

Network Setup Wizard, Internet Connection Sharing (ICS)
    broadband scheme configuration, 527–529
    dial-up scheme configuration, 523–526

network shares
    backups to, 866
    playing, WMP (Windows Media Player), 240

network-attached storage, 488

networked computers, passwords, changing, 493

networking. See also internetworking and networks
    home networking, sharing media files, 248–250
    hosts file, 512–513
    new features, 33–35
    optional network components, installing, 510–512
    shared folders, 542–546
    troubleshooting, 491
        carriage returns and line feeds, 499–500
        Macintosh files have lost application associations, 504
    with other operating systems, 488

Networking tab (Task Manager), 677

Networking with Microsoft Windows Vista, 585

networks. See also internetworking and networking
    ad hoc networks, 466
    adapters, 444
    bridging types, 484–485
    cabling systems, 447
        10/100BASE-T Ethernet, 448–449
        802.11g/n wireless networking, 451–452
        1000Mbps Ethernet (Gigabit Ethernet), 449
        fax machines, 453–454
        mixed networking, 453
        phoneline networking, 449–450
        powerline networking, 451

    printers, 453–454
    running, 447
    updating, 453
    computer identification
        checking, 587–588
        configuring, 476–477
    computers
        backing up over, 557
        searching for, 548
    configuration, checking, 581–582
    connections, checking, 588
    corporate networks, 41–42
    defenses, testing, 927, 929
    dial-up networking, RAS (Remote Access Services), 977
    domain networks, joining, 481–483
    Ethernet networks, cabling, 457–458
    fax machines, cabling, 453–454
    file permissions, 550–551
    file sharing, security, 550–552
    files
        In Use by Another User error message, 567
        searching for, 546–548
        sharing, 561–565
    folders
        searching for, 546–548
        sharing, 561–567
    hard drives, mapping to subfolders, 561
    homegroups
        alternatives to, 480–481
        configuring, 478–480
    hubs, non-working lights, 458
    infrastructure networks, 466
    Internet Connection Sharing, 454
    LANs (local area networks)
        documenting configuration, 420
        multiple connections, 998
        troubleshooting, 427–429
    managing, 571–572
        command line, 573–574

WSH (Windows Script Host), 836
multiple problems, 584
network adapters
  checking existing, 455
  installing, 454–455
  multiple installation, 456
Network and Sharing Center, 571–572
network cards, 444
network permissions, 552
offline files, 991
  encrypting, 997
  identifying for use, 992–993
  managing, 997
  synchronizing, 995–998
  troubleshooting, 992–995
  using, 993–995
optional components, installing, 510
outside access, enabling, 533–539
peer-to-peer networks, 443
  configuring, 472–476
planning, 444–445
  professional installation, 446–447
  servers, 445–446
printers, 552
  icon setup, 553–554
  installing, 556
  IPP (Internet Printing Protocol), 554–555
  LPR/LPD protocol (UNIX), 555–556
  naming, 554
  searching for, 548–549
  setting permissions, 569–570
Public folder, sharing, 565
RAS (Remote Access Services) dial-up networking
  advanced routing, 986–987
  configuring, 978–987
  connection properties, 980–982
  current location checks, 983

email connections, 986
ending connections, 986
establishing connections, 983–985
gateway settings, 981–982
incoming access, 987–990
monitoring connections, 986
multiple location management, 982–983
remote access, providing, 454
resources, managing, 573–574
searching, 546–550
security
  assessing personal risk, 914–915
  attacks, 915–916
  attacks, active defenses, 919–926
  attacks, defense measures, 917–919
  disaster planning, 929–932
  FTP folders, visibility of, 928
  holes, 914–915
  LAN guidelines, 934
  local policy configuration, 934–937
  sensitive web pages, visibility of, 928
  shared folders, visibility of, 928
  standalone guidelines, 933
  updates, 934
  Windows Firewall, configuring, 937–938
  Windows Firewall, enabling exceptions, 942
shared disk drives, enabling, 557–558
shared folders
  adding to libraries, 557
  availability, 997–998

monitoring use, 572
shared printers, 453–454
suspicious activities, monitoring, 929
Sync Center, 991
troubleshooting, 575
  common problems, 576–577
  configuration, 585–588
  connectivity, 588–589
  Device Manager, 584
  diagnostic tools, 577–584
  Event Viewer, 582–584
  file sharing, 589–590
  Network and Sharing Center, 577–578
  network cables, 585
  Network Diagnostics, 581–582
  Network Map, 579–581
  preparation, 576
  printer sharing, 589–590
  Windows Firewall, 582
UNC (Universal Naming Convention), 558–559
VPNs (virtual private networks), 977
  advanced routing, 986–987
  configuring, 978–987
  connection process, 977–978
  connection properties, 980–982
  data encapsulation, 977
  email connections, 986
  ending connections, 986
  establishing connections, 983–985
  gateway settings, 981–982
  incoming access, 987–990
  monitoring connections, 986
  RAS (Remote Access Services), 977
  tunnels, 977
Windows Firewall, configuring, 477

How can we make this index more useful? Email us at indexes@quepublishing.com

Windows Server, 445–446

wireless networks, 959
  ad hoc networks, 960, 965–966
  authentication, 464
  configuring, 464–466, 468–471, 966
  copying profiles, 968
  deleting profiles, 969
  domain networks, 961
  encryption, 464, 466–467
  evolution, 959
  home networks, 960
  infrastructure networks, 960
  installing, 463–472
  joining, 472, 961–965
  manually adding profiles, 968–969
  prioritizing connections, 967–968
  public networks, 960
  security, 960–961
  selecting preferred, 966
  SSIDs, 472, 968
  standards, 959
  switching between, 966–967
  troubleshooting, 964

wiring
  Ethernet crossover cables, 461–462
  in-wall wiring, 460–461
  installing, 457–463
  multiple switches, 462–463
  patch cables, 459–460

New Fax dialog box, 299

new features
  Windows 7, 13–14, 16–23, 25–38
    accessories, 31–32
    applications, 37
    configuration, 16–17
    corporate networks, 41–42
    data security, 29–30
    entertainment, 37–38
    installation, 16–17
    interface, 17–23, 25

  Internet Explorer, 27–28
    networking, 33–35
    performance, 30–31
    power management, 32–33
    services, 37
    stability, 35–36
    system management, 35–36
    system security, 25–26
    upgrades, 17
  Windows Explorer, 149–154

New Tab page (Tab Group), 363

news reader, Internet Explorer, setting, 381–383

news servers
  accessing, 408
  feeds, censorship of, 409
  FreeNews.net, 409
  locating, 409
  missing newsgroups, troubleshooting, 410
  monthly cost, 409
  Network News Transport Protocol (NNTP), 408
  Unix-to-Unix Copy Protocol (UUCP), 408
  Web-based, Newsguy.com, 409

newsgroups
  accounts, setting up, 410–411
  accessing, 408
  downloading lists, 411
  evolution of, 408
  locating, 412
  managing, 415–416
  messages
    new indicator, marking, 415
    unavailable after synchronization, 412–413
  missing from news servers, troubleshooting, 410
  posting messages to, 414–415
  reading, 412–415
  subscribing to, 412–414

Usenet
  compared, 409
  lack of oversight authority, 408

Newsguy.com Web-based news server, 409

Newton MessagePad 2000, 1030

NFS (network file system)
  Services for NFS, 512
  UNIX/Linux, internetworking, 500–501

NGM (non-genuine Windows mode), 72

NICs (network interface cards), 444
  10/100BASE-T Ethernet networks, 449

NNTP (Network News Transport Protocol), 408

nodes, Computer Management, 653

non-Aero mode, color schemes, 689–690

non-genuine Windows mode (NGM), 72

non-PnP hardware, installing, 785–787

notebook computers
  batteries
    cycling, 796
    optimization, 974–976
  DualView, 790
  extended view mode, 791
  mirror mode, 791
  Mobility Center, 972
    controls, 972–973
    Hardware and Sound Control Panel window, 973–974
    launching, 972
  power options, 796
  power usage profiles, 974
    creating, 975
    viewing, 974–976
  processors, clock speed, 974

remote computing
dial-up networking, 977–990
LANs (local area networks), 998
offline files, 991–998
Sync Center, 991
VPNs (virtual private networks), 977–990

Notepad, 225–226
troubleshooting, 226
WordPad, compared, 225

Notification Area, customizing, 683

Notification Area Icons (Control Panel), 602, 631–632

notification settings, Windows Firewall, changing, 940–941

Notify Me fax-receiving option (Windows Fax and Scan), 295

Novell NetWare, internetworking, 489

Now Playing (WMC), 253

NPR (National Public Radio) streaming broadcasts, 371

ntcmdprompt command (config.nt), 831

NTFS (Windows NT File System), 712
file permissions, 903–904
advanced settings, 906
assigning to groups, 908–909
auditing, 907–908
inheritance, 905
taking ownership of files, 908
viewing effective permissions, 907
partitions
converting, 780
FAT16/32, converting from, 722–723
printer permissions, 910

recovery keys, 751
volumes
EFS (Encrypted File System), 884
Properties tab, 723

ntvdm (Windows NT Virtual DOS Machine), 828–829

Numbers, Symbols, and Letters Recognition (Handwriting Recognition), 1042

numeric encryption, 886

O

objectionable content, controlling, Internet Explorer, 389–390

objects
drag-and-drop support, 163
properties, 124
right-clicking, 161–162
selecting multiple objects, 162–163
shortcuts, sending to, 123
Snipping Tool, 216–219
Start menu, adding to, 132
viewing, Folder view, 129–130

Off Line Files, 991–995

[iniI]Official Samba-3 HOWTO and Reference Guide, The[ffo], 497

offline files, 991
deleting, Disk Cleanup utility, 725
encrypting, 997
identifying for use, 992–995
managing, 997
synchronizing, 995–998
troubleshooting, 992–995

offline webpages, deleting, Disk Cleanup utility, 725

On-Screen Keyboard (Input Panel), 1037

onclick() method, 947

online meetings, third-party collaboration tools, 1010

online UPS (uninterruptible power supply), 797

opacity, gadgets, changing, 214–215

Open dialog box, 122

open door attacks, 916

OpenType font outline technology, 627–630

OpenType fonts, 628

operating systems, 488
crashes, troubleshooting, 144, 147–148
Microsoft desupport dates, 116
networking with other operating systems, 488–489

optimization
environment variables, setting, 825–827
hardware, 802–803

Options dialog box (Input Panel), 1039

organization, Registry, 805–806

organizational strategies, hard disks, 712–713

Organize menu, 160

ornamental fonts, 630

outgoing faxes, monitoring, 304–305

Outlook, 394

Output from the ipconfig /all Command listing (16.1), 428–429

outside network access, enabling, 533–539

Overview and Summary (Event Viewer), 657

ownership of files, taking, 908

P

packet filtering
function of, 921
network services, blocking,
921–922
routers, 921–923

packets, testing, ping
command, 434–435

packing files, 183–184

page file sizes, adjusting, 780

Page not available errors
(Internet Explorer),
troubleshooting, 360

Paint, 224–225
Internet Explorer, 383

panes. *See also* specific panes
toggling, 165–167

Parallel ATA (PATA) disk drives, 783

parallel printer ports, 191

parent locations, 155

Parental Controls, 602

Parental Controls (IE), 380
configuring, 388–389

partial screen capturing,
Snipping Tool, 216–219

Partition Commander
Professional 10 (Avanquest
Software), 710

partitions, 926
extended partitions, 710
NTFS
*converting FAT16/32
partitions to, 722–723
converting to, 780*
primary partitions, 710
separating applications
from data, 712

passphrases, encryption keys,
466–467

password cracking, 915

Password Protected
Sharing, 492

password protection,
internetworking with
Windows XP/2000/Vista,
491–494

password reset disks,
creating, 91–92

passwordless file sharing,
passwords, compared,
924–925

passwords
changing, networked
computers, 493
passwordless file sharing
versus, 924–925
policies, local settings,
935–936
requiring, 926
SPA (Secure Password
Authentication), 398
user accounts, 90–92

PATA (Parallel ATA) hard
disks, 783

patch cables, 457
installing, 459–460

PATH environment variable,
setting, 827

PC Magazine, 852

PC World
magazine, 852

PCIe (PCI Express) video
interface, 790–791

peeking, gadgets, 212

peer-to-peer networks,
configuring, 472
network locations, 475–476
TCP/IP protocol, 473–475

pels, 224

Pen and Touch dialog box,
1040, 1047–1049

pen flicks (Tablet PCs),
1034–1036, 1040–1041
customizing, 1048
Flip 3-D, triggering, 1041
troubleshooting, 1048

pen gestures (Tablet PCs),
1036–1040
Scratch-out gesture, 1040

pen-based computers. *See*
Tablet PCs

pen cursor,
troubleshooting, 1039

performance, hard disks,
defragmenting, 783

performance, improvements,
30–31

Performance Information and
Tools, 638
Adjust Indexing Options, 637
Adjust Visual Effects, 636
Advanced Tools option,
638–642
Window Experience Index,
633–636

Performance Information and
Tools (Control Panel), 602, 632

Performance Monitor, 639–640

Performance Options dialog
box, 650–651

Performance tab (Task
Manager), 675–677

permissions
advanced settings, 906
assigning to groups,
908–909
auditing, 907–908
file permissions, 550–551
*NTFS file permissions,
903–904*
inheritance, 905
for printers, 910
homegroups, setting,
563–565
network permissions, 552
restricted objects,
assigning, 910
taking ownership of files, 908
viewing effective
permissions, 907

personal firewalls, 856, 923

Personalization (Control
Panel), 602
desktop, icons
setting, 695–696
display properties,
customizing, 683–703

Phone and Modem (Control Panel), 602
property settings, 430–431

phoneline networking, 447–450

Photo Gallery, 294

photographs
burning to CD/DVD, 290–292, 325
fixing, Windows Media Player, 284–286
printing, 286–289
Windows Media Center, 269
scanning, 308
sharing electronically, 289–290
user accounts, changing, 90
Windows Pictures Library, 278
adding to, 278–279
digital cameras, 281–284
importing to, 279
organizing, 279
scanners, 279–281

Photoshop, scans, editing, 310

phrases, Control Panel, 82

Picasa.com, 281

PICS (Platform for Internet Content Selection) system, 390

pictures. *See* **photographs**

Pictures library, 141

ping command
Internet connections, troubleshooting, 434–435
LAN connections, testing, 427–429
network connectivity, testing, 588–589
PUT UNDER command-line tools, 821

pinning, 133

pixels, 224

PixelTrip, 234

Plain Text format, news messages, 415

planning networks, 444–445
professional installation, 446–447
servers, 445–446

Platform for Internet Content Selection (PICS) system, 390

Platinum Edition Using Windows XP, 13

Play tab (WMP), 235

Playback tab (Sound dialog box), 692–693

playing
audio, WMP (Windows Media Player), 239–240
CDs, WMP (Windows Media Player), 239
DVDs
troubleshooting, 232
WMP (Windows Media Player), 239
hard disk media files, WMP (Windows Media Player), 240

PNG (Portable Network Graphics) files, 320, 368

PnP (Plug and Play) hardware
drivers, providing, 787–789
installation, 784–787
installing, troubleshooting, 788–789
removing, 789–790

Pocket PCs, 1029

Point-to-Point Protocol over Ethernet (PPPoE), 347–348

points, fonts, 627

policies, Registry, 820

pop-up blocker (IE)
configuring, 386–387
enabling, 380

port settings, USB controllers, 790

portable media players
compatibility issues, 244
synchronizing with, 246–248

Portrait mode (Tablet PCs), 1046

Ports tab (printer properties dialog box), 199

posting newsgroup messages, Windows Live Mail, 414–415

power management, new features, 32–33

power options, laptops, 796

Power Options (Control Panel), 33, 602, 642

Power Options (Hardware and Sound Control Panel window), 973

Power Options Advanced Settings dialog box, 975–976

Power Saver power usage profile, 974

power usage profiles, laptop computers, 974–976

powerline networking, 451

PowerShell. *See* **WPS (Windows PowerShell)**

PPPoE (Point-to-Point Protocol over Ethernet), 347–348

Practical Network Cabling, 459

preferences, printing preferences, 196–197

preferred wireless networks, selecting, 966

preinstalled service packs, 768

preparation, attack defense measures, 917–919

Presentation Settings (Mobility Center), 973

pressure-sensitive touch screens, Tablet PCs, 1033

prestocked items, Start menu, 131

Preview pane, 166–167

previewing
faxes, 303
screen fonts, 704

How can we make this index more useful? Email us at indexes@quepublishing.com

previous versions of files, restoring, 901–902

primary displays, selection, troubleshooting, 792–793

primary IDE channels, hard disks, 783

primary partitions, hard disks, 710

Print Management tool, 205

Print Manager, 200–203

Print Setup dialog box, 201

printer icons, 188

Printer Properties dialog box, 198, 553

printer sharing
troubleshooting, 589–590
wireless networks, security, 960–961

printers
configuring, 189, 196–200
emulation mode, 195
installing, 189–195
local printers
  infrared port connection, 192
  installing, 191–192
  parallel port connection, 191
  serial port connection, 192
  troubleshooting, 192–195
mangled line feed/carriage returns, troubleshooting (UNIX), 499–500
multiple default settings, 198
networks, searching for, 548–549
permissions, 910
  setting, 569–570
Print Management tool, 205
properties, 196
removing, 200
server properties, 196
shared printers, 552
  cabling, 453–454
  icon setup, 553–554

installing, 556
IPP (Internet Printing Protocol), 554–555
LPR/LPD protocol (UNIX), 555–556
naming, 554
sharing, Macintosh OS X, 508, 510
troubleshooting, 201–202
UNIX, printing from, 499
UPS (uninterruptible power supply), 797

printing
Devices and Printers window, 187–189
from DOS applications, 202–203
photographs, Windows Media Center, 269
received faxes automatically, 305
setup windows, 418
UNIX queues from Windows, 499

printing preferences, 196–197

prioritizing wireless network connections, 967–968

privacy, Internet Explorer, 365
configuring, 384–386

Privacy tab (Internet Options), 380

Private Character Editor (System Tools folder), 670

private wireless networks, 960

privileges. *See also* **permissions**
Registry, 820

PrntScrn key, 418

problem reports and solutions, 752–753

problems. *See* **troubleshooting**

Process Explorer, 855

Processes tab (Task Manager), 674–675

Processor Power Management setting (Power Options Advanced Settings), 976

processors
laptops, clock speeds, 974
minimum requirements, 44
recommended specifications, 44

Product Keys, 57

profiles
scan profiles, 306–308
wireless networks, copying to other computers, 968

Program Compatibility Wizard, 774–776

program files, moving, 163

programs. *See also* **software**
crashes
  handling, 147
  troubleshooting, 147–148
default programs, 396
DLL Hell, 777
drive-by downloads, avoiding, 376–379
launching, 136
  Computer, 140
  Start button, 137
  Windows Explorer, 140
malware, protecting against, 374–375
third-party management tools, 677–678
uninstalling, 134–135, 643–644

programs (TV), recording, Windows Media Center, 264–265

Programs and Features (Control Panel), 602, 643–646
Features, disabling, 773–774
software, uninstalling, 772–774

Programs category (Category view), 597

Programs tab (Internet Options), 381–383

projectors, connecting to, 32

properties, printers, 196

Properties sheet, printer drivers, changing, 196–200

Properties tab, volumes, 723

proportionally spaced fonts, 629

protected mode, Internet Explorer, 932

Protocol Configuration dialog box, 419

Public folder, sharing, 565

public hot spots, wireless networks, joining, 964–965

public IP addresses, 518

Public networks, 475

public wireless networks, 960

purchasing routers, 520

Q-R

quad-link video adapter cards, 795

Quick Launch bar, 133

Quick Tabs page (Tab Group), 364

QuickTime, 370–371

RAID (Redundant Array of Independent Disks), 709
  arrays, 894
  dynamic disk information storage, 720
  mirroring, 783
  striping, 783

RAID 0, 894
  volumes, dynamic hard disks, 711

RAID 0+1, 894

RAID 1, 894
  volumes, dynamic hard disks, 711

RAID 5, 894
  volumes, dynamic hard disks, 711

RAM (random access memory)
  cost fluctuations, 784
  DDR SDRAM modules, 783
  DIMMs (dual in-line memory modules), 784
  maximum requirements, 784
  minimum requirements, 44, 783
  motherboards, compatibility, 784
  recommended specifications, 44
  SDRAM (synchronous dynamic RAM), 783
  starting addresses, 617
  troubleshooting, Windows Memory Diagnostic tool, 745–746
  upgrading, 45, 779, 783–784

RAS (Remote Access Services)
  dial-up networking, 977
    advanced routing, 986–987
    configuring, 978–987
    connection properties, 980–982
    current location checks, 983
    email connections, 986
    ending connections, 986
    establishing connections, 983–985
    gateway settings, 981–982
    incoming access, 987–990
    monitoring connections, 986
    multiple location management, 982–983
  VPNs (virtual private networks), 977

Rating Shortcuts (WMC), 254

Read & Execute NTFS permission, 891, 904

Read Attributes advanced NTFS permission, 892, 906

Read Extended Attributes advanced NTFS permission, 892, 906

Read NTFS permission, 891, 904

Read Permissions advanced NTFS permission, 906

reading
  incoming messages, Windows Live Mail, 398–399
  newsgroup messages, Windows Live Mail, 414–415
  newsgroups, Windows Live Mail, 412

ReadyBoost, 30, 780–781

real-time protection, 853–854

RealNetworks files, playing, 370

RealPlayer, downloading, 371

receiving faxes, 305

Recent Items, Documents, compared, 140

recipients, faxes, selecting, 301

recommended updates, 767

Recording tab (Sound dialog box), 692–693

recording television programs, Windows Media Center, 265

recordings, creating, Sound Recorder, 691–692

recovering. *See also* restoring
  data recovery, 751
    System Recovery Options menu, 755–756
  BitLocker encrypted drives, 899
  Files, Recycle Bin, 120–121
  NTFS, recovery keys, 751
  System Image Recovery, 743–745

Recovery (Control Panel), 603

recovery certificates
  backups of, 892–893
  securing, 889–892

How can we make this index more useful? Email us at indexes@quepublishing.com

recovery keys, 751

Recreational Software Advisory Council on the Internet (RSACi), 389

rectangular snips (Snipping Tool), 217, 320

Recycle bin
backups, 868
configuring, 707
files, deleting, 725

redirection, Registry, 808

Reduced Functionality Mode (RFM), 72

Redundant Array of Independent Disks (RAID). *See* RAID (Redundant Array of Independent Disks)

reflection, Registry, 808

Refresh command (View menu), 168

refresh rates, monitors, 702–703

Regedit, 747–748, 812
keys
adding, 815–816
adding values, 815
changing values, 815
Copy Key Name command, 816
deleting, 815–816
deleting values, 815
editing, 814–816
editing for other users, 816–817
renaming, 816
Registry
backing up, 810
restoring, 811–812
searching, 814
viewing, 812–814
security attributes, editing, 818–819
supported data types, 813

Region and Language (Control Panel), 603, 646

Registrar Registry Manager, Registry, editing, 820

registries, virtual registries, 777

Registry
associations, 805
backing up, 809
hard disk, 809
Regedit, 810
system restore, 810
third-party utilities, 809
editing
Regedit, 747–748
Registrar Registry Manager, 820
Registry Toolkit, 819
Tweak-7, 820
X-Setup Pro, 819
entries, editing for separate Windows installations, 817–818
exporting, 747
file corruption, signs, 811
hive files, 817–818
keys
adding, 815–816
adding values, 815
changing values, 815
Copy Key Name command, 816
deleting, 815–816
deleting values, 815
editing, 814–816
editing for other users, 816–817
renaming, 816
new features, 806–808
organization, 805–806
policies, 820
privileges, 820
redirection, 808
reflection, 808
restoring, 810–811
Regedit, 811–812
restore point, 811
searching, Regedit, 814
security attributes, editing, 818–819
top-level keys, 805–806
viewing, Regedit, 812–814
virtualization, 806–808

Registry Toolkit, Registry, editing, 819

REG_BINARY data type, 813

REG_DWORD data type, 813

REG_EXPAND_SZ data type, 813

REG_MULTI_SZ data type, 813

REG_QWORD data type, 813

REG_SZ data type, 813

reinstalling Windows 7, 751

Reliability Monitor (Action Center), 30–31, 606–607

Reliable Multicast Protocol, 512

remote access, networks, providing, 454

Remote Access Services (RAS). *See* RAS (Remote Access Services)

Remote Assistance
online meetings, 1010
Stop Sharing Control, 1006

remote computing, 972
battery optimization, 974–976
dial-up networking, RAS (Remote Access Services), 977
LANs (local area networks), multiple connections, 998
Mobility Center
controls, 972–973
Hardware and Sound Control Panel window, 973–974
launching, 972
offline files, 991
encrypting, 997
identifying for use, 992–993
managing, 997
synchronizing, 995–998
troubleshooting, 992–995
using, 993–995
RAS (Remote Access Services) dial-up networking

advanced routing, 986–987

configuring, 978–987

connection properties, 980–982

current location checks, 983

email connections, 986

establishing connections, 983–985

gateway settings, 981–982

incoming access, 987–990

monitoring connections, 986

multiple location management, 982–983

shared folders, availability, 997–998

Sync Center, 991

VPNs (virtual private networks), 977

advanced routing, 986–987

configuring, 978–987

connection process, 977–978

connection properties, 980–982

data encapsulation, 977

email connections, 986

ending connections, 986

establishing connections, 983–985

gateway settings, 981–982

incoming access, 987–990

monitoring connections, 986

RAS (Remote Access Services), 977

tunnels, 977

remote control, third-party remote control tools, 1027–1028

Remote Desktop, 1013–1014

advantages, 1014

keyboard shortcuts, 1027

local access, 1013

multiple users, 1027

Use All of My Monitors option, 1021

remote infrared (IR) sensors, Windows Media Center, 254

Remote Settings option (System Properties), 648–649

RemoteApp and Desktop Connections (Control Panel), 603

removable media

backups on, 871–872

USB flash drives, security, 910–911

removing

gadgets, 215–216

hardware, 789–790

software, 769–770, 772–774

wireless network profiles, 969

renaming, Registry keys, 816

Repair Your Computer advanced boot option, 749

repairing. *See also* **troubleshooting**

boot process, 738–739

command prompt, 746

hard disk errors, 728–730

reinstallation, 751

startup process, Regedit, 747–748

System Image Recovery, 743–745

system repair disc makers, 738

System Restore, 740

configuring, 740–741

restore point creation, 741–742

restore point restoration, 743

updates, Windows Update, 763–764

Windows Memory Diagnostic tool, 745–746

ReplayTV, 253

replying, incoming messages, Windows Live Mail, 399–400

residential gateways, Internet Connection Sharing (ICS), 518–520

resizing

desktop background images, 687

Taskbar, 683

resolution

desktop images, 687

faxes, 307

scan profiles, 308

screen resolution, setting, 697–700

resource conflicts, resolving, Device Manager, 618–619

resource data issues, Macintosh internetworking, 504

Resource Monitor, 641

resources, sharing, 561–565

restore point, Registry, restoring, 811

restore points

deleting, Disk Cleanup utility, 726

System Restore

creating, 741–742

restoring to, 743

restore procedures, maintaining for disaster planning, 930–931

restoring. *See also* **recovering**

encrypted files, 893

file and folder backups, 872–877

from System Recovery Options menu backups, 755–756

previous versions of files, 901–902

Registry, 810–812

system images, Backup and Restore Center, 883–884

WBADMIN command-line tool, 879–882

restricted objects, permissions, assigning, 910

restricting access controls, 926

reverse tracert tool, 439–440

Review Fax Status window (Fax and Scan), 304–305

Review Your Time and Date Settings dialog box, 57

RFM (Reduced Functionality Mode), 72

right-click context menus, 124–126

right-clicking objects, 161–162

right-clicks, stylus pen, 1039

RIP Listener, 511

ripping CDs, 240–242

Roland MPU-401 MIDI interface, 801

root folders, disk drives, sharing, 557–558

rootkits, 847–848

route command, router tables, managing, 437–438

routed service, 516

routed services, Internet connections, configuring LANs, 532

routers
blockages, checking (tracert), 435–437
configuration, troubleshooting, 420
connection-sharing routers, 518
DMZ hosts, forwarding, 537–539
external, versus Internet Connection Sharing (ICS), 520
filters, 532
locking down, 923–924
NetBIOS traffic, filtering, 532

network protection measures, 532
packet filtering, 921–923
purchasing advice, 520
shared, 529–531
traffic, checking (tracert), 437
wireless routers, 518

routing, 986–987

routing tables, managing, route command, 437–438

Roxio's Easy DVD Copy 4, 324

RSACi (Recreational Software Advisory Council on the Internet), 389

running
elevated privilege commands, 823–824
programs
Computer, 140
Start button, 137
Windows Explorer, 140

Russinovich, Mark, 87, 855

S

s.bat file, 833

Safe Mode advanced boot option, 749

Safe Mode with Command Prompt advanced boot option, 749

Safe Mode with Networking advanced boot option, 749

Safety button (IE), 949

Samba
client tools, 497–498
internetworking, 497–500
server tools, 498–500

sans-serif fonts, 629

SATA (Serial ATA) drives, 782
IDE drives, switching from, 713

SATA hard disks, 783

satellite dishes, 332

satellite service, Internet access, 332

saturation, colors, 690

Save dialog box, 122

scan profiles, 306–308

Scan Profiles dialog box, 308

scan service (Windows Fax and Scan), 293–294
adding scanned pages to faxes, 302
configuring, 305–306
emailing scans, 310
enabling, 293
faxing scans, 310
hardware requirements, 293
manipulating scanned images, 310
preparations, 294–295
scan profiles, 306–308
scanning images, 308
scanning pictures, 294
slides, faxing and scanning, 310–311
transparencies, faxing and scanning, 310–311

scanned pages, faxes, adding, 302

Scanner and Camera Wizard, 279

scanners
drivers, 295
preparing, Windows Fax and Scan, 294–295
speed, slowing, 308
testing, 302
troubleshooting, 281
WIA drivers, obtaining, 302
Windows Pictures Library, 279–281

scanning
documents, 305–306
slides, 310–311
transparencies, 310–311

scans, 308
editing, 310
emailing, 310
faxing, 310

scheduling hard disk defragmentation, 803

scheme D setup, 522

screen capturing, Snipping Tool, 216–219

screen flicker, reducing, 703

screen fonts
previewing, 704
resizing, 680
smoothing, 696

screen resolution, setting, 697–700

Screen Resolution window, 697–700
Advanced Settings link, 700
Color Management tab, 701
Monitor tab, 701
Troubleshoot tab, 701

Screen Rotation control (Mobility Center), 973

Screen Saver Settings dialog box, 693–695

screen savers
3D screen savers, 695
SETI (Search for Extraterrestrial Intelligence) screen saver project, 694
setting, 693–695

screen-capturing, Snipping Tool, 319–321

screens, Tablet PCs
calibrating, 1046
touch-sensitive screens, 1049

Script Host. *See* WSH (Windows Script Host)

scripting, WSH (Windows Script Host), 834

Scriptorium, fonts, 630

scripts
creating, WSH (Windows Script Host), 834–836
sample scripts, WSH (Windows Script Host), 836–837

SCSI hard disks, 782

SDRAM (synchronous dynamic RAM), 783

Search box (IE), 391–392

Search command (Start menu), 136

search engines, 392
Internet Explorer, setting default, 380

Search function, Start menu, 23–24

search paths, 822

searching
drivers, 787–789
networks, 546–550
computers, 548
files, 546–548
folders, 546–548
printers, 548–549
printer drivers, 194–195
Registry, Regedit, 814
Start menu, 180–181
Windows Explorer, 173–174
configuring, 174–177
deep searching, 174
grouping and stacking, 181–183
intermediate searching, 174
troubleshooting, 179
while typing, 177–181
WMP (Windows Media Player), 236–238

secondary display adapters, multiple monitors, 792

secondary IDE channels, hard disks, 783

secondary partitions, hard disks, 710

Secure Password Authentication (SPA), 398

Secure Startup. *See* BitLocker

securing
encrypted files, 891–893
recovery certificates, 887–893
routers, 923–924

security
access controls, restricting, 926
Action Center, 604–607
bulletins, subscribing, 918
cable services, Internet connections on LANs, 522
data security, new features, 29–30
encryption, 886
EFS (Encrypted File System), 884–894
file sharing, 550–552
files, 185
firewalls
configuring, 919–921
function of, 919–921
personal firewalls, 923
folders, 185
hackers, 845
Internet Explorer, 365
add-ons, 376–379
configuring, 384–386
Pop-Up Blocker, 386–387
web zones, 384
malware
avoiding, 862
preventing, 848–861
rootkits, 847–848
spyware, 847
viruses, 846
worms, 846–847
Microsoft E-Mail Updates Service, 934
NAT devices, 919, 923
networks
assessing personal risk, 914–915
attacks, 915–916
attacks, active defenses, 919–926
attacks, defense measures, 917–919
defenses, testing, 927, 929
disaster planning, 929–932
FTP folders, visibility of, 928
holes, 914–915

homegroups, *478–481*
LAN guidelines, *934*
local policy configuration,
  934–937
sensitive web pages,
  visibility of, *928*
shared folders, visibility
  of, *928*
standalone
  guidelines, *933*
suspicious activities,
  monitoring, *929*
updates, *934*
Windows Firewall, *477*
Windows Firewall,
  configuring, *937–938*
Windows Firewall,
  enabling
  exceptions, *942*
packet filtering, function
  of, *921*
permissions
  advanced settings, *906*
  assigning to groups,
    908–909
  auditing, *907–908*
  for printers, *910*
  NTFS file permissions,
    903–905
  taking ownership of
    files, *908*
  viewing effective
    permissions, *907*
RAID arrays, *894*
Registry, policies and
  privileges, *820*
routers
  locking down, *923–924*
  network protection
· measures, *532*
  packet filtering, *921–923*
system security, new
  features, *25–26*
USB flash drives, *910–911*
Web site resources, *934, 943*
wireless networks
  authentication, *464*
  encryption, *464–467*
  keys, *465*
  sharing, *960–961*

security attributes, Registry,
  editing, 818–819
Security log (Event
  Viewer), 656
Security tab (Internet
  Options), 380, 384–386
Security tab (printer
  properties dialog box), 199
sender information (Windows
  Fax and Scan),
  configuring, 296
sending
  faxes, 206, 299–304
  scans, 310
sensitive web pages, visibility
  of, 928
Sentences Recognition
  (Handwriting
  Recognition), 1043
Serial ATA (SATA) drives. *See*
  SATA (Serial ATA) drives
serial cables, UPS
  (uninterruptible power
  supply), 798
serial printer ports, 192
serif fonts, 629
server properties,
  printers, 196
server tools, Samba, 498–500
servers, choosing, 445–446
service hardening, 860–861
service packs, 767–768
  cumulative service
    packs, 768
  incremental service
    packs, 768
  installing, 768–769
  Microsoft Download Center,
    obtaining, 768
  preinstalled service
    packs, 768
  problems, 134
Services (Computer
  Management), 659–660

Services for NFS, 512
Services tab (Task
  Manager), 675
Set Associations option
  (Default Programs), 611
Set Program Access and
  Computer Defaults option
  (Default Programs), 612
Set Up a Network Wizard,
  468–470
Set Up Backup scheduler, 870
SETI (Search for
  Extraterrestrial Intelligence)
  screen saver project, 694
Setup log (Event Viewer), 656
setup windows, printing, 418
shadow copies. *See* volume
  shadow copies
shared connections,
  troubleshooting, 525
shared disk drives, enabling,
  557–558
shared fax machines, cabling
  system, 453–454
shared files
  managing, command-line,
    573–574
  searching for, 546–548
shared folders, 542
  availability, 997–998
  browsing, 544–545
    homegroups, *542–544*
    UNC (Universal Naming
      Convention), *545–546*
  libraries, adding to, 557
  managing, command-line,
    573–574
  monitoring use, 572
  Public folder, 565
  searching for, 546–548
  visibility of, 928
Shared Folders (Computer
  Management), 658–659
Shared Libraries (WMC), 254
shared modems, inability to
  access on LANs, 527

shared printers, 552
  cabling system, 453–454
  icons, setting, 553–554
  installing, 556
  IPP (Internet Printing
    Protocol), 554–555
  LPR/LPD protocol (UNIX),
    555–556
  permissions, setting,
    569–570
  pooling, 571
  spool directory, location
    changes, 570

shared resources, wireless
  networks, security, 960–961

shared routers
  broadband connections,
    configuring LANs,
    529–530
  dial-up connections,
    configuring LANs,
    529–530
  outside network access,
    enabling, 537–539
  Universal Plug and Play
    (UPnP), 531

sharing
  files
    Macintosh OS X,
      506–509
    passwords versus pass-
      wordless file sharing,
      924–925
  folders, 565–567
  media files, home
    networking, 248–250
  printers, Macintosh OS X,
    508, 510

sharing resources, 561–562, 565

Sharing tab (printer properties
  dialog box), 199

shortcut keys, 130–131

shortcuts
  Control Panel applets,
    creating, 595
  creating for desktop, 124
  objects, sending to, 123
  troubleshooting, 138

ShowStopper, 252

shrinking hard disks, 718

shuffling music files, WMP
  (Windows Media Player), 240

Shut Down button (Start
  menu), 132

shutdowns, 146

side-by-side installation,
  software, 776–777

Sidebar (Vista), 208

sight impairments, display
  settings, 626

signatures, email messages,
  setting up, 405–406

Simple File Sharing, 492

Simple Network Management
  Protocol (SNMP), 511

simple volumes, dynamic
  hard disks, 711

Simply Interactive PC
  (SIPC), 252

Single-Click setting,
  mouse, 703

SIPC (Simply Interactive
  PC), 252

slate Tablet PCs, 1031. See
  also Tablet PCs
  external keyboards, 1035
  limitations, 1035

Sleep option, shutdowns, 146

Sleep setting (Power Options
  Advanced Settings), 976

sleeping computers,
  encrypted files, risks,
  891, 895

slides, faxing and scanning,
  310–311

slow motion, monitors,
  troubleshooting, 698

Small Icons view (Control
  Panel), 595–604

small offices, wireless
  networks, joining, 961–964

ShowStopper, 252

SmartScreen antiphishing
  filter (IE), 356, 365, 947–949

Smith, David L., 846

smoothing screen fonts, 696

Snappy Fax Network
  Server, 454

Snipping Tool, 216–219
  desktop images, 319–321
  free-form snips, 217
  full-screen snips, 217
  quick access, 218
  rectangular snips, 217
  window snips, 217

SNMP (Simple Network
  Management Protocol), 511

Snopes.com, 955

social engineering, 916

software
  antivirus software, 850–852
  compatibility issues,
    774–776
  downloading, Internet
    Explorer, 373–379
  firewalls, 856
  installing, 769–770
    side-by-side installation,
      776–777
    via CD/DVD, 770
    via downloads, 771
  Internet configuration
    problems, 425
    cable modems, 426–427
    dial-up connections, 425
    DSL modems, 426–427
    LAN connections,
      427–429
  malware, 845
    avoiding, 862
    preventing, 848–861
    protecting against,
      374–375
    rootkits, 847–848
    spyware, 847
    viruses, 846
    worms, 846–847
  monitoring, 771
  removing, 769–774

third-party management tools, 677–678

uninstalling, 643–644

software DVD decoders, installing, 232

Software License Terms dialog box, 53

Software Protection Platform (SPP), hardware upgrades, 799

software updates. *See* updates

solid backgrounds, setting, 686

solid-state disks (SSDs), 31, 709

Sort By command (View menu), 167

sound, configuring, Ease of Access Center, 625

Sound (Control Panel), 603

Sound dialog box, 691
Communications tab, 693
Playback tab, 692–693
Recording tab, 692–693

Sound Recorder, recordings, creating, 691–692

Sound Sentry, 625

sounds
creating, Sound Recorder, 691–692
events, associating with, 690–693
playback, 692–693
recording, 692–693

SPA (Secure Password Authentication), 398

spam, Windows Live Mail, controlling, 407–408

Spangler, Brian, 234

spanned volumes
creating, Disk Management utility, 718
dynamic hard disks, 711

Special Edition Using DOS 6.22, Third Edition, 831

Special Edition Using Windows Vista, Second Edition, 13

Special Edition Using Windows XP Professional, 13

Specific People, homegroup permissions, editing, 564

Speech Recognition, 603
analog headsets, 1032
microphones, 1032
voice recognition, 1032

speech recognition software, Tablet PCs, 1032

Speed Check, Internet transfer monitor, 439

splitters, 346

SPP (Software Protection Program), hardware upgrades, 799

SPs (service packs), 767–768
cumulative service packs, 768
incremental service packs, 768
installing, 768–769
preinstalled service packs, 768

Spybot Search & Destroy, 388

SpyNet, 855

spyware, 845–847
preventing, Windows Defender, 852–856

SQL Slammer worm, 846

SSDs (solid-state disks), 31

SSDs (solid-state drives), 709

SSIDs, wireless networks, 472, 968

stability, new features, 35–36

stacking searches, 181–183

standalone computers, security guidelines, 933

standalone method, service pack installation, 769

standard definition aspect ratio, 323

Standard user accounts, 770

standards, wireless networks, 959

standby UPS (uninterruptible power supply), 797

start addresses, 617

Start button, programs, running from, 137

Start menu
accessing, 132
All Programs, 132
cascading elements, 707
customizing, 680–683
default settings, retuning to, 682
Help and Support, 143–144
items, adding to, 132
Jump Lists, 79–80
prestocked items, 131
Search function, 23–24
searching, 180–181
shortcuts, troubleshooting, 138
username, clicking on, 79
Windows Media Center, improvements, 253

Start menu commands
Search, 136
Switch User, 146

Start Windows Normally advanced boot option, 750

startup process. *See also* boot process
repairing, Regedit, 747–748
Startup Repair, 739
troubleshooting, creating backups from System Recovery Options menu, 755–756

Startup Repair, 739

static addresses, 473

Status Bar command (View menu), 167

Sticky Notes, 32, 226

Stop Sharing Control (Remote Assistant), 1006

storage
basic hard disks, 710
dynamic hard disks, 710–712
advantages, 711–712
converting to, 711
converting to basic disks, 710
mirrored volumes, 711
RAID-5 volumes, 711
simple volumes, 711
spanned volumes, 711
striped volumes, 711
Windows Backup, 871

streaming broadcasts, Internet Explorer, playing, 370–371

streaming video, frames per second (fps), 369

string value data type, 813

striped volumes
creating, Disk Management utility, 719–720
dynamic hard disks, 711

striping, RAID, 783

strokes, fonts, 629

stylus pens, 1038–1039
clicks, 1039
double-clicks, 1039
pen flicks, 1036, 1040–1041
customizing, 1048
triggering Flip 3-D, 1041
troubleshooting, 1048
pen gestures, 1036–1040
right-clicks, 1039
Tablet PCs, 1036

stylus pens, Tablet PCs, 1033

SUA (Subsystem for UNIX-based Applications), 501–503, 511
installing, 502

subfolders, hard drives, mapping to, 561

suboptions, removing, 134

subscribing to newsgroups, 412–414

subscription costs, antivirus software, 851

substitutions, fonts, 630–631

Suggested Sites (IE), 356

Switch User command (Start menu), 146

switches
10/100BASE-T Ethernet networks, 448
costs, 444
multiple switches, 448
installing, 462–463
uplink ports, 462–463

switching between wireless networks, 966–967

swivel screens, convertible Tablet PCs, 1033

Symantec antivirus software, 851

Symantec Norton Ghost, 911

symbolic links, user profile folder, 108

Sync Center, 603
offline files
encrypting, 997
managing, 997
reconciling changes, 995–996
synchronizing, 995–998
remote computing, 991
shared folders, availability, 997–998

Sync Center (Mobility Center), 973

Sync tab (WMP), 235

synchronization
newsgroups, message availability, 412–413
offline files, 995–998
portable media players, WMP (Windows Media Player), 246–248

synchronous dynamic RAM (SDRAM), 783

System (Control Panel), 603
Add Hardware applet, compared, 787

System and Maintenance category (Category view), 596

System and Security window, 82

system caches, 676

System Configuration (Administrative Tools), 664–666

System Diagnostics Report, 641–642

system files, hidden system files, 140

system image backups, 878–882

System Image Recovery, 743–745

system image restorations, Backup and Restore Center, 883–884

System Information (System Tools folder), 670–671

System log (Event Viewer), 656

system management, new features, 35–36

system performance, environment variables, setting, 825–827

System Properties dialog box, 647–651, 741
Advanced System Settings option, 650
Environment Variables button, 651–652
Remote Settings option, 648–649
System Protection option, 649

System Protection dialog box, 740

System Protection option (System Properties), 649

System Recovery, 738–739

system recovery disks, creating, 29

System Recovery Options menu, 755–756

system repair disc makers, 738

system requirements, BitLocker, 895

System Restore, 740
    configuring, 740–741
    Registry, backing up, 810
    restore points
        creating, 741–742
        restoring to, 743

system security, new features, 25–26

System Tools folder, 666
    Character Map, 667–669
    Private Character Editor, 670
    System Information, 670–671

system tray. See *Notification Area*

T

Tab Groups (IE), 28, 355, 361–364
    New Tab page, 363
    Quick Tabs page, 364

tabbed web pages, Internet Explorer
    browsing, 361–364
    enabling, 380

Tablet Input Panel, improvements, 1034

Tablet PC Settings (Control Panel), 37, 603

Tablet PC Settings dialog box, 1045–1047

Tablet PCs, 1029
    AutoComplete, 1043
    benefits, 1032
    choosing, 1035
    configuring, 1045–1049
        Pen and Touch dialog box, 1047–1049

Tablet PC Settings dialog box, 1045–1047
convertible Tablet PCs, 1031, 1036
    fragility, 1035
    troubleshooting, 1047
evolution, 1029–1031
handedness, specifying, 1046
handwriting recognition, 1034, 1041–1043, 1046
    Handwriting Personalization window, 1041–1042
    Numbers, Symbols, and Letters Recognition, 1042
    Sentences Recognition, 1043
Handwriting Recognizer, 1033
Input Panel, 1036–1037
    Options dialog box, 1039
    writing methods, 1037–1038
Landscape mode, 1047
Math Input Panel, 1034
multitouch capabilities, 1035
On-Screen Keyboard, 1037
PCs, compared, 1033–1036
pen flicks, 1034–1036, 1040–1041
    customizing, 1048
    triggering Flip 3-D, 1041
    troubleshooting, 1048
pen gestures, 1036–1040
    Scratch-out gesture, 1040
Portrait mode, 1046
pressure-sensitive touch screens, 1033
screens, calibrating, 1046
slate Tablet PCs, 1031
    external keyboards, 1035
    limitations, 1035
speech recognition software, 1032
stylus pens, 1033, 1036–1039
    clicks, 1039
    double-clicks, 1039
    right-clicks, 1039

swivel screens, 1033
Tablet Input Panel, improvements, 1034
taskbar, 1035
troubleshooting, pen cursor, 1039
touch-sensitive screens, configuring, 1049
Windows Journal, 1043–1045
Writing Pad, 1037

tabs, dialog boxes, 122

Take Ownership advanced NTFS permission, 906

Task Manager, 672, 675
    Applications tab, 672–674
    Networking tab, 677
    Performance tab, 675–677
    Processes tab, 674–675
    Services tab, 675
    Users tab, 677

Task Scheduler, 654, 839
    basic tasks, creating, 840–841
    tasks, 839
        creating, 841

taskbar, 95–96, 135
    Command Prompt window, pinning to, 822
    customizing, 682–683
    dragging, 683
    icons, 17–18
        organizing, 96
    items, drag-and-drop support, 163
    Jump List, 96–97
        adding to, 595
    Jump Lists, 18–19
    new features, 17–18
    Notification Area, customizing, 683
    Tablet PCs, 1035

Taskbar and Start Menu (Control Panel), 603

Taskbar and Start Menu Properties dialog box, 682

tasks (Task Scheduler), 839–841

TCP/IP
as default network protocol,
internetworking with
Windows XP and 2000, 490
peer-to-peer networks,
configuring, 473–475

**TCP/IP diagnostic tools,
433–438**
ipconfig tool, 419, 433–434
Network Connections,
419–420
pathping command, 437
ping command, 434–435
route command, 437–438
tracert, 418, 435–437

**telephone lines, fax signals,
confirming, 293**

**television, Windows Media
Center**
program selection, 264–265
recording, 265
skipping commercials, 265
TV Guide, 264–265
watching, 264–266

Telnet Client, 511

Telnet Server, 511

**temporary files, deleting, Disk
Cleanup utility, 725**

**temporary Internet files,
deleting**
Disk Cleanup utility, 725
Internet Explorer, 365

testing
fax modems, 300
LAN connections, 427–429
network cables, 585
network configuration,
585–588
*computer identification,
587–588*
connections, 588
ipconfig, 585–587
network connectivity,
588–589
network defenses, 927, 929
packets, ping command,
434–435

scanners, 302
UPS (uninterruptible power
supply), 799

text
converting handwriting
to, 1044
email messages,
aligning, 629
faxes, entering, 301–302

text captions, enabling, 625

text editors, 225

TFTP Client, 511

themes
downloading, 685
GUI display properties,
setting, 684–685
Windows Classic
theme, 684

third-party backup tools, 911

**third-party collaboration
tools, 1010**

**third-party disk management
tools, 732**

**third-party management
tools, 677–678**

**third-party remote control,
1027–1028**

third-party utilities
Internet connections,
troubleshooting, 439–440
Registry, backing up, 809

**threaded messages,
newsgroups, 414**

**thumbnails, deleting, Disk
Cleanup utility, 725**

TIFF files, 321

Tiles view (Computer), 140

TiVo, 252
Windows Media Center,
compared, 264–265

TiVo Desktop Plus, 246

toggling
features, 645–646
panes, 165–167

toolbars
Music library, 159
Windows Explorer, 151–152

**top-level keys (Registry),
805–806**

**touch-sensitive screens, Tablet
PCs, configuring, 1049**

**TPM (Trusted Platform
Module), enabling, 897–898**

**Traceroute.org, reverse tracert
tool, 439–440**

tracert tool
Internet connections,
troubleshooting, 418,
435–437
router blockages,
troubleshooting, 435–437
router traffic checks, 437

**traditional storage model,
hard disks, 710**

**transferring data between
computers, Windows Easy
Transfer, 101–104**

**transparencies, faxing and
scanning, 310–311**

**Traverse Folder/Execute File
advanced NTFS
permission, 906**

**Trend Micro antivirus
software, 851**

Trojan horses, 847, 916

**Troubleshoot tab (Screen
Resolution window), 701**

troubleshooters, 752–753

troubleshooting, 737. *See also*
repairing
application crashes,
147–148
backups, 875–878
BIOS, 782
BitLocker, 896
boot process, 748–751
Character Map, 669
CMOS, 782
command prompt, 746

convertible Tablet PCs, screen layout, 1047

dial-up process to ISPs, 344–345

digital photographs, print quality, 288–289

DVD playback, 232

DVDs, recording to, 325

EFS (Encrypted File System), 885

email servers, passwords, 398

file/folder deletion, Administrators account, 904

files, In Use by Another User error message, 567

hard disks, 733
  boot process, 736
  file structure problems, 735–736
  hardware problems, 735–736
  strategies, 733–734
  unrecognized hard disks, 735–736

hardware, installation, 788–789

hubs, non-working lights, 458

Internet connections, 345, 417–420
  dial-up settings, 420
  flowcharts, 422–423
  ipconfig tool, 419, 433–434
  ISP information, 418
  LAN connections, 427–429
  methodology, 420–422
  modems, 426–427, 430–433
  network cabling diagrams, 420
  Network Connections, 419–420
  network hardware problems, 429–433
  pathping command, 437
  ping command, 434–435
  reverse tracert, 439–440
  route command, 437–438
  router configuration, 420
  software configuration problems, 425–429
  Speed Check, 439
  TCP/IP diagnostic tools, 433–438
  third-party utilities, 439–440
  tracert, 435–437
  tracert tool, 418
  whois database, 439
  WS_Ping Pro Pack, 440

Internet Explorer
  add-on crashes, 379
  crashes, 358
  email links, 383
  Page not available errors, 360

Macintosh networking, lost application associations, 504

mangled line feed/carriage returns, UNIX networking, 499–500

memory, Windows Memory Diagnostic tool, 745–746

monitors
  blank monitors, 701
  blurry images, 701
  desktop item movement, 698–699
  screen flicker, 703
  slow motion, 698

multiple monitor installation, 791–793

network services, inability to block, 928

networking, 491
  carriage returns and line feeds, 499–500
  Macintosh files have lost application associations, 504

networks, 575
  common problems, 576–577
  configuration, 585–588
  connectivity, 588–589
  Device Manager, 584
  diagnostic tools, 577–584
  Event Viewer, 582–584
  file sharing, 589–590
  Network and Sharing Center, 577–578
  network cables, 585
  Network Diagnostics, 581–582
  Network Map, 579–581
  preparation, 576
  printer sharing, 589–590
  Windows Firewall, 582

newsgroups
  message availability after synchronization, 412–413
  missing from news servers, 410

Notepad, 226

offline files, 992–995

output to exterior televisions, 700

printers
  garbled text, 202
  lack of output, 201
  unfound, 192–194
  unlisted, 194–195

problem reports and solutions, 752–753

Registry, file corruption, 811

reinstallation, 751

scanners, 281

shared cable connections on LANs, 527

shared DSL connections on LANs, 527

shared Internet connections, 525

shared modem connections on LANs, 527

shortcuts, 138

small screen fonts, 680

startup process, creating backups from System Recovery Options menu, 755–756

Tablet PCs
  pen cursor, 1039
  pen flicks, 1048

tips, 753–755

troubleshooters, 752–753

Troubleshooting applet, 752–753

TV tuners, 261

USB backup devices, 874–875

video, Windows Media Center, 263

VPNs (virtual private networks)

  Error Number 629/720, 985

  missing certificates, 982

Windows Fax and Scan, 300

Windows Messenger, inability to send files, 943

Windows Update, 761

Windows XP, troubleshooters, 752

wireless networks, 963–964

WordPad, 227

Troubleshooting (Control Panel), 603, 752–753

TrueType font outline technology, 627–630

Trusted Platform Module (TPM), enabling, 897–898

Truth About Identity Theft, The, **921**

tunnels, VPNs (virtual private networks), 977

Turbo Scroll (WMC), 254

turning off. *See* disabling

TV Guide (WMC), setting up, 264–265

TV output jacks, Windows Media Center, 255

TV tuners, Windows Media Center, 255

TWAIN drivers, scanners, 295

Twain, Mark, 852

Tweak-7, Registry, editing, 820

TwistedPixel, 234

Type Your Windows Product Key dialog box, 56

typefaces, 627–630

  information sources, 630

  installing, 631

  points, 627

  substitutions, 630–631

  types, 629

Typography (Microsoft) website, 630

U

UAC (User Account Control), 26, 85–87, 594, 859–860, 932

UI (user interface)

  Aero

    Aero Peek, 133

    dialog boxes, 122–123

    gestures, 131

    Help and Support, 143–144

    libraries, 140–141

    putting items on, 123

    Quick Launch bar, 133

    shortcut keys, 130–131

    shortcuts, 124

  logon process, 117

  taskbar, 135

  Windows Explorer, file management, 129

UIs (user interfaces)

  file system

    navigating, 158–167

    right-clicking, 161–162

    selecting multiple items, 162–163

    viewing meta-information, 163–165

  file views, customizing, 167–168

  folder views, customizing, 167–170

  panes, toggling, 165–167

  Windows Explorer, 149–154

    Address bar, 155

    breadcrumbs, 155–158

    indexing, 174–177

    searching, 173–183

    user profiles, 158

    WebView, 152–154

Ultra DMA EIDE drives, 782

UMDF (User-Mode Driver Framework), 789

UNC (Universal Naming Convention), 558–559

  shared folders, browsing, 545–546

Unicode subranges, choosing from, 668–669

Uninstall or Change a Program applet, 771

uninstalling

  applications, 135

  programs, 643–644

  updates, Windows Update, 763–764

uninstalling programs, 134–135

uninstalling software, 769–774

uninterruptible power supply (UPS). *See* UPS (uninterruptible power supply)

Universal Plug and Play (UPnP), shared routers, 531

UNIX

  internetworking, 497

    NFS (network file system), 500–501

    Samba, 497–500

    SUA (Subsystem for UNIX-based Applications), 501–503

  mangled line feed/carriage returns, troubleshooting, 499–500

  printing from Windows, 499

  Samba

    client tools, 497–498

    server tools, 498–500

  Windows printers, printing to, 499

Unix-to-Unix Copy Protocol (UUCP), news server protocol, 408

How can we make this index more useful? Email us at indexes@quepublishing.com

Unread E-mail Quick View (Windows Live Mail), 399

unrecognized hard disks, troubleshooting, 735–736

unsigned ActiveX controls, 386

Update Driver Software window (Device Manager), 765

updates, 757
automatic updates, 857
drivers, 764–767
hotfixes, 767
hotpatching, 759
importance of, 918, 934
important updates, 767
Microsoft E-Mail Updates Service, 934
recommended updates, 767
service packs, 767–768
 cumulative service packs, 768
 incremental service packs, 768
 installing, 768–769
 preinstalled service packs, 768
viewing installed, 644–645
Windows Update, 758–760
 automatic updates, 758–759
 disabling updates, 762–763
 hiding updates, 761
 manually installing updates, 760–761
 repairing updates, 763–764
 troubleshooting, 761
 uninstalling updates, 763–764
 viewing updates, 762–764

updating networks, cabling systems, 453

upgrading
Anytime Upgrade, 17
CPUs, 45
dynamic hard disks, 717

hardware, 779–780
 BIOS settings, 781–782
 EULA (End User Licensing Agreement), 799–801
 hard disks, 702–703
 HCL (Hardware Compatibility List), 801–803
 page file sizes, 780
 RAM (random access memory), 779, 783–784
 ReadyBoost, 780–781
 SPP (Software Protection Program), 799
Microsoft desupport dates, 116
problems, 134
RAM, 45
Windows 7 versions, 65–66
 upgrade paths, 41

***Upgrading and Repairing PCs*, 50, 431, 780**

uplink ports, switches, 462–463

UPS (uninterruptible power supply)
choosing, 797
configuring, 798–799
installing, 795–799
intelligent UPS, 795
line interactive UPS, 797
online UPS, 797
printers, 797
serial cables, 798
standby UPS, 797
testing, 799

URLs (uniform resource locators), commonly recognized, 947

USB backup devices, troubleshooting, 874–875

USB controllers, BIOS settings, 790

USB flash drives, security, 910–911

Use All of My Monitors option (Remote Desktop), 1021

Usenet, 408–409

User Account Control (UAC), 26, 85–87, 859–860, 932

User Account Control warning, 419

user accounts
Computer Administrator accounts, 89
configuring, 88–92
creating, 89–90
Guest user accounts, 90
logon process, Welcome screen, 117
names, changing, 90
password reset disks, creating, 91–92
passwords, changing and creating, 90
pictures, changing, 90
Standard user accounts, 770
transferring, 88

User Accounts (Control Panel), 603

User Accounts and Family Safety view (Category view), 597

"user experience," 117–121

user groups
assigning permissions to, 908–909
restricted objects, permission assignments, 910

user interface
Aero Peek, 133
dialog boxes, 122–123
gestures, 131
Help and Support, 143–144
libraries, 140–141
Quick Launch bar, 133
shortcut keys, 130–131

user interfaces (UIs). *See* UIs (user interfaces)

user profile folder, directory structure, 101, 106–107
junction points, 107–108
symbolic links, 108
virtualization, 108–109

user profiles
backups and, 868
Windows Explorer, 158
User State Migration Tool (USMT), 16
User-Mode Driver Framework (UMDF), 789
user-mode drivers, 789
Users tab (Task Manager), 677
USMT (User State Migration Tool), 16
utilities. *See also* specific utilities
Action Center, 604–607
Administrative Tools, 660–666
AutoPlay, 607–608
Color Management, 609
Control Panel, shortcuts, 595
Date and Time, 609–611
Default Programs, 611–612
Device Manager, 612–619
Devices and Printers, 619–623
Ease of Access Center, 623–627
Event Viewer, 655–658
Fonts, 627–631
MMC (Microsoft Management Console), 653–654
Notification Area Icons, 631–632
Performance Information and Tools, 632–642
Power Options, 642
Programs and Features, 643–646
Region and Language, 646
Services, 659–660
Shared Folders, 658–659
System Properties, 647–652
System Tools folder, 666
Character Map, 667–669
Private Character Editor, 670
System Information, 670–671

Task Manager, 672, 675
Applications tab, 672–674
Networking tab, 677
Performance tab, 675–677
Processes tab, 674–675
Services tab, 675
Users tab, 677
Task Scheduler, 654
third-party utilities, 677–678
Utilities tab (printer properties dialog box), 199
UTP (unshielded twisted-pair) cabling, 10/100BASE-T Ethernet, 448–449
UUCP (UNIX-to-UNIX Copy Protocol), 408

V

values, Registry keys, 815
variables, environment variables, setting, 825–827
VBScript, 834
versions, Windows 7, 12
compared, 38–41
upgrading, 65–66
VHDs (virtual hard disks), 721–722
video
frames per second (fps), 369
Internet Explorer
downloading, 373–379
supported formats, 368–373
streaming video, 369
playing, 370–371
video cards
3D screen savers, 695
AGP video cards, 790
minimum requirements, 44
multiple monitors, 790–791
PCIe (PCI Express) video cards, 790–791
quad-link video adapter cards, 795

recommended specifications, 44
video files, burning to DVD, 325
video projectors, connecting to, 32
View Available Networks popup window, 962
View By drop-down list (Control Panel), 83
View Gadgets dialog box, 216
View menu (Windows Explorer), 167–168
View Options dialog box, 127
View tab, Folder Options Control Panel applet, 154
viewing
desktop images, Snipping Tool, 320–321
effective permissions, 907
event details, Event Viewer, 657–658
IE add-ons, 377–379
installed software, 771
installed updates, 644–645
meta-information, 163–165
Registry, Regedit, 812–814
updates, Windows Update, 762–764
views
Control Panel
Category view, 595–596, 598–599
Large Icons view, 595–596, 598–604
Small Icons view, 595–596, 598–604
files, customizing, 167–168
Folder, 127
folders, customizing, 167–170
Internet Explorer, expanding, 358
Windows Explorer, 151
Views command (View menu), 167
Views menu, 160

virtual folders, 777

virtual hard disks (VHDs). *See* VHDs (virtual hard disks)

virtual machines (VMs), 1051

Virtual PC, 1051
installing, 1052–1053
minimum requirements, 1052

virtual private networks (VPNs). *See* VPNs (virtual private networks)

virtual registries, 777

Virtual Windows XP. *See* Windows XP Mode

virtualization, 1051–1052
Registry, 806–808
user profile folder, 108–109
Virtual PC, 1051
installing, 1052–1053
minimum requirements, 1052
Windows XP Mode, 1052
installing, 1053–1055
Windows XP VM, installing applications on, 1055–1056

viruses, 845–846, 916
avoiding, 862
Melissa virus, 846
Michelangelo virus, 846
preventing, 848
antivirus software, 850–852
automatic updates, 857
DEP (Data Execution Prevention), 857–859
email attachments, 404–405
firewalls, 856
Internet Explorer, 861
service hardening, 860–861
UAC (User Account Control), 859–860
Windows Action Center, 848–850
Windows Defender, 852–856

Vista. *See* Windows Vista

visual effects, configuring, 636

visual effects tools, 705–706

visualizations, WMP (Windows Media Player), 234

VMs (virtual machines), 1051

voice recognition, Speech Recognition, 1032

Volume Mixer, 317

volume shadow copies, 864, 901

Volume Shadow Copy Service (VSS). *See* VSS (Volume Shadow Copy Service)

Volume slider (Mobility Center), 973

volumes
displaying, Disk Management utility, 713
FAT volumes, Properties tab, 723
grafting, 715–717
joining, 714–717
mirrored volumes, 711
NTFS volumes, Properties tab, 723
RAID-5 volumes, 711
simple volumes, 711
spanned volumes, 711
creating, 718
striped volumes, 711
creating, 719–720

VPN reconnect, 26

VPNs (virtual private networks), 977
advanced routing, 986–987
configuring, 978–987
connection failures
certificates, 982
Error Number 629/720, 985
connection process, 977–978
connection properties, 980–982
data encapsulation, 977

email connections, 986
ending connections, 986
establishing connections, 983–985
gateway settings, 981–982
incoming access, 987–990
monitoring connections, 986
offline files, 991
encrypting, 997
identifying for use, 992–993
managing, 997
synchronizing, 995–998
troubleshooting, 992–995
using, 993–995
RAS (Remote Access Services), 977
shared folders, availability, 997–998
Sync Center, 991
tunnels, 977

VSS (Volume Shadow Copy Service), 29, 740
Backup and Restore Center, 864

Vyew, 1011

W

Wacom stylus pens, 1033

wallpaper, desktop
setting, 685–687
solid backgrounds, 686
stretching, 687

warnings, User Account Control, 419

WAT (Windows Activation Technology), 800

WAV files, 242
size considerations, 691
storing, 692

WBADMIN command-line tool, 879–882

WDF (Windows Driver Foundation), 789

web addresses, commonly recognized, 947

web browsers. *See* Internet Explorer

web feeds, 356

web pages
enlarging view, Internet Explorer, 358
video, frames per second (fps), 369

Web Slices (IE), 27, 356–357, 381

web zones, Internet Explorer security, 384

web-based e-mail, backing up, 868

WebCrawler, 392

WebEx MeetMeNow, 1010

websites
connection problems, troubleshooting, 420–423
favorite websites, adding, 365–367
FreeNews.net, 409
navigating, 361
security resources, 943

WebView, 152–154

WEI (Windows Experience Index), 632–636

Welcome screen, 78
logging on from, 117

WEP (wired equivalency privacy)
hexadecimal format, 466
key formats, wireless networks, 466–467

Which Type of Installation Do You Want? dialog box, 53–55

whois database, domain registration information, 439

WIA drivers
obtaining, 302
scanners, 295

WiFi hot spots, wireless networks, joining, 964–965

Window Color and Appearance dialog box, 688–690

window snips (Snipping Tool), 217

windows
color schemes, 688–690
maximizing, gestures, 131

Windows, desupport dates, 116

Windows 7
code base, 14
exiting, Sleep, 146
improvements, 12
new features, 13–38
  accessories, 31–32
  applications, 37
  configuration, 16–17
  corporate networks, 41–42
  data security, 29–30
  entertainment, 37–38
  installation, 16–17
  interface, 17–25
  Internet Explorer, 27–28
  networking, 33–35
  performance, 30–31
  power management, 32–33
  services, 37
  stability, 35–36
  system management, 35–36
  system security, 25–26
  upgrades, 17
Product Keys, 57
upgrade paths, 41
versions, 12
  32-bit versions, 39
  64-bit versions, 39
  compared, 38–41
  upgrading, 63–66
Welcome screen, 78–79, 117
Windows Media Center, version based on, 257
Windows Server, compared, 445–446
Windows Vista, compared, 12–13
Windows XP, compared, 13

Windows 7 and Vista Guide to Scripting, Automation, and Command Line Tools, 821, 824, 832–833

Windows 7 Compatibility Center, 50

Windows 95
compatibility mode, 122
internetworking, 496–497

Windows 98, internetworking, 496–497

Windows 2000, internetworking, 489
password protection and simple file sharing, 491–494
TCP/IP as default network protocol, 490

Windows accounts, pictures, setting, 696

Windows Action Center, 848–850
balloon notifications, 117

Windows Activation Technology (WAT), 800

Windows Anytime Update, 66

Windows Backup, Disk Management, 882–883

Windows Backup schedule, 869

Windows Boot Manager, 748–751

Windows Calendar, Internet Explorer, 383

Windows CardSpace, 603

Windows Classic theme, 684

Windows Classic visual palette, 118

Windows Communication Foundation HTTP Activation, 511

Windows Contacts, Internet Explorer, 383

Windows Defender, 388, 603, 852–856, 932

Windows Desktop gadgets, 119, 212

Windows Disc Image Burner, Internet Explorer, 383

Windows Easy Transfer, 88, 101–104

Windows Event Log, event ID numbers, locating, 840

Windows Experience Index (WEI), 632–636, 705

Windows Explorer, 81
  Address bar, 155–156
  breadcrumbs, 81, 155, 158
  computer contents, displaying, 128
  configuring, 98–100
  Details pane, 152
  Favorites group, 152
  file system
    navigating, 158–167
    right-clicking, 161–162
    selecting multiple items, 162–163
    viewing meta-information, 163–165
  files
    security, 185
    views, customizing, 167–170
    zipping and packing, 183–184
  folders
    security, 185
    selecting, 129
    viewing, 129
  Get Help button, 152
  indexing, configuring, 174–177
  Layout flyout menu, 166
  libraries
    adding elements to, 172–173
    creating, 170–172
    managing, 170–173
    removing elements to, 173

Libraries folder, 150
Libraries group, 152
location, 149
menu bar, 150
networks
    managing, 571 573
    searching, 546–550
new features, 24, 149–154
panes, toggling, 165–167
pictures, burning to CD/DVD, 290–291
programs, running from, 140
searching, 173–174
    configuring, 174–177
    deep searching, 174
    grouping and stacking, 181–183
    intermediate searching, 174
    troubleshooting, 179
    while typing, 177–181
  shared folders, browsing, 542–546
  toolbar, 151–152
  user profiles, 158
  View menu, 167–168
  views, 151
  WebView, 152–154

Windows Fax and Scan, 293–294
  adding scanned pages to faxes, 302
  configuration, 295
    cover pages, 296–297
    fax receiving options, 295–296
    fax settings, 298–299
    sender information, 296
  configuring, 305–306
  dialing rules, 303–304
  emailing scans, 310
  enabling, 293
  faxing scans, 310
  hardware requirements, 293
  manipulating scanned images, 310
  monitoring outgoing faxes, 304–305
  preparations, 294–295
  previewing faxes, 303

printing faxes
    automatically, 305
  receiving faxes, 305
  scan profiles, 306–308
  scanning images, 308
  scanning pictures, 294
  sending faxes, 299–302, 304
  slides, faxing and scanning, 310–311
  transparencies, faxing and scanning, 310–311
  troubleshooting, 300
  Windows Firewall, Unblock option, 295

Windows File Protection, 776

Windows Firewall, 603, 932
  Advanced Security Administrative program, 941–943
  configuring, 477, 920–921, 937–938
  default settings, restoring, 941
  disabling, 938–939
  enabling, 938–939
  exceptions, enabling, 942
  features, allowing, 939–940
  function of, 920–921
  inadvertent blockages, checking for, 582
  logging, enabling, 929
  notification settings, changing, 940–941
  programs, allowing, 939–940
  satellite Internet connections, 332
  turning off, 940–941
  Unblock option, 295

Windows for Pen Computing, 1030

Windows Gallery, 279

Windows Journal, Tablet PCs, 1043–1045

Windows Live, 37
  Windows Update, compared, 758

Windows Live Essentials, 394
  downloading, 394–395

Windows Live gadgets, 212

Windows Live Mail, 394
accounts, configuring,
395–398
attachments
opening, 403
sending, 403
virus prevention,
404–405
Contacts, 406
adding entries, 406–407
deleting entries, 407
editing entries, 406
downloading, 394
incoming messages
deleting, 401
reading, 398–399
replying, 399–400
junk mail filter, 954
launching, 395–396
messages, signature setup,
405–406
multiple accounts,
checking, 401
new messages
addressing, 402
creating, 401–402
sending, 402–403
newsgroups, 408
accessing, 408
account setup, 410–411
downloading lists, 411
locating, 412
managing, 415–416
marking messages, 415
posting, 414–415
reading, 412, 414–415
subscribing to, 412–413
spam, controlling, 407–408

Windows Live Messenger
assistance requests,
responding to, 1008
files, inability to send, 943

Windows Live Spaces, 357

Windows Lockdown! Your XP
and Vista Guide Against
Hacks, Attacks, and Other
Internet Mayhem, 921

Windows Logo'd Products
List, 784, 801–803

Windows Management
Instrumentation (WMI), WSH
(Windows Script Host),
836–837

Windows ME,
internetworking, 496–497

Windows Media Audio
files, 242

Windows Media Audio Pro
files, 242

Windows Media Center, 37,
232, 251
Ambient Slideshow, 254, 267
hardware information, 258
Integrated TV Pack
Enhancements, 254
interface, 252
Internet Explorer, 383
Movies library, 264
Music library, 253
Music Now Playing, 254
new features, 253–254
Now Playing, 253
photographs, printing, 269
Rating Shortcuts, 254
Shared Libraries, 254
Start menu,
improvements, 253
Start screen, 262
television
program selection,
264–265
recording, 265
skipping
commercials, 265
watching, 264–266
TiVo, compared, 264–265
troubleshooting
TV tuners, 261
video, 263
Turbo Scroll, 254
TV Guide, 264–265
Windows 7 version based
on, 257

Windows Media Player
(WMP). See WMP (Windows
Media Player)

Windows Memory Diagnostic
tool, 745–746

Windows Mobility Center,
604, 972
controls, 972–973
Hardware and Sound
Control Panel window,
973–974
launching, 972
Presentation Settings, 973
Sync Center, 973
Wireless Network icon, 973

Windows NT, compatibility
mode, 122

Windows NT Virtual DOS
Machine. See ntvdm
(Windows NT virtual DOS
Machine)

Windows operating system,
determining, 704

Windows Photo Gallery, 294
Internet Explorer, 383

Windows Pictures Library, 278
adding pictures to, 278–279
digital cameras, 281–284
importing files to, 279
organizing, 279
pictures
burning to CD/DVD,
290–292
printing, 286–289
sharing electronically,
289–290
scanners, 279–281

Windows PowerShell, 837–839

Windows PowerShell 2.0
Unleashed, 839

Windows Print Manager, 188

Windows Script Host (WSH).
See WSH (Windows Script
Host)

Windows Search Explorer,
Internet Explorer, 383

Windows Server
domain networks, joining,
481–483
Windows 7, compared,
445–446

Windows Slideshow gadgets, 212

windows snips (Snipping Tool), 320

Windows Task Scheduler. *See* **Task Scheduler**

Windows Terminal Services, 1014

Windows Update, 604, 758–760
automatic updates, 758–759
Change Settings window, 762
Device Installation Settings window, 767
driver settings, 766
manually installing updates, 760–761
running frequently, 803
service packs, installation, 768–769
troubleshooting, 761
updates
disabling, 762–763
hiding, 761
repairing, 763–764
uninstalling, 763–764
viewing, 762–764
Windows Live, compared, 758

Windows Vista
design mandate, 12
internetworking, 489
homegroups, 494–495
password protection and simple file sharing, 491–494
setting TCP/IP as default network protocol, 490
Mojave, remarketing as, 11
problems, 11
Windows 7, compared, 12–13

Windows XP
internetworking, 489
homegroups, 494–495
installing LLDP responder, 491
password protection and simple file sharing, 491–494

setting TCP/IP as default network protocol, 490
troubleshooters, 752
Windows 7, compared, 13

Windows XP Mode, 37, 1052
installing, 1053–1055

Windows XP VM, applications, installing on, 1055–1056

Windows.old folder, 751

Wireless Adapter Settings setting (Power Options Advanced Settings), 975

wireless Internet access, 332

Wireless Network icon (Mobility Center), 973

wireless networks, 959
802.11g/n wireless networking, 451–452
ad hoc networks, 960
creating, 965–966
configuring, 464–466, 468–471, 966
Internet service, 471
manually, 470–471
manufacturer's setup program, 468
Set Up a Network Wizard, 469–470
connections, prioritizing, 967–968
domain networks, 961
evolution, 959
file sharing, cryptographic keys, 464
home networks, 960
infrastructure networks, 960
installing, 463–472
Internet connections on LANs, 521–522
joining, 472, 961
corporate environments, 961
home networks, 961–963
public hot spots, 964–965
small offices, 961–963
someone else's office, 963–964

preferred wireless networks, selecting, 966
printer sharing, cryptographic keys, 464
profiles
copying to other computers, 968
deleting, 969
manually adding, 968–969
public networks, 960
security
authentication, 464
encryption, 464–467
shared resources, security, 960–961
SSIDs, 472, 968
standards, 959
switching between, 966–967
troubleshooting, 964

wireless routers, 518

wiring (networks)
Ethernet crossover cables, 461–462
in-wall wiring, 460–461
installing, 457–463
multiple switches, 462–463

wiring systems, networks. *See* **cabling systems**

wizards
Add Hardware Wizard, 785–786
Add Printer Wizard, 554
Files and Settings Transfer Wizard, 16
Program Compatibility Wizard, 774–776
Scanner and Camera Wizard, 279
Set Up a Network Wizard, 468–470

WMC (Windows Media Center). *See* **Windows Media Center**

WMI (Windows Management Instrumentation), WSH (Windows Script Host), 836–837

WMI SNMP Provider, 511

WMP (Windows Media Player), 231
  audio, playing, 239–240
  browsing, 236–238
  CDs
    burning music to, 235
    ripping, 240–242
  customized CDs, burning, 244–246
  Full Screen option, 239
  hard disk media files, playing, 240
  home networking, 248–250
  interface, 233–238
  Internet Explorer, 383
  libraries, adding items to, 243
  menu breadcrumbs, 233–236
  Navigation pane, 250
  network shares, playing, 240
  pictures
    burning to CD/DVD, 291
    fixing, 284–286
  portable media players
    compatibility issues, 244
    synchronization, 246–248
  searching, 236–238
  shuffling playback, 240
  supported file types, 232
  video files, playing, 370
  visualizations, 234

WMV (Windows Media Video) files, playing, Internet Explorer, 370

word processors, 225

Word Viewer, 227

WordPad, 37, 227–228
  Internet Explorer, 383
  NotePad, compared, 225
  troubleshooting, 227

Work networks, 475

work wireless networks, 960

worms, 845–847
  avoiding, 862

  preventing, 848
    antivirus software, 850–852
    automatic updates, 857
    DEP (Data Execution Prevention), 857–859
    firewalls, 856
    Internet Explorer, 861
    service hardening, 860–861
    UAC (User Account Control), 859–860
    Windows Action Center, 848–850
    Windows Defender, 852–856
  SQL Slammer, 846

WOW64 emulation layer, 39

WPA key formats, wireless networks, 466–467

WPS (Windows PowerShell), 837–839

Write Attributes advanced NTFS permission, 893, 906

Write Extended Attributes advanced NTFS permission, 906

Write NTFS permission, 891, 904

writing methods, Tablet PC Input Panel, 1037–1038

Writing Pad (Input Panel), 1037

WSH (Windows Script Host), 832–834
  disk management, 836
  network management, 836
  scripting languages, support, 834
  scripts
    creating, 834–836
    sample scripts, 836–837
  WMI (Windows Management Instrumentation), 836–837

WS_Ping Pro Pack, 440

X-Y-Z

X-Setup Pro, Registry, editing, 819

Xbox 360, Media Center Extender, 261

XP Mode, 73

XPS Viewer, 221–222

Zen X-Fi portable media players, 244

zero configuration VPN system, 987

zipping files, 183–184

Your purchase of **Microsoft Windows 7 In Depth** includes access to a free online edition for 45 days through the Safari Books Online subscription service. Nearly every Que book is available online through Safari Books Online, along with more than 5,000 other technical books and videos from publishers such as Cisco Press, Exam Cram, IBM Press, O'Reilly, Prentice Hall, Addison-Wesley Professional, and Sams.

SAFARI BOOKS ONLINE allows you to search for a specific answer, cut and paste code, download chapters, and stay current with emerging technologies.

Activate your FREE Online Edition at www.informit.com/safarifree

> **STEP 1:** Enter the coupon code: SQVYWWA.

> **STEP 2:** New Safari users, complete the brief registration form. Safari subscribers, just log in.

If you have difficulty registering on Safari or accessing the online edition, please e-mail customer-service@safaribooksonline.com